ADVENTURES
IN READING

The *ADVENTURES IN LITERATURE* Program

ADVENTURES FOR READERS: BOOK ONE
Teacher's Manual
Tests
Reading/Writing Workshop A

ADVENTURES FOR READERS: BOOK TWO
Teacher's Manual
Tests
Reading/Writing Workshop B

ADVENTURES IN READING
Teacher's Manual
Tests
Reading/Writing Workshop C

ADVENTURES IN APPRECIATION
Teacher's Manual
Tests
Reading/Writing Workshop D

ADVENTURES IN AMERICAN LITERATURE
Teacher's Manual
Tests

ADVENTURES IN ENGLISH LITERATURE
Teacher's Manual
Tests

CURRICULUM
AND
WRITING

Fannie Safier
Formerly teacher of English
New York City Schools, New York, New York

Secondary English Editorial Staff
Harcourt Brace Jovanovich, Publishers

ADVENTURES
IN READING

HERITAGE EDITION REVISED

Harcourt Brace Jovanovich, Publishers
Orlando   New York   Chicago   San Diego   Atlanta   Dallas

Acknowledgments

For permission to reprint copyrighted material, grateful acknowledgment is given to the following sources:

Margaret Walker Alexander: "Lineage" in *For My People* by Margaret Walker, published by Yale University Press, 1942.

Samuel Allen: "To Satch" by Samuel Allen (Paul Vesey).

American-Scandinavian Foundation: "The Eclipse" by Selma Lagerlöf translated by Velma Swanston Howard in *American-Scandinavian Review,* December 1922.

Atheneum Publishers: "Lizards and Snakes" from *The Hard Hours* by Anthony Hecht. Copyright © 1967 by Anthony E. Hecht. "Metaphor" from *It Doesn't Always Have to Rhyme* by Eve Merriam. Copyright © 1964 by Eve Merriam.

Brandt & Brandt Literary Agents, Inc.: "The Most Dangerous Game" by Richard Connell. Copyright 1924 by Richard Connell. Copyright renewed © 1952 by Louise Fox Connell. "Mozart and the Gray Steward" from *The Angel That Troubled the Waters* by Thornton Wilder. Copyright © 1928 by Coward-McCann, Inc. Copyright renewed 1956 by Thornton Wilder. *All rights reserved. Caution:* "Mozart and the Gray Steward" is the sole property of the author and is fully protected by copyright. It may not be acted by professionals or amateurs without formal permission and the payment of a royalty. All rights including professional, amateur, stock, radio and television, broadcasting, motion picture, recitation, lecturing, public reading, and the rights of translation into foreign languages are reserved. All inquiries should be addressed to Harold Freedman, Brandt & Brandt Dramatic Department, Inc., 1501 Broadway, New York, N.Y. 10036.

Curtis Brown, Ltd.: "400-Meter Freestyle" by Maxine Kumin. Copyright © 1961 by Maxine Kumin.

Cambridge University Press: Excerpted material from *Shakespeare's Imagery and What It Tells Us* by Caroline F. E. Spurgeon.

Don Congdon Associates, Inc.: "All the Years of Her Life" by Morley Callaghan. Copyright © 1935 by Morley Callaghan, renewal © 1962 by Morley Callaghan.

Bill Cooper Associates, Inc.: "The Fifty-First Dragon" by Heywood Broun.

Delacorte Press/Seymour Lawrence: "Tom Edison's Shaggy Dog" excerpted from *Welcome to the Monkey House* by Kurt Vonnegut, Jr. Copyright © 1953 by Kurt Vonnegut, Jr. Originally published in *Collier's.*

Dell Publishing Co., Inc.: Excerpted from the Introduction to "Romeo and Juliet" by William Shakespeare, edited by Francis Fergusson, with a Commentary by W. H. Auden. Introduction and Bibliographies copyright © 1958 by Francis Fergusson.

Dodd, Mead & Company, Inc.: "The Death of a Tree" from *Dune Boy* by Edwin Way Teale. Copyright 1943, 1971 by Edwin Way Teale.

Doubleday & Company, Inc.: Excerpt from *The Odyssey* by Homer translated by Robert Fitzgerald. Copyright © 1961 by Robert Fitzgerald. "The Meadow Mouse" from *The Collected Poems of Theodore Roethke* by Theodore Roethke. Copyright © 1963 by Beatrice Roethke as Administratrix of the Estate of Theodore Roethke. "The Gift of the Magi" by O. Henry.

Norma Millay (Ellis): "An Ancient Gesture" by Edna St. Vincent Millay, copyright 1954 by Norma Millay Ellis, and "The Fawn" by Edna St. Vincent Millay, copyright 1934, 1962 by Edna St. Vincent Millay and Norma Millay Ellis from *Collected Poems* by Edna St. Vincent Millay. Published by Harper & Row, Publishers, Inc.

Farrar, Straus & Giroux, Inc.: "A Summer's Reading" from *The Magic Barrel* by Bernard Malamud. Copyright

Critical Readers and Contributors

Contents

See page xv for the contents of *Reading and Writing About Literature*

SHORT STORIES

NONFICTION

Essays

Biography and Personal Recollection

POETRY

The Speaker

Diction

Imagery

SHORT STORIES

It is customary to begin the study of short stories with the element of *plot*. Plot is the organized pattern of events in a story. Sometimes the plot is relatively simple and straightforward, as in "The Most Dangerous Game." Sometimes the plot is more complicated; there may be more than one action to follow. Occasionally, a plot is structured to lead to an ingenious surprise at the end, such as the famous surprise ending of "The Gift of the Magi."

In some stories, plot is the most important element. Readers keep reading to find out what will happen next. But in most stories, the *characters* are of primary importance. Generally, a story focuses on a main character. Although Jess and Enoch and even Samantha, the goose, are fully depicted in "The Pacing Goose," it is Eliza who is at the center of the action.

Another element is *point of view*. Point of view is like the camera in a movie, the lens through which you, the reader, view the action. "The Cask of Amontillado" is told from a first-person point of view, by the central character in the story. Other stories are told from the third-person point of view, as if the action were seen by an objective observer who merely records what happens. Still other stories are told by an omniscient (all-knowing) narrator, who tells not only what happens but what the characters think and feel.

Just as every story has a point of view, so every story has a *setting*, the time and place of the action. Some settings are strange and exotic, such as Ship-Trap Island in "The Most Dangerous Game." Some settings are familiar and ordinary, such as the neighborhood in "A Summer's Reading."

Finally, many short stories do more than excite or amuse. They also express a *theme*, an idea about life. Occasionally, a theme is expressed directly through the author's comments, but generally theme is not directly stated—it must be inferred from other elements in the story.

All the short stories in this unit are fine examples of the short-story writer's art. As you explore the basic elements of each story, you will gain skills that will help you read other stories with greater insight and enjoyment.

The Most Dangerous Game
Richard Connell

"Off there to the right—somewhere—is a large island," said Whitney. "It's rather a mystery——"

"What island is it?" Rainsford asked.

"The old charts call it 'Ship-Trap Island,' " Whitney replied. "A suggestive name, isn't it? Sailors have a curious dread of the place. I don't know why. Some superstition——"

"Can't see it," remarked Rainsford, trying to peer through the dank tropical night that was palpable as it pressed its thick warm blackness in upon the yacht.

"You've good eyes," said Whitney, with a laugh, "and I've seen you pick off a moose moving in the brown fall bush at four hundred yards, but even you can't see four miles or so through a moonless Caribbean night."

"Nor four yards," admitted Rainsford. "Ugh! It's like moist black velvet."

"It will be light in Rio," promised Whitney. "We should make it in a few days. I hope the jaguar guns have come from Purdey's.[1] We should have some good hunting up the Amazon. Great sport, hunting."

"The best sport in the world," agreed Rainsford.

"For the hunter," amended Whitney. "Not for the jaguar."

"Don't talk rot, Whitney," said Rainsford. "You're a big-game hunter, not a philosopher. Who cares how a jaguar feels?"

"Perhaps the jaguar does," observed Whitney.

"Bah! They've no understanding."

"Even so, I rather think they understand one thing—fear. The fear of pain and the fear of death."

"Nonsense," laughed Rainsford. "This hot weather is making you soft, Whitney. Be a realist. The world is made up of two classes—the hunters and the huntees. Luckily, you and I are hunters. Do you think we've passed that island yet?"

"I can't tell in the dark. I hope so."

"Why?" asked Rainsford.

"The place has a reputation—a bad one."

"Cannibals?" suggested Rainsford.

"Hardly. Even cannibals wouldn't live in such a Godforsaken place. But it's gotten into sailor lore, somehow. Didn't you notice that the crew's nerves seemed a bit jumpy today?"

"They were a bit strange, now you mention it. Even Captain Nielsen——"

"Yes, even that tough-minded old Swede, who'd go up to the devil himself and ask him

---

1. **Purdey:** a famous English manufacturer of hunting rifles and shotguns.

for a light. Those fishy blue eyes held a look I never saw there before. All I could get out of him was: 'This place has an evil name among seafaring men, sir.' Then he said to me, very gravely: 'Don't you feel anything?'—as if the air about us was actually poisonous. Now, you mustn't laugh when I tell you this—I did feel something like a sudden chill.

"There was no breeze. The sea was as flat as a plate-glass window. We were drawing near the island then. What I felt was a—a mental chill; a sort of sudden dread."

"Pure imagination," said Rainsford. "One superstitious sailor can taint the whole ship's company with his fear."

"Maybe. But sometimes I think sailors have an extra sense that tells them when they are in danger. Sometimes I think evil is a tangible thing—with wavelengths, just as sound and light have. An evil place can, so to speak, broadcast vibrations of evil. Anyhow, I'm glad were getting out of this zone. Well, I think I'll turn in now, Rainsford."

"I'm not sleepy," said Rainsford. "I'm going to smoke another pipe up on the afterdeck."

"Good night, then, Rainsford. See you at breakfast."

"Right. Good night, Whitney."

There was no sound in the night as Rainsford sat there, but the muffled throb of the engine that drove the yacht swiftly through the darkness, and the swish and ripple of the wash of the propeller.

Rainsford, reclining in a steamer chair, indolently puffed on his favorite brier. The sensuous drowsiness of the night was on him. "It's so dark," he thought, "that I could sleep without closing my eyes; the night would be my eyelids—"

An abrupt sound startled him. Off to the right he heard it, and his ears, expert in such matters, could not be mistaken. Again he heard the sound, and again. Somewhere, off in the blackness, someone had fired a gun three times.

Rainsford sprang up and moved quickly to the rail, mystified. He strained his eyes in the direction from which the reports had come, but it was like trying to see through a blanket. He leaped upon the rail and balanced himself there, to get greater elevation; his pipe, striking a rope, was knocked from his mouth. He lunged for it; a short, hoarse cry came from his lips as he realized he had reached too far and had lost his balance. The cry was pinched off short as the blood-warm waters of the Caribbean Sea closed over his head.

He struggled up to the surface and tried to cry out, but the wash from the speeding yacht slapped him in the face and the salt water in his open mouth made him gag and strangle. Desperately he struck out with strong strokes after the receding lights of the yacht, but he stopped before he had swum fifty feet. A certain coolheadedness had come to him; it was not the first time he had been in a tight place. There was a chance that his cries could be heard by someone aboard the yacht, but that chance was slender, and grew more slender as the yacht raced on. He wrestled himself out of his clothes, and shouted with all his power. The lights of the yacht became faint and ever-vanishing fireflies; then they were blotted out entirely by the night.

Rainsford remembered the shots. They had come from the right, and doggedly he swam in that direction swimming with slow, deliberate strokes, conserving his strength. For a seemingly endless time he fought the sea. He began to count his strokes; he could do possibly a hundred more and then——

Rainsford heard a sound. It came out of the darkness, a high screaming sound, the sound of an animal in an extremity of anguish and terror.

He did not recognize the animal that made the sound; he did not try to; with fresh vitality he swam toward the sound. He heard it again; then it was cut short by another noise, crisp, staccato.

"Pistol shot," muttered Rainsford, swimming on.

Ten minutes of determined effort brought another sound to his ears—the most welcome he had ever heard—the muttering and growling of the sea breaking on a rocky shore. He was almost on the rocks before he saw them; on a night less calm he would have been shattered against them. With his remaining strength he dragged himself from the swirling waters. Jagged crags appeared to jut up into the opaqueness; he forced himself upward, hand over hand. Gasping, his hands raw, he reached

a flat place at the top. Dense jungle came down to the very edge of the cliffs. What perils that tangle of trees and underbrush might hold for him did not concern Rainsford just then. All he knew was that he was safe from his enemy, the sea, and that utter weariness was on him. He flung himself down at the jungle edge and tumbled headlong into the deepest sleep of his life.

When he opened his eyes he knew from the position of the sun that it was late in the afternoon. Sleep had given him new vigor; a sharp hunger was picking at him. He looked about him, almost cheerfully.

"Where there are pistol shots, there are men. Where there are men, there is food," he thought. But what kind of men, he wondered, in so forbidding a place? An unbroken front of snarled and ragged jungle fringed the shore.

He saw no sign of a trail through the closely knit web of weeds and trees; it was easier to go along the shore, and Rainsford floundered along by the water. Not far from where he had landed, he stopped.

Some wounded thing, by the evidence a large animal, had thrashed about in the underbrush; the jungle weeds were crushed down and the moss was lacerated; one patch of weeds was stained crimson. A small, glittering object not far away caught Rainsford's eye and he picked it up. It was an empty cartridge.

"A twenty-two," he remarked. "That's odd. It must have been a fairly large animal too. The hunter had his nerve to tackle it with a light gun. It's clear that the brute put up a fight. I suppose the first three shots I heard was when the hunter flushed his quarry[2] and wounded it. The last shot was when he trailed it here and finished it."

He examined the ground closely and found what he had hoped to find—the print of hunting boots. They pointed along the cliff in the direction he had been going. Eagerly he hurried along, now slipping on a rotten log or a loose stone, but making headway; night was beginning to settle down on the island.

Bleak darkness was blacking out the sea and jungle when Rainsford sighted the lights. He came upon them as he turned a crook in the coastline, and his first thought was that he had come upon a village, for there were many lights. But as he forged along he saw to his great astonishment that all the lights were in one enormous building—a lofty structure with pointed towers plunging upward into the gloom. His eyes made out the shadowy outlines of a palatial château;[3] it was set on a high bluff, and on three sides of it cliffs dived down to where the sea licked greedy lips in the shadows.

"Mirage," thought Rainsford. But it was no mirage, he found, when he opened the tall spiked iron gate. The stone steps were real enough; the massive door with a leering gargoyle[4] for a knocker was real enough; yet about it all hung an air of unreality.

He lifted the knocker, and it creaked up stiffly, as if it had never before been used. He let it fall, and it startled him with its booming loudness. He thought he heard steps within; the door remained closed. Again Rainsford lifted the heavy knocker, and let it fall. The door opened then, opened as suddenly as if it were on a spring, and Rainsford stood blinking in the river of glaring gold light that poured out. The first thing Rainsford's eyes discerned was the largest man Rainsford had ever seen—a gigantic creature, solidly made and black-bearded to the waist. In his hand the man held a long-barreled revolver, and he was pointing it straight at Rainsford's heart.

Out of the snarl of beard two small eyes regarded Rainsford.

"Don't be alarmed," said Rainsford, with a smile which he hoped was disarming. "I'm no robber. I fell off a yacht. My name is Sanger Rainsford of New York City."

The menacing look in his eyes did not change. The revolver pointed as rigidly as if the giant were a statue. He gave no sign that he understood Rainsford's words, or that he had even heard them. He was dressed in uniform, a black uniform trimmed with gray astrakhan.[5]

"I'm Sanger Rainsford of New York," Rainsford began again. "I fell off a yacht. I am hungry."

The man's only answer was to raise with his thumb the hammer of his revolver. Then

---

2. **flushed his quarry:** forced the game that was being hunted into the open.
3. **château** (shă-tō′): castle or large country house.

4. **gargoyle** (gär′goil′): a grotesque carved figure, usually of an animal or mythical creature.
5. **astrakhan** (ăs′trə-kăn′): the curled fur of young lambs.

Rainsford saw the man's free hand go to his forehead in a military salute, and he saw him click his heels together and stand at attention. Another man was coming down the broad marble steps, an erect, slender man in evening clothes. He advanced to Rainsford and held out his hand.

In a cultivated voice marked by a slight accent that gave it added precision and deliberateness, he said: "It is a very great pleasure and honor to welcome Mr. Sanger Rainsford, the celebrated hunter, to my home."

Automatically Rainsford shook the man's hand.

"I've read your book about hunting snow leopards in Tibet, you see," explained the man. "I am General Zaroff."

Rainsford's first impression was that the man was singularly handsome; his second was that there was an original, almost bizarre quality about the general's face. He was a tall man past middle age, for his hair was a vivid white; but his thick eyebrows and pointed military mustache were as black as the night from which Rainsford had come. His eyes, too, were black and very bright. He had high cheek bones, a sharp-cut nose, a spare, dark face, the face of a man used to giving orders, the face of an aristocrat. Turning to the giant in uniform, the general made a sign. The giant put away his pistol, saluted, withdrew.

"Ivan is an incredibly strong fellow," remarked the general, "But he has the misfortune to be deaf and dumb. A simple fellow, but, I'm afraid, like all his race, a bit of a savage."

"Is he Russian?"

"He is a Cossack,"[6] said the general, and his smile showed red lips and pointed teeth. "So am I."

6. **Cossack:** Cossacks are a people of the southern Soviet Union noted for their horsemanship and their courage and fierceness in battle.

"Come," he said, "we shouldn't be chatting here. We can talk later. Now you want clothes, food, rest. You shall have them. This is a most restful spot."

Ivan had reappeared, and the general spoke to him with lips that moved but gave forth no sound.

"Follow Ivan, if you please, Mr. Rainsford," said the general. "I was about to have my dinner when you came. I'll wait for you. You'll find that my clothes will fit you, I think."

It was to a huge, beam-ceilinged bedroom with a canopied bed big enough for six men that Rainsford followed the silent giant. Ivan laid out an evening suit, and Rainsford, as he put it on, noticed that it came from a London tailor who ordinarily cut and sewed for none below the rank of duke.

The dining room to which Ivan conducted him was in many ways remarkable. There was a medieval magnificence about it; it suggested a baronial hall of feudal times with its oaken panels, its high ceiling, its vast refectory table where twoscore men could sit down to eat. About the hall were the mounted heads of many animals—lions, tigers, elephants, moose, bears; larger or more perfect specimens Rainsford had never seen. At the great table the general was sitting, alone.

"You'll have a cocktail, Mr. Rainsford," he suggested. The cocktail was surpassingly good; and, Rainsford noted, the table appointments were of the finest—the linen, the crystal, the silver, the china.

They were eating borsch, the rich, red soup with sour cream so dear to Russian palates. Half apologetically General Zaroff said: "We do our best to preserve the amenities of civilization here. Please forgive any lapses. We are well off the beaten track, you know. Do you think the champagne has suffered from its long ocean trip?"

"Not in the least," declared Rainsford. He

was finding the general a most thoughtful and affable host, a true cosmopolite. But there was one small trait of the general's that made Rainsford uncomfortable. Whenever he looked up from his plate he found the general studying him, appraising him narrowly.

"Perhaps," said General Zaroff, "you were surprised that I recognized your name. You see, I read all books on hunting published in English, French, and Russian. I have but one passion in my life, Mr. Rainsford, and it is the hunt."

"You have some wonderful heads here," said Rainsford as he ate a particularly well-cooked filet mignon. "That Cape buffalo is the largest I ever saw."

"Oh, that fellow. Yes, he was a monster."

"Did he charge you?"

"Hurled me against a tree," said the general. "Fractured my skull. But I got the brute."

"I've always thought," said Rainsford, "that the Cape buffalo is the most dangerous of all big game."

For a moment the general did not reply; he was smiling his curious red-lipped smile. Then he said slowly: "No. You are wrong, sir. The Cape buffalo is not the most dangerous big game." He sipped his wine. "Here in my preserve on this island," he said in the same slow tone, "I hunt more dangerous game."

Rainsford expressed his surprise. "Is there big game on this island?"

The general nodded. "The biggest."

"Really?"

"Oh, it isn't here naturally, of course. I have to stock the island."

"What have you imported, general?" Rainsford asked. "Tigers?"

The general smiled. "No," he said. "Hunting tigers ceased to interest me some years ago. I exhausted their possibilities, you see. No thrill left in tigers, no real danger. I live for danger, Mr. Rainsford."

The general took from his pocket a gold cigarette case and offered his guest a long black cigarette with a silver tip; it was perfumed and gave off a smell like incense.

"We will have some capital hunting, you and I," said the general. "I shall be most glad to have your society."

"But what game——" began Rainsford.

"I'll tell you," said the general. "You will be amused, I know. I think I may say, in all modesty, that I have done a rare thing. I have invented a new sensation. May I pour you another glass of port, Mr. Rainsford?"

"Thank you, general."

The general filled both glasses, and said: "God makes some men poets. Some He makes kings, some beggars. Me He made a hunter. My hand was made for the trigger, my father said. He was a very rich man with a quarter of a million acres in the Crimea, and he was an ardent sportsman. When I was only five years old he gave me a little gun, specially made in Moscow for me, to shoot sparrows with. When I shot some of his prize turkeys with it, he did not punish me; he complimented me on my marksmanship. I killed my first bear in the Caucasus when I was ten. My whole life has been one prolonged hunt. I went into the army—it was expected of noblemen's sons—and for a time commanded a division of Cossack cavalry, but my real interest was always the hunt. I have hunted every kind of game in every land. It would be impossible for me to tell you how many animals I have killed."

The general puffed at his cigarette.

"After the debacle[7] in Russia I left the country, for it was imprudent for an officer of the Czar to stay there. Many noble Russians lost everything. I, luckily, had invested heavily in

---

7. **debacle** (dĭ-bä′kəl): collapse; here, referring to the overthrow of the empire of the czars in 1917.

American securities, so I shall never have to open a tearoom in Monte Carlo or drive a taxi in Paris. Naturally, I continued to hunt — grizzlies in your Rockies, crocodiles in the Ganges, rhinoceroses in East Africa. It was in Africa that the Cape buffalo hit me and laid me up for six months. As soon as I recovered I started for the Amazon to hunt jaguars, for I had heard they were unusually cunning. They weren't." The Cossack sighed. "They were no match at all for a hunter with his wits about him, and a high-powered rifle. I was bitterly disappointed. I was lying in my tent with a splitting headache one night when a terrible thought pushed its way into my mind. Hunting was beginning to bore me! And hunting, remember, had been my life. I have heard that in America businessmen often go to pieces when they give up the business that has been their life."

"Yes, that's so," said Rainsford.

The general smiled. "I had no wish to go to pieces," he said. "I must do something. Now, mine is an analytical mind, Mr. Rainsford. Doubtless that is why I enjoy the problems of the chase."

"No doubt, General Zaroff."

"So," continued the general, "I asked myself why the hunt no longer fascinated me. You are much younger than I am, Mr. Rainsford, and have not hunted as much, but you perhaps can guess the answer."

"What was it?"

"Simply this: hunting had ceased to be what you call 'a sporting proposition.' It had become too easy. I always got my quarry. Always. There is no greater bore than perfection."

The general lit a fresh cigarette.

"No animal had a chance with me any more. That is no boast; it is a mathematical certainty. The animal had nothing but his legs and his instinct. Instinct is no match for reason. When I thought of this it was a tragic moment for me, I can tell you."

Rainsford leaned across the table, absorbed in what his host was saying.

"It came to me as an inspiration what I must do," the general went on.

"And that was?"

The general smiled the quiet smile of one who has faced an obstacle and surmounted it with success. "I had to invent a new animal to hunt," he said.

"A new animal? You're joking."

"Not at all," said the general. "I never joke about hunting. I needed a new animal. I found one. So I bought this island, built this house, and here I do my hunting. The island is perfect for my purposes — there are jungles with a maze of trails in them, hills, swamps — "

"But the animal, General Zaroff?"

"Oh," said the general, "it supplies me with the most exciting hunting in the world. No other hunting compares with it for an instant. Every day I hunt, and I never grow bored now, for I have a quarry with which I can match my wits."

Rainsford's bewilderment showed in his face.

"I wanted the ideal animal to hunt," explained the general. "So, I said: 'What are the attributes of an ideal quarry?' And the answer was, of course: 'It must have courage, cunning, and, above all, it must be able to reason.' "

"But no animal can reason," objected Rainsford.

"My dear fellow," said the general, "there is one that can."

"But you can't mean — " gasped Rainsford.

"And why not?"

"I can't believe you are serious, General Zaroff. This is a grisly joke."

"Why should I not be serious? I am speaking of hunting."

"Hunting? General Zaroff, what you speak of is murder."

The general laughed with entire good nature. He regarded Rainsford quizzically. "I refuse to believe that so modern and civilized a young man as you seem to be harbors romantic ideas about the value of human life. Surely your experiences in the war——"

"Did not make me condone cold-blooded murder," finished Rainsford stiffly.

Laughter shook the general. "How extraordinarily droll you are!" he said. "One does not expect nowadays to find a young man of the educated class, even in America, with such a naive, and, if I may say so, mid-Victorian point of view. It's like finding a snuffbox in a limousine. Ah, well, doubtless you had Puritan ancestors. So many Americans appear to have had. I'll wager you'll forget your notions when you go hunting with me. You've a genuine new thrill in store for you, Mr. Rainsford."

"Thank you, I'm a hunter, not a murderer."

"Dear me," said the general, quite unruffled. "Again that unpleasant word. But I think I can show you that your scruples are quite ill-founded."

"Yes?"

"Life is for the strong, to be lived by the strong, and, if need be, taken by the strong. The weak of the world were put here to give the strong pleasure. I am strong. Why should I not use my gift? If I wish to hunt, why should I not? I hunt the scum of the earth—sailors from tramp ships—lascars, blacks, Chinese, whites, mongrels—a thoroughbred horse or hound is worth more than a score of them."

"But they are men," said Rainsford hotly.

"Precisely," said the general. "That is why I use them. It gives me pleasure. They can reason, after a fashion. So they are dangerous."

"But where do you get them?"

The general's left eyelid fluttered down in a wink. "This island is called Ship-Trap," he answered. "Sometimes an angry god of the high seas sends them to me. Sometimes, when Providence is not so kind, I help Providence a bit. Come to the window with me."

Rainsford went to the window and looked out toward the sea.

"Watch! Out there!" exclaimed the general, pointing into the night. Rainsford's eyes saw only blackness, and then, as the general pressed a button, far out to sea Rainsford saw the flash of lights.

The general chuckled. "They indicate a channel," he said, "where there's none: giant rocks with razor edges crouch like a sea monster with wide-open jaws. They can crush a ship as easily as I crush this nut." He dropped a walnut on the hardwood floor and brought his heel grinding down on it. "Oh, yes," he said, casually, as if in answer to a question, "I have electricity. We try to be civilized here."

"Civilized? And you shoot down men?"

A trace of anger was in the general's black eyes, but it was there for but a second, and he said, in his most pleasant manner: "Dear me, what a righteous young man you are! I assure you I do not do the thing you suggest. That would be barbarous. I treat these visitors with every consideration. They get plenty of good food and exercise. They get into splendid physical condition. You shall see for yourself tomorrow."

"What do you mean?"

"We'll visit my training school," smiled the general. "It's in the cellar. I have about a dozen pupils down there now. They're from the Spanish bark *San Lucar* that had the bad luck to go on the rocks out there. A very inferior lot, I regret to say. Poor specimens and more accustomed to the deck than to the jungle."

He raised his hand, and Ivan, who served as waiter, brought thick Turkish coffee. Rainsford, with an effort, held his tongue in check.

"It's a game, you see," pursued the general blandly. "I suggest to one of them that we go hunting. I give him a supply of food and an excellent hunting knife. I give him three hours' start. I am to follow, armed only with a pistol of the smallest caliber and range. If my quarry eludes me for three whole days, he wins the game. If I find him" — the general smiled — "he loses."

"Suppose he refuses to be hunted?"

"Oh," said the general, "I give him his option, of course. He need not play that game if he doesn't wish to. If he does not wish to hunt, I turn him over to Ivan. Ivan once had the honor of serving as official knouter[8] to the Great White Czar, and he has his own ideas of sport. Invariably, Mr. Rainsford, invariably they choose the hunt."

"And if they win?"

The smile on the general's face widened. "To date I have not lost," he said.

Then he added, hastily: "I don't wish you to think me a braggart, Mr. Rainsford. Many of them afford only the most elementary sort of problem. Occasionally I strike a tartar. One almost did win. I eventually had to use the dogs."

"The dogs?"

"This way, please. I'll show you."

The general steered Rainsford to a window. The lights from the windows sent a flickering illumination that made grotesque patterns on the courtyard below, and Rainsford could see moving about there a dozen or so huge black shapes; as they turned toward him, their eyes glittered greenly.

"A rather good lot, I think," observed the general. "They are let out at seven every night. If anyone should try to get into my house — or out of it — something extremely

---

8. **knouter** (nout'ər): A knout is a leather whip that was used in Russia to punish criminals.

regrettable would occur to him." He hummed a snatch of song from the Folies Bergère.

"And now," said the general, "I want to show you my new collection of heads. Will you come with me to the library?"

"I hope," said Rainsford, "that you will excuse me tonight, General Zaroff. I'm really not feeling at all well."

"Ah, indeed?" the general inquired solicitously. "Well, I suppose that's only natural, after your long swim. You need a good, restful night's sleep. Tomorrow you'll feel like a new man, I'll wager. Then we'll hunt, eh? I've one rather promising prospect——"

Rainsford was hurrying from the room.

"Sorry you can't go with me tonight," called the general. "I expect rather fair sport— a big, strong fellow. He looks resourceful— Well, good night, Mr. Rainsford; I hope you have a good night's rest."

The bed was good, and the pajamas of the softest silk, and he was tired in every fiber of his being, but nevertheless Rainsford could not quiet his brain with the opiate of sleep. He lay, eyes wide open. Once he thought he heard stealthy steps in the corridor outside his room. He sought to throw open the door; it would not open. He went to the window and looked out. His room was high up in one of the towers. The lights of the château were out now, and it was dark and silent, but there was a fragment of sallow moon, and by its wan light he could see, dimly, the courtyard; there, weaving in and out in the pattern of shadow, were black, noiseless forms; the hounds heard him at the window and looked up, expectantly, with their green eyes. Rainsford went back to the bed and lay down. By many methods he tried to put himself to sleep. He had achieved a doze when, just as morning began to come, he heard, far off in the jungle, the faint report of a pistol.

General Zaroff did not appear until luncheon. He was dressed faultlessly in the tweeds of a country squire. He was solicitous about the state of Rainsford's health.

"As for me," sighed the general, "I do not feel so well. I am worried, Mr. Rainsford. Last night I detected traces of my old complaint."

To Rainsford's questioning glance the general said: "Ennui. Boredom."

Then, taking a second helping of crêpes suzette, the general explained: "The hunting was not good last night. The fellow lost his head. He made a straight trail that offered no problems at all. That's the trouble with these sailors; they have dull brains to begin with, and they do not know how to get about in the woods. They do excessively stupid and obvious things. It's most annoying. Will you have another glass of Chablis, Mr. Rainsford?"

"General," said Rainsford firmly, "I wish to leave this island at once."

The general raised his thickets of eyebrows; he seemed hurt. "But, my dear fellow," the general protested, "you've only just come. You've had no hunting——"

"I wish to go today," said Rainsford. He saw the dead black eyes of the general on him, studying him. General Zaroff's face suddenly brightened.

He filled Rainsford's glass with venerable Chablis from a dusty bottle.

"Tonight," said the general, "we will hunt —you and I."

Rainsford shook his head. "No, general," he said. "I will not hunt."

The general shrugged his shoulders and delicately ate a hothouse grape. "As you wish, my friend," he said. "The choice rests entirely with you. But may I not venture to suggest that you will find my idea of sport more diverting than Ivan's?"

He nodded toward the corner to where the giant stood, scowling, his thick arms crossed on his hogshead of chest.

"You don't mean——" cried Rainsford.

"My dear fellow," said the general, "have I not told you I always mean what I say about hunting? This is really an inspiration. I drink to a foeman worthy of my steel—at last."

The general raised his glass, but Rainsford sat staring at him.

"You'll find this game worth playing," the general said enthusiastically. "Your brain against mine. Your woodcraft against mine. Your strength and stamina against mine. Outdoor chess! And the stake is not without value, eh?"

"And if I win——" began Rainsford huskily.

"I'll cheerfully acknowledge myself defeated if I do not find you by midnight of the third day," said General Zaroff. "My sloop will place you on the mainland near a town."

The general read what Rainsford was thinking.

"Oh, you can trust me," said the Cossack. "I will give you my word as a gentleman and a sportsman. Of course you, in turn, must agree to say nothing of your visit here."

"I'll agree to nothing of the kind," said Rainsford.

"Oh," said the general, "in that case—— But why discuss that now? Three days hence we can discuss it over a bottle of Veuve Cliquot, unless——"

The general sipped his wine.

Then a businesslike air animated him. "Ivan," he said to Rainsford, "will supply you with hunting clothes, food, a knife. I suggest you wear moccasins; they leave a poorer trail. I suggest too that you avoid a big swamp in the southeast corner of the island. We call it Death Swamp. There's quicksand there. One foolish fellow tried it. The deplorable part of it was that Lazarus followed him. You can imagine my feelings, Mr. Rainsford. I loved Lazarus; he was the finest hound in my pack. Well, I must beg you to excuse me now. I always take a siesta after lunch. You'll hardly have time for a nap, I fear. You'll want to start, no doubt. I shall not follow till dusk. Hunting at night is so much more exciting than by day, don't you think? Au revoir,[9] Mr. Rainsford, au revoir."

General Zaroff, with a deep, courtly bow, strolled from the room.

From another door came Ivan. Under one arm he carried khaki hunting clothes, a haversack of food, a leather sheath containing a long-bladed hunting knife; his right hand rested on a cocked revolver thrust in the crimson sash about his waist. . . .

Rainsford had fought his way through the bush for two hours. "I must keep my nerve. I must keep my nerve," he said through tight teeth.

He had not been entirely clearheaded when the château gates snapped shut behind him. His whole idea at first was to put distance between himself and General Zaroff, and, to this end, he had plunged along, spurred on by the sharp rowels of something very like panic. Now he had got a grip on himself, had stopped, and was taking stock of himself and the situation.

He saw that straight flight was futile; inevitably it would bring him face to face with the sea. He was in a picture with a frame of water, and his operations, clearly, must take place within that frame.

"I'll give him a trail to follow," muttered Rainsford, and he struck off from the rude paths he had been following into the trackless wilderness. He executed a series of intricate loops; he doubled on his trail again and again, recalling all the lore of the fox hunt, and all the dodges of the fox. Night found him leg-

9. **Au revoir** (ō rə-vwàr′): French for "until we meet again."

weary, with hands and face lashed by the branches, on a thickly wooded ridge. He knew it would be insane to blunder on through the dark, even if he had the strength. His need for rest was imperative and he thought: "I have played the fox, now I must play the cat of the fable." A big tree with a thick trunk and outspread branches was nearby, and, taking care to leave not the slightest mark, he climbed up into the crotch, and stretching out on one of the broad limbs, after a fashion, rested. Rest brought him new confidence and almost a feeling of security. Even so zealous a hunter as General Zaroff could not trace him there, he told himself; only the devil himself could follow that complicated trail through the jungle after dark. But, perhaps, the general was a devil—

An apprehensive night crawled slowly by like a wounded snake, and sleep did not visit Rainsford, although the silence of a dead world was on the jungle. Toward morning when a dingy gray was varnishing the sky, the cry of some startled bird focused Rainsford's attention in that direction. Something was coming through the bush, coming slowly, carefully, coming by the same winding way Rainsford had come. He flattened himself down on the limb, and through a screen of leaves almost as thick as tapestry, he watched. The thing that was approaching was a man.

It was General Zaroff. He made his way along with his eyes fixed in utmost concentration on the ground before him. He paused, almost beneath the tree, dropped to his knees and studied the ground. Rainsford's impulse was to hurl himself down like a panther, but he saw that the general's right hand held something metallic—a small automatic pistol.

The hunter shook his head several times, as if he were puzzled. Then he straightened up and took from his case one of his black cigarettes; its pungent incenselike smoke floated up to Rainsford's nostrils.

Rainsford held his breath. The general's eyes had left the ground and were traveling inch by inch up the tree. Rainsford froze there, every muscle tensed for a spring. But the sharp eyes of the hunter stopped before they reached the limb where Rainsford lay; a smile spread over his brown face. Very deliberately he blew a smoke ring into the air; then he turned his back on the tree and walked carelessly away, back along the trail he had come. The swish of the underbrush against his hunting boots grew fainter and fainter.

The pent-up air burst hotly from Rainsford's lungs. His first thought made him feel sick and numb. The general could follow a trail through the woods at night; he could follow an extremely difficult trail; he must have uncanny powers; only by the merest chance had the Cossack failed to see his quarry.

Rainsford's second thought was even more terrible. It sent a shudder of cold horror through his whole being. Why had the general smiled? Why had he turned back?

Rainsford did not want to believe what his reason told him was true, but the truth was as evident as the sun that had by now pushed through the morning mists. The general was playing with him! The general was saving him for another day's sport! The Cossack was the cat; he was the mouse. Then it was that Rainsford knew the full meaning of terror.

"I will not lose my nerve. I will not."

He slid down from the tree, and struck off again into the woods. His face was set and he forced the machinery of his mind to function. Three hundred yards from his hiding place he stopped where a huge dead tree leaned precariously on a smaller, living one. Throwing off his sack of food, Rainsford took his knife from its sheath and began to work with all his energy.

The job was finished at last, and he threw himself down behind a fallen log a hundred feet away. He did not have to wait long. The cat was coming again to play with the mouse.

Following the trail with the sureness of a bloodhound came General Zaroff. Nothing escaped those searching black eyes, no crushed blade of grass, no bent twig, no mark, no matter how faint, in the moss. So intent was the Cossack on his stalking that he was upon the thing Rainsford had made before he saw it. His foot touched the protruding bough that was the trigger. Even as he touched it, the general sensed his danger and leaped back with the agility of an ape. But he was not quite quick enough; the dead tree, delicately adjusted to rest on the cut living one, crashed down and struck the general a glancing blow on the shoulder as it fell; but for his alertness, he must have been smashed beneath it. He staggered, but he did not fall; nor did he drop his revolver. He stood there, rubbing his injured shoulder, and Rainsford, with fear again gripping his heart, heard the general's mocking laugh ring through the jungle.

"Rainsford," called the general, "if you are within sound of my voice, as I suppose you are, let me congratulate you. Not many men know how to make a Malay man-catcher. Luckily, for me, I too have hunted in Malacca. You are proving interesting, Mr. Rainsford. I am going now to have my wound dressed; it's only a slight one. But I shall be back. I shall be back."

When the general, nursing his bruised shoulder, had gone, Rainsford took up his flight again. It was flight now, a desperate, hopeless flight, that carried him on for some hours. Dusk came, then darkness, and still he pressed on. The ground grew softer under his moccasins; the vegetation grew ranker, denser; insects bit him savagely. Then, as he stepped forward, his foot sank into the ooze. He tried to wrench it back, but the muck sucked viciously at his foot as if it were a giant leech. With a violent effort, he tore his foot loose. He knew where he was now. Death Swamp and its quicksand.

His hands were tight closed as if his nerve were something tangible that someone in the darkness was trying to tear from his grip. The softness of the earth had given him an idea. He stepped back from the quicksand a dozen feet or so and, like some huge prehistoric beaver, he began to dig.

Rainsford had dug himself in in France when a second's delay meant death. That had been a placid pastime compared to his digging now. The pit grew deeper; when it was above his shoulders, he climbed out and from some hard saplings cut stakes and sharpened them to a fine point. These stakes he planted in the bottom of the pit with the points sticking up. With flying fingers he wove a rough carpet of weeds and branches and with it he covered the mouth of the pit. Then, wet with sweat and aching with tiredness, he crouched behind the stump of a lightning-charred tree.

He knew his pursuer was coming; he heard the padding sound of feet on the soft earth, and the night breeze brought him the perfume of the general's cigarette. It seemed to Rainsford that the general was coming with unusual swiftness; he was not feeling his way along, foot by foot. Rainsford, crouching there, could not see the general, nor could he see the pit. He lived a year in a minute. Then

he felt an impulse to cry aloud with joy, for he heard the sharp crackle of the breaking branches as the cover of the pit gave way; he heard the sharp scream of pain as the pointed stakes found their mark. He leaped up from his place of concealment. Then he cowered back. Three feet from the pit a man was standing, with an electric torch in his hand.

"You've done well, Rainsford," the voice of the general called. "Your Burmese tiger pit has claimed one of my best dogs. Again you score. I think, Mr. Rainsford, I'll see what you can do against my whole pack. I'm going home for a rest now. Thank you for a most amusing evening."

At daybreak Rainsford, lying near the swamp, was awakened by a sound that made him know that he had new things to learn about fear. It was a distant sound, faint and wavering, but he knew it. It was the baying of a pack of hounds.

Rainsford knew he could do one of two things. He could stay where he was and wait. That was suicide. He could flee. That was postponing the inevitable. For a moment he stood there, thinking. An idea that held a wild chance came to him, and tightening his belt, he headed away from the swamp.

The baying of the hounds drew nearer, then still nearer, nearer, ever nearer. On a ridge Rainsford climbed a tree. Down a watercourse, not a quarter of a mile away, he could see the bush moving. Straining his eyes, he saw the lean figure of General Zaroff; just ahead of him Rainsford made out another figure whose wide shoulders surged through the tall jungle weeds; it was the giant Ivan, and he seemed pulled forward by some unseen force, Rainsford knew that Ivan must be holding the pack in leash.

They would be on him any minute now. His mind worked frantically. He thought of a native trick he had learned in Uganda. He slid down the tree. He caught hold of a springy young sapling and to it he fastened his hunting knife, with the blade pointing down the trail; with a bit of wild grapevine he tied back the sapling. Then he ran for his life. The hounds raised their voices as they hit the fresh scent. Rainsford knew now how an animal at bay feels.

He had to stop to get his breath. The baying of the hounds stopped abruptly, and Rainsford's heart stopped too. They must have reached the knife.

He shinnied excitedly up a tree and looked back. His pursuers had stopped. But the hope that was in Rainsford's brain when he climbed died, for he saw in the shallow valley that General Zaroff was still on his feet. But Ivan was not. The knife, driven by the recoil of the springing tree, had not wholly failed.

Rainsford had hardly tumbled to the ground when the pack took up the cry again.

"Nerve, nerve, nerve!" he panted, as he dashed along. A blue gap showed between the trees dead ahead. Ever nearer drew the hounds. Rainsford forced himself on toward that gap. He reached it. It was the shore of the sea. Across a cove he could see the gloomy gray stone of the château. Twenty feet below him the sea rumbled and hissed. Rainsford hesitated. He heard the hounds. Then he leaped far out into the sea. . . .

When the general and his pack reached the place by the sea, the Cossack stopped. For some minutes he stood regarding the blue-green expanse of water. He shrugged his shoulders. Then he sat down, took a drink of brandy from a silver flask, lit a perfumed cigarette, and hummed a bit from *Madame Butterfly*.[10]

General Zaroff had an exceedingly good dinner in his great paneled dining hall that evening. With it he had a bottle of Pol Roger and half a bottle of Chambertin. Two slight annoyances kept him from perfect enjoyment. One was the thought that it would be difficult to replace Ivan; the other was that his quarry escaped him; of course the American hadn't played the game—so thought the general as he tasted his after-dinner liqueur. In his library he read, to soothe himself, from the works of Marcus Aurelius.[11] At ten he went up to his bedroom. He was deliciously tired, he said to himself, as he locked himself in. There was a little moonlight, so, before turning on his light, he went to the window and looked down at the courtyard. He could see the great hounds, and he called: "Better luck another time," to them. Then he switched on the light.

A man, who had been hiding in the curtains of the bed, was standing there.

"Rainsford!" screamed the general. "How did you get here?"

"Swam," said Rainsford. "I found it quicker than walking through the jungle."

The general sucked in his breath and smiled. "I congratulate you," he said. "You have won the game."

Rainsford did not smile. "I am still a beast at bay," he said, in a low, hoarse voice. "Get ready, General Zaroff."

The general made one of his deepest bows. "I see," he said. "Splendid! One of us is to furnish a repast for the hounds. The other will sleep in this very excellent bed. On guard, Rainsford. . . ."

He had never slept in a better bed, Rainsford decided.

---

10. *Madame Butterfly:* an opera by Giacomo Puccini.

11. **Marcus Aurelius:** Roman emperor (161–180), whose book, *Meditations*, is considered a classic of philosophy.

FOR STUDY AND DISCUSSION

1. "The Most Dangerous Game" tells of a struggle between Sanger Rainsford and General Zaroff. Who are these two men, and what have they in common? Why would their struggle be less interesting if Rainsford were a doctor, for example, rather than a hunter?

2. Two parts of the story provide clues for the struggle that is to come: the discussion on ship between Rainsford and Whitney; and Rainsford's observations—what he sees and hears—as he swims to the island and as he walks to Zaroff's château. How do these episodes hint at the coming struggle?

3. The discussions about hunting between Rainsford and Zaroff are important for two reasons: (a) they provide information about the two men and about the coming struggle; and (b) they provide a contrast between them. What information is provided? What is the contrast?

4. Tell about the hunt itself. What incidents make you anxious for Rainsford's safety? What incidents show that he is a worthy foe?

5. Near the end of the story, Rainsford is forced to take a desperate chance. What is it? Why do you think the author suddenly leaves Rainsford at this point and begins to tell the story through Zaroff's eyes?

6. The conversation between Rainsford and Whitney at the opening of the story reveals Rainsford's attitude toward hunting. Do you think his attitude changes in the course of the story? Give evidence to support your answer.

CONFLICT

Conflict is an important element in stories, novels, and plays. A conflict is a struggle between opposing forces or points of view. A conflict may take place between two individ-uals, between an individual and an animal, or between an individual and some natural force. Conflicts in which individuals struggle against something outside themselves are known as *external conflicts*. A conflict that takes place within an individual is called *internal conflict*.

The most obvious conflict in "The Most Dangerous Game" is between Rainsford and Zaroff. Are there other external conflicts? Is there also an internal conflict?

SUSPENSE AND FORESHADOWING

Skillful writers can build interest in a story through *suspense*, the quality that makes readers eager to know what happens next. Notice how the author creates suspense about Rainsford's fate in this episode of the story:

Rainsford held his breath. The general's eyes had left the ground and were traveling inch by inch up the tree. Rainsford froze there, every muscle tensed for a spring. But the sharp eyes of the hunter stopped before they reached the limb where Rainsford lay; a smile spread over his brown face. Very deliberately he blew a smoke ring into the air; then he turned his back on the tree and walked carelessly away, back along the trail he had come. The swish of the underbrush against his hunting boots grew fainter and fainter.

To build up suspense, an author often plants clues early in the story that hint at what will come later. The planting of such clues is called *foreshadowing*. How is the major action of the story foreshadowed in the conversation between Rainsford and Whitney? In Rainsford's arrival at the island? How does this foreshadowing help create suspense?

LANGUAGE AND VOCABULARY

Finding Meaning from Context

Sometimes you may be able to derive the definition of an unfamiliar word (or a familiar word used in an unfamiliar way) by using *context clues*—clues supplied by other words within the sentence or paragraph:

> . . . Rainsford noted, the table *appointments* were of the finest—the linen, the crystal, the silver, the china.

The word *appointments,* meaning "equipment" or "furnishings" is made clear by the context.

Use context clues to determine the meaning of the italicized words in these sentences from the story. Check your answers in the glossary at the back of this book or in a dictionary.

> Whenever he looked up from his plate he found the general studying him, *appraising* him narrowly.

> His hands were tight closed as if his nerve were something *tangible* that someone in the darkness was trying to tear from his grip.

> "One of us is to furnish a *repast* for the hounds."

FOR COMPOSITION

Writing a Paragraph with Conflict and Suspense

Most of the suspense in Connell's story is related to the external conflict between Rainsford and Zaroff. The reader wants to know whether Rainsford will survive the ordeal.

Write a paragraph that could be part of a longer story. Introduce a conflict and create suspense about the outcome. You may write about an external conflict—between two persons, between a person and an animal, or between a person and nature—or an internal conflict—a struggle between opposing parts of a person's inner nature.

ABOUT THE AUTHOR

Richard Connell (1893–1949) began his writing career at an early age. He has said, "My first writing was done for the newspaper my father edited in Poughkeepsie, New York. I covered baseball games. I was ten years old and got ten cents a game."

Connell attended Harvard College, where he was an editor on the *Daily Crimson* and the *Lampoon,* Harvard's humor magazine. After college, he worked in New York City, first for a newspaper and then for an advertising firm. In 1919 he decided to make his living as a free-lance writer. He once estimated that he had sold about three hundred short stories to American and English magazines. He also wrote several novels and many screenplays. "The Most Dangerous Game" is his best-known story. It has appeared in numerous anthologies and has been adapted for the movies and television.

The Lady, or the Tiger?

Frank R. Stockton

In the very olden time, there lived a semibarbaric king who was a man of exuberant fancy and of an authority so irresistible that, at his will, he turned his varied fancies into facts. He was greatly given to self-communing; and when he and himself agreed upon anything, the thing was done. When everything moved smoothly, his nature was bland and genial; but whenever there was a little hitch, he was blander and more genial still, for nothing pleased him so much as to make the crooked straight, and crush down uneven places.

Among his borrowed notions was that of the public arena, in which, by exhibitions of manly and beastly valor, the minds of his subjects were refined and cultured.

But even here the exuberant and barbaric fancy asserted itself. This vast amphitheater,[1] with its encircling galleries, its mysterious vault, and its unseen passages, was an agent of poetic justice, in which crime was punished, or virtue rewarded, by the decrees of an impartial and incorruptible chance.

When a subject was accused of a crime of sufficient importance to interest the king, public notice was given that on an appointed day the fate of the accused person would be decided in the king's arena.

When all the people had assembled in the galleries, and the king, surrounded by his court, sat high up on his throne of royal state on one side of the arena, he gave a signal, a door beneath him opened, and the accused subject stepped out into the amphitheater. Directly opposite him, on the other side of the enclosed space, were two doors, exactly alike and side by side. It was the duty and the privilege of the person on trial to walk directly to these doors and open one of them. He could open either door he pleased. He was subject to no guidance or influence but that of the aforementioned impartial and incorruptible chance. If he opened the one, there came out of it a hungry tiger, the fiercest and most cruel that could be procured, which immediately sprang upon him and tore him to pieces, as a punishment for his guilt. The moment that the case of the criminal was thus decided, doleful iron bells were clanged, great wails went up from the hired mourners posted on the outer rim of the arena, and the vast audience, with bowed heads and downcast hearts, wended slowly their homeward way, mourning greatly that one so young and fair, or so old and respected, should have merited so dire a fate.

But if the accused person opened the other door, there came forth from it a lady, the most suitable to his years and station that His Majesty could select among his fair subjects; and to this lady he was immediately married, as a reward of his innocence. It mattered not that he might already possess a wife and family, or that his affections might be engaged upon an object of his own selection. The king allowed no such arrangements to interfere with his great scheme of punishment and

---

1. **amphitheater** (ăm'fə-thē'ə-tər): an open arena with rising tiers of seats.

reward. The exercises, as in the other instance, took place immediately, and in the arena. Another door opened beneath the king, and a priest, followed by a band of choristers, and dancing maidens blowing joyous airs on golden horns, advanced to where the pair stood, side by side; and the wedding was promptly and cheerily solemnized. Then the gay brass bells rang forth their merry peals, and the people shouted glad hurrahs, and the innocent man, preceded by children strewing flowers on his path, led his bride to his home.

This was the king's semibarbaric method of administering justice. Its perfect fairness is obvious. The criminal could not know out of which door would come the lady. He opened either he pleased, without having the slightest idea whether, in the next instant, he was to be devoured or married. On some occasions the tiger came out of one door, and on some, out of the other. The decisions were not only fair, they were positively decisive. The accused person was instantly punished if he found himself guilty; and, if innocent, he was rewarded on the spot, whether he liked it or not. There was no escape from the judgments of the king's arena.

The institution was a very popular one. When the people gathered together on one of the great trial days, they never knew whether they were to witness a bloody slaughter or a hilarious wedding. This element of uncertainty lent an interest to the occasion which it could not otherwise have attained. Thus, the masses were entertained and pleased, and the thinking part of the community could bring no charge of unfairness against this plan; for did not the accused person have the whole matter in his own hands?

This semibarbaric king had a daughter as blooming as his most florid fancies, and with a soul as fervent and imperious as his own. As is usual in such cases, she was the apple of his eye, and was loved by him above all humanity. Among his courtiers was a young man of that fineness of blood and lowness of station common to the heroes of romance who love royal maidens. This royal maiden was well satisfied with her lover, for he was handsome and brave to a degree unsurpassed in all this kingdom; and she loved him with an ardor that had enough of barbarism in it to make it exceedingly warm and strong. This love affair moved on happily for many months, until one day the king happened to discover its existence. He did not hesitate nor waver in regard to his duty. The youth was immediately cast into prison, and a day was appointed for his trial in the king's arena. This, of course, was an especially important occasion; and His Majesty, as well as all the people, was greatly interested in the workings and development of this trial. Never before had such a case occurred — never before had a subject dared to love the daughter of a king. In after years such things became commonplace enough; but then they were, in no slight degree, novel and startling.

The tiger cages of the kingdom were searched for the most savage and relentless beasts, from which the fiercest monster might be selected for the arena; and the ranks of maiden youth and beauty throughout the land were carefully surveyed by competent judges, in order that the young man might have a fitting bride in case fate did not determine for him a different destiny. Of course, everybody knew that the deed with which the accused was charged had been done. He had loved the princess, and neither he, she, nor anyone else thought of denying the fact. But the king would not think of allowing any fact of this kind to interfere with the workings of the court of judgment, in which he took such great delight and satisfaction. No matter how the affair turned out, the youth would be disposed of; and the king would take pleasure in watching the course of events, which would determine whether or not the young man had done wrong in allowing himself to love the princess.

The appointed day arrived. From far and near the people gathered, and thronged the great galleries of the arena; and crowds, unable to gain admittance, massed themselves against its outside walls. The king and his court were in their places, opposite the twin doors—those fateful portals, so terrible in their similarity.

All was ready. The signal was given. A door beneath the royal party opened, and the lover of the princess walked into the arena. Tall, beautiful, fair, his appearance was greeted with a low hum of admiration and anxiety. Half the audience had not known so grand a youth had lived among them. No wonder the princess loved him! What a terrible thing for him to be there!

As the youth advanced into the arena, he turned, as the custom was, to bow to the king. But he did not think at all of that royal personage; his eyes were fixed upon the princess, who sat to the right of her father. Had it not been for the barbarism in her nature, it is probable that lady would not have been there. But her intense and fervid soul would not allow her to be absent on an occasion in which she was so terribly interested. From the moment that the decree had gone forth that her lover should decide his fate in the king's arena, she had thought of nothing, night or day, but this great event and the various subjects connected with it. Possessed of more power, influence, and force of character than anyone who had ever before been interested in such a case, she had done what no other person had done—she had possessed herself of the secret of the doors. She knew in which of the two rooms that lay behind those doors stood the cage of the tiger, with its open front, and in which waited the lady. Through these thick doors, heavily curtained with skins on the inside, it was impossible that any noise or suggestion should come from within to the person who should approach to raise the latch of one of them. But gold, and the power of a woman's will, had brought the secret to the princess.

And not only did she know in which room stood the lady, ready to emerge, all blushing and radiant, should her door be opened, but she knew who the lady was. It was one of the fairest and loveliest of the damsels of the court who had been selected as the reward of the accused youth, should he be proved innocent of the crime of aspiring to one so far above him; and the princess hated her. Often had she seen, or imagined that she had seen, this fair creature throwing glances of admiration upon the person of her lover, and sometimes she thought these glances were perceived and even returned. Now and then she had seen them talking together. It was but for a moment or two, but much can be said in a brief space. It may have been on most unimportant topics, but how could she know that? The girl was lovely, but she had dared to raise her eyes to the loved one of the princess; and, with all the intensity of the savage blood transmitted to her through long lines of wholly barbaric ancestors, she hated the woman who blushed and trembled behind that silent door.

When her lover turned and looked at her, and his eye met hers as she sat there paler and whiter than anyone in the vast ocean of anxious faces about her, he saw, by that power of quick perception which is given to those whose souls are one, that she knew behind which door crouched the tiger, and behind which stood the lady. He had expected her to know it. He understood her nature, and his

soul was assured that she would never rest until she had made plain to herself this thing, hidden to all other lookers-on, even to the king. The only hope for the youth in which there was any element of certainty was based upon the success of the princess in discovering this mystery; and the moment he looked upon her, he saw she had succeeded.

Then it was that his quick and anxious glance asked the question: "Which?" It was as plain to her as if he shouted it from where he stood. There was not an instant to be lost. The question was asked in a flash; it must be answered in another.

Her right arm lay on the cushioned parapet before her. She raised her hand, and made a slight, quick movement toward the right. No one but her lover saw her. Every eye but his was fixed on the man in the arena.

He turned, and with a firm and rapid step he walked across the empty space. Every heart stopped beating, every breath was held, every eye was fixed immovably upon that man. Without the slightest hesitation, he went to the door on the right, and opened it.

Now, the point of the story is this: Did the tiger come out of that door, or did the lady?

The more we reflect upon this question, the harder it is to answer. It involves a study of the human heart which leads us through roundabout pathways of passion, out of which it is difficult to find our way. Think of it, fair reader, not as if the decision of the question depended upon yourself, but upon that hot-blooded, semibarbaric princess, her soul at a white heat beneath the combined fires of despair and jealousy. She had lost him, but who should have him?

How often, in her waking hours and in her

dreams, had she started in wild horror and covered her face with her hands as she thought of her lover opening the door on the other side of which waited the cruel fangs of the tiger!

But how much oftener had she seen him at the other door! How in her grievous reveries had she gnashed her teeth and torn her hair, when she saw his start of rapturous delight as he opened the door of the lady! How her soul had burned in agony when she had seen him rush to meet that woman, with her flushing cheek and sparkling eye of triumph; when she had seen him lead her forth, his whole frame kindled with the joy of recovered life; when she had heard the glad shouts from the multitude, and the wild ringing of the happy bells; when she had seen the priest, with his joyous followers, advance to the couple, and make them man and wife before her very eyes; and when she had seen them walk away together upon their path of flowers, followed by the tremendous shouts of the hilarious multitude, in which her one despairing shriek was lost and drowned!

Would it not be better for him to die at once, and go to wait for her in the blessed regions of semibarbaric futurity?

And yet, that awful tiger, those shrieks, that blood!

Her decision had been indicated in an instant, but it had been made after days and nights of anguished deliberation. She had known she would be asked, she had decided what she would answer, and, without the slightest hesitation, she had moved her hand to the right.

The question of her decision is one not to be lightly considered, and it is not for me to presume to set up myself as the one person able to answer it. And so I leave it with all of you: Which came out of the opened door—the lady, or the tiger?

FOR STUDY AND DISCUSSION

1. The author challenges you to guess the outcome of the story. From what you know of the princess, which do you think she would point to: the lady or the tiger? Give reasons to support your answer.

2. At one point you are told that the solution to the question lies in understanding the nature of the princess: "Think of it, fair reader, not as if the decision of the question depended upon yourself, but upon that hot-blooded, semibarbaric princess, . . ." Does the answer lie within the story or within the individual reader?

PLOT

Plot is the sequence of events or actions in a story. Plot includes the following: whatever the characters do; whatever they say; whatever they think; and whatever happens to them.

Often before the plot proper begins, a section of *exposition* is provided. The exposition is an introduction; it presents information that helps readers understand the situation of the story. In "The Lady, or the Tiger?" the exposition is given in the first eight paragraphs. What information is presented?

The action of a story generally evolves out of *conflict*. What external and internal conflicts are presented in "The Lady, or the Tiger?" Which do you consider the central conflict?

Complications are introduced that make it difficult to settle the conflict. What complications does Stockton introduce into his story? How do they add interest?

As the story becomes more complicated, it moves to a *climax*. A climax is the point of highest intensity in the story, the point that determines the outcome of the action. What is the climax of this story?

The final part of a story is its *resolution.* A resolution moves down from the high point of the climax and usually settles the conflict or conflicts. How does Stockton handle the resolution in this story?

The plots of many stories follow this pattern: exposition, conflict, complications, climax, resolution. If you have already read "The Most Dangerous Game," identify these elements in that story.

IRONY

There are several kinds of *irony.* All of them depend upon a contrast between appearance and reality. A common kind is *verbal irony.* Verbal irony is a way of saying or writing one thing and meaning the direct opposite. For example, imagine you are tramping through five feet of snow. The temperature is below freezing, and a twenty-mile-an-hour wind is scraping at your cheeks. You say to a friend, "What a lovely day!" By using verbal irony, you give emphasis to your real meaning: What a terrible day!

Writers often describe unpleasant characters or ideas ironically. By pretending to accept these characters or ideas at face value, writers force us to realize how bad they really are. Stockton calls the king's system "poetic justice," but he expects his readers to understand that his meaning is quite the opposite. In order to understand a writer's irony, we must first decide what the facts really are. If the way things seem to us is very different from the way the writer describes them, then the chances are that the writer is using verbal irony.

Explain why each of the following statements in "The Lady, or the Tiger?" is ironic. If the irony is not clear, reread each statement in its context in the selection.

[In] the public arena . . . the minds of his subjects were *refined and cultured.* (page 19)
This was the king's semibarbaric method of administering justice. *Its perfect fairness is obvious.* (page 20)

Find other ironic statements in the story. Point out the contrast between the apparent meaning and the intended meaning.

FOR COMPOSITION

Writing an Ending to the Story
Frank Stockton leaves it up to you, the reader, to decide what finally happens. Write your own version of the ending, telling what happens when the young man opens the door. To make your ending effective, you might want to show the princess' reaction as the door opens. Or, you might want to show the young man's reaction to what he finds.

ABOUT THE AUTHOR

Frank R. Stockton (1834–1902) was born in Philadelphia. His parents thought that he might become a doctor, but he became a wood engraver instead. By 1867 he began to devote more and more time to writing and less to engraving. First he contributed children's stories to the *Riverside Magazine for Young People.* Then he began to contribute many stories to adult magazines. Stockton's most famous story, "The Lady, or the Tiger?" appeared in 1882 in the *Century* magazine. It caused a great sensation. Debates were held all over the country to decide the ending.

Tom Edison's Shaggy Dog

Kurt Vonnegut

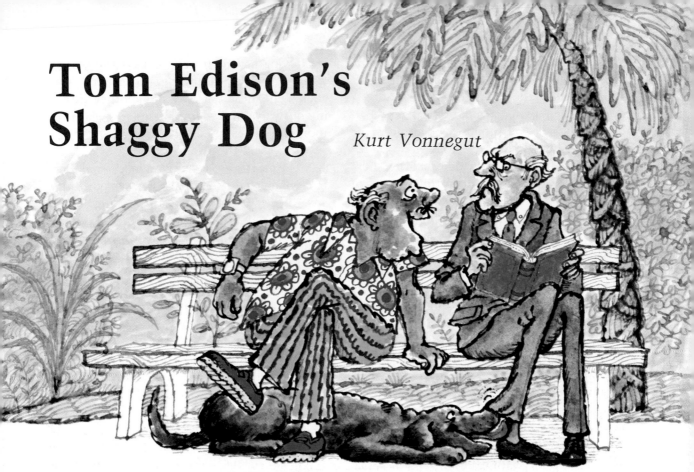

Two old men sat on a park bench one morning in the sunshine of Tampa, Florida—one trying doggedly to read a book he was plainly enjoying while the other, Harold K. Bullard, told him the story of his life in the full, round, head tones of a public address system. At their feet lay Bullard's Labrador retriever, who further tormented the aged listener by probing his ankles with a large, wet nose.

Bullard, who had been, before he retired, successful in many fields, enjoyed reviewing his important past. But he faced the problem that complicates the lives of cannibals—namely: that a single victim cannot be used over and over. Anyone who had passed the time of day with him and his dog refused to share a bench with them again.

So Bullard and his dog set out through the park each day in quest of new faces. They had had good luck this morning, for they had found this stranger right away, clearly a new arrival in Florida, still buttoned up tight in heavy serge, stiff collar and necktie, and with nothing better to do than read.

"Yes," said Bullard, rounding out the first hour of his lecture, "made and lost five fortunes in my time."

"So you said," said the stranger, whose name Bullard had neglected to ask. "Easy, boy. No, no, no, boy," he said to the dog, who was growing more aggressive toward his ankles.

"Oh? Already told you that, did I?" said Bullard.

"Twice."

"Two in real estate, one in scrap iron, and one in oil, and one in trucking."

"So you said."

"I did? Yes, guess I did. Two in real estate, one in scrap iron, one in oil, and one in trucking. Wouldn't take back a day of it."

"No, I suppose not," said the stranger. "Pardon me, but do you suppose you could move your dog somewhere else? He keeps——"

"Him?" said Bullard, heartily. "Friendliest dog in the world. Don't need to be afraid of him."

"I'm not afraid of him. It's just that he drives me crazy, sniffing at my ankles."

"Plastic," said Bullard, chuckling.

"What?"

"Plastic. Must be something plastic on your garters. By golly, I'll bet it's those little buttons. Sure as we're sitting here, those buttons must be plastic. That dog is nuts about plastic. Don't know why that is, but he'll sniff it out and find it if there's a speck around. Must be a deficiency in his diet, though, by gosh, he eats better than I do. Once he chewed up a whole plastic humidor. Can you beat it? *That's* the business I'd go into now, by glory, if the pill rollers hadn't told me to let up, to give the old ticker a rest."

"You could tie the dog to that tree over there," said the stranger.

"I get so darn' sore at all the youngsters these days!" said Bullard. "All of 'em mooning around about no frontiers any more. There never have been so many frontiers as there are today. You know what Horace Greeley[1] would say today?"

"His nose is wet," said the stranger, and he pulled his ankles away, but the dog humped forward in patient pursuit. "Stop it, boy!"

"His wet nose shows he's healthy," said Bullard. " 'Go plastic, young man!' That's what Greeley'd say. 'Go atom, young man!' "

---

1. **Horace Greeley** (1811–1872) an American journalist, founder of the New York *Tribune.* Many followed his advice, "Go West, young man, go West."

The dog had definitely located the plastic buttons on the stranger's garters and was cocking his head one way and another, thinking out ways of bringing his teeth to bear on those delicacies.

"Scat!" said the stranger.

" 'Go electronic, young man!' " said Bullard. "Don't talk to me about no opportunity any more. Opportunity's knocking down every door in the country, trying to get in. When I was young, a man had to go out and find opportunity and drag it home by the ears. Nowadays——"

"Sorry," said the stranger, evenly. He slammed his book shut, stood and jerked his ankle away from the dog. "I've got to be on my way. So good day, sir."

He stalked across the park, found another bench, sat down with a sigh and began to read. His respiration had just returned to normal, when he felt the wet sponge of the dog's nose on his ankles again.

"Oh—it's you!" said Bullard, sitting down beside him. "He was tracking you. He was on the scent of something, and I just let him have his head. What'd I tell you about plastic?" He looked about contentedly. "Don't blame you for moving on. It was stuffy back there. No shade to speak of and not a sign of a breeze."

"Would the dog go away if I bought him a humidor?" said the stranger.

"Pretty good joke, pretty good joke," said Bullard, amiably. Suddenly he clapped the stranger on his knee. "Sa-ay, you aren't in plastics, are you? Here I've been blowing off about plastics, and for all I know that's your line."

"My line?" said the stranger crisply, laying down his book. "Sorry—I've never had a line. I've been a drifter since the age of nine, since Edison set up his laboratory next to my home, and showed me the intelligence analyzer."

"Edison?" said Bullard. "Thomas Edison, the inventor?"

"If you want to call him that, go ahead," said the stranger.

"If I *want* to call him that?"—Bullard guffawed—"I guess I just will! Father of the light bulb and I don't know what all."

"If you want to think he invented the light bulb, go ahead. No harm in it." The stranger resumed his reading.

"Say, what is this?" said Bullard, suspiciously. "You pulling my leg? What's this about an intelligence analyzer? I never heard of that."

"Of course you haven't," said the stranger. "Mr. Edison and I promised to keep it a secret. I've never told anyone. Mr. Edison broke his promise and told Henry Ford,[2] but Ford made him promise not to tell anybody else—for the good of humanity."

Bullard was entranced. "Uh, this intelligence analyzer," he said, "it analyzed intelligence, did it?"

"It was an electric butter churn," said the stranger.

"Seriously now," Bullard coaxed.

"Maybe it *would* be better to talk it over with someone," said the stranger. "It's a terrible thing to keep bottled up inside me, year in and year out. But how can I be sure that it won't go any further?"

"My word as a gentleman," Bullard assured him.

"I don't suppose I could find a stronger guarantee than that, could I?" said the stranger, judiciously.

"There is no stronger guarantee," said Bullard, proudly. "Cross my heart and hope to die!"

"Very well." The stranger leaned back and closed his eyes, seeming to travel backward through time. He was silent for a full minute, during which Bullard watched with respect.

"It was back in the fall of eighteen seventy-nine," said the stranger at last, softly. "Back in the village of Menlo Park, New Jersey. I was a boy of nine. A young man we all thought was a wizard[3] had set up a laboratory next door to my home, and there were flashes and crashes inside, and all sorts of scary goings-on. The neighborhood children were warned to keep away, not to make any noise that would bother the wizard.

"I didn't get to know Edison right off, but his dog Sparky and I got to be steady pals. A dog a whole lot like yours, Sparky was, and we used to wrestle all over the neighborhood. Yes, sir, your dog is the image of Sparky."

"Is that so?" said Bullard, flattered.

"Gospel," replied the stranger. "Well, one day Sparky and I were wrestling around, and we wrestled right up to the door of Edison's laboratory. The next thing I knew, Sparky had pushed me in through the door, and bam! I was sitting on the laboratory floor, looking up at Mr. Edison himself."

"Bet he was sore," said Bullard, delighted.

"You can bet I was scared," said the stranger. "*I* thought I was face to face with Satan himself. Edison had wires hooked to his ears and running down to a little black box in his lap! I started to scoot, but he caught me by my collar and made me sit down.

" 'Boy,' said Edison, 'it's always darkest before the dawn. I want you to remember that.'

" 'Yes, sir,' I said,

" 'For over a year, my boy,' Edison said to

---

2. **Henry Ford** (1863–1947): American pioneer automobile manufacturer, who brought out an inexpensive, mass-produced car.

3. **wizard**: Edison was known as the Wizard of Menlo Park.

me, 'I've been trying to find a filament that will last in an incandescent lamp. Hair, string, splinters—nothing works. So while I was trying to think of something else to try, I started tinkering with another idea of mine, just letting off steam. I put this together,' he said, showing me the little black box. 'I thought maybe intelligence was a certain kind of electricity, so I made this intelligence analyzer here. It works! You're the first one to know about it, my boy. But I don't know why you shouldn't be. It will be your generation that will grow up in the glorious new era when people will be as easily graded as oranges.' "

"I don't believe it!" said Bullard.

"May I be struck by lightning this very instant!" said the stranger. "And it did work, too. Edison had tried out the analyzer on the men in his shop, without telling them what he was up to. The smarter a man was, by gosh, the farther the needle on the indicator in the little black box swung to the right. I let him try it on me, and the needle just lay where it was and trembled. But dumb as I was, then is when I made my one and only contribution to the world. As I say, I haven't lifted a finger since."

"Whadja do?" said Bullard, eagerly.

"I said, 'Mr. Edison, sir, let's try it on the dog.' And I wish you could have seen the show that dog put on when I said it! Old

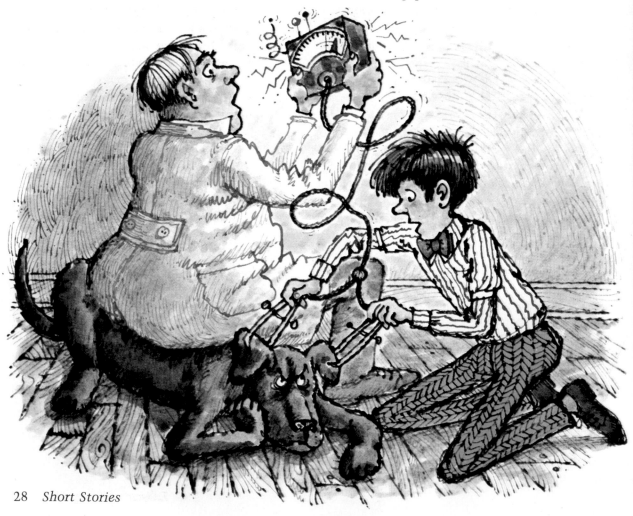

Sparky barked and howled and scratched to get out. When he saw we meant business, that he wasn't going to get out, he made a beeline right for the intelligence analyzer and knocked it out of Edison's hands. But we cornered him, and Edison held him down while I touched the wires to his ears. And would you believe it, that needle sailed clear across the dial, way past a little red pencil marker on the dial face!''

"The dog busted it," said Bullard.

" 'Mr. Edison, sir,' I said, 'what's the red mark mean?'

" 'My boy,' said Edison, 'it means that the instrument is broken, because that red mark is me.' "

"I'll say it was broken," said Bullard.

The stranger said gravely, "But it wasn't broken. No, sir. Edison checked the whole thing, and it was in apple-pie order. When Edison told me that, it was then that Sparky, crazy to get out, gave himself away."

"How?" said Bullard, suspiciously.

"We really had him locked in, see? There were three locks on the door — a hook and eye, a bolt, and a regular knob and latch. That dog stood up, unhooked the hook, pushed the bolt back and had the knob in his teeth when Edison stopped him."

"No!" said Bullard.

"Yes!" said the stranger, his eyes shining. "And then is when Edison showed me what a great scientist he was. He was willing to face the truth, no matter how unpleasant it might be.

" 'So!' said Edison to Sparky. 'Man's best friend, huh? Dumb animal, huh?'

"That Sparky was a caution. He pretended not to hear. He scratched himself and bit fleas and went around growling at ratholes — anything to get out of looking Edison in the eye.

" 'Pretty soft, isn't it, Sparky?' said Edison.

'Let somebody else worry about getting food, building shelters and keeping warm, while you sleep in front of a fire or go chasing after the girls or raise the devil with the boys. No mortgages, no politics, no war, no work, no worry. Just wag the old tail or lick a hand, and you're all taken care of.'

" 'Mr. Edison,' I said, 'do you mean to tell me that dogs are smarter than people?'

" 'Smarter?' said Edison. 'I'll tell the world! And what have I been doing for the past year? Slaving to work out a light bulb so dogs can play at night!' "

" 'Look, Mr. Edison,' said Sparky, 'why not —' "

"Hold on!" roared Bullard.

"Silence!" shouted the stranger, triumphantly. " 'Look, Mr. Edison,' said Sparky, 'why not keep quiet about this? It's been working out to everybody's satisfaction for hundreds of thousands of years. Let sleeping dogs lie. You forget all about it, destroy the intelligence analyzer, and I'll tell you what to use for a lamp filament.' "

"Hogwash!" said Bullard, his face purple.

The stranger stood. "You have my solemn word as a gentleman. That dog rewarded *me* for my silence with a stock-market tip that made me independently wealthy for the rest of my days. And the last words that Sparky ever spoke were to Thomas Edison. 'Try a piece of carbonized cotton thread,' he said. Later, he was torn to bits by a pack of dogs that had gathered outside the door, listening."

The stranger removed his garters and handed them to Bullard's dog. "A small token of esteem, sir, for an ancestor of yours who talked himself to death. Good day." He tucked his book under his arm and walked away.

FOR STUDY AND DISCUSSION

1. A shaggy-dog story is a joke that is spun out to a long, rambling tale. It is intended to lead on the listener, and generally involves absurd, unreal events. What is the shaggy-dog story the stranger tells Bullard? Why do you think he chooses to tell a story about Edison?

2. At what point does Bullard begin to realize that he has been taken in? What is the joke the stranger pulls on Bullard? Why is it an effective form of revenge?

THE STORY WITHIN A STORY

Sometimes an author chooses to tell a story within the *framework* of another story. In its simplest form, the framework can introduce a group of people discussing a particular topic. One of the group will then say, "Oh, yes. That reminds me of something that happened several years ago." And so, the inner story begins. In such a story, the inner story is usually much more important than the framework.

In other stories, the framework plays a much more important role. For example, "Tom Edison's Shaggy Dog" tells two stories that are almost equally important. The framework story and the story within a story reinforce one another, and each story adds meaning to the other.

In what way are the framework story and the inner story related? How does the inner story influence the outcome of the framework story?

ALLUSIONS

One of Bullard's annoying mannerisms is his transformation of well-known sayings to suit his own beliefs. For example, he changes Horace Greeley's famous statement, "Go West, young man, go West," to "Go atom, young man." Kurt Vonnegut depends upon the reader's recognizing the allusion to Greeley's actual quotation. To appreciate the humor of the revision, one needs to know the original.

Here are some other well-known sayings that appear in or are alluded to in the story. What humorous use is made of each?

Opportunity knocks only once.
It is always darkest just before the dawn.
Dog is man's best friend.
Let sleeping dogs lie.

FOR COMPOSITION

Writing an Imaginary Narrative
How was the wheel invented? How was fire discovered? Imagine how some invention or discovery came about. Treat your narrative as a shaggy-dog story if you wish.

ABOUT THE AUTHOR

Kurt Vonnegut (1922–   ) was born in Indianapolis. He attended Cornell, Carnegie Institute of Technology, and the universities of Tennessee and Chicago. During World War II he was a prisoner of war in Germany and witnessed the destruction of Dresden by allied bombers, an experience he later wrote about in his novels *Mother Night* and *Slaughterhouse-Five*. Some of his best-known books are *Cat's Cradle*, *The Sirens of Titan*, and *Breakfast of Champions*. He has published more than a hundred short stories, many of them science fiction. "Tom Edison's Shaggy Dog" is from *Welcome to the Monkey House*, a collection of his stories.

Character

The Secret Life of Walter Mitty

James Thurber

"We're going through!" The Commander's voice was like thin ice breaking. He wore his full-dress uniform, with the heavily braided white cap pulled down rakishly over one cold gray eye. "We can't make it, sir. It's spoiling for a hurricane, if you ask me." "I'm not asking you, Lieutenant Berg," said the Commander. "Throw on the power lights! Rev her up to 8,500! We're going through!" The pounding of the cylinders increased: ta - pocketa - pocketa - pocketa-*pocketa - pock-eta*. The Commander stared at the ice forming on the pilot window. He walked over and twisted a row of complicated dials. "Switch on No. 8 auxiliary!" he shouted. "Switch on No. 8 auxiliary!" repeated Lieutenant Berg. "Full strength in No. 3 turret!" shouted the Commander. "Full strength in No. 3 turret!" The crew, bending to their various tasks in the huge, hurtling eight-engined Navy hydroplane, looked at each other and grinned. "The Old Man'll get us through," they said to one another. "The Old Man ain't afraid of Hell!" . . .

"Not so fast! You're driving too fast!" said Mrs. Mitty. "What are you driving so fast for?"

"Hmm?" said Walter Mitty. He looked at his wife, in the seat beside him, with shocked astonishment. She seemed grossly unfamiliar, like a strange woman who had yelled at him in a crowd. "You were up to fifty-five," she said. "You know I don't like to go more than forty. You were up to fifty-five." Walter Mitty drove on toward Waterbury in silence, the roaring of the SN202 through the worst storm in twenty years of Navy flying fading in the remote, intimate airways of his mind. "You're tensed up again," said Mrs. Mitty. "It's one of your days. I wish you'd let Dr. Renshaw look you over."

Walter Mitty stopped the car in front of the building where his wife went to have her hair done. "Remember to get those overshoes while I'm having my hair done," she said. "I don't need overshoes," said Mitty. She put her mirror back into her bag. "We've been all through that," she said, getting out of the car. "You're not a young man any longer." He raced the engine a little. "Why don't you wear your gloves? Have you lost your gloves?" Walter Mitty reached in a pocket and brought out the gloves. He put them on, but after she had turned and gone into the building and he had driven on to a red light, he took them off again. "Pick it up, brother!" snapped a cop as the light changed, and Mitty hastily pulled on his gloves and lurched ahead. He drove

around the streets aimlessly for a time, and then he drove past the hospital on his way to the parking lot.

. . . "It's the millionaire banker, Wellington McMillan," said the pretty nurse. "Yes?" said Walter Mitty, removing his gloves slowly. "Who has the case?" "Dr. Renshaw and Dr. Benbow, but there are two specialists here, Dr. Remington from New York and Dr. Pritchard-Mitford from London. He flew over!" A door opened down a long cool corridor and Dr. Renshaw came out. He looked distraught and haggard. "Hello, Mitty," he said. "We're having the devil's own time with McMillan, the millionaire banker and close personal friend of Roosevelt. Obstreosis of the ductal tract. Tertiary. Wish you'd take a look at him." "Glad to," said Mitty.

In the operating room there were whispered introductions: "Dr. Remington, Dr. Mitty. Dr. Pritchard-Mitford, Dr. Mitty." "I've read your book on streptothricosis," said Pritchard-Mitford, shaking hands. "A brilliant performance, sir." "Thank you," said Walter Mitty. "Didn't know you were in the States, Mitty," grumbled Remington. "Coals to Newcastle,[1] bringing Mitford and me up here for a tertiary." "You are very kind," said Mitty. A huge, complicated machine, connected to the operating table, with many tubes and wires, began at this moment to go pocketa-pocketa-pocketa. "The new anesthetizer is giving way!" shouted an intern. "There is no one in the East who knows how to fix it!" "Quiet, man!" said Mitty, in a low, cool voice. He sprang to the machine, which was now going pocketa-pocketa-queep-pocketa-queep. He began fingering delicately a row of glistening dials. "Give me a fountain pen!" he snapped. Someone handed him a fountain pen. He pulled a faulty piston out of

---

1. **Coals to Newcastle:** a saying used to indicate unnecessary labor. Newcastle, a city in England, is famous for its production of coal.

the machine and inserted the pen in its place. "That will hold for ten minutes," he said. "Get on with the operation." A nurse hurried over and whispered to Renshaw, and Mitty saw the man turn pale. "Coreopsis has set in," said Renshaw nervously. "If you would take over, Mitty?" Mitty looked at him and at the craven figure of Benbow, who drank, and at the grave, uncertain faces of the two great specialists. "If you wish," he said. They slipped a white gown on him; he adjusted a mask and drew on thin gloves; nurses handed him shining . . .

"Back it up, Mac! Look out for that Buick!" Walter Mitty jammed on the brakes. "Wrong lane, Mac," said the parking-lot attendant, looking at Mitty closely. "Gee. Yeh," muttered Mitty. He began cautiously to back out of the lane marked "Exit Only." "Leave her sit there," said the attendant. "I'll put her away." Mitty got out of the car. "Hey, better leave the key." "Oh," said Mitty, handing the man the ignition key. The attendant vaulted into the car, backed it up with insolent skill, and put it where it belonged.

They're so cocky, thought Walter Mitty, walking along Main Street; they think they know everything. Once he had tried to take his chains off, outside New Milford, and he had got them wound around the axles. A man had had to come out in a wrecking car and unwind them, a young, grinning garageman. Since then Mrs. Mitty always made him drive to a garage to have the chains taken off. The next time, he thought, I'll wear my right arm in a sling; they won't grin at me then. I'll have my right arm in a sling and they'll see I couldn't possibly take the chains off myself. He kicked at the slush on the sidewalk. "Overshoes," he said to himself, and he began looking for a shoe store.

When he came out into the street again, with the overshoes in a box under his arm,

Walter Mitty began to wonder what the other thing was his wife had told him to get. She had told him twice before they set out from their house for Waterbury. In a way he hated these weekly trips to town—he was always getting something wrong. Kleenex, he thought, Squibb's, razor blades? No. Toothpaste, toothbrush, bicarbonate, carborundum, initiative and referendum?[2] He gave it up. But she would remember it. "Where's the what's-its-name?" she would ask. "Don't tell me you forgot the what's-its-name." A newsboy went by shouting something about the Waterbury trial.

. . . "Perhaps this will refresh your memory." The District Attorney suddenly thrust a heavy automatic at the quiet figure on the witness stand. "Have you ever seen this before?" Walter Mitty took the gun and examined it expertly. "This is my Webley-Vickers 50.80," he said calmly. An excited buzz ran around the courtroom. The Judge rapped for order. "You are a crack shot with any sort of firearms, I believe?" said the District Attorney, insinuatingly. "Objection!" shouted Mitty's attorney. "We have shown that the defendant could not have fired the shot. We have shown that he wore his right arm in a sling on the night of the fourteenth of July." Walter Mitty raised his hand briefly and the bickering attorneys were stilled. "With any known make of gun," he said evenly, "I could have killed Gregory Fitzhurst at three hundred feet *with my left hand*." Pandemonium broke loose in the courtroom. A woman's scream rose above the bedlam and suddenly a lovely, dark-haired girl was in Walter

2. **carborundum, initiative and referendum:** Carborundum is a hard, abrasive material. Initiative refers to the right of citizens to introduce new legislation. Referendum refers to the right of citizens to vote directly on laws. The association in Mitty's mind is one of sound, not of sense.

Mitty's arms. The District Attorney struck at her savagely. Without rising from his chair, Mitty let the man have it on the point of the chin. "You miserable cur!" . . .

"Puppy biscuit," said Walter Mitty. He stopped walking and the buildings of Waterbury rose up out of the misty courtroom and surrounded him again. A woman who was passing laughed. "He said 'Puppy biscuit,'" she said to her companion. "That man said 'Puppy biscuit' to himself." Walter Mitty hurried on. He went into an A & P, not the first one he came to but a smaller one farther up the street. "I want some biscuit for small, young dogs," he said to the clerk. "Any special brand, sir?" The greatest pistol shot in the world thought a moment. "It says 'Puppies Bark for It' on the box," said Walter Mitty.

His wife would be through at the hairdresser's in fifteen minutes, Mitty saw in looking at his watch, unless they had trouble drying it; sometimes they had trouble drying it. She didn't like to get to the hotel first; she would want him to be there waiting for her as usual. He found a big leather chair in the lobby, facing a window, and he put the overshoes and the puppy biscuit on the floor beside it. He picked up an old copy of *Liberty* and sank down into the chair. "Can Germany Conquer the World Through the Air?" Walter Mitty looked at the pictures of bombing planes and of ruined streets.

. . . "The cannonading has got the wind up in young Raleigh, sir," said the sergeant. Captain Mitty looked up at him through tousled hair. "Get him to bed," he said wearily, "with the others. I'll fly alone." "But you can't, sir," said the sergeant anxiously. "It takes two men to handle that bomber and the Archies[3]

are pounding hell out of the air. Von Richtman's circus[4] is between here and Saulier." "Somebody's got to get that ammunition dump," said Mitty. "I'm going over. Spot of brandy?" He poured a drink for the sergeant and one for himself. War thundered and whined around the dugout and battered at the door. There was a rending of wood and splinters flew through the room. "A bit of a near thing," said Captain Mitty carelessly. "The box barrage is closing in," said the sergeant. "We only live once, Sergeant," said Mitty, with his faint, fleeting smile. "Or do we?" He poured another brandy and tossed it off. "I never see a man could hold his brandy like you, sir," said the sergeant. "Begging your pardon, sir." Captain Mitty stood up and strapped on his huge Webley-Vickers automatic. "It's forty kilometers through hell, sir," said the sergeant. Mitty finished one last

---

3. **Archies:** allied troops' name for the antiaircraft guns in World War I.

4. **circus:** here, a squadron of planes flying in close formation.

brandy. "After all," he said softly, "what isn't?" The pounding of the cannon increased; there was the rat-tat-tatting of machine guns, and from somewhere came the menacing pocketa-pocketa-pocketa of the new flame-throwers. Walter Mitty walked to the door of the dugout humming "Auprès de Ma Blonde."[5] He turned and waved to the sergeant. "Cheerio!" he said. . . .

Something struck his shoulder. "I've been looking all over this hotel for you," said Mrs. Mitty. "Why do you have to hide in this old chair? How did you expect me to find you?" "Things close in," said Walter Mitty vaguely. "What?" Mrs. Mitty said. "Did you get the what's-its-name? The puppy biscuit? What's in that box?" "Overshoes," said Mitty. "Couldn't you have put them on in the store?" "I was thinking," said Walter Mitty. "Does it ever occur to you that I am sometimes thinking?" She looked at him. "I'm going to take your temperature when I get you home," she said.

They went out through the revolving doors that made a faintly derisive whistling sound when you pushed them. It was two blocks to the parking lot. At the drugstore on the corner she said, "Wait here for me. I forgot something. I won't be a minute." She was more than a minute. Walter Mitty lighted a cigarette. It began to rain, rain with sleet in it. He stood up against the wall of the drugstore, smoking. . . . He put his shoulders back and his heels together. "To hell with the handkerchief," said Walter Mitty scornfully. He took one last drag on his cigarette and snapped it away. Then, with that faint, fleeting smile playing about his lips, he faced the firing squad; erect and motionless, proud and disdainful, Walter Mitty the Undefeated, inscrutable[6] to the last.

---

5. **"Auprès de Ma Blonde"**: popular French song.

6. **inscrutable**: unknowable, mysterious.

FOR STUDY AND DISCUSSION

1. Contrast Walter Mitty's real life with his secret life. Why does he feel the need to escape from real life?

2. Each of Mitty's daydreams is sparked by some detail of everyday life. For example, Mitty drives past a hospital and imagines himself a famous doctor. Explain how his other daydreams grow out of actual events.

3. What kind of person is Mrs. Mitty?

4. The final incident of the story shows Walter Mitty dreaming of himself before a firing squad. How is this incident symbolic of his view of himself? Is this final daydream of Walter Mitty's an adequate summing-up of the total effect of the story? Why or why not?

5. Readers have found "The Secret Life of Walter Mitty" both funny and sad. How is it funny and how is it sad?

DIRECT AND INDIRECT CHARACTERIZATION

A writer can develop and reveal character in a number of ways: (1) through a physical description of the character; (2) through the character's actions; (3) through the character's thoughts, feelings, and speeches; (4) through the comments and reactions of other characters; (5) through direct statements giving the writer's opinion of the character. The first four methods are *indirect* methods of characterization; they *show* or *dramatize* character. The last method is *direct* characterization; it *tells* rather than dramatizes. Within a single passage, an author may use both direct and indirect methods of characterization.

James Thurber uses three of these methods of characterization to develop Walter Mitty. Tell which methods he uses and give examples of their use.

DRAMATIC IRONY

Irony contrasts what is real with what only seems to be real. A writer may say one thing and mean quite another. This kind of irony, which was discussed on page 24, is called *verbal irony*. Another kind of irony is *dramatic irony*. In dramatic irony, the contrast depends upon the difference between what a character believes and what readers know is true. For example, Mitty has a fantasy about being a flying ace, but the reader knows from Mitty's inept behavior in the parking lot that he has trouble just parking his car.

Find other examples of dramatic irony in "The Secret Life of Walter Mitty." How do the ironic contrasts in this story deepen your understanding of Mitty as a character?

LANGUAGE AND VOCABULARY

Recognizing Mock-Jargon

Jargon usually refers to the special language of a group of people, especially people in the same job. Engineers have their jargon, as do doctors, lawyers, and carpenters. Often, such language is necessary to communicate complex or technical ideas. But sometimes, special language is used simply to impress outsiders, to show that writers or speakers know more than their readers or listeners. Language used for this purpose fits another definition of jargon—"incomprehensible speech."

"The Secret Life of Walter Mitty" pokes fun at the jargon of several groups. Find examples of the mock-jargon of doctors. Can you find other examples of mock-jargon? What are they?

FOR COMPOSITION

Writing a Sequel to the Story

Write a sequel to "The Secret Life of Walter Mitty." Let Mitty have one more daydream of glory. Show how a detail of everyday life sparks his daydream. At the end of your story, show how his daydream is rudely interrupted.

Or, if you like, write a short, short story about another character who lives a double life—an everyday life and a secret life. Show why your character needs a secret life. Keep in mind that *showing* is a more effective way of developing a character than telling is.

ABOUT THE AUTHOR

James Thurber (1894–1961) achieved success as both a writer and a cartoonist. He is one of America's most highly regarded humorists. Part of his success lies in his gift for being funny and serious at the same time. His writings and drawings are populated by men and women who attempt to cope with one another and with modern life, and by puzzled, compassionate dogs who quietly observe the human scene.

Thurber grew up in Columbus, Ohio, and attended Ohio State University. Later he wrote about these early years in the wildly funny *My Life and Hard Times*. After working on newspapers in Columbus, Paris, and New York, he joined the staff of the *New Yorker* magazine. He was associated with the *New Yorker* for the rest of his life, first as an editor, then as a writer. He created essays, stories, and cartoons for the magazine and became one of its best-known contributors. Much of his work is collected in books with titles that reveal his ironic attitude toward the world at large: for example, *My World and Welcome to It*, *The Middle-Aged Man on the Flying Trapeze*, and *The Beast in Me and Other Animals*. He also collaborated on a play with Elliot Nugent, an old college friend. *The Male Animal* was a considerable success when first produced and is still occasionally revived. Some of his best satire appears in *Fables for Our Time* and *Further Fables for Our Time*. Thurber also wrote several children's books that are regarded as classics, among them *The White Deer* and *The Thirteen Clocks*.

All the Years of Her Life

Morley Callaghan

They were closing the drugstore, and Alfred Higgins, who had just taken off his white jacket, was putting on his coat and getting ready to go home. The little gray-haired man, Sam Carr, who owned the drugstore, was bending down behind the cash register, and when Alfred Higgins passed him, he looked up and said softly, "Just a moment, Alfred. One moment before you go."

The soft, confident, quiet way in which Sam Carr spoke made Alfred start to button his coat nervously. He felt sure his face was white. Sam Carr usually said, "Good night," brusquely, without looking up. In the six months he had been working in the drugstore Alfred had never heard his employer speak softly like that. His heart began to beat so loud it was hard for him to get his breath. "What is it, Mr. Carr?" he asked.

"Maybe you'd be good enough to take a few things out of your pocket and leave them here before you go," Sam Carr said.

"What things? What are you talking about?"

"You've got a compact and a lipstick and at least two tubes of toothpaste in your pocket, Alfred."

"What do you mean? Do you think I'm crazy?" Alfred blustered. His face got red and he knew he looked fierce with indignation. But Sam Carr, standing by the door with his blue eyes shining bright behind his glasses and his lips moving underneath his gray mustache, only nodded his head a few times, and then Alfred grew very frightened and he didn't know what to say. Slowly he raised his hand and dipped it into his pocket, and with his eyes never meeting Sam Carr's eyes, he took out a blue compact and two tubes of toothpaste and a lipstick, and he laid them one by one on the counter.

"Petty thieving, eh, Alfred?" Sam Carr said. "And maybe you'd be good enough to tell me how long this has been going on."

"This is the first time I ever took anything."

"So now you think you'll tell me a lie, eh? What kind of a sap do I look like, huh? I don't know what goes on in my own store, eh? I tell you you've been doing this pretty steady," Sam Carr said as he went over and stood behind the cash register.

Ever since Alfred had left school he had been getting in trouble wherever he worked. He lived at home with his mother and his father, who was a printer. His two older brothers were married and his sister had got married last year, and it would have been all right for his parents now if Alfred had only been able to keep a job.

While Sam Carr smiled and stroked the side of his face very delicately with the tips of his fingers, Alfred began to feel that familiar terror growing in him that had been in him every time he had got into such trouble.

"I liked you," Sam Carr was saying. "I liked you and would have trusted you, and now look what I got to do." While Alfred watched with his alert, frightened blue eyes, Sam Carr drummed with his fingers on the counter. "I don't like to call a cop in point-blank," he was saying as he looked very worried. "You're a fool, and maybe I should call your father and tell him you're a fool. Maybe I should let them know I'm going to have you locked up."

"My father's not at home. He's a printer. He works nights," Alfred said.

"Who's at home?"

"My mother, I guess."

"Then we'll see what she says." Sam Carr went to the phone and dialed the number. Alfred was not so much ashamed, but there was that deep fright growing in him, and he blurted out arrogantly, like a strong, full-grown man, "Just a minute. You don't need to draw anybody else in. You don't need to tell her." He wanted to sound like a swaggering, big guy who could look after himself, yet the old, childish hope was in him, the longing that someone at home would come and help him. "Yeah, that's right, he's in trouble," Mr. Carr was saying. "Yeah, your boy works for me. You'd better come down in a hurry." And when he was finished Mr. Carr went over to the door and looked out at the street and watched the people passing in the late summer night. "I'll keep my eye out for a cop," was all he said.

Alfred knew how his mother would come rushing in; she would rush in with her eyes blazing, or maybe she would be crying, and she would push him away when he tried to talk to her, and make him feel her dreadful contempt; yet he longed that she might come before Mr. Carr saw the cop on the beat passing the door.

While they waited—and it seemed a long time—they did not speak, and when at last they heard someone tapping on the closed door, Mr. Carr, turning the latch, said crisply, "Come in, Mrs. Higgins." He looked hard-faced and stern.

Mrs. Higgins must have been going to bed when he telephoned, for her hair was tucked in loosely under her hat, and her hand at her throat held her light coat tightly across her chest so her dress would not show. She came in, large and plump, with a little smile on her friendly face. Most of the store lights had been turned out and at first she did not see Alfred, who was standing in the shadow at the end of

As she listened Mrs. Higgins looked at Alfred sometimes and nodded her head sadly, and when Sam Carr had finished she said gravely, "Is it so, Alfred?"

"Yes."

"Why have you been doing it?"

"I been spending money, I guess."

"On what?"

"Going around with the guys, I guess," Alfred said.

Mrs. Higgins put out her hand and touched Sam Carr's arm with an understanding gentleness, and speaking as though afraid of disturbing him, she said, "If you would only listen to me before doing anything." Her simple earnestness made her shy; her humility made her falter and look away, but in a moment she was smiling gravely again, and she said with a kind of patient dignity, "What did you intend to do, Mr. Carr?"

"I was going to get a cop. That's what I ought to do."

"Yes, I suppose so. It's not for me to say, because he's my son. Yet I sometimes think a little good advice is the best thing for a boy when he's at a certain period in his life," she said.

Alfred couldn't understand his mother's quiet composure, for if they had been at home and someone had suggested that he was going to be arrested, he knew she would be in a rage and would cry out against him. Yet now she was standing there with that gentle, pleading smile on her face, saying, "I wonder if you don't think it would be better just to let him come home with me. He looks a big fellow, doesn't he? It takes some of them a long time to get any sense," and they both stared at Alfred, who shifted away with a bit of light shining for a moment on his thin face and the tiny pimples over his cheekbone.

But even while he was turning away uneasily Alfred was realizing that Mr. Carr had

the counter. Yet as soon as she saw him she did not look as Alfred thought she would look: she smiled, her blue eyes never wavered, and with a calmness and dignity that made them forget that her clothes seemed to have been thrown on her, she put out her hand to Mr. Carr and said politely, "I'm Mrs. Higgins. I'm Alfred's mother."

Mr. Carr was a little embarrassed by her lack of terror and her simplicity, and he hardly knew what to say to her, so she asked, "Is Alfred in trouble?"

"He is. He's been taking things from the store. I caught him red-handed. Little things like compacts and toothpaste and lipsticks. Stuff he can sell easily," the proprietor said.

become aware that his mother was really a fine woman; he knew that Sam Carr was puzzled by his mother, as if he had expected her to come in and plead with him tearfully, and instead he was being made to feel a bit ashamed by her vast tolerance. While there was only the sound of the mother's soft, assured voice in the store, Mr. Carr began to nod his head encouragingly at her. Without being alarmed, while being just large and still and simple and hopeful, she was becoming dominant there in the dimly lit store. "Of course, I don't want to be harsh," Mr. Carr was saying, "I'll tell you what I'll do. I'll just fire him and let it go at that. How's that?" and he got up and shook hands with Mrs. Higgins, bowing low to her in deep respect.

There was such warmth and gratitude in the way she said, "I'll never forget your kindness," that Mr. Carr began to feel warm and genial himself.

"Sorry we had to meet this way," he said. "But I'm glad I got in touch with you. Just wanted to do the right thing, that's all," he said.

"It's better to meet like this than never, isn't it?" she said. Suddenly they clasped hands as if they liked each other, as if they had known each other a long time. "Good night, sir," she said.

"Good night, Mrs. Higgins. I'm truly sorry," he said.

The mother and son walked along the street together, and the mother was taking a long, firm stride as she looked ahead with her stern face full of worry. Alfred was afraid to speak to her, he was afraid of the silence that was between them, so he only looked ahead too, for the excitement and relief was still pretty strong in him; but in a little while, going along like that in silence made him terribly aware of the strength and the sternness in her; he began to wonder what she was thinking of

as she stared ahead so grimly; she seemed to have forgotten that he walked beside her; so when they were passing under the Sixth Avenue elevated[1] and the rumble of the train seemed to break the silence, he said in his old blustering way, "Thank God it turned out like that. I certainly won't get in a jam like that again."

"Be quiet. Don't speak to me. You've disgraced me again and again," she said bitterly.

"That's the last time. That's all I'm saying."

"Have the decency to be quiet," she snapped. They kept on their way, looking straight ahead.

When they were at home and his mother took off her coat, Alfred saw that she was really only half dressed, and she made him feel afraid again when she said, without even looking at him, "You're a bad lot. God forgive you. It's one thing after another and always has been. Why do you stand there stupidly? Go to bed, why don't you?" When he was going, she said, "I'm going to make myself a cup of tea. Mind, now, not a word about tonight to your father."

While Alfred was undressing in his bedroom, he heard his mother moving around the kitchen. She filled the kettle and put it on the stove. She moved a chair. And as he listened there was no shame in him, just wonder and a kind of admiration of her strength and repose. He could still see Sam Carr nodding his head encouragingly to her; he could hear her talking simply and earnestly, and as he sat on his bed he felt a pride in her strength. "She certainly was smooth," he thought. "Gee, I'd like to tell her she sounded swell."

And at last he got up and went along to the kitchen, and when he was at the door he saw

---

1. **elevated:** a railway running above the street.

his mother pouring herself a cup of tea. He watched and he didn't move. Her face, as she sat there, was a frightened, broken face utterly unlike the face of the woman who had been so assured a little while ago in the drugstore. When she reached out and lifted the kettle to pour hot water in her cup, her hand trembled and the water splashed on the stove. Leaning back in the chair, she sighed and lifted the cup to her lips, and her lips were groping loosely as if they would never reach the cup. She swallowed the hot tea eagerly, and then she straightened up in relief, though the hand holding the cup still trembled. She looked very old.

It seemed to Alfred that this was the way it had been every time he had been in trouble before, that this trembling had really been in her as she hurried out half dressed to the drugstore. He understood why she had sat alone in the kitchen the night his young sister had kept repeating doggedly that she was getting married. Now he felt all that his mother had been thinking of as they walked along the street together a little while ago. He watched his mother, and he never spoke, but at that moment his youth seemed to be over; he knew all the years of her life by the way her hand trembled as she raised the cup to her lips. It seemed to him that this was the first time he had ever looked upon his mother.

FOR STUDY AND DISCUSSION

1. There are two major characters in the story: Alfred and his mother. Which one do you think is the main character? One way of answering this question is to identify the climax of the story. Is it Alfred escaping the consequences of his theft, or is it Alfred understanding his mother for the first time?

2. Tell what sort of person Alfred is. What methods does Callaghan use to characterize him?

3. How does Alfred's mother handle Mr. Carr? What does her handling of the druggist reveal about her?

4. Alfred's mother is seen chiefly through Alfred's eyes. How does his understanding of her change? How does he see her at the end of the story?

STATIC AND DYNAMIC CHARACTERS

Characters in fiction are often described as *static* or *dynamic*. Static characters remain the same throughout a story, novel, or play. Dynamic characters change in some important way.

Alfred undergoes an important change at the end of the story. How does insight into his mother's character cause him to change? Consider what this phrase means: "at that moment his youth seemed to be over." Does the change necessarily make Alfred a better person?

Is Walter Mitty in "The Secret Life of Walter Mitty" a static or dynamic character? How would you classify Sanger Rainsford in "The Most Dangerous Game"?

FOR COMPOSITION

Creating a Dominant Impression
Alfred begins to understand his mother's inner nature when he watches her pouring herself a cup of tea. Reread the passage on page 42 beginning, "Her face, as she sat there, was a frightened, broken face utterly unlike the face of the woman who had been so assured a little while ago in the drugstore." Note how Callaghan creates a single impression of Alfred's mother through the careful selection of details and through well-chosen modifiers and verbs. Which words are particularly effective?

Write a description of a real or an imaginary person. Convey a dominant impression through details of appearance and actions. Use appropriate verbs and modifiers.

ABOUT THE AUTHOR

Morley Callaghan (1903–   ) was born in Toronto and attended the University of Toronto and Osgoode Hall Law School. Between college and law school, he worked as a reporter on the Toronto *Star*. There he met Ernest Hemingway, who recognized Callaghan's talent and encouraged him to write. Callaghan's first short stories were published in small literary magazines. Later stories appeared in larger, general circulation magazines, such as the *New Yorker*. For nine consecutive years, stories by Callaghan were included in the annual collection *The Best Short Stories*. He has collected some of his stories in two books, *A Native Argosy* and *Now That April's Here*. In addition, he has written several novels, including *Broken Journey*, *More Joy in Heaven*, and *The Many-Colored Coat*. He is considered one of Canada's most distinguished writers.

Split Cherry Tree

Jesse Stuart

"I don't mind staying after school," I says to Professor Herbert, "but I'd rather you'd whip me with a switch and let me go home early. Pa will whip me anyway for getting home two hours late."

"You are too big to whip," says Professor Herbert, "and I have to punish you for climbing up in that cherry tree. You boys knew better than that! The other five boys have paid their dollar each. You have been the only one who has not helped pay for the tree. Can't you borrow a dollar?"

"I can't," I says. "I'll have to take the punishment. I wish it would be quicker punishment. I wouldn't mind."

Professor Herbert stood and looked at me. He was a big man. He wore a gray suit of clothes. The suit matched his gray hair.

"You don't know my father," I says to Professor Herbert. "He might be called a little old-fashioned. He makes us mind him until we're twenty-one years old. He believes if you spare the rod you spoil the child. I'll never be able to make him understand about the cherry tree. I'm the first of my people to go to high school."

"You must take the punishment," says Professor Herbert. "You must stay two hours after school today and two hours after school tomorrow. I am allowing you twenty-five cents an hour. That is good money for a high school student. You can sweep the school-house floor, wash the blackboards, and clean windows. I'll pay the dollar for you."

I couldn't ask Professor Herbert to loan me a dollar. He never offered to loan it to me. I had to stay and help the janitor and work out my fine at a quarter an hour.

I thought as I swept the floor, "What will Pa do to me? What lie can I tell him when I go home? Why did we ever climb that cherry tree and break it down for anyway? Why did we run crazy over the hills away from the crowd? Why did we do all of this? Six of us climbed up in a little cherry tree after one little lizard! Why did the tree split and fall with us? It should have been a stronger tree! Why did Eif Crabtree just happen to be below us plowing and catch us in his cherry tree? Why wasn't he a better man than to charge us six dollars for the tree?"

It was six o'clock when I left the school-house. I had six miles to walk home. It would be after seven when I got home. I had all my work to do when I got home. It took Pa and me both to do the work. Seven cows to milk. Nineteen head of cattle to feed, four mules, twenty-five hogs, firewood and stovewood to cut, and water to draw from the well. He would be doing it when I got home. He would be mad and wondering what was keeping me!

I hurried home. I would run under the dark, leafless trees. I would walk fast uphill. I would run down the hill. The ground was freezing. I had to hurry. I had to run. I reached the long ridge that led to our cow pasture. I ran along this ridge. The wind dried the sweat on my face. I ran across the pasture to the house.

I threw down my books in the chipyard. I ran to the barn to spread fodder on the ground for the cattle. I didn't take time to change my clean school clothes for my old work clothes. I ran out to the barn. I saw Pa spreading fodder on the ground to the cattle. That was my job. I ran up to the fence. I says, "Leave that for me, Pa. I'll do it, I'm just a little late."

"I see you are," says Pa. He turned and looked at me. His eyes danced fire. "What in th' world has kept you so? Why ain't you been here to help me with this work? Make a gentleman out'n one boy in th' family and this is what you get! Send you to high school and you get too onery fer th' buzzards to smell!"

I never said anything. I didn't want to tell why I was late from school. Pa stopped scattering the bundles of fodder. He looked at me. He says, "Why are you gettin' in here this time o' night? You tell me or I'll take a hickory withe[1] to you right here on th' spot!"

I says, "I had to stay after school." I couldn't lie to Pa. He'd go to school and find out why I had to stay. If I lied to him it would be too bad for me.

"Why did you haf to stay atter school?" says Pa.

I says, "Our biology class went on a field trip today. Six of us boys broke down a cherry tree. We had to give a dollar apiece to pay for the tree. I didn't have the dollar. Professor Herbert is making me work out my dollar. He gives me twenty-five cents an hour. I had to stay in this afternoon. I'll have to stay in tomorrow afternoon!"

"Are you telling me th' truth?" says Pa.

"I'm telling you the truth," I says. "Go and see for yourself."

"That's jist what I'll do in th' mornin'," says Pa. "Jist whose cherry tree did you break down?"

"Eif Crabtree's cherry tree!"

"What was you doin' clear out in Eif Crabtree's place?" says Pa. "He lives four miles

from th' county high school. Don't they teach you no books at that high school? Do they jist let you get out and gad over th' hillsides? If that's all they do I'll keep you at home, Dave. I've got work here fer you to do!"

"Pa," I says, "spring is just getting here. We take a subject in school where we have to have bugs, snakes, flowers, lizards, frogs, and plants. It is biology. It was a pretty day today. We went out to find a few of these. Six of us boys saw a lizard at the same time sunning on a cherry tree. We all went up the tree to get it. We broke the tree down. It split at the forks. Eif Crabtree was plowing down below us. He ran up the hill and got our names. The other boys gave their dollar apiece. I didn't have mine. Professor Herbert put mine in for me. I have to work it out at school."

"Poor man's son, huh," says Pa. "I'll attend to that myself in th' mornin'. I'll take keer o' 'im. He ain't from this county nohow. I'll go down there in th' mornin' and see 'im. Lettin' you leave your books and gallivant all over th' hills. What kind of a school is it nohow! Didn't do that, my son, when I's a little shaver in school. All fared alike, too."

"Pa, please don't go down there," I says, "just let me have fifty cents and pay the rest of my fine! I don't want you to go down there! I don't want you to start anything with Professor Herbert!"

"Ashamed of your old Pap, are you, Dave," says Pa, "atter th' way I've worked to raise you! Tryin' to send you to school so you can make a better livin' than I've made.

"I'll straighten this thing out myself! I'll take keer o' Professor Herbert myself! He ain't got no right to keep you in and let the other boys off jist because they've got th' money! I'm a poor man. A bullet will go in a professor same as it will any man. It will go in a rich man same as it will a poor man. Now you get into this work before I take one o'

---

1. **withe** (wĭth): a twig or branch.

these withes and cut the shirt off'n your back!"

I thought once I'd run through the woods above the barn just as hard as I could go. I thought I'd leave high school and home forever! Pa could not catch me! I'd get away! I couldn't go back to school with him. He'd have a gun and maybe he'd shoot Professor Herbert. It was hard to tell what he would do. I could tell Pa that school had changed in the hills from the way it was when he was a boy, but he wouldn't understand. I could tell him we studied frogs, birds, snakes, lizards, flowers, insects. But Pa wouldn't understand. If I did run away from home it wouldn't matter to Pa. He would see Professor Herbert anyway. He would think that high school and Professor Herbert had run me away from home. There was no need to run away. I'd just have to stay, finish foddering the cattle, and go to school with Pa the next morning.

I would take a bundle of fodder, remove the hickory-withe band from around it, and scatter it on rocks, clumps of green briers, and brush, so the cattle wouldn't tramp it under their feet. I would lean it up against the oak trees and the rocks in the pasture just above our pigpen on the hill. The fodder was cold and frosty where it had set out in the stacks. I would carry bundles of the fodder from the stack until I had spread out a bundle for each steer. Pa went to the barn to feed the mules and throw corn in the pen to the hogs.

The moon shone bright in the cold March sky. I finished my work by moonlight. Professor Herbert really didn't know how much work I had to do at home. If he had known he would not have kept me after school. He would have loaned me a dollar to have paid my part on the cherry tree. He had never lived in the hills. He didn't know the way the hill boys had to work so that they could go to school. Now he was teaching in a county high school where all the boys who attended were from hill farms.

After I'd finished doing my work I went to the house and ate my supper. Pa and Mom had eaten. My supper was getting cold. I heard Pa and Mom talking in the front room. Pa was telling Mom about me staying in after school.

"I had to do all th' milkin' tonight, chop th' wood myself. It's too hard on me atter I've turned ground all day. I'm goin' to take a day off tomorrow and see if I can't remedy things a little. I'll go down to that high school tomorrow. I won't be a very good scholar fer Professor Herbert nohow. He won't keep me in atter school. I'll take a different kind of lesson down there and make 'im acquainted with it."

"Now, Luster," says Mom, "you jist stay away from there. Don't cause a lot o' trouble. You can be jailed fer a trick like that. You'll get th' Law atter you. You'll just go down there and show off and plague your own boy Dave to death in front o' all th' scholars!"

"Plague or no plague," says Pa, "he don't take into consideration what all I haf to do here, does he? I'll show 'im it ain't right to keep one boy in and let the rest go scot-free. My boy is good as th' rest, ain't he? A bullet will make a hole in a schoolteacher same as it will anybody else. He can't do me that way and get by with it. I'll plug 'im first. I aim to go down there bright and early in the mornin' and get all this straight! I aim to see about bug larnin' and this runnin' all over God's creation huntin' snakes, lizards, and frogs. Ransackin' th' country and goin' through cherry orchards and breakin' th' trees down atter lizards! Old Eif Crabtree ought to a-poured th' hot lead to 'em instead o' chargin' six dollars fer th' tree! He ought to a-got old Herbert th' first one!"

I ate my supper. I slipped upstairs and lit the lamp. I tried to forget the whole thing. I studied planc geometry. Then I studied my biology lesson. I could hardly study for thinking about Pa. "He'll go to school with me in the morning. He'll take a gun for Professor Herbert! What will Professor Herbert think of me! I'll tell him when Pa leaves that I couldn't help it. But Pa might shoot him. I hate to go with Pa. Maybe he'll cool off about it tonight and not go in the morning."

Pa got up at four o'clock. He built a fire in the stove. Then he built a fire in the fireplace. He got Mom up to get breakfast. Then he got me up to help feed and milk. By the time we had our work done at the barn, Mom had breakfast ready for us. We ate our breakfast. Daylight came and we could see the bare oak trees covered white with frost. The hills were white with frost. A cold wind was blowing. The sky was clear. The sun would soon come out and melt the frost. The afternoon would be warm with sunshine and the frozen ground would thaw. There would be mud on the hills again. Muddy water would then run down the little ditches on the hills.

"Now, Dave," says Pa, "let's get ready fer school. I aim to go with you this mornin' and look into bug larnin', frog larnin', lizard and snake larnin', and breakin' down cherry trees! I don't like no sicha foolish way o' larnin' myself!"

Pa hadn't forgot. I'd have to take him to school with me. He would take me to school with him. We were going early. I was glad we were going early. If Pa pulled a gun on Professor Herbert there wouldn't be so many of my classmates there to see him.

I knew that Pa wouldn't be at home in the high school. He wore overalls, big boots, a blue shirt and a sheepskin coat, and a slouched black hat gone to seed at the top. He put his gun in its holster. We started trudging toward the high school across the hill.

It was early when we got to the county high school. Professor Herbert had just got there. I just thought as we walked up the steps into the schoolhouse, "Maybe Pa will find out Professor Herbert is a good man. He just doesn't know him. Just like I felt toward the Lambert boys across the hill. I didn't like them until I'd seen them and talked to them. After I went to school with them and talked to them, I liked them and we were friends. It's a lot in knowing the other fellow."

"You're th' Professor here, ain't you?" says Pa.

"Yes," says Professor Herbert, "and you are Dave's father."

"Yes," says Pa, pulling out his gun and laying it on the seat in Professor Herbert's office. Professor Herbert's eyes got big behind his black-rimmed glasses when he saw Pa's gun. Color came into his pale cheeks.

"Jist a few things about this school I want to know," says Pa. "I'm tryin' to make a scholar out'n Dave. He's the only one out'n eleven youngins I've sent to high school. Here he comes in late and leaves me all th' work to do! He said you's all out bug huntin' yesterday and broke a cherry tree down. He had to stay two hours atter school yesterday and work out money to pay on that cherry tree! Is that right?"

"Wwwwy," says Professor Herbert, "I guess it is."

He looked at Pa's gun.

"Well," says Pa, "this ain't no high school. It's a bug school, a lizard school, a snake school! It ain't no school nohow!"

"Why did you bring that gun?" says Professor Herbert to Pa.

"You see that little hole," says Pa as he picked up the long blue forty-four and put his finger on the end of the barrel, "a bullet can come out'n that hole that will kill a schoolteacher same as it will any other man. It will

kill a rich man same as a poor man. It will kill a man. But atter I come in and saw you, I know'd I wouldn't need it. This maul[2] o' mine could do you up in a few minutes."

Pa stood there, big, hard, brown-skinned, and mighty, beside of Professor Herbert. I didn't know Pa was so much bigger and harder. I'd never seen Pa in a schoolhouse before. I'd seen Professor Herbert. He always looked big before to me. He didn't look big standing beside of Pa.

"I was only doing my duty, Mr. Sexton," says Professor Herbert, "and following the course of study the state provided us with."

"Course o' study," says Pa, "what study, bug study? Varmint study? Takin' youngins to th' woods. Boys and girls all out there together a-gallivantin' in the brush and kickin' up their heels and their poor old Ma's and Pa's at home a-slavin' to keep 'em in school and give 'em a education! You know that's dangerous, too, puttin' a lot o' boys and girls out together like that!"

Students were coming into the schoolhouse now.

Professor Herbert says, "Close the door, Dave, so others won't hear."

I walked over and closed the door. I was shaking like a leaf in the wind. I thought Pa was going to hit Professor Herbert every minute. He was doing all the talking. His face was getting red. The red color was coming through the brown, weather-beaten skin on Pa's face.

"I was right with these students," says Professor Herbert. "I know what they got into and what they didn't. I didn't send one of the other teachers with them on this field trip. I went myself. Yes, I took the boys and girls together. Why not?"

"It jist don't look good to me," says Pa, "a-takin' all this swarm of youngins out to pil-

---

2. **maul:** a large, heavy hammer. Pa means his fist.

lage th' whole deestrict. Breakin' down cherry trees. Keepin' boys in atter school.''

"What else could I have done with Dave, Mr. Sexton?'' says Professor Herbert. "The boys didn't have any business all climbing that cherry tree after one lizard. One boy could have gone up in the tree and got it. The farmer charged us six dollars. It was a little steep, I think, but we had it to pay. Must I make five boys pay and let your boy off? He said he didn't have the dollar and couldn't get it. So I put it in for him. I'm letting him work it out. He's not working for me. He's working for the school!''

"I jist don't know what you could a-done with 'im,'' says Pa, "only a-larruped 'im with a withe! That's what he needed!''

"He's too big to whip,'' says Professor Herbert, pointing at me. "He's a man in size.''

"He's not too big fer me to whip,'' says Pa. "They ain't too big until they're over twenty-one! It jist didn't look fair to me! Work one and let th' rest out because they got th' money. I don't see what bugs has got to do with a high school! It don't look good to me nohow!''

Pa picked up his gun and put it back in its holster. The red color left Professor Herbert's face. He talked more to Pa. Pa softened a little. It looked funny to see Pa in the high school building. It was the first time he'd ever been there.

"We were not only hunting snakes, toads, flowers, butterflies, lizards,'' says Professor Herbert, "but, Mr. Sexton, I was hunting dry timothy grass to put in an incubator and raise some protozoa.''

"I don't know what that is,'' says Pa. "Th' incubator is th' newfangled way o' cheatin' th' hens and raisin' chickens. I ain't so sure about th' breed o' chickens you mentioned.''

"You've heard of germs, Mr. Sexton, haven't you?'' says Professor Herbert.

"Jist call me Luster, if you don't mind,'' says Pa, very casual like.

"All right, Luster, you've heard of germs, haven't you?''

"Yes,'' says Pa, "but I don't believe in germs. I'm sixty-five years old and I ain't seen one yet!''

"You can't see them with your naked eye,'' says Professor Herbert. "Just keep that gun in the holster and stay with me in the high school today. I have a few things I want to show you. That scum on your teeth has germs in it.''

"What,'' says Pa, "you mean to tell me I've got germs on my teeth!''

"Yes,'' says Professor Herbert. "The same kind as we might be able to find in a living black snake if we dissect it!''

"I don't mean to dispute your word,'' says Pa, "but I don't believe it. I don't believe I have germs on my teeth!''

"Stay with me today and I'll show you. I want to take you through the school anyway! School has changed a lot in the hills since you went to school. I don't guess we had high schools in this county when you went to school!''

"No,'' says Pa, "jist readin', writin', and cipherin'. We didn't have all this bug larnin', frog larnin', and findin' germs on your teeth and in the middle o' black snakes! Th' world's changin'.''

"It is,'' says Professor Herbert, "and we hope all for the better. Boys like your own there are going to help change it. He's your boy. He knows all of what I've told you. You stay with me today.''

"I'll shore stay with you,'' says Pa. "I want to see th' germs off'n my teeth. I jist want to see a germ. I've never seen one in my life. 'Seein' is believin',' Pap allus told me.''

Pa walks out of the office with the Professor Herbert. I just hoped Professor Herbert didn't have Pa arrested for pulling his gun. Pa's gun has always been a friend to him when he goes to settle disputes.

The bell rang. School took up. I saw the students when they marched in the schoolhouse look at Pa. They would grin and punch each other. Pa just stood and watched them pass in at the schoolhouse door. Two long lines marched in the house. The boys and girls were clean and well dressed. Pa stood over in the schoolyard under a leafless elm, in his sheepskin coat, his big boots laced in front with buckskin, and his heavy socks stuck above his boot tops. Pa's overalls legs were baggy and wrinkled between his coat and boot tops. His blue work shirt showed at the collar. His big black hat showed his gray-streaked black hair. His face was hard and weather-tanned to the color of a ripe fodder blade. His hands were big and gnarled like the roots of the elm tree he stood beside.

When I went to my first class I saw Pa and Professor Herbert going around over the schoolhouse. I was in my geometry class when Pa and Professor Herbert came in the room. We were explaining our propositions on the blackboard. Professor Herbert and Pa just quietly came in and sat down for a while. I heard Fred Wurts whisper to Glenn Armstrong, "Who is that old man? Lord, he's a rough-looking scamp." Glenn whispered back, "I think he's Dave's Pap." The students in geometry looked at Pa. They must have wondered what he was doing in school. Before the class was over, Pa and Professor Herbert got up and went out. I saw them together down on the playground. Professor Herbert was explaining to Pa. I could see the prints of Pa's gun under his coat when he'd walk around.

At noon in the high school cafeteria Pa and Professor Herbert sat together at the little table where Professor Herbert always ate by himself. They ate together. The students watched the way Pa ate. He ate with his knife instead of his fork. A lot of the students felt sorry for me after they found out he was my father. They didn't have to feel sorry for me. I wasn't ashamed of Pa after I found out he wasn't going to shoot Professor Herbert. I was glad they had made friends. I wasn't ashamed of Pa. I wouldn't be as long as he behaved. He would find out about the high school as I had found out about the Lambert boys across the hill.

In the afternoon when we went to biology Pa was in the class. He was sitting on one of the high stools beside the microscope. We went ahead with our work just as if Pa wasn't in the class. I saw Pa take his knife and scrape tartar from one of his teeth. Professor Herbert put it on the lens and adjusted the microscope for Pa. He adjusted it and worked awhile. Then he says: "Now Luster, look! Put your eye right down to the light. Squint the other eye!"

Pa put his head down and did as Professor Herbert said. "I see 'im," says Pa. "Who'd a ever thought that? Right on a body's teeth! Right in a body's mouth. You're right certain they ain't no fake to this, Professor Herbert?"

"No, Luster," says Professor Herbert. "It's there. That's the germ. Germs live in a world we cannot see with the naked eye. We must use the microscope. There are millions of them in our bodies. Some are harmful. Others are helpful."

Pa holds his face down and looks through the microscope. We stop and watch Pa. He sits upon the tall stool. His knees are against the table. His legs are long. His coat slips up behind when he bends over. The handle of his gun shows. Professor Herbert pulls his coat down quickly.

"Oh, yes," says Pa. He gets up and pulls his coat down. Pa's face gets a little red. He

knows about his gun and he knows he doesn't have any use for it in high school.

"We have a big black snake over here we caught yesterday," says Professor Herbert. "We'll chloroform him and dissect him and show you he has germs in his body, too."

"Don't do it," says Pa. "I believe you. I jist don't want to see you kill the black snake. I never kill one. They are good mousers and a lot o' help to us on the farm. I like black snakes. I jist hate to see people kill 'em. I don't allow 'em killed on my place."

The students look at Pa. They seem to like him better after he said that. Pa with a gun in his pocket but a tender heart beneath his ribs for snakes, but not for man! Pa won't whip a mule at home. He won't whip his cattle.

"Man can defend hisself," says Pa, "but cattle and mules can't. We have the drop on 'em. Ain't nothin' to a man that'll beat a good pullin' mule. He ain't got th' right kind o' a heart!"

Professor Herbert took Pa through the laboratory. He showed him the different kinds of work we were doing. He showed him our equipment. They stood and talked while we worked. Then they walked out together. They talked louder when they got out in the hall.

When our biology class was over I walked out of the room. It was our last class for the day. I would have to take my broom and sweep two hours to finish paying for the split cherry tree. I just wondered if Pa would want me to stay. He was standing in the hallway watching the students march out. He looked lost among us. He looked like a leaf turned brown on the tree among the treetop filled with growing leaves.

I got my broom and started to sweep. Professor Herbert walked up and says, "I'm going to let you do that some other time. You can go home with your father. He is waiting out there."

I laid my broom down, got my books, and went down the steps.

Pa says, "Ain't you got two hours o' sweepin' yet to do?"

I says, "Professor Herbert said I could do it some other time. He said for me to go home with you."

"No," says Pa. "You are goin' to do as he says. He's a good man. School has changed from my day and time. I'm a dead leaf, Dave. I'm behind. I don't belong here. If he'll let me I'll get a broom and we'll both sweep one hour. That pays your debt. I'll hep you pay it. I'll ast 'im and see if he won't let me hep you."

"I'm going to cancel the debt," says Professor Herbert. "I just wanted you to understand, Luster."

"I understand," says Pa, "and since I understand, he must pay his debt fer th' tree and I'm goin' to hep 'im."

"Don't do that," says Professor Herbert. "It's all on me."

"We don't do things like that," says Pa, "we're just and honest people. We don't want somethin' fer nothin'. Professor Herbert, you're wrong now and I'm right. You'll haf to listen to me. I've larned a lot from you. My boy must go on. Th' world has left me. It changed while I've raised my family and plowed th' hills. I'm a just and honest man. I don't skip debts. I ain't larned 'em to do that. I ain't got much larnin' myself but I do know right from wrong atter I see through a thing."

Professor Herbert went home. Pa and I stayed and swept one hour. It looked funny to see Pa use a broom. He never used one at home. Mom used the broom. Pa used the plow. Pa did hard work. Pa says, "I can't sweep. Durned if I can. Look at th' streaks o' dirt I leave on th' floor! Seems like no work a-tall fer me. Brooms is too light 'r somethin'. I'll jist do th' best I can, Dave. I've been wrong about th' school."

I says, "Did you know Professor Herbert can get a warrant out for you for bringing your pistol to school and showing it in his office! They can railroad[3] you for that!"

"That's all made right," says Pa. "I've made that right. Professor Herbert ain't goin' to take it to court. He likes me. I like 'im. We jist had to get together. He had the remedies. He showed me. You must go on to school. I am as strong a man as ever come out'n th' hills fer my years and th' hard work I've done. But I'm behind, Dave. I'm a little man. Your hands will be softer than mine. Your clothes will be better. You'll allus look cleaner than your old Pap. Jist remember, Dave, to pay your debts and be honest. Jist be kind to animals and don't bother th' snakes. That's all I got

3. **railroad:** slang for "send someone to prison on false charges."

agin th' school. Puttin' black snakes to sleep and cuttin' 'em open."

It was late when we got home. Stars were in the sky. The moon was up. The ground was frozen. Pa took his time going home. I couldn't run like I did the night before. It was ten o'clock before we got the work finished, our suppers eaten. Pa sat before the fire and told Mom he was going to take her and show her a germ sometime. Mom hadn't seen one either. Pa told her about the high school and the fine man Professor Herbert was. He told Mom about the strange school across the hill and how different it was from the school in their day and time.

FOR STUDY AND DISCUSSION

1. There are several conflicts in "Split Cherry Tree." The students get into trouble with Farmer Crabtree. Dave has difficulties with both Professor Herbert and his father. Pa confronts Professor Herbert. But the most important conflict is between two ways of life. Explain how the following sentence sums up the central conflict: "He looked like a leaf turned brown on the tree among the treetops filled with growing leaves."

2. A static character remains the same while a dynamic character changes in some significant way. The story that "Split Cherry Tree" tells is essentially about how Pa changes. Does Pa simply change his ideas or does he change in some deeper way? Explain.

3. Professor Herbert does not change, but your attitude toward him probably changes as you read the story. At the beginning he seems stiff and overbearing as he tells Dave, "You must take the punishment. You must stay two hours after school today and two hours after school tomorrow." Then he seems cowardly when he sees Pa's gun and his eyes widen. Point out later speeches and actions that change your initial impression of him.

4. How is the basic conflict of the story resolved?

COMPLEX CHARACTERIZATION

Perhaps you have known people who at first seemed cold and aloof, perhaps snobbish. After you got to know them better, you found they were actually warm and friendly. Their coldness was a mask for their shyness. Thus, as you learned more about them, your attitude toward them changed.

You sometimes go through this same process as you read a story or a novel. At the beginning, a character seems one kind of person. As you continue to read, you learn more about the character and your first impressions are modified. The writer has deliberately controlled your reaction by giving certain information at the beginning of the story and other information later on.

In "Split Cherry Tree" your attitude toward Pa changes as different facets of his character are revealed. When Dave tells Pa about the punishment and when Dave overhears Pa talking to Mom, Pa seems a stern, narrow-minded, violent man. Point out speeches by Pa that contribute to this impression.

Later in the story, Professor Herbert convinces Pa of the value of an education and other aspects of Pa's character emerge. How do the following incidents change your attitude toward Pa?

Pa pulling down his coat over the gun (page 50)

Pa's attitude toward snakes, mules, and cattle (page 51)

Pa's attempt to use a broom (page 52)

Pa's changed opinion of the value of an education (page 52)

The terms *flat* and *round* are sometimes used in distinguishing characters. A *flat character* is one-sided and often represents a stereotype. A *round character*, like Pa, is presented in depth from many angles.

As you learn more about Pa, you become an active participant in the story. Just as Pa's understanding of education and the modern world increases, so your understanding of him grows until he seems much more than a simple backwoods farmer. By the end of the story, you have come to know and appreciate a complex, many-sided character who has demonstrated the capacity to learn and change.

LANGUAGE AND VOCABULARY

Identifying Levels of Language

Jesse Stuart uses three levels of language to tell his story. Some passages are written in *formal standard English,* such as a person would use in a textbook, a business letter, or a formal speech. Some passages are in *informal standard English,* such as an educated person would use when speaking or in a friendly letter. Still other passages are in *dialect,* the special language of a specific region or group of people. Dave tells the story mostly in informal English, although he sometimes lapses into dialect. Which character tends to use formal English? Which character uses dialect? Why is it important in this particular story that different characters use different levels of language?

Find several examples of each level of language. Then take a passage written in dialect and rewrite it either as formal or informal English.

FOR COMPOSITION

Writing About Literature

1. Two central ideas run through this story: the idea of change from old ways to new, and the idea of peace through understanding. Tell how these ideas are developed and what connection is made between them in the story.

2. In "Split Cherry Tree" you see Pa at first as he *seems* to be. As the story unfolds, you come to understand his inner character. "All the Years of Her Life" (page 38) presents Mrs. Higgins at first as a confident woman who impresses Mr. Carr and then as the disconsolate mother alone in her kitchen. Choose one of these characters or a character in another story you have read and explore the contrasts in that character's nature.

ABOUT THE AUTHOR

Jesse Stuart (1907–1984) once said of himself, "I've always wanted to be a writer. I have fought for it; I have dreamed of it." He was born in a log cabin near Riverton, Kentucky. He attended a one-room county school and then a county high school between periods of work on farms. He put himself through Lincoln Memorial University in Tennessee by working at various jobs, including one in a stone quarry and another in a restaurant kitchen. After college, he became a teacher and then principal of a county high school. His first book was a collection of poems, *Man with a Bull Tongue Plow* (1934). His stories appeared in many magazines, and he published several novels. One of his best-known books is *The Thread That Runs So True,* an account of his experiences as a teacher in Kentucky and Ohio.

Gentleman of Río en Medio

Juan A. A. Sedillo

It took months of negotiation to come to an understanding with the old man. He was in no hurry. What he had the most of was time. He lived up in Río en Medio, where his people had been for hundreds of years. He tilled the same land they had tilled. His house was small and wretched, but quaint. The little creek ran through his land. His orchard was gnarled and beautiful.

The day of the sale he came into the office. His coat was old, green and faded. I thought of Senator Catron,[1] who had been such a power with these people up there in the mountains. Perhaps it was one of his old Prince Alberts.[2] He also wore gloves. They were old and torn and his fingertips showed through them. He carried a cane, but it was only the skeleton of a worn-out umbrella. Behind him walked one of his innumerable kin—a dark young man with eyes like a gazelle.

The old man bowed to all of us in the room. Then he removed his hat and gloves, slowly and carefully. Chaplin[3] once did that in a picture, in a bank—he was the janitor. Then he handed his things to the boy, who stood obediently behind the old man's chair.

There was a great deal of conversation about rain and about his family. He was very proud of his large family. Finally we got down to business. Yes, he would sell, as he had agreed, for twelve hundred dollars, in cash. We would buy, and the money was ready. "Don[4] Anselmo," I said to him in Spanish, "we have made a discovery. You remember that we sent that surveyor, that engineer, up there to survey your land so as to make the deed. Well, he finds that you own more than eight acres. He tells us that your land extends across the river and that you own almost twice as much as you thought." He didn't know that. "And now, Don Anselmo," I added, "these Americans are *buena gente,* they are good people, and they are willing to pay you for the additional land as well, at the same rate per acre, so that instead of twelve hundred dollars you will get almost twice as much, and the money is here for you."

The old man hung his head for a moment in thought. Then he stood up and stared at me. "Friend," he said, "I do not like to have you speak to me in that manner." I kept still and let him have his say. "I know these Americans are good people, and that is why I have agreed to sell to them. But I do not care to be

---

1. **Senator Catron:** Thomas Benton Catron, a Senator from New Mexico (1912–1917).
2. **Prince Alberts:** long, double-breasted coats named after Prince Albert, who later became King Edward VII of Great Britain.
3. **Chaplin:** Charlie Chaplin, a comic star of silent movies.

4. **Don:** a title of respect in Spanish, like *Sir* in English.

insulted. I have agreed to sell my house and land for twelve hundred dollars and that is the price."

I argued with him but it was useless. Finally he signed the deed and took the money but refused to take more than the amount agreed upon. Then he shook hands all around put on his ragged gloves, took his stick and walked out with the boy behind him.

A month later my friends had moved into Río en Medio. They had replastered the old adobe house, pruned the trees, patched the fence, and moved in for the summer. One day they came back to the office to complain. The children of the village were overrunning their property. They came every day and played under the trees, built little play fences around them, and took blossoms. When they were spoken to, they only laughed and talked back good-naturedly in Spanish.

I sent a messenger up to the mountains for Don Anselmo. It took a week to arrange another meeting. When he arrived he repeated his previous preliminary performance. He wore the same faded cutaway,[5] carried the same stick and was accompanied by the boy again. He shook hands all around, sat down with the boy behind his chair, and talked about the weather. Finally I broached the subject. "Don Anselmo, about the ranch you sold to these people. They are good people and want to be your friends and neighbors always. When you sold to them you signed a document, a deed, and in that deed you agreed to several things. One thing was that they were to have the complete possession of the property. Now, Don Anselmo, it seems that every day the children of the village overrun the orchard and spend most of their time there. We would like to know if you, as the most respected man in the village, could not stop them from doing so in order that these people may enjoy their new home more in peace."

Don Anselmo stood up. "We have all learned to love these Americans," he said, "because they are good people and good neighbors. I sold them my property because I knew they were good people, but I did not sell them the trees in the orchard."

This was bad. "Don Anselmo," I pleaded, "when one signs a deed and sells real property one sells also everything that grows on the land, and those trees, every one of them, are on the land and inside the boundaries of what you sold."

"Yes, I admit that," he said. "You know," he added, "I am the oldest man in the village. Almost everyone there is my relative and all the children of Río en Medio are my *sobrinos* and *nietos*,[6] my descendants. Every time a child has been born in Río en Medio since I took possession of that house from my mother I have planted a tree for that child. The trees in that orchard are not mine, *señor*, they belong to the children of the village. Every person in Río en Medio born since the railroad came to Santa Fe owns a tree in that orchard. I did not sell the trees because I could not. They are not mine."

There was nothing we could do. Legally we owned the trees but the old man had been so generous, refusing what amounted to a fortune for him. It took most of the following winter to buy the trees, individually, from the descendants of Don Anselmo in the valley of Río en Medio.

---

6. *sobrinos* (sō-brē′nōs) **and** *nietos* (nyĕ′tōs): Spanish for "nephews and nieces" and "grandchildren."

---

5. **cutaway:** a long coat with part of the lower front cut away, used for formal occasions.

FOR STUDY AND DISCUSSION

1. Don Anselmo and the Americans have different views about money and property. What surprising reply does Don Anselmo make when he is offered more money for his property?

2. The Americans believe they have a legal right to the entire property, but Don Anselmo has another surprise for them. Why does Don Anselmo feel he has no right to sell the trees?

3. Because of the unexpected turn of events, Don Anselmo's descendants receive some money at the end of this story. Do you think this solution is fair to everyone? Why or why not?

4. Don Anselmo is dressed in faded and tattered clothing. What details reveal that he wears these clothes like a dignified gentleman? In what other ways does Don Anselmo show that he is a true gentleman?

ABOUT THE AUTHOR

Juan A. A. Sedillo (1902–   ), who is now retired and living in Mexico, was born in New Mexico. He is a descendant of early Spanish colonists. As lawyer and judge, he has held several public offices. For a number of years he wrote a weekly article on Mexico for New Mexico newspapers. He describes himself as "principally a lawyer and only occasionally a writer." The story "Gentleman of Río en Medio" is based on an occurrence in his law office in Santa Fe.

Point of View

The Cask of Amontillado°

Edgar Allan Poe

The thousand injuries of Fortunato I had borne as I best could; but when he ventured upon insult, I vowed revenge. You, who so well know the nature of my soul, will not suppose, however, that I gave utterance to a threat. *At length* I would be avenged; this was a point definitively settled—but the very definitiveness with which it was resolved precluded the idea of risk. I must not only punish, but punish with impunity. A wrong is unredressed when retribution overtakes its redresser. It is equally unredressed when the avenger fails to make himself felt as such to him who has done the wrong.

It must be understood that neither by word nor deed had I given Fortunato cause to doubt my good will. I continued, as was my wont, to smile in his face, and he did not perceive that my smile *now* was at the thought of his immolation.[1]

He had a weak point—this Fortunato—although in other regards he was a man to be respected and even feared. He prided himself on his connoisseurship in wine. Few Italians have the true virtuoso spirit.[2] For the most part their enthusiasm is adopted to suit the time and opportunity—to practice imposture upon the British and Austrian millionaires. In painting and gemmary[3] Fortunato, like his countrymen, was a quack—but in the matter of old wines he was sincere. In this respect I did not differ from him materially; I was skillful in the Italian vintages myself, and bought largely whenever I could.

It was about dusk, one evening during the supreme madness of the carnival season,[4] that I encountered my friend. He accosted me with excessive warmth, for he had been drinking much. The man wore motley.[5] He had on a tight-fitting parti-striped dress, and his head was surmounted by the conical cap and bells. I was so pleased to see him that I thought I should never have done wringing his hand.

I said to him, "My dear Fortunato, you are luckily met. How remarkably well you are looking today! But I have received a pipe[6] of what passes for Amontillado, and I have my doubts."

"How?" said he. "Amontillado? A pipe? Impossible! And in the middle of the carnival!"

"I have my doubts," I replied; "and I was silly enough to pay the full Amontillado price

---

° **Amontillado** (ə-män′tə-lä′dō): a variety of sherry.
1. **immolation** (ĭm′ə-lā′shən): sacrifice.
2. **virtuoso spirit:** deep interest in and knowledge of the arts.
3. **gemmary** (jĕm′ə-rē′): knowledge of precious stones.
4. **carnival season:** the period of celebration before Lent, such as the Mardi Gras festival in New Orleans.
5. **motley:** a clown suit of many colors.
6. **pipe:** a large cask.

without consulting you in the matter. You were not to be found, and I was fearful of losing a bargain."

"Amontillado!"

"I have my doubts."

"Amontillado!"

"And I must satisfy them."

"Amontillado!"

"As you are engaged, I am on my way to Luchesi. If anyone has a critical turn, it is he. He will tell me——"

"Luchesi cannot tell Amontillado from sherry."[7]

"And yet some fools will have it that his taste is a match for your own."

"Come, let us go."

"Whither?"

"To your vaults."

"My friend, no; I will not impose upon your good nature. I perceive you have an engagement. Luchesi——"

"I have no engagement—come."

"My friend, no. It is not the engagement, but the severe cold with which I perceive you are afflicted. The vaults are insufferably damp. They are incrusted with niter."[8]

"Let us go, nevertheless. The cold is merely nothing. Amontillado! You have been imposed upon. And as for Luchesi, he cannot distinguish sherry from Amontillado."

Thus speaking, Fortunato possessed himself of my arm. Putting on a mask of black silk, and drawing a *roquelaure*[9] closely about my person, I suffered him to hurry me to my palazzo.[10]

There were no attendants at home; they had absconded to make merry in honor of the time. I had told them that I should not return until the morning, and had given them explicit orders not to stir from the house. These orders were sufficient, I well knew, to insure their immediate disappearance, one and all, as soon as my back was turned.

I took from their sconces two flambeaux,[11] and giving one to Fortunato, bowed him through several suites of rooms to the archway that led into the vaults. I passed down a long and winding staircase, requesting him to be cautious as he followed. We came at length to the foot of the descent, and stood together on the damp ground of the catacombs of the Montresors.

The gait of my friend was unsteady, and the bells upon his cap jingled as he strode.

"The pipe," said he.

"It is farther on," said I; "but observe the white webwork which gleams from these cavern walls."

He turned toward me, and looked into my eyes with two filmy orbs that distilled the rheum of intoxication.

"Niter?" he asked at length.

"Niter," I replied. "How long have you had that cough?"

"Ugh! ugh! ugh!—ugh! ugh! ugh!—ugh! ugh! ugh!—ugh! ugh! ugh!—ugh! ugh! ugh!"

My poor friend found it impossible to reply for many minutes.

"It is nothing," he said, at last.

"Come," I said, with decision, "we will go back; your health is precious. You are rich, respected, admired, beloved; you are happy, as once I was. You are a man to be missed. For me it is no matter. We will go back; you will be ill, and I cannot be responsible. Besides, there is Luchesi——"

---

7. **sherry:** Fortunato is probably using "sherry" for the sweet variety of sherry. Amontillado is a dry variety.
8. **niter** (nī′tər): white or gray salt deposit.
9. *roquelaure* (rŏk′ə-lôr): a short cloak.
10. **palazzo** (pə-lät′sō): a palace or very luxurious house.

11. **flambeaux** (flăm′bōz′): lighted torches.

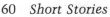

"Enough," he said; "the cough is a mere nothing; it will not kill me. I shall not die of a cough."

"True—true," I replied; "and, indeed, I had no intention of alarming you unnecessarily—but you should use all proper caution. A draft of this Medoc will defend us from the damps."

Here I knocked off the neck of a bottle which I drew from a long row of its fellows that lay upon the mold.

"Drink," I said, presenting him the wine.

He raised it to his lips with a leer. He paused and nodded to me familiarly, while his bells jingled.

"I drink," he said, "to the buried that repose around us."

"And I to your long life."

He again took my arm, and we proceeded.

"These vaults," he said, "are extensive."

"The Montresors," I replied, "were a great and numerous family."

"I forget your arms."[12]

"A huge human foot d'or, in a field azure; the foot crushes a serpent rampant[13] whose fangs are embedded in the heel."

"And the motto?"

"*Nemo me impune lacessit.*"[14]

"Good!" he said.

The wine sparkled in his eyes and the bells jingled. My own fancy grew warm with the Medoc. We had passed through walls of piled bones, with casks and puncheons[15] intermingling, into the inmost recesses of the catacombs. I paused again, and this time I made bold to seize Fortunato by an arm above the elbow.

"The niter!" I said; "see, it increases. It hangs like moss upon the vaults. We are below the river's bed. The drops of moisture trickle among the bones. Come, we will go back ere it is too late. Your cough——"

"It is nothing," he said; "let us go on. But first, another draft of the Medoc."

I broke and reached him a flagon of De Grâve. He emptied it at a breath. His eyes flashed with a fierce light. He laughed and threw the bottle upwards with a gesticulation I did not understand.

I looked at him in surprise. He repeated the movement—a grotesque one.

"You do not comprehend?" he said.

"Not I," I replied.

"Then you are not of the brotherhood."

"How?"

"You are not of the masons."[16]

12. **arms:** coat of arms, an insignia with several figures and a family motto.
13. **foot d'or . . . rampant:** The Montresor coat of arms shows a huge golden foot against a blue background, crushing a serpent that is rearing up.
14. *Nemo . . . lacessit:* Latin for "No one assails me with impunity." In other words: "No one can attack me without being punished."
15. **puncheons** (pŭn'chənz): large casks for beer or wine.

16. **masons:** the Freemasons, a secret fraternal order; also, bricklayers.

"Yes, yes," I said, "yes, yes."

"You? Impossible! A mason?"

"A mason," I replied.

"A sign," he said.

"It is this," I answered, producing a trowel from beneath the folds of my *roquelaure*.

"You jest," he exclaimed, recoiling a few paces. "But let us proceed to the Amontillado."

"Be it so," I said, replacing the tool beneath the cloak, and again offering him my arm. He leaned upon it heavily. We continued our route in search of the Amontillado. We passed through a range of low arches, descended, passed on, and, descending again, arrived at a deep crypt, in which the foulness of the air caused our flambeaux rather to glow than flame.

At the most remote end of the crypt there appeared another less spacious. Its walls had been lined with human remains, piled to the vault overhead, in the fashion of the great catacombs of Paris. Three sides of this interior crypt were still ornamented in this manner. From the fourth the bones had been thrown down, and lay promiscuously upon the earth, forming at one point a mound of some size. Within the wall thus exposed by the displacing of the bones, we perceived a still interior recess, in depth about four feet, in width three, in height six or seven. It seemed to have been constructed for no especial use within itself, but formed merely the interval between two of the colossal supports of the roof of the catacombs, and was backed by one of their circumscribing walls of solid granite.

It was in vain that Fortunato, uplifting his dull torch, endeavored to pry into the depth of the recess. Its termination the feeble light did not enable us to see.

"Proceed," I said; "herein is the Amontillado. As for Luchesi—"

"He is an ignoramus," interrupted my friend, as he stepped unsteadily forward, while I followed immediately at his heels. In an instant he had reached the extremity of the niche, and finding his progress arrested by the rock, stood stupidly bewildered. A moment more and I had fettered him to the granite. In its surface were two iron staples, distant from each other about two feet, horizontally. From one of these depended a short chain, from the other a padlock. Throwing the links about his waist, it was but the work of a few seconds to secure it. He was too much astounded to resist. Withdrawing the key I stepped back from the recess.

"Pass your hand," I said, "over the wall; you cannot help feeling the niter. Indeed it is *very* damp. Once more let me *implore* you to return. No? Then I must positively leave you. But I must first render you all the little attentions in my power."

"The Amontillado!" ejaculated my friend, not yet recovered from his astonishment.

"True," I replied; "the Amontillado."

As I said these words I busied myself among the pile of bones of which I have before spoken. Throwing them aside, I soon uncovered a quantity of building stone and mortar. With these materials and with the aid of my trowel, I began vigorously to wall up the entrance of the niche.

I had scarcely laid the first tier of the masonry when I discovered that the intoxication of Fortunato had in a great measure worn off. The earliest indication I had of this was a low moaning cry from the depth of the recess. It was *not* the cry of a drunken man. There was then a long and obstinate silence. I laid the second tier, and the third, and the fourth; and then I heard the furious vibrations of the chain. The noise lasted for several minutes, during which, that I might hearken to it with the more satisfaction, I ceased my labors and sat down upon the bones. When at last the clanking subsided, I resumed the trowel, and finished without interruption the fifth, the sixth, and the seventh tier. The wall was now nearly upon a level with my breast. I again paused, and holding the flambeaux over the masonwork, threw a few feeble rays upon the figure within.

A succession of loud and shrill screams, bursting suddenly from the throat of the chained form, seemed to thrust me violently back. For a brief moment I hesitated—I trembled. Unsheathing my rapier,[17] I began to grope with it about the recess; but the thought of an instant reassured me. I placed my hand upon the solid fabric of the catacombs, and felt satisfied. I reapproached the wall. I replied to the yells of him who clamored. I reechoed—I aided—I surpassed them in volume and in strength. I did this, and the clamorer grew still.

It was now midnight, and my task was drawing to a close. I had completed the eighth, the ninth, and the tenth tier. I had finished a portion of the last and the eleventh; there remained but a single stone to be fitted and plastered in. I struggled with its weight; I placed it partially in its destined position. But now there came from out the niche a low laugh that erected the hairs upon my head. It was succeeded by a sad voice, which I had difficulty in recognizing as that of the noble Fortunato. The voice said:

"Ha! ha! ha!—he! he!—a very good joke indeed—an excellent jest. We will have many a

---

17. **rapier** (rā′pē-ər): a long two-edged sword.

rich laugh about it at the palazzo—he! he! he!
—over our wine—he! he! he!"

"The Amontillado!" I said.

"He! he! he!—he! he! he!—yes, the Amontillado. But is it not getting late? Will not they be awaiting us at the palazzo—the Lady Fortunato and the rest? Let us be gone."

"Yes," I said, "let us be gone."

"*For the love of God, Montresor.*"

"Yes," I said, "for the love of God."

But to these words I hearkened in vain for a reply. I grew impatient. I called aloud:

"Fortunato!"

No answer. I called again:

"Fortunato!"

No answer still. I thrust a torch through the remaining aperture and let it fall within. There came forth in return only a jingling of the bells. My heart grew sick—on account of the dampness of the catacombs. I hastened to make an end of my labor. I forced the last stone into its position; I plastered it up. Against the new masonry I reerected the old rampart of bones. For the half of a century no mortal has disturbed them. *In pace requiescat!*[18]

---

18. *In . . . requiescat!:* Latin for "May he rest in peace!"

FOR STUDY AND DISCUSSION

1. In the opening paragraph Montresor speaks of carrying out his revenge with "impunity" —with freedom from risk or punishment. Give a step-by-step account of his plan.

2. The story takes place during the carnival season. During such a season there are many parties and costume balls. People often appear in the streets in costume, as Fortunato does. Why is it appropriate for Fortunato to wear a clown costume?

3. Montresor speaks of bearing the "thousand injuries of Fortunato." From what you learn of Fortunato through his words and actions, do you think he has deliberately injured Montresor? Explain. (For example, if he had, he would be cautious in his dealings with Montresor. Is he?) What does the mention of the "thousand injuries" tell you about Montresor?

4. Montresor ironically gives Fortunato hints of his intentions. Find examples. How does Fortunato react to these hints?

5. The last part of the story, after Montresor has chained Fortunato to the granite wall, is told in considerable detail to arouse the reader's horror. Point out some of the details. How does Montresor's matter-of-fact account of these details heighten the effect of horror?

6. Montresor is proud of his revenge and considers it an act of justice. Do you think the author meant you to share Montresor's attitude? Give details in the story to support your answer.

POINT OF VIEW

Point of View is the angle or position from which a story is told. Just as a movie camera remains at a distance to take in a large scene or moves in to concentrate on one face, so the point of view in a story determines the distance between readers and characters. A story can be told by an outside observer, by a single character, or by several characters within a story.

Edgar Allan Poe chose to tell "The Cask of Amontillado" from the inside, through the words of its principal character. This point of view, in which the narrator speaks in his own person as "I," is called the *first-person point of view*. Poe never steps outside of his narrator to tell you what he, the author, thinks about the characters or actions. Yet he does leave clues to indicate how his readers should regard Montresor. You probably concluded that Montresor is not a reliable narrator and that you should not take his word for the "thousand injuries" he had endured or for the justice of his revenge.

Why do you think Poe decided to limit the point of view so that you see the events through Montresor's eyes and mind? To answer this question, imagine that "The Cask of Amontillado" had been told by an outside observer, as in a police report or in a newspaper story. Would the story be as horrible or as shocking? Explain.

FOR COMPOSITION

Writing a Radio Play

"The Cask of Amontillado" has several times been adapted and performed as a radio play. Make your own adaptation for the medium of radio, providing narration, dialogue, and sound effects. Remember that a radio play appeals to the imagination through the mind's eye. Sound effects and pauses can be as effective as words in stirring your listeners' emotions. You may present your play already taped or perform it "live," making use of a narrator and a sound-effects technician.

ABOUT THE AUTHOR

The son of actors, Edgar Allan Poe (1809–1849) was orphaned at the age of two. He was taken in by a childless couple, Mr. and Mrs. John Allan of Richmond, Virginia. The Allans gave Poe a gentleman's education but never formally adopted him. Poe entered the University of Virginia and soon ran up large debts, which the Allans refused to pay. Poe left the University before his first academic year ended. Under an assumed name, he enlisted in the army and rose to the rank of sergeant major. After two years he entered West Point, but chafing under the restraints of military discipline, he deliberately provoked a court-martial and was expelled from the Academy. Thereafter, the Allans would no longer help him.

The rest of Poe's life was a struggle to support himself through writing and editing. His marriage to Virginia Clemm, his thirteen-year-old cousin, added to his financial burdens. She died of tuberculosis when she was twenty-five. Poe worked as an editor on several magazines, but the work was taxing and the pay small. Near the end of his life, he managed to gain control of a magazine, but it failed for lack of sufficient funds.

Today Poe is equally famous for his short stories and his poetry. Among his best-known poems are "The Raven," "Ulalume," "Annabel Lee," and "The Bells." Among his most famous short stories are "The Black Cat," "The Fall of the House of Usher," "The Pit and the Pendulum," and "The Murders in the Rue Morgue." Poe believed that a short story should be planned and written so that every word, every detail contributes toward a single, powerful impression.

Before the End of Summer

Grant Moss, Jr.

When Dr. Frazier came, Bennie's grandmother told him to run down to the spring and wade in the stream that flowed from it across the pasture field to Mr. Charley Miller's pond, or play under the big oak tree that stood between her field and Mr. Charley Miller's. He started along the path, but when he was about midway to the spring he stopped. He had waded in the stream and caught minnows all that morning. He had played under the oak tree all yesterday afternoon. He had asked his grandmother to let him walk the mile and a half down the road to James and Robert Lee Stewart's to play, but she had not let him go. There was nothing he wanted to do alone. He wanted someone to play with. He turned and went back and crept under the window of his grandmother's room. Their voices floated low and quiet out into the cool shade that lay over the house.

"How long will it be?" he heard his grandmother say.

"Before the end of summer."

"Are you sure?"

"Yes. You should have sent for me long ago."

"I've passed my threescore and ten years. I'm eighty-four."

What did they mean? Perhaps he ought not to be listening.

"How will it come? Tell me, Doctor. I can stand it."

"There will be sharp, quick pains like the ones you've been having. Your heart cannot stand many more attacks. It grows weaker with each one, even though you're able to go about your work as you did before the attack came. I'm going to leave you a prescription for some pills that will kill the pain almost instantly. But that's about all they will do. When an attack comes, take two with a glass of water. They'll make you drop off to sleep. One time you won't wake up."

Now Bennie understood. But he could not turn and run away.

There was a brief silence. Then his grandmother said, "Don't tell Birdie nor anybody else."

"But you can't stay here alone with the child all day long. Why, he's only ten years old."

"I know. . . . Doctor, there ain't anyone to come stay with me. Birdie must go to the Fieldses' to work. You know it's just Birdie, the boy, and me. I got no close kin. My husband, my three sons, and my other daughter's been dead for years now. You see, I know death, Doctor, I know it well. I'm just not use to it."

"No one is," Dr. Frazier said.

"Here's what I want to do. I'll go on just like before. There ain't nothin' else for me to do. When an attack comes, I'll take the two pills and I'll send Bennie runnin' down the road for May Mathis. She'll come. May will come. I know nobody I'd rather have set beside me than May. I knowed her all my life. Me and her done talked about this thing many times. It's July now. July the seventh. Then August—then September. But here I go runnin' on and on. Let me get your money. You've got to be paid. You've got to live."

"Please," Dr. Frazier said.

"No harm meant."

In a moment, Bennie heard them walking out onto the porch through the door of her room. Then he could see them as they crossed the yard to the gate, where Dr. Frazier's horse and buggy stood. He was a little man, with a skin that was almost black. He climbed into

his buggy and started up the road toward the town, which was three miles away, and she stood and looked after him. Her back was to the house. People said that Bennie's grandmother had Indian blood in her veins, for she had high cheekbones and her nose was long and straight, but her mouth was big. Her eyes seemed as though they were buried way back in her head, in a mass of wrinkles. They danced and twinkled whenever they looked at him. She was a big woman, and she wore long full skirts that came all the way to the ground.

She closed the gate and started back to the house, and it came to Bennie that he was alone with her, and that she was going to die soon. He turned and ran noiselessly across the backyard, through the back gate, and down the path to the spring.

When he reached the spring, he kept running. He ran across the pasture field and up the hill to the barbed-wire fence that divided his grandmother's land from Mr. Charley Miller's. He threw himself to the ground and rolled under the fence, picked himself up on the other side, and ran through Mr. Charley Miller's field of alfalfa and into the woods, until at last he fell exhausted in the cool damp grass of a shaded clearing.

His grandmother was going to die. She might even be dead now. She was going to lie cold and still, in a long black casket that would be put into a hearse that would take her to church in town. The Reverend Isaiah Jones would preach her funeral. People would cry, because people liked his grandmother. His mother would cry. He would cry. And now he was crying, and he could not stop crying.

But at last he did, and he sat up and took from his pocket the clean white rag that his grandmother had given him to use as a handkerchief and dried his eyes. He must get up and go back to the house. He would have to be alone with his grandmother until his mother came home from the Fieldses' after she had cooked their supper. And he must tell no one what he had heard Dr. Frazier say to his grandmother.

He found her sitting in her big rocking chair, her hands clasped in her lap. "You been gone a long time," she said. "The water bucket's empty. Take it and go fill it at the spring. Time for me to be gettin' up from here and cookin' supper."

When he got back from the spring, he found her laying a fire in the kitchen stove.

It was nearly dark when he saw his mother coming, and he ran to meet her. She looked at him closely and said, "Bennie, why on earth did you run so fast?"

He could only say breathlessly, "I don't know." He added quickly, "What did you bring me?" Sometimes she brought him a piece of cake or pie, or the leg of chicken from the Fieldses'. Today she did not have anything.

It was a long time before he went to sleep that night.

The next day, he stayed outdoors and only went into the house when his grandmother called him to do something for her. She did not notice.

On Sunday, his mother did not go to the Fieldses'. In the morning, they went to church. That afternoon, Mr. Joe Bailey drove up to the house in his horse and buggy to take Bennie's mother for a buggy ride. She had put on her pretty blue-flowered dress and her big wide-brimmed black straw hat with the red roses around its crown and the black ribbon that fell over the brim and down her back. She looked very pretty and as pleased as she could be. Bennie wanted to go riding with them. Once, he had asked Mr. Joe if he could go along, and Mr. Joe had grinned and said yes,

but Bennie's mother had not been pleased at all, for some reason. This Sunday, after they had gone, his grandmother let him walk the mile and a half down the road to play with James and Robert Lee Stewart.

He knew that his grandmother was preparing to die. He came upon her kneeling in prayer beside her bed and its high headboard that almost touched the ceiling. As she sat in her rocking chair, she said the Twenty-third Psalm. He knew only the first verse: "The Lord is my shepherd; I shall not want."

Now he felt toward his grandmother the way he felt toward certain people, only more so. There was a feeling that made people seem strange—a feeling that came from them to you—that made you stand away from them. There was Miss Sally Cannon, his teacher. You did not go close to Miss Sally. She made you sit still and always keep your reader or your spelling book open on your desk, or do your arithmetic problems. If she caught you whispering or talking, she called you up to the front of the room and gave you several stinging lashes on your leg or across your back with one of the long switches that always lay across her desk. You did not go close to Miss Sally unless you had to. You did not go close to Dr. Frazier or the Reverend Isaiah Jones. Teachers, doctors, and preachers were special people.

You did not go close to white people, either. Sometimes when he and his grandmother went to town, they would stop at the Fieldses'. They would walk up the long green yard and go around the big red brick house, with its tall white columns, to the kitchen, where his mother was; it always seemed a nice place to be, even on a hot summer day. His mother and his grandmother would chuckle over something that Miss Marion Fields or Mr. Ridley Fields had done. They would stop smiling the minute Miss Marion came into the room, and they would become like people waiting in the vestibule of a church for the prayer to be finished so they could go in. He knew that he acted the same way.

Miss Marion had light-brown hair and light-brown eyes. His grandmother said that she was like a sparrow, for she was a tiny woman. She always wore a dress that was pretty enough to wear to church. The last time he was at the Fieldses', Miss Marion came into the kitchen. After she had spoken to his grandmother, she turned to him. He was sitting in a chair near the window, and he felt himself stiffen both inside and outside. She said, "I declare, Birdie, Bennie's the prettiest colored child I ever did see. Lashes long as a girl's. Is he a good boy, Hannah?"

"He's a quiet child," his grandmother said. "Sometimes I think he's too quiet, but he's a good child—at least when I got my eyes on him." They all laughed.

"I'm sure Bennie's good," Miss Marion said. "Be a good boy, Bennie. Eat plenty and grow strong, and when you're big enough to work, Mr. Ridley will be glad to give you work here on his place. We're so glad to have your mother here with us. Now, be good, won't you?"

"Yes, Ma'am," he answered.

"Birdie, give him a piece of that lemon pie you baked for supper. Well, Hannah, it's been nice talking with you again. Always stop on your way to town."

Two weeks to the day after Dr. Frazier's visit, Miss May Mathis came to see his grandmother. She was much shorter than his grandmother—a plump woman, who always wore long black-and-white checked gingham dresses that fell straight down from her high full breasts to her knees and then flared outward. Her chin was sharp, with folds of flesh

around it. Her nose was wide and flat. She had small, snapping black eyes. Her skin was like cream that had been kept too long and into which hundreds of tiny black specks had fallen.

As she came into the yard, she asked Bennie if his grandmother was at home. She said she would sit on the porch, where it was cool. He ran into the house to tell his grandmother that she was there.

His grandmother put away her sewing and went out on the porch. "May, I'm glad you come. I've been lookin' for you," she said.

"I'd been here sooner, but my stomach's been givin' me trouble lately. Sometimes I think my time ain't long."

"Hush—hush! You'll live to see me put under the ground."

"Well, the day before yesterday I spent half the day in bed. I thought I'd have to send John for you," Miss May answered, and she went into a long account of the illness that troubled her.

Bennie got up from the edge of the porch and ran around the house. The two old women paid no attention to his going. He knew what his grandmother would say to Miss May. She would tell Miss May how she wanted to be dressed for burial. She would name the song she wanted to be sung over her. He had heard the same conversation many times. Now it was different. What they were talking about would soon "come to pass," as his grandmother would say. Miss May did not know, but he knew.

He went out of the back gate and down the path to the spring. He waded in the stream awhile, catching minnows in his hands and then letting them go. He went across the pasture field. He broke off a persimmon bush to use as a switch, and he chased his grandmother's cow about the pasture a bit. But the cow was old and soon grew tired of moving when he hit her with the switch. Then he went to the big oak tree that stood between the fields and sat down. He stayed there until he saw Miss May Mathis going out of the front gate.

The July days went slowly by, one much like another. It grew hotter and hotter.

One day when he walked into the house after playing a long time in the stream and the pasture field, he found his grandmother quietly sleeping in her big rocking chair. He saw a bottle full of big white pills on the dresser. It had not been there when he left the house. An empty glass stood beside the pills. He felt too frightened to move. Her breast was rising and falling evenly. She stirred and then opened her eyes.

She seemed dazed and not to see him for a moment. Then her lips curved into a queer smile, and a twinkle came into her eyes. "Must have dropped off to sleep like a baby," she said. "Run outdoors and play. I'll sct here awhile, and then I'll get up and start supper."

Later on, she called him and asked if he could make out with milk and cold food from dinner. She left the milking for his mother to do when she came home from the Fieldses'. But the next morning his grandmother was all right, and he thought she was not going to die that summer, after all.

One morning, a little after his mother had gone to the Fieldses', Mr. John Mathis drove up. He turned his horse and buggy around to face the way he had come. Then he walked up the path to the house. He was a tall, rawboned man with a bullet-shaped head, and he looked exactly like what he was—a deacon in a church.

"What is it, John?" Bennie's grandmother asked.

"It's May. She was sick all day yesterday. Last night I had to get the doctor for her. Jennie Stewart's there now."

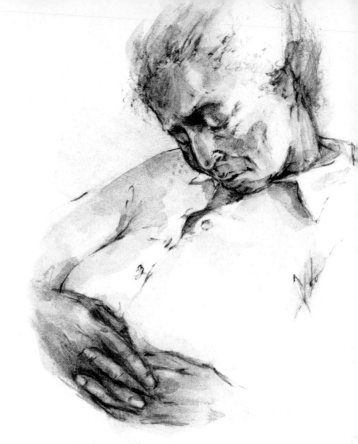

"I'll be ready to go in a minute," his grandmother said.

On the way to the Mathises', Bennie sat on the back of the buggy. His grandmother and Mr. John said only a few words. When they reached the house, his grandmother told him to keep very quiet and to be good, and she went inside at once. There were people on the porch, and people continued to come and go. It was midafternoon, and still his grandmother had not come from within the house. A Ford car drove up to the gate. In it were Philomena Jones and her mother. Philomena was a year younger than Bennie. She had a sharp little yellow face, big black eyes that went everywhere, and she wore her hair in two long plaits. "Come on," she said, "and let's play something." When they were out of hearing of the grown-up people, she said, "Miss May going to die."

"How do you know?"

"I heard my mama say she was. She's old. When you're old you have to die."

Next, Philomena said, "Your mama's tryin' to catch Mr. Joe Bailey for a husband. Mama said it's time she's getting another husband if she's ever going to get one."

"You stop talkin'!" Bennie told her.

"She said you pa's been dead nine years now and if your mama don't hurry and take Mr. Joe Bailey—that is, if she can get him—she may never get a chance to marry again."

"If you don't stop talkin', I'll hit you!"

"No, you won't. I'm not scared of you, even if you are a boy, and I'll say what I want to. Mama said, 'Birdie Wilson's in her forties, if she a day, and if a woman lets herself get into her forties without marryin', her chance are mightly slim after that.' I'm goin' to marry when I'm twenty."

"Nobody'd want you. You talk too much."

"I don't, either."

"I won't play with you. I'm goin' back to the porch," he said.

Philomena stayed in the yard a little longer. She carried on an imaginary conversation with a person who seemed as eager to talk as she. After a while, she ran back to the porch and sat down and gave her attention to what the grown-up people were saying, now and then putting in a word herself.

Then his grandmother came out from the house. People stopped talking at the sight of her face. "May's gone," she said.

The people on the porch bowed their heads, and their faces became as though they were already at Miss May Mathis's funeral.

His grandmother looked very tired. After a moment she said, "The Lord giveth and the Lord taketh. Blessed be the name of the Lord." There was a silence. Then she spoke again. "I thought May would do for me what I have to do for her now." She turned and went back into the house. Some of the women rose and followed her.

The people who remained on the porch spoke in low voices. Someone wondered when the funeral would be. Someone wondered if Miss May's sister Ethel, who lived in St. Louis, would come. Someone hoped it would not rain the day of the funeral.

Then Mr. John Mathis and Bennie's grandmother came out on the porch. Mr. John said, "Hannah, you done all you could do. May couldn't have had a better friend. You're tired now. I'll send you home."

At home, his grandmother seemed not to notice him. Her eyes seemed to be taking a great sad rest. She sent him to the spring to get water to cook supper.

As he walked down the path, he thought about his grandmother. He felt more sorry for her than he felt fear of her. Miss May Mathis was dead; he could not run and get her now.

On Sunday afternoon at two o'clock at the Baptist Church, Miss May Mathis's funeral service was held. There was a procession of buggies, surreys, and even a few automobiles from the house to the church. Mr. Joe Bailey came and took Bennie's mother, his grandmother, and him to church. The funeral was a long one. He sat beside his grandmother and listened to the prayers, the songs, and the sermon, all the time dreading the moment when the flowers would be taken from the gray casket, the casket would be opened, and the people would file by to see the body for the last time.

The Reverend Isaiah Jones described Heaven as a land flowing with milk and honey, a place where people ate fruit from the tree of life, wore golden slippers, long white robes, and starry crowns, and rested forever. The Reverend Isaiah Jones was certain that Miss May Mathis was there, resting in the arms of Jesus, done with the sins and sorrows of this world. Bennie wondered why Mr. John covered his face with his hands, and why Miss May's sister Ethel, who had come all the way from St. Louis, cried out, and why people cried, if Miss May was so happy in this land. It seemed that they would be glad for her, so glad they would not cry. Or did they cry because they were glad? He could not understand. The Reverend Jones said that they would see Miss May on the Resurrection morning. Bennie could not understand this, either.

At last the gray casket was opened, and people began to file by it. And at last he was close. His mother went by, and then Mr. Joe. Now his grandmother. The line of people stopped, waiting expectantly. His grandmother stood and looked down on Miss May for a long time. She did not cry out. She simply stood there and looked down, and finally she moved on. Now he was next. Miss May Mathis looked as though she had simply combed her hair and piled it on top of her head, put on her best black silk dress, pinned her big old brooch to its lace collar, picked up a white handkerchief with one hand, and then decided that instead of going to church she would sleep a little while. As he looked down on her, he was not as afraid as he'd thought he would be.

Outside the church, as the procession was forming to go to the graveyard, Dr. Frazier came up to his grandmother and asked how she was.

"As well as could be expected, Doctor," his grandmother said. And then, in a low voice, "I've had only one."

"You got through it all right."

"Yes."

"And this?"

"I've managed to get through it."

"You will be careful."

"Yes."

"Now?"

"He'll have to go to the Stewarts'."

They did not know that he understood what they were talking about, even if none of the other people around them did. He heard two women whispering. One said to the other, "It's wonderful the way Aunt Hannah took it." He felt very proud of his grandmother.

Now his grandmother's footsteps were slower as she moved about the house and yard. He kept the garden and the flower beds along the yard fences weeded, the stove box full of wood, the water bucket full all the time, without her having to ask him to do these things for her. He overheard her say to his mother, "Child does everything without being told. It ain't natural."

"Reckon he's not well?" his mother asked anxiously.

"Don't think so. He eats well. Maybe the trouble is the child don't have nobody to play with every day. He'll be all right when fall comes and school starts."

August came, and it grew hotter. The sun climbed up the sky in the morning and down the sky in the evening like a tired old man with a great load on his back going up and down a hill. Then one hot mid-August day dawned far hotter and sultrier than the one just past. It grew still hotter during the early part of the morning, but by midday there was a change, for there was a breeze, and in the west a few dark clouds gathered in the sky. His grandmother said, "I believe the rain will come at last."

About three o'clock, the wind rose suddenly. It bent the top of the big oak tree that stood in the yard. There were low rumbles of thunder.

"Bennie, Bennie, come! Let's get the chickens up!" his grandmother called to him.

By the time the chickens were safe in the henhouse and chicken coops, it was time to go into the house and put the windows down. The wind lifted the curtains almost to the ceiling. They got the windows down. His grandmother went into the kitchen. He went out on the porch. He wanted to watch the clouds, for he had never seen any bigger or blacker or quite so low to the earth—he was sure they must be touching the ground some-where. He wanted to see what the wind did to the trees, the corn, and the grass.

At last the rain fell, first in great drops that were blown onto the edge of the porch by the wind and felt cool and good as they touched his face. They made him want to run out into the yard. Then the rain came so quickly and so heavily, and with it so much wind, that it came up on the porch and almost pushed him back into the house. The thunder roared and there were flashes of lightning.

"Bennie, Bennie, where are you?" his grand-mother called, and when he went inside she said, "Set down—set down in the big chair there or come into my room if you want to. I'm goin' to just set in my rocker."

"I'll stay here," he said, and he went to the big chair near the fireplace and sat down.

"There—there—just set there. I'll leave the door open."

He tried to keep from thinking what might happen if his grandmother had one of her spells, but he could not. He went to the fireplace. The back of the fireplace was wet; water stood on it in drops that looked like tears on a face. He stood and looked at it awhile, then he sat down in the big chair. There was nothing else to do but to sit there.

He heard her cry out. The cry was sharp and quick. Then it was cut off.

She called him. "Bennie! Bennie!" Her voice was thick.

He could not move.

"Bennie!"

He went into the room where she was.

She sat on the side of her bed. She was breathing hard, and in one hand she had the bottle of white pills. "Get me a glass of water. One of my spells done come over me."

He went into the kitchen and got a glass from the kitchen safe and filled it with water from the bucket that sat on the side table. Then he went back to her and gave her the water.

She took it and put two pills in her mouth and gulped them down with the water. She was breathing hard. "Pull off my shoes," she said.

As he was unlacing the high-top shoes she always wore, she gave a little cry. He felt her body tremble. "Just a bit of pain. Don't worry. I'm all right," she said. "It's gone," she added a moment later.

When he got her shoes off, he lifted her legs onto the bed, and she lay back and closed her eyes. "Go into the front room," she said, "and close the door behind you and stay there until the storm is past. I'm goin' to drop off to sleep—and if I'm still asleep when the storm is over, just let me sleep until your mama comes. Don't come in here. Don't try to wake me. 'Twon't do me no harm to take me a long good sleep."

He could not move. He could only stand and stare at her.

"Hear me? Go on, I tell you. Go on—don't, I'll get up from here and skin you alive."

He crept from the room, closing the door after him.

He went to the big chair and sat down. He must not cry. Crying could not help him. There was nothing to do but to sit there until the storm was past.

The rain and the wind came steadily now. He sat back in the big chair. He wondered about his mother. Was she safe at the

Fieldses'? He wondered if the water had flowed into the henhouse and under the chicken coops, where the little chickens were. If it had, some of the little chickens might get drowned. The storm lasted so long that it began to seem to him that it had always been there.

At last he became aware that the room was growing lighter and the rain was not so hard. The thunder and lightning were gone. Then, almost as suddenly as it had begun, the storm was over.

He got up and went out on the porch. Everything was clean. Everything looked new. There were little pools of water everywhere, and it was cool. There were a few clouds in the sky, but they were white and light gray. He looked across the field toward Mr. Charley Miller's, and he opened his eyes wide when he saw that the storm had blown down the big oak tree. He started to run back into the house to tell his grandmother that the storm had blown the tree down, and then he stopped. After a minute, he stepped down from the porch. The wet grass felt good on his bare feet.

He felt his grandmother in the doorway even before he heard her call. He turned and looked at her. She had put on her shoes and the long apron she always wore. She came out on the porch, and he decided that she looked as though her sleep had done her good.

He remembered the tree, and he cried, "Look—look, Grannie! The storm blowed down the tree between your field and Mr. Charley Miller's."

"That tree was there when me and your grandpa came here years and years ago," she said. "The Lord saw fit to let it be blowed down in this storm. I—I—" She broke off and went back into the house.

He ran into the house and said to her, "I'm going down to the spring. I bet the stream's deep as a creek."

"Don't you get drowned like old Pharaoh's army," she said.

The storm drove away the heat, for the days were now filled with cool winds that came and rattled the cornstalks and the leaves on the oak tree in the yard. There were showers. The nights were long and cool; the wind came into the rooms, gently pushing aside the neat white curtains to do so.

One morning when he went into the kitchen to get hot water and soap to take to the back porch to wash his face and hands, he found his mother and grandmother busy talking. They stopped the moment they saw him. His mother's face seemed flushed and uncomfortable, but her eyes were very bright.

"Done forgot how to say good mornin' to a body?" his grandmother said.

"Good mornin', Grannie. Good mornin', Mama."

"That's more like it."

"Good mornin', Bennie," his mother said. She looked at him, and he had a feeling that she was going to come to him and take him in her arms the way she used to do when he was a little boy. But she did not.

His grandmother laughed. "Well, son, Mr. Joe Bailey went and popped the question to your mama last night."

His mother blushed. He did not know what to say to either of them. He just stood and looked at them.

"What you goin' to say to that?" his mother said.

All he could think to say was "It's all right."

His grandmother laughed again, and his mother smiled at him the way she did when he ran down the road to meet her and asked her to let him carry the packages that she had.

"When will they be married?" he asked.

"Soon," his mother said.

"Where will they live—here?"

"That ain't been settled yet," his grandmother said. "Nothin' been settled. They just got engaged last night while they were settin' in the front room and you was sleepin' in your bed. Things can be settled later." She gave a sigh that his mother did not hear. But he heard it.

He poured water from the teakettle into the wash pan and took the pan out on the back porch and washed and dried his hands. He looked across the fields and hills. The sun had not come up yet, but the morning lay clear and soft and quiet as far as his eyes could see.

His mother was going to marry Mr. Joe Bailey. He did mind a little. He knew that was what she wanted. He liked Mr. Joe. When Mr. Joe smiled at him, he always had to smile back at him; something seemed to make him do so.

After his mother had gone to the Fieldses', he and his grandmother sat down to breakfast at the table in the kitchen. His grandmother never ate a meal without saying grace. Usually she gave thanks just for the food that they were about to eat. This morning she asked the Lord to bless his mama, Mr. Joe, and him, and she thanked the Lord for answering all her prayers.

As they ate, she talked to him. She spoke as though she were talking to herself, expecting no answer from him, but he knew that she meant for him to listen to her words, and he knew why she was talking to him. "Joe Bailey will make your mama a good husband and you a good father to take the place of your father who you never knew. The Lord took your father when your father was still young, but that was the Lord's will. Joe Bailey will be good to you, for he is a good man. Mind him. Don't make trouble between him and your mama. Hear me?"

"Yes, Ma'am."

"Don't you worry about where you'll stay. You'll be with your mama. Hear me?"

"Yes'm."

She sat silent for a moment, and then she added, "Well, no matter if your mama is going to marry Mr. Joe Bailey. We got to work today just like we always has. No matter what comes, we have to do the little things that our hands find to do. Soon as you finish eatin', go to the spring and get water and fill the pot and the tubs."

August drew toward its close, but the soft cool days stayed on, and they were calm and peaceful. His grandmother cooked the meals, and washed and ironed their own clothes and those that his mother brought home from the Fieldses' and Mr. Charley Miller's. Sometimes Bennie wondered if she had put from her mind the things that Dr. Frazier had said to her that day he listened under the window. Sometimes it seemed to him that he had never crept close to the window and listened to her and Dr. Frazier. The summer seemed just like last summer and the summer before that.

One day near the end of the month, Mr. John Mathis stopped by the house on his way to town. He was on horseback, riding a big black horse whose sides glistened. He hailed Bennie's grandmother, and she came out on the porch to pass the time of day with him.

"Ever see such a fine summer day, John?" she said.

"It's not a summer day, Hannah. It's a fall day. It's going to be an early fall this year."

"Think so?" his grandmother asked. Her face changed, but Mr. John did not notice.

"I can feel it. I can feel it in the air. The smell of fall is here already." Then they fell to talking about the church and people they knew.

She stood on the porch and watched Mr. John ride up the road on his big black horse. Often that day, she came out on the porch and stood and looked across the fields and hills.

When Bennie went outside for the first time the next morning and looked around him, he did not see a single cloud in the sky. The quiet that lay about him felt like a nice clean sheet you pull over your head before you go to sleep at night that shuts out everything to make a space both warm and cool just for you. The day grew warm. A little after midday, clouds began to float across the sky, but for the most part it remained clear and very blue. He played in the yard under the oak tree, and then he went down to the spring and played. In the afternoon, he rolled his hoop up and down the road in front of the house. He grew tired of this and went and sat under the tree.

He was still sitting under the tree when his grandmother cried out. She gave a sharp sudden cry, like the cry people make when they've been stung by a bee or a wasp. He got to his feet. Then he heard her call. "Bennie! Bennie!"

He ran into the house and into her room.

She sat in her big rocking chair, leaning forward a little, her hands clutching the arms of the chair. She was breathing hard. He had never seen her eyes as they were now. "Water — the pills — in the dresser."

He ran into the kitchen and got a glass of water and ran back to the room and gave it to her and then went to the dresser and got the bottle of pills. He unscrewed the top and took out two of them and gave them to her.

She put the pills in her mouth and gulped them down with water. Then she leaned back and closed her eyes. At last she breathed easier, and in a few moments she opened her eyes. "Run and get—get Miss— No, go get your mama. Hurry! Your grandmother is very sick."

It was a long way to the Fieldses'—even longer than to the Stewarts'! He stood still and looked at her. She was a big woman, and the chair was a big chair. Now she seemed smaller—lost in the chair.

"Hurry—hurry, child."

"Grannie, I'll stay with you until you go to sleep, if you want me to," he heard himself say.

"No! No! Hurry!"

"I heard you and Dr. Frazier talking that day."

"Child! Child! You knew all the time?"

"Yes, Grannie."

"When I drop off to sleep, I won't wake up. Your grandmother won't wake up here."

"I know."

"You're not afraid?"

He shook his head.

She seemed to be thinking hard, and at last she said, "Set down, child. Set down beside me."

He pulled up the straight chair and sat down facing her.

"Seems like I don't know what to say to you, Bennie. Be a good boy. Seems like I can't think any more. Everything leavin' me—leavin' me."

"I'll set here until you go to sleep, and then I'll go and get Mama."

"That's a good boy," she said, and she closed her eyes.

He sat still and quiet until her breath came softly and he knew that she was asleep. It was not long. Then he got up and walked from the room and out of the house.

He did not look back, and he did not run until he was a good way down the road. Then suddenly he began to run, and he ran as fast as he could.

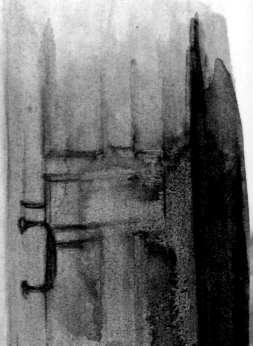

FOR STUDY AND DISCUSSION

1. At the beginning of the story, Bennie learns that his grandmother is expected to die before the end of summer. At the end of the story, Bennie witnesses her death. Compare his reactions in the opening and closing scenes of the story. What change would you say has taken place in his understanding of death?

2. Throughout the story Bennie is reminded of his grandmother's impending death. How does Miss May's funeral prepare Bennie to face the death of someone he loves?

3. This story is told from the point of view of a ten-year-old. How does the author convince you that Bennie's perceptions are those of a child? What aspects of the adult world are beyond Bennie's grasp?

LIMITED THIRD-PERSON POINT OF VIEW

A writer may sometimes tell a story in the third person from the point of view of a character in the story. "Before the End of Summer" is told from the point of view of Bennie.

Because Bennie is only ten years old, there are many things he does not understand. At the funeral service of May Mathis, he is confused by the mourners' grief when they are told that Miss May is in heaven:

Bennie wondered why Mr. John covered his face with his hands, and why Miss May's sister Ethel, who had come all the way from St. Louis, cried out, and why people cried, if Miss May was so happy in this land. It seemed that they should be glad for her, so glad they would not cry. Or did they cry because they were glad? He could not understand.

The language of the story is also carefully controlled so that Bennie's thoughts are conveyed realistically:

He went to the big chair and sat down. He must not cry: Crying could not help him. There was nothing to do but to sit there until the storm was past.

The rain and the wind came steadily now. He sat back in the big chair. He wondered about his mother. Was she safe at the Fieldses'? He wondered if the water had flowed into the henhouse and under the chicken coops, where the little chickens were. If it had, some of the little chickens might get drowned. The storm lasted so long that it began to seem to him that it had always been there.

In this story the author has chosen to use the *limited third-person point of view*. You know only what Bennie sees and feels. You are not told what the other characters are thinking and feeling. Why do you think the author chose to tell the story in this way? Would the story have been as effective if it had been told from the point of view of an adult? Explain.

ABOUT THE AUTHOR

Grant Moss, Jr. has had stories published in *Opportunity, The New Yorker,* and *Essence* magazines. He now teaches at Grambling College in Grambling, Louisiana.

A Mild Attack of Locusts

Doris Lessing

The rains that year were good; they were coming nicely just as the crops needed them — or so Margaret gathered when the men said they were not too bad. She never had an opinion of her own on matters like the weather, because even to know about what seems a simple thing like the weather needs experience. Which Margaret had not got. The men were Richard, her husband, and old Stephen, Richard's father, a farmer from way back; and these two might argue for hours whether the rains were ruinous or just ordinarily exasperating. Margaret had been on the farm three years. She still did not understand how they did not go bankrupt altogether, when the men never had a good word for the weather, or the soil, or the government. But she was getting to learn the language. Farmers' language. And they neither went bankrupt nor got very rich. They jogged along doing comfortably.

Their crop was maize.[1] Their farm was three thousand acres on the ridges that rise up toward the Zambesi[2] escarpment — high, dry, wind-swept country, cold and dusty in winter, but now, in the wet season, steamy with the heat rising in wet soft waves off miles of green foliage. Beautiful it was, with the sky blue and brilliant halls of air, and the bright green folds and hollows of country beneath, and the mountains lying sharp and bare twenty miles off across the rivers. The sky made her eyes ache; she was not used to it. One does not look so much at the sky in the city she came from. So that evening when Richard said: "The government is sending out warnings that locusts are expected, coming down from the breeding grounds up North," her instinct was to look about her at the trees. Insects — swarms of them — horrible! But Richard and the old man had raised their eyes and were looking up over the mountain. "We haven't had locusts in seven years," they said. "They go in cycles, locusts do." And then: "There goes our crop for this season!"

But they went on with the work of the farm just as usual until one day they were coming up the road to the homestead for the midday break, when old Stephen stopped, raised his finger and pointed: "Look, look, there they are!"

Out ran Margaret to join them, looking at the hills. Out came the servants from the kitchen. They all stood and gazed. Over the rocky levels of the mountain was a streak of rust-colored air. Locusts. There they came.

At once Richard shouted at the cookboy. Old Stephen yelled at the houseboy. The cookboy ran to beat the old plowshare hanging from a tree branch, which was used to summon the laborers at moments of crisis. The houseboy ran off to the store to collect tin cans, any old bit of metal. The farm was ringing with the clamor of the gong; and they could see the laborers come pouring out of the compound, pointing at the hills and shouting

---

1. **maize** (māz): corn.
2. **Zambesi** (zăm-bē′zē): a river in southern Africa.

excitedly. Soon they had all come up to the house, and Richard and old Stephen were giving them orders—Hurry, hurry, hurry.

And off they ran again, the two white men with them, and in a few minutes Margaret could see the smoke of fires rising from all around the farmlands. Piles of wood and grass had been prepared there. There were seven patches of bared soil, yellow and oxblood color and pink, where the new mealies were just showing, making a film of bright green; and around each drifted up thick clouds of smoke. They were throwing wet leaves onto the fires now, to make it acrid and black. Margaret was watching the hills. Now there was a long, low cloud advancing, rust-color still, swelling forward and out as she looked. The telephone was ringing Neighbors—quick, quick, there come the locusts. Old Smith had had his crop eaten to the ground. Quick, get your fires started. For of course, while every farmer hoped the locusts would overlook his farm and go on to the next, it was only fair to warn each other; one must play fair. Everywhere, fifty miles over the countryside, the smoke was rising from myriads[3] of fires. Margaret answered the telephone calls, and between calls she stood watching the locusts. The air was darkening. A strange darkness, for the sun was blazing—it was like the darkness of a veldt[4] fire, when the air gets thick with smoke. The sunlight comes down distorted, a thick, hot orange. Oppressive it was, too, with the heaviness of a storm. The locusts were coming fast. Now half the sky was darkened. Behind the reddish veils in front, which were the advance guards of the swarm, the main swarm showed in dense black cloud, reaching almost to the sun itself.

Margaret was wondering what she could do

---

3. **myriads** (mîr′ē-ədz): countless or vast numbers.
4. **veldt** (vĕlt): open grassy field in southern Africa, used for grazing.

to help. She did not know. Then up came old Stephen from the lands. "We're finished, Margaret, finished! Those beggars can eat every leaf and blade off the farm in half an hour! And it is only early afternoon—if we can make enough smoke, make enough noise till the sun goes down, they'll settle somewhere else perhaps. . . ." And then: "Get the kettle going. It's thirsty work, this."

So Margaret went to the kitchen, and stoked up the fire, and boiled the water. Now, on the tin roof of the kitchen she could hear the thuds and bangs of falling locusts, or a scratching slither as one skidded down. Here were the first of them. From down on the lands came the beating and banging and clanging of a hundred gasoline cans and bits of metal. Stephen impatiently waited while one gasoline can was filled with tea, hot, sweet and orange-colored, and the other with water. In the meantime, he told Margaret about how twenty years back he was eaten out, made bankrupt, by the locust armies. And then, still talking, he hoisted up the gasoline cans, one in each hand, by the wood pieces set cornerwise across each, and jogged off down to the road to the thirsty laborers. By now the locusts were falling like hail onto the roof of the kitchen. It sounded like a heavy storm. Margaret looked out and saw the air dark with a crisscross of the insects, and she set her teeth and ran out into it—what the men could do, she could. Overhead the air was thick, locusts everywhere. The locusts were flopping against her, and she brushed them off, heavy red-brown creatures, looking at her with their beady old-men's eyes while they clung with hard, serrated legs. She held her breath with disgust and ran through into the house. There it was even more like being in a heavy storm. The iron roof was reverberating, and the clamor of iron from the lands was like thunder. Looking out, all the trees were queer and still, clotted with insects, their boughs weighed to the ground. The earth seemed to be moving, locusts crawling everywhere, she could not see the lands at all, so thick was the swarm. Toward the mountains it was like looking into driving rain—even as she watched, the sun was blotted out with a fresh onrush of them. It was a half-night, a perverted blackness. Then came a sharp crack from the bush—a branch had snapped off. Then another. A tree down the slope leaned over and settled heavily to the ground. Through the hail of insects a man came running. More tea, more water was needed. She supplied them. She kept the fires stoked and filled cans with liquid, and then it was four in the afternoon, and the locusts had been pouring across overhead for a couple of hours. Up came old Stephen again, crunching locusts underfoot with every step, locusts clinging all over him; he was cursing and swearing, banging with his old hat at the air. At the doorway he stopped briefly, hastily pulling at the clinging insects and throwing them off, then he plunged into the locust-free living room.

"All the crops finished. Nothing left," he said.

But the gongs were still beating, the men still shouting, and Margaret asked: "Why do you go on with it, then?"

"The main swarm isn't settling. They are heavy with eggs. They are looking for a place to settle and lay. If we can stop the main body settling on our farm, that's everything. If they get a chance to lay their eggs, we are going to have everything eaten flat with hoppers later on." He picked a stray locust off his shirt and split it down with his thumbnail—it was clotted inside with eggs. "Imagine that multiplied by millions. You ever seen a hopper swarm on the march? Well, you're lucky."

Margaret thought an adult swarm was bad enough. Outside now the light on the earth was a pale, thin yellow, clotted with moving shadows; the clouds of moving insects thickened and lightened like driving rain. Old Stephen said, "They've got the wind behind them, that's something."

"Is it very bad?" asked Margaret fearfully, and the old man said emphatically: "We're finished. This swarm may pass over, but once they've started, they'll be coming down from the North now one after another. And then there are the hoppers—it might go on for two or three years."

Margaret sat down helplessly, and thought: Well, if it's the end, it's the end. What now? We'll all three have to go back to town. . . . But at this, she took a quick look at Stephen, the old man who had farmed forty years in this country, been bankrupt twice, and she knew nothing would make him go and become a clerk in the city. Yet her heart ached for him, he looked so tired, the worry lines deep from nose to mouth. Poor old man. . . . He had lifted up a locust that had got itself somehow into his pocket, holding it in the air by one leg. "You've got the strength of a steel spring in those legs of yours," he was telling the locust, good-humoredly. Then, although he had been fighting locusts, squashing locusts, yelling at locusts, sweeping them in great mounds into the fires to burn for the last three hours, nevertheless he took this one to the door and carefully threw it out to join its fellows, as if he would rather not harm a hair of its head. This comforted Margaret; all at once she felt irrationally cheered. She remembered it was not the first time in the last three years the man had announced their final and irremediable[5] ruin.

"Get me a drink, lass," he then said, and she set the bottle of whiskey by him.

In the meantime, out in the pelting storm of insects, her husband was banging the gong, feeding the fires with leaves, the insects clinging to him all over—she shuddered. "How can you bear to let them touch you?" she asked. He looked at her, disapproving. She felt suitably humble—just as she had when he had first taken a good look at her city self, hair waved and golden, nails red and pointed. Now she was a proper farmer's wife, in sensible shoes and a solid skirt. She might even get to letting locusts settle on her—in time.

Having tossed back a whiskey or two, old Stephen went back into the battle, wading now through glistening brown waves of locusts.

Five o'clock. The sun would set in an hour. Then the swarm would settle. It was as thick overhead as ever. The trees were ragged mounds of glistening brown.

Margaret began to cry. It was all so hopeless—if it wasn't a bad season, it was locusts; if it wasn't locusts, it was army worm[6] or veldt fires. Always something. The rustling of the locust armies was like a big forest in the storm; their settling on the roof was like the beating of the rain; the ground was invisible in a sleek, brown, surging tide—it was like being drowned in locusts, submerged by the loathsome brown flood. It seemed as if the roof might sink in under the weight of them, as if the door might give in under their pressure and these rooms fill with them—and it was getting so dark . . . she looked up. The air was thinner; gaps of blue showed in the dark, moving clouds. The blue spaces were cold and thin—the sun must be setting. Through the fog of insects she saw figures approaching. First old Stephen, marching bravely along, then her husband, drawn and haggard with

---

5. **irremediable** (ĭr'ĭ-mē'dē-ə-bəl): impossible to correct.

6. **army worm:** the larvae of certain moths that travel in large groups, devouring crops and grass.

weariness. Behind them the servants. All were crawling all over with insects. The sound of the gongs had stopped. She could hear nothing but the ceaseless rustle of a myriad wings.

The two men slapped off the insects and came in.

"Well," said Richard, kissing her on the cheek, "the main swarm has gone over."

"For heaven's sake," said Margaret angrily, still half crying, "what's here is bad enough, isn't it?" For although the evening air was no longer black and thick, but a clear blue, with a pattern of insects whizzing this way and that across it, everything else—trees, buildings, bushes, earth—was gone under the moving brown masses.

"If it doesn't rain in the night and keep them here—if it doesn't rain and weight them down with water, they'll be off in the morning at sunrise."

"We're bound to have some hoppers. But not the main swarm—that's something."

Margaret roused herself, wiped her eyes, pretended she had not been crying, and fetched them some supper, for the servants were too exhausted to move. She sent them down to the compound to rest.

She served the supper and sat listening. There is not one maize plant left, she heard. Not one. The men would get the planters out the moment the locusts had gone. They must start all over again.

But what's the use of that, Margaret wondered, if the whole farm was going to be crawling with hoppers? But she listened while they discussed the new government pamphlet that said how to defeat the hoppers. You must have men out all the time, moving over the farm to watch for movement in the grass. When you find a patch of hoppers, small lively black things, like crickets, then you dig trenches around the patch or spray them with poison from pumps supplied by the government. The government wanted them to cooperate in a world plan for eliminating this plague forever. You should attack locusts at the source. Hoppers, in short. The men were talking as if they were planning a war, and Margaret listened, amazed.

In the night it was quiet; no sign of the settled armies outside, except sometimes a branch snapped, or a tree could be heard crashing down.

Margaret slept badly in the bed beside Richard, who was sleeping like the dead, exhausted with the afternoon's fight. In the morning she woke to yellow sunshine lying across the bed—clear sunshine, with an occasional blotch of shadow moving over it. She went to the window. Old Stephen was ahead of her. There he stood outside, gazing down over the bush. And she gazed, astounded—and entranced, much against her will. For it looked as if every tree, every bush, all the earth, were lit with pale flames. The locusts were fanning their wings to free them of the night dews. There was a shimmer of red-tinged gold light everywhere.

She went out to join the old man, stepping carefully among the insects. They stood and watched. Overhead the sky was blue, blue and clear.

"Pretty," said old Stephen, with satisfaction.

Well, thought Margaret, we may be ruined, we may be bankrupt, but not everyone has seen an army of locusts fanning their wings at dawn.

Over the slopes, in the distance, a faint red smear showed in the sky, thickened and spread. "There they go," said old Stephen. "There goes the main army, off south."

And now from the trees, from the earth all round them, the locusts were taking wing. They were like small aircraft, maneuvering

for the takeoff, trying their wings to see if they were dry enough. Off they went. A reddish-brown steam was rising off the miles of bush, off the lands, the earth. Again the sunlight darkened.

And as the clotted branches lifted, the weight on them lightening, there was nothing but the black spines of branches, trees. No green left, nothing. All morning they watched, the three of them, as the brown crust thinned and broke and dissolved, flying up to mass with the main army, now a brownish-red smear in the southern sky. The lands which had been filmed with green, the new tender mealie plants, were stark and bare. All the trees stripped. A devastated landscape. No green, no green anywhere.

By midday the reddish cloud had gone. Only an occasional locust flopped down. On the ground were the corpses and the wounded. The African laborers were sweeping these up with branches and collecting them in tins.

"Ever eaten sun-dried locust?" asked old Stephen. "That time twenty years ago, when I went broke, I lived on mealie meal and dried locusts for three months. They aren't bad at all — rather like smoked fish, if you come to think of it."

But Margaret preferred not even to think of it.

After the midday meal the men went off to the lands. Everything was to be replanted. With a bit of luck another swarm would not come traveling down just this way. But they hoped it would rain very soon, to spring some new grass, because the cattle would die otherwise — there was not a blade of grass left on the farm. As for Margaret, she was trying to get used to the idea of three or four years of locusts. Locusts were going to be like bad weather, from now on, always imminent. She felt like a survivor after war — if this devastated and mangled countryside was not ruin, well, what then was ruin?

But the men ate their supper with good appetites.

"It could have been worse," was what they said. "It could be much worse."

FOR STUDY AND DISCUSSION

1. In the first paragraph of the story, you learn that although Margaret has been on the farm for three years, she has not yet learned "the language." The men have a habit of talking about being ruined but acting as if nothing out of the way has happened. How is this made evident during the attack of the locusts?

2. At one point Stephen lifts up a locust and speaks to it good-humoredly, then throws it outdoors carefully. Why does this action comfort Margaret? What does it reveal about Stephen's nature?

3. Margaret feels that farming is a hopeless business—some disaster is always imminent. What is the attitude of the men toward the land? How does the title of the story express this contrast in attitudes?

4. Do you think that Stephen and Richard behave foolishly or admirably? Explain.

5. Why do you think the author chose to tell the story from Margaret's point of view? Imagine the story told from the point of view of Stephen or Richard. How might it be different?

FIGURATIVE LANGUAGE

When writers choose to state a fact or an idea directly, they use *literal language*. Quite often, however, writers decide that an indirect statement is more effective than a direct statement. They then use *figurative language*. Compare these statements:

> The locusts were drying their wings in order to fly off.

> They were like small aircraft, maneuvering for the takeoff, trying their wings to see if they were dry enough.

The second sentence is an example of figurative language: it suggests that the locust attack has been like the invasion of an air force.

Writers frequently use figurative language to give emphasis to ideas and to make their style vivid. One kind of figurative language is the *simile*. A simile expresses a comparison between two unlike things. A word such as *like* or *as* is used to suggest the similarity.

Explain the comparisons expressed in each of these similes:

> By now the locusts were falling *like hail* onto the roof of the kitchen.

> The iron roof was reverberating, and the clamor of iron from the lands was *like thunder*.

> The rustling of the locust armies was *like a big forest in the storm* . . .

Metaphor is another kind of figurative language. Like simile, metaphor compares two things that are basically different. However, a metaphor does not use connecting words to express the comparison. A metaphor identifies the two things—that is, it says that one thing *is* another:

> Behind the reddish veils in front, which were the advance guards of the swarm, the main swarm showed . . .

The phrase *reddish veils* identifies the locusts with transparent material that partly conceals and protects what it covers. What comparison is implied by the phrase *advance guards*?

Find similes and metaphors that compare the locust attack to an army invasion, to a storm, and to a strong current. Explain why the author's use of figurative language is more effective than direct statement would be.

LANGUAGE AND VOCABULARY

Finding Meaning from Context

The *context* of a word refers to the words that surround it and to the total situation in which it is used. You often can use context clues to determine the meaning of an unfamiliar word. For example, the following passage provides clues to the meaning of *hopper* as it is used in the story:

> [Stephen] picked a stray locust off his shirt and split it down with his thumbnail—it was clotted inside with eggs. "Imagine that multiplied by millions. You ever seen a hopper swarm on the march? Well, you're lucky."
>
> Margaret thought an adult swarm was bad enough.

What clues in the passage tell you that hoppers are immature locusts? That they are more destructive than adult locusts? Hoppers are without wings and so must hop rather than fly. Find a clue to this in the passage.

Use context clues to define the italicized words in the following passages from the story. Then check your answers in the glossary or in a dictionary.

1. Their farm was three thousand acres on the ridges that rise up toward the Zambesi *escarpment*—high, dry, wind-swept country . . . (page 78)
2. There were seven patches of bared soil, . . . where the new *mealies* were just showing, making a film of bright green . . . (page 79)
3. The air was darkening. A strange darkness, for the sun was blazing . . . *Oppressive* it was, too, with the heaviness of a storm. (page 79)
4. Locusts were going to be like bad weather, from now on, always *imminent*. (page 83)

FOR COMPOSITION

Writing from a Different Point of View

"A Mild Attack of Locusts" is told from Margaret's point of view. Choose one of the episodes in the story and retell it from Stephen's point of view, revealing his thoughts and feelings as well as his external actions. Use first-person or third-person point of view.

ABOUT THE AUTHOR

Doris Lessing (1919–   ) was born in Persia, where her father worked as a bank manager. In 1924, her family settled on a farm in Rhodesia. She writes that she lived on "an enormous tract of bush dotted with lonely farms." The nearest neighbors were miles away. She spent her time reading or walking through the African bush. In 1949, she moved to England and began to establish herself as a writer. Today she is regarded as one of England's most important writers. She has written a number of novels, many short stories, and some poetry. She regards writing as a striving inward toward self-knowledge. "I am always surprised at what I find within myself, and this to me is the most rewarding part of being a writer."

The Pacing Goose

Jessamyn West

Jess sat in the kitchen at the long table by the west window where in winter he kept his grafting tools: the thin-bladed knife, the paper sweet with the smell of beeswax and the resin, the boxes of roots and scions.[1] Jess was a nurseryman and spring meant for him not only spirits' flowering – but the earth's. A week more of moderating weather and he'd be out, still in gum boots, but touching an earth that had thawed, whose riches were once again fluid enough to be sucked upward, toward those burgeonings which by summer would have swelled into Early Harvests, Permains, and Sweet Bows.[2]

Spring's a various season, Jess thought, no two years the same: comes in with rains, mud deep enough to swallow horse and rider; comes in cold, snow falling so fast it weaves a web; comes in with a warm wind blowing about thy ears and bringing a smell of something flowering, not here, but southaways, across the Ohio, maybe, in Kentucky. Nothing here now but a smell of melting snow – which is no smell at all, but a kind of prickle in the nose, like a bygone sneeze. Comes in so various, winter put by and always so welcome.

"And us each spring so much the same."

"Thee speaking to me, Jess?"

"Nothing thee'd understand, Eliza."

Spring made Jess discontented with the human race – and with women, if anything, more than men. It looked as if spring put them all in the shade: the season so resourceful and they each year meeting it with nothing changed from last year, digging up roots from the same sassafras thicket, licking sulfur and molasses[3] from the big-bowled spoon.

Behind him the table was set for supper, plates neatly turned to cover the bone-handled knives and forks, spoon vase aglitter with steel well burnished by brick dust, dishes of jam with more light to them than the sun, which was dwindling away, peaked and overcast, outside his window.

"Spring opening up," he said, "and nobody in this house so much as putting down a line of poetry."

Eliza, who was lifting dried-peach pies from a hot oven, said nothing. She set the four of them in a neat row on the edge of her kitchen cabinet to cool, and slid her pans of cornbread into the oven. Then she turned to Jess, her cheeks red with heat, and her black eyes warm with what she had to say. "Thee'd maybe relish a nice little rhyme for thy supper, Jess Birdwell."

Jess sighed, then sniffed the pies, so rich with ripe peach flavor that the kitchen smelled like a summer orchard, nothing lacking but the sound of bees. "Now, Eliza," he said, "thee knows I wouldn't have thee anyways altered. Thee . . ."

"Thee," Eliza interrupted him, "is like all men. Thee wants to have thy poetry and eat it too."

---

1. **scions** (sī'ənz): plant shoots prepared for grafting.
2. **Early . . . Bows:** varieties of apples.

3. **sulfur and molasses:** an old-time "spring tonic."

Detail from *Quaker Meeting*. Anonymous 19th-century American painting.
Museum of Fine Arts, Boston
Bequest of Maxim Karolik

Jess wondered how what he'd felt about spring, a season with the Lord's thumbprint fresh on it, could've led to anything so un-springlike as an argument about a batch of dried-peach pies.

"Eliza," he said firmly, "I didn't mean thee. Though it's crossed my mind sometimes as strange that none of the boys have ever turned, this time of year, to rhyming."

"Josh writes poems," Eliza said.

"Thee ever read what Josh writes, Eliza?" Eliza nodded.

Ah, well, Jess thought, no use at this late date to tell her what's the difference.

Eliza looked her husband over carefully. "Jess Birdwell," she said, "thee's full of humors. Thy blood needs thinning. I'll boil thee up a good cup of sassafras tea."

Jess turned away from the green and gold sunset and the patches of snow it was gilding and fairly faced the dried-peach pies and Eliza, who was dropping dumplings into a pot of beans.

"That's just it, Eliza," he said. "That's just the rub."

Eliza gave him no encouragement, but he went on anyway. "Earth alters, season to season, spring comes in never two times the same, only us pounding on steady as pump bolts and not freshened by so much as a grass blade."

"Jess, thee's got spring fever."

"I could reckon time and temperature, each spring, by the way thee starts honing[4] for geese. 'Jess, don't thee think we might have a few geese?' It's a tardy spring," Jess said. "Snow still on the ground and not a word yet from thee about geese."

Eliza pulled a chair out from the table and sat. "Jess, why's thee always been so set against geese?"

"I'm not set against geese. It's geese that's set against farming. They can mow down a half-acre of sprouting corn while thee's trying to head them off—and in two minutes they'll level a row of pie plant it's taken two years to get started. No, Eliza, it's the geese that's against me."

"If thee had tight fences . . ." Eliza said.

"Eliza, I got tight fences, but the goose's never been hatched that'll admit fences exist.

---

4. **honing:** yearning.

And an old gander'd just as soon go through a fence as hiss—and if he can't find a hole or crack in a fence he'll lift the latch.''

"Jess," said Eliza flatly, "thee don't like geese.''

"Well," said Jess, "I wouldn't go so far's to say I didn't like them, but I will say that if there's any meaner, dirtier animal, or one that glories in it more, I don't know it. And a thing I've never been able to understand about thee, Eliza, is what thee sees in the shifty-eyed birds.''

"Geese," said Eliza, with a dreaminess unusual to her, "march along so lordly like . . . they're pretty as swans floating down a branch . . . in fall they stretch out their necks and honk to geese passing overhead as if they's wild. My father never had any trouble raising geese and I've heard him say many a time that there's no better food for a brisk morning than a fried goose egg.''

Jess knew, with spring his topic, he'd ought to pass over Eliza's father and his fried goose egg but he couldn't help saying, "A fried goose egg always had a kind of bloated look to me, Eliza''—but then he went on fast. "The season's shaping up," he said. "I can see thee's all primed to say, 'Jess, let's get a setting of goose eggs.' ''

Eliza went over to the bean kettle and began to lift out dumplings. "It's a forwarder season than thee thinks, Jess," she said. "I got a setting under a hen now.''

Jess looked at his wife. He didn't know what had made him want spring's variety in a human being—nor Eliza's substituting doing for asking. And speaking of it just now, as he had, made opposition kind of ticklish.

"When'd thee set them?" he asked finally.

"Yesterday," said Eliza.

"Where'd thee get the eggs?"

"Overbys'," said Eliza. The Overbys were their neighbors to the south.

"Well, they got enough for a surety," Jess said, "to give a few away.''

"The Overbys don't give anything away, as thee knows. I paid for them. With my own money," Eliza added.

"How many?" Jess asked.

"Eight," Eliza said.

Jess turned back to his window. The sun had set, leaving a sad green sky and desolate black and white earth. "Five acres of corn gone," he calculated.

"Thee said," Eliza reminded him, "that what thee wanted was a little variety in me. 'Steady as a pump bolt,' were thy words.''

"I know I did," Jess admitted glumly. "I talk too much.''

"Draw up thy chair," Eliza said placidly, not contradicting him; "here's Enoch and the boys.''

Next morning after breakfast Jess and Enoch left the kitchen together. The sun was the warmest the year had yet produced and the farm roofs were steaming; south branch, swollen by melting snow, was running so full the soft lap of its eddies could be heard in the barnyard; a rooster tossed his voice into the bright air, loud and clear as if aiming to be heard by every fowl in Jennings County.

"Enoch," said Jess to his hired man, "what's thy feeling about geese?"

Enoch was instantly equipped, for the most part, with feelings on every subject. Geese was a homelier topic than he'd choose himself to enlarge upon, not one that could be much embellished nor one on which Mr. Emerson,[5] so far's he could recall, had ever expressed an opinion. "In the fall of the year," he said, "long about November or December,

---

5. **Mr. Emerson:** Ralph Waldo Emerson, American essayist and poet (1803–1882).

there's nothing tastier on the table than roast goose."

"Goose on the table's not what I mean," Jess said. "I was speaking of goose on the hoof. Goose nipping off a stand of corn, Enoch, goose roistering round, honking and hissing so's thee can't hear thyself think, goose eyeing thee like a snake on stilts."

Enoch gazed at his employer for a few seconds. "Mr. Birdwell," he said, "I think that if they's an ornery bird, it's a goose. Ornery and undependable."

"I'm glad we's so like-minded about them," Jess said. "Otherwise, I'd not like to ask thee to do this little job." He pulled a long darning needle from beneath the lapel of his coat.

Enoch eyed it with some mistrust. "I can't say's I've been handy with a needle, Mr. Birdwell."

"Thee'll be handy enough for this," Jess said with hearty conviction. "To come to it, Enoch, Eliza's set eight goose eggs. Next year with any luck she'd have two dozen. And so on. More and more. Feeling the way thee does, Enoch, about geese, it's no more'n fair to give thee a chance to put a stop to this before it goes too far. One little puncture in each egg with this and the goose project's nipped in the bud and Eliza none the wiser."

"I'm mighty awkward with my hands," said Enoch, "doing fine work. Ticklish job like this I might drop an egg and break it."

"Enoch," said Jess, "thee's not developing a weakness for geese, is thee?"

"It ain't the geese," said Enoch frankly, "it's your wife. She's been mighty clever[6] to me and if she's got her heart set on geese, it'd go against the grain to disappoint her. Whyn't you do it, Mr. Birdwell?"

"Same reason," said Jess, "only more of them—and if Eliza ever asks if I tampered

with that setting of eggs I figure on being able to say no." Jess held the needle nearer Enoch, who looked at it but still made no motion to take it.

"Likely no need to do a thing," Enoch said. "Two to one those eggs'll never hatch anyways. Overbys're such a fox-eared tribe they more'n likely sold her bad eggs to begin with."

"Thee's knowed about this," Jess asked, "all along?"

"Yes," Enoch said.

"Here's the needle," Jess said.

"You look at this," Enoch inquired, "not so much as a favor asked as a part of the day's work with orders from you?"

"Yes," Jess said, "that's about the way I look at it."

Enoch took the needle, held it somewhat gingerly, and with the sun glinting across its length walked slowly toward the chicken house.

It takes thirty days for a goose egg to hatch, and the time, with spring work to be done, went fast. The hen Eliza had picked was a good one and kept her mind strictly on her setting. Eliza kept her mind on the hen, and Jess and Enoch found their minds oftener than they liked on Eliza and her hoped-for geese.

At breakfast on the day the geese were due to break their shells Jess said, "If I's thee, Eliza, I wouldn't bank too much on them geese. I heard Enoch say a while back he wouldn't be surprised if not an egg hatched. Thought the eggs were likely no good."

Enoch was busy pouring coffee into a saucer, then busy cooling it, but Eliza waited until he was through. "Did thee say that, Enoch?"

Enoch looked at Jess. "Yes," he said, "I kind of recollect something of the sort."

"What made thee think so, Enoch?"

---

6. **clever:** kind (a local use of the word).

"Why," said Jess, for Enoch was busy with his coffee again, "it was the Overbys. Enoch's got a feeling they's kind of unreliable. Fox-eared, I think thee said, Enoch, didn't thee?"

Enoch's work took him outside almost at once and Jess himself said, "If thee'll just give me a little packet of food, Eliza, I won't trouble thee for anything at noon. I'm going to be over'n the south forty and it'll save time coming and going."

Eliza was surprised, for Jess'd usually come twice as far for a hot dinner at midday, but she made him fried-ham sandwiches and put them and some cold apple turnovers in a bag.

"It's a pity thee has to miss thy dinner," she told him, but Jess only said, "Press of work, press of work," and hurriedly departed.

Jess came home that evening through the spring twilight, somewhat late, and found a number of things to do at the barn before he went up to the house. When he entered the kitchen nothing seemed amiss — lamps ruddy, table set, stove humming, and beside the stove a small box over which Eliza was bending. Jess stopped to look — and listen; from inside the box was coming a kind of birdlike peeping, soft and not unpleasant. Reluctantly he walked to Eliza's side. There, eating minced boiled egg, and between bites lifting its beak to Eliza, it seemed, and making those chirping sounds he'd heard, was a gray-gold gosling.

Eliza looked up pleasantly. "Enoch was right," she said. "The eggs were bad. Only one hatched. I plan to call it Samantha," she told Jess. "It's a name I've always been partial to."

"Samantha," said Jess without any enthusiasm whatever for either name or gosling. "How's thee know it's a she?"

"I don't," said Eliza, "but if it's a gander it's a name easily changed to Sam."

Enoch came in just then with a load of wood for the kitchen woodbox. "Enoch," asked Jess, "has thee seen Samantha — or Sam?"

Enoch mumbled but Jess understood him to say he had.

"It was my understanding, Enoch, that thy opinion was that all those eggs were bad."

"Well, Mr. Birdwell," said Enoch, "a man could make a mistake. He could count wrong."

"A man ought to be able to count to eight without going astray," said Jess.

Eliza was paying no attention to either of them; she was making little tweeting sounds herself, bending over the chirping gosling. "Does thee know," she asked Jess, "that this is the first pet I ever had in my life?"

"Thee's got Ebony," Jess said.

"I don't mean a caged pet," Eliza said, "but one to walk beside thee. I'm reconciled the others didn't hatch. With eight I'd've had to raise geese for the table. With one only I can make Samantha a pure pet."

A pure pet was what she made of her: Samantha ate what the family ate, with the exception of articles which Eliza thought might be indigestible and would risk on humans but not on her goose. Cake, pie, corn on the cob, there was nothing too good for Samantha. From a big-footed, gold-downed gosling she swelled, almost at once, like a slack sail which gets a sudden breeze, into a full-rounded convexity.

"Emphasis on the vexity," Jess said when he thought of this. Samantha was everything he'd disliked in the general run of geese, with added traits peculiar to herself, which vexed him. Because she was fed at the doorstep, she was always underfoot. No shout, however loud, would move her before she's ready to move. If she's talked to too strong she'd flail you with her wings and pinch the calf of your leg until for some days it would look to be mortifying. She'd take food out of children's hands, and the pansies Jess had planted in a circle at the base of the Juneberry tree she sheared so close that there was not a naked stem left to show for all his work. And when not being crossed in any way, Jess simply looking at her and meditating, trying to fathom Samantha's fascination for Eliza, the goose would suddenly extend her snakelike neck, and almost touching Jess, hiss with such a hint of icy disapprobation that Jess would involuntarily recoil.

But she was Eliza's pure pet, no two ways about that, and would lift her head for Eliza to scratch, and walk beside her with the lordly roll of the known elect.[7]

"There was some goddess," Enoch remembered, "who always had a big bird with her." Jess supposed Enoch was thinking of Juno and her peacock, but the reference didn't convince him that a goose was a suitable companion for any goddess—let alone Eliza, and he couldn't honestly feel much regret when one evening toward the end of November Eliza told him Samantha was missing. "She'll turn up," Jess said. "That bird's too ornery to die young."

Eliza said nothing, but next evening she proved Jess was right. "Samantha's over at Overbys'," she said.

"Well, did thee fetch her home?" Jess asked.

"No," said Eliza with righteous indignation, "they wouldn't let me. They said they had forty geese—and forty's what they got now, and they don't think Samantha's there. They provoked me so, Jess, I told them they'd sold me seven bad eggs and now they try to take the eighth away from me."

Jess felt a little abashed at this, but he asked, "How can thee be so sure Samantha's

there? She might've been carried off by a varmint."

Eliza was scornful. "Thee forgets I hand-raised Samantha from a gosling. I'd know her among four hundred—let alone forty."

"Whyn't thee buy her back then," Jess asked, "if that's the only way?"

"After what I said about their eggs," Eliza answered sadly, "the Overbys say they don't want any more dealings with me."

Eliza mourned so for the lost Samantha that first Enoch and then Jess went over to the Overbys' but no one there would admit the presence of a visiting goose—forty they had, and forty you could see by counting was what they had now. Short of force there didn't seem any way of getting Samantha home again.

When Eliza heard the Overbys were going to sell geese for Christmas eating she was frantic. "Jess," she said, "I just can't bear to think of Samantha, plucked naked and resting on a table waiting to be carved. She used to sing as sweet as any bird when she was little, and she'd walk by my side taking the air. She's the only goose I ever heard of," Eliza remembered mournfully, "who'd drink tea."

In Jess's opinion a goose'd eat anything at either end of the scale, but he didn't suppose this was a suitable time to mention it to Eliza. "Eliza," he said, "short of me and Enoch's going over there and using force on old man Overby—or sneaking over at night and breaking into their chicken pen, I don't know how in the world we're going to get Samantha back for thee."

"We could sue," said Eliza.

"Thee mean go to law?" Jess asked, astounded. Quakers stayed out of courts, believing in amicable settlements without recourse to law.

"Yes," said Eliza. "I'd do it for Samantha. I'd think it my duty. Going to law'd be a misery for us . . . but not so lasting a misery as

---

7. **elect:** according to Calvinist doctrine, those who have been selected by God for salvation.

being roasted would be for Samantha."

Jess couldn't deny this, but he said, "I'd have to think it over. I've never been to law yet in my life and suing for a gone goose don't seem to me a very likely place to start."

Next morning Eliza served a good but silent breakfast, not sitting herself to eat with the rest of her family.

"Thee feeling dauncy,[8] Eliza?" Jess asked.

"I just can't eat," she said, "for thinking of Samantha."

Labe and Mattie had tears in their eyes. Little Jess was mournfully bellowing. Enoch looked mighty glum. Jess felt ashamed to be swallowing victuals in the midst of so much sorrow. Eliza stood at the end of the stove where the gosling's box had rested for the first few weeks of its life, looking down, as if remembering how it had sung and lifted its beak to her.

Jess couldn't stand it. "Eliza," he said, "if thee wants to go through with it I'll go to Vernon and fee a lawyer for thee. Thee'll have to go to court, be on the witness stand—and even then I misdoubt thee'll ever get thy goose back. Does thee still want me to do it?"

Eliza came to the table and stood with her hand on Jess's shoulder. "Yes, Jess," she said, "I want thee to do it."

Jess went to Vernon, fee'd a lawyer, had a restraining order put on the Overbys so they couldn't sell or kill the goose Eliza said was Samantha, and awaited with misgivings the day of the trial. It came in mid-December.

Eliza, Jess and Enoch rode to the trial through a fall of light, fresh snow. Brilliant sunlight, crisp air, glittering snow, and Rome's[9] spirited stepping made the occasion, in spite of its purpose, seem festive. Eliza made it seem festive. Jess, who did not forget its purpose, regarded her with some wonder. He couldn't say what it was about her—dress and bonnet appeared to be simply her First Day[10] best— but she had a holiday air.

He considered it his duty to warn her. "Eliza," he said, "thee understands thee's not going to Meeting?[11] They're not going to sit silent while thee tells them how much thee loves Samantha and how she sang when young and drank tea. Old man Overby'll have his say and he's got a lawyer hired for no other purpose than to trip thee up."

Eliza was unimpressed. "What's our lawyer fee'd for, Jess?" she asked.

Jess took another tack. "Eliza," he told her, "I don't figger thee's got a chance in a thousand to get Samantha back."

"This is a court of justice, isn't it?" Eliza asked.

"Yes," Jess said.

"Then there's no need for thee to fash[12] thyself, Jess Birdwell. I'll get Samantha back."

Not getting Samantha back wasn't what fashed Jess—he reckoned he could bear up under that mighty well. What fashed him was the whole shooting match. . . . In some few cases, matters of life and death, going to court might be necessary, and he could imagine such. But a suit over a goose named Samantha wasn't one of them. And poor Eliza. Law to her was all Greek and turkey tracks . . . and here she was bound for court as chipper as if she was Chief Justice Taney[13] himself. Jess sighed and shook his head. Getting shut of Samantha would be no hardship for him, but

---

8. **dauncy:** ill.
9. **Rome:** Rome Beauty, the Birdwells' carriage horse.

10. **First Day:** Quaker name for Sunday.
11. **Meeting:** Quaker church meeting.
12. **fash:** worry.
13. **Taney** (tā′nē): Roger B. Taney, a Chief Justice of the Supreme Court (1836–1864).

he was downcast for Eliza's sake and the way she'd have to turn homeward empty-handed.

In the courtroom hard, clear light reflected upward from the snow fell onto what Jess thought were hard faces: courthouse hangers-on; farmers whose slackening work made the diversion of a trial an inviting possibility; lovers of oddity who figured a tilt between a Quaker female, preacher to boot, and an old sinner like Milt Overby over the ownership of a goose ought to produce some enlivening quirks. They stared at Eliza, exchanged salutes with Milt Overby and inspected Samantha, who in her crate awaited the court's decision.

The two lawyers Jess considered to be on a par. Nothing fancy, either one . . . old roadsters both, gone gray in service and with a knowledge of their business. The circuit judge was something else, unaccountably young, jug-eared and dressed more sprightly than a groom for his own wedding. A city whippersnapper, born and trained north of the Mississinewa,[14] and now, in Jess's opinion, setting a squeamish foot in backwoods provinces, and irked to find himself trying so trifling a case. Didn't know a goose from a guinea hen, like as not, and would consider tossing a coin a more suitable manner of settling such a matter—just as near right in the end—and his valuable time saved.

Eliza, Jess saw, was of no such opinion. She, too, was scanning the young judge, and Jess, who knew her, saw from the look on her face that she was taken by him. A neat, thin, pious boy—far from home—he looked, no doubt, to her; a young man who could do with better cooking and more regular eating.

The young man rapped the court to order. Spitting and shuffling slackened and in a high, precise voice he read, "Birdwell versus Overby. Charge, petty larceny. Appropriation and willful withholding of goose named Samantha." The name Samantha seemed to somewhat choke him, but he got it out.

"Ready for Birdwell," said Mr. Abel Samp, Eliza's lawyer.

"Ready for Overby," said the defendant's lawyer.

Eliza was the first witness on the stand. Jess sometimes forgot what a good-looking woman Eliza was, but the interest shown on lifted faces all about him refreshed his memory.

"Swear the plaintiff in," the judge said.

Eliza, in her sweet voice, spoke directly to the judge. "I don't swear," she said.

The judge explained that profanity was not asked for. "I understood," said Eliza, "that thee wasn't asking for profanity. No one would think that of thee. But we Quakers do not take oaths in court. We affirm."

"Permit Mrs. Birdwell to affirm," said the judge. Eliza affirmed.

Mr. Samp then proceeded to question Eliza as to Samantha's birth and habits.

"Judge," Eliza began.

"Address the judge," Mr. Samp said, "as Your Honor."

"We Quakers," Eliza told the judge, gently, "do not make use of such titles. What is thy name? I think thee'll go far in our state and thy name's one I'd like to know."

The judge appeared somewhat distraught, undecided as to whether to make the tone of the court brisk and legal (if possible) or to follow Eliza's lead of urbane sociability.

"Pomeroy," he said and made a slight bow in Eliza's direction.

Eliza returned the bow, deeper and with more grace. "Friend Pomeroy," she said, "it is indeed a pleasure to know thee."

Samantha's story as Eliza told it to Friend

---

14. **Mississinewa** (mĭs-ĭs-sĭn'ĭ-wä): a small river flowing into the Wabash River in Indiana.

Detail from *Quaker Meeting*. Anonymous 19th-century
American painting.

Pomeroy was surprisingly terse. Affecting, and losing nothing by Eliza's telling, but to the point.

"Mrs. Birdwell," said Samp, "how long have you had an acquaintanceship with geese and their habits?"

"Since I was a child," Eliza said. "My father was a great fancier of geese."

"And you think you could identify this goose Samantha, which you admit in looks was similar to the defendant's?"

"I could," Eliza said with much authority.

Mr. Samp, to Jess's surprise, left the matter there. "Take the witness," he said to Overby's lawyer—but the counsel for the defendant was in no hurry to cross-examine Eliza. Instead he put his client on the stand.

"Farewell, Samantha," Jess said to Enoch.

"You relieved?" Enoch asked.

"Putting Eliza first," Jess said, "as I do, no."

Milt Overby, whose natural truculence was somewhat stimulated by a nip he'd had to offset snappy weather, bellowed his way through his testimony. At one juncture he set the judge aright when he asked some elementary questions concerning the habits and configurations of geese. "Where in tarnation you from?" he snorted. "What they mean sending us judges down here who don't know Toulouse from Wyandotte,[15] or goose from gander?"

The young judge used voice and gavel to quiet the guffawing which filled the courtroom and the trial proceeded. A number of witnesses for both sides were brought to the stand and while it was shown that Overbys had maybe eaten a goose or two and neglected out of pure fondness for the creatures to count them as among the departed, still nobody had

15. **Toulouse** (tōō-lōōz´) . . . **Wyandotte** (wī´ən-dŏt): breeds of fowl.

been able to positively identify Samantha.

Mr. Overby's lawyer seemed somewhat loath to cross-examine Eliza, but he put her on the stand. She'd said she knew geese and her testimony had been direct and positive. "Mrs. Birdwell," he said, "how can you be so sure your goose was with my client's geese?"

Eliza's black eyes rested confidingly upon the judge. "Friend Pomeroy," she said, "I raised Samantha from a gosling."

Jess sighed. "Here it comes," he said, "how that goose could sing and drink tea."

Eliza continued, "And there's one thing about her that always set her apart from every other goose."

"Yes, Mrs. Birdwell," said Judge Pomeroy, who was inclined to forget, with Eliza on the stand, that he was in a courtroom.

"Samantha," said Eliza, with much earnestness, "from the day she was born had a gait unlike any other goose I ever saw and one that set her apart from all her Overby connections. I picked her out at once when I went over there, because of it. Thee couldn't've missed it, Friend Pomeroy."

"Yes, Mrs. Birdwell," said the judge with interest in his voice.

"Samantha," said Eliza, "was a born pacer. Thee knows what a pacer is?"

"Certainly," said Judge Pomeroy. "A pacer," he repeated with no surprise — and with obvious pleasure that Eliza'd hit upon so clear and differentiating an aspect of her goose and one that made identification possible.

A titter was mounting through the courtroom — Judge Pomeroy lifted his head. He had no desire to be further instructed as to the history, habits, and breeds of geese, and he liked to see a trial settled by some such little and too often overlooked subtlety. Judge Pomeroy brought down his gavel. "The court awards decision in favor of the plaintiff. Case dismissed." While the silence that followed

on his words still prevailed Judge Pomeroy stepped briskly and with obvious pleasure out through the rear door.

Jess was also brisk about departure. No use lingering until Friend Pomeroy had been more thoroughly informed as to gaits in general and geese in particular. Midafternoon's a quiet time in any season. In winter with snow on the ground, no leaves to rustle and bare limbs rigid as rock against a cloudless sky, the hush is deepest of all. Nothing broke that hush in the surrey,[16] except the squeak of leather and snow, the muffled footfalls of Rome Beauty. Jess and Eliza, on the front seat, rode without speaking. Enoch, in the back, seemed to meditate. Even Samantha in her crate at Enoch's feet was silent.

Maple Grove Nursery was in sight before Jess spoke. "Eliza," he said, "would thee mind telling me — did thee ever see a trotting goose?"

Enoch ceased to meditate and listened. He had been wondering about this himself.

"Certainly not," said Eliza. "Thee knows as well as I, Jess Birdwell, an animal can't trot without hind feet and forefeet."

"So far, Eliza," Jess said, "we see eye to eye. Now maybe thee'd tell me — did thee ever see a goose that didn't pace?"

Eliza was truly amazed, it seemed. "Why, Jess," she said, "an ordinary goose just walks — but Samantha paces."

Jess was silent for a spell. "What'd thee say the difference is?"

"It's the swing, Jess Birdwell," said Eliza, "same as in a horse that nature's formed for a pacer . . . it's the natural bent, the way the spirit leads the beast to set his feet down, Samantha's a natural pacer."

That seemed as far as they'd likely get on

---

16. **surrey:** a light carriage.

the subject and Jess joined Enoch in meditation. In the barnyard, before she went up to the house, Eliza said, like an old hand at the business, "Attending court whettens the appetite. It's a little early but I thought if thee'd relish it"—and she looked at Jess and Enoch, never sparing a glance for Samantha, as if her menfolk's welfare was her sole concern—"I'd stir us up a bite to eat. Hot tea and fresh sweetcakes, say. Might fry a little sausage and open some cherry preserves. If thee'd relish it," she repeated.

Jess wasn't taken in, but he'd relish it, and so would Enoch, and they both said so. They hustled with the unhitching so they could uncrate Samantha and note her progress with eyes newly instructed as to what made a pacer. Jess dumped her in the snow, and Enoch tapped her with his hat. Samantha made for the back door.

"By sugar," said Jess, "Eliza's right. She paces." Samantha had the smooth roll of a racker[17]—there were no two ways about it. At heart she was a pacer, and what two legs could do in that line, Samantha accomplished.

"With four legs," Enoch said, "you could enter her in any county fair—rack on," he cried with enthusiasm. As they followed Samantha to the house, Enoch, for whom any event existed chiefly in its after aspects as a cud for rumination, asked. "How you feel in respect of court trials, now, Mr. Birdwell?"

"I'm still against them," Jess said, "though they's three things this trial's taught me I might never otherwise have learned. Two's about women."

Enoch revered all knowledge and he had a notion that information on this subject might have a more than transcendental[18] value. "What's the two things you learned about women, Mr. Birdwell?"

"Well, Enoch, I learned first, dependability's woman's greatest virtue. Steady as a pump bolt, day in, day out. When thee finds a woman like that, Enoch, don't try to change her. Not even in spring."

"No, sir," said Enoch, "I won't."

"Second, when it's a case of woman and the law—thee don't need to waste any worry on the woman."

"No, sir," said Enoch again.

When they reached the back steps, Enoch asked, "I understood you to say you'd learned three things, Mr. Birdwell. What's the third about?"

"Hired men," said Jess.

Enoch was taken aback, but he'd asked for it. "Yes, Mr. Birdwell," he said.

"Never hire one," Jess told him, "till thee finds out first if he can count to eight. Save thyself a lot of trouble that way, Enoch."

"How's I to know the eighth'd turn out to be Samantha?" Enoch asked.

Samantha herself, who was waiting at the doorstep for an expected tidbit, reached out and, unhampered by either boots or work pants, nipped Enoch firmly through his thin Sunday best.

"Thee say something, Enoch?" Jess asked.

Enoch had but he didn't repeat it. Instead he said, "Pacer or no pacer, that's Samantha," and the two of them stepped out of the snow into the warm kitchen, scented with baking sweetcakes and frying sausage.

---

17. **racker:** a horse that paces.

18. **transcendental:** here, abstract.

FOR STUDY AND DISCUSSION

1. When the story opens, Jess is feeling discontented. How is his discontent linked to the season of the year? Why does Eliza's announcement about the goose eggs come as a surprise?

2. Explain how the conflict between Jess and Eliza over Samantha is a result of their different personalities. Despite the conflict Jess and Eliza continue to live in harmony. What evidence is there, in their speech and action, of mutual love and esteem?

3. "The Pacing Goose" appears in a collection of stories about the Birdwells called *The Friendly Persuasion*. The title refers to Jess and Eliza being Quakers, since Quakers prefer to be known as the Society of Friends. Quakers believe in the importance of acting in accordance with the dictates of individual conscience. Why is Eliza's going to court a particularly significant act?

4. Jess is clearly surprised by the events in the courtroom. What does he think will happen? How does he underestimate Eliza's character?

5. Jess claims to have learned three things from the trial. What are they? In what way has his admiration for his wife deepened?

THE OMNISCIENT POINT OF VIEW

A story is sometimes told from the point of view of an outside observer who has complete knowledge of all the characters and who can therefore reveal not only their actions, their words, and their physical characteristics, but also their unspoken thoughts and feelings. Such an observer is *omniscient*, or "all-knowing," and the story is said to be told from the *omniscient point of view*.

This point of view allows readers to explore the internal as well as the external lives of characters. In "The Pacing Goose," for example, the conflict between Jess and Eliza is often expressed through thoughts:

> Spring made Jess discontented with the human race — and with women, if anything, more than men. It looked as if spring put them all in the shade: the season so resourceful and they each year meeting it with nothing changed from last year . . . (page 86)

> Ah, well, Jess thought, no use at this late date to tell her what's the difference. (page 87)

> Eliza kept her mind on the hen, and Jess and Enoch found their minds oftener than they liked on Eliza and her hoped-for geese. (page 89)

> Samantha was everything he'd disliked in the general run of geese, with added traits peculiar to herself, which vexed him. (page 90)

Find passages where the author makes known the thoughts and feelings of Enoch, Overby, and Judge Pomeroy.

This technique gives Jessamyn West considerable freedom. It allows her to tell more than any individual character in the story could tell about the action.

LANGUAGE AND VOCABULARY

Understanding Dialect

Dialects within a single language vary greatly in matters of pronunciation, sentence structure, and vocabulary, and writers make use of these differences in the realistic portrayal of character. Dave's father in "Split Cherry

Tree" (page 44) speaks a Kentucky dialect.

"The Pacing Goose" is set on a farm in Indiana during the Civil War, and Jessamyn West has reproduced characteristics of Quaker and regional speech. Look up each of the italicized words in the following list and tell what it means:

1. *Thee* speaking to me, Jess?
2. She might've been carried off by a *varmint*.
3. Nothing fancy, either one . . . old *roadsters* both . . .
4. Where in *tarnation* you from?
5. Attending court *whettens* the appetite.

FOR COMPOSITION

Describing a Season
At the opening of the story, Jess is sitting in the kitchen, musing about the coming of spring. To him, spring is a "various season," a season filled with variety. What details does he associate with spring? Consider what details he might have used to describe summer, winter, or fall. In a paragraph of your own, describe one of these other seasons, emphasizing its variety.

ABOUT THE AUTHOR

Jessamyn West (1907–1984) was born in Indiana but grew up in California. She studied at Whittier College, where she married a classmate. She continued her studies in England, then returned to the United States to attend the University of California. When she was confined to bed with tuberculosis, she began to write. Her first book was *The Friendly Persuasion*, a group of stories about a Quaker family (much like her mother's people), who lived on a farm in Indiana during the Civil War. The book was praised for its humor, its richness of language, and its fine sense of daily life. Some years later, she published another collection of stories about the Birdwell family, *Except for Me and Thee: a Companion to The Friendly Persuasion*. In addition, West wrote *Cress Delahanty*, a collection of stories about a teenage girl, and two other short-story collections: *Love, Death, and the Ladies' Drill Team* and *Crimson Ramblers of the World, Farewell*. She produced several novels, including *The Witch Diggers* and *The Massacre at Fall Creek*; and two autobiographical works: *Hide and Seek: A Continuing Journey* and *To See the Dream*, an account of her trip to Los Angeles to work on the script for the film version of *The Friendly Persuasion*.

Setting

War   *Jack London*

I

He was a young man, not more than twenty-four or -five, and he might have sat his horse with the careless grace of his youth had he not been so catlike and tense. His black eyes roved everywhere, catching the movements of twigs and branches where small birds hopped, questing ever onward through the changing vistas of trees and brush, and returning always to the clumps of undergrowth on either side. And as he watched, so did he listen, though he rode on in silence, save for the boom of heavy guns from far to the west. This had been sounding monotonously in his ears for hours, and only its cessation[1] would have aroused his notice. For he had business closer to hand. Across his saddlebow was balanced a carbine.

So tensely was he strung that a bunch of quail, exploding into flight from under his horse's nose, startled him to such an extent that automatically, instantly, he had reined in and fetched the carbine halfway to his shoulder. He grinned sheepishly, recovered himself, and rode on. So tense was he, so bent upon the work he had to do, that the sweat stung his eyes unwiped, and unheeded rolled down his nose and spattered his saddle pommel. The band of his cavalryman's hat was

---

1. **cessation** (sē-sā'shən): stopping, ceasing.

fresh-stained with sweat. The roan horse under him was likewise wet. It was high noon of a breathless day of heat. Even the birds and squirrels did not dare the sun, but sheltered in shady hiding places among the trees.

Man and horse were littered with leaves and dusted with yellow pollen, for the open was ventured no more than was compulsory. They kept to the brush and trees, and invariably the man halted and peered out before crossing a dry glade or naked stretch of upland pasturage. He worked always to the north, though his way was devious,[2] and it was from the north that he seemed most to apprehend[3] that for which he was looking. He was no coward, but his courage was only that of the average civilized man, and he was looking to live, not die.

Up a small hillside he followed a cowpath through such dense scrub that he was forced to dismount and lead his horse. But when the path swung around to the west, he abandoned it and headed to the north again along the oak-covered top of the ridge.

The ridge ended in a steep descent—so steep that he zigzagged back and forth across the face of the slope, sliding and stumbling among the dead leaves and matted vines and keeping a watchful eye on the horse above that threatened to fall down upon him. The sweat ran from him, and the pollen dust, settling pungently[4] in mouth and nostrils, increased his thirst. Try as he would, nevertheless the descent was noisy, and frequently he stopped, panting in the dry heat and listening for any warning from beneath.

At the bottom he came out on a flat,[5] so densely forested that he could not make out

its extent. Here the character of the woods changed, and he was able to remount. Instead of the twisted hillside oaks, tall, straight trees, big-trunked and prosperous, rose from the damp, fat soil. Only here and there were thickets, easily avoided, while he encountered winding, parklike glades where the cattle had pastured in the days before war had run them off.

His progress was more rapid now, as he came down into the valley, and at the end of half an hour he halted at an ancient rail fence on the edge of a clearing. He did not like the openness of it, yet his path lay across to the fringe of trees that marked the banks of the stream. It was a mere quarter of a mile across that open, but the thought of venturing out in it was repugnant.[6] A rifle, a score of them, a thousand, might lurk in that fringe by the stream.

Twice he essayed[7] to start, and twice he paused. He was appalled by his own loneliness. The pulse of war that beat from the west suggested the companionship of battling thousands; here was naught but silence, and himself, and possible death-dealing bullets from a myriad[8] ambushes. And yet his task was to find what he feared to find. He must go on, and on, till somewhere, sometime, he encountered another man, or other men, from the other side, scouting, as he was scouting, to make report, as he must make report, of having come in touch.

Changing his mind, he skirted inside the woods for a distance, and again peeped forth. This time, in the middle of the clearing, he saw a small farmhouse. There were no signs of life. No smoke curled from the chimney,

---

2. **devious** (dē′vē-əs): roundabout, not straight.
3. **apprehend** (ăp′rĭ-hĕnd′): fear, be afraid of.
4. **pungently** (pŭn′jənt-lē): in a way producing sharp sensations of taste and smell.
5. **flat:** a level surface.

6. **repugnant** (rĭ-pŭg′nənt): hateful.
7. **essayed:** tried; attempted.
8. **myriad** (mîr′ē-əd): a countless number of.

not a barnyard fowl clucked and strutted. The kitchen door stood open, and he gazed so long and hard into the black aperture[9] that it seemed almost that a farmer's wife must emerge at any moment.

He licked the pollen and dust from his dry lips, stiffened himself, mind and body, and rode out into the blazing sunshine. Nothing stirred. He went on past the house, and approached the wall of trees and bushes by the river's bank. One thought persisted maddeningly. It was of the crash into his body of a high-velocity bullet. It made him feel very fragile and defenseless, and he crouched lower in the saddle.

Tethering his horse in the edge of the wood, he continued a hundred yards on foot till he came to the stream. Twenty feet wide it was, without perceptible current, cool and inviting, and he was very thirsty. But he waited inside his screen of leafage, his eyes fixed on the screen on the opposite side. To make the wait endurable, he sat down, his carbine resting on his knees. The minutes passed, and slowly his tenseness relaxed. At last he decided there was no danger; but just as he prepared to part the bushes and bend down to the water, a movement among the opposite bushes caught his eye.

It might be a bird. But he waited. Again there was an agitation[10] of the bushes, and then, so suddenly that it almost startled a cry from him, the bushes parted and a face peered out. It was a face covered with several weeks' growth of ginger-colored beard. The eyes were blue and wide apart, with laughter-wrinkles in the corners that showed despite the tired and anxious expression of the whole face. All this he could see with microscopic

clearness, for the distance was no more than twenty feet. And all this he saw in such brief time that he saw it as he lifted his carbine to his shoulder. He glanced along the sights, and knew that he was gazing upon a man who was as good as dead. It was impossible to miss at such point-blank range.

But he did not shoot. Slowly he lowered the carbine and watched. A hand, clutching a water bottle, became visible, and the ginger beard bent downward to fill the bottle. He could hear the gurgle of the water. Then arm and bottle and ginger beard disappeared behind the closing bushes. A long time he waited, when, with thirst unslaked,[11] he crept back to his horse, rode slowly across the sunwashed clearing, and passed into the shelter of the woods beyond.

II

Another day, hot and breathless. A deserted farmhouse, large, with many outbuildings and an orchard, standing in a clearing. From the woods, on a roan horse, carbine across pommel, rode the young man with the quick black eyes. He breathed with relief as he gained the house. That a fight had taken place here earlier in the season was evident. Clips and empty cartridges, tarnished with verdigris,[12] lay on the ground, which, while wet, had been torn up by the hoofs of horses. Hard by the kitchen garden were graves, tagged and numbered. From the oak tree by the kitchen door, in tattered, weather-beaten garments, hung the bodies of two men. The faces, shriveled and defaced, bore no likeness to the faces of men. The roan horse snorted beneath them, and the rider caressed and soothed it and tied it farther away.

---

9. **aperture** (ăp′ər-chŏŏr′): opening.
10. **agitation** (ă′jĭ-tā′shən): disturbance.

11. **unslaked** (ŭn-slākd′): unsatisfied.
12. **verdigris** (vûr′də-grēs): a greenish coating that forms, like rust, on certain metals.

Entering the house, he found the interior a wreck. He trod on empty cartridges as he walked from room to room to reconnoiter[13] from the windows. Men had camped and slept everywhere, and on the floor of one room he came upon stains unmistakable where the wounded had been laid down.

Again outside, he led the horse around behind the barn and invaded the orchard. A dozen trees were burdened with ripe apples. He filled his pockets, eating while he picked. Then a thought came to him, and he glanced at the sun, calculating the time of his return to camp. He pulled off his shirt, tying the sleeves and making a bag. This he proceeded to fill with apples.

As he was about to mount his horse, the animal suddenly pricked up its ears. The man, too, listened, and heard, faintly, the thud of hoofs on soft earth. He crept to the corner of the barn and peered out. A dozen mounted men, strung out loosely, approaching from the opposite side of the clearing, were only a matter of a hundred yards or so away. They rode on to the house. Some dismounted, while others remained in the saddle as an earnest[14] that their stay would be short. They seemed to be holding a council, for he could hear them talking excitedly in the detested tongue of the alien invader. The time passed, but they seemed unable to reach a decision. He put the carbine away in its boot, mounted, and waited impatiently, balancing the shirt of apples on the pommel.

He heard footsteps approaching, and drove his spurs so fiercely into the roan as to force a surprised groan from the animal as it leaped forward. At the corner of the barn he saw the intruder, a mere boy of nineteen or twenty for all of his uniform, jump back to escape being

run down. At the same moment the roan swerved, and its rider caught a glimpse of the aroused men by the house. Some were springing from their horses, and he could see the rifles going to their shoulders. He passed the kitchen door and the dried corpses swinging in the shade, compelling his foes to run around the front of the house. A rifle cracked, and a second, but he was going fast, leaning forward, low in the saddle, one hand clutching the shirt of apples, the other guiding the horse.

The top bar of the fence was four feet high, but he knew his roan and leaped it at full career[15] to the accompaniment of several scattered shots. Eight hundred yards straight away were the woods, and the roan was cover-

---

13. **reconnoiter** (rē′kə-noi′tər): make a survey.
14. **earnest:** a pledge; an assurance.

15. **at full career:** at full speed.

ing the distance with mighty strides. Every man was now firing. They were pumping their guns so rapidly that he no longer heard individual shots. A bullet went through his hat, but he was unaware, though he did know when another tore through the apples on the pommel. And he winced and ducked even lower when a third bullet, fired low, struck a stone between his horse's legs and ricocheted off through the air, buzzing and humming like some incredible insect.

The shots died down as the magazines were emptied, until, quickly, there was no more shooting. The young man was elated. Through that astonishing fusillade he had come unscathed. He glanced back. Yes, they had emptied their magazines. He could see several reloading. Others were running back behind the house for their horses. As he looked, two, already mounted, came back into view around the corner, riding hard. And

at the same moment, he saw the man with the unmistakable ginger beard kneel down on the ground, level his gun, and coolly take his time for the long shot.

The young man threw his spurs into the horse, crouched very low, and swerved in his flight in order to distract the other's aim. And still the shot did not come. With each jump of the horse, the woods sprang nearer. They were only two hundred yards away, and still the shot was delayed.

And then he heard it, the last thing he was to hear, for he was dead ere he hit the ground in the long crashing fall from the saddle. And they, watching at the house, saw him fall, saw his body bounce when it struck the earth, and saw the burst of red-cheeked apples that rolled about him. They laughed at the unexpected eruption of apples, and clapped their hands in applause of the long shot by the man with the ginger beard.

FOR STUDY AND DISCUSSION

1. What details help you establish the time and place of the story?
2. What is the young cavalryman's quest? In what way is his task more fearful than being in the midst of battle?
3. Why do you think he decides not to shoot the man with the ginger-colored beard?
4. The young cavalryman is killed by the very man he spared earlier in the story. What does this ironic ending suggest about the nature of war?
5. Why do you suppose London does not identify his young soldier by name?

SETTING

The element of *setting* is the physical background of a story—its time and place. Sometimes an entire story is dependent on setting. Think, for example, of "The Most Dangerous Game" (page 2), where the conflict of Rainsford and Zaroff is confined to Ship-Trap Island. In a story such as "A Mild Attack of Locusts" (page 78), setting explains how characters live and why they act as they do. The setting can also lend atmosphere, as the underground crypt does in "The Cask of Amontillado" (page 58).

In "War" the setting is essential to the action of the story. The setting also allows London to build in certain ironic contrasts. In Part II of the story, for example, the young cavalryman comes to a deserted farmhouse where a fight had taken place earlier. There are signs of war everywhere: clips and empty cartridges, graves, corpses hanging from trees, the bloodstains of wounded men. Then the young man finds an orchard bursting with ripe fruit. What do you think is London's purpose in using these contrasts?

LANGUAGE AND VOCABULARY

Recognizing Word Origins

When we hear the word *magazine,* we usually think of a periodical like *Time* or *Family Circle,* which contains various articles and photographs. But *magazine* is also a military term meaning "a place to store ammunition or explosives." In this story, it refers to a clip or a small metal container for cartridges, which is inserted into a rifle.

What can you find out about the origins and meanings of these terms?

carbine   cavalry   fusillade
cartridge   clip

Which of these words also have meanings *not* directly associated with the military?

ABOUT THE AUTHOR

Born in poverty in San Francisco, Jack London (1876–1916) worked for ten cents an hour in a cannery as soon as he graduated from grammar school. By the time he published his first book at the age of twenty-four, he had been a hobo, a longshoreman, an oyster pirate, a seaman, and a gold prospector in Alaska. He had also been in jail twice—once for vagrancy in New York and once for speaking at a socialist meeting in California. London's participation in the gold rush to the Klondike in 1896 paid off—not in gold, but in material for stories. London soon became one of the most highly paid writers in the United States. Disciplined to write a thousand words a day, he turned out popular adventure fiction, such as the famous story "To Build a Fire" and the best-selling novel *The Call of the Wild.* London's fiction was realistic and often portrayed people in a grim struggle for survival.

Sliding

Leslie Norris

The cold had begun very suddenly on Tuesday night, when Bernard had gone out to play. The boys were playing kick-the-tin in the lamp-light at the top of the street, and nobody realized how cold it was until Randall Jenkins went home for his cap and scarf. Then they all felt the bitter weather—at their knees, their wrists, the tips of their ears. Bernard went indoors and borrowed his father's knitted scarf and found his own old gloves from last winter. Pretty soon, the game was on again and they forgot about the weather.

That night in bed, the sheets were hard and slippery, unfriendly as ice. Carefully, by an act of will, Bernard made warm a place in bed exactly the same shape as his body, thin and hunched under the covers. He extended it gradually, inch by inch, sending his toes gently into the cold until at last he was straight and comfortable. Everything was fine then, except that he had to pull the blankets firmly about his ears and shoulders. In the morning, the window was covered with frost-flowers, and the kitchen fire blazed ferociously against the Welsh winter. He called for Danny Kenyon, as usual, on the way to school. Danny was his best friend, and they ran all the way, although Danny was short and plump.

Bernard was used now to the ice. Out in the yard, the tap had been frozen for days and a tongue of glass poked out of its mouth. Every morning was gray and spiteful, churlish[1] light making the whole world dingy. Patches of hard grit gathered in the gutters and at the corners of streets, whipping against the boy's face and into his eyes. All day long, the shops kept their lights on, but there was nothing cheerful about them; only Mr. Toomey's shop was strong with color, because of the brilliant globes of his pyramids of oranges.

In school on Friday morning, Albert Evans began to cry. The teacher asked him why, but Albert wouldn't answer. It was Randall Jenkins who told about Albert's legs. The inside of his thighs was chafed raw—red all the way from his groin to his knees. The skin was hard and angry, and there were weeping cracks in it. The teacher let Albert sit in front, near the stove, and he didn't have to do any arithmetic. When Bernard told his mother about Albert's legs, she narrowed her mouth and said that Annie Evans had no more sense than the day she was born, and then she took a pot of ointment over to Albert's house. While she was out, Bernard's father told him it had been the coldest day in more than twenty years. It was funny about skin and cold weather. Some boys turned red because of the cold, and some rather blue, and Danny Kenyon's knees went a kind of mottled color—but he only laughed. When Bernard's mother came back, she was vexed. "Poor little scamp," she said. "It's agony for him to walk at all."

After breakfast on Saturday morning, Bernard climbed into his den, which was the room above the stable in the yard. His father had whitewashed the walls for him, and together they'd carried up some old chairs from the house. Two large kitchen tables, covered

---

1. **churlish**: here, stingy.

with paints and bits of models and old newspapers, stood side by side under the windows. His record player was there, too, and it was warm because of the oilstove. It was a fine room, with an enormous spider in the corner of the roof and a web thick and black against the white wall. Bernard sat in a chair near the stove and began to think of the things he would do when the summer came and he would be nine, going on ten. He and Danny Kenyon would go camping, they would find a field that nobody else knew about, and every day would be cloudless. He made the field in his head—the perfect green of its grass, its great protective tree in one corner, and its stream so pure that you could see every fragmentary pebble, every waving strand of weed in its bed. They were too young to go camping. He knew that.

And then Randall Jenkins climbed the stairs. He was grinning. He carried about his neck a pair of heavy boots, tied by their laces.

He took them off and dropped them proudly on the floor, where they stood bluntly on their uncouth soles, exactly as if they still had someone's feet in them and invisible legs climbing up from them. Randall held out his hands to the stove and danced slowly around it, revolving so that he warmed himself all over.

"Coming sliding?" he said. "This afternoon? We're all going—on the big pond; it's holding."

"I'll ask," said Bernard. "I expect it will be all right."

He thought of the big pond under the hills, its heavy acres hundreds of yards wide, the water cold and thick. It held in its silence fabulous pike, more than a yard long and twenty pounds in weight, although Bernard had never seen one. He didn't like the big pond.

"You'll need special boots," said Randall. "I've borrowed my brother's—take a look at them."

He lifted the great boots and held them for Bernard's inspection. The soles were an inch thick and covered with a symmetrical pattern of bold nails—flat squares shining like silver. Crescents of smooth metal were screwed at heel and toe into the leather, the edges worn thin as a razor.

Randall rubbed his sleeve over the scarred toecaps, breathing on them as he burnished.

"These are the ones," he said. "My brother's old working boots. They might have been made for sliding."

"They're too big for you," said Bernard.

"Size 7," said Randall with satisfaction. "My brother's grown out of them. Three or four pairs of socks and they'll fit me—you watch, I'll scream right across the pond."

He moved the boots through the air as if they were fighter planes.

"You'll need a pair like this," he said. "Otherwise you'll never go any distance."

Randall was lucky to have big brothers. Bernard thought dismally of his own boots—light, gentlemanly, with rubber soles and heels. His grandfather didn't like rubber soles and heels, either. Only thieves and policemen, he had said, two classes of society with much in common, wear rubber on their feet. Bernard didn't understand that.

"Is Danny Kenyon coming?" Bernard asked.

"Sure," Randall said. "We're all going. I told you."

After lunch, they all went to the pond, protected by layers of clothing against the wind's knives, their woolen hats pulled over their ears. Some of the boys had managed to borrow heavy boots, just to be like Randall Jenkins, and they clumped awkwardly up the hill as they learned to manage their erratic feet. Randall Jenkins turned out his toes, shuffling around corners like Charlie Chaplin,[2] and they all laughed.

Bernard began to feel very happy. He began to imagine the long quietness of his gliding over the ice. He thought of thick ice, clear as glass, beneath which the cold fish swam, staring up with their goggle eyes at the sliding boys. He thought of ice like a dazzling mirror set in the hills, on which they could skim above their own images, each brilliant slider like two perfect boys—one upside-down—joined at the feet. In his happiness he jostled and bumped against Danny Kenyon, and Danny charged right back at him, until they were both laughing and the wind blew away their white breath in clouds from their mouths.

But the pond was a disappointment. Winter had taken all the life from the hills, and the face of the ice was gray and blind—the color

of the flat sky above it. There were no reeds at the lake's edge. Featureless, the ice stretched on, swept by an unhindered wind. The boys bent their heads down against the brutal cold. Their voices were feeble; they felt small and helpless. Only Randall Jenkins was unaffected. Whooping and waving at the ice, he began to run, lifting his enormous boots in slow, high-stepping strides. He ran on, planting his laughable feet one after the other so heavily that Bernard imagined he could hear the whole bowl ringing; and then, his legs rigid, both arms raised for balance, he slid with comic dignity. They all rushed after him, sliding and calling. The afternoon was suddenly warm and vigorous.

---

2. **Charlie Chaplin:** a motion-picture comedian, famous for his characterization of the "little tramp" in silent films.

Bernard was a good runner, and he hurled himself along so that the momentum of his first slide would be memorable. He raced past two or three of the boys and then stopped, his legs braced wide, head up, arms raised. He was expecting something birdlike, something approaching flight, but nothing happened. His rubber soles clung wickedly to the surface of the ice and he slid no more than a few yards. He was inconsolable.

He shuffled cautiously along the margins of the ice, tentative and humble. Far out, in the wide middle of the pond, he could see the dark figures of his friends, freely sliding, gyrating, crouching, skating on one leg. Their voices came bouncing to him high and clear like the calling of sea gulls. But he ran alone at the edge of the lake, unable to slide. Then, unexpectedly, without warning, he found himself free of the binding friction that had held him. He had begun to glide. He sat on the bank, lifted one foot, and inspected the sole of his boot. A thin layer of polished ice, thinner than a postage stamp, had built itself onto the black rubber. He saw that the other boot was also transformed, and he ran jubilantly into the heart of the pond, far outstripping the loud boys, sliding far and fast, hearing their admiration and surprise. The pond was his.

Late in the afternoon came two young men, tall, with deep voices, all of seventeen years old. They strapped on their sharp and proper skates, and skated expertly. Briefly, the boys watched them, but soon Randall Jenkins had organized a game of follow-my-leader. Randall was a superb leader, his invention and audacity encouraging them to a skill and daring they had not known they possessed. The last dare was to run as fast as they could toward the ice from the shore itself, leaping from the bank at full speed. Randall raced forward, his long slow legs gathering pace as he ran, and then he leaped high outward from the bank, landing yards out. Rigid as a scarecrow, he sped on, stopping at last a prodigious way out, and standing absolutely still in the attitude of his sliding. One by one they followed him, although nobody was as brave as Randall, nobody would hurl himself as uninhibitedly from the steep bank. At last, only three boys were left. Bernard thought he had never seen anything as lovely as the dark ice, hardly lit at all as the light faded, and the still figures of his friends dotted about on it, not moving, their arms in a variety of postures, their bodies bent or upright. He took a great breath, and ran. He had never felt so light, he was full of fiery energy. He reached the bank and thrust himself so urgently, so powerfully, that the exhilaration of his leap made him gasp. He hit the ice beautifully, and felt at once the speed of his sliding, and he knew that nobody had ever slid so far. Stopping at last, he looked around. He was yards farther than Randall Jenkins, miles farther than the other boys. Jackie Phelps was slowing miserably a long way off, and only Danny was left to jump.

He could see Danny up on the bank, preparing to run, swaying from one foot to the other, bent forward at the waist. Cupping his hands, Bernard shouted, "You'll never reach me!"

Danny waved furiously. You could see that he was going to give it all he had by the way he set his shoulders. He ran forward and leaped wildly from the bank. Bernard could see him so clearly that everything seemed to happen in slow motion. He saw Danny hit the ice and knew that it was wrong. Danny landed on his heels, not on the flat of his feet, and his body was already tilting gently backward. He sped along, the slope of his body already irrevocably past the point of recovery. They saw his heels leave the ice, and for a perceptible moment he sailed through the unsupporting air before the back of his head cracked frighteningly against the surface. He lay broken and huddled. Bernard could not move. He could see Danny in a black heap, but he couldn't move toward him. It was Randall Jenkins who reached him first, and they all ran in behind him.

They crowded around Danny, looking down at him. His face was still and white, his eyes closed. As they looked, a little worm of blood appeared at one nostril and curled onto Danny's lip. What if he should die? Bernard bent, and in an urgency of terror lifted his friend. Randall helped him, and together they hauled Danny to the bank. Some of the boys were crying, and Randall set them to collect twigs, pieces of paper — anything that would burn. Bernard took off Danny's gloves and rubbed his hands in his own. Danny's fingers were very cold, but in a while he began to move and groan. Twice he opened his eyes, without recognizing them and without saying anything. Randall lit a fire, and it burned with a dull light, sullenly. He sent all the boys except Bernard to find more fuel, told them to rip branches from small trees. Bernard wiped the blood from Danny's nose, and after a while the bleeding stopped. It hadn't been very much, he comforted himself. His knees hurt from bending down so long. Behind him, Randall had whipped the fire into a huge blaze that pushed away the darkness, and the boys sat near it, not speaking. Danny moved heavily, sat up, and looked at Bernard.

"Oh, my God," said Danny Kenyon. "What happened?"

He was all right; everything was all right. The boys cheered, slapped each other on the back, put Danny to sit even nearer the fire. They danced and sang, released from fright, and they were pert and arrogant when one of the young men suddenly appeared.

"What's the matter with him?" he asked, bending over Danny.

"Nothing," said Randall airily. "Nothing at all."

"None of your business," said Jackie Phelps, out of the darkness.

"How old are you?" said the young man to Bernard.

"Ten," lied Bernard. He pointed to Randall. "And he's eleven," he said.

"Get that boy home," said the young man. "How do you feel, son?"

"Great," said Danny. "I feel great."

"Get home," said the young man. "And the rest of you see that this fire is out."

He skated into the darkness. Bernard could feel the iron shearing of his blades.

The fire was very hot. Bernard could imagine it warming a thin crust of frozen soil, then maybe deeper, a half-inch deep. Already he could hear the ice hiss in the released ground. He sat with his back up against Danny's back, so they were both comfortable. All the boys sat around. They were very quiet.

Bit by bit, the dark and the cold crept into the interstices of the flames, winning the night back for winter. Randall got up and stamped about. His feet had gone to sleep.

"Time to go, lads," he said. "Time to go."

They stood up and followed obediently behind Randall. Bernard was so tired that his legs were slow and stiff, and his mind was always about two steps in front of them, but in a little while they got better. The boys went down the lane past the old rectory and started down the hill toward the town. A night wind flew at them as if it cared nothing for people and meant to blow straight through them. Bernard began to shiver. What if Danny had died? He saw again Danny's face as he lay on the ice, as white and stiff as a candle. As he looked, an imaginary worm of blood crawled from Danny's nose and covered the side of his cheek. He closed his mind from the terror of it and put his arm over Danny's shoulder.

"How do you feel?" he whispered, but Randall heard him.

"He feels great," Randall Jenkins roared, his voice red as fire. "What's the matter with you? He feels fine!"

"I'm OK," said Danny. "Honest, I'm OK."

A few small flakes of snow fell out of the sky. The boys felt them hit their faces, light as cobwebs, and then vanish. It was intolerably dark and cold. As they entered the first streets of the town, the boys moved together for solace and started to run. They trotted close together, moving home as one boy through the darkness, united against whatever terror might threaten them.

FOR STUDY AND DISCUSSION

1. Point out specific details and sentences in the first four paragraphs that emphasize the bitterness of winter. How do these passages signal that something painful will happen later on?

2. When the group of boys sets out for the pond, Bernard feels very happy. Why is he disappointed when they arrive?

3. Bernard's mood (and the mood of the story) changes as he slides on the ice. Point out sentences that show his mood. What happens to shatter this mood? How has the description of the pond prepared you for this event?

4. The last sentence of the story states that the boys "trotted close together, moving home as one boy through the darkness, united against whatever terror might threaten them." What terror have the boys already experienced? What is the terror that might threaten them?

5. In some stories setting plays such an important role that it functions almost like a character. In what way is winter in this story an antagonist, or enemy? Cite some passages that contribute to this impression.

SETTING

Most of "Sliding" takes place at a pond. But the story also has a larger setting: winter. In "Sliding" winter is more than simply a time of year. It is an ominous presence, which makes bedsheets "unfriendly as ice" and attacks the body. Notice how, in the following sentences, winter is treated as if it has the thoughts and motives of a living being:

Winter had taken all the life from the hills and the face of the ice was gray and blind — the color of the flat sky above it.

Bit by bit, the dark and the cold crept back into the interstices of the flames, winning the night back for winter.

How does winter, as it is depicted in "Sliding," make Danny's mishap more than simply an unlucky accident?

FIGURATIVE LANGUAGE

One feature of Leslie Norris' style is his imaginative use of figurative language. Identify the similes and metaphors in each of the following excerpts from the story, and explain each comparison in your own words. For a review of figurative language, see page 84.

1. That night in bed, the sheets were hard and slippery, unfriendly as ice.
2. In the morning, the window was covered with frostflowers . . .
3. Out in the yard, the tap had been frozen for days and a tongue of glass poked out of its mouth.
4. The skin was hard and angry, and there were weeping cracks in it.
5. After lunch, they all went to the pond, protected by layers of clothing against the wind's knives . . .
6. He thought of ice like a dazzling mirror set in the hills, on which they could skim above their own images . . .
7. Their voices came bouncing to him high and clear like the calling of sea gulls.
8. A thin layer of polished ice, thinner than a postage stamp, had built itself onto the black rubber.
9. He saw again Danny's face as he lay on the ice, as white and stiff as a candle.
10. As he looked, an imaginary worm of blood crawled from Danny's nose and covered the side of his cheek.

FOR COMPOSITION

Writing About a Personal Experience
Leslie Norris depicts vividly his characters' exhilaration in sliding across a frozen pond. Recall an experience of your own in which you felt a similar excitement or happiness. Tell about that experience and re-create your feelings for the reader. Describe the setting, using vivid images and figures of speech.

ABOUT THE AUTHOR

Leslie Norris (1920–   ) a poet and short-story writer, was born in Merthyn Tydfil, Glamorganshire, Wales. He went to college in Coventry, England, and also studied at the University of Southampton Institute of Education. Since 1958, he has taught English at the Training College at Bognor Regis in Sussex, England. Mr. Norris has had many short stories and poems published in magazines. In 1976, *Sliding*, a collection of his stories, appeared. It was praised for powerfully evoking "all the atmosphere of an English or Welsh landscape."

A Summer's Reading

Bernard Malamud

George Stoyonovich was a neighborhood boy who had quit high school on an impulse when he was sixteen, run out of patience, and though he was ashamed every time he went looking for a job, when people asked him if he had finished and he had to say no, he never went back to school. This summer was a hard time for jobs and he had none. Having so much time on his hands, George thought of going to summer school, but the kids in his classes would be too young. He also considered registering in a night high school, only he didn't like the idea of the teachers always telling him what to do. He felt they had not respected him. The result was he stayed off the streets and in his room most of the day. He was close to twenty and had needs with the neighborhood girls, but no money to spend, and he couldn't get more than an occasional few cents because his father was poor, and his sister Sophie, who resembled George, a tall bony girl of twenty-three, earned very little and what she had she kept for herself. Their mother was dead, and Sophie had to take care of the house.

Very early in the morning George's father got up to go to work in a fish market. Sophie left at about eight for her long ride in the subway to a cafeteria in the Bronx.[1] George had his coffee by himself, then hung around in the house. When the house, a five-room railroad flat[2] above a butcher store, got on his nerves he cleaned it up—mopped the floors with a wet mop and put things away. But most of the time he sat in his room. In the afternoons he listened to the ball game. Otherwise he had a couple of old copies of the *World Almanac* he had bought long ago, and he liked to read in them and also the magazines and newspapers that Sophie brought home, that had been left on the tables in the cafeteria. They were mostly picture magazines about movie stars and sports figures, also usually the *News* and *Mirror*.[3] Sophie herself read whatever fell into her hands, although she sometimes read good books.

She once asked George what he did in his room all day and he said he read a lot too.

"Of what besides what I bring home? Do you ever read any worthwhile books?"

"Some," George answered, although he really didn't. He had tried to read a book or two that Sophie had in the house but found he was in no mood for them. Lately he couldn't stand made-up stories, they got on his nerves. He wished he had some hobby to work at—as a kid he was good in carpentry, but where could he work at it? Sometimes during the day he went for walks, but mostly he did his walking after the hot sun had gone down and it was cooler in the streets.

In the evening after supper George left the

---

1. **Bronx:** a borough of New York City.

2. **railroad flat:** an apartment of rooms in a line. Each room is entered from another.
3. ***News* and *Mirror*:** daily newspapers. The *Mirror* no longer exists.

house and wandered in the neighborhood. During the sultry days some of the storekeepers and their wives sat in chairs on the thick, broken sidewalks in front of their shops, fanning themselves, and George walked past them and the guys hanging out on the candy-store corner. A couple of them he had known his whole life, but nobody recognized each other. He had no place special to go, but generally, saving it till the last, he left the neighborhood and walked for blocks till he came to a darkly lit little park with benches and trees and an iron railing, giving it a feeling of privacy. He sat on a bench here, watching the leafy trees and the flowers blooming on the inside of the railing, thinking of a better life for himself. He thought of the jobs he had had since he had quit school—delivery boy, stock clerk, runner, lately working in a factory—and he was dissatisfied with all of them. He felt he would someday like to have a good job and live in a private house with a porch, on a

street with trees. He wanted to have some dough in his pocket to buy things with, and a girl to go with, so as not to be so lonely, especially on Saturday nights. He wanted people to like and respect him. He thought about these things often but mostly when he was alone at night. Around midnight he got up and drifted back to his hot and stony neighborhood.

One time while on his walk George met Mr. Cattanzara coming home very late from work. He wondered if he was drunk but then could tell he wasn't. Mr. Cattanzara, a stocky, baldheaded man who worked in a change booth on an IRT station,[4] lived on the next block after George's, above a shoe repair store. Nights, during the hot weather, he sat on his stoop[5] in an undershirt, reading the *New York*

---

4. **IRT station:** The IRT is one of the public-transportation systems in New York City.
5. **stoop:** staircase leading to the entrance of a building.

Times in the light of the shoemaker's window. He read it from the first page to the last, then went up to sleep. And all the time he was reading the paper, his wife, a fat woman with a white face, leaned out of the window, gazing into the street, her thick white arms folded under her loose breast, on the window ledge.

Once in a while Mr. Cattanzara came home drunk, but it was a quiet drunk. He never made any trouble, only walked stiffly up the street and slowly climbed the stairs into the hall. Though drunk, he looked the same as always, except for his tight walk, the quietness, and that his eyes were wet. George liked Mr. Cattanzara because he remembered him giving him nickels to buy lemon ice with when he was a squirt. Mr. Cattanzara was a different type than those in the neighborhood. He asked different questions than the others when he met you, and he seemed to know what went on in all the newspapers. He read them, as his fat sick wife watched from the window.

"What are you doing with yourself this summer, George?" Mr. Cattanzara asked. "I see you walkin' around at nights."

George felt embarrassed. "I like to walk."

"What are you doin' in the day now?"

"Nothing much just right now. I'm waiting for a job." Since it shamed him to admit he wasn't working, George said, "I'm staying home—but I'm reading a lot to pick up my education."

Mr. Cattanzara looked interested. He mopped his hot face with a red handkerchief.

"What are you readin'?"

George hesitated, then said, "I got a list of books in the library once, and now I'm gonna read them this summer." He felt strange and a little unhappy saying this, but he wanted Mr. Cattanzara to respect him.

"How many books are there on it?"

"I never counted them. Maybe around a hundred."

Mr. Cattanzara whistled through his teeth.

"I figure if I did that," George went on earnestly, "it would help me in my education. I don't mean the kind they give you in high school. I want to know different things than they learn there, if you know what I mean."

The change maker nodded. "Still and all, one hundred books is a pretty big load for one summer."

"It might take longer."

"After you're finished with some, maybe you and I can shoot the breeze about them?" said Mr. Cattanzara.

"When I'm finished," George answered.

Mr. Cattanzara went home and George continued on his walk. After that, though he had the urge to, George did nothing different from usual. He still took his walks at night, ending up in the little park. But one evening the shoemaker on the next block stopped George to say he was a good boy, and George figured that Mr. Cattanzara had told him all about the books he was reading. From the shoemaker it must have gone down the street, because George saw a couple of people smiling kindly at him, though nobody spoke to him personally. He felt a little better around the neighborhood and liked it more, though not so much he would want to live in it forever. He had never exactly disliked the people in it, yet he had never liked them very much either. It was the fault of the neighborhood. To his surprise, George found out that his father and Sophie knew about his reading too. His father was too shy to say anything about it—he was never much of a talker in his whole life—but Sophie was softer to George, and she showed him in other ways she was proud of him.

As the summer went on George felt in a good mood about things. He cleaned the house every day, as a favor to Sophie, and he enjoyed the ball games more. Sophie gave him a buck a week allowance, and though it still wasn't enough and he had to use it carefully, it was a helluva lot better than just having two bits now and then. What he bought with the money—cigarettes mostly, an occasional beer or movie ticket—he got a big kick out of. Life wasn't so bad if you knew how to appreciate it. Occasionally he bought a paperback book from the newsstand, but he never got around to reading it, though he was glad to have a couple of books in his room. But he read thoroughly Sophie's magazines and newspapers. And at night was the most enjoyable time, because when he passed the storekeepers sitting outside their stores, he could tell they regarded him highly. He walked erect, and though he did not say much to them, or they to him, he could feel approval on all sides. A couple of nights he felt so good that he skipped the park at the end of the evening. He just wandered in the neighborhood, where people had known him from the time he was a kid playing punchball whenever there was a game of it going; he wandered there, then came home and got undressed for bed, feeling fine.

For a few weeks he had talked only once with Mr. Cattanzara, and though the change maker had said nothing more about the books, asked no questions, his silence made George a little uneasy. For a while George didn't pass in front of Mr. Cattanzara's house any more, until one night, forgetting himself, he approached it from a different direction than he usually did when he did. It was already past midnight. The street, except for one or two people, was deserted, and George was surprised when he saw Mr. Cattanzara still reading his newspaper by the light of the streetlamp overhead. His impulse was to stop at the stoop and talk to him. He wasn't sure

what he wanted to say, though he felt the words would come when he began to talk; but the more he thought about it, the more the idea scared him, and he decided he'd better not. He even considered beating it home by another street, but he was too near Mr. Cattanzara, and the change maker might see him as he ran, and get annoyed. So George unobtrusively crossed the street, trying to make it seem as if he had to look in a store window on the other side, which he did, and then went on, uncomfortable at what he was doing. He feared Mr. Cattanzara would glance up from his paper and call him a dirty rat for walking on the other side of the street, but all he did was sit there, sweating through his undershirt, his bald head shining in the dim light as he read his *Times,* and upstairs his fat wife leaned out of the window, seeming to read the paper along with him. George thought she would spy him and yell out to Mr. Cattanzara, but she never moved her eyes off her husband.

George made up his mind to stay away from the change maker until he had got some of his softback books read, but when he started them and saw they were mostly storybooks, he lost his interest and didn't bother to finish them. He lost his interest in reading other things too. Sophie's magazines and newspapers went unread. She saw them piling up on a chair in his room and asked why he was no longer looking at them, and George told her it was because of all the other reading he had to do. Sophie said she had guessed that was it. So for most of the day, George had the radio on, turning to music when he was sick of the human voice. He kept the house fairly neat, and Sophie said nothing on the days when he neglected it. She was still kind and gave him his extra buck, though things weren't so good for him as they had been before.

But they were good enough, considering.

Also his night walks invariably picked him up, no matter how bad the day was. Then one night George saw Mr. Cattanzara coming down the street toward him. George was about to turn and run but he recognized from Mr. Cattanzara's walk that he was drunk, and if so, probably he would not even bother to notice him. So George kept on walking straight ahead until he came abreast of Mr. Cattanzara and though he felt wound up enough to pop into the sky, he was not surprised when Mr. Cattanzara passed him without a word, walking slowly, his face and body stiff. George drew a breath in relief at his narrow escape, when he heard his name called, and there stood Mr. Cattanzara at his elbow, smelling like the inside of a beer barrel. His eyes were sad as he gazed at George, and George felt so intensely uncomfortable he was tempted to shove the drunk aside and continue on his walk.

But he couldn't act that way to him, and, besides, Mr. Cattanzara took a nickel out of his pants pocket and handed it to him.

"Go buy yourself a lemon ice, Georgie."

"It's not that time any more, Mr. Cattanzara," George said, "I am a big guy now."

"No, you ain't," said Mr. Cattanzara, to which George made no reply he could think of.

"How are all your books comin' along now?" Mr. Cattanzara asked. Though he tried to stand steady, he swayed a little.

"Fine, I guess," said George, feeling the red crawling up his face.

"You ain't sure?" The change maker smiled slyly, a way George had never seen him smile.

"Sure I'm sure. They're fine."

Though his head swayed in little arcs, Mr. Cattanzara's eyes were steady. He had small blue eyes which could hurt if you looked at them too long.

"George," he said, "name me one book on that list that you read this summer, and I will drink to your health."

"I don't want anybody drinking to me."

"Name me one so I can ask you a question on it. Who can tell, if it's a good book maybe I might wanna read it myself."

George knew he looked passable on the outside, but inside he was crumbling apart.

Unable to reply, he shut his eyes, but when —years later—he opened them, he saw that Mr. Cattanzara had, out of pity, gone away, but in his ears he still heard the words he had said when he left: "George, don't do what I did."

The next night he was afraid to leave his room, and though Sophie argued with him he wouldn't open the door.

"What are you doing in there?" she asked.

"Nothing."

"Aren't you reading?"

"No."

She was silent a minute, then asked, "Where do you keep the books you read? I never see any in your room outside of a few cheap trashy ones."

He wouldn't tell her.

"In that case you're not worth a buck of my hard-earned money. Why should I break my back for you? Go on out, you bum, and get a job."

He stayed in his room for almost a week, except to sneak into the kitchen when nobody was home. Sophie railed at him, then begged him to come out, and his old father wept, but George wouldn't budge, though the weather was terrible and his small room stifling. He found it very hard to breathe, each breath was like drawing a flame into his lungs.

One night, unable to stand the heat anymore, he burst into the street at one A.M., a shadow of himself. He hoped to sneak to the park without being seen, but there were people all over the block, wilted and listless, waiting for a breeze. George lowered his eyes and walked, in disgrace, away from them, but before long he discovered they were still friendly to him. He figured Mr. Cattanzara hadn't told on him. Maybe when he woke up out of his drunk the next morning, he had forgotten all about meeting George. George felt his confidence slowly come back to him.

That same night a man on a street corner asked him if it was true that he had finished reading so many books, and George admitted he had. The man said it was a wonderful thing for a boy his age to read so much.

"Yeah," George said, but he felt relieved. He hoped nobody would mention the books any more, and when, after a couple of days, he accidentally met Mr. Cattanzara again, *he* didn't, though George had the idea he was the one who had started the rumor that he had finished all the books.

One evening in the fall, George ran out of his house to the library, where he hadn't been in years. There were books all over the place, wherever he looked, and though he was struggling to control an inward trembling, he easily counted off a hundred, then sat down at a table to read.

FOR STUDY AND DISCUSSION

1. What is George's problem at the opening of the story? How much of George's difficulty is caused by circumstances and how much by his own character?

2. This story takes place in New York City during the summer. What impression do you have of George's neighborhood and his neighbors? Why is it significant that this story takes place in the summer rather than, say, in the spring?

3. Why does George lie to Mr. Cattanzara about the books he is reading? How does this lie affect George's status in the neighborhood? How does his attitude toward the neighborhood change?

4. How is George made to face the consequences of his lie? What does Mr. Cattanzara mean when he says "George, don't do what I did"?

5. What do you think finally drives George to the library? Do you believe this action marks a change in his life? Why or why not? Why is it significant that the story ends in the fall?

LANGUAGE AND VOCABULARY

Distinguishing Informal English from Slang
Standard English can be formal or informal. Informal standard English is the language used most of the time in writing and speaking. Formal standard English is more elegant and elaborate. It is used in scholarly books, research papers, technical writing, and on formal occasions in public speaking.

Slang lies outside of standard usage and is generally used in very informal situations. Slang tends to be colorful, humorous, and fresh. Sometimes slang is made up or invented. Sometimes slang is the result of giving a new meaning to an established word or phrase: "in the doghouse." A slang expression may pass quickly from the language or it may become part of standard usage.

In this sentence from "A Summer's Reading," the italicized phrase is an example of informal standard English:

George had his coffee by himself, then *hung around* in the house.

In a formal context, instead of "hang around" you might use "loiter" or "linger indolently." The phrase *hang out* is slang:

. . . George walked past them and the guys *hanging out* on the candy-store corner.

In standard English you might use "spending time" or "frequenting."

Dictionaries often identify informal and nonstandard usage of words. Using your dictionary, find out if each of the italicized expressions listed here is classified as informal standard English or slang. Tell what each one means.

1. He wanted to have some *dough* in his pocket to buy things with . . .
2. George liked Mr. Cattanzara because he remembered him giving him nickels to buy lemon ice with when he was a *squirt.*
3. . . . it was a lot better than just having *two bits* now and then.
4. He even considered *beating it* home by another street . . .

FOR COMPOSITION

Comparing Characters
Compare George with Alfred Higgins in "All the Years of Her Life" (page 38). What similarity is there in the way both characters deal with their problems? What do you think each boy discovers about himself?

ABOUT THE AUTHOR

Bernard Malamud (1914–1986) was born in Brooklyn, New York. He attended the City College of New York and Columbia University. In 1952 his first novel, *The Natural,* was published. His second novel, *The Assistant,* appeared in 1957. "A Summer's Reading" is from a collection of stories called *The Magic Barrel,* which received the National Book Award for fiction in 1959. Malamud's other works include *A New Life* (1961), *Idiots First* (1963), *The Fixer* (1966), which received both a National Book Award and the Pulitzer Prize for fiction, *Pictures of Fidelman* (1969), and *The Tenants* (1971).

Lonesome Boy, Silver Trumpet

Arna Bontemps

When Bubber first learned to play the trumpet, his old grandpa winked his eye and laughed.

"You better mind how you blow that horn, sonny boy. You better mind."

"I like to blow loud, I like to blow fast, and I like to blow high," Bubber answered. "Listen to this, Grandpa." And he went on blowing with his eyes closed.

When Bubber was a little bigger, he began carrying his trumpet around with him wherever he went, so his old grandpa scratched his whiskers, took the corncob pipe out of his mouth, and laughed again.

"You better mind *where* you blow that horn, boy," he warned. "I used to blow one myself, and I know."

Bubber smiled. "Where did you ever blow music, Grandpa?"

"Down in New Orleans and all up and down the river. I blowed trumpet most everywhere in my young days, and I tell you, you better mind where you go blowing."

"I like to blow my trumpet in the school band when it marches, I like to blow it on the landing when the riverboats come in sight, and I like to blow it among the trees in the swamp," he said, still smiling. But when he looked at his grandpa again, he saw a worried look on the old man's face, and he asked, "What's the matter, Grandpa, ain't that all right?"

Grandpa shook his head. "I wouldn't do it if I was you."

That sounded funny to Bubber, but he was not in the habit of disputing his grandfather. Instead he said, "I don't believe I ever heard you blow the trumpet, Grandpa. Don't you want to try blowing on mine now?"

Again the old man shook his head. "My blowing days are long gone," he said. "I still got the lip, but I ain't got the teeth. It takes good teeth to blow high notes on a horn, and these I got ain't much good. They're store teeth."

That made Bubber feel sorry for his grandfather, so he whispered softly, "I'll mind where I blow my horn, Grandpa."

He didn't really mean it, though. He just said it to make his grandpa feel good. And the very next day he was half a mile out in the country blowing his horn in a cornfield. Two or three evenings later he was blowing it on a shady lane when the sun went down and not paying much attention where he went.

When he came home, his grandpa met him. "I heard you blowing your horn a long ways away," he said. "The air was still. I could hear it easy."

"How did it sound, Grandpa?"

"Oh, it sounded right pretty." He paused a moment, knocking the ashes out of his pipe, before adding, "Sounded like you mighta been lost."

That made Bubber ashamed of himself, because he knew he had not kept his word and that he was not minding where he blowed his trumpet. "I know what you mean, Grandpa," he answered. "But I can't do like you say. When I'm blowing my horn, I don't always look where I'm going."

Grandpa walked to the window and looked out. While he was standing there, he hitched his overalls up a little higher. He took a red handkerchief from his pocket and wiped his forehead. "Sounded to me like you might have been past Barbin's Landing."

"I was lost," Bubber admitted.

"You can end up in some funny places when you're just blowing a horn and not paying attention. I know," Grandpa insisted. "I know."

"Well, what do you want me to do, Grandpa?"

The old man struck a kitchen match on the seat of his pants and lit a kerosene lamp because the room was black dark by now. While the match was still burning, he lit his pipe. Then he sat down and stretched out his feet. Bubber was on a stool on the other side of the room, his trumpet under his arm. "When you go to school and play your horn in the band, that's all right," the old man said. "When you come home, you ought to put it in the case and leave it there. It ain't good to go traipsing around with a horn in your hand. You might get into devilment."

"But I feel lonesome without my trumpet, Grandpa," Bubber pleaded. "I don't like to go around without it anytime. I feel lost."

Grandpa sighed. "Well, there you are—lost with it and lost without it. I don't know what's going to become of you, sonny boy."

"You don't understand, Grandpa. You don't understand."

The old man smoked his pipe quietly for a few minutes and then went off to bed, but Bubber did not move. Later on, however, when he heard his grandpa snoring in the next room, he went outdoors, down the path, and around the smokehouse, and sat on a log. The night was still. He couldn't hear anything louder than a cricket. Soon he began wondering how his trumpet would sound on such a still night, back there behind the old smokehouse, so he put the mouthpiece to his lips very lightly and blew a few silvery notes. Immediately Bubber felt better. Now he knew for sure that Grandpa didn't understand how it was with a boy and a horn—a lonesome boy with a silver trumpet. Bubber lifted his horn toward the stars and let the music pour out.

Presently a big orange moon rose, and everything Bubber could see changed suddenly. The moon was so big it made the smokehouse and the trees and the fences seem small. Bubber blew his trumpet loud, he blew it fast, and he blew it high, and in just a few minutes he forgot all about Grandpa sleeping in the house.

He was afraid to talk to Grandpa after that. He was afraid Grandpa might scold him or warn him or try in some other way to persuade him to leave his trumpet in its case. Bubber was growing fast now. He knew what he liked, and he did not think he needed any advice from Grandpa.

Still he loved his grandfather very much, and he had no intention of saying anything that would hurt him. Instead he decided to leave home. He did not tell Grandpa what he was going to do. He just waited till the old man went to sleep in his bed one night. Then he quietly blew out the lamp, put his trumpet under his arm, and started walking down the road from Marksville to Barbin's Landing.

No boat was there, but Bubber did not mind. He knew one would come by before morning, and he knew that he wouldn't be lonesome so long as he had his trumpet with him. He found a place on the little dock where he could lean back against a post and swing his feet over the edge while playing, and the time passed swiftly. And when he finally went aboard a riverboat, just before morning, he found a place on the deck that suited him just as well and went right on blowing his horn.

Nobody asked him to pay any fare. The riverboatmen did not seem to expect it of a boy who blew a trumpet the way Bubber did. And in New Orleans the cooks in the kitchens where he ate and the people who kept the rooming houses where he slept did not seem to expect him to pay either. In fact, people seemed to think that a boy who played a trumpet where the patrons of a restaurant could hear him or for the guests of a rooming house should receive money for it. They began to throw money around Bubber's feet as he played his horn.

At first he was surprised. Later he decided it only showed how wrong Grandpa had been about horn blowing. So he picked up all the money they threw, bought himself fancy new clothes, and began looking for new places to play. He ran into boys who played guitars or bull fiddles or drums or other instruments, and he played right along with them. He went out with them to play for picnics or barbecues or boat excursions or dances. He played early in the morning and he played late at night, and he bought new clothes and dressed up so fine he scarcely knew himself in a mirror. He scarcely knew day from night.

It was wonderful to play the trumpet like that, Bubber thought, and to make all that money. People telephoned to the rooming house where he lived and asked for him nearly every day. Some sent notes asking if he would play his trumpet at their parties. Occa-

sionally one would send an automobile to bring him to the place, and this was the best of all. Bubber liked riding through the pretty part of the city to the ballrooms in which well-dressed people waited to dance to his music. He enjoyed even more the times when he was taken to big white-columned houses in the country, houses surrounded by old trees with moss on them.

But he went to so many places to play his trumpet, he forgot where he had been and he got into the habit of not paying much attention. That was how it was the day he received a strange call on the telephone. A voice that sounded like a very proper gentleman said, "I would like to speak to the boy from Marksville, the one who plays the trumpet."

"I'm Bubber, sir. I'm the one."

"Well, Bubber, I'm having a very special party tonight—very special," the voice said. "I want you to play for us."

Bubber felt a little drowsy because he had been sleeping when the phone rang, and he still wasn't too wide awake. He yawned as he answered, "Just me, sir? You want me to play by myself?"

"There will be other musicians, Bubber. You'll play in the band. We'll be looking for you?"

"Where do you live, sir?" Bubber asked sleepily.

"Never mind about that, Bubber. I'll send my chauffeur with my car. He'll bring you."

The voice was growing faint by this time, and Bubber was not sure he caught the last words. "Where did you say, sir?" he asked suddenly. "When is it you want me?"

"I'll send my chauffeur," the voice repeated and then faded out completely.

Bubber put the phone down and went back to his bed to sleep some more. He had played his trumpet very late the night before, and now he just couldn't keep his eyes open.

Something was ringing when he woke up again. Was it the telephone? Bubber jumped out of bed and ran to answer, but the phone buzzed when he put it to his ear. There was nobody on the line. Then he knew it must have been the doorbell. A moment later he heard the door open, and footsteps came down the dark hall toward Bubber's room. Before Bubber could turn on the light, the footsteps were just outside his room, and a man's voice said, "I'm the chauffeur. I've brought the car to take you to the dance."

"So soon?" Bubber asked, surprised.

The man laughed. "You must have slept all day. It's night now, and we have a long way to drive."

"I'll put on my clothes," Bubber said.

The streetlight was shining through the window, so he did not bother to switch on the light in his room. Bubber never liked to open his eyes with a bright light shining, and anyway he knew right where to put his hands on the clothes he needed. As he began slipping into them, the chauffeur turned away. "I'll wait for you on the curb," he said.

"All right," Bubber called. "I'll hurry."

When he finished dressing, Bubber took his trumpet off the shelf, closed the door of his room, and went out to where the tall driver was standing beside a long, shiny automobile. The chauffeur saw him coming and opened the door to the back seat. When Bubber stepped in, he threw a lap robe across his knees and closed it. Then the chauffeur went around to his place in the front seat, stepped on the starter, switched on his headlights, and sped away.

The car was finer than any Bubber had ridden in before; the motor purred so softly and the chauffeur drove it so smoothly that Bubber soon began to feel sleepy again. One thing puzzled him, however. He had not yet seen the driver's face, and he wondered what the man looked like. But now the chauffeur's cap was down so far over his eyes and his coat collar was turned up so high Bubber could not see his face at all, no matter how far he leaned forward.

After a while he decided it was no use. He would have to wait till he got out of the car to look at the man's face. In the meantime he would sleep. Bubber pulled the lap robe up over his shoulders, stretched out on the wide back seat of the car, and went to sleep again.

The car came to a stop, but Bubber did not wake up till the chauffeur opened the door and touched his shoulder. When he stepped out of the car, he could see nothing but dark, twisted trees with moss hanging from them. It was a dark and lonely place, and Bubber was so surprised he did not remember to look at the chauffeur's face. Instead, he followed the tall figure up a path covered with leaves to a white-columned house with lights shining in the windows.

Bubber felt a little better when he saw the big house with the bright windows. He had played in such houses before, and he was glad for a chance to play in another. He took his trumpet from under his arm, put the mouthpiece to his lips, and blew a few bright, clear notes as he walked. The chauffeur did not turn around. He led Bubber to a side entrance, opened the door, and pointed the boy to the room where the dancing had already started. Without ever showing his face, the chauffeur closed the door and returned to the car.

Nobody had to tell Bubber what do do now. He found a place next to the big fiddle that made the rhythms, waited a moment for the beat, then came in with his trumpet. With the bass fiddle, the drums, and the other stringed instruments backing him up, Bubber began to bear down on his trumpet. This was just what he liked. He played loud, he played fast, he played high, and it was all he could do to keep

from laughing when he thought about Grandpa and remembered how the old man had told him to mind how he played his horn. Grandpa should see him now, Bubber thought.

Bubber looked at the dancers swirling on the ballroom floor under the high swinging chandelier, and he wished that Grandpa could somehow be at the window and see how they glided and spun around to the music of his horn. He wished the old man could get at least one glimpse of the handsome dancers, the beautiful women in bright-colored silks, the slender men in black evening clothes.

As the evening went on, more people came and began dancing. The floor became more and more crowded, and Bubber played louder and louder, faster and faster, and by midnight the gay ballroom seemed to be spinning like a pinwheel. The floor looked like glass under the dancers' feet. The drapes on the windows resembled gold, and Bubber was playing his trumpet so hard and so fast his eyes looked like they were ready to pop out of his head.

But he was not tired. He felt as if he could go on playing like this forever. He did not even need a short rest. When the other musicians called for a break and went outside to catch a breath of fresh air, he kept right on blowing his horn, running up the scale and down, hitting high C's, swelling out on the notes and then letting them fade away. He kept the dancers entertained till the full band came back, and he blew the notes that started them to dancing again.

Bubber gave no thought to the time, and when a breeze began blowing through the tall windows, he paid no attention. He played as loud as ever, and the dancers swirled just as fast. But there was one thing that did bother him a little. The faces of the dancers began to look thin and hollow as the breeze brought streaks of morning mist into the room. What was the matter with them? Were they tired from dancing all night? Bubber wondered.

But the morning breeze blew stronger and stronger. The curtains flapped, and a gray light appeared in the windows. But this time Bubber noticed that the people who were dancing had no faces at all, and though they continued to dance wildly as he played his trumpet, they seemed dim and far away. Were they disappearing?

Soon Bubber could scarcely see them at all. Suddenly he wondered where the party had gone. The musicians too grew dim and finally disappeared. Even the room with the big chandelier and the golden drapes on the windows was fading away like a technicolor dream. Bubber was frightened when he realized that nothing was left, and he was alone. Yes, definitely, he was alone – but *where?* Where was he now?

He never stopped blowing his shiny trumpet. In fact, as the party began to break up in this strange way, he blew harder than ever to help himself feel brave again. He also closed his eyes. That was why he happened to notice how uncomfortable the place where he was sitting had become. It was about as unpleasant as sitting on a log. And it was while his eyes were closed that he first became aware of leaves nearby, leaves rustling and blowing in the cool breeze.

But he could not keep his eyes closed for long with so much happening. Bubber just had to peep eventually, and when he did, he saw only leaves around him. Certainly leaves were nothing to be afraid of, he thought, but it was a little hard to understand how the house and room in which he had been playing for the party all night had been replaced by branches and leaves like this. Bubber opened both his eyes wide, stopped blowing his horn for a moment, and took a good, careful look at his surroundings.

Only then did he discover for sure that he was not in a house at all. There were no dancers, no musicians, nobody at all with him, and what had seemed like a rather uncomfortable chair or log was a large branch. Bubber was sitting in a pecan tree, and now he realized that this was where he had been blowing his trumpet so fast and so loud and so high all night. It was very discouraging.

But where was the chauffeur who had brought him here and what had become of the party and the graceful dancers? Bubber climbed down and began looking around. He could see no trace of the things that had seemed so real last night, so he decided he had better go home. Not home to the rooming house where he slept while in New Orleans, but home to the country where Grandpa lived.

He carried his horn under his arm, but he did not play a note on the bus that took him back to Marksville next day. And when he got off the bus and started walking down the road to Grandpa's house in the country, he still didn't feel much like playing anything on his trumpet.

Grandpa was sleeping in a hammock under a chinaberry tree when he arrived, but he slept with one eye open, so Bubber did not have to wake him up. He just stood there, and Grandpa smiled.

"I looked for you to come home before now," the old man said.

"I should have come home sooner," Bubber answered, shamefaced.

"I expected you to be blowing on your horn when you came."

"That's what I want to talk to you about, Grandpa."

The old man sat up in the hammock and put his feet on the ground. He scratched his head and reached for his hat. "Don't tell me anything startling," he said. "I just woke up, and I don't want to be surprised so soon."

Bubber thought maybe he should not mention what had happened. "All right, Grandpa," he whispered, looking rather sad. He leaned against the chinaberry tree, holding the trumpet under his arm, and waited for Grandpa to speak again.

Suddenly the old man blinked his eyes as if remembering something he had almost forgotten. "Did you mind how you blew on that horn down in New Orleans?" he asked.

"Sometimes I did. Sometimes I *didn't*," Bubber confessed.

Grandpa looked hurt. "I hate to hear that, sonny boy," he said. "Have you been playing your horn at barbecues and boat rides and dances and all such as that?"

"Yes, Grandpa," Bubber said, looking at the ground.

"Keep on like that and you're apt to wind up playing for a devil's ball."

Bubber nodded sadly. "Yes, I know."

Suddenly the old man stood up and put his hand on Bubber's shoulder. "Did a educated gentleman call you on the telephone?"

"He talked so proper I could hardly make out what he was saying."

"Did the chauffeur come in a long, shiny car?"

Bubber nodded again. "I ended up in a pecan tree," he told Grandpa.

"I tried to tell you, Bubber, but you wouldn't listen to me."

"I'll listen to you from now on, Grandpa."

Grandpa laughed through his whiskers. "Well, take your trumpet in the house and put it on the shelf while I get you something to eat," he said.

Bubber smiled too. He was hungry, and he had not tasted any of Grandpa's cooking for a long time.

FOR STUDY AND DISCUSSION

1. Why does Bubber decide to leave home?
2. The central episode of the story takes place in New Orleans. Why is New Orleans an appropriate setting for a boy who plays a trumpet?
3. At the rooming house Bubber receives a telephone call that proves to be the beginning of a strange adventure. What gives Bubber's adventure a dreamlike quality?
4. This story has certain characteristics of a *folk tale*. A folk tale is a story of anonymous authorship that is handed down orally from one generation to another. Usually it contains legendary or mythological elements. What is the legend that this story is based on?

ABOUT THE AUTHOR

Arna Bontemps (1902–1973) was born in Louisiana and attended college in California. After teaching in several parts of the United States, he took a position as librarian of Fisk University in Nashville, Tennessee. At the time of his death, he was writer-in-residence.

Bontemps was one of the pioneers of the Harlem Renaissance, a flowering of black writing, art, music, and thought in the 1920's, which had its center in Harlem, New York City. He wrote poetry, short stories, novels, biographies, and books for children. Among his works are *Black Thunder, God Sends Sunday*, and *Free at Last: The Life of Frederick Douglass*. He also edited a number of anthologies including *Golden Slippers, American Negro Poetry*, and *Harlem Renaissance Remembered*. He collaborated with the poet Langston Hughes on *The Book of Negro Folklore* and *The Poetry of the Negro (1746–1970)*.

Theme

The Gift of the Magi *O. Henry*

One dollar and eighty-seven cents. That was all. And sixty cents of it was in pennies. Pennies saved one and two at a time by bulldozing the grocer and the vegetable man and the butcher until one's cheek burned with silent imputation of parsimony[1] that such close dealing implied. Three times Della counted it. One dollar and eighty-seven cents. And the next day would be Christmas.

There was clearly nothing to do but flop down on the shabby little couch and howl. So Della did it. Which instigates the moral reflection that life is made up of sobs, sniffles, and smiles, with sniffles predominating.

While the mistress of the home is gradually subsiding from the first stage to the second, take a look at the home. A furnished flat at eight dollars per week. It did not exactly beggar description, but it certainly had that word on the lookout for the mendicancy squad.[2]

In the vestibule below was a letter box into which no letter would go, and an electric button from which no mortal finger could coax a ring. Also appertaining thereunto was a card bearing the name "Mr. James Dillingham Young."

The "Dillingham" had been flung to the breeze during a former period of prosperity when its possessor was being paid thirty dollars per week. Now, when the income was shrunk to twenty dollars, the letters of "Dillingham" looked blurred, as though they were thinking seriously of contracting to a modest and unassuming *D*. But whenever Mr. James Dillingham Young came home and reached his flat above he was called "Jim" and greatly hugged by Mrs. James Dillingham Young, already introduced to you as Della. Which is all very good.

Della finished her cry and attended to her cheeks with the powder rag. She stood by the window and looked out dully at a gray cat walking a gray fence in a gray backyard. Tomorrow would be Christmas Day, and she had only one dollar and eighty-seven cents with which to buy Jim a present. She had been saving every penny she could for months, with this result. Twenty dollars a week doesn't go far. Expenses had been greater than she had calculated. They always are. Only one dollar and eighty-seven cents to buy a present for Jim. Her Jim. Many a happy hour she had spent planning for something nice for him. Something fine and rare and sterling—

---

1. **imputation** (ĭm'pyōō-tā'shən) **of parsimony** (pär'sə-mō'nē): accusation of stinginess.
2. **mendicancy** (mĕn'dĭ-kən'sē) **squad:** a police squad that picked up beggars.

Now there were two possessions of the James Dillingham Youngs in which they both took a mighty pride. One was Jim's gold watch that had been his father's and his grandfather's. The other was Della's hair. Had the Queen of Sheba[4] lived in the flat across the air shaft, Della would have let her hair hang out the window someday to dry, just to depreciate Her Majesty's jewels and gifts. Had King Solomon been the janitor, with all his treasures piled up in the basement, Jim would have pulled out his watch every time he passed, just to see him pluck at his beard from envy.

So now Dell's beautiful hair fell about her, rippling and shining like a cascade of brown waters. It reached below her knee and made itself almost a garment for her. And then she did it up again nervously and quickly. Once she faltered for a minute and stood still while a tear or two splashed on the worn red carpet.

On went her old brown jacket; on went her old brown hat. With a whirl of skirts and with the brilliant sparkle still in her eyes, she fluttered out the door and down the stairs to the street.

Where she stopped the sign read: "Mme. Sofronie. Hair Goods of All Kinds." One flight up Della ran—and collected herself, panting. Madame, large, too white, chilly, hardly looked the "Sofronie."

"Will you buy my hair?" asked Della.

"I buy hair," said Madame. "Take yer hat off and let's have a sight at the looks of it."

Down rippled the brown cascade.

"Twenty dollars," said Madame, lifting the mass with a practiced hand.

"Give it to me quick," said Della.

something just a little bit near to being worthy of the honor of being owned by Jim.

There was a pier glass[3] between the windows of the room. Perhaps you have seen a pier glass in an eight-dollar flat. A very thin and very agile person may, by observing his reflection in a rapid sequence of longitudinal strips, obtain a fairly accurate conception of his looks. Della, being slender, had mastered the art.

Suddenly she whirled from the window and stood before the glass. Her eyes were shining brilliantly, but her face had lost its color within twenty seconds. Rapidly she pulled down her hair and let it fall to its full length.

---

3. **pier glass:** a long, narrow mirror designed to fit between two windows.

4. **Queen of Sheba** (shē′bə): in the Bible, a queen from southern Arabia, famous for her wealth and beauty. When she heard of King Solomon's reputation for wisdom, she came to test him with hard questions.

Oh, and the next two hours tripped by on rosy wings. Forget the hashed metaphor. She was ransacking the stores for Jim's present.

She found it at last. It surely had been made for Jim and no one else. There was no other like it in any of the stores, and she had turned all of them inside out. It was a platinum fob chain simple and chaste in design, properly proclaiming its value by substance alone and not by meretricious[5] ornamentation—as all good things should do. It was even worthy of The Watch. As soon as she saw it she knew that it must be Jim's. It was like him. Quietness and value—the description applied to both. Twenty-one dollars they took from her for it, and she hurried home with the eighty-seven cents. With that chain on his watch Jim might be properly anxious about the time in any company. Grand as the watch was, he sometimes looked at it on the sly on account of the old leather strap that he used in place of a chain.

When Della reached home her intoxication gave way a little to prudence and reason. She got out her curling irons and lighted the gas and went to work repairing the ravages made by generosity added to love. Which is always a tremendous task, dear friends—a mammoth task.

Within forty minutes her head was covered with tiny, close-lying curls that made her look wonderfully like a truant schoolboy. She looked at her reflection in the mirror long, carefully, and critically.

"If Jim doesn't kill me," she said to herself, "before he takes a second look at me, he'll say I look like a Coney Island chorus girl. But what could I do—oh! what could I do with a dollar and eighty-seven cents?"

At seven o'clock the coffee was made and the frying pan was on the back of the stove hot and ready to cook the chops.

Jim was never late. Della doubled the fob chain in her hand and sat on the corner of the table near the door that he always entered. Then she heard his step on the stair away down on the first flight, and she turned white for just a moment. She had a habit of saying little silent prayers about the simplest everyday things, and now she whispered, "Please, God, make him think I am still pretty."

The door opened and Jim stepped in and closed it. He looked thin and very serious. Poor fellow, he was only twenty-two—and to be burdened with a family! He needed a new overcoat and he was without gloves.

5. **meretricious** (mĕr′ə-trĭsh′əs): attractive in a cheap, flashy way.

128   *Short Stories*

Jim stopped inside the door, as immovable as a setter at the scent of quail. His eyes were fixed upon Della; and there was an expression in them that she could not read, and it terrified her. It was not anger, nor surprise, nor disapproval, nor horror, nor any of the sentiments that she had been prepared for. He simply stared at her fixedly with that peculiar expression on his face.

Della wriggled off the table and went to him.

"Jim, darling," she cried, "don't look at me that way. I had my hair cut off and sold it because I couldn't have lived through Christmas without giving you a present. It'll grow out again—you won't mind, will you? I just had to do it. My hair grows awfully fast. Say 'Merry Christmas!' Jim, and let's be happy. You don't know what a nice—what a beautiful, nice gift I've got for you."

"You've cut off your hair?" asked Jim laboriously, as if he had not arrived at that patent fact yet even after the hardest mental labor.

"Cut it off and sold it," said Della. "Don't you like me just as well, anyhow? I'm me without my hair, ain't I?"

Jim looked about the room curiously.

"You say your hair is gone?" he said, with an air almost of idiocy.

"You needn't look for it," said Della. "It's sold, I tell you—sold and gone, too. It's Christmas Eve, boy. Be good to me, for it went for you. Maybe the hairs of my head were numbered," she went on with a sudden serious sweetness, "but nobody could ever count my love for you. Shall I put the chops on, Jim?"

Out of his trance Jim seemed quickly to wake. He enfolded his Della. For ten seconds let us regard with discreet scrutiny some inconsequential object in the other direction. Eight dollars a week or a million a year—what is the difference? A mathematician or a wit would give you the wrong answer. The Magi[6] brought valuable gifts, but that was not among them. This dark assertion will be illuminated later on.

Jim drew a package from his overcoat pocket and threw it upon the table.

"Don't make any mistake, Dell," he said, "about me. I don't think there's anything in the way of a haircut or a shave or a shampoo that could make me like my girl any less. But if you'll unwrap that package you may see why you had me going awhile at first."

White fingers and nimble tore at the string and paper. And then an ecstatic scream of joy; and then, alas! a quick feminine change to hysterical tears and wails, necessitating the immediate employment of all the comforting powers of the lord of the flat.

For there lay The Combs—the set of combs, side and back, that Della had worshiped for long in a Broadway window. Beautiful combs, pure tortoise shell, with jeweled rims—just the shade to wear in the beautiful vanished hair. They were expensive combs, she knew, and her heart had simply craved and yearned over them without the least hope of possession. And now they were hers, but the tresses that should have adorned the coveted adornments were gone.

But she hugged them to her bosom, and at length she was able to look up with dim eyes and a smile and say, "My hair grows so fast, Jim!"

And then Della leaped up like a little singed cat and cried, "Oh, oh!"

Jim had not yet seen his beautiful present. She held it out to him eagerly upon her open palm. The dull precious metal seemed to flash with a reflection of her bright and ardent spirit.

---

6. **Magi** (mā′jī′).

"Isn't it a dandy, Jim? I hunted all over town to find it. You'll have to look at the time a hundred times a day now. Give me your watch. I want to see how it looks on it."

Instead of obeying, Jim tumbled down on the couch and put his hands under the back of his head and smiled.

"Della," said he, "let's put our Christmas presents away and keep 'em awhile. They're too nice to use just at present. I sold the watch to get the money to buy your combs. And now suppose you put the chops on."

The Magi, as you know, were wise men — wonderfully wise men — who brought gifts to the Babe in the manger. They invented the art of giving Christmas presents. Being wise, their gifts were no doubt wise ones, possibly bearing the privilege of exchange in case of duplication. And here I have lamely related to you the uneventful chronicle of two foolish children in a flat who most unwisely sacrificed for each other the greatest treasures of their house. But in a last word to the wise of these days let it be said that of all who give gifts these two were the wisest. Of all who give and receive gifts, such as they are wisest. Everywhere they are wisest. They are the Magi.

FOR STUDY AND DISCUSSION

1. What is the author's attitude toward Della? For example, do his humorous comments about her indicate that he thinks she is silly and impractical? Or are these comments affectionate and good-natured? Explain.
2. An ironic situation is one in which the characters' actions bring about an unexpected result. What is ironic about the outcome of "The Gift of the Magi"? Often, an ironic situation tends to belittle characters, to make them seem foolish or contemptible. Is this the case with Della and Jim? Why or why not?
3. O. Henry is famous for the surprise endings in his stories. Some of his endings have been criticized as unfair tricks. Is the end of "The Gift of the Magi" unfair? Or is it a logical ending, considering what you know about Jim and Della? Explain.
4. What is the gift O. Henry refers to in the title and what has it to do with the Magi? Why, according to O. Henry, are people like Jim and Della "the wisest"?

THEME

As you read "The Gift of the Magi," you probably realized that O. Henry was not simply telling a story about a young married couple whose plans misfire. Behind his plot and its surprise ending there is a controlling idea about what is important and unimportant in life. In the last paragraph of the story, he explicitly states his controlling idea — that love such as Della's and Jim's is far more important than any material gift. Such a controlling idea — an expression of a point of view about life — is called a *theme*. How does the story's theme give significance to Della and Jim, who otherwise might be viewed as an insignificant poor couple living in a large city?

ALLUSIONS

In expressing his theme, O. Henry compares Della's and Jim's gifts to the gifts of the Magi. He expects his readers to know the story of the three wise men who made the journey to Bethlehem to pay homage to the Christ Child. According to tradition, the Magi were three kings named Melchior, Gaspar, and Balthazar; the gifts they brought were gold, frankincense, and myrrh. Understanding the story's theme depends to some extent on recognizing this *allusion* to the Biblical story.

An allusion is an indirect reference to literature, history, art, music, or the like, which a writer expects readers to recognize. When an allusion is used effectively, it helps the reader call up certain associations that clarify or enrich the writer's meaning. At one point in his narrative, O. Henry makes an allusion to the Biblical story of Solomon and Sheba. Locate this allusion and tell how it is important to the plot and theme.

FOR COMPOSITION

Writing a Story with a Theme

The theme of "The Gift of the Magi"—that the best gifts are the gifts of love and sacrifice—is stated in the last paragraph of the story. O. Henry leads up to his theme throughout the story, however, by stressing the unselfish love of Della and Jim. Choose a theme for a brief story of your own. If you like, use one of the following suggestions. Try to suggest your theme through the actions of the characters, then state it at the very end.

It is better to give than to receive.
We must get to know people before we can really like them.
True love is forgiving.

ABOUT THE AUTHOR

O. Henry's real name was William Sydney Porter (1862–1910). The son of a doctor, he grew up in Greensboro, North Carolina. When he was twenty, he moved to Texas for reasons of health. He settled in Austin, where he worked as a clerk, bookkeeper, and bank teller. To earn more money, he began contributing news items and sketches to newspapers throughout the country, and in 1895, he moved to Houston to work as a reporter for the Houston *Post*. Nine months later he was called back to Austin to stand trial for bank embezzlement. Porter was almost certainly innocent of the charge. The bank he had worked for was notoriously lax in its accounting procedures, and Porter himself had probably been no more than careless. He boarded a train to Austin, but on impulse he went to New Orleans instead, and then to Honduras in Central America. Three years later, the news that his wife was seriously ill brought him back to Texas. He stood trial, was convicted, and served five years in prison.

When he was released, he went to Pittsburgh, Pennsylvania, where he began once again to write. His editors encouraged him to move to New York. It was in New York that Porter adopted the pen name of O. Henry and became a famous writer of short stories. He was a prolific writer. In 1905 alone he wrote sixty-five short stories. In his stories, he drew on his experiences out West and in Latin America. Above all, he drew on his knowledge of and fascination with New York, whose streets he roamed in search of ideas. He called New York "Baghdad-on-the-Subway," comparing it to the fabulous city of Scheherazade's *A Thousand and One Nights*. Some of his best stories are collected in *The Four Million*, *The Voice of the City*, *Hearts of the West*, *The Gentle Grafter*, and *Whirligigs*.

The Balek Scales

Heinrich Böll
Translated by Leila Vennewitz

Where my grandfather came from, most of the people lived by working in the flax sheds. For five generations they had been breathing in the dust which rose from the crushed flax stalks, letting themselves be killed off by slow degrees, a race of long-suffering, cheerful people who ate goat cheese, potatoes, and now and then a rabbit; in the evening they would sit at home spinning and knitting; they sang, drank mint tea and were happy. During the day they would carry the flax stalks to the antiquated machines, with no protection from the dust and at the mercy of the heat which came pouring out of the drying kilns. Each cottage contained only one bed, standing against the wall like a closet and reserved for the parents, while the children slept all round the room on benches. In the morning the room would be filled with the odor of thin soup; on Sundays there was stew, and on feast days the children's faces would light up with pleasure as they watched the black acorn coffee turning paler and paler from the milk their smiling mother poured into their coffee mugs.

The parents went off early to the flax sheds; the housework was left to the children: they would sweep the room, tidy up, wash the dishes and peel the potatoes, precious pale-yellow fruit whose thin peel had to be produced afterwards to dispel any suspicion of extravagance or carelessness.

As soon as the children were out of school they had to go off into the woods and, depending on the season, gather mushrooms and herbs: woodruff and thyme, caraway, mint and foxglove, and in summer, when they had brought in the hay from their meager fields, they gathered hayflowers. A kilo[1] of hayflowers was worth one pfennig,[2] and they were sold by the apothecaries in town for twenty pfennigs a kilo to highly strung ladies. The mushrooms were highly prized: they fetched twenty pfennigs a kilo and were sold in the shops in town for one mark[3] twenty. The children would crawl deep into the green darkness of the forest during the autumn when dampness drove the mushrooms out of the soil, and almost every family had its own places where it gathered mushrooms, places which were handed down in whispers from generation to generation.

The woods belonged to the Baleks, as well as the flax sheds, and in my grandfather's village the Baleks had a château, and the wife of the head of the family had a little room next to the dairy where mushrooms, herbs and hayflowers were weighed and paid for. There on the table stood the great Balek scales, an old-fashioned, ornate bronze-gilt contraption, which my grandfather's grandparents had already faced when they were children, their grubby hands holding their lit-

---

1. **kilo** (kē′lō): short for *kilogram*, a unit of weight a little over two pounds.
2. **pfennig** (fĕn′ĭg): a coin like the United States penny.
3. **mark:** at one time, the monetary unit in several European countries; now the monetary unit in Germany. There are one hundred pfennigs to a mark.

tle baskets of mushrooms, their paper bags of hayflowers, breathlessly watching the number of weights Frau Balek had to throw on the scale before the swinging pointer came to rest exactly over the black line, that thin line of justice which had to be redrawn every year. Then Frau Balek would take the big book covered in brown leather, write down the weight, and pay out the money, pfennigs or ten-pfennig pieces and very, very occasionally, a mark. And when my grandfather was a child there was a big glass jar of lemon drops standing there, the kind that cost one mark a kilo, and when Frau Balek — whichever one happened to be presiding over the little room — was in a good mood, she would put her hand into this jar and give each child a lemon drop, and the children's faces would light up with pleasure, the way they used to when on feast days their mother poured milk into their coffee mugs, milk that made the coffee turn paler and paler

until it was as pale as the flaxen pigtails of the little girls.

One of the laws imposed by the Baleks on the village was: No one was permitted to have any scales in the house. The law was so ancient that nobody gave a thought as to when and how it had arisen, and it had to be obeyed, for anyone who broke it was dismissed from the flax sheds, he could not sell his mushrooms or his thyme or his hayflowers, and the power of the Baleks was so far-reaching that no one in the neighboring villages would give him work either, or buy his forest herbs. But since the days when my grandfather's parents had gone out as small children to gather mushrooms and sell them in order that they might season the meat of the rich people of Prague[4] or be baked into game pies, it had never occurred to anyone to

---

4. **Prague** (präg): the capital of Czechoslovakia.

break this law: flour could be measured in cups, eggs could be counted, what they had spun could be measured by the yard, and besides, the old-fashioned bronze-gilt, ornate Balek scales did not look as if there was anything wrong with them, and five generations had entrusted the swinging black pointer with what they had gone out as eager children to gather from the woods.

True, there were some among these quiet people who flouted the law, poachers bent on making more money in one night than they could earn in a whole month in the flax sheds, but even these people apparently never thought of buying scales or making their own. My grandfather was the first person bold enough to test the justice of the Baleks, the family who lived in the château and drove two carriages, who always maintained one boy from the village while he studied theology at the seminary in Prague, the family with whom the priest played taroc every Wednesday, on whom the local reeve,[5] in his carriage emblazoned with the Imperial coat of arms, made an annual New Year's Day call and on whom the Emperor[6] conferred a title on the first day of the year 1900.

My grandfather was hardworking and smart: he crawled further into the woods than the children of his clan had crawled before him, he penetrated as far as the thicket where, according to legend, Bilgan the Giant was supposed to dwell, guarding a treasure. But my grandfather was not afraid of Bilgan: he worked his way deep into the thicket, even when he was quite little, and brought out great quantities of mushrooms; he even found truffles, for which Frau Balek paid thirty pfennigs a pound. Everything my grandfather took

to the Baleks he entered on the back of a torn-off calendar page: every pound of mushrooms, every gram of thyme, and on the right-hand side, in his childish handwriting, he entered the amount he received for each item; he scrawled in every pfennig, from the age of seven to the age of twelve, and by the time he was twelve the year 1900 had arrived, and because the Baleks had been raised to the aristocracy by the Emperor, they gave every family in the village a quarter of a pound of real coffee, the Brazilian kind; there was also free beer and tobacco for the men, and at the château there was a great banquet; many carriages stood in the avenue of poplars leading from the entrance gates to the château.

But the day before the banquet the coffee was distributed in the little room which had housed the Balek scales for almost a hundred years, and the Balek family was now called Balek von Bilgan because, according to legend, Bilgan the Giant used to have a great castle on the site of the present Balek estate.

My grandfather often used to tell me how he went there after school to fetch the coffee for four families: the Cechs, the Weidlers, the Vohlas and his own, the Brüchers. It was the afternoon of New Year's Eve: there were the front rooms to be decorated, the baking to be done, and the families did not want to spare four boys and have each of them go all the way to the château to bring back a quarter of a pound of coffee.

And so my grandfather sat on the narrow wooden bench in the little room while Gertrud the maid counted out the wrapped four-ounce packages of coffee, four of them, and he looked at the scales and saw that the pound weight was still lying on the left-hand scale; Frau Balek von Bilgan was busy with preparations for the banquet. And when Gertrud was about to put her hand into the jar with the lemon drops to give my grandfather one, she

5. **reeve:** the chief officer of a district.
6. **Emperor:** William II (1888–1918), called Kaiser Wilhelm.

discovered it was empty: it was refilled once a year, and held one kilo of the kind that cost a mark.

Gertrud laughed and said: "Wait here while I get the new lot," and my grandfather waited with the four four-ounce packages which had been wrapped and sealed in the factory, facing the scales on which someone had left the pound weight, and my grandfather took the four packages of coffee, put them on the empty scale, and his heart thudded as he watched the black finger of justice come to rest on the left of the black line: the scale with the pound weight stayed down, and the pound of coffee remained up in the air; his heart thudded more than if he had been lying behind a bush in the forest waiting for Bilgan the Giant, and he felt in his pocket for the pebbles he always carried with him so he could use his catapult to shoot the sparrows which pecked away at his mother's cabbage plants—he had to put three, four, five pebbles beside the packages of coffee before the scale with the pound weight rose and the pointer at last came to rest over the black line. My grandfather took the coffee from the scale, wrapped the five pebbles in his kerchief, and when Gertrud came back with the big kilo bag of lemon drops which had to last for another whole year in order to make the children's faces light up with pleasure, when Gertrud let the lemon drops rattle into the glass jar, the pale little fellow was still standing there, and nothing seemed to have changed. My grandfather only took three of the packages, then Gertrud looked in startled surprise at the white-faced child who threw the lemon drop onto the floor, ground it under his heel, and said: "I want to see Frau Balek."

"Balek von Bilgan, if you please," said Gertrud.

"All right, Frau Balek von Bilgan," but Gertrud only laughed at him, and he walked back to the village in the dark, took the Cechs, the Weidlers and the Vohlas their coffee, and said he had to go and see the priest.

Instead he went out into the dark night with his five pebbles in his kerchief. He had to walk a long way before he found someone who had scales, who was permitted to have them; no one in the villages of Blaugau and Bernau had any, he knew that, and he went straight through them till, after two hours' walking, he reached the little town of Dielheim where Honig the apothecary lived. From Honig's house came the smell of fresh pancakes, and Honig's breath, when he opened the door to the half-frozen boy, already smelled of punch, there was a moist cigar between his narrow lips, and he clasped the boy's cold hands firmly for a moment, saying: "What's the matter, has your father's lung got worse?"

"No, I haven't come for medicine, I wanted . . ." My grandfather undid his kerchief, took out the five pebbles, held them out to Honig and said: "I wanted to have these weighed." He glanced anxiously into Honig's face, but when Honig said nothing and did not get angry, or even ask him anything, my grandfather said: "It is the amount that is short of justice," and now, as he went into the warm room, my grandfather realized how wet his feet were. The snow had soaked through his cheap shoes, and in the forest the branches had showered him with snow which was now melting, and he was tired and hungry and suddenly began to cry because he thought of the quantities of mushrooms, the herbs, the flowers, which had been weighed on the scales which were short five pebbles' worth of justice. And when Honig, shaking his head and holding the five pebbles, called his wife, my grandfather thought of the generations of his parents, his grandparents, who had all had to have their mushrooms, their flowers, weighed on the scales, and he was overwhelmed by a great wave of injustice, and began to sob louder than ever, and, without waiting to be asked, he sat down on a chair, ignoring the pancakes, the cup of hot coffee which nice plump Frau Honig put in front of him, and did not stop crying till Honig himself came out from the shop at the back and, rattling the pebbles in his hand, said in a low voice to his wife: "Fifty-five grams, exactly."

My grandfather walked the two hours home through the forest, got a beating at home, said nothing, not a single word, when he was asked about the coffee, spent the whole evening doing sums on the piece of paper on which he had written down everything he had sold to Frau Balek, and when midnight struck, and the cannon could be heard from the château, and the whole village rang with shouting and laughter and the noise of rattles, when

the family kissed and embraced all round, he said into the New Year silence: "The Baleks owe me eighteen marks and thirty-two pfennigs." And again he thought of all the children there were in the village, of his brother Fritz who had gathered so many mushrooms, of his sister Ludmilla; he thought of the many hundreds of children who had all gathered mushrooms for the Baleks, and herbs and flowers, and this time he did not cry but told his parents and brothers and sisters of his discovery.

When the Baleks von Bilgan went to High Mass on New Year's Day, their new coat of arms—a giant crouching under a fir tree—already emblazoned in blue and gold on their carriage, they saw the hard, pale faces of the people all staring at them. They had expected garlands in the village, a song in their honor,

cheers and hurrahs, but the village was completely deserted as they drove through it, and in church the pale faces of the people were turned toward them, mute and hostile, and when the priest mounted the pulpit to deliver his New Year's sermon he sensed the chill in those otherwise quiet and peaceful faces, and he stumbled painfully through his sermon and went back to the altar drenched in sweat. And as the Baleks von Bilgan left the church after Mass, they walked through a lane of mute, pale faces. But young Frau Balek von Bilgan stopped in front of the children's pews, sought out my grandfather's face, pale little Franz Brücher, and asked him, right there in the church: "Why didn't you take the coffee for your mother?" And my grandfather stood up and said: "Because you owe me as much money as five kilos of coffee would cost." And he pulled the five pebbles from his pocket, held them out to the young woman and said: "This much, fifty-five grams, is short in every pound of your justice"; and before the woman could say anything the men and women in the church lifted up their voices and sang: "The justice of this earth, O Lord, hath put Thee to death. . . ."

While the Baleks were at church, Wilhelm Vohla, the poacher, had broken into the little room, stolen the scales and the big fat leather-bound book in which had been entered every kilo of mushrooms, every kilo of hayflowers, everything bought by the Baleks in the village, and all afternoon of that New Year's Day the men of the village sat in my great-grandparents' front room and calculated, calculated one tenth of everything that had been bought —but when they had calculated many thousands of talers[7] and had still not come to an end, the reeve's gendarmes[8] arrived, made their way into my great-grandfather's front room, shooting and stabbing as they came, and removed the scales and the book by force. My grandfather's little sister Ludmilla lost her life, a few men were wounded, and one of the gendarmes was stabbed to death by Wilhelm Vohla the poacher.

Our village was not the only one to rebel: Blaugau and Bernau did too, and for almost a week no work was done in the flax sheds. But a great many gendarmes appeared, and the men and women were threatened with prison, and the Baleks forced the priest to display the scales publicly in the school and demonstrate that the finger of justice swing to and fro accurately. And the men and women went back to the flax sheds—but no one went to the school to watch the priest: he stood there all alone, helpless and forlorn with his weights, scales, and packages of coffee.

And the children went back to gathering mushrooms, to gathering thyme, flowers and foxglove, but every Sunday, as soon as the Baleks entered the church, the hymn was struck up: "The justice of this earth, O Lord, hath put Thee to death," until the reeve ordered it proclaimed in every village that the singing of the hymn was forbidden.

My grandfather's parents had to leave the village, and the new grave of their little daughter; they became basket weavers, but did not stay long anywhere because it pained them to see how everywhere the finger of justice swung falsely. They walked along behind their cart, which crept slowly over the country roads, taking their thin goat with them, and passers-by could sometimes hear a voice from the cart singing: "The justice of this earth, O Lord, hath put Thee to death." And those who wanted to listen could hear the tale of the Baleks von Bilgan, whose justice lacked a tenth part. But there were few who listened.

---

7. **talers** (tä′lərz): silver coins.
8. **gendarmes** (zhän′därmz): a semimilitary police force.

FOR STUDY AND DISCUSSION

1. The narrator is telling a story about his grandfather's boyhood in a small village in Europe. What impression do you get of these villagers and the way that they lived? How would you describe their attitude toward the laws imposed by the Baleks?

2. The Balek family becomes known as Balek von Bilgan, after the giant Bilgan. Recall what you know about wicked giants in folk stories. In what way is the Balek family like such giants? How does such a comparison make clear the narrator's attitude toward the Baleks?

3. In the central incident of the story, the narrator's grandfather, Franz Brücher, makes an important discovery. What does he learn about the Balek scales? What do you know about his character that prepares you for his subsequent actions?

4. After the villagers learn of Franz's discovery, what happens? Do you feel that the story's ending is the logical outcome of earlier events? Give reasons for your answer.

5. As you read "The Balek Scales," you probably began to realize that it is not simply about one group of people in one village. The story also expresses a *theme,* a general idea about life. Try to state the theme of this story in a sentence or two. As you formulate the theme, keep in mind the story's ending as well as the words of the hymn that the villagers sing.

6. Throughout the story the narrator uses irony to point up the contrast between appearance and reality. Find examples of this irony in the story and tell how it serves to reinforce the theme.

EXPRESSING A THEME

If you have already read "The Gift of the Magi," you have found that O. Henry explicitly states the theme of the story in the final paragraph. Heinrich Böll makes no such explicit statement. Yet passages and details throughout the story help make readers aware that a general idea is being expressed through specific incidents. The general idea, or theme, concerns justice and injustice on earth. Notice how, near the end of the story, a reference to Bilgan the Giant emphasizes the unjust relationship between the Baleks and the people in the village.

When the Baleks von Bilgan went to High Mass on New Year's Day, their new coat of arms—a giant crouching under a fir tree—already emblazoned in blue and gold on their carriage, they saw the hard, pale faces of the people all staring at them. (page 136)

The people have already learned how the Baleks have cheated them for five generations. The image of a wicked giant crouching under a tree, waiting to ambush the unwary traveler, suggests both the power and the unjust actions of the Baleks.

How do the following passages help express the story's theme?

There on the table stood the great Balek scales . . . which my grandfather's grandparents had already faced when they were children, . . . breathlessly watching the number of weights Frau Balek had to throw on the scale before the swinging pointer came to rest exactly over the black line, that thin line of justice which had to be redrawn every year. (pages 132–133)

One of the laws imposed by the Baleks on the village was: No one was permitted to have any scales in the house. The law was so ancient that nobody gave a thought as to when and how it had arisen . . . (page 133)

My grandfather undid his kerchief, took out the five pebbles, held them out to Honig and said: "I wanted to have these weighed." He glanced anxiously into Honig's face, but when Honig said nothing and did not get angry, or even ask him anything, my grandfather said: "It is the amount that is short of justice" . . . (page 135)

Find other passages in "The Balek Scales" that help make readers aware of the story's theme.

FOR COMPOSITION

Writing a Sentence That Builds to a Climax

When the narrator tells about his grandfather going home on New Year's Eve and finally declaring that the Baleks are dishonest, he does it all in one sentence.

My grandfather walked the two hours home through the forest, got a beating at home, said nothing, not a single word, when he was asked about the coffee, spent the whole evening doing some sums on the piece of paper on which he had written down everything he had sold to Frau Balek, and when midnight struck, and the cannon could be heard from the château, and the whole village rang with shouting and laughter and the noise of rattles, when the family kissed and embraced all round, he said into the New Year silence: "The Baleks owe me eighteen marks and thirty-two pfennigs."

Notice how all the details of the sentence build to a high point, the boy's outburst. You have a sense of the boy's outrage building up through the evening in dramatic contrast to the merriment of the villagers, who are still innocent of the truth.

Write your own climactic sentence, using details that build to a high point at the end. (Your sentence need not be as long as Böll's.) Choose your own subject or use one of the following:

A racer beginning slowly, gaining speed, and coming to the finish line

Two students trying to pass each other in a narrow school corridor

Paul Revere riding to warn the colonists about the British

The last few minutes of a basketball (hockey, football, tennis) game where the score is tied

ABOUT THE AUTHOR

Heinrich Böll (1917-1985) was born in Cologne, Germany. He served in the German army during World War II, mostly on the Russian front, and was wounded four times. After his release from a prisoner-of-war camp in 1945, he returned to Cologne. There he found a job with the city government and began to write. In his novels and short stories, Böll probed the nature of German society.

In 1972 Böll was awarded the Nobel Prize for Literature for his contributions "to a renewal of German literature." Critics have noted a strong vein of ironic humor that runs through his basically serious work. One German critic has called him "Germany's best as well as best-selling author whose work is both profound and eminently readable."

The Necklace *Guy de Maupassant*

She was one of those pretty and charming girls, born, as if by an accident of fate, into a family of clerks. With no dowry, no prospects, no way of any kind of being met, understood, loved, and married by a man both prosperous and famous, she was finally married to a minor clerk in the Ministry of Education.

She dressed plainly because she could not afford fine clothes, but was as unhappy as a woman who has come down in the world; for women have no family rank or social class. With them, beauty, grace, and charm take the place of birth and breeding. Their natural poise, their instinctive good taste, and their mental cleverness are the sole guiding principles which make daughters of the common people the equals of ladies in high society.

She grieved incessantly, feeling that she had been born for all the little niceties and luxuries of living. She grieved over the shabbiness of her apartment, the dinginess of the walls, the worn-out appearance of the chairs, the ugliness of the draperies. All these things, which another woman of her class would not even have noticed, gnawed at her and made her furious. The sight of the little Breton[1] girl who did her humble housework roused in her disconsolate regrets and wild daydreams. She would dream of silent chambers, draped with Oriental tapestries and lighted by tall bronze floor lamps, and of two handsome butlers in knee breeches, who, drowsy from the heavy warmth cast by the central stove, dozed in large overstuffed armchairs.

---

1. **Breton** (brĕt′n): a native of Brittany, a province in northwestern France.

She would dream of great reception halls hung with old silks, of fine furniture filled with priceless curios, and of small, stylish, scented sitting rooms just right for the four o'clock chat with intimate friends, with distinguished and sought-after men whose attention every woman envies and longs to attract.

When dining at the round table, covered for the third day with the same cloth, opposite her husband, who would raise the cover of the soup tureen, declaring delightedly, "Ah! a good stew! There's nothing I like better . . ." she would dream of fashionable dinner parties, of gleaming silverware, of tapestries making the walls alive with characters out of history and strange birds in a fairyland forest; she would dream of delicious dishes served on wonderful china, of gallant compliments whispered and listened to with a sphinxlike smile as one eats the rosy flesh of a trout or nibbles at the wings of a grouse.

She had no evening clothes, no jewels, nothing. But those were the things she wanted; she felt that was the kind of life for her. She so much longed to please, be envied, be fascinating and sought after.

She had a well-to-do friend, a classmate of convent-school days whom she would no longer go to see, simply because she would feel so distressed on returning home. And she would weep for days on end from vexation, regret, despair, and anguish.

Then one evening, her husband came home proudly holding out a large envelope.

"Look," he said, "I've got something for you."

She excitedly tore open the envelope and

pulled out a printed card bearing these words:

"The Minister of Education and Mme. Georges Ramponneau[2] beg M. and Mme. Loisel[3] to do them the honor of attending an evening reception at the Ministerial Mansion on Friday, January 18."

Instead of being delighted, as her husband had hoped, she scornfully tossed the invitation on the table, murmuring, "What good is that to me?"

"But, my dear, I thought you'd be thrilled to death. You never get a chance to go out, and this is a real affair, a wonderful one! I had an awful time getting a card. Everybody wants one; it's much sought after, and not many clerks have a chance at one. You'll see all the most important people there."

She gave him an irritated glance and burst out impatiently, "What do you think I have to go in?"

He hadn't given that a thought. He stammered, "Why, the dress you wear when we go to the theater. That looks quite nice, I think."

He stopped talking, dazed and distracted to see his wife burst out weeping. Two large tears slowly rolled from the corners of her eyes to the corners of her mouth; he gasped, "Why, what's the matter? What's the trouble?"

By sheer will power she overcame her outburst and answered in a calm voice while wiping the tears from her wet cheeks:

"Oh, nothing. Only I don't have an evening dress and therefore I can't go to that affair. Give the card to some friend at the office whose wife can dress better than I can."

He was stunned. He resumed, "Let's see, Mathilde.[4] How much would a suitable outfit cost—one you could wear for other affairs too—something very simple?"

She thought it over for several seconds, going over her allowance and thinking also of the amount she could ask for without bringing an immediate refusal and an exclamation of dismay from the thrifty clerk.

Finally, she answered hesitatingly, "I'm not sure exactly, but I think with four hundred francs[5] I could manage it."

He turned a bit pale, for he had set aside just that amount to buy a rifle so that, the following summer, he could join some friends who were getting up a group to shoot larks on the plain near Nanterre.[6]

However, he said, "All right. I'll give you four hundred francs. But try to get a nice dress."

As the day of the party approached, Mme. Loisel seemed sad, moody, and ill at ease. Her outfit was ready, however. Her husband said to her one evening, "What's the matter? You've been all out of sorts for three days."

And she answered, "It's embarrassing not to have a jewel or a gem—nothing to wear on my dress. I'll look like a pauper: I'd almost rather not go to that party."

He answered, "Why not wear some flowers? They're very fashionable this season. For ten francs you can get two or three gorgeous roses."

She wasn't at all convinced. "No. . . . There's nothing more humiliating than to look poor among a lot of rich women."

But her husband exclaimed, "My, but you're silly! Go see your friend Mme. Forestier[7] and ask her to lend you some jewelry.

---

2. **Mme. Georges Ramponneau** (mȧ-dȧm' zhôrzh rȧm'pə-nō).
3. **M. . . . Loisel** (mə-syûr' . . . lwȧ-zĕl').
4. **Mathilde** (mȧ-tēld').

5. **four-hundred francs:** at that time, about eighty dollars.
6. **Nanterre** (nȧN-târ'): a town near Paris.
7. **Forestier** (fô-rə-styā').

You and she know each other well enough for you to do that.''

She gave a cry of joy, ''Why, that's so! I hadn't thought of it.''

The next day she paid her friend a visit and told her of her predicament.

Mme. Forestier went toward a large closet with mirrored doors, took out a large jewel box, brought it over, opened it, and said to Mme. Loisel: ''Pick something out, my dear.''

At first her eyes noted some bracelets, then a pearl necklace, then a Venetian cross, gold and gems, of marvelous workmanship. She tried on these adornments in front of the mirror, but hesitated, unable to decide which to part with and put back. She kept on asking, ''Haven't you something else?''

''Oh, yes, keep on looking. I don't know just what you'd like.''

All at once she found, in a black satin box, a superb diamond necklace; and her pulse beat faster with longing. Her hands trembled as she took it up. Clasping it around her throat, outside her high-necked dress, she stood in ecstasy looking at her reflection.

Then she asked, hesitatingly, pleading, ''Could I borrow that, just that and nothing else?''

''Why, of course.''

She threw her arms around her friend, kissed her warmly, and fled with her treasure.

The day of the party arrived. Mme. Loisel was a sensation. She was the prettiest one there, fashionable, gracious, smiling, and wild with joy. All the men turned to look at her, asked who she was, begged to be introduced. All the Cabinet officials wanted to waltz with her. The minister took notice of her.

She danced madly, wildly, drunk with pleasure, giving no thought to anything in the triumph of her beauty, the pride of her success, in a kind of happy cloud composed of all the adulation, of all the admiring glances, of all the awakened longings, of a sense of complete victory that is so sweet to a woman's heart.

She left around four o'clock in the morning. Her husband, since midnight, had been dozing in a small empty sitting room with three other gentlemen whose wives were having too good a time.

He threw over her shoulders the wraps he had brought for going home, modest garments of everyday life whose shabbiness clashed with the stylishness of her evening clothes. She felt this and longed to escape, unseen by the other women who were draped in expensive furs.

Loisel held her back.

"Hold on! You'll catch cold outside. I'll call a cab."

But she wouldn't listen to him and went rapidly down the stairs. When they were on the street, they didn't find a carriage; and they set out to hunt for one, hailing drivers whom they saw going by at a distance.

They walked toward the Seine,[8] disconsolate and shivering. Finally on the docks they found one of those carriages that one sees in Paris only after nightfall, as if they were ashamed to show their drabness during daylight hours.

It dropped them at their door in the Rue des Martyrs, and they climbed wearily up to their apartment. For her, it was all over. For him, there was the thought that he would have to be at the Ministry at ten o'clock.

Before the mirror, she let the wraps fall from her shoulders to see herself once again in all her glory. Suddenly she gave a cry. The necklace was gone.

Her husband, already half undressed, said, "What's the trouble?"

She turned toward him despairingly, "I . . . I . . . I don't have Mme. Forestier's necklace."

"What! You can't mean it! It's impossible!"

They hunted everywhere, through the folds of the dress, through the folds of the coat, in the pockets. They found nothing.

He asked, "Are you sure you had it when leaving the dance?"

"Yes, I felt it when I was in the hall of the Ministry."

"But if you had lost it on the street we'd have heard it drop. It must be in the cab."

"Yes, Quite likely. Did you get its number?"

"No. Didn't you notice it either?"

"No."

They looked at each other aghast. Finally Loisel got dressed again.

"I'll retrace our steps on foot," he said, "to see if I can find it."

And he went out. She remained in her evening clothes, without the strength to go to bed, slumped in a chair in the unheated room, her mind a blank.

Her husband came in about seven o'clock. He had had no luck.

He went to the police station, to the newspapers to post a reward, to the cab companies, everywhere the slightest hope drove him.

That evening Loisel returned, pale, his face lined; still he had learned nothing.

"We'll have to write your friend," he said, "to tell her you have broken the catch and are having it repaired. That will give us a little time to turn around."

She wrote to his dictation.

At the end of a week, they had given up all hope.

8. **Seine** (sĕn): a river that runs through Paris.

And Loisel, looking five years older, declared, "We must take steps to replace that piece of jewelry."

The next day they took the case to the jeweler whose name they found inside. He consulted his records. "I didn't sell that necklace, madame," he said. "I only supplied the case."

Then they went from one jeweler to another hunting for a similar necklace, going over their recollections, both sick with despair and anxiety.

They found, in a shop in Palais Royal,[9] a string of diamonds which seemed exactly like the one they were seeking. It was priced at forty thousand francs. They could get it for thirty-six.

They asked the jeweler to hold it for them for three days. And they reached an agreement that he would take it back for thirty-four thousand if the lost one was found before the end of February.

Loisel had eighteen thousand francs he had inherited from his father. He would borrow the rest.

He went about raising the money, asking a thousand francs from one, four hundred from another, a hundred here, sixty there. He signed notes, made ruinous deals, did business with loan sharks, ran the whole gamut of moneylenders. He compromised the rest of his life, risked his signature without knowing if he'd be able to honor it, and then, terrified by the outlook for the future, by the blackness of despair about to close around him, by the prospect of all the privations of the body and tortures of the spirit, he went to claim the new necklace with the thirty-six thousand francs which he placed on the counter of the shopkeeper.

When Mme. Loisel took the necklace back, Mme. Forestier said to her frostily, "You should have brought it back sooner; I might have needed it."

She didn't open the case, an action her friend was afraid of. If she had noticed the substitution, what would she have thought? What would she have said? Would she have thought her a thief?

Mme. Loisel experienced the horrible life the needy live. She played her part, however, with sudden heroism. That frightful debt had to be paid. She would pay it. She dismissed her maid; they rented a garret under the eaves.

She learned to do the heavy housework, to perform the hateful duties of cooking. She washed dishes, wearing down her shell-pink nails scouring the grease from pots and pans; she scrubbed dirty linen, shirts, and cleaning rags which she hung on a line to dry; she took the garbage down to the street each morning and brought up water, stopping on each landing to get her breath. And, clad like a peasant woman, basket on arm, guarding sou[10] by sou her scanty allowance, she bargained with the fruit dealers, the grocer, the butcher, and was insulted by them.

Each month notes had to be paid, and others renewed to give more time.

Her husband labored evenings to balance a tradesman's accounts, and at night, often, he copied documents at five sous a page.

And this went on for ten years.

Finally, all was paid back, everything including the exorbitant rates of the loan sharks and accumulated compound interest.

Mme. Loisel appeared an old woman, now. She became heavy, rough, harsh, like one of the poor. Her hair untended, her skirts askew, her hands red, her voice shrill, she even

---

9. **Palais Royal** (pȧ-lä′ rwȧ-yȧl′): a section of Paris with fashionable stores.

10. **sou** (sōō): a coin then worth about one cent.

slopped water on her floors and scrubbed them herself. But, sometimes, while her husband was at work, she would sit near the window and think of that long-ago evening when, at the dance, she had been so beautiful and admired.

What would have happened if she had not lost that necklace? Who knows? Who can say? How strange and unpredictable life is! How little there is between happiness and misery!

Then one Sunday when she had gone for a walk on the Champs Élysées[11] to relax a bit from the week's labors, she suddenly noticed a woman strolling with a child. It was Mme. Forestier, still young-looking; still beautiful, still charming.

Mme. Loisel felt a rush of emotion. Should she speak to her? Of course. And now that everything was paid off, she would tell her the whole story. Why not?

She went toward her. "Hello, Jeanne."

The other, not recognizing her, showed astonishment at being spoken to so familiarly by this common person. She stammered, "But . . . madame . . . I don't recognize . . . You must be mistaken."

"No, I'm Mathilde Loisel."

Her friend gave a cry, "Oh, my poor Mathilde, how you've changed!"

"Yes, I've had a hard time since last seeing you. And plenty of misfortunes—and all on account of you!"

"Of me . . . How do you mean?"

"Do you remember that diamond necklace you loaned me to wear to the dance at the Ministry?"

"Yes, but what about it?"

"Well, I lost it."

"You lost it! But you returned it."

"I brought you another just like it. And we've been paying for it for ten years now. You can imagine that wasn't easy for us who had nothing. Well, it's over now, and I am glad of it."

Mme. Forestier stopped short. "You mean to say you bought a diamond necklace to replace mine?"

"Yes. You never noticed, then? They were quite alike."

And she smiled with proud and simple joy.

Mme. Forestier, quite overcome, clasped her by the hands. "Oh, my poor Mathilde. But mine was only paste.[12] Why, at most it was worth only five hundred francs!"

---

11. **Champs Élysées** (shän' zā-lē-zā'): the main avenue of Paris.

12. **paste:** a brilliant, glassy material used in imitiation diamonds.

FOR STUDY AND DISCUSSION

1. The first six paragraphs of the story tell about the life Madame Loisel wishes to lead and the life she really leads. What details bring out this contrast?

2. Madame Loisel wishes to have an expensive dress for the reception. How does her husband react to her wish? What does this incident reveal about the values of Madame Loisel and of her husband?

3. What reason does Madame Loisel give for needing a jewel to go with her dress? Do you think her concern is reasonable or foolish? Why does she choose the necklace rather than any of the other pieces of jewelry?

4. At the reception, what incident shows the contrast between Madame Loisel's apparent situation in life and her true situation? What incident contrasts her values with her husband's values? After the Loisels leave to go home, what incident suggests a return to her true life?

5. What actions do the Loisels take to replace the necklace? What qualities of character are revealed by these actions? Why do you think they do not tell Madame Forestier that they have lost the necklace?

6. How does Madame Loisel's character change as a result of the hardships she has to endure? Do you think her values change? Give reasons for your answer.

7. "The Necklace" is famous for its surprise ending. How does the surprise drive home the story's theme — the underlying idea about true and false values?

IMPLICIT THEME

The theme of "The Necklace" depends upon a contrast between true values and false values. Nowhere is the contrast directly stated, nor is the author's attitude toward Madame Loisel specifically declared. Yet readers can perceive this attitude as they learn more about Madame and Monsieur Loisel. For example, Madame Loisel's desire for an expensive evening dress shows that she values appearances and does not consider how such an extravagance will strain her husband's finances. Details such as this not only characterize Madame Loisel but also shape readers' attitudes toward her and her values.

Give at least three other details that de Maupassant uses to shape your attitude toward Madame Loisel and her values. Show how these details are related to the theme of the story.

LANGUAGE AND VOCABULARY

Using Words with Exactness

Often, looking up a word in a dictionary is only the first step to learning its exact meaning. We must also look at the way the word is used in a specific context. Look up each italicized word in the following passages from "The Necklace." Show that you understand the exact meaning of each word by using it in the same sense in a sentence of your own.

1. Their natural *poise,* their *instinctive* good taste . . . are the sole guiding principles which make daughters of the common people the equals of ladies in high society.
2. She grieved *incessantly* . . .
3. The sight of the little Breton girl who did her humble housework roused in her *disconsolate* regrets and wild daydreams.

4. She danced madly, wildly, drunk with pleasure, . . . in a kind of happy cloud composed of all the *adulation*, of all the admiring glances . . .

5. He threw over her shoulder the wraps he had brought for going home, modest garments of everyday life whose *shabbiness* clashed with the stylishness of her evening clothes.

FOR COMPOSITION

Comparing Themes

If you have already read "The Gift of the Magi," write a composition comparing the theme of that story with the theme of "The Necklace." In your composition, consider the following question: How does the theme of each story depend upon a contrast between true and false values?

Writing a Sequel

Write a sequel to "The Necklace." Tell how Madame Loisel reacts to the discovery that the necklace is paste. How does this discovery affect the lives of Madame Loisel and her husband?

ABOUT THE AUTHOR

Guy de Maupassant (1850–1893) was born in Normandy, a province of France. After he served in the French army during the Franco-Prussian War, he went to Paris and got a job as government clerk. An aspiring writer, he made friends with a number of distinguished French writers, among them Gustave Flaubert. De Maupassant became Flaubert's protégé and showed the older man many manuscripts before Flaubert decided that his young disciple was ready to publish. De Maupassant's first published story, "Ball of Fat," was acclaimed a masterpiece. By 1882, he had achieved success as a writer and was able to quit his government post. He wrote prolifically, producing sixteen volumes of short stories, six novels, and several volumes of travel sketches. It is for his short stories that De Maupassant is principally remembered. They are famous for their clear, smooth style, their compression, and their eye for telling detail. His stories reflect his knowledge of country life and small-town life in Normandy, and of fashionable and unfashionable life in Paris. Among his best-known stories are "The Piece of String," "The Duel," "At Sea," "Two Little Soldiers," and "The Diary of a Madman." De Maupassant's most famous story is "The Necklace"; it is one of the most anthologized stories of all time.

The Fifty-First Dragon

Heywood Broun

Of all the pupils at the knight school Gawaine le Cœur-Hardy[1] was among the least promising. He was tall and sturdy, but his instructors soon discovered that he lacked spirit. He would hide in the woods when the jousting class was called, although his companions and members of the faculty sought to appeal to his better nature by shouting to him to come out and break his neck like a man. Even when they told him that the lances were padded, the horses no more than ponies, and the field unusually soft for late autumn, Gawaine refused to grow enthusiastic. The Headmaster and the Assistant Professor of Pleasaunce[2] were discussing the case one spring afternoon

---

1. **Gawaine le Cœur-Hardy** (gä'wĭn lə kûr'här'dē): Gawaine the Boldhearted. *Cœur* is French for "heart."
2. **Pleasaunce** (plĕz'əns): Usually this word means "pleasure." Here, it probably means "courtesy."

and the Assistant Professor could see no remedy but expulsion.

"No," said the Headmaster, as he looked out at the purple hills which ringed the school, "I think I'll train him to slay dragons."

"He might be killed," objected the Assistant Professor.

"So he might," replied the Headmaster brightly, but he added, more soberly, "we must consider the greater good. We are responsible for the formation of this lad's character."

"Are the dragons particularly bad this year?" interrupted the Assistant Professor. This was characteristic. He always seemed restive when the head of the school began to talk ethics and the ideals of the institution.

"I've never known them worse," replied the Headmaster. "Up in the hills to the south last week they killed a number of peasants, two cows and a prize pig. And if this dry spell holds there's no telling when they may start a forest fire simply by breathing around indiscriminately."

"Would any refund on the tuition fee be necessary in case of an accident to young Cœur-Hardy?"

"No," the principal answered, judicially, "that's all covered in the contract. But as a matter of fact he won't be killed. Before I send him up in the hills I'm going to give him a magic word."

"That's a good idea," said the Professor. "Sometimes they work wonders."

From that day on Gawaine specialized in dragons. His course included both theory and practice. In the morning there were long lectures on the history, anatomy, manners and customs of dragons. Gawaine did not distinguish himself in these studies. He had a marvelously versatile gift for forgetting things. In the afternoon he showed to better advantage, for then he would go down to the South Meadow and practice with a battle-ax. In this exercise he was truly impressive, for he had enormous strength as well as speed and grace. He even developed a deceptive display of ferocity. Old alumni say that it was a thrilling sight to see Gawaine charging across the field toward the dummy paper dragon which had been set up for his practice. As he ran he would brandish his ax and shout, "A murrain[3] on thee!" or some other vivid bit of campus slang. It never took him more than one stroke to behead the dummy dragon.

Gradually his task was made more difficult. Paper gave way to papier-mâché[4] and finally to wood, but even the toughest of these dummy dragons had no terrors for Gawaine. One sweep of the ax always did the business. There were those who said that when the practice was protracted until dusk and the dragons threw long, fantastic shadows across the meadow, Gawaine did not charge so impetuously nor shout so loudly. It is possible there was malice in this charge. At any rate, the Headmaster decided by the end of June that it was time for the test. Only the night before, a dragon had come close to the school grounds and had eaten some of the lettuce from the garden. The faculty decided that Gawaine was ready. They gave him a diploma and a new battle-ax and the Headmaster summoned him to a private conference.

"Sit down," said the Headmaster. "Have a cigarette."

Gawaine hesitated.

"Oh, I know it's against the rules," said the Headmaster. "But after all, you have received your preliminary degree. You are no longer a

---

3. **murrain** (mûr′ĭn): plague.
4. **papier-mâché** (pā′pər-mə-shā′): a material made of paper pulp mixed with glue or rosin. It can be molded into different shapes when wet, and then hardens as it dries.

boy. You are a man. Tomorrow you will go out into the world, the great world of achievement."

Gawaine took a cigarette. The Headmaster offered him a match, but he produced one of his own and began to puff away with a dexterity which quite amazed the principal.

"Here you have learned the theories of life," continued the Headmaster, resuming the thread of his discourse, "but after all, life is not a matter of theories. Life is a matter of facts. It calls on the young and the old alike to face these facts, even though they are hard and sometimes unpleasant. Your problem, for example, is to slay dragons."

"They say that those dragons down in the south wood are five hundred feet long," ventured Gawaine, timorously.

"Stuff and nonsense!" said the Headmaster. "The curate saw one last week from the top of Arthur's Hill. The dragon was sunning himself down in the valley. The curate didn't have an opportunity to look at him very long because he felt it was his duty to hurry back to make a report to me. He said the monster — or shall I say, the big lizard? — wasn't an inch over two hundred feet. But the size has nothing at all to do with it. You'll find the big ones even easier than the little ones. They're far slower on their feet and less aggressive, I'm told. Besides, before you go I'm going to equip you in such fashion that you need have no fear of all the dragons in the world."

"I'd like an enchanted cap," said Gawaine.

"What's that?" asked the Headmaster, testily.

"A cap to make me disappear," explained Gawaine.

The Headmaster laughed indulgently. "You mustn't believe all those old wives' stories," he said. "There isn't any such thing. A cap to make you disappear, indeed! What would you do with it? You haven't even appeared yet.

Why, my boy, you could walk from here to London, and nobody would so much as look at you. You're nobody. You couldn't be more invisible than that."

Gawaine seemed dangerously close to a relapse into his old habit of whimpering. The Headmaster reassured him: "Don't worry; I'll give you something much better than an enchanted cap. I'm going to give you a magic word. All you have to do is to repeat this magic charm once and no dragon can possibly harm a hair of your head. You can cut off his head at your leisure."

He took a heavy book from the shelf behind his desk and began to run through it. "Sometimes," he said, "the charm is a whole phrase or even a sentence. I might, for instance, give you 'To make the' — no, that might not do. I think a single word would be best for dragons."

"A short word," suggested Gawaine.

"It can't be too short or it wouldn't be potent. There isn't so much hurry as all that. Here's a splendid magic word: 'Rumplesnitz.' Do you think you can learn that?"

Gawaine tried and in an hour or so he seemed to have the word well in hand. Again and again he interrupted the lesson to inquire, "And if I say 'Rumplesnitz' the dragon can't possibly hurt me?" And always the Headmaster replied, "If you only say 'Rumplesnitz,' you are perfectly safe."

Toward morning Gawaine seemed resigned to his career. At daybreak the Headmaster saw him to the edge of the forest and pointed him to the direction in which he should proceed. About a mile away to the southwest a cloud of steam hovered over an open meadow in the woods and the Headmaster assured Gawaine that under the steam he would find a dragon. Gawaine went forward slowly. He wondered whether it would be best to approach the dragon on the run as he did in his practice in the South Meadow or to walk slowly toward him, shouting "Rumplesnitz" all the way.

The problem was decided for him. No sooner had he come to the fringe of the meadow than the dragon spied him and began to charge. It was a large dragon and yet it seemed decidedly aggressive in spite of the Headmaster's statement to the contrary. As the dragon charged it released huge clouds of hissing steam through its nostrils. It was almost as if a gigantic teapot had gone mad. The dragon came forward so fast and Gawaine was so frightened that he had time to say "Rumplesnitz" only once. As he said it, he swung his battle-ax and off popped the head of the dragon. Gawaine had to admit that it was even easier to kill a real dragon than a wooden one if only you said "Rumplesnitz."

Gawaine brought the ears home and a small section of the tail. His schoolmates and the faculty made much of him, but the Headmaster wisely kept him from being spoiled by insisting that he go on with his work. Every clear day Gawaine rose at dawn and went out to kill dragons. The Headmaster kept him at home when it rained, because he said the woods were damp and unhealthy at such times and that he didn't want the boy to run needless risks. Few good days passed in which Gawaine failed to get a dragon. On one particularly fortunate day he killed three, a husband and a wife and a visiting relative. Gradually he developed a technique. Pupils who sometimes watched him from the hilltops a long way off said that he often allowed the dragon to come within a few feet before he said "Rumplesnitz." He came to say it with a mocking sneer. Occasionally he did stunts. Once when an excursion party from London was watching him he went into action with his right hand tied behind his back. The dragon's head came off just as easily.

As Gawaine's record of killings mounted higher the Headmaster found it impossible to keep him completely in hand. He fell into the habit of stealing out at night and engaging in long drinking bouts at the village tavern. It was after such a debauch that he rose a little before dawn one fine August morning and started out after his fiftieth dragon. His head was heavy and his mind sluggish. He was heavy in other respects as well, for he had adopted the somewhat vulgar practice of wearing his medals, ribbons and all, when he went out dragon hunting. The decorations began on his chest and ran all the way down to his abdomen. They must have weighed at least eight pounds.

Gawaine found a dragon in the same meadow where he had killed the first one. It was a fair-sized dragon, but evidently an old one. Its face was wrinkled and Gawaine thought he had never seen so hideous a countenance. Much to the lad's disgust, the monster refused to charge and Gawaine was obliged to walk toward him. He whistled as he went. The dragon regarded him hopelessly, but craftily. Of course it had heard of Gawaine. Even when the lad raised his battle-ax the dragon made no move. It knew that there was no salvation in the quickest thrust of the head, for it had been informed that this hunter was protected by an enchantment. It merely waited, hoping something would turn up.

Gawaine raised the battle-ax and suddenly lowered it again. He had grown very pale and he trembled violently.

The dragon suspected a trick. "What's the matter?" it asked, with false solicitude.

"I've forgotten the magic word," stammered Gawaine.

"What a pity," said the dragon. "So that was the secret. It doesn't seem quite sporting to me, all this magic stuff, you know. Not

cricket, as we used to say when I was a little dragon; but after all, that's a matter of opinion.''

Gawaine was so helpless with terror that the dragon's confidence rose immeasurably and it could not resist the temptation to show off a bit.

''Could I possibly be of any assistance?'' it asked. ''What's the first letter of the magic word?''

''It begins with an 'r,' '' said Gawaine weakly.

''Let's see,'' mused the dragon, ''that doesn't tell us much, does it? What sort of a word is this? Is it an epithet,[5] do you think?''

Gawaine could do no more than nod.

---

5. **epithet** (ĕp′ə-thĕt′): a word or phrase used to describe a person, thing, or idea. An epithet is sometimes used as a substitute for a name.

''Why, of course,'' exclaimed the dragon, ''reactionary Republican.''

Gawaine shook his head.

''Well, then,'' said the dragon, ''we'd better get down to business. Will you surrender?''

With the suggestion of a compromise Gawaine mustered up enough courage to speak.

''What will you do if I surrender?'' he asked.

''Why, I'll eat you,'' said the dragon.

''And if I don't surrender?''

''I'll eat you just the same.''

''Then it doesn't mean any difference, does it?'' moaned Gawaine.

''It does to me,'' said the dragon with a smile. ''I'd rather you didn't surrender. You'd taste much better if you didn't.''

The dragon waited for a long time for Gawaine to ask ''Why?'' but the boy was too frightened to speak. At last the dragon had to give the explanation without his cue line.

"You see," he said, "if you don't surrender you'll taste better because you'll die game."

This was an old and ancient trick of the dragon's. By means of some such quip he was accustomed to paralyze his victims with laughter and then to destroy them. Gawaine was sufficiently paralyzed as it was, but laughter had no part in his helplessness. With the last word of the joke the dragon drew back his head and struck. In that second there flashed into the mind of Gawaine the magic word "Rumplesnitz," but there was no time to say it. There was time only to strike and, without a word, Gawaine met the onrush of the dragon with a full swing. He put all his back and shoulders into it. The impact was terrific and the head of the dragon flew almost a hundred yards and landed in a thicket.

Gawaine did not remain frightened very long after the death of the dragon. His mood was one of wonder. He was enormously puzzled. He cut off the ears of the monster almost in a trance. Again and again he thought to himself, "I didn't say 'Rumplesnitz'!" He was sure of that and yet there was no question that he had killed the dragon. In fact, he had never killed one so utterly. Never before had he driven a head for anything like the same distance. Twenty-five yards was perhaps his best previous record. All the way back to the knight school he kept rumbling about in his mind seeking an explanation for what had occurred. He went to the Headmaster immediately and after closing the door told him what had happened. "I didn't say 'Rumplesnitz,' " he explained with great earnestness.

The Headmaster laughed. "I'm glad you've found out," he said. "It makes you ever so much more of a hero. Don't you see that? Now you know that it was you who killed all these dragons and not that foolish little word 'Rumplesnitz.' "

Gawaine frowned. "Then it wasn't a magic word after all?" he asked.

"Of course not," said the Headmaster, "you ought to be too old for such foolishness. There isn't any such thing as a magic word."

"But you told me it was magic," protested Gawaine. "You said it was magic and now you say it isn't."

"It wasn't magic in a literal sense," answered the Headmaster, "but it was much more wonderful than that. The word gave you confidence. It took away your fears. If I hadn't told you that, you might have been killed the very first time. It was your battle-ax did the trick."

Gawaine surprised the Headmaster by his attitude. He was obviously distressed by the explanation. He interrupted a long philosophic and ethical discourse by the Headmaster with "If I hadn't of hit 'em all mighty hard and fast any one of 'em might have crushed me like a, like a——" He fumbled for a word.

"Eggshell," suggested the Headmaster.

"Like a eggshell," assented Gawaine, and he said it many times. All through the evening meal people who sat near him heard him muttering, "Like a eggshell, like a eggshell."

The next day was clear, but Gawaine did not get up at dawn. Indeed, it was almost noon when the Headmaster found him cowering in bed, with the clothes pulled over his head. The principal called the Assistant Professor of Pleasaunce, and together they dragged the boy toward the forest.

"He'll be all right as soon as he gets a couple more dragons under his belt," explained the Headmaster.

The Assistant Professor of Pleasaunce agreed. "It would be a shame to stop such a fine run," he said. "Why, counting that one yesterday, he's killed fifty dragons."

They pushed the boy into a thicket above which hung a meager cloud of steam. It was obviously quite a small dragon. But Gawaine did not come back that night or the next. In fact, he never came back. Some weeks afterward brave spirits from the school explored the thicket, but they could find nothing to remind them of Gawaine except the metal parts of his medals. Even the ribbons had been devoured.

The Headmaster and the Assistant Professor of Pleasaunce agreed that it would be just as well not to tell the school how Gawaine had achieved his record and still less how he came to die. They held that it might have a bad effect on school spirit. Accordingly, Gawaine has lived in the memory of the school as its greatest hero. No visitor succeeds in leaving the building today without seeing a great shield which hangs on the wall of the dining hall. Fifty pairs of dragon's ears are mounted upon the shield and underneath in gilt letters is "Gawaine le Cœur-Hardy," followed by the simple inscription, "He killed fifty dragons." The record has never been equaled.

FOR STUDY AND DISCUSSION

1. A traditional tale about knights and dragons would not include, as one of its characters, an "Assistant Professor of Pleasaunce." Nor would the character ask "Would any refund on the tuition fee be necessary in case of an accident?" Such *anachronisms*—that is, events existing out of their proper time in history—add to the humor of the story. Cite other details in which the "knight school" is treated as if it were a school of today.

2. Explain the Headmaster's plan to turn Gawaine into a bold knight. What attitude toward human nature is behind this plan? Would you call it a cynical attitude? Explain.

3. Gawaine has several assets as a dragon-slaying knight: "enormous strength as well as speed and grace." But he also has a serious flaw. What is it? What other flaws in his character emerge after he becomes a famous dragon slayer?

4. The encounter with the fiftieth dragon, a key episode in the story, is both humorous and suspenseful. Point out humorous passages. What details contribute to the suspense?

5. When Gawaine tells the Headmaster about his encounter with the fiftieth dragon, the Headmaster reveals that there is no such thing as a magic word. What effect does this revelation have on Gawaine? If you were in Gawaine's place, would you have wanted to be told the truth about the magic word? Why or why not?

6. "The Fifty-First Dragon" can be understood on two levels. On the most obvious level, it is an amusing spoof of tales about knights and dragons. On a deeper level, it makes a serious comment about human beings and their need for beliefs. State the theme, using evidence from the story to support your answer.

FOR COMPOSITION

Recasting the Story

Write a modern equivalent of "The Fifty-First Dragon." Instead of making Gawaine a knight, choose some profession or trade he might follow today. Instead of an encounter with the fiftieth dragon, choose a comparable encounter as the key episode of your story. Here are some possibilities: Gawaine as an offensive football player—given false confidence by his coach's pep talks and finally encountering a 330-pound tackle; Gawaine as a supersalesman discovering that the product he sells is defective. In developing these or other possibilities, emphasize the character's need to believe and his collapse when the belief proves false.

ABOUT THE AUTHOR

Born in Brooklyn, New York, Heywood Broun (1888–1939) attended the Horace Mann School in Manhattan, where he edited the school newspaper. After attending Harvard, he got a job with the New York *Telegraph* as a sports writer. In 1912 he went to work for the New York *Tribune,* where he began his column, "It Seems to Me." In time, it became one of the most popular newspaper columns in America. Although Broun published several novels, he was best known as a newspaper columnist. He had strong, controversial opinions and did not hesitate to express them. One critic has written that Broun's work at its best shows "a depth, a warmth, and a power . . . that were the outward expression of the man himself."

Practice in Reading and Writing

DESCRIPTION AND NARRATION

Reading Description

The purpose of a descriptive passage is to give a clear picture or impression of a scene, character, or object. A good description contains specific details, all of which support a dominant impression. Sometimes a writer will state in the very first sentence the main impression he or she wishes to convey, as in this paragraph from "The Pacing Goose."

> Spring's a various season, Jess thought, no two years the same: comes in with rains, mud deep enough to swallow horse and rider; comes in cold, snow falling so fast as it weaves a web; comes in with a warm wind blowing about thy ears and bringing a smell of something flowering, not here, but southaways, across the Ohio, maybe in Kentucky. Nothing here now but a smell of melting snow—which is no smell at all, but a kind of prickle in the nose, like a bygone sneeze. Comes in so various, winter put by and always so welcome.

---

1. What impression does this paragraph give you?

2. What phrase in the last sentence reinforces the paragraph's dominant impression?

3. What details does Jessamyn West use to support the dominant impression? Which of these details give visual pictures? Which appeal to the other senses?

In reading a description, you should try to grasp the dominant impression given by the details the writer has chosen. Read the following paragraph from "All the Years of Her Life." Write a statement of the dominant impression you receive and list the details supporting this impression.

> Mrs. Higgins must have been going to bed when he telephoned, for her hair was tucked in loosely under her hat, and her hand at her throat held her light coat tightly across her

chest so her dress would not show. She came in, large and plump, with a little smile on her friendly face. Most of the store lights had been turned out and at first she did not see Alfred, who was standing in the shadow at the end of the counter. Yet as soon as she saw him she did not look as Alfred thought she would look: she smiled, her blue eyes never wavered, and with a calmness and dignity that made them forget that her clothes seemed to have been thrown on her, she put out her hand to Mr. Carr and said politely, "I'm Mrs. Higgins. I'm Alfred's mother."

Writing a Description

In writing a description, try to follow these steps:

---

1. *Look hard at the scene, character or object you are describing to get a definite impression of what you want your reader to feel or see.*

2. *State or suggest this main impression in your opening sentence.*
3. *Reinforce or develop this impression with a logical arrangement of details.*

Write a paragraph describing some place you have recently seen. State your dominant impression of the place in your first sentence, then support it with details arranged in a logical order such as left to right, up to down, or near to far.

In a single paragraph, communicate your impression of a person or thing. Suggest this impression with the details you select and the order in which you arrange them.

Sharpening Your Writing

Modifiers are words that change (modify) another word by restricting it (making it more exact) in meaning. In the phrase "Spring's a various season," *various* is a modifier of *season*. The modifier adds a fresh and interesting idea to what otherwise would be a dull and obvious statement. Note the effect of the following modifiers:

"snow falling *so fast it weaves a web*"
"with a *warm* wind blowing about thy ears"

Many writers fail to make their modifiers exact enough. Go back over the paragraphs you have just written. If any of your modifiers seem weak or stale, replace them with words that are more exact and accurate.

Reading Narration

Narration is storytelling, and a paragraph of narration, like a
story, is a series of events or actions. In a good paragraph, as in
a good story, the order of incidents is clear and logical: one action leads to another in a way that seems right and natural. The
most natural order for such a series of events is *chronological* — that is, in the same order as they would naturally occur
in time.

A good story begins — and a good paragraph may begin — in a
way that arouses your curiosity and anticipation. Once your
interest is aroused, you are more alert to all the details of the
actions and readier to draw your own conclusions. Reading
narration demands a special alertness and readiness to draw
conclusions. The author very often simply tells what happened, leaving it up to you to form your own opinion of the
character or characters involved and what their actions show
about them.

This paragraph from "The Most Dangerous Game" captures
the tension of the hunt. Note how the very first sentence
arouses your anticipation. Note how carefully the sequence of
events is conveyed.

> They would be on him any minute now. His mind worked
> frantically. He thought of a native trick he had learned in
> Uganda. He slid down the tree. He caught hold of a springy
> young sapling and to it he fastened his hunting knife, with
> the blade pointing down the trail; with a bit of wild grape-
> vine he tied back the sapling. Then he ran for his life. The
> hounds raised their voices as they hit the fresh scent. Rains-
> ford knew now how an animal at bay feels.

Narratives frequently include dialogue. Good dialogue is appropriate to the speakers and advances the action of the story.
Note how this dialogue from "Tom Edison's Shaggy Dog"
creates a vivid impression of the characters while it carries the
plot forward:

> "Yes," said Bullard, rounding out the first hour of his lec-
> ture, "made and lost five fortunes in my time."
> "So you said," said the stranger, whose name Bullard had
> neglected to ask. "Easy, boy. No, no, no, boy," he said
> to the dog, who was growing more aggressive toward his
> ankles.
> "Oh? Already told you that, did I?" said Bullard.

"Twice."

"Two in real estate, one in scrap iron, and one in oil, and one in trucking."

"So you said."

"I did? Yes, guess I did. Two in real estate, one in scrap iron, one in oil, and one in trucking. Wouldn't take back a day of it."

"No, I suppose not," said the stranger. "Pardon me, but do you suppose you could move your dog somewhere else? He keeps——"

"Him?" said Bullard heartily. "Friendliest dog in the world. Don't need to be afraid of him."

In reading narration, try to follow the sequence of events that lead to the climax of each episode. Read the following paragraph from "War" and outline the events in sequence:

The shots died down as the magazines were emptied, until, quickly, there was no more shooting. The young man was elated. Through that astonishing fusillade he had come unscathed. He glanced back. Yes, they had emptied their magazines. He could see several reloading. Others were running back behind the house for their horses. As he looked, two, already mounted, came back into view around the corner, riding hard. And at the same moment, he saw the man with the unmistakable ginger beard kneel down on the ground, level his gun, and coolly take his time for the long shot.

Writing Narration

In writing a narrative, keep these points in mind:

---

1. *Decide on what you want the climax of your story to be.*
2. *Plan a logical—and chronological—series of events that will lead up to your climax.*

3. *Use transitional expressions to relate and connect your sentences.*
4. *Try to interest your reader with the very first event of your story.*

Plan and write an account of some event or incident you saw or were involved in. Make sure your sequence of events leads logically to the climax of the episode.

Write a short story based on an exciting incident you saw or read or heard about. Work out a logical sequence of events and actions. Include dialogue if you wish.

For Further Reading

Bradbury, Ray, *Long After Midnight* (Knopf, 1976; paperback, Bantam)
 A master of science fiction presents twenty-two of his eerie tales.

Bradbury, Ray, editor, *Timeless Stories for Today and Tomorrow* (paperback, Bantam, 1952)
 These twenty-six stories of fantasy are written by such well-known authors as Shirley Jackson, Roald Dahl, Christopher Isherwood, John Cheever, E. B. White, and Ray Bradbury.

Corbin, Richard, and Ned E. Hoopes, editors, *Incredible Tales of Saki* (paperback, Dell, 1966)
 In this collection are thirty-one stories that reveal the author's special talent for blending humor and horror.

Fox, Austin McC., editor, *The Legend of Sleepy Hollow and Other Selections from Washington Irving* (paperback, Pocket Books, 1962)
 This book includes selections from *The Sketch Book, The Alhambra, Tales of a Traveller,* and other works that have become part of America's folklore.

Henry, O., *Best Short Stories of O. Henry* (Doubleday, 1965)
 Here is a varied collection of stories by the master of surprise endings.

Hughes, Langston, *Something in Common and Other Stories* (paperback, Hill & Wang, 1963)
 These thirty-seven stories, which were chosen for this book by Hughes, range in setting from Africa to Harlem and reveal a rare sense of humanity.

Neider, Charles, editor, *The Complete Short Stories of Mark Twain* (Doubleday, 1957; paperback, Bantam)
 Sixty stories cover the span of the great satirist's life and reflect the humor of the American frontier.

Serling, Rod, editor, *Rod Serling's Other Worlds* (paperback, Bantam, 1978)
 These tales of adventure in time and space were selected by the creator of *The Twilight Zone* and include "They" by Robert Heinlein, "I'm in Marsport Without Hilda" by Isaac Asimov, "Little Old Miss Macbeth" by Fritz Leiber, and eleven other stories.

Shefter, Harry, editor, *The Great Adventures of Sherlock Holmes* (paperback, Pocket Books)
 This anthology contains twelve stories by Sir Arthur Conan Doyle, the master of the classic detective story, and a Reader's Supplement with photographs of actors who have played the roles of Holmes and Watson.

Slater, Michael, editor, *The Christmas Books,* volumes 1 and 2 (paperback, Penguin, 1971)
 Here is a collection containing the famous story "A Christmas Carol" and other favorite works by Charles Dickens.

Sohn, David, A., editor, *Great Tales of Horror by Edgar Allan Poe* (paperback, Bantam, 1964)
 Readers will enjoy "The Tell-Tale Heart," "The Masque of the Red Death," and ten other chilling tales of suspense by the master of the supernatural.

Stern, Madeleine B., editor, *Behind a Mask: The Unknown Thrillers of Louisa May Alcott* (William Morrow, 1975; paperback, Bantam)
 The thrillers in this book were published in various weeklies more than a century ago, before *Little Women* was written. Alcott wrote these "blood and thunder" tales under the pseudonym A. M. Barnard.

Thurber, James, *My World—And Welcome to It* (paperback, Harcourt Brace Jovanovich, 1969)
 In this mixture of thirty stories, sketches, and articles, the famous humorist includes such stories as "The Whip-Poor-Will" and "You Could Look It Up."

The line between *fiction* and *nonfiction* is sometimes difficult to establish, but in general we can say that fiction deals with imaginary characters and events, nonfiction with real people, their experiences and ideas. Many different kinds of writing are classified as nonfiction. Two major categories—essays and true narratives—are represented in this unit.

The purpose of nonfiction may be to entertain, to inform, to explain, or to persuade. Whatever the purpose, writers make use of different forms of discourse: *description*, to give a picture of the subject and to communicate sensory impressions; *narration*, to tell about a series of events; *exposition*, to present information or to explain a subject; and *argumentation* or *persuasion*, to influence or change people's ideas or actions.

Essays

NONFICTION

It was Michel de Montaigne, the sixteenth-century French writer, who coined the word *essai* and who wrote the first modern essay. The essay for Montaigne was an attempt in prose (the French *J'essai* means "I try") to set forth his ideas in a limited and personal manner on a wide range of topics. Although the essay has taken many forms since Montaigne, his basic definition still holds true. Today an essay can be loosely defined as a piece of prose writing that deals with its subject briefly and from a personal point of view.

It is customary to classify essays as *formal* or *informal*. The formal essay is serious in tone, tightly organized, and generally objective. The informal, or *familiar*, essay may range freely over the subject; we are interested as much in the writer's personality and point of view as in what he or she has to say. Neither Montaigne nor Francis Bacon, the English writer and statesman whose *Essays* were first published in 1597, considered the essay to be a complete or thorough discussion of the subject, though the essay did become a treatise in the hands of later writers. In the hands of James Thurber, E. B. White, and other modern essayists, the essay continues to be what it was for Montaigne and Bacon. We are engaged by the writer's *style*—the way the writer uses language—as well as by the subject.

The American satirist James Thurber (1894–1961) was born and raised in Columbus, Ohio, where he later attended Ohio State University. Most of his sketches, stories, and illustrations first appeared in *The New Yorker* magazine, with which Thurber was closely associated throughout his writing career. Thurber lost the use of one eye as a boy, and by the time of his death he was almost completely blind; yet he continued to write with undiminished humor and vigor.

Thurber is a master of the informal essay. One of his methods as an essayist and satirist is to focus on a subject or area of experience, and to range freely, introducing ideas and experiences not always closely related to the subject he began with. This is the method of the conversationalist. Thurber shares with the reader his amusement over human foibles— the comic oddities of character rather than its faults. In doing so, he reveals much about himself, through direct comments and, indirectly, through the subjects of his essays and his personal handling of them.

How to Name a Dog

James Thurber

Every few months somebody writes me and asks if I will give him a name for his dog. Several of these correspondents in the past year have wanted to know if I would mind the use of my own name for their spaniels. Spaniel-owners seem to have the notion that a person could sue for invasion of privacy or defamation of character if his name were applied to a cocker without written permission, and one gentleman even insisted that we conduct our correspondence in the matter through a notary public. I have a way of letting communications of this sort fall behind my roll-top desk, but it has recently occurred to me that this is an act of evasion, if not, indeed, of plain cowardice. I have therefore decided to come straight out with the simple truth that it is as hard for me to think up a name for a dog as it is for anybody else. The idea that I am an expert in the business is probably the outcome of a piece I wrote several years ago, incautiously revealing the fact that I have owned forty or more dogs in my life. This is true, but it is also deceptive. All but five or six of my dogs were disposed of when they were puppies, and I had not gone to the trouble of giving to these impermanent residents of my house any names at all except Shut Up! and Cut That Out! and Let Go!

Names of dogs end up in 176th place in the

list of things that amaze and fascinate me. Canine cognomens should be designed to impinge on the ears of dogs and not to amuse neighbors, tradespeople, and casual visitors. I remember a few dogs from the past with a faint but lingering pleasure: a farm hound named Rain, a roving Airedale named Marco Polo, a female bull terrier known as Brody[1] because she liked to jump from moving motor cars and second-story windows, and a Peke called Darien;[2] but that's all.

Well, there is Poker, alias *Fantôme Noir*,[3] a miniature black poodle I have come to know since I wrote the preceding paragraphs. Poker, familiarly known as Pokey, belongs to Mr. and Mrs. J. G. Gude, of White Plains, and when they registered him with the American Kennel Club they decided he needed a more dignified name. It wasn't easy to explain this to their youngest child, David, and his parents never did quite clear it up for him. When he was only eight, David thought the problem over for a long while and then asked his father solemnly, "If he belongs to that club, why doesn't he ever go there?" Since I wrote this piece originally, I have also heard about a sheepdog named Jupiter, which used to belong to Jimmy Cannon, journalist, critic, and man about dog shows. He reported in a recent column of his that Jupiter used to eat geraniums. I have heard of other dogs that ate flowers, but I refuse to be astonished by this until I learn of one that's downed a nasturtium.

The only animals whose naming demands concentration, hard work, and ingenuity are the seeing-eye dogs. They have to be given unusual names because passers-by like to call to seeing-eyers—"Here, Sport" or "Yuh, Rags" or "Don't take any wooden nickels, Rin Tin Tin." A blind man's dog with an ordinary name would continually be distracted from its work. A tyro at naming these dogs might make the mistake of picking Durocher[4] or Teeftallow.[5] The former is too much like Rover and the latter could easily sound like "Here, fellow" to a dog. Ten years ago I met a young man in his twenties who had been mysteriously blind for nearly five years and had been led about by a seeing-eye German shepherd during all of that time, which included several years of study at Yale. Then

---

1. **Brody:** A man named Steven Brodie pretended to jump off the Brooklyn Bridge in 1886.
2. **Peke called Darien:** *Peke* is short for Pekingese. Thurber is punning on the phrase "a peak in Darien" from the sonnet "On First Looking into Chapman's Homer" by John Keats.
3. *Fantôme Noir* (fàn'tôm nwàr): French for "black phantom."

4. **Durocher:** Leo Durocher, a manager of the Brooklyn Dodgers.
5. **Teeftallow:** the title of a book by T. S. Stribling, published in the 1920's.

suddenly one night the dog's owner began to get his vision back, and within a few weeks was able to read the fine print of a telephone book. The effect on his dog was almost disastrous, and it went into a kind of nervous crackup, since these animals are trained to the knowledge, or belief, that their owners are permanently blind. After the owner regained his vision he kept his dog, of course, not only because they had become attached to each other but because the average seeing-eye dog cannot be transferred from one person to another.

Speaking of puppies, as I was a while back, I feel that I should warn inexperienced dog-owners who have discovered to their surprise and dismay a dozen puppies in a hall closet or under the floor of the barn, not to give them away. Sell them or keep them, but don't give them away. Sixty percent of persons who are given a dog for nothing bring him back sooner or later and plump him into the reluctant and unprepared lap of his former owner. The people say that they are going to Florida and can't take the dog, or that he doesn't want to go; or they point out that he eats first editions or lace curtains or spinets, or that he doesn't see eye to eye with them in the matter of housebreaking, or that he makes disparaging remarks under his breath about their friends. Anyway, they bring him back and you are stuck with him—and maybe six others. But if you charge ten or even five dollars for pups, the new owners don't dare return them. They are afraid to ask for their money back because they believe you might think they are hard up and need the five or ten dollars. Furthermore, when a mischievous puppy is returned to its former owner it invariably behaves beautifully, and the person who brought it back is likely to be regarded as an imbecile or a dog-hater or both.

Names of dogs, to get back to our subject,

have a range almost as wide as that of the violin. They run from such plain and simple names as Spot, Sport, Rex, Brownie to fancy appellations such as Prince Rudolph Hertenberg Gratzheim of Darndorf-Putzelhorst, and Darling Mist o' Love III of Heather-Light-Holyrood—names originated by adults, all of whom in every other way, I am told, have made a normal adjustment to life. In addition to the plain and fancy categories, there are the Cynical and the Coy. Cynical names are given by people who do not like dogs too much. The most popular cynical names during the war[6] were Mussolini, Tojo, and Adolf. I never have been able to get very far in my exploration of the minds of people who call their dogs Mussolini, Tojo, and Adolf, and I suspect the reason is that I am unable to associate with them long enough to examine what goes on in their heads. I nod, and I tell them the time of day, if they ask, and that is all. I never vote for them or ask them to have a drink. The great Coy category is perhaps the largest. The Coy people call their pets Bubbles and Boggles and Sparkles and Twinkles and Doodles and Puffy and Lovums and Sweetums and Itsy-Bitsy and Betsy-Bye-Bye and Sugarkins. I pass these dog-owners at a dogtrot, wearing a horrible fixed grin.

There is a special subdivision of the Coys that is not quite so awful, but awful enough. These people, whom we will call the Wits, own two dogs, which they name Pitter and Patter, Willy and Nilly, Helter and Skelter, Namby and Pamby, Hugger and Mugger, and even Wishy and Washy, Ups and Daisy, Fitz and Startz, Fetch and Carrie, and Pro and Connie. Then there is the Cryptic category. These people select names for some private reason or for no reason at all—except perhaps to arouse a visitor's curiosity, so that he will

---

6. **war:** World War II.

exclaim, "Why in the world do you call your dog *that?*" The Cryptic name their dogs October, Bennett's Aunt, Three Fifteen, Doc Knows, Tuesday, Home Fried, Opus 38, Ask Leslie, and Thanks for the Home Run, Emil. I make it a point simply to pat these unfortunate dogs on the head, ask no question of their owners, and go about my business.

This article has degenerated into a piece that properly should be entitled "How Not to Name a Dog." I was afraid it would. It seems only fair to make up for this by confessing a few of the names I have given my own dogs, with the considerable help, if not, indeed, the insistence, of their mistress. Most of my dogs have been females, and they have answered, with apparent gladness, to such names as Jennie, Tessa, Julie, and Sophie. I have never owned a dog named Pamela, Jennifer, Clarrisa, Jacqueline, Guinevere, or Shelmerdene.

About fifteen years ago, when I was looking for a house to buy in Connecticut, I knocked on the front door of an attractive home whose owner, my real-estate agent had told me, wanted to sell it and go back to Iowa to live. The lady agent who escorted me around had informed me that the owner of this place was a man named Strong, but a few minutes after arriving at the house, I was having a drink in the living room with Phil Stong,[7] for it was he. We went out into the yard after a while and I saw Mr. Stong's spaniel. I called to the dog and snapped my fingers, but he seemed curiously embarrassed, like his master. "What's his name?" I asked the latter. He was cornered and there was no way out of it. "Thurber," he said, in a small frightened voice. Thurber and I shook hands, and he didn't seem to me any more depressed than any other spaniel I have met. He had, however, the expression of a bachelor on his way to a party he has tried in vain to get out of, and I think it must have been this cast of countenance that had reminded Mr. Stong of the dog I draw. The dog I draw is, to be sure, much larger than a spaniel and not so shaggy, but I confess, though I am not a spaniel man, that there are certain basic resemblances between my dog and all other dogs with long ears and troubled eyes.

Perhaps I should suggest at least one name for a dog, if only to justify the title of this piece. All right, then, what's the matter with Stong? It's a good name for a dog, short, firm, and effective. I recommend it to all those who have written to me for suggestions and to all those who may be at this very moment turning over in their minds the idea of asking my advice in this difficult and perplexing field of nomenclature.

Since I first set down these not too invaluable rules for naming dogs, I have heard of at least a dozen basset hounds named Thurber, a Newfoundland called Little Bears Thurber and a bloodhound named Tiffany's Thurber. This is all right with me, so long as the owners of Thurbers do not bring them to call on me at my house in Connecticut without making arrangements in advance. Christabel, my old and imperious poodle, does not like unannounced dog visitors, and tries to get them out of the house as fast as she can. Two years ago a Hartford dog got lost in my neighborhood and finally showed up at my house. He hadn't had much, if anything, to eat for several days, and we fed him twice within three hours, to the high dismay and indignation of Christabel, who only gets one big meal a day. The wanderer was returned to its owner, through a story in the Hartford *Courant,* and quiet descended on my home until a handsome young male collie showed up one night. We had quite a time getting him

---

7. **Phil Stong:** American writer (1899–1957), author of *State Fair.*

out of the house. Christabel kept telling him how wonderful it was outdoors and trotting to the door, but the collie wasn't interested. I tried to pick him up, but I am too old to pick up a full-grown collie. In the end Christabel solved the problem herself by leading him outside on the promise of letting him chew one of the bones she had buried. He still keeps coming back to visit us from time to time, but Christabel has hidden her bones in new places. She will romp with the young visitor for about twenty seconds, then show her teeth and send him home. I don't do anything about the situation. After all, my home has been in charge of Christabel for a great many years now, and I never interfere with a woman's ruling a household.

FOR STUDY AND DISCUSSION

1. An informal essay may reveal as much about the personality of its author as it does about its subject. What impression do you get of Thurber from his various comments in the opening paragraph? Would you say that he is tolerant or intolerant of people's quirks and foibles? Does he have a sense of humor about himself as well as about others?

2. Thurber's essay points out that the naming of a dog reveals something of the owner's personality. What incident shows that Poker's owners are snobs? What is special about spaniel-owners? According to Thurber, what do the Cynical, Coy, and Cryptic categories of names tell about dog-owners?

3. An informal essay is often written in a conversational style complete with digressions and humorous anecdotes. At what points in the essay does Thurber let on that he has wandered from the subject? How does he make a return to the subject?

4. How does Thurber show that he credits his dogs with intelligence and with individual personalities? What do the names he chose for his own dogs tell you about him? Would you consider him a genuine dog-lover?

OPENING SENTENCES

Paragraphs usually begin with a *topic sentence,* a sentence that gives the central idea. Sometimes the central idea is not given until later in the paragraph. The opening sentence, then, states the subject of the paragraph only, and serves as a signpost to the reader.

The opening sentence of the third paragraph in Thurber's essay states the subject only:

Well, there is Poker . . . a miniature black poodle I have come to know since I wrote the preceding paragraphs.

The opening sentence of the fourth paragraph states the central idea:

The only animals whose naming demands concentration, hard work, and ingenuity are the seeing-eye dogs.

Which of Thurber's opening sentences resemble the first sentence, and which resemble the second?

LANGUAGE AND VOCABULARY

Recognizing Words Used for Humorous Effect

Thurber uses the fancy word *cognomen* in place of the simple word *name* for humorous effect in the following sentence:

Canine cognomens should be designed to impinge on the ears of dogs and not to amuse neighbors, tradespeople, and casual visitors.

Find other examples in the essay of words and names chosen or cited for their humor.

Determining Exact Meanings

Thurber chooses words for their exact meanings. The words *impinge on* in the sentence quoted above carry the meaning of "colliding with"—and that is the exact meaning Thurber wants in his sentence. The name should catch the attention of the dog, make its ears perk up—in short, collide with the dog. Look up the italicized words in the following sentences from Thurber's essay, and explain how each word or phrase is used:

1. I have a way of letting communications of this sort fall behind my roll-top desk, but it has recently occurred to me that this is an act of *evasion*, if not, indeed, of plain cowardice.
2. The only animals whose naming demands concentration, hard work, and *ingenuity* are the seeing-eye dogs.
3. . . . I feel that I should warn inexperienced dog-owners who have discovered to their surprise and *dismay* a dozen puppies in a hall closet or under the floor of the barn, not to give them away.
4. *Cynical* names are given by people who do not like dogs too much.

5. The great *Coy* category is perhaps the largest.
6. Then there is the *Cryptic* category.
7. This article has *degenerated* into a piece that properly should be entitled "How Not to Name a Dog."
8. . . . I think it must have been this *cast of countenance* that had reminded Mr. Stong of the dog I draw.

FOR COMPOSITION

Writing a Humorous Essay

Write a humorous essay on one of the following topics. In your opening paragraph, introduce yourself to your reader as Thurber does. Conclude your essay with a final anecdote or an observation about your experience.

Living with a family pet
The pleasures of raising and caring for a pet
Getting along with neighborhood pets
The personalities of neighborhood dogs or cats

E. B. White (1899–1985) was born in Mount Vernon, New York, and was educated at Cornell University. Through most of his writing career, he was associated with *The New Yorker*. His collection of short essays, *One Man's Meat*, is mainly concerned with country life in Maine, where White lived for many years.

An essayist frequently uses the methods of the storyteller to present an idea effectively. In "The Wings of Orville," White makes use of the fable form to explore certain characteristics in human nature. This work illustrates well his typical understated humor deriving from a keen observation of people and their sometimes strange dreams and actions. Though fables characteristically end with a statement of the moral, White lets his animal characters and their actions speak for themselves.

The Wings of Orville

E. B. White

All through the courtship, the building of the nest, and even the incubation of the eggs, Orville had acted in what to the hen sparrow seemed a normal manner. He had been fairly attentive, too, as cockbirds go. The first indication Orville's wife had of any quirk in his nature came one morning when he turned up before breakfast carrying a ginger ale bottle cap in his beak.

"I won't be home for lunch," he said. His mate looked at the bottle cap.

"What's that for?"

Orville tried to act preoccupied, but it wasn't a success. He knew he'd better make a direct answer. "Well," he said, "I'm going to fly to Hastings-upon-Hudson and back, carrying this bottle cap."

The hen looked at him. "What's the idea of carrying a bottle cap up the river and back?"

"It's a flight," replied Orville, importantly.

"What do you mean, it's a *flight*? How else would you get there if you didn't fly?"

"Well, this is different," said Orville. "I want to prove the practicability of a round-trip flight between Madison Square and Hastings-upon-Hudson carrying a bottle cap."

There wasn't anything she could say to that. Orville stayed around for a few minutes, then after what seemed to his wife a great deal of unnecessary fluttering on the edge of the nest, he gripped the bottle cap firmly in his bill and departed. She noticed that he was flying faster than his usual gait, and was keeping an unusually straight course. Dutifully she watched him out of sight. "He'll be all tuckered out when he gets back," she thought to herself.

Orville, as the hen sparrow had expected, was tired that evening; but he seemed pleased with the results of the day.

"How did it go?" asked his wife, after he had deposited the bottle cap on the base of the statue of Admiral Farragut.

"Fine," said Orville. "I ran into a little rain the other side of Yonkers, but kept right on into fair weather again. It was only bad once, when ice began to form on my wings."

His wife looked at him intently. "I don't believe for a minute," she said, "that any ice started to form on your wings."

"Yes, it did," replied Orville.

He mooched about the nest for a while, and went into a few details for the benefit of his three children.

The nest occupied by Orville's family was in a tree in Madison Square near the Farragut statue. It was no neater than most sparrows' nests, and had been constructed eagerly of a wide variety of materials, including a kite string that hung down. One morning, a few days after the Hastings affair, Orville came to his wife with a question. "Are you through with that string?" he asked, nodding toward the trailing strand.

"Are you crazy?" she replied, sadly.

"I need it for something."

His wife gazed at him. "You're going to wreck the nest if you go pulling important strings out."

"I can get it out without hurting anything," said Orville. "I want it for a towline."

"A what?"

"Listen," said Orville, "I'm going to fly to 110th Street tomorrow, towing a wren."

The hen sparrow looked at him in disgust. "Where are you going to get a wren?"

"I can get a wren," he said, wisely. "It's all

arranged. I'm going to tow it till we get up about three thousand feet and then I'm going to cut the wren loose and it will glide down to a landing. I think I can prove the feasibility of towing a wren behind a sparrow."

Orville's wife did not say anything more. Grudgingly she helped him pull the kite string from the nest. Pretty strange doings, it seemed to her.

That evening Orville experimented alone with his string, tying it first to one foot and then the other. Next morning he was up at the crack of dawn and had the string all lashed to his right leg before breakfast. Putting in the half hitches had occasioned an immense lot of kicking around and had been fairly uncomfortable for the youngsters.

"For goodness' sake, Orville," said the hen sparrow, "can't you take it down to the ground and tie it on there?"

"Do me a favor," said Orville. "Put your finger on this knot while I draw it tight."

When the towline was arranged to his complete satisfaction, he flew down to the Square. There he immediately became the center of attention. His wife, noticing how other birds gathered around, was a bit piqued to see all this fuss made over Orville. Sparrows, she told herself, will gape at anything queer. She didn't believe that Orville had actually located a wren, and was genuinely surprised when one showed up—a tiny brown bird, with sharp eyes and a long, excitable tail. Orville greeted the wren cordially, hopping briskly round and round dragging the line. When about fifty sparrows and pigeons had congregated, he took the wren to one side. "I don't want to take off," he said, "till we get a weather report."

The news that the flight was to be delayed pending a report on weather conditions increased the interest of the other birds, and one of them volunteered to fly up to Central Park and back to find out how things were. He was back in ten minutes, and said the weather was clear. Orville, without any hesitation, motioned to the wren, who seized the towline in its beak, spread its wings rigidly, and waited. Then, at a signal from Orville, they both ran as fast as they could along the grass and jumped wildly into the air, Orville beating his wings hard. One foot, two feet, three feet off the ground they soared. Orville was working like a horse. He put everything he had into it, but soon it became clear that they hadn't enough altitude to clear a park bench that loomed up directly ahead—and the crash came. Orville landed with the string tangled in one wing, and the wren fell to the ground, stunned.

No further attempt to tow a wren was made that day. Orville felt sick, and so did the wren.

The incident, however, was the talk of the Square, and the other birds were still discussing it when night fell. When Orville's wife settled herself on the roosting branch beside her mate for the twittering vespers, she turned to him and said: "I believe you could have made it, Orville, if that darn bench hadn't been there."

"Sure we could have."

"Are you going to try again tomorrow?" There was a note of expectation in her voice.

"Yes."

The hen sparrow settled herself comfortably beside him. He, if any sparrow could, would prove the feasibility of towing a wren. For a minute she roosted there, happily. Then, when Orville had dropped off to sleep, she stole quietly down to the kitchen and busied herself making two tiny sandwiches, which she tied up in wax paper.

"I'll give him these tomorrow," she murmured, "just before he takes off."

FOR STUDY AND DISCUSSION

1. Fables usually employ animals that are given human qualities; the story teaches a moral, sometimes stated at the end, by one of the animals or by the author. What human qualities does White give Orville? Do you think he is truly imaginative and ingenious or just bird-brained? How does he differ from other birds, including his wife?

2. What attitude does Orville's wife take toward his round-trip flight carrying the bottle cap? Is her attitude toward his second venture markedly different?

3. Is the implied comparison with the first human flight by Orville Wright intended to say something about human ventures? In general, what do you think White is saying in the fable?

LANGUAGE AND VOCABULARY

Distinguishing Denotative from Connotative Meanings

In addition to their literal, or *denotative,* meanings, words may have suggested, or *connotative,* meanings. The word *tiger,* for example, *denotes* or names a particular member of the cat family: we have given the *denotation* when we have stated all the ways the tiger is different from all members of the class of animals to which it belongs. The word *tiger* also *connotes* or suggests different feelings to people: beauty to some, terror and mystery to others. The English poet William Blake describes a tiger in the opening lines of one of his poems:

Tiger! Tiger! burning bright
In the forests of the night,
What immortal hand or eye
Could frame thy fearful symmetry!

Beauty, terror, mystery, perfection of form— all of these *connotations* are evoked by Blake. None of them is a quality or feeling we find in the dictionary definition of the tiger.

In these sentences, what do the words White chooses to describe the birds denote, and what additional feelings and qualities do they connote?

1. Orville stayed around for a few minutes, then after what seemed to his wife a great deal of unnecessary *fluttering* on the edge of the nest, he gripped the bottle cap firmly in his bill and departed.
2. "He'll be all *tuckered* out when he gets back," she thought to herself.
3. He *mooched* about the nest for a while, and went into a few details for the benefit of his three children.
4. His wife, noticing how other birds gathered around, was a bit *piqued* to see all this fuss made over Orville.

FOR COMPOSITION

Writing a Fable

Write a fable of your own, comparing a situation with animal characters to a situation involving human beings. State your moral at the end, through one of the characters or in your own person. Add descriptive words to your fable, choosing them for their connotations. Try to choose words that suggest human as well as animal characteristics.

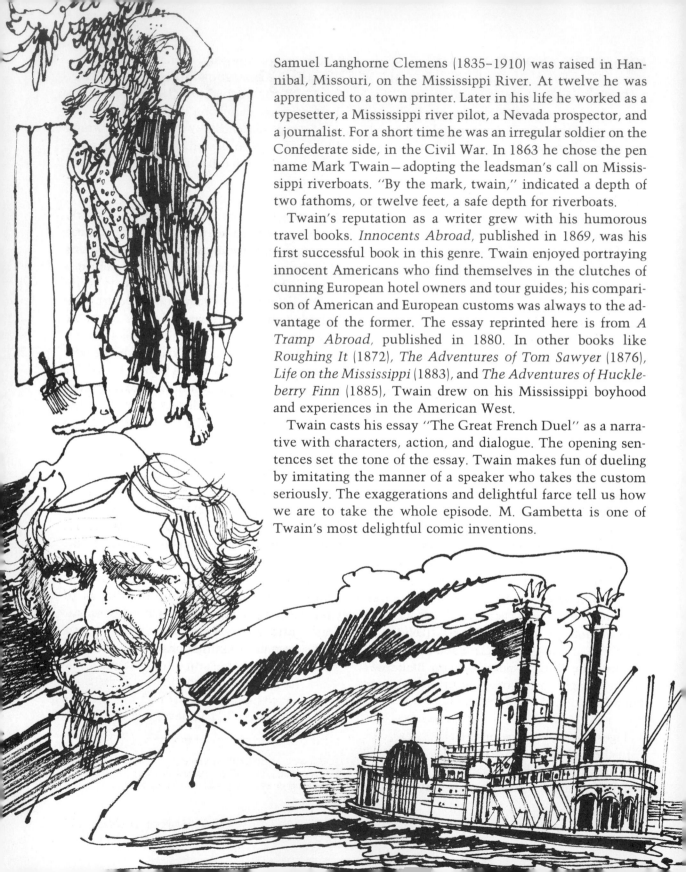

Samuel Langhorne Clemens (1835–1910) was raised in Hannibal, Missouri, on the Mississippi River. At twelve he was apprenticed to a town printer. Later in his life he worked as a typesetter, a Mississippi river pilot, a Nevada prospector, and a journalist. For a short time he was an irregular soldier on the Confederate side, in the Civil War. In 1863 he chose the pen name Mark Twain—adopting the leadsman's call on Mississippi riverboats. "By the mark, twain," indicated a depth of two fathoms, or twelve feet, a safe depth for riverboats.

Twain's reputation as a writer grew with his humorous travel books. *Innocents Abroad,* published in 1869, was his first successful book in this genre. Twain enjoyed portraying innocent Americans who find themselves in the clutches of cunning European hotel owners and tour guides; his comparison of American and European customs was always to the advantage of the former. The essay reprinted here is from *A Tramp Abroad,* published in 1880. In other books like *Roughing It* (1872), *The Adventures of Tom Sawyer* (1876), *Life on the Mississippi* (1883), and *The Adventures of Huckleberry Finn* (1885), Twain drew on his Mississippi boyhood and experiences in the American West.

Twain casts his essay "The Great French Duel" as a narrative with characters, action, and dialogue. The opening sentences set the tone of the essay. Twain makes fun of dueling by imitating the manner of a speaker who takes the custom seriously. The exaggerations and delightful farce tell us how we are to take the whole episode. M. Gambetta is one of Twain's most delightful comic inventions.

The Great French Duel

Mark Twain

Much as the modern French duel is ridiculed by certain smart people, it is in reality one of the most dangerous institutions of our day. Since it is always fought in the open air, the combatants are nearly sure to catch cold. M. Paul de Cassagnac, the most inveterate of the French duelists, has suffered so often in this way that he is at last a confirmed invalid; and the best physician in Paris has expressed the opinion that if he goes on dueling for fifteen or twenty years more—unless he forms the habit of fighting in a comfortable room where damps and drafts cannot intrude—he will eventually endanger his life. This ought to moderate the talk of those people who are so stubborn in maintaining that the French duel is the most health-giving of recreations because of the open-air exercise it affords. And it ought also to moderate that foolish talk about French duelists and socialist-hated monarchs being the only people who are immortal.

But it is time to get at my subject. As soon as I heard of the late fiery outbreak between M. Gambetta and M. Fourtou in the French Assembly, I knew that trouble must follow. I knew it because a long personal friendship with M. Gambetta had revealed to me the desperate and implacable nature of the man. Vast as are his physical proportions, I knew that the thirst for revenge would penetrate to the remotest frontiers of his person.

I did not wait for him to call on me, but went at once to him. As I had expected, I found the brave fellow steeped in a profound French calm. I say French calm, because

French calmness and English calmness have points of difference. He was moving swiftly back and forth among the debris of his furniture, now and then staving chance fragments of it across the room with his foot; grinding a constant grist of curses through his set teeth; and halting every little while to deposit another handful of his hair on the pile which he had been building of it on the table.

He threw his arms around my neck, bent me over his stomach to his breast, kissed me on both cheeks, hugged me four or five times, and then placed me in his own armchair. As soon as I had got well again, we began business at once.

I said I supposed he would wish me to act as his second, and he said, "Of course." I said I must be allowed to act under a French name, so that I might be shielded from obloquy[1] in my country, in case of fatal results. He winced here, probably at the suggestion that dueling was not regarded with respect in America. However, he agreed to my requirements. This accounts for the fact that in all the newspaper reports M. Gambetta's second was apparently a Frenchman.

First, we drew up my principal's[2] will. I insisted upon this, and stuck to my point. I said I had never heard of a man in his right mind going out to fight a duel without first making his will. He said he had never heard of a man

---

1. **obloquy** (ŏb′lə-kwē): disgrace.
2. **principal:** here, the combatant in a duel. The principal's aid or assistant is known as his second.

in his right mind doing anything of the kind. When he had finished the will, he wished to proceed to a choice of his "last words." He wanted to know how the following words, as a dying exclamation, struck me:

"I die for my God, for my country, for freedom of speech, for progress, and the universal brotherhood of man!"

I objected that this would require too lingering a death; it was a good speech for a consumptive, but not suited to the exigencies of the field of honor. We wrangled over a good many antemortem[3] outbursts, but I finally got him to cut his obituary down to this, which he copied into his memorandum book, purposing to get it by heart:

"I DIE THAT FRANCE MAY LIVE."

I said that this remark seemed to lack relevancy; but he said relevancy was a matter of no consequence in last words, what you wanted was thrill.

The next thing in order was the choice of weapons. My principal said he was not feeling well, and would leave that and the other details of the proposed meeting to me. Therefore I wrote the following note and carried it to M. Fourtou's friend:

> Sir: M. Gambetta accepts M. Fourtou's challenge, and authorizes me to propose Plessis-Piquet as the place of meeting; tomorrow morning at daybreak as the time; and axes as the weapons. I am, sir, with great respect,
>
> MARK TWAIN.

M. Fourtou's friend read this note, and shuddered. Then he turned to me, and said, with a suggestion of severity in his tone:

"Have you considered, sir, what would be the inevitable result of such a meeting as this?"

"Well, for instance, what *would* it be?"

"Bloodshed!"

"That's about the size of it," I said. "Now, if it is a fair question, what was your side proposing to shed?"

I had him there. He saw he had made a blunder, so he hastened to explain it away. He said he had spoken jestingly. Then he added that he and his principal would enjoy axes, and indeed prefer them, but such weapons were barred by the French code, and so I must change my proposal.

I walked the floor, turning the thing over in my mind, and finally it occurred to me that Gatling guns[4] at fifteen paces would be a likely way to get a verdict on the field of honor. So I framed this idea into a proposition.

But it was not accepted. The code was in the way again. I proposed rifles; then double-barreled shotguns; then, Colt's navy revolvers. These being all rejected, I reflected awhile, and sarcastically suggested brickbats at three quarters of a mile. I always hate to fool away a humorous thing on a person who has no perception of humor; and it filled me with bitterness when this man went soberly away to submit the last proposition to his principal.

He came back presently and said his principal was charmed with the idea of brickbats at three quarters of a mile, but must decline on account of the danger to disinterested parties passing between. Then I said:

"Well, I am at the end of my string, now. Perhaps *you* would be good enough to suggest a weapon? Perhaps you have even had one in your mind all the time?"

---

3. **antemortem:** made before death.

4. **Gatling gun:** an early kind of machine gun.

His countenance brightened, and he said with alacrity:

"Oh, without doubt, monsieur!"

So he fell to hunting in his pockets—pocket after pocket, and he had plenty of them—muttering all the while, "Now, what could I have done with them?"

At last he was successful. He fished out of his vest pocket a couple of little things which I carried to the light and ascertained to be pistols. They were single-barreled and silver-mounted, and very dainty and pretty. I was not able to speak for emotion. I silently hung one of them on my watch chain, and returned the other. My companion in crime now unrolled a postage stamp containing several cartridges, and gave me one of them. I asked if he meant to signify by this that our men were to be allowed but one shot apiece. He replied that the French code permitted no more. I then begged him to go on and suggest a distance, for my mind was growing weak and confused under the strain which had been put upon it. He named sixty-five yards. I nearly lost my patience. I said:

"Sixty-five yards, with these instruments? Squirt guns would be deadlier at fifty. Consider, my friend, you and I are banded together to destroy life, not make it eternal."

But with all my persuasions, all my arguments, I was only able to get him to reduce the distance to thirty-five yards; and even this concession he made with reluctance, and said with a sigh:

"I wash my hands of this slaughter; on your head be it."

There was nothing for me but to go home to my old lionheart and tell my humiliating story. When I entered, M. Gambetta was laying his last lock of hair upon the altar. He sprang toward me, exclaiming:

"You have made the fatal arrangements—I see it in your eye!"

"I have."

His face paled a trifle, and he leaned upon the table for support. He breathed thick and heavily for a moment or two, so tumultuous were his feelings; then he hoarsely whispered:

"The weapon, the weapon! Quick! what is the weapon?"

"This!" and I displayed that silver-mounted thing. He cast but one glance at it, then swooned ponderously to the floor.

When he came to, he said mournfully:

"The unnatural calm to which I have subjected myself has told upon my nerves. But away with weakness! I will confront my fate like a man and a Frenchman."

He rose to his feet, and assumed an attitude which for sublimity has never been approached by man, and has seldom been surpassed by statues. Then he said, in his deep bass tones:

"Behold, I am calm, I am ready; reveal to me the distance."

"Thirty-five yards." . . .

I could not lift him up, of course; but I rolled him over and poured water down his back. He presently came to, and said:

"Thirty-five yards—without a rest? But why ask? Since murder was that man's intentions, why should he palter with small details? But mark you one thing: in my fall the world shall see how the chivalry of France meets death."

After a long silence he asked:

"Was nothing said about that man's family standing up with him, as an offset to my bulk? But no matter; I would not stoop to make such a suggestion; if he is not noble enough to suggest it himself, he is welcome to this advantage, which no honorable man would take."

He now sank into a sort of stupor of reflection, which lasted some minutes; after which he broke silence with:

"The hour—what is the hour fixed for the collision?"

"Dawn, tomorrow."

He seemed greatly surprised, and immediately said:

"Insanity! I never heard of such a thing. Nobody is abroad at such an hour."

"That is the reason I named it. Do you mean to say you want an audience?"

"It is no time to bandy words. I am astonished that M. Fourtou should ever have agreed to so strange an innovation. Go at once and require a later hour."

I ran downstairs, threw open the front door, and almost plunged into the arms of M. Fourtou's second. He said:

"I have the honor to say that my principal strenuously objects to the hour chosen, and begs you will consent to change it to half past nine."

"Any courtesy, sir, which it is in our power to extend is at the service of your excellent principal. We agree to the proposed change of time."

"I beg you to accept the thanks of my client." Then he turned to a person behind him, and said, "You hear, M. Noir, the hour is altered to half past nine." Whereupon M. Noir bowed, expressed his thanks, and went away. My accomplice continued:

"If agreeable to you, your chief surgeons and ours shall proceed to the field in the same carriage, as is customary."

"It is entirely agreeable to me, and I am obliged to you for mentioning the surgeons, for I am afraid I should not have thought of them. How many shall I want? I suppose two or three will be enough?"

"Two is the customary number for each party. I refer to 'chief' surgeons; but considering the exalted positions occupied by our clients, it will be well and decorous that each of us appoint several consulting surgeons, from among the highest in the profession. These will come in their own private carriages. Have you engaged a hearse?"

"Bless my stupidity, I never thought of it! I will attend to it right away. I must seem very ignorant to you; but you must try to overlook that, because I have never had any experience of such a swell duel as this before. I have had a good deal to do with duels on the Pacific coast, but I see now that they were crude affairs. A hearse—sho! we used to leave the elected lying around loose, and let anybody cord them up and cart them off that wanted to. Have you anything further to suggest?"

"Nothing, except that the head undertakers shall ride together, as is usual. The subordinates and mutes[5] will go on foot, as is also usual. I will see you at eight o'clock in the morning, and we will then arrange the order of the procession. I have the honor to bid you a good day."

I returned to my client, who said, "Very well; at what hour is the engagement to begin?"

"Half past nine."

"Very good indeed. Have you sent the fact to the newspapers?"

"*Sir!* If after our long and intimate friendship you can for a moment deem me capable of so base a treachery——"

"Tut, tut! What words are these, my dear friend? Have I wounded you? Ah, forgive me; I am overloading you with labor. Therefore go on with the other details, and drop this one from your list. The bloody-minded Fourtou will be sure to attend to it. Or I myself—yes, to make certain, I will drop a note to my journalistic friend, M. Noir——"

"Oh, come to think of it, you may save yourself the trouble; that other second has informed M. Noir."

---

5. **mutes:** mourners hired by the undertaker.

"H'm! I might have known it. It is just like that Fourtou, who always wants to make a display."

At half past nine in the morning the procession approached the field of Plessis-Piquet in the following order: first came our carriage—nobody in it but M. Gambetta and myself; then a carriage containing M. Fourtou and his second; then a carriage containing two poet-orators, and these had MS.[6] funeral orations projecting from their breast pockets; then a carriage containing the head surgeons and their cases of instruments; then eight private carriages containing consulting surgeons; then a hack containing a coroner; then the two hearses; then a carriage containing the head undertakers; then a train of assistants and mutes on foot; and after these came plodding through the fog a long procession of camp followers, police, and citizens generally. It was a noble turnout, and would have made a fine display if we had had thinner weather.

There was no conversation. I spoke several times to my principal, but I judge he was not aware of it, for he always referred to his notebook and muttered absently, "I die that France may live."

Arrived on the field, my fellow second and I paced off the thirty-five yards, and then drew lots for choice of position. This latter was but an ornamental ceremony, for all the choices were alike in such weather. These preliminaries being ended, I went to my principal and asked him if he was ready. He spread himself out to his full width, and said in a stern voice, "Ready! Let the batteries be charged."

The loading was done in the presence of duly constituted witnesses. We considered it best to perform this delicate service with the assistance of a lantern, on account of the state of the weather. We now placed our men.

6. **MS.**: manuscript.

At this point the police noticed that the public had massed themselves together on the right and left of the field; they therefore begged a delay, while they should put these poor people in a place of safety. The request was granted.

The police having ordered the two multitudes to take positions behind the duelists, we were once more ready. The weather growing still more opaque, it was agreed between myself and the other second that before giving the fatal signal we should each deliver a loud whoop to enable the combatants to ascertain each other's whereabouts.

I now returned to my principal, and was distressed to observe that he had lost a good deal of his spirit. I tried my best to hearten him. I said, "Indeed, sir, things are not as bad as they seem. Considering the character of the weapons, the limited number of shots allowed, the generous distance, the impenetrable solidity of the fog, and the added fact that one of the combatants is one-eyed and the other cross-eyed and nearsighted, it seems to me that this conflict need not necessarily be fatal. There are chances that both of you may survive. Therefore, cheer up; do not be downhearted."

This speech had so good an effect that my principal immediately stretched forth his hand and said, "I am myself again; give me the weapon."

I laid it, all lonely and forlorn, in the center of the vast solitude of his palm. He gazed at it and shuddered. And still mournfully contemplating it, he murmured, in a broken voice:

"Alas, it is not death I dread, but mutilation."

I heartened him once more, and with such success that he presently said, "Let the tragedy begin. Stand at my back; do not desert me in this solemn hour, my friend."

I gave him my promise. I now assisted him to point his pistol toward the spot where I judged his adversary to be standing, and cautioned him to listen well and further guide himself by my fellow second's whoop. Then I propped myself against M. Gambetta's back, and raised a rousing "Whoop-ee!" This was answered from out the far distances of the fog, and I immediately shouted:

"One—two—three—*fire!*"

Two little sounds like *spit! spit!* broke upon my ear, and in the same instant I was crushed to the earth under a mountain of flesh. Bruised as I was, I was still able to catch a faint accent from above, to this effect:

"I die . . . for . . . perdition take it, what *is* it I die for? . . . oh, yes — FRANCE! I die that France may live!"

The surgeons swarmed around with their probes in their hands, and applied their microscopes to the whole area of M. Gambetta's person, with the happy result of finding nothing in the nature of a wound. Then a scene ensued which was in every way gratifying and inspiring.

The two gladiators fell upon each other's necks, with floods of proud and happy tears; that other second embraced me; the surgeons, the orators, the undertakers, the police, everybody embraced, everybody congratulated, everybody cried, and the whole atmosphere was filled with praise and with joy unspeakable.

It seemed to me then that I would rather be a hero of a French duel than a crowned and sceptered monarch.

When the commotion had somewhat subsided, the body of surgeons held a consultation, and after a good deal of debate decided that with proper care and nursing there was reason to believe that I would survive my injuries. My internal hurts were deemed the most serious, since it was apparent that a broken rib had penetrated my left lung, and that many of my organs had been pressed out so far to one side or the other of where they belonged, that it was doubtful if they would ever learn to perform their functions in such remote and unaccustomed localities. They then set my left arm in two places, pulled my right hip into its socket again, and reelevated my nose. I was an object of great interest, and even admiration; and many sincere and warm-hearted persons had themselves introduced to me, and said they were proud to know the only man who had been hurt in a French duel in forty years.

I was placed in an ambulance at the very head of the procession; and thus with gratifying éclat[7] I was marched into Paris, the most conspicuous figure in that great spectacle, and deposited at the hospital.

The cross of the Legion of Honor has been conferred upon me. However, few escape that distinction.

Such is the true version of the most memorable private conflict of the age.

I have no complaints to make against anyone. I acted for myself, and I can stand the consequences. Without boasting, I think I may say I am not afraid to stand before a modern French duelist, but as long as I keep in my right mind I will never consent to stand behind one again.

7. **éclat** (ā-klä′): show, brilliance.

FOR STUDY AND DISCUSSION

1. The first sentence of the essay leads the reader to think that Twain will treat the subject of dueling in a serious way. How does Twain comically deflate this idea in the rest of the first paragraph?

2. What does Twain show about the motives for dueling through the behavior of M. Gambetta? What does Twain find comical in M. Gambetta's discussion of his "obituary," "I die that France may live"?

3. What elements of exaggeration and ridicule does Twain introduce in the discussion of weapons?

4. Twain says: "I always hate to fool away a humorous thing on a person who has no sense of humor." What does this statement reveal about Twain's attitude toward dueling?

5. What does Twain find comical about the procession to the duel, as well as the duel itself? Events are ironic when their outcome is different from what is expected. What is ironic about the way the duel ends?

6. Satire seeks to correct or change a way of acting or thinking through exaggeration and ridicule. Twain is satirizing more than dueling. In what way are his other targets general human attitudes or traits, even professions?

7. An informal essay often reveals aspects of the author's personality. What personal qualities does Twain reveal in this essay? What would you say is his feeling about pompous behavior and pretentiousness?

LANGUAGE AND VOCABULARY

Recognizing Satirical Language

Successful writing depends on the choice of the right words, strategically placed in the sentence and paragraph. Twain, for example, saves the clinching comic phrase for the end of the sentence:

> Since it is always fought in the open air, the combatants are nearly sure to catch cold.

Compare Twain's sentence with this revision of it:

> The combatants are nearly sure to catch cold since it is always fought in the open air.

The humor has been deflated: the "punch" of the original sentence is gone. Find other examples in the essay of this strategic use of the end of the sentence.

What makes the language of M. Gambetta pompous? What would be equivalent words and expressions of people entering a fight today?

Twain says that he had "never had any experience of such a swell duel as this before." Use your dictionary to determine the meaning of *swell*. Do we use the word with this sense today?

Given the dictionary meaning of *gladiators*, what is comical about Twain's use of this word to describe the duellists?

FOR COMPOSITION

Writing a Humorous Sketch

Write a humorous sketch of an event, imitating a serious account of it, and deflating the people involved in the event through satirizing their language.

MacKinlay Kantor (1904–1977) was born and raised in Webster City, Iowa. He worked for newspapers and in advertising before becoming a novelist. His major fiction has been concerned with Midwestern life and with historical subjects; his novel, *Andersonville,* for which Kantor received the Pulitzer Prize in 1956, is about the Confederate prison camp in Andersonville, Georgia, during the Civil War. The essay reprinted here is from Kantor's essays on Hamilton County, Iowa, which Kantor shows to be typical of the Middle West. Kantor treats the essay as a highly personal form, connecting his various comments and reminiscences through his feelings of the moment. We listen to Kantor as we listen to an older friend or relative talk about his childhood, letting his imagination range freely over time and place.

The Basketball Game

MacKinlay Kantor

In most portions of Hamilton County, throughout the winter months, scholastic basketball occupies the attention and energy and emotion of young people to an extent which would have seemed unbelievable to those who lived in the days before basketball was invented by one nice Mr. James Naismith for his YMCA classes. That happened in Springfield, Massachusetts, in 1891.

In the United States alone, more than one hundred and twenty million people were spectators at the games last year. Thus it seems odd to realize that, statistically, there are many millions of Americans still living who are older than basketball itself.

(Maybe so. But I remember being guided over scorched terrain under the Yucatán[1] sun, until we stood on a paved court next to the ruins at Chichén-Itzá or Uxmal or one of those places. I asked our guide about a stone ring cemented against the ancient wall, and he said that the Maya used it in a game they played. The idea was to toss a ball through that stone ring; and the idea of the opposing team was to prevent you from doing so. Kind of like basketball, wasn't it? . . . Except that the captain of the losing team paid a gentle little forfeit: he had his heart cut out of his body. Those Maya really played for keeps, whether they called it basketball or no.)

In the days when this author went to school in his hometown in Hamilton County, we had a player named Merritt Creeley. He was a popular boy . . . for some reason his nickname was Dog. Dog Greeley was the star shooter of our school team. That was before rules were amended to compel any player who was

---

1. **Yucatán** (yōō′kə-tän′): the Yucatán Peninsula, a region including parts of Mexico, northern British Honduras, and Guatemala.

fouled—and thus gained a free throw—to try for that extra point *himself*. Not so in 1922. Whenever a team was awarded a free throw, some man on the team who specialized in this art could undertake the shot from the established free-throw line: fifteen feet from the basket.

Dog was an unimpressive figure—flat-chested, lounging in his gait. Not the beau ideal of a basketball player or any other sort of athlete. . . . Well, one day he had a little falling-out or a little run-in, whatever you want to call it, with the basketball coach. This seems mysterious now; but I can't call up Merritt Greeley on the telephone and ask him what that dispute was all about. He has gone to a Realm where Long Distance does not function.

He was in fact a mild-mannered youth, easygoing as to disposition. Maybe the coach, himself very young at the time, decided that he must establish an awesome reputation as a martinet. Whatever the reason, he banished Dog Greeley. Our best shooter, and he was thrown off the squad.

What it amounted to was wiping out our team's chances for the rest of the year. Oh, sure—there were a lot of good players still left on the squad. But since every team always had a specialist for free throws, we were handicapped. Our team went down to defeat, game after game.

People came around and pleaded with the coach to reinstate Greeley, but he said that they were just wasting their time.

Greeley went to all the games just the same. He sat in the audience on the sidelines and punished himself for whatever sins he'd committed, in watching the rival teams' triumph.

Until you've seen a high school basketball game with the crowd going wild. . . . Well, I guess you hain't seen nothing yet, far as young people are concerned.

Game and equipment as used in 1892. (From lecture material of Amos Alonzo Stagg)
Hickox Library

. . . So it was the end of the first half, with the home team behind, visitors leading. Say it was Visitors 34, Home Team 31. Had we been able to capitalize on free throws subsequent to the fouls, we would have been well ahead. But the boys who tossed the balls weren't displaying any accuracy. Each time a ball toppled clumsily off the backboard a groan would go up from the hometowners who clogged balconies and benches; and a shriek of glee would rise from the smaller mass of visiting fans in their special section.

. . . So the whistle had blown, and players went darting off to the locker rooms. And, for some reason or other, some official allowed the ball to get away from him. I guess he tossed it to another official, and the other official missed the catch.

Anyway the big lively round ball went rolling and bouncing all the way down the playing court to where Dog Greeley sat on a front row bench in his shabby sweater. The ball came and kissed against his ankle, as much as to say, "Hi, Greeley. Where you been lately?"

Dog sort of sighed. He leaned over and took the ball between his hands. He stood up and—

The basket at the far end of the court was over a hundred feet away as the crow might fly (if any crows had been flying in that gym). With the same easy motion, as he lifted the ball in his hands and as he rose, Dog tossed it the length of the playing court. The ball sailed high and far. It dropped through that basket so easily that it scarcely disturbed the mesh hanging from the ring.

You ought to have heard the wail which went up from local fans. Our coach, belatedly heading for the locker room, had turned around, and he saw the whole thing. He stood for a moment, hands on hips, glaring at Merritt Greeley. Then he turned toward the door. Greeley had slouched back on his bench once more, and gave a big yawn.

left: (Knicks–Hawks) Madison Square Garden, New York, 4/4/78

right: (Jazz–Bulls) Superdome, New Orleans, 10/31/78

The fury of the crowd followed the coach all the way to the door. Booooo . . . booooo . . . booooo!

Nearly fifty years later, another coach says, *I'm going to put you in there for Oscarsen. You remember to pop it to Fushard, underneath. I'll bet I've told Oscarsen to do that a hundred times, so that's why he's coming out of the game. Now listen, Buster. We're playing a three-two zone press, and dropping into a one-two-two. Get in there and do a job, see?*

A hometown crowd in Wright County watches the visiting team from Hamilton County, right next door. Too bad . . . they don't know it now, but the Hamilton County team is going to win.

The young, the oh so tender young, the bellowing, the squealing, the strong, the bright ones, the dullards, the way-out types, the square types; the ones just ready to graduate and thus achieve that momentary elation of maturity; little brothers and sisters fetched along; everybody's got to go to the game, everybody would die if they couldn't go to the game; pity the absent people at home with flu, or maybe they slipped on the ice and got a broken arm or a broken ankle, and they couldn't go to the game; look at them, try to hear them if you can, no you can't truly hear them, your ears won't accept the tempest, the whistles, the shrieks, the howls, the hullabaloo; it isn't the cheerleaders who are doing it . . . see them sitting up there on that barricade, watching, resting between bouts of more studied cheering, doing their personal yelling about the game.

Coach says, *Twelve always does the same thing. Get this now: he does a double pump left, then shoots or drives right. Don't follow his fake, and you'll have him bottled up. Make him prove he can drive left.*

Oh yes, get Wickstrom out of chaser, and back underneath the basket. It's only the second quarter, and he already has three fouls.

These players aren't from Drake or Tulsa, they're not from Purdue or UCLA, they're not any players from North Carolina. But—who knows? Maybe one of these times some of them will be starring for Drake University. You never know.

They might not look like All-Americans, but they all look like Americans.

Who can guess what blows will strike those youthful faces in the crowd, or estimate the joys that will charm them? What will life do to a bespectacled blonde cheerleader who somehow got mixed up with the audience; and what will she do to the lives around her? What will the years bring to a plump-faced girl with a wide-open mouth, to a meditative little boy in sneakers, to another blonde who presses her hands together in an agony of prayer; and, in turn, how will *they* affect the decades ahead?

(Let us laugh in unison, and discontinue such idle speculation. Neither you nor I know what life will offer us—next week, or next month, or tomorrow, or in the next ten minutes. Nor, in turn, do we know just whom we will hurt, or whom we will sustain.)

Switch to a four zone, with Brayce playing man-to-man on Twelve. You and Fushard get underneath, and McCool and Wickstrom outside. . . . If Twenty-two or Thirty-two prove they can hit, play a four man-to-man, with Wickstrom dropping off Forty and playing zone.

I can't win this game from the bench. It's up to you guys out there on the court. Just play like you have all year, and you can take this game.

FOR STUDY AND DISCUSSION

1. The first two paragraphs establish the background and popularity of basketball in the United States. Why do you think Kantor follows these paragraphs with the parenthetical information about the Mayan game that resembled basketball?

2. What is the difference between the coach who benches Dog Greeley and the coach who sends in the substitute for Oscarsen?

3. One of Kantor's themes is life's unpredictability: "Neither you nor I know what life will offer us—next week, or next month, or tomorrow, or in the next ten minutes." Can you suggest how this theme is related to basketball?

4. How does the form of Kantor's essay suggest life's unpredictability—its lack of continuity and its interruptions?

5. What impression do you get of Kantor as a person?

LANGUAGE AND VOCABULARY

Using Context Clues
Using context clues, explain the italicized word in each of the following sentences. Check your answers in a dictionary. Then use the word in a sentence of your own:

1. Dog was an unimpressive figure—flat-chested, *lounging* in his *gait*.
2. Maybe the coach, himself very young at the time, decided that he must establish an awesome reputation as a *martinet*.
3. . . . a shriek of *glee* would rise from the smaller mass of visiting fans in their special section.
4. Our coach, *belatedly* heading for the locker room, had turned around, and he saw the whole thing.

5. Greeley had *slouched* back on his bench once more, and gave a big yawn.
6. Let us laugh in *unison*, and discontinue such idle *speculation*.

Distinguishing Language Styles
Kantor writes from the viewpoint of many people—a man remembering basketball in his youth, an observer of a present-day basketball game, a teenager in the bleachers. For each of these people he creates a special language or "usage." The older man is formal in his words and sentences, though he can imitate the slang and rolling sentences of the teenager; the modern coach talks in a language different from both the older man and the teenager. Find examples of each of these differences in words and sentences.

Recognizing Jargon
Every sport has its special language or jargon—words, expressions, turns of phrases and idioms shared by players, coaches, and fans. What examples of this special language do you find in the essay?

FOR COMPOSITION

Describing an Event from Different Viewpoints
Describe a baseball, football, or hockey game or a comparable event from the viewpoint of several people—a player, the coach, a parent, a stranger, a teenager watching the game. Shift from one viewpoint to another, as Kantor does, conveying the change in viewpoint through a change in language.

The American naturalist Edwin Way Teale (1899–1980) was one of America's foremost authors of nature books. *The American Seasons*, his major work, consists of four volumes: *North with the Spring, Journey into Summer, Autumn Across America*, and *Wandering Through Winter*. The last of these volumes was awarded the Pulitzer Prize in 1966.

Teale was raised in Joliet, Illinois, but up to the age of sixteen lived most of his summers with his grandparents on their farm in northern Indiana, close to the dunes of Lake Michigan. It is this world that Teale describes in the essay reprinted here. Teale uses an important form of analysis, that of process—here, a natural process rather than an artificial or a historical one.

In reading this essay, notice that each paragraph focuses on a single idea and usually states that idea in the opening sentence. At every point in the essay, the reader sees where he or she is going. Yet Teale manages his transitions skillfully: he does not clutter the essays with signposts that detract attention from ideas and details. Teale writes in simple language, in a familiar style that never calls attention to itself. We hear always the voice of the speaking man—of a human being who communicates in writing as he would converse with us, seriously, about what he has observed in his lifetime.

The Death of a Tree

Edwin Way Teale

For a great tree death comes as a gradual transformation. Its vitality ebbs slowly. Even when life has abandoned it entirely it remains a majestic thing. On some hilltop a dead tree may dominate the landscape for miles around. Alone among living things it retains its character and dignity after death. Plants wither; animals disintegrate. But a dead tree may be as arresting, as filled with personality, in death as it is in life. Even in its final moments, when the massive trunk lies prone and it has moldered into a ridge covered with mosses and fungi, it arrives at a fitting and a noble end. It enriches and refreshes the earth. And later, as part of other green and growing things, it rises again.

The death of the great white oak which gave our Indiana homestead its name and which played such an important part in our daily lives was so gentle a transition that we never knew just when it ceased to be a living organism.

It had stood there, toward the sunset from the farmhouse, rooted in that same spot for two hundred years or more. How many generations of red squirrels had rattled up and down its gray-black bark! How many generations of robins had sung from its upper branches! How many humans, from how many lands, had paused beneath its shade!

The passing of this venerable giant made a profound impression upon my young mind. Just what caused its death was then a mystery. Looking back, I believe the deep drainage ditches, which had been cut through the dune-country marshes a few years before, had lowered the water table just sufficiently to affect the roots of the old oak. Millions of delicate root tips were injured. As they began to wither, the whole vast underground system of nourishment broke down and the tree was no longer able to send sap to the upper branches.

Like a river flowing into a desert, the life stream of the tree dwindled and disappeared before it reached the topmost twigs. They died first. The leaf at the tip of each twig, the last to unfold, was the first to wither and fall. Then, little by little, the twig itself became dead and dry. This process of dissolution, in the manner of a movie run backward, reversed the development of growth. Just as, cell by cell, the twig had grown outward toward the tip, so now death spread, cell by cell, backward from the tip.

Sadly we watched the blight work from twig to branch, from smaller branch to larger branch, until the whole top of the tree was dead and bare. For years those dry, barkless upper branches remained intact. Their wood became gray and polished by the winds. When thunderstorms rolled over the farm from the northwest the dead branches shone like silver against the black and swollen sky. Robins and veeries sang from these lofty perches, gilded by the sunset long after the purple of advancing dusk filled the spaces below.

Then, one by one, their resiliency gone, the topmost limbs crashed to earth, carried away by the fury of stormwinds. In fragments and patches, bark from the upper trunk littered the ground below. The protecting skin of the tree was broken. In through the gaps poured a host of microscopic enemies, the organisms of decay.

Ghostly white fungus penetrated into the sapwood. It worked its way downward along the unused tubes, those vertical channels through which had flowed the lifeblood of the oak. The continued flow of this sap might have kept out the fungus. But sap rises only to branches clothed with leaves. As each limb became blighted and leafless, the sap level dropped to the next living branch below. And close on the heels of this descending fluid followed the fungus. From branch to branch its silent, deadly descent continued.

Soft and flabby, so unsubstantial it can be crushed without apparent pressure between a thumb and forefinger, this pale fungus is yet able to penetrate through the hardest of woods. This amazing and paradoxical feat is accomplished by means of digestive enzymes which the fungus secretes and which dissolve the wood as strong acids might do. These fungus enzymes, science has learned, are virtually the same as those produced by the single-celled protozoa which live in the bodies of the termites and enable those insects to digest the cellulose in wood.

Advancing in the form of thin white threads, which branch again and again, the fungus works its way from side to side as well as downward through the trunk of a dying tree. Beyond the reach of our eyes the fungus kept spreading within the body of the old oak, branching into a kind of vast, interlacing root system of its own, pale and ghostly.

Behind the fungus, along the dead upper trunk, yellow hammers drummed on the dry wood. I saw them, with their chisel-bills, hewing out nesting holes which, in turn, admitted new organisms of decay. In effect, the dissolution of a great tree is like the slow turning of an immense wheel of life. Each stage of its decline and decay brings a whole new, interdependent population of dwellers and their parasites.

Even while the lower branches of the oak were still green, insect wreckers were already at work above them. First to arrive were the bark beetles. In the earliest stages their fare was the tender inner layer of the bark, the living bond between the trunk and its covering. As death spread downward in the oak, as freezing and storms loosened the bark, the beetles descended, foot by foot. Some of them left behind elaborate patterns, branching mazes of tunnels that took on the appearance of fantastic "thousand-leggers" engraved on wood.

During the winter when I was twelve years old a gale of abnormal force swept the Great Lakes region. Gusts reached almost hurricane proportions. Weakened by the work of the fungus, bacteria, woodpeckers, and beetles, the whole top of the tree snapped off some seventy feet from the ground. After that the progress of its dissolution was rapid.

Finally the last of the lower leaves disappeared. The green badge of life returned no more. On summer days the sound of the wind sweeping through the old oak had a winter shrillness. No more was there the rustling of a multitude of leaves above our hammock; no more was there the "plump!" of falling acorns. Leaves and acorns, life and progress, were at an end.

In the days that followed, as the bark loosened to the base, the wheel of life, which had its hub in the now-dead oak, grew larger.

I saw carpenter ants hurrying this way and that over the lower tree trunk. Ichneumon flies, trailing deadly, drill-like ovipositors,[1] hovered above the bark in search of buried larvae on which to lay their eggs. Carpenter bees, their black abdomens glistening like patent leather, bit their way into the dry wood of the dead branches. Click beetles and sow bugs and small spiders found security beneath fragments of the loosened bark. And around the base of the tree swift-legged carabid beetles hunted their insect prey under cover of darkness.

Yellowish-brown, the wood flour of the powder-post beetles began to sift about the foot of the oak. It, in turn, attracted the larvae of the darkling beetles. Thus, link by link, the chain of life expanded. To the expert eye the

1. **Ichneumon** (ĭk-nōō′mən); **ovipositor** (ō′və-pŏz′ə-tər).

condition of the wood, the bark, the ground about the base of the oak—all told of the action of the interrelated forms of life attracted by the death and decay of a tree.

But below all this activity, beyond the power of human sight to detect, other changes were taking place. The underground root system, comprising almost as much wood as was visible in the tree rising above ground, was also altering.

Fungus, entering the damaged root tips or working downward from the infected trunk, followed the sap channels and hastened decay. The great main roots, spreading out as far as the widest branches of the tree itself, altered rapidly. Their fibers grew brittle; their old pliancy disappeared; their bark split and loosened. The breakdown of the upper tree found its counterpart, within the darkness of the earth, in the dissolution of the lower roots.

I remember well the day the great oak came down. I was fourteen at the time. Gramp had measured distances and planned his cutting operations in advance. He chopped away for fully half an hour before he had a V-shaped bite cut exactly in position to bring the trunk crashing in the place desired. Hours filled with the whine of the crosscut saw followed.

Then came the great moment. A few last, quick strokes. A slow, deliberate swaying. The crack of parting fibers. Then a long "swoo-sh!" that rose in pitch as the towering trunk arced downward at increasing speed. There followed a vast tumult of crashing, crackling sound; the dance of splintered branches; a haze of dead, swirling grass. Then a slow settling of small objects and silence. All was over. Lone oak was gone.

Gram, I remember, brushed away what she remarked was dust in her eyes with a corner of her apron and went inside. She had known and loved that one great tree since she had come to the farm as a bride of sixteen. She had seen it under all conditions and through eyes colored by many moods. Her children had grown up under its shadow and I, a grandchild, had known its shade. Its passing was like the passing of an old, old friend. For all of us there seemed an empty space in our sky in the days that followed.

Gramp and I set to work, attacking the fallen giant. Great piles of cordwood, mounds of broken branches for kindling, grew around the prostrate trunk as the weeks went by. Eventually only the huge, circular table of the low stump remained—reddish-brown and slowly dissolving into dust.

For two winters wood from the old oak fed the kitchen range and the dining-room stove. It had a clean, well-seasoned smell. And it burned with a clear and leaping flame, continuing—unlike the quickly consumed poplar and elm—for an admirable length of time. Like the old tree itself, the fibers of these sticks had character and endurance to the very end.

FOR STUDY AND DISCUSSION

1. Teale states his central idea, or thesis, in his opening paragraph. Death comes to the tree as a "gradual transformation." How does this transformation make the death of the tree different from the death of plants and animals? What point is Teale making about the tree in the whole paragraph?

2. How do the details of the description illustrate the point that "Each stage of its decline and decay brings a whole new, interdependent population of dwellers and their parasites"? How does this process of dissolution explain the phrase, "the slow turning of an immense wheel of life"?

3. What are the three main stages in the death of the tree, and how does Teale keep them in focus for the reader?

4. How do the details of the final paragraphs relate the tree to the human world? How does Teale restate his thesis in the final paragraph?

FIGURES OF SPEECH

In discussing the possible cause of the tree's death, and the beginning of the process, Teale uses metaphor and simile. The tree is metaphorically a "venerable giant," as if it possessed human qualities. This particular kind of metaphor is called *personification*. How are these qualities suggested in the details of the living tree? What comparisons or similies does Teale use to make the process of dying concrete?

LANGUAGE AND VOCABULARY

Determining Exact Meanings
Use your dictionary to determine the exact meaning of each of the following words:

blight   dissolution   molder
disintegrate   dwindle   wither

Write sentences of your own, using each word to show its exact meaning.

Recognizing Parallelism
Teale occasionally arranges sentences in parallel order to stress the similarity in ideas:

How many generations of robins had sung from its upper branches!

How many humans, from how many lands, had paused beneath its shade!

Phrases and clauses within a sentence can be balanced in the same way: "How many humans, from how many lands." Find examples of other phrases or clauses balanced in the same way.

FOR COMPOSITION

Describing a Process
Describe a process you have performed many times—for example, repairing a bicycle tire or boning a fish. Write to an audience that has never performed this process and therefore needs to be informed about the tools needed and the details of each step in the process.

Writing an Outline of the Essay
Teale's essay has three main parts, corresponding to the stages in the death of the tree. The opening and concluding paragraphs provide an introduction and a final comment on these stages. Write an outline of the essay, making the first part (I) correspond to the first stage of the dying process. Present the opening paragraph as a thesis statement introducing the outline.

Anaïs Nin (1903–1977) wrote novels and short stories, but is probably best known for her diaries, which she began at the age of eleven. Her travel writing is particularly rich in sensory details that allow the reader to imagine fully the scene or place being described.

Travel literature combines narrative with description and therefore is often complex in its organization. Where narrative calls for events arranged in chronological order (the order of time), description calls for a spatial order. This means that the writer can begin with a panoramic or bird's-eye view of the scene: an impression of the scene from a distant point. Or the writer may begin with a part of the scene and move to other parts, gradually building the impression. At the same time, the requirements of narrative must be met: the reader must know at what time of the day or night the scene is being described; the reader must understand why the writer is shifting focus from one part of the scene to another. Anaïs Nin chooses to begin with an impression of the Moroccan city of Fez before she takes the reader into its streets and shops. Her topic sentences meet the needs of description and narrative perfectly; for they focus the reader's attention, at the same time indicating when and why the focus has shifted.

The Labyrinthine° City of Fez *Anaïs Nin*

Fez was created for the delight of our five senses. My first impression is a fragrant odor of cedarwood from the furniture of the Hotel Palais Jamai, a smell that reappears in the *souk*, or street, amidst the intense activity of the carpenters. My room already bears the colors of Fez: blue tile, copper tray, copper-colored draperies. When I open them, the whole city of Fez lies before my eyes. The earth-colored houses huddle together, following the sinuosities of the hills, encircling every now and then a mosque with its minaret of green tiles shining in the setting sun.

° **Labyrinthine** (lăb′ə-rĭn′thĭn′): having intricate winding passages like a maze.

On the terraces are draped what I mistook for trailing bougainvillea and which turned out to be dyed skins and wools drying in the sun, draped over the walls and ramparts of the city like bright cherry vines.

The minarets are numerous, three hundred or so, one for each quarter, giving the sense of protection and serenity so characteristic of the Islamic religion. Fez lies very still. It is a city of silence, which makes it appear more and more like an illustration from the Bible. The draped figures in their varicolored jellabas[1] keep their age and weight a secret. They could be sketched by a child who has never learned drawing: a blotch of color against the landscape, moved by the wind, women's faces hidden in *ltem*, or veils, the men's faces hidden by burnouses.[2] It is a life bent towards inner self-perfection, whose dynamic activity lies in the skill, the incredible creative activity of their hands.

The hotel is high above Fez because it was once the palace of the vizier, and he could see the entire city from his terrace. A new hotel has been added right next to the old, but the ancient one can be visited. It has a room with encrustations of gold in the ceiling; and the favorite's room in the garden, with its deep rose and red rugs like a carpet of flowers from Persian fairy tales, its dark, sumptuous bed with a shell-like headpiece encrusted with copper and mother-of-pearl, exhaling the perfume of cedarwood, its copper myriad-eyed lamps diffusing a soft jeweled light, the many pillows of damask and silk, the low divans, the ornamentation enriched by the lovingly carved wood, by stucco, and by meticulous tile work. There is a cabinet of cedarwood, deep and ample, for the favorite's jewels.

Because the souks of Fez are a maze, it is necessary to have a guide. Only those born in this ancient city can find their way. The streets were built narrow originally for coolness against the relentless sun. Some of the ninth-century streets are only a yard and a half wide. As soon as you step out of the hotel courtyard, with a handsome, tall guide dressed in a brown wool jellaba and bright canary-yellow *babouches*, or slippers, you enter the *medina*, or old Arab city. The beauty of this labyrinth is that it takes you into a world of crafts and arts and awakens your five senses every bit of the way. Every small boutique, sometimes as small as eight feet by eight, is a revelation of some skill. Men are sewing the embroidered caftans[3] worn by the women, with gold braids, embroidered edges, trimmings of colored

---

1. **jellaba:** long, loose outer garment, also spelled *djellaba* or *djellabah*.
2. **burnous** (bər-nōos′): long cloak with hood, also spelled *burnoose*.

3. **caftan** (kăf′tən): long-sleeved robe worn with a sash.

sequins. The transparent chiffon and gauze dresses worn by the dancers are made to shine like jewels, and as they hang in front of the boutiques they seem like pennants of exotic tribes. A man in a blue jellaba and a white skullcap is shaping the various colored babouches, made from the leather we saw drying on the walls and terraces of Fez.

Colors seep into your consciousness as never before: a sky-blue jellaba with a black face veil, a pearl-gray jellaba with a yellow veil, a black jellaba with a red veil, a shocking-pink jellaba with a purple veil. The clothes conceal the wearers' figures so that they remain elusive, with all the intensity and expression concentrated in the eyes. The eyes speak for the body, the self, for the age, conveying innumerable messages from their deep and rich existence.

After color and the graceful sway of robes, the flares, the stance, the swing of loose clothes, come the odors. One stand is devoted to sandalwood from Indonesia and the Philippines. It lies in huge round baskets and is sold by weight, for it is a precious luxury wood for burning as incense. The walls of the cubicle are lined with small bottles containing the essence of flowers—jasmine, rose, honeysuckle, and the rose water that is used to perfume guests. In the same baskets lie the henna leaves that the women distill and use on their hair and hands and feet. For the affluent, the henna comes in liquid form. And there is, too, the famous *kohl*, the dust from antimony that gives the women such a soft, iridescent, smoky radiance around their eyes.

The smell of fruit, the smell of perfumes, and the smell of leather intermingle with the smell of wet wool hanging outside of the shops to dry—gold bedspreads hanging like flags in the breeze, sheep's-wool rugs, the favored cherry-red wool blankets, and rose carpets, like fields of daisies, lilies, apple blos-

soms. Blue is the symbolic color of Fez, a sky blue, a transparent blue, the only blue that evokes the word long-forgotten and loved by the poets: *azure*. Fez is azure. You rediscover the word *azure*.

The smell of cedar grows stronger. We are now in the carpenters' quarter. It is spacious, high enough for the beams of wood, brought by the donkeys, to be turned into tables, chairs, trunks. The smell is delicious, comparable only to that of fresh-baked bread. The wood is blond, and the carpenters work with care and skill. The art of working mother-of-pearl encrustations is rare. Two members of the distinguished family that alone knows the art are teaching it to children. I watch them work in the aisle of the museum, with pieces as tiny as one eighth of an inch, shaping and fitting them to a sculptured rosewood box. It is not an art found in tourist bazaars. To watch hands at such delicate work is to understand the whole of the Moroccan character—patience, timelessness, care, devotion.

And now we are in the street of spices. They look beautiful in their baskets, like an array of painter's powders. There is the gold-red saffron, the silver herbs, the scarlet-red peppers, the sepia cinnamon, the ocher ginger, and the yellow curry. The smells surround you, enwrap you, drug you. You are tempted to dip your whole hand in the powdery colors. Later these herbs and spices will appear subtly in the local cooking.

The Moroccan can work in a small space because he knows the art of stillness, he is concentrated on his work, immobile. He does not know restlessness. He is unraveling silk skeins, rolling the silk onto bobbins, tying and braiding belts. But just as you begin to float on a dream of silk, muslins, embroidery, you are plunged into the hundreds of hammer blows of copperwork. Copper trays, copper-edged mirrors, candelabra, teapots, are being carved with a burin[4] and hammer. The men hold the large trays between their knees. The oldest and the best of the artists works with

---

4. **burin** (byŏŏr'ĭn): cutting tool used in engraving.

infinite precision, reproducing designs from famous mosques. His dishes shine like gold, and the designs open and flower and expand and proliferate like intoxicated nature. There are always children and young men in the background, learning the craft.

After the roar of copper works, the hammer strokes, comes a different tone of clatter. It is the work on pewter, iron caldrons for laundry, pots and pans for cooking.

The barber shop is a mysterious cavern, with four huge thronelike chairs taking the whole space. In ancient times the barber was also the circumciser and sometimes the surgeon.

Children pass by, giggling and running, carrying trays of dough prepared for the communal oven. Every quarter has its own mosque, its fountain, its school, its *hammam*, or bath, and its communal oven. The little girls of five and six carry the baby of the family tied to their backs with shawls. They manage to play in between their duties.

A small stand sells sugar loaves—the gift to bring when invited to dinner—sugar for the mint tea and for the sweet pastry, so flaky and light, that they bake.

Two women pass me in gold and silver caftans, on their way to a party or a wedding.

The only sights I miss from my former visit, many years ago, are the handsome cavaliers in their full regalia, white burnouses, red trimmings on the horses, gold knives in their belts. The rich families of sheiks have gone to live in Casablanca. So all I see now are donkeys and mules laden with wood for burning, with dried skins, with furniture, with fruit and garbage, with bolts of material, with potato sacks, with bricks. And when they come with a shout of warning you have to squeeze yourself against the walls.

Now we come to the dyers' souk. The whole crooked, serpentine street of cobblestones belongs to them, and your foot discovers first of all a river of colored water overflowing from the vats. The guide says: "Don't mind. Your shoes will be dyed in beautiful colors." In every dark cavernous lair there are caldrons with dyes of different hues. The men dip the wool and silk and then squeeze them dry. Their legs are bare, and both legs and hands are dyed the color they work with. Children are watching, learning, and helping when they can.

Glancing into one mosque, discreetly, I see a sumptuous blood-red rug given by the king. There is a separate prayer room for the women. Before entering, the faithful wash their feet and faces at the fountain.

Mosques, markets, souks, schools, baths, are all intertwined, giving a feeling of common humanity, or intimacy. Every trade is carried out in the open. Passing by the schools I hear the chorus of recitation from the Koran,[5] which children learn at the earliest age. Wooden trellised windows conceal them from the street, but some come to the door to smile. Learning the verses by heart is difficult, and the discipline severe.

There are no schools for women, but they learn their arts and crafts from the skilled workers who serve them: dressmaking, embroidery, painting, pottery, weaving. Their knowledge is not confined to housekeeping. In ancient days they excelled in poetry, philosophy, and music.

Inevitably the rug merchant invites you to drink mint tea and to glance at the rugs. They are spread on the floor of an ancient palace, now a warehouse for rugs. You learn to distinguish between the designs of Fez and the Berber. The Fez recall the flowery, intricate designs of Persia, but the Berber[6] rugs in nat-

ural wool with austere, abstract designs in pure colors, recall American Indian patterns in their simplicity.

The old inns, or *fondouks*, are still there, as they were in the Middle Ages. Donkeys and camels rest in the courtyard, and in the cells all around, the merchants who come from other cities sleep in their burnouses. But many of the inns have been turned over to the craftsmen and artisans. One is filled with sheepskins, which are being dipped in lye to make it easier to pull off the wool.

A heavy cedarwood gate, elaborately carved, with a heavy silver lock or a tree-sized bolt, indicates a wealthy home.

In a dark lair men are feeding the fires for the hammam, throwing into the furnaces chips left over from carpentry or bundles of odorous eucalyptus.

Baskets of mint are sold in abundance, sometimes by one solitary old woman. When

---

5. **Koran** (kô-răn′): the sacred book of Moslems.
6. **Berber** (bûr′bər): a Moslem people living in North Africa.

I stop at a very small and dark café, I see the samovar they keep going, and watch the ritual of making mint tea. I sit on a plain rough bench, and the boy in charge of pressing the mint into the teapot brings a tiny stool for the glasses.

The tall red hat the Moroccans love to wear, with its black tassel, came from Turkey and is called a *tarbouche* by the natives, a *fez* by the tourists.

I say to a merchant, persistently pointing inside his shop, which is filled with antiques: "I am not shopping. I am writing about Fez." He bows and replies in flowery French, "Come in for the pure delight of the eyes."

For the pure delight of the five senses!

The strong pungent smell of tanning is the only unpleasant one. Tanning occupies a

whole square all to itself, with immense vats holding a cement-colored liquid. The men work half naked, using hooks to handle the skins. Eight or ten vats are worked at the same time, and the skins hung on the wall to dry.

Knowing that Fez—one of Morocco's Four Imperial Cities—was the center of religious and cultural life from ancient times, I want to visit the library of the Karaouine University, which contains original Arabic manuscripts. For this visit I am given a guide called Ali. He is tall, handsome, dark-haired, with an olive complexion, and he speaks French with beautiful diction. He is dressed in the traditional brown jellaba and pointed yellow slippers. I know the Arabian love of poetry, the cult of the spoken word, the gift for storytelling. Ali transports me to the year 900 by his recitation of verses from the Koran, his chanting of the poetry of Omar Khayyám.[7] He is deeply concerned about the survival of Fez. He shows me the exquisite students' quarters, those which were opened and reconstructed by the Beaux Arts.[8] But he also shows me those which have been condemned for lack of repairs, with their sad, plain wood bolts drawn tight, and those which have been put to other uses such as the carving of cedarwood by an artist. He shows me the neglected fountain with the tile decoration partly eroded. He makes me fearful that this vision of other centuries might vanish, like a dream out of *A Thousand and One Nights,* through carelessness or indifference. He wants America the bountiful, America the rebuilder of Versailles, to intervene, to rescue the sculptured cedar beams, the subtle tile work, the lace patterns of the stucco, the delicate arches. In

---

7. **Omar Khayyám** (ō'mär'kī-yäm'): Persian poet, author of *The Rubáiyát.*
8. **Beaux Arts** (bō-zàr'): French for "fine arts."

between his canto[9] to the beauty of Fez, so much more refined, so much more intellectual, so much more spiritual than other cities, and his canto to its skilled artisans, Ali recited verses from Omar Khayyám:

Lo! Some we loved, the loveliest and best
That Time and Fate of all their Vintage prest,
Have drunk their Cup a Round or two before,
And one by one crept silently to rest.

He makes me aware of the fragility of Fez, that we should see it well before it vanishes, that we should learn the myriad gestures of its craftsmen's hands, their patience, their delight in transforming every stone, every piece of wood, every layer of stucco, into an object of beauty. He makes me lament the corroded woods, the broken tiles, the neglected palaces abandoned to time, and the fig tree cut down in the square in front of the library where the students once gathered for discussions, to read their poems and pin them to the tree for passers-by to judge.

The treasure of the library, the illuminated manuscripts, are locked away from my eyes, but Ali is a living spokesman for all I have read about Fez. His softly modulated voice comes from the intellectual and literary past of luminous Fez.

He reminds me of a storyteller I had seen in Fez years before. Ali says he will not be there in the winter. The square where sword swallowers, water carriers, rug sellers, dancers, acrobats, and storytellers gathered is too cold and no place to linger in. But I am stubborn, and on Friday, the Islamic holiday, I go to the square. Even though it has only fifty or a hundred visitors, I find my storyteller standing in the center of an attentive, rapt group of listeners of all ages. They squat on the ground, absolutely absorbed by him, not wavering in their attention for one moment. He is young, wears a heavy wool jellaba of black and white stripes, and a white skullcap, and he carries a stick for emphasis. He has huge glowing eyes, a swarthy skin, and regular features. He is telling the story of Ali Baba[10] with dramatic emphasis, with suspenseful pauses, with a flowing, incantatory style.

Because of Ali's emphasis on the ephemeral beauty of Fez and the possibility of its vanishing, my recurrent feeling that I am dreaming within other centuries, I seek with even more intensity to hold this dream close at least during my stay. I see the tiles broken into small pieces for the mosaic work, I see the lightness and clarity of the air, I see the old ramparts, the city's walls, covered with soft verdigris,[11] lichen, and moss. The secret essence of Fez is serenity. It is expressed in its stillness at night, the rare lights, in the tamarisk trees that never look disheveled, in the figures stirred by the wind, in Cézanne blues, Dufy[12] pinks, pearl whites, and charcoal blacks. The secret essence of Fez comes to me at five thirty in the morning when I awaken to the *muezzin*, the prayer call, from the minaret. Five times a day this prayer is chanted; it seems like both a lament and an invocation, a

---

9. **canto:** here, chanting.

10. **Ali Baba:** a character in *The Arabian Nights* who finds the treasure of the forty thieves. By saying "Open Sesame!" he causes the door of the treasure cave to open.
11. **verdigris** (vûr'də-grēs): a greenish-blue coating.
12. **Cézanne** (sā-zăn') . . . **Dufy** (dü-fē'): Paul Cézanne (1839–1906) and Raoul Dufy (1877–1953), French painters.

consolation and a lyrical thanksgiving. At five thirty in the morning it takes on a special quality, that of a lonely faith protecting the sleeping city, a prayer which is also a call to awaken those prodigious, dynamic hands, agile and supple, never still and never lazy, resting only at the moment of prayer.

It is Ali who tells me the legend of the name of Fez. It had its inception in the democratic spirit of the founder, Idriss II. When the site was chosen and building began, the king took a pick and gave the first stone-breaking blow. The word for pick was *fez*. During later excavations a gold pick was found, said to have been given to the founder as a symbol. When this legend is questioned, museum keepers are apt to answer with silence — respect for legends being as great as respect for fact.

Ali is not content with quoting Omar Khayyam and the Koran, but he recites his own poetry, poems to the beauty of Fez, naming its trees — araucaria, ginger, bamboo, date, monkey puzzle; its fruit; its flowers.

He has theories about visitors. They should not be treated as tourists. They should be invited as friends to weddings, funerals, birthdays, and feast days.

This makes me accept the invitation of the waiter at the Palais Jamai, who says his wife wants to cook a real couscous for me. We go to a tiny house, climb tiny stairs, and find her cooking in a tiny kitchen on the terrace. She is beautiful, with large eyes and a noble profile. She has been cooking all day. I sit in the living room, with its low divans all along the wall and the round copper table in the center. On the walls hang the blue Fez pottery dishes. Cookies are brought in, made like the domed pewter dish I saw being shaped in the souks. The wife's mother is visiting. She comes from the north. Neither woman speaks French, but we manage to convey friendliness, and I show my appreciation of the couscous, which is delicious: a mound of millet, saffron-colored, topped by vegetables, chicken, and raisins. We eat from the same dish. The mother's hands are hennaed, and I notice she is not eating. When I ask Mr. Lahlou why, he explains she cannot eat with spoon and fork. So I say we are the clumsy ones who do not know how to eat with our hands. Then the mother eats, skillfully and neatly, making little balls out of the millet. The meal ends with a large sweet orange, which the host peels and shares with all. And, of course, mint tea. When I am about to leave, the host takes down from the wall the blue pottery dishes and gives them to me. He explains that the tourists are not properly welcomed. The ancient ideal of hospitality is still in evidence. Hospitality is sacred among the people of Islam.

On this day of no wind the smoke of the communal ovens can be seen from the window of the hotel, a clean white smoke. And on such days the five golden balls on the tip of the minarets, symbolizing the five prayers, shine like suns.

When two little boys quarrel in the souks, wrestling angrily, Mustafa, the guide, not only separates them but insists they kiss each other's hair. The men greet each other also with a kiss on the hair when they meet in cafés, and hold hands in the streets as they talk. The whole of life exudes a fraternal tenderness.

"Now when it was the thousand and first night, Dunyayad said to her sister . . ."

FOR STUDY AND DISCUSSION

1. Anaïs Nin begins with an impression of the city—arising first from the furniture in the hotel, then from the window of her hotel room. How does the city as seen from the window delight the senses? What senses does the description most appeal to?

2. From the room Nin takes the reader into the streets. What features of the street suggest the age of the city? What senses does she appeal to in her description?

3. What examples does Nin use to illustrate the "patience, timelessness, care, devotion" of the Moroccan character? How does she show that hospitality and tenderness are important to Moroccans?

4. On page 196, Nin says she is fearful that Fez may vanish "like a dream out of *A Thousand and One Nights.*" *A Thousand and One Nights,* also known as *The Arabian Nights,* is a collection of entertaining stories, chiefly folk tales and fantasies. Why do you think Nin ends her essay with a quotation from this work?

5. A writer selects a focus for any piece of writing. Why do you think Anaïs Nin chooses to emphasize the beauty of Fez and the character of its people rather than, say, politics and economics? What impression do you get of her from what she chooses to tell you about Fez and her way of telling it?

LANGUAGE AND VOCABULARY

Recognizing Sensory and Concrete Language
Imagery is usually thought of as being visual—appealing to sight. But images can appeal to the other senses, and they take their names from them—auditory (hearing), gustatory (taste), olfactory (smell), and tactile (touch). Find examples of each type in the essay.

Reread Nin's description of the herbs and spices on page 194. Note that the second sentence in this passage begins with an abstract idea: the spices look beautiful. Nin then adds a comparison:

> And now we are in the street of spices. They look beautiful in their baskets, like an array of painter's powders.

The comparison makes the abstraction concrete. And, in the passage, Anaïs Nin proceeds to name the spices and their colors, and suggests their effect on the person in the street. Find other examples of how impressions are made concrete in this way.

FOR COMPOSITION

Writing a Description of a Place
Describe an unusual place you have visited, perhaps an unfamiliar neighborhood in your town or city. Let your reader experience this place through its sights, smells, and noises. Assume that your reader is seeing the place for the first time—through your eyes.

Before writing your essay, make a list of places and details and decide on an arrangement. In the actual writing, you need not stay with this plan; indeed, you will want to make changes in organization and add details. Consider your outline as a provisional plan of writing.

George Orwell (1903–1950) was born Eric Blair, of English parents in India. He was educated at private schools in England, and later served in the Indian Imperial Police in Burma. He lived in Paris for two years before returning to India, where he worked at various jobs until he became a journalist. His account of a British mining town, in *The Road to Wigan Pier*, and his account of his experiences in the Spanish Civil War, in *Homage to Catalonia*, are masterpieces of twentieth-century reporting. Orwell is probably best known for his satirical fiction—his animal fable about totalitarianism, *Animal Farm*, and his anti-Utopian novel set in a future time, *Nineteen Eighty-Four*.

"Why Do We Believe That the Earth Is Round?" is one of a series of short columns Orwell wrote for British periodicals in the 1940's. In it Orwell considers both sides of an argument, offering reasons to both support and refute a given point. Like all good essays it leads the reader to the subject, and it draws a conclusion from the discussion at the end. Orwell writes in a familiar style, writing as he would speak in ordinary conversation.

Why Do We Believe That the Earth Is Round?

George Orwell

Somewhere or other—I think it is in the preface to *Saint Joan*—Bernard Shaw remarks that we are more gullible and superstitious today than we were in the Middle Ages, and as an example of modern credulity he cites the widespread belief that the earth is round. The average man, says Shaw, can advance not a single reason for thinking that the earth is round. He merely swallows this theory because there is something about it that appeals to the twentieth-century mentality.

Now, Shaw is exaggerating, but there is something in what he says, and the question is worth following up, for the sake of the light it throws on modern knowledge. Just why *do* we believe that the earth is round? I am not speaking of the few thousand astronomers, geographers and so forth who could give ocular proof, or have a theoretical knowledge of the proof, but of the ordinary newspaper-reading citizen, such as you or me.

As for the Flat Earth theory, I believe I could refute it. If you stand by the seashore on a clear day, you can see the masts and funnels of invisible ships passing along the horizon. This phenomenon can only be explained by assuming that the earth's surface is curved. But it does not follow that the earth is spherical. Imagine another theory called the Oval Earth theory, which claims that the earth is shaped like an egg. What can I say against it?

Against the Oval Earth man, the first card I can play is the analogy of the sun and moon. The Oval Earth man promptly answers that I don't know, by my own observation, that those bodies are spherical. I only know that they are round, and they may perfectly well be flat discs. I have no answer to that one. Besides, he goes on, what reason have I for thinking that the earth must be the same shape as the sun and moon? I can't answer that one either.

My second card is the earth's shadow: when cast on the moon during eclipses, it appears to be the shadow of a round object. But how do I know, demands the Oval Earth man, that eclipses of the moon are caused by the shadow of the earth? The answer is that I don't know, but have taken this piece of information blindly from newspaper articles and science booklets.

Defeated in the minor exchanges, I now play my queen of trumps: the opinion of the experts. The Astronomer Royal, who ought to know, tells me that the earth is round. The Oval Earth man covers the queen with his king. Have I tested the Astronomer Royal's statement, and would I even know a way of testing it? Here I bring out my ace. Yes, I do

know one test. The astronomers can foretell eclipses, and this suggests that their opinions about the solar system are pretty sound. I am therefore justified in accepting their say-so about the shape of the earth.

If the Oval Earth man answers—what I believe is true—that the ancient Egyptians, who thought the sun goes round the earth, could also predict eclipses, then bang goes my ace. I have only one card left: navigation. People can sail ships round the world, and reach the places they aim at, by calculations which assume that the earth is spherical. I believe that finishes the Oval Earth man, though even then he may possibly have some kind of counter.

It will be seen that my reasons for thinking that the earth is round are rather precarious ones. Yet this is an exceptionally elementary piece of information. On most other questions I should have to fall back on the expert much earlier, and would be less able to test his pronouncements. And much the greater part of our knowledge is at this level. It does not rest on reasoning or on experiment, but on authority. And how can it be otherwise, when the range of knowledge is so vast that the expert himself is an ignoramus as soon as he strays away from his own specialty? Most people, if asked to prove that the earth is round, would not even bother to produce the rather weak arguments I have outlined above. They would start off by saying that "everyone knows" the earth to be round, and if pressed further, would become angry. In a way Shaw is right. This *is* a credulous age, and the burden of knowledge which we now have to carry is partly responsible.

FOR STUDY AND DISCUSSION

1. How does Orwell lead the reader to a statement of his subject? How does he try to persuade the reader that his subject is worth considering?

2. What reasons does Orwell give for believing that the earth is round? Why does he present these reasons in the order he has?

3. An analogy draws a comparison or finds points of similarity between two unlike things. What does Orwell mean by "the analogy of the sun and moon"?

4. In the final paragraph, Orwell states his thesis or central idea—that the greater part of our knowledge rests on authority rather than on reasoning. According to Orwell, why are we so dependent on experts for our knowledge?

5. Orwell's essay was written before the age of space exploration. What new evidence supplied by voyages into space could be used to support Orwell's argument?

LANGUAGE AND VOCABULARY

Distinguishing Meanings
Explain how the word in brackets would change the meaning of the preceding italicized word:

1. . . . we are more *gullible* [foolish] and superstitious today than we were in the Middle Ages . . .
2. . . . an example of modern *credulity* [faith] . . .
3. . . . the twentieth-century *mentality* [soul].
4. . . . my reasons for thinking that the earth is round are rather *precarious* [undependable] ones.
5. . . . the expert himself is an *ignoramus* [charlatan] as soon as he strays away from his own specialty.

FOR COMPOSITION

Writing a Persuasive Essay
Give your reasons for holding a belief like the one Orwell discusses. State whether you consider these reasons adequate and convincing. Introduce your essay as Orwell does—leading your reader to your subject. Conclude it as Orwell does—drawing conclusions from your analysis.

Explaining an Analogy
An analogy draws a point-by-point comparison between two things. An analogy is often drawn between love and war. Can you see the points of resemblance? Can you see the analogy between a human body and a machine? Write a paragraph explaining either of these analogies or another of your own choice.

Practice in Reading and Writing

EXPOSITION

Reading Exposition

Exposition is writing that gives information, explains something, or expresses an opinion. Exposition is generally built around a central, or *controlling*, idea, which the writer develops by details, examples, reason, or a combination of all three methods. Most expository writing follows this overall structure: the controlling idea is stated in the introductory paragraph or paragraphs, developed in the body of the piece, then summarized or reinforced in the conclusion.

A similar structure may be used for individual paragraphs. Very often the central idea of a paragraph is stated in a *topic sentence*. This idea is then supported by details, examples, or reasons.

Analyze the organization of this paragraph from "The Death of a Tree" by Edwin Way Teale:

> For a great tree death comes as a gradual transformation. Its vitality ebbs slowly. Even when life has abandoned it entirely, it remains a majestic thing. On some hilltop a dead tree may dominate the landscape for miles around. Alone among living things it retains its character and dignity after death. Plants wither; animals disintegrate. But a dead tree may be as arresting, as filled with personality, in death as it is in life. Even in its final moments, when the massive trunk lies prone and it has moldered into a ridge covered with mosses and fungi, it arrives at a fitting and a noble end. It enriches and refreshes the earth. And later, as part of other green and growing things, it rises again.

1. What is the controlling idea of the paragraph and where is it expressed?
2. How does Teale support this idea in the paragraph?
3. What transitional words help to make clear the movement of the author's thought?
4. Does the paragraph have a concluding, or "clincher," sentence?

Here is another paragraph from the same essay. What is the logic of organization?

Like a river flowing into a desert, the life stream of the tree dwindled and disappeared before it reached the topmost twigs. They died first. The leaf at the tip of each twig, the last to unfold, was the first to wither and fall. Then, little by little, the twig itself became dead and dry. This process of dissolution, in the manner of a movie run backward, reversed the development of growth. Just as, cell by cell, the twig had grown outward toward the tip, so now death spread, cell by cell, backward from the tip.

Writing Exposition

In writing exposition, you should try to do the following:

1. *Keep your controlling idea firmly in mind.*
2. *Think of details, examples, or reasons that will support or develop your central idea.*
3. *Arrange them in a logical order that will best express your point.*
4. *Write clearly and persuasively, making all shifts and turnings of your thought clear with transitional words.*

Write a paragraph of exposition developing one of these topics or a topic of your own:

How to Start a Stamp (Coin) Collection
Methods of Energy Conservation
Building a Classroom Terrarium
Recycling Clothes (Furniture)

"There is properly no history; only biography," said Ralph Waldo Emerson, the great American essayist and poet. He was echoing his British contemporary and friend, Thomas Carlyle, who wrote in his own essay on history, "History is the essence of innumerable biographies."

The interest in great men and women has brought readers to biography since ancient times. We desire to know how these people thought and felt, and what may have been the source of their success in life — and their failures. We also turn to biography to discover our "roots," to use a word Alex Haley has popularized. Perhaps more so than in any previous time, we enjoy reading about ordinary people whose lives helped shape the present world.

Biography and Personal Recollection

Manuscript page from Mark Twain's *Autobiography.*
Bancroft Library,
University of California, Berkeley
Mark Twain Papers

Charles Dickens (1812–1870) was born in a town on the south coast of England, where his father was a clerk in the Naval Pay Office. Charles spent his boyhood in various parts of southeast England, including London and Rochester; he described this world in his novel *Great Expectations*. His childhood was a happy one for a time, and he felt a special love for his father—"as kindhearted and generous a man as ever lived in the world," Dickens wrote of him. Dickens' father found it more and more difficult to take care of his growing family. Instead of going to school, Charles did odd jobs for his parents, was taught by his mother how to read, and played in the streets.

The Dickens family moved to London permanently when Charles was ten, and sank quickly into poverty and debt. People to whom John Dickens owed money often came to the house and demanded payment. To help support himself, Charles was sent to work at a blacking (shoe polish) warehouse near the Thames River; he was twelve years old. Shortly afterward his father was imprisoned for debt in the Marshalsea Prison, and the household soon broke up: Charles and his oldest sister were boarded out, and Mrs. Dickens and the younger children went to live with John Dickens in prison, a common practice in the early nineteenth century in England. Charles and his sister visited their parents on Sundays; Charles later moved to a small attic room to be closer to the prison. At the blacking warehouse he worked from eight in the morning to eight at night. Three months after being imprisoned, John Dickens came into a small inheritance and was able to leave prison. But Charles continued to work at the blacking warehouse a little longer.

Dickens found these experiences perhaps the most painful of his life—so painful that he never told his wife or children about them. He recorded them in an autobiography which he started to write; he did not complete it and instead used his experiences in his novel *David Copperfield*, in which David is sent to work at a blacking warehouse, "Murdstone and Grinby's." As the fragments of the autobiography show, the character David Copperfield is speaking for Charles Dickens when he tells his reader, "I know enough of the world now, to have almost lost the capacity of being much surprised by anything; but it is matter of some surprise to me, even now, that I can have been so easily thrown away at such an age."

Fragments of an Autobiography

Charles Dickens

Old Hungerford Stairs. Anonymous 19th-century drawing.
British Museum, London   Crace Collection

[It was] an evil hour for me, as I often bitterly thought. Its chief manager, James Lamert, the relative who had lived with us in Bayham Street, seeing how I was employed from day to day, and knowing what our domestic circumstances then were, proposed that I should go into the blacking warehouse, to be as useful as I could, at a salary, I think, of six shillings a week. I am not clear whether it was six or seven. I am inclined to believe, from my uncertainty on this head, that it was six at first, and seven afterwards. At any rate the offer was accepted very willingly by my father and mother, and on a Monday morning I went down to the blacking warehouse to begin my business life.

It is wonderful to me how I could have been so easily cast away at such an age. It is wonderful to me that, even after my descent into the poor little drudge I had been since we came to London, no one had compassion enough on me—a child of singular abilities, quick, eager, delicate, and soon hurt, bodily or mentally—to suggest that something might have been spared, as certainly it might have been, to place me at any common school. Our friends, I take it, were tired out. No one made any sign. My father and mother were quite satisfied. They could hardly have been more so, if I had been twenty years of age, distinguished at a grammar school, and going to Cambridge.

The blacking warehouse was the last house on the left-hand side of the way, at old Hungerford Stairs. It was a crazy, tumble-down old house, abutting of course on the river, and literally overrun with rats. Its wainscotted rooms, and its rotten floors and staircase, and the old gray rats swarming down in the cellars, and the sound of their squeaking and scuffling coming up the stairs at all times, and the dirt and decay of the place, rise up visibly before me, as if I were there again. The countinghouse was on the first floor, looking over the coal barges and the river. There was a recess in it, in which I was to sit and work. My work was to cover the pots of paste-blacking, first with a piece of oilpaper, and then with a piece of blue paper; to tie them round with a string; and then to clip the paper close and neat, all round, until it looked as smart as a pot of ointment from an apothecary's[1] shop. When a certain number of grosses of pots had attained this pitch of perfection, I was to paste on each a printed label, and then go on again with more pots. Two or three other boys were kept at similar duty downstairs on similar wages. One of them came up, in a ragged apron and a paper cap, on the first Monday morning, to show me the trick of using the string and tying the knot. His name was Bob Fagin; and I took the liberty of using his name, long afterwards, in *Oliver Twist*.

---

1. **apothecary** (ə-pŏth′ə-kĕr′ē): druggist.

Our relative had kindly arranged to teach me something in the dinner hour, from twelve to one, I think it was, every day. But an arrangement so incompatible with countinghouse business soon died away, from no fault of his or mine; and for the same reason, my small worktable, and my grosses of pots, my papers, string, scissors, pastepot, and labels, by little and little, vanished out of the recess in the countinghouse, and kept company with the other small worktables, grosses of pots, papers, string, scissors, and pastepots, downstairs. It was not long before Bob Fagin and I, and another boy whose name was Paul Green, but who was currently believed to have been christened Poll (a belief which I transferred, long afterwards again, to Mr. Sweedlepipe, in *Martin Chuzzlewit*), worked generally, side by side. Bob Fagin was an orphan, and lived with his brother-in-law, a waterman. Poll Green's father had the additional distinction of being a fireman, and was employed at Drury Lane Theater, where another relation of Poll's, I think his little sister, did imps in the pantomimes.

No words can express the secret agony of my soul as I sunk into this companionship; compared these everyday associates with those of my happier childhood; and felt my early hopes of growing up to be a learned and distinguished man, crushed in my breast. The deep remembrance of the sense I had of being utterly neglected and hopeless; of the shame I felt in my position; of the misery it was to my young heart to believe that, day by day, what I had learned, and thought, and delighted in, and raised my fancy and my emulation up by, was passing away from me, never to be brought back any more, cannot be written. My whole nature was so penetrated with the grief and humiliation of such considerations, that even now, famous and caressed and happy, I often forget in my dreams that I have a dear wife and children, even that I am a man, and wander desolately back to that time of my life.

My mother and my brothers and sisters (excepting Fanny in the Royal Academy of Music) were still encamped, with a young servant-girl from Chatham Workhouse, in the two parlors in the emptied house in Gower Street North. It was a long way to go and return within the dinner hour, and, usually, I either carried my dinner with me, or went and bought it at some neighboring shop. In the latter case, it was commonly a saveloy[2] and a penny loaf; sometimes, a fourpenny plate of beef from a cook's shop; sometimes, a plate of bread and cheese, and a glass of beer, from a miserable old public house over the way: The Swan, if I remember right, or The Swan and something else that I have forgotten. Once, I remember tucking my own bread (which I had brought from home in the morning) under my arm, wrapped up in a piece of paper like a book, and going into the best dining room in Johnson's a la mode beefhouse in Clare Court, Drury Lane, and magnificently ordering a small plate of a la mode beef to eat with it. What the waiter thought of such a strange little apparition coming in all alone, I don't know; but I can see him now, staring at me as I ate my dinner, and bringing up the other waiter to look. I gave him a halfpenny, and I wish now that he hadn't taken it.

The household broke up. Dickens' mother and the younger children went to live with John Dickens in the Marshalsea Prison.

The key of the house was sent back to the landlord, who was very glad to get it; and I (small Cain that I was, except that I had never done harm to anyone) was handed over as a lodger to a reduced old lady, long known to our family, in Little College Street, Camden Town, who took children in to board, and had once done so at Brighton; and who, with a few alterations and embellishments, unconsciously began to sit for Mrs. Pipchin in *Dombey* when she took in me.

She had a little brother and sister under her care then, somebody's natural children, who were very irregularly paid for, and a widow's little son. The two boys and I slept in the same room. My own exclusive breakfast, of a penny cottage loaf and a pennyworth of milk, I provided for myself. I kept another small loaf, and a quarter of a pound of cheese, on a particular shelf of a particular cupboard, to make my supper on when I came back at night. They made a hole in the six or seven shillings, I know well; and I was out at the blacking warehouse all day, and had to support myself upon that money all the week. I suppose my lodging was paid for, by my father. I certainly did not pay it myself; and I certainly had no other assistance whatever (the making of my clothes, I think, excepted), from Monday morning until Saturday night. No advice, no counsel, no encouragement, no consolation, no support, from anyone that I can call to mind, so help me God.

Sundays, Fanny and I passed in the prison. I was at the academy in Tenterden Street, Hanover Square, at nine o'clock in the morning, to fetch her; and we walked back there together, at night.

I was so young and childish, and so little qualified—how could I be otherwise?—to undertake the whole charge of my own existence, that, in going to Hungerford Stairs of a morning, I could not resist the stale pastry put out at half price on trays at the confectioners doors in Tottenham Court Road; and I often spent in that, the money I should have kept for my dinner. Then I went without my dinner, or bought a roll, or a slice of pudding.

---

2. **saveloy** (săv′ə-loi): spicy, dried sausage.

There were two pudding shops between which I was divided, according to my finances. One was in a court close to St. Martin's Church (at the back of the church) which is now removed altogether. The pudding at that shop was made with currants, and was rather a special pudding, but was dear: two penn'orth[3] not being larger than a penn'orth of more ordinary pudding. A good shop for the latter was in the Strand, somewhere near where the Lowther Arcade is now. It was a stout, hale pudding, heavy and flabby, with great raisins in it, stuck in whole, at great distances apart. It came up hot, at about noon every day; and many and many a day did I dine off it.

We had half an hour, I think, for tea. When I had money enough, I used to go to a coffee shop, and have half a pint of coffee, and a slice of bread and butter. When I had no money, I took a turn in Covent Garden market, and stared at the pineapples. The coffee shops to which I most resorted were, one in Maiden Lane; one in a court (nonexistent now) close to Hungerford Market; and one in St. Martin's Lane, of which I only recollect that it stood near the church, and that in the door there was an oval glass plate, with COFFEE ROOM painted on it, addressed towards the street. If I ever find myself in a very different kind of coffee room now, but where there is such an inscription on glass, and read it backward on the wrong side MOOR EEFFOC (as I often used to do then, in a dismal reverie), a shock goes through my blood.

---

3. **penn'orth:** pennyworth.

I know I do not exaggerate, unconsciously and unintentionally, the scantiness of my resources and the difficulties of my life. I know that if a shilling or so were given me by anyone, I spent it in a dinner or a tea. I know that I worked, from morning to night, with common men and boys, a shabby child. I know that I tried, but ineffectually, not to anticipate my money, and to make it last the week through, by putting it away in a drawer I had in the countinghouse, wrapped into six little parcels, each parcel containing the same amount, and labeled with a different day. I know that I have lounged about the streets, insufficiently and unsatisfactorily fed. I know that, but for the mercy of God, I might easily have been, for any care that was taken of me, a little robber or a little vagabond.

But I held some station at the blacking warehouse too. Besides that my relative at the countinghouse did what a man so occupied, and dealing with a thing so anomalous,[4] could, to treat me as one upon a different footing from the rest, I never said, to man or boy, how it was that I came to be there, or gave the least indication of being sorry that I was there. That I suffered in secret, and that I suffered exquisitely, no one ever knew but I. How much I suffered, it is, as I have said already, utterly beyond my power to tell. No man's imagination can overstep the reality. But I kept my own counsel, and I did my work. I knew from the first that if I could not do my work as well as any of the rest, I could not hold myself above slight and contempt. I soon became at least as expeditious and as skillful with my hands as either of the other boys. Though perfectly familiar with them, my conduct and manners were different enough from theirs to place a space between us. They, and the men, always spoke of me

as "the young gentleman." A certain man (a soldier once) named Thomas, who was the foreman, and another named Harry, who was the carman and wore a red jacket, used to call me "Charles" sometimes, in speaking to me; but I think it was mostly when we were very confidential, and when I had made some efforts to entertain them over our work with the results of some of the old readings, which were fast perishing out of my mind. Poll Green uprose once, and rebelled against the "young gentleman" usage; but Bob Fagin settled him speedily.

My rescue from this kind of existence I considered quite hopeless, and abandoned as such, altogether; though I am solemnly convinced that I never, for one hour, was reconciled to it, or was otherwise than miserably unhappy. I felt keenly, however, the being so cut off from my parents, my brothers, and sisters; and, when my day's work was done,

4. **anomalous** (ə-nŏm′ə-ləs): irregular.

211

going home to such a miserable blank; and *that*, I thought, might be corrected. One Sunday night I remonstrated with my father on this head, so pathetically and with so many tears that his kind nature gave way. He began to think that it was not quite right. I do believe he had never thought so before, or thought about it. It was the first remonstrance I had ever made about my lot, and perhaps it opened up a little more than I intended. A back attic was found for me at the house of an insolvent court agent, who lived in Lant Street in the borough, where Bob Sawyer lodged many years afterwards. A bed and bedding were sent over for me, and made up on the floor. The little window had a pleasant prospect of a timber yard; and when I took possession of my new abode, I thought it was a Paradise.

Bob Fagin was very good to me on the occasion of a bad attack of my old disorder. I suffered such excruciating pain that time, that they made a temporary bed of straw in my old recess in the countinghouse, and I rolled about on the floor, and Bob filled empty blacking bottles with hot water, and applied relays of them to my side, half the day. I got better, and quite easy towards evening; but Bob (who was much bigger and older than I) did not like the idea of my going home alone, and took me under his protection. I was too proud to let him know about the prison; and after making several efforts to get rid of him, to all of which Bob Fagin in his goodness was deaf, shook hands with him on the steps of a house near Southwark Bridge on the Surrey side, making believe that I lived there. As a finishing piece of reality in case of his looking back, I knocked at the door, I recollect, and asked, when the woman opened it, if that was Mr. Robert Fagin's house.

I am not sure that it was before this time, or after it, that the blacking warehouse was removed to Chandos Street, Covent Garden. It is no matter. Next to the shop at the corner of Bedford Street in Chandos Street, are two rather old-fashioned houses and shops adjoining one another. They were one then, or thrown into one, for the blacking business; and had been a butter shop. Opposite to them was, and is, a public house, where I got my ale, under these new circumstances. The stones in the street may be smoothed by my small feet going across to it at dinnertime and back again. The establishment was larger now, and we had one or two new boys. Bob Fagin and I had attained to great dexterity in tying up the pots. I forget how many we could do in five minutes. We worked, for the light's sake, near the second window as you come from Bedford Street; and we were so brisk at it that the people used to stop and look in. Sometimes there would be quite a little crowd there. I saw my father coming in at the door one day when we were very busy, and I wondered how he could bear it.

Now, I generally had my dinner in the warehouse. Sometimes I brought it from home, so I was better off. I see myself coming across Russell Square from Somers Town, one morning, with some cold hotchpotch[5] in a small basin tied up in a handkerchief. I had the same wanderings about the streets as I used to have, and was just as solitary and self-dependent as before; but I had not the same difficulty in merely living. I never, however, heard a word of being taken away, or of being otherwise than quite provided for.

At last, one day, my father, and the relative so often mentioned, quarreled; quarreled by letter, for I took the letter from my father to him which caused the explosion, but quar-

---

5. **hotchpotch:** a stew of meats and vegetables.

reled very fiercely. It was about me. It may have had some backward reference, in part, for anything I know, to my employment at the window. All I am certain of is that, soon after I had given him the letter, my cousin (he was a sort of cousin, by marriage) told me he was very much insulted about me; and that it was impossible to keep me, after that. I cried very much, partly because it was so sudden, and partly because in his anger he was violent about my father, though gentle to me. Thomas, the old soldier, comforted me, and said he was sure it was for the best. With a relief so strange that it was like oppression, I went home.

My mother set herself to accommodate the quarrel, and did so next day. She brought home a request for me to return next morning, and a high character of me, which I am very sure I deserved. My father said I should go back no more, and should go to school. I do not write resentfully or angrily: for I know how all these things have worked together to make me what I am: but I never afterwards forgot, I never shall forget, I never can forget, that my mother was warm for my being sent back.

From that hour until this at which I write, no word of that part of my childhood which I have now gladly brought to a close, has passed my lips to any human being. I have no idea how long it lasted, whether for a year, or much more, or less. From that hour until this, my father and my mother have been stricken dumb upon it. I have never heard the least allusion to it, however far off and remote, from either of them. I have never, until I now impart it to this paper, in any burst of confidence with anyone, my own wife not excepted, raised the curtain I then dropped, thank God.

Until old Hungerford Market was pulled down, until old Hungerford Stairs were destroyed, and the very nature of the ground changed, I never had the courage to go back to the place where my servitude began. I never saw it. I could not endure to go near it. For many years, when I came near to Robert Warren's in the Strand, I crossed over to the opposite side of the way, to avoid a certain smell of the cement they put upon the blacking corks, which reminded me of what I was once. It was a very long time before I liked to go up Chandos Street. My old way home by the borough made me cry, after my eldest child could speak.

In my walks at night I have walked there often, since then, and by degrees I have come to write this. It does not seem a tithe of what I might have written, or of what I meant to write.

FOR STUDY AND DISCUSSION

1. In this autobiographical fragment, Dickens views the most painful episode of his childhood from the vantage point of maturity. What impression do you form of Dickens as a child from his relationship with the other boys in the blacking warehouse? From the description of his meals and his lodgings? From his solitary walks through the city?

2. As a writer Dickens is well known for his evocative descriptions of settings. Where in this selection does he create vivid pictures of his surroundings?

3. In his novels Dickens created a gallery of memorable characters. Where does he show that early in his life he had keen insight into human nature?

LANGUAGE AND VOCABULARY

Explaining Phrases from Context
Explain the following phrases and state what they reveal about Dickens' feelings about himself:

1. What . . . raised my fancy and my emulation up by, was passing away from me . . .
2. . . . small Cain that I was . . .
3. . . . a shabby child.
4. . . . as expeditious and as skillful with my hands as either of the other boys.

Rewriting a Passage in Modern English
Had Dickens been writing his autobiography in the 1970's, he would have written different sentences and used different words. Rewrite the following sentence in your own language. Make your words communicate the same feelings and ideas:

> The deep remembrance of the sense I had of being utterly neglected and hopeless; of the shame I felt in my position; of the misery it was to my young heart to believe that, day by day, what I had learned, and thought, and delighted in, and raised my fancy and my emulation up by, was passing away from me, never to be brought back any more, cannot be written.

You might want to start your sentence, "I cannot write" or "I can't tell you," instead of delaying the verb phrase until the end of the sentence as Dickens does.

FOR COMPOSITION

Describing a Work Experience
Describe your first work experience—whether doing odd jobs in your neighborhood, or baby-sitting, or helping in a family business. Tell your reader the details of the following:

> your reasons for doing the work
> the nature and amount of work you did
> your feelings about the work
> the people you met, or the friends you made, or new experiences that working made possible
> the lessons you learned

Before you write, decide in what order you wish to present these details. Keep your reader in mind as you write. Let the reader see and feel these experiences as you did.

Writing About Literature
Dickens drew on his childhood experiences in the novels he wrote. In *Pickwick Papers,* for example, he describes life in a debtors' prison similar to the one in which his father was imprisoned. Read one or more of Chapters 41–45 in *Pickwick Papers,* and write a short essay on details that reveal to you the attitude in early nineteenth-century England toward poor people or those incapable of taking care of themselves. You might want to write about how Dickens reveals his own attitude toward debtors' prisons or the situation of poor people in them.

As she tells us in her narrative, Nancy Huddleston Packer (1925–   ) was raised in Washington, D. C., where her father served as Congressman from Alabama for twenty-two years. The world she describes is the Washington of the early 1930's: unemployment was widespread throughout the country, jobless war veterans marched on the city to secure immediate payment of war bonuses, and Congress voted a decrease in its salary. The events of the Great Depression seemed unimportant to a little girl embarking on her first Christmas shopping trip.

The author presents her experiences in narrative form, describing events as they occurred, and pausing to comment on her humiliation and embarrassment. As in exposition, personal narrative must establish and maintain a clear point of view. The author has the double job of letting the reader share the point of view of the little girl and at the same time the point of view of the grown woman remembering her past. As you read, notice how unobtrusive the transitions are from one point of view to the other.

Giving, Getting

Nancy Huddleston Packer

Early memories are cloudy, and often I can't separate myself from the other children in our family. Was it one of my sisters or I who cried when the Bonus Marchers[1] came to Washington? Did all five of us march through Union Station bearing placards that said "Be Kind to Dumb Animals — Pity Hoover the Elephant"? It's all very confusing. But in the Christmas of 1931, when I was six, I see myself separately

and unmistakably, for the story has been preserved intact by family ridicule and tenderness.

We were a frugal family in good times and bad. Our father was a member of Congress from Alabama, and though the pay was not "handsome" (the Congress had voted itself a decrease in pay from $10,000 to $9,000 after, I venture to say, a roll-call vote), we considered ourselves comfortably off. Reelection expenses surely totaled no more than a hundred dollars or so for gasoline and twenty-five dollars for printing. We had plenty, but nonetheless we took money seriously. Allowances

---

1. **Bonus Marchers:** The word *bonus* here means a government grant to veterans of the armed forces. In 1932, thousands of unemployed veterans of the First World War marched on Washington to secure payment of war bonuses.

and cash gifts were not bestowed merely to provide pleasure; they carried with them a test of virtue and a means to family standing.

Being the youngest, I was the last to be given money. My Saturday movie dime was entrusted to my brother George. As if poverty had made me mute, the ice-cream man would ask my sister Jane what flavor I wanted. But that Christmas, everything changed. Our father was an honorable, stern, and just man. On the Friday evening before Christmas Sunday, he gave each of my four brothers and sisters two dollars and fifty cents to spend on presents. After a slow, appraising gaze, he took two more dollars and a fifty-cent piece and gave them to me. For a moment no one spoke. Glances were exchanged between the older children. In a querulous voice that held no hope of prevailing, one of my sisters said, "Nancy hasn't got two dollars and fifty cents' worth of friends. The rest of us, like me. . . ."

"Hush," my father said. He smiled at her. "There's no halfway house to equality. Nancy is equal now."

My brother George was five years older than I and very careful with money. He owned a little file case in which he kept a stack of IOU's signed by his friends and family. When all of us went, say, to an amusement park, he chose his rides on the closely calculated basis of ride time to money. And so it was to him I went for advice on how to plan my Christmas spending.

"First you make a list," he said. He would do it for me since I couldn't really write. "Now you figure out how much to spend on everybody by how much you love them."

We commenced. By means of a private logic I cannot now recall, I settled on thirty-five cents for Mother and thirty for Father. Next came my brothers and sisters: Mary, George,

John, and Jane. Beside each name I directed George to write twenty cents.

"Everyone exactly the same, huh?" he said. "OK, what about Ida?"

Instinctively I read his meaning. If I cared no more for him than for the others, then he would make it tough for me. "I reckon you didn't even think about Ida," he said harshly. "Poor as she is, much as she loves you."

Ida worked for Mother and was very important to all of us, but I hadn't thought I would buy her a present, for our parents gave her a nice one from all of us. Nevertheless I fell before George's attack and said, "Ida: twenty-five cents."

George stared at me. "Twenty-five cents," I repeated. "How much have I got left?"

Grudgingly he informed me that I had eighty cents left. I directed him to write down ten cents beside the names of three school friends with whom I had agreed to exchange presents. That left Walter.

Walter lived next door and he was my hero. He was a year and a half older than I, the only child of a gay young larking couple. If we took pride in the penny saved, they took equal pleasure in the penny spent. Walter, who was not at all musical, had a grand piano, a trumpet in a leather case lined with blue velvet, and a real kettledrum.

"Forty cents for Walter," I said.

"You're even stupider than I thought," George said. "You won't have but a dime left for yourself." I ignored for the moment what this disclosed of George's plans for his own two dollars and fifty cents. I was too pleased with the windfall.

In addition to the traits that I've mentioned, Father was both proud and eccentric. Much that he did caused his children that peculiar double pain of embarrassment and shame for being embarrassed. We cringed doubly on the snowy afternoon when he walked home from the House Office Building with newspapers wrapped around his legs to protect his trousers. We were humiliated the time he walked out in the middle of a sermon because, as he said, "I tolerate a mighty lot of fools six days a week. A man has the right to rest on Sunday." When he decided on the spur of the moment to take us to do our shopping that Christmas Eve, we understood that his presence conferred an honor upon us. But beneath our false glad cries when he told us he was coming lurked the dull recalcitrance of inveterate criminals about to be handcuffed.

Our father hadn't had his daily walk, and so we walked to the nearest shopping area eight blocks away. Woolworth's was teeming with children, and not even our father's magnificent will would be able to hold us in a band. Quickly he calculated aptitudes and dispositions, paired and totaled them, and sent us out like snipers to distant corners. I was sent with George, who of course would not pursue his own pleasure in buying until he had exhausted mine.

Setting off at a dogtrot, round and round the store we went. At last we landed at Glassware. We were always breaking glasses, George insisted, wanting to get me started. My eye was caught by a set of thick blue glasses set in holes cut out of a tin tray.

"It says brandy," said George. "That's liquor."

"Mother doesn't drink brandy," I said.

"Look," he said impatiently, "she has a lot of flower vases, hasn't she? Does that mean she drinks dirty flower water? Get 'em."

I got them. Thirty-five cents. It was quite a moment, but George would not let me enjoy it. He hurried me off to the necktie counter. On my own I selected a red-and-yellow necktie for my father to replace the black bow tie he always wore. There was a slight hitch because the tie cost only twenty-nine cents.

"You're only cheating him by a penny," said George.

"I could put the penny in the package," I said.

"If you want to," he said, "stupid."

Ida was more of a problem. I knew nothing of her life outside our house. She did have boyfriends, tall, kindly dark men who came to sit with her when she stayed with us on those rare evenings when our parents went out. How did they entertain themselves, I wondered, once we'd all gone to bed? I bought a deck of playing cards for a quarter to tide them through their boredom in our absence.

We had circled the store many times and George's impatience was growing. He kept trying to work me over to the toy counter, but I would not be worked. In a sudden huff, he vanished. At once he returned, looking both vicious and contrite.

"If he found out I left you. . ."

"I promise I won't tell him."

After a searching look, he decided to trust me. He departed and I went at once, not to Toys but to Drugs. My brothers were only seventeen months apart and each measured his worth by the other one. For the sake of peace, everyone gave them the same presents. I knew what I wanted to buy for them because I knew what they wanted. Our eldest sister, Mary, fastidious to a fault, had a large bottle of Lavoris mouthwash that was the envy of us all. It was red and flavorful and mysterious, and we stole swigs from the bottle. Not a week before, my brother John had been caught with the bottle at his lips. With customary bravado he had said, "It ain't nearly as good as Listerine." I bought John and George each a twenty-cent bottle of Listerine.

Staying in that section of the store out of timidity and ignorance and victimized by impulse, I quickly bought vanishing cream and powdered rouge for my sisters, and for each of my three school friends a bottle of blood-red fingernail polish. These were exactly the kind of selections my father had expected George to prevent. But they cleared the way for the big moment: Walter's present.

Poor Walter was always deprived by excess. When the other boys played football they wore gray sweatshirts and dirty blue jeans and Keds. When Walter joined them, he looked like Frankenstein's monster, with padded pants that forced him to goose-step, regulation shoulder pads that held his arms spread-eagled, and an immense helmet that dropped across his vision at the moment of impact. And while the rest of us had pistols into which we inserted single torn-off caps, Walter had a repeater machine gun that consumed a roll of caps before he could get his finger off the trigger or his eye on the target. Only recently he had tried to swap his expensive gun for a cheaper one, but his desperation spoiled everything and no one would swap. I wanted to please him, and I had decided to get him a pistol.

The ordinary cap pistol cost twenty cents, and so I bought two, to use up the forty cents. I gave the saleswoman a fifty-cent piece, which was all I had left except the awkward penny left from Father's present. She gave me a sack containing the two pistols and a number of coins which I dropped into my coat pocket. As I stood there, I had a vague feeling that the coins amounted to more than the dime George had said I would have left. I went in search of advice.

Pushing and squeezing past adult backsides and children's shoulders, I wriggled my way through the store after George and found him paying for a large bottle of perfume. I held out the coins. "Count this," I said.

At that precise moment, the thundering

voice of our father crashed down upon us. He was stationed at the front of the store ready to go home, and he summoned us in the most efficacious manner he knew. Oblivious of our pain, our shameful pain, in his booming orator's voice and in chronological order he summoned us. At once the entire store grew silent.

"Mary!" he shouted. A slight reverberating pause. I imagined her collapsing in a heap across the pots and pans. "George!" George chewed his tongue, winced, cast darting glances right and left, cornered, little, quick. "John!" Cool, nonchalant, John would pretend to ignore the voice, would idly finger the goods for a rapid count of three, and then race to answer the summons. "Jane!" Jane had no doubt found a friend to whom she gave a glance that asked "Jane who?" She knew. "Nancy!" he shouted. I started to whimper.

We walked home in the cold, through cold streets, clutching our packages and our humiliation, no one daring to complain, no one old enough to laugh. Our father asked if we had had a successful trip. Yes, we murmured. When we got home, Mary burst into the house, shot Mother an I-told-you-so look, and rushed off to her room.

"What's wrong with her?" Father asked. Mother must have suspected what was wrong, but she said nothing. There was no point going into it, for that would have brought forth from our father a lecture on Posturing and Finickyness. We recovered at speeds becoming to our ages. I recovered most quickly, having my money still in mind, and I went in search of George.

"I gave her the fifty-cent piece," I said, showing him the coins, "and she gave me this."

"That's sixty cents," he said. Light appeared in his face. He looked at me with incredulity and admiration. "You pulled a fast

one, kid, you rooked 'em good. You're not so stupid after all."

Oh, but I was. Ignoring my brother's entreaties, beaming with pride, confident at last of status and praise, I went sailing back to my father. "They gave me too much change," I said. My halo fairly glittered. Without the slightest show of response, for he had an infinite capacity for patience, he asked me to tell him exactly what I had bought and how much I had paid. I produced my dog-eared list, and he insisted that I get my purchases so that he could see the prices. When he had carefully examined the sales slips, he said, "Get your coat."

By the time I fully understood the import of that, the news had flashed through the house. My brothers and sisters gathered behind the banisters, silently mocking me. What a dolt, what a simp! Although their epithets were mouthed or whispered, to avoid a reprimand from our father, I began to cry, recognizing their truth.

"Honor," my father said as he closed the front door. "Honesty," he said as we walked down the walk to the car. "Fair dealing," he said. We got in the car. "Honor. Honesty. Fair dealing," he repeated as he started the car. "These are virtues without which civilization cannot endure. Money," he said as we jerked away from the curb and headed toward Woolworth's, "is only a convention of society. Yet it tests virtue as it threatens it. Let this be an abiding lesson to you."

And it was.

By next morning, my brothers and sisters had forgotten me in the thrill of Christmas. My presents were hits for the most part, although it turned out that my brothers were not as fond of Listerine as I had thought. In fact, only after they found out that I had two cap pistols for Walter would they speak to me again.

Then they berated, cajoled, wheedled, nagged, begged, and ultimately persuaded me to exchange their presents for Walter's. They went roaring through the house shooting caps while I rewrapped the Listerine in fancy paper.

I had barely finished when Walter and his mother came knocking at our door. Walter had on a new baseball uniform with regulation shoes. He walked quite carefully across the floor. He had a large package for me, wrapped in navy-blue paper and tied with a gold ribbon. His mother was all smiles and elegance as she watched him give it to me.

"If it doesn't fit," she told my mother, "do exchange it."

It was a baby-blue sweater with a white angora yoke. My mother flushed and coughed and looked hopeless.

"It's lovely," she said. "You shouldn't have."

With flamboyance and pride—for had I not selected it all by myself?—I gave Walter his present. He felt, smelled, licked the package, and when he shook it and heard the faint gurgle, he began to dance a little jig of excitement on his spikes. No doubt he thought it was whiskey. Bits of paper and ribbon flew about the room. And then a dead silence fell among us. Walter held in each hand a bottle of Listerine. Though I had bought the Listerine, made the swap, and wrapped the package, I recoiled with shock.

"Well, Nancy," said his mother, "two bottles of Listerine. I hope Walter can take that big a hint."

She was laughing, of course, and my mother was laughing. But Walter was not laughing. With a whoop of rage, he threw the bottles onto the sofa where I was sitting, and on his spikes he went screeching, sliding, cutting, tearing out of the living room and out of the house.

Attracted by all the commotion, my father came to the doorway. When he saw me, he said, "Now, Nancy, how do you like being a full-fledged participant in the yearly giving and getting? What's your verdict?" He smiled most tenderly.

I could not answer him then, and I'm not sure I could now. Thirty-odd years later, I still make my list and by the secret scale of love decide approximately how much for whom. During the course of buying, I deceive myself and others. And on Christmas night, as certain as the season, after all the presents have been exchanged and the disappointments duly felt and recorded alongside the rare perfect success, after all the inequities have been laughed away or forgiven, then I ask myself why giving and getting, these simple pleasures, must end so often in comic failure.

FOR STUDY AND DISCUSSION

1. How does the opening paragraph identify the author and establish the point of view—the feeling about the past and the experience to be narrated?

2. What is the central idea of the narrative? Where is it stated? Why do you think the author waits until this point to state her main idea?

3. What details about family finances help us to know her father? How are we prepared for his behavior at Woolworth's, at the end of the shopping trip?

4. How do the details about Walter at the beginning of the essay prepare us for the ironic ending? What is ironic about what happens to Nancy?

LANGUAGE AND VOCABULARY

Recognizing Concrete Language

Packer is concrete in her statements. She does not merely state that her father "was both proud and eccentric," and that he embarrassed his children: she provides a concrete example—his walking home from the office, his legs wrapped in newspapers. How do later details also make this point concrete?

Packer states: "But beneath our false glad cries when he told us he was coming lurked the dull recalcitrance of inveterate criminals about to be handcuffed." What images does this sentence bring to mind? How would the meaning have been changed if Packer had referred to the "unwillingness of criminals about to be handcuffed"?

Distinguishing Meanings

Look up the following italicized words, and write down how the words in each group differ in meaning.

1. Quickly he calculated *aptitudes* and *dispositions*, paired and totaled them, and sent us out like snipers to distant corners.

2. There was no point going into it, for that would have brought forth from our father a lecture on *Posturing* and *Finickyness*.

3. With a whoop of rage, he threw the bottles onto the sofa where I was sitting, and on his spikes he went *screeching, sliding, cutting, tearing out* of the living room and out of the house.

Substituting Words

Rewrite the following sentences, substituting words of your own for the italicized phrases:

1. Our eldest sister, Mary, *fastidious to a fault,* had a large bottle of Lavoris mouthwash that was the envy of us all.

2. He was stationed at the front of the store ready to go home, and he summoned us *in the most efficacious manner he knew. Oblivious of our pain,* our shameful pain, in his *booming orator's voice* and in chronological order he summoned us.

FOR COMPOSITION

Writing from Different Points of View

1. Discuss how the shopping expedition looked to a salesperson in Woolworth's or to Nancy's father. In other words, present the episode from the viewpoint of another person. Or describe Walter's reaction to the Listerine from the viewpoint of another member of the family.

2. Describe a similar episode in your own life — your first shopping trip, your first Christmas list, an embarrassment you suffered. In your opening paragraph establish your point of view — your age, feelings and experience.

Harry Mark Petrakis (1923–   ) has written novels and short stories about Greek-American life. His characters are people who live with memories of another culture and seek to join the old ways with new customs and attitudes. Petrakis was born in St. Louis, Missouri, and worked at an assortment of jobs, in steel mills and driving trucks, before becoming a writer. The selection reprinted here is taken from his autobiography, *Stelmark*.

A Whole Nation and a People

Harry Mark Petrakis

There was one storekeeper I remember above all others in my youth. It was shortly before I became ill, spending a good portion of my time with a motley group of varied ethnic ancestry. We contended with one another to deride the customs of the old country. On our Saturday forays into neighborhoods beyond our own, to prove we were really Americans, we ate hot dogs and drank Cokes. If a boy didn't have ten cents for this repast he went hungry, for he dared not bring a sandwich from home made of the spiced meats our families ate.

One of our untamed games was to seek out the owner of a pushcart or a store, unmistakably an immigrant, and bedevil him with a chorus of insults and jeers. To prove allegiance to the gang it was necessary to reserve our fiercest malevolence for a storekeeper or peddler belonging to our own ethnic background.

For that reason I led a raid on the small, shabby grocery of old Barba Nikos, a short, sinewy Greek who walked with a slight limp and sported a flaring, handlebar mustache.

We stood outside his store and dared him to come out. When he emerged to do battle, we plucked a few plums and peaches from the baskets on the sidewalk and retreated across the street to eat them while he watched. He waved a fist and hurled epithets at us in ornamental Greek.

Aware that my mettle was being tested, I raised my arm and threw my half-eaten plum at the old man. My aim was accurate and the plum struck him on the cheek. He shuddered and put his hand to the stain. He stared at me across the street, and although I could not see his eyes, I felt them sear my flesh. He turned and walked silently back into the store. The boys slapped my shoulders in admiration, but it was a hollow victory that rested like a stone in the pit of my stomach.

At twilight, when we disbanded, I passed the grocery alone on my way home. There was a small light burning in the store and the shadow of the old man's body outlined against the glass. Goaded by remorse, I walked to the door and entered.

The old man moved from behind the narrow wooden counter and stared at me. I wanted to turn and flee, but by then it was too late. As he motioned for me to come closer, I braced myself for a curse or a blow.

"You were the one," he said, finally, in a harsh voice.

I nodded mutely.

"Why did you come back?"

I stood there unable to answer.

"What's your name?"

"Haralambos," I said, speaking to him in Greek.

He looked at me in shock. "You are Greek!" he cried. "A Greek boy attacking a Greek grocer!" He stood appalled at the immensity of my crime. "All right," he said coldly. "You are here because you wish to make amends." His great mustache bristled in concentration. "Four plums, two peaches," he said. "That makes a total of seventy-eight cents. Call it seventy-five. Do you have seventy-five cents, boy?"

I shook my head.

"Then you will work it off," he said. "Fifteen cents an hour into seventy-five cents makes"—he paused—"five hours of work. Can you come here Saturday morning?"

"Yes," I said.

"Yes, Barba Nikos," he said sternly. "Show respect."

"Yes, Barba Nikos," I said.

"Saturday morning at eight o'clock," he said. "Now go home and say thanks in your prayers that I did not loosen your impudent head with a solid smack on the ear." I needed no further urging and fled.

Saturday morning, still apprehensive, I returned to the store. I began by sweeping, raising clouds of dust in dark and hidden corners. I washed the windows, whipping the squeegee swiftly up and down the glass in a fever of fear that some member of the gang would see me. When I finished I hurried back inside.

For the balance of the morning I stacked cans, washed the counter, and dusted bottles of yellow wine. A few customers entered, and Barba Nikos served them. A little after twelve o'clock he locked the door so he could eat lunch. He cut himself a few slices of sausage, tore a large chunk from a loaf of crisp-crusted bread, and filled a small cup with a dozen black shiny olives floating in brine. He offered me the cup. I could not help myself and grimaced.

"You are a stupid boy," the old man said. "You are not really Greek, are you?"

"Yes, I am."

"You might be," he admitted grudgingly. "But you do not act Greek. Wrinkling your nose at these fine olives. Look around this store for a minute. What do you see?"

"Fruits and vegetables," I said. "Cheese and olives and things like that."

He stared at me with a massive scorn. "That's what I mean," he said. "You are a bonehead. You don't understand that a whole nation and a people are in this store."

I looked uneasily toward the storeroom in the rear, almost expecting someone to emerge.

"What about olives?" he cut the air with a sweep of his arm. "There are olives of many shapes and colors. Pointed black ones from Kalamata, oval ones from Amphissa, pickled green olives and sharp tangy yellow ones. Achilles[1] carried black olives to Troy and after a day of savage battle leading his Myrmidons, he'd rest and eat cheese and ripe black olives such as these right here. You have heard of Achilles, boy, haven't you?"

"Yes," I said.

---

1. **Achilles** (ə-kĭl′ēz): a legendary Greek warrior, hero of the epic poem *The Iliad.*

"Yes, Barba Nikos."

"Yes, Barba Nikos," I said.

He motioned at the row of jars filled with varied spices. "There is origanon there and basilikon and daphne and sesame and miantanos, all the marvelous flavorings that we have used in our food for thousands of years. The men of Marathon[2] carried small packets of these spices into battle, and the scents reminded them of their homes, their families, and their children."

He rose and tugged his napkin free from around his throat. "Cheese, you said. Cheese! Come closer, boy, and I will educate your abysmal ignorance." He motioned toward a wooden container on the counter. "That glistening white delight is feta, made from goat's milk, packed in wooden buckets to retain the flavor. Alexander the Great demanded it on his table with his casks of wine when he planned his campaigns."

He walked limping from the counter to the window where the piles of tomatoes, celery, and green peppers clustered. "I suppose all you see here are some random vegetables?" He did not wait for me to answer. "You are dumb again. These are some of the ingredients that go to make up a Greek salad. Do you know what a Greek salad really is? A meal in itself, an experience, an emotional involvement. It is created deftly and with grace. First, you place large lettuce leaves in a big, deep bowl." He spread his fingers and moved them slowly, carefully, as if he were arranging the leaves. "The remainder of the lettuce is shredded and piled in a small mound," he said. "Then comes celery, cucumbers, tomatoes sliced lengthwise, green peppers, origanon, green olives, feta, avocado, and anchovies. At the end you dress it with lemon, vinegar, and pure olive oil, glinting golden in the light."

He finished with a heartfelt sigh and for a moment closed his eyes. Then he opened one eye to mark me with a baleful intensity. "The story goes that Zeus[3] himself created the recipe and assembled and mixed the ingredients on Mount Olympus[4] one night when he had invited some of the other gods to dinner."

He turned his back on me and walked slowly again across the store, dragging one foot slightly behind him. I looked uneasily at the clock, which showed that it was a few minutes past one. He turned quickly and

---

2. **Marathon:** an ancient Greek village, site of a battle between the Greeks and the Persians in the fifth century B.C.

3. **Zeus:** in Greek mythology, the king of the gods.
4. **Mount Olympus:** the home of the ancient Greek gods and goddesses.

startled me. "And everything else in here," he said loudly. "White beans, lentils, garlic, crisp bread, kokoretsi, meatballs, mussels and clams." He paused and drew a deep, long breath. "And the wine," he went on, "wine from Samos, Santorini, and Crete, retsina and mavrodaphne, a taste almost as old as water . . . and then the fragrant melons, the pastries, yellow diples and golden loukoumades, the honey custard galatobouriko. Everything a part of our history, as much a part as the exquisite sculpture in marble, the bearded warriors, Pan[5] and the oracles at Delphi,[6] and the nymphs dancing in the shadowed groves under Homer's[7] glittering moon." He paused, out of breath again, and coughed harshly. "Do you understand now, boy?"

He watched my face for some response and then grunted. We stood silent for a moment until he cocked his head and stared at the clock. "It is time for you to leave," he motioned brusquely toward the door. "We are square now. Keep it that way."

I decided the old man was crazy and reached behind the counter for my jacket and cap and started for the door. He called me back. From a box he drew out several soft, yellow figs that he placed in a piece of paper. "A bonus because you worked well," he said. "Take them. When you taste them, maybe you will understand what I have been talking about."

I took the figs and he unlocked the door and I hurried from the store. I looked back once and saw him standing in the doorway, watching me, the swirling tendrils of food curling like mist about his head.

---

5. **Pan:** a god of fields and forests.
6. **oracles . . . Delphi:** The gods were consulted through oracles—priests and priestesses who uttered divine prophecies.
7. **Homer:** a Greek epic poet, author of the *Iliad* and the *Odyssey*.

Detail from Attic black-figured amphora
Museum of Fine Arts, Boston
Pierce Residuary Fund and Bartlett Collection

I ate the figs late that night. I forgot about them until I was in bed, and then I rose and took the package from my jacket. I nibbled at one, then ate them all. They broke apart between my teeth with a tangy nectar, a thick sweetness running like honey across my tongue and into the pockets of my cheeks. In the morning when I woke, I could still taste and inhale their fragrance.

I never again entered Barba Nikos' store. My spell of illness, which began some months later, lasted two years. When I returned to the streets I had forgotten the old man and the grocery. Shortly afterwards my family moved from the neighborhood.

Some twelve years later, after the war, I drove through the old neighborhood and passed the grocery. I stopped the car and for a moment stood before the store. The windows were stained with dust and grime, the interior bare and desolate, a store in a decrepit group of stores marked for razing so new structures could be built.

I have been in many Greek groceries since then and have often bought the feta and Kalamata olives. I have eaten countless Greek salads and have indeed found them a meal for the gods. On the holidays in our house, my wife and sons and I sit down to a dinner of steaming, buttered pilaf like my mother used to make and lemon-egg avgolemono and roast lamb richly seasoned with cloves of garlic. I drink the red and yellow wines, and for dessert I have come to relish the delicate pastries coated with honey and powdered sugar. Old Barba Nikos would have been pleased.

But I have never been able to recapture the halcyon flavor of those figs he gave me on that day so long ago, although I have bought figs many times. I have found them pleasant to my tongue, but there is something missing. And to this day I am not sure whether it was the figs or the vision and passion of the old grocer that coated the fruit so sweetly I can still recall their savor and fragrance after almost thirty years.

FOR STUDY AND DISCUSSION

1. In his opening paragraphs, Petrakis tells how he and his friends banded together to reject their own ethnic backgrounds. Why is this information important to understanding the experience he narrates?

2. What details characterize Barba Nikos? What shows his feelings about how children are raised in America?

3. Although the narrator wants the respect of his companions, he feels that the attack on the grocer is "a hollow victory." Why?

4. What role does ancient Greek culture play in Barba Nikos' life? How does that culture shape his values?

5. How does the concluding statement about the figs suggest a central point or thesis? Is the appearance of the store twelve years later important to what Petrakis is saying about Barba Nikos' values and world?

LANGUAGE AND VOCABULARY

Examining Phrases from Context
Explain these phrases from the selection:

1. . . . motley group . . .
2. . . . our fiercest malevolence . . .
3. . . . my mettle was being tested . . .
4. . . . your abysmal ignorance.
5. . . . created deftly and with grace.
6. . . . he motioned brusquely . . .
7. . . . swirling tendrils of food . . .
8. . . . decrepit group of stores . . .
9. . . . the halcyon flavor of those figs . . .

FOR COMPOSITION

Writing About a Personal Experience
Write an essay on someone who influenced your life in the way Barba Nikos influenced the narrator. Describe the person fully—physical appearance, manner of speech, values, attitude toward children, and other pertinent details. In your opening paragraph tell your readers who you are and why you are narrating the experience.

George Plimpton (1927–   ) attended Harvard University and King's College, Cambridge. He began his career in journalism as editor of the *Harvard Lampoon*, and later edited the *Paris Review*, *Horizon*, and *Sports Illustrated*. To discover how professional athletes, musicians, and other performers live and work, he has trained with them and actually participated in games and orchestral performances (with the New York Philharmonic Orchestra). Plimpton has investigated baseball, football, hockey, and boxing. His book *Paper Lion* describes his experiences with the Detroit Lions, with whom Plimpton trained, lived and played in 1963.

The reader of *Paper Lion* may expect an amusing account of the mishaps of an amateur player treated indulgently by professional football players. But Plimpton has surprises in store for the reader. For he discovered quickly that not all the Lions were prepared to welcome an amateur. Each player entering the team had to prove himself. Plimpton could not be sure how the team would treat him on the practice field, or how spectators even at an exhibition game would accept an amateur quarterback who knew five plays and never before had participated in a professional football game. Plimpton describes what happened in this lively narrative.

My Career as a Quarterback
George Plimpton

Jack Benny[1] used to say that when he stood on the stage in white tie and tails for his violin concerts and raised his bow to begin his routine scraping through "Love in Bloom"—

that he *felt* like a great violinist. He reasoned that, if he wasn't a great violinist, what was he doing dressed in tails, and about to play before a large audience?

At Pontiac I *felt* myself a football quarterback, not an interloper. My game plan was organized, and I knew what I was supposed to do. My nerves seemed steady, much steadier

---

1. **Jack Benny** (1894–1974): a comedian who appeared on radio, stage, film, and television. One of his comic routines was producing discordant sounds on his violin.

than they had been as I waited on the bench. I trotted along easily. I was keenly aware of what was going on around me.

I could hear Bud Erickson's voice over the loudspeaker system, a dim murmur, telling the crowd what was going on. He was telling them that number zero, coming out across the sidelines was not actually a rookie, but an amateur, a writer, who had been training with the team for three weeks and had learned five plays, which he was now going to run against the first-string Detroit defense. It was like a nightmare come true, he told them, as if one of *them*, rocking a beer around in a paper cup, with a pretty girl leaning past him to ask the hot-dog vendor in the aisle for mustard, were suddenly carried down underneath the stands by a sinister clutch of ushers. He would protest, but he would be encased in the accouterments, the silver helmet, with the two protruding bars of the cage, jammed down over his ears, and sent out to take over the team — that was the substance of Erickson's words, drifting across the field, swayed and shredded by the steady breeze coming up across the open end of Wisner Stadium from the vanished sunset. The crowd was interested, and I was conscious, just vaguely, of a steady roar of encouragement.

The team was waiting for me, grouped in the huddle watching me come. I went in among them. Their heads came down for the signal. I called out, "Twenty-six!" forcefully, to inspire them, and a voice from one of the helmets said, "Down, down, the whole stadium can hear you."

"Twenty-six," I hissed at them. "Twenty-six near oh pinch; on three. *Break!*" Their hands cracked as one, and I wheeled and started for the line behind them.

My confidence was extreme. I ambled slowly behind Whitlow, poised down over the ball, and I had sufficient presence to pause,

resting a hand at the base of his spine, as if on a windowsill — a nonchalant gesture I had admired in certain quarterbacks — and I looked out over the length of his back to fix in my mind what I saw.

Everything fine about being a quarterback — the embodiment of his power — was encompassed in those dozen seconds or so: giving the instructions to ten attentive men, breaking out of the huddle, walking for the line, and then pausing behind the center, dawdling amidst men poised and waiting under the trigger of his voice, cataleptic, until the deliverance of himself and them to the future. The pleasure of the sport was so often the chance to indulge the cessation of time itself — the pitcher dawdling on the mound, the skier poised at the top of a mountain trail, the basketball player with the rough skin of the ball against his palm preparing for a foul shot, the tennis player at set point over his opponent — all of them savoring a moment before committing themselves to action.

I had the sense of a portcullis[2] down. On the other side of the imaginary bars the linemen were poised, the light glistening off their helmets, and close in behind them were the linebackers, with Joe Schmidt just opposite me, the big number 56 shining on his white jersey, jumpjacking back and forth with quick choppy steps, his hands poised in front of him, and he was calling out defensive code words in a stream. I could sense the rage in his voice, and the tension in those rows of bodies waiting, as if coils had been wound overtight, which my voice, calling a signal, like a lever would trip to spring them all loose. "Blue! Blue! Blue!" I heard Schmidt shout.

Within my helmet, the schoolmaster's voice murmured at me: "Son, nothing to it, nothing at all . . ."

I bent over the center. Quickly, I went over what was supposed to happen—I would receive the snap and take two steps straight back, and hand the ball to the number-two back coming laterally across from right to left, who would then cut into the number-six hole. That was what was designated by 26—the two back into the six hole. The mysterious code words "near oh pinch" referred to blocking assignments in the line, and I was never sure exactly what was meant by them. The important thing was to hang on to the ball, turn, and get the ball into the grasp of the back coming across laterally.

I cleared my throat. "Set!" I called out—my voice loud and astonishing to hear, as if it belonged to someone shouting into the earholes of my helmet. "Sixteen, sixty-five, forty-four, *hut* one, *hut* two, *hut* three," and at three the ball slapped back into my palm, and Whitlow's rump bucked up hard as he went for the defensemen opposite.

2. **portcullis** (pôrt-kŭl′ĭs): a grating used to close a gateway.

The lines cracked together with a yawp and smack of pads and gear. I had the sense of quick, heavy movement, and as I turned for the backfield, not a second having passed, I was hit hard from the side, and as I gasped the ball was jarred loose. It sailed away, and bounced once, and I stumbled after it, hauling it under me five yards back, hearing the rush of feet, and the heavy jarring and wheezing of the blockers fending off the defense, a great roar up from the crowd, and above it, a relief to hear, the shrilling of the referee's whistle. My first thought was that at the snap of the ball, the right side of the line had collapsed just at the second of the handoff, and one of the tacklers, Brown or Floyd Peters, had cracked through to make me fumble. Someone, I assumed, had messed up on the assignments designated by the mysterious code words "near oh pinch." In fact, as I discovered later, my *own man* bowled me over—John Gordy, whose assignment as offensive guard was to pull from his position and join the interference on the far side of the center. He was required to pull back and travel at a great clip parallel to the line of scrimmage to get out in front of the runner, his route theoretically passing between me and the center. But the extra second it took me to control the ball, and the creaking execution of my turn, put me in his path, a rare sight for Gordy to see, his own quarterback blocking the way, like coming around a corner in a high-speed car to find a moose ambling across the center line, and he caromed off me, jarring the ball loose.

It was not new for me to be hit down by my own people. At Cranbrook I was knocked down all the time by players on the offense—the play patterns run with such speed along routes so carefully defined that if everything wasn't done right and at the proper speed, the play would break down in its making. I was often reminded of film clips in which the process of a porcelain pitcher, say, being dropped by a butler and smashed, is shown in reverse, so that the pieces pick up off the floor and soar up to the butler's hand, each piece on a predestined route, sudden perfection out of chaos. Often, it did not take more than an inch or so off line to throw a play out of kilter. On one occasion at the training camp, practicing handoff plays to the fullback, I had my chin hanging out just a bit too far, something wrong with my posture, and Pietrosante's shoulder pad caught it like a punch as he went by, and I spun slowly to the ground, grabbing at my jaw. Brettschneider had said that afternoon: "The defense is going to rack you up one of these days, if your own team'd let you *stand* long enough for us defense guys to get *at* you. It's aggravating to bust through and find that you've already been laid flat by your own offense guys."

My confidence had not gone. I stood up.

The referee took the ball from me. He had to tug to get it away, a faint look of surprise on his face. My inner voice was assuring me that the fault in the tumble had not been mine. "They let you down," it was saying. "The blocking failed." But the main reason for my confidence was the next play on my list—the 93 pass, a play which I had worked successfully in the Cranbrook scrimmages. I walked into the huddle and I said with considerable enthusiasm, "All right! All *right!* Here we *go!*"

"Keep the voice down," said a voice. "You'll be tipping them the play."

I leaned in on them and said: "Green right" ("Green" designated a pass play, "right" put the flanker to the right side), "three right" (which put the three back to the right), "ninety-three" (indicating the two primary receivers; nine, the right end, and three, the three back) "on *three . . . Break!*"—the clap of

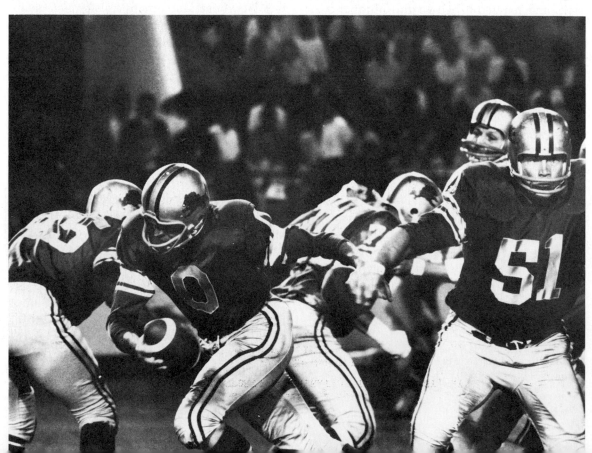

the hands again in unison, the team streamed past me up to the line, and I walked briskly up behind Whitlow.

Again, I knew exactly how the play was going to develop—back those seven yards into the defensive pocket for the three to four seconds it was supposed to hold, and Pietrosante, the three back, would go down in his pattern, ten yards straight, then cut over the middle, and I would hit him.

"Set! . . . sixteen! . . . eighty-eight . . . fifty-five . . . *hut* one . . . *hut* two . . . *hut* three . . ."

The ball slapped into my palm at "three." I turned and started back. I could feel my balance going, and two yards behind the line of scrimmage I *fell down*—absolutely flat, as if my feet had been pinned under a trip wire stretched across the field, not a hand laid on me. I heard a great roar go up from the crowd. Suffused as I had been with confidence, I could scarcely believe what had happened. Mud cleats catching in the grass? Slipped in the dew? I felt my jaw go ajar in my helmet. "Wha'? Wha'?"—the mortification beginning to come fast. I rose hurriedly to my knees at the referee's whistle, and I could see my team-mates' big silver helmets with the blue Lion decals turn toward me, some of the players rising from blocks they'd thrown to protect me, their faces masked, automaton, prognathous[3] with the helmet bars protruding toward me, characterless, yet the dismay was in the set of their bodies as they loped back for the huddle. The schoolmaster's voice flailed at me inside my helmet. "Ox!" it cried. "Clumsy oaf."

I joined the huddle. "Sorry, sorry," I said.

"Call the play, man," came a voice from one of the helmets.

"I don't know what happened," I said.

"Call it, man."

---

3. **prognathous** (prŏg′nə-thəs): with jaws projecting.

The third play on my list was the 42, an-other running play, one of the simplest in foot-ball, in which the quarterback receives the snap, makes a full spin, and shoves the ball into the four back's stomach—the fullback's. He has come straight forward from his posi-tion as if off starting blocks, his knees high, and he disappears with the ball into the number-two hole just to the left of the center—a straight power play, and one which, seen from the stands, seems to offer no difficulty.

I got into an awful jam with it. Once again, the jack-rabbit speed of the professional back-field was too much for me. The fullback—Danny Lewis—was past me and into the line before I could complete my spin and set the ball in his belly. And so I did what was required: I tucked the ball into my own belly and followed Lewis into the line, hoping that he might have budged open a small hole.

I tried, grimacing, my eyes squinted almost shut, and waiting for the impact, which came before I'd taken two steps—I was grabbed up by Roger Brown.

He tackled me high, and straightened me with his power, so that I churned against his three-hundred-pound girth like a comic bicy-clist. He began to shake me. I remained upright to my surprise, flailed back and forth, and I realized that he was struggling for the ball. His arms were around it, trying to tug it free. The bars of our helmets were nearly locked, and I could look through and see him inside—the first helmeted face I recognized that evening—the small, brown eyes surpris-ingly peaceful, but he was grunting hard, the sweat shining, and I had time to think, "It's Brown, it's *Brown!*" before I lost the ball to him, and flung to one knee on the ground I watched him lumber ten yards into the end zone behind us for a touchdown.

The referee wouldn't allow it. He said he'd blown the ball dead while we were struggling for it. Brown was furious. "You taking that away from *me*," he said, his voice high and squeaky. "Man, I took that ball in there good."

The referee turned and put the ball on the

ten-yard line. I had lost twenty yards in three attempts, and I had yet, in fact, to run off a complete play.

The veterans walked back very slowly to the next huddle.

I stood off to one side, listening to Brown rail at the referee. "I never scored like that befo'. You takin' that away from me?" His voice was peeved. He looked off toward the stands, into the heavy tumult of sound, spreading the big palms of his hands in grief.

I watched him, detached, not even moved by his insistence that I suffer the humiliation of having the ball stolen for a touchdown. If the referee had allowed him his score, I would not have protested. The shock of having the three plays go as badly as they had left me dispirited and numb, the purpose of the exercise forgotten. Even the schoolmaster's voice seemed to have gone—a bleak despair having set in so that as I stood shifting uneasily, watching Brown jawing at the referee, I was perfectly willing to trot in to the bench at that point and be done with it.

Then, by chance, I happened to see Brettschneider standing at his corner linebacker position, watching me, and beyond the bars of his cage I could see a grin working. That set my energies ticking over once again —the notion that some small measure of recompense would be mine if I could complete a pass in the Badger's territory and embarrass him. I had such a play in my series—a slant pass to the strong-side end, Jim Gibbons.

I walked back to the huddle. It was slow in forming. I said, "The Badger's asleep. He's fat and he's asleep."

No one said anything. Everyone stared down. In the silence I became suddenly aware of the feet. There are twenty-two of them in the huddle, after all, most of them very large, in a small area, and while the quarterback ruminates and the others await his instruction,

there's nothing else to catch the attention. The sight pricked at my mind, the oval of twenty-two football shoes, and it may have been responsible for my error in announcing the play. I forgot to give the signal on which the ball was to be snapped back by the center. I said: "Green right nine slant *break!*" One or two of the players clapped their hands, and as the huddle broke, some of them automatically heading for the line of scrimmage, someone hissed: "Well, the *signal*, what's the signal?"

I had forgotten to say "on two."

I should have kept my head and formed the huddle again. Instead, I called out "Two!" in a loud stage whisper, directing my call first to one side, then the other, *"two! two!"* as we walked up the line. For those that might have been beyond earshot, who might have missed the signal, I held out two fingers spread like a V, which I showed around furtively, trying to hide it from the defense, and hoping that my people would see.

The pass was incomplete. I took two steps back (the play was a quick pass, thrown without out a protective pocket) and I saw Gibbons break from his position, then stop, buttonhooking;[4] his hand, which I used as a target, came up, but I threw the ball over him. A yell came up from the crowd seeing the ball in the air (it was the first play of the evening which hadn't been "blown"—to use the player's expression for a missed play), but then a groan went up when the ball was overshot and bounced across the sidelines.

"Last play," George Wilson was calling. He had walked over with a clipboard in his hand and was standing by the referee. "The ball's on the ten. Let's see you take it all the way," he called out cheerfully.

---

4. **buttonhooking:** making a J-turn.

One of the players asked: "Which end zone is he talking about?"

The last play of the series was a pitchout—called a flip on some teams—a long lateral to the number-four back running parallel to the line and cutting for the eight hole at left end. The lateral, though long, was easy for me to do. What I had to remember was to keep on running out after the flight of the ball. The hole behind me as I lateraled was left unguarded by an offensive lineman pulling out from his position and the defensive tackle could bull through and take me from behind in his rush, not knowing I'd got rid of the ball, if I didn't clear out of the area.

I was able to get the lateral off and avoid the tackler behind me, but unfortunately the defense was keyed for the play. They knew my repertoire, which was only five plays or so, and they doubted I'd call the same play twice. One of my linemen told me later that the defensive man opposite him in the line, Floyd Peters, had said, "Well, here comes the forty-eight pitchout," and it *had* come, and they were able to throw the number-four back, Pietrosante, who had received the lateral, back on the one-yard line—just a yard away from the mortification of having moved a team backward from the thirty-yard line into one's own end zone for a safety.

As soon as I saw Pietrosante go down, I left for the bench on the sidelines at midfield, a long run from where I'd brought my team, and I felt utterly weary, shuffling along through the grass.

Applause began to sound from the stands, and I looked up, startled, and saw people standing, and the hands going. It made no sense at the time. It was not derisive; it seemed solid and respectful. "Wha'? Wha'?" I thought, and I wondered if the applause wasn't meant for someone else—if the mayor had come into the stadium behind me and

was waving from an open-topped car. But as I came up to the bench I could see the people in the stands looking at me, and the hands going.

I thought about the applause afterward. Some of it was, perhaps, in appreciation of the lunacy of my participation, and for the fortitude it took to do it; but most of it, even if subconscious, I decided was in *relief* that I had done as badly as I had: it verified the assumption that the average fan would have about an amateur blundering into the brutal world of professional football. He would get slaughtered. If by some chance I had uncorked a touchdown pass, there would have been wild acknowledgment—because I heard the groans go up at each successive disaster—but afterward the spectators would have felt uncomfortable. Their concept of things would have been upset. The outsider did not belong, and there was comfort in that being proved.

Some of the applause, as it turned out, came from people who had enjoyed the comic aspects of my stint. More than a few thought that they were being entertained by a professional comic in the tradition of baseball's Al Schacht, or the Charlie Chaplins, the clowns, of the bullfights. Bud Erickson told me that a friend of his had come up to him later: "Bud, that's one of the funniest . . . I mean that guy's *got* it," this man said, barely able to control himself.

I did not take my helmet off when I reached the bench. It was tiring to do and there was security in having it on. I was conscious of the big zero on my back facing the crowd when I sat down. Some players came by and tapped me on the top of the helmet. Brettschneider leaned down and said, "Well, you stuck it . . . that's the big thing."

The scrimmage began. I watched it for a while, but my mind returned to my own performance. The pawky[5] inner voice was at hand again. "You didn't stick it," it said testily. "You funked it."

At half time Wilson took the players down to the band shell at one end of the stadium. I stayed on the bench. He had his clipboards with him, and I could see him pointing and explaining, a big semicircle of players around him, sitting on the band chairs. Fireworks soared up into the sky from the other end of the field, the shells puffing out clusters of light that lit the upturned faces on the crowd in silver, then red, and then the reports would go off, reverberating sharply, and in the stands across the field I could see the children's hands flap up over their ears. Through the noise I heard someone yelling my name. I turned and saw a girl leaning over the rail of the grandstand behind me. I recognized her from the Gay Haven in Dearborn. She was wearing a mohair Italian sweater, the color of spun pink sugar, and tight pants, and she was holding a thick folding wallet in one hand along with a pair of dark glasses, and in the other a Lion banner, which she waved, her face alive with excitement, very pretty in a perishable, childlike way, and she was calling, "Beautiful; it was beautiful."

The fireworks lit her, and she looked up, her face chalk-white in the swift aluminum glare.

I looked at her out of my helmet. Then I lifted a hand, just tentatively.

---

5. **pawky** (pô′kē): tricky.

FOR STUDY AND DISCUSSION

1. How does the anecdote about Jack Benny and Plimpton's comments on his entry on the field help us to understand his feelings?

2. We know how the professional quarterback feels through what he does—"dawdling amidst men poised and waiting under the trigger of his voice." What other details help us to understand the work and feelings of the quarterback? What details help us to understand the work and feelings of linebackers?

3. How do Plimpton's feelings change during the course of the game?

4. How does Plimpton convey the difficulty of the various plays, and the difference between what the spectators see and what the players see and experience?

5. What point is Plimpton making about the crowd's response to his performance? What is his attitude toward the girl in the grandstand?

6. The word *tentative* means "hesitant" or "uncertain." What feelings does Plimpton want to convey about his experience in the final sentence of the selection, "Then I lifted a hand, just tentatively"?

LANGUAGE AND VOCABULARY

Noting How Style Relates to Subject

Words sometimes are chosen because their sounds seem to imitate the action they describe: we call this effect *onomatopoeia*. A *yawp* is a loud, harsh cry, and Plimpton uses the word to convey the effect of players crashing into one another: "The lines cracked together with a yawp and smack of pads and gear." Notice that the word sounds like the action it describes. What other words in this sentence and paragraph are onomatopoeic? What words later in the selection suggest the sound of action?

The movement of Plimpton's sentences often imitates the action being described:

> It sailed away, and bounced once, and I stumbled after it, hauling it under me five yards back, hearing the rush of feet, and the heavy jarring and wheezing of the blockers fending off the defense, a great roar up from the crowd, and above it, a relief to hear, the shrilling of the referee's whistle.

The sentence presents a series of connected actions and impressions in chronological order. Had Plimpton broken the sentence into several short ones, the sense of movement would have been interrupted: the sentence would no longer imitate the action. Find another sentence in the selection that imitates an action in the same way, and explain how it does so.

Long sentences like the above succeed through sentence parallelism. Words that perform the same function have the same form:

> *hauling* it . . . *hearing* the rush of feet

Find other examples of this use of parallelism in long sentences.

Plimpton often uses very short sentences to convey instantaneous actions and feelings: "I got into an awful jam with it." What other short sentences do you find performing the same function?

Plimpton uses the jargon of football players. He tells us that the "pitchout" is "called a flip on some teams." What other examples of football jargon do you find in the selection?

FOR COMPOSITION

Describing an Action from the Player's Viewpoint

Describe a scrimmage in football, fielding in baseball, serving in tennis, tending goal in ice hockey, or some other action from the viewpoint of the player. Make your details as specific and evocative of the sport as you can. Try writing a long sentence that imitates a connected action, but in doing so keep in mind that the reference of your words must be clear to your reader.

Explaining the Rules of a Game

Choose some indoor or outdoor game with which you are familiar. Write an essay explaining the rules of the game. To make sure your discussion is inclusive, prepare an outline before writing. For the game of football, your outline might look like this:

The Rules of Football

I. Football field
   A. Dimensions of the playing area
   B. Position of the goalposts
II. Players
   A. Composition of the teams
   B. Positions and functions of the players
III. Equipment
   A. Uniforms
   B. Ball
IV. Plays
   A. Scoring
   B. Offensive and defensive plays
      1. Kickoff
      2. Runback
      3. Tackle, etc.
   C. Fouls
   D. Length of game
   E. Time out
V. Officials
   A. Referee
   B. Lineman, etc.

Practice in Reading and Writing

DESCRIPTION, NARRATION, AND EXPOSITION

Most writing uses a combination of description, narration, and exposition, very often within a single passage. This paragraph from *The Life of Charles Dickens* illustrates the three kinds of writing. In the course of narrating his experiences in the blacking warehouse, Dickens gives a vivid description of the setting and explains the process of pasting labels on bottles:

The blacking warehouse was the last house on the left-hand side of the way, at old Hungerford Stairs. It was a crazy, tumbledown old house, abutting of course on the river, and literally overrun with rats. Its wainscotted rooms, and its rotten floors and staircase, and the old gray rats swarming down in the cellars, and the sound of their squeaking and scuffling coming up the stairs at all times, and the dirt and decay of the place, rise up visibly before me, as if I were there again. The countinghouse was on the first floor, looking over the coal barges and the river. There was a recess in it, in which I was to sit and work. My work was to cover the pots of paste-blacking, first with a piece of oilpaper, and then with a piece of blue paper; to tie them round with a string; and then to clip the paper close and neat, all round, until it looked as smart as a pot of ointment from an apothecary's shop. When a certain number of grosses of pots had attained this pitch of perfection, I was to paste on each a printed label, and then go on again with more pots. Two or three other boys were kept at similar duty downstairs on similar wages. One of them came up, in a ragged apron and a paper cap, on the first Monday morning, to show me the trick of using the string and tying the knot. His name was Bob Fagin; and I took the liberty of using his name, long afterwards, in *Oliver Twist.*

Read this paragraph from "The Labyrinthine City of Fez" by
Anaïs Nin and tell what its central idea is. Identify the kind
or kinds of writing the author uses and give the purpose each
kind of writing serves in the paragraph.

The Moroccan can work in a small space because he
knows the art of stillness, he is concentrated on his work,
immobile. He does not know restlessness. He is unraveling
silk skeins, rolling the silk onto bobbins, tying and braiding
belts. But just as you begin to float on a dream of silk,
muslins, embroidery, you are plunged into the hundreds of
hammer blows of copperwork. Copper trays, copper-edged
mirrors, candelabra, teapots, are being carved with a burin
and hammer. The men hold the large trays between their
knees. The oldest and the best of the artists works with infinite precision, reproducing designs from famous mosques.
His dishes shine like gold, and the designs open and flower
and expand and proliferate like intoxicated nature. There are
always children and young men in the background, learning
the craft.

Write an essay in which you analyze some experience in
your past. This might take the form of an encounter with an
adult, such as that narrated by Harry Petrakis in "A Whole
Nation and a People." It might be a childhood experience in
the manner of Nancy Huddleston Packer's "Giving, Getting." It might be an experience of performing before a
crowd, like that of George Plimpton in "My Career as a Quarterback." You may combine narration, description, and exposition in your essay.

For Further Reading

Asimov, Isaac, *The Beginning and the End* (Doubleday, 1977)
  Here are twenty-three discussions about the past, present, and future of the universe.

Bombeck, Erma, *If Life Is a Bowl of Cherries— What Am I Doing in the Pits?* (Mc-Graw-Hill, 1978)
  In a funny encore to her earlier books, Bombeck confronts and copes with the daily annoyances of suburban life.

Clarke, Arthur C., *Profiles of the Future: An Inquiry into the Limits of the Possible,* revised edition (Harper & Row, 1973; paperback, Popular Library)
  The author focuses on some possibilities and promises of a "fantastic" future.

Eiseley, Loren, *The Firmament of Time* (paperback, Atheneum, 1960)
  Eiseley discusses such subjects as "How the World Became Natural" and "How Life Became Natural."

Frank, Anne, *The Diary of a Young Girl,* translated by B. M. Mooyart (Doubleday, 1952; paperback, Pocket Books)
  Anne Frank kept this diary while she lived in hiding in Amsterdam during the Nazi Occupation in World War II.

Gemme, Leila B., *The New Breed of Athlete* (paperback, Pocket Books, 1975)
  Here are portraits of Joe Namath, Kareem Abdul-Jabbar, Billie Jean King, and nine other men and women who pay little attention to the old rules of the sports world.

Herriot, James, *All Creatures Great and Small* (St. Martin, 1972; paperback, Bantam)
  A country veterinary surgeon recounts the special problems and joys of his life and work with animals.

Plath, Aurelia S., editor, *Letters Home* (Harper & Row, 1975; paperback, Bantam)
  From her college days to her death, poet and novelist Sylvia Plath wrote nearly a thousand letters to her mother. Together they form a fascinating autobiography.

Read, Piers Paul, *Alive: The Story of the Andes Survivors* (Lippincott, 1974; paperback, Avon)
  This is the account of a plane crash in the snowbound Andes and of the young people who managed to survive seventy-two days under the most extreme conditions.

Steffens, Lincoln, *The Autobiography of Lincoln Steffens* (Harvest paperback, Harcourt Brace Jovanovich)
  Here is the life story of a great journalist who became famous in the reform movement called "muckraking," which exposed political and financial corruption early in this century.

Stuart, Jesse, *The Thread That Runs So True* (Scribner, 1968; paperback, Scribner)
  The novelist and poet recalls his unusual experiences as a young teacher in a one-room Kentucky schoolhouse.

Teale, Edwin Way, *A Walk Through the Year* (Dodd, Mead, 1978)
  The well-known naturalist sets down his experiences and discoveries as he walks through Trail Wood, his New England homestead.

Thomas, Lewis, *Lives of a Cell: Notes of a Biology Watcher* (Viking Press, 1974; paperback, Bantam)
  Thomas' reflections on language, music, ants and ecology, and other subjects form a bold vision of the world around us.

Thurber, James, *My Life and Hard Times* (paperback, Harper & Row, 1973)
  In this collection of incidents from his early days in Columbus, Ohio, Thurber satirizes the silly things people sometimes do when they think they are using good sense.

Twain, Mark, *Life on the Mississippi* (many editions)
  Twain reminisces about Mississippi riverboat life and his youthful experiences as an apprentice to a steamboat pilot.

White, E. B., *Essays of E. B. White* (Harper & Row, 1977)
  Chosen by White himself, these uncommonly amusing essays are grouped under such headings as "The Farm," "The Planet," and "The City."

We live in a fast-moving age that often forces us to move fast, too. It is the age of "speed-reading," and students are frequently encouraged to read quickly so they can take in large amounts of information in a short time. Many ads and articles are written in simple, stripped-down form so they can be read and digested swiftly. But poetry is a different kind of writing and demands a different kind of reading — reading that is more leisurely, more personal. A poem is not read like a newspaper, for quick information, but rather for an emotional and thought-provoking experience.

Sometimes a single sentence of poetry is as rich and complex as a whole paragraph of prose. Also, poetry pays great attention to sound. The words and lines are meant to be savored and enjoyed, not thoughtlessly gulped down. And the sounds may be more than simply pleasurable: they may add emotion and power to the poem's content. For all these reasons, it is a good idea to read a poem several times, and to read it more slowly than you would read prose. It is also helpful to read the poem aloud, to experience fully its language and rhythms.

POETRY

The Speaker

The poet Robert Frost once said that a poem is "spoken by a person in a scene—in character, in a setting." This person, or *speaker*, is often simply the poet, but may be someone or something altogether different from the poet. Through the ages, poets have delighted in disguising their voices, like actors, and speaking as characters.

One aid to understanding a poem is to identify its speaker. Your knowledge of who or what the speaker is will help you understand other things about the poem: where and when the poem is set, what situation it describes, what story it tells.

Ego   *Philip Booth*

When I was on Night Line,
flying my hands to park
a big-bird B-29,
I used to command the dark:
four engines were mine   5

to jazz; I was ground crew,
an unfledged pfc,
but when I waved planes through
that flight line in Tennessee,
my yonder was wild blue.   10

Warming up, I was hot
on the throttle, logging an hour
of combat, I was the pilot
who rogered the tower.
I used to take off a lot.   15

With a flat-hat for furlough
and tin wings to sleep on,
I fueled my high-octane ego:
I buzzed, I landed my jeep on
the ramp, I flew low.   20

When a cross-country hop
let down, I was the big deal
who signaled big wheels to stop.
That's how I used to feel.
I used to get all revved up.   25

FOR STUDY AND DISCUSSION

1. The speaker in this poem used to direct bomber planes to their parking places on the landing field. Although he was an "unfledged pfc," how did he feel? He says in lines 4–6, "I used to command the dark:/four engines were mine/to jazz." Which other lines in the poem indicate what he imagined himself doing?

2. Reread the last stanza of the poem. How does the speaker now feel about the job and about himself? Do you think that he is laughing at himself? That he is nostalgic? What evidence in the poem supports your answer?

3. The word *I* appears fourteen times in the poem. Why do you think the poet uses this word so frequently? Do you think that "Ego" is a good title for this poem? Explain.

LANGUAGE AND VOCABULARY

Recognizing Jargon

Jargon is the special language used by people who do the same kind of work or who have the same kind of hobby. Policemen have their own jargon; so do reporters and citizen-band radio enthusiasts. Jargon is also used as a derogatory term for any unintelligible speech.

In "Ego," Philip Booth uses military jargon. When the speaker says, "flying my hands to park/a big-bird B-29" (lines 2–3), he is referring to hand signals used to direct the B-29 airplanes to their parking places. What other examples of military jargon can you find in "Ego"? Given the amount of jargon in the poem, how deeply do you think the speaker was involved in his job?

*The Chattahoochee (chăt'ə-hoo'chē) River begins in the
Blue Ridge Mountains of northeastern Georgia and forms
the Georgia–Alabama and Georgia–Florida borders.
Habersham and Hall are counties in northeast Georgia
through which the Chattahoochee flows.*

Song of the Chattahoochee   *Sidney Lanier*

Out of the hills of Habersham,
  Down the valleys of Hall
I hurry amain° to reach the plain,   **3. amain:** energetically.
Run the rapid and leap the fall,
Split at the rock and together again,   5
Accept my bed, or narrow or° wide,   **6. or . . . or:** either . . . or.
And flee from folly on every side
With a lover's pain to attain the plain
  Far from the hills of Habersham,
  Far from the valleys of Hall.   10

All down the hills of Habersham,
  All through the valleys of Hall,
The rushes cried *Abide, abide,*°   **13. abide:** remain.
The willful waterweeds held me thrall,°   **14. thrall:** captive.
The laving° laurel turned my tide,   15   **15. laving:** washing.
The ferns and the fondling grass said *Stay,*
The dewberry dipped for to work delay,
And the little reeds sighed *Abide, abide,*
  Here in the hills of Habersham,
  Here in the valleys of Hall.   20

High o'er the hills of Habersham,
  Veiling the valleys of Hall,
The hickory told me manifold°   **23. manifold:** many kinds of.
Fair tales of shade, the poplar tall
Wrought me her shadowy self to hold,   25
The chestnut, the oak, the walnut, the pine,
Overleaning, with flickering meaning and sign,
Said, *Pass not, so cold, these manifold*
  Deep shades of the hills of Habersham,
  These glades in the valleys of Hall.   30

And oft in the hills of Habersham,
    And oft in the valleys of Hall,
The white quartz shone, and the smooth brook-stone
Did bar me of passage with friendly brawl,
And many a luminous jewel lone   35
—Crystals clear or a-cloud with mist,
Ruby, garnet and amethyst—
Made lures with the lights of streaming stone
    In the clefts of the hills of Habersham,
    In the beds of the valleys of Hall.   40

    But oh, not the hills of Habersham,
    And oh, not the valleys of Hall
Avail:° I am fain for to water the plain.   **43. Avail:** help, succeed.
Downward the voices of Duty call—
Downward, to toil and be mixed with the main;°   45   **45. main:** the sea.
The dry fields burn, and the mills are to turn,
And a myriad° flowers mortally yearn,   **47. myriad** (mîr′ē-əd): countless.
And the lordly main from beyond the plain
    Calls o'er the hills of Habersham,
    Calls through the valleys of Hall.   50

FOR STUDY AND DISCUSSION

1. The speaker of this poem is the Chattahoochee River. What is the river's destination? How do the plants and trees that grow along the banks and the stones in the riverbed try to stop the Chattahoochee?

2. Rivers can be said to have distinct personalities: some are wild and dangerous, some sluggish and placid. How would you describe the character of the Chattahoochee? Which lines in the poem make you imagine it this way?

FOR COMPOSITION

Creating a Speaker
Write a brief paragraph in which the speaker is something that does not really talk: an animal, a building, a school desk, or a street. Try to make your language appropriate to your speaker.

One Wants a Teller in a Time like This

Gwendolyn Brooks

One wants a Teller in a time like this.

One's not a man, one's not a woman grown,
To bear enormous business all alone.

One cannot walk this winding street with pride,
Straight-shouldered, tranquil-eyed,   5
Knowing one knows for sure the way back home.
One wonders if one has a home.

One is not certain if or why or how.
One wants a Teller now:

Put on your rubbers and you won't catch cold.   10
Here's hell, there's heaven. Go to Sunday School.
Be patient, time brings all good things—(and cool
Strong balm to calm the burning at the brain?)—
Behold,
Love's true, and triumphs; and God's actual.   15

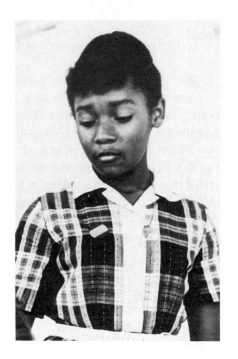

FOR STUDY AND DISCUSSION

1. The speaker says, "One's not a man, one's not a woman grown." Which other lines in the poem tell you that the speaker is a young person? What does the speaker mean by "a time like this" in line 1?

2. The speaker needs a "Teller" — someone to answer questions and give advice. What do you think the speaker means by "enormous business" in line 3? What is the meaning of line 8?

3. Most of the last stanza is written in italics. This indicates that the lines are spoken by someone else. What kind of information does this second speaker give? Why do you think the first speaker wants to be told this information?

4. The speaker in "Ego" uses military jargon. The speaker in "Song of the Chattahoochee" uses a more formal kind of language. In "One Wants a Teller in a Time like This," the speaker uses a conversational style. Look, for example, at line 6: "Knowing one knows for sure the way back home." Which other lines in the poem suggest a person talking directly to you as in a conversation?

FOR COMPOSITION

Writing an Eyewitness Account

Imagine yourself as an eyewitness to some dramatic historical event: for example, the eruption of Mount Vesuvius in A.D. 79; the arrival of the *Mayflower* at Plymouth Rock in 1620; the battle at the Alamo in 1836; the discovery of gold in California in 1848; the sinking of the luxury liner *Titanic* in 1912. Create an identity for yourself and tell your story in prose or verse. Before writing, consult an encyclopedia or other reference book for the facts.

ABOUT THE AUTHORS

Philip Booth (1925–   ) was born in Hanover, New Hampshire and attended Dartmouth. During World War II he served as a pilot in the Air Force. He now teaches at Syracuse University, where he is professor of English and poet-in-residence.

Sidney Lanier (1842–1881), whose name is pronounced lə-nîr′, was one of the first young poets to emerge from the South after the Civil War. Both poet and musician, Lanier sought to unite the two arts in his poems. Several of his works have been compared to musical compositions. Among his most famous poems are "The Marshes of Glynn," "The Symphony," and "Song of the Chattahoochee." A lake formed by the Chattahoochee is named Lake Sidney Lanier in the poet's honor.

Gwendolyn Brooks (1917–   ) grew up in Chicago's black community. This community and its people became one of the main subjects of her poetry. Her poems show a wide range of emotion, from quiet simplicity to fierce anger. She has written with great insight on both personal and social themes. In 1950 she won a Pulitzer Prize for *Annie Allen,* a series of poems about a black girl growing up. Gwendolyn Brooks is now Poet Laureate of Illinois.

Diction

In their *diction,* or choice of words, poets aim for clearness and effectiveness. They often prefer a concrete word to an abstract word. In "Song of the Chattahoochee," Lanier's diction is precise: instead of using the word *stone* in line 33, he uses *quartz.* Note also how he identifies the different plants in stanza 2 and the trees in stanza 3.

Poets also choose words that arouse particular sensations or moods. We would have a far different attitude toward the Chattahoochee had Lanier written these lines:

> With a gurgle and gush
> And a sloggish slush,
> I spray the logs and spatter the frogs,
>   Far from the hills of Maconville,
>   Far from the plains of Plains.

The diction of a poem may be formal and even elegant, or it may be informal to the point of being slangy. You will find that poets choose their words carefully in order to control the reader's response.

The "Satch" to whom this poem is dedicated was the phenomenal baseball pitcher Satchel Paige. Paige was one of the "iron men" of baseball. He was still pitching in the major leagues when most men his age had long retired from baseball. He was as well known for his sense of humor as for his genius with the change-up pitch.

To Satch
*Samuel Allen
(Paul Vesey)*

Sometimes I feel like I will *never* stop
Just go on forever
'Til one fine mornin'
I'm gonna reach up and grab me a handfulla stars
Swing out my long lean leg
And whip three hot strikes burnin' down the heavens
And look over at God and say
How about that!

FOR STUDY AND DISCUSSION

1. Who is the speaker of this poem? How do you know?
2. How does the speaker reveal confidence in his abilities? How does he also reveal a sense of humor?
3. This poem makes use of dialect, slang, and lively expressions. How is this language appropriate to the subject?

A Narrow Fellow in the Grass

Emily Dickinson

A narrow fellow in the grass
Occasionally rides;
You may have met him—did you not?
His notice sudden is.

The grass divides as with a comb,   5
A spotted shaft is seen;
And then it closes at your feet
And opens further on.

He likes a boggy acre,
A floor too cool for corn.   10
Yet when a boy, and barefoot,
I more than once, at noon,

Have passed, I thought, a whiplash
Unbraiding in the sun—
When, stopping to secure it,   15
It wrinkled, and was gone.

Several of nature's people
I know, and they know me;
I feel for them a transport°
Of cordiality;   20

But never met this fellow,
Attended or alone,
Without a tighter breathing,
And zero at the bone.

19. **transport:** strong feeling.

FOR STUDY AND DISCUSSION

1. Identify the "narrow fellow." What details in the poem supply clues to his identity?

2. What does the phrase "zero at the bone" tell you about the speaker's reaction to encountering the "narrow fellow"?

3. How can you tell that the speaker of this poem is not meant to be Emily Dickinson herself? From the information given in the poem, what can you tell about the speaker? Can you think of any reasons why Dickinson might choose to speak through this person, instead of speaking to the reader directly?

DICTION

Emily Dickinson's poetry is famous for its startling and original diction. Some of her words and phrases may at first seem unusual, but within the context of her poems prove to be fresh and appropriate. For example, in line 2, she uses the word *rides* to describe the movement of the "narrow fellow" through the grass. What more ordinary word or phrase might she have used? What kind of movement does the word *rides* make you imagine?

Reread the lines containing the following words. How does the diction, or choice of words, present a lively and vivid picture?

notice — line 4   wrinkled — line 16
whiplash — line 13   tighter — line 23

INVERTED WORD ORDER

Emily Dickinson often uses *inverted word order* in her poetry; that is, the words in a line are turned around so that they do not occur in the usual or expected position. Compare the first two lines of her poem with these lines:

Occasionally a narrow fellow
Rides in the grass —

What emphasis is gained when the poet changes the normal word order of these lines?

Another example of inverted word order occurs in the fourth line: "His notice sudden is." What special effect does the poet achieve by placing *sudden* before the verb?

What other examples of inverted word order can you find in the poem? What reasons do you think Emily Dickinson had for using inversion in these lines?

FOR COMPOSITION

Using Exact Words in Description
In Emily Dickinson's poetry, even the most familiar things seem to take on new significance and meaning because of the unexpected, yet remarkably accurate, words she uses. Choose some creature — a bird, an insect, a fish, or a four-legged animal — and observe it in some characteristic action. Describe its movements in exact and vivid pictures. If you wish, compose a poem.

The English poet John Masefield is best known for his poems about the sea, and the following poem is one of his most famous. Do not be put off by the strange words in the opening line: a quinquireme (kwĭn′kwī-rēm′) *was a galley ship of olden times;* Nineveh (nĭn′ə-və), *the galley's home port, was a city of ancient* Assyria (ə-sîr′ē-ə)*; and* Ophir (ō′fər) *was a Biblical land famed for its great stores of gold.*

The Armada (c. 1588). Anonymous oil painting, design for a tapestry.
National Maritime Museum, Greenwich, England

Cargoes   *John Masefield*

Quinquireme of Nineveh from distant Ophir,
Rowing home to haven in sunny Palestine,
With a cargo of ivory,
And apes and peacocks,
Sandalwood, cedarwood, and sweet white wine.   5

Stately Spanish galleon coming from the Isthmus,°
Dipping through the Tropics by the palm-green shores,
With a cargo of diamonds,
Emeralds, amethysts,
Topazes, and cinnamon, and gold moidores.°   10

Dirty British coaster with a salt-caked smokestack,
Butting through the Channel in the mad March days,
With a cargo of Tyne coal,°
Road rails, pig lead,
Firewood, ironware, and cheap tin trays.   15

6. **Isthmus** (is′məs): Panama.

10. **moidores** (moi′dôrz′): Portuguese gold coins.

13. **Tyne coal:** coal from the British mining center, Newcastle-upon-Tyne.

Recognizing Connotative Meanings

A word can have *denotative* and *connotative* meanings. Denotation is a word's literal, "dictionary" meaning. For example, the word *springtime* denotes the season between winter and summer. Connotations are the additional meanings a word gains because of its associations. *Springtime* has connotations of youth, rebirth, and romance.

A poet may draw on a word's connotations to arouse a special feeling in the reader. Each stanza of "Cargoes" ends with a list of things one of the ships carries. What connotations do the words in each list have? Suppose that line 3 read: "With a cargo of dead elephants' tusks" instead of "With a cargo of ivory." In what way would the effect of the line be different?

FOR STUDY AND DISCUSSION

1. Each stanza of this poem describes a ship from a different period in history. The ship in stanza 1 is from Biblical times. Identify the historical periods in stanzas 2 and 3.

2. Compare the first two lines of each stanza, which describe the ships' movements and locations. What differences do you find between the first two ships and the third one?

3. The cargoes of the first two ships are exotic, rich, and colorful. How do they differ from the cargo of the third ship? What is this poem implying about the differences between past times and modern times?

4. The poet's attitude toward each ship is different. How would you describe the poet's attitude toward the third ship and its cargo? Which words in the last stanza lead you to think so?

FOR COMPOSITION

Writing a Description

Imagine a modern cargo carried by modern means, such as a truck, train, or airplane. Write a short essay describing such a cargo, using words whose connotations reveal your attitude toward the cargo. For example, a truck full of poultry might be described as "a gleaming van full of fine, fat fowls," or as "a clattering old wreck with crates of half-dead chickens." If you like, try to write a fourth stanza to Masefield's poem, describing the kind of cargo a ship might carry today.

Dream Deferred *Langston Hughes*

What happens to a dream deferred?

Does it dry up
like a raisin in the sun?

Or fester like a sore—
And then run?   5

Does it stink like rotten meat?
Or crust and sugar over—
like a syrupy sweet?

Maybe it just sags
like a heavy load.   10

Or does it explode?

FOR STUDY AND DISCUSSION

1. Hughes's poem is organized as a series of questions. In lines 2–10 the questions are phrased as comparisons. How does this approach immediately engage your interest?
2. What words does the poet use that have unpleasant connotations? Why is this language effective? How would you describe the speaker's emotions?

FOR COMPOSITION

Analyzing Diction
Compare the diction in "Dream Deferred" with the diction of "A Narrow Fellow in the Grass" (page 250) and "Cargoes" (page 252). How would you characterize the diction in each poem? How is the diction of each poem suited to its subject? In your composition, cite examples that illustrate your point.

In this poem, Countee Cullen refers to two figures from Greek mythology: Tantalus and Sisyphus (sĭs′ĭ-fəs). As punishment for revealing secrets of Zeus, Tantalus was sent to Hades. He was forced to stand in water that receded when he tried to drink and under fruit-laden trees he could never reach. Sisyphus, a greedy king who also angered Zeus, was condemned forever to roll a great boulder to the top of a hill, only to have it roll down again.

Yet Do I Marvel   *Countee Cullen*

I doubt not God is good, well-meaning, kind,
And did He stoop to quibble could tell why
The little buried mole continues blind,
Why flesh that mirrors Him must some day die,
Make plain the reason tortured Tantalus   5
Is baited by the fickle fruit, declare
If merely brute caprice dooms Sisyphus
To struggle up a never-ending stair.
Inscrutable° His ways are, and immune
To catechism° by a mind too strewn   10
With petty cares to slightly understand
What awful° brain compels His awful hand.
Yet do I marvel at this curious thing:
To make a poet black, and bid him sing!

9. **Inscrutable:** beyond understanding.

9-10. **immune/To catechism:** not open to question or dispute.

12. **awful:** inspiring awe.

FOR STUDY AND DISCUSSION

1. In the first eight lines, Cullen cites some things that are beyond his understanding. What specific examples does he use? In a larger sense, what is he talking about?

2. An *allusion* is a reference to a person, place, or event in literature, art, history, or the like, which the author expects the reader to recognize. Allusions enrich a piece of writing and strengthen a point the writer is making. How do the allusions to Tantalus and Sisyphus in lines 5–8 reinforce the ide— pressed in lines 1–4?

3. What conclusion does Cull— lines 9–12? State this con— words.

4. To whom i— line of the — myst—

ABOUT THE AUTHORS

It was said of Emily Dickinson (1830–1886) that her life story could be told in very few words: she was born in Amherst, lived in Amherst, and died in Amherst, a small town in Massachusetts. She had an independent and intelligent mind, but was also extremely sensitive and shy. As she grew older, she withdrew more and more from the world, seldom meeting outsiders and rarely leaving her father's house and garden. She dressed only in white, and wrote her poetry on small scraps of paper that she stitched together into little packets and kept hidden in her room. Only a handful of these poems was published in her lifetime, none with her consent, and several without her name. It was only after her death that her many packets of poems were discovered. Today, these poems are recognized as some of the most original poetry of the nineteenth century, and Emily Dickinson, who died almost totally unknown to the public, is considered one of the great poets of her time.

John Masefield (1878–1967) was born in England. At the age of fourteen he ran away to sea. Three years later, when his ship docked in New York, he decided to live for a while in America. He supported himself through a variety of jobs: working in a bakery, a livery stable, a saloon, and a carpet mill. The sights he had seen and the experiences he had undergone made him want to read and write poetry, so during his stay in America, he eagerly read all the great English poets. He returned to England and worked for a time as a newspaperman, and, in 1902, he published his first book of poems, *Salt Water Ballads*. In addition to poetry he wrote dramas, such as *The Tragedy of Pompey the Great*, and novels, such as *Lost Endeavor*. In 1930, John Masefield made Poet Laureate of England.

Samuel Allen (1917–   ) was born in Columbus, Ohio. He attended Fisk University and Harvard, then continued his studies at the Sorbonne in Paris. Some of his early poems were published by Richard Wright, who was then living in Paris. In 1956, an edition of Allen's poems was published in Germany in both German and English. Allen's poetry has appeared in *American Negro Poetry*, *New Negro Poets: U.S.A.*, and other publications. He sometimes uses the pseudonym "Paul Vesey."

Langston Hughes (1902–1967) began traveling at the age of fourteen. He went to Mexico and then New York City, where he attended Columbia University for a year. He signed on as a crew member of a steamer and spent two years working his way around Africa and Europe. For his poetry, Hughes drew on modern folk and jazz rhythms, the kind of speech and music he heard in the black community. Hughes's work, down-to-earth and realistic, pointed the way to a new, distinctly American kind of poetry.

Countee Cullen (1903–1946) had his first collection of poems, *Color* (1925), published while he was an undergraduate student at New York University. Within four years, three more volumes of poetry appeared. His poems are generally written in traditional forms and often reflect a romantic outlook. Cullen was also influential as the editor of an important early anthology of black poetry, *Caroling Dusk* (1927). His other works include *The Lost Zoo* (1940), a highly imaginative book of poems for children.

Imagery

Although we do a great deal of our thinking with words, many of our thoughts come to us as pictures or as imagined sensations. For instance, if you think about riding a roller coaster, you may see a picture of long tracks stretching down before you, and imagine a lurching feeling in the pit of your stomach. Such imagined pictures or sensations are called *images*.

Poets attempt to share their experiences with us by appealing to our imaginations. One way in which a poet makes an experience seem real, vivid, and fresh to us is through the skillful use of *imagery*.

"Blackie, the Electric Rembrandt"

Thom Gunn

We watch through the shop-front while
Blackie draws stars—an equal

concentration on his and
the youngster's faces. The hand

is steady and accurate;   5
but the boy does not see it

for his eyes follow the point
that touches (quick, dark movement!)

a virginal° arm beneath   9. **virginal:** untouched, unmarked.
his rolled sleeve: he holds his breath.   10

. . . Now that it is finished, he
hands a few bills to Blackie

and leaves with a bandage on
his arm, under which gleam ten

stars, hanging in a blue thick   15
cluster. Now he is starlike.

FOR STUDY AND DISCUSSION

1. Rembrandt is the popular name for Rembrandt van Rijn (rīn), a seventeenth-century Dutch painter and etcher. He is considered one of the greatest artists who ever lived. What kind of artist is Blackie? Why do you think he is called "the Electric Rembrandt"?
2. Certain details of the scene are very clearly pictured. For example, the poet uses this image in lines 4–5 to describe the careful way in which Blackie works: "The hand/is steady and accurate." What other sharp visual images can you find?
3. The boy leaves with a design of stars on his arm. How does the poet describe these stars? Do you think the boy is proud of Blackie's work? How might the audience as well as the design make him feel "starlike"?
4. In what way is the pairing of Blackie's nickname with the great painter Rembrandt ironic? What does the phrase "the Electric Rembrandt" suggest about the speaker's attitude toward our society?

There Will Come Soft Rains   *Sara Teasdale*

War Time

There will come soft rains and the smell of the ground,
And swallows circling with their shimmering sound;

And frogs in the pools singing at night,
And wild plum-trees in tremulous° white.

Robins will wear their feathery fire   5
Whistling their whims on a low-fence-wire;

And not one will know of the war, not one
Will care at last when it is done.

Not one would mind, neither bird nor tree,
If mankind perished utterly;   10

And Spring herself, when she woke at dawn
Would scarcely know that we were gone.

4. **tremulous:** trembling.

FOR STUDY AND DISCUSSION

1. Images can appeal to all our senses. For example, the image of "soft rains" in line 1 appeals to our sense of touch. What other images do you find in the first stanza? To which senses do they appeal?

2. Which images in the poem help to create a quiet, peaceful atmosphere?

3. The last three stanzas contrast sharply with the first three. What event does the speaker mention in lines 7–8? What do the last three stanzas suggest about the relationship of human beings to nature?

FOR COMPOSITION

Describing a Scene

Imagine a scene without people: a city street at dawn, a zoo after closing time, or a deserted house in the country. Try to imagine the mood of the scene. It might be sad and lonely, or quiet and calm like the scene in Sara Teasdale's poem. Or it might be frightening, as if all people had suddenly disappeared. Write a short paragraph describing the scene, and include several specific images to help convey the mood. You may illustrate the scene if you wish.

The Meadow Mouse

Theodore Roethke

I

In a shoe box stuffed in an old nylon stocking
Sleeps the baby mouse I found in the meadow,
Where he trembled and shook beneath a stick
Till I caught him up by the tail and brought him in,
Cradled in my hand,   5
A little quaker, the whole body of him trembling,
His absurd whiskers sticking out like a cartoon-mouse,
His feet like small leaves,
Little lizard-feet,
Whitish and spread wide when he tried to struggle away,   10
Wriggling like a miniscule° puppy.

11. **miniscule:** tiny.

Now he's eaten his three kinds of cheese and drunk from
     his bottle-cap watering-trough—
So much he just lies in one corner,
His tail curled under him, his belly big
As his head; his batlike ears   15
Twitching, tilting toward the least sound.

Do I imagine he no longer trembles
When I come close to him?
He seems no longer to tremble.

II

But this morning the shoe-box house on the back porch is
    empty.   20
Where has he gone, my meadow mouse,
My thumb of a child that nuzzled in my palm?—
To run under the hawk's wing,
Under the eye of the great owl watching from the elm
    tree,
To live by courtesy of the shrike,° the snake, the tomcat.   25

I think of the nestling° fallen into the deep grass,
The turtle gasping in the dusty rubble of the highway,
The paralytic stunned in the tub, and the water rising—
All things innocent, hapless,° forsaken.

25. **shrike:** a violent, shrill-voiced bird of prey.

26. **nestling:** baby bird.

29. **hapless:** unfortunate.

FOR STUDY AND DISCUSSION

1. In line 7, the speaker describes the mouse as having whiskers "like a cartoon-mouse." What other comparisons does the speaker use to describe the mouse?
2. In the first part of the poem, the speaker describes the mouse several times as "trembling." What does he imagine in lines 17–19? How do you think the speaker feels toward the mouse?
3. The second part of the poem contrasts sharply with the first part. The images in the first part create a mood of playfulness and affection. What images in the second part create a mood of helplessness and terror? How does the speaker express compassion for all helpless creatures?

LANGUAGE AND VOCABULARY

Analyzing Word Structure
Many words in our language are made up of separate word elements. The word *innocent*, for example, is made up of two parts. The first part, *in-*, is a *prefix* from Latin meaning "not." The main part or *root* of the word is *nocens*, also from Latin, meaning "to do wrong to." *Innocent* means "not doing wrong to" or "guiltless." The word *whitish* is also made up of two parts. The root is the word *white* and the part at the end, *-ish*, is a *suffix* meaning "somewhat."

Identify the separate elements in each of these words, using a dictionary where necessary: *absurd, batlike, forsake, hapless, nestling, twitching.*

The Fawn   *Edna St. Vincent Millay*

There it was I saw what I shall never forget
And never retrieve.
Monstrous and beautiful to human eyes, hard to believe,
He lay, yet there he lay,
Asleep on the moss, his head on his polished cleft small
    ebony° hooves,   5   5. **ebony:** black.
The child of the doe, the dappled child of the deer.

Surely his mother had never said, "Lie here
Till I return," so spotty and plain to see
On the green moss lay he.
His eyes had opened; he considered me.   10

I would have given more than I care to say
To thrifty ears, might I have had him for my friend
One moment only of that forest day:

Might I have had the acceptance, not the love
Of those clear eyes;   15
Might I have been for him the bough above
Or the root beneath his forest bed,
A part of the forest, seen without surprise.

Was it alarm, or was it the wind of my fear lest° he depart   19. **lest:** that.
That jerked him to his jointy knees   20
And sent him crashing off, leaping and stumbling
On his new legs, between the stems of the white trees?

FOR STUDY AND DISCUSSION

1. The speaker in this poem sees a rare sight
—a lone fawn. What are her feelings when she
sees the fawn? What images does she use to
describe the fawn? What do you think she
means by the word *monstrous* in line 3?

2. In line 14, the speaker says she wished she
might have "the acceptance, not the love" of
the shy fawn. She knows it would be impossible for so wild a creature to love any human
being. Reread lines 16–18. What do you think
she means by "acceptance"?

FOR COMPOSITION

Comparing Two Poems

The situations in "The Meadow Mouse"
(page 260) and "The Fawn" are similar: a
speaker comes upon an animal unexpectedly,
wishes to befriend it, but instead frightens it
away. Although the subject of both poems is
the relationship of human beings to nature,
the focus in each poem is different. In
"The Meadow Mouse," the speaker's feelings
are directed toward the mouse and toward all
helpless things. In "The Fawn," the focus of
the experience is the speaker's sense of loss.

Compare the two poems, discussing similarities and differences in choice of details,
imagery, and attitudes toward nature.

Meeting at Night *Robert Browning*

The gray sea and the long black land;
And the yellow half-moon large and low;
And the startled little waves that leap
In fiery ringlets from their sleep,
As I gain the cove with pushing prow,   5
And quench its speed i' the slushy sand.

Then a mile of warm sea-scented beach;
Three fields to cross till a farm appears;
A tap at the pane, the quick sharp scratch
And blue spurt of a lighted match,   10
And a voice less loud, through its joys and fears,
Than the two hearts beating each to each!

FOR STUDY AND DISCUSSION

The speaker has come a long way for this meeting. What images show the distance he must cover and the path he takes? What images help create a mood of urgency and secrecy? What imagery suggests that the meeting is between two lovers?

FOR COMPOSITION

Analyzing Imagery
In line 1, there is an image of "gray sea" and an image of "long black land." What other visual images do you find in the poem? What images appeal to your senses of hearing, smell, and touch?

Empty House *Stephen Spender*

Then, when the child was gone,
I was alone
In the house, suddenly grown huge. Each noise
Explained its cause away,
Animal, vegetable, mineral,   5
Nail, creaking board, or mouse.
But mostly there was quiet of after battle
Where round the room still lay
The soldiers and the paintbox, all the toys.
    Then, when I went to tidy these away,   10
My hands refused to serve:°
My body was the house,
And everything he'd touched, an exposed nerve.

11. **to serve:** to do what the
speaker wants them to do.

FOR STUDY AND DISCUSSION

1. The child is no longer in the house, but we are not told why. What do you think happened to the child? What do the images in lines 7–9 suggest may have happened?

2. The speaker says that the house, with the child gone, has "suddenly grown huge." What does this phrase mean? The noises in the house are no longer made by the child. According to lines 3–6, what are the noises made by?

3. How would you describe the emotions of the speaker in this poem? Look at the last two lines of the poem. In what ways is the speaker's body like the house? Why does each thing the child touched seem like "an exposed nerve"?

The following poem uses imagery not to express a mood or tell a story, but to express an idea. The butterfly, with its "flying-crooked gift," may show us something about the way we move through our own lives.

Flying Crooked   *Robert Graves*

The butterfly, a cabbage-white,
(His honest idiocy of flight)
Will never now, it is too late,
Master the art of flying straight,
Yet has—who knows so well as I?—   5
A just sense of how not to fly;
He lurches here and here by guess
And God and hope and hopelessness.
Even the aerobatic° swift°
Has not his flying-crooked gift.   10

9. **aerobatic:** able to do spectacular aerial feats. **swift:** a fast-flying bird.

FOR STUDY AND DISCUSSION

1. The cabbage butterfly is known for the way it darts and skips about in the air. In what sense is its uneven flight a kind of "idiocy"?
2. According to lines 7–8, what guides the butterfly's flight?
3. In line 5, the speaker suggests that he is like this butterfly. What similarity might he see between his own life and the butterfly's flight? How would you describe his attitude toward the butterfly's flight?

Lament for the Non-Swimmers

David Wagoner

They never feel they can be well in the water,
Can come to rest, that their bodies are light.
When they reach out, their cupped hands hesitate:
What they wanted runs between their fingers.
Their fluttering, scissoring legs sink under.   5

Their bones believe in heaviness, their ears
Shake out the cold invasion of privacy,
Their eyes squeeze shut. Each breath,
Only half air, is too breath-taking.
The dead man's float seems strictly for dead men.   10

They stand in the shallows, their knees touching,
Their feet where they belong in the sand.
They wade as carefully as herons, but hope for nothing
Under the surface, that wilderness
Where eels and sharks slip out of their element.   15

Those who tread water and call see their blurred eyes
Turn distant,° not away from a sky's reflection
As easy to cross as the dependable earth
But from a sight as blue as drowned men's faces.
They splash ashore, pretending to feel buoyant.°   20

16–17. **see . . . distant:** see the nonswimmers look away from the water.

20. **buoyant:** able to float; happy and confident.

FOR STUDY AND DISCUSSION

What images does the speaker use to convey the nonswimmers' fear, frustration, and awkwardness? How are the images appropriate to the subject of the poem?

ABOUT THE AUTHORS

Thom(son William) Gunn (1929–) was born in Gravesend, England, and attended Cambridge University. He has published *Fighting Terms, The Sense of Movement,* and *My Sad Captains.* He has also collaborated with his brother Ander on a book of photographs and poems called *Positives.* He now lives in California and teaches at the University of California at Berkeley.

Sara Teasdale (1884–1933) was born in St. Louis, Missouri. Her childhood was quiet and almost secluded. Her parents taught her at home and then sent her to private schools. She was not allowed to travel about without a guardian. But her family encouraged her writing, and an influential editor, Harriet Monroe, took an interest in her work. Success as a poet came quickly. Her most mature work appears in the collections *Flame and Shadow* (1920), *Dark of the Moon* (1926), and *Strange Victory* (1933).

Theodore Roethke (1908–1963), whose name is pronounced rĕt′kē, was born in Saginaw, Michigan, and spent much of his youth exploring the wild countryside or observing the mysterious processes of growth and life in his father's greenhouses. His poetry is rich in observations of the natural world and covers a wide range of moods. He won many awards for poetry, including a Pulitzer Prize and two National Book Awards.

Edna St. Vincent Millay (1892–1950) was born in Rockland, Maine. She began publishing poetry when she was still in high school, and her first long poem, ''Renascence,'' was written when she was barely nineteen. After graduating from college, she moved to New York City, where she made her living as an actress and playwright for the Provincetown Players.

In 1923, her collection of poems, *The Harp-Weaver,* was awarded the Pulitzer Prize.

Robert Browning (1812–1889) was born in England. He grew up surrounded by books. His father, who greatly valued education, was his teacher. Browning went to college for only a few months, having learned at home most of the things the university taught. Browning is perhaps second only to Shakespeare in the creation of lively characters in poetry. He portrayed a wide variety of human types. Both his personality and his poetry were marked by a lively mind and a zest for life.

Stephen Spender (1909–) was born in London. As a young man, he became well-known for his poems of political protest and for his sympathy for the underdog. His later poetry is less public and more personal: it explores the private worlds of people rather than the political world outside. His poetry has been praised for its compassionate pictures of human emotions and needs.

Robert Graves (1895–1985) was born in Wimbledon near London. During World War I he served in the Royal Welch Fusiliers, went to France, and was wounded in action. After the war he studied at Oxford. Graves had a long and distinguished writing career. Apart from poetry, he wrote critical essays, translations, mythological studies, and historical novels.

David Wagoner (1926–) was born in Massillon, Ohio, and attended Pennsylvania State College and Indiana University. His collections of poetry include *Dry Sun, Dry Wind; A Place to Stand; The Nesting Ground; Staying Alive;* and *Sleeping in the Woods.* He is a Professor of English at the University of Washington and editor of *Poetry Northwest.*

Figurative Language

In our everyday speech, we often use *figurative language*—language that represents one thing in terms of another. We may describe an action or a feeling by comparing it to something else: "I felt like a worm"; "We ate like kings"; "That test was murder." Expressions that describe one thing in terms of another are called *figures of speech*.

Figures of speech help to make language richer in meaning and more imaginative. In *Macbeth*, William Shakespeare describes a storm in which the sky grows so dreary that it seems as though "dark night strangles" the sun. Emily Dickinson, describing a violent storm, uses this figure of speech to evoke the sound of a shrill wind: "There came a wind like a bugle." Through figurative language poets can express fresh, exciting, or unusual relationships between things, and so give us new insights into what we see and feel.

The Day Is Done   *Henry Wadsworth Longfellow*

The day is done, and the darkness
  Falls from the wings of night,
As a feather is wafted downward
  From an eagle in his flight.

I see the lights of the village
  Gleam through the rain and the mist,
And a feeling of sadness comes o'er me,
  That my soul cannot resist:

A feeling of sadness and longing,
  That is not akin to pain,   10
And resembles sorrow only
  As the mist resembles the rain.

Come, read to me some poem,
  Some simple and heartfelt lay,°
That shall soothe this restless feeling,   15
  And banish the thoughts of day.

Not from the grand old masters,
  Not from the bards sublime,°
Whose distant footsteps echo
  Through the corridors of time.   20

For, like strains of martial music,
  Their mighty thoughts suggest
Life's endless toil and endeavor;
  And tonight I long for rest.

Read from some humbler poet,   25
  Whose songs gushed from his heart,
As showers from the clouds of summer,
  Or tears from the eyelids start;

Who, through long days of labor,
  And nights devoid of ease,   30
Still heard in his soul the music
  Of wonderful melodies.

Such songs have power to quiet
  The restless pulse of care,
And come like the benediction°   35
  That follows after prayer.

Then read from the treasured volume
  The poem of thy choice,
And lend to the rhyme of the poet
  The beauty of thy voice.   40

And the night shall be filled with music,
  And the cares, that infest the day,
Shall fold their tents, like the Arabs,
  And as silently steal away.

14. **lay:** a ballad or story poem.

18. **bards sublime:** poets who wrote lofty, exalted poems.

35. **benediction:** state of blessedness or grace.

SIMILES

A simile is a figure of speech that compares two unlike things, using a word such as *like, as,* or *than* to suggest the similarity. Simple similes occur in our everyday speech:

He runs *like* the wind.
Her sunburn made her face red *as* a beet.
Superman is faster *than* a speeding bullet.

In "The Day Is Done," Longfellow uses several striking similes. Look, for example, at the comparison in the sixth stanza:

For, like strains of martial music,
  Their mighty thoughts suggest
Life's endless toil and endeavor;

The word *martial* means "military" or "warlike." What is Longfellow comparing to the sounds of martial music?

Look at the simile in stanza 9. What two things are being compared? A famous and often-quoted comparison is found in the last stanza. What is Longfellow comparing his cares to?

Find other similes in the poem and explain the comparison in each one.

I'll Tell You How the Sun Rose

Emily Dickinson

I'll tell you how the sun rose—
A ribbon at a time.
The steeples swam in amethyst,
The news like squirrels ran.

The hills untied their bonnets,   5
The bobolinks begun.
Then I said softly to myself,
"That must have been the sun!"

But how he set, I know not.
There seemed a purple stile°   10   10. **stile:** steps enabling a person
Which little yellow boys and girls   to climb over a fence or wall.
Were climbing all the while

Till when they reached the other side,
A dominie° in gray   14. **dominie:** clergyman.
Put gently up the evening bars,   15
And led the flock away.

FOR STUDY AND DISCUSSION

1. The speaker describes the sun rising "a ribbon at a time." What image does this phrase give you?

2. What is the color of amethyst? In what way might the steeples appear to *swim* "in amethyst"?

3. What does the word *news* refer to in line 4? How might the spreading of the news look like squirrels running?

4. Notice the colors the speaker uses to describe the "stile" (line 10), the children (line 11), and the "dominie" (line 14). How do these colors and the actions described in lines 10–16 help to suggest the setting sun?

METAPHORS

Like a simile, a metaphor points out a resemblance between two unlike things. A simile makes the comparison through the use of connecting words such as *like* or *as:* Jim growled *like* a bear. A metaphor identifies the two things as one: Jim is a bear.

Emily Dickinson is famous for her unusual metaphors. In line 5 of this poem, she says that the hills "untied their bonnets." A bonnet, like any other kind of hat, hides part of the wearer's head and also keeps the head warm. What is she comparing the hills to? Why is it appropriate that the hills should "untie their bonnets" when the sun rises?

Moon Tiger   *Denise Levertov*

The moon tiger.
In the room, here.
It came in, it is
prowling sleekly
under and over   5
the twin beds.
See its small head,
silver smooth,
hear the pad of its
large feet. Look,   10
its white stripes
in the light that slid
through the jalousies.°
It is sniffing our
clothes, its cold nose   15
nudges our bodies.
The beds are narrow,
but I'm coming in with you.

13. **jalousies** (jăl′ə-sēz): a type of
window or door that is made of adjustable slats.

FOR STUDY AND DISCUSSION

1. "I'll Tell You How the Sun Rose" contains
several different metaphors, but "Moon
Tiger" is based on one central metaphor. To
what thing is the moon compared? What does
this comparison tell you about the speaker's
feelings toward the moon?
2. What phrases and details make the comparison strong? How might moonlight seem
to prowl, sniff, or nudge bodies?

IMPLIED METAPHOR

Sometimes a metaphor is suggested or *implied*. It does not directly state that one thing
is another, different thing. What comparisons are implied by the following metaphors?

The wind drove the galloping storm clouds
across the sky.

Carefully, cleverly, the spy wove his web of
deceit and waited to entrap his victim.

The windows of the old house stared out
into the night, and the open door seemed
to grin.

It Bids Pretty Fair   *Robert Frost*

The play seems out for an almost infinite run.
Don't mind a little thing like the actors fighting.
The only thing I worry about is the sun.
We'll be all right if nothing goes wrong with the lighting.

FOR STUDY AND DISCUSSION

1. This poem consists of a single metaphor. What is the play referred to in the first line? Why does this play have "an almost infinite run"? Who are the actors and why are they fighting?

2. The poem's title, "It Bids Pretty Fair," means "It looks pretty good." How is the title ironic? Do you think the speaker really believes that "we'll be all right"? What does the metaphor of the play tell you about the speaker's attitude?

FOR COMPOSITION

Analyzing Figurative Language
Reread Emily Dickinson's poem "A Narrow Fellow in the Grass" (page 250). Analyze the similes and metaphors in the poem, explaining each comparison in your own words.

Silver   *Walter de la Mare*

Slowly, silently, now the moon
Walks the night in her silver shoon;°
This way, and that, she peers, and sees
Silver fruit upon silver trees;
One by one the casements° catch   5
Her beams beneath the silvery thatch;
Couched in his kennel, like a log,
With paws of silver sleeps the dog;
From their shadowy cote° the white breasts peep
Of doves in a silver-feathered sleep;   10
A harvest mouse goes scampering by,
With silver claws and a silver eye;
And moveless fish in the water gleam,
By silver reeds in a silver stream.

2. **shoon:** shoes.

5. **casements:** window frames.

9. **cote:** coop.

FOR STUDY AND DISCUSSION

1. How are objects and animals transformed by the moonlight?
2. The first line of the poem sets a still and silent mood. What images in the poem add to this mood?
3. The word *silver* is repeated throughout the poem. What is the effect of this repetition? Would the word *golden* have been equally effective? Explain.
4. Reread the poem and listen closely to its sounds. What sounds are repeated? How do these sounds help to create a quiet, still mood?

PERSONIFICATION

Personification is a figure of speech that gives human qualities to something nonhuman. At the New Year, cartoonists depict the old year as a toothless old man and the new year as a sturdy baby. Death is often portrayed as a grim and bony figure in a hooded robe, carrying a scythe. The natural world is personified as Mother Nature. Through personification, a writer can describe a quality or idea in a concrete, yet imaginative way. In "Silver," Walter de la Mare personifies the moon. Which words and phrases in the poem suggest that the moon is human?

Close-up

A. R. Ammons

Are all these stones
    yours
I said
and the mountain
pleased   5

but reluctant to
admit my praise could move it much

shook a little
and rained a windrow° ring of stones
to show   10
that it was so

Stonefelled I got
up addled° with dust

and shook
    myself   15
without much consequence

Obviously I said it doesn't pay
to get too
close up to
    greatness   20
and the mountain friendless wept
    and said
it couldn't help
itself

---

9. **windrow:** a row, usually of leaves or dust, made
by the wind. 13. **addled:** confused.

FOR STUDY AND DISCUSSION

1. Describe the personality of the mountain. How does the mountain answer the speaker's opening question? The mountain is reluctant to admit "praise could move it much." Considering the mountain's action after that statement, what two meanings does the word *move* have?

2. What does the speaker learn about the mountain's power? What does he learn about his own power?

3. Why does the speaker find it undesirable to "get too/close up to/greatness"? Why do you suppose the mountain is friendless? How is the great mountain's final remark ironic?

FOR COMPOSITION AND ARTWORK

Using Personification

Write a short paragraph in which you personify some familiar object. Imagine, for example, what kind of personality your family car or your house might have. Or, if you like, use personification to portray an idea such as love, beauty, time, or truth.

Cartoonists often personify political ideas or issues. Try drawing a simple cartoon that uses a person or persons to represent some contemporary problem or issue.

Mending Wall   *Robert Frost*

Something there is that doesn't love a wall,
That sends the frozen-ground-swell under it
And spills the upper boulders in the sun,
And makes gaps even two can pass abreast.
The work of hunters is another thing: 5
I have come after them and made repair
Where they have left not one stone on a stone,
But they would have the rabbit out of hiding,
To please the yelping dogs. The gaps I mean,
No one has seen them made or heard them made,   10
But at spring mending-time we find them there.
I let my neighbor know beyond the hill;
And on a day we meet to walk the line
And set the wall between us once again.
We keep the wall between us as we go.   15
To each the boulders that have fallen to each.
And some are loaves and some so nearly balls
We have to use a spell to make them balance:
"Stay where you are until our backs are turned!"
We wear our fingers rough with handling them.   20
Oh, just another kind of outdoor game,
One on a side. It comes to little more:
There where it is we do not need the wall:
He is all pine and I am apple orchard.
My apple trees will never get across   25
And eat the cones under his pines, I tell him.
He only says, "Good fences make good neighbors."
Spring is the mischief in me, and I wonder
If I could put a notion in his head:
"*Why* do they make good neighbors? Isn't it   30
Where there are cows? But here there are no cows.
Before I built a wall I'd ask to know
What I was walling in or walling out,
And to whom I was like to give offense.

Something there is that doesn't love a wall,   35
That wants it down." I could say "Elves" to him,
But it's not elves exactly, and I'd rather
He said it for himself. I see him there,
Bringing a stone grasped firmly by the top
In each hand, like an old-stone savage armed.   40
He moves in darkness as it seems to me,
Not of woods only and the shade of trees.
He will not go behind his father's saying,
And he likes having thought of it so well
He says again, "Good fences make good neighbors."   45

FOR STUDY AND DISCUSSION

1. Although the speaker meets with his neighbor each spring to mend the wall, he thinks that the wall is unnecessary. Why? What is his neighbor's attitude toward mending the wall? What do these attitudes reveal about the speaker and his neighbor?

2. What does the speaker think people should consider before they put up walls?

3. What simile does the speaker use near the end of the poem to describe his neighbor? In what sense does the neighbor "move in darkness" (line 41)?

4. In the first four lines, the speaker suggests that there is "Something"—a force or drive—that insists on breaking down walls. This "Something" can make a gap so wide that "even two can pass abreast." What does this image of two people walking side by side through a broken wall suggest to you?

5. What is your impression of the speaker? Where does he exhibit a sense of humor? Do you think he has a good grasp of human nature? Explain.

SYMBOLS

Symbols are a part of our everyday lives. The eagle is a symbol of America; the skull and crossbones on a bottle is a symbol of poison; the dove is a symbol of peace.

Symbolism is one of the most powerful devices that a writer can use. It enables a writer to compress a very complex idea or set of ideas into one image or even one word. Certain symbols occur again and again in literature. For example, the butterfly is frequently used to symbolize the human soul; night, the sea, and winter often symbolize death; a journey often symbolizes the journey through life.

Writers often create their own symbols. Robert Frost seems to be talking about a simple and familiar process—mending a wall with a neighbor in spring. Yet, by the end of the poem, the wall, the neighbor, and the act of putting up a wall become symbolic; they come to represent things larger than themselves. What does the "wall" symbolize? What is the "Something . . . that doesn't love a wall"?

ABOUT THE AUTHORS

Henry Wadsworth Longfellow (1807–1882) was born in Portland, Maine. Four of his ancestors were pilgrims at Plymouth. Longfellow became the most famous American poet of his day and one of the most productive. He emphasized the values of freedom and wrote fearlessly against slavery at a time when many, less courageous, were silent. He was one of the first American writers to celebrate American events, and his historical poems are among his most famous: "Paul Revere's Ride," *Hiawatha, The Courtship of Miles Standish,* and *Evangeline.* Europeans as well as Americans were enthusiastic about his work; it was translated into twenty-four languages. Longfellow was the first American poet to have his bust placed in London's Westminster Abbey, where memorials are placed to England's greatest writers.

Denise Levertov (1923–   ) was born in Essex, England, and educated at home. Her early poetry was traditional, but after the publication of her first book, *The Double Image,* she turned to freer and less conventional forms. She is married to an American writer, Mitchell Goodman, and lives in New York.

Walter de la Mare (1873–1956) was born in Kent, England, and spent most of his life around London. His first volume of poetry, *Songs of Childhood,* was published under the pseudonym of "Walter Ramal." De la Mare is a master of mood. One of his most famous poems, "The Listeners," conveys an eerie sense of the supernatural.

A. R. Ammons (1926–   ) was born in Whiteville, North Carolina. He went to Wake Forest College and then to the University of California. His books include *Expressions of Sea Level, Corsons Inlet, Tape for the Turn of the Year,* and *Northfield Poems.* In 1973, he was awarded the National Book Award for his volume *Collected Poems: 1951–1971.* He now lives in Ithaca, New York, and teaches at Cornell University.

Robert Frost (1874–1963) was born in San Francisco, California. When he was eleven years old his father died, and he moved with his mother to Lawrence, Massachusetts. Though Frost was determined to write poetry, no one seemed interested in or impressed with his work. He worked as a farmer in New England to support himself, but he did not like farming and was not successful at it. Still, Frost managed to scratch out a living, and he refused to believe he was not a good poet. His courage and determination were finally rewarded. He became one of America's best-known and most-respected poets, and the winner of four Pulitzer Prizes. His poems are distinguished for their wisdom and wit and for the different levels of meaning that lie beneath their surfaces.

Sound Patterns

"To take sound away from poetry," said one poet, "is like tearing the wings from a bird." Poets, like musicians, are sensitive to the effects of sound. By varying rhythms, they can excite different emotions in the reader. They may use harsh or melodious sounds to convey a particular mood. Rhyme and other devices of repetition can make a poem pleasant, forceful, or comic. In combination, these devices can give a poem a rich texture of sound, which is pleasurable in itself and which also enhances the poem's meaning.

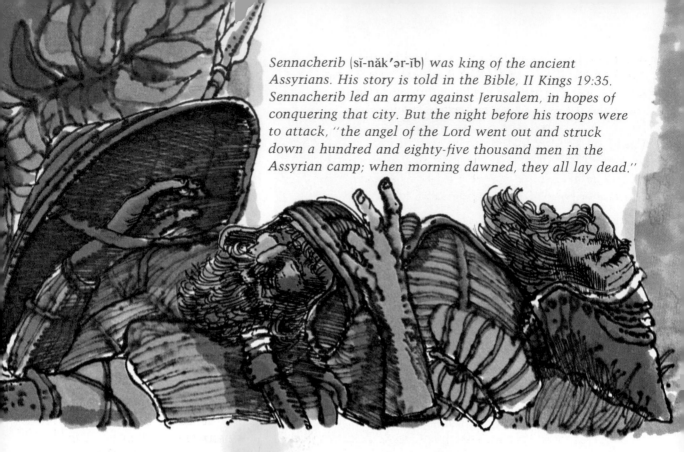

Sennacherib (sĭ-năk′ər-ĭb) was king of the ancient Assyrians. His story is told in the Bible, II Kings 19:35. Sennacherib led an army against Jerusalem, in hopes of conquering that city. But the night before his troops were to attack, "the angel of the Lord went out and struck down a hundred and eighty-five thousand men in the Assyrian camp; when morning dawned, they all lay dead."

The Destruction of Sennacherib

George Gordon, Lord Byron

The Assyrian came down like the wolf on the fold,°
And his cohorts were gleaming in purple and gold;
And the sheen of their spears was like stars on the sea,
When the blue wave rolls nightly on deep Galilee.

Like the leaves of the forest when Summer is green,   5
That host with their banners at sunset were seen:
Like the leaves of the forest when Autumn hath blown,
That host on the morrow lay withered and strown.°

For the Angel of Death spread his wings on the blast,°
And breathed in the face of the foe as he passed;   10
And the eyes of the sleepers waxed° deadly and chill,
And their hearts but once heaved, and forever grew still!

1. **fold:** flock of sheep, or place where sheep are kept.

8. **strown:** strewn, scattered.

9. **blast:** wind.

11. **waxed:** grew.

And there lay the steed with his nostril all wide,
But through it there rolled not the breath of his pride;
And the foam of his gasping lay white on the turf,   15
And cold as the spray of the rock-beating surf.

And there lay the rider distorted and pale,
With the dew on his brow, and the rust on his mail:
And the tents were all silent, the banners alone,
The lances unlifted, the trumpet unblown.   20

And the widows of Ashur° are loud in their wail,
And the idols are broke in the temple of Baal;°
And the might of the Gentile,° unsmote by the sword,
Hath melted like snow in the glance of the Lord!

21. **Ashur** (ä′shŏŏr′): Assyria.

22. **Baal** (bā′əl): chief Assyrian god.

23. **Gentile:** non-Jew; here, the Assyrian Sennacherib.

FOR STUDY AND DISCUSSION

1. What similes in the first stanza help you picture the power of the Assyrians? How is the change in their power described in the second stanza?

2. The destruction of the Assyrians is related in detail in stanzas 3–6. Tell in your own words what each stanza describes. How does each stanza build toward the climax of the poem?

RHYTHM AND METER

Rhythm occurs everywhere in nature: in the phases of the moon, in the tides, in the beating of our hearts. And rhythm has always had a profound effect on human beings. From the earliest times, people have sung, danced, chanted, and made music out of an instinctive love of rhythm.

The rhythm of a poem may be compared to a person's heartbeat. Rhythm may beat slowly, swiftly, or irregularly, but it gives movement and vitality to the poem. In English poetry, rhythm is based on a pattern of stressed and unstressed syllables. The stressed syllables are marked ′ and the unstressed syllables ˘.

When the rhythm of a poem has a regular and pronounced pattern, we call it *meter*. The metrical pattern in ''The Destruction of Sennacherib'' looks like this:

The Assyrian came down like the wolf on the fold,
And his cohorts were gleaming in purple and gold;

Two unstressed syllables are followed by a stressed syllable. How many stressed syllables do you find in each line? Analyze the meter of lines 5–8. What variety has Byron introduced in the pattern?

Byron has chosen a swift meter for this poem. Why is such a meter appropriate to his subject?

Jazz Fantasia   *Carl Sandburg*

Drum on your drums, batter on your banjoes,
sob on the long cool winding saxophones.
Go to it, O jazzmen.

Sling your knuckles on the bottoms of the happy
tin pans,° let your trombones ooze, and go husha-   5
husha-hush with the slippery sandpaper.°

Moan like an autumn wind high in the lonesome treetops, moan soft like
you wanted somebody terrible, cry like a racing car slipping away from a
motorcycle cop, bang-bang! you jazzmen, bang altogether drums, traps,°
banjoes, horns, tin cans—make two people fight on top of a stairway   10
and scratch each other's eyes in a clinch tumbling down the stairs.

Can the rough stuff . . . now a Mississippi steamboat pushes up the night
river with a hoo-hoo-hoo-oo . . . and the green lanterns calling to the high
soft stars . . . a red moon rides on the humps of the low river hills . . .
go to it, O jazzmen.   15

---

5. **tin pans:** In early years jazz players often improvised instruments, using tin pans, coconuts, or anything else that could make interesting sounds.   6. **slippery sandpaper:** Sandpaper, too, was used as an instrument.   9. **traps:** percussion instruments.

FOR STUDY AND DISCUSSION

1. Father of the blues and grandfather of rock music, jazz came into being in the late nineteenth and early twentieth centuries. Freer and livelier than traditional music, it created a new style and influenced modern composers. What images in the poem convey the intensity and roughness of jazz? What images indicate that jazz can be soft and serene as well?

2. The word *fantasia* in the title refers to a musical composition without a fixed form. Its structure is invented by the composer. Jazz is often created by improvisation. How does the last stanza give the impression of being improvised? In what way is the poem like a "jazz fantasia"?

3. Unlike "The Destruction of Sennacherib," this poem has an irregular rhythm. Why is irregular rhythm appropriate? At what points in the poem can you feel the rhythm change?

During the sixteenth century, many explorers came to the New World in search of El Dorado, the legendary kingdom of fabulous wealth. The name El Dorado has come to have another meaning—that of an unattainable ideal.

Eldorado   *Edgar Allan Poe*

Gaily bedight,°
A gallant knight,
In sunshine and in shadow,
  Had journeyed long,
  Singing a song,   5
In search of Eldorado.

But he grew old—
This knight so bold—
And o'er his heart a shadow
  Fell as he found   10
  No spot of ground
That looked like Eldorado.

And, as his strength
Failed him at length,
He met a pilgrim° shadow—   15
  "Shadow," said he,
  "Where can it be—
This land of Eldorado?"

"Over the Mountains
  Of the Moon,   20
Down the Valley of the Shadow,
  Ride, boldly ride,"
  The shade° replied—
"If you seek for Eldorado!"

1. **bedight:** dressed.

15. **pilgrim:** wanderer.

23. **shade:** ghost.

FOR STUDY AND DISCUSSION

1. The first two stanzas of this poem tell how the knight grew old on his quest. What is about to happen to the knight near the end of the poem?

2. What pair of rhyming words is repeated in each stanza? Does the word *shadow* mean exactly the same thing in each stanza? Explain.
3. The shade's reply to the knight is mysterious. What is the shade telling the knight about his quest for Eldorado?

Next! *Ogden Nash*

I thought that I would like to see
The early world that used to be,
That mastodonic° mausoleum,°
The Natural History Museum.
On iron seat in marble bower,   5
I slumbered through the closing hour.
At midnight in the vasty hall
The fossils gathered for a ball.
High above notices and bulletins
Loomed up the Mesozoic° skeletons.   10
Aroused by who knows what elixirs,
They ground along like concrete mixers.
They bowed and scraped in reptile pleasure,
And then began to tread the measure.
There were no drums or saxophones,   15
But just the clatter of their bones,
A rolling, rattling, carefree circus
Of mammoth polkas and mazurkas.
Pterodactyls° and brontosauruses°
Sang ghostly prehistoric choruses.   20
Amid the megalosauric° wassail°
I caught the eye of one small fossil.
Cheer up, old man, he said, and winked—
It's kind of fun to be extinct.

3. **mastodonic** (măs′tə-dŏn′ĭk): referring to certain extinct elephantlike mammals. **mausoleum** (mô′sə-lē′əm): here, a large building that houses animal remains.

10. **Mesozoic** (mĕz′ə-zō′ĭk): in prehistoric times, the age of reptiles.

19. **Pterodactyls** (tĕr′ə-dăk′tĭlz): flying reptiles. **brontosauruses** (brŏn′tə-sôr′əs-əs): plant-eating dinosaurs.
21. **megalosauric** (mĕg′ə-lə-sôr′ĭk): The megalosaur was a meat-eating dinosaur. **wassail** (wŏs′əl): here, a revel or festivity.

FOR STUDY AND DISCUSSION

1. In medieval times, people believed that there was a substance called the "elixir of life," which could give eternal life. What humorous use does Nash make of this idea in the poem?

2. Polkas and mazurkas are lively dances that require agility and lightness of movement. Why is it particularly comical to have these dances performed by "Mesozoic skeletons"?

3. Nash is known for his clever and humorous rhymes. He often pairs words in unusual and unexpected combinations. For example, in lines 19–20, Nash rhymes *brontosauruses* with *choruses*. Find other examples of comic rhymes in the poem.

4. What lines in the poem suggest that the narrator is dreaming?

5. What do you think the title means?

RHYME AND RHYME SCHEME

Rhyme is the correspondence of sounds in words or phrases that appear close to each other in a poem. Most rhymes are *end rhymes,* that is, the rhyme occurs on final syllables:

Gaily be*dight*
A gallant *knight*

Find other examples of end rhyme in Poe's poem.

Sometimes rhyme occurs within a line of poetry:

The splendor *falls* on castle *walls.*

This is called *internal rhyme.*

One reason a poet uses rhyme is to give a poem structure. Usually rhyme words are arranged in a pattern called a *rhyme scheme.* Consider the pattern in the first stanza of "Eldorado":

Gaily bedight,	*a*
A gallant knight,	*a*
In sunshine and in shadow,	*b*
Had journeyed long,	*c*
Singing a song,	*c*
In search of Eldorado.	*b*

This stanza has an *aabccb* rhyme scheme (each new rhyme is indicated by a different letter of the alphabet). In which stanza does the rhyme scheme change? Look at "The Destruction of Sennacherib" (page 282). What is the rhyme scheme of the first two stanzas?

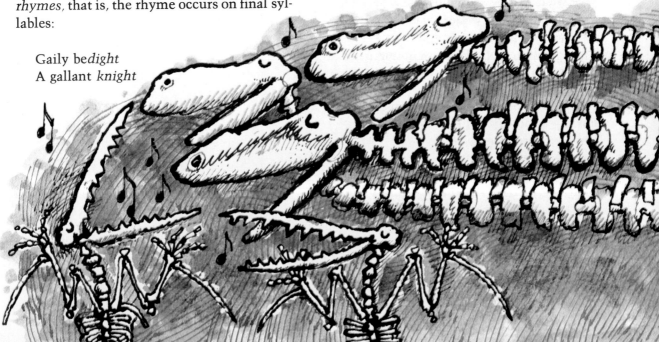

The Shell   *James Stephens*

And then I pressed the shell
Close to my ear
And listened well,
And straightway like a bell
Came low and clear   5
The slow, sad murmur of the distant seas,
Whipped by an icy breeze
Upon a shore
Wind-swept and desolate.
It was a sunless strand° that never bore   10   10. **strand:** beach.
The footprint of a man,
Nor felt the weight
Since time began
Of any human quality or stir
Save what the dreary winds and waves incur.°   15   15. **incur:** here, cause.
And in the hush of waters was the sound
Of pebbles rolling round,
Forever rolling with a hollow sound.
And bubbling seaweeds as the waters go
Swish to and fro   20
Their long, cold tentacles of slimy gray.
There was no day,
Nor ever came a night
Setting the stars alight
To wonder at the moon: 25
Was twilight only and the frightened croon,°   26. **croon:** a murmuring sound.
Smitten° to whimpers, of the dreary wind   27. **Smitten:** struck.
And waves that journeyed blind—
And then I loosed° my ear . . . O, it was sweet   29. **loosed:** moved away.
To hear a cart go jolting down the street.   30

FOR STUDY AND DISCUSSION

1. Describe the place that the speaker imagines as he holds the seashell to his ear. What is the only sound of life? What other sounds does he hear?

2. In lines 22–28, what strange and forbidding images are we given of this place? How does the mood of the poem suddenly change in lines 29–30?

3. The speaker brings us closer to his experience by using words whose sounds suggest the whistling wind, the rush of waves, and the murmur of the sea. Find examples of words whose sounds echo the sounds of the wind and the sea. What sounds are repeated most often? How do these sounds help us to imagine the scene more clearly?

ONOMATOPOEIA, ALLITERATION, AND ASSONANCE

One technique that is commonly used by poets is *onomatopoeia* (ŏn′ə-măt′ə-pē′ə), in which the sound of a word imitates a natural sound. For example, the word *crack* sounds like something cracking. Which word in line 6 of "The Shell" is onomatopoetic? Which other words in the poem are onomatopoetic?

Sometimes a poet creates special sound effects by *alliteration*—the repetition of consonant sounds, usually at the beginning of words. Many familiar expressions employ alliteration: *w*ild and *w*ooly, *s*weet *s*ixteen, *th*rough *th*ick and *th*in. Find an example of alliteration in the poem and explain its effect.

The name *assonance* is sometimes used for the repetition of vowel sounds. Assonance occurs in line 27:

Sm*i*tten to wh*i*mpers, of the dreary w*i*nd

How does the assonance in lines 17–18 echo the meaning of those lines?

The Book of Psalms in the Bible is composed of one hundred fifty poems in praise of God. The word psalm *comes from a Greek word meaning "song sung to a harp," and it indicates the musical nature of these early poems.*

Psalm 96   from *The King James Bible*

O sing unto the Lord a new song:
Sing unto the Lord, all the earth.
Sing unto the Lord, bless his name;
Show forth his salvation from day to day.
Declare his glory among the heathen,   5
His wonders among all people.
For the Lord is great, and greatly to be praised:
He is to be feared above all gods.
For all the gods of the nations are idols:
But the Lord made the heavens.   10
Honor and majesty are before him:
Strength and beauty are in his sanctuary.
Give unto the Lord, O ye kindreds of people,
Give unto the Lord glory and strength.
Give unto the Lord the glory due unto his name: 15
Bring an offering, and come into his courts.
O worship the Lord in the beauty of holiness:
Fear before him, all the earth.
Say among the heathen that the Lord reigneth:
The world also shall be established that it shall not be
     moved: 20
He shall judge the people righteously.
Let the heavens rejoice, and let the earth be glad;
Let the sea roar, and the fullness thereof.
Let the field be joyful, and all that is therein:
Then shall all the trees of the wood rejoice   25
Before the Lord: for he cometh,
For he cometh to judge the earth:
He shall judge the world with righteousness,
And the people with his truth.

FOR STUDY AND DISCUSSION

1. How are the first three lines of Psalm 96 similar in meaning and in structure? How are lines 4–6 alike?

2. What reasons does the poet give for praising the Lord? According to the poet, in what ways can people praise the Lord?

3. The ancient Hebrew poets were fond of using images from nature. According to this poet, how will nature respond to the knowledge of God? How does the poet use nature imagery to build to a joyful climax?

PARALLELISM

One of the devices most frequently used in the poetry of the Psalms is *parallelism*—the repetition of phrases or sentences that are similar in meaning or in structure. Look, for example, at lines 22–24:

> Let the heavens rejoice, and let the earth be glad;
> Let the sea roar, and the fullness thereof.
> Let the field be joyful, and all that is therein:

The three lines are related in meaning: they call for universal rejoicing. The lines are also parallel in structure: each line is broken in the middle by a comma, and each begins with the words *let the*. The structure of the lines also gives rise to a parallel rhythm, so that the lines seem to balance and echo one another. This rhythmic parallelism gives the lines a special emphasis when they are read aloud. What other examples of parallelism can you find in the Psalm?

Because of its often stirring emotional impact, parallelism has been used in diverse forms of literature. You are probably familiar with this famous example of parallelism in "The Gettysburg Address": "government of the people, by the people, for the people."

FOR COMPOSITION

Analyzing a Psalm
Choose one of the Psalms in the Bible and analyze its musical devices. Some of the best-known Psalms are 23, 24, and 121.

ABOUT THE AUTHORS

George Gordon, Lord Byron (1788–1824) has been called "the most interesting personality in the history of the world." He was a dashing, rebellious genius, as famous for the scandals he was involved in as for his poems. When he was a student at Cambridge, he objected to a rule prohibiting students from keeping dogs. He protested by buying a bear—an animal not prohibited—to keep as a pet. His rebelliousness alienated him from many of his peers, and he left England forever in 1816. Thereafter, he devoted himself to various international revolutionary causes. He became an officer in the Greek revolutionary army, which sought independence for Greece from Turkish rule. However, he never participated in the revolution, for shortly after he arrived in Greece, at the age of thirty-six, he died of a fever. Byron created not only a body of enduring poetry but also a legend and a new kind of hero: the young rebel.

Carl Sandburg (1878–1967), the son of Swedish immigrant parents, had to quit school at thirteen to help support his family. He held almost every kind of job—from washing pop bottles to harvesting wheat. At the start of the Spanish-American War in 1898, he joined the army. After the war, he returned to his native Illinois where he worked as a firefighter to put himself through college. Later, he worked in politics and as a reporter. His ramblings across the country, his wide experience in working with ordinary people, and his deep interest in America's past combined to make him a poet who celebrated everyday life and average people. An author of children's books and a historian as well as a poet, Sandburg won a Pulitzer Prize in 1940 for his biography of Abraham Lincoln, and another Pulitzer Prize in 1950 for his *Complete Poems.*

Before Ogden Nash (1902–1971) began writing poetry, he was a schoolteacher, a salesman, and a copywriter for a publisher. After his first poem was accepted by *The New Yorker* in 1931, he joined the staff of the magazine and turned to writing as a full-time career. Nash is generally acknowledged to be America's foremost humorous poet. He published more than twenty books of poetry and prose. He also collaborated with S. J. Perelman on the libretto for *One Touch of Venus,* a musical comedy.

James Stephens (1882–1950) lacked a formal education, but through his own reading he made himself an authority on art and folk music, as well as a successful novelist and poet. His first success was a book of fairy stories, *The Crock of Gold.* All of his writing is full of fantasy and deep imagination. Stephens could hold a group spellbound for hours with Irish stories, legends, and poetry.

Structures

If a poem is to work, it must have the right kind of structure to carry it. One of the poet's most difficult tasks is to match the content of a poem to the form that is best suited for it. The basic unit of structure in most poems is the *stanza*. A stanza is any group of lines that forms a division of a poem. It may be based on the number of lines, rhyme scheme, rhythm, or other devices of repetition.

Four Little Foxes   *Lew Sarett*

Speak gently, Spring, and make no sudden sound;
For in my windy valley yesterday I found
Newborn foxes squirming on the ground—
    Speak gently.

Walk softly, March, forbear the bitter blow;   5
Her feet within a trap, her blood upon the snow,
The four little foxes saw their mother go—
    Walk softly.

Go lightly, Spring, Oh give them no alarm;
When I covered them with boughs to shelter them from
        harm,   10
The thin blue foxes suckled at my arm—
    Go lightly.

Step softly, March, with your rampant hurricane;
Nuzzling one another, and whimpering with pain,
The new little foxes are shivering in the rain—   15
    Step softly.

FOR STUDY AND DISCUSSION

1. Why are the cubs in a perilous situation?
2. What is the stanza pattern of this poem? Are line length and number, rhyme scheme, and rhythm the same from stanza to stanza?

3. A new stanza generally marks a division in thought, so that each one works something like a paragraph. How does each stanza in this poem make the plight of the fox cubs clearer? Why is each stanza almost like a prayer, chant, or spell to protect the foxes?

The Sound of the Sea

Henry Wadsworth Longfellow

Rhyme Scheme	
a	The sea awoke at midnight from its sleep,
b	And round the pebbly beaches far and wide
b	I heard the first wave of the rising tide
a	Rush onward with uninterrupted sweep;
a	A voice out of the silence of the deep, 5
b	A sound mysteriously multiplied
b	As of a cataract° from the mountain's side,
a	Or roar of winds upon a wooded steep.
c	So comes to us at times, from the unknown
d	And inaccessible° solitudes of being, 10
e	The rushing of the sea-tides of the soul;
c	And inspirations, that we deem° our own,
d	Are some divine foreshadowing and foreseeing
e	Of things beyond our reason or control.

7. **cataract:** huge, crashing waterfall.

10. **inaccessible:** (ĭn′ăk-sĕs′ə-bəl) impossible to reach.

12. **deem:** judge.

THE PETRARCHAN SONNET

One of the most popular poetic forms is the *sonnet*—a fourteen-line poem with a traditional rhyme scheme. "The Sound of the Sea" is an example of a *Petrarchan* sonnet. It consists of two parts. The first part is eight lines long and has a rhyme scheme of *abbaabba*. It is called the *octave*, from the Latin word for "eight." The second, six-line part usually has a *cdecde* rhyme scheme, and is called a *sestet*, from the Latin word for "six." Where does the first sentence of the poem end? How does this strengthen the two-part division of the poem?

Sometimes in a Petrarchan sonnet the octave raises an idea that the sestet extends. In the octave of this poem, the speaker describes the sea tide as sounding awesome. In the sestet, what does he compare to the sea tide? What, according to the speaker, is the true source of our inspirations? How do the speaker's attitudes toward the sea and toward inspiration help to unify the sonnet?

Sonnet 55   *William Shakespeare*

*Rhyme
Scheme*

a	Not marble, nor the gilded monuments
b	Of princes, shall outlive this powerful rime;
a	But you shall shine more bright in these contents°
b	Than unswept stone, besmeared with sluttish time.
c	When wasteful war shall statues overturn, 5
d	And broils° root out the work of masonry,
c	Nor Mars his sword° nor war's quick fire shall burn
d	The living record of your memory.
e	'Gainst death and all-oblivious enmity°
f	Shall you pace forth; your praise shall still find room 10
e	Even in the eyes of all posterity
f	That wear this world out to the ending doom.
g	So, till the judgment that yourself° arise,
g	You live in this, and dwell in lovers' eyes.

---

3. **these contents:** the contents of this poem.   6. **broils:** fights, brawls.   7. **Mars his sword:** Mars's sword.   9. **all-oblivious enmity:** war which sends all to oblivion.   12–13. These lines refer to the belief that the world will come to an end with a final day of judgment, when all the dead will arise;   **that yourself:** when you yourself.

FOR STUDY AND DISCUSSION

Each of Shakespeare's sonnets presents an "argument" in verse. How do the first twelve lines develop the idea that this poem is a more permanent tribute than a stone monument? How do the last two lines summarize the argument?

THE SHAKESPEAREAN SONNET

A sonnet usually has fourteen iambic pentameter lines— that is, ten syllables with a stress on every other syllable:

When wásteful wár shall státues óvertúrn

The Italian, or Petrarchan, form of the sonnet, as you have seen, is divided into the *octave* and the *sestet*. The structure of the Shakespearean sonnet is different. It contains three *quatrains*—four-line stanzas—and a *couplet* —a pair of rhyming lines. The rhyme scheme is *abab cdcd efef gg.* In the Petrarchan sonnet, the last six lines usually present a comment on or a summary of the argument that has been presented in the first eight lines. In the Shakespearean sonnet, by contrast, the conclusion or resolution is generally delivered in the final two lines.

Manhole Covers *Karl Shapiro*

The beauty of manhole covers—what of that?
Like medals struck by a great savage kahn,°
Like Mayan calendar stones, unliftable, indecipherable,
Not like old electrum, chased and scored,°
Mottoed and sculptured to a turn,   5
But notched and whelked° and pocked and smashed
With the great company names:
Gentle Bethlehem, smiling United States.
This rustproof artifact of my street,
Long after roads are melted away, will lie   10
Sidewise in the grave of the iron-old world,
Bitten at the edges,
Strong with its cryptic° American,
Its dated beauty.

2. **khan:** Asian ruler, such as Genghis Khan.

4. **chased and scored:** delicately etched and marked.

6. **whelked:** twisted.

13. **cryptic:** mysterious.

FOR STUDY AND DISCUSSION

1. How do the comparisons in lines 2–3 of this poem make the manhole covers seem exotic and mysterious? According to the speaker, what will finally become of manhole covers? Why will they be *cryptic?*

2. Where in the poem do you find the devices of parallelism and simile? Look carefully at the structure of the poem. The first eight lines describe the manhole covers, the last six comment on their significance. What kind of poem does this pattern resemble?

FREE VERSE

In your reading, you have seen that not all poems are organized by stanzas, and many poems do not seem to have a fixed rhythm, rhyme scheme, or line length. This kind of poetry, called *free verse*, has become a popular form in the twentieth century. It is called free verse because no set pattern controls it. It may rhyme in some places and not in others, or not rhyme at all. Its lines may be of different lengths. It may have no dominant rhythm, or it may switch rhythms as it progresses.

Free verse enables poets to create effects that are not possible within the restrictions of a set pattern. Poets are freer to fit sounds and rhythms more closely to the meaning of a poem. They can use everyday language and natural speech rhythms. In what ways does "Manhole Covers" illustrate these characteristics?

The danger of free verse is that it looks easy to write, but it is actually very difficult to write well. Like other poetry, it must have structure. In free verse, with no traditional guidelines for direction, the poet must create and develop a special structure for each poem.

As easy as it seems to be, free verse is considered by many poets to be the hardest kind of verse to write.

Although there is no fixed pattern of rhythm in free verse, it sometimes uses very strong rhythms. Listen to "Manhole Covers" being read aloud. Would you call the rhythm light and graceful, or heavy? Is the rhythm appropriate to the subject? Lines that end with a stressed syllable tend to be more forceful than lines that do not. How many lines in the poem end with a stressed syllable? Poetry, free verse or otherwise, usually contains more stressed syllables than ordinary language. What lines can you find in the poem that contain many stressed syllables?

FOR COMPOSITION

Finding Beauty in the Commonplace

Write a poem or brief paragraph in which you describe some ordinary object so that your readers will see it in a new light and appreciate its uniqueness. To do this, you will have to look at something in a different way yourself. For example, people frequently complain that our cities are unclean and unsafe and our highways are cluttered with ugly gas stations, fast-food restaurants, and billboards. Can you find anything in such scenes as these that has a special sort of beauty people usually do not notice?

Poetry is meant to be heard, but poets have experimented with how it looks on the page as well. Modern poets in particular take delight in playing with the shapes of poems, experimenting with strange arrangements of lines and print. A poem may be written so that its shape on the page resembles its subject; there are poems shaped like swans, wineglasses, Christmas trees, and sets of wings. If the appearance of the following poem puzzles you at first, just imagine the movements of a swimmer back and forth across a pool.

400-meter Freestyle   *Maxine W. Kumin*

THE GUN full swing the swimmer catapults and cracks
                        s
                        i
                        x
feet away onto that perfect glass he catches at
a
n
d
throws behind him scoop after scoop cunningly moving
                        t
                        h
                        e
water back to move him forward. Thrift is his wonderful
s
e
c
ret; he has schooled out all extravagance. No muscle
                        r
                        i
                        p
ples without compensation wrist cock to heel snap to
h
i
s

mobile mouth that siphons in the air that nurtures
                                                    h
                                                     i
                                                      m
at half an inch above the sea level so to speak.
   T
 h
   e
astonishing whites of the soles of his feet rise
                                                   a
                                                    n
                                                     d
salute us on the turns. He flips, converts, and is gone
   a
 l
 l
in one. We watch him for signs. His arms are steady at
                                                       t
                                                        h
                                                         e
catch, his cadent feet tick in the stretch, they know
   t
 h
   e
lesson well. Lungs know, too; he does not list for
                                                   a
                                                    i
                                                     r
he drives along on little sips carefully expended
   b
 u
   t
that plum red heart pumps hard cries hurt how soon
                                                    i
                                                     t
                                                      s
near one more and makes its final surge TIME: 4:25:9

FOR STUDY AND DISCUSSION

1. What do the words in capitals at the beginning and end of the poem signify? How does the arrangement of the lines imitate the movement of the swimmer in the pool?

2. What does the poet mean when she says of the swimmer "Thrift is his wonderful secret"? What examples does she give of this "thrift"?

3. Show how the poet uses alliteration and assonance to make the lines move with force and strenuousness, like the swimmer. What lines do you think vividly capture the movements and feelings of the swimmer?

FOR COMPOSITION

Experimenting with Line Arrangements

Write a few lines of your own that form a recognizable shape on the page. Have the lines express some thought or idea, and be sure that the shape you create has something to do with your subject. Imagination is all you need for this kind of expression; you may write some lines in a shape that is as simple as a box or as complicated as a plate of spaghetti.

Getting Across *Carter Revard*

Hanging
      out under the bridge
   by fingertips and a toe
        between ledge and girder, high
over deep water and thinking.   5
        I can't swim,
    unreachable by the older boys
        who've made it across, he watches
the steel-blue flash of wings
      and chestnut bellies of barnswallows   10
shooting and swirling around him,
                below him,
   a two-foot gar's black shadow
      in the green-brown water beneath,
and before he weakens has   15
   let the toe slip gently and
    swung down
   like a pendulum, hand
  over hand along the girder to
       where the others perch   20
          on the concrete ledge,
has kicked up his right leg onto the ledge and
    been pulled to its safety,
can look back now at the swallow's easy
   curve upward,   25
      its flutter and settling
    gently into the cup
of feather-lined mud there nestling
   on the shining girder's side
    where he has passed his death.   30

FOR STUDY AND DISCUSSION

1. What does the title of the poem refer to?
2. Compare the description of the swallow in lines 24–30 with that of the barnswallows in lines 9–11. How do these descriptions mirror the boy's state of mind?
3. How is the idea of "getting across" conveyed by the arrangement of lines in the poem?

ABOUT THE AUTHORS

Lew Sarett (1888–1954) was born in Chicago, Illinois. During his career as educator, poet, and lecturer, he served as advisory editor to *Poetry* and was Professor of Speech at Northwestern University. His books include *Many Many Moons* (1920), *The Box of God* (1922), *Slow Smoke* (1925), *Wings Against the Moon* (1931), and *Collected Poems* (1941).

William Shakespeare (1564–1616) is generally considered the greatest writer in the English language. He was born in an English town called Stratford-on-Avon. He left for London sometime in his early twenties and joined a company of actors. He soon became the company's chief playwright, and by the time he retired to Stratford-on-Avon, he had written thirty-seven plays — a great body of tragedies, comedies, histories, and romances. Ben Jonson, a contemporary and a great dramatist in his own right, said this of Shakespeare: "He was not of an age, but for all time." Jonson's prophecy has turned out to be true, for today, Shakespeare's works are read and performed all over the world. His infinite variety never grows stale.

Karl Jay Shapiro (1913–   ) was born in Baltimore, Maryland, and attended the University of Virginia. He left school for a time and tried various jobs. He then entered Johns Hopkins University. When World War II broke out, he was inducted into the Army and sent to the South Pacific. He wrote poetry during his years in the service, and his fiancée had this work published while Shapiro was overseas. His volume *Person, Place, and Thing* (1942) won high praise from critics, and *V-Letter and Other Poems* (1944) was awarded the Pulitzer Prize. Shapiro has also worked as an editor of *Poetry* magazine and *Prairie Schooner.*

Maxine (Winokur) Kumin (1925–   ) was born in Philadelphia, Pennsylvania, and attended Radcliffe College. She has been an instructor in English at Tufts University and a fellow at the Radcliffe Institute for Independent Study. In addition to several volumes of poetry, she has written novels and books for children. *No One Writes a Letter to the Snail* is a collection of poems for children. In 1973 she won the Pulitzer Prize for *Up Country: Poems of New England.*

Carter Revard is part Osage (ō'sāj') on his father's side. His Osage name, Nompewathe, means "fear-inspiring." Revard grew up in Oklahoma. He won a radio quiz scholarship to the University of Tulsa, then a Rhodes Scholarship to Oxford University in England. He holds a Ph.D. from Yale and teaches English at Washington University in St. Louis.

Tone

People speak in many tones of voice: angry, thoughtful, joking, tired, and so on. Tone shows the speaker's mood, the emotion behind the words. Poets, too, speak in a variety of tones. The tone of a poem shows its speaker's attitude toward the subject as well as toward the audience. It results from all the different parts of the poem working together. Although there may be shifts of mood within a work, poets generally aim for uniformity of tone.

Diction, or choice of words, affects tone. The words *ladies and gentlemen* convey a tone different from that of *guys and dolls*. If an automotive mechanic says, "Your car could use some repair," the statement indicates a measure of respect for both the car and its owner. Compare the tone of that statement with the tone carried by these words: "Your clunker of a car is falling apart."

Imagery, too, can affect tone. If, for instance, you were describing the food in a cafeteria, the details you select would help convey your attitude. Images such as "the sizzle of frying chicken" and "the aroma of fresh strawberries" convey altogether different feelings from such images as "an overripe tomato slice on a wilted lettuce leaf" and "a cold hot dog on a stale bun."

Even the sounds of the words within a poem help shape its tone. Repetition, as you have seen, can have an emphatic, hypnotic, or haunting emotional effect. Such devices as alliteration, assonance, and onomatopoeia help communicate the poet's attitude toward subject and audience. Rhythm, like words, can affect tone, and so can rhyme or lack of rhyme. A poem with a tightly controlled rhythm and rhyme scheme creates a more formal tone than does a poem that imitates the rhythms of ordinary speech.

Sentence structure, too, can color the tone of a poem. The more complicated the sentence structure, usually the more formal the poem. Parallelism can help determine the tone of a poem as can stanzaic form and organization.

At Woodward's Gardens
Robert Frost

A boy, presuming on his intellect,
Once showed two little monkeys in a cage
A burning-glass they could not understand
And never could be made to understand.
Words are no good: to say it was a lens   5
For gathering solar rays would not have helped.
But let him show them how the weapon worked.
He made the sun a pinpoint on the nose
Of first one, then the other, till it brought
A look of puzzled dimness to their eyes   10
That blinking could not seem to blink away.
They stood arms laced together at the bars,
And exchanged troubled glances over life.
One put a thoughtful hand up to his nose
As if reminded—or as if perhaps   15
Within a million years of an idea.
He got his purple little knuckles stung.

The already known had once more been confirmed
By psychological experiment,
And that were all the finding to announce 20
Had the boy not presumed too close and long.
There was a sudden flash of arm, a snatch,
And the glass was the monkeys', not the boy's.
Precipitately° they retired back-cage

24. **Precipitately:** hurriedly.

And instituted an investigation 25
On their part, though without the needed insight.
They bit the glass and listened for the flavor.
They broke the handle and the binding off it.
Then none the wiser, frankly gave it up,
And having hid it in their bedding straw 30
Against the day of prisoners' ennui,°

31. **ennui** (än'wē'): boredom.

Came dryly forward to the bars again
To answer for themselves: Who said it mattered
What monkeys did or didn't understand?
They might not understand a burning-glass. 35
They might not understand the sun itself.
It's knowing what to do with things that counts.

FOR STUDY AND DISCUSSION

1. What is the "burning-glass"?

2. What does Frost mean when he says the boy is "presuming on his intellect"? How would you describe this attitude in everyday language? What tone is conveyed by Frost's elegant phrase?

3. How would you describe the poet's attitude toward the boy's experiment? Toward the monkeys?

4. For what different purposes do the boy and the monkeys try to use the burning-glass? What comment does the poem make on our use of scientific discoveries?

5. How would you describe the poem's overall tone? Would you characterize it as serious, mocking, comic, ironic? Explain.

FOR COMPOSITION

Communicating Tone in a Description
In a brief paragraph describe some animal or thing in such a way that your attitude is clear. Do not say directly what you think of your subject. Let your choice of words convey your attitude.

Writing a Fable
Choose a well-known saying such as "All that glitters is not gold" or "The grass is always greener on the other side of the fence" and write a fable that illustrates the wisdom of that saying. You may use animal characters or human characters. If you wish, compose your fable in verse. Accompany the fable with illustrations if you like.

Art Review   *Kenneth Fearing*

Recently displayed at the Times Square° Station, a new
    Vandyke° on the face-cream girl.
(Artist unknown. Has promise, but lacks the brilliance
    shown by the great masters of the Elevated age°)
The latest wood carving in a Whelan° telephone booth,
    titled "O Mortal Fools WA 9-5090," shows two
    winged hearts above an ace of spades.
(His meaning is not entirely clear, but this man will go
    far)
A charcoal nude in the rear of Flatbush° Ahearn's Bar &
    Grill, "Forward to the Brotherhood of Man," has been
    boldly conceived in the great tradition.   5
(We need more, much more of this)
Then there is the chalk portrait, on the walls of a wa-
    terfront warehouse, of a gentleman wearing a derby
    hat: "Bleecker Street° Mike is a double-crossing rat."
(Morbid, but powerful. Don't miss)

Know then by these presents, know all men by these
    signs and omens, by these simple thumbprints on the
    throat of time,
Know that Pete, the people's artist, is ever watchful,   10
That Tuxedo Jim has passed among us, and was much
    displeased, as always,
That George the Ghost (no man has ever seen him) and
    Billy the Bicep boy will neither bend nor break,
That Mr. Harkness of Sunnyside still hopes for the best,
    and has not lost his human touch,
That Phantom Phil, the master of them all, has come and
    gone, but will return, and all is well.

1. **Times Square:** a colorful section of Manhattan in New York City. **Vandyke:** a pointed beard named after the Flemish painter Vandyke.

2. **Elevated age:** of elevated trains.

3. **Whelan:** the name of a chain of drugstores.

5. **Flatbush:** a community in Brooklyn, New York.

7. **Bleecker Street:** a street in downtown Manhattan.

FOR STUDY AND DISCUSSION

1. The art that forms the subject of this poem is *graffiti* (grə-fē′tē), crude drawings on walls and doors in public places. What different kinds of graffiti does the speaker itemize?

2. Part of the mock-serious tone of this poem comes from treating the subject of graffiti in elegant language. For instance, the beard scribbled on the "face-cream girl" is described as being "recently displayed," as if it were a work of art. The person who drew it is described as an unknown artist, as if the work were listed in a museum guide. What other examples can you find of ordinary subjects described in lofty language?

3. This poem, like a play, has a cast of characters. The characters' names help describe them and also define the poet's attitude toward them. What tone do the names create?

4. Do you think the poet is more critical of the artists or of the world they portray in their art? Explain. How does the title help convey the poem's tone?

Lizards and Snakes   *Anthony Hecht*

On the summer road that ran by our front porch
  Lizards and snakes came out to sun.
It was hot as a stove out there, enough to scorch
  A buzzard's foot. Still, it was fun
To lie in the dust and spy on them. Near but remote,   5
  They snoozed in the carriage ruts, a smile
In the set of the jaw, a fierce pulse in the throat
Working away like Jack Doyle's after he'd run the mile.

Aunt Martha had an unfair prejudice
  Against them (as well as being cold   10
Toward bats). She was pretty inflexible in this,
  Being a spinster and all, and old.
So we used to slip them into her knitting box.
  In the evening she'd bring in things to mend
And a nice surprise would slide out from under the socks.   15
It broadened her life, as Joe said. Joe was my friend.

But we never did it again after the day
  Of the big wind when you could hear the trees
Creak like rocking chairs. She was looking away
  Off, and kept saying, "Sweet Jesus, please   20
Don't let him near me. He's as like as twins.
  He can crack us like lice with his fingernail.
I can see him plain as a pikestaff.° Look how he grins
And swinges° the scaly horror of his folded tail."

23. **plain as a pikestaff:** quite clearly.

24. **swinges** (swĭn′jəz): beats, whips (archaic).

FOR STUDY AND DISCUSSION

1. How does the speaker's description of lizards and snakes in the first stanza suggest his attitude toward them?

2. What is the difference between the way the speaker feels about lizards and snakes and the way Aunt Martha feels? How does the speaker's attitude toward Aunt Martha change by the end of the poem? What causes this change?

3. The last line is from John Milton's poem "On the Morning of Christ's Nativity." The reference is to Satan, the Devil. What is the traditional connection between reptiles and evil?

4. Examine the similes in the last stanza. Tell how each one contributes to the poem's tone.

FOR COMPOSITION

Analyzing Tone
Choose one of the poems in this unit and analyze its tone. Show how the poet's use of different elements helps create the tone.

ABOUT THE AUTHORS

Kenneth Fearing (1902–1961) was born in Oak Park, Illinois, a suburb of Chicago. After attending the University of Wisconsin, he worked at various jobs before turning to writing as a career. Much of Fearing's poetry is about life in the modern American city.

Anthony Hecht (1923–   ) was born in New York City and attended Bard College and Columbia University. His volumes of poetry include *A Summoning of Stones* and *The Hard Hours,* which was awarded the Pulitzer Prize in 1968. He now teaches at the University of Rochester.

Types of Poetry

The following section covers three major types of poetry: *lyric, narrative,* and *dramatic.* Although these categories frequently overlap (a narrative poem may also be dramatic, for instance), each type has distinctive characteristics. Lyric poems are generally short poems that express an intense emotional response of the speaker to some person, place, object, or idea. Narrative poems tell a story. Dramatic poems present characters who speak to other characters or to an implied audience.

In ancient Greece, lyrics were sung to the music of a lyre, a sort of harp. We still call the words of a song its lyrics. Lyric poems are rich in musical devices. There are many different kinds of lyric poems, including sonnets, hymns, songs, odes, and elegies.

John Anderson My Jo   *Robert Burns*

John Anderson my jo,° John,
  When we were first acquent,°
Your locks were like the raven,
  Your bonny brow was brent,°
But now your brow is beld,° John,   5
  Your locks are like the snow;
But blessings on your frosty pow,°
  John Anderson my jo.

John Anderson my jo, John,
  We clamb the hill thegither;   10
And mony a canty° day, John,
  We've had wi' ane anither:
Now we maun° totter down, John,
  And hand in hand we'll go,
And sleep thegither at the foot,   15
  John Anderson my jo.

1. **jo:** joy, sweetheart.
2. **acquent:** acquainted.
4. **brent:** unwrinkled.
5. **beld:** bald.
7. **pow:** head.
11. **canty:** happy.
13. **maun:** must.

1. Who is the speaker in this poem? How have she and her sweetheart changed? What does the speaker recall about their days together?
2. What symbolic meaning is suggested by the phrases "clamb the hill" and "totter down"? What do you think is the meaning of line 15?

3. Read the poem aloud, paying attention to the words in Scottish dialect. How do the rhyme, alliteration, and repetition of words and phrases contribute to the music of the poem?
4. Although this poem is written in Scottish dialect, it is one of the best-known love poems in our language. What do you think is the source of its wide appeal? Why would it appeal to both young and old readers?

O Mistress Mine   *William Shakespeare*

O mistress mine, where are you roaming?
O, stay and hear, your true-love's coming,
  That can sing both high and low.
Trip no further, pretty sweeting;
Journeys end in lovers meeting,   5
  Every wise man's son doth know.

What is love? 'Tis not hereafter;
Present mirth hath present laughter;
  What's to come is still unsure:
In delay there lies no plenty;   10
Then come and kiss me, sweet and twenty,
  Youth's a stuff will not endure.

FOR STUDY AND DISCUSSION

In this poem the speaker pleads with his beloved to return his love quickly, since the time of youth is short. Which lines express this idea? What is the argument of lines 7–10?

FOR COMPOSITION

Comparing Tone
Compare the tones of "John Anderson My Jo" and "O Mistress Mine." What attitude toward love is expressed in each poem?

I Wandered Lonely as a Cloud

William Wordsworth

I wandered lonely as a cloud
  That floats on high o'er vales° and hills,
When all at once I saw a crowd,
  A host, of golden daffodils,
Beside the lake, beneath the trees,   5
Fluttering and dancing in the breeze.

Continuous as the stars that shine
  And twinkle on the Milky Way,
They stretched in never-ending line
  Along the margin of a bay:°   10
Ten thousand saw I at a glance,
Tossing their heads in sprightly dance.

The waves beside them danced; but they
  Outdid the sparkling waves in glee;
A poet could not but be gay,   15
  In such a jocund° company;
I gazed—and gazed—but little thought
What wealth the show to me had brought:

For oft, when on my couch I lie
  In vacant or in pensive mood,   20
They flash upon that inward eye
  Which is the bliss of solitude;
And then my heart with pleasure fills,
And dances with the daffodils.

2. **vales:** valleys.

10. **margin of a bay:** edge of the water.

16. **jocund:** merry.

FOR STUDY AND DISCUSSION

1. What was the poet's mood before he encountered the great wild garden of flowers? How did his discovery change his mood?
2. Did the poet realize, at the time he saw the flowers, how important the sight would become to him? How do the flowers continue to be a thing of beauty even when he can no longer see them? What is the "inward eye" Wordsworth refers to in line 21?
3. Which lines in the poem contain similes and personifications? Which lines strike you as particularly melodious? Notice the very regular rhyme scheme. Where in the poem does the poet use inversion? How does inverted word order enable him to keep a tight rhyme scheme?

Loveliest of Trees   *A. E. Housman*

Loveliest of trees, the cherry now
Is hung with bloom along the bough,
And stands about the woodland ride°
Wearing white for Eastertide.

3. **woodland ride:** a forest path, usually for riding horses.

Now, of my threescore years and ten,°   5
Twenty will not come again,
And take from seventy springs a score,
It only leaves me fifty more.

5. **threescore years and ten:** seventy years, a Biblical allusion to the average human life span. See Psalm 90 : 10.

And since to look at things in bloom
Fifty springs are little room,   10
About the woodlands I will go
To see the cherry hung with snow.

FOR STUDY AND DISCUSSION

1. How old does the speaker say he is in stanza 2? What do lines 7–8 mean?

2. What does the speaker mean by saying "Fifty springs are little room"? Why does he go to see the trees?

3. Both this poem and "I Wandered Lonely as a Cloud" (page 312) express delight in nature. How are the speakers' attitudes toward nature similar? Are their attitudes different in any way? If so, how?

We usually think of a desert as a hot, sandy, sun-baked land. But the word also means any barren, desolate place. As this poem shows, a desert can be a state of mind as well.

Desert Places   *Robert Frost*

Snow falling and night falling fast, oh, fast
In a field I looked into going past,
And the ground almost covered smooth in snow,
But a few weeds and stubble showing last.

The woods around it have it—it is theirs.   5
All animals are smothered° in their lairs.
I am too absent-spirited to count;
The loneliness includes me unawares.

6. **smothered**: here, asleep or hibernating.

And lonely as it is, that loneliness
Will be more lonely ere it will be less—   10
A blanker whiteness of benighted° snow
With no expression, nothing to express.

11. **benighted**: overtaken by the night or darkness.

They cannot scare me with their empty spaces
Between stars—on stars where no human race is.
I have it in me so much nearer home   15
To scare myself with my own desert places.

FOR STUDY AND DISCUSSION

1. What mood is evoked in the first two stanzas of the poem? Which details of scene contribute to this mood?
2. What is the meaning of lines 7–8?
3. In stanza 3, the speaker looks into the future. What change does he foresee in the scene? In his mood?
4. In stanza 4, who do you think "They" are? What does the speaker mean by his "own desert places"?

FOR COMPOSITION

Describing a Scene in Nature
"I Wandered Lonely as a Cloud" and "Loveliest of Trees" are about spring and the emotions nature evokes in the speakers. "Desert Places" is about a winter scene and the speaker's reaction to it. Write a brief essay describing a scene in summer or fall, and the emotions it stirs in you. Make your description as specific as you can, using words that communicate your feelings to the reader.

A recessional is the hymn that is sung as the choir and clergy are leaving the church at the end of a service. Rudyard Kipling wrote this poem in 1897, the year of England's celebration of the sixtieth anniversary—the Diamond Jubilee—of the reign of Queen Victoria. In that year, England was at its height as a world power.

Recessional *Rudyard Kipling*

God of our fathers, known of old,
   Lord of our far-flung battle line,
Beneath whose awful Hand we hold
   Dominion over palm and pine—
Lord God of Hosts, be with us yet,   5
Lest we forget—lest we forget!

The tumult and the shouting dies;
   The captains and the kings depart:
Still stands Thine ancient sacrifice,
   An humble and a contrite heart.   10
Lord God of Hosts, be with us yet,
Lest we forget—lest we forget!

Far-called, our navies melt away;
   On dune and headland sinks the fire:
Lo, all our pomp of yesterday   15
   Is one with Nineveh and Tyre!°
Judge of the Nations, spare us yet,
Lest we forget—lest we forget!

16. **Nineveh** (nĭn′ə-və) **and Tyre** (tīr): great centers of ancient civilizations. According to the Bible, they neglected God's commandments and decayed.

If, drunk with sight of power, we loose
   Wild tongues that have not Thee in awe,   20
Such boasting as the Gentiles° use,
   Or lesser breeds without the Law°—
Lord God of Hosts, be with us yet,
Lest we forget—lest we forget!

For heathen heart that puts her trust   25
   In reeking tube and iron shard,°
All valiant dust that builds on dust,
   And guarding, calls not Thee to guard,
For frantic boast and foolish word—
Thy Mercy on Thy People, Lord!   30

21. **Gentiles** (jĕn′tīlz): here, in the Biblical sense of "outsider"—those who did not obey God's Law.
22. **the Law:** the Hebrew Law of the Old Testament.

26. **shard:** a hard or brittle fragment—here, a bullet from the "reeking tube" of a gun.

FOR STUDY AND DISCUSSION

1. In what things does Kipling say his nation should not put its trust? Why should it reject these sources of power? On what would Kipling have his country rely?

2. What examples does Kipling give to prove that success in war and conquest will not keep a nation great? Why, as an empire expands, might its power tend to "melt away"?

How might a nation's puffing up with a sense of its own importance hasten this process?

3. A word, a phrase, a line, or a group of lines that reappears from stanza to stanza is called a *refrain*. What lines does Kipling use as a refrain? How does the refrain grow in effect and meaning each time it is repeated in the poem? Where does Kipling vary the refrain and what new ideas are introduced in these variations?

ABOUT THE AUTHORS

Robert Burns (1759–1796) is sometimes called the national poet of Scotland. He was born in Ayr in southwestern Scotland. His family was poor and Burns received little formal schooling. He learned old Scottish songs and stories, and while he worked as a plowboy on his family's farm, he composed many of his poems to the tunes of traditional Scottish songs. Burns is one of the greatest songwriters in English literature. Many of his poems have been set to music. Some well-known love poems are "Highland Mary," "Sweet Afton," and "The Banks o' Doon."

William Wordsworth (1770–1850) is generally considered to be the first major Romantic poet in English literature and the greatest nature poet in the language. He was a leader in the rebellion against the content and technique of eighteenth-century poetry. His idea of poetry is set forth in a famous document, the preface to the second edition of *Lyrical Ballads*, a collection of poetry that marks the beginning of the Romantic period in English literature. In this preface, Wordsworth rejected the idea that the subject matter or language of poetry need be exalted or elegant. He emphasized that the language of poetry should be natural and that its subject matter should be drawn from everyday life.

A. E. Housman (1859–1936), a renowned classical scholar, was professor of Latin at University College, London, and then at Trinity College, Cambridge. His literary reputation is largely founded on *A Shropshire Lad*, a collection of sixty-three poems he published in 1896. The speaker in these poems is a farm lad of Shropshire whom Housman described as "an imaginary figure, with something of my own temper and view of life." The poems are famous for their simple diction, their melody, and their craftsmanship.

Rudyard Kipling (1865–1936) was born in Bombay, India. When he was not quite six years old, he was sent to England for his education. He stayed there until he was seventeen, then returned to India where he worked as a journalist. When he was twenty-one, he published a volume of light verse called *Departmental Ditties*, and a year later he published a collection of stories, *Plain Tales from the Hills*. By the time he returned to England from India in his mid-twenties, he was famous. Kipling's work is characterized by its power and vitality. Some of his best-known novels are *The Light That Failed*, *Captains Courageous*, and *Kim*. Among his well-known poems are "If," "The Ballad of East and West," "Gunga Din," "Danny Deever," and "Mandalay." In 1907 he was awarded the Nobel Prize for literature.

This old version of a famous folk ballad tells a story through the dialogue of Lord Randal and his mother. Though the spelling may look strange, most of the words will be clear if pronounced aloud, and the lines will rhyme more closely than they appear to on the page.

Lord Randal

"O where hae° ye been, Lord Randal my son?
O where hae ye been, my handsome young man?"
  "I hae been to the wild wood; mother, make my bed
    soon,
  For I'm weary wi' hunting, and fain wald° lie down."

1. **hae:** have.

4. **wi':** with.   **fain wald:** gladly would.

"Where got ye your dinner, Lord Randal my son?   5
Where got ye your dinner, my handsome young man?"
  "I dined wi' my true-love; mother, make my bed soon,
  For I'm weary wi' hunting, and fain wald lie down."

"What got ye to your dinner, Lord Randal my son?
What got ye to your dinner, my handsome young man?"   10
  "I got eels boiled in broo;° mother, make my bed soon,
  For I'm weary wi' hunting, and fain wald lie down."

11. **eels boiled in broo:** eels in broth, a soup.

"What became of your bloodhounds, Lord Randal my
    son?
What became of your bloodhounds, my handsome young
    man?"
  "O they swelled and they died; mother, make my bed
    soon,   15
  For I'm weary wi' hunting, and fain wald lie down."

"O I fear ye are poisoned, Lord Randal my son!
O I fear ye are poisoned, my handsome young man!"
  "O yes, I am poisoned; mother, make my bed soon,
  For I'm sick at the heart, and I fain wald lie down."   20

FOR STUDY AND DISCUSSION

1. Sometimes we must read between the lines of a poem to tell exactly what happens. This poem is like a short murder mystery. Who has poisoned Lord Randal? Which of the mother's questions indicate that she suspects, from the beginning, that something bad has happened?

2. Why do you think Lord Randal does not immediately tell his mother that he has been poisoned? In what ways is he "sick at the heart"?

3. Like most songs, folk ballads use repetition freely. Where do you find alliteration in this poem?

4. Which phrases and lines form refrains (see page 317)? What variations occur in these refrains? How do the refrains help to build drama and suspense in the poem?

THE BALLAD

One of the most enduring types of narrative poetry is the ballad. The earliest ballads we have are called *folk ballads* or *popular ballads*. These poems were composed to be sung, and they survived by being passed along orally for generations. In the process, they were altered by storytellers, and over the years appeared in many different versions.

A ballad is usually composed in four-line rhymed stanzas, with strong, simple rhythm. Frequently the story is told through the dialogue of the characters. There is generally one central dramatic or tragic incident, told simply and briefly. Ballads often shift rapidly from scene to scene, or leave gaps in the story that must be filled in by the audience.

All in green went my love riding

e e cummings

All in green went my love riding
on a great horse of gold
into the silver dawn.

four lean hounds crouched low and smiling   5
the merry deer ran before.

Fleeter be they than dappled° dreams
the swift sweet deer
the red rare° deer.

Four red roebuck° at a white water   10
the cruel bugle sang before.

6. **dappled:** speckled.

8. **rare:** very fine.

9. **roebuck:** male roe deer, a type of small, swift deer.

Cains Marius Cimbri Camp.
Fragment of tapestry.
Museum of Fine Arts, Boston
Maria Antoinette Evans Fund

Horn at hip went my love riding
riding the echo down
into the silver dawn.

four lean hounds crouched low and smiling
the level meadows ran before.   15

Softer be they than slippered sleep
the lean lithe deer
the fleet flown deer.

Four fleet does at a gold valley
the famished arrow sang before.   20

Bow at belt went my love riding
riding the mountain down
into the silver dawn.

four lean hounds crouched low and smiling
the sheer peaks ran before.   25

Paler be they than daunting° death
the sleek slim deer
the tall tense deer.

Four tall stags at a green mountain
the lucky hunter sang before.   30

All in green went my love riding
on a great horse of gold
into the silver dawn.

four lean hounds crouched low and smiling
my heart fell dead before.   35

26. **daunting:** frightening.

FOR STUDY AND DISCUSSION

1. This poem is a *literary ballad*. A literary ballad has a known author and is intended to be read rather than sung. It has several characteristics in common with folk ballads. Which lines and images in Cummings' poem establish the setting as far off in the past?
2. Certain images, such as those of the smiling dogs and the silver dawn, give the poem a strange, almost supernatural atmosphere. What other words and phrases give the landscape and animals an air of mystery?
3. Ballads often shift scenes rapidly, leaving gaps in the action. In this poem there are several abrupt shifts of scene as the hunter pursues different groups of deer. Where do these shifts occur?
4. In many old poems, the lover is described as a hunter pursuing the beloved. Who is the hunter's last "victim" in this poem? What is meant by the last line?
5. Like many ballads, this poem uses repetition and refrain. Which lines appear in exactly the same form from stanza to stanza? Which lines are repeated with slight variations?

FOR COMPOSITION

Writing a Ballad
Ballads have been composed about various subjects: love, death, adventure, mystery, war. Many ballads deal with a famous figure from history or legend. A number of American ballads, for example, grew up around the exploits of the Western desperado Billy the Kid.

Choose a subject for a ballad. It may be based on a historical or legendary incident. You may choose some character in a television series or a cartoon strip as the hero or heroine of your ballad. If you wish, write a humorous ballad. Try to incorporate repetition and refrains in your ballad.

The Castle   *Edwin Muir*

The Hunt of the Unicorn VI (c. 1500). Tapestry.
The Cloisters Collection, Metropolitan Museum of Art, New York   Gift of John D. Rockefeller, Jr., 1937

All through that summer at ease we lay,
And daily from the turret° wall   2. **turret:** tower.
We watched the mowers in the hay
And the enemy half a mile away.
They seemed no threat to us at all.   5

For what, we thought, had we to fear
With our arms and provender, load on load,
Our towering battlements, tier on tier,
And friendly allies drawing near
On every leafy summer road.   10

Our gates were strong, our walls were thick,
So smooth and high, no man could win
A foothold there, no clever trick
Could take us, have us dead or quick.°   14. **quick:** alive.
Only a bird could have got in.   15

What could they offer us for bait?
Our captain was brave and we were true. . . .
There was a little private gate,
A little wicked wicket gate.
The wizened° warder let them through.   20   20. **wizened:** (wĭz′ənd) wrinkled.

Oh then our maze of tunneled stone°   21. **maze . . . stone:** the stone
Grew thin and treacherous as air.   castle, designed to confuse and
The cause was lost without a groan,   repel enemies.
The famous citadel° overthrown,   24. **citadel:** fortress.
And all its secret galleries° bare.   25   25. **galleries:** halls.

How can this shameful tale be told?
I will maintain until my death
We could do nothing, being sold;
Our only enemy was gold,
And we had no arms to fight it with.   30

FOR STUDY AND DISCUSSION

1. What made the inhabitants of the castle feel safe, even though the enemy was near? What deed or action caused the castle to fall into enemy hands?

2. What does the fifth stanza mean? What "cause" was lost? In what sense was it lost "without a groan"?

3. You are never told what castle, what battle, or what war the speaker refers to. Why do you think the poet deliberately refrains from setting the narrative in a specific locale at a specific time?

4. The speaker's story has a moral. Which lines in the poem might be taken as a statement of that moral? Tell in your own words what they mean.

ABOUT THE AUTHORS

Edward Estlin Cummings (1894–1962) was born in Cambridge, Massachusetts. He attended Harvard University. During World War I he enlisted in the French Ambulance Corps, then served in the United States Infantry. After the war he divided his time between New York and Paris. Unlike many poets, he was able to support himself entirely through the sale and reading of his poems. Cummings experimented with visual and verbal devices to communicate to his readers the beauty and freshness of what he saw around him.

Edwin Muir (1887–1959) was born in Orkney, Scotland. For many years, Muir was known as a critic, teacher, and translator. Not until he was almost sixty did he publish a book of poems, *The Voyager.* This book, and the following one, *The Labyrinth,* established him as a major poet.

The Seven Ages of Man   *William Shakespeare*

Flemish Country Festival. Oil painting by Pieter Brueghel
the Younger (c. 1564–1638).
Sabauda Gallery, Turin, Italy

Art Resource

All the world's a stage,

And all the men and women merely players.
They have their exits and their entrances,
And one man in his time plays many parts.
His acts being seven ages. At first the infant,   5
Mewling° and puking in the nurse's arms.
Then the whining schoolboy, with his satchel
And shining morning face, creeping like snail
Unwillingly to school. And then the lover,
Sighing like furnace, with a woeful ballad   10
Made to his mistress' eyebrow. Then a soldier,
Full of strange oaths and bearded like the pard,°

6. **Mewling:** whimpering, whining.

12. **pard:** leopard.

Jealous in honor, sudden and quick in quarrel,
Seeking the bubble reputation
Even in the cannon's mouth. And then the justice,   15
In fair round belly with good capon° lined,   16. **capon:** chicken.
With eyes severe and beard of formal cut,
Full of wise saws and modern instances,°   18. **saws and modern instances:**
And so he plays his part. The sixth age shifts   old sayings and obvious examples.
Into the lean and slippered Pantaloon°   20   20. **Pantaloon:** a foolish old man.
With spectacles on nose and pouch on side,   Pantaloon was a stock character in
His youthful hose, well saved, a world too wide   Italian comedies.
For his shrunk shank,° and his big manly voice,   23. **shrunk shank:** shrunken legs.
Turning again toward childish treble, pipes
And whistles in his sound. Last scene of all,   25
That ends this strange eventful history,
Is second childishness and mere oblivion,°   27. **oblivion:** forgetfulness.
Sans° teeth, sans eyes, sans taste, sans everything.   28. **Sans:** without.

FOR STUDY AND DISCUSSION

1. The speaker of this poem is a character named Jaques (jā′kwēz) from one of Shakespeare's comedies, *As You Like It*. In the speech Jaques tells what life is like: a great stage on which people play a variety of roles as they age. How does Jaques' description make each age sound unpleasant, silly, or futile? What words and images create these impressions about each age?

2. Some of Jaques' descriptions are comic. Point out lines, such as that of the lover "sighing like furnace," that make fun of some of the "characters" people play. Does the last line strike you as humorous? If not, what tone does it have?

3. Shakespeare uses several vivid similes and metaphors that show us how Jaques feels about life. Jaques shows his contempt for fame by referring to reputation as a "bubble." Point out some other figures of speech and tell how they are effective in revealing Jaques' attitudes.

DRAMATIC POETRY

Dramatic poetry is poetry that resembles a play in some way. A dramatic poem may be in the form of a dialogue between two or more people, or the speaker may be talking to someone who does not answer but whose presence is understood. Many narrative poems are also dramatic. "Lord Randal" (page 319) is a dialogue between two characters. Who are the speakers? Who is the speaker in "The Castle" (page 323)? To whom do you think he is telling his shameful tale?

Uphill *Christina Rossetti*

Does the road wind uphill all the way?
    Yes, to the very end.
Will the day's journey take the whole long day?
    From morn to night, my friend.

But is there for the night a resting place?   5
    A roof for when the slow dark hours begin.
May not the darkness hide it from my face?
    You cannot miss that inn.

Shall I meet other wayfarers at night?
    Those who have gone before.   10
Then must I knock, or call when just in sight?
    They will not keep you standing at that door.

Shall I find comfort, travel-sore and weak?
    Of labor you shall find the sum.
Will there be beds for me and all who seek?   15
    Yea, beds for all who come.

FOR STUDY AND DISCUSSION

1. At first this poem seems to be simply about a traveler preparing for a journey. But the poem has a symbolic level too. What might this journey stand for? What might the inn symbolize? What clues in the poem point to these symbolic meanings?

2. How would you describe the attitude of the questioner? What is the tone of the answers? Are they optimistic, reassuring, frightening, cynical?

3. How does the poet use line length, indentation, and punctuation to show that there are two speakers in the poem? What is the rhyme scheme of the poem? How does it help identify the speakers?

4. Explain the title of the poem.

ABOUT THE AUTHOR

Christina Rossetti (1830–1894) came from one of the most remarkable artistic families in England. Her father was an Italian poet whose political verses so angered his enemies that he had to flee to England for his life. Her brother Dante Gabriel was a leading poet and painter, and another brother, Michel, was a writer, editor, and influential art critic. Her sister Maria was a teacher and critic who later became a nun. Christina Rossetti, like her father and brothers, was artistic, and like her sister, intensely religious. She spent the last fifteen years of her life almost totally withdrawn from the world, performing devotional acts and writing. She died, as she probably would have wished, while at prayer.

Practice in Reading and Writing

POETRY

Reading Poetry

Reading poetry often requires more concentration and greater care than reading prose. Here are suggestions to follow in studying a poem:

1. *Read in sentences rather than lines.* Do not stop automatically at the end of each line. Such a practice may break up sentences and thereby break up meaning. Follow the punctuation of the poem. At least once, read aloud.

2. *Check the meaning of any unfamiliar word.* Study words carefully in the context of the lines in which they appear. Many words have more than one meaning, and poets are unusually sensitive to the multiple meanings and shades of meaning in words.

3. *Analyze the structure (syntax) of unclear sentences.* Look for key words and the central idea. Punctuation often gives important clues to meaning, so pay special attention to the punctuation of a complicated or troublesome sentence. Sometimes it is helpful to put the sentence into your own words to see if your version makes sense within the context of the poem.

4. *Note poetic devices and their purpose.* Determine how imagery and figurative language help to convey ideas and feelings. Identify the speaker and the point of view or tone expressed by the poem. Find out how devices of sound are related to meaning. Look for other techniques and their purpose.

5. *Try to get at the overall idea or purpose of the poem.* Look for statements that express or imply the main ideas of the poem. Determine if the poem has more than one level of meaning. Note how the ideas are developed and how they are related to the form or structure of the poem.

Read the following poem by William Wordsworth, using the suggestions outlined above.

She Dwelt Among the Untrodden Ways

She dwelt among the untrodden ways
  Beside the springs of Dove,
A maid whom there were none to praise
  And very few to love:

A violet by a mossy stone   5
    Half hidden from the eye!
—Fair as a star, when only one
    Is shining in the sky.

She lived unknown, and few could know
    When Lucy ceased to be;   10
But she is in her grave, and, oh,
    The difference to me!

---

1. *Sentences.* How many sentences are there in the poem? Where are the important breaks in punctuation? How does the punctuation in lines 7 and 11 affect your reading of the poem?

2. *Words.* The language of the poem is simple, but you may need to check the meanings of *ways* and *untrodden*. (The Dove is a river in the north of England.)

3. *Syntax.* What is the subject of stanza 2? Rephrase lines 5–8 in your own words, supplying any ideas or phrases that are implied.

4. *Poetic devices.* What images and figures of speech does the speaker use to give us a striking picture of Lucy? What do they reveal about his feelings?

5. *Overall idea.* On one level this poem is making a statement about the death of a young woman. On a second level the poem is a love poem, expressing the speaker's feelings. Which lines in the poem are statements of fact? Which lines are expressions of personal feeling?

Writing About Poetry

Paraphrasing a Poem

To paraphrase a poem means to restate it in your own words. Paraphrase is often a convenient way to simplify a poem's content. To test your paraphrase of a line or sentence, check that it makes sense within the context of the poem. A paraphrase is helpful in learning what a poem means, but should never be substituted for the poem itself.

Here is a short lyric by George Gordon, Lord Byron, noted for its musical qualities:

So We'll Go No More a Roving

So we'll go no more a roving
    So late into the night,
Though the heart be still as loving
    And the moon be still as bright.

For the sword outwears the sheath,   5
   And the soul wears out the breast,
And the heart must pause to breathe,
   And love itself have rest.

Though the night was made for loving,
   And the day returns too soon,   10
Yet we'll go no more a roving
   By the light of the moon.

This poem laments that time, circumstances, and fatigue force the speaker to slow down and live less fully than he did in his youth. The first stanza might be paraphrased thus: "We won't go roaming about until it's quite late any more, even though our hearts are still capable of love and joy, and the moon still shines brightly." The *sense* of the lines is there, but not their music.

Paraphrase the remaining two stanzas of the poem so that their content is clear and perfectly understandable. Then return to the poem itself to see how Byron has expressed these ideas with great economy and beauty.

Comparing Two Poems

One way to understand a poem better is by comparing it with a poem that is similar in subject, theme, or meaning. You may have read "Uphill" by Christina Rossetti (page 327). Compare that poem with this poem by Emily Dickinson:

What Inn Is This

What inn is this
Where for the night
Peculiar traveler comes?
Who is the landlord?
Where the maids?   5
Behold, what curious rooms!
No ruddy fires on the hearth,
No brimming tankards flow.
Necromancer, landlord,
Who are these below?   10

Read and reread these poems carefully, using the procedures you have learned. Look up any unfamiliar words. Paraphrase any lines or sentences that seem difficult or obscure. When you feel you understand both poems, compare them in an essay. In your essay, include answers to the following questions:

1. What is similar about the subjects of the poems?
2. What is similar or dissimilar about the moods or tones created by the two poems?
3. Who are the speakers in the poems? How do the speakers and their situations resemble or differ from one another?
4. What other similarities and differences can you find in the ideas and methods used in the two poems?

What Is Poetry?

Below are a number of statements by critics and poets about the nature of poetry. Use one (or more) of them as the main idea in any essay about the poetry you have read, referring to two or three of the poems in this book as examples. You may, of course, either agree or disagree with any of these ideas.

1. "Poetry is the spontaneous overflow of powerful feelings."
2. "A poem begins in delight and ends in wisdom."
3. "Poetry is the rhythmical creation of beauty in words."
4. "Poetry is the art of uniting pleasure with truth."
5. "Poetry is simply the most beautiful, impressive, and widely effective mode of saying things."
6. "The success of the poem is determined not by how much the poet felt in writing it, but by how much the reader feels in reading it."

For Further Reading

Adoff, Arnold, editor, *Celebrations: A New Anthology of Black American Poetry* (Follett, 1977)
> Eighty-five black poets—including Arna Bontemps, Gwendolyn Brooks, Robert Hayden, and Langston Hughes—write about the tradition and future of black Americans. The poems are arranged around themes such as "The Idea of Ancestry," "The Southern Road," and "For Each of You."

Bierhorst, John, editor, *In the Trail of the Wind: American Indian Poems and Ritual Orations* (Farrar, Straus & Giroux, 1971; paperback, many editions)
> Here are omens, battle songs, love lyrics, prayers, and mysterious incantations translated from more than forty languages and representing the best-known Indian cultures of North and South America.

Brinnin, John Malcolm, editor, *Emily Dickinson* (paperback, Dell, 1960)
> Collected here are more than one hundred and seventy poems by this witty poet.

Cole, William, editor, *The Fireside Book of Humorous Poetry* (Simon & Schuster, 1959)
> Lighthearted poems are organized around themes such as "The Other Animals," "Bores and Boors," "Races, Places, and Dialects," and "In Praise and Dispraise of Love."

De la Mare, Walter, *Peacock Pie* (Faber & Faber, 1958)
> This collection includes fun-to-read poems.

Dunning, Stephen, et al., editors, *Reflections on a Gift of Watermelon Pickle . . . And Other Modern Verse* (Scott, Foresman, 1966)
> The three hundred poems in this anthology have been compiled especially for young people. The book begins with Eve Merriam's advice on "How to Eat a Poem."

Henderson, Harold G., editor and translator, *An Introduction to Haiku: An Anthology of Poems and Poets from Bashō to Shiki* (Doubleday, 1958)
> Collected here are fine examples of haiku by masters of this lyric form.

Knudson, Rozanne, and P. K. Ebert, editors, *Sports Poems* (paperback, Dell, 1971)
> This anthology includes poems about football, baseball, basketball, and many other sports by such poets as May Swenson, James Dickey, Ogden Nash, and Carl Sandburg.

Leach, MacEdward, editor, *The Ballad Book* (A. S. Barnes, 1955)
> Here are two hundred and fifty English, Scottish, and American storytelling poems.

Millay, Edna St. Vincent, *Collected Sonnets* (paperback, Harper & Row, 1959)
> This book includes the first sonnet the author wrote, when she was fifteen years old.

Morse, David, *Grandfather Rock: The New Poetry and the Old* (paperback, Dell, 1972)
> This collection offers an interesting comparison of rock lyrics with classical poetry.

Peck, Richard, editor, *Pictures That Sound Inside My Head* (paperback, Avon, 1976)
> In poems and themes selected for young people, this anthology presents works by such poets as Sylvia Plath, Ted Hughes, James Dickey, Marianne Moore, and E. E. Cummings.

Sandburg, Carl, *The American Songbag* (paperback, Harcourt Brace Jovanovich, 1970)
> Here are the words and music to two hundred and eighty songs and ballads sung in the making of America.

Sohn, David A., and Richard H. Tyre, editors, *Frost: The Poet and His Poetry* (Holt, Rinehart and Winston, 1967; paperback, Bantam)
> Twenty-six major poems are accompanied by an outline of Frost's life that incorporates his personal memoirs.

Untermeyer, Louis, editor, *This Singing World* (Harcourt Brace Jovanovich, 1951)
> This is an anthology of modern poems chosen especially for young people and selected from the works of the world's best-loved poets. The poems are arranged under such intriguing titles as "Fables in Foolscap," "Rhyme Without Reason," and "Stars to Hitch to."

DRAMA

Drama, like poetry, is a very old literary genre that developed long before the novel and short story. The oldest dramas that have survived in Western literature—those of the Greek playwrights Aeschylus, Sophocles, and Euripides—were composed and performed twenty-five hundred years ago. Some people believe these early plays have never been surpassed.

The two major forms of drama are tragedy and comedy. The word *tragedy* comes from a Greek word meaning "goat song." No one knows what the association with goat means, but it is generally agreed that the drama had some connection with religious rituals. Perhaps a goat was sacrificed to one of the gods, or perhaps the actors wore goatskins. The word *comedy* also comes from the Greek. Roughly translated, it means "a singer in the revels," indicating that it was associated with a joyous festival of some kind.

Within each major type of drama there are subtypes, each with its own traditions. It is possible to distinguish different kinds of tragedy: Greek classical tragedy, Shakespearean tragedy, domestic tragedy, heroic tragedy, and the like. *Romeo and Juliet* (page 386) is a Shakespearean tragedy. Comedy, likewise, may be subdivided into categories: romantic comedy, comedy of humors, comedy of manners, for example. *A Marriage Proposal* by Anton Chekhov (chĕk'ôf') (page 334) is a type of comedy known as *farce,* which depends on improbable situations and exaggerated characters.

In earlier times, plays were written almost exclusively for performance in a theater—whether that theater was outdoors or indoors. In our own time we have had plays developed for different media. *Orpheus* by Ted Hughes (page 367) was originally created for radio. As you read the play, you will see how the playwright has made use of special sound effects that would be effective for a radio audience. *Visit to a Small Planet* by Gore Vidal (page 344) was written for television. In reading the play you will find special sets of directions governing the position of the television cameras.

Many of the elements that you have already studied in connection with short stories are relevant to the study of drama. Throughout this unit you will have opportunity to examine the dramatist's art.

People walking down the road to happiness often trip over their own feet. This is the message of A Marriage Proposal, *a wild, fast-paced farce set in nineteenth-century Russia. The play is about a landowner who decides to marry the girl next door. She likes the idea and so does her father. What could go wrong? You are about to find out.*

A Marriage Proposal

Anton Chekhov

Characters

Stepan Stepanovitch Tschubukov (stĕ-pän′ stĕ-pä′nô-vĭch chōō-bōō-kôf′), a country farmer

Natalia Stepanovna (nä-täl′yə stĕ-pä′nôv-nə), his daughter, age twenty-five

Ivan Vassiliyitch Lomov (ĭ-vän′ vä-sĭl′ē-yĭch lô′môf), Tschubukov's neighbor

Scene: *Reception room in Tschubukov's country home, Russia. Tschubukov discovered as the curtain rises. Enter* Lomov, *wearing a dress suit.*

Tschubukov (*going toward him and greeting him*). Who is this I see? My dear fellow! Ivan Vassiliyitch! I'm so glad to see you! (*Shakes hands*) But this is a surprise! How are you?

Lomov. Thank you! And how are you?

Tschubukov. Oh, so-so, my friend. Please sit down. It isn't right to forget one's neighbor. But tell me, why all this ceremony? Dress clothes, white gloves and all? Are you on your way to some engagement, my good fellow?

Lomov. No, I have no engagement except with you, Stepan Stepanovitch.

Tschubukov. But why in evening clothes, my friend? This isn't New Year's!

Lomov. You see, it's simply this, that—(*composing himself*) I have come to you, Stepan Stepanovitch, to trouble you with a request. It is not the first time I have had the honor of turning to you for assistance, and you have always, that is—I beg your pardon, I am a bit excited! I'll take a drink of water first, dear Stepan Stepanovitch. (*He drinks.*)

Tschubukov (*aside*). He's come to borrow money! I won't give him any! (*To* Lomov) What is it, then, dear Lomov?

Lomov. You see—dear—Stepanovitch, pardon me, Stepan—Stepan—dearvitch—I mean—I am terribly nervous, as you will be so good as to see—! I What I mean to say—you are the only one who can help me, though I don't deserve it, and—and I have no right whatever to make this request of you.

Tschubukov. Oh, don't beat about the bush, my dear fellow. Tell me!

Lomov. Immediately—in a moment. Here it is, then: I have come to ask for the hand of your daughter, Natalia Stepanovna.

Tschubukov (*joyfully*). Angel! Ivan Vassiliyitch! Say that once again! I didn't quite hear it!

Lomov. I have the honor to beg——

Tschubukov (*interrupting*). My dear, dear man! I am so happy that everything is so—everything! (*Embraces and kisses him*) I have wanted this to happen for so long. It has been my dearest wish! (*He represses a tear.*) And I have always loved you, my dear fellow, as my own son! May God give you His blessings and His grace and—I always wanted it to happen. But why am I standing here like a blockhead? I am completely dumbfounded with pleasure, completely dumbfounded. My whole being—I'll call Natalia——

Lomov. Dear Stepan Stepanovitch, what do you think? May I hope for Natalia Stepanovna's acceptance?

Tschubukov. Really! A fine boy like you—and you think she won't accept on the minute? Lovesick as a cat and all that—! (*He goes out right.*)

Lomov. I'm cold. My whole body is trembling as though I was going to take my examination! But the chief thing is to settle matters! If a person meditates too much, or hesitates, or talks about it, waits for an ideal or for true love, he never gets it. Brrr! It's cold! Natalia is an excellent housekeeper, not at all bad-looking, well educated—what more could I ask? I'm so excited my ears are roaring! (*He drinks water.*) And not to marry, that won't do! In the first place, I'm thirty-five—a critical age, you might say. In the second place, I must live a well-regulated life. I have a weak heart, continual palpitation, and I am very sensitive and always getting excited. My lips begin to tremble and the pulse in my right temple throbs terribly. But the worst of all is sleep! I hardly lie down and begin to doze before something in my left side begins to pull and tug, and something begins to hammer in my left shoulder—and in my head, too! I jump up like a madman, walk about a little, lie down again, but the moment I fall asleep I have a terrible cramp in the side. And so it is all night long!

[*Enter* Natalia Stepanovna.]

Natalia. Ah! It's you. Papa said to go in: there was a dealer in there who'd come to buy something. Good afternoon, Ivan Vassiliyitch.

Lomov. Good day, my dear Natalia Stepanovna.

Natalia. You must pardon me for wearing my apron and this old dress: we are working today. Why haven't you come to see us oftener? You've not been here for so long! Sit down. (*They sit down.*) Won't you have something to eat?

Lomov. Thank you, I have just had lunch.

Natalia. Smoke, do, there are the matches. Today it is beautiful and only yesterday it rained so hard that the workmen couldn't do a stroke of work. How many bricks have you cut? Think of it! I was so anxious that I had the whole field mowed, and now I'm sorry I did it, because I'm afraid the hay will rot. It would have been better if I had waited. But what on earth is this? You are in evening clothes! The latest cut! Are you on your way to a ball? And you seem to be looking better, too—really. Why are you dressed up so gorgeously?

Lomov (*excited*). You see, my dear Natalia Stepanovna—it's simply this: I have decided to ask you to listen to me—of course it will be a surprise, and indeed you'll be angry, but I ——(*Aside*) How fearfully cold it is!

Natalia. What is it? (*A pause*) Well?

Lomov. I'll try to be brief. My dear Natalia Stepanovna, as you know, for many years, since my childhood, I have had the honor to know your family. My poor aunt and her husband, from whom, as you know, I inherited the estate, always had the greatest respect for your father and your poor mother. The Lomovs and the Tschubukovs have been for decades on the friendliest, indeed the closest, terms with each other, and furthermore my property, as you know, adjoins your own. If you will be so good as to remember, my meadows touch your birchwoods.

Natalia. Pardon the interruption. You said "my meadows"—but are they yours?

Lomov. Yes, they belong to me.

Natalia. What nonsense! The meadows belong to us—not to you!

Lomov. No, to me! Now, my dear Natalia Stepanovna!

Natalia. Well, that is certainly news to me. How do they belong to you?

Lomov. How? I am speaking of the meadows lying between your birchwoods and my brick earth.

Natalia. Yes, exactly. They belong to us.

Lomov. No, you are mistaken, my dear Natalia Stepanovna, they belong to me.

Natalia. Try to remember exactly, Ivan Vassiliyitch. Is it so long ago that you inherited them?

Lomov. Long ago! As far back as I can remember they have always belonged to us.

Natalia. But that isn't true! You'll pardon my saying so.

Lomov. It is all a matter of record, my dear Natalia Stepanovna. It is true that at one time the title to the meadows was disputed, but now everyone knows they belong to me. There is no room for discussion. Be so good as to listen: my aunt's grandmother put these meadows, free from all costs, into the hands of your father's grandfather's peasants for a certain time while they were making bricks for my grandmother. These people used the meadows free of cost for about forty years, living there as they would on their own property. Later, however, when—

Natalia. There's not a word of truth in that! My grandfather, and my great-grandfather, too, knew that their estate reached back to the swamp, so that the meadows belong to us. What further discussion can there be? I can't understand it. It is really most annoying.

Lomov. I'll show you the papers, Natalia Stepanovna.

Natalia. No, either you are joking, or trying to lead me into a discussion. That's not at all nice! We have owned this property for nearly three hundred years, and now all at once we hear that it doesn't belong to us. Ivan Vassiliyitch, you will pardon me, but I really can't believe my ears. So far as I am concerned, the meadows are worth very little. In all they don't contain more than five acres and they are worth only a few hundred rubles, say three hundred, but the injustice of the thing is what affects me. Say what you will, I can't bear injustice.

Lomov. Only listen until I have finished, please! The peasants of your respected father's grandfather, as I have already had the honor to tell you, baked bricks for my grandmother. My aunt's grandmother wished to do them a favor—

Natalia. Grandfather! Grandmother! Aunt! I know nothing about them. All I know is that the meadows belong to us, and that ends the matter.

Lomov. No, they belong to me!

Natalia. And if you keep on explaining it for two days, and put on five suits of evening clothes, the meadows are still ours, ours, ours! I don't want to take your property, but I refuse to give up what belongs to us!

Lomov. Natalia Stepanovna, I don't need the meadows, I am only concerned with the principle. If you are agreeable, I beg of you, accept them as a gift from me!

Natalia. But I can give them to you, because they belong to me! That is very peculiar, Ivan Vassiliyitch! Until now we have considered you as a good neighbor and a good friend; only last year we lent you our threshing machine, so that we couldn't thresh until November, and now you treat us like thieves! You offer to give me my own land. Excuse me, but neighbors don't treat each other that way. In my opinion, it's a very low trick—to speak frankly—

Lomov. According to you I'm a usurper, then, am I? My dear lady, I have never appropriated other people's property, and I shall permit no one to accuse me of such a thing! (*He goes quickly to the bottle and drinks water.*) The meadows are mine!

Natalia. That's not the truth! They are mine!

Lomov. Mine!

Natalia. Eh? I'll prove it to you! This afternoon I'll send my reapers into the meadows.

Lomov. W—h—a—t?

Natalia. My reapers will be there today!

Lomov. And I'll chase them off!

Natalia. If you dare!

Lomov. The meadows are mine, you understand? Mine!

Natalia. Really, you needn't scream so! If you want to scream and snort and rage you may do it at home, but here please keep yourself within the limits of common decency.

Lomov. My dear lady, if it weren't that I were suffering from palpitation of the heart and hammering of the arteries in my temples, I would deal with you very differently! (*In a loud voice*) The meadows belong to me!

Natalia. Us!

Lomov. Me!

[*Enter* Tschubukov, *right.*]

Tschubukov. What's going on here? What is he yelling about?

Natalia. Papa, please tell this gentleman to whom the meadows belong, to us or to him?

Tschubukov (*to* Lomov). My dear fellow, the meadows are ours.

Lomov. But, merciful heavens, Stepan Stepanovitch, how do you make that out? You at least might be reasonable. My aunt's grandmother gave the use of the meadows free of cost to your grandfather's peasants; the peasants lived on the land for forty years and used it as their own, but later when —

Tschubukov. Permit me, my dear friend. You forget that your grandmother's peasants never paid, because there had been a lawsuit over the meadows, and everyone knows that the meadows belong to us. You haven't looked at the map.

Lomov. I'll prove to you that they belong to me!

Tschubukov. Don't try to prove it, my dear fellow.

Lomov. I will!

Tschubukov. My good fellow, what are you shrieking about? You can't prove anything by yelling, you know. I don't ask for anything that belongs to you, nor do I intend to give up anything of my own. Why should I? If it has gone so far, my dear man, that you really intend to claim the meadows, I'd rather give them to the peasants than you, and I certainly shall!

Lomov. I can't believe it! By what right can you give away property that doesn't belong to you?

Tschubukov. Really, you must allow me to decide what I am to do with my own land! I'm not accustomed, young man, to have people address me in that tone of voice. I, young man, am twice your age, and I beg you to address me respectfully.

Lomov. No! No! You think I'm a fool! You're making fun of me! You call my property yours and then expect me to stand quietly by and talk to you like a human being. That isn't the way a good neighbor behaves, Stepan Stepanovitch! You are no neighbor, you're no better than a land-grabber. That's what you are!

Tschubukov. Wh—at? What did he say?

Natalia. Papa, send the reapers into the meadows this minute!

Tschubukov (*to* Lomov). What was that you said, sir?

Natalia. The meadows belong to us and I won't give them up! I won't give them up! I won't give them up!

Lomov. We'll see about that! I'll prove in court that they belong to me.

Tschubukov. In court! You may sue in court, sir, if you like! Oh, I know you, you are only waiting to find an excuse to go to law! You're an intriguer, that's what you are! Your whole family were always looking for quarrels. The whole lot!

Lomov. Kindly refrain from insulting my family. The entire race of Lomov has always been honorable! And never has one been brought to trial for embezzlement, as your dear uncle was!

Tschubukov. And the whole Lomov family were insane!

Natalia. Every one of them!

Tschubukov. Your grandmother was a dipsomaniac, and the younger aunt, Nastasia Michailovna, ran off with an architect.

Lomov. And your mother limped. (*He puts his hand over his heart.*) Oh, my side pains! My temples are bursting! Water!

Tschubukov. And your dear father was a gambler—and a glutton!

Natalia. And your aunt was a gossip like few others!

Lomov. And you are an intriguer. Oh, my heart! And it's an open secret that you cheated at the elections—my eyes are blurred! Where is my hat?

Natalia. Oh, how low! Liar! Disgusting thing!

Lomov. Where's the hat—? My heart! Where shall I go? Where is the door—? Oh—it seems—as though I were dying! I can't—my legs won't hold me——(*Goes to the door*)

Tschubukov (*following him*). May you never darken my door again!

Natalia. Bring your suit to court! We'll see!

[Lomov *staggers out, center.*]

Tschubukov (*angrily*). The devil!

Natalia. Such a good-for-nothing! And then they talk about being good neighbors!

Tschubukov. Loafer! Scarecrow! Monster!

Natalia. A swindler like that takes over a piece of property that doesn't belong to him and then dares to argue about it!

Tschubukov. And to think that this fool dares to make a proposal of marriage!

Natalia. What? A proposal of marriage?

Tschubukov. Why, yes! He came here to make you a proposal of marriage.

Natalia. Why didn't you tell me that before?

Tschubukov. That's why he had on his evening clothes! The poor fool!

Natalia. Proposal for me? Oh! (*Falls into an armchair and groans*) Bring him back! Bring him back!

Tschubukov. Bring whom back?

Natalia. Faster, faster, I'm sinking! Bring him back! (*She becomes hysterical.*)

Tschubukov. What is it? What's wrong with you? (*His hands to his head*) I'm cursed with bad luck! I'll shoot myself! I'll hang myself!

Natalia. I'm dying! Bring him back!

Tschubukov. Bah! In a minute! Don't bawl! (*He rushes out, center.*)

Natalia (*groaning*). What have they done to me? Bring him back! Bring him back!

Tschubukov (*comes running in*). He's coming at once! The devil take him! Ugh! Talk to him yourself, I can't.

Natalia (*groaning*). Bring him back!

Tschubukov. He's coming, I tell you! What a task it is to be the father of a grown daughter! I'll cut my throat! I really will cut my throat!

We've argued with the fellow, insulted him, and now we've thrown him out!—and you did it all, you!

Natalia. No, you! You haven't any manners, you are brutal! If it weren't for you, he wouldn't have gone!

Tschubukov. Oh, yes, I'm to blame! If I shoot or hang myself, remember *you'll* be to blame. You forced me to it! You! (Lomov *appears in the doorway.*) There, talk to him yourself! (*He goes out.*)

Lomov. Terrible palpitation!—My leg is lamed! My side hurts me—

Natalia. Pardon us, we were angry, Ivan Vassiliyitch. I remember now—the meadows really belong to you.

Lomov. My heart is beating terribly! My meadows—my eyelids tremble—— (*They sit down.*) We were wrong. It was only the principle of the thing—the property isn't worth much to me, but the principle is worth a great deal.

Natalia. Exactly, the principle! Let us talk about something else.

Lomov. Because I have proofs that my aunt's grandmother had, with the peasants of your good father—

Natalia. Enough, enough. (*Aside*) I don't know how to begin. (*To* Lomov) Are you going hunting soon?

Lomov. Yes, heath-cock shooting, respected Natalia Stepanovna. I expect to begin after the harvest. Oh, did you hear? My dog, Ugadi,[1] you know him—limps!

Natalia. What a shame! How did that happen?

Lomov. I don't know. Perhaps it's a dislocation, or maybe he was bitten by some other dog. (*He sighs.*) The best dog I ever had—to say nothing of his price! I paid Mironov a hundred and twenty-five rubles[2] for him.

Natalia. That was too much to pay, Ivan Vassiliyitch.

Lomov. In my opinion it was very cheap. A wonderful dog!

Natalia. Papa paid eighty-five rubles for his Otkatai[3], and Otkatai is much better than your Ugadi.

Lomov. Really? Otkatai is better than Ugadi? What an idea! (*He laughs.*) Otkatai better than Ugadi!

Natalia. Of course he is better. It is true Otkatai is still young; he isn't full-grown yet, but in the pack or on the leash with two or three, there is no better than he, even—

Lomov. I really beg your pardon, Natalia Stepanovna, but you quite overlooked the fact that he has a short lower jaw, and a dog with a short lower jaw can't snap.

Natalia. Short lower jaw? That's the first time I ever heard that!

Lomov. I assure you, his lower jaw is shorter than the upper.

Natalia. Have you measured it?

Lomov. I have measured it. He is good at running, though.

Natalia. In the first place, our Otkatai is a purebred, a full-blooded son of Sapragavas and Stameskis,[4] and as for your mongrel, nobody could ever figure out his pedigree; he's old and ugly, and as skinny as an old hag.

Lomov. Old, certainly! I wouldn't take five of your Otkatais for him! Ugadi is a dog and Otkatai is—it is laughable to argue about it! Dogs like your Otkatai can be found by the dozens at any dog dealer's, a whole poundful!

Natalia. Ivan Vassiliyitch, you are very contrary today. First our meadows belong to you and then Ugadi is better than Otkatai. I don't like it when a person doesn't say what he really thinks. You know perfectly well that

---

1. **Ugadi** (ōō-gä-dī′).
2. **ruble:** The Russian unit of money.

3. **Otkatai** (ät-kä-tī′).
4. **Sapragavas** (sä-prə-gä′vəs); **Stameskis** (stä-měs′kĭs).

Otkatai is a hundred times better than your silly Ugadi. What makes you keep on saying he isn't?

Lomov. I can see, Natalia Stepanovna, that you consider me either a blindman or a fool. But at least you may as well admit that Otkatai has a short lower jaw!

Natalia. It isn't so!

Lomov. Yes, a short lower jaw!

Natalia (*loudly*). It's not so!

Lomov. What makes you scream, my dear lady?

Natalia. What makes you talk such nonsense? It's disgusting! It is high time that Ugadi was shot, and yet you compare him with Otkatai!

Lomov. Pardon me, but I can't carry on this argument any longer. I have palpitation of the heart!

Natalia. I have always noticed that the hunters who do the most talking know the least about hunting.

Lomov. My dear lady, I beg of you to be still. My heart is bursting! (*He shouts.*) Be still!

Natalia. I won't be still until you admit that Otkatai is better!

[*Enter* Tschubukov.]

Tschubukov. Well, has it begun again?

Natalia. Papa, say frankly, on your honor, which dog is better: Otkatai or Ugadi?

Lomov. Stepan Stepanovitch, I beg of you, just answer this: has your dog a short lower jaw or not? Yes or no?

Tschubukov. And what if he has? Is it of such importance? There is no better dog in the whole country.

Lomov. My Ugadi is better. Tell the truth, now!

Tschubukov. Don't get so excited, my dear fellow! Permit me. Your Ugadi certainly has his good points. He is from a good breed, has a good stride, strong haunches, and so forth. But the dog, if you really want to know it, has two faults; he is old and he has a short lower jaw.

Lomov. Pardon me, I have palpitation of the heart!—Let us keep to facts—just remember in Maruskins' meadows, my Ugadi kept ear to ear with the Count Rasvachai and your dog.

Tschubukov. He was behind, because the Count struck him with his whip.

Lomov. Quite right. All the other dogs were on the fox's scent, but Otkatai found it necessary to bite a sheep.

Tschubukov. That isn't so!—I am sensitive about that and beg you to stop this argument. He struck him because everybody looks on a strange dog of good blood with envy. Even you, sir, aren't free from the sin. No sooner do you find a dog better than Ugadi than you begin to—this, that—his, mine—and so forth! I remember distinctly.

Lomov. I remember something, too!

Tschubukov (*mimicking him*). I remember something, too! What do you remember?

Lomov. Palpitation! My leg is lame—I can't—

Natalia. Palpitation! What kind of hunter are you? You ought to stay in the kitchen by the stove and wrestle with the potato peelings, and not go fox-hunting! Palpitation!

Tschubukov. And what kind of hunter are you? A man with your diseases ought to stay at home and not jolt around in the saddle. If you were a hunter—! But you only ride around in order to find out about other people's dogs, and make trouble for everyone. I am sensitive! Let's drop the subject. Besides, you're no hunter.

Lomov. You only ride around to flatter the Count!—My heart! You intriguer! Swindler!

Tschubukov. And what of it? (*Shouting*) Be still!

Lomov. Intriguer!

Tschubukov. Baby! Puppy! Walking drug-store!

Lomov. Old rat! Oh, I know you!

Tschubukov. Be still! Or I'll shoot you — with my worst gun, like a partridge! Fool! Loafer!

Lomov. Everyone knows that — oh, my heart! — that your poor late wife beat you. My leg — my temples — Heavens — I'm dying — I——

Tschubukov. And your housekeeper wears the trousers in your house!

Lomov. Here — here — there — there — my heart has burst! My shoulder is torn apart. Where is my shoulder? I'm dying! (*He falls into a chair.*) The doctor! (*Faints*)

Tschubukov. Baby! Half-baked clam! Fool!

Natalia. Nice sort of hunter you are! You can't even sit on a horse. (*To Tschubukov*) Papa, what's the matter with him? (*She screams.*) Ivan Vassiliyitch! He is dead!

Lomov. I'm ill! I can't breathe! Air!

Natalia. He is dead! (*She shakes Lomov in the chair.*) Ivan Vassiliyitch! What have we done! He is dead! (*She sinks into a chair.*) The doctor — doctor! (*She goes into hysterics.*)

Tschubukov. Ahh! What is it? What's the matter with you?

Natalia (*groaning*). He's dead! — Dead!

Tschubukov. Who is dead? Who? (*Looking at* Lomov) Yes, he is dead! Water! The doctor! (*Holding the glass to* Lomov's *lips*) Drink! No, he won't drink! He's dead! What a terrible situation! Why didn't I shoot myself? Why have I never cut my throat? What am I waiting for now? Only give me a knife! Give me a pistol! (Lomov *moves.*) He's coming to! Drink some water — there!

Lomov. Sparks! Mists! Where am I?

Tschubukov. Get married! Quick, and then go to the devil! She's willing! (*He joins the hands of* Lomov *and* Natalia.) She's agreed! Only leave me in peace!

Lomov. Wh — what? (*Getting up*) Whom?

Tschubukov. She's willing! Well? Kiss each other and — the devil take you both!

Natalia (*groans*). He lives! Yes, yes, I'm willing!

Tschubukov. Kiss each other!

Lomov. Eh? Whom? (Natalia *and* Lomov *kiss.*) Very nice — ! Pardon me, but what is this for? Oh, yes, I understand! My heart — sparks — I am happy, Natalia Stepanovna. (*He kisses her hand.*) My leg is lame!

Natalia. I'm happy, too!

Tschubukov. Ahh! A load off my shoulders! Ahh!

Natalia. And now at least you'll admit that Ugadi is worse than Otkatai!

Lomov. Better!

Natalia. Worse!

Tschubukov. Now the domestic joys have begun. — Champagne!

Lomov. Better!

Natalia. Worse, worse, worse!

Tschubukov (*trying to drown them out*). Champagne, champagne!

[*Curtain.*]

FOR STUDY AND DISCUSSION

1. Why does Lomov want to marry Natalia? What does he think her qualifications are? Does he think she is his ideal love?
2. Considering the purpose of Lomov's visit, why is his argument with Natalia over the meadows particularly absurd?
3. Just when the characters seem to have patched up their quarrel, there is another disagreement. What causes this new conflict?
4. How does Lomov's state of health affect the outcome of the play?
5. What is ironic about the title of the play?

FARCE

Farces begin with an absurd situation: an unimportant lie gets someone into big trouble, or something crucial left unsaid causes a ruckus. The farcical basis of *A Marriage Proposal* is Lomov's inability to propose.

Other types of comedy begin with absurd situations. What makes a farce different is the element of exaggeration. While farce stops short of the pie-in-the-face physical humor of slapstick comedy, it can get fairly wild. Lomov's shrieking and fainting is a fair example.

In farce, characters are painted in broad, uncomplicated strokes. A character's every gesture and reaction is typical of that character. The characters do not have subtle internal contradictions.

Choose one of the episodes in the play and describe the farcical elements of character and situation.

FOR COMPOSITION

Writing a Character Sketch

Write a character sketch of one character in *A Marriage Proposal*. Take care that you do not simply list traits. Instead, organize your information into three or four general categories (for example, appearance, behavior, background) and write a series of linked paragraphs, each exploring one category.

ABOUT THE AUTHOR

Anton Chekhov (1860–1904) was born in Taganrog, a tiny Russian town he later described as "dirty and dull, with deserted streets and a lazy, ignorant population." His father was a shopkeeper who loved the arts, tyrannized his family, and neglected his business so much that Anton and his brothers and sister grew up in poverty. In 1879, Chekhov moved to Moscow to study medicine. But most of his time was spent writing short stories and sketches, which he sold to literary magazines to support his family. Gradually, Chekhov practiced medicine less and less and began writing plays. First came a series of one-act comedies. *A Marriage Proposal* was among them. *Ivanov*, his first major play, was produced in 1887. It was followed by *The Sea Gull, Uncle Vanya, The Three Sisters*, and *The Cherry Orchard*.

In Chekhov's best writing, human nature is explored with scientific precision and loving compassion simultaneously. This is no small accomplishment. His characters frequently stop listening to each other, constantly contradict themselves, and always make up excuses for their own failings. Yet Chekhov was able to use these shortcomings in human nature to make his audiences laugh, and perhaps understand themselves a little better.

Can it be that only a creature from outer space can see the world as it really is? This is the question that Gore Vidal's science fiction teleplay asks. The answer contains a number of surprises, not the least of which is the alien's diabolical plan for redesigning the earth.

Visit to a Small Planet

Gore Vidal

Characters

Kreton	Aide
Roger Spelding	Paul Laurent
Ellen Spelding	Second Visitor
Mrs. Spelding	President of Paraguay
John Randolph	Technicians
General Powers	Soldiers

Act One

Stock Shot:[1] *The night sky, stars. Then slowly a luminous object arcs into view. As it is almost upon us,* dissolve to[2] *the living room of the Spelding house in Maryland.*

Superimpose card: "The Time: The Day After Tomorrow"

The room is comfortably balanced between the expensively decorated and the homely. Roger Spelding *is concluding his TV broadcast. He is middle-aged, unctuous[3], resonant. His wife, bored and vague, knits passively while he talks at his desk. Two Technicians are on hand, operating the equipment. His daughter,* Ellen, *a lively girl of twenty, fidgets as she listens.*

---

1. **Stock shot:** film footage taken from the television studio's library rather than made specifically for the project at hand.
2. **dissolve to:** to cause one image to disappear while a second image appears simultaneously.
3. **unctuous** (ŭngk′chōō-əs): falsely earnest.

Spelding (*into microphone*). . . . and so, according to General Powers . . . who should know if anyone does . . . the flying object which has given rise to so much irresponsible conjecture is nothing more than a meteor passing through the earth's orbit. It is not, as many believe, a secret weapon of this country. Nor is it a spaceship as certain lunatic elements have suggested. General Powers has assured me that it is highly doubtful there is any form of life on other planets capable of building a spaceship. "If any traveling is to be done in space, we will do it first." And those are his exact words. . . . Which winds up another week of news. (*Crosses to pose with wife and daughter*) This is Roger Spelding, saying good night to Mother and Father America, from my old homestead in Silver Glen, Maryland, close to the warm pulsebeat of the nation.

Technician. Good show tonight, Mr. Spelding.

Spelding. Thank you.

Technician. Yes sir, you were right on time.

[Spelding *nods wearily, his mechanical smile and heartiness suddenly gone.*]

Mrs. Spelding. Very nice, dear. Very nice.

Technician. See you next week, Mr. Spelding.

Spelding. Thank you, boys.

[Technicians *go.*]

Spelding. Did you like the broadcast, Ellen?
Ellen. Of course I did, Daddy.
Spelding. Then what did I say?
Ellen. Oh, that's not fair.
Spelding. It's not very flattering when one's own daughter won't listen to what one says while millions of people . . .
Ellen. I always listen, Daddy, you know that.
Mrs. Spelding. We love your broadcasts, dear. I don't know what we'd do without them.
Spelding. Starve.
Ellen. I wonder what's keeping John?
Spelding. Certainly not work.
Ellen. Oh, Daddy, stop it! John works very hard and you know it.
Mrs. Spelding. Yes, he's a perfectly nice boy, Roger. I like him.
Spelding. I know, I know; he has every virtue except the most important one: he has no get-up-and-go.
Ellen (*precisely*). He doesn't want to get up and he doesn't want to go because he's already where he wants to be on his own farm, which is exactly where *I'm* going to be when we're married.
Spelding. More thankless than a serpent's tooth is an ungrateful child.[4]
Ellen. I don't think that's right. Isn't it "more deadly . . ."
Spelding. Whatever the exact quotation is, I stand by the sentiment.
Mrs. Spelding. Please don't quarrel. It always gives me a headache.
Spelding. I never quarrel. I merely reason, in my simple way, with Miss Know-it-all here.
Ellen. Oh, Daddy! Next you'll tell me I should marry for money.

---

4. **More . . . child:** The Speldings are misquoting lines from *King Lear* by William Shakespeare. The correct quotation is "How sharper than a serpent's tooth it is/ To have a thankless child!" (I, 4, 312)

Spelding. There is nothing wrong with marrying a wealthy man. The horror of it has always eluded me. However, my only wish is that you marry someone hard-working, ambitious, a man who'll make his mark in the world. Not a boy who plans to sit on a farm all his life, growing peanuts.
Ellen. English walnuts.
Spelding. Will you stop correcting me?
Ellen. But, Daddy, John grows walnuts . . .

[John *enters, breathlessly.*]

John. Come out! Quickly. It's coming this way. It's going to land right here!
Spelding. *What's* going to land?
John. The spaceship. Look!
Spelding. Apparently you didn't hear my broadcast. The flying object in question is a meteor, not a spaceship.

[John *has gone out with* Ellen. Spelding *and* Mrs. Spelding *follow.*]

Mrs. Spelding. Oh, my! Look! Something *is* falling! Roger, you don't think it's going to hit the house, do you?
Spelding. The odds against being hit by a falling object that size are, I should say, roughly ten million to one.
John. Ten million to one or not, it's going to land right here and it's *not* falling.
Spelding. I'm sure it's a meteor.
Mrs. Spelding. Shouldn't we go down to the cellar?
Spelding. If it's not a meteor, it's an optical illusion . . . mass hysteria.
Ellen. Daddy, it's a real spaceship. I'm sure it is.
Spelding. Or maybe a weather balloon. Yes, that's what it is. General Powers said only yesterday . . .
John. It's landing!

Spelding. I'm going to call the police . . . the army! (*Bolts inside*)

Ellen. Oh, look how it shines!

John. Here it comes!

Mrs. Spelding. Right in my rose garden!

Ellen. Maybe it's a balloon.

John. No, it's a spaceship and right in your own backyard.

Ellen. What makes it shine so?

John. I don't know but I'm going to find out. (*Runs off toward the light*)

Ellen. Oh, darling, don't! John, please! John, John, come back!

[Spelding, *wide-eyed, returns.*]

Mrs. Spelding. Roger, it's landed right in my rose garden.

Spelding. I got General Powers. He's coming over. He said they've been watching this thing. They . . . they don't know what it is.

Ellen. You mean it's nothing of ours?

Spelding. They believe it . . . (*swallows hard*) . . . it's from outer space.

Ellen. And John's down there! Daddy, get a gun or something.

Spelding. Perhaps we'd better leave the house until the army gets here.

Ellen. We can't leave John.

Spelding. I can. (*Peers nearsightedly*) Why, it's not much larger than a car. I'm sure it's some kind of meteor.

Ellen. Meteors are blazing hot.

Spelding. This is a cold one . . .

Ellen. It's opening . . . the whole side's opening! (*Shouts*) John! Come back! Quick. . . .

Mrs. Spelding. Why, there's a man getting out of it! (*Sighs*) I feel much better already. I'm sure if we ask him, he'll move that thing for us. Roger, you ask him.

Spelding (*ominously*). If it's really a man?

Ellen. John's shaking hands with him. (*Calls*) John darling, come on up here . . .

Mrs. Spelding. And bring your friend . . .

Spelding. There's something wrong with the way that creature looks . . . if it is a man and not a . . . not a monster.

Mrs. Spelding. He looks perfectly nice to me.

[John *and the* Visitor *appear. The* Visitor *is in his forties, a mild, pleasant-looking man with side whiskers and dressed in the fashion of 1860. He pauses when he sees the three people, in silence for a moment. They stare back at him, equally interested.*]

Visitor. I seem to've made a mistake. I *am* sorry. I'd better go back and start over again.

Spelding. My dear sir, you've only just arrived. Come in, come in. I don't need to tell you what a pleasure this is . . . Mister . . . Mister . . .

Visitor. Kreton . . . This *is* the wrong costume, isn't it?

Spelding. Wrong for what?

Kreton. For the country, and the time.

Spelding. Well, it's a trifle old-fashioned.

Mrs. Spelding. But really awfully handsome.

Kreton. Thank you.

Mrs. Spelding (*to husband*). Ask him about moving that thing off my rose bed.

[Spelding *leads them all into living room.*]

Spelding. Come on in and sit down. You must be tired after your trip.

Kreton. Yes, I am a little. (*Looks around delightedly*) Oh, it's better than I'd hoped!

Spelding. Better? What's better?

Kreton. The house . . . that's what you call it? Or is this an apartment?

Spelding. This is a house in the State of Maryland, U.S.A.

Kreton. In the late twentieth century! To think this is really the twentieth century. I must sit down a moment and collect myself. The *real* thing! (*He sits down.*)

Ellen. You . . . you're not an American, are you?

Kreton. What a nice thought! No, I'm not.

John. You sound more English.

Kreton. Do I? Is my accent very bad?

John. No, it's quite good.

Spelding. Where *are* you from, Mr. Kreton?

Kreton (*evasively*). Another place.

Spelding. On this earth, of course.

Kreton. No, not on this planet.

Ellen. Are you from Mars?

Kreton. Oh dear, no, not Mars. There's nobody on Mars . . . at least no one I know.

Ellen. I'm sure you're testing us and this is all some kind of publicity stunt.

Kreton. No, I really am from another place.

Spelding. I don't suppose you'd consent to my interviewing you on television?

Kreton. I don't think your authorities will like that. They are terribly upset as it is.

Spelding. How do you know?

Kreton. Well, I . . . pick up things. For instance, I know that in a few minutes a couple of people from your army will be here to question me and they . . . like you . . . are torn by doubt.

Spelding. How extraordinary!

Ellen. Why did you come here?

Kreton. Simply a visit to your small planet. I've been studying it for years. In fact, one might say, you people are my hobby. Especially this period of your development.

John. Are you the first person from your . . . your planet to travel in space like this?

Kreton. Oh my, no! Everyone travels who wants to. It's just that no one wants to visit you. I can't think why. *I* always have. You'd be surprised what a thorough study I've made. (*Recites*) The planet, Earth, is divided into five continents with a number of large islands. It is mostly water. There is one moon. Civilization is only just beginning. . . .

Spelding. Just beginning! My dear sir, we have had . . .

Kreton (*blandly*). You are only in the initial

stages, the most fascinating stage as far as I'm concerned . . . I do hope I don't sound patronizing.

Ellen. Well, we are very proud.

Kreton. I know, and that's one of your most endearing, primitive traits. Oh, I can't believe I'm here at last!

[General Powers, *a vigorous product of the National Guard, and his* Aide *enter.*]

Powers. All right, folks. The place is surrounded by troops. Where is the monster?

Kreton. I, my dear General, am the monster.

Powers. What are you dressed up for, a fancy-dress party?

Kreton. I'd hoped to be in the costume of the period. As you see, I am about a hundred years too late.

Powers. Roger, who is this joker?

Spelding. This is Mr. Kreton . . . General Powers. Mr. Kreton arrived in that thing outside. He is from another planet.

Powers. I don't believe it.

Ellen. It's true. We saw him get out of the flying saucer.

Powers (*to* Aide). Captain, go down and look at that ship. But be careful. Don't touch anything. And don't let anybody else near it. (Aide *goes.*) So you're from another planet.

Kreton. Yes. My, that's a very smart uniform but I prefer the ones made of metal, the ones you used to wear, you know: with the feathers on top.

Powers. That was five hundred years ago . . . Are you *sure* you're not from the Earth?

Kreton. Yes.

Powers. Well, I'm not. You've got some pretty tall explaining to do.

Kreton. Anything to oblige.

Powers. All right, which planet?

Kreton. None that you have ever heard of.

Powers. Where is it?

Kreton. You wouldn't know.

Powers. This solar system?

Kreton. No.

Powers. Another system?

Kreton. Yes.

Powers. Look, Buster, I don't want to play games: I just want to know where you're from. The law requires it.

Kreton. It's possible that I could explain it to a mathematician but I'm afraid I couldn't explain it to you, not for another five hundred years and by then of course *you'd* be dead because you people do die, don't you?

Powers. What?

Kreton. Poor fragile butterflies, such brief little moments in the sun. . . . You see, *we* don't die.

Powers. You'll die all right if it turns out you're a spy or a hostile alien.

Kreton. I'm sure you wouldn't be so cruel.

[Aide *returns; he looks disturbed.*]

Powers. What did you find?

Aide. I'm not sure, General.

Powers (*heavily*). Then do your best to describe what the object is like.

Aide. Well, it's elliptical, with a fourteen-foot diameter. And it's made of an unknown metal which shines and inside there isn't anything.

Powers. Isn't anything?

Aide. There's nothing inside the ship: no instruments, no food, nothing.

Powers (*to* Kreton). What did you do with your instrument board?

Kreton. With my what? Oh, I don't have one.

Powers. How does the thing travel?

Kreton. I don't know.

Powers. You don't know. Now look, mister, you're in pretty serious trouble. I suggest you do a bit of cooperating. You claim you traveled here from outer space in a machine with no instruments . . .

Kreton. Well, these cars are rather common in my world and I suppose, once upon a time, I must've known the theory on which they operate but I've long since forgotten. After all, General, we're not mechanics, you and I.

Powers. Roger, do you mind if we use your study?

Spelding. Not at all. Not at all, General.

Powers. Mr. Kreton and I are going to have a chat. (*To* Aide) Put in a call to the Chief of Staff.

Aide. Yes, General.

[Spelding *rises, leads* Kreton *and* Powers *into next room, a handsomely furnished study, many books and a globe of the world.*]

Spelding. This way, gentlemen.

[Kreton *sits down comfortably beside the globe, which he twirls thoughtfully. At the door,* Spelding *speaks in a low voice to* Powers.]

I hope I'll be the one to get the story first, Tom.

Powers. There isn't any story. Complete censorship. I'm sorry but this house is under martial law. I've a hunch we're in trouble.

[*He shuts the door.* Spelding *turns and rejoins his family.*]

Ellen. I think he's wonderful, whoever he is.

Mrs. Spelding. I wonder how much damage he did to my rose garden . . .

John. It's sure hard to believe he's really from outer space. No instruments, no nothing . . . boy, they must be advanced scientifically.

Mrs. Spelding. Is he spending the night, dear?

Spelding. What?

Mrs. Spelding. Is he spending the night?

Spelding. Oh yes, yes, I suppose he will be.

Mrs. Spelding. Then I'd better go make up the bedroom. He seems perfectly nice to me. I like his whiskers. They're so very . . . comforting. Like Grandfather Spelding's. (*She goes.*)

Spelding (*bitterly*). I *know* this story will leak out before I can interview him. I just know it.

Ellen. What does it mean, we're under martial law?

Spelding. It means we have to do what General Powers tells us to do. (*He goes to the window as a* Soldier *passes by.*) See?

John. I wish I'd taken a closer look at that ship when I had the chance.

Ellen. Perhaps he'll give us a ride in it.

John. Traveling in space! Just like those stories. You know: intergalactic drive stuff.

Spelding. *If* he's not an impostor.

Ellen. I have a feeling he isn't.

John. Well, I better call the family and tell them I'm all right.

[*He crosses to telephone by the door which leads into hall.*]

Aide. I'm sorry, sir, but you can't use the phone.

Spelding. He certainly can. This is my house . . .

Aide (*mechanically*). This house is a military reservation until the crisis is over: order General Powers. I'm sorry.

John. How am I to call home to say where I am?

Aide. Only General Powers can help you. You're also forbidden to leave this house without permission.

Spelding. You can't do this!

Aide. I'm afraid, sir, we've done it.

Ellen. Isn't it exciting!

[*Cut to*[5] *study.*]

---

5. **Cut to:** to change the camera angle or scene abruptly, without using a dissolve.

Powers. Are you deliberately trying to confuse me?

Kreton. Not deliberately, no.

Powers. We have gone over and over this for two hours now and all that you've told me is that you're from another planet in another solar system . . .

Kreton. In another dimension. I think that's the word you use.

Powers. In another dimension and you have come here as a tourist.

Kreton. Up to a point, yes. What did you expect?

Powers. It is my job to guard the security of this country.

Kreton. I'm sure that must be very interesting work.

Powers. For all I know, you are a spy, sent here by an alien race to study us, preparatory to invasion.

Kreton. Oh, none of my people would *dream* of invading you.

Powers. How do I know that's true?

Kreton. You don't, so I suggest you believe me. I should also warn you: I can tell what's inside.

Powers. What's inside?

Kreton. What's inside your mind.

Powers. You're a mind reader?

Kreton. I don't really read it. I hear it.

Powers. What am I thinking?

Kreton. That I am either a lunatic from the earth or a spy from another world.

Powers. Correct. But then you could've guessed that. (*Frowns*) What am I thinking now?

Kreton. You're making a picture. Three silver stars. You're pinning them on your shoulder, instead of the two stars you now wear.

Powers (*startled*). That's right. I was thinking of my promotion.

Kreton. If there's anything I can do to hurry it along, just let me know.

Powers. You can. Tell me why you're here.

Kreton. Well, we don't travel much, my people. We used to, but since we see everything through special monitors and re-creators, there is no particular need to travel. However, I am a hobbyist. I love to gad about.

Powers (*taking notes*). Are you the first to visit us?

Kreton. Oh, no! We started visiting you long before there were people on the planet. However, we are seldom noticed on our trips. I'm sorry to say I slipped up, coming in the way I did . . . but then this visit was all rather impromptu. (*Laughs*) I am a creature of impulse, I fear.

[Aide *looks in*.]

Aide. Chief of Staff on the telephone, General.

Powers (*picks up phone*). Hello, yes, sir. Powers speaking. I'm talking to him now. No, sir. No, sir. No, we can't determine what method of power was used. He won't talk. Yes, sir. I'll hold him there. I've put the house under martial law . . . belongs to a friend of mine, Roger Spelding, the TV commentator. Roger Spelding, the TV . . . What? Oh, no, I'm sure he won't say anything. Who . . . oh, yes, sir. Yes, I realize the importance of it. Yes, I will. Goodbye. (*Hangs up*) The President of the United States wants to know all about you.

Kreton. How nice of him! And I want to know all about him. But I do wish you'd let me rest a bit first. Your language is still not familiar to me. I had to learn them all, quite exhausting.

Powers. You speak *all* our languages?

Kreton. Yes, all of them. But then it's easier than you might think since I can see what's inside.

Powers. Speaking of what's inside, we're going to take your ship apart.

Kreton. Oh, I wish you wouldn't.

Powers. Security demands it.

Kreton. In that case *my* security demands you leave it alone.

Powers. You plan to stop us?

Kreton. I already have. . . . Listen.

[*Far-off shouting.* Aide *rushes into the study.*]

Aide. Something's happened to the ship, General. The door's shut and there's some kind of wall all around it, an invisible wall. We can't get near it.

Kreton (*to camera*). I hope there was no one inside.

Powers (*to* Kreton). How did you do that?

Kreton. I couldn't begin to explain. Now if you don't mind, I think we should go in and see our hosts.

[*He rises, goes into living room.* Powers *and* Aide *look at each other.*]

Powers. Don't let him out of your sight.

[Cut to *living room as* Powers *picks up phone.* Kreton *is with* John *and* Ellen.]

Kreton. I don't mind curiosity but I really can't permit them to wreck my poor ship.

Ellen. What do you plan to do, now you're here?

Kreton. Oh, keep busy. I have a project or two. . . . (*Sighs*) I can't believe you're real.

John. Then we're all in the same boat.

Kreton. Boat? Oh, yes! Well, I should have come ages ago but I . . . I couldn't get away until yesterday.

John. Yesterday? It only took you a *day* to get here?

Kreton. One of *my* days, not yours. But then you don't know about time yet.

John. Oh, you mean relativity.

Kreton. No, it's much more involved than

that. You won't know about time until . . . now let me see if I remember . . . no, I don't, but it's about two thousand years.

John. What do we do between now and then?

Kreton. You simply go on the way you are, living your exciting primitive lives . . . you have no idea how much fun you're having now.

Ellen. I hope you'll stay with us while you're here.

Kreton. That's very nice of you. Perhaps I will. Though I'm sure you'll get tired of having a visitor underfoot all the time.

Ellen. Certainly not. And Daddy will be deliriously happy. He can interview you by the hour.

John. What's it like in outer space?

Kreton. Dull.

Ellen. I should think it would be divine!

[Powers *enters.*]

Kreton. No, General, it won't work.

Powers. What won't work?

Kreton. Trying to blow up my little force field.[6] You'll just plow up Mrs. Spelding's garden.

[Powers *snarls and goes into study.*]

Ellen. Can you tell what we're *all* thinking?

Kreton. Yes. As a matter of fact, it makes me a bit giddy. Your minds are not at all like ours. You see, we control our thoughts while you . . . well, it's extraordinary the things you think about!

Ellen. Oh, how awful! You can tell *everything* we think?

Kreton. Everything! It's one of the reasons I'm here, to intoxicate myself with your primitive minds . . . with the wonderful rawness of your emotions! You have no idea how it excites me! You simply seethe with unlikely emotions.

Ellen. I've never felt so sordid.

John. From now on I'm going to think about agriculture.

Spelding (*entering*). You would.

Ellen. Daddy!

Kreton. No, no. You must go right on thinking about Ellen. Such wonderfully *purple* thoughts!

Spelding. Now see here, Powers, you're carrying this martial law thing too far . . .

Powers. Unfortunately, until I have received word from Washington as to the final disposition of this problem, you must obey my orders: no telephone calls, no communication with the outside.

Spelding. This is unsupportable.

Kreton. Poor Mr. Spelding! If you like, I shall go. That would solve everything, wouldn't it?

Powers. You're not going anywhere, Mr. Kreton, until I've had my instructions.

Kreton. I sincerely doubt if you could stop me. However, I put it up to Mr. Spelding. Shall I go?

Spelding. Yes! (Powers *gestures a warning.*) Do stay, I mean, we want you to get a good impression of us . . .

Kreton. And of course you still want to be the first journalist to interview me. Fair enough. All right, I'll stay on for a while.

Powers. Thank you.

Kreton. Don't mention it.

Spelding. General, may I ask our guest a few questions?

Powers. Go right ahead, Roger. I hope you'll do better than I did.

Spelding. Since you read our minds, you probably already know what our fears are.

Kreton. I do, yes.

Spelding. We are afraid that you represent a hostile race.

Kreton. And I have assured General Powers that my people are not remotely hostile. Except for me, no one is interested in this planet's present stage.

Spelding. Does this mean you might be interested in a *later* stage?

Kreton. I'm not permitted to discuss your future. Of course my friends think me perverse to be interested in a primitive society, but there's no accounting for tastes, is there? You are my hobby. I love you. And that's all there is to it.

Powers. So you're just here to look around . . . sort of going native.

---

6. **force field:** a space inside of which electrical or magnetic energies are active.

Kreton. What a nice expression! That's it exactly. I am going native.

Powers (*grimly*). Well, it is my view that you have been sent here by another civilization for the express purpose of reconnoitering prior to invasion.

Kreton. That *would* be your view! The wonderfully primitive assumption that all strangers are hostile. You're almost too good to be true, General.

Powers. You deny your people intend to make trouble for us?

Kreton. I deny it.

Powers. Then are they interested in establishing communication with us? Trade? That kind of thing?

Kreton. We have always had communication with you. As for trade, well, we do not trade . . . that is something peculiar only to your social level. (*Quickly*) Which I'm not criticizing! As you know, I approve of everything you do.

Powers. I give up.

Spelding. You have no interest then in . . . well, trying to dominate the earth.

Kreton. Oh, yes!

Powers. I thought you just said your people weren't interested in us.

Kreton. *They're* not, but *I* am.

Powers. You!

Kreton. Me . . . I mean I. You see, I've come here to take charge.

Powers. Of the United States?

Kreton. No, of the whole world. I'm sure you'll be much happier and it will be great fun for me. You'll get used to it in no time.

Powers. This is ridiculous. How can one man take over the world?

Kreton (*gaily*). Wait and see!

Powers (*to* Aide). Grab him!

[Powers *and* Aide *rush* Kreton *but within a foot of him, they stop, stunned.*]

Kreton. You can't touch me. That's part of the game. (*He yawns.*) Now, if you don't mind, I shall go up to my room for a little lie-down.

Spelding. I'll show you the way.

Kreton. That's all right, I know the way. (*Touches his brow*) Such savage thoughts! My head is vibrating like a drum. I feel quite giddy, all of you thinking away. (*He starts to the door; he pauses beside* Mrs. Spelding.) No, it's not a dream, dear lady. I shall be here in the morning when you wake up. And now, good night, dear, wicked children. . . .

[*He goes as we* fade out.]

FOR STUDY AND DISCUSSION

1. How does the setting of Spelding's newscast differ from that of a typical newscast today? What is the significance of setting the play in Maryland, close to "the warm pulse-beat of the nation"?

2. Compare the reactions of the different characters to the landing of the spaceship. Of these reactions, which do you think is the most appropriate and why?

3. "I do hope I don't sound patronizing," Kreton says at one point. List some instances in which Kreton does behave in a patronizing manner. What powers or qualities does Kreton have that make him superior to people on Earth? Why is his playfulness both amusing and sinister?

4. What is absurd about Powers' angry, threatening attitude? What is ironic about Powers' belief that Kreton represents a hostile race?

5. At the end of the act, the conflict of the play becomes apparent. State the conflict in terms of who wants what.

Act Two

Fade in on[1] *Kreton's bedroom next morning. He lies fully clothed on bed with cat in his lap.*

Kreton. Poor cat! Of course I sympathize with you. Dogs *are* distasteful. What? Oh, I can well believe they do: yes, yes, how disgusting. They don't ever groom their fur! But you do *constantly,* such a fine coat. No, no, I'm not just saying that, I really mean it: exquisite texture. Of course, I wouldn't say it was *nicer* than skin but even so . . . What? Oh, no! They *chase* you! Dogs chase you for no reason at all except pure malice? You poor creature. Ah, but you *do* fight back! That's right! Give it to them: slash, bite, scratch! Don't let them get away with a trick. . . . No!

---

1. **Fade in on:** to cause an image to appear gradually on the screen in place of darkness.

Do dogs really do that? Well, I'm sure *you* don't. What . . . oh, well, yes, I completely agree about mice. They *are* delicious! (Ugh!) Pounce, snap, and there is a heavenly dinner. No, I don't know any mice yet . . . they're not very amusing? But, after all, think how you must terrify them because you are so bold, so cunning, so beautifully predatory! (*Knock at door*) Come in.

Ellen (*enters*). Good morning. I brought you your breakfast.

Kreton. How thoughtful! (*Examines bacon*) Delicious, but I'm afraid my stomach is not like yours, if you'll pardon me. I don't eat. (*Removes pill from his pocket and swallows it*) This is all I need for the day. (*Indicates cat*) Unlike this creature, who would eat her own weight every hour, given a chance.

Ellen. How do you know?

Kreton. We've had a talk.

Ellen. You can *speak* to the cat?

Kreton. Not speak exactly, but we communicate. I look inside and the cat cooperates. Bright red thoughts, very exciting, though rather on one level.

Ellen. Does kitty like us?

Kreton. No, I wouldn't say she did. But then she has very few thoughts not connected with food. Have you, my quadruped criminal? (*He strokes the cat, which jumps to the floor.*)

Ellen. You know you've really upset everyone.

Kreton. I supposed that I would.

Ellen. Can you really take over the world, just like that?

Kreton. Oh, yes.

Ellen. What do you plan to do when you *have* taken over?

Kreton. Ah, that is my secret.

Ellen. Well, I think you'll be a very nice President, *if* they let you, of course.

Kreton. What a sweet girl you are! Marry him right away.

Ellen. Marry John?

Kreton. Yes. I see it in your head *and* in his. He wants you very much.

Ellen. Well, we plan to get married this summer, if Father doesn't fuss too much.

Kreton. Do it before then. I shall arrange it all if you like.

Ellen. How?

Kreton. I can convince your father.

Ellen. That sounds awfully ominous. I think you'd better leave poor Daddy alone.

Kreton. Whatever you say. (*Sighs*) Oh, I love it so! When I woke up this morning I had to pinch myself to prove I was really here.

Ellen. We were all doing a bit of pinching too. Ever since dawn we've had nothing but visitors and phone calls and troops outside in the garden. No one has the faintest idea what to do about you.

Kreton. Well, I don't think they'll be confused much longer.

Ellen. How do you plan to conquer the world?

Kreton. I confess I'm not sure. I suppose I must make some demonstration of strength, some colorful trick that will frighten everyone . . . though I much prefer taking charge quietly. That's why I've sent for the President.

Ellen. The President? *Our* President?

Kreton. Yes, he'll be along any minute now.

Ellen. But the President just doesn't go around visiting people.

Kreton. He'll visit me. (*Chuckles*) It may come as a surprise to him, but he'll be in this house in a very few minutes. I think we'd better go downstairs now. (*To cat*) No, I will not give you a mouse. You must get your own. Be self-reliant. Beast!

[*Dissolve to* the study. Powers *is reading book entitled* The Atom and You. *Muffled explosions offstage.*]

Aide (*entering*). Sir, nothing seems to be working. Do we have the General's permission to try a fission bomb on the force field?

Powers. No . . . no. We'd better give it up.

Aide. The men are beginning to talk.

Powers (*thundering*). Well, keep them quiet! (*Contritely*) I'm sorry, Captain. I'm on edge. Fortunately, the whole business will soon be in the hands of the World Council.

Aide. What will the World Council do?

Powers. It will be interesting to observe them.

Aide. You don't think this Kreton can really take over the world, do you?

Powers. Of course not. Nobody can.

[*Dissolve to* living room. Mrs. Spelding *and* Spelding *are talking.*]

Mrs. Spelding. You still haven't asked Mr. Kreton about moving that thing, have you?

Spelding. There are too many *important* things to ask him.

Mrs. Spelding. I hate to be a nag but you know the trouble I have had getting anything to grow in that part of the garden . . .

John (*enters*). Good morning.

Mrs. Spelding. Good morning, John.

John. Any sign of your guest?

Mrs. Spelding. Ellen took his breakfast up to him a few minutes ago.

John. They don't seem to be having much luck, do they? I sure hope you don't mind my staying here like this.

[*Spelding glowers.*]

Mrs. Spelding. Why, we love having you! I just hope your family aren't too anxious.

John. One of the GI's finally called them, said I was staying here for the weekend.

Spelding. The rest of our *lives,* if something isn't done soon.

John. Just how long do you think that'll be, Dad?

Spelding. Who knows?

[Kreton *and* Ellen *enter.*]

Kreton. Ah, how wonderful to see you again! Let me catch my breath. . . . Oh, your minds! It's not easy for me, you know. So many crude thoughts blazing away! Yes, Mrs. Spelding, I will move the ship off your roses.
Mrs. Spelding. That's awfully sweet of you.
Kreton. Mr. Spelding, if any interviews are to be granted, you will be the first. I promise you.
Spelding. That's very considerate, I'm sure.
Kreton. So you can stop thinking *those* particular thoughts. And now where is the President?
Spelding. The President?
Kreton. Yes, I sent for him. He should be here. (*He goes to the terrace window.*) Ah, that must be he. (*A swarthy* Man *in uniform with a sash across his chest is standing, bewildered, on the terrace.* Kreton *opens the glass doors.*) Come in, sir, come in, Your Excellency. Good of you to come on such short notice.

[Man *enters.*]

Man (*in Spanish accent*). Where am I?
Kreton. You *are* the President, aren't you?
Man. Of course I am the President. What am I doing here? I was dedicating a bridge and I find myself . . .
Kreton (*aware of his mistake*). Oh, dear! *Where* was the bridge?
Man. Where do you think, you idiot, in Paraguay!
Kreton (*to others*). I seem to've made a mistake. Wrong President. (*Gestures and the* Man *disappears.*) Seemed rather upset, didn't he?
John. You can make people come and go just like that?

Kreton. Just like that.

[Powers *looks into room from the study.*]

Powers. Good morning, Mr. Kreton. Could I see you for a moment?
Kreton. By all means. (*He crosses to the study.*)
Spelding. I believe I am going mad.

[Cut to *study. The* Aide *stands at attention while* Powers *addresses* Kreton.]

Powers. . . . and so we feel, the government of the United States feels, that this problem is too big for any one country; therefore we are turning the whole affair over to Paul Laurent, the Secretary-General of the World Council.
Kreton. Very sensible, I should've thought of that myself.
Powers. Mr. Laurent is on his way here now. And I may add, Mr. Kreton, you've made me look singularly ridiculous.
Kreton. I'm awfully sorry. (*Pause*) No, you can't kill me.
Powers. You were reading my mind again.
Kreton. I can't really help it, you know. And such *black* thoughts today, but intense, very intense.
Powers. I regard you as a menace.
Kreton. I know you do and I think it's awfully unkind. I do mean well.
Powers. Then go back where you came from and leave us alone.
Kreton. I'm afraid I can't do that just yet . . .

[*Phone rings;* the Aide *answers it.*]

Aide. He's outside? Sure, let him through. (*To* Powers) The Secretary-General of the World Council is here, sir.
Powers (*to* Kreton). I hope you'll listen to *him*.
Kreton. Oh, I shall, of course. I love listening.

[*The door opens and* Paul Laurent, *middle-aged and serene, enters.* Powers *and his* Aide *stand to attention.* Kreton *goes forward to shake hands.*]

Laurent. Mr. Kreton?
Kreton. At your service, Mr. Laurent.
Laurent. I welcome you to this planet in the name of the World Council.
Kreton. Thank you, sir, thank you.
Laurent. Could you leave us alone for a moment, General?
Powers. Yes, sir.

[Powers *and* Aide *go.* Laurent *smiles at* Kreton.]

Laurent. Shall we sit down?
Kreton. Yes, yes, I love sitting down. I'm afraid my manners are not quite suitable, yet.

[*They sit down.*]

Laurent. Now, Mr. Kreton, in violation of all the rules of diplomacy, may I come to the point?

Kreton. You may.
Laurent. Why are you here?
Kreton. Curiosity. Pleasure.
Laurent. You are a tourist then in this time and place?
Kreton (*nods*). Yes. Very well put.
Laurent. We have been informed that you have extraordinary powers.
Kreton. By your standards, yes, they must seem extraordinary.
Laurent. We have also been informed that it is your intention to . . . to take charge of this world.
Kreton. That is correct. . . . What a remarkable mind you have! I have difficulty looking inside it.
Laurent (*laughs*). Patience. I've attended so many conferences. . . . May I say that your conquest of our world puts your status of tourist in a rather curious light?

Kreton. Oh, I said nothing about *conquest*.

Laurent. Then how else do you intend to govern? The people won't allow you to direct their lives without a struggle.

Kreton. But I'm sure they will if I ask them to.

Laurent. You believe you can do all this without, well, without violence?

Kreton. Of course I can. One or two demonstrations and I'm sure they'll do as I ask. (*Smiles*) Watch this.

[*Pause. Then shouting.* Powers *bursts into room.*]

Powers. Now what've you done?

Kreton. Look out the window, Your Excellency.

[Laurent *goes to window. A rifle floats by, followed by an alarmed* Soldier.]

Nice, isn't it? I confess I worked out a number of rather melodramatic tricks last night. Incidentally, all the rifles of the soldiers in all the world are now floating in the air. (*Gestures*) Now they have them back.

Powers (*to* Laurent). You see, sir, I didn't exaggerate in my report.

Laurent (*awed*). No, no, you certainly didn't.

Kreton. You were skeptical, weren't you?

Laurent. Naturally. But now I . . . now I think it's possible.

Powers. That this . . . this gentleman is going to run everything?

Laurent. Yes, yes I do. And it might be wonderful.

Kreton. You *are* more clever than the others. You begin to see that I mean only good.

Laurent. Yes, only good. General, do you realize what this means? We can have one government . . .

Kreton. With innumerable bureaus, and intrigue. . . .

Laurent (*excited*). And the world could be incredibly prosperous, especially if he'd help us with his superior knowledge.

Kreton (*delighted*). I will, I will. I'll teach you to look into one another's minds. You'll find it devastating but enlightening: all that self-interest, those *lurid* emotions . . .

Laurent. No more countries. No more wars . . .

Kreton (*startled*). Oh, but I like a lot of countries. Besides, at this stage of your development you're supposed to have lots of countries and lots of wars . . . innumerable wars . . .

Laurent. But you can help us change all that.

Kreton. *Change* all that! My dear sir, I am your friend.

Laurent. What do you mean?

Kreton. Why, your deepest pleasure is violence. How can you deny that? It is the whole point to you, the whole point to my hobby . . . and you are my hobby, all mine.

Laurent. But our lives are devoted to *controlling* violence, and not creating it.

Kreton. Now, don't take me for an utter fool. After all, I can see into your minds. My dear fellow, don't you *know* what you are?

Laurent. What are we?

Kreton. You are savages. I have returned to the dark ages of an insignificant planet simply because I want the glorious excitement of being among you and reveling in your savagery! There is murder in all your hearts and I love it! It intoxicates me!

Laurent (*slowly*). You hardly flatter us.

Kreton. I didn't mean to be rude but you did ask me why I am here and I've told you.

Laurent. You have no wish then to . . . to help us poor savages.

Kreton. I couldn't even if I wanted to. You won't be civilized for at least two thousand years and you won't reach the level of my people for about a million years.

Laurent (*sadly*). Then you have come here only to . . . to observe?

Kreton. No, more than that. I mean to regulate your pastimes. But don't worry: I won't upset things too much. I've decided I don't want to be known to the people. You will go right on with your countries, your squabbles, the way you always have, while I will *secretly* regulate things through you.

Laurent. The World Council does not govern. We only advise.

Kreton. Well, I shall advise you and you will advise the governments and we shall have a lovely time.

Laurent. I don't know what to say. You obviously have the power to do as you please.

Kreton. I'm glad you realize that. Poor General Powers is now wondering if a hydrogen bomb might destroy me. It won't, General.

Powers. Too bad.

Kreton. Now, Your Excellency, I shall stay in this house until you have laid the groundwork for my first project.

Laurent. And what is that to be?

Kreton. A war! I want one of your really splendid wars, with all the trimmings, all the noise and the fire . . .

Laurent. A war! You're joking. Why, at this moment we are working as hard as we know how *not* to have a war.

Kreton. But secretly you want one. After all, it's the one thing your little race does well. You'd hardly want me to deprive you of your simple pleasures, now would you?

Laurent. I think you must be mad.

Kreton. Not mad, simply a philanthropist. Of course I myself shall get a great deal of pleasure out of a war (the vibrations must be incredible!) but I'm doing it mostly for you. So, if you don't mind, I want you to arrange a few incidents, so we can get one started spontaneously.

Laurent. I refuse.

Kreton. In that event, I shall select someone else to head the World Council. Someone who *will* start a war. I suppose there exist a few people here who might like the idea.

Laurent. How can you do such a horrible thing to us? Can't you see that we don't want to be savages?

Kreton. But you have no choice. Anyway, you're just pulling my leg! I'm sure you want a war as much as the rest of them do and that's what you're going to get: the biggest war you've ever had!

Laurent (*stunned*). Heaven help us!

Kreton (*exuberant*). Heaven won't! Oh, what fun it will be! I can hardly wait! (*He strikes the globe of the world a happy blow as we fade out.*)

FOR STUDY AND DISCUSSION

1. Kreton converses with the cat almost as if he were conversing with a person. What is the significance of his remarks to the cat?

2. What two things does the incident with the President of Paraguay show us about Kreton's powers?

3. What does the remark Laurent makes as he sits down with Kreton imply about the rules of diplomacy? Why does Kreton find it difficult to look into Laurent's mind?

4. What benefits does Laurent at first see in Kreton's plan to dominate the world? What does Kreton's first project turn out to be?

5. Kreton states that the deepest pleasure for human beings is violence. What evidence does he give for his conclusion?

Act Three

Fade in on *the study, two weeks later. Kreton is sitting at desk on which a map is spread out. He has a pair of dividers, some models of jet aircraft. Occasionally he pretends to dive-bomb, imitating the sound of a bomb going off. Powers enters.*

Powers. You wanted me, sir?

Kreton. Yes, I wanted those figures on radio-active fallout.

Powers. They're being made up now, sir. Anything else?

Kreton. Oh, my dear fellow, why do you dislike me so?

Powers. I am your military aide, sir: I don't have to answer that question. It is outside the sphere of my duties.

Kreton. Aren't you at least happy about your promotion?

Powers. Under the circumstances, no, sir.

Kreton. I find your attitude baffling.

Powers. Is that all, sir?

Kreton. You have never once said what you thought of my war plans. Not once have I got a single word of encouragement from you, a single compliment . . . only black thoughts.

Powers. Since you read my mind, sir, you know what I think.

Kreton. True, but I can't help but feel that deep down inside of you there is just a twinge of professional jealousy. You don't like the idea of an outsider playing your game better than you do. Now confess!

Powers. I am acting as your aide only under duress.

Kreton (*sadly*). Bitter, bitter . . . and to think I chose you especially as my aide. Think of all the other generals who would give anything to have your job.

Powers. Fortunately, they know nothing about my job.

Kreton. Yes, I do think it wise not to advertise my presence, don't you?

Powers. I can't see that it makes much difference, since you seem bent on destroying our world.

Kreton. I'm not going to destroy it. A few dozen cities, that's all, and not very nice cities either. Think of the fun you'll have building new ones when it's over.

Powers. How many millions of people do you plan to kill?

Kreton. Well, quite a few, but they love this sort of thing. You can't convince me they don't. Oh, I know what Laurent says. But he's a misfit, out of step with his time. Fortunately, my new World Council is more reasonable.

Powers. Paralyzed is the word, sir.

Kreton. You don't think they like me either?

Powers. You *know* they hate you, sir.

Kreton. But love and hate are so confused in your savage minds and the vibrations of the one are so very like those of the other that I can't always distinguish. You see, we neither love nor hate in my world. We simply have hobbies. (*He strokes the globe of the world tenderly.*) But now to work. Tonight's the big night: first, the sneak attack, then: boom! (*He claps his hands gleefully.*)

[Dissolve to *the living room*, to John *and* Ellen.]

Ellen. I've never felt so helpless in my life.

John. Here we all stand around doing nothing while he plans to blow up the world.

Ellen. Suppose we went to the newspapers.

John. He controls the press. When Laurent resigned they didn't even print his speech.

[*A gloomy pause*]

Ellen. What are you thinking about, John?

John. Walnuts.

[*They embrace.*]

Ellen. Can't we do anything?

John. No, I guess there's nothing.

Ellen (*vehemently*). Oh! I could kill him!

[Kreton *and* Powers *enter.*]

Kreton. Very good, Ellen, *very* good! I've never felt you so violent.

Ellen. You heard what I said to John?

Kreton. Not in words, but you were absolutely bathed in malevolence.

Powers. I'll get the papers you wanted, sir. (Powers *exits.*)

Kreton. I don't think he likes me very much but your father does. Only this morning he offered to handle my public relations and I said I'd let him. Wasn't that nice of him?

John. I think I'll go get some fresh air. (*He goes out through the terrace door.*)

Kreton. Oh, dear! (*Sighs*) Only your father is really entering the spirit of the game. He's a much better sport than you, my dear.

Ellen (*exploding*). Sport! That's it! You think we're sport. You think we're animals to be played with: well, we're not. We're people and we don't want to be destroyed.

Kreton (*patiently*). But *I* am not destroying you. You will be destroying one another of your own free will, as you have always done. I am simply a . . . a kibitzer.

Ellen. No, you are a vampire!

Kreton. A vampire? You mean I drink blood? Ugh!

Ellen. No, you drink emotions, our emotions. You'll sacrifice us all for the sake of your . . . your vibrations!

Kreton. Touché.[1] Yet what harm am I really doing? It's true I'll enjoy the war more than anybody; but it will be *your* destructiveness, after all, not mine.

Ellen. You could stop it.

Kreton. So could you.

Ellen. I?

Kreton. Your race. They could stop altogether but they won't. And I can hardly intervene in their natural development. The most I can do is help out in small, practical ways.

Ellen. We are not what you think. We're not so . . . so primitive.

Kreton. My dear girl, just take this one household: your mother dislikes your father but she is too tired to do anything about it, so she knits and she gardens and she tries not to think about him. Your father, on the other hand, is bored with all of you. Don't look shocked; he doesn't like you any more than you like him . . .

Ellen. Don't say that!

Kreton. I am only telling you the truth. Your

---

1. *Touché* (too-shā'): a French fencing term meaning "touched"; that is, "You have scored a point."

father wants you to marry someone important; therefore he objects to John, while you, my girl . . .

Ellen (*with a fierce cry*, Ellen *grabs vase to throw*). You devil! (*Vase breaks in her hand.*)

Kreton. You see? That proves my point perfectly. (*Gently*) Poor savage, I cannot help what you are. (*Briskly*) Anyway, you will soon be distracted from your personal problems. Tonight is the night. If you're a good girl, I'll let you watch the bombing.

[*Dissolve to* study. *Eleven forty-five.* Powers *and the* Aide *gloomily await the war.*]

Aide. General, isn't there anything we can do?

Powers. It's out of our hands.

[Kreton, *dressed as a hussar*[2] *with shako,*[3] *enters.*]

Kreton. Everything on schedule?

Powers. Yes, sir. Planes left for their targets at twenty-two hundred.

Kreton. Good . . . good. I, myself, shall take off shortly after midnight to observe the attack firsthand.

Powers. Yes, sir.

[Kreton *goes into the living room, where the family is gloomily assembled.*]

Kreton (*enters from study*). And now the magic hour approaches! I hope you're all as thrilled as I am.

Spelding. You still won't tell us who's attacking whom?

Kreton. You'll know in exactly . . . fourteen minutes.

---

2. **hussar** (hŏŏ-zär′): a European cavalry soldier in a brightly colored uniform.
3. **shako** (shăk′ō): a fancy, cylindrical military hat with a plume on top.

Ellen (*bitterly*). Are we going to be killed too?

Kreton. Certainly not! You're quite safe, at least in the early stages of the war.

Ellen. Thank you.

Mrs. Spelding. I suppose this will mean rationing again.[4]

Spelding. Will . . . will we see anything from here?

Kreton. No, but there should be a good picture on the monitor in the study. Powers is tuning in right now.

John (*at window*). Hey look, up there! Coming this way!

[Ellen *joins him.*]

Ellen. What is it?

John. Why . . . it's *another* one! And it's going to land.

Kreton (*surprised*). I'm sure you're mistaken. No one would dream of coming here. (*He has gone to the window, too.*)

Ellen. It's landing!

Spelding. Is it a friend of yours, Mr. Kreton?

Kreton (*slowly*). No, no, not a friend . . . (Kreton *retreats to the study; he inadvertently*[5] *drops a lace handkerchief beside the sofa.*)

John. Here he comes.

Ellen (*suddenly bitter*). Now we have two of them.

Mrs. Spelding. My poor roses.

[*The new* Visitor *enters in a gleam of light from his ship. He is wearing a most futuristic costume. Without a word, he walks past the awed family into the study.* Kreton *is cowering behind the globe.* Powers *and the* Aide *stare, bewildered, as the* Visitor *gestures*

---

4. **rationing again:** Mrs. Spelding is remembering World War II, when gasoline and food consumption were restricted in the United States.
5. **inadvertently** (in′əd-vûr′tənt-lē): through an oversight.

sternly and Kreton *reluctantly removes shako and sword. They communicate by odd sounds.*]

Visitor (*to* Powers). Please leave us alone.

[Cut to *living room as* Powers *and the* Aide *enter from the study.*]

Powers (*to* Ellen). Who on earth was that?
Ellen. It's another one, another visitor.
Powers. Now we're done for.
Ellen. I'm going in there.
Mrs. Spelding. Ellen, don't you dare!
Ellen. I'm going to talk to them. (*Starts to door*)
John. I'm coming, too.
Ellen (*grimly*). No, alone. I know what I want to say.

[Cut to *interior of the study,* to Kreton *and the other* Visitor *as* Ellen *enters.*]

Ellen. I want you both to listen to me . . .
Visitor. You don't need to speak. I know what you will say.
Ellen. That you have no right here? That you mustn't . . .
Visitor. I agree. Kreton has no right here. He is well aware that it is forbidden to interfere with the past.
Ellen. The past?
Visitor (*nods*). You are the past, the dark ages: we are from the future. In fact, we are *your* descendants on another planet. We visit you from time to time but we never interfere because it would change *us* if we did. Fortunately, I arrived in time.
Ellen. There won't be a war?

Visitor. There will be no war. And there will be no memory of any of this. When we leave here you will forget Kreton and me. Time will turn back to the moment before his arrival.

Ellen. Why did you want to hurt us?

Kreton (*heartbroken*). Oh, but I didn't! I only wanted to have . . . well, to have a little fun, to indulge my hobby . . . against the rules, of course.

Visitor (*to* Ellen). Kreton is a rarity among us. Mentally and morally he is retarded. He is a child and he regards your period as his toy.

Kreton. A child, now really!

Visitor. He escaped from his nursery and came back in time to you . . .

Kreton. And *everything* went wrong, everything! I wanted to visit 1860 . . . that's my *real* period but then something happened to the car and I ended up here, not that I don't find you nearly as interesting but . . .

Visitor. We must go, Kreton.

Kreton (*to* Ellen). You did like me just a bit, didn't you?

Ellen. Yes, yes, I did, until you let your hobby get out of hand. (*To* Visitor) What is the future like?

Visitor. Very serene, very different . . .

Kreton. Don't believe him: it is dull, dull, dull beyond belief! One simply floats through eternity: no wars, no excitement . . .

Visitor. It is forbidden to discuss these matters.

Kreton. I can't see what difference it makes, since she's going to forget all about us anyway.

Ellen. Oh, how I'd love to see the future . . .

Visitor. It is against . . .

Kreton. Against the rules: how tiresome you are. (*To* Ellen) But, alas, you can never pay us a call because you aren't born yet! I mean where we are you are not. Oh, Ellen, dear, think kindly of me, until you forget.

Ellen. I will.

Visitor. Come. Time has begun to turn back. Time is bending.

[*He starts to door.* Kreton *turns conspiratorially to* Ellen.]

Kreton. Don't be sad, my girl. I shall be back one bright day, but a bright day in 1860. I dote on the Civil War, so exciting . . .

Visitor. Kreton!

Kreton. Only next time I think it'll be more fun if the *South* wins! (*He hurries after the* Visitor.)

[Cut to *clock as the hands spin backwards.* Dissolve to *the living room, exactly the same as the first scene:* Spelding, Mrs. Spelding, Ellen.]

Spelding. There is nothing wrong with marrying a wealthy man. The horror of it has always eluded me. However, my only wish is that you marry someone hard-working, ambitious, a man who'll make his mark in the world. Not a boy who is content to sit on a farm all his life, growing peanuts . . .

Ellen. English walnuts! And he won't just sit there.

Spelding. Will you stop contradicting me?

Ellen. But, Daddy, John grows walnuts . . .

[John *enters.*]

John. Hello, everybody.

Mrs. Spelding. Good evening, John.

Ellen. What kept you, darling? You missed Daddy's broadcast.

John. I saw it before I left home. Wonderful broadcast, sir.

Spelding. Thank you, John.

[John *crosses to window.*]

John. That meteor you were talking about, well, for a while it looked almost like a spaceship or something. You can just barely see it now.

[Ellen *joins him at window. They watch, arms about one another.*]

Spelding. Spaceship! Nonsense! Remarkable what some people will believe, *want* to believe. Besides, as I said in the broadcast: if there's any traveling to be done in space, we'll do it first.

[*He notices* Kreton's *handkerchief on sofa and picks it up. They all look at it, puzzled, as* we *cut to stock shot of the starry night, against which two spaceships vanish in the distance, one serene in its course, the other erratic, as we* fade out.]

FOR STUDY AND DISCUSSION

1. What difference is there in the way Laurent and General Powers react to Kreton's plans? Why does Kreton keep Paul Laurent's speech from appearing in the press?

2. How and why does Ellen's attitude toward Kreton change? Why is it logical that Mr. Spelding wants to work for Kreton, now that Kreton is in command?

3. Kreton's speech about the Spelding household is a key speech in the play. What primitive anger does he see in each family member? Which human capacity does he dismiss?

4. What does the Visitor mean when he says that Kreton is morally retarded? Why is it forbidden for the visitors to interfere with what happens on Earth?

5. Why is Kreton's forgotten handkerchief crucial to the ending of the play?

LANGUAGE AND VOCABULARY

Using Combining Forms

Many words have been created by combining older words or word fragments. Often it is possible to figure out the original meaning of a word simply by separating it into parts — provided you know what the parts mean.

inter-

> **John.** Traveling in space! Just like those stories. You know: intergalactic drive stuff.

Inter- is a prefix meaning "between or among." Therefore, *intergalactic* travel means "travel between galaxies." What is an *interfaith* conference? An *intercollegiate* football game? An *interplanetary* mission? An *interdepartmental* meeting?

mal-

> **Kreton.** . . . you were absolutely bathed in malevolence.

Mal- is a combining form meaning "bad or badly, wrong or ill." The remainder of the word *malevolence* is related to the word *voluntary*. A voluntary action is something you do because you wish to do it or have a will to do it. Therefore, *malevolence* is ill will. What is *malnutrition*? What does *malodorous* mean? What is a *malfunction*? What is *malpractice*?

philo- and *anthropo-*

> **Laurent.** I think you must be mad.
> **Kreton.** Not mad, simply a philanthropist.

You probably know that a philanthropist is a giver of charity. In the quotation above, Kreton means more than that.

Philo- (*phil-* before a vowel) means "loving or liking."

Anthropo (*anthrop-* before a vowel) means "human."

A philanthropist, therefore, is a lover of human beings.

Use your dictionary to find out what the second part of each of the following words means. You will find the answers in the derivation entries for the words in question, not in the definitions. You may have to do some cross-referencing. Read the definitions after you have found the answers.

anthropocentric
anthropology
anthropometry
anthropomorphism

philharmonic
Philip
philology
philosophy

FOR COMPOSITION

Analyzing Satirical Elements

A satire is a literary work that points up or attacks follies or vices in human nature. Satire can range in tone from lighthearted wit to scorching ironic bitterness. Almost all comic writers use some satirical elements in their work.

Choose one of the following aspects of Vidal's satire for analysis, and develop a short paper, using evidence from the play to support your conclusions.

What are some examples of hypocrisy that occur in the play? Why is Kreton particularly suited to expose them?

Kreton tends to emphasize the negative rather than the positive aspects of humanity. Are his observations useful, destructive, or both? Apply your answer to satire in general as you elaborate.

Gore Vidal's original plan when he was writing *Visit to a Small Planet* was to end the play with the entire world blowing up. Which ending better suits the satirical points that the author has to make? Explain.

ABOUT THE AUTHOR

Gore Vidal (1926–   ) wrote his first novel at the age of nineteen. This was during the Second World War; Vidal was first mate of an army ship. His first few novels were successful, but from 1954 to 1956, Vidal turned to television writing for his livelihood. *Visit to a Small Planet* was first telecast on May 8, 1955. Vidal later rewrote the teleplay for Broadway, where it had a long run. In the mid-sixties, Vidal returned to novel writing and surpassed his earlier record by writing five best sellers in little more than ten years.

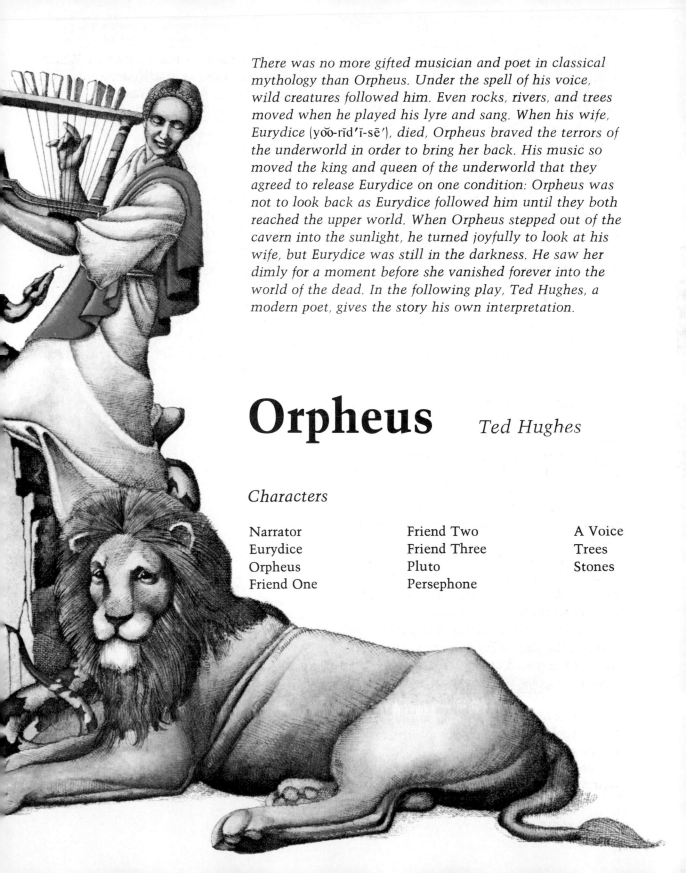

There was no more gifted musician and poet in classical mythology than Orpheus. Under the spell of his voice, wild creatures followed him. Even rocks, rivers, and trees moved when he played his lyre and sang. When his wife, Eurydice (yŏŏ-rĭd′ĭ-sē′), died, Orpheus braved the terrors of the underworld in order to bring her back. His music so moved the king and queen of the underworld that they agreed to release Eurydice on one condition: Orpheus was not to look back as Eurydice followed him until they both reached the upper world. When Orpheus stepped out of the cavern into the sunlight, he turned joyfully to look at his wife, but Eurydice was still in the darkness. He saw her dimly for a moment before she vanished forever into the world of the dead. In the following play, Ted Hughes, a modern poet, gives the story his own interpretation.

Orpheus   *Ted Hughes*

Characters

Narrator	Friend Two	A Voice
Eurydice	Friend Three	Trees
Orpheus	Pluto	Stones
Friend One	Persephone	

Orpheus from Politian's *La Giostra di Giuliano de Medici* (1498). Anonymous woodcut.
Museum of Fine Arts, Boston

Narrator. This is the story
  Of Orpheus the Magician, whose magic was music.

[*Music—guitar—Pop.*]

  This is the dance of the trees.
  His music is so magic, he makes the trees dance.
  The oaks unknot; they toss their limbs   5
  And the willows whirl in a ring.
  This is the dance of the trees.

[*Music stops. Giant sigh from all trees.*]

  And this is the dance of the stones.

[*Music for stones—still Pop.*]

368 *Drama*

His music is so magic the stones dance.
The rocks uproot and caper in their places,   10
The pebbles skip like mice,
The ordinary stones bounce like footballs.
This is the dance of the stones.

[*Music stops. Sigh from all stones.*]

His music reaches out to the bears in the forest.

[*Bear music — still Pop.*]

It reaches up to the deer in the wrinkles of the hills.   15

[*Deer music.*]

It reaches down to the salmon in the pools below the
    falls.

[*Salmon music.*]

And wherever his music is heard, the dancing begins.

[*Music.*]

His music has a name. Its name is happiness.
Every living thing loves Orpheus
Because his music is happiness.   20

[Eurydice *becomes visible.*]

And this is the cause of Orpheus' happiness:
This is his wife, for her he makes his music.
Orpheus. Why shouldn't I be happy?
The world is beautiful.
Day after day the huge gift of the world   25
Is beautiful as ever.
More beautiful than the whole world is my wife
    Eurydice.
This is the secret of my music.
It is all for Eurydice, my happiness.

[*Music.*]

Narrator. Nevertheless, there keeps coming a voice   30
  To Orpheus — a voice which he does not like.
Voice. Beware, Orpheus, beware.
Narrator. He dare not listen to the voice. He plays louder.

[*Music louder, to drown out the voice.*]

  Is it the voice of a bird? Or a spider? Or a serpent?
Voice *(very loud).* Beware, Orpheus, beware.   35

[*Music stops.*]

(Very soft) Beware, beware, beware.
Orpheus. What should I beware of? Why should I beware?
Voice. In the world of the trees,
  In the world of the stones,
  In the world of the frog,° of the vole,° of the linnet°—   40
  Every song has to be paid for.
Orpheus. Nonsense!
  The world is a gift.
  The brave take it with thanks and greet it with song.
  Only the fearful peer at it with suspicion,   45
  Thinking about the payment.
Voice. Beware, Orpheus, beware.

[Orpheus *drowns the voice with a storm of his music.*]

Narrator. Orpheus hammers his guitar nevertheless.
  And the trees dance once again
  And the stones dance.   50
  The deer on the hills, and the salmon in the weirs°
  And the bears in the holes of the forest
  And the travelers out on the roads
  Dance, dance when they hear it.
  The world dances with happiness.   55
  But suddenly —

[*Music falters and stops.*]

Orpheus. My hand! Something has happened to my hand.
Narrator. Orpheus' hand suddenly becomes numb.

[*Sudden terrible cry in distance; voice coming nearer; a*
Friend *bringing the news.*]

40. **vole:** a rodent. **linnet:** a song-bird.

51. **weirs:** fences built in a river to catch fish.

Friend. Orpheus! *(Nearer)* Orpheus!

Orpheus. Who is that?   60

Friend *(nearer).* Orpheus!

Orpheus. Here.

Friend *(very close, entering).* Orpheus!

Orpheus. Your face is terrifying. So is your voice.
What is your news?   65

Friend. Eurydice is dead.

[*Magnified crash of strings, as if instruments smashed;
light effects — sudden darkening.*]

Narrator. Eurydice lies dead in the orchard, bitten by a
snake.
Her soul has left her body. Her body is cold.
Her voice has been carried away to the land of the dead.

Orpheus. Eurydice!   70

[*He lies prostrate. His music — now erratic and discordant — struggles to tormented climax and again collapses
as if all instruments smashed. Light effects.*]

Narrator. Orpheus mourns for a month and his music is
silent.
The trees droop their boughs; they weep leaves.
The stones in the wall weep.
The river runs silent with sorrow under its willows.
The birds sit mourning in silence on the ridge of the
house.   75
Orpheus lies silent and face downwards.
His friends try to rouse him.

Friend. Orpheus, you are mourning too long. The dead
are dead.
Remember the living. Let your own music heal your
sorrow.
Play for us.   80

Narrator. The trees know better.

Trees. We shall never dance again. Eurydice is dead. Now
we return to the ancient sadness of the forest.

Narrator. And the stones know better.

Stones. We are the stones, older than life. We have stood   85
by many graves. We know grief to the bottom. We
danced for a while because Orpheus was happy.

Eurydice is dead. Now we return to the ancient sadness of the hills.

Narrator. But still, his friends try to rouse him. 90

Friends One, Two, and **Three.** Eurydice did not want you to grieve so long, Orpheus. Play your music again. Deceive your grief. Defeat evil fortunes. The dead belong to the dead, the living to the living. Play for us.

Narrator. Have they succeeded? 95
At last! Orpheus reaches for the magic strings.

[One note, repeated, gathering volume and impetus — insane.]

Friends One, Two, and **Three.** Horrible! Is this music? He has forgotten how to play. Grief has damaged his brain. This is not music.

Orpheus. I am going down to the underworld. 100
To find Eurydice.

Friends. Mad! He is mad! Orpheus has gone mad!

Orpheus. I am going to the bottom of the underworld. I am going to bring Eurydice back.

Friend One. Nobody ever came back from the land of the 105 dead.

Orpheus. I am going. And I shall come back. With Eurydice.

Friends. Mad! He is mad! Orpheus has gone mad! Nobody ever returns from the land of the dead. 110

[Their voices fade. His crazy note strengthens, modulating into electronic infernal accompaniments. Major light effects through what follows.]

Narrator (*speaking with greatly magnified voice over the music — not declaiming so much as a giant whisper*).
Where is the land of the dead? Is it everywhere? Or nowhere?
How deep is the grave?
What is the geography of death?
What are its frontiers?
Perhaps it is a spider's web. Perhaps it is a single grain of dirt. 115

A million million souls can sit in an atom.
Is that the land of the dead?
A billion billion ghosts in the prison of an atom
Waiting for eternity to pass.

[*Orpheus' music louder. Light effects.*]

Orpheus beats his guitar. He is no longer making 120
music. He is making a road of sound. He is making a
road through the sky. A road to Eurydice.
Orpheus. Eurydice! Eurydice! Eurydice!
Narrator. He flies on his guitar. His guitar is carrying
him. It has lifted him off the earth. It lifts him over the 125
treetops.

[*Music continuing, the monotonous note like a drum
note insistent.*]

Friends. Orpheus, come back! Orpheus, come back!
Orpheus. Eurydice!
Narrator. It carries him into a cloud.

[*Light and sound effects through what follows, his music
continuing throughout.*]

Through the thunder he flies. Through the lightning. 130
It carries him
Through the storm of cries,
The last cries of all who have died on earth,
The jealous, screaming laments
Of all who have died on earth and cannot come back. 135

[*Storm of cries.*]

Orpheus. Eurydice!
Narrator. He lays his road of sound across the heavens.
His guitar carries him
Into the storm of blood,
The electrical storm of all the blood of all who have
died on earth. 140
He is whirled into the summit of the storm.
Lightnings strike through him, he falls —
Orpheus. Eurydice!

Narrator. He falls into the mouth of the earth.
　　He falls through the throat of the earth, he recovers.　145
　　He rides his serpent of sound through the belly of the
　　　earth.
　　He drives his spear of sound through the bowels of the
　　　earth.
　　Mountains under the earth fall on him, he dodges.
　　He flies through walls of burning rock and ashes.
　　His guitar carries him.　　　　　　　　　　　　150

[*Music continuing monotonous and insane.*]

　　He hurtles towards the centermost atom of the earth.
　　He aims his beam of sound at the last atom.
Orpheus. Eurydice!
Narrator. He smashes through the wall of the last atom.
　　He falls　　　　　　　　　　　　　　　　155
　　He falls
　　At the feet of Pluto, king of the kingdom of the dead.

[*Silence. Appropriate light effects.*]

Pluto. So you have arrived. At first I thought it was a fly.
　　Then I thought it was a meteorite. But now I see—it is a
　　man. A living man, in the land of the dead. Stand. I am　160
　　Pluto, king of the underworld. And you, I think, are
　　Orpheus.
Narrator. Orpheus stands on the floor of the hall of
　　judgment, like a mouse on the floor of a cathedral.
　　Pluto's face, vast on his vast throne, is made of black　165
　　iron, and it is the face of a spider. The face of
　　Persephone, his wife and queen, vast on her vast
　　throne, beside him, is made of white ivory, and it is the
　　pointed, eyeless face of a maggot.
Pluto. Orpheus! I have heard of you. What is it, Orpheus,　170
　　brings you alive to the land of the dead?
Orpheus. You took away my wife Eurydice.
Pluto. That is true.
Orpheus. What can I do to get her back?
Pluto. Get her back?　　　　　　　　　　　　175

[*Laughs—Plutonic laughter in hell.*]

　　Alas, your wife has gone into the vaults of the dead.

You cannot have her back.

Orpheus. Release her. You are a god. You can do as you like.

Pluto. Some things are not in my power, Orpheus. Here is 180
my wife, for instance, Persephone. Perhaps you have
heard about her. Six months she spends with me, here
in the underworld. Six months she is up on earth, in the
woods and meadows, with her mother. That is the
arrangement. Up on the earth she is a flower-face, she 185
laughs and sings; everybody adores her. But now you
see her. Here in the underworld she is quite different.
She never makes a sound. Never speaks, never sings.
And you see her face? It is the peaked face of a maggot.
Yet it is not a maggot. It is the white beak of the 190
first sprout of a flower. I have never seen it open. Here in
the underworld it is closed—white, pointed and
closed—the face of a maggot.

Here is something I cannot alter.

There is another thing, Orpheus. Here in the 195
underworld, the accounting is strict. A payment was
due from you.

Orpheus. Payment.

Pluto. Nothing is free. Everything has to be paid for. For
every profit in one thing—payment in some other 200
thing. For every life—a death. Even your music—of
which we have heard so much—that had to be paid for.
Your wife was the payment for your music. Hell is now
satisfied.

Orpheus. You took my wife— 205

Pluto. To pay for your music.

Orpheus. But I had my music from birth. I was born
with it.

Pluto. You had it on credit. You were living in debt.
Now you have paid, and the music is yours. 210

Orpheus. Then take back my music. Give me my wife.

Pluto. Too late.

Orpheus. What good is my music without my wife?
What can I do to make you give me my wife?

Pluto. Nothing can open hell. 215

[Orpheus *strikes a chord—no longer Pop—solemn Handel,
Bach, Vivaldi, or earlier. Light effects.*]

Now what are you doing?
Your music is even more marvelous in hell
Than ever on earth. But it cannot help you.

[*Music.*]

Orpheus. Look at your wife, Pluto. Look at Persephone,
your queen.   220

[*Music.*]

Pluto. Her face is opening.
Orpheus. A wife for a wife, Pluto. Shall I continue to
play?
Pluto. Keep playing. Keep playing.

[*Music stops.*]

Keep playing. Why have you stopped?   225
Orpheus. It is in my power to release the flower
In your wife's face and awake her. Release my wife.
Pluto. Play.
Orpheus. A wife for a wife.
Pluto. Whatever you wish. Only play. You can have your 230
wife.

[*Music.*]

Beautiful as the day I plucked her off the earth!

[*Music stops.*]

Orpheus. You have your wife, Pluto.
Persephone. Keep your promise to Orpheus. Give him his
wife.   235
Pluto. I cannot.
Orpheus. Cannot? A god cannot break his promise. A
god's promise is stronger than the god.
Pluto. I cannot. Your wife's body is crumbling to dust.
Persephone. Give him her soul.   240
Pluto. I can only give you her soul.
Orpheus. Let it be so. Let my wife's soul come with me.

[*Light effects. Dance and mime through what follows.*]

Pluto. You who have awakened the queen of hell,
　　Return to the world. Your wife's soul will be with
　　　you.

[Orpheus' *new music very soft.*]

Narrator. Orpheus returns to the earth. It is not far. It is
　　only a step.　　　　　　　　　　　　　　　　245
　A step, a step, and a step,
　A step — and he turns. He looks for his wife. The air is
　　empty.

[*Music stops.*]

Orpheus.　Eurydice?
Eurydice. I am here.
Orpheus. Eurydice, where are you? Eurydice?　　　250
Eurydice. Here at your side, Orpheus.
Narrator. He cannot see her. He cannot touch her. He can
　　only hear her. He listens.
Eurydice. Play for me, Orpheus.

[Orpheus *plays his new music.*]

Narrator. Orpheus' friends come running. They listen to　255
　　his music. It is no longer the same music.
Friend One. This won't make anybody dance.
Friend Two. This is queer music. He's gone to the dogs.
　　This is dreary.
Friend Three. Play as you used to play, Orpheus. Make us　260
　　dance.

[*Music continues.*]

Narrator. The trees did not dance. But the trees listened.
　The music was not the music of dancing
　But of growing and withering,
　Of the root in the earth and the leaf in the light,　　265
　The music of birth and of death.
　And the stones did not dance. But the stones listened.
　The music was not the music of happiness

But of everlasting, and the wearing away of the hills,
The music of the stillness of stones, 270
Of stones under frost, and stones under rain, and stones
  in the sun,
The music of the seabed drinking at the stones of the
  hills.
The music of the floating weight of the earth.
And the bears in their forest holes
Heard the music of bears in their forest holes, 275
The music of bones in the starlight,
The music of many a valley trodden by bears,
The music of bears listening on the earth for bears.
And the deer on the high hills heard the crying of
  wolves,
And the salmon in the deep pools heard the whisper of
  the snows, 280
And the traveler on the road
Heard the music of love coming and love going
And love lost forever,
The music of birth and of death.
The music of the earth, swaddled in heaven, kissed by
  its cloud and watched by its ray. 285
And the ears that heard it were also of leaf and of stone.
The faces that listened were flesh of cliff and of river.
The hands that played it were fingers of snakes and a
  tangle of flowers.

FOR STUDY AND DISCUSSION

1. At the opening of the play, the Narrator says that Orpheus is a magician. What magic does he perform with his music?

2. Orpheus' music reflects his feelings throughout the play. At the beginning of the play, Orpheus is happy and so is his music. What kind of music does Orpheus play when he decides to pursue Eurydice to the underworld? What does this music reveal about his feelings?

3. What two things does Orpheus offer Pluto in exchange for Eurydice? In what form does Eurydice return with Orpheus?

4. In the last speech of the play, the Narrator describes the new kind of music that Orpheus is playing. Explain how the new music differs from the old.

FOR COMPOSITION

Creating Background in a Play

1. Suppose you were the technician assigned to producing the sound effects for *Orpheus*. Tell what equipment you would need and how you would create the right atmosphere for the play.

2. If you were writing a radio script for one of these settings, what sound effects would you need to create a realistic background?

a jungle safari
rush hour on the freeway
noon in the school cafeteria

ABOUT THE AUTHOR

Ted Hughes (1930–   ) is widely regarded as one of the outstanding poets of his generation. He was born in a quiet town in Yorkshire, England. From an early age he had a strong feeling for nature. He loved to roam the moors and farms, under the shadow of a great cliff called Scout Rock. Before entering Cambridge University, he served two years in the Royal Air Force as a ground wireless operator. During that time, he says, he had "nothing to do but read and reread Shakespeare and watch the grass grow."

Hughes has produced several collections of poetry, including *The Hawk in the Rain, The Earth-Owl and Other Moon-People,* and *Crow.* He has also written books for children. Among them are *How the Whale Became, The Iron, Giant,* and *Poetry Is.* The play *Orpheus* was originally written for radio.

Practice in
Reading and Writing

DRAMA

Reading Drama

A play, or a drama, is a story that is supposed to be performed in front of an audience. All three ingredients — story,
performance, and audience — are essential elements. There
must be a story, or no one will bother to sit quietly for any
length of time; the story must be performed by actors, or
puppets, or moving pictures of actors, otherwise we are simply in the realm of fiction, not drama; and finally, we, as
readers or playgoers, must have the sense of being part of an
audience, part of a group experiencing the play together and
simultaneously, or else one of the great aspects and effects of
drama is lost.

We must always remember that drama is intended to be performed. A play may seem, in its printed form, to be merely a
number of people saying a number of words. To see it staged,
to see these people come alive and move on the stage, to
hear their pauses as well as their words, is to experience
drama. When we read plays, we should try to stage them as
much as possible in our own minds. Our imaginations must
create the theater for us, cast the characters, design their
costumes and the scenery. The more the visual side, this
theatricality, comes alive for us, the more we will appreciate
the play.

Here are some points to consider about the plays you have
studied in this unit:

1. *A playwright usually provides the audience with essential background early in the play. The characters are identified and the situation clarified during the* exposition *of the play. How does Chekhov make his exposition develop naturally out of the dialogue in* A Marriage Proposal?

2. *The* climax *of a play is the point of greatest excitement or tension. Which scene would you say is the climax of* Visit to a Small Planet? *Tell why.*

3. *A play normally ends with the resolution of a conflict. In classical drama, a resolution was often provided by the intervention of a god, who was brought in by stage machinery. Such a figure was known as a* deus ex machina *(god from a machine). In what way is* Visit to a Small Planet *resolved by a* deus ex machina?

4. *A playwright makes effective use of* props *and* costumes *to underscore the meaning of dialogue and action. What props and costumes does Vidal make use of? How do they emphasize important aspects of his play?*

5. *Sound effects can be as important as dialogue in a play. How does Hughes make use of sound effects in* Orpheus *to emphasize the mythical nature of his play?*

Writing a Play

Try your hand at a farce. Remember that farce depends on some ludicrous or improbable situation and exaggeration of character and action. Consider these possibilities:

The central character is mistaken for someone else and is unable to establish his or her identity.

An English-speaking traveler on vacation abroad tries to order a meal in a restaurant but does not speak the language.

The central character has made two dates for the same evening and is unable to get out of either commitment.

Choose a story from myth, legend, or folklore for dramatization. You may give the story a contemporary setting with modern-day characters if you wish. If you know the myth of Hercules and his twelve labors, you might create modern equivalents for the Nemean Lion, the Hydra, the bull of Minos, and so on.

Write a pilot for a new science fiction series for television. If you wish, design the costumes for your characters and the sets for your teleplay.

Romeo and Juliet

Romeo and Juliet is probably the most popular romantic tragedy in the English-speaking world. It has had a long and successful stage history (nearly four hundred years), and in our own time has been produced on film and on television as well as on stage. So powerful is Shakespeare's concept of the "star-crossed lovers" that his tragedy has inspired composers, artists, and choreographers to create original works based on the play.

Shakespeare did not invent the story of Romeo and Juliet. It was already well known and popular when he came to write the play sometime around 1594. But in Shakespeare's hands the narrative was skillfully transformed into a magnificent poetic drama, the most lyrical of the tragedies Shakespeare was to write.

A scene from Franco Zeffirelli's film production of *Romeo and Juliet.*
Culver Pictures, Inc.

*The Chandos Portrait of
Shakespeare.* Anonymous oil
painting.
National Portrait Gallery, London

Shakespeare's Life

Comparatively little is known about Shakespeare's early life.
He was born in 1564 in Stratford-on-Avon, a small English
town in Warwickshire. He married Anne Hathaway when he
was eighteen and she twenty-six. The couple had three children.

Sometime in his twenties Shakespeare went to London and
became involved in the theater, acting in and writing plays. In
1594 he became a shareholder in a company of actors called
the Lord Chamberlain's Men. Shakespeare wrote *Romeo and
Juliet* for this company. When James became King of England
in 1603, he renamed the Chamberlain's Men the "King's
Men." About 1610 Shakespeare retired to Stratford-on-Avon,
where he died on April 23, 1616.

The White Hart Inn. Anonymous print.
Folger Shakespeare Library, Washington, D.C.

The interior of a private theater, frontispiece from *The Wits,* a 17th-century collection of skits. Falstaff, shown here in the foreground, was one of Shakespeare's most popular characters.
The Folger Shakespeare Library, Washington, D.C.

Shakespeare's Theater

In Shakespeare's day London had several theaters, all well attended. Competition among rival theaters was keen. Because literary property was not protected by law, it was common for popular plays to be pirated.

The sixteenth-century theater resembled the open courtyard of an inn. There was no roof. The stage was a large platform without a curtain or stage setting. At the back of the stage were two large doors. In the center of the platform was a recess or inner stage, which was usually concealed by a curtain. In *Romeo and Juliet* this inner stage could serve as Friar Laurence's cell or Juliet's tomb. Above the recess was a balcony. In *Romeo and Juliet* it would serve for the garden scene.

Since there was no front curtain, the actors had to make their entrances and exits in full view of the audience. There was no scenery and no artificial lighting. Plays were held in the afternoon. In order to create atmosphere, playwrights and actors had to rely on words and actions. In the great balcony scene in *Romeo and Juliet,* the feeling of a moonlit night is evoked by the language. The lack of elaborate equipment had other advantages. Because no scenery had to be changed, the action of the play could flow more quickly.

There were no actresses in Shakespeare's day. The young women's parts were played by boys. There were usually about fifteen full members in a company of players, who shared in the profits of their performances. In such a small company, certain roles became specialized, and playwrights frequently wrote parts tailored to the talents of their star actors.

The audience was made up of individuals from every walk of life. Few members of the audience could afford to buy seats. Most spectators stood in the yard around the platform stage. They were known as groundlings. The well-to-do customers sat in covered galleries around the stage.

The audience demanded action and excitement. They liked their action gory. The majority of people could not read, but they loved the music of good language. They responded to the dignity and grandeur of poetry, and they liked puns and word games. Shakespeare was able to satisfy the many different tastes of his audience. In *Romeo and Juliet* he included vigorous action, boisterous humor, and splendid poetry.

Model of Globe Theater by John Cranford Adams.
Folger Shakespeare Library, Washington, D.C.
Courtesy, John Cranford Adams

Romeo and Juliet

Characters

The Montagues

Lord Montague
Lady Montague
Romeo, son of Montague
Benvolio, nephew of Montague
   and friend of Romeo
Balthasar, servant of Romeo
Abraham, servant of Montague

The Capulets

Lord Capulet
Lady Capulet
Juliet, daughter of Capulet
Tybalt, nephew of Lady Capulet
Nurse to Juliet
Peter, servant of the Nurse
Sampson ⎫
Gregory ⎭ servants of Capulet
An Old Man of the Capulet family

Prince Escalus, ruler of Verona
Mercutio, kinsman of the Prince and friend of Romeo
Friar Laurence, a Franciscan priest
Friar John, another Franciscan priest
Count Paris, a young nobleman, kinsman of the Prince
Apothecary
Page to Paris
Chief Watchman
Three Musicians
An Officer

Citizens of Verona, Kinsfolk of both houses, Maskers, Guards, Watchmen, and Attendants

The Time: The fourteenth century
The Place: Verona; Mantua, in northern Italy

Prologue

[*From the back of the stage the* Chorus° *enters to introduce and explain the theme of the play.*

Chorus. Two households, both alike in dignity,°
    In fair Verona, where we lay our scene,
  From ancient grudge break to new mutiny,°
    Where civil blood makes civil hands unclean.
  From forth the fatal loins of these two foes   5
    A pair of star-crossed° lovers take their life,
  Whose misadventured piteous overthrows
    Do with their death bury their parents' strife.
  The fearful passage of their death-marked love,
    And the continuance of their parents' rage,   10
  Which, but their children's end, naught could remove,
    Is now the two hours' traffic° of our stage;
  The which if you with patient ears attend,
  What here shall miss, our toil shall strive to mend.°

Act One

Scene 1

[*Verona. A public place. Enter* Sampson *and* Gregory, *of the House of Capulet, with swords and bucklers.*°]

Sampson. Gregory, on my word, we'll not carry coals.° ~~put up with insults~~
Gregory. No, for then we should be colliers.° ~~(coal-dealers)~~
Sampson. I mean, an° we be in choler,° we'll draw.
Gregory. Aye, while you live, draw your neck out o' the collar.° ~~save yourself~~
Sampson. I strike quickly, being moved.   5
Gregory. But thou art not quickly moved to strike.
Sampson. A dog of the house of Montague moves me. ~~a Montague angers me~~
Gregory. To move is to stir, and to be valiant is to stand. Therefore if thou are moved, thou
    runn'st away.
Sampson. A dog of that house shall move me to stand.   10
Gregory. The quarrel is between our masters and us their men.
Sampson. 'Tis all one, I will show myself a tyrant.
Gregory. Draw thy tool. Here comes two of the house of Montagues.

Prologue. Chorus: an actor who addresses the audience directly and comments on the action. 1. **dignity:** rank.
3. **mutiny:** riot. 6. **star-crossed:** doomed by unlucky stars. 12. **traffic:** business. 14. **mend:** make clearer.
    S.D. (The abbreviation S.D. stands for *stage direction.*) **bucklers:** small shields. 1. **carry coals:** put up with insults.
2. **colliers:** coal-dealers. 3. **an:** if. **choler:** anger. 4. **collar:** hangman's noose. The characters are punning on the
words *collier, choler,* and *collar.* For a discussion of puns, see page 477.

[Enter Abraham and Balthasar, servants of Montague.]

Sampson. My naked weapon is out. Quarrel—I will back thee.

Gregory. How! Turn thy back and run? 15

Sampson. Fear me not.

Gregory. No, marry,° I fear thee!

Sampson. Let us take the law of our sides.° Let them begin.

Gregory. I will frown as I pass by, and let them take it as they list.°

Sampson. Nay, as they dare. I will bite my thumb° at them, which is a disgrace to them, if 20
they bear it.

Abraham. Do you bite your thumb at us, sir?

Sampson. I do bite my thumb, sir.

Abraham. Do you bite your thumb at us, sir?

Sampson. *[Aside to Gregory]* Is the law of our side, if I say aye? 25

Gregory. No.

Sampson. No, sir, I do not bite my thumb at you, sir; but I bite my thumb, sir.

Gregory. Do you quarrel, sir?

Abraham. Quarrel, sir! No, sir.

Sampson. But if you do, sir, I am for you. I serve as good a man as you. 30

Abraham. No better.

Sampson. Well, sir.

[Enter Benvolio, nephew of Montague.]

Gregory. *[Aside to Sampson]* Say "Better." Here comes one of my master's kinsmen.

Sampson. Yes, better, sir.

Abraham. You lie. 35

Sampson. Draw, if you be men. Gregory, remember thy swashing° blow.

[They fight.]

Benvolio. Part, fools *[Beating down their weapons.]* Put up your swords. You know not
what you do.

[Enter Tybalt, hot-tempered nephew of Lady Capulet, with sword drawn.]

Tybalt. What, art thou drawn among these heartless hinds?°
Turn thee, Benvolio, look upon thy death. 40

Benvolio. I do but keep the peace. Put up thy sword,
Or manage it to part these men with me.

---

17. **marry:** by the Virgin Mary.   18. **take . . . sides:** be legally in the right.   19. **list:** please.   20. **bite my thumb:** an
insulting gesture.   36. **swashing:** slashing.   39. **heartless hinds:** cowardly servants.

Tybalt. What, drawn, and talk of peace! I hate the word
    As I hate Hell, all Montagues, and thee.
    Have at thee, coward! 45

                    [*They fight.*]

[*Enter several of both houses, who join the fray; then enter* Citizens *and* Peace Officers, *with clubs.*]

First Officer. Clubs, bills, and partisans!° Strike! Beat them down!
    Down with the Capulets! Down with the Montagues!

            [*Enter old* Capulet *in his gown, and* Lady Capulet.]

Capulet. What noise is this? Give me my long sword, ho!
Lady Capulet. A crutch, a crutch! Why call you for a sword?
Capulet. My sword, I say! Old Montague is come, 50
    And flourishes his blade in spite of° me.

           [*Enter old* Montague *and* Lady Montague.]

---

46. **bills . . . partisans:** different kinds of spears.   51. **in spite of:** to spite.

Montague. Thou villain Capulet!—Hold me not, let me go.

Lady Montague. Thou shalt not stir one foot to seek a foe.

[*Enter* Prince Escalus, *with* Attendants. *At first no one hears him.*]

Prince. Rebellious subjects, enemies to peace,
    Profaners of this neighbor-stainèd steel°—   55
    Will they not hear? What ho! You men, you beasts,
    That quench the fire of your pernicious rage
    With purple fountains issuing from your veins,
    On pain of torture, from those bloody hands
    Throw your mistempered° weapons to the ground,   60
    And hear the sentence of your movèd prince.
    Three civil brawls, bred of an airy° word,
    By thee, old Capulet and Montague,
    Have thrice disturbed the quiet of our streets,
    And made Verona's ancient citizens   65
    Cast by their grave beseeming ornaments°
    To wield old partisans, in hands as old,
    Cankered with peace, to part your cankered° hate.
    If ever you disturb our streets again,
    Your lives shall pay the forfeit of the peace.   70
    For this time, all the rest depart away.
    You, Capulet, shall go alone with me,
    And, Montague, come you this afternoon,
    To know our further pleasure in this case,
    To old Freetown, our common judgment place.   75
    Once more, on pain of death, all men depart.

[*Exeunt°* all but Montague, Lady Montague, *and* Benvolio.]

Montague. Who set this ancient quarrel new abroach°
    Speak, Nephew, were you by when it began?

Benvolio. Here were the servants of your adversary
    And yours close fighting ere I did approach.   80
    I drew to part them. In the instant came
    The fiery Tybalt, with his sword prepared,
    Which as he breathed defiance to my ears,
    He swung about his head and cut the winds,
    Who, nothing hurt withal,° hissed him in scorn.   85
    While we were interchanging thrusts and blows,

---

55. **neighbor-stainèd steel:** swords stained with the blood of neighbors. 60. **mistempered:** ill-made and ill-used. 62. **airy:** light. 66. **grave . . . ornaments:** dignified ornaments of peace, suitable to aged citizens. 68. **cankered:** rusted, corroded. S.D. **Exeunt:** plural form of *Exit.* 77. **abroach:** afoot, astir. 85. **withal:** by this.

Came more and more, and fought on part and part
Till the Prince came, who parted either part.

Lady Montague. Oh, where is Romeo? Saw you him today?
Right glad I am he was not at this fray.   90

Benvolio. Madam, an hour before the worshiped sun
Peered forth the golden window of the east,
A troubled mind drave me to walk abroad,
Where, underneath the grove of sycamore
That westward rooteth from the city's side,   95
So early walking did I see your son.
Towards him I made; but he was ware° of me,
And stole into the covert° of the wood.
I, measuring his affections by my own,
That most are busied when they're most alone,   100
Being one too many by my weary self,
Pursued my humor,° not pursuing his,
And gladly shunned who gladly fled from me.

Montague. Many a morning hath he there been seen,
With tears augmenting the fresh morning's dew,   105
Adding to clouds more clouds with his deep sighs.
But all so soon as the all-cheering sun
Should in the farthest east begin to draw
The shady curtains from Aurora's° bed,
Away from light steals home my heavy° son,   110
And private in his chamber pens himself,
Shuts up his windows, locks fair daylight out,
And makes himself an artificial night.
Black and portentous must this humor prove.
Unless good counsel may the cause remove.   115

Benvolio. My noble uncle, do you know the cause?

Montague. I neither know it nor can learn of him.

Benvolio. Have you impórtuned° him by any means?

Montague. Both by myself and many other friends.
But he, his own affections' counselor,   120
Is to himself—I will not say how true—
But to himself so secret and so close,
So far from sounding and discovery,
As is the bud bit with an envious° worm
Ere he can spread his sweet leaves to the air,   125
Or dedicate his beauty to the sun.

---

97. **ware:** aware. 98. **covert:** covering. 102. **humor:** mood. 109. **Aurora:** goddess of the dawn. 110. **heavy:** melancholy. 118. **impórtuned:** asked insistently. 124. **envious:** hateful.

Could we but learn from whence his sorrows grow,
We would as willingly give cure as know.

[*Enter* Romeo *in a melancholy mood.*]

Benvolio. See where he comes. So please you, step aside.
    I'll know his grievance, or be much denied.   130
Montague. I would thou wert so happy° by thy stay
    To hear true shrift.° Come, madam, let's away.

                                    [*Exeunt* Montague *and* Lady.]

Benvolio. Good morrow,° Cousin.
Romeo.   Is the day so young?
Benvolio. But new struck nine.
Romeo.   Aye me, sad hours seem long!   135
    Was that my father that went hence so fast?
Benvolio. It was. What sadness lengthens Romeo's hours?
Romeo. Not having that which, having, makes them short.
Benvolio. In love?
Romeo. Out—
Benvolio. Of love?   140
Romeo. Out of her favor where I am in love.
Benvolio. Alas that love,° so gentle in his view,°
    Should be so tyrannous and rough in proof!
Romeo. Alas that love, whose view is muffled still,°
    Should without eyes see pathways to his will!   145
    Where shall we dine? Oh me! What fray was here?
    Yet tell me not, for I have heard it all.
    Here's much to do with hate, but more with love.
    Why then, O brawling love! O loving hate!
    O heavy lightness! Serious vanity!   150
    Misshapen chaos of well-seeming forms!
    Feather of lead, bright smoke, cold fire, sick health!
    Still-waking sleep, that is not what it is!
    This love feel I, that feel no love in this.
    Dost thou not laugh?
Benvolio.   No, Coz,° I rather weep.   155
Romeo. Good heart, at what?
Benvolio.   At thy good heart's oppression.
Romeo. Why, such is love's transgression.

---

131. **happy:** fortunate. 132. **shrift:** confession. 133. **Good morrow:** Good morning. "Cousin" is a name used for
any relative. 142. **love:** here, Cupid, god of love. **view:** appearance. 144. **muffled still:** always blindfolded. 155. **Coz:** cousin.

Griefs of mine own lie heavy in my breast,
Which thou wilt propagate,° to have it pressed°
With more of thine. This love that thou has shown
Doth add more grief to too much of mine own.
Love is a smoke raised with the fume of sighs;
Being purged, a fire sparkling in lovers' eyes;
Being vexed, a sea nourished with lovers' tears.
What is it else? A madness most discreet,   165
A choking gall and a preserving sweet.
Farewell, my coz.

Benvolio.   Soft!° I will go along.
And if you leave me so, you do me wrong.

Romeo. Tut, I have lost myself, I am not here.
This is not Romeo, he's some other where.   170

Benvolio. Tell me in sadness,° who is that you love?

Romeo. What, shall I groan and tell thee?

Benvolio.   Groan! Why, no,
But sadly tell me who.

Romeo. Bid a sick man in sadness make his will.
Ah, word ill urged to one that is so ill!   175
In sadness, Cousin, I do love a woman.

Benvolio. I aimed so near when I supposed you loved.

Romeo. A right good mark-man! And she's fair I love.

Benvolio. A right fair mark, fair Coz, is soonest hit.

Romeo. Well, in that hit you miss. She'll not be hit   180
With Cupid's arrow. She hath Dian's° wit,
And in strong proof° of chastity well armed,
From love's weak childish bow she lives unharmed.
She will not stay the siege of loving terms,
Nor bide the encounter of assailing eyes,   185
Nor ope her lap to saint-seducing gold.
Oh, she is rich in beauty, only poor
That when she dies, with beauty dies her store.°
She hath forsworn° to love, and in that vow
Do I live dead, that live to tell it now.   190

Benvolio. Be ruled by me, forget to think of her.

Romeo. Oh, teach me how I should forget to think.

Benvolio. By giving liberty unto thine eyes
Examine other beauties.

---

159. **propagate** (prŏp′ə-gāt′): increase. **pressed:** burdened. 167. **Soft:** an exclamation meaning "Wait." 171. **sadness:** seriousness. 181. **Dian:** Diana was the Roman goddess of chastity, hunting, and the moon. 182. **proof:** armor; power. 188. **with . . . store:** She will leave no children to pass on her beauty. 189. **forsworn to:** sworn not to.

Romeo.   'Tis the way

    To call hers exquisite, in question more.°   195

    These happy masks° that kiss fair ladies' brows,

    Being black, put us in mind they hide the fair.

    He that is stricken blind cannot forget

    The precious treasure of his eyesight lost.

    Show me a mistress that is passing° fair,   200

    What doth her beauty serve but as a note

    Where I may read who passed that passing fair?°

    Farewell. Thou canst not teach me to forget.

Benvolio. I'll pay that doctrine,° or else die in debt.

                                                  [Exeunt.]

Scene 2

    [*A street. Enter* Capulet *with* Paris, *a kinsman of the* Prince, *and* Servant.]

Capulet. But Montague is bound° as well as I,

    In penalty alike, and 'tis not hard, I think,

    For men so old as we to keep the peace.

Paris. Of honorable reckoning° are you both,

    And pity 'tis you lived at odds so long.   5

    But now, my lord, what say you to my suit?

Capulet. But saying o'er what I have said before.

    My child is yet a stranger in the world—

    She hath not seen the change of fourteen years.

    Let two more summers wither in their pride   10

    Ere we may think her ripe to be a bride.

Paris. Younger than she are happy mothers made.

Capulet. And too soon marred are those so early made.

    The earth hath swallowed all my hopes but she,

    She is the hopeful lady of my earth.°   15

    But woo her, gentle Paris, get her heart.

    My will to her consent is but a part;

    An° she agree, within her scope° of choice

    Lies my consent and fair according° voice.

    This night I hold an old accustomed feast,   20

    Whereto I have invited many a guest

---

195. **in question more:** by comparing her beauty more with others.   196. **masks:** Elizabethan women wore masks to protect their faces from the sun. 200. **passing:** very. 202. **passed . . . fair:** surpassed those who are very pretty.   204. **pay that doctrine:** pay for that teaching.

    1. **bound:** pledged to keep the peace. 4. **reckoning:** reputation. 15. **earth:** body, "flesh and blood." 18. **An:** if. **scope:** range. 19. **according:** agreeing.

Such as I love, and you among the store,
One more, most welcome, makes my number more.
At my poor house look to behold this night
Earth-treading stars that make dark heaven light.   25
Such comfort as do lusty young men feel
When well-appareled April on the heel
Of limping winter treads, even such delight
Among fresh female buds shall you this night
Inherit° at my house. Hear all, all see,   30
And like her most whose merit most shall be.
Which on more view, of many mine, being one,
May stand in number, though in reckoning none.°
Come, go with me. [*To* Servant, *giving a paper*] Go, sirrah,° trudge about
Through fair Verona. Find those persons out   35
Whose names are written there, and to them say
My house and welcome on their pleasure stay.

                           [*Exeunt* Capulet *and* Paris.]

Servant. [*Who cannot read*] Find them out whose names are written here! It is written
that the shoemaker should meddle with his yard° and the tailor with his last, the
fisher with his pencil and the painter with his nets; but I am sent to find those per-   40
sons whose names are here writ, and can never find what names the writing person
hath here writ. I must to the learned. In good time.°

                      [*Enter* Benvolio *and* Romeo.]

Benvolio. Tut, man, one fire burns out another's burning,
    One pain is lessened by another's anguish.
Turn giddy, and be holp° by backward turning,   45
    One desperate grief cures with another's languish.
Take thou some new infection to thy eye,
And the rank poison of the old will die.
Romeo. Your plantain° leaf is excellent for that.
Benvolio. For what, I pray thee?
Romeo.   For your broken° shin.   50
Benvolio. Why, Romeo, art thou mad?
Romeo. Not mad, but bound more than a madman is,
    Shut up in prison, kept without my food,
    Whipped and tormented and —— Godden,° good fellow,

---

30. **Inherit:** have. 33. **reckoning none:** not worth considering. 34. **sirrah:** a term used in addressing servants.
39. **yard:** measure. The servant mixes his metaphors. He means that people ought to stick to what they can do
best. 42. **In good time:** What luck! Just in time! 45. **holp:** helped. 49. **plantain:** a weed used to stop bleeding. 50. **broken:** scratched. 54. **Godden:** good evening, a greeting used in the afternoon.

Servant. God gi' godden. I pray, sir, can you read?   55

Romeo. Aye, mine own fortune in my misery.

Servant. Perhaps you have learned it without a book, but I pray, can you read anything you see?

Romeo. Aye, if I know the letters and the language.

Servant. Ye say honestly. Rest you merry!°   60

Romeo. Stay, fellow, I can read. [*Reads.*]

> "Signior Martino and his wife and daughters; County° Anselme and his beauteous
> sisters; the lady widow of Vitruvio; Signior Placentio and his lovely nieces; Mercu-
> tio and his brother Valentine; mine uncle Capulet, his wife and daughters; my fair
> niece Rosaline; Livia; Signior Valentio and his cousin Tybalt; Lucio and the lively   65
> Helena."

A fair assembly. Whither should they come?

Servant. Up.

Romeo. Whither?

Servant. To supper, to our house.   70

Romeo. Whose house?

Servant. My master's.

Romeo. Indeed I should have asked you that before.

Servant. Now I'll tell you without asking. My master is the great rich Capulet, and if you
be not of the House of Montagues, I pray come and crush° a cup of wine. Rest you   75
merry!

                                                                           [*Exit.*]

Benvolio. At this same ancient° feast of Capulet's
Sups the fair Rosaline whom thou so lovest,
Go thither, and with unattainted° eye
Compare her face with some that I shall show,   80
And I will make thee think thy swan a crow.

Romeo. One fairer than my love! The all-seeing sun
Ne'er saw her match since first the world begun.

Benvolio. Tut, you saw her fair, none else being by,
Herself poised° with herself in either eye.   85
But in that crystal scales° let there be weighed
Your lady's love against some other maid
That I will show you shining at this feast,
And she shall scant° show well that now seems best.

Romeo. I'll go along, no such sight to be shown,   90
But to rejoice in splendor of mine own.   [*Exeunt.*]

---

60. **Rest you merry:** God keep you merry. 62. **County:** Count. 75. **crush:** drink. 77. **ancient:** that is, established
by tradition. 79. **unattainted:** unprejudiced. 85. **poised:** balanced. 86. **crystal scales:** Romeo's eyes. 89. **scant:**
scarcely, hardly.

Scene 3

[*A room in* Capulet's *house. Enter* Lady Capulet *and* Nurse.]

Lady Capulet. Nurse, where's my daughter? Call her forth to me.
Nurse. I bade her come. What, lamb! What, ladybird!° —
    Where's this girl? What, Juliet!

[*Enter* Juliet.]

Juliet. How now! Who calls?
Nurse. Your mother.   5
Juliet. Madam, I am here. What is your will?
Lady Capulet. This is the matter. Nurse, give leave° awhile,
    We must talk in secret — Nurse, come back again,
    I have remembered me, thou'st° hear our counsel.
    Thou know'st my daughter's of a pretty age.   10
Nurse. Faith, I can tell her age unto an hour.

---

2. **ladybird:** a small insect with bright red spots; a pretty little thing.   7. **give leave:** leave us alone.   9. **thou'st:** thou shalt.

Lady Capulet. She's not fourteen.

Nurse.   I'll lay fourteen of my teeth—
And yet, to my teen° be it spoken, I have but four—
She is not fourteen. How long is it now
To Lammastide?°

Lady Capulet.   A fortnight and odd days.   15

Nurse. Even or odd, of all days in the year,
Come Lammas Eve at night shall she be fourteen,
Susan and she—God rest all Christian souls!—
Were of an age. Well, Susan is with God.
She was too good for me.—But, as I said,   20
On Lammas Eve at night shall she be fourteen.
That shall she, marry, I remember it well.
'Tis since the earthquake now eleven years,°
And she was weaned—I never shall forget it—
Of all the days of the year, upon that day.   25
My lord and you were then at Mantua.—
For then she could stand high-lone°—nay, by the rood,°
She could have run and waddled all about,
For even the day before, she broke° her brow,
And then my husband—God be with his soul!   30
A'° was a merry man—took up the child.
"Yea," quoth he, "dost thou fall upon thy face?

Lady Capulet. Enough of this. I pray thee hold thy peace.

Nurse. Peace, I have done. God mark° thee to His grace!
Thou wast the prettiest babe that e'er I nursed.   35
An I might live to see thee married once,
I have my wish.

Lady Capulet. Marry,° that "marry" is the very theme
I came to talk of. Tell me, daughter Juliet,
How stands your disposition to be married?   40

Juliet. It is an honor that I dream not of.

Lady Capulet. Well, think of marriage now. Younger than you
Here in Verona, ladies of esteem,
Are made already mothers. By my count,
I was your mother much upon these years°   45
That you are now a maid. Thus then in brief—
The valiant Paris seeks you for his love.

---

13. **teen:** sorrow.   15. **Lammastide:** a church festival celebrated August 1.   23. **'Tis . . . years:** An earthquake occurred in England in 1580.   27. **high-lone:** unaided.   **rood:** cross, crucifix.   29. **broke:** cut, broke the skin of.   31. **A':** he.   34. **mark:** select, choose.   38. **Marry:** indeed.   45. **much upon these years:** at much the same age.

Nurse. A man, young lady! Lady, such a man
As all the world—Why, he's a man of wax.°
Lady Capulet. Verona's summer hath not such a flower. 50
Nurse. Nay, he's a flower, in faith, a very flower.
Lady Capulet. What say you? Can you love the gentleman?
This night you shall behold him at our feast.
Read o'er the volume° of young Paris' face,
And find delight writ there with beauty's pen. 55
Examine every married lineament,°
And see how one another lends content,
And what obscured in this fair volume lies
Find written in the margent° of his eyes.
This precious book of love, this unbound lover, 60
To beautify him, only lacks a cover.
That book in many's eyes doth share the glory
That in gold clasps locks in the golden story.
So shall you share all that he doth possess,
By having him making yourself no less. 65
Speak briefly. Can you like of Paris' love?
Juliet. I'll look to like, if looking liking move.°
But no more deep will I endart mine eye
Than your consent° gives strength to make it fly.

[*Enter a* Servingman.]

Servant. Madam, the guests are come, supper served up, you called, my young lady asked 70
for, the nurse cursed in the pantry, and everything in extremity.° I must hence to wait.
I beseech you, follow straight.°
Lady Capulet. We follow thee. [*Exit* Servingman.]
Juliet, the County stays.°

[*Exeunt.*]

Scene 4

[*A street. Enter* Romeo, Mercutio, Benvolio, *with five or six other* Maskers, *and* Torch-
bearers *on their way to* Capulet's *house.*]

Romeo. Give me a torch. I am not for this ambling.°
Being but heavy,° I will bear the light

---

49. **man of wax:** perfect, like a wax model.   54–63. **volume . . . story:** In these lines, Shakespeare compares Paris to a
book.   56. **married lineament:** perfectly united part.   59. **margent:** margin.   67. **move:** arouse.   69. **consent:**
approval.   71. **extremity:** confusion.   72. **straight:** right away, at once.   74. **stays:** waits for you.
   1. **ambling:** mincing.   2. **heavy:** sad.

Mercutio. Nay, gentle Romeo, we must have you dance.

Romeo. Not I, believe me. You have dancing shoes
    With nimble soles. I have a soul of lead   5
    So stakes me to the ground I cannot move.

Mercutio. You are a lover. Borrow Cupid's wings,
    And soar with them above a common bound.°

Romeo. I am too sore enpiercèd° with his shaft°
    To soar with his light feathers, and so bound,   10
    I cannot bound a pitch° above dull woe.
    Under love's heavy burden do I sink.

Mercutio. And to sink in it, should you burden love,
    Too great oppression for a tender thing.

Romeo. Is love a tender thing? It is too rough,   15
    Too rude, too boisterous, and it pricks like thorn.

Mercutio. If love be rough with you, be rough with love.
    Give me a case to put my visage° in.
    A visor for a visor!° What care I
    What curious eye doth quote° deformities?   20
    Here are the beetle° brows shall blush for me.

Benvolio. Come, knock and enter, and no sooner in
    But every man betake him to his legs.°

Romeo. A torch for me. Let wantons light of heart
    Tickle the senseless rushes° with their heels,   25
    For I am proverbed with a grandsire phrase.°
    I'll be a candleholder,° and look on.
    The game was ne'er so fair, and I am done.°
    I dreamed a dream tonight.

Mercutio.   And so did I.

Romeo. Well, what was yours?

Mercutio.   That dreamers often lie.   30

Romeo. In bed asleep, while they do dream things true.

Mercutio. Oh then, I see Queen Mab° hath been with you.
    She is the fairies' midwife, and she comes
    In shape no bigger than an agate stone°
    On the forefinger of an alderman,   35
    Drawn with a team of little atomies°
    Athwart men's noses as they lie asleep—

---

8. **bound:** leap.   9. **enpiercèd** (pronounced as 3 syllables): pierced, wounded.   **shaft:** arrow.   11. **bound a pitch:** leap in flight.   18. **visage:** face. Mercutio covers his face with a mask.   19. **visor for a visor:** mask for an ugly face.   20. **quote:** note.   21. **beetle:** overhanging.   23. **betake him to his legs:** begin to dance.   25. **rushes:** Floors were covered with rushes, grasslike plants.   26. **grandsire phrase:** old proverb.   27. **candleholder:** onlooker.   28. **The game . . . done:** I am too tired for the game no matter how fair it is.   32. **Queen Mab:** the fairy queen.   34. **agate** (ăg'ĭt) **stone:** large seal ring.   36. **atomies:** tiny creatures.

Her wagon spokes made of long spinners'° legs;
The cover, of the wings of grasshoppers;
Her traces,° of the smallest spider's web;   40
Her collars, of the moonshine's watery beams;
Her whip, of cricket's bone; the lash, of film;°
Her wagoner,° a small gray-coated gnat
Not half so big as a round little worm
Pricked from the lazy finger of a maid.°   45
Her chariot is an empty hazelnut,
Made by the joiner° squirrel or old grub,
Time out o' mind the fairies' coachmakers.
And in this state° she gallops night by night
Through lovers' brains, and then they dream of love; 50
O'er courtiers' knees, that dream on curtseys straight;
O'er lawyers' fingers, who straight dream on fees;
O'er ladies' lips, who straight on kisses dream,
Which oft the angry Mab with blisters plagues
Because their breaths with sweetmeats° tainted are. 55
Sometime she gallops o'er a courtier's nose,
And then dreams he of smelling out a suit.°
And sometime comes she with a tithe pig's° tail
Tickling a parson's nose as a' lies asleep,
Then dreams he of another benefice.°   60
Sometime she driveth o'er a soldier's neck,
And then dreams he of cutting foreign throats,
Of breaches, ambuscadoes,° Spanish blades,
Of healths° five fathom deep; and then anon
Drums in his ear, at which he starts and wakes, 65
And being thus frighted swears a prayer or two,
And sleeps again. This is that very Mab
That plaits the manes of horses in the night,
And bakes the elflocks° in foul sluttish hairs,
Which once untangled much misfortune bodes. 70
This is she——

Romeo.   Peace, peace, Mercutio, peace!
Thou talk'st of nothing.

Mercutio.   True, I talk of dreams,

---

38. **spinners:** spiders. 40. **traces:** harness. 42. **film:** spider's thread. 43. **wagoner:** coachman. 44–45. **worm . . . maid:** In Shakespeare's time, it was a popular superstition that lazy maids grew worms in their fingers. 47. **joiner:** carpenter. 49. **state:** grand style. 55. **sweetmeats:** sweets; candy, cakes. 57. **suit:** a petition for special favor. 58. **tithe** (tīth) **pig:** the parson was often paid in goods, such as a pig, instead of money. 60. **benefice:** church appointment, source of income. 63. **ambuscadoes:** ambushes. 64. **healths:** toasts. 69. **elflocks:** Mischievous fairies were supposed to make knots in horses' manes and to tangle human hair.

Which are the children of an idle brain,
Begot of nothing but vain fantasy,°
Which is as thin of substance as the air   75
And more inconstant than the wind, who woos
Even now the frozen bosom of the North,
And, being angered, puffs away from thence,
Turning his face to the dew-dropping South.
Benvolio. This wind you talk of blows us from ourselves.   80
Supper is done, and we shall come too late.
Romeo. I fear, too early. For my mind misgives°
Some consequence, yet hanging in the stars,
Shall bitterly begin his fearful date°
With this night's revels, and expire the term   85
Of a despisèd life° closed in my breast
By some vile forfeit of untimely death.
But He that hath the steerage of my course
Direct my sail! On, lusty gentlemen.
Benvolio. Strike, drum.   90

[*Exeunt.*]

Scene 5

[*A hall in* Capulet's *house. Musicians waiting. Enter* Servingmen, *with napkins.*]

First Servant. Where's Potpan, that he helps not to take away? He shift a trencher!° He
scrape a trencher!
Second Servant. When good manners shall lie all in one or two men's hands, and they
unwashed too, 'tis a foul thing.
First Servant. Away with the joint stools,° remove the court cupboard,° look to the plate.° 5
Good thou, save me a piece of marchpane.° And, as thou lovest me, let the porter let in
Susan Grindstone and Nell. Antony, and Potpan!
Second Servant. Aye, boy, ready.
First Servant. You are looked for and called for, asked for and sought for, in the great
chamber.°   10
Third Servant. We cannot be here and there too. Cheerly, boys. Be brisk a while, and the
longer liver take all.°

[*They retire behind.*]

---

74. **fantasy:** fancy. 82. **misgives:** fears. 84. **date:** time, period. 85–86. **expire . . . life:** cause the lease of my life to
come to an end.
   1. **trencher:** wooden platter. 5. **joint stools:** stools made by a joiner (carpenter). **cupboard:** sideboard. **plate:** silver
plate. 6. **marchpane:** marzipan, a mixture made of almond paste. 9–10. **great chamber:** used for dining and social occasions. 12. **longer liver take all:** The last survivor takes all.

[*Enter* Capulet, *with* Juliet *and others of his house, meeting the* Guests *and* Maskers.]

Capulet. Welcome, gentlemen! Ladies that have their toes
    Unplagued with corns will have a bout with you.
    Ah ha, my mistresses! Which of you all   15
    Will now deny to dance? She that makes dainty,°
    She, I'll swear, hath corns—am I come near ye now?°
    Welcome, gentlemen! I have seen the day
    That I have worn a visor,° and could tell
    A whispering tale in a fair lady's ear   20
    Such as would please. 'Tis gone, 'tis gone, 'tis gone.
    You are welcome, gentlemen! Come, musicians, play.
    A hall, a hall!° Give room! And foot it, girls. [*Music plays, and they dance.*]
    More light, you knaves, and turn the tables up,
    And quench the fire, the room is grown too hot.   25
    Ah, sirrah, this unlooked-for sport° comes well.
    Nay, sit, nay, sit, good Cousin Capulet,
    For you and I are past our dancing days.
    How long is 't now since last yourself and I
    Were in a mask?

Second Capulet.   By 'r Lady, thirty years.   30

Capulet. What, man! 'Tis not so much, 'tis not so much.
    'Tis since the nuptial of Lucentio,
    Come Pentecost° as quickly as it will,
    Some five and twenty years, and then we masked.

Second Capulet. 'Tis more, 'tis more. His son is elder, sir,   35
    His son is thirty.

Capulet.   Will you tell me that?
    His son was but a ward° two years ago.

[Romeo, *masked and unrecognized, sees* Juliet *and instantly falls in love with her.*]

Romeo. [*To a* Servingman] What lady's that which doth enrich the hand
    Of yonder knight?

Servant. I know not, sir.   40

Romeo. Oh, she doth teach the torches to burn bright!
    It seems she hangs upon the cheek of night
    Like a rich jewel in an Ethiop's ear—
    Beauty too rich for use, for earth too dear!°

---

16. **makes dainty:** pretends to be shy. 17. **come near ye now:** touching a tender spot. 19. **worn a visor:** worn a mask
—that is, has been a dancer. 23. **A hall, a hall:** that is, clear the hall for dancing. 26. **unlooked-for sport:** Capulet had
not expected the maskers. 33. **Pentecost:** the seventh Sunday after Easter. 37. **ward:** a minor in the charge of a guardian. 44. **dear:** precious.

So shows a snowy dove trooping with crows   45
As yonder lady o'er her fellows shows.
The measure° done, I'll watch her place of stand,
And, touching hers, make blessèd my rude hand.
Did my heart love till now? Forswear it, sight!
For I ne'er saw true beauty till this night.   50
Tybalt. This, by his voice, should be a Montague.
Fetch me my rapier, boy. What dares the slave
Come hither, covered with an antic face,°
To fleer° and scorn at our solemnity?°
Now, by the stock and honor of my kin,   55
To strike him dead I hold it not a sin.
Capulet. Why, how now, kinsman! Wherefore storm you so?
Tybalt. Uncle, this is a Montague, our foe,
A villain, that is hither come in spite
To scorn at our solemnity this night.   60
Capulet. Young Romeo, is it?
Tybalt.   'Tis he, that villain Romeo.
Capulet. Content thee, gentle Coz, let him alone,
He bears him like a portly° gentleman,
And, to say truth, Verona brags of him
To be a virtuous and well-governed youth.   65
I would not for the wealth of all this town
Here in my house do him disparagement.°
Therefore be patient, take no note of him.
It is my will, the which if thou respect,
Show a fair presence and put off these frowns,   70
An ill-beseeming semblance° for a feast.
Tybalt. It fits when such a villain is a guest.
I'll not endure him.
Capulet. [*Losing his temper*] He shall be endured.
What, goodman boy° I say he shall. Go to,°
Am I the master here, or you? Go to.   75
You'll make a mutiny among my guests!
Tybalt. Why, Uncle, 'tis a shame.
Capulet.   Go to, go to,
You are a saucy boy. Is't so, indeed?
This trick° may chance to scathe° you, I know what.
You must contrary me! Marry, 'tis time.   80

---

47. **measure:** dance.   53. **antic face:** grotesque mask.   54. **fleer:** sneer.   **solemnity:** celebration.   63. **portly:** dignified.   67. **disparagement** (dĭs-pălʹĭj-mənt): disrespect, insult.   71. **semblance:** appearance.   74. **goodman boy:** an insulting phrase. Goodman is a man under the rank of gentleman. **Go to:** an exclamation showing impatience.   79. **trick:** habit (of quarreling).   **scathe:** injure.

Well said, my hearts! You are a princox,° go.
Be quiet, or—— More light, more light! For shame!
I'll make you quiet. What, cheerly, my hearts!

Tybalt. Patience perforce° with willful choler° meeting
Makes my flesh tremble in their different greeting.   85
I will withdraw. But this intrusion shall,
Now seeming sweet, convert to bitterest gall.

                                                              [*Exit.*]

Romeo. [*To* Juliet] If° I profane with my unworthiest hand
    This holy shrine, the gentle fine° is this,
My lips, two blushing pilgrims, ready stand   90
    To smooth that rough touch with a tender kiss.
Juliet. Good pilgrim, you do wrong your hand too much,
    Which mannerly devotion° shows in this;
For saints have hands that pilgrims' hands do touch,
    And palm to palm is holy palmers'° kiss.   95
Romeo. Have not saints lips, and holy palmers too?
Juliet. Aye, pilgrim, lips that they must use in prayer.
Romeo. Oh then, dear saint, let lips do what hands do.
    They pray. Grant thou, lest faith turn to despair.
Juliet. Saints do not move, though grant for prayers' sake.   100
Romeo. Then move not while my prayer's effect I take.
    Thus from my lips by thine my sin is purged.

                              [*Kissing her.*]

Juliet. Then have my lips the sin that they have took.
Romeo. Sin from my lips? Oh, trespass sweetly urged!°
    Give me my sin again.
Juliet.   You kiss by the book.°   105
Nurse. Madam, your mother craves a word with you.
Romeo. What is her mother?
Nurse.   Marry, bachelor,
    Her mother is the lady of the house,
    And a good lady, and a wise and virtuous.
    I nursed her daughter, that you talked withal.°   110
    I tell you, he that can lay hold of her
    Shall have the chinks.°

---

81. **princox:** conceited boy. 84. **perforce:** forced (on me). **choler** (kŏl'ər): anger. 88–101. **If . . . take:** These fourteen
lines are a Shakespearean sonnet. The dialogue is based on the metaphor that Romeo is a pilgrim and Juliet a
saint. 89. **fine:** punishment. 93. **devotion:** the pilgrim's vow. 95. **palmer:** a pilgrim who carried a palm leaf to show
that he or she had been to the Holy Land. 104. **urged:** argued. 105. **by the book:** according to the book; that is, you
are merely being gallant. 110. **withal:** with. 112. **chinks:** cash.

Romeo.   Is she a Capulet?
  Oh, dear account! My life is my foe's debt.°
Benvolio. Away, be gone. The sport is at the best.
Romeo. Aye, so I fear. The more is my unrest.   115
Capulet. Nay, gentlemen, prepare not to be gone,
  We have a trifling foolish banquet toward.°
  Is it e'en so? Why then, I thank you all,
  I thank you, honest gentlemen. Good night.
  More torches here! Come on, then, let's to bed.   120
  Ah, sirrah, by my fay,° it waxes° late.
  I'll to my rest.

  [*Exeunt all but* Juliet *and* Nurse. *At first* Juliet *hides her feelings for* Romeo.]

Juliet. Come hither, Nurse. What is yond gentleman?
Nurse. The son and heir of old Tiberio.
Juliet. What's he that now is going out of door?   125

---

113. **is my foe's debt:** belongs to my enemy. 117. **toward:** in preparation. 121. **fay:** faith. **waxes:** grows.

Nurse. Marry, that, I think, be young Petruchio.

Juliet. What's he that follows there, that would not dance?

Nurse. I know not.

Juliet. Go ask his name. If he be marrièd,
My grave is like to be my wedding bed.   130

Nurse. His name is Romeo, and a Montague,
The only son of your great enemy.

Juliet. My only love sprung from my only hate!
Too early seen unknown, and known too late!
Prodigious° birth of love it is to me,   135
That I must love a loathèd enemy.

Nurse. What's this? What's this?

Juliet.   A rhyme I learned even now
Of one I danced withal. [*One calls within,* "Juliet."]

Nurse.   Anon, anon!
Come, let's away, the strangers all are gone.

                                                          [*Exeunt.*]

---

135. **Prodigious:** monstrous, unnatural.

FOR STUDY AND DISCUSSION

1. In fourteen lines the Prologue gives the setting and background of the play and prepares the audience for what is to come. Which words in the Prologue point to the influence of fate in the deaths of Romeo and Juliet? What effect will their deaths have on their parents' quarrel?

2. Why do you think Shakespeare never explains how the quarrel between the Montagues and the Capulets began? What does the Prince think has caused "three civil brawls"? How does he intend to punish any future outbreaks of violence?

3. Describe Romeo's mood when he first enters. What has caused him to feel as he does?

4. Paris wishes to marry Juliet. Why is Capulet reluctant to accept the Count's offer?

What do you learn about Capulet's feelings for his daughter?

5. For what reason does Benvolio urge Romeo to attend Capulet's feast? Why does Romeo want to go?

6. How would you characterize Juliet's behavior toward her mother? What is Juliet's feeling about marriage? Do you think her answer (Scene 3, lines 67–69) pleases her mother?

7. What do you learn about the Nurse's character in Scene 3? How does she provide humor in the scene?

8. How does Mercutio attempt to cheer Romeo in Scene 4? Does he really believe in Queen Mab? What is his purpose in describing Queen Mab to Romeo?

9. Reread Tybalt's lines in Scene 1. How is his behavior at Capulet's feast consistent with his behavior in the earlier scene?

10. In Scene 1, Capulet calls for a sword when he sees his enemy Montague. Yet when Tybalt wishes to attack Romeo, Capulet restrains him. Why?

11. The first fourteen lines that Romeo and Juliet speak to each other form a sonnet (see page 405) in which Romeo sees himself as a pilgrim and Juliet as the saint he worships. What does the language show about their feelings for each other?

12. How does Shakespeare keep you aware of the bitter hatred between the Montagues and the Capulets throughout Act One? Which characters do you think will come into conflict in later scenes?

DRAMATIC STRUCTURE: THE FOIL

To examine how a play has been put together, we analyze its *structure*. The most important structural device in *Romeo and Juliet* is *juxtaposition for contrast.* Shakespeare repeatedly places two people or words or actions side by side in order to heighten the differences between them.

A character who serves as a contrast for another character is called a *foil.* Originally, "foil" meant a thin sheet of metal (remember aluminum foil) that was placed under a jewel to make it appear brighter.

In the first scene of the play, Benvolio is a foil for Tybalt. Benvolio attempts to keep the peace but Tybalt insists on fighting. Each character is intensified by the other's presence.

In Scene 3, how does the Nurse serve as a foil for Lady Capulet? In Scene 4, how does Mercutio serve as a foil for Romeo? In Scene 5, Tybalt's discovery of Romeo at the Capulet party almost leads to conflict. This episode is followed by the meeting of Romeo and Juliet. Tell how these sequences make for dramatic contrast.

PERSONIFICATION

Personification is a figure of speech in which an animal, object, or idea is treated as if it were human. Many characters in *Romeo and Juliet* speak of love (an idea) as a person.

> Alas that love, whose view is muffled still,
> Should without eyes see pathways to his will!

Romeo in this speech has in mind the old saying "Love is blind," which really means that those who are in love do not see the faults of those they love. Romeo personifies love, saying it is like a person who can see how to get what he wants even though he is blindfolded.

Explain what is being personified in each of these quotations from Act One:

> In the instant came
> The fiery Tybalt, with his sword prepared,
> Which as he breathed defiance to my ears,
> He swung about his head and cut the winds,
> Who, nothing hurt withal, hissed him in scorn.
>
> (1, 81–85)

> Madam, an hour before the worshiped sun
> Peered forth the golden window of the east,
> A troubled mind drave me to walk abroad. . . .
>
> (1, 91–94)

> Such comfort as do lusty young men feel
> When well-appareled April on the heel
> Of limping winter treads . . .
>
> (2, 26–28)

> One fairer than my love! The all-seeing sun
> Ne'er saw her match since first the world begun.
>
> (2, 83–84)

Act Two

Scene 1

[*A lane by the wall of* Capulet's *orchard. Enter* Romeo, *alone.*]

Romeo. Can I go forward when my heart is here?
　Turn back, dull earth,° and find thy center° out.

[Exit.]

[*Enter* Benvolio *with* Mercutio.]

Benvolio. Romeo! My cousin Romeo!
Mercutio.　　　　　　　　　He is wise,
　And, on my life, hath stol'n him home to bed.
Benvolio. He ran this way, and leaped this orchard wall.　　　　5
　Call, good Mercutio.
Mercutio.　　　　　　　Nay, I'll conjure° too.
　Romeo! Humors! Madman! Passion! Lover!
　Appear thou in the likeness of a sigh.
　Speak but one rhyme, and I am satisfied,
　Cry but "aye me!" pronounce but "love" and "dove."　　　　10
　He heareth not, he stirreth not, he moveth not.
　The ape is dead, and I must conjure him.
　I conjure thee by Rosaline's bright eyes,
　By her high forehead and her scarlet lip,
　That in thy likeness thou appear to us!　　　　15
Benvolio. An if he hear thee, thou wilt anger him.
Mercutio. This cannot anger him. My invocation
　Is fair and honest, and in his mistress' name
　I conjure only but to raise up him.
Benvolio. Come, he hath hid himself among these trees,　　　　20
　To be consorted° with the humorous° night.
　Blind is his love, and best befits the dark.
Mercutio. If love be blind, love cannot hit the mark.
　Romeo, good night. I'll to my truckle bed,°
　This field bed is too cold for me to sleep.　　　　25
　Come, shall we go?
Benvolio.　　　　　　Go then, for 'tis in vain
　To seek him here that means not to be found.

[Exeunt.]

---

2. **earth:** body. **center:** the center of the universe—that is, Juliet. 6. **conjure:** call up a spirit. 21. **consorted:** associated. **humorous:** moody. 24. **truckle bed:** trundle bed, a baby bed pushed under the great bed during the daytime.

Scene 2

[Capulet's *orchard. Enter* Romeo.]

Romeo. He jests° at scars that never felt a wound.

[Juliet *appears above at a window.*]

But, soft! What light through yonder window breaks?
It is the east, and Juliet is the sun!
Arise, fair sun, and kill the envious moon,
Who is already sick and pale with grief   5
That thou her maid art far more fair than she.
Be not her maid, since she is envious.
Her vestal livery° is but sick and green,
And none but fools do wear it. Cast it off.
It is my lady, oh, it is my love!   10
Oh, that she knew she were!
She speaks, yet she says nothing. What of that?
Her eye discourses,° I will answer it.
I am too bold, 'tis not to me she speaks.
Two of the fairest stars in all the heaven,   15
Having some business, do entreat her eyes
To twinkle in their spheres° till they return.
What if her eyes were there, they in her head?
The brightness of her cheek would shame those stars
As daylight doth a lamp; her eyes in heaven   20
Would through the airy region stream so bright
That birds would sing and think it were not night.
See how she leans her cheek upon her hand!
Oh, that I were a glove upon that hand,
That I might touch that cheek!
Juliet.   Aye me!
Romeo. [*Softly, to himself*]   She speaks.   25
Oh, speak again, bright angel! For thou art
As glorious to this night, being o'er my head,
As is a wingèd messenger of Heaven
Unto the white-upturnèd wondering eyes
Of mortals that fall back to gaze on him   30
When he bestrides the lazy-pacing clouds
And sails upon the bosom of the air.

---

1. **jests:** laughs, jokes.   8. **vestal livery:** maiden's dress.   13. **discourses:** speaks.   17. **spheres:** orbits.

Juliet. O Romeo, Romeo, wherefore° art thou Romeo?
    Deny thy father and refuse thy name,
    Or, if thou wilt not, be but sworn my love   35
    And I'll no longer be a Capulet.
Romeo. [*Aside*] Shall I hear more, or shall I speak at this?
Juliet. 'Tis but thy name that is my enemy.
    Thou art thyself, though not° a Montague.
    What's Montague? It is nor hand, nor foot,   40
    Nor arm, nor face, nor any other part
    Belonging to a man. Oh, be some other name!
    What's in a name? That which we call a rose
    By any other name would smell as sweet.
    So Romeo would, were he not Romeo called,   45
    Retain that dear perfection which he owes°
    Without that title. Romeo, doff° thy name,
    And for thy name, which is not part of thee,
    Take all myself.
Romeo. [*Aloud*]   I take thee at thy word.
    Call me but love, and I'll be new baptized.   50
    Henceforth I never will be Romeo.
Juliet. What man art thou that, thus bescreened in night,
    So stumblest on my counsel?°
Romeo.   By a name
    I know not how to tell thee who I am.
    My name, dear saint, is hateful to myself   55
    Because it is an enemy to thee.
    Had I it written, I would tear the word.
Juliet. My ears have yet not drunk a hundred words
    Of thy tongue's uttering, yet I know the sound.
    Art thou not Romeo, and a Montague?   60
Romeo. Neither, fair saint, if either thee dislike.°
Juliet. How camest thou hither, tell me, and wherefore?
    The orchard walls are high and hard to climb,
    And the place death, considering who thou art,
    If any of my kinsmen find thee here.   65
Romeo. With love's light wings did I o'erperch° these walls,
    For stony limits cannot hold love out.
    And what love can do, that dares love attempt,
    Therefore thy kinsmen are no let° to me.
Juliet. If they do see thee, they will murder thee.   70

---

33. **wherefore:** why. 39. **though not:** even if you were not. 46. **owes:** owns. 47. **doff:** remove. 53. **counsel:** innermost thoughts. 61. **dislike:** displease 66. **o'erperch:** climb over. 69. **let:** hindrance, obstacle.

Romeo. Alack, there lies more peril in thine eye
    Than twenty of their swords. Look thou but sweet,
    And I am proof° against their enmity.
Juliet. I would not for the world they saw thee here.
Romeo. I have night's cloak to hide me from their eyes,   75
    And but° thou love me, let them find me here.
    My life were better ended by their hate
    Than death proroguèd,° wanting of° thy love.
Juliet. By whose direction found'st thou out this place?
Romeo. By love, that first did prompt me to inquire.   80
    He lent me counsel, and I lent him eyes.
    I am no pilot, yet wert thou as far
    As that vast shore washed with the farthest sea,
    I would adventure for such merchandise.
Juliet. Thou know'st the mask of night is on my face,   85
    Else would a maiden blush bepaint my cheek
    For that which thou hast heard me speak tonight.
    Fain° would I dwell on form,° fain, fain deny
    What I have spoke. But farewell compliment!°
    Dost thou love me? I know thou wilt say "Aye,"   90
    And I will take thy word. Yet if thou swear'st,
    Thou mayst prove false. At lovers' perjuries
    They say Jove° laughs. O gentle Romeo,
    If thou dost love, pronounce it faithfully.
    Or if thou think'st I am too quickly won,   95
    I'll frown and be perverse and say thee nay,
    So° thou wilt woo; but else, not for the world.
    In truth, fair Montague, I am too fond,°
    And therefore thou mayst think my 'havior light.
    But trust me, gentleman, I'll prove more true   100
    Than those that have more cunning to be strange.°
    I should have been more strange, I must confess,
    But that thou overheard'st, ere I was ware,°
    My true love's passion. Therefore pardon me,
    And not impute this yielding to light love,   105
    Which the dark night hath so discovered.°
Romeo. Lady, by yonder blessed moon I swear,
    That tips with silver all these fruit-tree tops——

---

73. **proof:** armored, safe. 76. **And but:** unless: 78. **proroguèd** (prō-rōg'əd): postponed. **wanting of:** lacking. 88. **Fain:** gladly. **dwell on form:** behave in the customary way. 89. **compliment:** polite manners. 93. **Jove** (jōv): in classical mythology, the ruler of the gods. 97. **So:** so long as. 98. **fond:** foolishly affectionate. 101. **strange:** cold, distant. 103. **ware:** aware. 106. **discovered:** revealed.

Juliet. Oh, swear not by the moon, th' inconstant moon,
That monthly changes in her circled orb,° 110
Lest that thy love prove likewise variable.
Romeo. What shall I swear by?
Juliet.   Do not swear at all.
Or, if thou wilt, swear by thy gracious self,
Which is the god of my idolatry,
And I'll believe thee.
Romeo.   If my heart's dear love— 115
Juliet. Well, do not swear. Although I joy in thee,
I have no joy of this contráct° tonight.
It is too rash, too unadvised, too sudden,
Too like the lightning, which doth cease to be
Ere one can say "It lightens." Sweet, good night! 120
This bud of love, by summer's ripening breath,
May prove a beauteous flower when next we meet.
Good night, good night! As sweet repose and rest
Come to thy heart as that within my breast!
Romeo. Oh, wilt thou leave me so unsatisfied? 125
Juliet. What satisfaction canst thou have tonight?
Romeo. The exchange of thy love's faithful vow for mine.
Juliet. I gave thee mine before thou didst request it,
And yet I would it were to give again.
Romeo. Wouldst thou withdraw it? For what purpose, love? 130
Juliet. But to be frank,° and give it thee again.
And yet I wish but for the thing I have.
My bounty° is as boundless as the sea,
My love as deep; the more I give to thee,
The more I have, for both are infinite. 135
I hear some noise within. Dear love, adieu!

                        [Nurse *calls within.*°]

Anon,° good Nurse! Sweet Montague, be true.
Stay but a little, I will come again.

                                         [*Exit.*]

Romeo. Oh, blessed, blessed night! I am afeard,
Being in night, all this is but a dream, 140
Too flattering-sweet to be substantial.°

                      [*Reenter* Juliet, *above.*]

---

110. **orb:** orbit. 117. **contráct:** betrothal. 131. **frank:** generous. 133. **bounty:** generosity. S.D. **within:** off stage. 137. **Anon:** in a minute. 141. **substantial:** real.

Juliet. Three words, dear Romeo, and good night indeed.
 If that thy bent° of love be honorable,
 Thy purpose marriage, send me word tomorrow
 By one that I'll procure to come to thee,   145
 Where and what time thou wilt perform the rite,
 And all my fortunes at thy foot I'll lay,
 And follow thee my lord throughout the world.
Nurse. [*Within*] Madam!
Juliet. I come, anon.—But if thou mean'st not well, I do beseech thee——   150
Nurse. [*Within*] Madam!
Juliet.   By and by, I come—
 To cease thy suit, and leave me to my grief.
 Tomorrow will I send.
Romeo.   So thrive my soul——

Juliet. A thousand times good night!   [*Exit.*]
Romeo. A thousand times the worse, to want thy light.   155
 Love goes toward love as schoolboys from their books,
 But love from love toward school with heavy looks.

                                                          [*Retiring slowly.*]

                [*Reenter* Juliet, *above.*]

Juliet. Hist! Romeo, hist!—Oh, for a falconer's° voice,
 To lure this tassel-gentle° back again!
 Bondage is hoarse,° and may not speak aloud,   160
 Else would I tear the cave where Echo° lies
 And make her airy tongue more hoarse than mine
 With repetition of my Romeo's name.
Romeo. It is my soul that calls upon my name.
 How silver-sweet sound lovers' tongues by night,   165
 Like softest music to attending° ears!
Juliet. Romeo!
Romeo.   My dear?
Juliet.   At what o'clock tomorrow
 Shall I send to thee?
Romeo.   At the hour of nine.
Juliet. I will not fail. 'Tis twenty years till then.
 I have forgot why I did call thee back.   170

---

143. **bent:** intention.   158. **falconer:** keeper of hawks.   159. **tassel-gentle:** male falcon.   160. **Bondage is hoarse:** that is, being under the control of my parents, I must whisper.   161. **Echo:** in classical mythology, a wood nymph. Rejected by the man she loved, Echo retired to a cave and pined away until all that was left of her was her voice.   166. **attending:** attentive.

Romeo. Let me stand here till thou remember it.

Juliet. I shall forget, to have thee still stand there,
Remembering how I love thy company.

Romeo. And I'll still stay, to have thee still forget,
Forgetting any other home but this.   175

Juliet. 'Tis almost morning. I would have thee gone,
And yet no farther than a wanton's° bird,
Who lets it hop a little from her hand,
Like a poor prisoner in his twisted gyves,°
And with a silk thread plucks it back again,   180
So loving-jealous of his liberty.

Romeo. I would I were thy bird.

Juliet.   Sweet, so would I.
Yet I should kill thee with much cherishing.
Good night, good night! Parting is such sweet sorrow
That I shall say good night till it be morrow.   185

[Exit.]

Romeo. Sleep dwell upon thine eyes, peace in thy breast!
Would I were sleep and peace, so sweet to rest!
Hence will I to my ghostly° father's cell,
His help to crave and my dear hap° to tell.

[Exit.]

Scene 3

[Friar Laurence's cell. Enter Friar Laurence, *with a basket.]*

Friar Laurence. The gray-eyed morn smiles on the frowning night,
Checkering the eastern clouds with streaks of light,
And fleckèd° darkness like a drunkard reels
From forth day's path and Titan's° fiery wheels.
Now, ere the sun advance his burning eye,   5
The day to cheer and night's dank dew to dry,
I must upfill° this osier cage° of ours
With baleful° weeds and precious-juicèd flowers.
Oh, mickle° is the powerful grace° that lies
In herbs, plants, stones, and their true qualities.   10
For naught so vile that on the earth doth live,
But to the earth some special good doth give;

---

177. **wanton:** spoiled child.   179. **gyves** (jīvz): fetters.   188. **ghostly:** spiritual.   189. **hap:** luck.
  3. **fleckèd:** spotted.   4. **Titan:** the sun. In classical mythology, the sun god drove his chariot across the sky.   7. **up-fill:** fill up.   **osier cage:** wicker basket.   8. **baleful:** poisonous.   9. **mickle:** great.   **grace:** goodness.

Nor aught so good but, strained° from that fair use,
Revolts from true birth,° stumbling on abuse.°
Virtue itself turns vice, being misapplied,   15
And vice sometime's by action dignified.
Within the infant rind of this small flower
Poison hath residence, and medicine power.
For this, being smelt, with that part cheers each part,
Being tasted, slays all senses with the heart.°   20
Two such opposèd kings encamp them still°
In man as well as herbs, grace and rude will°;
And where the worser is predominant,°
Full soon the canker° death eats up that plant.

[*Enter* Romeo.]

Romeo. Good morrow, Father.
Friar Laurence.   Benedicite!   25
What early tongue so sweet saluteth me?
Young son, it argues a distempered° head
So soon to bid good morrow to thy bed.
Care keeps his watch in every old man's eye,
And where care lodges, sleep will never lie;   30
But where unbruisèd youth with unstuffed brain
Doth couch his limbs, there golden sleep doth reign.
Therefore thy earliness doth me assure
Thou art uproused by some distemperature.°
Or if not so, then here I hit it right,   35
Our Romeo hath not been in bed tonight.
Romeo. That last is true. The sweeter rest was mine.
Friar Laurence. God pardon sin! Wast thou with Rosaline?
Romeo. With Rosaline, my ghostly father? No.
I have forgot that name and that name's woe.   40
Friar Laurence. That's my good son. But where hast thou been, then?
Romeo. I'll tell thee ere thou ask it me again.
I have been feasting with mine enemy,
Where on a sudden one hath wounded me
That's by me wounded. Both our remedies   45
Within thy help and holy physic° lies.

---

13. **strained:** turned aside.   14. **Revolts from true birth:** turns away from its true function. **abuse:** misuse.   18–20. **Poison . . . heart:** The plant can be used as a poison or as a restorative: if smelled, it acts as a stimulant; if tasted, it is deadly.   21. **still:** always.   22. **rude will:** the natural desire for evil.   23. **predominant:** stronger.   24. **canker:** worm.   27. **distempered:** disturbed.   34. **distemperature:** sickness.   46. **physic:** remedy.

I bear no hatred, blessed man, for, lo,
My intercession° likewise steads° my foe.
Friar Laurence. Be plain, good son, and homely° in thy drift.°
    Riddling° confession finds but riddling shrift.°   50
Romeo. Then plainly know my heart's dear love is set
    On the fair daughter of rich Capulet.
    As mine on hers, so hers is set on mine,
    And all combined° save what thou must combine
    By holy marriage. When, and where, and how,   55
    We met, we wooed and made exchange of vow,
    I'll tell thee as we pass; but this I pray,
    That thou consent to marry us today.
Friar Laurence. Holy Saint Francis, what a change is here!
    Is Rosaline, that thou didst love so dear,   60
    So soon forsaken? Young men's love then lies
    Not truly in their hearts, but in their eyes.
    Jesu Maria, what a deal of brine
    Hath washed thy sallow cheeks for Rosaline!
    How much salt water thrown away in waste,   65
    To season° love, that of it doth not taste!
    The sun not yet thy sighs from heaven clears,
    Thy old groans ring yet in mine ancient ears.
    Lo, here upon thy cheek the stain doth sit
    Of an old tear that is not washed off yet.   70
    If e'er thou wast thyself and these woes thine,
    Thou and these woes were all for Rosaline.
    And art thou changed? Pronounce this sentence° then—
    Women may fall when there's no strength in men.
Romeo. Thou chid'st° me oft for loving Rosaline.   75
Friar Laurence. For doting, not for loving, pupil mine.
Romeo. And bad'st me bury love.
Friar Laurence.   Not in a grave
    To lay one in, another out to have.
Romeo. I pray thee, chide not. She whom I love now
    Doth grace for grace and love for love allow.   80
    The other did not so.
Friar Laurence.   Oh, she knew well
    Thy love did read by rote° and could not spell.
    But come, young waverer, come, go with me,

---

48. **intercession:** prayer, plea. **steads:** benefits. 49. **homely:** simple, plain. **drift:** speech. 50. **Riddling:** speaking in riddles. **shrift:** forgiveness. 54. **combined:** united. 66. **season:** keep fresh, as meat is preserved by salt. 73. **sentence:** proverb. 75. **chid'st:** scolded. 82. **by rote:** by heart.

In one respect I'll thy assistant be;
For this alliance may so happy prove,   85
To turn your households' rancor° to pure love.
Romeo. Oh, let us hence. I stand on sudden haste.°
Friar Laurence. Wisely and slow. They stumble that run fast.

[Exeunt.]

Scene 4

[A street. Enter Benvolio and Mercutio.]

Mercutio. Where the devil should this Romeo be?
   Came he not home tonight?
Benvolio. Not to his father's, I spoke with his man.°
Mercutio. Ah, that same pale hardhearted wench, that Rosaline,
   Torments him so that he will sure run mad.   5
Benvolio. Tybalt, the kinsman of old Capulet,
   Hath sent a letter to his father's house.
Mercutio. A challenge, on my life.
Benvolio. Romeo will answer it.
Mercutio. Any man that can write may answer a letter.   10
Benvolio. Nay, he will answer the letter's master, how he dares, being dared.
Mercutio. Alas, poor Romeo, he is already dead! Stabbed with a white wench's black eye, shot thorough the ear with a love song, the very pin° of his heart cleft with the blind bowboy's butt shaft.° And is he a man to encounter Tybalt?
Benvolio. Why, what is Tybalt?   15
Mercutio. More than Prince of Cats,° I can tell you. Oh, he's the courageous captain of compliments.° He fights as you sing, keeps time, distance, and proportion; rests me his minim° rest, one, two, and the third in your bosom. The very butcher of a silk button, a duelist, a duelist, a gentleman of the very first house,° of the first and second cause.° Ah, the immortal passado! The punto reverso! The hai!°   20

[Enter Romeo, no longer melancholy.]

Benvolio. Here comes Romeo, here comes Romeo.
Mercutio. You gave us the counterfeit° fairly last night.

---

86. **rancor:** hatred.   87. **stand on sudden haste:** am impatient.
  3. **man:** servant.   13. **pin:** center of the target.   13–14. **blind bowboy's butt shaft:** Cupid's blunt arrow. A butt shaft, an unpointed arrow, was used in target practice.   16. **Prince of Cats:** In stories of Reynard the fox, Tybalt is Prince of Cats.   16–17. **captain of compliments:** expert in fashionable behavior.   18. **minim rest:** the shortest rest.   19. **first house:** finest school.   **first and second cause:** the reasons that caused a gentleman to issue a challenge to a duel.   20. **passado . . . hai:** dueling terms. The *passado* is a lunge; *punto reverso* is a backhand stroke; *hai* is the cry as the fencer thrusts home.   22–24. **counterfeit:** A counterfeit coin was called a slip.

Romeo. Good morrow to you both. What counterfeit did I give you?

Mercutio. The slip, sir, the slip.

Romeo. Pardon, good Mercutio, my business was great, and in such a case as mine a man   25
may strain courtesy. Here's goodly gear!°

[*Enter* Nurse *and* Peter.]

Mercutio. A sail, a sail!

Benvolio. Two, two—a shirt and a smock.°

Nurse. Peter!

Peter. Anon?   30

Nurse. My fan, Peter.

Mercutio. Good Peter, to hide her face, but her fan's the fairer face.

Nurse. God ye good morrow, gentlemen. Can any of you tell me where I may find the
young Romeo?

Romeo. I can tell you, but young Romeo will be older when you have found him than he   35
was when you sought him. I am the youngest of that name, for fault of a worse.

Nurse. You say well.

Mercutio. Yea, is the worst well? Very well took,° i' faith—wisely, wisely.

Nurse. If you be he, sir, I desire some confidence° with you.

Mercutio. Romeo, will you come to your father's? We'll to dinner thither.   40

Romeo. I will follow you.

Mercutio. Farewell, ancient lady, farewell.

[*Exeunt* Mercutio *and* Benvolio.]

Nurse. Marry, farewell! I pray you, sir, what saucy merchant was this, that was so full of
his ropery?°

Romeo. A gentleman, Nurse, that loves to hear himself talk, and will speak more in a min-   45
ute than he will stand to in a month.

Nurse. An a' speak anything against me, I'll take him down, an a' were lustier than he is,
and twenty such Jacks;° and if I cannot, I'll find those that shall. Scurvy knave! Pray
you, sir, a word. And as I told you, my young lady bade me inquire you out—what she
bade me say, I will keep to myself. But first let me tell ye, if ye should lead her into a   50
fool's paradise, as they say, it were a very gross kind of behavior, as they say. For the
gentlewoman is young, and therefore if you should deal double with her, truly it were
an ill thing to be offered to any gentlewoman, and very weak dealing.

Romeo. Nurse, commend me to thy lady and mistress. I protest° unto thee—

Nurse. Good heart, and i' faith, I will tell her as much. Lord, Lord, she will be a joyful   55
woman.

---

26. **gear:** stuff.   28. **a shirt and a smock:** a man and a woman.   38. **took:** understood.   39. **confidence:** for "conference." The Nurse frequently confuses words that have a similar sound.   44. **ropery:** for "roguery."   48. **Jacks:**
knaves.   54. **protest:** declare.

Romeo. What wilt thou tell her, Nurse? Thou dost not mark° me.

Nurse. I will tell her, sir, that you do protest, which, as I take it, is a gentlemanlike offer.

Romeo. Bid her devise
    Some means to come to shrift° this afternoon,   60
    And there she shall at Friar Laurence' cell
    Be shrived and married. Here is for thy pains.

Nurse. No, truly, sir, not a penny.

Romeo. Go to, I say you shall.

Nurse. This afternoon, sir? Well, she shall be there.   65

Romeo. And stay, good Nurse, behind the abbey wall.
    Within this hour my man shall be with thee,
    And bring thee cords made like a tackled stair,°
    Which to the high topgallant° of my joy
    Must be my convoy in the secret night.   70
    Farewell. Be trusty, and I'll quit thy pains.°
    Farewell, commend me to thy mistress.

Nurse. Now God in Heaven bless thee! Hark you, sir.

Romeo. What say'st thou, my dear nurse?

Nurse. Is your man secret? Did you ne'er hear say   75
    Two may keep counsel, putting one away?°

Romeo. I warrant thee, my man's as true as steel.

Nurse. Well, sir, my mistress is the sweetest lady—Lord, Lord, when 'twas a litle prating thing—Oh, there is a nobleman in town, one Paris, that would fain lay knife aboard;° but she, good soul, had as lieve° see a toad, a very toad, as see him. I anger her some-   80 times, and tell her that Paris is the properer° man. But I'll warrant you, when I say so, she looks as pale as any clout° in the versal world.° Doth not rosemary and Romeo begin both with a letter?

Romeo. Aye, Nurse, what of that? Both with an R.

Nurse. Ah, mocker! That's the dog's name.° R is for the——No, I know it begins with some   85 other letter—and she hath the prettiest sententious° of it, of you and rosemary, that it would do you good to hear it.

Romeo. Commend me to thy lady.

Nurse. Aye, a thousand times. [*Exit* Romeo.] Peter!

Peter. Anon?   90

Nurse. Peter, take my fan, and go before, and apace.°

                                         [*Exeunt.*]

---

57. **mark:** pay attention to.   60. **shrift:** confession.   68. **tackled stair:** rope ladder.   69. **topgallant:** topmast.   71. **quit thy pains:** reward your trouble.   76. **Two . . . away:** Two can keep a secret—if only one of them knows of it.   79. **lay knife aboard:** get her for himself.   80. **lieve:** soon.   81. **properer:** more handsome.   82. **clout:** cloth.   **versal world:** universe.   85. **dog's name:** The letter *R* because it suggests a growling sound.   86. **sententious:** for "sentence" or proverb.   91. **apace:** quickly.

Scene 5

[*Capulet's orchard. Enter* Juliet, *waiting impatiently for the* Nurse.]

Juliet. The clock struck nine when I did send the nurse.
In half an hour she promised to return.
Perchance she cannot meet him. That's not so.
Oh, she is lame! Love's heralds should be thoughts,
Which ten times faster glide than the sun's beams,   5
Driving back shadows over lowering° hills.
Therefore do nimble-pinioned° doves draw love,
And therefore hath the wind-swift Cupid wings.
Now is the sun upon the highmost hill
Of this day's journey, and from nine till twelve   10
Is three long hours; yet she is not come.
Had she affections and warm youthful blood,
She would be as swift in motion as a ball,
My words would bandy° her to my sweet love,
And his to me.   15
But old folks, many feign as they were dead,
Unwieldy, slow, heavy and pale as lead.

[*Enter* Nurse, *with* Peter.]

Oh, God, she comes! O honey Nurse, what news?
Hast thou met with him? Send thy man away.
Nurse. Peter, stay at the gate.   20

[*Exit* Peter.]

Juliet. Now, good sweet Nurse—Oh, Lord, why look'st thou sad?
Though news be sad, yet tell them merrily;
If good, thou shamest the music of sweet news
By playing it to me with so sour a face.
Nurse. I am aweary, give me leave° a while.   25
Fie, how my bones ache! What a jaunce° have I had!
Juliet. I would thou hadst my bones and I thy news.
Nay, come, I pray thee, speak, good, good Nurse, speak.
Nurse. Jesu, what haste? Can you not stay° a while?
Do you not see that I am out of breath?   30
Juliet. How art thou out of breath when thou hast breath
To say to me that thou art out of breath?

---

6. **lowering:** frowning. 7. **nimble-pinioned:** swift-winged. 14. **bandy:** bat, hit (like a tennis ball). 25. **give me leave:** let me alone. 26. **jaunce:** running back and forth. 29. **stay:** wait.

The excuse that thou dost make in this delay
Is longer than the tale thou dost excuse.
Is thy news good, or bad? Answer to that.   35
Say either, and I'll stay the circumstance.°
Let me be satisfied, is 't good or bad?

Nurse. Well, you have made a simple° choice. You know not how to choose a man. Romeo!
No, not he, though his face be better than any man's, yet his leg excels all men's; and
for a hand, and a foot, and a body, though they be not to be talked on, yet they are past   40
compare. He is not the flower of courtesy,° but, I'll warrant him, as gentle as a lamb.
Go thy ways, wench, serve God. What, have you dined at home?

Juliet. No, no. But all this did I know before.
What says he of our marriage? What of that?

Nurse. Lord, how my head aches! What a head have I!   45
It beats as it would fall in twenty pieces.
My back o' t' other side—ah, my back, my back!
Beshrew° your heart for sending me about
To catch my death with jauncing up and down!

Juliet. I' faith, I am sorry that thou art not well.   50
Sweet, sweet, sweet Nurse, tell me, what says my love?

Nurse. Your love says, like an honest gentleman, and a courteous, and a kind, and a handsome, and, I warrant, a virtuous——Where is your mother?

Juliet. Where is my mother! Why, she is within,
Where should she be? How oddly thou repliest!   55
"Your love says, like an honest gentleman,
Where is your mother?"

Nurse.   Oh, God's Lady dear!°
Are you so hot°? Marry, come up, I trow.°
Is this the poultice° for my aching bones?
Henceforth do your messages yourself.   60

Juliet. Here's such a coil!° Come, what says Romeo?

Nurse. Have you got leave to go to shrift today?

Juliet. I have.

Nurse. Then hie° you hence to Friar Laurence' cell,
There stays a husband to make you a wife.   65
Now comes the wanton blood up in your cheeks,
They'll be in scarlet straight at any news.
Hie you to church, I must another way,
To fetch a ladder by the which your love

---

36. **stay the circumstance:** wait for details. 38. **simple:** foolish. 41. **flower of courtesy:** perfect gentleman. 48. **Beshrew:** a plague on. 57. **God's Lady dear:** by God's dear Mother (the Virgin Mary).' 58. **hot:** impatient. **Marry . . . trow:** Come, come, you're too impatient, I say. 59. **poultice:** remedy. 61. **coil:** fuss. 64. **hie:** hurry.

Must climb a bird's nest soon when it is dark.   70
  Go, I'll to dinner, hie you to the cell.
Juliet. Hie to high fortune! Honest Nurse, farewell.

[Exeunt.]

Scene 6

[Friar Laurence's *cell. Enter* Friar Laurence *and* Romeo.]

Friar Laurence. So smile the Heavens upon this holy act
  That afterhours with sorrow chide us not!
Romeo. Amen, amen! But come what sorrow can,
  It cannot countervail° the exchange of joy
  That one short minute gives me in her sight.   5
  Do thou but close our hands with holy words,
  Then love-devouring death do what he dare,
  It is enough I may but call her mine.
Friar Laurence. These violent delights have violent ends,
  And in their triumph die, like fire and powder°   10
  Which as they kiss consume. The sweetest honey
  Is loathsome in his own deliciousness,
  And in the taste confounds the appetite.
  Therefore, love moderately, long love doth so,
  Too swift arrives, as tardy as too slow.   15

[*Enter* Juliet.]

  Here comes the lady. Oh, so light a foot
  Will ne'er wear out the everlasting flint.°
  A lover may bestride the gossamer°
  That idles in the wanton° summer air,
  And not yet fall, so light is vanity.°   20
Juliet. Good even to my ghostly confessor.
Friar Laurence. Romeo shall thank thee, daughter, for us both.
Juliet. As much° to him, else is his thanks too much.
Romeo. Ah, Juliet, if the measure of thy joy
  Be heaped like mine, and that thy skill be more   25
  To blazon° it, then sweeten with thy breath
  This neighbor air, and let rich music's tongue

---

   4. **countervail:** counterbalance, outweigh. 10. **powder:** gunpowder. 17. **flint:** hard stone. 18. **gossamer:** a spider's web. 19. **wanton:** playful. 20. **vanity:** unreality. 23. **As much:** the very same greeting. 26. **blazon** (blā′zən): describe.

Unfold the imagined happiness that both
Receive in either by this dear encounter.

Juliet. Conceit, more rich in matter than in words,   30
Brags of his substance, not of ornament.°
They are but beggars that can count their worth,
But my true love is grown to such excess,
I cannot sum up sum of half my wealth.

Friar Laurence. Come, come with me, and we will make short work,   35
For, by your leaves, you shall not stay alone
Till Holy Church incorporate two in one.

[*Exeunt.*]

30–31. **Conceit . . . ornament:** True understanding (conceit) does not need words.

FOR STUDY AND DISCUSSION

1. To whom does Romeo refer in Scene 2 when he says, "He jests at scars that never felt a wound"? What does this remark mean?

2. Scene 2 takes place in the Capulet orchard late at night after the party. In what two ways does darkness influence what happens in the scene?

3. The balcony scene is famous for its poetry. Which lover uses images of light? Which one uses images of flowers and birds? Find lines in which they express their feelings for each other through these images.

4. In what ways does Juliet exhibit more common sense and practicality than Romeo?

5. Why is the Friar surprised at Romeo's confession of a new love? Why does he consent to marry Romeo and Juliet?

6. Although Mercutio teases Romeo in Scene 4, he is actually worried for him. Why?

7. Look closely at the Nurse's description of Romeo in Scene 5. Is she praising him or finding fault? Is she really tired when she enters or is she just teasing Juliet?

8. What concern does the Friar express in Scene 6 about the relationship of Romeo and Juliet?

DRAMATIC STRUCTURE: CONVENTIONS

Prose and Poetry

At different times in the history of the theater, dramatists have adopted certain *conventions*, or practices that become established and accepted by players and audiences. Shakespeare wrote most of his plays in verse. This was a convention of the Elizabethan theater. Prose is generally reserved for comic passages. Most of the prose passages in *Romeo and*

Juliet are spoken by servants and by the Nurse, but Mercutio's comic banter is written in prose too. Prose, as a rule, is used for the "lighter" moments of the play.

The most common form of verse in Shakespeare's play is *blank verse*. Blank verse is unrhymed iambic pentameter. In a line that is perfectly regular, an unstressed syllable is always followed by a stressed syllable. This pattern is called iambic.

Bŭt sóft! / Whăt líght / thrŏugh yón/dĕr

wín/dŏw breáks?

The meter is called pentameter because there are five feet in each line, indicated above by slash marks.

A blank verse line is sometimes divided between two speakers:

Jul. Take all myself.
Rom.   I take thee at thy word.

Not all lines are perfectly regular. Without variety in rhythm, the speeches would become monotonous.

A pair of rhymed lines in iambic pentameter is called a *heroic couplet*. Shakespeare often closes a scene with a couplet:

Farewell. Thou canst not teach me to
   forget.
I'll pay that doctrine, or else die in debt.
                            (I, 1)

Hence will I to my ghostly father's cell,
His help to crave and my dear hap to tell.
                            (II, 2)

For, by your leaves, you shall not stay alone
Till Holy Church incorporate two in one.
                            (II, 6)

Soliloquy, Monologue, and Aside

When the Friar stands alone on the stage at the beginning of Act Two, Scene 3, and talks to himself, we understand that he is speaking his thoughts aloud so that we can hear them. This is another convention known as *soliloquy*. A soliloquy is spoken by a character who is alone on stage.

Mercutio's famous speech on Queen Mab in Act One, Scene 4, is a *monologue*. A monologue is a long, virtually uninterrupted speech that is spoken in the presence of other characters.

An *aside* is a short remark usually directed to the audience and not intended to be heard by the other characters on stage. Sometimes, however, an aside is directed at another character. In the first scene of Act One, the servants Gregory and Sampson speak to each other in asides that are not intended to be overheard by Abraham and Balthasar.

Act Three

Scene 1

[*A public place. Enter* Mercutio, Benvolio, Page, *and* Servants.]

Benvolio. I pray thee, good Mercutio, let's retire.
  The day is hot, the Capulets abroad,
  And if we meet, we shall not 'scape a brawl;
  For now these hot days is the mad blood stirring.
Mercutio. Thou art like one of those fellows that when he enters the confines of a tavern   5
  claps me his sword upon the table and says, "God send me no need of thee!" and by the
  operation of the second cup draws it on the drawer,° when indeed there is no need.
Benvolio. Am I like such a fellow?
Mercutio. Come, come, thou art as hot a Jack in thy mood as any in Italy, and as soon
  moved to be moody,° and as soon moody to be moved.   10
Benvolio. And what to?
Mercutio. Nay, an there were two such, we should have none shortly, for one would kill
  the other. Thou! Why, thou wilt quarrel with a man that hath a hair more, or a hair
  less, in his beard than thou hast. Thou wilt quarrel with a man for cracking nuts, having no other reason but because thou hast hazel eyes. What eye but such an eye would   15
  spy out such a quarrel? Thy head is as full of quarrels as an egg is full of meat, and yet
  thy head hath been beaten as addle as an egg for quarreling. Thou hast quarreled with a
  man for coughing in the street, because he hath wakened thy dog that hath lain asleep
  in the sun. Didst thou not fall out with a tailor for wearing his new doublet° before
  Easter? With another for tying his new shoes with old ribbon? And yet thou wilt tutor   20
  me from quarreling!°
Benvolio. An I were so apt to quarrel as thou art, any man should buy the fee simple° of my
  life for an hour and a quarter.
Mercutio. The fee simple! Oh, simple!

[*Enter* Tybalt *and others.*]

Benvolio. By my head, here come the Capulets.   25
Mercutio. By my heel, I care not.
Tybalt. Follow me close, for I will speak to them.
  Gentlemen, good-den—a word with one of you.
Mercutio. And but one word with one of us? Couple it with something—make it a word
  and a blow.   30
Tybalt. You shall find me apt enough to that, sir, an you will give me occasion.
Mercutio. Could you not take some occasion without giving?

---

7. **drawer:** waiter.   10. **moody:** angry.   19. **doublet:** short, close-fitting jacket.   20–21. **tutor me from quarreling:**
teach me how to avoid quarreling.   22. **fee simple:** absolute possession.

Tybalt. Mercutio, thou consort'st° with Romeo—

Mercutio. Consort! What, dost thou make us minstrels?° An thou make minstrels of us, look to hear nothing but discords. Here's my fiddlestick,° here's that shall make you 35 dance. 'Zounds,° consort!

Benvolio. We talk here in the public haunt of men.
Either withdraw unto some private place,
And reason coldly of your grievances,
Or else depart. Here all eyes gaze on us. 40

Mercutio. Men's eyes were made to look, and let them gaze.
I will not budge for no man's pleasure, I.

[*Enter* Romeo, *now kinsman by marriage to the* Capulets.]

Tybalt. Well, peace be with you, sir. Here comes my man.°

Mercutio. But I'll be hanged, sir, if he wear your livery.°
Marry, go before to field,° he'll be your follower. 45
Your worship in that sense may call him man.

Tybalt. Romeo, the hate I bear thee can afford
No better term than this—thou art a villain.

Romeo. Tybalt, the reason that I have to love thee 50
Doth much excuse the appertaining rage°
To such a greeting. Villain am I none,
Therefore farewell. I see thou know'st me not.°

Tybalt. Boy, this shall not excuse the injuries
That thou hast done me, therefore turn and draw. 55

Romeo. I do protest I never injured thee,
But love thee better than thou canst devise°
Till thou shalt know the reason of my love.
And so, good Capulet—which name I tender°
As dearly as mine own—be satisfied. 60

Mercutio. Oh, calm, dishonorable, vile submission!
Alla stoccata° carries it away. [*Draws his sword.*]
Tybalt, you ratcatcher, will you walk?

Tybalt. What wouldst thou have with me?

Mercutio. Good King of Cats,° nothing but one of your nine lives, that I mean to make bold 65
withal, and, as you shall use me hereafter, dry-beat° the rest of the eight. Will you
pluck your sword out of his pilcher° by the ears? Make haste, lest mine be about your
ears ere it be out.

---

33. **consort'st:** are friendly with. 34. **minstrels:** Mercutio puns on another meaning of consort—a party of musicians. 35. **fiddlestick:** rapier, his sword. 36. **'Zounds:** by God's wounds. 43. **my man:** the man I want. 44. **your livery:** servant's uniform. Mercutio interprets *man* in its other sense of "servant." 45. **field:** dueling place. 51. **appertaining rage:** the anger with which I would otherwise respond. 53. **know'st me not:** Tybalt does not know they are now kinsmen because Romeo has married Juliet. 57. **devise:** guess, imagine. 59. **tender:** regard, care for. 62. **Alla stoccata:** a thrust in fencing. Mercutio uses this term as a name for Tybalt. 65. **King of Cats:** See note 16 on page 418. 66. **dry-beat:** bruise. 67. **pilcher:** scabbard, a case for a sword.

Tybalt. I am for you. [*Drawing.*]
Romeo. Gentle Mercutio, put thy rapier up.   70
Mercutio. Come, sir, your passado.°

[*They fight.*]

Romeo. Draw, Benvolio, beat down their weapons.
    Gentlemen, for shame, forbear this outrage!
    Tybalt, Mercutio, the Prince expressly hath
    Forbid this bandying° in Verona streets.   75
    Hold, Tybalt, good Mercutio!

[Tybalt *under* Romeo's *arm stabs* Mercutio *and flies with his followers.*]

Mercutio.   I am hurt.
    A plague o' both your houses! I am sped.°
    Is he gone, and hath nothing?
Benvolio.   What, art thou hurt?
Mercutio. Aye, aye, a scratch, a scratch—marry, 'tis enough.
    Where is my page? Go, villain,° fetch a surgeon.   80

[*Exit* Page.]

---

71. **passado:** lunge.   75. **bandying:** quarreling.   77. **sped:** done for.   80. **villain:** term used in addressing a servant.

Romeo. Courage, man, the hurt cannot be much.

Mercutio. No, 'tis not so deep as a well nor so wide as a church door, but 'tis enough, 'twill serve. Ask for me tomorrow and you shall find me a grave man.° I am peppered,° I warrant, for this world. A plague o' both your houses! 'Zounds, a dog, a rat, a mouse, a cat, to scratch a man to death! A braggart, a rogue, a villain, that fights by the book of arithmetic!° Why the devil came you between us! I was hurt under your arm.

Romeo. I thought all for the best.

Mercutio. Help me into some house, Benvolio,
Or I shall faint. A plague o' both your houses!
They have made worms' meat of me. I have it,
And soundly too—your houses!

                                  [Exeunt Mercutio *and* Benvolio.]

Romeo. This gentleman, the Prince's near ally,
My very friend, hath got his mortal hurt
In my behalf, my reputation stained
With Tybalt's slander—Tybalt, that an hour
Hath been my kinsman. O sweet Juliet,
Thy beauty hath made me effeminate,°
And in my temper softened valor's steel!

85

90

95

---

83. **grave man:** Mercutio's last pun. The two meanings of grave are "serious" and "dead." **peppered:** shot, wounded. 85–86. **book of arithmetic:** textbook on fencing; by exact rules. 97. **effeminate:** womanly.

Benvolio. O Romeo, Romeo, brave Mercutio's dead!
　That gallant spirit hath aspired° the clouds,　　　　　　　　　100
　Which too untimely here did scorn the earth.
Romeo. This day's black fate on more days doth depend,°
　This but begins the woe others must end.

[*Reenter* Tybalt.]

Benvolio. Here comes the furious Tybalt back again.
Romeo. Alive, in triumph! And Mercutio slain!　　　　　　　105
　Away to Heaven, respective lenity,°
　And fire-eyed fury be my conduct° now!
　Now, Tybalt, take the "villain" back again
　That late thou gavest me; for Mercutio's soul
　Is but a little way above our heads,　　　　　　　　　　　110
　Staying for thine to keep him company.
　Either thou, or I, or both, must go with him.
Tybalt. Thou, wretched boy, that didst consort him here,
　Shalt with him hence.
Romeo. 　　　　　　　　This shall determine that.

[*They fight; Tybalt falls dead.*]

Benvolio. Romeo, away, be gone!　　　　　　　　　　　115
　The citizens are up, and Tybalt slain.
　Stand not amazed. The Prince will doom thee death
　If thou art taken. Hence, be gone, away!
Romeo. Oh, I am fortune's fool!°
Benvolio. 　　　　　　　Why dost thou stay?

[*Exit* Romeo.]

[*Enter* Citizens.]

First Citizen. Which way ran he that killed Mercutio?　　120
　Tybalt, that murderer, which way ran he?
Benvolio. There lies that Tybalt.
First Citizen. 　　　　　　　Up, sir, go with me.
　I charge thee in the Prince's name, obey.

---

100. **aspired:** soared to.　102. **on more days doth depend:** will be followed by more fatal days.　106. **respective lenity:** considerate mercy (which Romeo has shown to Tybalt).　107. **conduct:** guide.　119. **fortune's fool:** fooled by fortune.

[*Enter* Prince, *attended;* Montague, Capulet, *their* Wives, *and others.*]

Prince. Where are the vile beginners of this fray?

Benvolio. O noble Prince, I can discover° all   125
    The unlucky manage° of this fatal brawl.
    There lies the man, slain by young Romeo,
    That slew thy kinsman, brave Mercutio.

Lady Capulet. Tybalt, my cousin! Oh, my brother's child!
    O Prince! O Cousin! Husband! Oh, the blood is spilt   130
    Of my dear kinsman! Prince, as thou art true,
    For blood of ours shed blood of Montague.
    O Cousin, Cousin!

Prince. Benvolio, who began this bloody fray?

Benvolio. Tybalt, here slain, whom Romeo's hand did slay—   135
    Romeo that spoke him fair, bade him bethink
    How nice° the quarrel was, and urged withal
    Your high displeasure. All this uttered
    With gentle breath, calm look, knees humbly bowed,
    Could not take truce with the unruly spleen°   140
    Of Tybalt deaf to peace, but that he tilts
    With piercing steel at bold Mercutio's breast,
    Who, all as hot, turns deadly point to point,
    And, with a martial scorn, with one hand beats
    Cold death aside and with the other sends   145
    It back to Tybalt, whose dexterity
    Retorts it. Romeo, he cries aloud,
    "Hold, friends! Friends, part!" and, swifter than his tongue,
    His agile arm beats down their fatal points,
    And 'twixt them rushes. Underneath whose arm   150
    An envious° thrust from Tybalt hit the life
    Of stout Mercutio, and then Tybalt fled,
    But by and by comes back to Romeo,
    Who had but newly entertained revenge,
    And to 't they go like lightning. For ere I   155
    Could draw to part them was stout Tybalt slain,
    And as he fell, did Romeo turn and fly.
    This is the truth, or let Benvolio die.

Lady Capulet. He is a kinsman to the Montague,
    Affection makes him false, he speaks not true.   160
    Some twenty of them fought in this black strife,

---

125. **discover:** reveal.   126. **manage:** circumstances.   137. **nice:** trifling, trivial.   140. **spleen:** fiery temper.   151. **envious:** hateful.

And all those twenty could but kill one life.
I beg for justice, which thou, Prince, must give.
Romeo slew Tybalt, Romeo must not live.

Prince. Romeo slew him, he slew Mercutio.   165
Who now the price of his dear blood doth owe?

Montague. [*Pleading*] Not Romeo, Prince, he was Mercutio's friend.
His fault concludes but what the law should end,
The life of Tybalt.

Prince. [*His anger roused*] And for that offense
Immediately we do exile him hence.   170
I have an interest° in your hate's proceeding,
My blood for your rude brawls doth lie a-bleeding.
But I'll amerce° you with so strong a fine
That you shall all repent the loss of mine.
I will be deaf to pleading and excuses,   175
Nor tears nor prayers shall purchase out° abuses.
Therefore use none. Let Romeo hence in haste,
Else, when he's found, that hour is his last.
Bear hence this body, and attend our will.°
Mercy but murders, pardoning those that kill.   [*Exeunt.*]   180

Scene 2

[Capulet's *orchard. Enter* Juliet.]

Juliet. Gallop apace, you fiery-footed steeds,
Toward Phoebus° lodging. Such a wagoner
And Phaëton° would whip you to the west,
And bring in cloudy night immediately.
Come, gentle night, come, loving, black-browed night,   5
Give me my Romeo; and when he shall die,
Take him and cut him out in little stars,
And he will make the face of heaven so fine
That all the world will be in love with night,
And pay no worship to the garish° sun.   10
Oh, here comes my nurse,
And she brings news, and every tongue that speaks
But Romeo's name speaks heavenly eloquence.

---

171. **interest:** concern. Mercutio was the Prince's kinsman. 173. **amerce:** punish. 176. **purchase out:** pay
for. 179. **attend our will:** come to receive my judgment.

2. **Phoebus** (fē′bəs): the sun god, Phoebus Apollo, who according to mythology was drawn across the sky in his
chariot every day. 3. **Phaëton** (fā′ə-tən): the son of Phoebus. He tried to drive his father's chariot, but was unable to
control the horses. 10. **garish:** gaudy

[*Enter* Nurse, *with ladder of cords.*]

Now, Nurse, what news? What hast thou there? The cords
That Romeo bid thee fetch?   15
Nurse. Aye, aye, the cords. [*Throws them down.*]
Juliet. Aye me! What news? Why dost thou wring thy hands?
Nurse. Ah, welladay! He's dead, he's dead, he's dead.
   We are undone, lady, we are undone.
   Alack the day! He's gone, he's killed, he's dead.   20
Juliet. Can Heaven be so envious?
Nurse.   Romeo can,
   Though Heaven cannot, O Romeo, Romeo!
   Who ever would have thought it? Romeo!
Juliet. What devil art thou that dost torment me thus?
   This torture should be roared in dismal Hell.   25
   Hath Romeo slain himself?
Nurse. I saw the wound, I saw it with mine eyes—
   God save the mark!—here on his manly breast.
   A piteous corse,° a bloody piteous corse,
   Pale, pale as ashes, all bedaubed in blood,   30
   All in gore blood. I swounded° at the sight.
Juliet. Oh, break, my heart! Poor bankrupt, break at once!
   To prison, eyes, ne'er look on liberty!
   Vile earth° to earth resign, end motion here,
   And thou and Romeo press one heavy bier!   35
Nurse. O Tybalt, Tybalt, the best friend I had!
   O courteous Tybalt! Honest gentleman!
   That ever I should live to see thee dead!
Juliet. What storm is this that blows so contrary?
   Is Romeo slaughtered, and is Tybalt dead?   40
   My dear-loved cousin, and my dearer lord?
   Then, dreadful trumpet,° sound the general doom!
   For who is living if those two are gone?
Nurse. Tybalt is gone, and Romeo banishèd—
   Romeo that killed him, he is banishèd.   45
Juliet. Oh, God! Did Romeo's hand shed Tybalt's blood?
Nurse. It did, it did. Alas the day, it did!
Juliet. Oh, serpent heart, hid with a flowering face!
   Did ever dragon keep so fair a cave?
   Was ever book containing such vile matter   50

---

29. **corse:** corpse. 31. **swounded:** swooned, fainted. 34. **Vile earth:** Juliet refers to herself. 42. **dreadful trumpet:** the trumpet that is supposed to announce the end of the world.

So fairly bound? Oh, that deceit should dwell
In such a gorgeous palace!

Nurse.   There's no trust,
No faith, no honesty in men—all perjured,
All forsworn, all naught, all dissemblers.°
Ah, where's my man? Give me some aqua vitae.°   55
These griefs, these woes, these sorrows, make me old.
Shame come to Romeo!

Juliet.   Blistered be thy tongue
For such a wish! He was not born to shame.
Upon his brow shame is ashamed to sit,
For 'tis a throne where honor may be crowned   60
Sole monarch of the universal earth.
Oh, what a beast was I to chide at him!

Nurse. Will you speak well of him that killed your cousin?

Juliet. Shall I speak ill of him that is my husband?
Ah, poor my lord, what tongue shall smooth thy name   65
When I, thy three-hours wife, have mangled it?
But wherefore, villain, didst thou kill my cousin?
That villain cousin would have killed my husband.
Back, foolish tears, back to your native spring,
Your tributary drops belong to woe   70
Which you mistaking offer up to joy.
My husband lives, that Tybalt would have slain,
And Tybalt's dead, that would have slain my husband.
All this is comfort, wherefore weep I, then?
Some word there was, worser than Tybalt's death,   75
That murdered me. I would forget it fain,°
But, oh, it presses to my memory
Like damnèd guilty deeds to sinners' minds.
"Tybalt is dead, and Romeo banishèd."
That "banishèd," that one word "banishèd,"   80
Hath slain ten thousand Tybalts. Tybalt's death
Was woe enough if it had ended there.
Or, if sour woe delights in fellowship,
And needly° will be ranked with other griefs,
Why followed not, when she said "Tybalt's dead,"   85
Thy father, or thy mother, nay, or both,
Which modern° lamentation might have moved?
But with a rearward following Tybalt's death,

---

54. **dissemblers:** pretenders, hypocrites.   55. **aqua vitae** (vī′tē): spirits.   76. **fain:** willingly.   84. **needly:** necessarily.
87. **modern:** ordinary.

"Romeo is banishèd." To speak that word
Is father, mother, Tybalt, Romeo, Juliet,   90
All slain, all dead. "Romeo is banishèd."
There is no end, no limit, measure, bound,
In that word's death; no words can that woe sound.
Where is my father, and my mother, Nurse?
Nurse. Weeping and wailing over Tybalt's corse.   95
Will you go to them? I will bring you thither.
Juliet. Wash they his wounds with tears. Mine shall be spent,
When theirs are dry, for Romeo's banishment.
Nurse. Hie to your chamber. I'll find Romeo
To comfort you. I wot° well where he is.   100
Hark ye, your Romeo will be here at night.
I'll to him—he is hid at Laurence' cell.
Juliet. Oh, find him! Give this ring to my true knight,
And bid him come to take his last farewell.   [*Exeunt.*]

Scene 3

[Friar Laurence's *cell. Enter* Friar Laurence.]

Friar Laurence. Romeo, come forth, come forth, thou fearful° man.
Affliction is enamored of thy parts,°
And thou art wedded to calamity.

[*Enter* Romeo.]

Romeo. Father, what news? What is the Prince's doom?°
What sorrow craves acquaintance at my hand   5
That I yet know not?
Friar Laurence.   Too familiar
Is my dear son with such sour company.
I bring thee tidings of the Prince's doom.
Romeo. What less than Doomsday is the Prince's doom?
Friar Laurence. A gentler judgment vanished° from his lips,   10
Not body's death, but body's banishment.
Romeo. Ha, banishment! Be merciful, say "death,"
For exile hath more terror in his look,
Much more, than death. Do not say "banishment."

---

100. **wot:** know.
    1. **fearful:** full of fear.   2. **Affliction . . . parts:** Misfortune has fallen in love with your good qualities (and so follows wherever you go).   4. **doom:** sentence.   10. **vanished:** escaped.

Friar Laurence. Hence from Verona art thou banishèd. 15
　Be patient, for the world is broad and wide.

Romeo. There is no world without° Verona walls,
　But Purgatory, torture, Hell itself.
　Hence banishèd is banished from the world,
　And world's exile is death. Then "banishèd," 20
　Is death mistermed. Calling death "banishèd"
　Thou cut'st my head off with a golden ax,
　And smilest upon the stroke that murders me.

Friar Laurence. Oh, deadly sin! Oh, rude unthankfulness!
　Thy fault our law calls death, but the kind Prince, 25
　Taking thy part, hath rushed° aside the law,
　And turned that black word "death" to "banishment."
　This is dear° mercy, and thou seest it not.

Romeo. 'Tis torture, and not mercy. Heaven is here,
　Where Juliet lives, and every cat and dog 30
　And little mouse, every unworthy thing,
　Live here in Heaven and may look on her,
　But Romeo may not. More validity,
　More honorable state, more courtship, lives
　In carrion flies than Romeo. They may seize 35
　On the white wonder of dear Juliet's hand,
　And steal immortal blessing from her lips,
　But Romeo may not, he is banishèd.
　This may flies do, but I from this must fly.
　They are free men, but I am banishèd. 40
　And say'st thou yet that exile is not death?
　Hadst thou no poison mixed, no sharp-ground knife,
　No sudden means of death, though ne'er so mean,
　But "banishèd" to kill me?— "Banishèd"?
　O Friar, the damnèd use that word in Hell, 45
　Howling attends it. How hast thou the heart,
　Being a divine, a ghostly confessor,
　A sin-absolver, and my friend professed,
　To mangle me with that word "banishèd"?

Friar Laurence. Thou fond° madman, hear me but speak a word. 50

Romeo. Oh, thou wilt speak again of banishment.

Friar Laurence. I'll give thee armor to keep off that word,
　Adversity's sweet milk, philosophy,
　To comfort thee, though thou art banishèd.

Romeo. Yet "banishèd"? Hang up philosophy! 55

---

17. **without:** outside.　26. **rushed:** brushed.　28. **dear:** precious.　50. **fond:** foolish.

Unless philosophy can make a Juliet,
Displant° a town, reverse a Prince's doom,
It helps not, it prevails not. Talk no more.
Friar Laurence. Oh, then I see that madmen have no ears.
Romeo. How should they when that wise men have no eyes?   60
Friar Laurence. Let me dispute° with thee of thy estate.°
Romeo. Thou canst not speak of that thou dost not feel.
    Wert thou as young as I, Juliet thy love,
    An hour but married, Tybalt murderèd,
    Doting like me, and like me banishèd,   65
    Then mightst thou speak, then mightst thou tear thy hair
    And fall upon the ground, as I do now,
    Taking the measure of an unmade grave.

      [As he falls to the ground, someone knocks within.]

Friar Laurence. Arise, one knocks. Good Romeo, hide thyself.
Romeo. Not I, unless the breath of heartsick groans   70
    Mistlike enfold me from the search of eyes. *[Knocking.]*
Friar Laurence. Hark how they knock! Who's there? Romeo, arise,
    Thou wilt be taken. — Stay while! — Stand up, *[Knocking.]*
    Run to my study. — By and by!° — God's will,
    What simpleness is this! — I come, I come! *[Knocking.]*   75
    Who knocks so hard? Whence come you? What's your will?
Nurse. *[Within]* Let me come in, and you shall know my errand.
    I come from Lady Juliet.
Friar Laurence.   Welcome, then.

      [Enter Nurse.]

Nurse. O holy Friar, oh, tell me, holy Friar,
    Where is my lady's lord, where's Romeo?   80
Friar Laurence. There on the ground, with his own tears made drunk.
Nurse. Oh, he is even in my mistress' case,
    Just in her case!
Friar Laurence.   Oh, woeful sympathy!
    Piteous predicament!
Nurse.   Even so lies she,
    Blubbering and weeping, weeping and blubbering.   85
    Stand up, stand up, stand, an you be a man.

---

57. **Displant:** uproot.   61. **dispute:** discuss.   **estate:** circumstances.   74. **By and by:** Wait a moment.

For Juliet's sake, for her sake, rise and stand.
Why should you fall into so deep an O?°
Romeo. Nurse!
Nurse. Ah sir, ah sir! Well, death's the end of all.   90
Romeo. Spakest thou of Juliet? How is it with her?
Doth she not think me an old° murderer,
Now I have stained the childhood of our joy
With blood removed but little from her own?
Where is she? And how doth she? And what says   95
My concealed lady° to our canceled love?
Nurse. Oh, she says nothing, sir, but weeps and weeps,
And now falls on her bed, and then starts up
And Tybalt calls, and then on Romeo cries,
And then down falls again.
Romeo.   As if that name,   100
Shot from the deadly level° of a gun,
Did murder her, as that name's cursèd hand
Murdered her kinsman. Oh, tell me, Friar, tell me,
In what vile part of this anatomy°
Doth my name lodge? Tell me, that I may sack°   105
The hateful mansion. [*Drawing his dagger.*]
Friar Laurence.   Hold thy desperate hand.
Art thou a man? Thy form cries out thou art.
Thy tears are womanish, thy wild acts denote
The unreasonable fury of a beast.
Unseemly woman in a seeming man!   110
Or ill-beseeming beast in seeming both!°
Thou hast amazed me. By my holy order,
I thought thy disposition better tempered.°
Hast thou slain Tybalt? Wilt thou slay thyself?
And slay thy lady too that lives in thee,   115
By doing damnèd hate upon thyself?
Why rail'st thou on thy birth, the Heaven and earth?
Since birth and Heaven and earth all three do meet
In thee at once, which thou at once wouldst lose.
What, rouse thee, man! Thy Juliet is alive,   120
For whose dear sake thou wast but lately dead.
There art thou happy. Tybalt would kill thee,
But thou slew'st Tybalt. There art thou happy too.

---

88. **O:** cry of grief.   92. **old:** experienced.   96. **concealed lady:** secret bride.   101. **level:** aim.   104. **anatomy:**
body.   105. **sack:** destroy.   111. **Or . . . both:** a shameful beast for you are neither man nor woman.   113. **tempered:**
mixed.

The law, that threatened death, becomes thy friend
And turns it to exile. There art thou happy.   125
A pack of blessings lights upon thy back,
Happiness courts thee in her best array;
But, like a misbehaved and sullen wench,
Thou pout'st upon thy fortune and thy love.
Take heed, take heed, for such die miserable.   130
Go, get thee to thy love, as was decreed,
Ascend her chamber—hence and comfort her.
But look thou stay not till the watch be set,°
For then thou canst not pass to Mantua,
Where thou shalt live till we can find a time   135
To blaze° your marriage, reconcile your friends,
Beg pardon of the Prince, and call thee back
With twenty hundred thousand times more joy
Than thou went'st forth in lamentation.
Go before, Nurse. Commend me to thy lady,   140
And bid her hasten all the house to bed,
Which heavy sorrow makes them apt unto.
Romeo is coming.
Nurse. Oh Lord, I could have stayed here all the night
To hear good counsel. Oh, what learning is!   145
My lord, I'll tell my lady you will come.
Romeo. Do so, and bid my sweet prepare to chide.
Nurse. Here, sir, a ring she bid me give you, sir.
Hie you, make haste, for it grows very late.

[Exit.]

Romeo. How well my comfort is revived by this!   150
Friar Laurence. Go hence, good night, and here stands all your state.°
Either be gone before the watch be set,
Or by the break of day disguised from hence.
Sojourn° in Mantua. I'll find out your man,
And he shall signify from time to time   155
Every good hap° to you that chances here.
Give me thy hand, 'tis late. Farewell, good night.
Romeo. But that a joy past joy calls out on me,
It were a grief so brief to part with thee.
Farewell.   160

[Exeunt.]

---

133. **watch be set:** watchmen go on duty at the gates.   136. **blaze:** make public.   151. **here . . . state:** on this depends
all your good fortune.   154. **Sojourn:** remain.   156. **hap:** happening.

Scene 4

[*A room in* Capulet's house.]

Capulet. Things have fall'n out, sir, so unluckily,
That we have had no time to move° our daughter.
Look you, she loved her kinsman Tybalt dearly,
And so did I. Well, we were born to die.
'Tis very late, she'll not come down tonight.   5
I promise you, but for your company
I would have been abed an hour ago.

Paris. These times of woe afford no time to woo.
Madam, good night. Commend me to your daughter.

Lady Capulet. I will, and know her mind early tomorrow;   10
Tonight she's mewed up to her heaviness.°

Capulet. Sir Paris, I will make a desperate tender°
Of my child's love. I think she will be ruled
In all respects by me—nay, more, I doubt it not.
Wife, go you to her ere you go to bed,   15
Acquaint her here of my son° Paris' love,
And bid her, mark you me, on Wednesday next—
But, soft! what day is this?

Paris.   Monday, my lord.

Capulet. Monday! Ha, ha! Well, Wednesday is too soon.
O' Thursday let it be. O' Thursday, tell her,   20
She shall be married to this noble Earl.
Will you be ready? Do you like this haste?
We'll keep no great ado, a friend or two;
For, hark you, Tybalt being slain so late,°
It may be thought we held him carelessly,°   25
Being our kinsman, if we revel much.
Therefore we'll have some half a dozen friends,
And there an end. But what say you to Thursday?

Paris. My lord, I would that Thursday were tomorrow.

Capulet. Well, get you gone. O' Thursday be it, then.   30
Go you to Juliet ere you go to bed,
Prepare her, wife, against° this wedding day.
Farewell, my lord. Light to my chamber, ho!
Afore me,° it is so very late

---

2. **move:** make your proposal to.   11. **mewed . . . heaviness:** shut up in seclusion with her sorrow.   12. **desperate tender:** bold offer.   16. **son:** future son-in-law.   24. **late:** lately, recently.   25. **held him carelessly:** did not care about him.   32. **against:** in readiness for.   34. **Afore me:** an oath meaning "before God."

That we may call it early by and by.   35
Good night.

[Exeunt.]

Scene 5

[Capulet's *orchard. Enter* Romeo *and* Juliet, *above, at the window.*]

Juliet. Wilt thou be gone? It is not yet near day.
    It was the nightingale, and not the lark,°
    That pierced the fearful hollow of thine ear.
    Nightly she sings on yond pomegranate tree.
    Believe me, love, it was the nightingale.   5
Romeo. It was the lark, the herald of the morn,
    No nightingale. Look, love, what envious streaks
    Do lace° the severing clouds in yonder east.
    Night's candles° are burnt out, and jocund day
    Stands tiptoe on the misty mountaintops.   10
    I must be gone and live, or stay and die.
Juliet. Yond light is not daylight, I know it, I.
    It is some meteor that the sun exhales,°
    To be to thee this night a torchbearer
    And light thee on thy way to Mantua.   15
    Therefore stay yet—thou need'st not to be gone.
Romeo. Let me be ta'en, let me be put to death,
    I am content, so thou wilt have it so.
    I'll say yon gray is not the morning's eye,
    'Tis but the pale reflex° of Cynthia's° brow;   20
    Nor that is not the lark whose notes do beat
    The vaulty heaven so high above our heads.
    I have more care to stay than will to go.
    Come, death, and welcome! Juliet wills it so.
    How is 't, my soul? Let's talk. It is not day.   25
Juliet. It is, it is. Hie hence, be gone, away!
    It is the lark that sings so out of tune,
    Straining harsh discords and unpleasing sharps.
    Some say the lark makes sweet division.°
    This doth not so, for she divideth us.   30
    Some say the lark and loathèd toad change eyes.°

---

2. **nightingale . . . lark:** The nightingale sings at night; the lark sings in the early morning.   8. **lace:** stripe.   9. **Night's candles:** the stars.   13. **exhales:** gives out.   20. **reflex:** reflection.   **Cynthia's:** the moon's.   29. **division:** melody.   31. **change eyes:** People believed that the toad and lark had once exchanged eyes. This belief would explain why larks are beautiful but have ugly eyes while toads are ugly but have beautiful eyes.

Oh, now I would they had changed voices too!
Since arm from arm that voice doth us affray,°
Hunting thee hence with hunt's-up° to the day.
Oh, now be gone, more light and light it grows.   35
Romeo. More light and light. More dark and dark our woes!

[*Enter* Nurse, *to the chamber.*]

Nurse. Madam!
Juliet. Nurse?
Nurse. Your lady mother is coming to your chamber.
    The day is broke, be wary, look about.   40

                                                                          [*Exit.*]

Juliet. Then, window, let day in, and let life out.
Romeo. Farewell, farewell! One kiss, and I'll descend.

                          [*He climbs down by the ladder of cords.*]

Juliet. Art thou gone so? Love, lord, aye, husband, friend!
    I must hear from thee every day in the hour,
    For in a minute there are many days.   45
    Oh, by this count I shall be much in years
    Ere I again behold my Romeo!
Romeo. Farewell!
    I will omit no opportunity
    That may convey my greetings, love, to thee.   50
Juliet. Oh, think'st thou we shall ever meet again?
Romeo. I doubt it not, and all these woes shall serve
    For sweet discourses in our time to come.
Juliet. Oh God! I have an ill-divining° soul.
    Methinks I see thee, now thou art below,   55
    As one dead in the bottom of a tomb.
    Either my eyesight fails or thou look'st pale.
Romeo. And trust me, love, in my eye so do you.
    Dry sorrow drinks° our blood. Adieu, adieu!

                                                                          [*Exit.*]

Juliet. O Fortune, Fortune, all men call thee fickle.   60
    If thou art fickle, what dost thou with him
    That is renowned for faith? Be fickle, Fortune,
    For then, I hope, thou wilt not keep him long,
    But send him back.
Lady Capulet. [*Within*] Ho, daughter! Are you up?   65

---

33. **affray:** frighten.   34. **hunt's-up:** hunters' morning song.   54. **ill-divining:** fearful, foreseeing evil.   59. **drinks:** drains. Sorrow was believed to drain the blood.

Juliet. Who is 't that calls? It is my lady mother!
    Is she not down so late, or up so early?
    What unaccustomed cause procures her hither?

[Enter Lady Capulet.]

Lady Capulet. Why, how now, Juliet!
Juliet.   Madam, I am not well.
Lady Capulet. Evermore weeping for your cousin's death?   70
    What, wilt thou wash him from his grave with tears?
    And if thou couldst, thou couldst not make him live,
    Therefore have done. Some grief shows much of love,
    But much of grief shows still some want of wit.
Juliet. Yet let me weep for such a feeling° loss.   75
Lady Capulet. So shall you feel the loss, but not the friend
    Which you weep for.
Juliet.   Feeling so the loss,
    I cannot choose but ever weep the friend.
Lady Capulet. Well, girl, thou weep'st not so much for his death
    As that the villain lives which slaughtered him.   80
Juliet. What villain, madam?
Lady Capulet.   That same villain, Romeo.
Juliet. *(Aside)* Villain and he be many miles asunder.
    God pardon him! I do, with all my heart,
    And yet no man like° he doth grieve my heart.
Lady Capulet. That is because the traitor murderer lives.   85
Juliet. Aye, madam, from the reach of these my hands.
    Would none but I might venge my cousin's death!
Lady Capulet. We will have vengeance for it, fear thou not.
    Then weep no more. I'll send to one in Mantua,
    Where that same banished runagate° doth live,   90
    Shall give him such an unaccustomed dram°
    That he shall soon keep Tybalt company.
    And then I hope thou wilt be satisfied.
Juliet. Indeed I never shall be satisfied
    With Romeo till I behold him—dead—   95
    Is my poor heart so for a kinsman vexed.
    Madam, if you could find out but a man
    To bear a poison, I would temper° it,
    That Romeo should, upon receipt thereof,

---

75. **feeling:** deeply felt. 84. **like:** as much as. 90. **runagate:** runaway. 91. **unaccustomed dram:** unexpected dose. 98. **temper:** mix.

Soon sleep in quiet. Oh, how my heart abhors   100
To hear him named and cannot come to him,
To wreak° the love I bore my cousin
Upon his body that hath slaughtered him!

Lady Capulet. Find thou the means, and I'll find such a man.
But now I'll tell thee joyful tidings, girl.   105

Juliet. And joy comes well in such a needy time.
What are they, I beseech your ladyship?

Lady Capulet. Well, well, thou hast a careful° father, child,
One who, to put thee from thy heaviness,
Hath sorted° out a sudden day of joy,   110
That thou expect'st not, nor I looked not for.

Juliet. Madam, in happy time,° what day is that?

Lady Capulet. Marry, my child, early next Thursday, morn,
The gallant, young, and noble gentleman,
The County Paris, at Saint Peter's Church,   115
Shall happily make thee there a joyful bride.

Juliet. Now, by Saint Peter's Church, and Peter too,
He shall not make me there a joyful bride.
I wonder at this haste, that I must wed
Ere he that should be husband comes to woo.   120
I pray you tell my lord and father, madam,
I will not marry yet. And when I do, I swear
It shall be Romeo, whom you know I hate,
Rather than Paris. These are news indeed!

Lady Capulet. Here comes your father, tell him so yourself   125
And see how he will take it at your hands.

[*Enter* Capulet *and* Nurse.]

Capulet. When the sun sets, the air doth drizzle dew,
But for the sunset of my brother's son
It rains downright.
How now! A conduit,° girl? What, still in tears?   130
Evermore showering? In one little body
Thou counterfeit'st° a bark,° a sea, a wind.
For still thy eyes, which I may call the sea,
Do ebb and flow with tears; the bark thy body is,
Sailing in this salt flood, the winds, thy sighs,   135

---

102. **wreak:** revenge.   108. **careful:** considerate.   110. **sorted:** chosen.   112. **in happy time:** indeed.   130. **conduit:** fountain.   132. **Thou counterfeit'st:** You imitate.   **bark:** boat.

Who raging with thy tears, and they with them,
Without a sudden calm will overset
Thy tempest-tossed body. How now, wife!
Have you delivered to her our decree?

Lady Capulet. Aye, sir, but she will none, she gives you thanks.   140
I would the fool were married to her grave!

Capulet. Soft! Take me with you, take me with you,° wife.
How! Will she none? Doth she not give us thanks?
Is she not proud? Doth she not count her blest,
Unworthy as she is, that we have wrought   145
So worthy a gentleman to be her bridegroom?

Juliet. Not proud you have, but thankful that you have.
Proud can I never be of what I hate,
But thankful even for hate that is meant love.

Capulet. How, how! How, how! Chop-logic!° What is this?   150
"Proud," and "I thank you," and "I thank you not,"
And yet "not proud." Mistress minion,° you,
Thank me no thankings, nor proud me no prouds,
But fettle° your fine joints 'gainst Thursday next,
To go with Paris to Saint Peter's Church,   155
Or I will drag thee on a hurdle° thither.
Out, you green-sickness carrion!° Out, you baggage!
You tallow-face!

Lady Capulet. [*To* Capulet] Fie, fie! What are you mad!

Juliet. Good Father, I beseech you on my knees,
Hear me with patience but to speak a word.   160

Capulet. Hang thee, young baggage! Disobedient wretch!
I tell thee what. Get thee to church o' Thursday
Or never after look me in the face.
Speak not, reply not, do not answer me.
My fingers itch. Wife, we scarce thought us blest   165
That God had lent us but this only child,
But now I see this one is one too much,
And that we have a curse in having her.
Out on her, hilding!°

Nurse: God in Heaven bless her!
You are to blame, my lord, to rate° her so.   170

Capulet. And why, my lady wisdom? Hold your tongue,
Good prudence. Smatter° with your gossips,° go.

---

142. **Take me with you:** What do you mean?   150. **Chop-logic:** hair-splitting.   152. **Mistress minion:** saucy miss.   154. **fettle:** make ready.   156. **hurdle:** a frame used to carry condemned criminals to execution.   157. **green-sickness carrion:** anemic lump of flesh.   169. **hilding:** worthless girl.   170. **rate:** scold.   172. **Smatter:** chatter. **gossips:** cronies.

Nurse. I speak no treason.

Capulet. Oh, God ye godden.

Nurse. May not one speak?

Capulet. Peace, you mumbling fool!
    Utter your gravity° o'er a gossip's bowl, 175
    For here we need it not.

Lady Capulet. You are too hot.

Capulet. [*To* Juliet] God's bread!° It makes me mad.
    Day, night, hour, tide, time, work, play,
    Alone, in company, still° my care hath been
    To have her matched. And having now provided 180
    A gentleman of noble parentage,
    Of fair demesnes,° youthful, and nobly trained,
    Stuffed,° as they say, with honorable parts,°
    Proportioned as one's thought would wish a man—
    And then to have a wretched puling° fool, 185
    A whining mammet,° in her fortune's tender,°
    To answer "I'll not wed, I cannot love,
    I am too young, I pray you, pardon me."

---

175. **gravity:** wise words. 177. **God's bread:** by the sacred host. 179. **still:** always. 182. **demesnes** (dĭ-mānz′): estates, wealth. 183. **stuffed:** full. **parts:** qualities. 185. **puling:** whining. 186. **mammet:** doll. **in her fortune's tender:** when good fortune is offered to her.

But an you will not wed, I'll pardon you.
Graze where you will, you shall not house with me.   190
Look to 't, think on 't, I do not use to° jest.
Thursday is near. Lay hand on heart, advise.°
An you be mine, I'll give you to my friend.
An you be not, hang, beg, starve, die in the streets,
For, by my soul, I'll ne'er acknowledge thee,   195
Nor what is mine shall never do thee good—
Trust to 't, bethink you, I'll not be forsworn.°

                                                                    [*Exit.*]

Juliet. Is there no pity sitting in the clouds
    That sees into the bottom of my grief?
    O sweet my mother, cast me not away!   200
    Delay this marriage for a month, a week;
    Or, if you do not, make the bridal bed
    In that dim monument where Tybalt lies.
Lady Capulet. Talk not to me, for I'll not speak a word.
    Do as thou wilt, for I have done with thee.   205

                                                                    [*Exit.*]

Juliet. Oh, God!—O Nurse, how shall this be prevented?
    My husband is on earth, my faith in Heaven.
    How shall that faith return again to earth
    Unless that husband send it me from Heaven
    By leaving earth? Comfort me, counsel me.   210
    Alack, alack, that Heaven should practice stratagems°
    Upon so soft a subject as myself!
    What say'st thou? Hast thou not a word of joy?
    Some comfort, Nurse.
Nurse.   Faith, here it is.
    Romeo is banished, and all the world to nothing°   215
    That he dares ne'er come back to challenge° you;
    Or if he do, it needs must be by stealth.
    Then, since the case so stands as now it doth,
    I think it best you married with the County.
    Oh, he's a lovely gentleman!   220
    Romeo's a dishclout to him.° An eagle, madam,
    Hath not so green, so quick, so fair an eye
    As Paris hath. Beshrew° my very heart,
    I think you are happy in this second match,

---

191. **use to:** usually. 192. **advise:** be careful. 197. **be forsworn:** break my vow. 211. **stratagems:** violent deeds. 215. **all the world to nothing:** the odds are overwhelming. 216. **challenge:** claim. 221. **to him:** compared to him. 223. **Beshrew:** curse.

For it excels your first. Or if it did not, 225
Your first is dead, or 'twere as good he were
As living here and you no use of him.
Juliet. Speakest thou from thy heart?
Nurse. And from my soul too, else beshrew them both.
Juliet. Amen!
Nurse.   What?
Juliet.   Well, thou hast comforted me marvelous much 230
Go in, and tell my lady I am gone,
Having displeased my father, to Laurence' cell,
To make confession and to be absolved.
Nurse. Marry, I will, and this is wisely done.

[*Exit.*]

Juliet. Ancient damnation!° Oh, most wicked fiend! 235
Is it more sin to wish me thus forsworn,°
Or to dispraise my lord with that same tongue
Which she hath praised him with above compare
So many thousand times? Go, counselor.
Thou and my bosom° henceforth shall be twain. 240
I'll to the Friar, to know his remedy.
If all else fail, myself have power to die.

[*Exit.*]

235. **Ancient damnation:** old devil.   236. **forsworn:** perjured.   240. **bosom:** inner thoughts.

FOR STUDY AND DISCUSSION

1. How has the audience been prepared for the dueling scene at the opening of Act Three? What have you learned about Tybalt and Mercutio that makes their actions in this scene consistent with their characters?
2. Why does Romeo refuse to accept Tybalt's challenge? How does Mercutio interpret Romeo's action? Why does he decide to fight Tybalt?
3. How does Juliet first react when she learns that Romeo has killed Tybalt? Why does she then change her mind? What do these reactions show about her?

4. At the opening of Scene 3, Romeo is in despair. What happens to raise his spirits? Where else in the play has Romeo shown a sudden change in spirits?
5. In Act One Capulet was not eager to see Juliet married. Why has he suddenly decided to accept Paris' offer?
6. Why are Capulet and his wife surprised by Juliet's refusal to marry? How do they react? How has Shakespeare prepared you for Capulet's reaction in earlier scenes of the play?
7. What is the Nurse's advice to Juliet? Why do you suppose Juliet pretends to be comforted by the Nurse? What has she realized she must do?

DRAMATIC STRUCTURE: PLOT

Most plays begin with an *exposition,* an introduction to the situation and setting of the action. The first act of *Romeo and Juliet* presents the conflict between the Montagues and Capulets. Out of the enmity between these two houses will grow misfortune for all the major characters in the play. When the lovers meet at the Capulet party, the main action is set into motion.

The exposition of a play is followed by the *rising action,* a sequence of events that lead to a *turning point,* or *crisis.* During the second act, Romeo and Juliet declare their love and get married. They have not been struck by tragedy. There is even a possibility, nursed by Friar Laurence, that the marriage of the lovers will serve to unite the warring factions. But in Act Three, Tybalt kills Mercutio, and Romeo kills Tybalt. This is the turning point of the play; it determines how the action will come out.

Following the turning point is the *falling action,* which ends with the *resolution,* or conclusion of the play. The fortunes of the lovers steadily decline. Romeo is banished. The lovers must separate. Juliet finds herself alone, without the support of her parents or the Nurse. The action from this point on will lead directly to the final catastrophe. The *climax,* the point of greatest emotional intensity, usually comes at the end of a Shakespearean play.

LANGUAGE AND VOCABULARY

Recognizing Classical Allusions
The heroes and gods of ancient Greek and Roman mythology, largely forgotten during Medieval times, were of great interest during the Renaissance, when Shakespeare lived. References to these ancient heroes and gods are known as *classical allusions.*

Here is a classical allusion from Act Three, Scene 2:

> Gallop apace you fiery-footed steeds,
> Toward Phoebus' lodging.

The allusion, as the footnote tells, is to the horses of Phoebus (Apollo) the sun god, who, as the myth would have it, drove his chariot (the sun) across the sky each day. Juliet is urging the sun to hurry across the sky and set.

Using a dictionary or a book of mythology, explain the allusion in each of these quotations:

> But all so soon as the all-cheering sun
> Should in the farthest east begin to draw
> The shady curtains from *Aurora*'s bed.
> (I, 1, 107–109)

> She'll not be hit
> With *Cupid*'s arrow.
> (I, 1, 180–181)

> Bondage is hoarse, and may not speak aloud,
> Else would I tear the cave where *Echo* lies
> And make her airy tongue more hoarse than
>   mine
> With repetition of my Romeo's name.
> (II, 2, 160–163)

> I'll say yon gray is not the morning's eye,
> 'Tis but the pale reflex of *Cynthia*'s brow.
> (III, 5, 19–20)

Act Four

Scene 1

[Friar Laurence's *cell. Enter* Friar Laurence *and* Paris.]

Friar Laurence. On Thursday, sir? the time is very short.
Paris. My father° Capulet will have it so,
  And I am nothing slow to slack his haste.°
Friar Laurence. You say you do not know the lady's mind.
  Uneven is the course,° I like it not.   5
Paris. Immoderately she weeps for Tybalt's death,
  And therefore have I little talked of love,
  For Venus smiles not in a house of tears.
  Now, sir, her father counts it dangerous
  That she doth give her sorrow so much sway,   10
  And in his wisdom hastes our marriage,
  To stop the inundation° of her tears,
  Which, too much minded° by herself alone,
  May be put from her by society.°
  Now do you know the reason of this haste.   15
Friar Laurence. [*Aside*] I would I knew not why it should be slowed.
  Look, sir, here comes the lady toward my cell.

[*Enter* Juliet.]

Paris. Happily met, my lady and my wife!
Juliet. That may be, sir, when I may be a wife.
Paris. That may be must be, love, on Thursday next.   20
Juliet. What must be shall be.
Friar Laurence.   That's a certain text.
Paris. Come you to make confession to this Father?
Juliet. To answer that, I should confess to you.
Paris. Do not deny to him that you love me.
Juliet. I will confess to you that I love him.   25
Paris. So will ye, I am sure, that you love me.
Juliet. If I do so, it will be of more price
  Being spoke behind your back than to your face.
Paris. Poor soul, thy face is much abused with tears.

---

2. **father:** future father-in-law.   3. **And . . . haste:** I am as eager as he to hasten the marriage.   5. **Uneven is the course:** a rough proceeding.   12. **inundation:** flood.   13. **minded:** brooded over.   14. **society:** the company of others.

Juliet. The tears have got small victory by that,   30
    For it was bad enough before their spite.°
Paris. Thou wrong'st it more than tears with that report.
Juliet. That is no slander, sir, which is a truth,
    And what I spake, I spake it to my face.
Paris. Thy face is mine, and thou hast slandered it.   35
Juliet. It may be so, for it is not mine own.
    Are you at leisure, holy Father, now,
    Or shall I come to you at evening mass?
Friar Laurence. My leisure serves me, pensive° daughter, now.
    My lord, we must entreat the time alone.   40
Paris. God shield° I should disturb devotion!
    Juliet, on Thursday early will I rouse ye.
    Till then, adieu, and keep this holy kiss.

                                                     [Exit.]

Juliet. Oh, shut the door, and when thou hast done so,
    Come weep with me—past hope, past cure, past help!   45
Friar Laurence. Ah, Juliet, I already know thy grief,
    It strains me past the compass° of my wits.
    I hear thou must, and nothing may prorogue° it,
    On Thursday next be married to this County.
Juliet. Tell me not, Friar, that thou hear'st of this,   50
    Unless thou tell me how I may prevent it.
    If in thy wisdom thou canst give no help,
    Do thou but call my resolution wise, *[Draws a dagger]*
    And with this knife I'll help it presently.°
    God joined my heart and Romeo's, and thou our hands,   55
    And ere this hand, by thee to Romeo's sealed,
    Shall be the label to another deed,°
    Or my true heart with treacherous revolt
    Turn to another, this shall slay them both.
    Therefore, out of thy long-experienced time,   60
    Give me some present counsel; or, behold,
    'Twixt my extremes° and me this bloody knife
    Shall play the umpire, arbitrating that
    Which the commission° of thy years and art
    Could to no issue of true honor bring.   65
    Be not so long to speak, I long to die
    If what thou speak'st speak not of remedy.

---

31. **spite:** injury. 39. **pensive:** thoughtful, solemn. 41. **shield:** forbid. 47. **compass:** reach. 48. **prorogue:** postpone. 54. **presently:** immediately. 56–57. **ere . . . deed:** before my hand agrees to another contract. 62. **extremes:** misfortunes. 64. **commission:** authority.

Friar Laurence. Hold, daughter. I do spy a kind of hope,
　　Which craves as desperate an execution
　　As that is desperate which we would prevent. 70
　　If, rather than to marry County Paris,
　　Thou hast the strength of will to slay thyself,
　　Then it is likely thou wilt undertake
　　A thing like death to chide away this shame,
　　That copest° with death himself to 'scape from it. 75
　　And, if thou darest, I'll give thee remedy.
Juliet. Oh, bid me leap, rather than marry Paris,
　　From off the battlements of yonder tower;
　　Or walk in thievish ways; or bid me lurk
　　Where serpents are; chain me with roaring bears; 80
　　Or shut me nightly in a charnel house,°
　　O'ercover'd quite with dead men's rattling bones,
　　With reeky° shanks and yellow chapless° skulls;
　　Or bid me go into a new-made grave,
　　And hide me with a dead man in his shroud— 85
　　Things that to hear them told have made me tremble—
　　And I will do it without a fear or doubt,
　　To live an unstained wife to my sweet love.
Friar Laurence. Hold, then, go home, be merry, give consent
　　To marry Paris. Wednesday is tomorrow. 90
　　Tomorrow night look that thou lie alone,
　　Let not thy nurse lie with thee in thy chamber.
　　Take thou this vial, being then in bed,
　　And this distillèd liquor drink thou off,
　　When presently through all thy veins shall run 95
　　A cold and drowsy humor;° for no pulse
　　Shall keep his native° progress, but surcease.°
　　No warmth, no breath, shall testify thou livest.
　　The roses in thy lips and cheeks shall fade
　　To paly ashes, thy eyes' windows fall, 100
　　Like death when he shuts up the day of life.
　　Each part, deprived of supple government,°
　　Shall, stiff and stark and cold, appear like death.
　　And in this borrowed likeness of shrunk death
　　Thou shalt continue two and forty hours, 105
　　And then awake as from a pleasant sleep.
　　Now, when the bridegroom in the morning comes

---

75. **copest:** deals.　81. **charnel house:** shed for bones from old graves.　83. **reeky:** stinking.　**chapless:** without jaws.　96. **humor:** moisture, fluid.　97. **native:** natural.　**surcease:** cease.　102. **supple government:** ability to move.

To rouse thee from thy bed, there art thou dead.
Then, as the manner of our country is,
In thy best robes uncovered on the bier   110
Thou shalt be borne to that same ancient vault
Where all the kindred of the Capulets lie.
In the meantime, against° thou shalt awake,
Shall Romeo by my letters know our drift,°
And hither shall he come, and he and I   115
Will watch thy waking, and that very night
Shall Romeo bear thee hence to Mantua.
And this shall free thee from this present shame,
If no inconstant toy° nor womanish fear
Abate thy valor in the acting it.   120

Juliet. [*Taking the vial*] Give me, give me! Oh, tell not me of fear!
Friar Laurence. Hold, get you gone, be strong and prosperous
    In this resolve. I'll send a friar with speed
    To Mantua, with my letters to thy lord.
Juliet. Love give me strength! And strength shall help afford.   125
    Farewell, dear Father!

                                                    [*Exeunt.*]

Scene 2

[*Hall in* Capulet's house. *Enter* Capulet, Lady Capulet, Nurse, *and two* Servingmen.]

Capulet. So many guests invite as here are writ.

                                  [*Exit* First Servant.]

    Sirrah, go hire me twenty cunning cooks.
Second Servant. You shall have none ill, sir, for I'll try if they can lick their fingers.
Capulet. How can'st thou try them so?
Second Servant. Marry, sir, 'tis an ill cook that cannot lick his own fingers. Therefore, he   5
    that cannot lick his fingers goes not with me.
Capulet. Go, be gone.

                                  [*Exit* Second Servant.]

    We shall be much unfurnished° for this time.
    What, is my daughter gone to Friar Laurence?
Nurse. Aye, forsooth.   10
Capulet. Well, he may chance to do some good on her.
    A peevish self-willed harlotry° it is.

---

113. **against:** before.   114. **drift:** purpose, intention.   119. **inconstant toy:** fickle fancy, foolish whim.
  8. **unfurnished:** unprepared.   12. **harlotry:** hussy.

[*Enter* Juliet.]

Nurse. See where she comes from shrift with merry look.

Capulet. How now, my headstrong! Where have you been gadding?

Juliet. Where I have learned me to repent the sin   15
    Of disobedient opposition
    To you and your behests, and am enjoined
    By holy Laurence to fall prostrate here,
    To beg your pardon. [*Kneeling*] Pardon, I beseech you!
    Henceforward I am ever ruled by you.   20

Capulet. Send for the County, go tell him of this.
    I'll have this knot knit up tomorrow morning.

Juliet. I met the youthful lord at Laurence' cell,
    And gave him what becomèd° love I might,
    Not stepping o'er the bounds of modesty.   25

Capulet. Why, I am glad on 't, this is well. Stand up.
    This is as 't should be. Let me see the County.
    Aye, marry, go, I say, and fetch him hither.
    Now, afore God, this reverend holy Friar,
    All our whole city is much bound° to him.   30

Juliet. Nurse, will you go with me into my closet,°
    To help me sort° such needful ornaments
    As you think fit to furnish me tomorrow?

Lady Capulet. No, not till Thursday, there is time enough.

Capulet. Go, Nurse, go with her. We'll to church tomorrow.   35

[*Exeunt* Juliet *and* Nurse.]

Lady Capulet. We shall be short in our provision.
    'Tis now near night.

Capulet.   Tush, I will stir about,
    And all things shall be well, I warrant thee, wife.
    Go thou to Juliet, help to deck up her.
    I'll not to bed tonight, let me alone,   40
    I'll play the housewife for this once. What ho!°
    They are all forth. Well, I will walk myself
    To County Paris, to prepare him up
    Against tomorrow. My heart is wondrous light
    Since this same wayward girl is so reclaimed.   45

[*Exeunt.*]

---

24. **becomèd**: suitable, proper.   30. **bound**: in debt.   31. **closet**: small private room.   32. **sort**: select.   41. **What ho!**: Capulet calls for a servant.

Scene 3

[Juliet's *chamber. Enter* Juliet *and* Nurse.]

Juliet. Aye, those attires are best. But, gentle Nurse,
    I pray thee leave me to myself tonight;
    For I have need of many orisons°
    To move the Heavens to smile upon my state,°
    Which, well thou know'st, is cross° and full of sin.   5

[*Enter* Lady Capulet.]

Lady Capulet. What, are you busy, ho? Need you my help?
Juliet. No, madam, we have culled° such necessaries
    As are behooveful° for our state tomorrow.
    So please you, let me now be left alone,
    And let the nurse this night sit up with you,   10
    For I am sure you have your hands full all
    In this so sudden business.
Lady Capulet.   Goodnight.
    Get thee to bed and rest, for thou hast need.

                      [*Exeunt* Lady Capulet *and* Nurse.]

Juliet. Farewell! God knows when we shall meet again.
    I have a faint cold fear thrills through my veins   15
    That almost freezes up the heat of life.
    I'll call them back again to comfort me.
    Nurse!—What should she do here?
    My dismal scene I needs must act alone.
    Come, vial.   20
    What if this mixture do not work at all?
    Shall I be married then tomorrow morning?
    No, no, this shall forbid it. Lie thou there.

[*Laying down a dagger.*]

    What if it be a poison which the Friar
    Subtly hath ministered° to have me dead,   25
    Lest in this marriage he should be dishonored
    Because he married me before to Romeo?
    I fear it is. And yet methinks it should not,

---

3. **orisons:** prayers. 4. **state:** condition. 5. **cross:** amiss. 7. **culled:** selected. 8. **behooveful:** fit. 25. **ministered:** provided.

For he hath still been tried° a holy man.
How if, when I am laid into the tomb,   30
I wake before the time that Romeo
Come to redeem me? There's a fearful point.
Shall I not then be stifled in the vault,
To whose foul mouth no healthsome air breathes in,
And there die strangled ere my Romeo comes?   35
Or if I live, it is not very like,
The horrible conceit° of death and night,
Together with the terror of the place,
As in a vault, an ancient receptacle,
Where for this many hundred years the bones   40
Of all my buried ancestors are packed;
Where bloody Tybalt, yet but green in earth,°
Lies festering in his shroud; where, as they say,
At some hours in the night spirits resort—
Alack, alack, is it not like that I   45
So early waking, what with loathsome smells
And shrieks like mandrakes'° torn out of the earth,
That living mortals hearing them run mad?
Oh, if I wake, shall I not be distraught,
Environèd with all these hideous fears,   50
And madly play with my forefathers' joints,
And pluck the mangled Tybalt from his shroud,
And in this rage, with some great kinsman's bone,
As with a club, dash out my desperate brains?
Oh, look! Methinks I see my cousin's ghost   55
Seeking out Romeo, that did spit his body
Upon a rapier's point. Stay, Tybalt, stay!
Romeo, I come! This do I drink to thee.

[*She falls upon her bed, within the curtains.*]

Scene 4

[*Hall in* Capulet's *house. Enter* Lady Capulet *and* Nurse.]

Lady Capulet. Hold, take these keys, and fetch more spices, Nurse.
Nurse. They call for dates and quinces in the pastry.°

---

29. **tried:** found to be. 37. **conceit:** idea. 42. **green in earth:** newly buried. 47. **mandrakes:** plants with forked roots, which, according to superstition, screamed when dug up.
  2. **pastry:** the room where baking was done.

[*Enter* Capulet.]

Capulet. Come, stir, stir, stir! The second cock hath crowed,
    The curfew bell hath rung, 'tis three o'clock.
    Look to the baked meats, good Angelica.   5
    Spare not for cost.
Nurse.   Go, you cotquean,° go,
    Get you to bed. Faith, you'll be sick tomorrow
    For this night's watching.

---

6. **cotquean** (kŏt′kwēn): a man who meddles with women's affairs.

Capulet. No, not a whit. What! I have watched ere now
    All night for lesser cause, and ne'er been sick.   10
Lady Capulet. Aye, you have been a mousehunt° in your time,
    But I will watch you from such watching now.
                                  [Exeunt Lady Capulet *and* Nurse.]

Capulet. A jealoushood,° a jealoushood!

    [Enter three or four Servingmen, *with spits, and logs, and baskets.]*

                        Now, fellow, What's there?
First Servingman. Things for the cook, sir, but I know not what.
Capulet. Make haste, make haste. *[Exit* First Servingman.] Sirrah, fetch drier logs.   15
    Call Peter, he will show thee where they are.
Second Servingman. I have a head, sir, that will find out logs
    And never trouble Peter for the matter.
Capulet. Mass,° and well said, ha!
    Thou shalt be loggerhead.° *[Exit* Second Servingman.] Good faith, 'tis day.   20
    The County will be here with music straight,
    For so he said he would. *[Music within.]* I hear him near.
    Nurse! Wife! What ho! What, Nurse, I say!

                  [Reenter Nurse.]

    Go waken Juliet, go and trim her up.
    I'll go and chat with Paris. Hie, make haste,   25
    Make haste. The bridegroom he is come already.
    Make haste, I say.

                                         [Exeunt.]

Scene 5

    [Juliet's *chamber. Curtains drawn around her bed. Enter* Nurse.]

Nurse. Mistress! What, mistress! Juliet! Fast,° I warrant her, she.
    Why, lamb! Why, lady! Fie, you slugabed!
    Why, love, I say! Madam! Sweetheart! Why, bride!
    What, not a word?

                [Undraws the curtains.]

---

11. **mousehunt:** in today's slang, "a wolf."   13. **jealoushood:** jealousy.   19. **Mass:** by the mass.   20. **loggerhead:** blockhead.
  1. **Fast:** fast asleep.

What, dressed! And in your clothes! And down again!   5
I must needs wake you. Lady, lady, lady!
Alas, alas! Help, help! My lady's dead!
Oh, welladay that ever I was born!
Some aqua vitae, ho! My lord! My lady!

[*Enter* Lady Capulet.]

Lady Capulet. What noise is here?
Nurse.   Oh, lamentable day!   10
Lady Capulet. What is the matter?
Nurse.   Look, look! Oh, heavy day!
Lady Capulet. Oh me, oh me! My child, my only life,
   Revive, look up, or I will die with thee.
   Help! help! Call help.

[*Enter* Capulet.]

Capulet. For shame, bring Juliet forth, her lord is come.   15
Nurse. She's dead, deceased, she's dead, alack the day!
Lady Capulet. Alack the day, she's dead, she's dead, she's dead!
Capulet. Ha! Let me see her. Out, alas! She's cold.
   Her blood is settled and her joints are stiff.
   Life and these lips have long been separated.   20
   Death lies on her like an untimely frost
   Upon the sweetest flower of all the field.
Nurse. Oh, lamentable day!
Lady Capulet.   Oh, woeful time!
Capulet. Death, that hath ta'en her hence to make me wail,
   Ties up my tongue and will not let me speak.   25

[*Enter* Friar Laurence *and* Paris *with* Musicians.]

Friar Laurence. Come, is the bride ready to go to church?
Capulet. Ready to go, but never to return.
   Death is my son-in-law, Death is my heir,
   My daughter he hath wedded. I will die,
   And leave him all—life, living, all is Death's.   30
Paris. Have I thought long to see this morning's face
   And doth it give me such a sight as this?
Lady Capulet. Accurst, unhappy, wretched, hateful day!
   Most miserable hour that e'er time saw

In lasting labor of his pilgrimage!   35
But one, poor one, one poor and loving child,
But one thing to rejoice and solace° in,
And cruel death hath catched it from my sight!

Nurse. Oh, woe! Oh, woeful, woeful, woeful day!
Most lamentable day, most woeful day,   40
That ever, ever, I did yet behold!
Oh, day, oh, day, oh, day! Oh, hateful day!
Never was seen so black a day as this.
Oh, woeful day, oh, woeful day!

Paris. Beguiled, divorced, wronged, spited, slain!   45
Most detestable death, by thee beguiled,
By cruel cruel thee quite overthrown!
Oh, love! Oh, life! Not life, but love in death!

Capulet. Despised, distressed, hated, martyred, killed!
Uncomfortable° time, why camest thou now   50
To murder, murder our solemnity?
O child! O child! My soul, and not my child!
Dead art thou! Alack, my child is dead,
And with my child my joys are burièd!

Friar Laurence. Peace ho, for shame! Confusion's cure lives not   55
In these confusions. Heaven and yourself
Had part in this fair maid, now Heaven hath all,
And all the better is it for the maid.
Your part in her you could not keep from death,
But Heaven keeps his part in eternal life.   60
The most you sought was her promotion,
For 'twas your heaven she should be advanced.
And weep ye now, seeing she is advanced
Above the clouds, as high as Heaven itself?
Oh, in this love, you love your child so ill   65
That you run mad, seeing that she is well.°
She's not well married that lives married long,
But she's best married that dies married young.
Dry up your tears, and stick your rosemary°
On this fair corse, and, as the custom is,   70
In all her best array bear her to church.
For though fond nature° bids us all lament,
Yet nature's tears are reason's merriment.°

---

37. **solace:** take comfort.   50. **Uncomfortable:** distressing.   66. **well:** that is, in heaven.   69. **rosemary:** Rosemary was used for weddings and funerals.   72. **nature:** human nature.   73. **nature's tears . . . merriment:** though natural to weep, there is also reason to rejoice (because Juliet is in heaven).

Capulet. All things that we ordainèd° festival
    Turn from their office to black funeral.   75
    Our instruments to melancholy bells,
    Our wedding cheer to a sad burial feast,
    Our solemn hymns to sullen dirges change,
    Our bridal flowers serve for a buried corse,
    And all things change them to the contrary.   80
Friar Laurence. Sir, go you in, and, madam, go with him.
    And go, Sir Paris, everyone prepare
    To follow this fair corse into her grave.
    The Heavens do lour° upon you for some ill;
    Move them no more by crossing their high will.   85
                    [*Exeunt* Capulet, Lady Capulet, Paris, *and* Friar.]

---

74. **ordainèd:** intended for. 84. **lour:** frown, scowl.

FOR STUDY AND DISCUSSION

1. Why do you think the Friar doesn't tell Paris or the Capulets that Juliet is already married to Romeo?

2. How does Juliet respond to Paris' gallantries when she meets him at Friar Laurence's cell? Is Paris aware of her true feelings for him? How do you know?

3. What is the Friar's scheme for reuniting Romeo and Juliet? How is Romeo to be told of this plan?

4. How and why does Capulet's mood change during Scene 2? What important change does he make in the wedding plans? How will this change affect the timing of the Friar's plan?

5. What doubts does Juliet have before drinking the Friar's potion? What are her fears? What finally causes her to drink the potion?

6. How does the mood of Scene 4 differ from that of Scenes 3 and 5?

7. What argument does the Friar use to comfort Paris, Juliet's parents, and the Nurse? What "ill" is he probably referring to in line 84 in Scene 5?

8. From the point of view of her parents, the Nurse, and Paris, what must have been the cause of Juliet's death?

DRAMATIC STRUCTURE: DRAMATIC IRONY

In Scene 4 we watch Capulet happily making preparations for Juliet's wedding. We know that at any moment he will discover that Juliet is dead. We know something that he does not.

This is an example of *dramatic irony*. We are outside the play, yet we possess special knowledge that would affect the characters if they were aware of it. But, of course, there is no way we can affect the action on stage.

Dramatic irony is one of the most powerful tools playwrights have at their disposal. Dramatic irony heightens suspense. It involves us in the action and increases our sympathy for the characters.

Look back through the first four acts of the play and locate some moments of dramatic irony. Jot down what piece of information you had that the characters lacked.

LANGUAGE AND VOCABULARY

Noting Obsolete and Archaic Meanings

Look at the word *and* in this quotation:

Nay, and there were two such, we should have none shortly, for one would kill the other.

Nowadays we would say *if* rather than *and*. But in Shakespeare's time, *if* was one of the meanings of *and*. The dictionary tells us that *if* is an *obsolete* meaning of *and*. Obsolete means "out of date, no longer used." The word *archaic* also means "out of date." However, there is this difference: an archaic meaning might still be used, but rarely, and only for special purposes.

Try to define the italicized words in the following passages without looking back at the footnotes. Then consult the notes to check your answers.

And then my husband—God be with his
    soul!
'*A* was a merry man—took up the child.
                    (I, 3, 30-31)

Therefore pardon me,
And not impute this yielding to light love,
Which the dark night hath so *discovered*.
                (II, 2, 104-105)

Tybalt would kill thee,
But thou slew'st Tybalt. There art thou
    happy too.
                (III, 3, 122-123)

Take thou this vial, being then in bed,
And this distillèd liquor drink thou off,
When presently through all thy veins shall
    run
A cold and drowsy *humor* . . .
                (IV, 1, 93-96)

What if it be a poison which the Friar
Subtly hath ministered to have me dead . . .
I fear it is; and yet methinks it should not,
For he hath *still* been tried a holy man.
         (IV, 3, 24-25, 28-29)

Act Five

Scene 1

[*Mantua. A street. Enter* Romeo.]

Romeo. If I may trust the flattering truth of sleep,°
   My dreams presage° some joyful news at hand.
   My bosom's lord° sits lightly in his throne,
   And all this day an unaccustomed spirit
   Lifts me above the ground with cheerful thoughts.   5
   I dreamed my lady came and found me dead—
   Strange dream, that gives a dead man leave to think!—
   And breathed such life with kisses in my lips
   That I revived and was an emperor.
   Ah me, how sweet is love itself possessed   10
   When but love's shadows are so rich in joy!

[*Enter* Balthasar, Romeo's *servant, booted.*°]

   News from Verona! How now, Balthasar!
   Dost thou not bring me letters from the Friar?
   How doth my lady? Is my father well?
   How fares my Juliet? That I ask again;   15
   For nothing can be ill if she be well.
Balthasar. Then she is well, and nothing can be ill.
   Her body sleeps in Capels' monument,°
   And her immortal part with angels lives.
   I saw her laid low in her kindred's vault,   20
   And presently took post° to tell it you.
   Oh, pardon me for bringing these ill news,
   Since you did leave it for my office,° sir.
Romeo. Is it e'en so? Then I defy you, stars!
   Thou know'st my lodging. Get me ink and paper,   25
   And hire post horses. I will hence tonight.
Balthasar. I do beseech you, sir, have patience.
   Your looks are pale and wild, and do import°
   Some misadventure.°

---

1. **flattering truth of sleep:** happy dreams that seemed true. 2. **presage** (prĭ-sāj′): foretell. 3. **bosom's lord:** heart. S.D. **booted:** in riding boots. 18. **monument:** tomb. 21. **took post:** rode fast. 23. **office:** duty. 28. **import:** suggest, imply. 29. **misadventure:** misfortune.

Romeo. Tush, thou art deceived.
    Leave me, and do the thing I bid thee do.   30
    Hast thou no letters to me from the Friar?
Balthasar. No, my good lord.
Romeo.   No matter. Get thee gone,
    And hire those horses. I'll be with thee straight.

                                            [Exit Balthasar.]

    Well, Juliet, I will lie with thee tonight.
    Let's see for means—O mischief, thou art swift   35
    To enter in the thoughts of desperate men!
    I do remember an apothecary,
    And hereabouts he dwells, which late I noted
    In tattered weeds,° with overwhelming° brows,
    Culling of simples.° Meager were his looks,   40
    Sharp misery had worn him to the bones.
    And in his needy shop a tortoise hung,
    An alligator stuffed and other skins
    Of ill-shaped fishes; and about his shelves
    A beggarly account° of empty boxes,   45
    Green earthen pots, bladders, and musty seeds,
    Remnants of packthread and old cakes of roses,°
    Were thinly scattered, to make up a show.
    Noting this penury, to myself I said,
    "An if a man did need a poison now,   50
    Whose sale is present death in Mantua,
    Here lives a caitiff° wretch would sell it him."
    Oh, this same thought did but forerun my need,
    And this same needy man must sell it me.
    As I remember, this should be the house.   55
    Being holiday, the beggar's shop is shut.
    What ho! Apothecary!

                        [Enter Apothecary.]

Apothecary.   Who calls so loud?
Romeo. Come hither, man. I see that thou art poor.
    Hold, there is forty ducats. Let me have
    A dram of poison, such soon-speeding gear°   60
    As will disperse itself through all the veins,
    That the life-weary taker may fall dead.

---

39. **weeds:** clothes. **overwhelming:** overhanging. 40. **simples:** herbs. 45. **account:** number. 47. **cakes of roses:** dried rose leaves compressed into cakes, used for perfume. 52. **caitiff** (kā′tĭf): miserable. 60. **gear:** stuff.

Apothecary. Such mortal drugs I have, but Mantua's law
    Is death to any he that utters° them.
Romeo. Art thou so bare and full of wretchedness,   65
    And fear'st to die? Famine is in thy cheeks,
    Need and oppression starveth in thy eyes,
    Contempt and beggary hangs upon thy back,
    The world is not thy friend, nor the world's law.
    The world affords no law to make thee rich,   70
    Then be not poor, but break it, and take this.
Apothecary. My poverty, but not my will, consents.
Romeo. I pay thy poverty and not thy will.
Apothecary. Put this in any liquid thing you will,
    And drink it off, and if you had the strength   75
    Of twenty men, it would dispatch you straight.
Romeo. There is thy gold, worse poison to men's souls,
    Doing more murder in this loathsome world
    Than these poor compounds that thou mayst not sell.
    I sell thee poison, thou hast sold me none.   80
    Farewell. Buy food, and get thyself in flesh.
    Come, cordial° and not poison, go with me
    To Juliet's grave, for there must I use thee.

                                                           [Exeunt.]

Scene 2

                          [Friar Laurence*'s cell.*]

Friar John. Holy Franciscan friar! Brother, ho!

                        [*Enter* Friar Laurence.]

Friar Laurence. This same should be the voice of Friar John.
    Welcome from Mantua. What says Romeo?
    Or if his mind be writ, give me his letter.
Friar John. Going to find a barefoot brother out,   5
    One of our order, to associate° me
    Here in this city visiting the sick,
    And finding him, the searchers° of the town,
    Suspecting that we both were in a house
    Where the infectious pestilence° did reign,   10

---

64. **utters:** sells. 82. **cordial:** restorative medicine.
  6. **associate:** accompany. 8. **searchers:** health officers. 10. **pestilence:** plague. When a case of plague was discovered, all persons in the house were locked in to prevent the disease from spreading.

Sealed up the doors and would not let us forth,
So that my speed to Mantua there was stayed.
Friar Laurence. Who bare my letter, then, to Romeo?
Friar John. I could not send it—here it is again—
    Nor get a messenger to bring it thee,   15
    So fearful were they of infection.
Friar Laurence. Unhappy fortune! By my brotherhood,
    The letter was not nice,° but full of charge°
    Of dear import,° and the neglecting it
    May do much danger. Friar John, go hence.   20
    Get me an iron crow° and bring it straight
    Unto my cell.
Friar John. Brother, I'll go and bring it thee.

                                                    [*Exit.*]

Friar Laurence. Now must I to the monument alone.
    Within this three hours will fair Juliet wake.   25
    She will beshrew° me much that Romeo
    Hath had no notice of these accidents.
    But I will write again to Mantua,
    And keep her at my cell till Romeo come.
    Poor living corse, closed in a dead man's tomb!   30
                                                    [*Exit.*]

Scene 3

[*A churchyard; in it a monument belonging to the* Capulets. *Enter* Paris *and his* Page, *bearing flowers and a torch.*]

Paris. Give me thy torch, boy. Hence, and stand aloof.
    Yet put it out, for I would not be seen.
    Under yond yew trees lay thee all along,°
    Holding thine ear close to the hollow ground.
    So shall no foot upon the churchyard tread,   5
    Being loose, unfirm, with digging up of graves,
    But thou shalt hear it. Whistle then to me,
    As signal that thou hear'st something approach.
    Give me those flowers. Do as I bid thee, go.
Page. [*Aside*] I am almost afraid to stand alone   10
    Here in the churchyard, yet I will adventure.   [*Retires.*]

---

18. **nice:** trivial. **full of charge:** weighty, important.   19. **dear import:** great importance.   21. **crow:** crowbar.
26. **beshrew:** blame.
  3. **all along:** at full length.

Paris. Sweet flower, with flowers thy bridal bed I strew —
    Oh, woe! Thy canopy is dust and stones —
    Which with sweet water nightly I will dew,
      Or, wanting that, with tears distilled by moans.   15
    The obsequies° that I for thee will keep
    Nightly shall be to strew thy grave and weep.

                [The Page *whistles.]*

    The boy gives warning something doth approach.
    What cursèd foot wanders this way tonight,
    To cross° my obsequies and true love's rite?   20
    What, with a torch! Muffle° me, night, awhile.   *[Retires.]*

      [Enter Romeo *and* Balthasar, *with a torch, mattock,° etc.]*

Romeo. Give me that mattock and the wrenching iron.
    Hold, take this letter. Early in the morning
    See thou deliver it to my lord and father.
    Give me the light. Upon thy life, I charge thee,   25
    Whate'er thou hear'st or seest, stand all aloof,
    And do not interrupt me in my course.
    Why I descend into this bed of death
    Is partly to behold my lady's face,
    But chiefly to take thence from her dead finger   30
    A precious ring, a ring that I must use
    In dear employment.° Therefore hence, be gone.
    But if thou, jealous,° dost return to pry
    In what I farther shall intend to do,
    By Heaven, I will tear thee joint by joint   35
    And strew this hungry churchyard with thy limbs.
    The time and my intents are savage-wild,
    More fierce and more inexorable far
    Than empty° tigers or the roaring sea.
Balthasar. I will be gone, sir, and not trouble you.   40
Romeo. So shalt thou show me friendship. Take thou that. *[Giving money]*
    Live, and be prosperous, and farewell, good fellow.
Balthasar. *[Aside]* For all this same, I'll hide me hereabout.
    His looks I fear, and his intents I doubt.°   *[Retires.]*

---

16. **obsequies** (ob′sə-kwēz): funeral rites. 20. **cross:** thwart, interrupt. 21. **Muffle:** hide. S.D. **mattock:** a tool like a pick, with a broad end. 32. **in dear employment:** for an important purpose. 33. **jealous:** curious. 39. **empty:** hungry. 44. **doubt:** suspect.

Romeo. Thou detestable maw,° thou womb of death, 45
    Gorged with the dearest morsel of the earth,
    Thus I enforce thy rotten jaws to open,
    And in despite° I'll cram thee with more food.

[Opens the tomb.]

Paris. This is that banished haughty Montague
    That murdered my love's cousin, with which grief 50
    It is supposèd the fair creature died,
    And here is come to do some villainous shame
    To the dead bodies. I will apprehend° him.

[Comes forward.]

    Stop thy unhallowed toil, vile Montague!
    Can vengeance be pursued further than death? 55
    Condemnèd villain, I do apprehend thee.
    Obey, and go with me, for thou must die.
Romeo. I must indeed, and therefore came I hither.
    Good gentle youth, tempt not a desperate man.
    Fly hence and leave me. Think upon these gone, 60
    Let them affright thee. I beseech thee, youth,
    Put not another sin upon my head,
    By urging me to fury. Oh, be gone!
    By Heaven, I love thee better than myself,
    But I come hither armed against myself. 65
    Stay not, be gone. Live, and hereafter say
    A madman's mercy bid thee run away.
Paris. I do defy thy conjurations°
    And apprehend thee for a felon here.
Romeo. Wilt thou provoke me? Then have at thee, boy! 70
Page. Oh, Lord, they fight! I will go call the watch.

[Exit.]

Paris. Oh, I am slain! *[Falls.]* If thou be merciful,
    Open the tomb, lay me with Juliet.

[Dies.]

Romeo. In faith, I will. Let me peruse this face.
    Mercutio's kinsman, noble County Paris! 75
    What said my man, when my betossèd° soul

---

45. **maw:** stomach. 48. **despite:** scorn, defiance. 53. **apprehend:** arrest. 68. **conjurations:** spells. 76. **betossèd:** upset.

Did not attend° him as we rode? I think
He told me Paris should have married Juliet.
Said he not so? Or did I dream it so?
Or am I mad, hearing him talk of Juliet,   80
To think it was so? Oh, give me thy hand,
One writ with me in sour misfortune's book!
I'll bury thee in a triumphant grave—
A grave? Oh, no, a lantern,° slaughtered youth;
For here lies Juliet, and her beauty makes   85
This vault a feasting presence° full of light.
Death, lie thou there, by a dead man interred.

[*Laying* Paris *in the monument.*]

How oft when men are at the point of death
Have they been merry! Which their keepers call
A lightning° before death. Oh, how may I   90
Call this a lightning? [*Sees* Juliet.] O my love! My wife!
Death, that hath sucked the honey of thy breath,
Hath had no power yet upon thy beauty.
Thou art not conquered; beauty's ensign° yet
Is crimson in thy lips and in thy cheeks,   95
And death's pale flag is not advancèd there.
Tybalt, liest thou there in thy bloody sheet?
Oh, what more favor can I do to thee
Than with that hand that cut thy youth in twain
To sunder° his that was thine enemy?   100
Forgive me, Cousin! Ah, dear Juliet,
Why art thou yet so fair? Shall I believe
That unsubstantial death is amorous,
And that the lean abhorrèd monster keeps
Thee here in dark to be his paramour?   105
For fear of that, I still will stay with thee,
And never from this palace of dim night
Depart again. Here, here will I remain
With worms that are thy chambermaids. Oh, here
Will I set up my everlasting rest,   110
And shake the yoke of inauspicious° stars
From this world-wearied flesh. Eyes, look your last!

---

77. **attend:** listen to.   84. **lantern:** dome with windows that gives additional light to a hall.   86. **a feasting presence:** a hall lit brightly for a feast.   90. **lightning:** brightening.   94. **ensign:** flag.   100. **sunder:** cut off.   111. **inauspicious:** unlucky.

Arms, take your last embrace! And lips, O you
The doors of breath, seal with a righteous kiss
A dateless° bargain to engrossing° death!   115
Come, bitter conduct,° come unsavory guide!
Thou desperate pilot,° now at once run on
The dashing rocks thy seasick weary bark.°
Here's to my love! [*Drinks the poison.*] O true apothecary!
Thy drugs are quick. Thus with a kiss I die.   120

                                                                        [*Dies.*]

[*Enter, at the other end of the churchyard,* Friar Laurence, *with a lantern, crowbar, and*
  spade.]

Friar Laurence. Saint Francis be my speed!° How oft tonight
    Have my old feet stumbled° at graves! Who's there?
Balthasar. Here's one a friend, and one that knows you well.
Friar Laurence. Bliss be upon you! Tell me, good my friend,
    What torch is yond that vainly lends his light   125
    To grubs and eyeless skulls? As I discern,
    It burneth in the Capel's monument.
Balthasar. It doth so, holy sir, and there's my master,
    One that you love.
Friar Laurence.   Who is it?
Balthasar.   Romeo.
Friar Laurence. How long hath he been there?
Balthasar.   Full half an hour.   130
Friar Laurence. Go with me to the vault.
Balthasar.   I dare not, sir.
    My master knows not but I am gone hence,
    And fearfully did menace me with death
    If I did stay to look on his intents.
Friar Laurence. Stay, then, I'll go alone. Fear comes upon me—   135
    Oh, much I fear some ill unlucky thing.
Balthasar. As I did sleep under this yew tree here,
    I dreamed my master and another fought,
    And that my master slew him.
Friar Laurence.   Romeo! [*Advances.*]
    Alack, alack, what blood is this which stains   140
    The stony entrance of this sepulcher?
    What mean these masterless and gory swords
    To lie discolored by this place of peace?

---

115. **dateless:** unending. **engrossing:** self-encompassing. 116. **conduct·** guide. 117. **desperate pilot:** Romeo.
118. **bark:** ship. 121. **speed:** help. 122. **stumbled:** Stumbling was consi͟   ͟vil omen.

[*Enters the tomb.*] Romeo! Oh, pale! Who else? What, Paris too? 145
And steeped in blood? Ah, what an unkind hour
Is guilty of this lamentable chance!
The lady stirs.

[Juliet *wakes.*]

Juliet. O comfortable° Friar! Where is my lord?
I do remember well where I should be,
And there I am. Where is my Romeo? 150

[*Noise within.*]

Friar Laurence. I hear some noise, Lady, come from that nest
Of death, contagion, and unnatural sleep.
A greater power than we can contradict
Hath thwarted our intents. Come, come away.
Thy husband in thy bosom there lies dead, 155
And Paris, too. Come, I'll dispose of thee
Among a sisterhood of holy nuns.
Stay not to question, for the watch is coming.
Come, go, good Juliet, I dare no longer stay.
Juliet. Go, get thee hence, for I will not away. 160

[*Exit* Friar Laurence.]

What's here? A cup, closed in my true love's hand?
Poison, I see, hath been his timeless° end.
O churl! Drunk all, and left no friendly drop
To help me after? I will kiss thy lips—
Haply° some poison yet doth hang on them 165
To make me die with a restorative.

[*Kisses him.*]

Thy lips are warm.
First Watchman. [*Within*] Lead, boy. Which way?
Juliet. Yea, noise? Then I'll be brief. O happy dagger!

[*Snatching* Romeo's *dagger.*]

This is thy sheath. [*Stabs herself.*] There rust, and let me die. 170

[*Falls on* Romeo's *body, and dies.*]

[*Enter* Watch, *with the* Page *of* Paris.]

148. **comfortable:** comforting.   162. **timeless:** untimely.   165. **Haply:** perhaps.

Page. This is the place—there, where the torch doth burn.
First Watchman. The ground is bloody. Search about the churchyard.
    Go, some of you, whoe'er you find attach.°
    Pitiful sight! Here lies the County slain,
    And Juliet bleeding, warm, and newly dead,   175
    Who here hath lain this two days burièd.
    Go tell the Prince. Run to the Capulets,
    Raise up the Montagues. Some others search.
    We see the ground whereon these woes do lie,
    But the true ground of all these piteous woes   180
    We cannot without circumstance° descry.°

        [Reenter some of the Watch, *with* Balthasar.]

Second Watchman. Here's Romeo's man. We found him in the churchyard.
First Watchman. Hold him in safety till the Prince come hither.

        [Reenter Friar Laurence, *and another* Watchman.]

---

173. **attach:** arrest. 181. **circumstance:** knowledge of the facts. **descry:** understand.

Third Watchman. Here is a friar that trembles, sighs, and weeps.
    We took this mattock and this spade from him   185
    As he was coming from this churchyard's side.
First Watchman. A great suspicion. Stay the friar too.

[*Enter the* Prince *and* Attendants.]

Prince. What misadventure is so clearly up
    That calls our person from our morning rest?

[*Enter* Capulet, Lady Capulet, *and others.*]

Capulet. What should it be that they so shriek abroad?   190
Lady Capulet. The people in the street cry Romeo,
    Some Juliet, and some Paris, and all run
    With open outcry toward our monument.
Prince. What fear is this which startles in our ears?
First Watchman. Sovereign, here lies the County Paris slain,   195
    And Romeo dead, and Juliet, dead before,
    Warm and new-killed.
Prince. Search, seek, and know how this foul murder comes.
First Watchman. Here is a friar, and slaughtered Romeo's man,
    With instruments upon them fit to open   200
    These dead men's tombs.
Capulet. Oh, heavens! O wife, look how our daughter bleeds!
    This dagger hath mista'en, for, lo, his house°
    Is empty on the back of Montague,
    And it missheathèd in my daughter's bosom!   205
Lady Capulet. Oh me! This sight of death is as a bell°
    That warns my old age to a sepulcher.

[*Enter* Montague *and others.*]

Prince. Come, Montague, for thou art early up,
    To see thy son and heir more early down.
Montague. Alas, my liege, my wife is dead tonight,   210
    Grief of my son's exile hath stopped her breath.
    What further woe conspires against mine age?
Prince. Look, and thou shalt see.
Montague. O thou untaught! What manners is in this,
    To press before thy father to a grave?   215

---

203. **house:** here, sheath.   206. **bell:** Church bells tolled for the dead.

Prince. Seal up the mouth of outrage° for a while
Till we can clear these ambiguities
And know their spring,° their head, their true descent.
And then will I be general of your woes,
And lead you even to death. Meantime forbear,   220
And let mischance be slave to patience.
Bring forth the parties of suspicion.°
Friar Laurence. I am the greatest, able to do least,
Yet most suspected, as the time and place
Doth make against me, of this direful murder.   225
And here I stand, both to impeach° and purge°
Myself condemnèd and myself excused.
Prince. Then say at once what thou dost know in this.
Friar Laurence. I will be brief, for my short date of breath°
Is not so long as is a tedious tale.   230
Romeo, there dead, was husband to that Juliet,
And she, there dead, that Romeo's faithful wife.
I married them, and their stol'n marriage day
Was Tybalt's doomsday, whose untimely death
Banished the new-made bridegroom from this city,   235
For whom, and not for Tybalt, Juliet pined.
You, to remove that siege of grief from her,
Betrothed and would have married her perforce
To County Paris. Then comes she to me,
And with wild looks bid me devise some mean   240
To rid her from this second marriage,
Or in my cell there would she kill herself.
Then gave I her, so tutored by my art,
A sleeping potion, which so took effect
As I intended, for it wrought on her   245
The form of death. Meantime I writ to Romeo
That he should hither come as this° dire night,
To help to take her from her borrowed° grave,
Being the time the potion's force should cease.
But he which bore my letter, Friar John,   250
Was stayed by accident, and yesternight
Returned my letter back. Then all alone
At the prefixèd hour of her waking
Came I to take her from her kindred's vault,

---

216. **mouth of outrage:** the tomb where violent deeds were done. At this point the curtains at the back of the stage would be closed to hide the bodies.   218. **spring:** source.   222. **parties of suspicion:** suspected persons.   226. **impeach:** accuse.   **purge:** clear (of guilt).   229. **my short date of breath:** the little life left me.   247. **as this:** this same. 248. **borrowed:** temporary.

Meaning to keep her closely° at my cell   255
Till I conveniently could send to Romeo.
But when I came, some minute ere the time
Of her awaking, here untimely lay
The noble Paris and true Romeo dead.
She wakes, and I entreated her come forth,   260
And bear this work of Heaven with patience.
But then a noise did scare me from the tomb,
And she too desperate would not go with me,
But, as it seems, did violence on herself.
All this I know, and to the marriage   265
Her nurse is privy.° And if aught in this
Miscarried by my fault, let my old life
Be sacrificed some hour before his time
Unto the rigor of severest law.

Prince. We still° have known thee for a holy man.   270
    Where's Romeo's man? What can he say in this?

Balthasar. I brought my master news of Juliet's death,
    And then in post he came from Mantua
    To this same place, to his same monument.
    This letter he early bid me give his father,   275
    And threatened me with death, going in the vault,
    If I departed not and left him there.

Prince. Give me the letter, I will look on it.
    Where is the County's page, that raised the watch?
    Sirrah, what made° your master in this place?   280

Page. He came with flowers to strew his lady's grave,
    And bid me stand aloof, and so I did.
    Anon comes one with light to ope the tomb,
    And by and by my master drew on him,
    And then I ran away to call the watch.   285

Prince. This letter doth make good the Friar's words,
    Their course of love, the tidings of her death.
    And here he writes that he did buy a poison
    Of a poor 'pothecary, and therewithal
    Came to this vault to die and lie with Juliet.   290
    Where be these enemies? Capulet! Montague!
    See what a scourge° is laid upon your hate
    That Heaven finds means to kill your joys with love!
    And I, for winking° at your discords too,

---

255. **closely** secretly.　266. **is privy:** shares the secret.　270. **still:** always.　280. **made:** did.　292. **scourge:** punishment.　294. **winking:** shutting my eyes.

Have lost a brace° of kinsmen. All are punished.   295
Capulet. O Brother Montague, give me thy hand.
    This is my daughter's jointure,° for no more
    Can I demand.
Montague.   But I can give thee more.
    For I will raise her statue in pure gold,
    That whiles Verona by that name is known   300
    There shall no figure at such rate° be set
    As that of true and faithful Juliet.
Capulet. As rich shall Romeo's by his lady's lie,
    Poor sacrifices of our enmity!
Prince. A glooming° peace this morning with it brings,   305
    The sun for sorrow will not show his head.
    Go hence, to have more talk of these sad things.
    Some shall be pardoned and some punishèd.
    For never was a story of more woe
    Than this of Juliet and her Romeo.   310

                                      [*Exeunt.*]

---

295. **brace:** pair.   297. **jointure:** wedding gift.   301. **rate:** value.   305. **glooming:** cloudy, overcast.

FOR STUDY AND DISCUSSION

1. When Romeo says "I defy you, stars!" he challenges fate to do its worst. How is his reaction at this point similar to some of his reactions earlier in the play?

2. Why does Romeo think he will be able to convince the Apothecary to break the law of Mantua? What substance does Romeo consider to be more harmful than poison and why?

3. What circumstances kept Friar John from delivering the letter to Romeo?

4. Why does Paris come to Juliet's tomb? What effect does Paris' last request have on Romeo?

5. Why does the Friar run away, leaving Juliet behind?

6. How are Juliet's last actions in the play typical of her? Where else has she acted with such decisiveness?

7. What does the Prince mean when he says "all are punished"? What does he see as his own mistake?

8. What good has come from the deaths of Romeo and Juliet?

LANGUAGE AND VOCABULARY

Understanding Puns

A pun is a play on words. Shakespeare was fond of puns and his plays are full of them, even in serious moments.

Sometimes a pun plays on different meanings of a single word. When Mercutio refers to himself as a "grave man," he puns on two meanings of *grave*: "serious" and "ready for the grave." Sometimes a pun plays on different words that sound alike but that have different meanings. *Romeo and Juliet* begins with a triple pun on the word *collier* (coal vendor), which sounds like *choler* (anger) and *collar* (hangman's noose).

Identify the puns in the following quotations and state what different meanings are intended for each one.

Give me a torch. I am not for this ambling.
Being but heavy, I will bear the light.
(I, 4, 1–2)

Not I, believe me. You have dancing shoes
With nimble soles. I have a soul of lead
So stakes me to the ground I cannot move.
(I, 4, 4–6)

. . . What, dost thou make us minstrels? An thou make minstrels of us, look to hear nothing but discords.
(III, 1, 34–35)

We see the ground whereon these woes do lie,
But the true ground of all these piteous woes
We cannot without circumstance descry.
(V, 3, 179–181)

FOR FURTHER DISCUSSION

1. From 1660 to 1845, *Romeo and Juliet* was most often performed with an altered ending in which the young lovers did not die, but lived happily ever after. Would you have preferred the play to end happily? How does a happy ending alter the meaning of the play?

2. Is Romeo's love for Rosaline different from his love for Juliet? Does Romeo's character change during the play? Cite specific evidence to defend your answer.

3. Does Juliet develop a will of her own during the play, or does she merely shift her obedience from her parents to Romeo? Support your answer with quotations.

4. As the play is presented, do you think that Romeo and Juliet are responsible for what happens, or are they just the playthings of fate?

5. At the end of the play, Prince Escalus announces that "all are punished." Does everyone deserve to be punished? Does anyone get off too easily? Discuss.

Practice in
Reading and Writing

READING AND WRITING ABOUT SHAKESPEARE

Read each of the following comments on *Romeo and Juliet*.
Then write a paragraph or two supporting or contradicting
the writer's argument with quotations and evidence from the
play.

[Shakespeare saw the story] as a tale of the passions of youth.
His lovers are very young and innocent when love over-
whelms them. So are the bored young men, loafing about
town, in whom the passions of the feuding Capulets and
Montagues explode so fatally. The old Capulets and Montagues, and the worried Prince of Verona, feel partly responsible for the feud and try to control it. The Friar, when
Romeo and Juliet confide in him, does his best to guide their
love to life and safety. But the moving force which Shakespeare saw in the old story is that glamorous and dangerous
passion which everyone feels in youth, and no one fully understands at any age.

> Frances Fergusson
> Introduction to *Romeo and Juliet*
> Laurel Edition

The tragedy of *Romeo and Juliet* . . . is not simply a tragedy
of two individuals, but the tragedy of a city. Everybody in the
city is in one way or another involved in and responsible for
what happens.

> W. H. Auden
> Commentary on *Romeo and Juliet*
> Laurel Edition

In a tragedy like this, where love is the theme that is treated
under its manifold aspects, the contrast of joking and laughter should not be forgotten. Through the whole piece, as in a

many-voiced musical symphony, the voices of the young people at one time mingle in unison, then separate and flow onward in contrast; Benvolio the sedate, Tybalt the furious, Mercutio the witty, Romeo the enthusiast, Paris the tender, refined youth . . . .

Johann Ludwig Tieck
reprinted in *Romeo and Juliet*
New Variorum Edition

The Nurse, whatever her age, is a triumphant and complete achievement. She stands foursquare, and lives and breathes in her own right from the moment she appears. You may, indeed, take any sentence the Nurse speaks throughout the play, and only she could speak it.

Harley Granville-Barker
Prefaces to Shakespeare

Juliet begins as a demure girl who is prepared to listen respectfully to the advice of her mother. When she has fallen in love, she becomes suddenly a woman of great courage and resource, who will face even death and fantastic horror to regain her husband.

G. B. Harrison
Shakespeare: The Complete Works

In *Romeo and Juliet* the beauty and ardor of young love are seen by Shakespeare as the irradiating glory of sunlight and starlight in a dark world. The dominating image is *light* . . . the sun, moon, stars, fire, lightning, the flash of gunpowder, and the reflected light of beauty and of love; while by contrast we have night, darkness, clouds, rain, mist, and smoke. Each of the lovers thinks of the other as light . . .

Caroline Spurgeon
Shakespeare's Imagery

For Further Reading

Barrie, Sir James Matthew, *The Admirable Crichton* in *English Drama in Transition 1880–1920*, edited by Henry Frank Salerno (paperback, Pegasus, 1968)

A British lord and his butler change places when their party is shipwrecked on an island.

Blinn, William, *Brian's Song* (paperback, Bantam, 1972)

Highly acclaimed as a television drama, this true story depicts the friendship of two football players, Gale Sayers and Brian Piccolo. Piccolo died of cancer in 1970.

Chekhov, Anton, *The Bear* (or *The Boor*) in *Ten Great One-Act Plays*, edited by Morris Sweetkind (paperback, Bantam, 1968)

In this play, subtitled "A Jest in One Act," a retired lieutenant of the artillery, who believes in equal rights, challenges a pretty widow to a duel.

Chute, Marchette, *Stories from Shakespeare* (Collins-World, 1956; paperback, New American Library)

Shakespeare's tragedies, comedies, and histories are retold simply and clearly in prose.

Gilbert, W. S., *The Pirates of Penzance* in *The Complete Plays of Gilbert and Sullivan* (paperback, Norton, 1976)

In this comic opera, the reader discovers an ingenious paradox: Frederick, who has been apprenticed to a band of pirates until his twenty-first birthday, discovers he was born on February 29 and is therefore only five years old.

Hansberry, Lorraine, *To Be Young, Gifted and Black*, adapted by Robert Nemiroff (paperback, New American Library, 1969)

The author of *A Raisin in the Sun* presents her autobiography in dramatic form.

Kaufman, William I., editor, *Great Television Plays*, volume I (paperback, Dell, 1969)

This collection contains six plays, including *Requiem for a Heavyweight* by Rod Serling and *Twelve Angry Men* by Reginald Rose.

Koch, Howard, *The Invasion from Mars* in *The Panic Broadcast* (paperback, Avon, 1970)

This famous radio play, based on H. G. Wells's novel *The War of the Worlds*, caused a panic when it was broadcast in 1938.

Mersand, Joseph, editor, *Three Comedies of American Life* (paperback, Pocket Books, 1961)

Included are *I Remember Mama* by John van Druten, *Life with Father* by Howard Lindsay and Russel Crouse, and *You Can't Take It with You* by Moss Hart and George S. Kaufman.

Miller, Arthur, *The Crucible* (Viking Press, 1953; paperback, many editions)

Miller based this play on the witchcraft trials in Salem, Massachusetts, in 1692.

Rose, Reginald, *Thunder on Sycamore Street* in *The Mentor Book of Short Plays*, edited by Richard H. Goldstone and Abraham H. Lass (paperback, New American Library, 1969)

In addition to Rose's melodrama of suburban life, this anthology includes eleven short plays written for stage, radio, and television.

Rostand, Edmund, *Cyrano de Bergerac* (many editions)

Cyrano, legendary for his wit, his swordsmanship, and his huge nose, wins the love of the beautiful Roxane.

Shakespeare, William, *A Midsummer Night's Dream* (many editions)

This comedy about love and its comic confusions includes a hilarious performance of "Pyramus and Thisbe" by a troupe of amateur actors.

Sohn, David A., and Richard H. Tyre, editors, *Nine Modern Short Plays: Outstanding Works from Stage, Radio, and Television* (paperback, Bantam, 1977)

Included in this collection are works by Gore Vidal and Lucille Fletcher.

Wilder, Thornton, *Three Plays by Thornton Wilder* (Harper & Row, 1957; paperback, Avon)

The plays are *Our Town*, *The Skin of Our Teeth*, and *The Matchmaker*.

An *epic* is a long narrative poem about a national or legendary hero. Ancient Greece produced two epics—the *Iliad* and the *Odyssey*—which are considered the first great works of Western literature. The *Odyssey* is named for its hero, Odysseus, who is also known as Ulysses. The *Iliad* is not named for its hero, Achilles, but for Ilium, or Troy, the setting of the action.

Since classical times, both epics have been attributed to a poet named Homer. We know almost nothing about him. Seven different cities claimed to be his birthplace, but none could prove the claim. There is a tradition that Homer was blind, and an ancient bust shows him to be so. If he was blind, he must have had his sight at one time, for the poems are so rich in visual imagery that they are clearly the creation of someone who had observed the world carefully.

AN EPIC POEM: THE ODYSSEY

Head of Homer. Greek, Hellenistic period. Marble.
Museum of Fine Arts, Boston
H. L. Pierce Fund

Protesilaos, the first Greek killed at the landing before Troy. Silver coin from Macedonia, 500-490 B.C.
Museum of Fine Arts, Boston
Theodora Wilbour Fund in memory of Zoë Wilbour

Scholars have established that the *Iliad* was composed sometime between 900 and 700 B.C. and that it preceded the *Odyssey* by some years. The raw material of both epics was a well-known body of legend about the most famous event in Greek history, the Trojan War, which had occurred several centuries earlier, about 1200 B.C. The probable cause of the Trojan War was economic. Troy's location enabled it to control all trade and shipping through the Dardanelles: once Troy was destroyed, the Greeks could expand their trade routes as much as they pleased. According to legend, however, the war began when Helen, the most beautiful woman in the world and wife of King Menelaus of Sparta, was kidnapped by Paris, a young Trojan prince. It took several years for the outraged Menelaus to assemble an army, for Greece was not a unified nation at that time. Kings and soldiers from all over Greece—Achilles and Odysseus among them—sailed to Troy to bring back Helen. The war went on for ten years, and finally the Trojans were defeated.

Ruins of the ancient city of Troy, Turkey.
Art Resource

Homer used this legendary material as the basis for his poems. He added an original plot structure, realistic characters, dialogue and detail, and tales of fabulous monsters. Against the drama on earth he set the drama of the Olympian gods and goddesses, who were interested in human affairs and who often intervened to protect or punish mortals. Homer's portrayal of the gods made them seem human. They quarreled and loved and were jealous of each other. Although Homer occasionally treats the gods lightly, he is always respectful. A pervasive theme throughout these epics is that respect for the gods is essential to survival.

Hector Charges into Battle.
Bronze coin of Ilion (Troy),
struck under the Roman
Emperor Gallienus (253–268).
Museum of Fine Arts, Boston
Theodora Wilbour Fund
in Memory of Zoë Wilbour

When the poems were first composed, they were not written down. They were passed orally from one generation to the next. They were memorized by traveling poets called *rhapsodes,* who recited the epics in the banquet halls of kings and noble families. Both poems were recited in public every four years in Athens at the festival of Athena, goddess of wisdom and patron of the city. In time, the study of Homer's epics became the basis of Greek education. From Homer, Greek youths learned how to tell a story, to portray character, to give a speech, and to express the Greek ideals of thought and action. The *Iliad* and the *Odyssey* became models for later writers, notably the Roman poet Virgil, author of the *Aeneid.*

*Thetis Brings the Arms to Achilles, Who Is
Attended by Phoinix.* Vase painting, c. 540 B.C.
by the Amasis painter.
Museum of Fine Arts, Boston H. L. Pierce Fund

Trojan Horse. Relief on a wine jar, from Mykonos, first half of 7th century B.C.
Mykonos Museum, Greece
Erich Lessing, Magnum Photos

Detail from *Mourning Women.* Early Attic plaque, about 600 B.C.
Museum of Fine Arts, Boston
Charles Amos Cummings Fund

The *Iliad* opens in the tenth—and last—year of the Trojan War. The war is at a stalemate, and in the Greek camp there is much dissension. Achilles, the greatest warrior among the Greeks, and Agamemnon, the leader of the Greeks, have had a bitter quarrel over a captive slave girl. Achilles has withdrawn from the war and is sulking in his tent. His absence from the field gives the Trojans an advantage in the war. Only after Hector, the great Trojan hero, kills Achilles' friend Patroclus does Achilles return to combat. He kills Hector, and his victory demoralizes the Trojans. The *Iliad* ends with a twelve-day truce in which both sides bury and mourn their dead.

Homer tells about the last days of the Trojan War in his second epic. The man responsible for the fall of Troy is Odysseus, the shrewdest of the Greeks. He conceives a plan to leave a huge wooden horse filled with Greek warriors outside the gates of Troy. Believing that the Greek ships have sailed for home and that this wooden horse is an offering to the gods, the Trojans bring the horse within their gates. When the Trojans are off guard, the Greeks slip out of the horse and open the city gates to their own army.

The Odyssey 485

Return of Odysseus. Greek, 5th century B.C. Terracotta relief.
The Metropolitan Museum of Art, New York   Mr. and Mrs. Isaac D. Fletcher Collection, Fletcher Fund, 1930

Because Odysseus is instrumental in the destruction of Troy, he angers the gods who are sympathetic to Troy. They vow that he will have a long and difficult journey home. This homeward journey—which takes ten years—is the subject of the *Odyssey.*

The *Odyssey* is a very long poem—11,300 lines divided into twenty-four books. The poem has three major plot strands. First, there is the story of what happens in Ithaca to Odysseus' wife and son as they await his return. The second story is the tale of Odysseus' wanderings during the ten years following the Trojan War. These two strands come together when Odysseus returns to Ithaca and joins forces with his son, Telemachus, to destroy their enemies.

The Blinding of Polyphemus. Early Attic vase from Eleusis, second quarter of the 7th century B.C.
Eleusis Museum, Greece   Erich Lessing, Magnum Photos

People have interpreted the *Odyssey* in many different ways. Some read it simply as an exciting adventure story. In this sense, with its emphasis on character and plot, it has been rightly called a forerunner of the novel. Others interpret the *Odyssey* as the story of every human being, who must overcome temptations and obstacles in the journey through life and in the effort to find a place of peace and joy.

You will be reading some of the best-known excerpts from the poem. In Part 1 of the unit, you will read about the adventures of Odysseus and his crew as they attempt to return to Ithaca. In Part 2, you will read how Odysseus takes his place as rightful king of Ithaca. The text is a translation from the Greek by the American poet Robert Fitzgerald.

Ulysses and the Sirens. Attic vase from Vulci, c. 475 B.C. British Museum, London

487

The Odyssey

Homer

Translated by Robert Fitzgerald

PART 1   FAR FROM HOME

"I Am Odysseus"

Odysseus is in the banquet hall of Alcinous (ăl-sĭn′ō-əs),
King of Phaeacia (fē-ā′shə), who helps him on his way after
all his comrades have been killed and his last vessel destroyed. Odysseus tells the story of his adventures thus far.

"I am Laertes′° son, Odysseus.
                    Men hold me
formidable for guile in peace and war:
this fame has gone abroad to the sky's rim.
My home is on the peaked sea-mark of Ithaca°
under Mount Neion's wind-blown robe of leaves,   5
in sight of other islands—Dulichium,
Same, wooded Zacynthus—Ithaca
being most lofty in that coastal sea,
and northwest, while the rest lie east and south.
A rocky isle, but good for a boy's training;   10

1. **Laertes** (lā-ûr′tēz).

4. **Ithaca** (ĭth′ə-kə): an island off the west coast of Greece.

I shall not see on earth a place more dear,
though I have been detained long by Calypso,°
loveliest among goddesses, who held me
in her smooth caves, to be her heart's delight,
as Circe of Aeaea,° the enchantress,
desired me, and detained me in her hall.
But in my heart I never gave consent.
Where shall a man find sweetness to surpass
his own home and his parents? In far lands
he shall not, though he find a house of gold.
What of my sailing, then, from Troy?
                              What of those years
of rough adventure, weathered under Zeus?°
The wind that carried west from Ilion°
brought me to Ismarus, on the far shore,
a strongpoint on the coast of the Cicones.°
I stormed that place and killed the men who fought.
Plunder we took, and we enslaved the women,
to make division, equal shares to all—
but on the spot I told them: 'Back, and quickly!
Out to sea again!' My men were mutinous,
fools, on stores of wine. Sheep after sheep
they butchered by the surf, and shambling cattle,
feasting—while fugitives went inland, running
to call to arms the main force of Cicones.
This was an army, trained to fight on horseback
or, where the ground required, on foot. They came
with dawn over that terrain like the leaves
and blades of spring. So doom appeared to us,
dark word of Zeus for us, our evil days.
My men stood up and made a fight of it—
backed on the ships, with lances kept in play,
from bright morning through the blaze of noon
holding our beach, although so far outnumbered;
but when the sun passed toward unyoking time,
then the Achaeans,° one by one, gave way.
Six benches were left empty in every ship
that evening when we pulled away from death,
And this new grief we bore with us to sea:
our precious lives we had, but not our friends.
No ship made sail next day until some shipmate
had raised a cry, three times, for each poor ghost
unfleshed by the Cicones on that field.

15

20

25

30

35

40

45

50

12. **Calypso** (kə-lĭp′sō).

15. **Circe** (sûr′sē) of **Aeaea** (ē′ē-ə).

22. **Zeus** (zo͞os): king of the gods.

23. **Ilion** (ĭl′ē-ŏn): Troy.

25. **Cicones** (sĭ-kō′nēz).

45. **Achaeans** (ə-kē′ənz): Greeks
(Odysseus' men).

The Lotus-Eaters

Now Zeus the lord of cloud roused in the north
a storm against the ships, and driving veils
of squall moved down like night on land and sea.   55
The bows went plunging at the gust; sails
cracked and lashed out strips in the big wind.
We saw death in that fury, dropped the yards,
unshipped the oars, and pulled for the nearest lee:°
then two long days and nights we lay offshore   60
worn out and sick at heart, tasting our grief,
until a third Dawn came with ringlets shining.
Then we put up our masts, hauled sail, and rested,
letting the steersmen and the breeze take over.

I might have made it safely home, that time,   65
but as I came round Malea the current
took me out to sea, and from the north
a fresh gale drove me on, past Cythera.

59. **lee:** place sheltered from the wind.

Nine days I drifted on the teeming sea
before dangerous high winds. Upon the tenth   70
we came to the coastline of the Lotus-Eaters,
who live upon that flower. We landed there
to take on water. All ships' companies
mustered alongside for the midday meal.
Then I sent out two picked men and a runner   75
to learn what race of men that land sustained.
They fell in, soon enough, with Lotus-Eaters,
who showed no will to do us harm, only
offering the sweet Lotus to our friends—
but those who ate this honeyed plant, the Lotus,   80
never cared to report, nor to return:
they longed to stay forever, browsing on
that native bloom, forgetful of their homeland.
I drove them, all three wailing, to the ships,
tied them down under their rowing benches,   85
and called the rest: 'All hands aboard;
come, clear the beach and no one taste
the Lotus, or you lose your hope of home.'
Filing in to their places by the rowlocks
my oarsmen dipped their long oars in the surf,   90
and we moved out again on our seafaring.

The Cyclops

In the next land we found were Cyclopes,°
giants, louts, without a law to bless them.
In ignorance leaving the fruitage of the earth in mystery
to the immortal gods, they neither plow   95
nor sow by hand, nor till the ground, though grain—
wild wheat and barley—grows untended, and
wine grapes, in clusters, ripen in heaven's rain.
Cyclopes have no muster and no meeting,
no consultation or old tribal ways,   100
but each one dwells in his own mountain cave
dealing out rough justice to wife and child,
indifferent to what the others do. . . .

As we rowed on, and nearer to the mainland,
at one end of the bay, we saw a cavern   105
yawning above the water, screened with laurel,
and many rams and goats about the place
inside a sheepfold—made from slabs of stone
earthfast between tall trunks of pine and rugged
towering oak trees.
         A prodigious° man   110
slept in this cave alone, and took his flocks
to graze afield—remote from all companions,
knowing none but savage ways, a brute
so huge, he seemed no man at all of those
who eat good wheaten bread; but he seemed rather   115
a shaggy mountain reared in solitude.
We beached there, and I told the crew
to stand by and keep watch over the ship;
as for myself I took my twelve best fighters
and went ahead. I had a goatskin full   120
of that sweet liquor that Euanthes' son,
Maron, had given me. He kept Apollo's°
holy grove at Ismarus; for kindness
we showed him there, and showed his wife and child,
he gave me seven shining golden talents°   125
perfectly formed, a solid silver winebowl,
and then this liquor—twelve two-handled jars
of brandy, pure and fiery. Not a slave
in Maron's household knew this drink; only
he, his wife and the storeroom mistress knew;   130

92. **Cyclopes** (sī-klō′pēz), plural form of Cyclops (sī′-klŏps); a race of one-eyed Giants.

110. **prodigious** (prə-dĭj′əs): gigantic.

122. **Apollo** (ə-pŏl′ō): god of music, prophecy, and medicine.

125. **talent:** a unit of money in ancient Greece.

and they would put one cupful—ruby-colored,
honey-smooth—in twenty more of water,
but still the sweet scent hovered like a fume
over the winebowl. No man turned away
when cups of this came round.
                              A wineskin full   135
I brought along, and victuals in a bag,
for in my bones I knew some towering brute
would be upon us soon—all outward power,
a wild man, ignorant of civility.

We climbed, then, briskly to the cave. But Cyclops   140
had gone afield, to pasture his fat sheep,
so we looked round at everything inside:
a drying rack that sagged with cheeses, pens
crowded with lambs and kids, each in its class:
firstlings apart from middlings, and the 'dewdrops,'   145
or newborn lambkins, penned apart from both.
And vessels full of whey were brimming there—
bowls of earthenware and pails for milking.
My men came pressing round me, pleading:
                              'Why not
take these cheeses, get them stowed, come back,   150
throw open all the pens, and make a run for it?
We'll drive the kids and lambs aboard. We say
put out again on good salt water!'
                              Ah,
how sound that was! Yet I refused. I wished
to see the cave man, what he had to offer—   155
no pretty sight, it turned out, for my friends.

We lit a fire, burnt an offering,
and took some cheese to eat; then sat in silence
around the embers, waiting. When he came
he had a load of dry boughs on his shoulder   160
to stoke his fire at suppertime. He dumped it
with a great crash into that hollow cave,
and we all scattered fast to the far wall.
Then over the broad cavern floor he ushered
the ewes he meant to milk. He left his rams   165
and he-goats in the yard outside, and swung
high overhead a slab of solid rock
to close the cave. Two dozen four-wheeled wagons,

with heaving wagon teams, could not have stirred
the tonnage of that rock from where he wedged it   170
over the doorsill. Next he took his seat
and milked his bleating ewes. A practiced job
he made of it, giving each ewe her suckling;
thickened his milk, then, into curds and whey,
sieved out the curds to drip in withy° baskets,   175
and poured the whey to stand in bowls
cooling until he drank it for his supper.
When all these chores were done, he poked the fire,
heaping on brushwood. In the glare he saw us.

'Strangers,' he said, 'who are you? And where from?   180
What brings you here by seaways—a fair traffic?
Or are you wandering rogues, who cast your lives
like dice, and ravage other folk by sea?'

We felt pressure on our hearts, in dread
of that deep rumble and that mighty man.   185
But all the same I spoke up in reply:

175. **withy** (wĭth′ē): made of slender twigs.

'We are from Troy, Achaeans, blown off course
by shifting gales on the Great South Sea;
homeward bound, but taking routes and ways
uncommon; so the will of Zeus would have it.   190
We served under Agamemnon,° son of Atreus—
the whole world knows what city
he laid waste, what armies he destroyed.
It was our luck to come here; here we stand,
beholden for your help, or any gifts   195
you give—as custom is to honor strangers.
We would entreat you, great Sir, have a care
for the gods' courtesy; Zeus will avenge
the unoffending guest.'
                          He answered this
from his brute chest, unmoved:
                                  'You are a ninny, 200
or else you come from the other end of nowhere,
telling me, mind the gods! We Cyclopes
care not a whistle for your thundering Zeus
or all the gods in bliss; we have more force by far.
I would not let you go for fear of Zeus—   205
you or your friends—unless I had a whim to.
Tell me, where was it, now, you left your ship—
around the point, or down the shore, I wonder?'

191. **Agamemnon** (ăg′ə-mĕm′nŏn′):
Greek king who led the Greeks
against the Trojans.

He thought he'd find out, but I saw through this,
and answered with a ready lie:
                         'My ship?   210
Poseidon° Lord, who sets the earth a-tremble,
broke it up on the rocks at your land's end.
A wind from seaward served him, drove us there.
We are survivors, these good men and I.'

Neither reply nor pity came from him,   215
but in one stride he clutched at my companions
and caught two in his hands like squirming puppies
to beat their brains out, spattering the floor.
Then he dismembered them and made his meal,
gaping and crunching like a mountain lion—   220
everything: innards, flesh, and marrowbones.
We cried aloud, lifting our hands to Zeus,
powerless, looking on at this, appalled;
but Cyclops went on filling up his belly
with manflesh and great gulps of whey,   225
then lay down like a mast among his sheep.
My heart beat high now at the chance of action,
and drawing the sharp sword from my hip I went
along his flank to stab him where the midriff
holds the liver. I had touched the spot   230
when sudden fear stayed me: if I killed him
we perished there as well, for we could never
move his ponderous doorway slab aside.
So we were left to groan and wait for morning.

When the young Dawn with fingertips of rose   235
lit up the world, the Cyclops built a fire
and milked his handsome ewes, all in due order,
putting the sucklings to the mothers. Then,
his chores being all dispatched, he caught
another brace° of men to make his breakfast,   240
and whisked away his great door slab
to let his sheep go through—but he, behind,
reset the stone as one would cap a quiver.
There was a din of whistling as the Cyclops
rounded his flock to higher ground, then stillness.   245
And now I pondered how to hurt him worst,
if but Athena° granted what I prayed for.
Here are the means I thought would serve my turn:

211. **Poseidon** (pō-sī′dən): god of
the sea and of earthquakes.

240. **brace:** pair.

247. **Athena** (ə-thē′nə): goddess of
wisdom.

A club, or staff, lay there along the fold—
an olive tree, felled green and left to season   250
for Cyclops' hand. And it was like a mast
a lugger of twenty oars, broad in the beam—
a deep-sea-going craft—might carry:
so long, so big around, it seemed. Now I
chopped out a six-foot section of this pole   255
and set it down before my men, who scraped it;
and when they had it smooth, I hewed again
to make a stake with pointed end. I held this
in the fire's heart and turned it, toughening it,
then hid it, well back in the cavern, under   260
one of the dung piles in profusion there.
Now came the time to toss for it: who ventured
along with me? whose hand could bear to thrust
and grind that spike in Cyclops' eye, when mild
sleep had mastered him? As luck would have it,   265
the men I would have chosen won the toss—
four strong men, and I made five as captain.

At evening came the shepherd with his flock,
his woolly flock. The rams as well, this time,
entered the cave: by some sheepherding whim—   270
or a god's bidding—none were left outside.
He hefted his great boulder into place
and sat him down to milk the bleating ewes
in proper order, put the lambs to suck,
and swiftly ran through all his evening chores.   275
Then he caught two more men and feasted on them.
My moment was at hand, and I went forward
holding an ivy bowl of my dark drink,
looking up, saying:
                        'Cyclops, try some wine.
Here's liquor to wash down your scraps of men.   280
Taste it, and see the king of drink we carried
under our planks. I meant it for an offering
if you would help us home. But you are mad,
unbearable, a bloody monster! After this,
will any other traveler come to see you?'   285

He seized and drained the bowl, and it went down
so fiery and smooth he called for more:

'Give me another, thank you kindly. Tell me,
how are you called? I'll make a gift will please you.
Even Cyclopes know the wine grapes grow   290
out of grassland and loam in heaven's rain,
but here's a bit of nectar and ambrosia!'°

Three bowls I brought him, and he poured them down.
I saw the fuddle and flush come over him,
then I sang out in cordial tones:
                                    'Cyclops,   295
you ask my honorable name? Remember
the gift you promised me, and I shall tell you.
My name is Nohbdy: mother, father, and friends,
everyone calls me Nohbdy.'
                            And he said:
'Nohbdy's my meat, then, after I eat his friends.   300
Others come first. There's a noble gift, now.'

292. **nectar and ambrosia** (ăm-brō′zhə): drink and food of the Olympian gods.

Even as he spoke, he reeled and tumbled backward,
his great head lolling to one side; and sleep
took him like any creature. Drunk, hiccuping,
he dribbled streams of liquor and bits of men.   305

Now, by the gods, I drove my big hand spike
deep in the embers, charring it again,
and cheered my men along with battle talk
to keep their courage up: no quitting now.
The pike of olive, green though it had been,   310
reddened and glowed as if about to catch.
I drew it from the coals and my four fellows
gave me a hand, lugging it near the Cyclops
as more than natural force nerved them; straight
forward they sprinted, lifted it, and rammed it   315
deep in his crater eye, and I leaned on it
turning it as a shipwright turns a drill
in planking, having men below to swing
the two-handled strap that spins it in the groove.
So with our brand we bored that great eye socket   320
while blood ran out around the red-hot bar.
Eyelid and lash were seared; the pierced ball
hissed broiling, and the roots popped.
                              In a smithy
one sees a white-hot axhead or an adz
plunged and wrung in a cold tub, screeching steam—   325
the way they make soft iron hale and hard:
just so that eyeball hissed around the spike.
The Cyclops bellowed and the rock roared round him,
and we fell back in fear. Clawing his face
he tugged the bloody spike out of his eye,   330
threw it away, and his wild hands went groping;
then he set up a howl for Cyclopes
who lived in caves on windy peaks nearby.
Some heard him; and they came by divers° ways   334. **divers** (dī′vərz): various.
to clump around outside and call:
                              'What ails you,   335
Polyphemus?° Why do you cry so sore   336. **Polyphemus** (pol′ə-fe′məs).
in the starry night? You will not let us sleep.
Sure no man's driving off your flock? No man
has tricked you, ruined you?'
                              Out of the cave
the mammoth Polyphemus roared in answer: 340

'Nohbdy, Nohbdy's tricked me, Nohbdy's ruined me!'

To this rough shout they made a sage reply:

'Ah well, if nobody has played you foul
there in your lonely bed, we are no use in pain
given by great Zeus. Let it be your father,   345
Poseidon Lord, to whom you pray.'
                So saying
they trailed away. And I was filled with laughter
to see how like a charm the name deceived them.
Now Cyclops, wheezing as the pain came on him,
fumbled to wrench away the great doorstone   350
and squatted in the breach with arms thrown wide
for any silly beast or man who bolted—
hoping somehow I might be such a fool.
But I kept thinking how to win the game:
death sat there huge; how could we slip away?   355
I drew on all my wits, and ran through tactics,
reasoning as a man will for dear life,
until a trick came—and it pleased me well.
The Cyclops' rams were handsome, fat, with heavy
fleeces, a dark violet.
                Three abreast   360
I tied them silently together, twining
cords of willow from the ogre's bed;
then slung a man under each middle one
to ride there safely, shielded left and right.
So three sheep could convey each man. I took   365
the woolliest ram, the choicest of the flock,
and hung myself under his kinky belly,
pulled up tight, with fingers twisted deep
in sheepskin ringlets for an iron grip.
So, breathing hard, we waited until morning.   370

When Dawn spread out her fingertips of rose
the rams began to stir, moving for pasture,
and peals of bleating echoed round the pens
where dams with udders full called for a milking.
Blinded, and sick with pain from his head wound,   375
the master stroked each ram, then let it pass,
but my men riding on the pectoral° fleece
the giant's blind hands blundering never found.

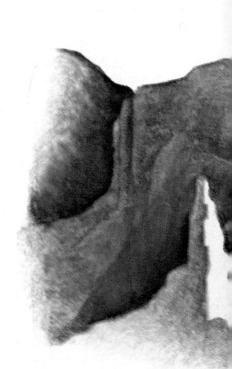

377. **pectoral** (pĕk′tər-əl): on the chest.

Last of them all my ram, the leader, came,
weighted by wool and me with my meditations. 380
The Cyclops patted him, and then he said:

'Sweet cousin ram, why lag behind the rest
in the night cave? You never linger so,
but graze before them all, and go afar
to crop sweet grass, and take your stately way 385
leading along the streams. until at evening
you run to be the first one in the fold.
Why, now, so far behind? Can you be grieving
over your Master's eye? That carrion rogue°
and his accurst companions burnt it out 390
when he had conquered all my wits with wine.
Nohbdy will not get out alive, I swear.
Oh, had you brain and voice to tell
where he may be now, dodging all my fury!
Bashed by this hand and bashed on this rock wall 395
his brains would strew the floor, and I should have
rest from the outrage Nohbdy worked upon me.'

389. **carrion** (kăr′ē-ən) **rogue:** rotten scoundrel.

He sent us into the open, then. Close by,
I dropped and rolled clear of the ram's belly,
going this way and that to untie the men.   400
With many glances back, we rounded up
his fat, stiff-legged sheep to take aboard,
and drove them down to where the good ship lay.
We saw, as we came near, our fellows' faces
shining; then we saw them turn to grief   405
tallying those who had not fled from death.
I hushed them, jerking head and eyebrows up,
and in a low voice told them: 'Load this herd;
move fast, and put the ship's head toward the breakers.'
They all pitched in at loading, then embarked   410
and struck their oars into the sea. Far out,
as far offshore as shouted words would carry,
I sent a few back to the adversary:

'O Cyclops! Would you feast on my companions?
Puny, am I, in a cave man's hands?   415
How do you like the beating that we gave you,
you damned cannibal? Eater of guests
under your roof! Zeus and the gods have paid you!'

The blind thing in his doubled fury broke
a hilltop in his hands and heaved it after us.   420
Ahead of our black prow it struck and sank
whelmed in a spuming geyser, a giant wave
that washed the ship stern foremost back to shore.
I got the longest boathook out and stood
fending us off, with furious nods to all   425
to put their backs into a racing stroke—
row, row, or perish. So the long oars bent
kicking the foam sternward, making head
until we drew away, and twice as far.
Now when I cupped my hands I heard the crew   430
in low voices protesting:
                          'Godsake, Captain!
Why bait the beast again? Let him alone!'

'That tidal wave he made on the first throw
all but beached us.'
                          'All but stove us in!'

'Give him our bearing with your trumpeting,   435
he'll get the range and lob a boulder.'
                                      'Aye!
He'll smash our timbers and our heads together!'

I would not heed them in my glorying spirit,
but let my anger flare and yelled:
                                   'Cyclops,
if ever mortal man inquire   440
how you were put to shame and blinded, tell him
Odysseus, raider of cities, took your eye:
Laertes' son, whose home's on Ithaca!'

At this he gave a mighty sob and rumbled:

'Now comes the weird° upon me, spoken of old.   445   445. **weird:** fate or destiny.
A wizard, grand and wondrous, lived here—Telemus,
a son of Eurymus; great length of days
he had in wizardry among the Cyclopes,
and these things he foretold for time to come:
my great eye lost, and at Odysseus' hands.   450
Always I had in mind some giant, armed
in giant force, would come against me here.
but this, but you—small, pitiful and twiggy—
you put me down with wine, you blinded me.
Come back, Odysseus, and I'll treat you well,   455
praying the god of earthquake° to befriend you—   456. **god of earthquake:** Poseidon.
his son I am, for he by his avowal
fathered me, and, if he will, he may
heal me of this black wound—he and no other
of all the happy gods or mortal men.'   460

Few words I shouted in reply to him:

'If I could take your life I would and take
your time away, and hurl you down to hell!
The god of earthquake could not heal you there!'

At this he stretched his hands out in his darkness   465
toward the sky of stars, and prayed Poseidon:

'O hear me, lord, blue girdler of the islands,
if I am thine indeed, and thou art father:

grant that Odysseus, raider of cities, never
see his home: Laertes' son, I mean,   470
who kept his hall on Ithaca. Should destiny
intend that he shall see his roof again
among his family in his fatherland,
far be that day, and dark the years between.
Let him lose all companions, and return   475
under strange sail to bitter days at home.'

In these words he prayed, and the god heard him.
Now he laid hands upon a bigger stone
and wheeled around, titanic for the cast,
to let it fly in the black-prowed vessel's track.   480
But it fell short, just aft the steering oar,
and whelming seas rose giant above the stone
to bear us onward toward the island.
                                  There
as we ran in we saw the squadron waiting,
the trim ships drawn up side by side, and all   485
our troubled friends who waited, looking seaward.
We beached her, grinding keel in the soft sand,
and waded in, ourselves, on the sandy beach.
Then we unloaded all the Cyclops' flock
to make division, share and share alike,   490
only my fighters voted that my ram,
the prize of all, should go to me. I slew him
by the seaside and burnt his long thighbones
to Zeus beyond the stormcloud, Cronus' son,
who rules the world. But Zeus disdained my offering: 495
destruction for my ships he had in store
and death for those who sailed them, my companions.
Now all day long until the sun went down
we made our feast on mutton and sweet wine,
till after sunset in the gathering dark   500
we went to sleep above the wash of ripples.

When the young Dawn with fingertips of rose
touched the world, I roused the men, gave orders
to man the ships, cast off the mooring lines;
and filing in to sit beside the rowlocks   505
oarsmen in line dipped oars in the gray sea.
So we moved out, sad in the vast offing,
having our precious lives, but not our friends.

FOR STUDY AND DISCUSSION

1. Odysseus begins his narrative when he and his men set sail from Troy. What does the episode of the Cicones reveal about Odysseus and his men?

2. Almost all of the adventures in the *Odyssey* illustrate some aspect of Odysseus' character. What specific characteristics are revealed in the episode of the Lotus-Eaters?

3. The land of the Lotus-Eaters has been said to symbolize *escapism* — that is, withdrawal from reality into a dream world. Do you agree? If you do, point out lines that support your view. If you do not, give reasons for your opinion.

4. Why does Odysseus consider the Cyclopes barbarians?

5. Hospitality to strangers is a theme that recurs throughout the *Odyssey*. The ancient Greeks believed that the gods themselves sometimes came to earth disguised as humble strangers. How does the Cyclops respond to Odysseus' plea for hospitality?

6. Twice in the Cyclops episode Odysseus brings misfortune upon himself and his men by ignoring their good advice. Identify both instances and tell why Odysseus acts as he does.

7. Odysseus devises a plan that enables him and his men to escape from the Cyclops' cave and to prevent anyone coming to the Cyclops' aid. What is each stage of the plan?

8. What aspects of Odysseus' character are revealed in the incident with the Cyclops?

9. Reread the Cyclops' prayer to Poseidon (lines 467–476). What lines suggest that Odysseus will have to face other trials? How does this foreshadowing add to the suspense of the poem?

The Sirens

Odysseus and his crew arrive next at the island of Aeolus (ē′ə-ləs), god of the winds, who helps them homeward by bottling up unfavorable winds and sending them a fair breeze. After nine days' sail, with Ithaca in sight, the men untie the bag of winds, and their ships are blown straight back to Aeolus' island. Realizing that their voyage is cursed by the gods, Aeolus drives them away.

In the land of the Laestrygonians (lĕs′trĭ-gō′nē-ənz), a race of cannibals, all the ships but one are destroyed and their crews devoured. Odysseus' own ship escapes and proceeds to the island of Aeaea, where the goddess Circe transforms Odysseus' men into swine. After Circe releases his men from the spell, Odysseus spends a year with her. He longs, however, to return to Ithaca. Odysseus sails to the land of the dead, where the ghost of the blind prophet Tiresias (tī-rē′sē-əs) tells him what he must do to reach home. Before setting sail for Ithaca, Odysseus returns briefly to Circe's island. She warns him of the dangers that lie ahead, and Odysseus tells his men what Circe has predicted.

As Circe spoke, Dawn mounted her golden throne,
and on the first rays Circe left me, taking   510
her way like a great goddess up the island.
I made straight for the ship, roused up the men
to get aboard and cast off at the stern.
They scrambled to their places by the rowlocks
and all in line dipped oars in the gray sea.   515
But soon an offshore breeze blew to our liking—
a canvas-bellying breeze, a lusty shipmate
sent by the singing nymph with sunbright hair.°   518. **nymph . . . hair:** Circe.
So we made fast the braces, and we rested,
letting the wind and steersman work the ship.   520
The crew being now silent before me, I
addressed them, sore at heart:
                'Dear friends,
more than one man, or two, should know those things
Circe foresaw for us and shared with me,
so let me tell her forecast: then we die   525
with our eyes open, if we are going to die,
or know what death we baffle if we can. Sirens
weaving a haunting song over the sea

we are to shun, she said, and their green shore
all sweet with clover; yet she urged that I   530
alone should listen to their song. Therefore
you are to tie me up, tight as a splint,
erect along the mast, lashed to the mast,
and if I shout and beg to be untied,
take more turns of the rope to muffle me.'   535

I rather dwelt on this part of the forecast
while our good ship made time, bound outward down
the wind for the strange island of Sirens.
Then all at once the wind fell, and a calm
came over all the sea, as though some power   540
lulled the swell.
          The crew were on their feet
briskly, to furl the sail, and stow it; then,
each in place, they poised the smooth oar blades
and sent the white foam scudding by. I carved
a massive cake of beeswax into bits   545
and rolled them in my hands until they softened—
no long task, for a burning heat came down
from Helios,° lord of high noon. Going forward
I carried wax along the line, and laid it
thick on their ears. They tied me up, then, plumb   550
amidships, back to the mast, lashed to the mast,
and took themselves again to rowing. Soon,
as we came smartly within hailing distance,
the two Sirens, noting our fast ship
off their point, made ready, and they sang: 555

    'This way, oh turn your bows,
      Achaea's glory,
  As all the world allows—
      Moor and be merry.

    Sweet coupled airs we sing.   560
      No lonely seafarer
  Holds clear of entering
      Our green mirror.

    Pleased by each purling note
      Like honey twining   565
  From her throat and my throat,
      Who lies a-pining?

548. Helios (hē′lē-ŏs′): the sun god.

Sea rovers here take joy
  Voyaging onward,
As from our song of Troy   570
Graybeard and rower-boy
  Goeth more learnèd.

All feats on that great field
  In the long warfare,
Dark days the bright gods willed,   575
  Wounds you bore there,

Argos' old soldiery°
  On Troy beach teeming,
Charmed out of time we see.
No life on earth can be   580
  Hid from our dreaming.'

577. **Argos' old soldiery:** the
soldiers from Argos, a city in ancient Greece, who fought in the
Trojan War.

The lovely voices in ardor appealing over the water
made me crave to listen, and I tried to say
'Untie me!' to the crew, jerking my brows;
but they bent steady to the oars. Then Perimedes° 585
got to his feet, he and Eurylochus,°
and passed more line about, to hold me still.
So all rowed on, until the Sirens
dropped under the sea rim, and their singing
dwindled away.
        My faithful company 590
rested on their oars now, peeling off
the wax that I had laid thick on their ears;
then set me free.

585. **Perimedes** (pĕr′ə-mē′dēz).
586. **Eurylochus** (yōō-rĭl′ə-kəs).

Scylla and Charybdis

Circe has warned Odysseus of another sea peril. He and his
crew must pass between Scylla (sĭl'ə) and Charybdis
(kə-rĭb'dĭs). Scylla is a terrifying monster with six heads.
She dwells in a high rocky cave, devouring sailors in ships
that pass close by. Charybdis is a whirlpool. Three times a
day she swallows the sea, then vomits it up fiery hot. Circe
has advised Odysseus to sail toward Scylla's crag, for it is better to lose six of his men—one to each of her heads—than for
all to perish in the whirlpool.

But scarcely had that island
faded in blue air than I saw smoke
and white water, with sound of waves in tumult—   595
a sound the men heard, and it terrified them.
Oars flew from their hands; the blades went knocking
wild alongside till the ship lost way,
with no oarblades to drive her through the water.

Well, I walked up and down from bow to stern,   600
trying to put heart into them, standing over
every oarsman, saying gently,
                  'Friends,
have we never been in danger before this?
More fearsome is it now, than when the Cyclops
penned us in his cave? What power he had!   605
Did I not keep my nerve, and use my wits
to find a way out for us?
                Now I say
by hook or crook this peril too shall be
something that we remember.
                  Heads up, lads!
We must obey the orders as I give them,   610
Get the oarshafts in your hands, and lay back
hard on your benches; hit these breaking seas.
Zeus help us pull away before we founder.
You at the tiller, listen, and take in
all that I say—the rudders are your duty;   615
keep her out of the combers and the smoke;
steer for that headland; watch the drift, or we
fetch up in the smother, and you drown us.'

That was all, and it brought them round to action.
But as I sent them on toward Scylla, I 620
told them nothing, as they could do nothing.
They would have dropped their oars again, in panic,
to roll for cover under the decking. Circe's
bidding against arms had slipped my mind,
so I tied on my cuirass° and took up 625
two heavy spears, then made my way along
to the foredeck — thinking to see her first from there,
the monster of the gray rock, harboring
torment for my friends. I strained my eyes
upon that cliffside veiled in cloud, but nowhere 630
could I catch sight of her.

625. **cuirass** (kwĭ-răs′): armor for the chest and back.

                    And all this time,
in travail, sobbing, gaining on the current,
we rowed into the strait—Scylla to port
and on our starboard beam Charybdis, dire
gorge° of the salt-sea tide. By heaven! when she   635   635. **gorge:** devouring mouth.
vomited, all the sea was like a caldron
seething over intense fire, when the mixture
suddenly heaves and rises.
                    The shot spume
soared to the landside heights, and fell like rain.

But when she swallowed the sea water down   640
we saw the funnel of the maelstrom,° heard   641. **maelstrom** (māl'strəm) violent
the rock bellowing all around, and dark   whirlpool.
sand raged on the bottom far below.
My men all blanched against the gloom, our eyes
were fixed upon that yawning mouth in fear   645
of being devoured.
                    Then Scylla made her strike,
whisking six of my best men from the ship.
I happened to glance aft at ship and oarsmen
and caught sight of their arms and legs, dangling
high overhead. Voices came down to me   650
in anguish, calling my name for the last time.

A man surf-casting on a point of rock
for bass or mackerel, whipping his long rod
to drop the sinker and the bait far out,
will hook a fish and rip it from the surface   655
to dangle wriggling through the air:
                              so these
were borne aloft in spasms toward the cliff.

She ate them as they shrieked there, in her den,
in the dire grapple, reaching still for me—
and deathly pity ran me through   660
at that sight—far the worst I ever suffered,
questing the passes of the strange sea.
                              We rowed on.
The Rocks were now behind; Charybdis, too,
and Scylla dropped astern. . . .

The Cattle of the Sun God

Odysseus urges his exhausted crew to bypass Thrinacia (thrĭn-ā'shə), the island of the sun god. The men, however, insist on landing. Odysseus makes them swear not to touch the god's cattle, for both Circe and Tiresias have warned him of disaster if the cattle are harmed.

In the small hours of the third watch, when stars 665
that shone out in the first dusk of evening
had gone down to their setting, a giant wind
blew from heaven, and clouds driven by Zeus
shrouded land and sea in a night of storm;
so just as Dawn with fingertips of rose 670
touched the windy world, we dragged our ship
to cover in a grotto, a sea cave
where nymphs had chairs of rock and sanded floors.
I mustered all the crew and said:

        'Old shipmates,
our stores are in the ship's hold, food and drink; 675
the cattle here are not for our provision,
or we pay dearly for it.

      Fierce the god is
who cherishes these heifers and these sheep:
Helios; and no man avoids his eye.'

To this my fighters nodded. Yes. But now 680
we had a month of onshore gales, blowing
day in, day out—south winds, or south by east.
As long as bread and good red wine remained
to keep the men up, and appease their craving,
they would not touch the cattle. But in the end, 685
when all the barley in the ship was gone,
hunger drove them to scour the wild shore
with angling hooks, for fishes and seafowl,
whatever fell into their hands; and lean days
wore their bellies thin.

       The storms continued. 690
So one day I withdrew to the interior
to pray the gods in solitude, for hope
that one might show me some way of salvation.
Slipping away, I struck across the island
to a sheltered spot, out of the driving gale. 695

I washed my hands there, and made supplication
to the gods who own Olympus,° all the gods—
but they, for answer, only closed my eyes
under slow drops of sleep.

697. **Olympus** (ō-lĭm′pəs): Mount Olympus, believed to be the home of the gods.

                Now on the shore Eurylochus
made his insidious plea:

                'Comrades,' he said,   700
'You've gone through everything; listen to what I say.
All deaths are hateful to us, mortal wretches,
but famine is the most pitiful, the worst
end that a man can come to.

                Will you fight it?
Come, we'll cut out the noblest of these cattle   705
for sacrifice to the gods who own the sky;
and once at home, in the old country of Ithaca,
if ever that day comes—
we'll build a costly temple and adorn it
with every beauty for the Lord of Noon.°   710
But if he flares up over his heifers lost,
wishing our ship destroyed, and if the gods
make cause with him, why, then I say: Better
open your lungs to a big sea once for all
than waste to skin and bones on a lonely island!'   715

710. **Lord of Noon:** Helios.

Thus Eurylochus; and they murmured 'Aye!'
trooping away at once to round up heifers.
Now, that day tranquil cattle with broad brows
were grazing near, and soon the men drew up
around their chosen beasts in ceremony. 720
They plucked the leaves that shone on a tall oak—
having no barley meal—to strew the victims,
performed the prayers and ritual, knifed the kine° 723. **kine:** cattle.
and flayed each carcass, cutting thighbones free
to wrap in double folds of fat. These offerings, 725
with strips of meat, were laid upon the fire.
Then, as they had no wine, they made libation° 727. **libation:** ritual pouring of
with clear spring water, broiling the entrails first; wine or other liquid.
and when the bones were burnt and tripes shared,
they spitted the carved meat.
                              Just then my slumber 730
left me in a rush, my eyes opened,
and I went down the seaward path. No sooner
had I caught sight of our black hull, than savory
odors of burnt fat eddied around me;
grief took hold of me, and I cried aloud: 735

'O Father Zeus and gods in bliss forever,
you made me sleep away this day of mischief!
O cruel drowsing, in the evil hour!
Here they sat, and a great work they contrived.'

Lampetia° in her long gown meanwhile   740
had borne swift word to the Overlord of Noon:
'They have killed your kine.'
                              And the Lord Helios
burst into angry speech amid the immortals:

'O Father Zeus and gods in bliss forever,
punish Odysseus' men! So overweening,   745
now they have killed my peaceful kine, my joy
at morning when I climbed the sky of stars,
and evening, when I bore westward from heaven.
Restitution or penalty they shall pay—
and pay in full—or I go down forever   750
to light the dead men in the underworld.'

Then Zeus who drives the stormcloud made reply:

'Peace, Helios: shine on among the gods,
shine over mortals in the fields of grain.
Let me throw down one white-hot bolt, and make   755
splinters of their ship in the winedark sea.'

—Calypso later told me of this exchange,
as she declared that Hermes° had told her.

Well, when I reached the sea cave and the ship,
I faced each man, and had it out; but where   760
could any remedy be found? There was none.
The silken beeves of Helios were dead.
The gods, moreover, made queer signs appear:
cowhides began to crawl, and beef, both raw
and roasted, lowed like kine upon the spits.   765

Now six full days my gallant crew could feast
upon the prime beef they had marked for slaughter
from Helios' herd; and Zeus, the son of Cronus,°
added one fine morning.

740. **Lampetia** (lăm-pē′shə): a nymph.

758. **Hermes** (hûr′mēz′): the messenger of the gods.

768. **Cronus** (krō′nəs): a Titan who ruled the universe before Zeus.

                        All the gales
had ceased, blown out, and with an offshore breeze   770
we launched again, stepping the mast and sail,
to make for the open sea. Astern of us
the island coastline faded, and no land
showed anywhere, but only sea and heaven,
when Zeus Cronion piled a thunderhead   775
above the ship, while gloom spread on the ocean.
We held our course, but briefly. Then the squall
struck whining from the west, with gale force, breaking
both forestays, and the mast came toppling aft
along the ship's length, so the running rigging   780
showered into the bilge.
                        On the afterdeck
the mast had hit the steersman a slant blow
bashing the skull in, knocking him overside,
as the brave soul fled the body, like a diver.
With crack on crack of thunder, Zeus let fly   785
a bolt against the ship, a direct hit,
so that she bucked, in reeking fumes of sulfur,
and all the men were flung into the sea.
They came up round the wreck, bobbing awhile
like petrels° on the waves.

790. petrels (pĕt'rəlz): small sea birds.

                        No more seafaring   790
homeward for these, no sweet day of return;
the god had turned his face from them.
                        I clambered
fore and aft my hulk until a comber
split her, keel from ribs, and the big timber
floated free; the mast, too, broke away.   795
A backstay floated dangling from it, stout
rawhide rope, and I used this for lashing
mast and keel together. These I straddled,
riding the frightful storm.
                        Nor had I yet
seen the worst of it: for now the west wind   800
dropped, and a southeast gale came on—one more
twist of the knife—taking me north again,
straight for Charybdis. All that night I drifted,
and in the sunrise, sure enough, I lay
off Scylla mountain and Charybdis deep.   805
There, as the whirlpool drank the tide, a billow
tossed me, and I sprang for the great fig tree,

catching on like a bat under a bough.
Nowhere had I to stand, no way of climbing,
the root and bole° being far below, and far   810   810. **bole:** tree trunk.
above my head the branches and their leaves,
massed, overshadowing Charybdis pool.
But I clung grimly, thinking my mast and keel
would come back to the surface when she spouted.
And ah! how long, with what desire, I waited!   815
till, at the twilight hour, when one who hears
and judges pleas in the marketplace all day
between contentious men, goes home to supper,
the long poles at last reared from the sea.

Now I let go with hands and feet, plunging   820
straight into the foam beside the timbers,
pulled astride, and rowed hard with my hands
to pass by Scylla. Never could I have passed her
had not the Father of gods and men,° this time,   824. **Father of gods and men:** Zeus.
kept me from her eyes. Once through the strait,   825
nine days I drifted in the open sea
before I made shore, buoyed up by the gods,
upon Ogygia° Isle. The dangerous nymph   828. **Ogygia** (ō-jĭj′ē-ə).
Calypso lives and sings there, in her beauty,
and she received me, loved me.
                                   But why tell   830
the same tale that I told last night in hall
to you and to your lady? Those adventures
made a long evening, and I do not hold
with tiresome repetition of a story."

FOR STUDY AND DISCUSSION

1. Odysseus maneuvers his men safely past the Sirens while he alone listens to their song. How do the Sirens tempt him?

2. Faced with a choice between Scylla and Charybdis, Odysseus does as Circe advises and chooses Scylla. He knows that six of his men will die, yet he withholds this information from his crew. Is this a strength or weakness in his character? Explain.

3. Consider each of the episodes you have read so far. How well does Odysseus control his men in each episode? How effective and responsible is he as a leader? Cite specific lines to support your answer.

4. Before Odysseus' men feast on the cattle of the sun god, they perform a ritual of sacrifice to the gods. Why does the ritual fail to please the gods? How are the men punished?

5. Odysseus alone survives. How is he aided by Zeus?

PART 2   ODYSSEUS IN ITHACA

Father and Son

After hearing the story of Odysseus' wanderings, the king of Phaeacia offers him a boat and crew to take him home to Ithaca. Thus Odysseus returns to his own land after an absence of twenty years.

The goddess Athena appears to Odysseus and tells him to proceed cautiously. Believing that he is dead, many suitors have besieged his palace, eager to marry his beautiful wife, Penelope. Penelope does not believe that Odysseus is dead, but she is unable to make the suitors leave. They remain in Ithaca, eating and drinking at her expense. They are even plotting to murder her son, Telemachus (tə-lĕm′ə-kəs), before he is old enough to inherit his father's lands. Telemachus, who hopes for his father's return, has gone to Sparta to ask for news of him.

Athena disguises Odysseus as a ragged old beggar and sends him to the hut of Eumaeus (yōō-mē′əs), an old and loyal swineherd. She then directs Telemachus to return to Ithaca and tells Odysseus that it is time to reveal his identity to his son.

>   . . . From the air   835
> she walked, taking the form of a tall woman,
> handsome and clever at her craft, and stood
> beyond the gate in plain sight of Odysseus,
> unseen, though, by Telemachus, unguessed,
> for not to everyone will gods appear.   840
> Odysseus noticed her; so did the dogs,
> who cowered whimpering away from her. She only
> nodded, signing to him with her brows,
> a sign he recognized. Crossing the yard,
> he passed out through the gate in the stockade   845
> to face the goddess. There she said to him:
>
> "Son of Laertes and the gods of old,
> Odysseus, master of landways and seaways,
> dissemble to your son no longer now.
> The time has come: tell him how you together   850
> will bring doom on the suitors in the town.

I shall not be far distant then, for I
myself desire battle.''
                    Saying no more,
she tipped her golden wand upon the man,
making his cloak pure white, and the knit tunic   855
fresh around him. Lithe and young she made him,
ruddy with sun, his jawline clean, the beard
no longer gray upon his chin. And she
withdrew when she had done.
                    Then Lord Odysseus
reappeared—and his son was thunderstruck.   860
Fear in his eyes, he looked down and away
as though it were a god, and whispered:
                              ''Stranger,
you are no longer what you were just now!
Your cloak is new; even your skin! You are
one of the gods who rule the sweep of heaven!   865
Be kind to us, we'll make you fair oblation°   866. **oblation:** an offering to a god.
and gifts of hammered gold. Have mercy on us!''

The noble and enduring man replied:

"No god. Why take me for a god? No, no.
I am that father whom your boyhood lacked   870
and suffered pain for lack of. I am he."

Held back too long, the tears ran down his cheeks
as he embraced his son.
                Only Telemachus,
uncomprehending, wild
with incredulity, cried out:
                     "You cannot   875
be my father Odysseus! Meddling spirits
conceived this trick to twist the knife in me!
No man of woman born could work these wonders
by his own craft, unless a god came into it
with ease to turn him young or old at will.   880
I swear you were in rags and old,
and here you stand like one of the immortals!"

Odysseus brought his ranging mind to bear
and said:
        "This is not princely, to be swept
away by wonder at your father's presence.   885
No other Odysseus will ever come,
for he and I are one, the same; his bitter
fortune and his wanderings are mine.
Twenty years gone, and I am back again
on my own island.
             As for my change of skin,   890
that is a charm Athena, Hope of Soldiers,
uses as she will; she has the knack
to make me seem a beggar man sometimes
and sometimes young, with finer clothes about me.
It is no hard thing for the gods of heaven   895
to glorify a man or bring him low."

When he had spoken, down he sat
               Then, throwing
his arms around this marvel of a father
Telemachus began to weep. Salt tears
rose from the wells of longing in both men,   900
and cries burst from both as keen and fluttering

as those of the great taloned hawk,
whose nestlings farmers take before they fly.
So helplessly they cried, pouring out tears,
and might have gone on weeping so till sundown,   905
had not Telemachus said:
                              "Dear father! Tell me
what kind of vessel put you here ashore
on Ithaca? Your sailors, who were they?
I doubt you made it, walking on the sea!"

Then said Odysseus, who had borne the barren sea: 910

"Only plain truth shall I tell you, child.
Great seafarers, the Phaeacians, gave me passage
as they give other wanderers. By night
over the open ocean, while I slept,
they brought me in their cutter, set me down   915
on Ithaca, with gifts of bronze and gold
and stores of woven things. By the gods' will
these lie all hidden in a cave. I came
to this wild place, directed by Athena,
so that we might lay plans to kill our enemies.   920
Count up the suitors for me, let me know
what men at arms are there, how many men.
I must put all my mind to it, to see
if we two by ourselves can take them on
or if we should look round for help."
                              Telemachus   925
replied:
            "O Father, all my life your fame
as a fighting man has echoed in my ears—
your skill with weapons and the tricks of war—
but what you speak of is a staggering thing,
beyond imagining, for me. How can two men   930
do battle with a houseful in their prime?
For I must tell you this is no affair
of ten or even twice ten men, but scores,
throngs of them. You shall see, here and now.
The number from Dulichium alone   935
is fifty-two, picked men, with armorers,
a half-dozen; twenty-four came from Same,
twenty from Zacynthus; our own island
accounts for twelve, high-ranked, and their retainers,

Medon the crier, and the Master Harper,   940
besides a pair of handymen at feasts.
If we go in against all these
I fear we pay in salt blood for your vengeance.
You must think hard if you would conjure up
the fighting strength to take us through."

                                 Odysseus   945
who had endured the long war and the sea
answered:

         "I'll tell you now.
Suppose Athena's arm is over us, and Zeus
her father's, must I rack my brains for more?"

Clearheaded Telemachus looked hard and said:　　　950
"Those two are great defenders, no one doubts it,
but throned in the serene clouds overhead;
other affairs of men and gods they have
to rule over."
　　　　　　And the hero answered:

"Before long they will stand to right and left of us　　955
in combat, in the shouting, when the test comes—
our nerve against the suitors' in my hall.
Here is your part: At break of day tomorrow
home with you, go mingle with our princes.
The swineherd later on will take me down　　　960
the port-side trail—a beggar, by my looks,
hangdog and old. If they make fun of me
in my own courtyard, let your ribs cage up
your springing heart, no matter what I suffer,
no matter if they pull me by the heels　　　965
or practice shots at me, to drive me out.
Look on, hold down your anger. You may even
plead with them, by heaven! in gentle terms
to quit their horseplay—not that they will heed you,
rash as they are, facing their day of wrath.　　　970
Now fix the next step in your mind.
　　　　　　　　Athena,
counseling me, will give me word, and I
shall signal to you, nodding: at that point
round up all armor, lances, gear of war
left in our hall, and stow the lot away　　　975
back in the vaulted storeroom. When the suitors
miss those arms and question you, be soft
in what you say—answer:
　　　　　　　　'I thought I'd move them
out of the smoke. They seemed no longer those
bright arms Odysseus left us years ago　　　980
when he went off to Troy. Here where the fire's
hot breath came, they had grown black and drear.
One better reason, too, I had from Zeus:
Suppose a brawl starts up when you are drunk,
you might be crazed and bloody one another,　　　985
and that would stain your feast, your courtship.
　　　Tempered
iron can magnetize a man.

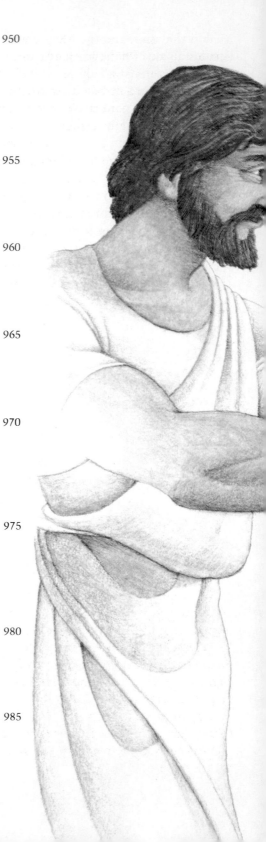

524　*An Epic Poem*

Say that.
But put aside two broadswords and two spears
for our own use, two oxhide shields nearby
when we go into action. Pallas Athena   990
and Zeus All-Provident will see you through,
bemusing our young friends.

                    Now one thing more.
If son of mine you are and blood of mine,
let no one hear Odysseus is about.
Neither Laertes, nor the swineherd here,   995
nor any slave, nor even Penelope.
But you and I alone must learn how far
the women are corrupted; we should know
how to locate good men among our hands,
the loyal and respectful, and the shirkers   1000
who take you lightly, as alone and young."

FOR STUDY AND DISCUSSION

1. What makes Telemachus think that Odysseus must be a god? How does Odysseus convince Telemachus that he is his father?

2. Telemachus warns Odysseus that there are far too many suitors for the two of them to fight. How does Odysseus persuade Telemachus that they can win?

3. Odysseus outlines his plan in lines 958–990. What is Telemachus' part in the plan?

4. Why does Odysseus want to keep his return a secret?

The Suitors

The next day, disguised once more as a beggar, Odysseus
enters the hall of his home and passes among the suitors to
beg. Antinous (ăn-tĭn′ō-əs), the most arrogant and outspoken
of the suitors, breaks into a rage.

But here Antinous broke in, shouting:
"God!
What evil wind blew in this pest?
Get over,
stand in the passage! Nudge my table, will you?
Egyptian whips are sweet   1005
to what you'll come to here, you nosing rat,
making your pitch to everyone!
These men have bread to throw away on you
because it is not theirs. Who cares? Who spares
another's food, when he has more than plenty?"   1010

With guile Odysseus drew away, then said:

"A pity that you have more looks than heart.
You'd grudge a pinch of salt from your own larder
to your own handyman. You sit here, fat
on others' meat, and cannot bring yourself   1015
to rummage out a crust of bread for me!"

Then anger made Antinous' heart beat hard,
and, glowering under his brows, he answered:
"Now!
You think you'll shuffle off and get away
after that impudence? Oh, no you don't!"   1020

The stool he let fly hit the man's right shoulder
on the packed muscle under the shoulder blade—
like solid rock, for all the effect one saw.
Odysseus only shook his head, containing
thoughts of bloody work, as he walked on,   1025
then sat, and dropped his loaded bag again
upon the doorsill. Facing the whole crowd
he said, and eyed them all:
"One word only,
my lords, and suitors of the famous queen.

One thing I have to say.   1030
There is no pain, no burden for the heart
when blows come to a man, and he defending
his own cattle—his own cows and lambs.
Here it was otherwise. Antinous
hit me for being driven on by hunger—   1035
how many bitter seas men cross for hunger!
If beggars interest the gods, if there are Furies°

1037. **Furies:** three goddesses who
punished those crimes that went
unavenged.

pent in the dark to avenge a poor man's wrong, then
     may
Antinous meet his death before his wedding day!"

Then said Eupeithes' son, Antinous:
                              "Enough.   1040
Eat and be quiet where you are, or shamble elsewhere,
unless you want these lads to stop your mouth
pulling you by the heels, or hands and feet,
over the whole floor, till your back is peeled!"

But now the rest were mortified, and someone   1045
spoke from the crowd of young bucks to rebuke him:

"A poor show, that—hitting this famished tramp—
bad business, if he happened to be a god.
You know they go in foreign guise, the gods do,
looking like strangers, turning up   1050
in towns and settlements to keep an eye
on manners, good or bad."
                              But at this notion
Antinous only shrugged.
                              Telemachus,
after the blow his father bore, sat still
without a tear, though his heart felt the blow.   1055
Slowly he shook his head from side to side,
containing murderous thoughts.
                              Penelope
on the higher level of her room had heard
the blow, and knew who gave it. Now she murmured:

"Would god you could be hit yourself, Antinous—   1060
hit by Apollo's bowshot!"

         And Eurynome,°
her housekeeper, put in:

             "He and no other?
If all we pray for came to pass, not one
would live till dawn!"

         Her gentle mistress said:

"Oh, Nan, they are a bad lot; they intend   1065
ruin for all of us; but Antinous
appears a blacker-hearted hound than any.
Here is a poor man come, a wanderer,
driven by want to beg his bread, and everyone
in hall gave bits, to cram his bag—only   1070
Antinous threw a stool, and banged his shoulder!"

So she described it, sitting in her chamber
among her maids—while her true lord was eating.
Then she called in the forester and said:

"Go to that man on my behalf, Eumaeus,   1075
and send him here, so I can greet and question him.
Abroad in the great world, he may have heard
rumors about Odysseus—may have known him!"

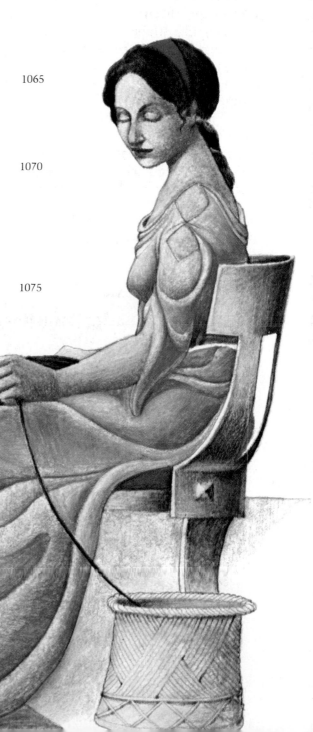

1061. **Eurynome** (yōō-rĭn′ə-mē).

Penelope

Later that night Penelope meets secretly with the old beggar.
She asks him if he has heard any news of her husband.

"Friend, let me ask you first of all:
who are you, where do you come from, of what nation 1080
and parents were you born?"
                                    And he replied:

"My lady, never a man in the wide world
should have a fault to find with you. Your name
has gone out under heaven like the sweet
honor of some god-fearing king, who rules   1085
in equity over the strong: his back lands bear
both wheat and barley, fruit trees laden bright,
new lambs at lambing time—and the deep sea
gives great hauls of fish by his good strategy,
so that his folk fare well.

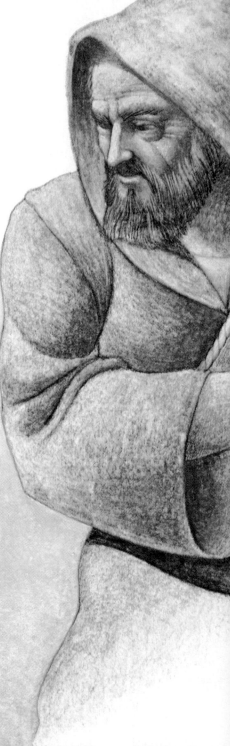

O my dear lady,   1090
this being so, let it suffice to ask me
of other matters—not my blood, my homeland.
Do not enforce me to recall my pain.
My heart is sore; but I must not be found
sitting in tears here, in another's house: 1095
it is not well forever to be grieving.
One of the maids might say—or you might think—
I had got maudlin over cups of wine."

And Penelope replied:
                        "Stranger, my looks,
my face, my carriage, were soon lost or faded   1100
when the Achaeans crossed the sea to Troy,
Odysseus my lord among the rest.
If he returned, if he were here to care for me,
I might be happily renowned!
But grief instead heaven sent me—years of pain.   1105
Sons of the noblest families on the islands,
Dulichium, Same, wooded Zacynthus,
with native Ithacans, are here to court me,
against my wish; and they consume this house.
Can I give proper heed to guest or suppliant   1110
or herald on the realm's affairs?
                        How could I?
wasted with longing for Odysseus, while here
they press for marriage.
                        Ruses served my turn
to draw the time out—first a close-grained web
I had the happy thought to set up weaving   1115
on my big loom in hall. I said, that day:
'Young men—my suitors, now my lord is dead,
let me finish my weaving before I marry,
or else my thread will have been spun in vain.
It is a shroud I weave for Lord Laertes   1120
when cold Death comes to lay him on his bier.
The country wives would hold me in dishonor
if he, with all his fortune, lay unshrouded.'
I reached their hearts that way, and they agreed.
So every day I wove on the great loom,   1125
but every night by torchlight I unwove it;
and so for three years I deceived the Achaeans.
But when the seasons brought a fourth year on,

as long months waned, and the long days were spent,
through imprudent folly in the slinking maids   1130
they caught me—clamored up to me at night;
I had no choice then but to finish it.
And now, as matters stand at last,
I have no strength left to evade a marriage,
cannot find any further way; my parents   1135
urge it upon me, and my son
will not stand by while they eat up his property.
He comprehends it, being a man full-grown,
able to oversee the kind of house
Zeus would endow with honor.
                              But you too   1140
confide in me, tell me your ancestry.
You were not born of mythic oak or stone.''

The beggar invents a tale of how he had seen Odysseus
twenty years ago in Crete, when Odysseus was bound for
Troy. He convinces Penelope that the story is true by describing Odysseus' clothes in detail. Then he tells her he has heard
that Odysseus is about to set sail for Ithaca.

"You see, then, he is alive and well, and headed
homeward now, no more to be abroad
far from his island, his dear wife and son.   1145
Here is my sworn word for it. Witness this,
god of the zenith,° noblest of the gods,
and Lord Odysseus' hearthfire, now before me:
I swear these things shall turn out as I say.
Between this present dark and one day's ebb,   1150
after the wane, before the crescent moon,
Odysseus will come.''

1147. **god of the zenith:** Zeus.

FOR STUDY AND DISCUSSION

1. A number of years have passed since Odysseus' adventure with the Cyclops. How has
Odysseus changed?

2. Penelope represents characteristics that
the Greeks admired in women. What qualities does she reveal about herself in her discussion with her housekeeper (lines 1065–

1071)? In her interview with the beggar? How
was she able to trick the suitors for three
years? What does this ruse show about her?

3. The scene in which Penelope meets her
husband Odysseus disguised as a beggar is an
example of *dramatic irony*, for the reader
knows something that Penelope does not
know. Why do you think Odysseus keeps his
identity a secret from his wife?

The Challenge

The suitors summon Penelope to the hall and demand that she choose one of them at once. Penelope announces a challenge: she will marry whoever can string Odysseus' great bow and shoot an arrow through a row of twelve ax-handle sockets, as Odysseus used to do. One by one the suitors try but fail to even bend the bow. The old beggar then asks for a turn. The suitors protest until both Penelope and Telemachus insist that he be given the bow.

    . . . And Odysseus took his time,
turning the bow, tapping it, every inch,
for borings that termites might have made   1155
while the master of the weapon was abroad.
The suitors were now watching him, and some
jested among themselves:
                  "A bow lover!"

"Dealer in old bows!"

        "Maybe he has one like it
at home!"

        "Or has an itch to make one for himself."   1160

"See how he handles it, the sly old buzzard!"

And one disdainful suitor added this:

"May his fortune grow an inch for every inch he
    bends it!"

But the man skilled in all ways of contending,
satisfied by the great bow's look and heft,   1165
like a musician, like a harper, when
with quiet hand upon his instrument
he draws between his thumb and forefinger
a sweet new string upon a peg: so effortlessly
Odysseus in one motion strung the bow.   1170
Then slid his right hand down the cord and plucked it,
so the taut gut vibrating hummed and sang
a swallow's note.

        In the hushed hall it smote the suitors
and all their faces changed. Then Zeus thundered
overhead, one loud crack for a sign.   1175
And Odysseus laughed within him that the son
of crooked-minded Cronus had flung that omen down.
He picked one ready arrow from his table
where it lay bare: the rest were waiting still
in the quiver for the young men's turn to come.   1180
He nocked° it, let it rest across the handgrip,
and drew the string and grooved butt of the arrow,
aiming from where he sat upon the stool.

        Now flashed
arrow from twanging bow clean as a whistle
through every socket ring, and grazed not one,   1185
to thud with heavy brazen head beyond.

        Then quietly
Odysseus said:

    "Telemachus, the stranger
you welcomed in your hall has not disgraced you.
I did not miss, neither did I take all day

1181. **nocked:**
placed an
arrow against
the string of
the bow.

stringing the bow. My hand and eye are sound,   1190
not so contemptible as the young men say.
The hour has come to cook their lordships' mutton—
supper by daylight. Other amusements later,
with song and harping that adorn a feast."

He dropped his eyes and nodded, and the prince   1195
Telemachus, true son of King Odysseus,
belted his sword on, clapped hand to his spear,
and with a clink and glitter of keen bronze
stood by his chair, in the forefront near his father.

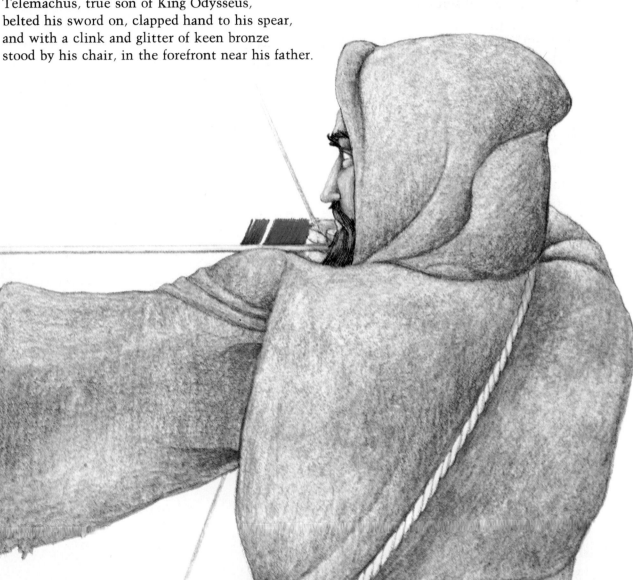

Odysseus' Revenge

Now shrugging off his rags the wiliest fighter of the
    islands   1200
leapt and stood on the broad doorsill, his own bow in
    his hand.
He poured out at his feet a rain of arrows from the
    quiver
and spoke to the crowd:
           "So much for that. Your clean-cut game is over.
Now watch me hit a target that no man has hit before,
if I can make this shot. Help me, Apollo."   1205

He drew to his fist the cruel head of an arrow
    for Antinous
just as the young man leaned to lift his beautiful
    drinking cup,
embossed, two-handled, golden: the cup was in his
    fingers:
the wine was even at his lips: and did he dream of
    death?
How could he? In that revelry amid his throng of
    friends   1210
who would imagine a single foe—though a strong foe
    indeed—
could dare to bring death's pain on him and darkness
    on his eyes?
Odysseus' arrow hit him under the chin
and punched up to the feathers through his throat.

Backward and down he went, letting the winecup fall   1215
from his shocked hand. Like pipes his nostrils jetted
crimson runnels, a river of mortal red,
and one last kick upset his table
knocking the bread and meat to soak in dusty blood.
Now as they craned to see their champion where he lay   1220
the suitors jostled in uproar down the hall,
everyone on his feet. Wildly they turned and scanned
the walls in the long room for arms; but not a shield,
not a good ashen spear was there for a man to take
    and throw.
All they could do was yell in outrage at Odysseus: 1225

"Foul! to shoot at a man! That was your last shot!"

"Your own throat will be slit for this!"
                                   "Our finest lad is down!
You killed the best on Ithaca."
                                   "Buzzards will tear your eyes out!"

For they imagined as they wished—that it was a
        wild shot,
an unintended killing—fools, not to comprehend   1230
they were already in the grip of death.
But glaring under his brows Odysseus answered:

"You yellow dogs, you thought I'd never make it
home from the land of Troy. You took my house
        to plunder.
                        . . . You dared
bid for my wife while I was still alive.   1235
Contempt was all you had for the gods who rule
        wide heaven,
contempt for what men say of you hereafter.
Your last hour has come. You die in blood."

As they all took this in, sickly green fear
pulled at their entrails, and their eyes flickered   1240
looking for some hatch or hideaway from death.
Eurymachus° alone could speak. He said:

1242. **Eurymachus** (yōō-rī′mə-kəs).

"If you are Odysseus of Ithaca come back,
all that you say these men have done is true.
Rash actions, many here, more in the countryside.   1245
But here he lies, the man who caused them all.
Antinous was the ringleader, he whipped us on
to do these things. He cared less for a marriage
than for the power Cronion has denied him
as king of Ithaca. For that   1250
he tried to trap your son and would have killed him.
He is dead now and has his portion. Spare
your own people. As for ourselves, we'll make
restitution of wine and meat consumed,
and add, each one, a tithe of twenty oxen   1255
with gifts of bronze and gold to warm your heart.
Meanwhile we cannot blame you for your anger."

Odysseus glowered under his black brows
and said:
          "Not for the whole treasure of your fathers,
all you enjoy, lands, flocks, or any gold   1260
put up by others, would I hold my hand.
There will be killing till the score is paid.
You forced yourselves upon this house. Fight your
      way out,
or run for it, if you think you'll escape death.
I doubt one man of you skins by."   1265

They felt their knees fail, and their hearts—but heard
Eurymachus for the last time rallying them.

"Friends," he said, "the man is implacable.
Now that he's got his hands on bow and quiver
he'll shoot from the big doorstone there   1270
until he kills us to the last man.
                              Fight, I say,
let's remember the joy of it. Swords out!
Hold up your tables to deflect his arrows.

After me, everyone: rush him where he stands.
If we can budge him from the door, if we can pass   1275
into the town, we'll call out men to chase him.
This fellow with his bow will shoot no more.''

He drew his own sword as he spoke, a broadsword of
     fine bronze,
honed like a razor on either edge. Then crying hoarse
     and loud
he hurled himself at Odysseus. But the kingly man let
     fly   1280
an arrow at that instant, and the quivering feathered
     butt
sprang to the nipple of his breast as the barb stuck in
     his liver.
The bright broadsword clanged down. He lurched and
     fell aside,
pitching across his table. His cup, his bread and meat,
were spilt and scattered far and wide, and his
     head slammed on the ground.   1285
Revulsion, anguish in his heart, with both feet
     kicking out,
he downed his chair, while the shrouding wave
     of mist closed on his eyes.

Amphinomus now came running at Odysseus,
broadsword naked in his hand. He thought to make
the great soldier give way at the door.   1290
But with a spear throw from behind Telemachus hit
    him
between the shoulders, and the lancehead drove
clear through his chest. He left his feet and fell
forward, thudding, forehead against the ground.
Telemachus swerved around him, leaving the long
    dark spear   1295
planted in Amphinomus. If he paused to yank it out
someone might jump him from behind or cut him
    down with a sword
at the moment he bent over. So he ran—ran from the
    tables
to his father's side and halted, panting, saying:

"Father let me bring you a shield and spear,   1300
a pair of spears, a helmet.
I can arm on the run myself; I'll give
outfits to Eumaeus and this cowherd.
Better to have equipment."
                    Said Odysseus:

"Run then, while I hold them off with arrows
as long as the arrows last. When all are gone
if I'm alone they can dislodge me."
                            Quick
upon his father's word Telemachus
ran to the room where spears and armor lay.
He caught up four light shields, four pairs of spears,
four helms of war high-plumed with flowing manes,
and ran back, loaded down, to his father's side.
He was the first to pull a helmet on
and slide his bare arm in a buckler strap.
The servants armed themselves, and all three took
    their stand
beside the master of battle.
                        While he had arrows
he aimed and shot, and every shot brought down
one of his huddling enemies.
But when all barbs had flown from the bowman's fist,
he leaned his bow in the bright entryway   1320

540   *An Epic Poem*

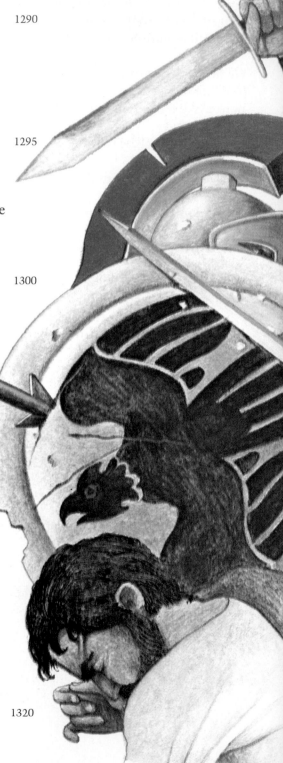

beside the door, and armed: a four-ply shield
hard on his shoulder, and a crested helm,
horsetailed, nodding stormy upon his head,
then took his tough and bronze-shod spears. . . .

Odysseus, Telemachus, and the two faithful servants kill
every suitor. Several times Athena saves Odysseus' life by
turning aside the suitors' deadly blows.

And Odysseus looked around him, narrow-eyed,   1325
for any others who had lain hidden
while death's black fury passed.
                              In blood and dust
he saw that crowd all fallen, many and many slain.

Think of a catch that fishermen haul in to a half-moon
        bay
in a fine-meshed net from the whitecaps of the sea: 1330
how all are poured out on the sand, in throes for the salt
        sea,
twitching their cold lives away in Helios' fiery air:
so lay the suitors heaped on one another.

FOR STUDY AND DISCUSSION

1. At what point in this episode does Odysseus reveal his identity to the suitors?
2. Eurymachus tries to convince Odysseus to spare the suitors' lives. Restate his arguments in your own words. What reason does Odysseus give for refusing?
3. Do you think Odysseus' revenge is excessive? Give reasons for your opinion.
4. Why are the stringing of Odysseus' bow and the slaying of the suitors considered the climax of the *Odyssey?*

Penelope Tests Odysseus

After twenty years of waiting for Odysseus, Penelope hesitates to acknowledge the stranger as her husband. She tests
him with a secret only Odysseus could know.

Greathearted Odysseus, home at last,
was being bathed now by Eurynome   1335
and rubbed with golden oil, and clothed again
in a fresh tunic and a cloak. Athena
lent him beauty, head to foot. She made him
taller, and massive, too, with crisping hair
in curls like petals of wild hyacinth   1340
but all red-golden. Think of gold infused
on silver by a craftsman, whose fine art
Hephaestus° taught him, or Athena—one
whose work moves to delight: just so she lavished
beauty over Odysseus' head and shoulders.   1345
He sat then in the same chair by the pillar,
facing his silent wife, and said:

                "Strange woman,
the immortals of Olympus made you hard,
harder than any. Who else in the world
would keep aloof as you do from her husband   1350
if he returned to her from years of trouble,
cast on his own land in the twentieth year?

Nurse, make up a bed for me to sleep on.
Her heart is iron in her breast."

                  Penelope
spoke to Odysseus now. She said:

                  "Strange man,   1355
if man you are . . . This is no pride on my part
nor scorn for you—not even wonder, merely.
I know so well how you—how he—appeared
boarding the ship for Troy. But all the same . . .

Make up his bed for him, Eurycleia.   1360
Place it outside the bedchamber my lord
built with his own hands. Pile the big bed
with fleeces, rugs, and sheets of purest linen."

1343. **Hephaestus** (hĭ-fĕs′təs): god
of metalworking.

With this she tried him to the breaking point,
and he turned on her in a flash raging: 1365

"Woman, by heaven you've stung me now!
Who dared to move my bed?
No builder had the skill for that—unless
a god came down to turn the trick. No mortal
in his best days could budge it with a crowbar.   1370
There is our pact and pledge, our secret sign,
built into that bed—my handiwork
and no one else's!
               An old trunk of olive
grew like a pillar on the building plot,
and I laid out our bedroom round that tree,   1375
lined up the stone walls, built the walls and roof,
gave it a doorway and smooth-fitting doors.
Then I lopped off the silvery leaves and branches,
hewed and shaped that stump from the roots up
into a bedpost, drilled it, let it serve   1380
as model for the rest. I planed them all,
inlaid them all with silver, gold and ivory,
and stretched a bed between—a pliant web
of oxhide thongs dyed crimson.
                    There's our sign!
I know no more. Could someone else's hand   1385
have sawn that trunk and dragged the frame away?"

Their secret! as she heard it told, her knees
grew tremulous and weak, her heart failed her.
With eyes brimming tears she ran to him,
throwing her arms around his neck, and kissed him,   1390
murmuring:
            "Do not rage at me, Odysseus!
No one ever matched your caution! Think
what difficulty the gods gave: they denied us
life together in our prime and flowering years,
kept us from crossing into age together.   1395
Forgive me, don't be angry. I could not
welcome you with love on sight! I armed myself
long ago against the frauds of men,
impostors who might come—and all those many
whose underhanded ways bring evil on! . . .   1400

But here and now, what sign could be so clear
as this of our own bed?
No other man has ever laid eyes on it —
only my own slave, Actoris, that my father
sent with me as a gift — she kept our door.   1405
You make my stiff heart know that I am yours."

Now from his breast into his eyes the ache
of longing mounted, and he wept at last,
his dear wife, clear and faithful, in his arms,
longed for as the sunwarmed earth is longed for by
    a swimmer   1410
spent in rough water where his ship went down
under Poseidon's blows, gale winds and tons of sea.
Few men can keep alive through a big surf
to crawl, clotted with brine, on kindly beaches
in joy, in joy, knowing the abyss behind: 1415
and so she too rejoiced, her gaze upon her husband,
her white arms round him pressed as though forever.

Postscript

The following morning Odysseus and Telemachus set out for
the country estate of Laertes, Odysseus' father. Their happy
reunion is interrupted by the arrival of angry relatives of the
slain suitors, armed for battle. Athena appears and commands
them to make peace. So ends the *Odyssey*, with Odysseus
restored to his family and to his kingdom.

FOR STUDY AND DISCUSSION

1. What does Penelope imply by the phrase
"if man you are" in line 1356?
2. What test does Penelope devise to tell
whether the stranger is really Odysseus?
3. How does Penelope show that she and
Odysseus are well-matched?

CHARACTERISTICS OF THE EPIC

Homeric Simile
As you know, a simile is a comparison of two
dissimilar actions or objects that are usually
linked by *like, as,* or some other connecting
word. A Homeric simile is an extended comparison of two actions or objects that develops

mounting excitement and usually ends in a climax. In this passage, Scylla seizing Odysseus' men is compared to a fisherman landing a fish:

> A man surf-casting on a point of rock
> for bass or mackerel, whipping his long rod
> to drop the sinker and the bait far out,
> will hook a fish and rip it from the surface
> to dangle wriggling through the air:
>   so these
> were borne aloft in spasms toward the cliff.

Notice how the simile is extended by describing the actions of a fisherman and the parallel actions of the monster. How does Homer's choice of details make the action rise in excitement?

Look at the simile Homer uses to describe Odysseus' stringing of the bow (lines 1166–1170). Why is this simile strikingly effective?

Find other examples of Homeric similes and tell how the comparisons make the actions more vivid and gripping.

The Epithet

Like the extended simile, the epithet is a favorite device of the ancient epic poets. An epithet is a word or phrase used to characterize someone or something, as in "the *wine-dark* sea." Homer refers to Odysseus as "raider of cities," "the wiliest fighter of the islands," and "Laertes' son." The gods and goddesses are often identified by epithets. Zeus, for example, is called "Father of gods and men," "god of the zenith," "the lord of cloud," and "All Provident." Find other epithets Homer uses in the *Odyssey*

FOR COMPOSITION

Analyzing Odysseus as Epic Hero

In the opening lines of this translation of the *Odyssey*, Odysseus describes himself as "formidable for guile in peace and war." Do you think Odysseus characterizes himself accurately? Why or why not?

The hero of an epic is generally larger than life. He is stronger, braver, and more clever than the other characters. Sometimes his powers are superhuman. Write a brief composition in which you analyze Odysseus as an epic hero. Use evidence from the poem to support your analysis.

Analyzing the Role of the Olympians

In Homer's epics the Olympian gods and goddesses frequently intervene in human affairs. In the *Iliad*, they join the battle of the Greeks and the Trojans on the plains outside Troy. They take sides: Athena and Hera fight for the Greeks, Apollo and Aphrodite for the Trojans. The gods intervene in several ways — by starting arguments, by shielding warriors, or by changing the course of an arrow.

How do the gods and goddesses affect the action of the *Odyssey*? Choose several episodes that illustrate *divine intervention* and tell in a brief composition the motives for these interventions and their consequences.

*You have read the episode of the Lotus-Eaters (lines 65–91).
After Odysseus' men eat the lotus plant, they have no
desire to go home and must be forced back to the ships.*

*Alfred, Lord Tennyson expanded the incident into a
famous poem. In the first section of the poem, which
follows, Odysseus speaks to his men as they first sight the
shore. How does Tennyson suggest a mood of indolence?*

The Lotus-Eaters   *Alfred, Lord Tennyson*

"Courage!" he said, and pointed toward the land,
"This mounting wave will roll us shoreward soon."
In the afternoon they came unto a land
In which it seemèd always afternoon.
All round the coast the languid air did swoon,   5
Breathing like one that hath a weary dream.
Full-faced above the valley stood the moon;
And, like a downward smoke, the slender stream
Along the cliff to fall and pause and fall did seem.

A land of streams! some, like a downward smoke,   10
Slow-dropping veils of thinnest lawn,° did go;
And some through wavering lights and shadows broke,
Rolling a slumbrous sheet of foam below.
They saw the gleaming river seaward flow.
From the inner land; far off, three mountaintops,   15
Three silent pinnacles of aged snow,
Stood sunset-flushed; and, dewed with showery drops,
Up-clomb° the shadowy pine above the woven copse.°

11. **lawn:** a thin, sheer fabric.

18. **clomb:** climbed. **copse:** a thick
growth of small trees.

The charmèd sunset lingered low adown
In the red west; through mountain clefts the dale   20
Was seen far inland, and the yellow down°
Bordered with palm, and many a winding vale
And meadow, set with slender galingale,°
A land where all things always seemed the same!
And round about the keel with faces pale,   25
Dark faces pale against that rosy flame,
The mild-eyed melancholy Lotus-eaters came.

21. **down:** rolling, upland
countryside.

23. **galingale** (găl'ĭn-gāl'): an aromatic
plant of the ginger family.

Branches they bore of that enchanted stem,
Laden with flower and fruit, whereof they gave
To each, but whoso did receive of them   30
And taste, to him the gushing of the wave
Far, far away did seem to mourn and rave
On alien shores; and if his fellow spake,
His voice was thin, as voices from the grave;
And deep asleep he seemed, yet all awake,   35
And music in his ears his beating heart did make.

They sat them down upon the yellow sand,
Between the sun and moon upon the shore;
And sweet it was to dream of fatherland,
Of child, and wife, and slave; but evermore   40
Most weary seemed the sea, weary the oar,
Weary the wandering fields of barren foam.
Then someone said, "We will return no more";
And all at once they sang, "Our island home
Is far beyond the wave; we will no longer roam."   45

*In this poem Edna St. Vincent Millay draws on the story of
Penelope's web. What contrast is drawn between Penelope
and Odysseus in the second stanza?*

An Ancient Gesture   *Edna St. Vincent Millay*

I thought, as I wiped my eyes on the corner of my apron:
Penelope did this too.
And more than once: you can't keep weaving all day
And undoing it all through the night;
Your arms get tired, and the back of your neck gets tight;   5
And along towards morning, when you think it will
          never be light,
And your husband has been gone, and you don't know
          where, for years,
Suddenly you burst into tears;
There is simply nothing else to do.

And I thought, as I wiped my eyes on the corner of my
          apron: 10
This is an ancient gesture, authentic, antique,
In the very best tradition, classic, Greek;
Ulysses did this too.
But only as a gesture,—a gesture which implied
To the assembled throng that he was much too moved
          to speak.   15
He learned it from Penelope . . .
Penelope, who really cried.

People and Places in The Odyssey

Achaeans (ə-kē′ənz): Greeks; specifically, the people of Achaea in northeastern Greece.

Aeaea (ē-ē′ə): island home of Circe, the enchantress.

Agamemnon (ăg′ə-měm′nŏn′): commander of the Greeks during the Trojan War.

Alcinous (ăl-sĭn′ō-əs): King of Phaeacia.

Antinous (ăn-tĭn′ō-əs): an Ithacan noble, most arrogant of the suitors.

Apollo (ə-pŏl′ō): in Greek mythology, god of poetry, music, and prophecy.

Argo (är′gō): the ship manned by Jason and his crew of Greek heroes on their quest for the Golden Fleece.

Athena (ə-thē′nə): Greek goddess of wisdom, crafts, and war.

Calypso (kə-lĭp′sō): beautiful sea nymph, who kept Odysseus on her island for seven years.

Charybdis (kə-rĭb′dĭs): a whirlpool in the Straits of Messina, personified as a female monster.

Cicones (sĭ-kō′nēz): a people living on the southwestern coast of Thrace, who were attacked by Odysseus' men on their way home from Troy.

Circe (sûr′sē): beautiful witch-goddess who transformed Odysseus' men into beasts.

Cronus (krō′nəs): in Greek mythology, a Titan and ruler of the universe until he was overthrown by his son, Zeus.

Cyclops (sī′klŏps): member of a race of one-eyed giants. The Cyclopes (sī-klō′pēz) were said to have lived as shepherds on the island of Sicily.

Eumaeus (yōō-mē′əs): a swineherd, an old and loyal servant to Odysseus.

Eurycleia (yōō-rĭ-klē′yə): Penelope's servant and Odysseus' old nurse.

Eurylochus (yōo-rĭl′ə-kəs): one of Odysseus' crew.

Eurymachus (yōo-rĭm′ə-kəs): one of Penelope's suitors, an Ithacan noble.

Eurynome (yōo-rĭn′ə-mē): Penelope's maid.

Helios (hē′lē-ŏs′): in early Greek mythology, the sun god.

Ithaca (ĭth′ə-kə): Odysseus' home, an island off the western coast of Greece.

Laertes (lā-ûr′tēz): Odysseus' father.

Laestrygonians (lĕs′trĭ-gō′nē-ənz): race of mean-eating giants.

Odysseus (ō-dĭs′yōos′, ō-dĭs′ē-əs): king of Ithaca and hero of the *Odyssey*.

Penelope (pə-nĕl′ə-pē): Odysseus' wife.

Phaeacia (fē-ā′shə): an island kingdom inhabited by seafarers and traders.

Polyphemus (pŏl′ə-fē′məs): a Cyclops, son of Poseidon.

Poseidon (pō-sī′dən): Greek god of the sea; identified with the Roman god Neptune.

Scylla (sĭl′ə): a dangerous rock in the Straits of Messina, personified as a female monster with six heads who devoured passing sailors.

Sirens (sī′rənz): sea nymphs who lured sailors to destruction with their songs.

Telemachus (tə-lĕm′ə-kəs): son of Odysseus and Penelope.

Zeus (zōos): ruler of the gods and goddesses on Mount Olympus.

Practice in Reading and Writing

THE ODYSSEY

In a short essay, develop the ideas presented in one of these quotations. Cite specific passages in the poem to support your statements.

The *Odyssey* takes its name from its hero, Odysseus . . . The name itself signifies "the man of all-odds," of every chance and circumstance. Odysseus' resourcefulness is the wonder of men and gods alike. . . . No wonder others admire him, and he admires himself in an engagingly frank way.

W. H. D. Rouse, Preface to *The Odyssey*

Odysseus is a good example of a man who indulges in his share of folly but who wins through successfully by faith in the gods and the employment of as much self-control and intelligence as he can command.

Ennis Rees, *The Iliad of Homer*

This tale of adventure built on a sound moral foundation is the story of a man striving against obstacles within and without himself to get back to his home. It is also the narrative of the home which is in desperate need of [the man] who has been absent for twenty years.

Andre Michalopoulos, *Homer*

If Homer was blind . . . he remembered well what he once saw. Few poets have the gift of conveying visible things so clearly as he can.

C. M. Bowra, *Ancient Greek Literature*

For Further Reading

Homeric Epics

Finley, Moses I., *The World of Odysseus* (Viking Press, 1977; paperback, Penguin)
In this study of ancient Greek civilization, Finley uses Homer's poems as historical evidence of what the world of Odysseus was really like.

Fitzgerald, Robert, translator, *The Odyssey* (paperback, Doubleday, 1961)
This verse translation contains an interesting postscript on the art of translating and helpful notes on the background of the poem.

Lattimore, Richmond, translator, *The Iliad* (University of Chicago Press, 1975)
The action of this epic, set in the tenth year of the Trojan War, reaches its climax in the battle between Hector, champion of the Trojans, and Achilles, greatest of the Greek warriors. This translation is in verse.

Rouse, W. H. D., translator, *The Iliad* (paperback, New American Library, 1954)
The great epic of the Trojan War is told in vivid prose.

Classical Mythology

Asimov, Isaac, *Words from the Myths* (paperback, New American Library, 1969)
The author retells the Greek myths simply and clearly, and explains the influence of myths on modern language and life.

Bulfinch, Thomas, *Bulfinch's Mythology* (Crowell, 1970; paperback, New American Library)
Here, in two volumes, is the author's retelling of the Greek and Roman myths, Norse sagas, and European legends of chivalry.

Hamilton, Edith, *Mythology* (Little, Brown, 1942; paperback, New American Library)
The renowned classicist retells the great Greek, Roman, and Norse myths in a way that preserves the excitement of the originals.

Other Epics

The Aeneid of Virgil, translated by Allen Mandelbaum (paperback, Bantam, 1972)
Here is a vigorous, modern version of the famous epic that records and celebrates the adventures of Aeneas and the founding of Rome.

Beowulf, translated by Michael Alexander (paperback, Penguin, 1973)
In this Old English epic, the hero Beowulf slays the monster Grendel in hand-to-hand combat, then destroys Grendel's mother in an exciting underwater struggle.

The Epic of Gilgamesh, translated by Nancy K. Sandars (paperback, Penguin, 1960)
The earliest known epic recounts the adventures of King Gilgamesh in his search for glory and the secret of eternal life.

Ramayana: A Shortened Modern Prose Version, translated by R. K. Narayan (Viking Press, 1972)
This great Indian epic is said to have been composed in the first century A.D.

Ancient Civilizations

Carcopino, Jerome, *Daily Life in Ancient Rome* (Yale University Press, 1940; paperback, Yale University Press)
Here are illuminating accounts of the Romans and their city at the height of the Roman Empire.

Bowra, Cecil, M., *The Greek Experience* (paperback, New American Library, 1957)
The author provides a fascinating interpretation of life in Greece from the time of Homer to the fall of Athens.

Cottrell, Leonard, *The Anvil of Civilization* (paperback, New American Library, 1957)
Here is an archaeological history of the ancient cultures of the world: Egyptian, Sumerian, Babylonian, Assyrian, Cretan, Hebrew, Phoenician, Persian, and Greek.

Novels are so familiar to us that we might easily assume that they have been in existence for as long as, for example, the drama, which dates back for centuries. However, the novel is one of the most recent forms of literature. It came into being only about three hundred years ago. Essentially a novel is a long story, often with many characters and more than one story line.

The novel and the short story, both of which are classified as fiction, make use of the same basic elements: plot, character, setting, point of view, and theme. Because of its greater length and scope, a novel makes more extensive use of these elements. The plot is frequently more complicated than in a short story, and there may be one or more subplots related to the main action. In a novel there are generally more characters than in a short story, and the characters are portrayed in greater depth. The setting of a novel can reflect the background, ideas, and customs of a historical period, and since the novel is a long work, there is time and space to explore and develop important themes.

THE NOVEL

Charles Dickens (1859).
Oil painting by W. P. Frith.
Victoria and Albert Museum, London

Great Expectations, the novel in this unit, is by Charles Dickens. Dickens' books have been consistently popular for more than a hundred years. Dickens is one of the greatest storytellers who ever lived, and, with the single exception of Shakespeare, no writer of the English-speaking world has had a greater gift for creating sharply individualized characters.

Dickens was born at Portsmouth on February 7, 1812. In 1823 his family moved to London. John Dickens, his father, was arrested for debt. In order to support himself, Charles, who was twelve, went to work in a blacking warehouse, labeling bottles for six shillings a week. This experience was to haunt him for the rest of his life. After his father was released from Marshalsea Debtors' Prison, Dickens was able to leave his job and return to school.

At fifteen Dickens took a job as a law clerk. He taught himself shorthand and began working as a free-lance newspaper reporter. Dickens' first literary work, *Sketches by Boz,* appeared in 1833 ("Boz" was a pseudonym Dickens used to sign his prose sketches). His first novel, *The Pickwick Papers* (1836–1837), like his subsequent novels, appeared in serial form. Shortly after the first installment of the book was published, Dickens married Catherine Hogarth, the daughter of a journalist.

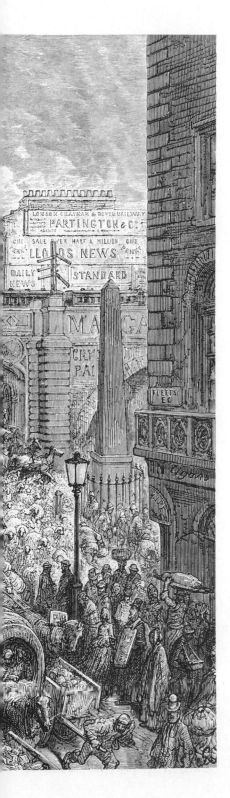

During the next thirty years, Dickens produced an extraordinary series of books: *Oliver Twist* (1837); *Nicholas Nickleby* (1838–1839); *The Old Curiosity Shop* (1840–1841); *Barnaby Rudge* (1841); *A Christmas Carol* (1843); *Martin Chuzzlewit* (1843–1844); *Dombey and Son* (1846–1848); *David Copperfield* (1849–1850); *Bleak House* (1852–1853); *Hard Times* (1854); *Little Dorrit* (1855–1857); *A Tale of Two Cities* (1859); *Great Expectations* (1860–1861); and *Our Mutual Friend* (1864–1865). When he died in 1870, Dickens was working on another novel, *Edwin Drood*.

Great Expectations is the last of Dickens' great novels. In the book we follow the development of Pip, the central character (and narrator), from childhood to manhood. When we first meet Pip, he is a frightened, sensitive boy who aspires to a world outside his reach. Through a strange twist of fate, he is allowed to fulfill his early dreams, and he learns what kind of life he truly wishes to lead.

Many critics feel that Dickens never wrote anything better than the opening chapters of *Great Expectations*. George Gissing, a novelist, particularly admired the narrative technique of this book: "No story in the first person was ever better told." You may agree as you follow Pip's adventures through the three stages of his expectations.

Great Expectations

Charles Dickens

Chapter 1

In this chapter we meet Pip, who meets a convict in a graveyard.

My father's family name being Pirrip, and my Christian name Philip, my infant tongue could make of both names nothing more explicit than Pip. So I called myself Pip, and came to be called Pip.

I gave Pirrip as my father's family name, on the authority of his tombstone and my sister —Mrs. Joe Gargery, who married the blacksmith. I never saw my father or my mother, and never saw a picture of either of them.

Ours was the marsh country, down by the river, within twenty miles of the sea. My first vivid impression of things seems to me to have been gained on a memorable raw afternoon toward evening. At such a time I found out for certain that this bleak place was the churchyard; and that Philip Pirrip, late of this parish, and Georgiana, wife of the above, were dead and buried. I knew that the dark flat wilderness beyond was the marshes; and that the low leaden line beyond was the river; and that the distant savage lair from which the wind was rushing was the sea; and that the small bundle of shivers growing afraid of it all and beginning to cry was Pip.

"Hold your noise!" cried a terrible voice, as a man started up from among the graves. "Keep still, you little devil, or I'll cut your throat!"

A fearful man, all in coarse gray, with a great iron on his leg. A man with no hat, and with broken shoes, and with an old rag tied around his head. A man who had been soaked in water, and smothered in mud, and lamed by stones, and cut by flints, and stung by nettles, and torn by briars; who limped and shivered, and glared and growled; and whose teeth chattered in his head as he seized me by the chin.

"Oh! Don't cut my throat, sir," I pleaded in terror. "Pray don't do it, sir."

"Tell us your name!" said the man. "Quick!"

"Pip, sir."

"Once more," said the man, staring at me. "Give it mouth!"

"Pip. Pip, sir."

"Show us where you live," said the man. "Pint out the place!"

I pointed to where our village lay, a mile or more from the church.

The man, after looking at me for a moment, turned me upside down and emptied my pockets. There was nothing in them but a piece of bread. He ate the bread ravenously.

"You young dog," said the man, licking his lips. "What fat cheeks you ha' got. Darn me if I couldn't eat 'em, and if I han't half a mind to't!"

I held tighter to the tombstone on which he had put me; partly, to keep myself upon it; partly, to keep myself from crying.

"Now lookee here!" said the man. "Where's your mother?"

"There, sir!" said I.

He started, made a short run, and stopped and looked over his shoulder.

"There, sir!" I timidly explained. "Also Georgiana. That's my mother."

"Oh!" said he, coming back. "And is that your father alonger your mother?"

"Yes, sir," said I; "him too."

"Ha!" he muttered. "Who d'ye live with—supposin' you're kindly let to live, which I han't made up my mind about?"

"My sister, sir—Mrs. Joe Gargery—wife of Joe Gargery, the blacksmith, sir."

"Blacksmith, eh?" said he. And looked down at his leg.

After darkly looking at his leg and at me several times, he came closer, took me by both arms, and tilted me back as far as he could hold me.

"Now lookee here," he said, "the question being whether you're to be let to live. You know what a file is?"

"Yes, sir."

"And you know what wittles[1] is?"

"Yes, sir."

After each question he tilted me over a little more, so as to give me a greater sense of helplessness and danger.

"You get me a file." He tilted me again. "And you get me wittles." He tilted me again. "You bring 'em both to me." He tilted me again. "Or I'll have your heart and liver out."

I was dreadfully frightened, and so giddy that I clung to him with both hands and said, "If you would kindly please to let me keep upright, sir, perhaps I shouldn't be sick, and perhaps I could attend more."

He gave me a tremendous dip and roll. Then he held me by the arms in an upright position and went on in these fearful terms:

"You bring me, tomorrow morning early, that file and them wittles to that old Battery[2] over yonder. You do it, and you never dare to say a word or dare to make a sign concerning your having seen such a person as me, or any person sumever, and you shall be let to live. You fail, or you go from my words in any particler, no matter how small it is, and your heart and your liver shall be tore out, roasted, and ate. Now, I ain't alone, as you may think I am. There's a young man hid with me. That young man hears the words I speak. That young man has a secret way of getting at a boy, and at his heart, and at his liver. It is in wain for a boy to attempt to hide himself from that young man. A boy may lock his door, may be warm in bed, may tuck himself up, may draw the clothes over his head, may think himself comfortable and safe, but that young man will creep his way to him and tear him open. I am a-keeping that young man from harming of you at the present moment, with great difficulty. I find it wery hard to hold that young man off of your inside. Now, what do you say?"

I said that I would get him the file, and I would get him what broken bits of food I could, and I would come to him at the Battery early in the morning.

"Say, Lord strike you dead if you don't!" said the man.

I said so, and he took me down.

"Now," he pursued, "you remember what you've undertook, and you remember that young man, and you get home."

He hugged his shuddering body in both his arms and limped toward the low church wall. He got over it, like a man whose legs were numbed and stiff, and then turned round to look for me. I looked all around for the horrible young man, and could see no signs of him. But now I was frightened again, and ran home without stopping.

---

1. **wittles:** victuals (vĭt'lz), food. The convict and other characters pronounce v like w.

2. **Battery:** a bank of earth on which large guns are mounted.

Chapter 2

We now meet Mrs. Joe Gargery, Pip's sister, and Joe Gargery the blacksmith, his brother-in-law.

My sister, Mrs. Joe Gargery, was more than twenty years older than I, and had established a great reputation with herself and the neighbors because she had brought me up "by hand." Knowing her to have a hard and heavy hand, and to be much in the habit of laying it upon her husband as well as upon me, I supposed that Joe Gargery and I were both brought up by hand.

She was not a good-looking woman, my sister; and I had a general impression that she must have made Joe Gargery marry her by hand. Joe was a fair man, with curls of flaxen hair on each side of his smooth face, and with eyes of a very undecided blue. He was a mild, good-natured, sweet-tempered, easygoing, foolish, dear fellow—a sort of Hercules in strength, and also in weakness. My sister, Mrs. Joe, with black hair and eyes, was tall and bony, and almost always wore a coarse apron, fastened over her figure behind with two loops.

Joe's forge adjoined our house, which was a wooden house, as many of the dwellings in our country were. When I ran home from the churchyard, the forge was shut up, and Joe was sitting alone in the kitchen. Joe and I being fellow sufferers, Joe imparted a confidence to me the moment I raised the latch of the door and peeped in at him.

"Mrs. Joe has been out a dozen times looking for you, Pip. And she's out now making it a baker's dozen."

"Is she?"

"Yes, Pip," said Joe, "and what's worse, she's got Tickler with her."

At this dismal intelligence,[1] I twisted the only button on my waistcoat round and round, and looked in great depression at the fire. Tickler was a wax-ended piece of cane, worn smooth by collision with my tickled frame.

"She sot down," said Joe, "and she got up, and she made a grab at Tickler, and she Ram-paged[2] out. That's what she did," said Joe, "she Ram-paged out, Pip."

"Has she been gone long, Joe?" I always treated him as a larger child, and as no more than my equal.

"Well," said Joe, "she's been on the Rampage, this last spell, about five minutes, Pip. She's a-coming! Get behind the door, old chap."

I took the advice. My sister, Mrs. Joe, throwing the door wide open, and finding an obstruction behind it, immediately divined the cause, and applied Tickler. She concluded by throwing me at Joe, who passed me on into the chimney and quietly fenced me up there with his great leg.

"Where have you been, you young monkey?" said Mrs. Joe, stamping her foot. "Tell me directly what you've been doing to wear me away with fret and fright and worrit, or I'd have you out of that corner if you was fifty Pips, and he was five hundred Gargerys."

"I have only been to the churchyard," said I, from my stool, crying and rubbing myself.

"Churchyard!" repeated my sister. "If it warn't for me you'd have been to the churchyard long ago, and stayed there. Who brought you up by hand?"

"You did," said I.

"And why did I do it, I should like to know?" exclaimed my sister.

I whimpered, "I don't know."

---

1. **intelligence:** here, news.
2. **Ram-paged:** Joe is giving emphasis to the word *rampage*, to storm about in a fit of anger.

"*I* don't!" said my sister. "I'd never do it again! I know that. It's bad enough to be a blacksmith's wife, and him a Gargery, without being your mother."

My thoughts strayed from that question as I looked disconsolately at the fire. For, the fugitive out on the marshes with the ironed leg, the mysterious young man, the file, the food, and the dreadful pledge I was under to commit a larceny on those sheltering premises, rose before me in the avenging coals.

My sister had a way of cutting our bread and butter for us that never varied. First, with her left hand she jammed the loaf hard against her bib. Then she took some butter (not too much) and spread it on the loaf, then sawed a very thick round off the loaf and hewed it into two halves, of which Joe got one, and I the other. Though I was hungry, I dared not eat my slice. I felt that I must have something in reserve for my dreadful acquaintance and his ally, the still more dreadful young man. I resolved to put my hunk of bread and butter down the leg of my trousers.

Joe was about to take a bite when his eye fell on me, and he saw that my bread and butter was gone.

The wonder and consternation with which Joe stopped and stared at me were too evident to escape my sister's observation.

"What's the matter now?" said she.

"I say, you know!" muttered Joe, shaking his head at me in a very serious remonstrance. "Pip, old chap! You'll do yourself a mischief. It'll stick somewhere. You can't have chawed it, Pip."

"What's the matter *now*?" repeated my sister, more sharply than before.

"If you can cough any trifle of it up, Pip, I'd recommend you to do it," said Joe, all aghast. "Manners is manners, but still your 'elth's your 'elth."

By this time, my sister was quite desperate, so she pounced on Joe, and, taking him by the two whiskers, knocked his head for a little while against the wall behind him while I sat in the corner looking guiltily on.

"Now, perhaps you'll mention what's the matter," said my sister, out of breath, "you staring great stuck pig."

Joe looked at her in a helpless way; then took a helpless bite and looked at me again.

"Been bolting his food, has he?" cried my sister.

"You know, old chap," said Joe, "I bolted, myself, when I was your age, but I never see your bolting equal yet, Pip."

My sister made a dive at me, and fished me up by the hair, saying nothing more than the awful words, "You come along and be dosed."

Some medical beast had revived tar-water[3] in those days as a fine medicine, and Mrs. Joe always kept a supply of it in the cupboard. The urgency of my case demanded a pint of this mixture, which was poured down my throat while Mrs. Joe held my head under her arm.

Conscience is a dreadful thing. The guilty knowledge that I was going to rob Mrs. Joe—I never thought I was going to rob Joe, for I never thought of any of the housekeeping property as his—united to the necessity of always keeping one hand on my bread and butter as I sat, or when I was ordered about the kitchen on any small errand, almost drove me out of my mind.

It was Christmas Eve, and I had to stir the pudding for the next day with a copper stick. I tried it with the load upon my leg (and that made me think afresh of the man with the load on *his* leg), and found the tendency of exercise to bring the bread and butter out at my ankle quite unmanageable. Happily I slipped

---

3. **tar-water:** a solution of tar and water regarded as a cure-all and also used as a tonic.

away and deposited that part of my conscience in my garret bedroom.

"Hark!" said I, when I had done my stirring, and was taking a final warm in the chimney corner before being sent up to bed. "Was that great guns, Joe?"

"Ah!" said Joe. "There's another conwict off."

"What does that mean, Joe?" said I.

"There was a conwict off last night," said Joe," after sunset gun. And they fired warning of him. And now it appears they're firing warning of another."

"*Who's* firing?" said I.

"Drat that boy," interposed my sister, frowning at me over her work; "what a questioner he is. Ask no questions, and you'll be told no lies."

"Mrs. Joe," said I, "I should like to know—if you wouldn't much mind—where the firing comes from?"

"Lord bless the boy!" exclaimed my sister, as if she didn't quite mean that but rather the contrary. "From the Hulks!"

"And please what's Hulks?" said I.

"That's the way with this boy!" exclaimed my sister, pointing me out with her needle and thread, and shaking her head at me. "Answer him one question, and he'll ask you a dozen directly. Hulks are prison ships, right 'cross th' meshes." We always used that name for marshes in our country.

"I wonder who's put into prison ships, and why they're put there?" said I, in a general way, and with quiet desperation.

It was too much for Mrs. Joe, who immediately rose. "I tell you what, young fellow," said she; "I didn't bring you up by hand to badger people's lives out. People are put in the Hulks because they murder, and because they rob, and forge, and do all sorts of bad; and they always begin by asking questions. Now, you get along to bed!"

I was never allowed a candle to light me to bed, and, as I went upstairs in the dark, I was in mortal terror of the young man who wanted my heart and liver; I was in mortal terror of the man with the iron leg; I was in mortal terror of myself, from whom an awful promise had been extracted.

As soon as the great black velvet pall outside my little window was shot with gray, I got up and went downstairs, every board upon the way, and every crack in every board, calling after me, "Stop thief!" and "Get up, Mrs. Joe!" I had no time to spare. I stole some bread, some rind of cheese, and about half a jar of mincemeat (which I tied up in my pocket handkerchief with my last night's slice), some brandy from a stone bottle, diluting the stone bottle from a jug in the kitchen cupboard, a meat bone with very little on it, and a beautiful round compact pork pie.

There was a door in the kitchen communicating with the forge; I unlocked and unbolted that door and got a file from among Joe's tools. Then I put the fastenings as I had found them, opened the door at which I had entered when I ran home last night, shut it, and ran for the misty marshes.

Chapter 3

A second convict appears.

It was a rimy morning and very damp. On every rail and gate, wet lay clammy, and the marsh mist was thick. However fast I went, I couldn't warm my feet, to which the damp cold seemed riveted as the iron was riveted to the leg of the man I was running to meet. I knew my way to the Battery, for I had been down there with Joe, and Joe had told me that, when I was apprenticed[1] to him, we would have such larks[2] there! I had just crossed a ditch which I knew to be very near the Battery, and had just scrambled up the mound beyond, when I saw the man sitting before me. His back was toward me, and he had his arms folded and was nodding forward, heavy with sleep, so I went forward softly and touched him on the shoulder. He instantly jumped up, and it was not the same man, but another man!

And yet this man was dressed in coarse gray, too, and had a great iron on his leg, and was lame, and hoarse, and cold, and everything that the other man was except that he had not the same face, and had a flat, broad-brimmed, low-crowned felt hat on. He swore an oath at me and then he ran into the mist, stumbling twice as he went.

"It's the young man!" I thought, feeling my heart shoot as I identified him. I dare say I should have felt a pain in my liver, too, if I had known where it was.

I was soon at the Battery, and there was the right man—hugging himself and limping to and fro, as if he had never all night left off hugging and limping—waiting for me. He was awfully cold, to be sure. His eyes looked awfully hungry, too. He did not turn me upside down this time, but left me right side upward while I opened the bundle and emptied my pockets.

"What's in the bottle, boy?" said he.

"Brandy," said I.

He was already handing mincemeat down his throat in the most curious manner—more like a man who was putting it away somewhere in a violent hurry, than a man who was eating it—but he left off to take some of the liquor. He shivered all the while so violently that it was quite as much as he could do to keep the neck of the bottle between his teeth without biting it off.

"I think you have got the ague,"[3] said I.

"I'm much of your opinion, boy," said he.

"It's bad about here," I told him. "You've been lying out on the meshes."

"I'll eat my breakfast afore they're the death of me," said he. "I'd do that if I was going to be strung up to that there gallows over there, directly arterward. I'll beat the shivers so far, *I'll* bet you."

He was gobbling mincemeat, meat bone, bread, cheese, and pork pie, all at once; staring distrustfully while he did so at the mist all around us, and often stopping to listen. Some real or fancied sound, some clink upon the river or breathing of beast upon the marsh, now gave him a start, and he said, suddenly:

"You're not a deceiving imp? You brought no one with you?"

"No, sir! No!"

"Well," said he, "I believe you. You'd be but a fierce young hound indeed, if at your time of life you could help to hunt a wretched warmint, hunted as near death as this poor wretched warmint is!"

Something clicked in his throat as if he had works in him like a clock, and was going to strike. And he smeared his ragged rough sleeve over his eyes.

Pitying his desolation, and watching him as

---

1. **apprenticed:** In former times, apprenticeship was the most common way to learn a trade. A boy (with his parents or guardian) signed a contract, called "indentures," by which he was bound to serve a master workman without pay for five to seven years. In return for this service, he was taught the workman's trade.
2. **larks:** fun.

3. **ague** (ā'gyōō): chills and fever.

he gradually settled down upon the pie, I made bold to say, "I am glad you enjoy it."

"Thankee, my boy. I do."

"I am afraid you won't leave any of it for him," said I, timidly. "There's no more to be got where that came from."

"Leave any for him? Who's him?" said my friend, stopping in his crunching of piecrust.

"The young man. That you spoke of. That was hid with you."

"Oh, ah!" he returned, with something like a gruff laugh. "Him? Yes, yes! *He* don't want no wittles."

"I thought he looked as if he did," said I.

The man stopped eating and regarded me with the keenest scrutiny and the greatest surprise.

"Looked? When?"

"Just now."

"Where?"

"Yonder," said I, pointing; "over there, where I found him nodding asleep, and thought it was you."

He held me by the collar and stared at me so that I began to think his first idea about cutting my throat had revived.

"Dressed like you, you know, only with a hat," I explained, trembling; "and—and—" I was very anxious to put this delicately—"and with—the same reason for wanting to borrow a file. Didn't you hear the cannon last night?"

"When a man's alone on these flats, with a light head and a light stomach, perishing of cold and want, he hears nothin' all night but guns firing and voices calling. But this man— did you notice anything in him?"

"He had a badly bruised face," said I.

"Not here?" exclaimed the man, striking his left cheek.

"Yes, there!"

"Where is he?" He crammed what little food was left into the breast of his gray jacket. "Show me the way he went. I'll pull him down, like a bloodhound. Curse this iron on my sore leg! Give us hold of the file, boy."

He was down on the rank wet grass, filing at his iron like a madman, and not minding me or minding his own leg, which had an old chafe upon it and was bloody, but which he handled as roughly as if it had no more feeling in it than the file.

I was very much afraid of him again, now that he had worked himself into this fierce hurry, and I was likewise very much afraid of keeping away from home any longer. I told him I must go, but he took no notice, so I thought the best thing I could do was to slip off. The last I saw of him, his head was bent over his knee and he was working hard at his fetter, muttering impatient imprecations at it and his leg. The last I heard of him, I stopped in the mist to listen, and the file was still going.

Chapter 4

We meet the Christmas dinner guests: Mr. Wopsle, the parish clerk; Mr. and Mrs. Hubble, a wheelwright and his wife; and Mr. Pumblechook, Joe's uncle, a corn merchant.

I fully expected to find a constable in the kitchen, waiting to take me up. But not only was there no constable there, but no discovery had yet been made of the robbery. Mrs. Joe was prodigiously busy in getting the house ready for the festivities of the day.

"And where the deuce ha' *you* been?" was Mrs. Joe's Christmas salutation, when I and my conscience showed ourselves.

I said I had been down to hear the carols. "Ah, well!" observed Mrs. Joe. "You might ha' done worse." Joe secretly crossed his two forefingers and exhibited them to me as our token that Mrs. Joe was in a cross temper.

We were to have a superb dinner, consisting of a leg of pickled pork and greens, and a pair of roast stuffed fowls. A handsome mince pie had been made yesterday morning (which accounted for the mincemeat not being missed), and the pudding was already on the boil. My sister, having so much to do, was going to church vicariously; that is to say, Joe and I were going. In his working clothes, Joe was a well-knit, characteristic-looking blacksmith; in his holiday clothes, he was more like a scarecrow in good circumstances than anything else. Nothing that he wore then fitted him or seemed to belong to him. As to me, when I was taken to have a new suit of clothes, the tailor had orders to make them like a kind of reformatory, and on no account to let me have the free use of my limbs. Joe and I going to church, therefore, must have been a moving spectacle for compassionate minds. Yet what I suffered outside was nothing to what I underwent within. The terrors that had assailed me whenever Mrs. Joe had gone near the pantry were only to be equaled by the remorse with which my mind dwelt on what my hands had done.

Mr. Wopsle, the clerk[1] at church, was to dine with us; and Mr. Hubble, the wheelwright, and Mrs. Hubble; and Uncle Pumblechook, who was a well-to-do corn chandler[2] in the nearest town, and drove his own chaise-cart.[3] The dinner hour was half past one. When Joe and I got home, we found the table laid, and Mrs. Joe dressed, and the dinner dressing, and the front door unlocked (it never was at any other time) for the company to enter by, and everything most splendid. And still, not a word of the robbery.

1. **clerk:** an official who assists the minister at church services and who teaches in the local school.
2. **corn chandler:** a person who buys and sells corn.
3. **chaise-cart** (shāz-kärt): a two-wheeled, one-horse carriage with a folding top.

The time came, without bringing with it any relief to my feelings, and the company came. Mr. Wopsle, united to a Roman nose and a large, shining, bald forehead, had a deep voice which he was uncommonly proud of. He punished the *amens* tremendously; and when he gave out the psalm, he looked all round the congregation first, as much as to say, "You have heard our friend overhead; oblige me with your opinion of this style!"

I opened the door to the company, first to Mr. Wopsle, next to Mr. and Mrs. Hubble, and last of all to Uncle Pumblechook. (*I* was not allowed to call him "uncle," under the severest penalties.)

"Mrs. Joe," said Uncle Pumblechook—a large, hard-breathing, middle-aged, slow man, with a mouth like a fish, dull staring eyes, and sandy hair standing upright on his head, so that he looked as if he had just been all but choked, and had that moment come to—"I have brought you as the compliments of the season—I have brought you, mum, a bottle of sherry wine—and I have brought you, mum, a bottle of port wine." Every Christmas Day he presented himself, as a profound novelty, with exactly the same words, and carrying the two bottles like dumbbells.

We dined on these occasions in the kitchen, and adjourned, for the nuts and oranges and apples, to the parlor. Among this good company I should have felt myself, even if I hadn't robbed the pantry, in a false position. I should not have minded that if they would only have left me alone. But they wouldn't leave me alone. They seemed to think the opportunity lost if they failed to point the conversation at me, every now and then, and stick the point into me.

It began the moment we sat down to dinner. Mr. Wopsle said grace with theatrical declamation and ended with the very proper aspiration that we might be truly grateful.

Upon which my sister fixed me with her eyes and said in a low reproachful voice. "Do you hear that? Be grateful."

"Especially," said Mr. Pumblechook, "be grateful, boy, to them which brought you up by hand."

Joe always aided and comforted me when he could, in some way of his own, and he always did so at dinnertime by giving me gravy, if there were any. There being plenty of gravy today, Joe spooned into my plate, at this point, about half a pint.

"He was a world of trouble to you, ma'am," said Mrs. Hubble, commiserating my sister.

"Trouble?" echoed my sister. "Trouble?" And then entered on a fearful catalogue of all the illnesses I had been guilty of, and all the acts of sleeplessness I had committed, and all the high places I had tumbled from, and all the low places I had tumbled into, and all the injuries I had done myself, and all the times she had wished me in my grave, and I had contumaciously[4] refused to go there. Everybody looked at me with indignation and abhorrence.

"Have a little brandy, uncle," said my sister.

O Heavens, it had come at last! He would find it was weak, he would say it was weak, and I was lost! I held tight to the leg of the table with both hands and awaited my fate.

My sister went for the stone bottle, came back with the stone bottle, and poured his brandy out; no one else taking any. The wretched man trifled with his glass—took it up, looked at it through the light, put it down—prolonged my misery. All this time Mrs. Joe and Joe were briskly clearing the table for the pie and pudding.

I couldn't keep my eyes off him. I saw the

miserable creature finger his glass playfully, take it up, smile, throw his head back, and drink the brandy off. Instantly, the company was seized with unspeakable consternation, owing to his springing to his feet, turning round several times in an appalling, spasmodic whooping-cough dance, and rushing out at the door; he then became visible through the window, making the most hideous faces and apparently out of his mind.

I held on tight, while Mrs. Joe and Joe ran to him. I didn't know how I had done it, but I had no doubt I had murdered him somehow. In my dreadful situation, it was a relief when

---

4. **contumaciously** (kŏn′tŏŏ-mā′shəs-lē): stubbornly, disobediently.

he was brought back, and, surveying the company all round as if *they* had disagreed with him, sank down into his chair with the one significant gasp, "Tar!"

I had filled up the bottle from the tar-water jug!

"Tar!" cried my sister, in amazement. "Why, how ever could tar come there?"

But Uncle Pumblechook, who was omnipotent in that kitchen, wouldn't hear the word, wouldn't hear of the subject, imperiously waved it all away with his hand, and asked for hot gin-and-water. My sister, who had begun to be alarmingly meditative, had to employ herself actively in getting the gin, the hot water, the sugar, and the lemon peel, and mixing them. For the time at least, I was saved. I still held on to the leg of the table, but clutched it now with the fervor of gratitude.

By degrees, I became calm enough to release my grasp and partake of pudding. Mr. Pumblechook partook of pudding. All partook of pudding. I began to think I should get over the day, when my sister said to Joe, "Clean plates — cold."

I clutched the leg of the table again immediately. I foresaw what was coming, and I felt that this time I really was gone.

"You must taste," said my sister, addressing the guests with her best grace, "you must taste, to finish with, a pie; a savory pork pie."

My sister went out to get it. I heard her steps proceed to the pantry. I saw Mr. Pumblechook balance his knife. I heard Joe say, "You shall have some, Pip." I felt that I could bear no more, and that I must run away. I released the leg of the table and ran for my life.

But I ran no farther than the house door, for there I ran head foremost into a party of soldiers with their muskets, one of whom held out a pair of handcuffs to me, saying: "Here you are, look sharp, come on!"

Chapter 5

The sergeant finds the two convicts.

The apparition of a file of soldiers ringing down the butt ends of their loaded muskets on our doorstep caused the dinner party to rise from table in confusion, and caused Mrs. Joe, reentering the kitchen empty-handed, to stop short and stare in her wondering lament of "Gracious goodness gracious me, what's gone — with the — pie!"

The sergeant and I were in the kitchen when Mrs. Joe stood staring. It was the sergeant who had spoken to me, and he was now looking round at the company, with his handcuffs invitingly extended toward them in his right hand, and his left on my shoulder.

"Excuse me, ladies and gentlemen," said the sergeant, "but I want the blacksmith. You see, blacksmith," said the sergeant, who had by this time picked out Joe with his eye, "we have had an accident with these, and I find the lock of one of 'em goes wrong. As they are wanted for immediate service, will you throw your eye over them?"

Joe threw his eye over them and pronounced that the job would necessitate the lighting of his forge fire, and would take nearer two hours than one. "Will it? Then will you set about it at once, blacksmith?" said the offhand sergeant, "as it's on His Majesty's service." With that he called to his men, who came trooping into the kitchen one after another and piled their arms in a corner.

I was in an agony of apprehension. But, beginning to perceive that the handcuffs were not for me, and that the military had so far got the better of the pie as to put it in the background, I collected a little more of my scattered wits.

"How far might you call yourselves from the marshes, hereabouts? Not above a mile, I reckon?"

"Just a mile," said Mrs. Joe.

"That'll do. We begin to close in upon 'em about dusk. That'll do."

"Convicts, sergeant?" asked Mr. Wopsle, in a matter-of-course way.

"Aye!" returned the sergeant. "Two. They're pretty well known to be out on the marshes still, and they won't try to get clear of 'em before dusk. Anybody here seen anything of any such game?"

Everybody, myself excepted, said no, with confidence. Nobody thought of me.

"Well," said the sergeant, "they'll find themselves trapped in a circle. Now, blacksmith! If you're ready, His Majesty the King is."

Joe had got his coat and waistcoat and cravat[1] off, and his leather apron on, and passed into the forge. One of the soldiers opened its wooden windows, another lighted the fire, another turned to at the bellows, the rest stood round the blaze, which was soon roaring. Then Joe began to hammer and clink, hammer and clink, and we all looked on.

At last Joe's job was done, and the ringing and roaring stopped. As Joe got on his coat, he mustered courage to propose that some of us should go down with the soldiers and see what came of the hunt. Mr. Wopsle said he would go, if Joe would. Joe said he was agreeable and would take me.

The sergeant took a polite leave of the ladies, and his men resumed their muskets and fell in. Mr. Wopsle, Joe, and I received strict charge to keep in the rear and to speak no word after we reached the marshes. When we were all out in the raw air and were steadily moving toward our business, I treasonably whispered to Joe, "I hope, Joe, we shan't find them." And Joe whispered to me, "I'd give a shilling if they had cut and run, Pip."

We were joined by no stragglers from the village, for the weather was cold and threatening, the way dreary, the footing bad, darkness coming on, and the people had good fires indoors, and were keeping the day.[2] We struck out on the open marshes, through the gate at the side of the churchyard. A bitter sleet came rattling against us here on the east wind, and Joe took me on his back.

Now that we were out upon the dismal wilderness where they little thought I had been within eight or nine hours, and had seen both men hiding, I considered for the first time, with great dread, if we should come upon them, would my particular convict suppose that it was I who had brought the soldiers there? He had asked me if I was a deceiving imp, and he said I should be a fierce young hound if I joined the hunt against him. Would he believe that I was both imp and hound in treacherous earnest, and had betrayed him?

It was of no use asking this question now. There I was, on Joe's back, and there was Joe beneath me, charging at the ditches like a hunter. The soldiers were in front of us, extending into a pretty wide line with an interval between man and man.

With my heart thumping like a blacksmith at Joe's broad shoulder, I looked all about for any sign of the convicts. I could see none, I could hear none. The soldiers were moving on in the direction of the old Battery, and we were moving on a little way behind them, when, all of a sudden, we all stopped. For there had reached us, on the wings of the wind and rain, a long shout. It was repeated. The sergeant, a decisive man, ordered that the sound should not be answered, but that the course should be changed, and that his men should make toward it "at the double."

It was a run indeed now. Down banks and

---

1. **cravat** (krə-văt'): necktie.

2. **keeping the day:** observing Christmas Day.

up banks, and over gates, and splashing into dikes, and breaking among coarse rushes, no man cared where he went. As we came nearer to the shouting, it became more and more apparent that it was made by more than one voice. After a while, we could hear one voice calling "Murder!" and another voice, "Convicts! Runaways! Guard! This way for the runaway convicts!" Then both voices would seem to be stifled in a struggle, and then would break out again. And when it had come to this, the soldiers ran like deer, and Joe too.

The sergeant ran in first, and two of his men ran in close upon him. Their pieces[3] were cocked and leveled when we all ran in.

"Here are both men!" panted the sergeant, struggling at the bottom of a ditch. "Surrender, you two! and confound you for two wild beasts! Come asunder!"

Water was splashing, and mud was flying, and oaths were being sworn, and blows were being struck, when some more men went down into the ditch to help the sergeant, and dragged out, separately, my convict and the other one. Both were bleeding and panting and execrating and struggling; but of course I knew them both directly.

"Mind," said my convict, wiping blood from his face with his ragged sleeves, and shaking torn hair from his fingers, "*I* took him! *I* give him up to you! Mind that!"

"It's not much to be particular about," said the sergeant. "It'll do you small good, my man, being in the same plight yourself. Handcuffs there!"

"I don't expect it to do me any good. I don't want it to do me more good than it does now," said my convict, with a greedy laugh. "I took him. He knows it. That's enough for me."

The other convict, in addition to the old

bruised left side of his face, seemed to be bruised and torn all over. He could not so much as get his breath to speak, until they were both separately handcuffed, but leaned upon a soldier to keep himself from falling.

"Take notice, guard—he tried to murder me," were his first words.

"Tried to murder him?" said my convict disdainfully. "Try, and not do it? I took him, and giv' him up, that's what I done. I not only prevented him getting off the marshes, but I dragged him here. He's a gentleman if you please, this villain. Now the Hulks has got its gentleman again, through me. Murder him? When I could do worse and drag him back!"

The other one still gasped, "He tried—he tried—to—murder me. Bear—bear witness."

"Lookee here!" said my convict to the sergeant. "Singlehanded I got clear of the prison ship; I made a dash and I done it. I could ha' got clear of these death-cold flats likewise—look at my leg; you won't find much iron on it—if I hadn't made discovery that *he* was here. Let *him* go free? Let *him* profit by means as I found out? Let *him* make a tool of me afresh and again? Once more? No, no, no. If I had died at the bottom there," and he made an emphatic swing at the ditch with his manacled hands, "I'd have held to him with that grip, that you should have been safe to find him in my hold."

The other fugitive, who was evidently in extreme horror of his companion, repeated, "He tried to murder me. I should have been a dead man if you had not come up."

"He lies!" said my convict, with fierce energy. "He's a liar born, and he'll die a liar. Look at his face: ain't it written there? Let him turn those eyes of his on me. I defy him to do it."

The other looked at the soldiers, and looked about at the marshes and at the sky, but certainly did not look at the speaker.

---

3. **pieces**: muskets.

"Do you see him?" pursued my convict. "Do you see what a villain he is? Do you see those groveling and wandering eyes? That's how he looked when we were tried together. He never looked at me."

The other, turning his eyes restlessly about him far and near, did at last turn them for a moment on the speaker, with the words, "You are not much to look at," and with a half-taunting glance at the bound hands. At that point, my convict became so frantically exasperated that he would have rushed upon him but for the interposition of the soldiers. "Didn't I tell you," said the other convict then, "that he would murder me, if he could?" And anyone could see that he shook with fear, and that there broke out upon his lips curious white flakes, like thin snow.

"Enough of this parley," said the sergeant. "Light those torches."

As one of the soldiers, who carried a basket, went down on his knee to open it, my convict looked round him for the first time and saw me. I had alighted from Joe's back on the brink of the ditch when we came up, and had not moved since. I looked at him eagerly when he looked at me, and slightly moved my hands and shook my head. I had been waiting for him to see me, that I might try to assure him of my innocence. He gave me a look that I did not understand, and it all passed in a moment. But if he had looked at me for an hour or for a day, I could not have remembered his face ever afterwards, as having been more attentive.

The soldier with the basket soon lighted three or four torches. Before we departed from that spot, four soldiers, standing in a ring, fired twice into the air. Presently we saw other torches kindled at some distance behind us, and others on the marshes on the opposite bank of the river. "All right," said the sergeant. "March."

We had not gone far when three cannon were fired ahead of us with a sound that seemed to burst something inside my ear. "You are expected on board," said the sergeant to my convict. "They know you are coming. Don't straggle, my man. Close up here."

The two were kept apart, and each walked surrounded by a separate guard. I had hold of Joe's hand now, and Joe carried one of the torches. Mr. Wopsle had been for going back, but Joe was resolved to see it out, so we went on with the party. The two prisoners limped along in the midst of the muskets. We could not go fast, because of their lameness; and they were so spent, that two or three times we had to halt while they rested.

After an hour or so, we came to a rough wooden hut and a landing place. Then we went into the hut, where there was a smell of tobacco and whitewash, and a bright fire, and a lamp.

My convict never looked at me, except that once. While we stood in the hut, he turned to the sergeant and remarked:

"I wish to say something respecting this escape. It may prevent some persons laying under suspicion alonger me."

"You can say what you like," returned the sergeant, standing coolly looking at him with his arms folded, "but you have no call to say it here. You'll have opportunity enough to say about it, and hear about it, before it's done with, you know."

"I know, but this is another matter. A man can't starve; at least *I* can't. I took some wittles, up at the village over yonder."

"You mean stole," said the sergeant.

"And I'll tell you where from. From the blacksmith's."

"Halloa!" said the sergeant, staring at Joe.

"Halloa, Pip!" said Joe, staring at me.

"It was some broken wittles—that's what it

was—and a dram of liquor, and a pie."

"Have you happened to miss such an article as a pie, blacksmith?" asked the sergeant confidentially.

"My wife did, at the very moment when you came in. Don't you know, Pip?"

"So," said my convict, turning his eyes on Joe in a moody manner, and without the least glance at me; "so you're the blacksmith, are you? Then I'm sorry to say, I've eat your pie."

"God knows you're welcome to it—so far as it was ever mine," returned Joe, with a saving remembrance of Mrs. Joe. "We don't know what you have done, but we wouldn't have you starved to death for it, poor miserable fellow creature. Would us, Pip?"

The something that I had noticed before clicked in the man's throat again, and he turned his back. The boat had returned, and his guard were ready, so we followed him to the landing place, and saw him put into the boat, which was rowed by a crew of convicts like himself. No one seemed surprised to see him, or interested in seeing him, or glad to see him, or sorry to see him, or spoke a word except that somebody in the boat growled as if to dogs, "Give way, you!" which was the signal for the dip of the oars. By the light of the torches, we saw the black Hulk lying out a little way from the mud of the shore, like a wicked Noah's ark. Cribbed and barred and moored by massive rusty chains, the prison ship seemed in my young eyes to be ironed like the prisoners. We saw the boat go alongside, and we saw him taken up the side and disappear. Then, the ends of the torches were flung hissing into the water, and went out, as if it were all over with him.

I do not recall that I felt any tenderness of conscience in reference to Mrs. Joe, when the fear of being found out was lifted off me. But I loved Joe—perhaps for no better reason in those days than because the dear fellow let me love him—and it was much on my mind that I ought to tell Joe the whole truth. Yet I did not, and for the reason that I mistrusted that if I did, he would think me worse than I was. The fear of losing Joe's confidence tied up my tongue. In a word, I was too cowardly to do what I knew to be right, as I had been too cowardly to avoid doing what I knew to be wrong.

Chapter 6

We meet Mr. Wopsle's great-aunt and Biddy, her granddaughter.

When I was old enough, I was to be apprenticed to Joe, and until I could assume that dignity I was not to be what Mrs. Joe called "Pompeyed," or (as I render it) pampered. Therefore, I was not only odd boy about the forge, but if any neighbor happened to want an extra boy to frighten birds, or pick up stones, or do any such job, I was favored with the employment. A money box was kept on the kitchen mantel shelf, into which it was publicly made known that all my earnings were dropped, but I had no hope of any personal participation in the treasure.

Mr. Wopsle's great-aunt kept an evening school in the village. She was a ridiculous old woman who used to go to sleep from six to seven every evening, in the society of youth who paid twopence[1] per week each for the improving opportunity of seeing her do it. She rented a small cottage, and Mr. Wopsle had the room upstairs, where we students used to overhear him reading aloud in a most dignified and terrific manner, and occasionally bumping on the ceiling. There was a fiction

---

1. **twopence** (tŭp'əns): about four cents in American money in Dickens' time.

that Mr. Wopsle "examined" the scholars once a quarter. What he did on those occasions was to turn up his cuffs, stick up his hair, and give us Mark Antony's oration over the body of Caesar.[2]

Mr. Wopsle's great-aunt, besides keeping this educational institution, kept — in the same room — a little general shop. She had no idea what stock she had, or what the price of anything in it was; but there was a little greasy memorandum book kept in a drawer, which served as a catalogue of prices, and by this oracle Biddy arranged all the shop transactions. Biddy was Mr. Wopsle's great-aunt's granddaughter. She was an orphan like myself; like me, too, had been brought up by hand. Her hair always wanted brushing, her hands always wanted washing, and her shoes always wanted mending and pulling up at heel.

More by the help of Biddy than of Mr. Wopsle's great-aunt, I struggled through the alphabet as if it had been a bramblebush, getting considerably worried and scratched by every letter. After that, I fell among those thieves, the nine figures,[3] who seemed every evening to do something new to disguise themselves and baffle recognition. But at last I began, in a groping way, to read, write, and cipher,[4] on the very smallest scale.

One night, I was sitting in the chimney corner with my slate, expending great efforts on the production of a letter to Joe. I think it must have been a full year after our hunt upon the marshes, for it was a long time after, and it was winter and a hard frost. With an alphabet on the hearth at my feet for reference, I contrived in an hour or two to print and smear this epistle:

---

2. **Mark . . . Caesar:** a famous speech from William Shakespeare's play *Julius Caesar.*
3. **the nine figures:** the numbers one through nine.
4. **cipher:** to do arithmetic.

MI DEER JO i OPE U r KRWITE WELL i OPE i SHAL SON B HABELL 4 2 TEEDGE U JO AN THEN WE SHORL B SO GLODD AN WEN i M PRENGTD 2 U JO WOT LARX AN BLEVE ME INF XN PIP.

There was no necessity for my communicating with Joe by letter, inasmuch as he sat beside me and we were alone. But I delivered this written communication (slate and all) with my own hand, and Joe received it as a miracle of erudition.

"I say, Pip, old chap!" cried Joe, opening his blue eyes wide. "What a scholar you are! Ain't you?"

"I should like to be," said I, glancing at the slate as he held it, with a misgiving that the writing was rather hilly.

"Why, here's a J," said Joe, "and a O equal to anythink! Here's a J and a O, Pip, and a J-O, Joe."

I had never heard Joe read aloud to any greater extent than this monosyllable, and I had observed at church last Sunday, when I accidentally held our prayer book upside down, that it seemed to suit his convenience quite as well as if it had been all right. Wishing to embrace the present occasion of finding out whether, in teaching Joe, I should have to begin quite at the beginning, I said, "Ah! But read the rest, Joe."

"The rest, eh, Pip?" said Joe, looking at it with a slowly searching eye. "One, two, three. Why, here's three J's, and three O's, and three J-O, Joe's, in it, Pip!"

I leaned over Joe, and, with the aid of my forefinger, read him the whole letter.

"Astonishing!" said Joe, when I had finished. "You *are* a scholar."

"How do you spell Gargery, Joe?" I asked.

"I don't spell it at all," said Joe.

"But supposing you did?"

"It *can't* be supposed," said Joe. "Tho' I'm oncommon fond of reading, too."

"Are you, Joe?"

"Oncommon. Give me," said Joe, "a good book, or a good newspaper, and sit me down afore a good fire, and I ask no better. Lord!" he continued, after rubbing his knees a little, "when you *do* come to a J and a O, and says you, 'Here, at last, is a J-O, Joe,' how interesting reading is!"

I derived from this last, that Joe's education, like steam, was yet in its infancy. Pursuing the subject, I inquired:

"Didn't you ever go to school, Joe, when you were as little as me?"

"No, Pip."

"Why didn't you ever go to school, Joe, when you were as little as me?"

"Well, Pip," said Joe, taking up the poker, and settling himself to his usual occupation, when he was thoughtful, of slowly raking the fire between the lower bars, "I'll tell you. My father, Pip, he were given to drink, and when he were overtook with drink, he hammered away at my mother most onmerciful. My mother and me we ran away from my father several times; and then my mother she'd go out to work, and she'd say, 'Joe,' she'd say, 'now, please God, you shall have some schooling, child,' and she'd put me to school. But my father were that good in his heart that he couldn't a-bear to be without us. So, he took us home and hammered us. Which, you see, Pip," said Joe, "were a drawback on my learning."

"Certainly, poor Joe!"

"Though mind you, Pip," said Joe, "rendering unto all their doo, and maintaining equal justice betwixt man and man, my father were that good in his heart, don't you see?"

I didn't see; but I didn't say so.

"'Consequence, my father didn't make objections to my going to work; so I went to work at my present calling, and I worked tolerable hard, I assure *you*, Pip. In time I were able to keep him, and I kep him till he went off in a purple leptic fit.[5] My mother, she were in poor 'elth, and quite broke. She weren't long of following, poor soul, and her share of peace come round at last."

Joe's blue eyes turned a little watery. "It were but lonesome then," said Joe, "living here alone, and I got acquainted with your sister. Now, Pip," Joe looked firmly at me, as if he knew I was not going to agree with him, "your sister is a fine figure of a woman."

I could not help looking at the fire, in an ob-

---

5. **purple leptic fit:** Joe means an *apoplectic* (ăp'ə-plĕk'tĭk) *fit. Apoplexy* (ăp'ə-plĕk'sē) is a sudden paralysis or loss of consciousness, sometimes called a *stroke.*

vious state of doubt.

"Whatever family opinions, or whatever the world's opinions, on that subject may be, Pip, your sister is," Joe tapped the top bar with the poker after every word following, "a —fine—figure—of—a—woman!"

I could think of nothing better to say than "I am glad you think so, Joe."

"So am I," returned Joe. "When I offered to your sister to keep company, and to be asked in church, at such times as she was willing and ready to come to the forge, I said to her, 'And bring the poor little child. God bless the poor little child,' I said to your sister, 'there's room for *him* at the forge!'"

I broke out crying and hugged Joe round the neck, who dropped the poker to hug me, and to say, "Ever the best of friends; ain't us, Pip? Don't cry, old chap!"

When this little interruption was over, Joe resumed:

"Well, you see, Pip, and here we are! Now, when you take me in hand in my learning, Pip (and I tell you beforehand I am awful dull, most awful dull), Mrs. Joe mustn't see too much of what we're up to. It must be done, as I may say, on the sly. I'll tell you why, Pip.

"Your sister is given to government," said Joe. "Which I meantersay the government of you and myself."

"Oh!"

"And she ain't overpartial to having scholars on the premises," Joe continued, "and in partickler would not be overpartial to my being a scholar, for fear as I might rise. Like a sort of rebel, don't you see?"

Young as I was, I believe that I dated a new admiration of Joe from that night. We were equals afterward, as we had been before; but afterward, at quiet times when I sat looking at Joe and thinking about him, I had a new sensation of feeling conscious that I was looking up to Joe in my heart.

"However," said Joe, rising to replenish the fire, "here's the Dutch clock a-working himself up to being equal to strike eight of 'em, and she's not home yet!"

Mrs. Joe made occasional trips with Uncle Pumblechook on market days to assist him in buying such household stuffs and goods as required a woman's judgment, Uncle Pumblechook being a bachelor. This was market day, and Mrs. Joe was out on one of these expeditions.

Joe made the fire and swept the hearth, and then we went to the door to listen for the chaise-cart. It was a dry, cold night.

"Here comes the mare," said Joe, "ringing like a peal of bells!"

Mrs. Joe was soon landed, and Uncle Pumblechook was soon down too, and we were soon all in the kitchen, carrying so much cold air with us that it seemed to drive all the heat out of the fire.

"Now," said Mrs. Joe, unwrapping herself with haste and excitement, and throwing her bonnet back on her shoulders, where it hung by the strings, "if this boy ain't grateful this night, he never will be!"

I looked as grateful as any boy possibly could who was wholly uninformed why he ought to assume that expression.

"It's only to be hoped," said my sister, "that he won't be Pompeyed. But I have my fears."

"She ain't in that line, mum," said Mr. Pumblechook. "She knows better."

She? I looked at Joe, making the motion with my lips and eyebrows. "She?" Joe looked at me, making the motion with *his* lips and eyebrows. "She?" My sister catching him in the act, he drew the back of his hand across his nose with his usual conciliatory air on such occasions, and looked at her.

"Well?" said my sister, in her snappish way. "What are you staring at? Is the house afire?"

"Which some individual," Joe politely hinted, "mentioned she."

"And she is a she, I suppose?" said my sister. "Unless you call Miss Havisham a he. And I doubt if even you'll go so far as that."

"Miss Havisham uptown?" said Joe.

"Is there any Miss Havisham downtown?" returned my sister. "She wants this boy to go and play there. And of course he's going. And he had better play there," said my sister, shaking her head at me as an encouragement to be extremely light and sportive, "or I'll work him."

I had heard of Miss Havisham uptown—everybody for miles round had heard of Miss Havisham uptown—as an immensely rich and grim lady who lived in a large and dismal house barricaded against robbers, and who led a life of seclusion.

"Well, to be sure!" said Joe, astounded. "I wonder how she comes to know Pip!"

"Noodle!" cried my sister. "Who said she knew him?"

"Which some individual," Joe again politely hinted, "mentioned that she wanted him to go and play there."

"And couldn't she ask Uncle Pumblechook if he knew of a boy to go and play there? Isn't it just barely possible that Uncle Pumblechook may be a tenant of hers, and that he may sometimes go there to pay his rent? And couldn't she then ask Uncle Pumblechook if he knew of a boy to go and play there? And couldn't Uncle Pumblechook—being always considerate and thoughtful for us, though you may not think it, Joseph, then mention this boy that I have forever been a willing slave to?"

"Good again!" cried Uncle Pumblechook. "Well put! Good indeed! Now, Joseph, you know the case."

"No, Joseph," said my sister, in a reproachful manner, "you do not yet—though you may not think it—know the case. Uncle Pumblechook, being sensible that this boy's fortune may be made by his going to Miss Havisham's, has offered to take him into town tonight in his own chaise-cart and to keep him tonight and to take him with his own hands to Miss Havisham's tomorrow morning. And Lor-a-mussy[6] me!" cried my sister, casting off her bonnet in sudden desperation, "here I stand talking to mere mooncalfs, with Uncle Pumblechook waiting, and the mare catching cold at the door, and the boy grimed with crock and dirt from the hair of his head to the sole of his foot!"

With that she pounced on me, like an eagle on a lamb, and my face was squeezed into wooden bowls in sinks, and my head was put under taps of water butts, and I was soaped, and kneaded, and toweled, and thumped, and harrowed, and rasped, until I really was quite beside myself.

When my ablutions were completed, I was put into clean linen of the stiffest character, and was trussed up in my tightest and fearfulest suit. I was then delivered over to Mr. Pumblechook, who formally received me as if he were the sheriff, and who let off upon me the speech that I knew he had been dying to make all along: "Boy, be forever grateful to all friends, but especially unto them which brought you up by hand!"

"Goodbye, Joe!"

"God bless you, Pip, old chap!"

I had never parted from him before, and what with my feelings and what with soap-suds, I could at first see no stars from the chaise-cart. But they twinkled out one by one, without throwing any light on the questions why on earth I was going to play at Miss Havisham's, and what on earth I was expected to play at.

---

6. **Lor-a-mussy:** Lord have mercy (on).

Chapter 7

We are introduced to Miss Havisham and her ward Estella.

Mr. Pumblechook's premises in the High Street of the market town were of a peppercorny character, as the premises of a corn chandler and seedsman should be. It was in the early morning after my arrival that I entertained this speculation. On the previous night, I had been sent straight to bed in an attic with a sloping roof, which was so low in the corner where the bedstead was that I calculated the tiles as being within a foot of my eyebrows.

Mr. Pumblechook and I breakfasted at eight o'clock in the parlor behind the shop while his shopman took his mug of tea and hunch of bread and butter on a sack of peas in the front premises. I considered Mr. Pumblechook wretched company. Besides giving me as much crumb as possible in combination with as little butter, and putting a great quantity of warm water in my milk, his conversation consisted of nothing but arithmetic. On my politely bidding him good morning, he said pompously, "Seven times nine, boy?" And how should *I* be able to answer, dodged in that way, in a strange place, on an empty stomach! I was hungry, but before I had swallowed a morsel, he began a running sum that lasted all through the breakfast. "Seven?" "And four?" "And eight?" "And six?" "And two?" "And ten?" And so on.

I was very glad when ten o'clock came and we started for Miss Havisham's. Within a quarter of an hour we came to Miss Havisham's house, which was of old brick, and dismal, and had a great many iron bars to it. Some of the windows had been walled up; of those that remained, all the lower were rustily barred. There was a courtyard in front,

and that was barred; so we had to wait, after ringing the bell, until someone should come to open it. While we waited at the gate, I saw that at the side of the house there was a large brewery. No brewing was going on in it, and none seemed to have gone on for a long time.

A window was raised, and a clear voice demanded, "What name?" To which my conductor replied, "Pumblechook." The voice returned, "Quite right," and the window was shut again, and a young lady came across the courtyard, with keys in her hand.

"This," said Mr. Pumblechook, "is Pip."

"This is Pip, is it?" returned the young lady, who was very pretty, and seemed very proud. "Come in, Pip."

Mr. Pumblechook was coming in also, when she stopped him with the gate.

"Oh!" she said. "Did you wish to see Miss Havisham?"

"If Miss Havisham wished to see me," returned Mr. Pumblechook, discomfited.

"Ah!" said the girl. "But you see she don't."

She said it so finally, that Mr. Pumblechook could not protest. But he eyed me severely—as if *I* had done anything to him!—and departed with the words reproachfully delivered: "Boy! Let your behavior here be a credit unto them which brought you up by hand!"

My young conductress locked the gate, and we went across the courtyard. It was paved and clean, but grass was growing in every crevice. The brewery beyond stood open, and all was empty and disused. The cold wind seemed to blow colder there than outside the gate; and it made a shrill noise in howling in and out at the open sides of the brewery, like the noise of the wind in the rigging of a ship at sea.

"What is the name of this house, miss?"

"Its name was Satis; which is Greek, or Latin, or Hebrew, or all three—or all one to me—for enough."

"Enough House!" said I. "That's a curious name, miss."

"Yes," she replied, "but it meant more than it said. It meant, when it was given, that whoever had this house, could want nothing else. They must have been easily satisfied in those days, I should think. But don't loiter, boy."

Though she called me "boy" so often, and with a carelessness that was far from complimentary, she was of about my own age. She seemed much older than I, of course, being a girl, and beautiful and self-possessed; and she was as scornful of me as if she had been one-and-twenty, and a queen.

We went into the house by a side door—the great front entrance had two chains across it outside—and the first thing I noticed was that the passages were all dark, and that she had left a candle burning there. She took it up, and we went through more passages and up a staircase, and still it was all dark, and only the candle lighted us.

At last we came to the door of a room, and she said, "Go in."

I answered, more in shyness than politeness, "After you, miss."

To this she returned, "Don't be ridiculous, boy; I am not going in." And scornfully walked away, and—what was worse—took the candle with her.

This was very uncomfortable, and I was half afraid. However, the only thing to be done being to knock at the door, I knocked, and was told from within to enter. I entered, therefore, and found myself in a pretty large room, well lighted with wax candles. No glimpse of daylight was to be seen in it. It was a dressing room, as I supposed from the furniture. But prominent in it was a draped table with a gilded looking glass, and that I made out at first sight to be a fine lady's dressing table.

In an armchair, with an elbow resting on the table and her head leaning on that hand, sat the strangest lady I have ever seen, or shall ever see.

She was dressed in rich materials—satins, and lace, and silks—all of white. Her shoes were white. And she had a long white veil dependent from her hair, and she had bridal flowers in her hair, but her hair was white. Some bright jewels sparkled on her neck and on her hands, and some other jewels lay sparkling on the table. Dresses and half-packed trunks were scattered about. She had not quite finished dressing, for she had but one shoe on—the other was on the table near her hand—her veil was but half arranged, her watch and chain were not put on, and some lace for her bosom lay with those trinkets, and with her handkerchief, and gloves, and some flowers, and a prayer book, all confusedly heaped about the looking glass.

But I saw that everything within my view which ought to be white had lost its luster, and was faded and yellow. I saw that the bride within the bridal dress had withered like the dress, and like the flowers, and had no brightness left but the brightness of her sunken eyes. I saw that the dress had been put upon the rounded figure of a young woman, and that the figure upon which it now hung loose had shrunk to skin and bone.

"Who is it?" said the lady at the table.

"Pip, ma'am."

"Pip?"

"Mr. Pumblechook's boy, ma'am. Come—to play."

"Come nearer; let me look at you. Come closer."

It was when I stood before her, avoiding her eyes, that I took note of the surrounding objects in detail, and saw that her watch had stopped at twenty minutes to nine, and that a clock in the room had stopped at twenty minutes to nine.

"Look at me," said Miss Havisham. "You are not afraid of a woman who has never seen the sun since you were born?"

I regret to state that I was not afraid of telling the enormous lie comprehended in the answer, "No."

"Do you know what I touch here?" she said, laying her hands, one upon the other, on her left side.

"Yes, ma'am."

"What do I touch?"

"Your heart."

"Broken!"

She uttered the word with an eager look, and with strong emphasis, and with a weird smile that had a kind of boast in it.

"I am tired," said Miss Havisham. "I sometimes have sick fancies, and I have a sick

fancy that I want to see some play. There, there!" with an impatient movement of the fingers of her right hand, "play, play, play!"

I stood looking at Miss Havisham in what I suppose she took for a stubborn manner, inasmuch as she said, when we had taken a good look at each other:

"Are you sullen and obstinate?"

"No ma'am, I am very sorry for you, and very sorry I can't play just now. If you complain of me, I shall get into trouble with my sister, so I would do it if I could; but it's so new here, and so strange, and so fine — and melancholy —" I stopped, fearing I might say too much, or had already said it, and we took another look at each other.

Before she spoke again, she turned her eyes from me, and looked at the dress she wore,

and at the dressing table, and finally at herself in the looking glass.

"So new to him," she muttered, "so old to me; so strange to him, so familiar to me; so melancholy to both of us! Call Estella."

As she was still looking at the reflection of herself, I thought she was still talking to herself, and kept quiet.

"Call Estella," she repeated, flashing a look at me. "You can do that. Call Estella. At the door."

To stand in the dark in a mysterious passage of an unknown house, bawling Estella to a scornful young lady neither visible nor responsive, and feeling it a dreadful liberty so to roar out her name, was almost as bad as playing to order. But, she answered at last, and her light came along the dark passage like a star.

Miss Havisham beckoned her to come close, and took up a jewel from the table, and tried its effect against her pretty brown hair. "Your own, one day, my dear, and you will use it well. Let me see you play cards with this boy."

"With this boy! Why, he is a common laboring boy!"

I thought I overheard Miss Havisham answer—only it seemed so unlikely—"Well? You can break his heart."

"What do you play, boy?" asked Estella of me, with the greatest disdain.

"Nothing but beggar my neighbor, miss."

"Beggar him," said Miss Havisham to Estella. So we sat down to cards.

It was then I began to understand that everything in the room had stopped, like the watch and the clock, a long time ago. I noticed that Miss Havisham put down the jewel exactly on the spot from which she had taken it up. As Estella dealt the cards, I glanced at the dressing table again, and saw that the shoe upon it, once white, now yellow, had never been worn. I glanced down at the foot from

which the shoe was absent, and saw that the silk stocking on it, once white, now yellow, had been trodden ragged.

Miss Havisham sat, corpselike, as we played at cards.

"He calls the knaves jacks, this boy!" said Estella with disdain, before our first game was out. "And what coarse hands he has! And what thick boots!"

I had never thought of being ashamed of my hands before; but her contempt for me was so strong that it became infectious, and I caught it.

She won the game, and I dealt. I misdealt, as was only natural when I knew she was lying in wait for me to do wrong; and she denounced me for a stupid, clumsy, laboring boy.

"You say nothing of her," remarked Miss Havisham to me, as she looked on. "She says many hard things of you, yet you say nothing of her. What do you think of her?"

"I don't like to say," I stammered.

"Tell me in my ear," said Miss Havisham, bending down.

"I think she is very proud," I replied, in a whisper.

"Anything else?"

"I think she is very pretty."

"Anything else?"

"I think she is very insulting." (She was looking at me then with a look of supreme aversion.)

"Anything else?"

"I think I should like to go home."

"And never see her again, though she is so pretty?"

"I am not sure that I shouldn't like to see her again, but I should like to go home now."

"You shall go soon," said Miss Havisham aloud. "Play the game out."

I played the game to an end with Estella, and she beggared me. She threw the cards down on the table when she had won them all, as if she despised them for having been won of me.

"When shall I have you here again?" said Miss Havisham. "Let me think. Come again after six days. You hear?"

"Yes, ma'am."

"Estella, take him down. Let him have something to eat, and let him roam and look about him while he eats. Go, Pip."

I followed the candle down, as I had followed the candle up, and she stood it in the place where we had found it.

"You are to wait here, you boy," said Estella. She disappeared and closed the door.

I took the opportunity of being alone to look at my coarse hands and my common boots. They had never troubled me before, but they troubled me now. I determined to ask Joe why he had ever taught me to call those picture cards jacks, which ought to be called knaves. I wished Joe had been rather more genteelly brought up, and then I should have been so too.

She came back, with some bread and meat and a little mug of beer. She put the mug down on the stones of the yard, and gave me the bread and meat without looking at me, as insolently as if I were a dog in disgrace. I was so humiliated, hurt, spurned, offended, angry, sorry, that tears started to my eyes. The moment they sprang there, the girl looked at me with a quick delight in having been the cause of them. This gave me power to keep them back and to look at her; so she gave a contemptuous toss—but with a sense, I thought, of having made too sure that I was so wounded—and left me.

But, when she was gone, I got behind one of the gates in the brewery lane, and leaned my sleeve against the wall there, and leaned my forehead on it, and cried. As I cried, I kicked the wall, and took a hard twist at my hair, so bitter were my feelings.

I got rid of my injured feelings for the time, by kicking them into the brewery wall, and twisting them out of my hair, and then I smoothed my face with my sleeve, and came from behind the gate. The bread and meat were acceptable, and the beer was warming and tingling.

Even with those aids, I might not have come to myself as soon as I did, but that I saw Estella approaching with the keys to let me out. She gave me a triumphant glance in passing me, as if she rejoiced that my hands were so coarse and my boots were so thick, and she opened the gate and stood holding it. I was passing out without looking at her when she touched me with a taunting hand.

"Why don't you cry?"

"Because I don't want to."

"You do," said she. "You have been crying till you are half blind, and you are near crying again now."

She laughed contemptuously, pushed me out, and locked the gate upon me. I went straight to Mr. Pumblechook's, and was immensely relieved to find him not at home. So, leaving word with the shopman on what day I was wanted at Miss Havisham's again, I set off on the four-mile walk to our forge, pondering, as I went along, on all I had seen, and that I was a common laboring boy; that my hands were coarse; that my boots were thick; that I was much more ignorant than I had considered myself last night; and generally that I was in a low-lived, bad way.

Chapter 8

Pip tells some tall tales.

When I reached home, my sister was very curious to know all about Miss Havisham's, and asked a number of questions. And I soon found myself getting heavily bumped from behind in the nape of the neck and the small of the back, and having my face ignominiously shoved against the kitchen wall, because I did not answer those questions at sufficient length.

I felt convinced that if I described Miss Havisham's as my eyes had seen it, I should not be understood. Not only that, but I felt convinced that Miss Havisham too would not be understood; and although she was perfectly incomprehensible to me, I entertained an impression that there would be something coarse and treacherous in my dragging her as she really was (to say nothing of Miss Estella) before the contemplation of Mrs. Joe. Consequently, I said as little as I could, and had my face shoved against the kitchen wall.

The worst of it was that bullying old Pumblechook, preyed upon by a devouring curiosity to be informed of all I had seen and heard, came gaping over in his chaise-cart at teatime, to have the details divulged to him.

"Well, boy," Uncle Pumblechook began, as soon as he was seated in the chair of honor by the fire. "How did you get on uptown?"

I answered, "Pretty well, sir," and my sister shook her fist at me.

"Pretty well?" Mr. Pumblechook repeated. "Pretty well is no answer. Tell us what you mean by pretty well, boy?"

My sister with an exclamation of impatience was going to fly at me—I had no shadow of defense, for Joe was busy in the forge—when Mr. Pumblechook interposed with "No! Don't lose your temper. Leave this lad to me, ma'am; leave this lad to me." Mr. Pumblechook then turned me toward him, as if he were going to cut my hair, and said: "Boy! What like is Miss Havisham?" Mr. Pumblechook began, folding his arms tight on his chest.

"Very tall and dark," I told him.

"Is she, uncle?" asked my sister.

Mr. Pumblechook winked assent, from which I at once inferred that he had never seen Miss Havisham, for she was nothing of the kind.

"Good!" said Mr. Pumblechook, conceitedly. "This is the way to have him! We are beginning to hold our own, I think, mum?"

"I am sure, uncle," returned Mrs. Joe; "I wish you had him always; you know so well how to deal with him."

"Now, boy! What was she a-doing of, when you went in today?" asked Mr. Pumblechook.

"She was sitting," I answered, "in a black velvet coach."

Mr. Pumblechook and Mrs. Joe stared at one another—as they well might—and both repeated, "In a black velvet coach?"

"Yes," said I. "And Miss Estella—that's her niece, I think—handed her in cake and wine at the coach window, on a gold plate. And we all had cake and wine on gold plates. And I got up behind the coach to eat mine, because she told me to."

Mr. Pumblechook and Mrs. Joe stared at one another again, in utter amazement. I was perfectly frantic—a reckless witness under the torture—and would have told them anything.

"Did you ever see her in it, uncle?" asked Mrs. Joe.

"How could I," he returned, forced to the admission, "when I never see her in my life? Never clapped eyes upon her!"

"Goodness, uncle! And yet you have spoken to her?"

"Why, don't you know," said Mr. Pumblechook testily, "that when I have been there, I have been took up to the outside of her door, and the door has stood ajar, and she has spoken to me that way. What did you play at, boy?"

"We played with flags," I said. (I beg to observe that I think of myself with amazement, when I recall the lies I told on this occasion.)

"Flags!" echoed my sister.

"Yes," said I. "Estella waved a blue flag, and I waved a red one, and Miss Havisham waved one sprinkled all over with little gold stars, out at the coach window. And then we all waved our swords and hurrahed."

If they had asked me any more questions, I should undoubtedly have betrayed myself. The subject still held them when Joe came in from his work to have a cup of tea. To whom my sister, more for the relief of her own mind than for the gratification of his, related my pretended experiences.

Now, when I saw Joe open his blue eyes and roll them all round the kitchen in helpless amazement, I was overtaken by penitence. Toward Joe, and Joe only, I considered myself a young monster, while they sat debating what results would come to me from Miss Havisham's acquaintance and favor. They had no doubt that Miss Havisham would "do something" for me. My sister stood out for "property." Mr. Pumblechook was in favor of a handsome premium[1] for binding me apprentice to some genteel trade—say, the corn and seed trade, for instance.

After Mr. Pumblechook had driven off, and when my sister was washing up, I stole into the forge to Joe, and remained by him until he had done for the night. Then I said, "Before the fire goes out, Joe, I should like to tell you something."

"Should you, Pip?" said Joe, drawing his shoeing stool near the forge. "Then tell us. What is it, Pip?"

"Joe," said I, taking hold of his rolled-up shirt sleeve, and twisting it between my fin-

ger and thumb, "you remember all that about Miss Havisham's?"

"Remember?" said Joe. "I believe you! Wonderful!"

"It's a terrible thing, Joe; it ain't true."

"What are you telling of, Pip?" cried Joe, falling back in the greatest amazement. "You don't mean to say it's——"

"Yes, I do; it's lies, Joe."

As I fixed my eyes hopelessly on Joe, Joe contemplated me in dismay. "Pip, old chap! This won't do, old fellow! I say! Where do you expect to go to?"

"It's terrible, Joe; ain't it?"

"Terrible?" cried Joe. "Awful! What possessed you?"

"I don't know what possessed me, Joe," I replied, letting his shirt sleeve go, and sitting down in the ashes at his feet, hanging my head; "but I wish you hadn't taught me to call knaves at cards jacks, and I wish my boots weren't so thick nor my hands so coarse."

And then I told Joe that I felt very miserable, and that I hadn't been able to explain myself to Mrs. Joe and Pumblechook, who were so rude to me, and that there had been a beautiful young lady at Miss Havisham's who was dreadfully proud, and that she had said I was common, and that I knew I was common, and that I wished I was not common, and that the lies had come of it somehow, though I didn't know how.

"There's one thing you may be sure of, Pip," said Joe, "namely, that lies is lies. Howsever they come, they didn't ought to come, and they come from the father of lies, and work round to the same. Don't you tell me no more of 'em, Pip. *That* ain't the way to get out of being common, old chap. And as to being common, I don't make it out at all clear. You are oncommon in some things. You're oncommon small. Likewise you're a oncommon scholar."

---

1. **premium:** a fee paid to a master workman by a prospective apprentice.

"No, I am ignorant and backward, Joe."

"Why, see what a letter you wrote last night! Wrote in print even! I've seen letters— ah! and from gentlefolks!—that I'll swear weren't wrote in print," said Joe.

"I have learned next to nothing, Joe. You think much of me. It's only that."

"Well, Pip," said Joe, "you must be a common scholar afore you can be a oncommon one, I should hope!"

"You are not angry with me, Joe?"

"No, old chap. That's all, old chap, and don't never do it no more."

When I got up to my little room and said my prayers, my young mind was in that disturbed and unthankful state that I thought long after I laid me down, how common Estella would consider Joe, a mere blacksmith, how thick his boots, and how coarse his hands. I thought how Joe and my sister were then sitting in the kitchen, and how I had come up to bed from the kitchen, and how Miss Havisham and Estella never sat in a kitchen, but were far above the level of such common doings. I fell asleep recalling what I "used to do" when I was at Miss Havisham's; as though I had been there weeks or months, instead of hours.

That was a memorable day to me, for it made great changes in me. But it is the same with any life. Imagine one selected day struck out of it, and think how different its course would have been. Pause, you who read this, and think for a moment of the long chain of iron or gold, of thorns or flowers, that would never have bound you, but for the formation of the first link on one memorable day.

Chapter 9

A mysterious stranger appears with a surprise for Pip.

The felicitous idea occurred to me a morning or two later when I woke, that the best step I could take toward making myself uncommon was to get out of Biddy everything she knew. I mentioned to Biddy when I went to Mr. Wopsle's great-aunt's at night, that I had a particular reason for wishing to get on in life, and that I should feel very much obliged to her if she would impart all her learning to me. Biddy, who was the most obliging of girls, immediately said she would, and indeed began to carry out her promise within five minutes.

The educational scheme or course established by Mr. Wopsle's great-aunt may be resolved into the following synopsis. The pupils ate apples and put straws down one another's backs until Mr. Wopsle's great-aunt collected her energies and made an indiscriminate totter at them with a birch rod. After receiving the charge with every mark of derision, the pupils formed in line and buzzingly passed a ragged book from hand to hand. The book had an alphabet in it, some figures and tables, and a little spelling. Biddy gave out the number of the page, and then we all read aloud in a frightful chorus, Biddy leading with a high, shrill, monotonous voice, and none of us having the least notion of, or reverence for, what we were reading about.

It appeared to me that it would take time to become uncommon under these circumstances; nevertheless, I resolved to try it, and that very evening Biddy entered on our special agreement by lending me, to copy at home, a large Old English *D* which she had imitated from the heading of some newspaper, and which I supposed, until she told me what it was, to be a design for a buckle.

Of course there was a public house[1] in the village, and of course Joe liked sometimes to smoke his pipe there. I had received strict orders from my sister to call for him at the Three Jolly Bargemen that evening, on my way from school, and bring him home at my peril. To the Three Jolly Bargemen, therefore, I directed my steps.

Joe was smoking his pipe in company with Mr. Wopsle and a stranger. Joe greeted me as usual with "Halloa, Pip, old chap!" and the moment he said that, the stranger turned his head and looked at me.

He was a secret-looking man whom I had never seen before. His head was all on one side, and one of his eyes was half shut up, as if he were taking aim at something with an invisible gun. He had a pipe in his mouth, and he took it out, and, after slowly blowing all his smoke away and looking hard at me all the time, nodded. So I nodded, and then he nodded again, and made room on the settle[2] beside him that I might sit down there.

But, as I was used to sit beside Joe whenever I entered that place of resort, I said, "No, thank you, sir," and fell into the space Joe made for me on the opposite settle. The strange man, after glancing at Joe, and seeing that his attention was otherwise engaged, nodded to me again when I had taken my seat, and then rubbed his leg—in a very odd way, as it struck me.

"You were saying," said the strange man, turning to Joe, "that you was a blacksmith. What'll you drink, Mr. Gargery? At my expense? To top up with?"

"Well," said Joe, "to tell you the truth, I ain't much in the habit of drinking at anybody's expense but my own."

---

1. **public house:** in England, a bar or tavern, often called a *pub*.
2. **settle:** bench.

"Habit? No," returned the stranger, "but once and away, and on a Saturday night, too. Come! Put a name to it, Mr. Gargery."

"I wouldn't wish to be stiff company," said Joe. "Rum."

"Rum," repeated the stranger. "And will the other gentleman originate a sentiment?"

"Rum," said Mr. Wopsle.

"Three rums!" cried the stranger, calling to the landlord. "Glasses round!"

The stranger put his legs up on the settle that he had to himself. He wore a flapping broad-brimmed traveler's hat and under it a handkerchief tied over his head in the manner of a cap, so that he showed no hair.

"I am not acquainted with this country, gentlemen, but it seems a solitary country toward the river."

"Most marshes is solitary," said Joe.

"No doubt, no doubt. Do you find any gypsies, now, or tramps, or vagrants of any sort, out there?"

"No," said Joe; "none but a runaway convict now and then. And we don't find *them* easy."

"Seems you have been out after such?" asked the stranger.

"Once," returned Joe. "Not that we wanted to take them, you understand; we went out as lookers-on, me and Mr. Wopsle and Pip. Didn't us, Pip?"

"Yes, Joe."

The stranger looked at me again and said, "He's a likely young parcel of bones, that. What is it you call him?"

"Pip," said Joe.

"Christened Pip?"

"No, not christened Pip."

"Surname Pip?"

"No," said Joe; "it's a kind of a family name what he gave himself when a infant, and is called by."

"Son of yours?"

"Well—" said Joe meditatively, "well—no. No, he ain't."

"Nevvy?"[3] said the strange man.

"Well," said Joe, "he is not—no, not to deceive you, he is *not*—my nevvy."

"What the blue blazes is he?" asked the stranger.

Mr. Wopsle expounded the ties between me and Joe. All this while the strange man looked at nobody but me, and looked at me as if he were determined to have a shot at me at last, and bring me down. But he said nothing until the glasses were brought: and then he made his shot, and a most extraordinary shot it was.

He stirred his rum-and-water pointedly at me, and he tasted his rum-and-water pointedly at me—not with a spoon that was brought to him, but *with a file.*

He did this so that nobody but I saw the file; and when he had done it, he wiped the file and put it in a breast pocket. I knew it to be Joe's file, and I knew that he knew my convict, the moment I saw the instrument. I sat gazing at him, spellbound. Joe got up to go, and took me by the hand.

"Stop half a moment, Mr. Gargery," said the strange man. "I think I've got a bright new shilling somewhere in my pocket, and if I have, the boy shall have it."

He looked it out from a handful of small change, folded it in some crumpled paper, and gave it to me. "Yours!" said he. "Mind! Your own."

I thanked him, staring at him far beyond the bounds of good manners, and holding tight to Joe. On the way home I was in a manner stupefied by this turning up of my old misdeed and old acquaintance, and could think of nothing else.

My sister was not in a very bad temper when we presented ourselves in the kitchen, and Joe was encouraged by that unusual circumstance to tell her about the bright shilling. "A bad un, I'll be bound," said Mrs. Joe triumphantly, "or he wouldn't have given it to the boy. Let's look at it."

I took it out of the paper, and it proved to be a good one. "But what's this?" said Mrs. Joe, throwing down the shilling and catching up the paper. "Two one-pound notes?"[4]

Joe caught up his hat again, and ran with them to the Jolly Bargemen to restore them to their owner. While he was gone I sat down on my usual stool and looked vacantly at my sister, feeling pretty sure that the man would not be there.

Presently Joe came back, saying that the man was gone, but that he, Joe, had left word at the Three Jolly Bargemen concerning the notes. Then my sister sealed them up in a piece of paper, and put them under some dried rose leaves in an ornamental teapot on the top of a press in the parlor. There they remained a nightmare to me many and many a night and day.

I had sadly broken sleep when I got to bed, through thinking of the strange man and of the guiltily coarse and common thing it was to be on secret terms of conspiracy with convicts—a feature in my low career that I had previously forgotten. I was haunted by the file too. A dread possessed me that when I least expected it, the file would reappear. I coaxed myself to sleep by thinking of Miss Havisham's next Wednesday; and in my sleep I saw the file coming at me out of a door, without seeing who held it, and I screamed myself awake.

---

3. **Nevvy:** nephew.

4. **Two one-pound notes:** forty shillings, or almost ten dollars in American money, which was a considerable sum of money in Dickens' time.

Chapter 10

We meet Camilla and her husband, Miss Sarah Pocket, Georgiana, and a pale young gentleman.

At the appointed time I returned to Miss Havisham's, and my hesitating ring at the gate brought out Estella. She locked it after admitting me, as she had done before, and took me to quite another part of the house, a small paved courtyard, the opposite side of which was formed by a detached dwelling house. There was a clock in the outer wall of this house. Like the clock in Miss Havisham's room, and like Miss Havisham's watch, it had stopped at twenty minutes to nine.

We went in at the door, which stood open, and into a gloomy room with a low ceiling, on the ground floor at the back. There was some company in the room, and Estella said, "You are to go and stand there, boy, till you are wanted." "There" being the window, I crossed to it and stood "there," in a very uncomfortable state of mind, looking out.

I divined that my coming had stopped conversation in the room, and that its other occupants were looking at me. There were three ladies in the room and one gentleman. Before I had been standing at the window five minutes, they somehow conveyed to me that they were all toadies and humbugs.[1] ~~fakes~~

They all had a listless and dreary air of waiting somebody's pleasure. The most talkative of the ladies, whose name was Camilla, very much reminded me of my sister, with the difference that she was older and of a blunter cast of features.

"Poor dear soul!" said this lady. "Nobody's enemy but his own!" *you are your own worst enemy*

---

1. **toadies and humbugs:** flatterers and people who are not what they pretend to be.

"It would be much more commendable to be somebody else's enemy," said the gentleman; "far more natural." *picking on Pip*

"Cousin Raymond," observed another lady, "we are to love our neighbor."

"Sarah Pocket," returned Cousin Raymond, "if a man is not his own neighbor, who is?" *Weds.*

"Poor soul!" Camilla presently went on (I knew they had all been looking at me in the meantime), "he is so very strange! Would anyone believe that when Tom's wife died, he actually could not be induced to see the importance of the children's having the deepest of trimmings to their mourning? 'Good Lord!' says he, 'Camilla, what can it signify so long as the poor bereaved little things are in black?' So like Matthew! The idea!" *kids should be dressed properly for a family funeral*

"Good points in him, good points in him," said Cousin Raymond, "but he never had and he never will have any sense of the proprieties." *manners*

The ringing of a distant bell, combined with the echoing of some cry or call along the passage by which I had come, interrupted the conversation and caused Estella to say to me, "Now, boy!"

As we were going with our candle along the dark passage, Estella stopped all of a sudden and, facing round, said in her taunting manner, with her face quite close to mine:

"Well?"

"Well, miss," I answered, almost falling over her and checking myself.

She stood looking at me, and of course I stood looking at her.

"Am I pretty?"

"Yes; I think you are very pretty."

"Am I insulting?"

"Not as much as you were last time," said I.

"Not so much so?"

"No."

She slapped my face with such force as she had.

"Now?" said she. "You little coarse monster, what do you think of me now?"

"I shall not tell you."

"Because you are going to tell upstairs. Is that it?"

"No," said I, "that's not it."

"Why don't you cry again, you little wretch?"

"Because I'll never cry for you again," said I. Which was, I suppose, as false a declaration as ever was made; for I was inwardly crying for her then, and I know what I know of the pain she cost me afterward.

We went on our way upstairs after this episode; and, as we were going up, we met a gentleman groping his way down.

"Whom have we here?" asked the gentleman, stopping and looking at me.

"A boy," said Estella.

He was a burly man of an exceedingly dark complexion, with an exceedingly large head. He took my chin in his large hand and turned up my face to have a look at me by the light of the candle. He was prematurely bald on the top of his head, and had bushy black eyebrows that wouldn't lie down, but stood up bristling. His eyes were set very deep in his head, and were disagreeably sharp and suspicious. He had a large watch chain, and strong black dots where his beard and whiskers would have been if he had let them. He was nothing to me, and I could have had no foresight then that he ever would be anything to me, but it happened that I had this opportunity of observing him well.

"Boy of the neighborhood? Hey?" said he.

"Yes, sir," said I.

"How do *you* come here?"

"Miss Havisham sent for me, sir," I explained.

"Well! Behave yourself. I have a pretty large experience of boys, and you're a bad set of fellows. Now mind!" said he, biting the side of his great forefinger, as he frowned at me, "you behave yourself!"

With these words he released me—which I was glad of, for his hand smelt of scented soap—and went his way downstairs. We were soon in Miss Havisham's room. Estella left me standing near the door, and I stood there until Miss Havisham cast her eyes upon me from the dressing table.

"So!" she said. "The days have worn away, have they?"

"Yes, ma'am. Today is——"

"There, there, there!" with the impatient movement of her fingers. "I don't want to know. Are you ready to play?"

I was obliged to answer in some confusion, "I don't think I am, ma'am."

"Not at cards again?" she demanded with a searching look.

"Yes, ma'am; I could do that, if I was wanted."

"Since this house strikes you old and grave, boy," said Miss Havisham impatiently, "and you are unwilling to play, are you willing to work?"

I could answer this inquiry with a better heart than I had been able to find for the other question, and I said I was quite willing.

"Then go into that opposite room," said she, pointing at the door behind me with her withered hand, "and wait there till I come."

I crossed the staircase landing and entered the room she indicated. From that room, too, the daylight was completely excluded, and it had an airless smell that was oppressive. Every discernible thing in it was covered with dust and mold, and dropping to pieces. The most prominent object was a long table with a tablecloth spread on it, as if a feast had been in preparation when the house and the clocks all stopped together. A centerpiece of some kind was in the middle of this cloth; it was so heavily overhung with cobwebs that its form

thumbnail sketch

was quite undistinguishable. I saw speckled-legged spiders with blotchy bodies running home to it, and running out from it.

I heard the mice, too, rattling behind the panels.

These crawling things had fascinated my attention, and I was watching them from a distance when Miss Havisham laid a hand upon my shoulder. In her other hand she had a crutch-headed stick on which she leaned, and she looked like the witch of the place.

"This," said she, pointing to the long table with her stick, "is where I will be laid when I am dead. They shall come and look at me here."

"What do you think that is," she asked me, again pointing with her stick; "that, where those cobwebs are?"

"I can't guess, ma'am."

"It's a great cake. A bride cake. Mine!"

She looked all round the room in a glaring manner, and then said, leaning on me while her hand twitched my shoulder, "Come, come, come! Walk me, walk me!"

I made out from this that the work I had to do was to walk Miss Havisham round and round the room. Accordingly, she leaned on my shoulder and we went away at a pace.

After a while she said, "Call Estella," so I went out on the landing and roared that name as I had done on the previous occasion. When her light appeared, I returned to Miss Havisham, and we started away again round and round the room.

If only Estella had come to be a spectator of our proceedings, I should have felt sufficiently discontented; but, as she brought with her the three ladies and the gentleman whom I had seen below, I didn't know what to do. I would have stopped; but Miss Havisham twitched my shoulder and we posted on.

"Dear Miss Havisham," said Miss Sarah Pocket. "How well you look!"

"I do not," returned Miss Havisham. "I am yellow skin and bone."

Camilla brightened when Miss Pocket met with this rebuff; and she murmured, as she plaintively contemplated Miss Havisham, "Poor dear soul! Certainly not to be expected to look well, poor thing. The idea!"

"And how are *you?*" said Miss Havisham to Camilla. As we were close to Camilla then, I would have stopped as a matter of course, only Miss Havisham wouldn't stop. We swept on, and I felt that I was highly obnoxious to Camilla.

"Thank you, Miss Havisham," she returned. "I am as well as can be expected."

"Why, what's the matter with you?" asked Miss Havisham, with exceeding sharpness.

"Nothing worth mentioning," replied Camilla. "I don't wish to make a display of my feelings, but I have habitually thought of you more in the night than I am quite equal to."

"Then don't think of me," retorted Miss Havisham.

"Oh!" cried Camilla. "It's a weakness to be so affectionate, but I can't help it."

Miss Havisham and I kept going round and round the room; now brushing against the skirts of the visitors; now giving them the whole length of the dismal chamber.

"There's Matthew!" said Camilla. "Never mixing with any natural ties, never coming here to see how Miss Havisham is!"

When this same Matthew was mentioned, Miss Havisham stopped me and herself, and stood looking at the speaker. This change had a great influence in bringing Camilla's chemistry to a sudden end.

"Matthew will come and see me at last," said Miss Havisham sternly, "when I am laid on that table. That will be his place—there," striking the table with her stick, "at my head! And yours will be there! And your husband's there! And Sarah Pocket's there! And Georgiana's there! Now you all know where to take your stations when you come to feast upon me.[2] And now go!"

At the mention of each name, she had struck the table with her stick in a new place. She now said, "Walk me, walk me!" and we went on again.

While Estella was away lighting them down, Miss Havisham still walked with her hand on my shoulder, but more and more slowly. At last she stopped before the fire and said, after muttering and looking at it some seconds:

"This is my birthday, Pip."

I was going to wish her many happy returns, when she lifted her stick.

"I don't suffer it to be spoken of. I don't suffer those who were here just now, or anyone, to speak of it. They come here on the day, but they dare not refer to it."

Of course I made no further effort to refer to it.

"On this day of the year, long before you were born, this heap of decay," stabbing with her crutched stick at the pile of cobwebs on the table, but not touching it, "was brought here. It and I have worn away together. The mice have gnawed at it, and sharper teeth than teeth of mice have gnawed at me."

She held the head of her stick against her heart as she stood looking at the table; she in her once white dress, all yellow and withered; the once white cloth all yellow and withered; everything around in a state to crumble under a touch.

"When the ruin is complete," said she, with a ghastly look, "and when they lay me dead, in my bride's dress on the bride's table — which shall be done, and which will be the finished curse upon him — so much the better if it is done on this day!"

I remained quiet. Estella returned, and she too remained quiet. At length, Miss Havisham said, "Let me see you two play at cards; why have you not begun?" With that, we returned to her room, and sat down as before; I was beggared as before, and again, as before, Miss Havisham watched us all the time, directed my attention to Estella's beauty, and made me notice it the more by trying her jewels on Estella's breast and hair.

Estella, for her part, likewise treated me as before, except that she did not condescend to speak. When we had played some half-dozen games, a day was appointed for my return, and I was taken down into the yard to be fed in the former doglike manner. There, too, I was again left to wander about as I liked.

I strolled into the garden and found myself in the dismal corner upon which I had looked out of a window. Never questioning for a moment that the house was now empty, I looked in at another window, and found myself, to my great surprise, exchanging a broad stare with a pale young gentleman with red eyelids and light hair.

This pale young gentleman quickly disappeared and reappeared beside me. He had been at his books when I had found myself staring at him, and I now saw that he was inky.

"Who let *you* in?" said he.

"Miss Estella."

"Who gave you leave to prowl about?"

"Miss Estella."

"Come and fight," said the pale young gentleman.

What could I do but follow him? I have often asked myself the question since; but, what else could I do? His manner was so final and I was so astonished that I followed where he led, as if I had been under a spell.

"Stop a minute, though," he said, wheeling

2. **feast . . . me:** that is, to collect their shares of her will after her death.

round before we had gone many paces. "I ought to give you a reason for fighting, too. There it is!" In a most irritating manner he instantly slapped his hands against one another, daintily flung one of his legs up behind him, pulled my hair, slapped his hands again, dipped his head, and butted it into my stomach.

I hit out at him, and was going to hit out again, when he said, "Aha! Would you?" and began dancing backward and forward in a manner quite unparalleled within my limited experience.

"Laws of the game!" said he. Here, he skipped from his left leg on to his right. "Regular rules!" Here, he skipped from his right leg on to his left. "Come to the ground, and go through the preliminaries!" Here, he dodged backward and forward, and did all sorts of things while I looked helplessly at him.

I was secretly afraid of him when I saw him so dexterous; but I followed him without a word to a retired nook of the garden. On his asking me if I was satisfied with the ground, and on my replying "Yes," he begged my leave to absent himself for a moment, and quickly returned with a bottle of water and a sponge dipped in vinegar. "Available for both," he said, and fell to pulling off, not only his jacket and waistcoat, but his shirt, too, in a manner at once lighthearted, businesslike, and bloodthirsty. Although he did not look very healthy, these dreadful preparations quite appalled me. I judged him to be about my own age, but he was much taller.

My heart failed me when I saw him squaring at me with every demonstration of mechanical nicety, and eyeing my anatomy as if he were minutely choosing his bone. I never have been so surprised in my life as I was when I let out the first blow and saw him lying on his back, looking up at me with a bloody nose.

But he was on his feet directly, and after sponging himself began squaring again. The second greatest surprise I have ever had in my life was seeing him on his back again, looking up at me out of a black eye.

His spirit inspired me with great respect. He seemed to have no strength, and he never once hit me hard, and he was always knocked down. He got heavily bruised, but he came up again and again until at last he got a bad fall with the back of his head against the wall. Even after that, he got up and turned round confusedly a few times; but finally went on his knees to his sponge and threw it up, panting out, "That means you have won."

He seemed so brave and innocent that although I had not proposed the contest, I felt but a gloomy satisfaction in my victory. However, I got dressed and said, "Can I help you?" and he said, "No, thankee," and I said, "Good afternoon," and *he* said, "Same to you."

When I got into the courtyard, I found Estella waiting with the keys. But she neither asked me where I had been, nor why I had kept her waiting; and there was a bright flush upon her face, as though something had happened to delight her. Instead of going straight to the gate, too, she stepped back into the passage and beckoned me.

"Come here! You may kiss me if you like."

I kissed her cheek as she turned it to me. I think I would have gone through a great deal to kiss her cheek. But I felt that the kiss was given to the coarse common boy as a piece of money might have been, and that it was worth nothing.

What with the birthday visitors, and what with the cards, and what with the fight, my stay had lasted so long that when I neared home, the light off the point on the marshes was gleaming against a black night sky, and Joe's furnace was flinging a path of fire across the road.

Chapter 11

Pip becomes Joe's apprentice.

My mind grew very uneasy on the subject of the pale young gentleman. The more I thought of the fight, and recalled the pale young gentleman on his back, the more certain it appeared that something would be done to me. When the day came round for my return to the scene of the deed of violence, my terrors reached their height. However, go to Miss Havisham's I must, and go I did. And behold! nothing came of the late struggle. It was not alluded to in any way, and no pale young gentleman was to be discovered on the premises.

On the broad landing between Miss Havisham's own room and that other room in which the long table was laid out, I saw a garden-chair—a light chair on wheels, that you pushed from behind. I entered, that same day, on a regular occupation of pushing Miss Havisham in this chair (when she was tired of walking with her hand upon my shoulder) round her own room, and across the landing, and round the other room. Over and over and over again, we would make these journeys, and sometimes they would last as long as three hours at a stretch. I fall into a general mention of these journeys as numerous, because it was at once settled that I should return every alternate day at noon, and because I am now going to sum up a period of at least eight or ten months.

As we began to be more used to one another, Miss Havisham talked more to me, and asked me such questions as what had I learned and what was I going to be? I told her I was going to be apprenticed to Joe, I believed; and I enlarged upon my knowing nothing and wanting to know everything, in the hope that she might offer some help toward that desirable end. But she did not; on the contrary, she seemed to prefer my being ignorant. Neither did she ever give me any money or anything but my daily dinner—nor even stipulate that I should be paid for my services.

Estella was always about, and always let me in and out, but never told me I might kiss her again. Sometimes, she would be quite familiar with me; sometimes, she would tell me energetically that she hated me. Miss Havisham would often ask me in a whisper, or when we were alone, "Does she grow prettier and prettier, Pip?" And when I said "Yes" (for indeed she did), would seem to enjoy it greedily. Also, when we played at cards, Miss Havisham would look on, with a miserly relish of Estella's moods, whatever they were. And sometimes, when her moods were so many and so contradictory that I was puzzled what to say or do, Miss Havisham would embrace her with lavish fondness, murmuring something in her ear that sounded like "Break their hearts, my pride and hope, break their hearts and have no mercy!"

Perhaps I might have told Joe about the pale young gentleman if I had not previously been betrayed into those enormous inventions to which I had confessed. I reposed complete confidence in no one but Biddy; but I told poor Biddy everything. Why it came natural for me to do so, and why Biddy had a deep concern in everything I told her, I did not know then, though I think I know now.

Meanwhile, councils went on in the kitchen at home. Pumblechook and my sister would pair off in nonsensical speculations about Miss Havisham, and about what she would do with me and for me. In these discussions, Joe bore no part. But he was often talked at, while they were in progress, by reason of Mrs. Joe's perceiving that he was not favorable to my being taken from the forge.

We went on in this way for a long time, when, one day, Miss Havisham stopped short as she and I were walking and said with some displeasure:

"You are growing tall, Pip!"

She said no more at the time, but she presently stopped and looked at me again; and after that looked frowning and moody. On the next day of my attendance, she stayed me with a movement of her impatient fingers:

"Tell me the name again of that blacksmith of yours."

"Joe Gargery, ma'am."

"Meaning the master you were to be apprenticed to?"

"Yes, Miss Havisham."

"You had better be apprenticed at once. Would Gargery come here with you, and bring your indentures,[1] do you think?"

"At any particular time, Miss Havisham?"

"There, there! I know nothing about times. Let him come soon, and come along with you."

When I delivered this message at home, my sister "went on the Ram-page," threw a candlestick at Joe, got out the dustpan—which was always a very bad sign—and cleaned us out of house and home so that we stood shivering in the backyard. It was ten o'clock at night before we ventured to creep in again.

It was a trial to my feelings, on the next day but one, to see Joe arraying himself in his Sunday clothes to accompany me to Miss Havisham's. At breakfast time, my sister declared her intention of going to town with us, and being left at Uncle Pumblechook's and called for "when we had done with our fine ladies."

The forge was shut up for the day, and Joe inscribed in chalk upon the door (as it was his custom to do on the very rare occasions when he was not at work) the monosyllable HOUT,[2] accompanied by a sketch of an arrow supposed to be flying in the direction he had taken. When we came to Pumblechook's, my sister bounced in and left us. As it was almost noon, Joe and I held straight on to Miss Havisham's house. Estella opened the gate as usual, and led us the way that I knew so well.

Estella told me we were both to go in, so I took Joe by the coat cuff and conducted him into Miss Havisham's presence. She was seated at her dressing table, and looked round at us immediately.

"Oh!" said she to Joe. "You are the husband of the sister of this boy?"

I could hardly have imagined dear old Joe looking so unlike himself or so like some extraordinary bird, standing, as he did, speechless, with his tuft of feathers ruffled, and his mouth open as if he wanted a worm.

"You are the husband," repeated Miss Havisham, "of the sister of this boy?"

It was very aggravating; but, throughout the interview, Joe persisted in addressing me instead of Miss Havisham. It was quite in vain for me to make him sensible that he ought to speak to Miss Havisham. The more I made faces and gestures to him to do it, the more confidential, argumentative, and polite he persisted in being to me.

"Have you brought his indentures with you?" asked Miss Havisham.

"Well, Pip, you know," replied Joe, as if that were a little unreasonable, "you yourself see me put 'em in my 'at, and therefore you know as they are here." With which he took them out, and gave them, not to Miss Havisham, but to me. I am afraid I was ashamed of the dear good fellow—I *know* I was ashamed of him—when I saw that Estella stood at the

1. **indentures:** a contract binding an apprentice to a master. See footnote on page 562.

2. **Hout:** out.

back of Miss Havisham's chair, and that her eyes laughed mischievously. I took the indentures out of his hand and gave them to Miss Havisham.

"You expected," said Miss Havisham, as she looked them over, "no premium with the boy?"

"Joe!" I remonstrated; for he made no reply at all. "Why don't you answer——"

"Pip," returned Joe, cutting me short as if he were hurt, "which I meantersay that were not a question requiring a answer betwixt yourself and me, and which you know the answer to be full well 'No.' You know it to be 'No,' Pip, and wherefore should I say it?"

Miss Havisham glanced at him as if she understood what he really was, better than I had thought possible; and took up a little bag from the table beside her.

"Pip has earned a premium here," she said, "and here it is. There are five-and-twenty guineas[3] in this bag. Give it to your master, Pip."

Joe, even at this pass, persisted in addressing me. "This is very liberal on your part, Pip," said Joe, "and it is as such received and grateful welcome, though never looked for. And now, old chap," said Joe, "may you and me do our duty, both on us by one and another."

"Goodbye, Pip!" said Miss Havisham. "Let them out, Estella."

"Am I to come again, Miss Havisham?" I asked.

"No. Gargery is your master now. Gargery! One word!"

Thus calling him back as I went out of the door, I heard her say to Joe, in a distinct emphatic voice, "The boy has been a good boy

---

3. **guinea** (gĭn′ē): a gold coin worth twenty-one shillings, a little more than five dollars in American money at that time.

here, and that is his reward. Of course, as an honest man, you will expect no other and no more.''

In another minute we were outside the gate, and it was locked, and Estella was gone. When we stood in the daylight alone again, Joe backed up against a wall and said to me, ''Astonishing!'' And there he remained so long, saying ''Astonishing'' at intervals so often that I began to think his senses were never coming back. At length he prolonged his remark into, ''Pip, I do assure *you* this is as-TON-ish-ing!'' and so, by degrees, became conversational and able to walk away.

''Well!'' cried my sister, addressing us both at once, when we arrived at Pumblechook's. ''I wonder you condescend to come back to such poor society as this, I am sure I do! And, what did she give young Rantipole[4] here?''

''She giv' him,'' said Joe, handing the bag to my sister, ''five-and-twenty pound.''

''It's five-and-twenty pound, mum,'' echoed that basest of swindlers, Pumblechook, rising to shake hands with her; ''and it's no more than your merits (as I said when my opinion was asked), and I wish you joy of the money!''

''Goodness knows, Uncle Pumblechook,'' said my sister (grasping the money), ''we're deeply beholden to you.''

''Never mind me, mum,'' returned that diabolical corn chandler. ''A pleasure's a pleasure all the world over. But this boy, you know; we must have him bound. I said I'd see to it—to tell you the truth.''

The justices were sitting in the town hall near at hand, and we at once went over to have me bound apprentice to Joe. I say we went over, but I was pushed over by Pumblechook, exactly as if I had that moment picked a pocket or fired a rick.[5] Indeed, it was the general impression in court that I had been taken red-handed; for, as Pumblechook shoved me before him through the crowd, I heard some people say, ''What's he done?'' and others, ''He's a young 'un, too, but looks bad, don't he?'' One person of mild and benevolent aspect even gave me a tract entitled, TO BE READ IN MY CELL.

When we had come out again, we went back to Pumblechook's. And there my sister became so excited by the twenty-five guineas that nothing would serve her but we must have a dinner at the Blue Boar, and that Mr. Pumblechook must go over in his chaise-cart and bring the Hubbles and Mr. Wopsle.

My only remembrances of the great festival are that they wouldn't let me go to sleep, but whenever they saw me dropping off, woke me up and told me to enjoy myself and that when I got into my little bedroom, I was truly wretched, and had a strong conviction on me that I should never like Joe's trade. I had liked it once, but once was not now.

It is a most miserable thing to feel ashamed of home. Home had never been a very pleasant place to me, because of my sister's temper. But Joe had sanctified it, and I believed in it. I had believed in the best parlor as a most elegant saloon;[6] I had believed in the kitchen as a chaste though not magnificent apartment; I had believed in the forge as the glowing road to manhood and independence. Within a single year all this was changed. Now, it was all coarse and common, and I would not have had Miss Havisham and Estella see it on any account.

How much of my ungracious condition of mind may have been my own fault, how much Miss Havisham's, how much my sister's, is now of no moment to me or anyone.

---

4. **Rantipole:** a wild and unruly person.
5. **fired a rick:** set fire to a haystack.

6. **saloon:** large room.

The change was made in me; the thing was done. Well or ill done, it was done.

Once it had seemed to me that when I should at last roll up my shirt sleeves and go into the forge, Joe's 'prentice, I should be distinguished and happy. Now I only felt that I was dusty with the dust of the small coal, and that I had a weight upon my daily remembrance to which the anvil was a feather. There have been occasions in my later life when I have felt for a time as if a thick curtain had fallen on all its interest and romance, to shut me out from anything save dull endurance any more. Never has that curtain dropped so heavy and blank, as when my way in life lay stretched out straight before me through the newly entered road of apprenticeship to Joe.

But I am glad to know that I never breathed a murmur to Joe while my indentures lasted. It is about the only thing I *am* glad to know of myself in that connection. It was not because I was faithful, but because Joe was faithful, that I never ran away and went for a soldier or a sailor. It was not because I had a strong sense of the virtue of industry, but because Joe had a strong sense of the virtue of industry, that I worked with tolerable zeal against the grain. It is not possible to know how far the influence of any amiable, honest-hearted, duty-doing man flies out into the world, but I know right well that any good that intermixed itself with my apprenticeship came of plain, contented Joe, and not of restless, aspiring, discontented me.

What I dreaded was that in some unlucky hour I, being at my grimiest and commonest, should lift up my eyes and see Estella looking in at one of the wooden windows of the forge. I was haunted by the fear that she would, sooner or later, find me out, with a black face and hands, doing the coarsest part of my work, and would exult over me and despise me. Often after dark, when I was pulling the bellows for Joe, I would fancy that I saw her just drawing her face away, and would believe that she had come at last.

After that, when we went in to supper, the place would have a more homely look than ever, and I would feel more ashamed of home than ever, in my own ungracious breast.

Chapter 12

Introducing Orlick.

As I was getting too big for Mr. Wopsle's great-aunt's room, my education under that preposterous female terminated; not, however, until Biddy had imparted to me everything she knew, from the little catalogue of prices to a comic song she had once bought for a halfpenny. Although the only coherent part of the latter piece of literature was the opening lines,

> When I went to Lunnon town, sirs,
> > Too rul loo rul!
> > Too rul loo rul!
> Wasn't I done very brown, sirs?
> > Too rul loo rul!
> > Too rul loo rul!

—still, in my desire to be wiser, I got this composition by heart with the utmost gravity. In my hunger for information, I made proposals to Mr. Wopsle to bestow some intellectual crumbs upon me; with which he kindly complied. As it turned out, however, that he only wanted me for a dramatic lay figure,[1] to be contradicted and embraced and wept over and bullied and clutched and stabbed and knocked about in a variety of ways, I soon declined that course of instruction, though not until Mr. Wopsle in his poetic fury had severely mauled me.

---

1. **lay figure:** a puppet or dummy; here used in its secondary meaning of an unimportant or servile person.

Whatever I acquired, I tried to impart to Joe. This statement sounds so well that I cannot in my conscience let it pass unexplained. I wanted to make Joe less ignorant and common, that he might be worthier of my society and less open to Estella's reproach.

The old Battery out on the marshes was our place of study, and a broken slate and a short piece of slate pencil were our educational implements, to which Joe always added a pipe of tobacco. I never knew Joe to remember anything from one Sunday to another, or to acquire, under my tuition, any piece of information whatever. Yet he would smoke his pipe at the Battery with a far more sagacious air than anywhere else—even with a learned air—as if he considered himself to be advancing immensely. Dear fellow, I hope he did.

It was pleasant and quiet out there with the sails on the river. Whenever I watched the vessels standing out to sea with their white sails spread, I somehow thought of Miss Havisham and Estella. One Sunday I resolved to mention a thought concerning them that had been much in my head.

"Joe," said I, "don't you think I ought to pay Miss Havisham a visit?"

"Well, Pip," returned Joe, slowly considering. "What for?"

"What for, Joe? What is any visit made for?"

"There is some wisits p'r'aps," said Joe, "as forever remains open to the question, Pip. But in regard of wisiting Miss Havisham. She might think you wanted something—expected something of her."

I had thought of that too, and it was very far from comforting to me to find that he had thought of it; for it seemed to render it more probable.

"But, Joe."

"Yes, old chap."

"Here am I, getting on in the first year of my time, and since the day of my being bound I have never thanked Miss Havisham, or asked after her, or shown that I remember her."

"Well," said Joe, "if I was yourself, Pip, I wouldn't. No, I would *not*."

"But, Joe; what I wanted to say was, that as we are rather slack just now, if you would give me a half holiday tomorrow, I think I would go uptown and make a call on Miss Est—Havisham."

"Which her name," said Joe gravely, "ain't Estavisham, Pip, unless she has been rechris'ened."

"I know, Joe. It was a slip. What do you think of it, Joe?"

In brief, Joe thought that if I thought well of it, he thought well of it. But he was particular in stipulating that if I were not received with cordiality, or if I were not encouraged to repeat my visit, as a visit which had no ulterior object, but was simply one of gratitude for a favor received, then this experimental trip should have no successor. By these conditions I promised to abide.

Now, Joe kept a journeyman[2] at weekly wages whose name was Orlick. He was a broad-shouldered, loose-limbed, swarthy fellow of great strength, never in a hurry, and always slouching. He never even seemed to come to his work on purpose, but would slouch in as if by mere accident. He lodged at a sluice keeper's[3] out on the marshes, and on working days would come slouching from his hermitage, with his hands in his pockets and his dinner loosely tied in a bundle round his neck and dangling on his back.

This morose journeyman had no liking for

---

2. **journeyman** (jûr′nē-mən): a person who has learned a trade and is no longer an apprentice, but who still works for a master craftsman.

3. **sluice** (slōōs) **keeper:** a person in charge of a gate that regulates the flow of water in a sluice, an artificial stream used for drainage and irrigation.

me. When I was very small and timid, he gave me to understand that the Devil lived in a black corner of the forge, and that he knew the fiend very well; also that it was necessary to make up the fire, once in seven years, with a live boy, and that I might consider myself fuel. When I became Joe's 'prentice, Orlick was perhaps confirmed in some suspicion that I should displace him; howbeit he liked me still less.

Orlick was at work and present, next day, when I reminded Joe of my half holiday. He said nothing at the moment, for he and Joe had just got a piece of hot iron between them, and I was at the bellows; but by and by he said, leaning on his hammer:

"Now, master! Sure you're not a-going to favor only one of us. If Young Pip has a half holiday, do as much for Old Orlick." I suppose he was about five-and-twenty, but he usually spoke of himself as an ancient person.

"Why, what'll you do with a half holiday if you get it?" said Joe.

"What'll *I* do with it? What'll *he* do with it? I'll do as much with it as *him*," said Orlick.

"As to Pip, he's going uptown," said Joe.

"Well then, as to Old Orlick, *he's* a-going uptown," retorted that worthy. "Two can go uptown. 'Tain't only one wot can go uptown."

"Don't lose your temper," said Joe.

"Shall if I like," growled Orlick, "Now, master! Come. No favoring in this shop. Be a man!"

"Then, as in general you stick to your work as well as most men," said Joe, "let it be a half holiday for all."

My sister had been standing silent in the yard, within hearing—she was a most unscrupulous spy and listener—and she instantly looked in at one of the windows

"Like you, you fool!" said she to Joe, "giving holidays to great idle hulkers like that.

You are a rich man, upon my life, to waste wages in that way. I wish *I* was his master!"

"You'd be everybody's master if you durst," retorted Orlick, with an ill-favored grin.

"Let her alone," said Joe.

"I'd be a match for all noodles and all rogues," returned my sister, beginning to work herself into a mighty rage. "And I couldn't be a match for the noodles without being a match for your master, who's the dunderheaded king of the noodles. And I couldn't be a match for the rogues without being a match for you, who are the meanest-looking and the worst rogue between this and France. Now!"

"You're a foul shrew, Mother Gargery," growled the journeyman. "If that makes a judge of rogues, you ought to be a good 'un."

"Let her alone, will you?" said Joe.

"What did you say?" cried my sister, beginning to scream. "What did you say? What did that fellow Orlick say to me, Pip? What did he call me, with my husband standing by? Oh! Oh! Oh!" Each of these exclamations was a shriek. "Oh! Hold me! Oh!"

"Ah-h-h!" growled the journeyman, between his teeth. "I'd hold you, if you was my wife. I'd hold you under the pump and choke it out of you."

"I tell you, let her alone," said Joe.

"Oh! To hear him!" cried my sister, with a clap of her hands and a scream together. "To hear the names he's giving me! That Orlick! In my own house! Me, a married woman! With my husband standing by! Oh! Oh!"

What could the wretched Joe do now but stand up to his journeyman? They went at one another like two giants. But if any man in that neighborhood could stand up long against Joe, I never saw the man. Orlick was very soon among the coal dust, and in no hurry to come out of it. Then Joe picked up my sister, who had dropped insensible at the window, and carried her into the house. Afterward came that calm and silence which succeed all uproars—and I went upstairs to dress.

When I came down again, I found Joe and Orlick sweeping up, without any other traces of discomposure than a slit in one of Orlick's nostrils. A pot of beer had appeared from the Jolly Bargemen, and they were sharing it by turns in a peaceable manner. Joe followed me out into the road to say, as a parting observation that might do me good, "On the Rampage, Pip, and off the Ram-page, Pip—such is life!"

With what absurd emotions (for, we think the feelings that are very serious in a man quite comical in a boy) I found myself again going to Miss Havisham's, matters little here. Nor, how I passed and repassed the gate many times before I could make up my mind to ring.

Miss Sarah Pocket came to the gate. No Estella.

"How, then? You here again?" said Miss Pocket. "What do you want?"

When I said that I only came to see how Miss Havisham was, Sarah let me in, and presently brought the sharp message that I was to "come up."

Everything was unchanged, and Miss Havisham was alone.

"Well!" said she, fixing her eyes upon me. "I hope you want nothing? You'll get nothing."

"No indeed, Miss Havisham. I only wanted you to know that I am doing very well in my apprenticeship, and am always much obliged to you."

"There, there!" with the old restless fingers. "Come now and then; come on your birthday.—Aye!" she cried suddenly, turning herself and her chair toward me. "You are looking round for Estella? Hey?"

I had been looking round—in fact, for Estella—and I stammered that I hoped she was well.

"Abroad," said Miss Havisham; "educating for a lady; far out of reach; prettier than ever; admired by all who see her. Do you feel that you have lost her?"

There was such a malignant enjoyment in her utterance of the last words, and she broke into such a disagreeable laugh, that I was at a loss what to say. She spared me the trouble of considering, by dismissing me. When the gate was closed upon me, I felt more than ever dissatisfied with my home and with my trade and with everything.

As I was loitering along the High Street, looking at the shop windows and thinking what I would buy if I were a gentleman, who should come out of the bookshop but Mr. Wopsle. He insisted on my accompanying him to the Pumblechookian parlor. I made no great resistance; consequently, we turned into Pumblechook's just as the street and shops were lighting up.

It was a very dark night when I set out with Mr. Wopsle on the walk home. Beyond town we found a heavy mist out, and it fell wet and thick. The turnpike lamp was a blur, and its rays looked solid substance on the fog. We were noticing this when we came upon a man, slouching under the lee of the turnpike house.

"Halloa!" we said, stopping. "Orlick there?"

"Ah!" he answered, slouching out. "I was standing by a minute on the chance of company."

"You are late," I remarked.

Orlick not unnaturally answered, "Well? And *you're* late."

"We have been," said Mr. Wopsle, "indulging, Mr. Orlick, in an intellectual evening."

Old Orlick growled, as if he had nothing to

say about that, and we all went on together. I asked him presently whether he had been spending his half holiday up and down town?

"Yes," said he, "all of it. I come in behind yourself. I didn't see you, but I must have been pretty close behind you. By the bye, the guns is going again."

"At the Hulks?" said I.

"Aye! There's some of the birds flown from the cages. The guns have been going since dark, about. You'll hear one presently."

In effect, we had not walked many yards further when the well-remembered boom came toward us, deadened by the mist.

"A good night for cutting off in," said Orlick. "We'd be puzzled how to bring down a jailbird on the wing tonight." Orlick, with his hands in his pockets, slouched heavily at my side. I thought he had been drinking, but he was not drunk.

Thus we came to the village. The way by which we approached it took us past the Three Jolly Bargemen, which we were surpised to find—it being eleven o'clock—in a state of commotion, with the door wide open, and lights scattered about. Mr. Wopsle dropped in to ask what was the matter (surmising that a convict had been taken), but came running out in a great hurry.

"There's something wrong," said he, without stopping, "up at your place, Pip. Run all!"

"What is it?" I asked, keeping up with him. So did Orlick, at my side.

"I can't quite understand. The house seems to have been violently entered when Joe Gargery was out. Supposed by convicts. Somebody has been attacked and hurt."

We were running too fast to admit of more being said, and we made no stop until we got into our kitchen. It was full of people; the whole village was there or in the yard, and there was a surgeon, and there was Joe, and there was a group of women, all on the floor in the midst of the kitchen. The unemployed bystanders drew back when they saw me, and so I became aware of my sister—lying without sense or movement on the bare boards where she had been knocked down by a tremendous blow on the back of the head, dealt by some unknown hand when her face was turned toward the fire—destined never to be on the Ram-page again, while she was the wife of Joe.

Joe had been at the Three Jolly Bargemen, smoking his pipe, from a quarter after eight o'clock to a quarter before ten. While he was there, my sister had been seen standing at the kitchen door and had exchanged good night with a farm laborer going home. When Joe went home at five minutes before ten, he found her struck down on the floor, and promptly called in assistance.

Nothing had been taken away from any part of the house. But there was one remarkable piece of evidence on the spot. She had been struck with something blunt and heavy, on the head and spine; after the blows were dealt, something heavy had been thrown down at her with considerable violence, as she lay on her face. And on the ground beside her, when Joe picked her up, was a convict's leg iron which had been filed asunder.

Now, Joe, examining this iron with a smith's eye, declared it to have been filed asunder some time ago. The hue and cry going off to the Hulks, and people coming thence to examine the iron, Joe's opinion was corroborated. They claimed to know for certain that that particular manacle had not been worn by either of two convicts who had escaped last night. Further, one of those two was already retaken, and had not freed himself of his iron.

Knowing what I knew, I believed the iron to be my convict's iron—the iron I had seen and heard him filing at, on the marshes—but my mind did not accuse him of having put it to its latest use. For I believed one of two other persons to have become possessed of it, and to have turned it to this cruel account. Either Orlick, or the strange man who had shown me the file.

Now, as to Orlick; he had gone to town exactly as he told us when we picked him up at the turnpike, he had been seen about town all the evening, he had been in several public houses, and he had come back with myself and Mr. Wopsle. There was nothing against him, save the quarrel; and my sister had quarreled with him, and with everybody else about her, ten thousand times. As to the strange man: if he had come back for his two bank notes, there could have been no dispute about them, because my sister was fully prepared to restore them. Besides, there had been no altercation; the assailant had come in so silently and suddenly that she had been felled before she could look round.

The constables were about the house for a week or two. They took up several obviously wrong people, and they ran their heads very hard against wrong ideas, and persisted in trying to fit the circumstances to the ideas, instead of trying to extract ideas from the circumstances.

Long after these constitutional powers had dispersed, my sister lay ill in bed. Her sight was disturbed, so that she saw objects multiplied; her hearing was greatly impaired; her memory also; and her speech was unintelligible. It was necessary to keep my slate always by her, that she might indicate in writing what she could not indicate in speech.

However, her temper was greatly improved, and she was patient. We were at a loss to find a suitable attendant for her, until a circumstance happened conveniently to relieve us. Mr. Wopsle's great-aunt conquered a confirmed habit of living into which she had fallen,[4] and Biddy became part of our establishment. Biddy came to us with a small speckled box containing the whole of her worldly effects and became a blessing to the household. Above all she was a blessing to Joe, for the dear old fellow was sadly cut up by the constant contemplation of the wreck of his wife. Biddy instantly taking the cleverest charge of her, Joe became able in some sort to appreciate the greater quiet of his life, and to get down to the Jolly Bargemen now and then for a change that did him good.

Biddy's first triumph in her new office was to solve a difficulty that had completely vanquished me. Again and again and again, my sister had traced upon the slate a character that looked like a curious *T*, and then with the utmost eagerness had called our attention to it as something she particularly wanted. I had in vain tried everything producible that began with a *T*, from tar to toast and tub. At length it had come into my head that the sign looked like a hammer, and on my lustily calling that word in my sister's ear, she had begun to hammer on the table and had expressed a qualified assent. Thereupon, I had brought in all our hammers, one after another, but without avail.

When my sister found that Biddy was very quick to understand her, this mysterious sign reappeared on the slate. Biddy looked thoughtfully at it, heard my explanation, looked thoughtfully at Joe (who was always represented on the slate by his initial letter), and ran into the forge, followed by Joe and me.

"Why, of course!" cried Biddy with an exultant face. "Don't you see? It's *him!*"

Orlick, without a doubt! She had lost his name, and could only signify him by his hammer. We told him why we wanted him to come into the kitchen, and he slowly laid

---

4. **conquered . . . fallen:** died.

down his hammer, wiped his brow with his arm, took another wipe at it with his apron, and came slouching out.

I confess that I expected to see my sister denounce him, and that I was disappointed by the different result. She manifested the greatest anxiety to be on good terms with him, was evidently much pleased by his being at length produced, and motioned that she would have him given something to drink. She watched his countenance as if she were particularly wishful to be assured that he took kindly to his reception. After that, a day rarely passed without her drawing the hammer on her slate, and without Orlick's slouching in and standing doggedly before her, as if he knew no more than I did what to make of it.

Chapter 13

Pip opens his heart to Biddy.

I now fell into a regular routine of apprenticeship life, which was varied, beyond the limits of the village and the marshes, by no more remarkable circumstance than the arrival of my birthday and my paying another visit to Miss Havisham. The interview lasted but a few minutes, and she gave me a guinea when I was going, and told me to come again on my next birthday. I may mention at once that this became an annual custom. I tried to decline taking the guinea on the first occasion, causing her to ask me angrily if I expected more. Then, and after that, I took it. So unchanging was the dull old house, it bewildered me, and under its influence I continued at heart to hate my trade and to be ashamed of home.

Imperceptibly I became conscious of a change in Biddy, however. Her shoes came up at the heel, her hair grew bright and neat, her hands were always clean. She was not beautiful—she was common, and could not be like Estella—but she was pleasant and wholesome and sweet-tempered. I observed to myself one evening that she had curiously thoughtful and attentive eyes; eyes that were very pretty and very good. I laid down my pen, and Biddy stopped in her needlework without laying it down.

"Biddy," said I, "how do you manage it? Either I am very stupid, or you are very clever."

"What is it that I manage? I don't know," returned Biddy, smiling.

She managed her whole domestic life, and wonderfully too; but I did not mean that, though that made what I did mean more surprising.

"How do you manage, Biddy," said I, "to learn everything that I learn, and always to keep up with me?" I was beginning to be rather vain of my knowledge, for I spent my birthday guineas on it and the greater part of my pocket money.

"I suppose I must catch it—like a cough," said Biddy quietly, and went on with her sewing.

"You are one of those, Biddy," said I, "who make the most of every chance. You never had a chance before you came here, and see how improved you are!"

Biddy looked at me for an instant and went on with her sewing. "I was your first teacher, though, wasn't I?" said she, as she sewed.

"Yes, Biddy," I observed, "you were my first teacher, and that at a time when we little thought of ever being together like this in this kitchen. I must consult you a little more, as I used to do. Let us have a quiet walk on the marshes next Sunday, Biddy, and a long chat."

My sister was never left alone now; and Joe more than readily undertook the care of her on that Sunday afternoon, and Biddy and I went out together. It was summertime and lovely weather. When we came to the river-side and sat down on the bank, I resolved that it was a good time and place for the admission of Biddy into my inner confidence.

"Biddy," said I, after binding her to secrecy, "I want to be a gentleman."

"Oh, I wouldn't, if I was you!" she returned. "I don't think it would be right."

"Biddy," said I, with some severity, "I have particular reasons for wanting to be a gentleman."

"You know best, Pip; but don't you think you are happier as you are?"

"Biddy," I exclaimed impatiently, "I am not at all happy as I am. I am disgusted with my calling and with my life. Don't be absurd."

"Was I absurd?" said Biddy, quietly raising her eyebrows. "I am sorry for that; I didn't mean to be. I only want you to do well and be comfortable."

"Well, then, understand once for all that I never shall or can be comfortable—or anything but miserable—there, Biddy!—unless I can lead a very different sort of life from the life I lead now."

"That's a pity!" said Biddy, shaking her head with a sorrowful air.

"If I could have settled down," I said to Biddy, "I know it would have been much better for me. You and I and Joe would have wanted nothing then, and Joe and I would perhaps have gone partners when I was out of my time, and I might even have grown up to keep company with you. I should have been good enough for *you;* shouldn't I, Biddy?"

Biddy sighed and returned for an answer, "Yes; I am not overparticular." It scarcely sounded flattering, but I knew she meant well.

"Instead of that, see how I am going on. Dissatisfied and uncomfortable, and—what would it signify to me, being coarse and common, if nobody had told me so!"

Biddy turned her face suddenly toward mine and looked attentively at me.

"It was neither a very true nor a very polite thing to say," she remarked. "Who said it?"

"The beautiful young lady at Miss Havisham's, and she's more beautiful than anybody ever was, and I admire her dreadfully, and I want to be a gentleman on her account."

"Do you want to be a gentleman to spite her or to gain her over?" Biddy quietly asked me, after a pause.

"I don't know," I moodily answered.

"Because, if it is to spite her," Biddy pursued, "I should think—but you know best—that might be better and more independently done by caring nothing for her words. And if it is to gain her over, I should think—but you know best—she was not worth gaining over."

"It may be all quite true," said I to Biddy, "but I admire her dreadfully."

I turned over on my face when I came to that, and got a good grasp on the hair on each side of my head, and wrenched it well. Biddy was the wisest of girls, and she tried to reason no more with me. She put her hand, which was a comfortable hand though roughened by work, upon my hands and gently took them out of my hair. Then she softly patted my shoulder in a soothing way, while with my face upon my sleeve I cried a little—exactly as I had done in the brewery yard—and felt vaguely convinced that I was very much ill-used by somebody, or by everybody; I can't say which.

"I am glad of one thing," said Biddy, "and that is, that you have felt you could give me your confidence, Pip." So, with a quiet sigh for me, Biddy rose from the bank and said, with a fresh and pleasant change of voice, "Shall we walk a little farther or go home?"

"Biddy," I cried, getting up, putting my arm around her neck, and giving her a kiss, "I shall always tell you everything."

"Till you're a gentleman," said Biddy.

"You know I never shall be, so that's always. Not that I have any occasion to tell you anything, for you know everything I know—as I told you at home the other night."

"Ah!" said Biddy, quite in a whisper, and then repeated, with her former pleasant change, "shall we walk a little farther or go home?"

We talked a good deal as we walked, and all that Biddy said seemed right. Biddy was never insulting, or capricious, or Biddy today and somebody else tomorrow; she would have derived only pain, and no pleasure, from giving me pain.

I began to consider whether I was not more naturally and wholesomely situated, after all, in these circumstances, than playing beggar my neighbor by candlelight in the room with the stopped clocks, and being despised by Estella. How could it be, then, that I did not like her much the better of the two?

"Biddy," said I, when we were walking homeward, "I wish you could put me right."

"I wish I could!" said Biddy.

"If I could only get myself to fall in love with you—you don't mind my speaking so openly to such an old acquaintance?"

"Oh, dear, not at all!" said Biddy. "Don't mind me."

"If I could only get myself to do it, *that* would be the thing for me."

"But you never will, you see," said Biddy.

When we came near the churchyard, we had to cross an embankment and get over a stile near a sluice gate. There started up, from the rushes, Old Orlick.

"Halloa!" he growled. "Where are you two going?"

"Where should we be going, but home?"

"Well, then," said he, "I'm jiggered if I don't see you home!"

Biddy said to me in a whisper, "Don't let him come; I don't like him." As I did not like him either, I took the liberty of saying that we thanked him, but we didn't want seeing home. He dropped back, but came slouching after us at a little distance.

Curious to know whether Biddy suspected him of having had a hand in that murderous attack of which my sister had never been able to give any account, I asked her why she did not like him.

"Oh," she replied, glancing over her shoulder as he slouched after us, "because I—I am afraid he likes me!"

"Did he ever tell you he liked you?" I asked indignantly.

"No," said Biddy, glancing over her shoulder again, "he never told me so; but he dances at me whenever he can catch my eye."

I kept an eye on Orlick after that night. He had struck root in Joe's establishment, by reason of my sister's sudden fancy for him, or I should have tried to get him dismissed. He quite understood and reciprocated my good intentions, as I had reason to know thereafter.

And now my mind was confused. At times, I would decide that my disaffection to dear old Joe and the forge was gone, and that I was growing up in a fair way to be partners with Joe and to keep company with Biddy—when all in a moment some remembrance of the Havisham days would fall upon me and scatter my wits again. Scattered wits take a long time picking up; and often they would be dispersed in all directions by one stray thought, that perhaps after all Miss Havisham was going to make my fortune when my time was out.

If my time had run out, it would have left me still at the height of my perplexities, I dare say. It never did run out, however, but was brought to a premature end, as I proceed to relate.

Chapter 14

Mr. Jaggers, a lawyer, brings astonishing news.

It was in the fourth year of my apprenticeship to Joe, and it was a Saturday night. There was a group assembled round the fire at the Three Jolly Bargemen, attentive to Mr. Wopsle as he read the newspaper aloud. Of that group I was one.

I became aware of a strange gentleman leaning over the back of the settle opposite me, looking on. There was an expression of contempt on his face, and he bit the side of a great forefinger as he watched the group of faces.

"Well!" said the stranger to Mr. Wopsle, when the reading was done. "You have settled it all to your own satisfaction, I have no doubt?"

The strange gentleman, with an air of authority not to be disputed, and a manner expressive of knowing something secret about every one of us came into the space between the two settles, in front of the fire.

"From information I have received," said he, looking round at us as we all quailed before him, "I have reason to believe there is a blacksmith among you, by name Joseph — or Joe — Gargery. Which is the man?"

"Here is the man," said Joe.

The strange gentleman beckoned him out of his place, and Joe went.

"You have an apprentice," pursued the stranger, "commonly known as Pip? Is he here?"

"I am here!" I cried.

The stranger did not recognize me, but I recognized him as the gentleman I had met on the stairs on the occasion of my second visit to Miss Havisham. I had known him the moment I saw him looking over the settle. I checked off again in detail his large head, his dark complexion, his deep-set eyes, his bushy black eyebrows, his large watch chain, his strong black dots of beard and whisker, and even the smell of scented soap on his great hand.

"I wish to have a private conference with you two," said he, when he had surveyed me at his leisure. "It will take a little time. Perhaps we had better go to your place of residence."

Amidst a wondering silence, we three walked out of the Jolly Bargemen and in a wondering silence walked home. Joe went on ahead to open the front door. Our conference was held in the parlor, which was feebly lighted by one candle.

It began with the strange gentleman's sitting down at the table, drawing the candle to him, and looking over some entries in his pocketbook.

"My name," he said, "is Jaggers, and I am a lawyer in London. I am pretty well known. I have unusual business to transact with you, and I commence by explaining that it is not of my originating. If my advice had been asked, I should not have been here. It was not asked, and you see me here. What I have to do as the confidential agent of another, I do. No less, no more.

"Now, Joseph Gargery, I am the bearer of an offer to relieve you of this young fellow, your apprentice. You would not object to cancel his indentures at his request and for his good? You would want nothing for so doing?"

"Lord forbid that I should want anything for not standing in Pip's way," said Joe, staring.

"Lord forbidding is pious, but not to the purpose," returned Mr. Jaggers. "The question is, would you want anything? Do you want anything?"

"The answer is," returned Joe sternly, "no."

I thought Mr. Jaggers glanced at Joe, as if he considered him a fool for his disinterestedness. But I was too much bewildered between breathless curiosity and surprise to be sure of it.

"Very well," said Mr. Jaggers. "Now, I return to this young fellow. And the communication I have got to make is that he has Great Expectations."

Joe and I gasped and looked at one another.

"I am instructed to communicate to him," said Mr. Jaggers, throwing his finger at me sideways, "that he will come into a handsome property. Further, that it is the desire of the present possessor of that property that he be immediately removed from his present sphere of life and from this place and be brought up as a gentleman—in a word, as a young fellow of great expectations."

My dream was out; my wild fancy was surpassed by sober reality; Miss Havisham was going to make my fortune on a grand scale.

"Now, Mr. Pip," pursued the lawyer, "I address the rest of what I have to say to you. You are to understand, first, that it is the request of the person from whom I take my instructions that you always bear the name of Pip. You will have no objection, I dare say, but if you have any objection, this is the time to mention it."

My heart was beating so fast, and there was such a singing in my ears, that I could scarcely stammer I had no objection.

"I should think not! Now you are to understand, secondly, Mr. Pip, that the name of the person who is your liberal benefactor remains a profound secret until the person chooses to reveal it at firsthand by word of mouth to yourself. When or where that intention may be carried out, no one can say. It may be years hence. It is not the least to the purpose what the reasons of this prohibition are; they may

be the strongest and gravest reasons, or they may be a mere whim. This is not for you to inquire into. The condition is laid down. Your acceptance of it, and your observance of it as binding, is the only remaining condition that I am charged with by the person from whom I take my instructions. That person is the person from whom you derive your expectations, and the secret is solely held by that person and by me. If you have any objection to it, this is the time to mention it. Speak out."

Once more, I stammered that I had no objection.

"I should think not! Now, Mr. Pip, I have done with stipulations. We come next to mere details of arrangement. You must know that although I have used the term 'expectations' more than once, you are not endowed with expectations only. There is already lodged in my hands a sum of money amply sufficient for your suitable education and maintenance. You will please consider me your guardian.

"Oh!" for I was going to thank him. "I tell you at once, I am paid for my services, or I shouldn't render them. It is considered that you must be better educated, in accordance with your altered position."

I said I had always longed for it.

"Never mind what you have always longed for, Mr. Pip," he retorted. "Keep to the record. If you long for it now, that's enough. Am I answered that you are ready to be placed at once under some proper tutor? Is that it?"

I stammered yes, that was it.

"There is a certain tutor who I think might suit the purpose," said Mr. Jaggers. "The gentleman I speak of is one Mr. Matthew Pocket."

Ah! I caught at the name directly. Miss Havisham's relation. The Matthew whom Mr. and Mrs. Camilla had spoken of. The Matthew whose place was to be at Miss Havisham's head when she lay dead in her bride's dress on the bride's table.

"You know the name?" said Mr. Jaggers, looking shrewdly at me. "What do you say of it?"

I said that I was much obliged to him for his mention of Mr. Matthew Pocket, and that I would gladly try that gentleman.

"Good. You had better try him in his own house. The way shall be prepared for you, and you can see his son first, who is in London. When will you come to London?"

I said (glancing at Joe, who stood looking on, motionless) that I supposed I could come directly.

"First," said Mr. Jaggers, "you should have some new clothes to come in, and they should not be working clothes. Say this day week.[1] You'll want some money. Shall I leave you twenty guineas?"

---

1. **this day week:** a week from today.

He produced a long purse, with the greatest coolness, and counted them out on the table and pushed them over to me, and sat swinging his purse and eyeing Joe.

"Well, Joseph Gargery? You look dumfoundered?"

"I *am!*" said Joe, in a very decided manner.

"It was understood that you wanted nothing for yourself, remember?"

"It were understood," said Joe. "And it are understood. And it ever will be similar according."

"But what," said Mr. Jaggers, swinging his purse, "what if it was in my instructions to make you a present, as compensation?"

"As compensation what for?" Joe demanded.

"For the loss of his services."

Joe laid his hand upon my shoulder with the touch of a woman. "Pip is that hearty welcome," said Joe, "to go free with his services, to honor and fortun', as no words can tell him. But if you think as money can make compensation to me for the loss of the little child — what come to the forge — and ever the best of friends! — "

Oh, dear good Joe, whom I was so ready to leave and so unthankful to, I see you again, with your muscular blacksmith's arm before your eyes, and your broad chest heaving, and your voice dying away.

But I encouraged Joe at the time. I begged Joe to be comforted, for (as he said) we had ever been the best of friends, and (as I said) we ever would be so. Joe scooped his eyes with his wrist, but said not another word.

Mr. Jaggers, had looked on at this, as one who recognized in Joe the village idiot, and in me his keeper. When it was over, he said, "Now, Joseph Gargery, I warn you this is your last chance. If you mean to take a present that I have in charge to make you, speak out, and you shall have it. If on the contrary you mean

to say — " Here, to his great amazement, he was stopped by Joe's suddenly working round him with every demonstration of a pugilistic purpose.[2]

"Which I meantersay," cried Joe, "that if you come into my place bull-baiting and badgering me, come out! Which I meantersay as sech if you're a man, come on!"

I drew Joe away, and he immediately became placable. Mr. Jaggers backed near the door and there delivered his valedictory remarks:

"Well, Mr. Pip, I think the sooner you leave here, the better. Let it stand for this day week, and you shall receive my printed address in the meantime. You can take a hackney coach at the stagecoach office in London, and come straight to me."

Something came into my head which induced me to run after him.

"I beg your pardon, Mr. Jaggers."

"Halloa!" said he. "What's the matter?"

"I wish to be quite right, Mr. Jaggers. Would there be any objection to my taking leave of anyone I know about here, before I go away?"

"No," said he, looking as if he hardly understood me.

"I don't mean the village only, but uptown?"

"No," said he. "No objection."

I thanked him and ran home again, and there I found that Joe had already locked the front door and was seated by the kitchen fire with a hand on each knee, gazing intently at the burning coals. I too sat down before the fire and gazed at the coals, and nothing was said for a long time.

My sister was in her cushioned chair in her corner, and Biddy sat at her needlework before the fire, and Joe sat next to Biddy.

---

2. **pugilistic** (pyo͞o′jə-lĭs′tĭk) **purpose:** intention of fighting.

At length I got out, "Joe, have you told Biddy?"

"No, Pip," returned Joe, "I left it to yourself, Pip."

"I would rather you told, Joe."

"Pip's a gentleman of fortun', then," said Joe, "and God bless him in it!"

Biddy dropped her work and looked at me. Joe held his knees and looked at me. I looked at both of them. After a pause they both heartily congratulated me; but there was a certain touch of sadness in their congratulations that I rather resented.

I took it upon myself to impress Biddy (and through Biddy, Joe) with the grave obligation I considered my friends under, to know nothing and say nothing about the maker of my fortune. Biddy nodded her head thoughtfully at the fire and said she would be very particular; and Joe said, "Aye, aye, I'll be ekervally partickler, Pip," and then they congratulated me again, and went on to express so much wonder at the notion of my being a gentleman that I didn't half like it.

"Saturday night," said I, when we sat at our supper of bread-and-cheese and beer. "Five more days, and then the day before *the* day! They'll soon go."

"Yes, Pip," observed Joe, whose voice sounded hollow in his beer mug. "They'll soon go."

"I have been thinking, Joe, that when I go downtown on Monday and order my new clothes, I shall tell the tailor that I'll come and put them on there, or that I'll have them sent to Mr. Pumblechook's. It would be very disagreeable to be stared at by all the people here."

"Mr. and Mrs. Hubble might like to see you in your new genteel figure, too, Pip," said Joe. "So might Wopsle. And the Jolly Bargemen might take it as a compliment."

"That's just what I don't want, Joe. They would make such a business of it—such a coarse and common business—that I couldn't bear myself."

Biddy asked me here, "Have you thought about when you'll show yourself to Mr. Gargery, and your sister, and me? You will show yourself to us, won't you?"

"Biddy," I returned with some resentment, "you are so exceedingly quick that it's difficult to keep up with you. I shall bring my clothes here in a bundle one evening—most likely on the evening before I go away."

Biddy said no more. Handsomely forgiving her, I soon exchanged an affectionate good night with her and Joe, and went up to bed. When I got into my little room, I sat down and took a long look at it, as a mean little room that I should soon be parted from and raised above forever.

As I put the window open and stood looking out, I saw Joe come slowly forth at the dark door below and take a turn or two in the air; and then I saw Biddy come and bring him a pipe and light it for him. He never smoked so late, and it seemed to hint to me that he wanted comforting, for some reason or other. I drew away from the window and sat down in my one chair by the bedside, feeling it very sorrowful and strange that this first night of my bright fortunes should be the loneliest I had ever known.

I put my light out and crept into bed; and it was an uneasy bed now, and I never slept the old sound sleep in it any more.

Chapter 15

Pip visits Trabb, the tailor, and has a brief encounter with Trabb's boy.

Morning made a considerable difference in my general prospect of life. After breakfast, Joe brought out my indentures from the press in the best parlor, and we put them in the fire, and I felt that I was free.

After our early dinner, I strolled out alone. As I passed the church, I thought — with something akin to shame — of my companionship with the fugitive whom I had once seen limping among those graves. My comfort was that he had doubtless been transported a long way off, and that he was dead to me, and might be veritably[1] dead into the bargain. I made my way to the old Battery, and, lying down there to consider the question whether Miss Havisham intended me for Estella, fell asleep.

When I awoke, I was much surprised to find Joe sitting beside me, smoking his pipe. He greeted me with a cheerful smile on my opening my eyes, and said:

"As being the last time, Pip, I thought I'd foller."

"And, Joe, I am very glad you did so."

"Thankee, Pip."

"You may be sure, dear Joe," I went on, after we had shaken hands, "that I shall never forget you."

"No, no, Pip!" said Joe, in a comfortable tone. "*I'm* sure of that. Aye, aye, old chap!"

"It's a pity now, Joe," said I, "that you did not get on a little more when we had our lessons here, isn't it?"

"Well, I don't know," returned Joe. "I'm so awful dull. I'm only master of my own trade. It were always a pity as I was so awful dull; but it's no more of a pity now than it was — this day twelvemonth[2] — don't you see!"

What I had meant was that when I came into my property and was able to do something for Joe, it would have been much more agreeable if he had been better qualified for a rise in station. He was so perfectly innocent of my meaning, however, that I thought I would mention it to Biddy in preference.

So, when we had walked home and had had tea, I took Biddy into our little garden and said I had a favor to ask of her.

"And it is, Biddy," said I, "that you will not omit any opportunity of helping Joe on a little."

"How helping him on?" asked Biddy, with a steady sort of glance.

"Well! Joe is a dear good fellow — in fact, I think he is the dearest fellow that ever lived — but he is rather backward in some things. For instance, Biddy, in his learning and his manners."

"Oh, his manners! Won't his manners do, then?" asked Biddy, plucking a black-currant leaf.

"My dear Biddy, they do very well here — "

"Oh! they *do* very well here?" interrupted Biddy, looking closely at the leaf in her hand.

"Hear me out — but if I were to remove Joe into a higher sphere, as I shall hope to remove him when I fully come into my property, they would hardly do him justice."

"And don't you think he knows that?" asked Biddy.

It was such a provoking question (for it had never in the most distant manner occurred to me) that I said, snappishly, "Biddy, what do you mean?"

"Have you never considered that he may be proud?"

"Proud?" I repeated, with disdainful emphasis.

"Oh! there are many kinds of pride," said Biddy, looking full at me and shaking her head; "pride is not all of one kind — "

"Well? What are you stopping for?" said I.

"Not all of one kind," resumed Biddy. "He may be too proud to let anyone take him out of a place that he is competent to fill, and fills well and with respect."

---

1. **veritably** (vĕr′ə-tə-blē): actually.
2. **this day twelvemonth:** a year ago today.

"Now, Biddy," said I, "I am very sorry to see this in you. You are envious, Biddy, and grudging. You are dissatisfied on account of my rise in fortune, and you can't help showing it."

"If you have the heart to think so," returned Biddy, "say so. Say so over and over again, if you have the heart to think so."

"If you have the heart to be so, you mean, Biddy," said I, in a virtuous and superior tone. "Don't put it off upon me. I am extremely sorry to see this in you, Biddy. It's a—it's a bad side of human nature."

I walked away from Biddy, and Biddy went into the house, and I went out at the garden gate and took a dejected stroll until supper-time, again feeling it very sorrowful and strange that this, the second night of my bright fortunes, should be as lonely and unsatisfactory as the first.

But morning once more brightened my view, and I extended my clemency to Biddy, and we dropped the subject. Putting on the best clothes I had, I went into town as early as I could hope to find the shops open, and presented myself before Mr. Trabb, the tailor, who was having his breakfast in the parlor behind his shop, and who did not think it worth his while to come out to me, but called me in to him.

"Well!" said Mr. Trabb, in a hail-fellow-well-met kind of way. "How are you, and what can I do for you?"

"Mr. Trabb," said I, "it's an unpleasant thing to have to mention, because it looks like boasting, but I have come into a handsome property."

A change passed over Mr. Trabb. He got up from the bedside and wiped his fingers on the tablecloth, exclaiming, "Lord bless my soul!"

"I am going up to my guardian in London," said I, casually drawing some guineas out of my pocket and looking at them, "and I want a fashionable suit of clothes to go in. I wish to pay for them," I added, "with ready money."

"My dear sir," said Mr. Trabb, "may I venture to congratulate you? Would you do me the favor of stepping into the shop?"

Mr. Trabb's boy was the most audacious boy in all that countryside. When I had entered, he was sweeping the shop, and he had sweetened his labors by sweeping over me. He was still sweeping when I came out into the shop with Mr. Trabb, and he knocked the broom against all possible corners and obstacles, to express equality with any blacksmith, alive or dead.

"Hold that noise," said Mr. Trabb with the greatest sternness, "or I'll knock your head off! Do me the favor to be seated, sir. Now," said Mr. Trabb, taking down a roll of cloth.

I selected the materials for a suit, and reentered the parlor to be measured. When he had at last done and had appointed to send the articles to Mr. Pumblechook's, he said, "I know, sir, that London gentlemen cannot be expected to patronize local work, as a rule; but if you would give me a turn now and then, I should greatly esteem it. Good morning, sir, much obliged.—Door!"

The last word was flung at the boy, who had not the least notion what it meant. But I saw him collapse as his master rubbed me out with his hands, and my first decided experience of the stupendous power of money was that it had morally laid upon his back Trabb's boy.

After this memorable event I went to the hatter's, and the bootmaker's, and the hosier's, and felt rather like Mother Hubbard's dog whose outfit required the services of so many trades. I also went to the coach office and took my place for seven o'clock on Saturday morning. When I had ordered everything I wanted, I directed my steps toward Pumblechook's, and, as I approached that gentleman's place of business, I saw him standing at his door.

He was waiting for me with great impatience. He had been out early with the chaise-cart, and had called at the forge and heard the news. He had prepared a collation[3] for me in the parlor, and he too ordered his shopman to "come out of the gangway" as my sacred person passed.

"To think," said Mr. Pumblechook, after snorting admiration at me for some moments, "that I should have been the humble instrument of leading up to this, is a proud reward."

I begged Mr. Pumblechook to remember that nothing was to be ever said or hinted on that point. I mentioned that I wished to have my new clothes sent to his house, and he was ecstatic on my so distinguishing him. I mentioned my reason for desiring to avoid observation in the village, and he lauded it to the skies. There was nobody but himself, he intimated, worthy of my confidence. Then he asked me tenderly if I remembered our boyish games at sums, and how we had gone together to have me bound apprentice, and, in effect, how he had ever been my favorite fancy and my chosen friend. If I had taken ten times as many glasses of wine, I should have known that he never stood in that relation to me, and should in my heart of hearts have repudiated the idea. Yet for all that, I remember feeling convinced that I had been much mistaken in him, and that he was a sensible, practical, good-hearted, prime fellow.

Tuesday, Wednesday, and Thursday passed, and on Friday morning I went to Mr. Pumblechook's to put on my new clothes and pay my visit to Miss Havisham. My clothes were rather a disappointment, of course. Probably every new and eagerly expected garment ever put on fell a trifle short of the wearer's expectation. But after I had had my new suit on some half an hour, it seemed to fit me better.

I went to Miss Havisham's by all the back ways, and rang at the bell. Sarah Pocket came to the gate and positively reeled back when she saw me so changed.

"You?" said she. "You? Good gracious! What do you want?"

"I am going to London, Miss Pocket," said I, "and want to say goodbye to Miss Havisham."

I was not expected, for she left me locked in the yard while she went to ask if I were to be admitted. After a very short delay, she returned and took me up, staring at me all the way.

Miss Havisham was taking exercise in the room with the long spread table, leaning on her crutch stick. The room was lighted as of yore, and at the sound of our entrance, she stopped and turned. She was then just abreast of the rotted bride cake.

"Don't go, Sarah," she said. "Well, Pip?"

"I start for London, Miss Havisham, tomorrow." I was exceedingly careful what I said. "And I thought you would kindly not mind my taking leave of you."

"This is a gay figure, Pip," said she, making her crutch stick play round me, as if she, the fairy godmother who had changed me, were bestowing the finishing gift.

"I have come into such good fortune since I saw you last, Miss Havisham," I murmured. "And I am so grateful for it, Miss Havisham!"

"Aye, aye!" said she, looking at the envious Sarah with delight. "I have seen Mr. Jaggers. *I* have heard about it, Pip. So you go tomorrow?"

"Yes, Miss Havisham."

"And are you adopted by a rich person?"

"Yes, Miss Havisham."

---

3. **collation** (kə-lā′shən): a light meal, usually served cold.

"Not named?"

"No, Miss Havisham."

"And Mr. Jaggers is made your guardian?"

"Yes, Miss Havisham."

She quite gloated on these questions and answers, so keen was her enjoyment of Sarah Pocket's jealous dismay. "Well!" she went on. "You have a promising career before you. Be good—deserve it—and abide by Mr. Jaggers' instructions." She looked at me, and looked at Sarah, and Sarah's countenance wrung out of her watchful face a cruel smile. "Goodbye, Pip!—you will always keep the name of Pip, you know."

"Yes, Miss Havisham."

"Goodbye, Pip!"

She stretched out her hand, and I went down on my knee and put it to my lips. I had not considered how I should take leave of her; it came naturally to me at the moment to do this. She looked at Sarah Pocket with triumph in her weird eyes, and so I left my fairy godmother, with both her hands on her crutch stick, standing in the midst of the dimly lighted room beside the rotten bride cake that was hidden in cobwebs.

And now, those six days which were to have run out so slowly had run out fast and were gone, and tomorrow looked me in the face more steadily than I could look at it. As the six evenings had dwindled away, I had become more and more appreciative of the society of Joe and Biddy. On this last evening, I dressed myself out in my new clothes for their delight and sat in my splendor until bedtime. We had a hot supper on the occasion, graced by the inevitable roast fowl. We were all very low, and none the higher for pretending to be in spirits.

I was to leave our village at five in the morning, and I had told Joe that I wished to walk away all alone. I am afraid that this purpose originated in my sense of the contrast there would be between me and Joe if we went to the coach together. I had pretended with myself that there was nothing of this taint in the arrangement; but when I went up to my little room on this last night, I felt compelled to admit that it might be so, and had an impulse upon me to go down again and entreat Joe to walk with me in the morning. I did not.

It was a hurried breakfast with no taste in it. I got up from the meal, saying with a sort of briskness, as if it had only just occurred to me, "Well! I suppose I must be off!" and then I kissed my sister, who was nodding and shaking in her usual chair, and kissed Biddy, and threw my arms around Joe's neck. The last I saw of them was when dear old Joe waved his strong right arm above his head, crying huskily, "Hoo-roar!" and Biddy put her apron to her face.

I walked away at a good pace, thinking it was easier to go than I had supposed it would

be. The village was very peaceful and quiet, and all beyond was so unknown and great that in a moment with a strong heave and sob I broke into tears. I was better after I had cried than before—more sorry, more aware of my own ingratitude, more gentle. If I had cried before, I should have had Joe with me then.

When I was on the coach, and it was clear of the town, I deliberated with an aching heart whether I would not get down when we changed horses and walk back, and have another evening at home, and a better parting.

We changed, and I had not made up my mind, and still reflected for my comfort that it would be quite practicable to get down and walk back, when we changed again. We changed again, and yet again, and it was now too late, and too far to go back, and I went on. And the mists had all solemnly risen now, and the world lay spread before me.

This Is the End of the First Stage of Pip's Expectations.

FOR STUDY AND DISCUSSION

Characters

1. In the first stage of his expectations, Pip is involved in events in three very different "worlds": the forge, the marsh, and the strange mansion of Miss Havisham. Make a list of the main characters in each of these "worlds" and identify each one in a sentence or two.

2. What do you learn about Pip from his encounters with the convict on the marsh? Is Pip generous? Is he honest? Does he feel sympathy for those who are less fortunate than he is? Explain.

3. When Pip encounters each of the two convicts, the first one frightens him, and the second is frightened by him. Despite this, Pip likes the first convict better. Why? Why does the first convict tell the sergeant he stole the food Pip brought him? What does this show about his feelings toward Pip?

4. What impression do you receive of "Mrs. Joe" from Pip's description of her? Why do you think she treats Pip so harshly?

5. Pip's opinion of himself, his home, and his family changes after his first visit to Miss Havisham's mansion. What is the inner conflict that results from Pip's exposure to Miss Havisham and Estella?

6. Miss Havisham is one of Dickens' great eccentric characters. From the objects in her rooms and the things she says about them, what can you infer about her past? What do you think is her purpose in sending for Pip? What kinds of feelings does she seem to enjoy arousing in other people? Why do you think she takes pleasure in doing this?

7. What are Joe's feelings toward Pip? When Mr. Jaggers offers Joe money for releasing Pip from his apprenticeship, how does Joe react? What does his reaction show about his attitude toward life?

8. The nature of Pip's relationship with Joe is one of the important threads in the novel. Consider this relationship during the first part of the novel. How does Pip's attitude toward Joe change? What does this change reveal about Pip's character?

9. Compare Biddy and Estella. How are they different? How does each one influence Pip? Why does Pip choose Estella over Biddy?

10. What do Mrs. Joe and Mr. Pumblechook expect that Miss Havisham will do for Pip? From what you know of Miss Havisham and her attitude toward people, do you think these expectations are realistic and reasonable or foolish and unfounded? Why?

11. Compare the Pip of the first few chapters with the Pip who leaves for London. How has he developed and changed?

Plot

12. The plot of the novel is built around Pip's "great expectations." What is the meaning of this phrase? Who first uses it in the novel? What facts and circumstances lead Pip to believe that the source of his "great expectations" is Miss Havisham?

13. *Great Expectations* was first published in weekly installments in a magazine, which was edited by Dickens, called *All the Year Round.* To keep people interested in the story —and eager to buy the next issue of the magazine—Dickens made skillful use of mystery and suspense. Look back at the chapter endings in Stage 1 and note how often many of them arouse your curiosity about what will happen next. At the end of Stage 1, several questions have been left unanswered, such as "Who was the pale young gentleman?" and "Who attacked Mrs. Joe?" What are some other unanswered questions?

14. In *Great Expectations*, as in many novels, there is a main plot and several subplots. The main plot focuses on how Pip grows and

changes. The subplots are skillfully interwoven with this main plot. The story of the convicts in the marsh is one of the subplots. At first, the convicts seem to be only a passing episode in Pip's life. But the appearance of the man with the file, who gives Pip two one-pound notes, suggests that we will hear more about the convicts. What other subplots has Dickens connected with Pip's story in the first part of the novel?

15. Throughout the novel, Dickens deliberately introduces some comic scenes to lighten the tone of the narrative. What makes the Christmas dinner with Uncle Pumblechook such a funny scene?

Setting

16. The action of the story begins very dramatically with Pip's encounter with the convict in the graveyard. How does the setting in the graveyard add to the excitement and suspense of this scene? Which details of the setting and of the convict's appearance are especially effective in creating an atmosphere of mystery and terror?

17. Throughout the novel, the atmosphere of the marshes suggests loneliness and gloom. What might Dickens have intended the atmosphere of the marshes to symbolize? What other settings are associated with a specific mood? What influence on Pip do you think is symbolized by each?

Point of View

18. *Great Expectations* is told from the first-person point of view. We are able to share Pip's reactions to the other characters and everything they do. We also have Pip's insights into his own actions and thoughts from the vantage point of an adult looking back at his early life. How does Pip judge his own behavior toward Joe? Toward Biddy? Toward Estella?

Theme

19. Pip is quick to notice that some people treat him differently the minute they learn he has come into money. Mr. Pumblechook, Trabb the tailor, and Trabb's foolish boy—who seems to be the village clown—are among the first to alter their manner toward Pip. That money has power to change people's attitudes toward one another was a favorite subject of Dickens'. Tell how he develops this theme in the early part of *Great Expectations*. Choose several episodes from Stage 1 that illustrate different characters' attitudes toward money. Or, if you wish, focus on two characters whose attitudes are strikingly different.

LANGUAGE AND VOCABULARY

Learning Word Histories

As a blacksmith, Joe has two helpers, Pip and Orlick. They are his *apprentice* and his *journeyman,* respectively, and Joe is their *master.* In the England of Pip's day, a boy's apprenticeship (or period of training) had to be paid for. A legal contract called his *indentures* provided that his master be paid a certain sum, in return for which the boy received his room and board and training in the master's craft or trade.

Then, as now, a journeyman was a worker who had completed the term of apprenticeship. A master was an experienced worker who was capable of doing work of the highest quality.

We still use these old terms and titles. A *master* plumber is the person you would want to install a new sink, and you would probably not choose an *apprentice* carpenter to build your furniture. We also use such expressions as "journeyman playwright" and "master architect." What do these expressions mean?

FOR COMPOSITION

Writing a Character Description

Although the characters in a novel are more fully developed than those in a short story, the techniques for revealing character are the same in both forms of fiction. The author may comment directly on a character or use several means of indirect characterization: through description; through words, actions, and thoughts; through the reactions of other characters. Authors frequently use both direct and indirect characterization.

In direct characterization, the author summarizes a character's traits. In this passage, Dickens tells us directly the kind of person Joe is:

> He was a mild, good-natured, sweet-tempered, easygoing, foolish, dear fellow—a sort of Hercules in strength, and also in weakness.

In indirect characterization, the author implies what a character is like. Dickens gives us insight into Mr. Pumblechook's character when he tells us that at breakfast, Mr. Pumblechook gave Pip "as much crumb as possible in combination with as little butter." Dickens does not say directly that Mr. Pumblechook is stingy, but we can infer this trait from his actions.

Choose one of the characters introduced in Stage 1 of the novel and write a composition showing how Dickens reveals that character through direct and indirect characterization.

LOOKING AHEAD TO STAGE 2

In many ways the problems that Pip faces are much like those a young man or woman might face today. In Stage 1 he has already begun to change under the pressures of the world around him. Do you think Pip is satisfied with the change in his life and his new expectations? Will he become a "gentleman" and win Estella as his love? Will he renew his bonds with Joe and Biddy? What do you think lies ahead for Pip in London?

The Second Stage
of Pip's Expectations

Chapter 16

Pip meets Wemmick, Mr. Jaggers' clerk, and Herbert Pocket.

The journey from our town to the metropolis was a journey of about five hours. It was a little past midday when the four-horse stage-coach by which I was a passenger got into the ravel of traffic frayed out about the Cross Keys, Wood Street, Cheapside, London. We Britons had at that time particularly settled that it was treasonable to doubt our having and our being the best of everything; otherwise, while I was scared by the immensity of London, I think I might have had some faint doubts whether it was not rather ugly, crooked, narrow, and dirty.

Mr. Jaggers had duly sent me his address: it was Little Britain. A hackney coachman packed me up in his coach and hemmed me in with a folding and jingling barrier of steps, as if he were going to take me fifty miles. I had scarcely had time to enjoy the coach when I observed the coachman beginning to get down, as if we were going to stop presently. And stop we presently did, in a gloomy street, at certain offices with an open door, whereon was painted Mr. Jaggers.

I went into the front office and asked was Mr. Jaggers at home?

"He is not," returned the clerk. "He is in court at present. Am I addressing Mr. Pip?"

I signified that he was addressing Mr. Pip.

"Mr. Jaggers left word would you wait in his room. He couldn't say how long he might be, having a case on. But it stands to reason, his time being valuable, that he won't be longer than he can help."

With those words, the clerk opened a door and ushered me into an inner chamber at the back. Mr. Jaggers' room was lighted by a skylight only, and was a most dismal place. I sat wondering and waiting in Mr. Jaggers' close room, until I really could not bear it and got up and went out.

I told the clerk that I would take a turn in the air while I waited, and turned into a street where I saw the great black dome of Saint Paul's[1] bulging at me from behind a grim stone building which a bystander said was Newgate Prison. Following the wall of the jail, I found the roadway covered with straw to deaden the noise of passing vehicles; and from this and from the quantity of people standing about smelling strongly of spirits and beer, I inferred that the trials were on.

I dropped into the office to ask if Mr. Jaggers had come in yet, and I found he had not, and I strolled out again. I became aware that other people were waiting about for Mr. Jaggers, as well as I. There were two men of secret appearance lounging in Bartholemew Close, one of whom said to the other when they first passed me that "Jaggers would do it if it was to be done." There was a knot of three men and two women standing at a corner, and one of the women was crying on her dirty shawl, and the other comforted her by saying as she pulled her own shawl over her shoulders, "Jaggers is for him, 'Melia, and what more *could* you have?" These testimonies to the popularity of my guardian made a deep impression on me, and I admired and wondered more than ever.

At length I saw Mr. Jaggers coming across the road toward me. All the others who were waiting saw him at the same time, and there was quite a rush at him. Mr. Jaggers addressed himself to his followers.

First, he took the two secret men.

"Now, I have nothing to say to *you*," said Mr. Jaggers. "I told you from the first it was a tossup. Have you paid Wemmick?"

"Yes, sir," said both the men together.

"Very well; then you may go. If you say a word to me, I'll throw up the case."

"We thought, Mr. Jaggers—" one of the men began, pulling off his hat.

"That's what I told you not to do," said Mr. Jaggers. "*You* thought! I think for you; that's enough for you.

"And now *you!*" said Mr. Jaggers, suddenly stopping and turning on the two women with the shawls. "Once for all; if you come here, bothering about your Bill, I'll make an example of both your Bill and you, and let him slip through my fingers. Have you paid Wemmick?"

"Oh, yes, sir! Every farthing."

"Very well. Say another word—one single word—and Wemmick shall give you your money back." This terrible threat caused the two women to fall off immediately.

Without further interruption we reached the front office. My guardian then took me into his own room, and while he lunched, informed me what arrangements he had made for me. I was to go to Barnard's Inn, to young Mr. Pocket's rooms, where a bed had been sent in for my accommodation; I was to remain with young Mr. Pocket until Monday; on Monday I was to go with him to his father's house on a visit. Also, I was told what my allowance was to be—it was a very liberal one—and had handed to me the cards of certain tradesmen with whom I was to deal for all kinds of clothes and such other things as I could in reason want. "You will find your credit good, Mr. Pip," said my guardian, "but I shall by this means be able to check your bills, and to pull you up if I find you outrunning the constable. Of course you'll go wrong somehow, but that's no fault of mine."

After I had pondered a little over this encouraging sentiment, I asked Mr. Jaggers if I could send for a coach. He said it was not

---

1. **Saint Paul's:** a famous church designed by the English architect Christopher Wren (1632–1723).

worthwhile, I was so near my destination; Wemmick should walk round with me, if I pleased.

I then found that Wemmick was the clerk in the next room. I accompanied him into the street, after shaking hands with my guardian. We found a new set of people lingering outside, but Wemmick made a way among them by saying coolly yet decisively, "I tell you it's no use; he won't have a word to say to one of you"; and we soon got clear of them and went on side by side.

Casting my eyes on Mr. Wemmick as we went along, to see what he was like in the light of day, I found him to be a dry man, rather short in stature, with a square wooden face. He wore his hat on the back of his head, and looked straight before him, walking in a self-contained way as if there were nothing in the streets to claim his attention. His mouth was such a post office of a mouth that he had a mechanical appearance of smiling.

"Do you know where Mr. Matthew Pocket lives?" I asked Mr. Wemmick.

"Yes," said he, nodding in the direction. "At Hammersmith, west of London."

"Is that far?"

"Well! Say five miles."

"Do you know him?"

"Why, you are a regular cross-examiner!" said Mr. Wemmick, looking at me with an approving air. "Yes, I know him. *I* know him!"

There was an air of toleration about these words that rather depressed me; and I was still looking sideways at his block of a face in search of any encouraging note when he said here we were at Barnard's Inn. I had supposed that establishment to be a hotel kept by Mr. Barnard, to which the Blue Boar in our town was a mere public house. Whereas I now found Barnard to be a fiction and his inn the dingiest collection of shabby buildings ever squeezed together in a rank corner as a club for tomcats. We entered a melancholy little square that looked to me like a flat burying ground. I thought it had the most dismal trees in it, and the most dismal sparrows, and the most dismal cats, and the most dismal houses that I had ever seen. The windows of the houses were in every stage of dilapidated blind and curtain, crippled flowerpot, cracked glass, dusty decay, and miserable makeshift.

So imperfect was this realization of the first of my great expectations that I looked in dismay at Mr. Wemmick. He led me up a flight of stairs, which appeared to be slowly collapsing into sawdust, to a set of chambers on the top floor. MR. POCKET, JUN., was printed on the door, and there was a label on the letter box, "Return shortly."

"He hardly thought you'd come so soon," Mr. Wemmick explained. "You don't want me any more?"

"No, thank you," said I.

"As I keep the cash," Mr. Wemmick observed, "we shall most likely meet pretty often. Good day."

When he was gone, I opened the staircase window and had nearly beheaded myself, for the lines had rotted away, and it came down like the guillotine.[2] After this escape, I was content to stand dolefully looking out, saying to myself that London was decidedly overrated.

Mr. Pocket, Junior's, idea of "shortly" was not mine, for I had nearly maddened myself with looking out for half an hour, and had written my name with my finger several times in the dirt of every pane in the window, before I heard footsteps on the stairs. Gradually there arose before me the hat, head, waistcoat, trousers, boots, of a member of society of about my own standing. He had a

---

2. **guillotine** (gĭl′ə-tēn): a machine with a heavy blade, used to cut off a person's head.

paper bag under each arm and a pottle[3] of strawberries in one hand, and was out of breath.

"Mr. Pip?" said he.

"Mr. Pocket?" said I.

"Dear me!" he exclaimed, "I am extremely sorry; but I knew there was a coach from your part of the country at midday, and I thought you would come by that one. The fact is, I have been out on your account—not that that is any excuse—for I thought, coming from the country, you might like a little fruit after dinner, and I went to Covent Garden Market to get it."

For a reason that I had, I felt as if my eyes would start out of my head. I began to think this was a dream.

"Pray come in," said Mr. Pocket, Junior. "Allow me to lead the way. I am rather bare here, but I hope you'll be able to make out tolerably well till Monday. My father thought you would get on more agreeably through tomorrow with me than with him, and might like to take a walk about London. I am sure I shall be very happy to show London to you. As to our table, it will be supplied from our coffeehouse here, and (it is only right I should add) at your expense, such being Mr. Jaggers' directions. As to our lodging, it's not by any means splendid, because I have my own bread to earn, and my father hasn't anything to give me, and I shouldn't be willing to take it if he had. This is our sitting room—just such chairs and tables and carpet and so forth, you see, as they could spare from home. This is my little bedroom; rather musty, but Barnard's *is* musty. This is your bedroom; the furniture's hired for the occasion, but I trust it will answer the purpose, if you should want anything, I'll go and fetch it. The chambers are retired,[4] and we shall be alone together, but we shan't fight, I dare say."

As I stood opposite to Mr. Pocket, Junior, I saw the starting appearance come into his own eyes that I knew to be in mine, and he said, falling back:

"Lord bless me, you're the prowling boy!"

"And you," said I, "are the pale young gentleman!"

Chapter 17

Pip gets a new name.

The pale young gentleman and I stood contemplating one another in Barnard's Inn, until we both burst out laughing.

"The idea of its being you!" said he. "The idea of its being *you!*" said I. And then we contemplated one another afresh, and laughed again. "Well!" said the pale young gentleman, reaching out his hand good-humoredly, "it's all over now, I hope, and it will be magnanimous in you if you'll forgive me for having knocked you about so."

I derived from this speech that Mr. Herbert Pocket (for Herbert was the pale young gentleman's name) still rather confounded his intention with his execution. But I made a modest reply, and we shook hands warmly.

"You hadn't come into your good fortune at that time?" said Herbert Pocket.

"No," said I.

"No," he acquiesced. "I heard it had happened very lately. *I* was rather on the lookout for good fortune then."

"Indeed?"

"Yes. Miss Havisham had sent for me, to see if she could take a fancy to me. But she couldn't—at all events, she didn't."

---

3. **pottle** (pŏt′l): a small basket used for holding fruit (British).

4. **retired:** secluded; having few neighbors.

I thought it polite to remark that I was surprised to hear that.

"Bad taste," said Herbert, laughing, "but a fact. Yes, she had sent for me on a trial visit, and if I had come out of it successfully, I suppose I should have been provided for; perhaps I should have been what-you-may-called-it to Estella."

"What's that?" I asked, with sudden anxiety.

He was arranging his fruit in plates while we talked, which divided his attention, and was the cause of his having made this lapse of a word. "Affianced," he explained, still busy with the fruit. "Engaged. Betrothed."

"How did you bear your disappointment?" I asked.

"Pooh!" said he. "I didn't care much for it. *She's* a tartar."[1]

"Miss Havisham?"

"I don't say no to that, but I meant Estella. That girl's hard and haughty and capricious to the last degree, and has been brought up by Miss Havisham to wreak revenge on all the male sex."

"What relation is she to Miss Havisham?"

"None," said he. "Only adopted."

"Why should she wreak revenge on all the male sex? What revenge?"

"Lord, Mr. Pip!" said he. "Don't you know?"

"No," said I.

"Dear me! It's quite a story, and shall be saved till dinnertime. Mr. Jaggers is your guardian, I understand?" he went on.

"Yes."

"You know he is Miss Havisham's man of business and solicitor,[2] and has her confidence when nobody else has?"

This was bringing me (I felt) toward dangerous ground. I answered with a constraint I made no attempt to disguise that I had seen Mr. Jaggers in Miss Havisham's house on the very day of our combat, but never at any other time, and that I believed he had no recollection of having ever seen me there.

"He was so obliging as to suggest my father for your tutor, and he called on my father to propose it. Of course he knew about my father from his connection with Miss Havisham. My father is Miss Havisham's cousin; not that that implies familiar intercourse between them, for he is a bad courtier and will not propitiate[3] her."

Herbert Pocket had a frank and easy way with him that was very taking. I have never seen anyone who more strongly expressed to me, in every look and tone, a natural incapacity to do anything secret and mean. There was something wonderfully hopeful about his general air, and something that at the same time whispered to me he would never be very successful or rich. He was still a pale young gentleman, without much strength. He had not a handsome face, but it was better than handsome, being extremely amiable and cheerful.

As he was so communicative, I told him my small story, and laid stress on my being forbidden to inquire who my benefactor was. I further mentioned that as I had been brought up a blacksmith in a country place, and knew very little of the ways of politeness, I would take it as a great kindness in him if he would give me a hint whenever he saw me at a loss or going wrong.

"With pleasure," said he, "though I venture to prophesy that you'll want very few hints.

---

1. **tartar** (tär′tər): one with a cruel, ferocious nature.
2. **solicitor** (sə-lĭs′ə-tər): in England, a lawyer who handles a client's legal affairs, as distinguished from a barrister (băr′ĭ-stər), who pleads cases in court.

3. **propitiate** (prō-pĭsh′ē-āt): court the favor of.

Will you begin at once to call me by my Christian name, Herbert?"

I thanked him and said I would, I informed him in exchange that my Christian name was Philip.

"I don't take to Philip," said he, smiling, "for it sounds like a moral boy out of the spelling book. Would you mind Handel for a familiar name? There's a charming piece of music by Handel[4] called the Harmonious Blacksmith."

"I should like it very much."

"Then, my dear Handel," said he, turning round as the door opened, "here is the dinner."

We had made some progress in the dinner, when I reminded Herbert of his promise to tell me about Miss Havisham.

"True," he replied. "Let me introduce the topic, Handel, by mentioning that in London it is not the custom to put the knife in the mouth—for fear of accidents—and that while the fork is reserved for that use, it is not put farther in than necessary. It is scarcely worth mentioning, only it's as well to do as other people do. Also, the spoon is not generally used overhand, but under. This has two advantages. You get at your mouth better (which after all is the object), and you save a good deal of the attitude of opening oysters on the part of the right elbow."

He offered these friendly suggestions in such a lively way that we both laughed.

"Now," he pursued, "Miss Havisham was a spoiled child. Her mother died when she was a baby, and her father denied her nothing. He was very rich and very proud. So was his daughter."

"Miss Havisham was an only child?" I hazarded.

"Stop a moment, I am coming to that. No, she was not an only child; she had a half brother. Her father privately married again—his cook, I rather think."

"I thought he was proud," said I.

"My good Handel, so he was. He married his second wife privately, because he *was* proud, and in the course of time *she* died. When she was dead, I apprehend he first told his daughter what he had done, and then the son became a part of the family, residing in the house you are acquainted with. As the son became a young man, he turned out riotous, extravagant, undutiful—altogether bad. At last his father disinherited him; but he softened when he was dying and left him well off, though not nearly so well off as Miss Havisham.

"Miss Havisham was now an heiress, and was looked after as a great match. Her half brother had now ample means again, but wasted them most fearfully. There were strong differences between him and her, and it is suspected that he cherished a deep and mortal grudge against her. Now, I come to the cruel part of the story.

"There appeared upon the scene a certain man, who made love to Miss Havisham. I have heard my father mention that he was a showy man, and the kind of man for the purpose. But he was not to be mistaken for a gentleman. Well! This man pursued Miss Havisham closely and professed to be devoted to her. There is no doubt that she perfectly idolized him. He got great sums of money from her, and he induced her to buy her brother out of a share in the brewery (which had been weakly left him by his father) at an immense price, on the plea that when he was her husband he must hold and manage it all. Your guardian was not at that time in Miss Havisham's councils, and she was too haughty and too much in love to be advised by anyone. Her relations were poor and

---

4. **Handel** (hăn′d'l): George Frederick Handel (1685–1759).

scheming, with the exception of my father; he was poor enough, but not time-serving or jealous. The only independent one among them, he warned her that she was doing too much for this man, and was placing herself too unreservedly in his power. She took the first opportunity of angrily ordering my father out of the house, in his presence, and my father has never seen her since."

I thought of her having said, "Matthew will come and see me at last when I am laid dead upon that table."

"To return to the man and make an end of him. The marriage day was fixed, the wedding dresses were bought, the wedding guests were invited. The day came, but not the bridegroom. He wrote a letter—"

"Which she received," I struck in, "when she was dressing for her marriage? At twenty minutes to nine?"

"At the hour and minute," said Herbert, nodding, "at which she afterward stopped all the clocks. What was in it, further than that it most heartlessly broke the marriage off, I can't tell you, because I don't know. When she recovered from a bad illness, she laid the whole place waste, as you have seen it, and she has never since looked upon the light of day."

"Is that all the story?" I asked, after considering it.

"All I know of it. But I have forgotten one thing. It has been supposed that the man to whom she gave her misplaced confidence acted throughout in concert with her half brother; that it was a conspiracy between them; and that they shared the profits."

"What became of the two men? Are they alive now?"

"I don't know."

"You said just now that Estella was not related to Miss Havisham, but adopted. When adopted?"

Herbert shrugged his shoulders. "There has always been an Estella, since I have heard of a Miss Havisham. I know no more."

"And all I know," I replied, "you know."

"I fully believe it. And as to the condition on which you hold your advancement in life —namely, that you are not to inquire or discuss to whom you owe it—you may be very sure that it will never be even approached by me."

He said this with so much delicacy that I felt he as perfectly understood Miss Havisham to be my benefactress as I understood the fact myself.

We were very gay and sociable, and I asked him in the course of conversation what he was. He replied, "An insurer of ships. I shall not rest satisfied with merely insuring ships. I think I shall trade," said he, leaning back in his chair, "to the East Indies for shawls, spices, dyes, drugs, and precious woods. It's an interesting trade."

Quite overpowered by the magnificence of these transactions, I asked him where the ships he insured mostly traded to at present.

"I haven't begun insuring yet," he replied. "I am looking about me."

Somehow, that pursuit seemed more in keeping with Barnard's Inn. I said (in a tone of conviction), "Ah-h!"

"Yes. I am in a countinghouse,[5] and looking about me."

"Is a countinghouse profitable?" I asked.

"Why, n-no; not to me. Not directly profitable. That is, it doesn't pay me anything, and I have to—keep myself. But the thing is, that you look about you. *That's* the grand thing. You are in a countinghouse, you know, and you look about you."

---

5. **countinghouse:** an office or building where a company handles accounts and correspondence.

This was very like his way of conducting that encounter in the garden; very like. His manner of bearing his poverty, too, exactly corresponded to his manner of bearing that defeat. It seemed to me that he took all blows and buffets now, with just the same air as he had taken mine then. It was evident that he had nothing around him but the simplest necessaries, for everything that I remarked upon turned out to have been sent in on my account from the coffeehouse or somewhere else. Yet, having already made his fortune in his own mind, he was so unassuming that I felt quite grateful to him for not being puffed up. It was a pleasant addition to his naturally pleasant ways, and we got on famously.

Chapter 18

Pip meets Mr. Matthew Pocket.

On Monday morning at a quarter before nine, Herbert went to the countinghouse to report himself—to look around him, too, I suppose—and I bore him company. He was to come away in an hour or two to attend me to Hammersmith, and I was to wait about for him. When Herbert came, we went and had lunch and then took coach for Hammersmith. We arrived at two or three o'clock in the afternoon. Lifting the latch of a gate, we passed into a garden overlooking the river, where Mr. Pocket's children were playing about.

Mr. Pocket came out to make my acquaintance. He was a gentleman with a rather perplexed expression of face, and with his very gray hair disordered on his head, as if he didn't quite see his way to putting anything straight. Mr. Pocket said he was glad to see me, and he hoped I was not sorry to see him. "For I am

really not," he added, with his son's smile, "an alarming personage." He was a young-looking man, in spite of his perplexities and his very gray hair, and his manner seemed quite natural.

Mr. Pocket took me into the house and showed me my room, which was a pleasant one. He then knocked at the doors of two other similar rooms and introduced me to their occupants, by name Drummle and Startop. Drummle, an old-looking young man of a heavy order of architecture,[1] was whistling. Startop, younger in years and appearance, was reading and holding his head, as if he thought himself in danger of exploding it with too strong a charge of knowledge.

By degrees I learned, chiefly from Herbert, that Mr. Pocket had been educated at Harrow and Cambridge,[2] where he had distinguished himself. He had come to London and here, after gradually failing in loftier hopes, he had turned his acquirements to the account of literary compilation[3] and correction.

In the evening there was rowing on the river. As Drummle and Startop had each a boat, I resolved to set up mine, and to cut them both out. I was pretty good at most exercises in which country boys are adepts, but as I was conscious of wanting elegance of style for the Thames,[4] I at once engaged to place myself under the tuition of the winner of a prize wherry[5] who plied at our stairs, and to whom I was introduced by my new allies.

After two or three days, when I had established myself in my room and had gone

---

1. **heavy . . . architecture:** a large and heavyset physique.
2. **Harrow and Cambridge:** Harrow is a preparatory school, and Cambridge a famous university in England.
3. **compilation:** the gathering of materials from different sources for a book such as an anthology.
4. **Thames** (tĕmz): a river that passes through London.
5. **wherry** (hwĕr′ē): a light, fast rowboat, sometimes used for racing.

backward and forward to London several times, Mr. Pocket and I had a long talk together. He knew more of my intended career than I knew myself, for his having been told by Mr. Jaggers that I was not designed for any profession, and that I should be well enough educated for my destiny if I could "hold my own" with the average of young men in prosperous circumstances.

When I had begun to work in earnest, it occurred to me that if I could retain my bedroom in Barnard's Inn, my life would be agreeably varied, while my manners would be none the worse for Herbert's society; so I went off to Little Britain and imparted my wish to Mr. Jaggers.

"If I could buy the furniture now hired for me," said I, "and one or two other little things, I should be quite at home there."

"Go it!" said Mr. Jaggers, with a short laugh. "I told you you'd get on. Well! How much do you want?"

I said I didn't know how much.

"Come!" retorted Mr. Jaggers. "How much? Fifty pounds?"

"Oh, not nearly so much."

"Five pounds?" said Mr. Jagger.

This was such a great fall, that I said in discomfiture, "Oh! more than that."

"More than that, eh!" retorted Mr. Jaggers. "How much more?"

"It is so difficult to fix a sum," said I, hesitating.

"Wemmick!" said Mr. Jaggers, opening his office door. "Take Mr. Pip's written order, and pay him twenty pounds."

This strongly marked way of doing business made a strongly marked impression on me, and that not of an agreeable kind. As he happened to go out now, and as Wemmick was brisk and talkative, I said to Wemmick that I hardly knew what to make of Mr. Jaggers' manner.

"Tell him that, and he'll take it as a compliment," answered Wemmick. "He don't mean that you *should* know what to make of it. —Oh!" for I looked surprised, "it's not personal; it's professional, only professional."

He went on to say in a friendly manner:

"If at any odd time when you have nothing better to do, you wouldn't mind coming over to see me at Walworth, I could offer you a bed, and I should consider it an honor. I have not much to show you but such two or three curiosities as I have and a bit of garden and a summerhouse."

I said I should be delighted to accept his hospitality.

"Thankee," said he. "Then we'll consider that it's to come off, when convenient to you. Have you dined with Mr. Jaggers yet?"

"Not yet."

"Well," said Wemmick, "he'll give you wine, and good wine. I'll give you punch, and not bad punch. And now I'll tell you something. When you go to dine with Mr. Jaggers, look at his housekeeper."

"Shall I see something very uncommon?"

"Well," said Wemmick, "you'll see a wild beast tamed. It won't lower your opinion of Mr. Jaggers' powers. Keep your eye on it."

I told him I would do so, with all the interest and curiosity that his preparation awakened.

Chapter 19

Pip's friendships increase.

Bentley Drummle, who was so sulky a fellow that he even took up a book as if its writer had done him an injury, did not take up an acquaintance in a more agreeable spirit. Heavy in figure, movement, and comprehension, he was idle, proud, niggardly, reserved, and suspicious. He came of rich people who had nursed this combination of qualities until they made the discovery that it was just of age and a blockhead. Thus, Bentley Drummle had come to Mr. Pocket when he was a head taller than that gentleman, and half a dozen heads thicker than most gentlemen.

Startop had been spoiled by a weak mother and kept at home when he ought to have been at school, but he was devotedly attached to her and admired her beyond measure. He had a woman's delicacy of feature. It was but natural that I should take to him much more kindly than to Drummle, and that even in the earliest evenings of our boating, he and I should pull homeward abreast of one another, conversing from boat to boat, while Bentley Drummle came up in our wake alone.

Herbert was my intimate companion and friend. I presented him with a half share in my boat, which was the occasion of his often coming down to Hammersmith; and my possession of a half share in his chambers often took me up to London. We used to walk between the two places at all hours.

These were the surroundings among which I settled down and applied myself to my education. I soon contracted expensive habits and began to spend an amount of money that within a few short months I should have thought almost fabulous. But through good and evil I stuck to my books. Between Mr. Pocket and Herbert I got on fast.

I had not seen Mr. Wemmick for some weeks when I thought I would write him a note and propose to go home with him on a certain evening. He replied that it would give him much pleasure, and that he would expect me at the office at six o'clock. Thither I went, and found him, putting the key of his safe down his back as the clock struck.

"Did you think of walking down to Walworth?" said he.

"Certainly," said I, "if you approve."

"Very much," was Wemmick's reply, "for I have had my legs under the desk all day, and shall be glad to stretch them. Now I'll tell you what I've got for supper—a cold roast fowl. You don't object to an aged parent, I hope?"

I really thought he was still speaking of the fowl, until he added, "Because I have got an aged parent at my place." I then said what politeness required.

"So you haven't dined with Mr. Jaggers yet?" he pursued, as we walked along.

"Not yet."

"He told me so this afternoon. I expect you'll have an invitation tomorrow. He's going to ask your pals, too. Three of 'em, ain't there? Well, he's going to ask the whole gang."

Mr. Wemmick and I beguiled the time talking, until he gave me to understand that we had arrived in the district of Walworth. It appeared to be a collection of black lanes, ditches, and little gardens. Wemmick's house was a little wooden cottage in the midst of plots of garden, and the top of it was cut out and painted like a battery mounted with guns.

"My own doing," said Wemmick. "Looks pretty, don't it?"

I highly commended it. I think it was the smallest house I ever saw.

"That's a real flagstaff, you see," said Wemmick, "and on Sundays I run up a real flag. Then look here. After I have crossed this bridge, I hoist it up—so—and cut off the communication."

The bridge was a plank, and it crossed a chasm about four feet wide and two deep. But it was very pleasant to see the pride with which he hoisted it up and made it fast, smiling as he did so, with a relish and not merely mechanically.

"At nine o'clock every night, Greenwich

time,"[1] said Wemmick, "the gun fires. There
he is, you see! And when you hear him go, I
think you'll say he's a Stinger."

The piece of ordnance referred to was
mounted in a separate fortress, constructed of
latticework. It was protected from the
weather by an ingenious little tarpaulin umbrella.

"Then, at the back," said Wemmick,
"there's a pig, and there are fowls and rabbits;
and I grow cucumbers. So, sir," said Wemmick, smiling again, but seriously, too, as he
shook his head, "if you can suppose the little
place besieged, it would hold out a devil of a
time in point of provisions."

Then he conducted me to a bower about a
dozen yards off, and in this retreat our glasses
were already set forth.

"I am my own engineer, and my own carpenter, and my own plumber, and my own
gardener, and my own Jack-of-all-trades," said
Wemmick, in acknowledging my compliments. "Well, it's a good thing, you know. It
brushes the Newgate[2] cobwebs away, and
pleases the Aged. You wouldn't mind being at
once introduced to the Aged, would you? It
wouldn't put you out?"

I expressed the readiness I felt, and we went
into the castle. There we found, sitting by a
fire, a very old man in a flannel coat; clean,
cheerful, comfortable, and well cared for, but
intensely deaf.

"Well, Aged Parent," said Wemmick, shaking hands with him in a cordial way, "how am
you?"

"All right, John; all right!" replied the old
man.

"Here's Mr. Pip, Aged Parent," said Wemmick, "and I wish you could hear his name.

---

1. **Greenwich** (grĭn´ĭj) **time:** the official basis of standard
time throughout the world.

2. **Newgate:** Newgate Prison. Wemmick's dealings as
Mr. Jaggers' clerk were largely with persons who were
trying to get out or keep out of Newgate.

Nod away at him, Mr. Pip; that's what he likes. Nod away at him, if you please."

"This is a fine place of my son's, sir," cried the old man, while I nodded as hard as I possibly could.

"You're as proud of it as Punch; ain't you, Aged?" said Wemmick, contemplating the old man, with his hard face really softened; "*there's* a nod for you," giving him a tremendous one; "*there's* another for you," giving him a still more tremendous one; "you like that, don't you? If you're not tired, Mr. Pip— though I know it's tiring to strangers—will you tip him one more? You can't think how it pleases him."

I tipped him several more, and he was in great spirits. We left him bestirring himself to feed the fowls, and we sat down to our punch in the arbor, where Wemmick told me, as he smoked a pipe, that it had taken him a good many years to bring the property up to its present pitch of perfection.

"I hope Mr. Jaggers admires it," I said.

"Never seen it," said Wemmick. "Never heard of it. Never seen the Aged. Never heard of him. No; the office is one thing, and private life is another. When I go into the office, I leave the Castle behind me, and when I come into the Castle, I leave the office behind me. If it's not in any way disagreeable to you, you'll oblige me by doing the same. I don't wish it professionally spoken about."

Of course I felt my good faith involved in the observance of his request. The punch being very nice, we sat there drinking it and talking until it was almost nine o'clock. "Getting near gunfire," said Wemmick then, as he laid down his pipe. "It's the Aged's treat."

Proceeding into the Castle again, we found the Aged heating the poker, with expectant eyes, as a preliminary to the performance of this great nightly ceremony. Wemmick stood with his watch in his hand until the moment was come for him to take the red-hot poker from the Aged, and repair[3] to the Battery. He took it, and went out, and presently the Stinger went off with a bang that shook the crazy little box of a cottage as if it must fall to pieces, and made every glass and teacup in it ring. Upon this the Aged—who I believe would have been blown out of his armchair but for holding on by the elbows—cried out exultingly, "He's fired! I heared him!" and I nodded at the old gentleman until I absolutely could not see him.

The supper was excellent. I was heartily pleased with my whole entertainment. Nor was there any drawback to my little turret bedroom.

Our breakfast was as good as the supper, and at half past eight we started for Little Britain. By degrees, Wemmick seemed to get drier and harder as we went along. At last when we got to his place of business and he pulled out his key, he looked as unconscious of his Walworth property as if the Castle and the drawbridge and the arbor and the Aged had all been blown into space together by the last discharge of the Stinger.

Chapter 20

Pip has dinner at Mr. Jaggers' and observes his housekeeper.

It fell out, as Wemmick had told me it would, that my guardian gave me the invitation for myself and friends. "No ceremony," he stipulated, "and no dinner dress, and say tomorrow."

When I and my friends repaired to him at six o'clock next day, he conducted us to Gerrard Street, Soho, to a house on the south side

---

3. **repair:** go.

of that street, rather a stately house of its kind, but dolefully in want of painting, and with dirty windows. We went up a dark brown staircase into a series of three dark brown rooms on the first floor.

Dinner was laid in the best of these rooms. The table was comfortably laid and at the side of his chair was a dumbwaiter,[1] with a variety of bottles and decanters on it and four dishes of fruit for dessert. I noticed throughout that he kept everything under his own hand, and distributed everything himself.

As he had scarcely seen my three companions until now—for he and I had walked together—he stood on the hearthrug, after ringing the bell, and took a searching look at them. To my surprise, he seemed at once to be principally, if not solely, interested in Drummle.

"Pip," said he, putting his large hand on my shoulder and moving me to the window, "I don't know one from the other. Who's the Spider?"

"The Spider?" said I.

"The blotchy, sprawly, sulky fellow."

"That's Bentley Drummle," I replied. "The one with the delicate face is Startop."

Not taking the least account of "the one with the delicate face," he returned, "Bentley Drummle is his name, is it? I like the look of that fellow."

He immediately began to talk to Drummle. I was looking at the two when there came between me and them the housekeeper, with the first dish for the table.

She was a woman of about forty, tall, of a lithe, nimble figure, extremely pale, with large faded eyes and a quantity of streaming hair. She set the dish on, touched my guardian quietly on the arm with a finger to notify that dinner was ready, and vanished. No other attendant appeared.

Induced to take particular notice of the housekeeper, both by her own striking appearance and by Wemmick's preparation, I observed that whenever she was in the room, she kept her eyes attentively on my guardian. I fancied that I could detect in his manner a purpose of always holding her in suspense.

Dinner went off gaily, and although my guardian seemed to follow rather than originate subjects, I knew that he wrenched the weakest part of our dispositions out of us. I found that I was expressing my tendency to lavish expenditure, and to patronize Herbert, and to boast of my great prospects. It was so with all of us, but with no one more than Drummle. He informed our host that he much preferred our room to our company, and that as to skill he was more than our master, and that as to strength he could scatter us like chaff. He fell to baring and spanning his arm to show how muscular it was, and we all fell to baring and spanning our arms in a ridiculous manner.

Now the housekeeper was at that time clearing the table, my guardian taking no heed of her. Suddenly, he clapped his large hand on the housekeeper's like a trap, as she stretched it across the table.

"If you talk of strength," said Mr. Jaggers, "I'll show you a wrist. Molly, let me see your wrist."

Her entrapped hand was on the table, but she had already put her other hand behind her waist. "Master," she said, in a low voice, with her eyes attentively and entreatingly fixed upon him. "Don't."

"I'll show you a wrist," repeated Mr. Jaggers, with an immovable determination to show it. "Molly, let them see your wrist."

"Master," she again murmured. "Please!"

"Molly," said Mr. Jaggers, not looking at

---

1. **dumbwaiter:** small, movable table used for serving food.

her, "let them see *both* your wrists. Show them. Come!"

He took his hand from hers, and turned that wrist up on the table. She brought her other hand from behind her, and held the two out side by side. The last wrist was much disfigured—deeply scarred and scarred across and across. When she held her hands out, she took her eyes from Mr. Jaggers, and turned them watchfully on every one of the rest of us in succession.

"There's power here," said Mr. Jaggers, coolly tracing out the sinews with his forefinger. "Very few men have the power of wrist that this woman has. It's remarkable what mere force of grip there is in these hands. I have had occasion to notice many hands; but I never saw stronger in that respect, man's or woman's, than these. That'll do, Molly. You have been admired, and can go." She withdrew her hands and went out of the room, and Mr. Jaggers filled his glass and passed round the wine.

"At half past nine, gentlemen," said he, "we must break up. Pray make the best use of your time. I am glad to see you all. Mr. Drummle, I drink to you."

If his object in singling out Drummle were to bring him out still more, it perfectly succeeded. In a sulky triumph Drummle showed his morose depreciation of the rest of us in a more and more offensive degree, until he became downright intolerable. Through all his states, Mr. Jaggers followed him with the same strange interest.

In our boyish want of discretion I dare say we took too much to drink, and I know we talked too much. We became particularly hot upon some boorish sneer of Drummle's to the effect that we were too free with our money. Startop tried to turn the discussion aside with some small pleasantry that made us all laugh. Resenting this little success more than any-

thing, Drummle, without any threat or warning, pulled his hands out of his pockets, dropped his round shoulders, swore, took up a large glass, and would have flung it at his adversary's head, but for our entertainer's dexterously seizing it at the instant it was raised.

"Gentlemen," said Mr. Jaggers, deliberately putting down the glass, "I am exceedingly sorry to announce that it's half past nine."

On this hint we all rose to depart. Before we got to the street door, Startop was cheerily calling Drummle "old boy," as if nothing had happened. But the old boy would not even walk to Hammersmith on the same side of the way; so Herbert and I, who remained in town, saw them going down the street on opposite sides, Startop leading, and Drummle lagging behind in the shadow of the houses.

In about a month after that, the Spider's time with Mr. Pocket was up for good, and, to the great relief of all the house, he went home to the family hole.

Chapter 21

Pip has a visitor.

MY DEAR MR. PIP:

I write this by request of Mr. Gargery, for to let you know that he is going to London in company with Mr. Wopsle and would be glad if agreeable to be allowed to see you. He would call at Barnard's Hotel Tuesday morning at nine o'clock, when if not agreeable please leave word. Your poor sister is much the same as when you left. We talk of you in the kitchen every night, and wonder what you are saying and doing. If now considered in the light of a liberty, excuse it for the love of poor old days. No more, dear Mr. Pip, from

Your ever obliged,
and affectionate servant,
Biddy.

P.S. He wishes me most particular to write *what larks.* He says you will understand. I hope and do not doubt it will be agreeable to see him even though a gentleman, for you had ever a good heart, and he is a worthy man. I have read him all excepting only the last little sentence, and he wishes me most particular to write again *what larks.*

I received this letter by post on Monday morning, and therefore its appointment was for next day. Let me confess exactly with what feelings I looked forward to Joe's coming.

Not with pleasure, though I was bound to him by so many ties; no, with considerable disturbance and some mortification. If I could have kept him away by paying money, I certainly would have paid money. My greatest reassurance was that he was coming to Barnard's Inn, not to Hammersmith. I had little objection to his being seen by Herbert or his father, for both of whom I had respect; but I had the sharpest sensitiveness as to his being seen by Drummle, whom I held in contempt. So throughout life, our worst weaknesses and meannesses are usually committed for the sake of the people whom we most despise.

I had got on so fast of late that I had even started a boy in boots[1] — top boots — and had clothed him with a blue coat, canary waistcoat, white cravat, creamy breeches, and the boots already mentioned. I had to find him a little to do and a great deal to eat; and with both of these horrible requirements he haunted my existence.

I came into town on Monday night to be ready for Joe, and I got up early in the morning, and caused the sitting room and breakfast table to assume their most splendid appearance.

Presently I heard Joe on the staircase. I knew it was Joe by his clumsy manner of coming upstairs. When at last he stopped outside our door, I could hear his finger tracing over the painted letters of my name. Finally he gave a faint single rap, and Pepper[2] announced, "Mr. Gargery!"

"Joe, how are you, Joe?"

"Pip, how AIR you, Pip?"

With his good honest face all glowing and shining, and his hat put down on the floor between us, he caught both my hands and worked them straight up and down.

"I am glad to see you, Joe. Give me your hat."

But Joe, taking it up carefully with both hands, like a bird's nest with eggs in it, wouldn't hear of parting with that piece of property.

"Which you have that growed," said Joe, "and that gentlefolked," Joe considered a little before he discovered this word; "as to be a honor to your king and country."

"And you, Joe, look wonderfully well."

"Thank God," said Joe, "I'm ekerval to most. And your sister, she's no worse than she were. And Biddy, she's ever right and ready."

Herbert had entered the room, so I presented Joe to Herbert. Joe, being invited to sit down to table, looked all round the room for a suitable spot on which to deposit his hat and ultimately stood it on an extreme corner of the chimney piece, from which it ever afterward fell off at intervals.

"Do you take tea or coffee, Mr. Gargery?" asked Herbert, who always presided of a morning.

"Thankee, sir," said Joe, stiff from head to foot, "I'll take whichever is most agreeable to yourself."

---

1. **started . . . boots:** hired a serving boy.

2. **Pepper:** the servant.

"What do you say to coffee?"

"Thankee, sir," said Joe, evidently dispirited by the proposal, "since you *are* so kind as to make chice of coffee, I will not run contrairy to your own opinions. But don't you never find it a little 'eating?"

"Say tea, then," said Herbert, pouring it out.

Here Joe's hat tumbled off the mantelpiece, and he started out of his chair and picked it up, and fitted it to the same exact spot.

"When did you come to town, Mr. Gargery?"

"Were it yesterday afternoon?" said Joe, after coughing behind his hand. "Not it were not. Yes it were. Yes. It were yesterday afternoon" (with an appearance of mingled wisdom, relief, and strict impartiality).

"Have you seen anything of London, yet?"

"Why, yes, sir," said Joe, but his attention was attracted by his hat, which was toppling. Indeed, it demanded from him a constant attention. He made extraordinary play with it, and showed the greatest skill, now rushing at it and catching it neatly as it dropped; now merely stopping it midway, beating it up, finally splashing it into the slop basin, where I took the liberty of laying hands upon it.

Then he fell into such unaccountable fits of meditation, with his fork midway between his plate and his mouth; had his eyes attracted in such strange directions; was afflicted with such remarkable coughs; sat so far from the table; and dropped so much more than he ate, and pretended that he hadn't dropped it; that I was heartily glad when Herbert left us for the city.

I had neither the good sense nor the good feeling to know that this was all my fault, and that if I had been easier with Joe, Joe would have been easier with me. I felt impatient of him and out of temper with him.

"Us two being now alone, sir—" began Joe.

"Joe," I interrupted pettishly, "How can you call me sir?"

Joe looked at me for a single instant with something faintly like reproach. I was conscious of a sort of dignity in the look.

"Us two being now alone," resumed Joe, "and me having the intentions and abilities to stay not many minutes more, I will now conclude—leastways begin—to mention what have led to my having had the present honor.

"Well, sir, this is how it were. I were at the Bargemen t'other night, Pip" (whenever he subsided into affection, he called me Pip, and whenever he relapsed into politeness he called me sir), "when there come up in his shay-cart Pumblechook. Well, Pip; this same identical come to me at the Bargemen and his word were, 'Joseph, Miss Havisham she wish to speak to you.' "

"Miss Havisham, Joe?"

" 'She wished,' were Pumblechook's word, 'to speak to you.' " Joe sat and rolled his eyes at the ceiling.

"Yes, Joe? Go on, please."

"Next day, sir," said Joe, looking at me as if I were a long way off, "having cleaned myself, I go and I see Miss A."[3]

"Miss A., Joe? Miss Havisham?"

"Which I say, sir," replied Joe, with an air of legal formality, as if he were making his will, "Miss A., or otherways Havisham. Her expression air then as follering: 'Mr. Gargery. You air in correspondence with Mr. Pip?' Having had a letter from you, I were able to say 'I am.' 'Would you tell him, then' said she, 'that which Estella has come home, and would be glad to see him.' "

I felt my face fire up as I looked at Joe.

"Biddy," pursued Joe, "when I got home and asked her fur to write the message to you,

---

3. **Miss A.:** Joe pronounces Havisham as "'avisham."

a little hung back. Biddy says, 'I know he will be very glad to have it by word of mouth; it is holiday time, you want to see him, go!' I have now concluded, sir," said Joe, rising from his chair, "and, Pip, I wish you ever well and ever prospering to a greater and greater height."

"But you are not going now, Joe?"

"Yes I am," said Joe.

"But you are coming back to dinner, Joe?"

"No I am not," said Joe.

Our eyes met, and all the "sir" melted out of that manly heart as he gave me his hand.

"Pip, dear old chap, life is made of ever so many partings welded together, as I may say, and one man's a blacksmith, and one's a whitesmith,[4] and one's a goldsmith, and one's a coppersmith. Diwisions among such must come, and must be met as they come. If there's been any fault at all today, it's mine. You and me is not two figures to be together in London; nor yet anywheres else but what is private, and beknown, and understood among friends. It ain't that I am proud, but that I want to be right, as you shall never see me no more in these clothes. I'm wrong in these clothes. I'm wrong out of the forge, the kitchen, or off th' meshes. You won't find half so much fault in me if you think of me in my forge dress, with my hammer in my hand, or even my pipe. You won't find half so much fault in me if, supposing as you should ever wish to see me, you come and put your head in at the forge window and see Joe the blacksmith, there at the old anvil, in the old burned apron, sticking to the old work. I'm awful dull, but I hope I've beat out something nigh the rights of this at last. And so God bless you, dear old Pip, old chap, God bless you!"

I had not been mistaken in my fancy that there was a simple dignity in him. The fashion of his dress could no more come in its way

---

4. **whitesmith**: a tinsmith.

when he spoke these words than it could come in its way in Heaven. He touched me gently on the forehead, and went out. As soon as I could recover myself sufficiently, I hurried out after him and looked for him in the neighboring streets; but he was gone.

Chapter 22

The mysterious stranger returns, and so does Orlick.

It was clear that I must repair to our town next day, and in the first flow of my repentance it was equally clear that I must stay at Joe's. But when I secured my box-place by tomorrow's coach, I began to invent reasons for putting up at the Blue Boar. All other swindlers upon earth are nothing to the self-swindlers, and with such pretenses did I cheat myself. I settled that I must go to the Blue Boar.

At that time it was customary to carry convicts down to the dockyards by stagecoach. As I had often seen them on the highroad dangling their ironed legs over the coach roof, I had no cause to be surprised when Herbert came up and told me there were two convicts going down with me. But I had a reason that was an old reason now for faltering whenever I heard the word convict.

"You don't mind them, Handel?" said Herbert.

"Oh, no!"

"I thought you seemed as if you didn't like them?"

"I can't pretend that I do like them, and I suppose you don't particularly. But I don't mind them."

"See! There they are," said Herbert, "and what a degraded and vile sight it is!"

The two convicts were handcuffed together, and had irons on their legs—irons of a pattern that I knew well. They wore the dress that I likewise knew well. One was a taller and stouter man than the other, and his attire disguised him, but I knew his half-closed eye at one glance. There stood the man whom I had seen on the settle at the Three Jolly Bargemen on a Saturday night!

But this was not the worst of it. It came out that the whole of the back of the coach had been taken by a family, and that there were no places for the two prisoners but on the seat in front, behind the coachman. The convict I had recognized sat behind me with his breath on the hair of my head.

"Goodbye, Handel!" Herbert called out as we started. I thought what a blessed fortune it was that he had found another name for me than Pip.

The weather was miserably raw. I dozed off myself in considering the question whether I ought to restore a couple of pounds sterling to this creature before losing sight of him, and how it could best be done. In the act of dipping forward, I woke in a fright and took the question up again. Cowering forward for warmth and to make me a screen against the wind, the convicts were closer to me than before. The very first words I heard them interchange, as I became conscious, were the words of my own thought, "Two one-pound notes."

"How did he get 'em?" said the convict I had never seen.

"How should I know?" returned the other. "He had 'em stowed away somehows. Give him by friends, I expect."

"I wish," said the other, with a bitter curse upon the cold, "that I had 'em here."

"Two one-pound notes, or friends?"

"Two one-pound notes. I'd sell all the friends I ever had, for one, and think it a blessed good bargain. Well? So he says—?"

"So he says," resumed the convict I had recognized "—it was all said and done in half a minute, behind a pile of timber in the dockyards—'You're a-going to be discharged!' Yes, I was. Would I find out that boy that had fed him and kep' his secret, and give him them two one-pound notes? Yes, I would. And I did."

"More fool you," growled the other. "I'd have spent 'em on wittles and drink. He must have been a green one. Mean to say he knowed nothing of you?"

"Not a ha'porth.[1] Different gangs and different ships. He was tried again for prison breaking, and got made a lifer."[2]

"And was that the only time you worked out, in this part of the country?"

"The only time."

"What might have been your opinion of the place?"

"A most beastly place. Mudbank, mist, swamp, and work; work, swamp, mist, and mudbank."

They both execrated the place in very strong language, and gradually growled themselves out, and had nothing left to say.

After overhearing this dialogue, I resolved to alight as soon as we touched the town and put myself out of his hearing. This device I executed successfully. As to the convicts, they went their way with the coach, and I knew at what point they would be spirited off to the river. In my fancy, I saw the boat with its convict crew waiting for them at the slime-washed stairs—again heard the gruff "Give way, you!" like an order to dogs—again saw the wicked Noah's Ark[3] lying out on the

---

1. **ha'porth:** ha'penny worth; in other words, very little.
2. **got made a lifer:** was sentenced to life imprisonment.
3. **Noah's Ark:** the Hulks, the prison boat.

black water. I could not have said what I was afraid of, but there was great fear upon me.

Betimes in the morning I was up and out. It was too early yet to go to Miss Havisham's, so I loitered into the country on Miss Havisham's side of town—which was not Joe's side; I could go there tomorrow—thinking about my patroness, and painting brilliant pictures of her plans for me.

She had adopted Estella, she had as good as adopted me, and it could not fail to be her intention to bring us together. I loved Estella with the love of a man; I loved her simply because I found her irresistible. I knew to my sorrow, often and often, if not always, that I loved her against reason, against promise, against peace, against hope, against happiness, against all discouragement that could be. I loved her none the less because I knew it, and it had no more influence in restraining me than if I had devoutly believed her to be human perfection.

I so shaped out my walk as to arrive at the gate at my old time. I heard the side door open, and steps come across the courtyard, and started to find myself confronted by a man in a sober gray dress—the last man I should have expected to see in that place of porter at Miss Havisham's door.

"Orlick!"

"Ah, young master, there's more changes than yours. But come in, come in. It's opposed to my orders to hold the gate open."

I entered and he swung it, and locked it, and took the key out. "Yes!" said he, facing round. "Here I am!"

"How did you come here?"

"I come here," he retorted, "on my legs."

"Are you here for good?"

"I ain't here for harm, young master, I suppose."

I was not so sure of that. "Then you have left the forge?" I said.

"Do this look like a forge?" replied Orlick.

I had gone up the staircase in the dark, many a time. I ascended it now and tapped in my old way at the door of Miss Havisham's room. "Pip's rap," I heard her say, immediately; "come in, Pip."

She was in her chair near the old table, in the old dress, with her two hands crossed on her stick, her chin resting on them. Sitting near her was an elegant lady whom I had never seen.

"Come in, Pip," Miss Havisham continued. "Come in, Pip. How do you do, Pip? So you kiss my hand as if I were a queen, eh?— Well?"

"I heard, Miss Havisham," said I, rather at a loss, "that you were so kind as to wish me to come and see you, and I came directly."

"Well?"

The lady whom I had never seen before lifted up her eyes and looked archly at me,

and then I saw that the eyes were Estella's eyes. But she was so much changed, was so much more beautiful, so much more womanly, that I slipped hopelessly back into the coarse and common boy again. Oh, the sense of distance and disparity that came upon me, and the inaccessibility that came about her!

"Do you find her much changed, Pip?" asked Miss Havisham, with her greedy look, and striking her stick upon a chair that stood between them as a sign for me to sit down there.

"When I came in, Miss Havisham, I thought there was nothing of Estella in the face or figure; but now it all settles down so curiously into the old—"

"What? You are not going to say into the old Estella?" Miss Havisham interrupted. "She was proud and insulting, and you wanted to go away from her. Don't you remember?"

I said confusedly that that was long ago, and that I knew no better then. Estella smiled with perfect composure and said she had no doubt of my having been quite right, and of her having been very disagreeable.

"Is *he* changed?" Miss Havisham asked her.

"Very much," said Estella, looking at me.

"Less coarse and common?" said Miss Havisham, playing with Estella's hair.

Estella laughed. She treated me as a boy still, but she lured me on.

It was settled that I should stay there all the rest of the day, and return to the hotel at night, and to London tomorrow. When we had conversed for a while, Miss Havisham sent us two out to walk. Estella and I went into the garden, I trembling in spirit and worshiping the very hem of her dress; she, quite composed and decidedly not worshiping the hem of mine.

As the garden was too overgrown and rank

for walking, we came out again into the brewery yard. I showed her where I had seen her walking that first old day, and she said with a cold and careless look in that direction, "Did I?" I reminded her where she had come out of the house and given me my meat and drink, and she said, "I don't remember." "Not remember that you made me cry?" said I. "No," said she, and shook her head and looked about her. I verily believe that her not remembering and not minding in the least made me cry again, inwardly—and that is the sharpest crying of all.

"You must know," said Estella, condescending to me as a brilliant and beautiful woman might, "that I have no heart—if that has anything to do with my memory. I have no softness there, no—sympathy—sentiment—nonsense. If we are to be thrown much together, you had better believe it at once."

Her handsome dress had trailed upon the ground. She held it in one hand now, and with the other lightly touched my shoulder as we walked. We walked round the ruined garden twice or thrice more. At last we went back into the house, and there I heard with surprise that my guardian had come down to see Miss Havisham on business, and would come back to dinner. Estella left us to prepare herself, and Miss Havisham turned to me and said in a whisper:

"Is she beautiful, graceful, well grown? Do you admire her?"

"Everybody must who sees her, Miss Havisham."

She put an arm around my neck and drew my head close down to hers as she sat in the chair. "Love her, love her, love her! How does she use you?"

Before I could answer (if I could have answered so difficult a question at all), she repeated, "Love her, love her, love her! If she favors you, love her. If she wounds you, love her. If she tears your heart to pieces—and as it gets older and stronger it will tear deeper—love her, love her! Hear me, Pip! I adopted her to be loved. I bred her and educated her to be loved. I developed her into what she is, that she might be loved. Love her!"

"I'll tell you," said she in the same hurried passionate whisper, "what real love is. It is blind devotion, unquestioning self-humiliation, utter submission, trust and belief against yourself and against the whole world, giving up your whole heart and soul to the smiter—as I did!"

She rose up in the chair, in her shroud of a dress, and struck at the air as if she would as soon have struck herself against the wall and fallen dead. All this passed in a few seconds. As I drew her down into her chair, I turned and saw my guardian in the room.

Miss Havisham had seen him as soon as I, and was (like everybody else) afraid of him. She made a strong attempt to compose herself, and stammered that he was as punctual as ever.

"As punctual as ever," he repeated. "And so you are here, Pip?"

I told him when I had arrived, and how Miss Havisham wished me to come and see Estella.

"Well, Pip! How often have you seen Miss Estella before?" said he.

"How often?"

"Jaggers," interposed Miss Havisham, much to my relief; "leave my Pip alone, and go with him to your dinner."

He complied, and we groped our way down the dark stairs together.

"Pray, sir," said I, "may I ask you a question?"

"You may," said he, "and I may decline to answer it. Put your question."

"Estella's name, is it Havisham or—?" I had nothing to add.

"Or what?" said he.

"Is it Havisham?"

"It is Havisham."

This brought us to the dinner table, where she and Sarah Pocket awaited us. Mr. Jaggers scarcely directed his eyes to Estella's face once during dinner. When she spoke to him, he listened, and in due course answered, but never looked at her that I could see. On the other hand, she often looked at him, with interest and curiosity, if not distrust, but his face never showed the least consciousness.

Afterward we went up to Miss Havisham's room, and we four played at whist.[4] We played until nine o'clock, and then it was arranged that when Estella came to London I should be forewarned of her coming and should meet her at the coach; and then I took leave of her, and touched her and left her.

My guardian slept at the Boar in the next room to mine. Far into the night, Miss Havisham's words, "Love her, love her, love her!" sounded in my ears. I said to my pillow, "I love her, I love her, I love her!" hundreds of times.

Ah me! I thought those were high and great emotions. But I never thought there was anything low and small in my keeping away from Joe, because I knew she would be contemptuous of him. It was but a day gone, and Joe had brought the tears into my eyes; they had soon dried, God forgive me! soon dried.

Chapter 23

Trabb's boy has some fun with Pip.

After well considering the matter while I was dressing at the Blue Boar in the morning, I resolved to tell my guardian that I doubted Orlick's being the right sort of man to fill a

---

4. **whist** (hwĭst): a card game, the forerunner of bridge.

post of trust at Miss Havisham's. He listened in a satisfied manner while I told him what knowledge I had of Orlick. "Very good, Pip," he observed, when I had concluded. "I'll go round presently and pay our friend off." Rather alarmed by this summary action, I was for a little delay, and even hinted that our friend himself might be difficult to deal with. "Oh, no, he won't," said my guardian. "I should like to see him argue the question with *me*."

As we were going back together to London by the midday coach, and as I breakfasted under such terrors of Pumblechook that I could scarcely hold my cup, this gave me an opportunity of saying that I wanted a walk, and that I would go on along the London road while Mr. Jaggers was occupied, if he would let the coachman know that I would get into my place when overtaken. I was thus enabled to fly from the Blue Boar immediately after breakfast. By then making a loop of about a couple of miles into the open country at the back of Pumblechook's premises, I got round into the High Street again, a little beyond that pitfall, and felt myself in comparative security.

It was interesting to be in the quiet old town once more, and it was not disagreeable to be here and there suddenly recognized and stared after. My position was a distinguished one, and I was not at all dissatisfied with it, until Fate threw me in the way of that unlimited miscreant, Trabb's boy.

Casting my eyes along the street at a certain point of my progress, I beheld Trabb's boy approaching. Suddenly the knees of Trabb's boy smote together, his hair uprose, his cap fell off, he staggered out into the road, and crying to the populace, "Hold me! I'm so frightened!" feigned to be in a paroxysm of terror occasioned by the dignity of my appearance. As I passed him, his teeth loudly chattered in his head, and with every mark of extreme humiliation, he prostrated himself in the dust.

This was a hard thing to bear, but this was nothing. I had not advanced another two hundred yards, when, to my inexpressible amazement and indignation, I again beheld Trabb's boy approaching. He was coming round a narrow corner. He staggered round and round me with knees more afflicted, and with uplifted hands as if beseeching for mercy. His sufferings were hailed with the greatest joy by a knot of spectators, and I felt utterly confounded.

I had not got as much farther down the street as the post office when I again beheld Trabb's boy shooting round by a back way attended by a company of delighted young friends to whom he exclaimed, with a wave of his hand, "Don't know yah!" The disgrace attendant on his immediately afterwards taking to crowing and pursuing me across the bridge, culminated the disgrace with which I left town.

The coach, with Mr. Jaggers inside, came up in due time, and I took my box-seat again, and arrived in London safe—but not sound, for my heart was gone. As soon as I arrived, I sent a penitential codfish and a barrel of oysters to Joe (as reparation for not having gone myself), and then went on to Barnard's Inn.

I found Herbert dining on cold meat, and delighted to welcome me back, and I felt that I must open my breast that very evening to my friend and chum. Dinner done and we sitting with our feet upon the fender, I said to Herbert, "My dear Herbert, I have something very particular to tell you."

"My dear Handel," he returned, "I shall respect your confidence."

"It concerns myself, Herbert," said I, "and one other person."

Herbert looked at the fire with his head on one side, and looked at me because I didn't go on.

"Herbert," said I, laying my hand upon his knee. "I love—I adore—Estella. I have never left off adoring her. And she has come back, a most beautiful and most elegant creature. And I saw her yesterday. And if I adored her before, I now doubly adore her."

"Lucky for you then, Handel," said Herbert, "that you are picked out for her and allotted to her. Have you any idea yet of Estella's views on the adoration question?"

I shook my head gloomily. "Oh! She is thousands of miles away from me," said I.

"Patience, my dear Handel; time enough, time enough. But you have something more to say?"

"I am ashamed to say it," I returned, "and yet it's no worse to say it than to think it. You call me a lucky fellow. Of course, I am. I was a blacksmith's boy but yesterday; I am—what shall I say I am—today?"

"Say a good fellow, if you want a phrase," returned Herbert, smiling, "a good fellow, with impetuosity and hesitation, boldness and diffidence, action and dreaming, curiously mixed in him."

"Herbert," I went on, "you say I am lucky, and yet, when I think of Estella, I cannot tell you how dependent and uncertain I feel. I may say that on the constancy of one person (naming no person) all my expectations depend. And at the best, how indefinite and unsatisfactory, only to know so vaguely what they are!"

"Now, Handel," Herbert replied, in his gay, hopeful way, "it seems to me that we are looking into our gift horse's mouth with a magnifying glass. Didn't you tell me that your guardian, Mr. Jaggers, told you in the beginning that you were not endowed with expectations only? And even if he had not told you so, could you believe that of all men in London, Mr. Jaggers is the man to hold his present relations toward you unless he was sure of his ground?"

"What a hopeful disposition you have!" said I, gratefully admiring his cheery ways.

"I ought to have," said Herbert, "for I have not much else. And now, I want to make myself seriously disagreeable to you for a moment—positively repulsive."

"You won't succeed," said I.

"Oh, yes, I shall!" said he. "I have been thinking that Estella cannot surely be a condition of your inheritance, if she was never referred to by your guardian. Am I right in so understanding what you have told me, as that he never referred to her, directly or indirectly, in any way? Never even hinted, for instance, that your patron might have views as to your marriage ultimately?"

"Never."

"Now, Handel, I am quite free from the flavor of sour grapes, upon my soul and honor! Not being bound to her, can you not detach yourself from her?—I told you I should be disagreeable."

I turned my head aside, for, with a rush and a sweep, a feeling like that which had subdued me on the morning when I left the forge, smote upon my heart again. There was silence between us for a little while.

"My dear Handel," Herbert went on, "think of her bringing-up, and think of Miss Havisham. Think of what she is herself. This may lead to miserable things."

"I know it, Herbert," said I, with my head still turned away, "but I can't help it."

"Well!" said Herbert, getting up with a lively shake as if he had been asleep, and stirring the fire. "Now I'll endeavor to make myself agreeable again! I was going to say a word or two, Handel, concerning my father and my father's son. May I ask you if you have ever had an opportunity of remarking that the children of not exactly suitable marriages are always most particularly anxious to be married? Indeed, I think we are all engaged, except the baby."

"Then you are?" said I.

"I am," said Herbert; "but it's a secret."

"May I ask the name?" I said.

"Name of Clara," said Herbert.

"Live in London?"

"Yes. Her father had to do with the victualing[1] of passenger ships. I think he was a species of purser."

"What is he now?" said I.

"He's an invalid now," replied Herbert. "I have never seen him, for he has always kept his room overhead since I have known Clara. But I have heard him constantly. He makes tremendous rows—roars, and pegs at the floor with some frightful instrument." In looking at me and then laughing heartily, Herbert for the time recovered his usual hearty manner.

"Don't you expect to see him?" said I.

"Oh, yes, I constantly expect to see him," returned Herbert, "because I never hear him, without expecting him to come tumbling through the ceiling. But I don't know how long the rafters may hold."

When he had once more laughed heartily, he became meek and told me that the moment he began to realize Capital,[2] it was his intention to marry this young lady. He added, "But you *can't* marry, you know, while you're looking about you."

Chapter 24

Estella arrives in London.

One day when I was busy with my books and Mr. Pocket, I received a note by the post. It

---

1. **victualing:** supplying of food (victuals).
2. **realize Capital:** obtain some money.

had no set beginning, as Dear Mr. Pip, or Dear Pip, or Dear Sir, or Dear Anything, but ran thus:

I am to come to London the day after tomorrow by the midday coach. I believe it was settled you should meet me? At all events Miss Havisham has that impression, and I write in obedience to it. She sends you her regard.

— Yours, ESTELLA.

My appetite vanished instantly, and I knew no peace or rest until the day arrived. Then I was worse than ever, and began haunting the coach office in Wood Street, Cheapside, before the coach had left the Blue Boar in our town. I felt as if it were not safe to let the coach office be out of my sight longer than five minutes at a time, and in this condition of unreason I performed the first half-hour of a watch of four or five hours.

In her furred traveling dress, Estella seemed more delicately beautiful than she had ever seemed yet, even in my eyes. Her manner was more winning than before, and I thought I saw Miss Havisham's influence in the change.

"I am going to Richmond," she told me. "The distance is ten miles. I am to have a carriage, and you are to take me. This is my purse, and you are to pay my charges out of it. Oh, you must take the purse! We have no choice, you and I, but to obey our instructions. We are not free to follow our own devices, you and I."

As she looked at me in giving me the purse, I hoped there was an inner meaning in her words. She said them slightingly, but not with displeasure.

"A carriage will have to be sent for, Estella. Will you rest here a little?"

"Yes, I am to rest here a little, and I am to drink some tea, and you are to take care of me the while."

She drew her arm through mine, as if it must be done, and I requested a waiter to show us a private sitting room. Upon that, he pulled out a napkin, as if it were a magic clue without which he couldn't find the way upstairs, and led us to the black hole of the establishment. On my objecting to this retreat, he took us into another room with a dinner table for thirty. I was sensible that the air of this chamber, in its strong combination of stable with soup stock, might have led one to infer that the coaching department was not doing well, and that the enterprising proprietor was boiling down the horses for the refreshment department. Yet the room was all in all to me, Estella being in it. I thought that with her I could have been happy there for life. (I was not at all happy there at the time, observe, and I knew it well.)

"Where are you going to, at Richmond?" I asked Estella.

"I am going to live," said she, "at a great expense, with a lady there, who has the power— or says she has—of taking me about and introducing me and showing people to me and showing me to people. How do you thrive with Mr. Pocket?"

"I live quite pleasantly there; at least——" It appeared to me that I was losing a chance.

"At least?" repeated Estella.

"As pleasantly as I could anywhere, away from you."

"You silly boy," said Estella, quite composedly, "how can you talk such nonsense? Your friend Mr. Matthew, I believe, is superior to the rest of his family?"

"Very superior indeed."

"He really is disinterested, and above small jealousy and spite I have heard?"

"I am sure I have every reason to say so."

"You have not every reason to say so of the rest of his people," said Estella, "for they beset Miss Havisham with reports to your disadvantage. They watch you, misrepresent you, write letters about you (anonymous sometimes), and you are the torment and occupation of their lives. You can scarcely realize the hatred those people feel for you."

"They do me no harm, I hope?"

"No, no, you may be sure of that," said Estella. "Oh, what satisfaction it gives me to see those people thwarted! Two things I can tell you. First, these people never will impair your ground with Miss Havisham, in any particular, great or small. Second, I am beholden to you as the cause of their being so busy and so mean in vain, and there is my hand upon it."

As she gave it me playfully, I held it and put it to my lips. "You ridiculous boy," said Estella, "will you never take warning? Or do you kiss my hand in the same spirit in which I once let you kiss my cheek?"

"If I say yes, may I kiss the cheek again?"

"You should have asked before you touched the hand. But, yes, if you like."

I leaned down, and her calm face was like a statue's. "Now," said Estella, gliding away the instant I touched her cheek, "you are to take care that I have some tea, and you are to take me to Richmond."

Her reverting to this tone as if our association were forced upon us and we were mere puppets, gave me pain; but everything in our intercourse did give me pain. Whatever her tone with me happened to be, I could put no trust in it, and build no hope on it; and yet I went on against trust and against hope. Why repeat it a thousand times? So it always was.

I rang for the tea, and the waiter brought in by degrees some fifty adjuncts to that refreshment, but of tea not a glimpse. A teaboard, cups and saucers, plates, knives and forks, spoons, saltcellars, a meek little muffin confined with the utmost precaution under a strong iron cover, a fat family urn. After a prolonged absence he came in with a casket of

precious appearance containing twigs. These I steeped in hot water and extracted one cup of I don't know what, for Estella.

The bill paid, and the waiter remembered, and the chambermaid taken into consideration—in a word, the whole house bribed into a state of contempt and animosity, and Estella's purse much lightened—we got into our post coach and drove away. Turning into Cheapside and rattling up Newgate Street, we were soon under the walls of which I was so ashamed.[1]

"Mr. Jaggers," said I, "has the reputation of being more in the secrets of that dismal place than any man in London."

"He is more in the secrets of every place, I think," said Estella, in a low voice.

"You have been accustomed to see him often, I suppose?"

1. **the walls . . . ashamed:** Newgate Prison.

"I have been accustomed to see him at uncertain intervals ever since I can remember. But I know him no better now than I did before I could speak plainly. What is your own experience of him?"

"Once habituated to his distrustful manner," said I, "I have done very well."

"Are you intimate?"

"I have dined with him at his private house."

"I fancy," said Estella, shrinking, "that must be a curious place."

"It is a curious place."

I should have been chary[2] of discussing my guardian too freely even with her; but I should have gone on with the subject so far as to describe the dinner in Gerrard Street, if we had not then come into a sudden glare of gas.[3] When we were out of it, we fell into other talk, principally about the way by which we were traveling and about London.

It was impossible for me to avoid seeing that she cared to attract me; that she made herself winning; and would have won me even if the task had needed pains. Yet this made me none the happier, for I felt that she held my heart in her hand because she willfully chose to do it, and not because it would have wrung any tenderness in her to crush it and throw it away.

When we passed through Hammersmith, I showed her where Mr. Matthew Pocket lived, and said it was no great way from Richmond, and that I hoped I should see her sometimes.

"Oh, yes, you are to see me; you are to come when you think proper; you are to be mentioned to the family; indeed you are already mentioned."

I inquired was it a large household she was going to be a member of?

"No, there are only two, mother and daughter. The mother is a lady of some station, though not averse to increasing her income."

"I wonder Miss Havisham could part with you again so soon."

"It is a part of Miss Havisham's plans for me, Pip," said Estella, with a sigh, as if she were tired. "I am to write to her constantly and see her regularly, and report how I go on—I and the jewels—for they are nearly all mine now."

It was the first time she had ever called me by name. Of course she did so purposely, and knew that I should treasure it up.

We came to Richmond all too soon, and at our destination two cherry-colored maids came fluttering out to receive Estella. The doorway soon absorbed her boxes, and she gave me her hand and a smile, and said good night, and was absorbed likewise. And still I stood looking at the house, thinking how happy I should be if I lived there with her, and knowing that I never was happy with her, but always miserable.

Chapter 25

Pip and Herbert examine their affairs.

As I had grown accustomed to my expectations, I had insensibly begun to notice their effect upon myself and those around me. Their influence on my own character I disguised from my recognition as much as possible, but I knew very well that it was not all good. I lived in a state of chronic uneasiness respecting my behavior to Joe. My conscience was not by any means comfortable about Biddy. When I woke up in the night I used to think, with a weariness in my spirits, that I should have been happier and better if I had never seen Miss Havisham's face, and had risen to manhood content to be partners with

---

2. **chary** (châr′ē): hesitant; cautious.
3. **gas:** gaslight.

Joe in the honest old forge. Many a time of an evening, when I sat alone looking at the fire, I thought, after all, there was no fire like the forge fire and the kitchen fire at home.

Now, concerning the influence of my position on others, I perceived it was not beneficial to anybody, and above all, that it was not beneficial to Herbert. My lavish habits led his easy nature into expenses that he could not afford, corrupted the simplicity of his life, and disturbed his peace with anxieties and regrets. I began to contract a quantity of debt. I could hardly begin but Herbert must begin too, so he soon followed.

In my confidence in my own resources, I would willingly have taken Herbert's expenses on myself; but Herbert was proud, and I could make no such proposal to him. So he got into difficulties in every direction, and continued to look about him. When we gradually fell into keeping late hours and late company, I noticed that he looked about him with a desponding eye at breakfast time; that he began to look about him more hopefully about midday; that he drooped when he came in to dinner; that he seemed to descry[1] Capital in the distance rather clearly after dinner; that he all but realized Capital toward midnight; and that about two o'clock in the morning he became so deeply despondent again as to talk of buying a rifle and going to America, with a general purpose of compelling buffaloes to make his fortune.

We spent as much money as we could, and got as little for it as people could make up their minds to give us. We were always more or less miserable, and most of our acquaintance were in the same condition. There was a gay fiction among us that we were constantly enjoying ourselves, and a skeleton truth that we never did. To the best of my belief, our case was in the last aspect a rather common one.

At certain times I would say to Herbert, as if it were a remarkable discovery:

"My dear Herbert, we are getting on badly."

"My dear Handel," Herbert would say to me, in all sincerity, "if you will believe me, those very words were on my lips, by a strange coincidence."

"Then, Herbert," I would respond, "let us look into our affairs."

We always derived profound satisfaction from making an appointment for this purpose. Dinner over, we produced a bundle of pens, a copious supply of ink, and a goodly show of writing and blotting paper. For there was something very comfortable in having plenty of stationery.

I would then take a sheet of paper, and write across the top of it, in a neat hand, the heading, "Memorandum of Pip's debts." Herbert would also take a sheet of paper, and write across it, "Memorandum of Herbert's debts."

Each of us would then refer to a confused heap of papers at his side. The sound of our pens going refeshed us exceedingly, insomuch that I sometimes found it difficult to distinguish between this edifying business proceeding and actually paying the money.

When we had written a little while, I would ask Herbert how he got on.

"They are mounting up, Handel," Herbert would say; "upon my life they are mounting up."

"Be firm, Herbert," I would retort. "Look the thing in the face. Look into your affairs. Stare them out of countenance."

"So I would, Handel, only they are staring *me* out of countenance."

However, my determined manner would have its effect, and Herbert would fall to work again. After a time he would give up once

---

1. **descry** (dĭ-skrī'): see.

more, on the plea that he had not got Cobbs's bill, or Lobbs's, or Nobbs's, as the case might be.

"Then, Herbert, estimate; estimate it in round numbers, and put it down."

"What a fellow of resource you are!" my friend would reply, with admiration. "Really, your business powers are very remarkable."

I thought so too. I established with myself, on these occasions, the reputation of a first-rate man of business—prompt, decisive, energetic, clear, cool-headed. When I had got all my responsibilities down upon my list, I compared each with the bill, and ticked it off. My self-approval when I ticked an entry was quite a luxurious sensation. When I had no more ticks to make, I folded all my bills up uniformly, docketed[2] each on the back, and tied the whole into a symmetrical bundle. Then I did the same for Herbert (who modestly said he had not my administrative genius), and felt that I had brought his affairs into focus for him.

But there was a calm, a rest, a virtuous hush, consequent on these examinations of our affairs, that gave me, for the time, an admirable opinion of myself. Soothed by my exertions, my method, and Herbert's compliments, I would sit with his symmetrical bundle and my own on the table before me among the stationery, and feel like a bank of some sort, rather than a private individual.

We shut our outer door on these solemn occasions in order that we might not be interrupted. I had fallen into my serene state one evening, when we heard a letter drop through the slit in the said door and fall on the ground. "It's for you, Handel," said Herbert, going out and coming back with it, "and I hope there is nothing the matter." This was in allusion to its heavy black seal and border.

---

2. **docketed**: labeled.

The letter was signed TRABB & CO., and its contents were to inform me that Mrs. J. Gargery had departed this life on Monday last at twenty minutes past six in the evening, and that my attendance was requested at the interment on Monday next at three o'clock in the afternoon.

Chapter 26

Pip returns to the forge.

It was the first time that a grave had opened in my road of life, and the figure of my sister in her chair by the kitchen fire haunted me night and day. Whatever my fortunes might have been, I could scarcely have recalled my sister with much tenderness. But I suppose there is a shock of regret which may exist without much tenderness. I went down early in the morning and alighted at the Blue Boar, in good time to walk over to the forge. At last I came within sight of the house, and saw that Trabb and Co. had taken possession. Poor dear Joe, entangled in a little black cloak tied in a large bow under his chin, was seated apart at the upper end of the room, where, as chief mourner, he had evidently been stationed by Trabb. When I bent down and said to him, "Dear Joe, how are you?" he said, "Pip, old chap, you know'd her when she were a fine figure of a—" and clasped my hand and said no more.

Biddy, looking very neat and modest in her black dress, went quietly here and there, and was very helpful. When I had spoken to Biddy, as I thought it not a time for talking, I went and sat down near Joe.

"Pocket handkerchiefs out, all!" cried Mr. Trabb at this point, in a depressed business-like voice—"Pocket handkerchiefs out! We are ready!"

So, we all put our pocket handkerchiefs to our faces and filed out two and two: Joe and I, Biddy and Pumblechook, Mr. and Mrs. Hubble, the remains of my poor sister being carried by six bearers.

We went through the village, and now the range of marshes lay clear before us, and we went into the churchyard, close to the graves of my unknown parents, Philip Pirrip, late of this parish, and Also Georgiana, Wife of the Above. And there my sister was laid quietly in the earth while the larks sang high above it, and the light wind strewed it with beautiful shadows of clouds and trees.

When we got back and when they were all gone, Biddy, Joe, and I had a cold dinner together; but we dined in the best parlor, not in the old kitchen, and Joe was so exceedingly particular what he did with his knife and fork and the saltcellar and what not, that there was great restraint upon us. But after dinner, when I made him take his pipe, and when I had loitered with him about the forge, and when we sat down together on the great block of stone outside it, we got on better.

He was very much pleased by my asking if I might sleep in my own little room, and I was pleased too; for I felt that I had done rather a great thing in making the request.

When the shadows of evening were closing in, I took an opportunity of getting into the garden with Biddy for a little talk.

"Biddy," said I, "I think you might have written to me about these sad matters."

"Do you, Mr. Pip?" said Biddy. "I should have written if I had thought that."

She was so quiet, and had such an orderly, good, and pretty way with her that I did not like the thought of making her cry again. After looking a little at her downcast eyes as she walked beside me, I gave up that point.

"I suppose it will be difficult for you to remain here now, Biddy, dear?"

"Oh! I can't do so, Mr. Pip," said Biddy, in a tone of regret, but still of quiet conviction. "I have been speaking to Mrs. Hubble, and I am going to her tomorrow. I hope we shall be able to take some care of Mr. Gargery together until he settles down."

"How are you going to live, Biddy? If you want any mo——"

"How am I going to live?" repeated Biddy, striking in, with a momentary flush upon her face. "I'll tell you, Mr. Pip. I am going to try to get the place of mistress in the new school nearly finished here. I can be well recommended by all the neighbors, and I hope I can be industrious and patient, and teach myself while I teach others. The new schools are not like the old, but I learned a good deal from you after that time, and have had time since then to improve."

"I think you would always improve, Biddy, under any circumstances." I walked a little farther with Biddy, looking silently at her downcast eyes. "I have not heard the particulars of my sister's death, Biddy."

"They are very slight, poor thing. She had been in one of her bad states for four days, when she came out of it in the evening, just at teatime, and said quite plainly, 'Joe.' As she had never said any word for a long while, I ran and fetched in Mr. Gargery from the forge. She made signs to me that she wanted him to sit down close to her, and wanted me to put her arms round his neck. So I put them round his neck, and she laid her head down on his shoulder quite content and satisfied. And so she presently said 'Joe' again, and once 'Pardon,' and once 'Pip.' And so she never lifted her head up any more, and it was just an hour later when we laid it down on her own bed, because we found she was gone."

Biddy cried; the darkening garden, and the lane, and the stars that were coming out, were blurred in my own sight.

"Nothing was ever discovered, Biddy?"

"Nothing."

"Do you know what is become of Orlick?"

"I should think from the color of his clothes that he is working in the quarries."

"Of course you have seen him then? Why are you looking at that dark tree in the lane?"

"I saw him there on the night she died."

"That was not the last time either, Biddy?"

"No; I have seen him there since we have been walking here. It is of no use," said Biddy, laying her hand upon my arm, as I was for running out. "You know I would not deceive you; he was not there a minute, and he is gone."

It revived my utmost indignation to find that she was still pursued by this fellow, and I told her that I would spend any money or take any pains to drive him out of that country. By degrees she led me into more temperate talk, and she told me how Joe loved me, and how Joe never complained of anything—she didn't say, of me; she had no need; I knew what she meant—but ever did his duty in his way of life, and with a strong hand, a quiet tongue, and a gentle heart.

"Indeed, it would be hard to say too much for him," said I, "and of course I shall be often down here now. I am not going to leave poor Joe alone."

"Are you quite sure, then, that you *will* come to see him often?" asked Biddy, stopping in the narrow garden walk, and looking at me with a clear and honest eye.

"Oh, dear me!" said I as I found myself compelled to give up Biddy in despair. "This really is a very bad side of human nature! Don't say any more, if you please, Biddy. This shocks me very much."

For which cogent reason I kept Biddy at a distance during supper, and when I went up to my own little room, took as stately a leave of her as I could. As often as I was restless in the night, and that was every quarter of an hour, I reflected what an unkindness, what an injury, what an injustice, Biddy had done me.

Early in the morning I was to go. Early in the morning I was out, and looking in, unseen, at one of the wooden windows of the forge. There I stood, for minutes, looking at Joe, already at work with a glow of health and strength upon his face that made it show as if the bright sun of the life in store for him were shining on it.

"Goodbye, dear Joe! No, don't wipe it off—give me your blackened hand! I shall be down soon and often."

"Never too soon, sir," said Joe, "and never too often, Pip!"

Biddy was waiting for me at the kitchen door, with a mug of new milk and a crust of bread. "Biddy," said I, when I gave her my hand at parting, "I am not angry, but I am hurt."

"No, don't be hurt," she pleaded quite pathetically, "let only me be hurt, if I have been ungenerous."

Once more, the mists were rising as I walked away. If they disclosed to me, as I suspect they did, that I should *not* come back, and that Biddy was quite right, all I can say is—they were quite right too.

Chapter 27

Miss Skiffins helps serve tea.

Herbert and I went on from bad to worse, in the way of increasing our debts; and time went on; and I came of age. Herbert himself had come of age, eight months before me. As he had nothing else than his majority[1] to come into, the event did not make a profound sensation in Barnard's Inn. But we had looked

---

1. **majority:** here, legal age.

forward to my one-and-twentieth birthday with a crowd of speculations and anticipations, for we had both considered that my guardian could hardly help saying something definite on that occasion.

I had taken care to have it well understood in Little Britain when my birthday was. On the day before it, I received an official note from Wemmick, informing me that Mr. Jaggers would be glad if I would call upon him at five in the afternoon of the auspicious day. This convinced us that something great was to happen, and threw me into an unusual flutter when I repaired to my guardian's office, a model of punctuality.

Wemmick offered me his congratulations, and incidentally rubbed the side of his nose with a folded piece of tissue paper that I liked the look of. It was November, and my guardian was standing before his fire with his hands under his coattails.

"Well, Pip," said he, "I must call you Mr. Pip today. Congratulations, Mr. Pip."

We shook hands and I thanked him.

"Take a chair, Mr. Pip," said my guardian.

As I sat down, I felt at a disadvantage which reminded me of that old time when I had been put upon a tombstone.

"Now, my young friend," my guardian began, as if I were a witness in the box, "I am going to have a word or two with you."

"If you please, sir."

"What do you suppose," said Mr. Jaggers, "you are living at the rate of?"

"At the rate of, sir?"

"At," repeated Mr. Jaggers, "the—rate—of?"

Reluctantly, I confessed myself quite unable to answer the question. This reply seemed agreeable to Mr. Jaggers, who said, "I thought so! Now, I have asked *you* a question, my friend. Have you anything to ask *me?*"

"Of course it would be a great relief to me to ask you several questions, sir."

"Ask one," said Mr. Jaggers.

"Is my benefactor to be made known to me today?"

"No. Ask another."

"Is that confidence to be imparted to me soon?"

"Waive that a moment," said Mr. Jaggers, "and ask another."

"Have—I—anything to receive, sir?" On that, Mr. Jaggers said, triumphantly, "I thought we should come to it!" and called to Wemmick to give him that piece of paper. Wemmick appeared, handed it in, and disappeared.

"Now, Mr. Pip," said Mr. Jaggers, "attend if you please. You have been drawing pretty freely here; your name occurs pretty often in Wemmick's cashbook; but you are in debt, of course?"

"I am afraid I must say yes, sir."

"You know you must say yes, don't you?" said Mr. Jaggers.

"Yes, sir."

"I don't ask you what you owe, because you don't know; and if you did know, you wouldn't tell me; you would say less. Yes, yes, my friend," cried Mr. Jaggers, waving his forefinger to stop me, as I made a show of protesting; "it's likely enough that you think you wouldn't, but you would. Now, take this piece of paper in your hand. Now, unfold it and tell me what it is."

"This is a bank note," said I, "for five hundred pounds."

"You consider it, undoubtedly, a handsome sum of money. Now, that handsome sum of money, Pip, is your own. It is a present to you on this day, in earnest of your expectations. And at the rate of that handsome sum of money per annum,[2] and at no higher rate, you

---

2. **per annum** (ăn′əm): by the year (Latin).

are to live until the donor of the whole appears. That is to say, you will now take your money affairs entirely into your own hands, and you will draw from Wemmick one hundred and twenty-five pounds per quarter until you are in communication with the fountainhead[3] and no longer with the mere agent. As I have told you before, I am the mere agent. I execute my instructions, and I am paid for doing so. I think them injudicious, but I am not paid for giving any opinion on their merits."

After a pause, I hinted:

"There was a question just now, Mr. Jaggers, which you desired me to waive for a moment. I hope I am doing nothing wrong in asking it again?"

"What is it?" said he.

"Is it likely," I said, after hesitating, "that my patron, Mr. Jaggers, will soon come to London," said I, "or summon me anywhere else?"

"Now here," replied Mr. Jaggers, fixing me for the first time with his dark deep-set eyes, "we must revert to the evening when we first encountered one another in your village. What did I tell you then, Pip?"

"You told me, Mr. Jaggers, that it might be years hence when that person appeared."

"Just so," said Mr. Jaggers. "That's my answer."

"Do you suppose it will still be some years hence, Mr. Jaggers?"

"Come!" said Mr. Jaggers. "I'll be plain with you, my friend Pip. That's a question I must not be asked. When that person discloses, you and that person will settle your own affairs. My part in this business will cease. And that's all I have got to say."

"If that is all you have to say, sir," I re-marked," there can be nothing left for me to say."

He nodded assent and asked me where I was going to dine. I replied at my own chambers, with Herbert. As a necessary sequence, I asked him if he would favor us with his company, and he promptly accepted the invitation. But first he had a letter or two to write, and I said I would go into the outer office and talk to Wemmick.

The fact was that when the five hundred pounds had come into my pocket, a thought had come into my head which had been often there before; and it appeared to me that Wemmick was a good person to advise with.

"Mr. Wemmick," said I, "I want to ask your opinion. I am very desirous to serve a friend. This friend is trying to get on in commercial life, but has no money and finds it difficult and disheartening to make a beginning. Now, I want somehow to help him to a beginning."

"With money down?" said Wemmick, in a tone drier than any sawdust.

"With *some* money down," I replied, for an uneasy remembrance shot across me of that symmetrical bundle of papers at home; "with *some* money down, and perhaps some anticipation of my expectations."

"Mr. Pip," said Wemmick, "pitch your money into the Thames and you know the end of it. Serve a friend with it, and you may know the end of it too—but it's a less pleasant and profitable end."

"And that," said I, "is your deliberate opinion, Mr. Wemmick?"

"That," he returned, "is my deliberate opinion in this office."

"Ah!" said I, pressing him, for I thought I saw him near a loophole here; "but would that be your opinion at Walworth?"

"Mr. Pip," he replied with gravity, "Walworth is one place, and this office is another. Much as the Aged is one person, and Mr.

---

3. **fountainhead:** source.

Jaggers is another. They must not be confounded together. My Walworth sentiments must be taken at Walworth; none but my official sentiments can be taken in this office."

"Very well," said I, much relieved, "then I shall look you up at Walworth, you may depend upon it."

"Mr. Pip," he returned, "you will be welcome there, in a private and personal capacity."

We had held this conversation in a low voice, well knowing my guardian's ears to be the sharpest of the sharp. As he now appeared in his doorway, we all three went into the street together, and from the doorstep Wemmick turned his way, and Mr. Jaggers and I turned ours.

I devoted the next Sunday afternoon to a pilgrimage to the Castle. On arriving before the battlements, I found the Union Jack flying and the drawbridge up, but undeterred by this show of defiance and resistance, I rang at the gate, and was admitted by the Aged.

"My son, sir," said the old man, after securing the drawbridge, "left word that he would soon be home from his afternoon's walk. He is very regular in his walks, is my son. Very regular in everything, is my son."

I nodded at the old gentleman, and we went in and sat down by the fireside.

"You made acquaintance with my son, sir," said the old man, in his chirping way, while he warmed his hands at the blaze, "at his office, I expect?" I nodded. "Hah! I have heered that my son is a wonderful hand at his business."

I was startled by a sudden click in the wall on one side of the chimney, and the ghostly tumbling open of a little wooded flap with "JOHN" upon it. The old man, following my eyes, cried with great triumph, "My son's come home!" and we both went out to the drawbridge. The Aged was so delighted to work the drawbridge that I made no offer to assist him, but stood quiet until Wemmick had come across, and had presented me to Miss Skiffins, a lady by whom he was accompanied.

Miss Skiffins was of a wooden appearance, like her escort. The cut of her dress from the waist upward, both before and behind, made her figure very like a boy's kite, and I might have pronounced her gown a little too decidedly orange and her gloves a little too intensely green; but she seemed to be a good sort of fellow, and showed a high regard for the Aged. I was not long in discovering that she was a frequent visitor at the Castle.

While Miss Skiffins was taking off her bonnet (she retained her green gloves during the evening as an outward and visible sign that there was company), Wemmick invited me to take a walk with him round the property and see how the island looked in wintertime. Thinking that he did this to give me an opportunity of taking his Walworth sentiments, I seized the opportunity as soon as we were out of the Castle.

I informed Wemmick that I was anxious in behalf of Herbert Pocket, and I told him how we had first met, and how we had fought. I alluded to the advantages I had derived in my first ignorance from his society, and I confessed that I feared I had but ill repaid them, and that he might have done better without me and my expectations. For all these reasons (I told Wemmick), and because he was my young companion and friend, I sought advice how I could best help Herbert to some present income—say of a hundred a year, to keep him in good hope and heart—and gradually to buy him onto some small partnership. I begged Wemmick to understand that my help must always be rendered without Herbert's knowledge or suspicion, and that there was no one else in the world with whom I could advise. I wound up by laying my hand upon his shoulder and saying, "I can't help confiding in you, though I know it must be troublesome to you; but that is your fault in having ever brought me here."

Wemmick was silent for a little while, and then said, "Mr. Pip, I'll put on my considering cap, and I think all you want to do may be done by degrees. Skiffins (that's her brother) is an accountant and agent. I'll look him up and go to work for you."

After a little further conversation to the same effect, we returned into the Castle, where we found Miss Skiffins preparing tea. The responsible duty of making the toast was delegated to the Aged, and that excellent old gentleman prepared such a haystack of buttered toast that I could scarcely see him over it. We ate the whole of the toast and drank tea in proportion, and it was delightful to see how warm and greasy we all got after it. The Aged especially might have passed for some clean old chief of a savage tribe, just oiled. Then we drew round the fire, and Wemmick said, "Now, Aged Parent, read us the paper."

Wemmick explained to me while the Aged got his spectacles out that this was according to custom, and that it gave the old gentleman infinite satisfaction to read the news aloud. "I won't offer an apology," said Wemmick, "for he isn't capable of many pleasures—are you, Aged P.?"

"All right, John, all right," returned the old man, seeing himself spoken to.

"Only tip him a nod every now and then when he looks off his paper," said Wemmick, "and he'll be as happy as a king. We are all attention, Aged One."

As Wemmick and Miss Skiffins sat side by side, I observed him slowly and gradually stealing his arm round Miss Skiffins' waist. In course of time I saw his hand appear on the other side of Miss Skiffins; but at that mo-ment Miss Skiffins neatly stopped him with the green glove, unwound his arm again as if it were an article of dress, and with the greatest deliberation laid it on the table before her. Miss Skiffins' composure while she did this was one of the most remarkable sights I have ever seen.

At last the Aged read himself into a light slumber. Of course I knew better than to offer to see Miss Skiffins home, and under the circumstances I thought I had best go first; which I did, taking a cordial leave of the Aged, and having passed a pleasant evening.

Before a week was out, I received a note from Wemmick, dated Walworth, stating that he hoped he had made some advance in that matter appertaining to our private and personal capacities. The upshot was that we found a worthy young merchant, not long established in business, who wanted intelligent help, and who wanted capital, and who in due course of time would want a partner. Between him and me secret articles were signed of which Herbert was the subject, and I paid him half of my five hundred pounds down, and engaged for other payments; some to fall due at certain dates out of my income; some contingent on my coming into my property. Miss Skiffins' brother conducted the negotiation.

The whole business was so cleverly managed that Herbert had not the least suspicion of my hand being in it. I never shall forget the radiant face with which he came home one afternoon, and told me, as a mighty piece of news, of his having fallen in with one Clarriker (the young merchant's name), and of his belief that the opening had come at last. Day by day as his hopes grew stronger and his face brighter, he must have thought me a more and more affectionate friend, for I had the greatest difficulty in restraining my tears of triumph when I saw him so happy.

At length, the thing being done, and he having that day entered Clarriker's House, and he having talked to me for a whole evening in a flush of pleasure and success, I did really cry in good earnest when I went to bed, to think that my expectations had done some good to somebody.

A great event in my life, the turning point of my life, now opens on my view. But, before I proceed to narrate it, and before I pass on to all the changes it involved, I must give one chapter to Estella. It is not much to give to the theme that so long filled my heart.

Chapter 28

Estella warns Pip.

The lady with whom Estella was placed, Mrs. Brandley by name, was a widow, with one daughter several years older than Estella. They were in what is called a good position, and they visited, and were visited by, numbers of people.

In Mrs. Brandley's house and out of Mrs. Brandley's house, I suffered every kind and degree of torture that Estella could cause me. She made use of me to tease other admirers; and she turned the very familiarity between herself and me to the account of putting a constant slight on my devotion to her. And while I think it likely that it almost maddened her other lovers, I knew too certainly that it almost maddened me. She had admirers without end. No doubt my jealousy made an admirer of everyone who went near her; but there were more than enough of them without that.

I saw her often at Richmond, I heard of her often in town, and I used often to take her and the Brandleys on all sorts of pleasures—and they were all miseries to me. I never had one hour's happiness in her society, and yet my mind all round the four-and-twenty hours was harping on the happiness of having her with me unto death. She habitually reverted to that tone which expressed that our association was forced upon us. There were other times when she would come to a sudden check in this tone and in all her many tones and would seem to pity me.

"Pip, Pip," she said one evening, when we sat apart at a darkening window of the house in Richmond; "will you never take warning?"

"Of what?"

"Of me."

"Warning not to be attracted by you, do you mean, Estella?"

"Do I mean! If you don't know what I mean, you are blind."

"At any rate," said I, "I have no warning given me just now, for you wrote to me to come to you this time."

"That's true," said Estella, with a cold careless smile that always chilled me. "The time has come round when Miss Havisham wishes to have me for a day at Satis. You are to take me there, and bring me back, if you will. She would rather I did not travel alone, and objects to receiving my maid, for she has a sensitive horror of being talked of by such people. Can you take me?"

"Can I take you, Estella!"

"You can then? The day after tomorrow, if you please. You are to pay all charges out of my purse. You hear the condition of your going?"

"And must obey," said I.

We went down on the next day but one, and we found Miss Havisham in the room where I had first beheld her. She hung upon Estella's beauty, hung upon her words, hung upon her gestures, and looked at her, as though she were devouring the beautiful creature she had reared.

From Estella she looked at me, with a searching glance that seemed to pry into my heart and probe its wounds. "How does she use you, Pip, how does she use you?" she asked me again, with her witchlike eagerness, even in Estella's hearing. But when we sat by the flickering fire at night, she was most weird, for then, keeping Estella's hand drawn through her arm and clutched in her own hand, she extorted from her by dint of referring back to what Estella had told her in her regular letters the names and conditions of the men she had fascinated. I saw in this that Estella was set to wreak Miss Havisham's revenge on men. I, too, was tormented even while the prize was reserved for me. I saw in this the reason for my being staved off so long, and the reason for my late guardian's declining to commit himself to the formal knowledge of such a scheme.

The candles that lighted that room were placed in sconces on the wall.

They were high from the ground, and they burned with the steady dullness of artificial light in air that is seldom renewed. As I looked round at them, and at the pale gloom they made, and at the stopped clock, and at the withered articles of bridal dress upon the table and the ground, and at her own awful figure with its ghostly reflection thrown large by the fire upon the ceiling and the wall, I saw in everything the construction that my mind had come to, repeated and thrown back to me.

It happened on the occasion of this visit that some sharp words arose between Estella and Miss Havisham. It was the first time I had ever seen them opposed.

Miss Havisham still clutched Estella's hand in hers, when Estella gradually began to detach herself. She had shown a proud impatience more than once before, and had rather endured that fierce affection than accepted or returned it.

"What!" said Miss Havisham, flashing her eyes upon her. "Are you tired of me?"

"Only a little tired of myself," replied Estella, disengaging her arm.

"Speak the truth, you ingrate!" cried Miss Havisham, passionately striking her stick upon the floor. "You are tired of me."

Estella looked at her with perfect composure, and again looked down at the fire. Her graceful figure and her beautiful face expressed a self-possessed indifference to the wild heat of the other that was almost cruel.

"You stock and stone!" exclaimed Miss Havisham. "You cold, cold heart!"

"What!" said Estella. "Do you reproach me for being cold? You?"

"Are you not?" was the fierce retort.

"You should know," said Estella. "I am what you have made me."

"So proud, so proud!" moaned Miss Havisham, pushing away her gray hair with both her hands.

"Who taught me to be proud?" returned Estella. "Who praised me when I learned my lesson?"

"So hard, so hard!" moaned Miss Havisham, with her former action.

"Who taught me to be hard?" returned Estella. "Who praised me when I learned my lesson?"

"But to be proud and hard to *me!*" Miss Havisham quite shrieked, as she stretched out her arms. "Estella, Estella, Estella, to be proud and hard to *me!*"

"So," said Estella, "I must be taken as I have been made. The success is not mine, the failure is not mine, but the two together make me."

Miss Havisham had settled down, upon the floor, among the faded bridal relics with which it was strewn. I took advantage of the moment—I had sought one from the first—to leave the room, after beseeching Estella's attention to her with a movement of my hand. When I left, Estella was yet standing by the great chimney piece, just as she had stood throughout. Miss Havisham's gray hair was all adrift upon the ground, among the other bridal wrecks, and was a miserable sight to see.

It was with a depressed heart that I walked in the starlight for an hour and more, about the courtyard, and about the brewery, and about the ruined garden. When I at last took courage to return to the room, I found Estella sitting at Miss Havisham's knee. Afterward Estella and I played cards, as of yore—only we were skillful now, and played French games—and so the evening wore away, and I went to bed.

I lay in that separate building across the courtyard. It was the first time I had ever lain down to rest in Satis House, and sleep refused to come near me. At last I felt that I absolutely must get up. I put on my clothes and went out across the yard into the long stone passage. But I was no sooner in the passage than I extinguished my candle, for I saw Miss Havisham going along it in a ghostly manner, making a low cry. I followed her at a distance and saw her go up the staircase. She carried a bare candle in her hand and was a most unearthly object by its light. Standing at the bottom of the staircase, I heard her walking across into her own room, never ceasing the low cry. After a time, I tried in the dark both to get out and to go back, but I could do neither until some streaks of day strayed in and showed me where to lay my hands. During the whole interval, I heard her footstep, saw her candle pass above, and heard her ceaseless low cry.

Before we left next day, there was no revival of the difference between her and Estella, nor was it ever revived on any similar occasions; and there were four similar occasions, to the best of my remembrance.

It is impossible to turn this leaf of my life without putting Bentley Drummle's name upon it, or I would, very gladly.

On a certain occasion when the Finches[1] were assembled, the presiding Finch called the Grove to order, forasmuch as Mr. Drummle had not yet toasted a lady, it was the brute's turn to do so that day. What was my indignant surprise when he called upon the company to pledge him to "Estella!"

I tell this lightly, but it was no light thing to me. For I cannot express what pain it gave me to think that Estella should show any favor to a contemptible, clumsy, sulky booby, so very far below the average.

It was easy for me to find out, and I did soon find out, that Drummle had begun to follow her closely, and that she allowed him to do it. A little while, and he was always in pursuit of her, and Estella held him on; now with encouragement, now with discouragement, now almost flattering him, now openly despising him. The Spider, as Mr. Jaggers had called him, was used to lying in wait, however, and had the patience of his tribe.

At a certain Assembly Ball at Richmond, I resolved to speak to her concerning him. I took the opportunity when she was waiting for Mrs. Brandley to take her home.

"Are you tired, Estella?"

"Rather, Pip."

"You should be."

"Say, rather, I should not be; for I have my letter to Satis House to write before I go to sleep."

"Recounting tonight's triumph?" said I. "Surely a very poor one, Estella."

"What do you mean?"

"Estella," said I, "do look at that fellow in the corner yonder who is looking over here at us."

"Why should I look at him?" returned Estella. "What is there in that fellow in the corner that I need look at?"

"Indeed, that is the very question I want to ask you," said I. "For he has been hovering about you all night."

"Moths and all sorts of ugly creatures," replied Estella with a glance toward him, "hover about a lighted candle. Can the candle help it?"

"But, Estella, do hear me speak. It makes me wretched that you should encourage a

---

1. **Finches:** a social club to which Pip, Herbert, and Drummle belonged.

man so generally despised as Drummle. You know he is despised."

"Well?" said she.

"You know he is an ill-tempered, lowering, stupid fellow."

"Well?" said she.

"You know he has nothing to recommend him but money, don't you?"

"Pip," said Estella, casting her glance over the room, "don't be foolish about its effect on you. It may have its effect on others, and may be meant to have. It's not worth discussing."

"Yes, it is," said I, "because I cannot bear that people should say, 'she throws away her graces and attractions on a mere boor, the lowest in the crowd.' "

"I can bear it," said Estella.

"Oh! don't be so proud, Estella, and so inflexible."

"Calls me proud and inflexible in this breath!" said Estella, opening her hands. "And in his last breath reproached me for stooping to a boor!"

"There is no doubt you do," said I, "for I have seen you give him looks and smiles this very night, such as you never gave to—me."

"Do you want me then," said Estella, turning suddenly with a fixed and serious look, "to deceive and entrap you?"

"Do you deceive and entrap him, Estella?"

"Yes, and many others—all of them but you. Here is Mrs. Brandley. I'll say no more."

And now that I have given the one chapter to the theme that so filled my heart, and so often made it ache and ache again, I pass on unhindered to the event that had impended over me longer yet; the event that had begun to be prepared for before I knew that the world held Estella.

All the work, near and afar, that tended to the end, had been accomplished; and in an instant the blow was struck, and the roof of my stronghold dropped upon me.

Chapter 29

Pip has a midnight caller.

I was three-and-twenty years of age. Not another word had I heard to enlighten me on the subject of my expectations. We had left Barnard's Inn a year before, and lived in the Temple.[1] Our chambers were in Garden Court, down by the river. Mr. Pocket and I had for some time parted company as to our original relations, though we continued on the best terms.

Business had taken Herbert on a journey to Marseilles. I was alone, and had a dull sense of being alone. I sadly missed the cheerful face and ready response of my friend. It was wretched weather; stormy and wet, stormy and wet; mud, mud, mud, deep in all the streets. We lived at the top of the last house, and the wind rushing up the river shook the house that night, like discharges of cannon or breakings of a sea. I saw that the lamps in the court were blown out, and that the lamps on the bridges and the shore were shuddering, and that the coal fires in barges on the river were being carried away before the wind like red-hot splashes in the rain.

I read with my watch upon the table, purposing to close my book at eleven o'clock. As I shut it, all the church clocks in the city struck that hour. The sound was curiously flawed by the wind; and I was listening, when I heard a footstep on the stair.

What nervous folly made me start, and awfully connect it with the footstep of my dead sister, matters not. It was past in a moment, and I listened again and heard the footstep stumble in coming on. Remembering then

---

1. **Temple:** group of buildings near the Thames River, which were occupied by lawyers, court officials, and clerks.

that the staircase lights were blown out, I took up my reading lamp and went out to the stairhead. Whoever was below had stopped on seeing my lamp, for all was quiet.

"There is someone down there, is there not?" I called out, looking down.

"Yes," said a voice from the darkness beneath.

"What floor do you want?"

"The top, Mr. Pip."

"That is my name. There is nothing the matter?"

"Nothing the matter," returned the voice. And the man came on.

I stood with my lamp held out over the stair rail, and he came slowly within its light. I saw a face that was strange to me, looking up with an incomprehensible air of being touched and pleased by the sight of me.

Moving the lamp as the man moved, I made out that he was substantially dressed, but roughly, like a voyager by sea. That he had long iron-gray hair. That his age was about sixty. That he was a muscular man, strong on his legs, and that he was browned and hardened by exposure to weather. As he ascended the last stair or two, I saw, with a stupid kind of amazement, that he was holding out both his hands to me.

"Pray what is your business?" I asked him.

"My business?" he repeated, pausing. "Ah! Yes, I will explain my business, by your leave."

"Do you wish to come in?"

"Yes," he replied. "I wish to come in, master."

I took him into the room I had just left and, having set the lamp on the table, asked him as civilly as I could to explain himself.

He looked about him with the strangest air—an air of wondering pleasure, as if he had some part in the things he admired—and he pulled off a rough outer coat, and his hat.

Then I saw that his head was furrowed and bald, and that the long iron-gray hair grew only on its sides. But I saw nothing that in the least explained him. On the contrary, I saw him next moment once more holding out both his hands to me.

"What do you mean?" said I, half suspecting him to be mad.

He stopped in his looking at me and slowly rubbed his right hand over his head. "It's disappointing to a man," he said, in a coarse broken voice, "arter having looked for'ard so distant, and come so fur; but you're not to blame for that—neither on us is to blame for that. I'll speak in half a minute. Give me half a minute, please."

He sat down on a chair that stood before the fire, and covered his forehead with his large brown hands. I looked at him attentively then, and recoiled a little from him; but I did not know him.

"There's no one nigh," said he, looking over his shoulder, "is there?"

"Why do you, a stranger coming into my rooms at this time of the night, ask that question?" said I.

"You're a game one," he returned. "I'm glad you've grow'd up a game one! But don't catch hold of me. You'd be sorry afterwards to have done it."

I relinquished the intention he had detected, for I knew him! Even yet I could not recall a single feature, but I knew him! If the wind and the rain had driven away the intervening years, had swept us to the churchyard where we first stood face to face on such different levels, I could not have known my convict more distinctly than I knew him now, as he sat in the chair before the fire. No need to take a file from his pocket and show it to me; no need to take the handkerchief from his neck and twist it round his head; no need to hug himself with both his arms, and take a shivering turn across the room, looking back at me for recognition. I knew him before he gave me one of those aids, though a moment before I had not been conscious of remotely suspecting his identity.

He came back to where I stood and again held out both his hands. Not knowing what to do — for in my astonishment I had lost my self-possession — I reluctantly gave him my hands. He grasped them heartily, raised them to his lips, kissed them, and still held them.

"You acted nobly, my boy," said he. "Noble Pip! And I have never forgot it!"

At a change in his manners as if he were even going to embrace me, I laid a hand upon his breast and put him away.

"Stay!" said I. "Keep off! If you are grateful to me for what I did when I was a little child, I hope you have shown your gratitude by mending your way of life. If you have come here to thank me, it was not necessary. There must be something good in the feeling that has brought you here, and I will not repulse you; but surely you must understand — I — "

My attention was so attracted by the singularity of his fixed look at me that the words died away on my tongue.

"You was a-saying," he observed, when we had confronted one another in silence, "that surely I must understand. What surely must I understand?"

"That I cannot wish to renew that chance intercourse with you of long ago, under these different circumstances. I am glad to believe you have repented and recovered yourself. I am glad to tell you so. I am glad that, thinking I deserve to be thanked, you have come to thank me. But our ways are different ways, none the less. You are wet, and you look weary. Will you drink something before you go?"

He had replaced his neckerchief loosely, and had stood, keenly observant of me, biting a long end of it. "I think," he answered, still observant of me, "that I *will* drink (I thank you) afore I go."

I made him some hot rum-and-water. I tried to keep my hand steady while I did so. When at last I put the glass to him, I saw with amazement that his eyes were full of tears. I was softened by the softened aspect of the man, and felt a touch of reproach. "I hope," said I, "that you will not think I spoke harshly to you just now. I had no intention of doing it, and I am sorry for it if I did. I wish you well and happy!"

As I put my glass to my lips, he stretched out his hand. I gave him mine, and then he drank, and drew his sleeve across his eyes and forehead.

"How are you living?" I asked him.

"I've been a sheep farmer, stockbreeder, other trades besides, away in the new world," said he; "many a thousand mile of stormy water off from this."

"I hope you have done well?"

"I've done wonderful well. No man has done nigh as well as me. I'm famous for it."

"I'm glad to hear it."

"I hope to hear you say so, my dear boy."

Without stopping to try to understand those words or the tone in which they were spoken, I turned off to a point that had just come into my mind.

"Have you ever seen a messenger you once sent to me," I inquired, "since he undertook that trust?"

"Never set eyes upon him. I warn't likely to."

"He came faithfully, and he brought me the two one-pound notes. I was a poor boy then, as you know, and to a poor boy they were a little fortune. But, like you, I have done well since, and you must let me pay them back. You can put them to some other poor boy's use." I took out my purse.

He watched me as I laid my purse upon the table and opened it, and he watched me as I separated two one-pound notes from its contents. They were clean and new, and I spread them out and handed them over to him. Still watching me, he laid them one upon the other, folded them longwise, gave them a twist, set fire to them at the lamp, and dropped the ashes into the tray.

"May I make so bold," he said then, with a smile that was like a frown, and with a frown that was like a smile, "as to ask you *how* you have done well, since you and me was out on them lone shivering marshes?"

He emptied his glass, got up, and stood at the side of the fire, with his heavy brown hand on the mantelshelf. He put a foot up to the bars to dry and warm it, and the wet boot began to steam; but he neither looked at it nor at the fire, but steadily looked at me. It was only now that I began to tremble.

When my lips had parted, I forced myself to tell him that I had been chosen to succeed to some property.

"Might a mere warmint ask what property?" said he.

I faltered, "I don't know."

"Might a mere warmint ask whose property?" said he.

I faltered again, "I don't know."

"Could I make a guess, I wonder," said the convict, "at your income since you come of age? As to the first figure, now. Five?"

With my heart beating like a heavy hammer of disordered action, I rose out of my chair, and stood with my hand upon the back of it, looking wildly at him.

"Concerning a guardian," he went on. "There ought to have been some guardian or such-like, whiles you was a minor. Some lawyer, maybe. As to the first letter of that lawyer's name, now. Would it be J?"

All the truth of my position came flashing on me; and its disappointments, dangers, disgraces, consequences of all kinds, rushed in in such a multitude that I was borne down by them and had to struggle for every breath I drew. "Put it," he resumed, "as the employer of that lawyer whose name begun with a J, and might be Jaggers—put it as he had come over sea to Portsmouth, and had landed there, and had wanted to come on to you. Well! however did I find you out? Why, I wrote from Portsmouth to a person in London for particulars of your address. That person's name? Why, Wemmick."

I could not have spoken one word, though it had been to save my life. I stood, with a hand on the chair back and a hand on my breast, where I seemed to be suffocating—I stood so, looking wildly at him, until I grasped at the chair, when the room began to surge and turn. He caught me, drew me to the sofa, put me up against the cushions, and bent on one knee before me: bringing the face that I now well remembered, and that I shuddered at, very near to mine.

"Yes, Pip, dear boy, I've made a gentleman on you! It's me wot has done it! I swore that time, sure as ever I earned a guinea, that guinea should go to you. I swore arterwards, such as ever I spec'lated and got rich, you should get rich. I lived rough, that you should live smooth; I worked hard that you should be above work. What odds, dear boy? Do I tell it fur you to feel a obligation? Not a bit. I tell it fur you to know as that there hunted dog wot you kept life in got his head so high that he could make a gentleman—and, Pip, you're him!"

The abhorrence in which I held the man, the dread I had of him, the repugnance with which I shrank from him, could not have been exceeded if he had been some terrible beast.

"Look'ee here, Pip. I'm your second father. You're my son—more to me nor any son. I've put away money, only for you to spend. When I was a hired-out shepherd in a solitary hut, not seeing no faces but faces of sheep till I half forgot wot men's and women's faces wos like, I see yourn. I drops my knife many a time in that hut when I was a-eating my dinner or my supper, and I says, 'Here's the boy again, a-looking at me whiles I eats and drinks!' I see you there a many times as plain as ever I see you on them misty marshes. I says each time, 'If I gets liberty and money, I'll make that boy a gentleman!' And I done it. Why, look at you, dear boy! Look at these here lodgings of yourn, fit for a lord! A lord? Ah! You shall show money with lords for wagers, and beat 'em!''

In his heat and triumph, and in his knowledge that I had been nearly fainting, he did not remark on my reception of all this. It was the one grain of relief I had. Again he took both my hands and put them to his lips, while my blood ran cold within me.

"Don't you mind talking, Pip," said he. "You ain't looked slowly forward to this as I have; you wosn't prepared for this, as I wos. But didn't you never think it might be me?"

"Oh no, no, no," I returned. "Never, never!"

"Well, you see it *wos* me, and single-handed. Never a soul in it but my own self and Mr. Jaggers."

"Was there no one else?" I asked.

"No," said he, with a glance of surprise. "Who else should there be? And, dear boy, how good-looking you have growed! There's bright eyes somewheres—eh? Isn't there bright eyes somewheres, wot you love the thoughts on?"

O Estella, Estella!

"They shall be yourn, dear boy, if money can buy 'em. Let me finish wot I was a-telling you, dear boy. From that there hut and that there hiring-out, I got money left me by my

master (which died, and had been the same as me), and got my liberty and went for myself. It all prospered wonderful. As I giv' you to understand just now, I'm famous for it. It was the money left me and gains of the first few years wot I sent home to Mr. Jaggers—all for you—when he first come arter you, agreeable to my letter."

Oh, that he had never come! That he had left me at the forge—far from contented, yet, by comparison, happy!

"And, then, dear boy, I held steady afore my mind that I would for certain come one day and see my boy, and make myself known to him, on his own ground."

He laid his hand on my shoulder. I shuddered at the thought that for anything I knew his hand might be stained with blood.

"Where will you put me?" he asked presently. "I must be put somewheres, dear boy."

"To sleep?" said I.

"Yes. And to sleep long and sound," he answered, "for I've been sea-tossed and sea-washed, months and months."

"My friend and companion," said I, rising from the sofa, "is absent; you must have his room."

"He won't come back tomorrow, will he?"

"No," said I, answering almost mechanically, "not tomorrow."

"Because, look'ee here, dear boy," he said, dropping his voice, and laying a long finger on my breast in an impressive manner, "caution is necessary."

"How do you mean? Caution?"

"It's death!"

"What's death?"

"I was sent for life. It's death to come back. There's been overmuch coming back of late years, and I should of a certainty be hanged if took."

Nothing was needed but this; the wretched

man, after loading me with his wretched gold and silver chains for years, had risked his life to come to me, and I held it there in my keeping!

My first care was to close the shutters so that no light might be seen from without, and then to close and make fast the doors. He asked me for some of my "gentleman's linen" to put on in the morning. I brought it out, and laid it ready for him, and my blood again ran cold when he again took me by both hands to give me good night.

I got away from him, without knowing how I did it, and for an hour or more I remained too stunned to think. It was not until I began to think that I began fully to know how wrecked I was, and how the ship which I had sailed was gone to pieces.

Miss Havisham's intentions toward me, all a mere dream; Estella not designed for me; I only suffered in Satis House as a convenience, a sting for the greedy relations, a model with a mechanical heart to practice on when no other practice was at hand. But sharpest and deepest pain of all—it was for the convict, guilty of I knew not what crimes, that I had deserted Joe.

In every rage of wind and rush of rain, I heard pursuers. Twice I could have sworn there was a knocking and whispering at the outer door. With these fears upon me, I began to either imagine or recall that I had had mysterious warnings of this man's approach. Crowding up with these reflections came the reflection that I had seen him with my childish eyes to be a desperately violent man; that I had heard that other convict reiterate that he had tried to murder him; that I had seen him down in the ditch, tearing and fighting like a wild beast. Out of such remembrances, I brought into the light of the fire a half-formed terror that it might not be safe to be shut up there with him in the dead of the wild, solitary night. This impelled me to take a candle and go in and look at my dreadful burden.

He had rolled a handkerchief round his head, his face was set and lowering in his sleep. But he was asleep, and quietly, too, though he had a pistol lying on the pillow. I softly removed the key to the outside of his door, and turned it on him before I again sat down by the fire. Gradually I slipped from the chair and lay on the floor. When I awoke, the clocks were striking five, the candles were wasted out, the fire was dead, and the wind and rain intensified the thick black darkness.

This Is the End of the Second Stage of Pip's Expectations.

FOR STUDY AND DISCUSSION

Characters

1. Dickens introduces several new characters in Stage 2 of the novel. One of the most interesting is Bentley Drummle. How does Dickens' description of Drummle make you immediately dislike him? What character from Pip's past does Bentley Drummle remind you of in physical appearance and personality?

2. Another character prominent in Stage 2 is Mr. Jaggers. What is intriguing about his behavior when Pip first sees him in London? What new facts does Pip later learn that make Jaggers seem even more mysterious?

3. Where had Pip encountered Herbert Pocket in Stage 1 of the novel? What characteristics shown by Herbert in that encounter are still evident in him? Which of his qualities are a good influence on Pip? Which of his weaknesses does Pip pick up too easily?

4. The novels of Charles Dickens are filled with memorable portraits of characters, many of whom are eccentric, like Wemmick. Wemmick, his Aged Parent, and Miss Skiffins provide much of the humor in *Great Expectations*. What is amusing about the Aged? About Miss Skiffins? About Wemmick's "Castle" and its customs?

5. When Pip first arrives in London, Mr. Jaggers predicts, "Of course you'll go wrong somehow, but that's no fault of mine." What mistakes does Pip make in London? Do you think Pip is happy with his life there? Explain why or why not.

6. When they meet in London, Estella says to Pip: "We have no choice, you and I, but to obey our instructions. We are not free to follow our own devices, you and I." Is this true? Is Pip becoming a gentleman because he enjoys being one or because his benefactor expects him to become one?

7. Has Estella changed? If so, how? How do you think she really feels about Pip?

8. Describe Pip's relationship with Estella in this part of the novel. How are the hopes he has of being happy with her different from the way he actually feels when he is with her?

9. How does Miss Havisham's relationship to Estella change in Stage 2 of the novel? What does Miss Havisham realize about Estella? How does she react to this realization? How does this incident gain sympathy for her?

10. Pip has become a snob. How is this shown in his treatment of Joe? After visiting Miss Havisham at Satis House, why does Pip decide to return immediately to London? What is the real reason he wants to stay at the Blue Boar instead of at the forge?

11. When Pip learns that it is the convict who has been his benefactor, how does he react? Do you find his reaction one of weakness or strength? Explain.

12. Where in the novel does Pip for the first time make up his own mind to do something for someone else? What does this act show about Pip's character?

Plot

13. By the end of Stage 1, most of the subplots have been revealed. In Stage 2, each of the subplots is expanded—Pip and the convict, the injury to Mrs. Joe, Pip's love for Estella. How are these subplots brought farther along in the second part of the novel? What new subplots are introduced?

Setting

14. Compare Dickens' description of the weather on the night Pip's convict arrives at his London lodgings with the description of the marshes on the day of their first meeting. How are the two descriptions similar? What words are used in both descriptions? How does setting help to connect the two episodes?

Theme

15. In *Great Expectations,* Dickens explores different kinds of love. Miss Havisham tells Pip that real love is "blind devotion, unquestioning self-humiliation, utter submission, trust . . . giving up your whole heart and soul to the smiter—as I did!" Would you say that Pip's love for Estella is of the same kind? What other examples of love relationships are illustrated in the novel? What statement does Dickens seem to be making about love through the different relationships he presents?

LANGUAGE AND VOCABULARY

Differentiating Meanings

Herbert Pocket says about his father's relationship to Miss Havisham, "He is a bad courtier and will not *propitiate* her." What is the meaning of *propitiate?* Some words that Dickens might have used instead are *appease, conciliate, mollify, pacify,* or *placate.* In your dictionary, check the exact meaning of each of these words. Why does *propitiate* best suggest the exact relationship between Matthew Pocket and Miss Havisham? If you had to replace *propitiate* in this sentence with a synonym, which of the other five words would you choose?

Although the English language has many synonyms, few words have exactly the same meaning. Nearly every word has a unique shade of meaning that makes it more suitable in a given context than any other word. In your speaking and writing, always try to use the word that most exactly fits your meaning.

Use a dictionary to find at least two synonyms for each of the italicized words in the following passages. Then explain the different shades of meaning in each group of synonyms.

1. I should have been *chary* of discussing my guardian too freely even with her . . .
2. I lived in a state of *chronic* uneasiness respecting my behavior to Joe.
3. . . . I noticed that he looked about him with a *desponding* eye at breakfast time . . .

At one point Pip speaks of "the *hypocritical* Pumblechook." Earlier in the novel he refers to Miss Havisham's greedy relatives as "toadies and humbugs." The word *hypocritical* is from the Greek word *hypokritēs,* and refers to someone who tries to give the impression of being better (kinder or perhaps more honest) than he or she really is.

A *toady* plays up to people who are influential or rich. (Some dictionaries define a toady as a "toadeater.") A *humbug* is someone whose actions are deliberately deceptive and misleading.

Today we would be more likely to use the word *snob* than either *toady* or *humbug* to describe the Havisham relatives. A snob is someone who seeks to associate with those regarded as his or her superiors and who is quite cool toward those considered inferior in social position and wealth.

Which of these four words do you think most exactly describes Mr. Pumblechook?

LOOKING AHEAD TO STAGE 3

At the end of Stage 2, Pip faces the dilemma of what to do with his benefactor, who is a condemned criminal. He also has two shattering realizations that will change the course of his life: he has deserted Joe and life at the forge for expectations that have vanished; and Miss Havisham has never intended for him and Estella to marry. How do you think Pip's life will change as a result of these realizations?

The Third Stage of Pip's Expectations

Chapter 30

Pip confronts Jaggers.

It was fortunate for me that I had to take precautions to insure (so far as I could) the safety of my dreaded visitor; for, this thought pressing on me when I awoke held other thoughts at a distance. The impossibility of keeping him concealed in the chambers was self-evident. I was looked after by an inflammatory old female, assisted by an animated rag-bag whom she called her niece; and to keep a room secret from them would be to invite curiosity. I resolved to announce in the morning that my uncle had unexpectedly come from the country.

This course I decided on while I was yet groping about in the darkness for the means of getting a light. Not stumbling on the means after all, I was fain to go out to get the watchman to come with his lantern. Now, in groping my way down the black staircase, I fell over something, and that something was a man crouching in a corner. As the man made no answer when I asked him what he did there, I ran to the lodge and urged the watchman to come quickly. We examined the staircase from the bottom to the top and found no one there.

It troubled me that there should have been a lurker on the stairs on that night of all nights in the year, and I asked the watchman whether he had admitted at his gate any gentleman who had been dining out.

"The night being so bad, sir," said the watchman, "uncommon few have come in at my gate. Besides them three gentlemen that I know, I don't call to mind another since about eleven o'clock, when a stranger asked for you."

"My uncle," I muttered. "Yes."

"You saw him, sir?"

"Yes. Oh, yes."

"Likewise the person with him?"

"Person with him!" I repeated. "What sort of person?"

The watchman had not particularly noticed; he should say a working person; to the best of his belief, he had a dust-colored kind of clothes on, under a dark coat.

My mind was much troubled by these two circumstances taken together. I lighted my fire, which burned with a raw pale flare at that time of the morning, and fell into a doze before it. I was not able to consider my own situation, nor could I do so yet. At last the old woman and the niece came in. I imparted how my uncle had come in the night and was then asleep, and how the breakfast preparations were to be modified accordingly.

By and by, his door opened and he came out. I could not bring myself to bear the sight of him, and I thought he had a worse look by daylight.

"I do not even know," said I, speaking low as he took his seat at the table, "by what name to call you. I have given out that you are my uncle."

"That's it, dear boy! Call me uncle."

"You assumed some name, I suppose, on board ship?"

"Yes, dear boy. I took the name of Provis."

"Do you mean to keep that name?"

"Why, yes, dear boy, it's as good as another — unless you'd like another."

"What is your real name?" I asked him in a whisper.

"Magwitch," he answered in the same tone; "chrisen'd Abel."

"When you came into the Temple last

He ate in a ravenous way that was very disagreeable, and all his actions were uncouth,
noisy, and greedy. Some of his teeth had failed
him since I saw him eat on the marshes, and
as he turned his food in his mouth, and turned
his head sideways to bring his strongest fangs
to bear upon it, he looked terribly like a
hungry old dog. "I'm a heavy grubber, dear
boy," he said, as a polite kind of apology when
he had made an end of his meal. "Similarly, I
must have my smoke." He got up and brought
out a short black pipe and a handful of loose
tobacco. Having filled his pipe, he took a live
coal from the fire with the tongs and lighted
his pipe at it, and turned round on the
hearthrug with his back to the fire. He took
out of his pocket a great thick pocketbook,
bursting with papers, and tossed it on the
table.

"There's something worth spending in that
there book, dear boy. It's yourn. All I've got
ain't mine; it's yourn. Don't you be afeerd on
it. There's more where that come from. I've
come to the old country fur to see my gentle-

night," said I, "and asked the watchman the
way here, had you anyone with you?"

"With me? No, dear boy."

"But there was someone there?"

"I didn't take particular notice," he said
dubiously, "not knowing the ways of the
place. But I think there *was* a person, too,
come in alonger me."

"Are you known in London?"

"I hope not," said he, giving his neck a jerk
with his forefinger that made me turn hot and
sick.

"Were you known in London once?"

"Not over and above, dear boy. I was in the
provinces mostly."

"Were you—tried—in London?"

"Which time?" said he, with a sharp look.

"The last time."

He nodded. "First knowed Mr. Jaggers that
way. Jaggers was for me. And what I done is
worked out and paid for!"

man spend his money *like* a gentleman. That'll be *my* pleasure. *My* pleasure 'ull be fur to see him do it. And blast you all!" he wound up. "Blast you every one, from the judge in his wig to the colonist a-stirring up the dust, I'll show a better gentleman than the whole kit on you put together!"

"Stop!" said I, almost in a frenzy of fear and dislike. "I want to speak to you. I want to know what is to be done. I want to know how you are to be kept out of danger, how long you are going to stay, what projects you have."

"Look'ee here, Pip," said he, laying his hand on my arm in a suddenly altered and subdued manner. "I forgot myself half a minute ago. What I said was low; that's what it was; low. Look'ee here, Pip. Look over it. I ain't a-going to be low."

"First," I resumed, half groaning, "what precautions can be taken against your being recognized and seized?"

"Well, dear boy, the danger ain't so great. Without I was informed agen, the danger ain't so much to signify. There's Jaggers, and there's Wemmick, and there's you. Who else is there to inform?"

"Is there no chance person who might identify you in the street?" said I.

"Well," he returned, "there ain't many. Still, look'ee here, Pip. If the danger had been fifty times as great, I should ha' come to see you, mind you, just the same."

"And how long do you remain?"

"How long?" said he, taking his black pipe from his mouth and dropping his jaw as he stared at me. "I'm not a-going back. I've come for good."

"Where are you to live?" said I. "What is to be done with you? Where will you be safe?"

"Dear boy," he returned, "there's disguising wigs can be bought for money, and there's hair powder, and spectacles, and black clothes — and what not. As to the where and how of living, dear boy, give me your own opinions on it."

It appeared to me that I could do no better than secure him some quiet lodging hard by. That the secret must be confided to Herbert was plain to me. But it was by no means so plain to Mr. Provis (I resolved to call him by that name), who reserved his consent to Herbert's participation until he should have seen him. "And even then, dear boy," said he, pulling a greasy little clasped black Testament out of his pocket, "we'll have him on his oath." The book had the appearance of having been stolen from some court of justice.

There being a respectable loading house in Essex Street, almost within hail of my windows, I repaired to that house and was so fortunate as to secure the second floor for my uncle, Mr. Provis. I then went from shop to shop, making such purchases as were necessary to change his appearance. This business transacted, I turned my face, on my own account, to Little Britain. Mr. Jaggers was at his desk, but seeing me enter, got up immediately and stood before his fire.

"Now, Pip," said he, "be careful."

"I will, sir," I returned.

"Don't commit yourself," said Mr. Jaggers, "and don't commit anyone. You understand — anyone."

Of course I saw that he knew the man was come.

"I merely want, Mr. Jaggers," said I, "to assure myself what I have been told is true. I have been informed by a person named Abel Magwitch that he is the benefactor so long unknown to me."

"That is the man," said Mr. Jaggers, "— in New South Wales."[1]

---

1. **New South Wales:** a state in Australia; formerly a territory to which many convicts were transported, or exiled. Magwitch had been sentenced there for life.

"And only he?" said I.

"And only he," said Mr. Jaggers.

"I am not so unreasonable, sir, as to think you at all responsible for my wrong conclusions; but I always supposed it was Miss Havisham."

"As you say, Pip," returned Mr. Jaggers, "I am not at all responsible for that."

"And yet it looked so like it, sir," I pleaded with a downcast heart.

"Not a particle of evidence, Pip," said Mr. Jaggers. "Take nothing on its looks; take everything on evidence. There's no better rule."

"I have no more to say," said I, with a sigh, after standing silent for a little while. "I have verified my information, and there's an end."

"I communicated to Magwitch—in New South Wales—when he first wrote to me—from New South Wales—the caution that he was not at all likely to obtain a pardon, that he was expatriated for the term of his natural life, and that his presenting himself in this country would be an act of felony, rendering him liable to the extreme penalty of the law. I gave Magwitch that caution," said Mr. Jaggers, looking hard at me. "I wrote it to New South Wales. He guided himself by it, no doubt."

"No doubt," said I.

"I have been informed by Wemmick," pursued Mr. Jaggers, still looking hard at me, "that he has received a letter, from a colonist of the name of Purvis, or——"

"Or Provis," I suggested.

"Or Provis—thank you, Pip. Perhaps it is Provis? Perhaps you know it's Provis?"

"Yes," said I.

"You know it's Provis. A letter from a colonist of the name of Provis, asking for the particulars of your address, on behalf of Magwitch. Wemmick sent him the particulars, I understand, by return of post. Probably it is through Provis that you have received the explanation of Magwitch—in New South Wales?"

"It came through Provis," I replied.

"Good day, Pip," said Mr. Jaggers, offering his hand. "Glad to have seen you. In writing by post to Magwitch—in New South Wales—or in communicating with him through Provis, have the goodness to mention that the particulars and vouchers of our long account shall be sent to you, together with the balance; for there is still a balance remaining. Good day, Pip!"

Next day the clothes I had ordered all came home, and he put them on. To my thinking there was something in him that made it hopeless to attempt to disguise him. The more I dressed him, and the better I dressed him, the more he looked like the slouching fugitive on the marshes. He dragged one of his legs as if there were still a weight of iron on it, and from head to foot there was convict in the very grain of the man.

For five days, expecting Herbert all the time, I dared not go out except when I took Provis for an airing after dark. At length, one evening when dinner was over and I had dropped into a slumber quite worn out, I was roused by the welcome footstep on the staircase. Provis, who had been asleep too, staggered up at the noise I made, and in an instant I saw his jackknife shining in his hand.

"Quiet! It's Herbert!" I said.

"Handel, my dear fellow, how are you, and again how are you, and again how are you? I seem to have been gone a twelvemonth! Why, so I must have been, for you have grown quite thin and pale! Handel, my—— Halloa! I beg your pardon."

He was stopped in his running on and in his shaking hands with me, by seeing Provis. Provis, regarding him with a fixed attention, was slowly putting up his jackknife and groping in another pocket for something else.

"Herbert, my dear friend," said I, shutting the double doors, while Herbert stood staring and wondering, "something very strange has happened. This is—a visitor of mine."

"It's all right, dear boy!" said Provis, coming forward, with his little clasped black book, and then addressing himself to Herbert. "Take it in your right hand. Lord strike you dead on the spot if ever you split[2] in any way sumever. Kiss it!"

"Do so, as he wishes it," I said to Herbert. So Herbert, looking at me with a friendly uneasiness and amazement, complied, and Provis immediately shaking hands with him, said, "Now you're on your oath, you know. And never believe me on mine, if Pip shan't make a gentleman on you!"

Chapter 31

Two men, named Compeyson and Arthur, step out of the past.

In vain should I attempt to describe the astonishment and disquiet of Herbert, when he and I and Provis sat down before the fire, and I recounted the whole of the secret. Enough that I saw my own feelings reflected in Herbert's face, and, not least among them, my repugnance toward the man who had done so much for me.

"Look'ee here, Pip's comrade," he said to Herbert, after having discoursed for some time, "I know very well that once since I come back I've been low. But don't you fret yourself on that score. I ain't made Pip a gentleman, and Pip ain't a-goin' to make you a gentleman, not fur me not to know what's due to ye both."

---

2. **split:** slang for "inform."

Herbert said, "Certainly," but remained perplexed and dismayed. We were anxious for the time when he would go to his lodging and leave us together, but it was midnight before I saw him safely in at his own dark door. When it closed upon him, I experienced the first moment of relief I had known since the night of his arrival.

Herbert received me with open arms, and I had never felt before so blessedly what it is to have a friend. When he had spoken some sound words of sympathy and encouragement, we sat down to consider the question, What was to be done?

"What," said I to Herbert, "what is to be done? He is intent upon various new expenses—horses, and carriages, and lavish appearances of all kinds. He must be stopped somehow."

"You mean that you can't accept—"

"How can I?" I interposed, as Herbert paused. "Think of him! Look at him!"

An involuntary shudder passed over both of us.

"Then," said I, "after all, stopping short here, never taking another penny from him, think what I owe him already! Then again, I am heavily in debt—very heavily for me, who have now no expectations—and I have been bred to no calling, and I am fit for nothing."

"Well, well, well!" Herbert remonstrated, "Don't say fit for nothing."

"What am I fit for? I know only one thing that I am fit for, and that is to go for a soldier."

"You would be infinitely better in Clarriker's house, small as it is. I am working up toward a partnership, you know."

Poor fellow! He little suspected with whose money.

"But there is another question," said Herbert. "This is an ignorant determined man, who has long had one fixed idea. More than that, he seems to me (I may misjudge him) to be a man of a desperate and fierce character. Think of this! He comes here at the peril of his life, for the realization of his fixed idea. After all his toil and waiting, you destroy his idea, and make his gains worthless to him. Do you see nothing that he might do under the disappointment?"

"I have seen it, Herbert. Nothing has been in my thoughts so distinctly as his putting himself in the way of being taken."

"Then you may rely upon it," said Herbert. "That would be his reckless course if you forsook him. The first and the main thing to be done is to get him out of England. You will have to go with him, and then he may be induced to go. That done, extricate yourself, in Heaven's name, and we'll see it out together, dear old boy."

Provis came round at the appointed time, took out his jackknife, and sat down to his meal. He was full of plans "for his gentleman's coming out strong and like a gentleman" and urged me to begin speedily upon the pocketbook, which he had left in my possession. When he had made an end of his breakfast, and was wiping his knife on his leg, I said to him, without a word of preface:

"After you were gone last night, I told my friend of the struggle that the soldiers found you engaged in on the marshes. You remember?"

"Remember!" said he. "I think so!"

"We want to know something about that man—and about you. It is strange to know no more about either, and particularly you, than I was able to tell last night. Is not this as good a time as another for our knowing more?"

"Well," he said, after consideration. "You're on your oath, you know, Pip's comrade?"

"Assuredly," replied Herbert.

"And look'ee here! Wotever I done, is worked out and paid for," he insisted again.

He stuck his pipe in a buttonhole of his coat, spread a hand on each knee, and, after turning an angry eye on the fire for a few silent moments, looked around at us and said what follows:

"Dear boy and Pip's comrade, I am not a-going fur to tell you my life, like a song or a storybook. But to give it you short and handy, I'll put it at once into a mouthful of English. In jail and out of jail, in jail and out of jail, in jail and out of jail. There, you've got it. That's *my* life pretty much, down to such times as I got shipped off, arter Pip stood my friend.

"I've been done everything to, pretty well—except hanged. I've been locked up, and stuck in the stocks, and whipped and worried and drove. I've no more notion where I was born than you have. I first became aware of myself down in Essex, a-thieving turnips for my living. Summun had run away from me—a man—a tinker—and he'd took the fire with him, and left me wery cold. I knowed my name to be Magwitch, christened Abel. So fur as I could find, there warn't a soul that see young Abel Magwitch, with as little on him as in him, but wot caught fright at him, and either drove him off or took him up.[1] When I was a ragged little creetur as much to be pitied as ever I see, I got the name of being hardened. 'This is a terrible hardened one,' they says to prison visitors, picking out me. 'May be said to live in jails, this boy.' They always went on agen me about the Devil. But what the devil was I to do? I must put something into my stomach, mustn't I?

"Tramping, begging, thieving, working sometimes when I could—though that warn't as often as you may think, till you put the question whether you would ha' been overready to give me work yourselves—a bit of a poacher, a bit of a laborer, a bit of a wagoner, a

---

1. **took him up:** put him under arrest.

bit of a haymaker, a bit of a hawker, a bit of most things that don't pay and lead to trouble, I got to be a man.'

"At Epsom races, a matter of over twenty years ago, I got acquainted wi' a man whose skull I'd crack wi' this poker, like the claw of a lobster, if I'd got it on this hob. His right name was Compeyson; and that's the man, dear boy, what you see me a-pounding in the ditch. He set up fur a gentleman, this Compeyson, and had learning. He was a smooth one to talk and was a dab at the ways of gentlefolks. He was good-looking too.

"Compeyson took me on to be his man and pardner. And what was Compeyson's business in which we was to go pardners? Compeyson's business was the swindling, handwriting forging, stolen bank note passing, and suchlike. All sorts of traps as Compeyson could set with his head, and let another man in for, was Compeyson's business. He'd no more heart than a iron file, he was as cold as death, and he had the head of the Devil.

"There was another in with Compeyson, as was called Arthur. Him and Compeyson had been in a bad thing with a rich lady some years afore, and they made a pot of money by it; but Compeyson betted and gamed, and he'd have run through the king's taxes. So, Arthur was a-dying and a-dying poor and with the horrors on him, and Compeyson's wife was a-having pity on him when she could and Compeyson was a-having pity on nothing and nobody.

"I might a-took warning by Arthur, but I didn't. I begun wi' Compeyson, and a poor tool I was in his hands. Arthur lived at the top of Compeyson's house. The second or third time as ever I see him, he came a-tearing down into Compeyson's parlor late at night, in only a flannel gown, with his hair all in a sweat, and he says to Compeyson's wife, 'Sally, she really is upstairs alonger me, now, and I can't get rid of her. She's all in white,' he says, 'wi' white flowers in her hair, and she's awful mad, and she's got a shroud hanging over her arm, and she says she'll put it on me at five in the morning.'

"Says Compeyson: 'Why, you fool, don't you know she's got a living body? And how should she be up there, without coming through the door, or in at the window, and up the stairs?'

" 'I don't know how she's there,' says Arthur, shivering dreadful with the horrors, 'but she's standing in the corner at the foot of the bed. And over where her heart's broke — *you* broke it! — there's drops of blood.'

"Compeyson's wife and me took him up to bed agen, and he raved most dreadful. 'Why, look at her!' he cries out. 'She's a-shaking the shroud at me! She'll put it on me, and then I'm done for! Take it away from her, take it away!' And then he kep on a-talking to her, and answering of her, till I half believed I see her myself.

"He rested pretty quiet till it might want a few minutes of five, and then he screams out, 'Here she is! She's got the shroud again. She's unfolding it. She's coming out of the corner. She's coming to the bed. Hold me, both of you — one on each side — don't let her touch me with it.' Then he lifted himself up hard, and was dead.

"Compeyson took it easy as a good riddance for both sides. Him and me was soon busy, and I'll simply say to you, dear boy, and Pip's comrade, that that man got me into such nets as made me his slave. I was always in debt to him, always under his thumb, always a-working, always a-getting into danger. My missis as I had the hard time wi'——Stop though! I ain't brought *her* in——"

He looked about him in a confused way, turned his face to the fire, and spread his hands broader on his knees. "There ain't no need to go into it," he said, looking round once more. "At last, me and Compeyson was both committed for felony — on a charge of putting stolen notes in circulation. Compeyson says to me, 'Separate defenses, no communication,'[2] and that was all. And I was so miserable poor that I sold all the clothes I had, except what hung on my back, afore I could get Jaggers.

"When he was put in the dock,[3] I noticed first of all what a gentleman Compeyson looked, wi' his curly hair and his black clothes and his white pocket handkercher, and what a common sort of a wretch I looked. When the prosecution opened, I noticed how heavy it all bore on me, and how light on him. When the evidence was giv in the box,[4] I noticed how it was always me that had come for'ard, and could be swore to, how it was always me that the money had been paid to, how it was always me that had seemed to work the thing and get the profit. But when the defense come on, then I see the plan plainer; for, says the counselor for Compeyson, 'My lord and gentlemen, here you have afore you, side by side, two persons as your eyes can separate wide; one well brought up, one ill brought up.'

"And when the verdict come, warn't it Compeyson as was recommended to mercy on account of good character and bad company, and giving up all the information he could agen me, and warn't it me as got never a word but guilty? And when I says to Compeyson, 'Once out of this court, I'll smash that face of yourn!' ain't it Compeyson as prays the judge to be protected, and gets two

---

2. **Separate . . . communication:** Each man would handle his own case, and there would be no communication between them while defending themselves.
3. **dock:** the place where prisoners stand before the court.
4. **box:** the witness chair.

turnkeys stood betwixt us? And when we're sentenced, ain't it him as gets seven year, and me fourteen, and ain't it him as the judge is sorry for, because he might a-done so well, and ain't it me as the judge perceives to be a old offender of wiolent passion, likely to come to worse?"

He had worked himself into a state of great excitement, but he checked it, and stretching out his hand toward me, said, "I ain't a-going to be low, dear boy!

"We was in the same prison ship, but I couldn't get at him for long, though I tried. At last I come behind him and hit him on the cheek to turn him round and get a smashing one at him, when I was seen and seized. The black hole of that ship warn't a strong one. I escaped to the shore, and I was a-hiding among the graves there, envying them as was in 'em and all over, when I first see my boy!"

He regarded me with a look of affection that made him almost abhorrent to me again, though I had felt great pity for him.

"By my boy, I was giv to understand as Compeyson was out on them marshes too. Upon my soul, I half believed he escaped in his terror to get quit of me, not knowing it was me as had got ashore. I hunted him down. I smashed his face. 'And now,' says I, 'as the worst thing I can do, caring nothing for myself, I'll drag you back.' And I'd have swum off, towing him by the hair, if it had come to that, and I'd a got him aboard without the soldiers.

"Of course he'd much the best of it to the last and his punishment was light. I was put in irons, brought to trial again, and sent for life. I didn't stop for life, dear boy and Pip's comrade, being here."

He slowly took his tangle of tobacco from his pocket, plucked his pipe from his buttonhole, slowly filled it, and began to smoke.

"Is he dead?" I asked after a silence.

"Is who dead, dear boy?"

"Compeyson."

"He hopes *I* am, if he's alive, you may be sure," with a fierce look. "I never heard no more of him."

Herbert had been writing with his pencil in the cover of a book. He softly pushed the book over to me, as Provis stood smoking with his eyes on the fire, and I read in it:

"Young Havisham's name was Arthur. Compeyson is the man who professed to be Miss Havisham's lover."

I shut the book and nodded slightly to Herbert, and put the book by; but we neither of us said anything, and both looked at Provis as he stood smoking by the fire.

Chapter 32

Pip and Drummle exchange sharp words.

A new fear had entered in my mind by his narrative. If Compeyson were alive and should discover his return, I could hardly doubt the consequence. That Compeyson would hesitate to release himself for good from a dreaded enemy by the safe means of becoming an informer, was scarcely to be imagined.

Never had I breathed, and never would I breathe — or so I resolved — a word of Estella to Provis. But I said to Herbert that before I could go abroad, I must see both Estella and Miss Havisham. On my presenting myself at Mrs. Brandley's, Estella's maid was called to tell me that Estella had gone into the country. Where? To Satis House. She had never gone there before without me, and I went home again in complete discomfiture.

Next day, I had the meanness to feign that I was under a binding promise to go down to Joe. Provis was to be strictly careful while I was gone, and Herbert was to take the charge of him that I had taken.

Having thus cleared the way for my expedition to Miss Havisham's, I set off by the early morning coach. When we drove up to the Blue Boar, whom should I see come out under the gateway, toothpick in hand, to look at the coach, but Bentley Drummle!

As he pretended not to see me, I pretended not to see him. It was a very lame pretense on both sides; the lamer because we both went into the coffee room. I sat at my table while he stood before the fire. By degrees it became an enormous injury to me that he stood before the fire, and I got up, determined to have my share of it. I had to put my hands behind his legs for the poker when I went up to the fireplace to stir the fire, but still pretended not to know him.

"Is this a cut?"[1] said Mr. Drummle.

"Oh?" said I, poker in hand. "It's you, is it? How do you do? I was wondering who it was who kept the fire off."

With that I poked tremendously, and having done so, planted myself side by side with Mr. Drummle, my shoulders squared, and my back to the fire.

"Large tract of marshes about here, I believe?" said Drummle.

"Yes. What of that?" said I.

Mr. Drummle looked at me and laughed.

"Are you amused, Mr. Drummle?"

"No," said he, "not particularly. I am going out for a ride in the saddle. I mean to explore those marshes for amusement. Out-of-the-way villages there, they tell me. Curious little public houses — and smithies, and that. Waiter!"

"Yes, sir."

"Is that horse of mine ready?"

---

1. **cut:** a deliberate refusal to recognize someone.

"Brought round to the door, sir."

"I say. Look here. The lady won't ride today; the weather won't do."

"Very good, sir."

"And I don't dine, because I am going to dine at the lady's."

"Very good, sir."

Then Drummle glanced at me with an insolent triumph. One thing was manifest to both of us, and that was that until relief came, neither of us could relinquish the fire. There we stood, well squared up before it, shoulder to shoulder and foot to foot, with our hands behind us, not budging an inch.

After glancing at him once or twice, in an increased state of smoldering ferocity, I said:

"Mr. Drummle, I did not seek this conversation, and I don't think it's an agreeable one."

"I am sure it's not," said he superciliously, over his shoulder.

"And therefore," I went on, "with your leave, I will suggest that we hold no kind of communication in future."

"Quite my opinion," said Drummle. "But don't lose your temper. Haven't you lost enough without that?"

"What do you mean, sir?"

"Waiter," said Drummle, by way of answering me.

The waiter reappeared.

"Look here, you sir. You quite understand that the young lady don't ride today, and that I dine at the young lady's?"

"Quite so, sir!"

How long we might have remained in this ridiculous position it is impossible to say, but for the incursion of three thriving farmers, who came into the coffee room unbuttoning their greatcoats and rubbing their hands, and before whom, as they charged at the fire, we were obliged to give way. I saw him through the window, seizing his horse's mane, and mounting in his blundering brutal manner, and calling for a light for the cigar in his mouth. A man in a dust-colored dress appeared, and as Drummle leaned down from the saddle and lighted his cigar and laughed, with a jerk of his head toward the coffee-room windows, the slouching shoulders and ragged hair of this man, whose back was toward me, reminded me of Orlick.

Too heavily out of sorts to care, I washed the weather and the journey from my face and hands and went out to the memorable old house that it would have been so much the better for me never to have entered, never to have seen.

In the room where the dressing table stood, and where the wax candles burned on the wall, I found Miss Havisham and Estella; Miss Havisham seated on a settee near the fire, and Estella on a cushion at her feet. Estella was knitting and Miss Havisham was looking on. They both raised their eyes as I went in, and both saw an alteration in me. I derived that from the look they interchanged.

"And what wind," said Miss Havisham, "blows you here, Pip?"

Though she looked steadily at me, I saw that she was rather confused. Estella paused a moment in her knitting with her eyes upon me.

"Miss Havisham," said I, "I went to Richmond yesterday to speak to Estella; and finding that some wind had blown *her* here, I followed. What I had to say to Estella, Miss Havisham, I will say before you presently—in a few moments. It will not surprise you; it will not displease you. I am as unhappy as you can ever have meant me to be."

Miss Havisham continued to look steadily at me. I could see in the action of Estella's fingers as they worked that she attended to what I said, but she did not look up.

"I have found out who my patron is. It is

not a fortunate discovery, and is not likely ever to enrich me in reputation, station, fortune, anything. There are reasons why I must say no more of that. It is not my secret, but another's. When you first caused me to be brought here, Miss Havisham; when I belonged to the village over yonder, that I wish I had never left; I suppose I did really come here, as any other chance boy might have come—as a kind of servant, to gratify a want or a whim, and to be paid for it?"

"Aye, Pip," replied Miss Havisham, steadily nodding her head, "you did."

"And that Mr. Jaggers——"

"Mr. Jaggers," said Miss Havisham, taking me up in a firm tone, "had nothing to do with it, and knew nothing of it. His being my lawyer, and his being the lawyer of your patron is a coincidence."

"But when I fell into the mistake I have so long remained in, at least you led me on?" said I.

"Yes," she returned, again nodding steadily, "I let you go on."

"Was that kind?"

"Who am I," cried Miss Havisham, striking her stick upon the floor and flashing into wrath so suddenly that Estella glanced up at her in surprise, "who am I that I should be kind?"

"I was liberally paid for my old attendance here," I said, to soothe her, "in being apprenticed, and I have asked these questions only for my own information. What follows has another purpose. In humoring my mistake, Miss Havisham, you punished your self-seeking relations?"

"I did. Why, they would have it so! So would you. You made your own snares. *I* never made them."

Waiting until she was quiet again—for this, too, flashed out of her in a wild and sudden way—I went on.

"I have been thrown among one family of your relations, Miss Havisham, since I went to London. And I should be false and base if I did not tell you that you deeply wrong both Mr. Matthew Pocket and his son Herbert, if you suppose them to be otherwise than generous, upright, open, and incapable of anything designing or mean."

"They are your friends," said Miss Havisham.

"They made themselves my friends," said I, "when Sarah Pocket, Miss Georgiana, and Mistress Camilla were not my friends, I think."

This contrasting of them with the rest seemed, I was glad to see, to do them good with her. She looked at me keenly for a little while, and then said quietly:

"What do you want for them?"

"I do want something, Miss Havisham. If you could spare the money to do my friend Herbert a lasting service in life, but which from the nature of the case must be done without his knowledge, I could show you how."

"Why must it be done without his knowledge?" she asked, settling her hands upon her stick that she might regard me the more attentively.

"Because," said I, "I began the service myself, more than two years ago, without his knowledge, and I don't want to be betrayed. Why I fail in my ability to finish it, I cannot explain. It is a part of the secret which is another person's and not mine."

"What else?"

"Estella," said I, turning to her now, and trying to command my trembling voice, "you know I love you. You know that I have loved you long and dearly."

She raised her eyes to my face on being thus addressed, and her fingers plied their work, and she looked at me with an unmoved countenance. I saw that Miss Havisham glanced from me to her, and from her to me.

"I should have said this sooner, but for my long mistake. It induced me to hope that Miss Havisham meant us for one another. But I must say it now."

Preserving her unmoved countenance, and with her fingers still going, Estella shook her head.

"I know," said I, in answer to that action; "I know. I have no hope that I shall ever call you mine, Estella. I am ignorant what may become of me very soon, how poor I may be, or where I may go. Still, I love you. I have loved you ever since I first saw you in this house."

Looking at me perfectly unmoved and with her fingers busy, she shook her head again.

"It would have been cruel in Miss Havisham to torture me through all these years with a vain hope and an idle pursuit, if she had reflected on the gravity of what she did. But I think she did not. I think that in the endurance of her own trial, she forgot mine, Estella."

I saw Miss Havisham put her hand to her heart and hold it there, as she sat looking by turns at Estella and at me.

"It seems," said Estella very calmly, "that there are sentiments, fancies—I don't know how to call them—which I am not able to comprehend. When you say you love me, I know what you mean, as a form of words, but nothing more. You address nothing in my breast, you touch nothing there."

"Is it not true," said I, "that Bentley Drummle is in town here, and pursuing you?"

"It is quite true," she replied, referring to him with the indifference of utter contempt.

"That you encourage him, and ride out with him, and that he dines with you this very day?"

She seemed a little surprised that I should know it, but again replied, "Quite true."

"You cannot love him, Estella?"

Her fingers stopped for the first time, as she retorted rather angrily, "What have I told you? Do you still think, in spite of it, that I do not mean what I say?"

"You would never marry him, Estella?"

She looked toward Miss Havisham. Then she said, "Why not tell you the truth? I am going to be married to him."

I dropped my face into my hands, but was able to control myself better than I could have expected, considering what agony it gave me to hear her say those words.

"Estella, dearest, dearest Estella, do not let Miss Havisham lead you into this fatal step. Put me aside forever—you have done so, I well know—but bestow yourself on some worthier person than Drummle. Miss Havisham gives you to him, as the greatest slight and injury that could be done to the many far better men who admire you, and to the few who truly love you. Among those few, there may be one who loves you even as dearly, though he has not loved you as long, as I. Take him, and I can bear it better for your sake!"

My earnestness awoke a wonder in her.

"I am going," she said again, in a gentler voice, "to be married to him. The preparations for my marriage are making, and I shall be married soon. Why do you injuriously introduce the name of my mother by adoption? It is my own act."

"Your own act, Estella, to fling yourself away upon a brute?"

"On whom should I fling myself away?" she retorted, with a smile. "Should I fling myself away upon the man who would the soonest feel that I took nothing to him? I shall do well enough, and so will my husband. As to leading me into what you call this fatal step, Miss Havisham would have had me wait, and not marry yet; but I am tired of the life I have led, which has very few charms for me, and I am willing enough to change it. Say no more. We shall never understand each other."

"Such a mean brute, such a stupid brute!" I urged in despair.

"Don't be afraid of my being a blessing to him," said Estella. "I shall not be that. Come! Here is my hand."

"Oh, Estella!" I answered, as my bitter tears fell fast on her hand, do what I would to restrain them. "Even if I remained in England and could hold my head up with the rest, how could I see you Drummle's wife?"

"Nonsense," she returned, "nonsense. This will pass in no time."

"Never, Estella!"

"You will get me out of your thoughts in a week."

"Out of my thoughts! You are part of my existence, part of myself. You have been in every line I have ever read, since I first came here, the rough common boy whose poor heart you wounded even then. Estella, to the last hour of my life, you cannot choose but remain part of my character, part of the little good in me, part of the evil. But I associate you only with the good, for you must have done me far more good than harm. Oh, God bless you, God forgive you!"

I held her hand to my lips some lingering moments, and so I left her. But ever afterward, I remembered that the spectral figure of Miss Havisham, her hand still covering her heart, seemed all resolved into a ghastly stare of pity and remorse.

It was past midnight when I crossed London Bridge. I was not expected till tomorrow, but I had my keys, and, if Herbert were gone to bed, could get to bed myself without disturbing him.

The night porter examined me with much attention as he held the gate a little way open for me to pass in. To help his memory I mentioned my name.

"I was note quite sure, sir, but I thought so. Here's a note, sir. The messenger that brought it said would you be so good as to read it by my lantern?"

Much surprised by the request, I took the note. It was directed to Philip Pip, Esquire, and on the top of the superscription were the words, "PLEASE READ THIS HERE." I opened it, the watchman holding up his light, and read inside, in Wemmick's writing:

"DON'T GO HOME."

Chapter 33

Pip meets Clara, Herbert's fiancée.

Turning from the Temple gate as soon as I had read the warning, I made the best of the way to Fleet Street, and there got a late hackney chariot[1] and drove to the Hummums in Covent Garden. In those times a bed was always to be got there at any hour of the night, and the chamberlain, letting me in at his ready wicket, lighted the candle next in order on his shelf, and showed me straight into the bedroom next on his list.

1. **hackney chariot:** a horse-drawn cab.

What a doleful night! How anxious, how dismal, how long! The closet whispered, the fireplace sighed, the little washing-stand ticked, and one guitar string played occasionally in the chest of drawers. Why I was not to go home, and what had happened at home, and when I should go home, and whether Provis was safe at home, were questions occupying my mind so busily that one might have supposed there could be no more room in it for any other theme. Even when I thought of Estella, and how we had parted that day forever, I was pursuing here and there and everywhere the caution DON'T GO HOME. At last I dozed, in sheer exhaustion of mind and body.

I had left directions that I was to be called at seven; for it was plain that I must see Wemmick before seeing anyone else, and equally plain that this was a case in which his Walworth sentiments only could be taken.

The Castle battlements arose upon my view at eight o'clock. The little servant happening to be entering the fortress with two hot rolls, I crossed the drawbridge in her company and so came without announcement into the presence of Wemmick as he was making tea for himself and the Aged.

"Halloa, Mr. Pip!" said Wemmick. "You did come home, then?"

"Yes," I returned, "but I didn't go home."

"That's all right," said he, rubbing his hands. "I left a note for you at each of the Temple gates, on the chance. Which gate did you come to?"

I told him.

"I'll go round to the others in the course of the day and destroy the notes," said Wemmick. "It's a good rule never to leave documentary evidence if you can help it. Now, Mr. Pip, you and I understand one another. I accidentally heard, yesterday morning, that a certain person not altogether of uncolonial pursuits, and not unpossessed of portable property—we won't name this person—"

"Not necessary," said I.

"—had made some little stir in a certain part of the world where a good many people go, not always in gratification of their own inclination, by disappearing from such place and being no more heard of thereabouts. I also have heard that you at your chambers in Garden Court, Temple had been watched, and might be watched again."

"By whom?" said I.

"I wouldn't go into that," said Wemmick evasively. "It might clash with official responsibilities. I heard it."

As I saw that he was restrained by fealty to Little Britain from saying as much as he could, I could not press him. But I told him, after a little meditation over the fire, that I would like to ask him a question, subject to his answering or not answering, as he deemed right.

"You have heard of a man of bad character, whose true name is Compeyson?"

He answered with one nod.

"Is he living?"

One other nod.

"Is he in London?"

He gave me one last nod and went on with his breakfast.

"Now," said Wemmick, "questioning being over," which he emphasized and repeated for my guidance; "I come to what I did, after hearing what I heard. I went to Garden Court to find you; not finding you, I went to Clarriker's to find Mr. Herbert."

"And him you found?" said I, with great anxiety.

"And I found him. Without mentioning any names or going into any details, I gave him to understand that if he was aware of anybody—Tom, Jack, or Richard—being about the chambers, or about the immediate neighborhood, he had better get Tom, Jack, or Richard out of the way while you were out of the way."

"He would be greatly puzzled what to do?"

"He *was* puzzled what to do; not the less because I gave him my opinion that it was not safe to try to get Tom, Jack, or Richard too far out of the way at present. Mr. Pip, I'll tell you something. Under existing circumstances there is no place like a great city when you are once in it. Don't break cover too soon. Lie close. Wait till things slacken before you try the open, even for foreign air."

I thanked him for his valuable advice, and asked him what Herbert had done.

"Mr. Herbert," said Wemmick, "after being all of a heap for half an hour, struck out a plan. He mentioned to me as a secret that he is courting a young lady who has, as no doubt you are aware, a bedridden pa. Which pa, having been in the purser line of life, lies a-bed in a bow window where he can see the ships sail up and down the river. You are acquainted with the young lady, most probably?"

"Not personally," said I.

"The house with the bow window," said Wemmick, "being kept, it seems, by a very respectable widow, who has a furnished upper floor to let, Mr. Herbert put it to me, what did I think of that as a temporary tenement for Tom, Jack, or Richard? Now, I thought very well of it, for three reasons. Firstly. It is well away from the usual heap of streets. Secondly. Without going near it yourself, you could always hear of the safety of Tom, Jack, or Richard, through Mr. Herbert. Thirdly. After a while, and when it might be prudent, if you should want to slip Tom, Jack, or Richard on board a foreign packet boat,[2] there he is—ready."

---

2. **packet boat:** a steamship that carries mail, freight, and passengers along a regular route, in this case, from England to the Continent.

Much comforted by these considerations, I thanked Wemmick again and again, and begged him to proceed.

"Well, sir! Mr. Herbert threw himself into the business with a will, and by nine o'clock last night he housed Tom, Jack, or Richard—whichever it may be—you and I don't want to know—quite successfully. At the old lodgings it was understood that he was summoned to Dover. Now, another advantage of all this is that it was done without you. This diverts suspicion and confuses it, and you want confusion."

Wemmick, having finished his breakfast, here looked at his watch, and began to get his coat on.

"And now, Mr. Pip," said he, with his hands still in the sleeves, "I have probably done the most I can do. Here's the address. There can be no harm in your going here tonight and seeing for yourself that all is well with Tom, Jack, or Richard, before you go home. I must be off. If you had nothing more pressing to do than to keep here till dark that's what I should advise."

I soon fell asleep before Wemmick's fire, and the Aged and I enjoyed one another's society by falling asleep before it more or less all day. Eight o'clock had struck before I got into the air that was scented, not disagreeably, by the chips and shavings of the longshore boatbuilders, and mast, oar, and blockmakers. All that waterside region of the upper and lower Pool below London Bridge was unknown ground to me, and when I struck down by the river, I found that the spot I wanted was anything but easy to find. It was called Mill Pond Bank, Chinks's Basin; and I had no other guide to Chinks's Basin than the Old Green Copper Rope-Walk.

Selecting from the few queer houses upon Mill Pond Bank a house with a wooden front and three stories of bow window, I looked at the plate upon the door, and read there Mrs. Whimple. That being the name I wanted, I knocked, and an elderly woman of a pleasant and thriving appearance responded. She was immediately deposed, however, by Herbert, who silently led me into the parlor and shut the door.

"All is well, Handel," said Herbert, "and he is quite satisfied, though eager to see you. My dear girl is with her father, and if you'll wait till she comes down, I'll make you known to her, and then we'll go upstairs.—*That's* her father."

I had become aware of an alarming growling overhead, and had probably expressed the fact in my countenance.

"I am afraid he is a sad old rascal," said Herbert, smiling, "but I have never seen him. Don't you smell rum? He is always at it." While he thus spoke, the growling noise became a prolonged roar, and died away.

"To have Provis for an upper lodger is quite a godsend to Mrs. Whimple," said Herbert, "for of course people in general won't stand that noise."

As we were thus conversing, a very pretty, slight, dark-eyed girl of twenty or so came in with a basket in her hand, whom Herbert tenderly relieved of the basket, and presented, blushing, as "Clara." There was something confiding, loving, and innocent in her modest manner of yielding herself to Herbert's embracing arm. I was looking at her with pleasure and admiration when suddenly the growl swelled into a roar again, and a frightful bumping noise was heard above, as if a giant with a wooden leg were trying to bore it through the ceiling to come at us. Upon this, Clara said to Herbert, "Papa wants me, darling!" and ran away.

Clara returned soon afterward, and Herbert accompanied me upstairs to see our charge. I found Provis comfortably settled. He expressed no alarm, and seemed to feel none that was worth mentioning; but it struck me that he was softened—indefinably, for I could not have said how.

The opportunity that the day's rest had given me for reflection had resulted in my fully determining to say nothing to him respecting Compeyson. For anything I knew, his animosity toward the man might otherwise lead to his seeking him out and rushing on his own destruction. Therefore, when Herbert and I sat down with him by his fire, I asked him first of all whether he relied on Wemmick's judgment and sources of information.

"Aye, aye, dear boy!" he answered with a grave nod. "Jaggers knows."

"Then I have talked with Wemmick," said I, "and have come to tell you what caution he gave me and what advice."

I told him how Wemmick had heard in Newgate Prison that he was under some suspicion, and that my chambers had been watched; how Wemmick had recommended his keeping close for a time, and my keeping away from him; and what Wemmick had said about getting him abroad. I added that of course I should go with him. What was to follow that, I did not touch upon; neither indeed was I at all clear or comfortable about it in my own mind, now that I saw him in that softer condition, and in declared peril for my sake.

He was very reasonable throughout. His coming back was a venture, he said, and he had always known it to be a venture, and he had very little fear of his safety with such good help.

Herbert, who had been looking at the fire and pondering, here said, "We are both good watermen, Handel, and could take him down the river ourselves when the right time comes. No boat would then be hired for the purpose, and no boatmen; that would save at least a chance of suspicion, and any chance is worth saving. Don't you think it might be a good thing if you began at once to keep a boat at the Temple stairs, and were in the habit of rowing up and down the river? You fall into that habit, and then who notices or minds? Do it twenty or fifty times, and there is nothing special in your doing it the twenty-first or fifty-first."

I liked this scheme, and Provis was quite elated by it. We agreed that it should be carried into execution, and that Provis should never recognize us if we came below Bridge and rowed past Mill Pond Bank. But we further agreed that he should pull down the blind in that part of his window which faced upon the east whenever he saw us and all was right.

Our conference being now ended, and everything arranged, I rose to go, remarking to Herbert that he and I had better not go home together, and that I would take half an hour's start of him. "I don't like to leave you here," I said to Provis, "though I cannot doubt your being safer here than near me. Goodbye!"

"Dear boy," he answered, clasping my hands, "I don't know when we may meet again, and I don't like goodbye. Say good night!"

"Good night! Herbert will go regularly between us, and when the time comes, you may be certain I shall be ready. Good night, good night!" Looking back at him, I thought of the first night of his return, when our positions were reversed, and when I little supposed my heart could ever be as heavy and anxious at parting from him as it was now.

Next day, I set myself to get the boat. It was soon done, and the boat was brought round to the Temple stairs, and lay where I could reach her within a minute or two. Then I began to go out as for training and practice, sometimes alone, sometimes with Herbert. I was often out in cold, rain, and sleet, but nobody took much note of me after I had been out a few times. At first, I kept above Blackfriars Bridge; but as the hours of the tide changed, I took toward London Bridge. The first time I passed Mill Pond Bank, Herbert and I were pulling a pair of oars; and, both in going and returning, we saw the blind toward the east come down. Herbert was rarely there less frequently than three times in a week, and he never brought me a single word of intelligence that was at all alarming.

Still, I was always full of fears for the rash man who was in hiding. Herbert had sometimes said to me that he found it pleasant to stand at one of our windows after dark, when the tide was running down, and to think that it was flowing, with everything it bore, toward Clara. But I thought with dread that it was flowing toward Magwitch, and that any black mark on its surface might be his pursuers, going swiftly, silently, and surely to take him.

Chapter 34

Wemmick tells Pip the story of Molly.

Some weeks passed without bringing any change. We waited for Wemmick, and he made no sign. My worldly affairs began to wear a gloomy appearance, and I was pressed for money by more than one creditor. Even I myself began to know the want of ready money in my own pocket, and to relieve it by converting some easily spared articles of jewelry into cash. But I had quite determined that it would be a heartless fraud to take more money from my patron in the existing state of my uncertain thoughts and plans. Therefore, I had sent him the unopened pocketbook by

Herbert, to hold in his own keeping, and I felt a kind of satisfaction in not having profited by his generosity since his revelation of himself.

It was an unhappy life that I lived. Condemned to inaction and a state of constant restlessness and suspense, I rowed about in my boat, and waited, waited, waited, as I best could.

One afternoon, late in February, I came ashore at the wharf at dusk. I had pulled down as far as Greenwich with the ebb tide and had turned with the tide. It had been a fine bright day, but had become foggy as the sun dropped, and I had had to feel my way back among the shipping pretty carefully. Both in going and returning, I had seen the signal in his window, all well.

I had strolled up into Cheapside when a large hand was laid upon my shoulder, by someone overtaking me. It was Mr. Jaggers' hand, and he passed it through my arm.

"As we are going in the same direction, Pip, we may walk together. Come and dine with me."

I was going to excuse myself, when he added, "Wemmick's coming." So I changed my excuse into an acceptance.

We went to Gerrard Street, all three together, and as soon as we got there, dinner was served.

"Did you send that note of Miss Havisham's to Mr. Pip, Wemmick?" Mr. Jaggers asked, soon after we began dinner.

"No, sir," returned Wemmick; "it was going by post, when you brought Mr. Pip into the office. Here it is." He handed it to his principal, instead of to me.

"It's a note of two lines, Pip," said Mr. Jaggers, handing it on, "sent up to me by Miss Havisham, on account of her not being sure of your address. She tells me that she wants to see you on a little matter of business you mentioned to her. You'll go down?"

"Yes," said I, casting my eyes over the note, which was exactly in those terms.

"When do you think of going down?"

"I have an impending engagement," said I, glancing at Wemmick, "that renders me rather uncertain of my time. At once, I think."

"If Mr. Pip has the intention of going at once," said Wemmick to Mr. Jaggers, "he needn't write an answer, you know."

Receiving this as an intimation that it was best not to delay, I settled that I would go tomorrow, and said so. Wemmick drank a glass of wine and looked with a grimly satisfied air at Mr. Jaggers, but not at me.

"So, Pip! Our friend the Spider," said Mr. Jaggers, "has played his cards. He has won the pool."

It was as much as I could do to assent.

"So, here's to Mrs. Bentley Drummle," said Mr. Jaggers, taking a decanter of choicer wine from his dumbwaiter, and filling for each of us and for himself. "Now, Molly, Molly, Molly, Molly, how slow you are today!"

She was at his elbow when he addressed her, putting a dish upon the table. As she withdrew her hands from it, she fell back a step or two, nervously muttering some excuse. And a certain action of her fingers as she spoke arrested my attention.

"What's the matter?" said Mr. Jaggers.

"Nothing. Only the subject we were speaking of," said I, "was rather painful to me."

The action of her fingers was like the action of knitting. She stood looking at her master, not understanding whether she was free to go, or whether he had more to say to her and would call her back if she did go. Her look was very intent. Surely, I had seen exactly such eyes and such hands on a memorable occasion very lately!

He dismissed her, and she glided out of the room. But she remained before me, as plainly as if she were still there. I looked at those hands, I looked at those eyes, I looked at that flowing hair; and I compared them with other hands, other eyes, other hair, that I knew of, and with what those might be after twenty years of a brutal husband and a stormy life. I looked again at those hands and eyes of the housekeeper. And I felt absolutely certain that this woman was Estella's mother. Only twice more did the housekeeper reappear, and then her stay in the room was very short, and Mr. Jaggers was sharp with her. But her hands were Estella's hands, and her eyes were Estella's eyes, and if she had reappeared a hundred times I could have been neither more sure nor less sure that my conviction was the truth.

Wemmick and I took our leave early, and left together. I asked him if he had ever seen Miss Havisham's adopted daughter, Mrs. Bentley Drummle? He said no. To avoid being too abrupt, I then spoke of the Aged, and of Miss Skiffins. He looked rather sly when I mentioned Miss Skiffins.

"Wemmick," said I, "do you remember telling me, before I first went to Mr. Jaggers' private house, to notice that housekeeper?"

"Did I?" he replied. "Ah, I dare say I did."

"I wish you would tell me her story. I feel a particular interest in being acquainted with it. You know that what is said between you and me goes no further."

"Well!" Wemmick replied. "I don't know her story—that is, I don't know all of it. But what I do know, I'll tell you. We are in our private and personal capacities, of course."

"Of course."

"A score or so of years ago that woman was tried at the Old Bailey for murder and was acquitted. She was a very handsome young woman, and I believe had some gypsy blood in her. Anyhow, it was hot enough when it was up, as you may suppose."

"But she was acquitted."

"Mr. Jaggers was for her," pursued Wemmick, with a look full of meaning, "and worked the case in a way quite astonishing. It was a desperate case. The murdered person was a woman, a good ten years older, very much larger, and very much stronger. It was a case of jealousy. They both led tramping lives, and this woman in Gerrard Street here had been married very young to a tramping man, and was a perfect fury in point of jealousy. The murdered woman—more a match for the man, certainly, in point of years—was found dead in a barn. There had been a violent struggle, perhaps a fight. She was bruised and scratched and torn, and had been held by the throat at last and choked. Now, there was no reasonable evidence to implicate any person but this woman, and on the physical improbabilities of her having been able to do it, Mr. Jaggers principally rested his case. You may be sure," said Wemmick, touching me on the sleeve, "that he never dwelt upon the strength of her hands then, though he sometimes does now."

I had told Wemmick of his showing us her wrists that day of the dinner party.

"Well, sir!" Wemmick went on. "This woman was so artfully dressed from the time of her apprehension that she looked much slighter than she really was; her sleeves are always remembered to have been so skillfully contrived that her arms had a delicate look. But the backs of her hands were lacerated, and the question was, was it with fingernails? Now, Mr. Jaggers showed that she had struggled through a great lot of brambles which she could not have got through and kept her hands out of; and bits of those brambles were actually found in her skin and put in evidence. But the boldest point he made was this. It was attempted to be set up in proof of her jealousy that she was under strong suspi-cion of having, at about the time of the murder, frantically destroyed her child by this man—some three years old—to revenge herself upon him. Mr. Jaggers worked that in this way. 'We say these are not marks of fingernails, but marks of brambles, and we show you the brambles. You say they are marks of fingernails, and you set up the hypothesis that she destroyed her child. You must accept all consequences of that hypothesis. For anything we know, she may have destroyed her child, and the child in clinging to her may have scratched her hands. What then? You are not trying her for the murder of her child; why don't you? As to this case, if you *will* have scratches, we say that, for anything we know, you may have accounted for them, assuming for the sake of argument that you have not invented them.' To sum up, sir," added Wemmick, "Mr. Jaggers was altogether too many for the jury, and they gave in."

"Has she been in his service ever since?"

"Yes," said Wemmick, "she went into his service immediately after her acquittal, tamed as she is now."

"Do you remember the sex of the child?"

"Said to have been a girl."

"You have nothing more to say to me tonight?"

"Nothing."

We exchanged a cordial good night, and went home, with new matter for my thoughts, though with no relief from the old.

Chapter 35

Pip visits Miss Havisham for the last time.

Putting Miss Havisham's note in my pocket, I went down by coach next day. The best light of the day had gone when I passed the High Street. The cathedral chimes had at once a sadder and more remote sound to me; they seemed to call to me that the place was changed, and that Estella was gone out of it forever.

Miss Havisham was not in her own room, but was in the larger room across the landing. Looking in at the door, after knocking in vain, I saw her sitting on the hearth in a ragged chair, close before the ashy fire. I went in and stood where she could see me when she raised her eyes. There was an air of utter loneliness upon her. As I stood compassionating her,[1] and thinking how in the progress of time I too had come to be a part of the wrecked fortunes of that house, her eyes rested on me. She stared and said in a low voice, "Is it real?"

"It is I, Pip. Mr. Jaggers gave me your note yesterday, and I have lost no time."

"Thank you. Thank you.

"I want," she said, "to pursue that subject you mentioned to me when you were last here, and to show you that I am not all stone. You said, speaking for your friend, that you could tell me how to do something useful and good. Something that you would like done, is it not?"

"Something that I would like done very, very much."

"What is it?"

I began explaining to her that secret history of the partnership. I told her how I had hoped to complete the transaction out of my means, but how in this I was disappointed.

"So!" said she, assenting with her head, but not looking at me. "And how much money is wanting to complete the purchase?"

I was rather afraid of stating it, for it sounded a large sum. "Nine hundred pounds."

---

1. **compassionating her:** sympathizing deeply with her; being compassionate.

"If I give you the money for this purpose, will you keep my secret as you have kept your own?"

"Quite as faithfully."

"And your mind will be more at rest?"

"Much more at rest."

"Are you very unhappy now?"

"I am far from happy, Miss Havisham; but I have other causes of disquiet than any you know of. They are the secrets I have mentioned."

After a little while, she raised her head and looked at the fire again.

"Can I only serve you, Pip, by serving your friend? Regarding that as done, is there nothing I can do for you yourself?"

"Nothing. I thank you for the question. I thank you even more for the tone of the question. But, there is nothing."

She presently rose from her seat and looked about for the means of writing. There were none there, and she took from her pocket a yellow set of ivory tablets, mounted in tarnished gold, and wrote upon them with a pencil in a case of tarnished gold that hung from her neck.

"You are still on friendly terms with Mr. Jaggers?"

"Quite. I dined with him yesterday."

"This is an authority to him to pay you that money, to lay out at your discretion for your friend. I keep no money here; but if you would rather Mr. Jaggers knew nothing of the matter, I will send it to you."

"Thank you, Miss Havisham; I have not the least objection to receiving it from him."

She read me what she had written, and it was direct and clear, and evidently intended to absolve me from any suspicion of profiting by the receipt of the money. I took the tablets from her hand and it trembled as she took off the chain to which the pencil was attached, and put it in mine.

"My name is on the first leaf. If you can ever write under my name, 'I forgive her,' though ever so long after my broken heart is dust—pray do it!"

"Oh, Miss Havisham," said I, "I can do it now. I want forgiveness and direction far too much to be bitter with you."

She turned her face to me for the first time since she had averted it, and to my amazement, I may even add to my terror, dropped on her knees at my feet with her folded hands raised. To see her with her white hair and her worn face, kneeling at my feet, gave me a shock through all my frame.

"Oh!" she cried despairingly. "What have I done! What have I done!"

"If you mean, Miss Havisham, what have you done to injure me, let me answer. Very little. I should have loved her under any circumstances. Is she married?"

"Yes!"

It was a needless question, for a new desolation in the desolate house had told me so.

"What have I done! What have I done!" She wrung her hands, and crushed her white hair, and returned to this cry over and over again. "What have I done! Until you spoke to her the other day, and until I saw in you a looking glass that showed me what I once felt myself, I did not know what I had done. What have I done! What have I done!"

"Miss Havisham," I said, when her cry had died away, "you may dismiss me from your mind and conscience. But Estella is a different case, and if you can ever undo any scrap of what you have done amiss in keeping a part of her right nature away from her, it will be better to do that than to bemoan the past through a hundred years."

"Yes, yes, I know it. But, Pip—my dear!" There was an earnest womanly compassion for me in her new affection. "My dear! Believe this: when she first came to me, I meant to save her from misery like my own. At first I meant no more. But as she grew, and promised to be very beautiful, I gradually did worse, and with my praises, and with my jewels, and with my teachings, I stole her heart away and put ice in its place."

"Better," I could not help saying, "to have left her a natural heart, even to be bruised or broken."

"If you knew all my story," she pleaded, "you would have some compassion for me and a better understanding of me."

"Miss Havisham," I answered, as delicately as I could, "I believe I may say that I do know your story, and have known it ever since I first left this neighborhood. Does what has passed between us give me any excuse for asking you a question relative to Estella?"

She was seated on the ground, with her arms on the ragged chair, and her head leaning on them. She looked full at me and replied, "Go on."

"Whose child was Estella?"

She shook her head.

"You don't know?"

She shook her head again.

"But Mr. Jaggers brought her here, or sent her here?"

"Brought her here."

"Will you tell me how that came about?"

She answered in a low whisper and with caution, "I had been shut up in these rooms a long time when I told him that I wanted a little girl to rear and love, and save from my fate. He told me that he would look about him for such an orphan child. One night he brought her here asleep, and I called her Estella."

"Might I ask her age then?"

"Two or three. She herself knows nothing, but that she was left an orphan and I adopted her."

So convinced I was of that woman's being her mother that I wanted no evidence to establish the fact in my mind. But, to any mind, the connection here was clear and straight.

What more could I hope to do by prolonging the interview? I had succeeded on behalf of Herbert, Miss Havisham had told me all she knew of Estella, I had said and done what I could to ease her mind.

Twilight was closing in when I went downstairs into the natural air. I called to the woman who had opened the gate when I entered that I would not trouble her just yet, but would walk round the place before leaving. For I had a presentiment that I should never be there again, and I felt that the dying light was suited to my last view of it.

I made my way to the ruined garden. I went all round it; round by the corner where Herbert and I had fought our battle; round by the paths where Estella and I had walked. So cold, so lonely, so dreary all!

Passing on into the front courtyard, I hesitated whether to call the woman to let me out at the locked gate, of which she had the key, or first to go upstairs and assure myself that Miss Havisham was as safe and well as I had left her. I took the latter course and went up.

I looked into the room where I had left her, and I saw her seated in the ragged chair upon the hearth close to the fire, with her back toward me. In the moment when I was withdrawing my head to go quietly away, I saw a great flaming light spring up. In the same moment I saw her running at me, shrieking, with a whirl of fire blazing all about her, and soaring at least as many feet about her head as she was high.

I had a double-caped greatcoat on, and over

my arm another thick coat. I got them off, closed with her, threw her down, and got them over her; I dragged the great cloth from the table for the same purpose, and with it dragged down the heap of rottenness in the midst and all the ugly things that sheltered there. The closer I covered her, the more wildly she shrieked and tried to free herself. I knew that we were on the floor by the great table, and that patches of tinder yet alight were floating in the smoky air, which a moment ago had been her faded bridal dress.

Then I looked round and saw the disturbed beetles and spiders running away over the floor, and the servants coming in with breathless cries at the door. She was insensible, and I was afraid to have her moved, or even touched. Assistance was sent for, and I held her until it came, as if I unreasonably fancied that if I let her go, the fire would break out again and consume her. When I got up, on the surgeon's coming to her with other aid, I was astonished to see that both my hands were burned; for I had no knowledge of it through the sense of feeling.

On examination it was pronounced that she had received serious hurts, but that the danger lay mainly in the nervous shock. By the surgeon's directions, her bed was carried into that room and laid upon the great table, which happened to be well suited to the dressing of her injuries. When I saw her again, an hour afterward, she lay indeed where I had seen her strike her stick, and had heard her say she would lie one day.

Toward midnight she began to wander in her speech and said innumerable times, in a low solemn voice, "What have I done!" And then, "When she first came, I meant to save her from misery like mine." And then, "Take the pencil and write under my name, 'I forgive her'!" She never changed the order of these three sentences.

As I could do no service there, and as I had, nearer home, that pressing reason for anxiety and fear, I decided that I would return by the early morning coach. At about six o'clock of the morning, therefore, I leaned over her and touched her lips with mine, just as they said, "Take the pencil and write under my name, 'I forgive her.'"

Chapter 36

Pip hears more about Provis.

My hands had been dressed twice or thrice in the night, and again in the morning. My left arm was a good deal burned to the elbow, and less severely as high as the shoulder; it was very painful, but I felt thankful it was no worse. My right hand was not so badly burned but that I could move the fingers. My left hand and arm I carried in a sling; and I could only wear my coat like a cloak, loose over my shoulders and fastened at the neck.

Herbert devoted the day to attending on me. He was the kindest of nurses, and at stated times took off the bandages and steeped them in the cooling liquid that was kept ready, and put them on again, with a patient tenderness that I was deeply grateful for.

Neither of us spoke of the boat, but we thought of it. That was made apparent by our avoidance of the subject and by our agreeing—without agreement—to make my recovery of the use of my hands a question of so many hours, not of so many weeks.

My first question when I saw Herbert had been, of course, whether all was well down the river.

"I sat with Provis last night, Handel, two good hours. Do you know, Handel, he improves?"

"I said to you I thought he was softened when I last saw him."

"So you did. And so he is. He was very communicative last night, and told me more of his life. You remember his breaking off here about some woman that he had had great trouble with? He went into that part of his life, and a dark wild part it is. Shall I tell you?"

"Tell me by all means!"

"It seems, that the woman was a young woman, and a jealous woman, and a revengeful woman; revengeful, Handel, to the last degree."

"To what last degree?"

"Murder! She was tried for it, and Mr. Jaggers defended her, and the reputation of that defense first made his name known to Provis. It was another and a stronger woman who was the victim, and there had been a struggle—in a barn."

"Was the woman brought in guilty?"

"No; she was acquitted. This acquitted young woman and Provis had a little child, a little child of whom Provis was exceedingly fond. On the evening of the very night when the object of her jealousy was strangled, the young woman presented herself before Provis for one moment, and swore that she would destroy the child (which was in her possession), and he should never see it again; then she vanished. You don't think your breathing is affected, my dear boy? You seem to breathe quickly."

"Perhaps I do, Herbert. Did the woman keep her oath?"

"There comes the darkest part of Provis' life. She did."

"That is, he says she did."

"Why, of course, my dear boy," returned Herbert, in a tone of surprise, and again bending forward to get a nearer look at me. "He says it all. I have no other information."

"No, to be sure."

"Now, whether," pursued Herbert, "he had used the child's mother ill or well, Provis doesn't say; but she had shared some four or five years of the wretched life he described to us at this fireside, and he seems to have felt pity for her. Therefore, fearing he should be called upon to depose[1] about this destroyed child, and so be the cause of her death, he hid himself (much as he grieved for the child), kept himself dark, as he says, out of the way and out of the trial, and was only vaguely talked of as a certain man called Abel, out of whom the jealousy arose. After the acquittal she disappeared, and thus he lost the child and the child's mother."

"I want to ask——"

"A moment, my dear boy, and I have done. That evil genius, Compeyson, the worst of scoundrels, knowing of his keeping out of the way at that time, of course afterward held the knowledge over his head as a means of keeping him poorer and working him harder."

"I want to know," said I, "and particularly, Herbert, whether he told you when this happened?"

"Particularly? Let me remember, then, what he said as to that. His expression was, 'a round score o' year ago, and a'most directly after I took up wi' Compeyson.' How old were you when you came upon him in the little churchyard?"

"I think in my seventh year."

"Aye. It had happened some three or four years then, he said, and you brought into his mind the little girl so tragically lost, who would have been about your age."

"Herbert," said I, after a short silence, "the man we have hiding down the river is Estella's father."

---

1. **depose** (dĭ-pōz'): here used in the legal sense, to testify under oath.

Chapter 37

Pip receives a mysterious letter.

Early next morning I took my way to Little Britain. Although I had sent Mr. Jaggers a brief account of the accident as soon as I had arrived in town, yet I had to give him all the details now. My narrative finished, I then produced Miss Havisham's authority to receive the nine hundred pounds for Herbert. Mr. Jaggers' eyes retired a little deeper into his head when I handed him the tablets, but he presently handed them over to Wemmick with instructions to draw the check for his signature. From Little Britain I went, with my check in my pocket, to Miss Skiffins' brother, the accountant; and he going straight to Clarriker's and bringing Clarriker to me, I had the great satisfaction of concluding that arrangement. It was the only good thing I had done, and the only completed thing I had done, since I was first apprised of my great expectations.

Clarriker informed me that he would now be able to establish a small branch house in the East and that Herbert in his new partnership capacity would go out and take charge of it. And now indeed I felt as if my last anchor were loosening its hold, and I should soon be driving with the winds and waves.

We had now got into the month of March. My left arm took in the natural course so long to heal that I was still unable to get a coat on. My right arm was tolerably restored—disfigured, but fairly serviceable.

On a Monday morning, when Herbert and I were at breakfast, I received the following letter from Wemmick by the post.

Walworth. Burn this as soon as read. Early in the week, or say Wednesday, you might do what you know of, if you felt disposed to try it. Now burn.

When I had shown this to Herbert and had put it in the fire—but not before we had both got it by heart—we considered what to do. For, of course, my being disabled could now be no longer kept out of view.

"I have thought it over again and again," said Herbert, "and I think I know a better course than taking a Thames waterman. Take Startop. A good fellow, a skilled hand, fond of us, and enthusiastic and honorable."

I had thought of him more than once.

"But how much would you tell him, Herbert?"

"It is necessary to tell him very little. Let him suppose it a mere freak, but a secret one, until the morning comes; then let him know that there is urgent reason for your getting Provis aboard and away. You go with him?"

"No doubt."

"Where?"

It seemed to me almost indifferent what port we made for—Hamburg, Rotterdam, Antwerp—the place signified little, so that he was out of England. Any foreign steamer that fell in our way and would take us up would do. I had always proposed to myself to get him well down the river in the boat; certainly well beyond Gravesend, which was a critical place for search or inquiry if suspicion were afoot. As foreign steamers would leave London at about the time of high water, our plan would be to get down the river by a previous ebb tide, and lie by in some quiet spot until we could pull off to one. The time when one would be due where we lay, wherever that might be, could be calculated pretty nearly, if we made inquiries beforehand.

Herbert assented to all this, and we went out immediately after breakfast to pursue our investigations. We found that a steamer for Hamburg was likely to suit our purpose best, and we directed our thoughts chiefly to that vessel. But we noted down what other foreign steamers would leave London with the same tide, and we satisfied ourselves that we knew the build and color of each. We then separated for a few hours; I to get at once such passports as were necessary; Herbert, to see Startop at his lodgings. When we met again at one o'clock I, for my part, was prepared with passports; Herbert had seen Startop, and he was more than ready to join.

Those two would pull a pair of oars, we settled, and I would steer; our charge would be sitter, and keep quiet. We arranged that Herbert should prepare Provis to come down to some stairs hard by the house, on Wednesday, when he saw us approach, and not sooner; that all arrangements with him should be concluded that Monday night. These precautions well understood by both of us, I went home.

On opening the outer door of our chambers with my key, I found a letter in the box, directed to me—a very dirty letter, though not ill written. It had been delivered by hand and its contents were these:

If you are not afraid to come to the old marshes tonight or tomorrow night at nine, and to come to the little sluice house by the limekiln, you had better come. If you want information regarding *your uncle Provis*, you had better come and tell no one and lose no time. *You must come alone.* Bring this with you.

What to do now, I could not tell. And the worst was that I must decide quickly, or I should miss the afternoon coach, which would take me down in time for tonight. Tomorrow night I could not think of going, for it would be too close upon the time of the flight. For anything I knew, the information might have some important bearing on the flight itself. I resolved to go.

I had to read this mysterious epistle again, twice, before its injunction to me to be secret got into my mind. Yielding to it, I left a note in pencil to Herbert, telling him that I had decided to hurry down and back to ascertain for myself how Miss Havisham was faring. I caught the coach just as it came out of the yard. I was the only inside passenger, jolting away knee-deep in straw. And now I began to wonder at myself for being in the coach, and to doubt whether I had sufficient reason for being there, and to consider whether I should get out presently and go back, and to argue against ever heeding an anonymous communication, and, in short, to pass through all those phases of contradiction and indecision to which I suppose very few hurried people are strangers. Still, the reference to Provis by name mastered everything. I reasoned that in case any harm should befall him through my not going, how could I ever forgive myself!

It was dark before we got down. Avoiding the Blue Boar, I put up at an inn of minor reputation down the town and ordered some dinner. While it was preparing, I went to Satis House and inquired for Miss Havisham; she was still very ill, though considered something better.

As I was not able to cut my dinner, the old landlord with a shining bald head did it for me. This bringing us into conversation, he was so good as to entertain me with my own story—of course with the popular feature that Pumblechook was my earliest benefactor and the founder of my fortunes.

"Do you know the young man?" said I.

"Know him?" repeated the landlord. "Ever since he was—no height at all."

"Does he ever come back to this neighborhood?"

"Aye, he comes back," said the landlord, "to his great friends, now and again, and gives the cold shoulder to the man that made him."

"What man is that?"

"Him that I speak of," said the landlord. "Mr. Pumblechook."

"Is he ungrateful to no one else?"

"No doubt he would be, if he could," returned the landlord, "but he can't. And why? Because Pumblechook done everything for him."

"Does Pumblechook say so?"

"Say so!" replied the landlord. "He han't no call to say so."

"But does he say so?"

"It would turn a man's blood to white wine winegar to hear him tell of it, sir," said the landlord.

I thought, "Yet Joe, dear Joe, *you* never tell of it. Long-suffering and loving Joe, *you* never complain. Nor you, sweet-tempered Biddy!"

I had never been struck at so keenly for my thanklessness to Joe, as through the brazen impostor Pumblechook. The falser he, the truer Joe; the meaner he, the nobler Joe.

My heart was deeply and most deservedly humbled as I mused over the fire for an hour or more. The striking of the clock aroused me, and I got up and had my coat fastened round my neck, and went out. I had previously sought in my pockets for the letter, that I might refer to it again, but I could not find it, and was uneasy to think that it must have been dropped in the straw of the coach. I knew very well, however, that the appointed place was the little sluice house by the lime-kiln on the marshes, and the hour nine. Toward the marshes I now went straight, having no time to spare.

Chapter 38

Trabb's boy leads a rescue party.

It was a dark night, there was a melancholy wind, and the marshes were very dismal. A stranger would have found them insupportable, and even to me they were so oppressive that I hesitated, half inclined to go back. It was a half hour before I drew near to the kiln. The lime was burning with a sluggish, stifling smell, but the fires were made up and left, and no workmen were visible. Hard by was a small stone quarry.

Coming up to the marsh level out of this excavation, I saw a light in the old sluice house. I quickened my pace and knocked at the door. There was no answer, and I knocked again. No answer still, and I tried the latch.

The door yielded. Looking in, I saw a lighted candle on a table, a bench, and a mattress on a truckle bedstead.[1] As there was a loft above, I called, "Is there anyone here?" but no voice answered. Then I looked at my watch, and finding that it was past nine, called again, "Is there anyone here?" There being still no answer, I went out at the door, irresolute what to do.

It was beginning to rain fast. Seeing nothing, I turned back into the house. While I was considering that someone must have been there lately and must soon be coming back, or the candle would not be burning, it came into my head to look if the wick were long. I had taken up the candle in my hand, when it was extinguished by some violent shock, and the next thing I comprehended was that I had been caught in a strong running noose, thrown over my head from behind.

"Now," said a suppressed voice with an oath, "I've got you!"

"What is this?" I cried, struggling. "Who is it? Help, help, help!"

Not only were my arms pulled close to my sides, but the pressure on my bad arm caused me exquisite pain. A strong man's hand was

---

1. **truckle bedstead:** low bed on wheels, usually rolled underneath another bed.

set against my mouth to deaden my cries, and with a hot breath always close to me, I struggled ineffectually in the dark until I was fastened tight to the wall. "And now," said the suppressed voice with another oath, "call out again, and I'll make short work of you!"

Faint and sick with pain, I tried to ease my arm, but I was bound too tight. After groping about for a little, he began to strike a light. Presently I saw his lips breathing on the tinder, and then a flare of light flashed up and showed me Orlick.

Whom I had looked for, I don't know. I had not looked for him. Seeing him, I felt that I was in a dangerous strait indeed, and I kept my eyes upon him.

He lighted the candle from the flaring match with great deliberation, and dropped the match, and trod it out. Then he put the candle away from him on the table, so that he could see me, and sat with his arms folded on the table, and looked at me. I made out that I was fastened to a stout perpendicular ladder a few inches from the wall — a fixture there — the means of ascent to the loft above.

"Now," said he, when we had surveyed one another for some time, "I've got you."

"Why have you lured me here?"

"Don't you know?" said he, with a deadly look.

"Why have you set upon me in the dark?"

"Because I mean to do it all myself. One keeps a secret better than two. Oh, you enemy, you enemy!"

His enjoyment of the spectacle I furnished, as he sat with his arms folded on the table, shaking his head at me, made me tremble. As I watched him in silence, he put his hand into the corner at his side, and took up a gun with a brass-bound stock.

"Do you know this?" said he, making as if he would take aim at me. "Do you know where you saw it afore? Speak, wolf!"

"Yes," I answered.

"You cost me that place.[2] You did. Speak!"

"What else could I do?"

"You did that, and that would be enough, without more. How dared you come betwixt me and a young woman I liked?"

"When did I?"

"When didn't you? It was you as always give Old Orlick a bad name to her."

"You gave it to yourself; you gained it for yourself. I could have done you no harm, if you had done yourself none."

"You're a liar. And you'll take any pains, and spend any money, to drive me out of this country, will you?" said he, repeating my words to Biddy in the last interview I had with her. "Now, I'll tell you a piece of information. It was never so worth your while to get me out of this country as it is tonight." As he shook his heavy hand at me, with his mouth snarling like a tiger's, I felt that it was true.

"What are you going to do to me?"

"I'm a-going," said he, bringing his fist down upon the table with a heavy blow, and rising as the blow fell, to give it greater force, "I'm a-going to have your life!"

He leaned forward staring at me, slowly unclenched his hand and drew it across his mouth as if his mouth watered for me, and sat down again.

"You was always in Old Orlick's way since ever you was a child. You goes out of his way this present night. He'll have no more on you. You're dead."

I felt that I had come to the brink of my grave. For a moment I looked wildly round my trap for any chance of escape; but there was none.

"More than that," said he, "I won't have a

---

2. **that place:** Orlick's position at Miss Havisham's house.

rag of you, I won't have a bone of you, left on earth. I'll put your body in the kiln—I'd carry two such to it, on my shoulders—and, let people suppose what they may of you, they shall never know nothing."

My mind with inconceivable rapidity followed out all the consequences of such a death. Estella's father would believe I had deserted him, would be taken, would die accusing me; even Herbert would doubt me when he compared the letter I had left for him with the fact that I had called at Miss Havisham's gate for only a moment; Joe and Biddy would never know how sorry I had been that night.

Orlick had been drinking, and his eyes were red and bloodshot. Around his neck was slung a tin bottle. He brought the bottle to his lips and took a fiery drink from it.

"Wolf!" said he, folding his arms again. "Old Orlick's a-going to tell you somethink. It was you as did for your shrew sister."

"It was you, villain," said I.

"I tell you it was your doing—I tell you it was done through you," he retorted, catching up the gun, and making a blow with the stock at the vacant air between us. "I come upon her from behind, as I come upon you tonight. I giv' it her! I left her for dead, and if there had been a limekiln as nigh her as there is now nigh you, she shouldn't have come to life again. But it warn't Old Orlick as did it; it was you. You was favored, and he was bullied and beat. Old Orlick bullied and beat, eh? Now you pays for it. You done it; now you pays for it."

He drank again, and became more ferocious. He took up the candle, and shading it with his murderous hand so as to throw its light on me, stood before me, looking at me and enjoying the sight.

"Wolf, I'll tell you something more. It was Old Orlick as you tumbled over on your stairs

that night. And why was Old Orlick there? I'll tell you something more, wolf. You and her *have* pretty well hunted me out of this country, so far as getting a easy living in it goes, and I've took up with new companions and new masters. Some of 'em writes my letters when I wants 'em wrote. They writes fifty hands; they're not like sneaking you as writes but one. I've had a firm mind and a firm will to have your life, since you was down here at your sister's burying. I han't seen a way to get you safe, and I've looked arter you to know your ins and outs. For, says Old Orlick to himself, 'Somehow or another I'll have him!' What! When I looks for you, I finds your Uncle Provis, eh?

"*You* with a uncle, too! But when Old Orlick come for to hear that your Uncle Provis had mostlike wore the leg iron wot Old Orlick had picked up on these meshes ever so many year ago, and wot he kept by him till he dropped your sister with it—when he come to hear that—hey?—"

In his savage taunting, he flared the candle so close at me that I turned my face aside to save it from the flame.

"Ah!" he cried, laughing, after doing it again. "The burned child dreads the fire! Old Orlick knowed you was burned, Old Orlick knowed you was a-smuggling your Uncle Provis away, Old Orlick's a match for you and knowed you'd come tonight! Now I'll tell you something more, wolf, and this ends it. There's them that's as good a match for your Uncle Provis as Old Orlick has been for you. There's them that can't and that won't have Magwitch—yes, *I* know the name!—alive in the same land with them, and that's had sure information of him when he was alive in another land, as that he shouldn't leave it unbeknown and put them in danger. P'raps it's them that writes fifty hands, and that's not like sneaking you as writes but one. 'Ware

Compeyson, Magwitch, and the gallows!"

There was a clear space of a few feet between the table and the opposite wall. Within this space he now slouched backward and forward with his hands hanging loose and heavy at his sides, and with his eyes scowling at me. I had no grain of hope left.

Of a sudden he stopped, took the cork out of his bottle, and tossed it away. Light as it was, I heard it fall like a plummet.[3] He swallowed slowly, tilting up the bottle by little and little, and now he looked at me no more. The last few drops of liquor he poured into the palm of his hand and licked up. Then with a sudden hurry of violence and swearing horribly, he threw the bottle from him, and stooped; and I saw in his hand a stone hammer with a long heavy handle.

I shouted out with all my might, and struggled with all my might. It was only my head and my legs that I could move, but to that extent I struggled with all the force that was within me. In the same instant I heard responsive shouts, saw figures and a gleam of light dash in at the door, heard voices and tumult, and saw Orlick emerge from a struggle of men, clear the table at a leap, and fly out into the night!

After a blank, I found that I was lying unbound on the floor, in the same place, with my head on someone's knee. My eyes were fixed on the ladder against the wall when there came between me and it, a face. The face of Trabb's boy!

"I think he's all right!" said Trabb's boy, in a sober voice. "But ain't he just pale, though!"

At these words, the face of him who supported me looked over into mine, and I saw my supporter to be——

"Herbert! Great Heaven!"

"Softly," said Herbert. "Gently, Handel. Don't be too eager."

"And our old comrade, Startop!" I cried, as he too bent over me.

"Remember what he is going to assist us in," said Herbert, "and be calm."

The allusion made me spring up, though I dropped again from the pain in my arm. "The time has not gone by, Herbert, has it? What night is tonight? How long have I been here?"

"The time has not gone by. It is still Monday night."

"Thank God!"

"And you have all tomorrow, Tuesday, to rest in," said Herbert. "Can you stand?"

---

3. **plummet:** a lead weight attached to a string, used by carpenters to test the straightness of a wall.

"Yes, yes," said I, "I can walk, I have no hurt but in this throbbing arm."

They did what they could until we could get to the town and obtain some cooling lotion to put upon it. Trabb's boy—Trabb's overgrown young man now—went before us with a lantern. But the moon was a good two hours higher than when I had last seen the sky, and the night though rainy was much lighter.

Entreating Herbert to tell me how he had come to my rescue, I learned that I had in my hurry dropped the letter, open, in our chambers, where he, coming home to bring with him Startop, found it very soon after I was gone. Its tone made him uneasy, and he set off for the coach office with Startop. Finding that the afternoon coach was gone, he resolved to follow in a post chaise. So he and Startop arrived at the Blue Boar, fully expecting there to find me, or tidings of me; but, finding neither, went on to Miss Havisham's, where they lost me. Hereupon they went back to the hotel to refresh themselves and to get someone to guide them upon the marshes. Among the loungers under the Boar's archway happened to be Trabb's boy. Thus Trabb's boy became their guide, and with him they went out to the sluice house. Herbert left his guide and Startop on the edge of the quarry, and went on by himself, and stole round the house two or three times. As he could hear nothing but indistinct sounds of one deep rough voice, he began to doubt whether I was there, when suddenly I cried out loudly, and he answered the cries, and rushed in, closely followed by the other two.

We relinquished all thoughts of pursuing Orlick at that time. For the present, under the circumstances, we deemed it prudent to make rather light of the matter to Trabb's boy. When we parted, I presented him with two guineas (which seemed to meet his views),

and told him that I was sorry ever to have had an ill opinion of him (which made no impression on him at all).

It was daylight when we reached the Temple, and I went at once to bed, and lay in bed all day.

My terror, as I lay there, of falling ill and being unfitted for tomorrow, was so besetting that I wonder it did not disable me of itself. I started at every footstep and every sound, believing that he was discovered and taken, and this was the messenger to tell me so. I persuaded myself that I knew he was taken. It happened sometimes that in the mere escape of a fatigued mind, I dozed for some moments or forgot; then I would say to myself with a start, "Now it has come, and I am turning delirious!"

They kept me very quiet all day, and kept my arm constantly dressed, and gave me cooling drinks. Whenever I fell asleep, I awoke with the notion I had had in the sluice house, that a long time had elapsed, and the opportunity to save him was gone. About midnight I got out of bed and went to Herbert with the conviction that I had been asleep for four-and-twenty hours, and that Wednesday was past. It was the last self-exhausting effort of my fretfulness, for after that, I slept soundly.

Wednesday morning was dawning when I looked out of the window. Herbert lay asleep in his bed, and our old fellow student lay asleep on the sofa. I could not dress myself without help, but I made up the fire, which was still burning, and got some coffee ready for them. In good time they too started up strong and well, and we admitted the sharp morning air at the windows, and looked at the tide that was still flowing toward us.

"When it turns at nine o'clock," said Herbert cheerfully, "look out for us, and stand ready, you over there at Mill Pond Bank!"

Chapter 39

An informer goes to his death.

It was one of those March days when the sun shines hot and the wind blows cold: when it is summer in the light, and winter in the shade. We had our peacoats[1] with us, and I took a bag. Of all my worldly possessions, I took no more than the few necessaries that filled the bag. Where I might go, what I might do, or when I might return, were questions utterly unknown to me; nor did I vex my mind with them, for it was wholly set on Provis' safety. We loitered down to the Temple stairs, and stood loitering there, as if we were not quite decided to go upon the water at all. Of course I had taken care that the boat should be ready, and everything in order. After a little show of indecision, we went on board and cast off; Herbert in the bow, I steering. It was then about high water—half-past eight.

Our plan was this. The tide, beginning to run down at nine, and being with us until three, we intended still to creep on after it had turned, and row against it until dark. We should then be well in those long reaches below Gravesend, between Kent and Essex, where the river is broad and solitary, where the waterside inhabitants are very few, and where lone public houses are scattered here and there, of which we could choose one for a resting place. There, we meant to lie by all night. The steamer for Hamburg and the steamer for Rotterdam would start from London at about nine on Thursday morning. We should know at what time to expect them and would hail the first; so that if by any accident we were not taken aboard, we should have another chance. We knew the distinguishing marks of each vessel.

Old London Bridge was soon passed, and old Billingsgate market with its oyster boats and Dutchmen, and we were in among the tiers of shipping. Here were steamers, loading and unloading goods, and here, at her moorings, was tomorrow's steamer for Rotterdam, of which we took good notice; and here tomorrow's for Hamburg, under whose bowsprit[2] we crossed. And now I, sitting in the stern, could see, with a faster beating heart, Mill Pond Bank and Mill Pond stairs.

"Is he there?" said Herbert.

"Not yet."

"Right! He was not to come down till he saw us. Can you see his signal!"

"Not well from here; but I think I see it. Now I see him! Pull both. Easy, Herbert. Oars!"

We touched the stairs lightly for a single moment, and he was on board and we were off again. He had a boat cloak with him, and a black canvas bag, and he looked as like a river pilot as my heart could have wished.

"Dear boy!" he said, putting his arm on my shoulder, as he took his seat. "Faithful dear boy, well done. Thank'ee, thank'ee!"

Again among the tiers of shipping, in and out, avoiding rusty chain cables, frayed hempen hawsers,[3] and bobbing buoys, sinking for the moment, floating broken baskets, scattering floating chips of wood and shaving, cleaving floating scum of coal in and out—upon the clearer river, where the ships' boys might take their fenders[4] in, no longer fishing in

---

1. **peacoats:** thick, woolen jackets, often worn by seamen.

2. **bowsprit** (bou'sprĭt'): a pole or spar projecting from the bow (front) of a ship.
3. **hawsers** (hô'zərz): ropes.
4. **fenders:** anything used as padding against the sides of ships, to protect them from damage in bumping against wharves or other ships.

troubled waters with them over the side, and where the festooned sails might fly out to the wind.

At the stairs where we had taken him aboard, and ever since, I had looked warily for any token of our being suspected. I had seen none. He had his boat cloak on him, and looked, as I have said, a natural part of the scene. It was remarkable that he was the least anxious of any of us.

"If you knowed, dear boy," he said to me, "what it is to sit here alonger my dear boy and have my smoke, arter having been day by day betwixt four walls, you'd envy me. But you don't know what it is."

"I think I know the delights of freedom," I answered.

"Ah," said he, shaking his head gravely. "But you don't know it equal to me. You must have been under lock and key, dear boy, to know it equal to me — but I ain't a-going to be low."

"If all goes well," said I, "you will be perfectly free and safe again, within a few hours."

"Well," he returned, drawing a long breath, "I hope so."

We made what way we could until the sun went down. At length we descried a light and a roof, and presently afterward ran alongside a little causeway made of stones. I stepped ashore, and found the light to be in the window of a public house. It was a dirty place enough, and I dare say not unknown to smuggling adventurers; but there was a good fire in the kitchen, and there were eggs and bacon to eat. Also, there were two double-bedded rooms — "such as they were," the landlord said. No other company was in the house than the landlord, his wife, and a grizzled male creature, the "Jack"[5] of the little causeway.

---

5. **Jack:** a sailor.

With this assistant, I went down to the boat again, and we all came ashore, and brought out the oars, and rudder, and boathook, and all else, and hauled her up for the night. We made a very good meal by the kitchen fire, and then apportioned the bedrooms: Herbert and Startop were to occupy one; I and our charge the other. We considered ourselves well off, for a more solitary place we could not have found.

While we were comforting ourselves by the fire after our meal, the Jack asked me if we had seen a four-oared galley going up with the tide. When I told him no, he said she must have gone down then, and yet she "took up too," when she left there.

"They must ha' thought better on't for some reason or another," said the Jack, "and gone down."

"A four-oared galley did you say?" said I.

"A four," said the Jack, "and two sitters."

"Did they come ashore here?"

"They put in with a stone two-gallon jar for some beer."

This dialogue made us all uneasy, and me very uneasy. The dismal wind was muttering round the house, the tide was flapping at the shore, and I had a feeling that we were caged and threatened. A four-oared galley hovering about in so unusual a way as to attract this notice was an ugly circumstance that I could not get rid of. When I had induced Provis to go up to bed, I went outside with my two companions (Startop by this time knew the state of the case) and held council. On the whole we deemed it the better course to lie where we were, until within an hour or so of the steamer's time, and then to get out in her track, and drift easily with the tide. Having settled to do this, we returned into the house and went to bed.

I lay down with the greater part of my clothes on, and slept well for a few hours.

When I awoke, the wind had risen. I looked out of the window. It commanded the causeway where we had hauled up our boat, and I saw two men looking into her. They passed by under the window, looking at nothing else, and they did not go down to the landing place but struck across the marshes. In that light, however, I soon lost them, and feeling very cold, lay down to think of the matter and fell asleep again.

We were up early. As we walked to and fro, all four together, I deemed it right to recount what I had seen. Again our charge was the least anxious of the party. However, I proposed that he and I should walk away together to a distant point, and that the boat should take us aboard there. This being considered a good precaution, soon after breakfast he and I set forth, without saying anything at the tavern.

He smoked his pipe as we went along, and sometimes stopped to clap me on the shoulder. One would have supposed that it was I who was in danger, not he, and that he was reassuring me. We spoke very little.

We waited until we saw our boat coming round. We got aboard easily and rowed out into the track of the steamer. By that time it wanted but ten minutes of one o'clock, and we began to look out for her smoke.

But it was half past one before we saw her smoke, and soon after we saw behind it the smoke of another steamer. As they were coming on at full speed, we got the two bags ready, and took that opportunity of saying goodbye to Herbert and Startop. We had all shaken hands cordially, and neither Herbert's eyes nor mine were quite dry, when I saw a four-oared galley shoot out from under the bank but a little way ahead of us, and row out into the same track.

I called to Herbert and Startop to keep before the tide, that the steamer might see us lying by for her, and adjured Provis to sit quite still, wrapped in his cloak. He answered cheerily, "Trust to me, dear boy," and sat like a statue. Meanwhile the galley, which was skillfully handled, had crossed us, let us come up with her, and fallen alongside. Leaving just room enough for the play of the oars, she kept alongside, drifting when we drifted, and pulling a stroke or two when we pulled. Of the two sitters, one held the rudder lines, and looked at us attentively—as did all the rowers; the other sitter was wrapped up, much as Provis was, and seemed to shrink and whisper some instruction to the steerer as he looked at us. Not a word was spoken in either boat.

Startop could make out, after a few minutes, which steamer was first, and gave me the word "Hamburg," in a low voice as we sat face to face. She was nearing us very fast, and the beating of her paddles grew louder and louder. I felt as if her shadow were absolutely upon us, when the galley hailed us. I answered.

"You have a returned transport there," said the man who held the lines. "That's the man, wrapped in the cloak. His name is Abel Magwitch, otherwise Provis. I apprehend that man, and call upon him to surrender, and you to assist."

At the same moment, without giving any audible direction to his crew, he ran the galley aboard of us. They had pulled one sudden stroke ahead, had got their oars in, had run athwart us, and were holding on to our gunwale before we knew what they were doing. This caused great confusion on board of the steamer, and I heard them calling to us, and heard the order given to stop the paddles, and heard them stop, but felt her driving down upon us irresistibly. In the same moment, I saw the steersman of the galley lay his hand on his prisoner's shoulder, and saw that both boats were swinging round with the force of the tide, and saw that all hands on board the steamer were running forward frantically. Still in the same moment, I saw the prisoner start up, lean across his captor, and pull the cloak from the neck of the shrinking sitter in the galley. Still in the same moment, I saw that the face disclosed was the face of the other convict of long ago. Still in the same moment, I saw the face tilt backward with a white terror on it that I shall never forget, and heard a great cry on board the steamer and a loud splash in the water, and felt the boat sink from under me.

It was but for an instant that I seemed to struggle; that instant past I was taken on board the galley. Herbert was there, and Startop was there; but our boat was gone, and the two convicts were gone.

What with the cries aboard the steamer, and the furious blowing off of her steam, and her driving on, and our driving on, I could not at first distinguish sky from water or shore from shore; but the crew of the galley righted her with great speed, and, pulling certain swift strong strokes ahead, lay upon their oars, every man looking silently and eagerly at the water astern. Presently a dark object was seen in it, bearing toward us on the tide. No man spoke, but the steersman kept the boat straight and true before it. As it came nearer, I saw it to be Magwitch, swimming, but not freely. He was taken on board, and instantly manacled at the wrists and ankles.

The galley was kept steady, and the silent eager lookout at the water was resumed. But the Rotterdam steamer now came up, and apparently not understanding what had happened, came on at speed. By the time she had been hailed and stopped, both steamers were drifting away from us, and we were rising and falling in a troubled wake of water. The lookout was kept long after all was still again, and the two steamers were gone; but everybody knew that it was hopeless now.

At length we gave it up, and pulled under the shore toward the tavern we had lately left. Here, I was able to get some comforts for Magwitch—Provis no longer—who had received some very severe injury in the chest and a deep cut in the head.

He told me that he believed himself to have gone under the keel of the steamer, and to have been struck on the head in rising. The injury to his chest (which rendered his breathing extremely painful) he thought he had received against the side of the galley. He added that he did not pretend to say what he might have done to Compeyson, but that in the moment of his laying his hand on his cloak to identify him, that villain had staggered up and back, and they had both gone overboard together; when the sudden wrenching of Magwitch out of our boat had capsized us. He told me in a whisper that they had gone down, fiercely locked in each other's arms, and that there had been a struggle underwater, and that he had disengaged himself, struck out, and swum away.

I never had any reason to doubt the exact truth of what he had told me. The officer who steered the galley gave the same account of their going overboard.

When I asked this officer's permission to change the prisoner's wet clothes by purchasing any spare garments I could get at the public house, he gave it readily, merely observing that he must take charge of everything his prisoner had about him. So the pocketbook which had once been in my hands passed into the officer's. He further gave me leave to accompany the prisoner to London, but declined to accord that grace to my two friends.

We remained at the public house until the tide turned, and then Magwitch was carried down to the galley and put on board. Herbert and Startop were to get to London by land, as soon as they could. We had a doleful parting, and when I took my place by Magwitch's side, I felt that that was my place henceforth while he lived.

For now my repugnance to him had all melted away, and in the hunted, wounded, shackled creature who held my hand in his, I only saw a man who had meant to be my benefactor, and who had felt affectionately, gratefully, and generously toward me with great constancy through a series of years. I only saw in him a much better man than I had been to Joe.

His breathing became more difficult and painful as the night drew on, and often he could not repress a groan. I tried to rest him on the arm I could use, in any easy position; but it was dreadful to think that I could not be sorry at heart for his being badly hurt, since it was unquestionably best that he should die. That there were, still living, people enough who were able and willing to identify him, I could not doubt. That he would be leniently treated, I could not hope—he who had been presented in the worst light at his trial, who had since broken prison and been tried again, who had returned from transportation under a life sentence, and who had occasioned the death of the man who was the cause of his arrest.

As we returned toward the setting sun we had yesterday left behind us, and as the stream of our hopes seemed all running back, I told him how grieved I was to think he had come home for my sake.

"Dear boy," he answered, "I'm quite content to take my chance. I've seen my boy, and he can be a gentleman without me."

No. I had thought about that while we had been there side by side. I foresaw that, being convicted, his possessions would be forfeited to the Crown.[6]

"Look'ee here, dear boy," said he. "It's best

as a gentleman should not be knowed to belong to me now. Only come to see me as if you come by chance alonger Wemmick. Sit where I can see you when I am swore to, for the last o' many times, and I don't ask no more."

"I will never stir from your side," said I, "when I am suffered to be near you. Please God, I will be as true to you as you have been to me!"

I felt his hand tremble as it held mine, and he turned his face away as he lay in the bottom of the boat, and I heard that old sound in his throat—softened now, like all the rest of him. It was a good thing that he had touched this point, for it put into my mind what I might not otherwise have thought of until too late: that he need never know how his hopes of enriching me had perished.

Chapter 40

Mr. Wemmick takes a walk.

He was taken to the Police Court next day, and would have been immediately committed for trial, but that it was necessary to send down for an old officer of the prison ship from which he had once escaped, to speak to his identity. Nobody doubted it; but Compeyson, who had meant to depose to it, was dead. I had gone direct to Mr. Jaggers at his private house, on my arrival overnight, to retain his assistance, but he told me that no power on earth could prevent its going against us.

I imparted to Mr. Jaggers my design of keeping him in ignorance of the fate of his wealth. Mr. Jaggers was angry with me for having "let it slip through my fingers," and said we must try at all events for some of it. But he did not conceal from me that although there might be many cases in which forfeiture would not be

---

6. **forfeited** (fôr'fĭt-əd) **to the Crown:** taken by the government, which had the legal right to the possessions of a prisoner in Magwitch's position.

exacted, there were no circumstances in this case to make it one of them. I understood that very well. I was not related to the outlaw, or connected with him by any recognizable tie. I had no claim, and I resolved that my heart should never be sickened with the hopeless task of attempting to establish one.

There appeared to be reason for supposing that the drowned informer had hoped for a reward, and had obtained some accurate knowledge of Magwitch's affairs. When his body was found, many miles from the scene of his death, notes were still legible, folded in a case he carried. Among these were the name of a banking house in New South Wales where a sum of money was, and the designation of certain lands of considerable value. Both those heads of information were in a list that Magwitch, while in prison, gave to Mr. Jaggers, of the possessions he supposed I should inherit. His ignorance, poor fellow, at last served him; he never mistrusted but that my inheritance was quite safe, with Mr. Jaggers' aid.

After three days' delay, he was committed to take his trial at the next session, which would come on in a month.

It was at this dark time of my life that Herbert returned home one evening, a good deal cast down, and said:

"My dear Handel, I fear I shall soon have to leave you."

His partner having prepared me for that, I was less surprised than he thought.

"We shall lose a fine opportunity if I put off going to Cairo, and I am very much afraid I must go, Handel, when you most need me."

"Herbert, I shall always need you, because I shall always love you; but my need is no greater now than at another time."

"You will be so lonely."

"I have not leisure to think of that," said I. "You know that I am always with him to the full extent of the time allowed, and that I should be with him all day long, if I could. And when I come away from him, you know that my thoughts are with him."

"My dear fellow," said Herbert, "let the near prospect of our separation be my justification for troubling you about yourself. Have you thought of your future? In this branch house of ours, Handel, we must have a——"

I saw that his delicacy was avoiding the right word, so I said, "A clerk."

"A clerk. And I hope it is not at all unlikely that he may expand into a partner. Now, Handel—in short, my dear boy, will you come to me? Clara and I have talked about it again and again," Herbert pursued, "and the dear little thing begged me only this evening to say that if you will live with us when we come together, she will do her best to make you happy."

I thanked her heartily, and I thanked him heartily, but said I could not yet make sure of joining him.

"But if you thought, Herbert, that you could, without doing any injury to your business, leave the question open for a little while——"

"For any while," cried Herbert. "Six months, a year!"

"Not so long as that," said I. "Two or three months at most."

Herbert was highly delighted when we shook hands on this arrangement, and said he could now take courage to tell me that he believed he must go away at the end of the week.

On the Saturday in that same week, I took my leave of Herbert as he sat on one of the seaport mail coaches. I then went to my lonely home—if it deserved the name, for it was now no home to me, and I had no home anywhere.

On the stairs I encountered Wemmick. I had not seen him alone since the disastrous issue of the attempted flight; and he had come, in his private and personal capacity, to say a few words in reference to that failure.

"The late Compeyson," said Wemmick, "had by little and little got at the bottom of half of the regular business now transacted, and it was from the talk of some of his people in trouble that I heard what I did. I kept my ears open until I heard that he was absent, and I thought that would be the best time for making the attempt. I can only suppose now that it was a part of his policy, as a very clever man, habitually to deceive his own instruments. You don't blame me, I hope, Mr. Pip? I'm sure I tried to serve you, with all my heart."

"I am as sure of that, Wemmick, as you can be, and I thank you most earnestly for all your interest and friendship."

I invited Wemmick to come upstairs and refresh himself with a glass of grog before walking to Walworth. He accepted but appeared rather fidgety.

"What do you think of my meaning to take a holiday on Monday, Mr. Pip?"

"Why, I suppose you have not done such a thing these twelve months."

"These twelve years, more likely," said Wemmick. "Yes. I'm going to take a holiday. More than that; I'm going to take a walk. More than that; I'm going to ask you to take a walk with me. It ain't a long walk, and it's an early one. Say it might occupy you (including breakfast on the walk), from eight to twelve. Couldn't you stretch a point and manage it?"

He had done so much for me that this was very little to do for him. I said I could manage it—would manage it—and he was so very much pleased that I was pleased too.

Punctual to my appointment, I rang at the Castle gate on the Monday morning, and was received by Wemmick himself, who struck me as looking tighter[1] than usual, and having a sleeker hat on.

When we had fortified ourselves with biscuits and were going out for the walk, I was considerably surprised to see Wemmick take up a fishing rod and put it over his shoulder. "Why, we are not going fishing!" said I. "No," returned Wemmick, "but I like to walk with one."

I thought this odd; however, I said nothing, and we set off. We went toward Camberwell Green, and when we were thereabouts, Wemmick said suddenly:

"Halloa! Here's a church!"

There was nothing very surprising in that; but again, I was rather surprised when he said, as if he were animated by a brilliant idea:

"Let's go in!"

We went in, Wemmick leaving his fishing rod in the porch, and looked all round. In the meantime, Wemmick was diving into his coat pockets and getting something out of paper there.

"Halloa!" said he. "Here's a couple of pair of gloves! Let's put 'em on!"

As the gloves were white kid gloves, I now began to have my strong suspicions. They were strengthened into certainty when I beheld the Aged enter at a side door, escorting a lady.

"Halloa!" said Wemmick. "Here's Miss Skiffins! Let's have a wedding."

The clerk and clergyman then appeared, and true to his notion of seeming to do it all without preparation, I heard Wemmick say to himself as he took something out of his waistcoat pocket before the service began, "Halloa! Here's a ring!"

I acted in the capacity of best man to the bridegroom, while the responsibility of giving

---

1. **tighter:** neater.

the lady away devolved upon the Aged.

"Now, Mr. Pip," said Wemmick, triumphantly shouldering the fishing rod as we came out, "let me ask you whether anybody would suppose this to be a wedding party!"

Breakfast had been ordered at a pleasant little tavern a mile or so away. We had an excellent breakfast, and when anyone declined anything on the table, Wemmick said, "Provided by contract, you know; don't be afraid of it!" I drank to the new couple, drank to the Aged, drank to the Castle, saluted the bride at parting, and made myself as agreeable as I could.

Chapter 41

Pip takes final leave of Magwitch.

He lay in prison very ill during the whole interval between his committal for trial and the coming round of the sessions. He had broken two ribs, they had wounded one of his lungs, and he breathed with great pain and difficulty, which increased daily. Being far too ill to remain in the common prison, he was removed, after the first day or so, into the infirmary. This gave me opportunities of being with him that I could not otherwise have had. And but for his illness he would have been put into irons, for he was regarded as a determined prison breaker, and I know not what else.

Although I saw him every day, it was for only a short time. I do not recollect that I once saw any change in him for the better; he wasted and became slowly weaker and worse day by day from the day when the prison door closed upon him.

When the sessions came round, Mr. Jaggers caused an application to be made for the postponement of his trial and was refused. The trial came on at once, and when he was put to the bar, he was seated in a chair. No objection was made to my getting close to the dock and holding the hand that he stretched out to me.

The trial was very short and very clear. Such things as could be said for him were said — how he had taken to industrious habits, and had thriven[1] lawfully and reputably. But nothing could unsay the fact that he had returned, and was there in presence of the judge and jury. It was impossible not to try him for that, and do otherwise than find him guilty.

At that time it was the custom (as I learned from my terrible experience of that sessions) to devote a concluding day to the passing of sentences, and to make a finishing effect with the sentence of death. I saw two-and-thirty men and women put before the judge to receive that sentence together. Foremost among the two-and-thirty was he; seated, that he might get breath enough to keep life in him.

Penned in the dock, as I again stood outside it at the corner with his hand in mine, were the two-and-thirty men and women; some defiant, some stricken with terror, some sobbing and weeping, some covering their faces, some staring gloomily about. There had been shrieks from among the women convicts, but they had been stilled, and a hush had succeeded.

Then, the judge addressed them. Among the wretched creatures before him whom he must single out for special address, was one who almost from his infancy had been an offender against the laws; who, after repeated imprisonments and punishments, had been at length sentenced to exile for a term of years; and who, under circumstances of great violence and daring, had made his escape and been resentenced to exile for life. That miserable man would seem for a time to have

---

1. **thriven** (thrīv′ən): thrived; succeeded; prospered.

become convinced of his errors, when far removed from the scenes of his old offenses, and to have lived a peaceable and honest life. But in a fatal moment, he had quitted his haven of rest and repentance, and had come back to the country where he was proscribed.[2] Being here presently denounced, he had for a time succeeded in evading the officers of justice, but being at length seized while in the act of flight, he had resisted them, and had — he best knew whether by express design, or in the blindness of his hardihood — caused the death of his denouncer, to whom his whole career was known. The appointed punishment for his return to the land that had cast him out being death, he must prepare himself to die.

The sun was striking in at the great windows of the court, through the glittering drops of rain upon the glass, and it made a broad shaft of light between the two-and-thirty and the judge. Rising for a moment, a distinct speck of face in this way of light, the prisoner said, "My Lord, I have received my sentence of death from the Almighty, but I bow to yours," and sat down again.

I began that night to write out a petition to the Home Secretary of State, setting forth my knowledge of him and how it was that he had come back for my sake. I wrote as fervently and pathetically as I could, and when I had finished it and sent it in, I wrote out other petitions to such men in authority as I hoped were the most merciful, and drew up one to the Crown itself. For several days and nights after he was sentenced I took no rest, except when I fell asleep in my chair, but was wholly absorbed in these appeals. The daily visits I could make him were shortened now, and he was more strictly kept. Nobody was hard with him or with me. There was duty to be done, and it was done, but not harshly. Sometimes

_____
2. **proscribed:** banished.

he was almost unable to speak; then, he would answer me with slight pressures on my hand, and I grew to understand his meaning very well.

The number of days had risen to ten, when I saw a greater change in him than I had seen yet. His eyes were turned toward the door, and lighted up as I entered.

"Dear boy," he said, as I sat down by his bed, "I thought you was late. But I knowed you couldn't be that."

"It is just the time," said I. "I waited for it at the gate."

"You always waits at the gate; don't you, dear boy?"

"Yes. Not to lose a moment of the time."

"Thank'ee, dear boy, thank'ee. God bless you! You've never deserted me, dear boy."

I pressed his hand in silence, for I could not forget that I had once meant to desert him.

"And what's the best of all," he said, "you've been more comfortable alonger me since I was under a dark cloud, than when the sun shone. That's best of all."

He lay on his back, breathing with great difficulty. Do what he would, and love me though he did, the light left his face ever and again, and a film came over the placid look at the white ceiling.

"Are you in much pain today?"

"I don't complain of none, dear boy."

"You never do complain."

He had spoken his last words. He smiled, and I understood his touch to mean that he wished to lift my hand, and lay it on his breast. I laid it there, and he smiled again, and put both his hands upon it.

The allotted time ran out while we were thus; but, looking round, I found the governor of the prison standing near me, and he whispered, "You needn't go yet." I thanked him gratefully, and asked, "Might I speak to him, if he can hear me?"

The governor stepped aside and beckoned the officer away. The change, though it was made without noise, drew back the film from the placid look at the white ceiling, and he looked most affectionately at me.

"Dear Magwitch, I must tell you, now, at last. You understand what I say?"

A gentle pressure on my hand.

"You had a child once, whom you loved and lost."

A stronger pressure on my hand.

"She lived and found powerful friends. She is living now. She is a lady and very beautiful. And I love her!"

With a last faint effort, which would have been powerless but for my yielding to it, and assisting it, he raised my hands to his lips. Then he gently let it sink upon his breast again, with his own hands lying on it. The placid look at the white ceiling came back, and passed away, and his head dropped quietly on his breast.

I thought of the two men who went up into the Temple to pray, and I knew there were no better words that I could say beside his bed than, "O Lord, be merciful to him, a sinner!"[3]

Chapter 42

An old friend comes to Pip's rescue.

Now that I was left wholly to myself, I gave notice of my intention to quit the chambers in the Temple as soon as my tenancy could legally determine, and in the meanwhile to underlet them.[1] I was in debt, and had scarcely any money, and I began to be seriously alarmed by the state of my affairs.

---

3. **"O Lord, . . . sinner!":** From Luke 18:10.
1. **I gave . . . them:** Pip gave notice that he would leave his apartment as soon as his lease could be terminated and in the meantime would sublet the rooms.

Moreover, I was falling very ill. The late stress upon me had enabled me to put off illness, but not to put it away; I knew that it was coming on me now.

For a day or two I lay on the sofa, or on the floor—anywhere, according as I happened to sink down—with a heavy head and aching limbs, and no purpose, and no power. Then there came one night which appeared of great duration, and which teemed with anxiety and horror; and when in the morning I tried to sit up in my bed and think of it, I found I could not do so. Then I saw two men looking at me.

"What do you want?" I asked, starting. "I don't know you."

"Well, sir," returned one of them, bending down and touching me on the shoulder, "you're arrested."

"What is the debt?"

"Hundred and twenty-three pound, fifteen, six. Jeweler's account, I think."

I made some attempt to get up and dress myself. When I next attended to them, they were standing a little off from the bed, looking at me. I still lay there.

"You see my state," said I. "I would come with you if I could; but indeed I am quite unable. If you take me from here, I think I shall die by the way."

As they hang in my memory by only this one slender thread, I don't know what they did, except that they forbore to[2] remove me.

That I had a fever and was avoided, that I suffered greatly, I know of my own remembrance, and did in some sort know at the time. I was delirious and sometimes struggled with real people, in the belief that they were murderers, but above all, I knew that there was a constant tendency in all these people to settle down into the likeness of Joe.

---

2. **forbore to**: refrained from; did not.

After I had turned the worst point of my illness, I opened my eyes in the night, and I saw in the great chair at the bedside, Joe. I opened my eyes in the day, and, sitting on the window seat, smoking his pipe in the shaded open window, still I saw Joe. I asked for cooling drink, and the dear hand that gave it me was Joe's. I sank back on my pillow after drinking, and the face that looked so hopefully and tenderly upon me was the face of Joe.

At last one day I took courage, and said, "*Is it Joe?*"

And the dear old home voice answered, "Which it air, old chap."

"Oh, Joe, you break my heart! Look angry at me, Joe. Strike me, Joe. Tell me of my ingratitude. Don't be so good to me!"

For Joe had actually laid his head down on the pillow at my side and put his arm round my neck, in his joy that I knew him.

"Which dear old Pip, old chap," said Joe, "you and me was ever friends. And when you're well enough to go out for a ride—what larks!"

After which, Joe withdrew to the window and stood with his back toward me, wiping his eyes. And as my extreme weakness prevented me from getting up and going to him, I lay there, penitently whispering, "O God, bless him! O God, bless this gentle Christian man!"

Joe's eyes were red when I next found him beside me, but I was holding his hand and we both felt happy.

"Have you been here all the time, dear Joe?"

"Pretty nigh, old chap. For, as I says to Biddy when the news of your being ill were brought by letter, you might be amongst strangers, and you and me having been ever friends, a wisit at such a moment might not prove unacceptabobble. And Biddy, her word were, 'Go to him, without loss of time.'"

There Joe cut himself off short, and informed me I was to be talked to in great moderation. So I lay quiet while he proceeded to indite a note to Biddy, with my love in it.

Evidently Biddy had taught Joe to write. As I lay in bed looking at him, it made me, in my weak state, cry with pleasure to see the pride with which he set about his letter. He got on very well indeed, and when he had signed his name, he got up and hovered about the table, trying the effect of his performance from various points of view, with unbounded satisfaction.

Not to make Joe uneasy by talking too much, even if I had been able to talk much, I deferred asking him about Miss Havisham until next day. He shook his head when I then asked him if she had recovered.

"Is she dead, Joe?"

"Why, you see, old chap," said Joe, by way of getting at it by degrees, "I wouldn't go so far as to say that, for that's a deal to say; but she ain't living."

"Did she linger long, Joe?"

"Arter you was took ill, pretty much about what you might call a week," said Joe, still determined, on my account, to come at everything by degrees.

"Dear Joe, have you heard what becomes of her property?"

"Well, old chap," said Joe, "it do appear that she had settled the most of it on Miss Estella. But she had wrote out a little coddleshell[3] in her own hand a day or two afore the accident, leaving a cool four thousand to Mr. Matthew Pocket. And why do you suppose, above all things, Pip, she left that cool four thousand unto him? 'Because of Pip's account of him the said Matthew.' I am told by Biddy, that air the writing," said Joe.

---

3. **coddleshell:** Joe means *codicil* (kŏd′ə-sĭl), an item of instruction added to a will.

This account gave me great joy, as it perfected the only good thing I had done. I asked Joe whether any of the other relations had any legacies.

"Miss Sarah," said Joe, "she has twenty-five pound perannium fur to buy pills. Miss Georgiana, she has twenty, Mrs.—what's the name of them wild beasts with humps?"

"Camels?" said I, wondering why he could want to know.

Joe nodded. "Mrs. Camels," by which I understood he meant Camilla, "she have five pounds fur to buy rushlights to put her in spirits when she wake up in the night. And now," said Joe, "you can take in one more shovelful today. Old Orlick he's been a-bustin' open a dwelling 'ouse."

"Whose?" said I.

"Not, I grant you, but what his manners is given to blusterous. Still, an Englishman's 'ouse is his castle, and castles must not be busted 'cept when done in wartime. And wotsume'er the failings on his part, he were a corn and seedsman in his heart."

"Is it Pumblechook's house that has been broken into, then?"

"That's it, Pip," said Joe, "and they took his till, and they took his cashbox, and they drinked his wine, and they partook of his wittles, and they slapped his face, and they pulled his nose, and they tied him up to his bedpust, and they stuffed his mouth full of flowering annuals to perwent his crying out. But he knowed Orlick, and Orlick's in the county jail."

By these approaches we arrived at unrestricted conversation. I was slow to gain strength, but I did slowly and surely become less weak, and Joe stayed with me, and I fancied I was little Pip again.

For the tenderness of Joe was so beautifully proportioned to my need that I was like a child in his hands. He would sit and talk to me in the old confidence, and with the old simplicity, and in the old unassertive protecting way, so that I would half believe that all my life since the days of the old kitchen was one of the mental troubles of the fever that was gone.

We looked forward to the day when I should go out for a ride. And when the day came and an open carriage was got into the lane, Joe wrapped me up, took me in his arms, and carried me down to it, as if I were still the small helpless creature to whom he had so abundantly given of the wealth of his great nature. When we got back again and he carried me across the court and up the stairs, I thought of that eventful Christmas Day when he had carried me over the marshes. We had not yet made any allusion to my change of fortune, nor did I know how much of my late history he was acquainted with.

"Have you heard, Joe," I asked him that evening, as he smoked his pipe at the window, "who my patron was?"

"I heered," returned Joe, "as it were not Miss Havisham, old chap."

"Did you hear who it was, Joe?"

"Well! I heered as it were a person what sent the person what give you the bank notes at the Jolly Bargemen, Pip."

"So it was."

"Astonishing!" said Joe, in the placidest way.

"Did you hear that he was dead, Joe?"

"Which? Him as sent the bank notes, Pip?"

"Yes."

"I think," said Joe, after meditating a long time, and looking rather evasively at the window seat, "as I *did* hear tell that how he were something or another in a general way in that direction."

"Did you hear anything of his circumstances, Joe?"

"Not partickler, Pip."

"If you would like to hear, Joe—" I was beginning, when Joe got up and came to my sofa.

"Look'ee here, old chap," said Joe, bending over me. "Ever the best of friends; ain't us, Pip?"

I was ashamed to answer him.

"Wery good, then," said Joe, as if I *had* answered, "that's all right; that's agreed upon. Then why go into subjects, old chap, which as betwixt two sech must be forever onnecessary?"

The delicacy with which Joe dismissed this theme made a deep impression on my mind. But whether Joe knew how poor I was, and how my great expectations had all dissolved, like our own marsh mists before the sun, I could not understand.

Another thing in Joe that I could not understand when it first began to develop itself, was this. As I became stronger and better, Joe became a little less easy with me. In my weakness and entire dependence on him, the dear fellow had fallen into the old tone, and called me by the old names, the dear "old Pip, old chap," that now were music in my ears. I too had fallen into the old ways, only happy and thankful that he let me. But imperceptibly, though I held by them fast, Joe's hold upon them began to slacken; and I soon began to understand that the fault of it was all mine.

It was on the third or fourth occasion of my going out walking that I saw this change in him very plainly. We had been sitting in the bright warm sunlight, looking at the river, and I chanced to say as we got up:

"See, Joe! I can walk quite strongly. Now, you shall see me walk back by myself."

"Do not overdo it, Pip," said Joe; "but I shall be happy fur to see you able, sir."

The last word grated on me; but how could I remonstrate! I walked no farther than the gate of the gardens, and then pretended to be weaker than I was, and asked Joe for his arm. Joe gave it me, but was thoughtful.

I, for my part, was thoughtful too. I was ashamed to tell him exactly how I was placed. He would want to help me out of his little savings, I knew, and I knew that he ought not to help me, and that I must not suffer him to do it.

It was a thoughtful evening with both of us. Before we went to bed, I had resolved that I would wait over tomorrow, tomorrow being Sunday, and would begin my new course with the new week. On Monday morning I would speak to Joe and tell him what I had in my thoughts.

We had a quiet day on the Sunday, and we rode out into the country, and then walked in the fields. At night, when I had gone to bed, Joe came into my room as he had done all through my recovery. He asked me if I felt sure that I was as well as in the morning.

"Yes, dear Joe, quite."

"And are always a-getting stronger, old chap?"

"Yes, dear Joe, steadily."

Joe patted the coverlet on my shoulder with his great good hand and said, in what I thought a husky voice, "Good night!"

When I got up in the morning, refreshed and stronger yet, I was full of my resolution to tell Joe all, without delay. I went to his room, and he was not there. Not only was he not there, but his box was gone.

I hurried then to the breakfast table and on it found a letter. These were its brief contents.

Not wishful to intrude I have departured fur you are well again dear Pip and will do better without

Jo.

P.S. Ever the best of friends.

Enclosed in the letter was a receipt for the debt and costs on which I had been arrested.

Down to that moment I had vainly supposed that my creditor had withdrawn until I should be quite recovered. I had never dreamed of Joe's having paid the money; but Joe had paid it, and the receipt was in his name.

What remained for me now, but to follow him to the dear old forge and there to have out my disclosure to him, and my penitent remonstrance with him, and there to relieve my mind and heart of another idea, which had begun as a vague something lingering in my thoughts and had formed into a settled purpose.

The purpose was that I would go to Biddy, that I would show her how humbled and repentant I came back, that I would tell her how I had lost all I once hoped for. Then I would say to her, "Biddy, I think you once liked me very well, when my errant heart, even while it strayed away from you, was quieter and better with you than it ever has been since. If you can like me only half as well once more, if you can take me with all my faults and disappointments on my head, if you can receive me like a forgiven child, I hope I am a little worthier of you than I was—not much, but a little. And, Biddy, it shall rest with you to say whether I shall work at the forge with Joe, or whether I shall try for any different occupation down in this country, or whether we shall go away to a distant place where an opportunity awaits me which I set aside when it was offered, until I knew your answer. And now, dear Biddy, if you can tell me that you will go through the world with me, you will surely make it a better world for me, and me a better man for it, and I will try hard to make it a better world for you."

Such was my purpose. After three days more of recovery, I went down to the old place, to put it in execution. And how I sped in it is all I have left to tell.

Chapter 43

Biddy and Joe have news for Pip.

The tidings of my high fortunes having had a heavy fall had got down to my native place and its neighborhood before I got there. I found the Blue Boar in possession of the intelligence, and I found that it made a great change in the Boar's demeanor.

It was evening when I arrived, much fatigued by the journey. The Boar could not put me into my usual bedroom, which was engaged (probably by someone who had expectations), and could only assign me a very indifferent chamber among the pigeons. But I had as sound a sleep and the quality of my dreams was about the same as in the best bedroom.

Early in the morning I strolled round by Satis House. There were printed bills on the gate announcing a sale by auction of the household furniture and effects next week. The house itself was to be sold as old building materials, and pulled down. The ivy had been torn down, and much of it trailed low in the dust and was withered already. Stepping in for a moment at the open gate and looking around me with the uncomfortable air of a stranger who had no business there, I saw the auctioneer's clerk walking on the casks and telling them off for the information of a catalogue compiler, pen in hand, who made a temporary desk of the wheeled chair I had so often pushed along.

It was the pleasanter to turn to Biddy and to Joe. I went toward them slowly, for my limbs were weak, but with a sense of increasing relief as I drew nearer to them, and a sense of leaving arrogance and untruthfulness farther and farther behind.

The June weather was delicious. The sky was blue, the larks were soaring high over the green corn. I thought all that countryside more beautiful and peaceful by far than I had ever known it to be yet. Many pleasant pictures of the life that I would lead there, and of the change for the better that would come over my character when I had a guiding spirit at my side whose simple faith and clear home wisdom I had proved, beguiled my way. They awakened a tender emotion in me, for my heart was softened by my return, and such a change had come to pass that I felt like one who was toiling home barefoot from distant travel, and whose wanderings had lasted many years.

The schoolhouse where Biddy was mistress, I had never seen, but the little roundabout lane by which I entered the village for quietness' sake took me past it. I was disappointed to find that the day was a holiday, no children were there, and Biddy's house was closed. Some hopeful notion of seeing her, busily engaged in her daily duties, before she saw me, had been in my mind and was defeated.

But the forge was a very short distance off, and I went toward it under the sweet green limes, listening for the clink of Joe's hammer. But the clink of Joe's hammer was not in the midsummer wind.

Almost fearing without knowing why to come in view of the forge, I saw it at last, and saw that it was closed. No gleam of fire, no glittering shower of sparks, no roar of bellows; all shut up, and still.

But the house was not deserted, and the best parlor seemed to be in use, for there were white curtains fluttering in its window, and the window was open and gay with flowers. I went softly toward it, meaning to peep over the flowers, when Joe and Biddy stood before me, arm in arm.

At first Biddy gave a cry, as if she thought it was my apparition, but in another moment

she was in my embrace. I wept to see her, and she wept to see me; I, because she looked so fresh and pleasant; she, because I looked so worn and white.

"But, dear Biddy, how smart you look!"

"Yes, dear Pip."

"And, Joe, how smart *you* look!"

"Yes, dear old Pip, old chap."

I looked at both of them, from one to the other, and then—

"It's my wedding day," cried Biddy, in a burst of happiness, "and I am married to Joe!"

They had taken me into the kitchen, and I had laid my head down on the old deal table. Biddy held one of my hands to her lips, and Joe's restoring touch was on my shoulder. "Which he warn't strong enough, my dear, to be surprised," said Joe. And Biddy said, "I ought to have thought of it, dear Joe, but I was

too happy." They were both so overjoyed to see me, so proud to see me, so touched by my coming to them, so delighted that I should have come by accident to make their day complete!

My first thought was one of great thankfulness that I had never breathed this last baffled hope to Joe. How often, while he was with me in my illness, had it risen to my lips.

"Dear Biddy," said I, "you have the best husband in the whole world, and if you could have seen him by my bed you would have— But no, you couldn't love him better than you do."

"No, I couldn't indeed," said Biddy.

"And, dear Joe, you have the best wife in the whole world, and she will make you as happy as even you deserve to be, you dear, good, noble Joe!"

Joe looked at me with a quivering lip, and fairly put his sleeve before his eyes.

"And Joe and Biddy both, receive my humble thanks for all you have done for me, and all I have so ill repaid! And when I say that I am going away within the hour, for I am soon going abroad, and I shall never rest until I have worked for the money with which you have kept me out of prison, and have sent it to you, don't think, dear Joe and Biddy, that if I could repay it a thousand times over, I suppose I could cancel a farthing of the debt I owe you, or that I would do so if I could!"

They were both melted by these words, and both entreated me to say no more.

"But I must say more. Dear Joe, I hope you will have children to love, and that some little fellow will sit in this chimney corner of a winter night who may remind you of another little fellow gone out of it forever. Don't tell him, Joe, that I was thankless; don't tell him, Biddy, that I was ungenerous and unjust; only tell him that I honored you both, because you were both so good and true, and that, as your child, I said it would be natural to him to grow up a much better man than I did."

"I ain't a-going," said Joe, from behind his sleeve, "to tell him nothink o' that natur, Pip. Nor Biddy ain't."

"And now, though I know you have already done it in your own kind hearts, pray tell me, both, that you forgive me! Pray let me hear you say the words, that I may carry the sound of them away with me, and then I shall be able to believe that you can trust me, and think better of me, in the time to come!"

"Oh, dear old Pip, old chap," said Joe. "God knows as I forgive you, if I have anythink to forgive!"

"Amen! And God knows I do!" echoed Biddy.

"Now let me go up and look at my old little room and rest there a few minutes by myself. And then when I have eaten and drunk with you, go with me as far as the fingerpost,[1] dear Joe and Biddy, before we say goodbye!"

I sold all I had, and put aside as much as I could for my creditors—who gave me ample time to pay them in full—and I went out and joined Herbert. Within a month, I had quitted England, and within two months I was clerk to Clarriker and Co., and within four months I assumed my first undivided responsibility. For the beam across the parlor ceiling at Mill Pond Bank had then ceased to tremble under the old purser's growls and was at peace, and Herbert had gone away to marry Clara, and I was left in sole charge of the Eastern Branch until he brought her back.

Many a year went round before I was a partner in the house; but I lived happily with Herbert and his wife, and lived frugally, and paid my debts, and maintained a constant correspondence with Biddy and Joe. It was not until I became third in the firm that Clarriker betrayed me to Herbert; but he then declared that the secret of Herbert's partnership had been long enough upon his conscience, and he must tell it. So he told it, and Herbert was as much moved as amazed, and the dear fellow and I were not the worse friends for the long concealment. I must not leave it to be supposed that we were ever a great house, or that we made mints of money. We were not in a grand way of business, but we had a good name, and worked for our profits, and did very well. We owed so much to Herbert's ever cheerful industry and readiness that I often wondered how I had conceived that old idea of his inaptitude, until I was one day enlightened by the reflection that perhaps the inaptitude had never been in him at all, but had been in me.

---

1. **fingerpost:** a signpost, often shaped like a pointing hand or finger.

Chapter 44

Pip and Estella meet again.

For eleven years I had not seen Joe nor Biddy when, upon an evening in December, an hour or two after dark, I laid my hand softly on the latch of the old kitchen door. I touched it so softly that I was not heard, and I looked in unseen. There, smoking his pipe in the old place by the kitchen firelight, as hale and as strong as ever, though a little gray, sat Joe; and there, fenced into the corner with Joe's leg, and sitting on my own little stool looking at the fire, was—I again!

"We giv' him the name of Pip for your sake, dear old chap," said Joe, delighted when I took another stool by the child's side, "and we hoped he might grow a little bit like you, and we think he do."

I thought so too, and I took him out for a walk next morning, and we talked immensely, understanding one another to perfection. And I took him down to the churchyard, and set him on a certain tombstone there, and he showed me from that elevation which stone was sacred to the memory of Philip Pirrip, late of this parish, and Also Georgiana, Wife of the Above.

"Biddy," said I, when I talked with her after dinner, as her little girl lay sleeping in her lap, "you must give Pip to me, one of these days; or lend him, at all events."

"No, no," said Biddy gently. "You must marry."

"So Herbert and Clara say, but I don't think I shall, Biddy. I have so settled down in their home that it's not at all likely, I am already quite an old bachelor."

Biddy looked down at her child, and put its little hand to her lips, and then put the good matronly hand with which she had touched it into mine. There was something in the action and in the light pressure of Biddy's wedding ring that had a very pretty eloquence in it.

"Dear Pip," said Biddy, "you are sure you don't fret for her?"

"Oh, no—I think not, Biddy."

"Tell me as an old friend. Have you quite forgotten her?"

"My dear Biddy, I have forgotten nothing in my life that ever had a foremost place there, and little that ever had any place there. But that poor dream, as I once used to call it, has all gone by, Biddy, all gone by!"

Dickens originally wrote only two more paragraphs to end the story, but because so many of his friends were dissatisfied with the conclusion, he rewrote the final paragraphs of the novel to read as follows. You will find the original ending on page 715.

Nevertheless, I knew while I said those words that I secretly intended to revisit the site of the old house that evening, alone, for her sake. Yes, even so. For Estella's sake.

I had heard of her as leading a most unhappy life, and as being separated from her husband, who had used her with great cruelty, and who had become quite renowned as a compound of pride, avarice, brutality, and meanness. And I had heard of the death of her husband, from an accident consequent on his ill treatment of a horse. This release had befallen her some two years before; for anything I knew she was married again.

The early dinner hour at Joe's left me time to walk over to the old spot before dark. There was no house now, no brewery, no building whatever left, but the wall of the old garden. The cleared space had been enclosed with a rough fence, and looking over it, I saw that some of the old ivy had struck root anew and was growing green on low quiet mounds of ruin. A gate in the fence standing ajar, I pushed it open and went in.

A cold silvery mist had veiled the afternoon, and the moon was not yet up to scatter it. But the stars were shining beyond the mist, and the moon was coming, and the evening was not dark. I could trace out where every part of the old house had been and was looking along the desolate garden walk, when I beheld a solitary figure in it.

The figure showed itself aware of me as I advanced. It had been moving toward me, but it stood still. As I drew nearer, I saw it to be the figure of a woman. Then, it faltered as if much surprised, and uttered my name, and I cried out:

"Estella!"

"I am greatly changed. I wonder you know me."

The freshness of her beauty was indeed gone, but its majesty and its charm remained. Those attractions in it, I had seen before; what I had never seen before was the saddened softened light of the once proud eyes; what I had never felt before was the friendly touch of the once insensible hand.

We sat down on a bench that was near, and I said, "After so many years, it is strange that we should thus meet again, Estella, here where our first meeting was! Do you often come back?"

"I have never been here since."

"Nor I."

The moon began to rise, and I thought of the placid look at the white ceiling, which had passed away. The moon began to rise, and I thought of the pressure on my hand when I had spoken the last words he had heard on earth.

Estella was the next to break the silence.

"I have very often hoped and intended to come back, but have been prevented by many circumstances. Poor, poor old place!"

The silvery mist was touched with the first rays of the moonlight, and the same rays touched the tears that dropped from her eyes. Not knowing that I saw them, and setting herself to get the better of them, she said quietly:

"Were you wondering, as you walked along, how it came to be left in this condition?"

"Yes, Estella."

"The ground belongs to me. It is the only possession I have not relinquished. Everything else has gone from me, little by little, but I have kept this. It was the subject of the only determined resistance I made in all the wretched years."

"Is it to be built on?"

"At last it is. I came here to take leave of it before its change. And you," she said, in a voice of touching interest to a wanderer, "you live abroad still."

"Still."

"And do well, I am sure?"

"I work pretty hard for a sufficient living, and therefore—yes, I do well!"

"I have often thought of you," said Estella.

"Have you?"

"Of late, very often."

"You have always held your place in *my* heart," I answered.

And we were silent again until she spoke.

"I little thought," said Estella, "that I should take leave of you in taking leave of this spot. I am very glad to do so."

"Glad to part again, Estella? To me, parting is a painful thing. To me, the remembrance of our last parting has been ever mournful and painful."

"But you said to me," returned Estella, very earnestly, " 'God bless you, God forgive you!' And if you could say that to me then, you will not hesitate to say that to me now—now, when suffering has been stronger than all other teaching, and has taught me to understand what your heart used to be. I have been bent and broken, but—I hope—into a better shape. Be as considerate and good to me as you were, and tell me we are friends."

"We are friends," said I, rising and bending over her, as she rose from the bench.

"And will continue friends apart," said Estella.

I took her hand in mine, and we went out of the ruined place; and as the morning mists had risen long ago when I first left the forge, so the evening mists were rising now, and in all the broad expanse of tranquil light they showed to me, I saw no shadow of another parting from her.

Great Expectations originally ended with the following two paragraphs. In the original version, the final chapter was the same as the present one, up to the point where Pip tells Biddy, "that poor dream, as I once used to call it, has all gone by, Biddy, all gone by!" (See page 713.) From that point on, the original ending was as follows:

It was two years more before I saw Estella. I had heard of her as leading a most unhappy life, and as being separated from her husband, who had used her with great cruelty, and who had become quite renowned as a compound of pride, brutality, and meanness. I had heard of the death of her husband from an accident consequent on ill treating a horse, and of her being married again to a Shropshire doctor who, against his interest, had once very manfully interposed on an occasion when he was in professional attendance on Mr. Drummle, and had witnessed some outrageous treatment of her. I had heard that the Shropshire doctor was not rich, and that they lived on her own personal fortune. I was in England again —in London, and walking along Piccadilly with little Pip—when a servant came running after me to ask would I step back to a lady in a carriage who wished to speak to me. It was a little pony carriage which the lady was driving, and the lady and I looked sadly enough on one another.

"I am greatly changed, I know; but I thought you would like to shake hands with Estella too, Pip. Lift up that pretty child and let me kiss it!" (She supposed the child, I think, to be my child.) I was very glad afterward to have had the interview; for in her face and in her voice, and in her touch, she gave me the assurance that suffering had been stronger than Miss Havisham's teaching, and had given her a heart to understand what my heart used to be.

FOR STUDY AND DISCUSSION

Characters

1. In the first two stages of the novel, Pip does what other people tell him to do. Which of his actions in Stage 3 show a new independence of spirit?

2. How has Pip changed from the snob he had become? What is his new attitude toward those who had been kind to him in the past? How is this change shown in Pip's actions toward Magwitch during and after his trial?

3. In the third stage, which of Pip's experiences teach him the value of real friendship and affection? In particular, what does he learn from each of the following: meeting Clara, Herbert's fiancée; hearing the story Pumblechook has told about him; being held prisoner by Orlick; being cared for by Joe?

4. During his last visit to Satis House, Pip says to Estella, ". . . you cannot choose but remain part of my character, part of the little good in me, part of the evil. But I associate you only with the good, for you must have done me far more good than harm." Do you agree with Pip that Estella has been the source of more good than harm? Explain.

5. Although Magwitch is a criminal, Dickens treats him with compassion, and he emerges as a character of great dignity. In what way has Magwitch been the victim of injustice? How does Dickens show the good as well as the evil in Magwitch's nature?

6. In *Great Expectations*, there are a number of characters who are *foils*—that is, these characters set each other off by contrast. Biddy and Estella are foils; clearly, the reader is intended to compare their natures and their influence on Pip. In what way are Magwitch and Miss Havisham foils? Pip and Herbert? Estella and Clara? Estella and Pip?

7. Characters who do not change in the course of a literary work are *static* characters.

Characters who grow and develop are *dynamic* characters. How would you classify the following characters: Estella, Miss Havisham, Jaggers, Orlick, Herbert, Magwitch?

Plot

8. Dickens' masterful handling of plot and suspense is especially evident in his treatment of Molly. What clues does he provide to Molly's real identity? How does Molly's behavior, as observed by Pip, help to make Wemmick's story of the past convincing?

9. In this last stage of the novel, the threads of the plot come together as a logical design. Whom does Magwitch turn out to be related to? How did the other convict, Compeyson, swindle Miss Havisham? Who is Estella's mother?

10. The *climax* of a novel is usually the most exciting or dramatic part of the plot, the point at which the conflict is resolved and the outcome of the action decided. Which incident would you identify as the climax of *Great Expectations*? How does Dickens build suspense as he leads up to the climax?

11. Which of Dickens' two endings do you prefer? Why? Which do you think is most faithful to the nature of the characters involved? Does Pip, by the end of the novel, still want to marry Estella? Does Estella, because of what she has experienced, deserve to be forgiven by Pip? Is it believable that she could have come to love him? Do you think these two can still care for each other?

Setting

12. In a way, Satis House is a symbol of Miss Havisham. How has she made it reflect her own state of mind? What is suggested by the stopped clocks? The dark passageways? The yellowed bridal gown? When Pip pulls the tablecloth off the table, spiders and beetles run out of the wedding cake. What does this suggest about Miss Havisham's lost love?

Theme

13. Throughout the novel Dickens deals with the contrast between appearance and reality, illusion and substance. After Pip learns who his benefactor is, Mr. Jaggers tells him: "Take nothing on its looks; take everything on evidence. There's no better rule" (page 666). Where in the novel has Pip been influenced by "looks" rather than by "evidence"?

14. While ill with fever, Pip realizes, "My great expectations had all dissolved, like our own marsh mists before the sun." How is this statement, in a way, a summing-up of all that Pip has learned? In your own words, state what you think is the overall theme of *Great Expectations*.

LANGUAGE AND VOCABULARY

Analyzing Words from Latin Roots

Pip's first feeling toward Magwitch is one of *repugnance*—a strong dislike. The word comes from the Latin prefix *re-*, which means "back," and the verb *pugnare*, which means "to fight." From the same root come the words *pugnacious*, *pugilism*, and *impugn*. What does each of these words have to do with the original meaning "to fight"? Use a dictionary to find the answer.

Compeyson had meant to *depose* to the real identity of Magwitch. *Depose* in this sense means "to testify under oath"; a *deposition* is a person's testimony. Both words come from the Latin word *deponere*, which itself is composed of the prefix *de-*, meaning "down" and the verb *ponere*, meaning "to place or put." *Deponere* means "to put down." Tell what meaning the word *depose* has in this sentence: "Richard II was *deposed* by his cousin, Henry Bolingbroke." How are both meanings of *depose* related to the Latin meaning "to put down"?

In English the root word *ponere* often appears as *pos-*, *pose-*, *pon-* or *pone-*. Find the meanings of each of the following words by analyzing its structure. Use a dictionary if necessary.

composure   impose   postponement
depository   interpose   propose

FOR COMPOSITION

Expressing an Opinion

Write a short paper evaluating *Great Expectations* as a novel. Here are some questions to consider before you begin:

> Was the plot exciting? Did it hold your interest?
> Did you care about the characters and what happened to them?
> Were the characters and actions believable, given the setting and circumstances of the novel?
> Was the ending satisfying?
> Did the novel give you a better understanding of people and of life?

If you wish, devote a single paragraph to each of these questions. Give specific reasons based on events and characters in the novel.

Comparing the Short Story with the Novel

Reading *Great Expectations* has placed before you some examples of the qualities and characteristics of the novel as a "type," in comparison with the short story. The novel generally has more characters, for instance, and their lives can be studied in greater detail than those of the characters in a short story. Whereas the plot of a short story is usually limited to one major action, a novel may have several subplots. Compare elements of the two forms, noting their similarities and differences.

Practice in Reading and Writing

THE NOVEL

The following quotations represent brief critical comments on certain aspects of *Great Expectations*. After reading these statements of opinion, write a short essay supporting or refuting one of them on the basis of your own interpretation of the novel.

Great Expectations is in the first place a fantasy. It is a fantasy of a sort that many children have; perhaps all children have it, and certainly all lonely children, all children who feel too little wanted or appreciated, who feel the powerlessness of childhood. . . . It is a fantasy of sudden translation or sudden transformation, the fantasy of arrival at a point where yearning is magically fulfilled, commonly expressed in such phrases as "when I get rich" or "when my ship comes in." It is a fantasy of a beneficent if unpredictable universe that will someday shower us with gold without any effort or indeed any merit on our part.

> Paul Pickrel
> "Great Expectations"

[Dickens'] idea of Pip was . . . a young man who could be interpreted in detail as his character deteriorates under the stimulus of "great" or "undeserved" expectations of wealth and position. Dickens invented a series of events which would let Pip come close to ruin as a person because of his expectations, reach a climax of disappointment when they turn out to be "false" (false in the sense of caste and prestige), achieve maturity in the experience, then find gradual regeneration by learning to work for proper rewards in life. *Great Expectations* is planned on this concept of character, and all the action revolves around it.

> Earle Davis
> *The Flint and the Flame: The*
> *Artistry of Charles Dickens*

The attitude of Pip toward Magwitch in *Great Expectations* is extremely interesting. Pip is conscious all along of his ingratitude toward Joe, but far less so of his ingratitude toward Magwitch. When he discovers that the person who had loaded him with benefits for years is actually a transported convict, he falls into frenzies of disgust.

George Orwell
"Charles Dickens"

Great Expectations is the perfect expression of a phase of English society: it is a statement, to be taken as it stands, of what money can do, good and bad; of how it can change and make distinctions of class; how it can pervert virtue, sweeten manners, open up new fields of enjoyment and suspicion.

Humphrey House
The Dickens World

In "A Debt to Dickens," Pearl Buck tells how her discovery of Dickens' novels affected her life:

He opened my eyes to people, he taught me to love all sorts of people, high and low, rich and poor, the old and little children. He taught me to hate hypocrisy and pious mouthing of unctuous words. He taught me that beneath gruffness there may be kindness, and that kindness is the sweetest thing in the world, and goodness is the best thing in the world. He taught me to despise money grubbing. People today say he is obvious and sentimental and childish in his analysis of character. It may be so, and yet I have found people surprisingly like those he wrote about—the good a little less undiluted, perhaps, and the evil a little more mixed. And I do not regret that simplicity of his, for it had its own virtue. The virtue was a great zest for life. If he saw everything black and white, it was because life rushed out of him strong and clear, full of love and hate. He gave me that zest, that immense joy in life and in people, and in their variety

Do you think *Great Expectations* bears out this analysis of Dickens' work?

For Further Reading

Brontë, Charlotte, *Jane Eyre* (many editions)
> Engaged as a governess at Thornfield, Jane Eyre falls in love with her employer, a strange, moody man who harbors a tragic secret.

Buck, Pearl S., *The Good Earth* (Crowell, 1931; paperback, Pocket Books)
> This story of a peasant family, set in China during the early twentieth century, gives the reader a glimpse into a vanished way of life.

Christie, Agatha, *The Mysterious Affair at Styles* (Dodd, Mead, 1975; paperback, Bantam)
> Here is the first case solved by Hercule Poirot, Christie's most memorable sleuth.

Cooper, James Fenimore, *The Last of the Mohicans* (many editions)
> Natty Bumppo, a frontier scout (also known as Hawkeye), and his Mohican friends Chingachgook and Uncas, are the heroes, and Magua, a renegade Huron, is the villain in this exciting adventure set during the French and Indian War.

Dickens, Charles, *David Copperfield* (many editions)
> This novel, the most autobiographical of Dickens' works, is famous for its great character portraits: the impecunious Mr. Micawber, the unctuous Uriah Heep, the eccentric Betsy Trotwood, among others.

Dumas, Alexandre, *The Count of Monte-Cristo* (many editions)
> Edmond Dantès, imprisoned on a trumped-up charge, escapes from prison and returns to Marseilles as the Count of Monte-Cristo to carry out his revenge.

Golding, William, *Lord of the Flies* (Coward-McCann, 1962; paperback, Putnam)
> When they become stranded on an island after an air crash, a group of English schoolboys revert to primitive behavior.

Hemingway, Ernest, *The Old Man and the Sea* (Scribner, 1961; paperback, Scribner)
> An old fisherman pits his courage and endurance against the sea in a heroic struggle.

Kipling, Rudyard, *Kim* (many editions)
> Set in India during the period of British rule, this story tells the adventures of a young orphan, Kimball O'Hara, known as Kim.

Lipsyte, Robert, *The Contender* (Harper & Row, 1967; paperback, Bantam)
> A young boy struggles to grow up in Harlem and become a champion boxer.

Nordhoff, Charles, and James Norman Hall, *Mutiny on the Bounty* (Little, Brown, 1932; paperback, Pocket Books)
> Based on fact, this narrative tells of the voyage of the *Bounty* to the South Seas in 1787, and of the mutiny against the tyrannical and cruel Captain Bligh.

Richter, Conrad, *The Light in the Forest* (Knopf, 1953; paperback, Bantam)
> This novel, which tells of the conflicting loyalties of a white boy raised by Indians, is based on factual records of frontier life in Pennsylvania.

Steinbeck, John, *The Red Pony* (Viking Press, 1959)
> This novel contains four stories about the "coming of age" of Jody Tiflin, a boy who lives on a California ranch.

Stevenson, Robert Louis, *The Black Arrow* (Macmillan, 1962; paperback, Airmont)
> This story of adventure, romance, and intrigue takes place in fifteenth-century England during the struggle between the houses of York and Lancaster.

Twain, Mark, *The Prince and the Pauper* (many editions)
> Two look-alikes, a royal prince and a pauper's son, exchange clothes and roles in this novel set in sixteenth-century England.

Verne, Jules, *Twenty Thousand Leagues Under the Sea* (many editions)
> Aboard his submarine *Nautilus*, Captain Nemo and his crew live in isolation from society, all their needs provided by the riches of the ocean.

Reading and Writing About Literature

INTRODUCTION

Many of the compositions you will be asked to write in English class will be about the literature you read. The writing may be in response to an examination question, a homework assignment, or a research project. At times you may be assigned a topic to work on; at other times you may be instructed to choose your own subject.

In writing about literature, you make an effort to understand and respond to some aspect of a literary work or group of works. For example, you may discuss the conflict that is developed in a short story; you may give your impression of a character in a play or novel; you may compare the images in two poems; you may state the main idea of an essay. Such writing assignments are an important part of literary study, which aims at greater understanding and appreciation of the works you read.

Writing about a literary work is a way of getting to know it better. Before you write a composition about a story, a poem, a play, or a group of works, you must read and reread the material carefully. You must sort out your thoughts, consider the evidence, and reach conclusions. In putting your thoughts down on paper, you become more fully involved with the literature.

Throughout your studies you will become familiar with many elements that are useful in analyzing literary works. You can assume that your readers will understand what you mean when you refer to such elements as *plot, conflict, symbol,* or *irony*. These words are part of a common vocabulary used in writing about literature. (See the *Guide to Literary Terms and Techniques,* page 793.)

The material on the following pages offers help in planning and writing papers about literature. Here you will find suggestions for reading and analyzing literature, answering examination questions, choosing topics, gathering evidence, organizing essays, and writing and revising papers. Also included are model essays and several new selections for analysis along with suggested writing topics.

READING LITERATURE

When you read a chapter in a social studies or science textbook, you read primarily to get the facts. Your purpose may be to discover why England became a leader in the Industrial Revolution or how electricity and magnetism are related. You read chiefly to gather information that is stated *directly* on the page.

Reading literature calls for more than understanding what all the words mean and getting the facts straight. Much of the meaning of a literary work may be stated *indirectly*. For example, a writer may not *tell* you directly that a story takes place in Paris during the time of the French Revolution. However, by supplying important details, such as a description of a Paris mob storming the Bastille prison or a reference to a tumbrel (or cart) carrying aristocrats to the guillotine for execution, the writer establishes the setting for you. In other words, when you read literature, you depend a good deal on *inference*, drawing conclusions from different kinds of evidence. To read literature critically and grasp its meaning, you have to be an active reader, aware of *what* the author is doing, *how* the author is doing it, and *why*.

When you are asked to write about a literary work, be sure to read it carefully before you begin writing. Read actively, asking yourself questions as you work through the selection.

Close Reading of a Short Story

A reader who enters imaginatively into a short story reacts to the interplay of different elements: plot (the sequence of related events); characters (persons, animals, or things presented as persons); point of view (the vantage point of the narrative); setting (the time and place of the action); and theme (the underlying idea about human life). The better you, as an individual reader, understand how these elements work together, the better you will understand and appreciate the author's intent and meaning.

Here is a brief story that has been read carefully by an experienced reader. The notes in the margin show how this reader thinks in working through a story. Read the story at least twice before proceeding to the commentary on page 725. You may wish to make notes of your own on a separate sheet of paper.

The Death of the Dauphin° *Alphonse Daudet*

The little Dauphin is sick; the little Dauphin is going to die. In all the churches of the realm the Blessed Sacrament[1] is exposed night and day, and tall candles are burning for the recovery of the royal child. The streets in the old residence are sad and silent, the bells no longer ring, and carriages go at a footpace. About the palace the curious citizens watch, through the iron grilles, the porters with gilt paunches talking in the courtyards with an air of importance.

> The opening paragraph makes known the situation—the critical illness of the crown prince.
>
> It identifies the setting—France, long ago.
>
> It emphasizes the importance of the events. The entire realm is in mourning.

The whole château is in commotion. Chamberlains, major-domos,[2] run hastily up and down the marble staircases. The galleries are full of pages and courtiers in silk garments, who go from group to group asking news in undertones. On the broad steps weeping maids of honor greet one another with low courtesies,[3] wiping their eyes with pretty embroidered handkerchiefs.

> The scene shifts to the palace.
>
> Details emphasize the luxury of court life—marble staircases, silk garments, embroidered handkerchiefs.

In the orangery[4] there is a great assemblage of long-robed doctors. Through the windows they can be seen flourishing their long black sleeves and bending majestically their hammerlike wigs. The little Dauphin's governor[5] and equerry[6] walk back and forth before the door, awaiting the decision of the faculty. Scullions pass them by without saluting[7] them. The equerry swears like a heathen, the governor recites lines from Horace.[8] And meanwhile, in the direction of the stables one hears a long, plaintive neigh. It is the little Dauphin's horse, calling sadly from his empty manger.

> We now see how many people personally attend the Dauphin and how they are affected.
>
> The Dauphin's horse is neglected.

And the king? Where is *monseigneur*[9] the king? The king is all alone in a room at the end of the château. Majesties do not like to be seen weeping. As for the queen, that is a different matter. Seated at the little Dauphin's pillow, her lovely face is bathed in tears, and she sobs aloud before them all, as a linen draper's wife might do.

> We see how members of the royal family are affected.

In his lace-bedecked crib the little Dauphin, whiter than the cushions upon which he lies, is resting now with closed eyes. They think that he sleeps; but no. The little Dauphin is not asleep. He

> Main character is introduced last. Details focus on the child's privileged position and his deathly pallor.

° **Dauphin** (dō-făn′): a title used from 1349 to 1830 for the French crown prince.
1. **Blessed Sacrament:** the consecrated bread or wafer used in Holy Communion.
2. **Chamberlains, major-domos:** officials in charge of the household.
3. **courtesies:** curtseys.
4. **orangery** (ôr′ĭnj-rē): hothouse.
5. **governor:** tutor.
6. **equerry** (ĕk′wə-rē): official in charge of horses.
7. **saluting:** here, greeting.
8. **Horace:** a famous Roman poet (65–8 B.C.).
9. *monseigneur* (môn-sĕ-nyœr′): my lord.

turns to his mother, and seeing that she is weeping, he says to her:

"Madame queen, why do you weep? Is it because you really believe that I am going to die?"

The queen tries to reply. Sobs prevent her from speaking.

"Pray do not weep, madame queen; you forget that I am the Dauphin, and that dauphins cannot die like this."

Child's dialogue with his mother shows his innocence and his haughtiness. He refuses to die and believes he can defend himself from death.

The queen sobs more bitterly than ever, and the little Dauphin begins to be alarmed.

"I say," he says, "I don't want Death to come and take me and I will find a way to prevent his coming here. Let them send at once forty very strong troopers to stand guard around our bed! Let a hundred big guns watch night and day with matches lighted, under our windows! And woe to Death if it dares approach us!"

The Dauphin throws up another defense against death.

To please the royal child the queen makes a sign. In a moment they hear the big guns rumbling through the courtyard; and forty tall troopers, halberds in hand, take their places about the room. They are all old soldiers with gray mustaches. The little Dauphin claps his hands when he sees them. He recognizes one of them and calls him:

The Dauphin's whims are indulged.

"Lorrain! Lorrain!"

The soldier steps forward toward the bed.

"I love you dearly, my old Lorrain. Let me see your big sword. If Death tries to take me you must kill him, won't you?"

"Yes, *monseigneur,*" Lorrain replies. And two great tears roll down his bronzed cheeks.

The Dauphin seeks another defense against death in the loyalty of a trooper.

At that moment the chaplain approaches the little Dauphin and talks with him for a long time in a low voice, showing him a crucifix. The little Dauphin listens with an expression of great surprise, then, abruptly interrupting him, he says:

"I understand what you say, *monsieur l'abbé;*[10] but tell me, couldn't my little friend Beppo die in my place, if I gave him a lot of money?"

The chaplain is preparing the Dauphin for death, but the child still does not grasp what death means. He believes in still another defense—that someone else can take his place.

The chaplain continues to speak in a low voice, and the little Dauphin's expression becomes more and more astonished.

When the chaplain has finished, the little Dauphin replies with a deep sigh:

The child has discovered to his surprise that he cannot cheat death.

"All this that you tell me is very sad, *monsieur l'abbé;* but one thing consoles me, and that is that up yonder, in the paradise of the stars, I shall still be the Dauphin. I know that the good Lord is my cousin, and that He cannot fail to treat me according to my rank."

Then he adds, turning to his mother:

The Dauphin now understands that death is inevitable, but he thinks the special treatment due to royalty will prevail after death.

---

10. *monsieur l'abbé* (mə-syœ′ lä-bā′): my lord the abbé, a title given to a priest.

"Let them bring me my richest clothes, my doublet[11] of white ermine, and my velvet slippers! I wish to make myself handsome for the angels, and to enter paradise in the costume of a Dauphin."

The child still has illusions about his position.

A third time the chaplain leans toward the little Dauphin and talks to him for a long time in a low voice. In the midst of his harangue,[12] the royal child angrily interrupts:

Apparently, the chaplain informs the Dauphin that he will have no special privileges in paradise.

"Why, then, to be Dauphin is to be nothing at all!"

And refusing to listen to anything more, the little Dauphin turns toward the wall and weeps bitterly.

The Dauphin, completely disillusioned, now realizes that his wealth and power mean nothing in the face of death.

---

11. **doublet:** a closefitting jacket.
12. **harangue** (hə-răng'): scolding speech.

Commentary on "The Death of the Dauphin"

The title and the very first sentence of the story tell us that the Dauphin will die. Since the author gives us this information at the outset, it is clear that his purpose is not to keep us in suspense about the fate of the crown prince. Obviously he wishes to direct our attention to other things.

The opening paragraph tells us how the kingdom is affected by the Dauphin's critical illness. The author selects a few important details to convey this information. In all the churches of the kingdom, prayers are being said for the prince's recovery. The streets are quiet; the bells do not ring; even carriages move slowly through the street. An air of mourning surrounds the palace, where citizens watch and wait for news.

The author now moves us into the palace so that we can observe the effect of the news on the palace staff. We get an impression of anxiety and despair among the officials and court attendants. We also get an impression of the luxury of court life: the staircases are of marble; the courtiers are dressed in silk; the maids of honor carry embroidered handkerchiefs. What is implied in these details is that rank and privilege are no protection against death.

We learn from the third paragraph how large a staff personally attends the Dauphin. A large number of physicians are conferring about the case. From the showy movements of their hands ("flourishing their long black sleeves") and their bowing to one another ("bending majestically their hammerlike wigs"), we get an impression of their exaggerated opinion of their own importance. We also see those closer to the Dauphin: his tutor, who seeks comfort in reciting poetry, and his equerry, who swears in rage. A plaintive note is sounded by the neighing of the Dauphin's little horse, neglected by the grooms ("empty manger").

These opening paragraphs are important to the story. They tell us about the elegant and indulgent atmosphere in which the Dauphin lives.

The author next shows us how members of the royal family are affected. Although he does not explore the inner thoughts of the king and queen, he conveys their grief movingly. The king has withdrawn to a room at the farther end of the castle so that he will not be seen weeping. The queen grieves openly beside the Dauphin's bed. Death is a great equalizer, as the comparison to the linen draper's wife implies.

Finally we see the little Dauphin on his deathbed. Again, as in the second paragraph of the story, the author sets the richness of privileged position alongside the stark reality of death. The Dauphin lies in a "lace-bedecked crib," his pallor deathlike ("whiter than the cushions upon which he lies").

All that we have learned thus far is preparation for the scene that follows, in which the Dauphin learns a bitter truth about life. Having been raised in an atmosphere of luxury and shielded from the harsh realities of life, the Dauphin does not grasp the meaning of death. Step by step, as his illusions are stripped away, he realizes that his rank and position are ultimately powerless.

The child's first reaction is one of denial. He comforts his mother by telling her "dauphins cannot die like this." His statement is both innocent and haughty; he has contempt for death.

He becomes alarmed when his mother continues weeping, and offers another defense. Thinking of death as a human being, he calls for an armed guard to stand watch and protect him. In keeping with the make-believe atmosphere in which the Dauphin has lived, the Queen indulges this whim and sends for the troopers. The pretense is hard to keep up; the old soldier Lorrain has difficulty restraining his tears.

This deception does not last long. The chaplain comes in to prepare the Dauphin for death. Startled by this news, the Dauphin seeks another defense. He believes it is possible to pay someone else to die in his place. Learning to his astonishment that this is not possible, the Dauphin seeks consolation in his rank. He thinks that the special treatment due to royalty will prevail after death (". . . in the paradise of the stars, I shall still be the Dauphin"). Holding on to this illusion, the child calls for his most elegant clothes.

The final blow descends. The chaplain speaks a third time to the child, stripping him of his last illusion. The Dauphin, realizing that he will have no special privileges in paradise, is stunned: "Why, then, to be Dauphin is to be nothing at all!" He now knows that his wealth and power mean nothing in the face of death.

What you are *not* told in a story is often as important as what you are told. In "The Death of the Dauphin," there is very little information given about the characters. You do not know what the Dauphin looks like, how old he is, what has caused his illness, or even what his name is. One of the questions you should ask yourself is why the author has chosen to omit this information.

One answer might be that in this story Daudet has deliberately chosen to emphasize a thematic idea rather than character. Instead of trying to interest you in a particular event or person, Daudet wishes to dramatize a *universal* experience. Underlying the events of the story is the powerful idea that human power is illusory in the conflict with death. By focusing on a royal child as victim, Daudet stresses the point that no human being, however innocent, wealthy, or highborn, is invulnerable to death.

With practice, you can develop skill in reading and analyzing a literary work. Here are some rules to guide you in reading fiction.

Guidelines for Reading Fiction

1. *Look up unfamiliar words and references.* In Daudet's story, the word *Dauphin* (defined in a footnote) tells you that the story is set in France a long time ago. A careful reader would check any such words in a standard dictionary or other reference book.

2. *Learn to probe beneath the surface.* When you are told that the Dauphin's horse is calling from the empty manger, you infer that the manger (the trough that holds feed) is empty because the stable grooms, in their sorrow or neglect, have forgotten to fill it.

3. *Actively question the author's purpose and method.* Daudet, as we have seen, has a reason for giving more emphasis to the external details of court life than to the inner thoughts of his characters.

4. *Probe for the central idea or theme—the underlying meaning of the work.* Daudet's story, as we have noted, is not merely about the death of a royal child; it has a great deal to say about the illusions of privilege and rank, and the breakdown of these illusions in the struggle with death.

Practice in Close Reading

The following passages are from short stories you are not likely to have read. Each passage is accompanied by a set of questions. Read carefully before answering the questions. If you need to, look up unfamiliar words or references.

I

The red sunset, with narrow, black cloud strips like threats across it, lay on the curved horizon of the prairie. The air was still and cold, and in it settled the mute darkness and greater cold of night. High in the air there was wind, for through the veil of the dusk the clouds could be seen gliding rapidly south and changing shapes. A sensation of torment, of two-sided, unpredictable nature, arose from the stillness of the earth air beneath the violence of the upper air. Out of the sunset, through the dead, matted grass and isolated weed stalks of the prairie, crept the narrow and deeply rutted remains of a road. In the road, in places, there were crusts of shallow, brittle ice. There were little islands of an old oiled pavement in the road too, but most of it was mud, now frozen rigid. The frozen mud still bore the toothed impress of great tanks, and a wanderer on the neighboring undulations might have stumbled, in this light, into large, partially filled-in and weed-grown cavities, their banks channeled and beginning to spread into badlands.[1] These pits were such as might have been made by falling meteors, but they were not. They were the scars of gigantic bombs, their rawness already made a little natural by rain, seed and time. Along the road there were rakish remnants of fence. There was also, just visible, one portion of tangled and multiple barbed wire still erect, behind which was a shelving ditch with small caves, now very quiet and empty, at intervals in its back wall. Otherwise there was no structure or remnant of a structure visible over the dome of the darkling earth, but only, in sheltered hollows, the darker shadows of young trees trying again.

Walter Van Tilburg Clark
from "The Portable Phonograph"

---

1. **badlands:** sections of barren land where erosion has cut the soil into ridges and peaks.

1. Judging from details in this description of setting, what event has occurred?
2. This passage creates an ominous, or threatening, mood. Which words and phrases contribute to this emotional effect?

II

Although Bertha Young was thirty she still had moments like this when she wanted to run instead of walk, to take dancing steps on and off the pavement, to bowl a hoop, to throw something up in the air and catch it again, or to stand still and laugh at—nothing—at nothing, simply.

What can you do if you are thirty and, turning the corner of your own street, you are overcome, suddenly, by a feeling of bliss—absolute bliss!—as though you'd suddenly swallowed a bright piece of that late afternoon sun and it burned in your bosom, sending out a little shower of sparks into every particle, into every finger and toe? . . .

Oh, is there no way you can express it without being "drunk and disorderly"? How idiotic civilization is! Why be given a body if you have to keep it shut up in a case like a rare, rare fiddle?

"No, that about the fiddle is not quite what I mean," she thought, running up the steps and feeling in her bag for the key—she'd forgotten it, as usual—and rattling the letter box. "It's not what I mean, because—Thank you, Mary"—she went into the hall. "Is nurse back?"

"Yes, M'm."

"And has the fruit come?"

"Yes, M'm. Everything's come."

"Bring the fruit up to the dining room, will you? I'll arrange it before I go upstairs."

It was dusky in the dining room and quite chilly. But all the same Bertha threw off her coat; she could not bear the tight clasp of it another moment, and the cold air fell on her arms.

But in her bosom there was still that bright glowing place—that shower of little sparks coming from it. It was almost unbearable. She hardly dared to breathe for fear of fanning it higher, and yet she breathed deeply, deeply. She hardly dared to look into the cold mirror—but she did look, and it gave her back a woman, radiant,

with smiling, trembling lips, with big, dark eyes and an air of listening, waiting for something . . . divine to happen . . . that she knew
must happen . . . infallibly.

Katherine Mansfield
from "Bliss"

FOR STUDY AND DISCUSSION

1. This passage gives us insight into Bertha Young's mood. Which
details most vividly evoke her feelings?
2. How do you know Bertha is attempting to restrain her feelings?
Why do you suppose she controls her impulses?
3. What insight does this passage give you into Bertha's social status
and background?
4. Where does the author hint at Bertha's childlike nature?

Close Reading of a Poem

To experience a poem fully is to be aware of its special language
and structure. Poets rely on the suggestive powers of language and
choose words for their connotative as well as their denotative
values. Through imagery, figurative language, and symbols, poets
appeal to both the intellect and the senses. The meaning of a poem
is conveyed not only through its words but through its sounds. To
intensify meaning, poets choose patterns of sound, including rhyme
and rhythm. Poets achieve their effects, also, through special kinds
of organization, in structures called stanzas, and in conventional
forms such as sonnets and ballads.

It is a good idea to read a poem several times, and aloud at least
once. Read slowly and distinctly, paying attention to meaning as
well as to sound. Often it is helpful to write a prose paraphrase of a
poem, restating all its ideas in plain language (see page 806). A
paraphrase is no substitute for the "meaning" of a poem, but it
helps you clarify and simplify the author's text.

Read the following poem several times. Then turn to the explication on page 731. An *explication* is a line-by-line examination
of the content and technique of a work.

A Bird Came Down the Walk   *Emily Dickinson*

A bird came down the walk:
He did not know I saw;
He bit an angleworm° in halves   3. **angleworm:** earthworm.
And ate the fellow, raw.

And then he drank a dew   5
From a convenient grass,
And then hopped sidewise to the wall
To let a beetle pass.

He glanced with rapid eyes
That hurried all abroad—   10
They looked like frightened beads, I thought.
He stirred his velvet head

Like one in danger; cautious,
I offered him a crumb,
And he unrolled his feathers   15
And rowed him softer home

Than oars divide the ocean,
Too silver for a seam,
Or butterflies, off banks of noon,
Leap, plashless,° as they swim.   20   20. **plashless:** without a splash.

Explication of "A Bird Came Down the Walk"

In "A Bird Came Down the Walk," Emily Dickinson shows that she is extremely responsive to the natural world, in her careful attention to the creatures in the garden, her sensitivity to the bird's fear, and her admiration of the bird's graceful flight. The poet also implies that there is no mutual sympathy or concern between the natural world and the human world. The bird is indifferent to the poet's feelings. Her presence is not only of no consequence, but is felt instinctively to be an alien element.

In the opening stanza the poet observes the movements of a bird closely and quietly. At first, the bird is not aware of being watched (line 2). Unlike the poet, who has affection for natural creatures, the bird has a matter-of-fact attitude toward nature. He wastes no time cutting the angleworm in half and swallowing it "raw." He uses a "convenient" grass—whatever is at hand—to refresh himself with the dew that has condensed from the night air. Since the beetle is of no practical interest, he hops lightly out of its way.

In the third stanza, the poet conveys the bird's wariness. Lines 9–10 give us an effective image of the bird's extreme caution:

> He glanced with rapid eyes
> That hurried all abroad—

These lines show us the bird's eyes taking in the scene around him swiftly. We can see the small dark eyes of the bird, which are compared to "frightened beads," filled with fear.

The sentence beginning in the last line of stanza 3 and running over into stanza 4 describes the bird's head. The poet compares its softness to "velvet" and again emphasizes the bird's sense of danger.

Now the poet tries to approach the bird, offering to feed him. She acts cautiously to avoid frightening him, but she is unsuccessful. The last six lines of the poem use original metaphors to describe the flight of the bird. The words "he unrolled his feathers" tell that the bird began to fly. Although birds do not literally unroll their feathers, this metaphor is highly effective in suggesting the way a bird's wings open out and extend in flight. The last five lines show the bird moving through the air. The comparisons stress the softness and smoothness of the bird's flight. The movement of the bird's wings is compared to oars parting the water. The lines

> And rowed him softer home

> Than oars divide the ocean,
> Too silver for a seam,

suggest that the bird does not disturb the air, the natural element in which it moves. As the oars of a boat part the water ("divide the ocean"), the water immediately reunites so that there is no line or mark ("seam"). The word *silver* seems to refer to *quicksilver*, or liquid mercury. If it is divided, the two parts immediately come together without a seam.

The softness and smoothness of the bird's movements are also conveyed by the sounds in lines 15–18. The alliteration of *softer*, *silver*, and *seam*, and the subtle repetition of the soft consonant sounds *f, l, m, n, r,* and *v* (*A*nd, u*nr*olled, *f*eathers, *A*nd, *r*owed, hi*m*, so*ft*er, ho*m*e, *Th*an, oars, di*v*ide, ocean, si*lv*er, *f*or, sea*m*) make the lines flow smoothly. The assonance of long *o*'s in unrolled, rowed, home, and ocean is not just melodious; the repetition of the long vowel tends to slow up the lines, to emphasize the grace and control of the bird's flight.

In the final two lines, the bird's movement is compared to that of butterflies. Butterflies don't swim, but the lines suggest that they glide through the air as easily as fish move through the water. A *bank* is a stretch of land at the edge of a river or stream. The "banks of noon" suggest the butterflies springing into the warm air without the slightest noise ("plashless").

The imagery of the poem is quite wonderful. The picture of the bird with eyes "like frightened beads," rowing itself home soundlessly through the air, lingers in the memory as does the image of butterflies leaping off imaginary banks as they "swim" in the warm, midday air. By the power of her observation and imagination, Dickinson transforms a rather ordinary occurrence into something extraordinary and memorable.

Guidelines for Reading a Poem

1. *Read the poem several times, and aloud at least once, trying to follow the thought.* Commas, semicolons, colons, dashes, and periods tell you where to pause. The reader is not expected to pause automatically at the end of each line. Sometimes a complete thought runs over into a new stanza. In some lines more than one pause may be signaled.

2. *Be alert to key words and references.* In poetry, a word is often used in an unfamiliar or unusual way. The word *silver,* for example, is not the precious metal used for jewelry and tableware; it stands for *quicksilver,* another name for mercury.

3. *Write a paraphrase of any lines that need clarification or simplification.* A paraphrase helps a reader understand figurative language. For example, one paraphrase of lines 15–18 might read: The bird spread out his wings and began flying home. His wings moved through the air more smoothly than oars cleave the ocean, the water parting and reuniting without appearing to be disturbed.

4. *Arrive at the central idea or meaning of the poem.* Try to state this idea in one or two sentences: *"A Bird Came Down the Walk" reveals how much wonder a sensitive observer can find in simple, common aspects of nature.*

Practice in Close Reading

Each of the following poems is accompanied by a set of questions. Read each poem carefully before answering the questions. Remember to read each poem aloud at least once, paying attention to the sound as well as to the sense. Look up any unfamiliar words or references. Write a paraphrase of any lines that require clarification. Try to state the central idea of the poem.

I

Daffodils   *May Swenson*

Yellow telephones
in a row in the garden
are ringing,
shrill with light.

Old-fashioned spring   5
brings earliest models out
each April the same,
naïve° and classical.   8. **naïve** (nä-ēv′): here, simple.

Look into the yolk-
colored mouthpieces   10
alert with echoes.
Say hello to time.

FOR STUDY AND DISCUSSION

1. The poet compares daffodils to yellow telephones. What do you think is the "message" these telephones communicate?
2. Explain the meaning of the phrase "shrill with light" in line 4.
3. Daffodils appear in early spring. Which lines allude to this fact?
4. What are the "echoes" referred to in line 11?
5. Does the word *time* in the last line refer to a specific time or to a general idea of time? In what way do the flowers enable us to "speak" to time?

II

Interior   *Dorothy Parker*

Her mind lives in a quiet room,
  A narrow room, and tall,
With pretty lamps to quench the gloom
  And mottoes on the wall.

There all the things are waxen neat   5
  And set in decorous lines;
And there are posies, round and sweet,
  And little, straightened vines.

Her mind lives tidily, apart
  From cold and noise and pain,   10
And bolts the door against her heart,
  Out wailing in the rain.

FOR STUDY AND DISCUSSION

1. The room in this poem is a metaphor for a woman's life. What is suggested by the image of "a narrow room"? What might the "mottoes on the wall" be?
2. Which images in stanza 2 suggest that the woman has deceived herself into choosing an orderly but vacant existence?
3. How does the last stanza suggest the emptiness of her life?

Close Reading of a Play

Drama has its own conventions, or traditions, including stage directions, sound effects, soliloquies, monologues, and asides. Generally, however, dialogue is the dramatist's most important device for presenting character and for moving the action along.

    The following passage is from *Mozart and the Gray Steward,* a play by Thornton Wilder, a major American playwright. Wilder got the idea for his play from an incident in the composer's life. Shortly before his death, Mozart was visited by a stranger, who commissioned him to compose a requiem. Read the passage several times, and aloud at least once. Then turn to the commentary on page 738.

from Mozart and the Gray Steward

Thornton Wilder

Mozart *is seated at a table in a mean room in Vienna orchestrating The Magic Flute.*[1] *Leaves of ruled paper are strewn about the floor. His wife enters in great excitement.*

> Financial hardship revealed by shabbiness and disorder.

Constanze. There's someone come to see you, someone important. Pray God, it's a commission from Court.

Mozart (*unmoved*). Not while Salieri's[2] alive.

> Mozart is dependent on commissions.

Constanze. Put on your slippers, dear. It's someone dressed all in gray, with a gray mask over his eyes, and he's come in a great coach with its coat of arms all covered up with gray cloth. Pray God, it's a commission from Court for a *Te Deum*[3] or something. (*She tidies up the room in six gestures.*)

> The visitor wishes to conceal his identity.

Mozart. Not while Salieri's alive.

Constanze. But, now, do be nice, 'Gangl,[4] please. We must have some money, my treasure. Just listen to him and say "yes" and "thank you" and then you and I'll talk it over after he's gone. (*She holds his coat.*) Come, put this on. Step into your slippers.

> A hint that Mozart is not adept at court intrigue.

> Desperate financial situation is confirmed.

Mozart (*sighing*). I'm not well. I'm at home. I'm at work. There's not a single visitor in the whole world that could interest me. Bring him in.

> Mozart gives in, reluctantly.

[*She hurries out and presently reenters preceding the visitor. The visitor is dressed from head to foot in gray silk. His bright eyes look out through the holes in a narrow gray silk mask. He holds to his nose a gray perfumed handkerchief. One would say: an elegant undertaker.*]

> Visitor is elegantly dressed.

> He has an air of affectation.

The Gray Steward. Kapellmeister[5] Mozart, *servus.*[6] Gracious lady, *servus.*

Mozart. *Servus.*

The Gray Steward. Revered and noble master, wherever music reigns, wherever genius is valued, the name of Wolfgang Amadeus Mozart is . . .

---

1. *The Magic Flute:* an opera completed in 1791, the year of the composer's death.
2. **Salieri:** Antonio Salieri (1750–1825), an Italian composer who became prominent in Viennese musical life. He was the supposed enemy of Mozart.
3. *Te Deum* (tā'dā'əm, tē'dē'əm): a Latin hymn. The opening words are *Te Deum Laudamus,* meaning "We praise Thee, O God."
4. **'Gangl:** a shortened form of Wolfgang, Mozart's given name.
5. **Kapellmeister** (kä-pĕl'mīs'tər): German for "choir master."
6. *servus* (sûr'vŭs): Latin for "your servant."

Mozart. Sir, I have always been confused by compliments and beg you to spare me that mortification by proceeding at once to the cause of your visit . . . the . . . the honor of your visit.

The Gray Steward. Revered master, before I lay my business before you, may I receive your promise that—whether you accept my commission or not—you both will . . .

Mozart. I promise you our secrecy, unless our silence would prove dishonorable to me or injurious to someone else. Pray continue.

The Gray Steward. Know then, gracious and revered genius, that I come from a prince who combines all the qualities of birth, station, generosity, and wisdom.

Mozart. Ha! a European secret.

The Gray Steward. His Excellency moreover has just sustained a bitter misfortune. He has lately lost his wife and consort, a lady who was the admiration of her court and the sole light of her bereaved husband's life. Therefore, his Excellency, my master, commissions you to compose a Requiem Mass in honor of this lady. He asks you to pour into it the height of your invention and that wealth of melody and harmony that have made you the glory of our era. And for this music he asks leave to pay you the sum of four hundred crowns—two hundred now, and the second two hundred crowns when you deliver the first four numbers.

Mozart. Well, Constanze, I must not be proud.

The Gray Steward. There is but one proviso.[7]

Mozart. Yes, I heard it. The work must represent the height of my invention.

The Gray Steward. That was an easy assumption, master. The proviso is this: You shall let his Excellency have this music as an anonymous work, and you shall never by any sign, by so much as the nod of your head, acknowledge that the work is yours.

Mozart. And his Excellency is not aware that the pages I may compose at the height of my invention may be their own sufficient signature?

The Gray Steward. That may be. Naturally my master will see to it that no other composer will ever be able to claim the work as his.

Mozart. Quick, give me your paper and I will sign it. Leave your two hundred crowns with my wife at the foot of the stairs. Come back in August and you will have the first four numbers, *Servus. Servus.*

The Gray Steward (*backing out*). *Servus,* master. *Servus,* madame.

---

7. **proviso** (prə-vī′zō): condition.

Commentary on Scene from *Mozart and the Gray Steward*

This brief excerpt from Wilder's play is more than dramatized biography. It gives us insight into the way the arts were supported in eighteenth-century Europe. Artists of Mozart's stature were at the mercy of wealthy patrons or the Court, and could not afford the luxury of pride.

Wilder quickly establishes the situation in Mozart's household. It is the last year of Mozart's life. Despite his reputation as a musical genius, Mozart and his wife are living shabbily, in desperate financial straits. The two references to Salieri's influence suggest that Mozart is not adept at court intrigue. Constanze's anxiety for him to be civil to the visitor indicates that he has a rebellious temperament; he is not in the habit of being courteous or tactful.

The visitor, the steward of a great and wealthy household, appears masked in order to conceal his identity. Despite his elegant costume, there is something sinister about his appearance; he is described as an "elegant undertaker." His manners and excessive compliments offend Mozart, who interrupts him impatiently and scoffs at his inflated praise of his master. There is a discrepancy between the courtly, refined language of the steward and the base proposal he offers Mozart. His patron wishes to commission a Requiem Mass with the proviso that it remain anonymous. Clearly he intends to pass the work off as his own.

As the scene ends, Mozart lays aside his pride and accepts the commission. Although he signs away his right to claim the work as his own, he has the ironic satisfaction of knowing that the music he composes will be its own "sufficient signature."

Guidelines for Reading a Play

1. *Note any information that establishes the setting and the situation that will start the plot moving.* The opening of the play establishes the time and place of the action as eighteenth-century Vienna. We learn that Mozart and his wife are in desperate need of money and that they are hopeful of receiving a commission from Court.

2. *Note clues that tell you what the players are doing or how the lines are spoken.* Wilder uses stage directions to convey some of this information to you. Other instructions are built into the dialogue. For example, it is clear that Mozart is impatient with the

visitor and his flattery. He interrupts the Gray Steward twice, urging him to get down to business. His tone very likely would be abrupt, almost rude.

3. *Anticipate the action that will develop out of each scene.* There are hints in Constanze's speeches that Mozart has been rude to his patrons and too proud to accept their commissions. What might be the outcome of Mozart's accepting a commission that calls for his work to be anonymous?

4. *Be alert to the mood of the play.* The serious nature of the play is immediately evident in the references to financial hardship and in Constanze's concern for a commission from Court. There is a note of foreboding in the costume of the Gray Steward, who is described as "an elegant undertaker."

Practice in Close Reading

Here is the conclusion of Wilder's play. The action resumes after Constanze sees the visitor out.

[Constanze *returns in a moment and looks anxiously towards her husband.*]

Constanze. A visit from Heaven, 'Gangl. Now you can go into the country. Now you can drink all the Bohemian water in the world.

Mozart (*bitterly*). Good. And just at a time when I was contemplating a Requiem Mass. But for *myself.* However, I must not be proud.

Constanze (*trying to divert him*). Who can these people be? Try and think.

Mozart. Oh, there's no mystery about that. It's the Count von Walsegg. He composes himself. But for the most part he buys string quartets from us; he erases the signatures and has them played in his castle. The courtiers flatter him and pretend that they have guessed him to be the composer. He does not deny it. He tries to appear confused. And now he has succeeded in composing a Requiem. But that will reduce my pride.

Constanze. You know he will only be laughed at. The music will speak for itself. Heaven wanted to give us four hundred crowns—

Mozart. And Heaven went about it humorously.

Constanze. What was his wife like?

Mozart. Her impudences smelt to Heaven. She dressed like a page and called herself Cherubin.[1] Her red cheeks and her black teeth and her sixty years are in my mind now.

Constanze (*after a pause*). We'll give back the money. You can write the music, without writing it for them.

Mozart. No, I like this game. I like it for its very falseness. What does it matter who signs such music or to whom it is addressed? (*He flings himself upon the sofa and turns his face to the wall.*) For whom do we write music? for musicians? Salieri!—for patrons? Von Walsegg!—for the public? The Countess von Walsegg! I shall write this Requiem, but it shall be for myself, since I am dying.

Constanze. My beloved, don't talk so! Go to sleep. (*She spreads a shawl over his body.*) How can you say such things? Imagine even thinking such a thing! You will live many years and write countless beautiful pages. We will return the money and refuse the commission. Then the matter will be closed. Now go to sleep, my treasure.

[*She goes out, quietly closing the door behind her.* Mozart, *at the mercy of his youth, his illness, and his genius, is shaken by a violent fit of weeping. The sobs gradually subside and he falls asleep. In his dream* The Gray Steward *returns.*]

The Gray Steward. Mozart! Turn and look at me. You know who I am.

Mozart (*not turning*). You are the steward of the Count von Walsegg. Go tell him to write his own music. I will not stain my pen to celebrate his lady, so let the foul bury the foul.

The Gray Steward. Lie then against the wall, and learn that it is Death itself that commissions. . . .

Mozart. Death is not so fastidious. Death carries no perfumed handkerchief.

The Gray Steward. Lie then against the wall. Know first that all the combinations of circumstance can suffer two interpretations, the apparent and the real.

Mozart. Then speak, sycophant,[2] I know the apparent one. What other reading can this humiliation bear?

The Gray Steward. It is Death itself that commands you this Requiem. You are to give a voice to all those millions sleeping, who have no one but you to speak for them. There lie the captains and the thieves, the queens and the drudges, while the evening of their earthly remembrance shuts in, and from that great field rises an

---

1. **Cherubin** (kä-rŏŏ-bēn′): presumably after Cherubino, a character in Mozart's opera *The Marriage of Figaro*.
2. **sycophant** (sĭk′ə-fənt): a servile flatterer.

eternal *miserere nobis.*[3] Only through the intercession[4] of great love, can that despairing cry be eased. Was that not sufficient cause for this commission to be anonymous?

Mozart (*drops trembling on one knee beside the couch*). Forgive me.

The Gray Steward. And it was for this that the pretext and mover was chosen from among the weakest and vainest of humans. Death has her now, and all her folly has passed into the dignity and grandeur of her state. Where is your pride now? Here are her slippers and her trinkets. Press them against your lips. Again! Again! Know henceforth that only he who has kissed the leper[5] can enter the kingdom of art.

Mozart. I have sinned, yet grant me one thing. Grant that I may live to finish the Requiem.

The Gray Steward. No! No!

[*And it remains unfinished.*]

---

3. *miserere nobis* (mĭz′ə rârʹē nōʹbĭs): Latin for "Have mercy upon us."
4. **intercession** (ĭn′tər-sĕshʹən): mediation; interceding on behalf of others.
5. **he . . . leper:** This may be an allusion to a story about Saint Francis of Assisi (1182–1226). In order to do God's will, he overcame his repugnance for lepers and forced himself to greet a leper with the kiss of peace.

FOR STUDY AND DISCUSSION

1. How does Mozart guess that the commission for the Requiem has come from Count von Walsegg?

2. Why does Mozart feel that this commission is a humiliation?

3. In Mozart's dream, The Gray Steward returns as a messenger of Death. He says that there are two interpretations for circumstances. According to him, what is the "real" interpretation for the commission?

4. In what way does The Gray Steward answer Mozart's question, "For whom do we write music?"

5. Why does Mozart feel that he has sinned against the kingdom of art?

WRITING ABOUT LITERATURE

The Writing Process

We often refer to writing an essay as a *process*, which consists of three key stages or phases: **prewriting, writing,** and **revising.** In this process, much of the crucial work precedes the actual writing of an essay. In the prewriting stage, the writer makes decisions about what to say and how to say it. Prewriting activities include choosing and limiting a topic, gathering ideas, organizing ideas, and arriving at a *thesis*—the controlling idea for the paper. In the next stage, the writer uses the working plan to write a first draft of the essay. In the revising stage, the writer rewrites the draft, several times perhaps, adding or deleting ideas, rearranging order, rephrasing for clarity, and correcting errors in spelling, punctuation, and grammar. The steps in this process are interdependent. For example, as ideas are developed on paper, the writer may find that the central idea of the paper needs to be restated or that a different organization is needed. The amount of time devoted to each stage will vary with individual assignments. During a classroom examination you may have only minutes to think about and plan your essay. For a term paper you may have weeks or months to prepare.

On the following pages the steps in this process are illustrated through the development of several model essays.

Answering Examination Questions

From time to time you will be asked to demonstrate your understanding of a literary work or topic by writing a short essay in class. Usually, your teacher will select the subject of the essay. How well you do will depend not only on how carefully you have prepared for the examination but on how carefully you read and interpret the essay question.

Before you begin to answer an examination question, be sure you understand what the question calls for. If a question requires that you discuss the *theme* of a story, you will not fulfill the requirements of the question if you give a summary of the story's plot. If you are asked to compare two *humorous* essays, your answer will be unacceptable if you mistakenly write about two *serious* essays. No matter how good your essay is, it will be unsatisfactory if you do not respond to the question accurately. Always take some time to read the essay question carefully in order to determine how it should be answered.

Remember that you are expected to demonstrate specific knowledge of the literature. Any general statement should be supported by evidence. If you wish to show a character's internal conflict, for example, refer to specific actions, dialogue, thoughts and feelings, or direct comments by the author in order to illustrate your point. If you are allowed to use your textbook during the examination, you may occasionally quote short passages or refer to a specific page in order to provide supporting evidence.

At the start, it may be helpful to jot down some notes to guide you in writing the essay. If you have several points to make, decide what the most effective order of presentation will be. You might build up to your strongest point, or you might present your points to develop a striking contrast. Aim for a logical organization.

Also remember that length alone is not satisfactory. Your answer must be relevant, and it must be presented in acceptable, correct English. Always take time to proofread your paper.

The key word in examination questions is the *verb*. Let us look briefly at some common instructions used in examinations.

ANALYSIS A question may ask you to *analyze* some aspect of a literary work or topic. When you analyze something, you take it apart to see how each part works. On an examination, you will generally be directed to focus on some limited but essential aspect of a work in order to demonstrate your knowledge and understanding. A common type of exercise is *character analysis,* in which you draw on the most significant details of characterization in order to reach conclusions about a specific figure. For example, you might be asked to analyze the character of Odysseus as an epic hero, taking into account the traditional elements of characterization in classical epics (page 488). You might be asked to analyze the imagery in the poem "Meeting at Night" (page 264). You might be asked to analyze the satirical elements in the play *Visit to a Small Planet* (page 344). Analysis may be applied to form, technique, or ideas.

COMPARISON
CONTRAST A question may ask that you *compare* (or *contrast*) two things, such as techniques, ideas, characters, or works. When you *compare,* you point out likenesses; when you *contrast,* you point out differences. At times you will be asked to *compare and contrast.* In

that event, you will be expected to deal with similarities and differences. You might be asked to compare the themes of O. Henry's "The Gift of the Magi" (page 126) and De Maupassant's "The Necklace" (page 140). You might be asked to contrast Walter Mitty's fantasy life with his real life (page 31). You might compare and contrast the characteristics of the short story and the novel. Sometimes the instruction to *compare* implies both comparison and contrast. Always check with your teacher to make sure how inclusive the term *compare* is intended to be.

DESCRIPTION   If a question asks you to *describe* a setting or a character, you are expected to give a picture in words. In describing a setting, include not only features that establish the historical period and locale, but those features that help to evoke a mood. In describing a character, deal with both direct and indirect methods of characterization (see page 796). You might be asked to describe the setting in the opening scene of *Great Expectations* (page 556) in order to demonstrate how Dickens creates an atmosphere of mystery and terror. You might be asked to describe the eccentric character of Miss Havisham in that novel. You might be asked to describe the sensuous beauty of Fez emphasized in Anaïs Nin's essay "The Labyrinthine City of Fez" (page 191).

DISCUSSION   The word *discuss* in a question is much more general than the other words we've looked at. When you are asked to discuss a subject, you are expected to examine it in detail. A question might direct you to discuss the characteristics of the informal essay that apply to James Thurber's "How to Name a Dog" (page 162) and E. B. White's "The Wings of Orville" (page 168). You might be asked to discuss the tone of Twain's "The Great French Duel" (page 173). You might be asked to discuss the use of dramatic irony in Shakespeare's *Romeo and Juliet* (page 386).

EXPLANATION   A question may ask you to *explain* something. When you explain, you give reasons for something being the way it is. You make clear a character's actions, or you show how something has come about. You might, for example, be asked to explain the relation between Mitty's daydreams and actual events in "The Secret Life of Walter Mitty" (page 31). You might be asked to explain Kreton's plan for world domination in *Visit to a Small Planet* (page 344). You might be asked to explain the concept of vengeance in the *Odyssey* (page 488) or how the subplots are connected to the main plot of *Great Expectations* (page 556).

ILLUSTRATION	The word *illustrate, demonstrate,* or *show* asks that you provide examples to support a point. You might be asked to give examples of anachronisms in Heyward Broun's "The Fifty-first Dragon" (page 148). You might be asked to illustrate Emily Dickinson's use of startling and original diction to present fresh images in her poetry (pages 250, 272, 330). You might be asked to demonstrate musical effects in James Stephens' "The Shell" (page 288). Or you might be asked to show that in the *Odyssey* Homer mixes real and fabulous elements (page 488).
INTERPRETATION	The word *interpret* in a question asks that you give the meaning or significance of something. For example, you might be asked to provide an interpretation for a symbol, such as the journey in Christina Rossetti's "Uphill" (page 327). You might be asked to interpret the meaning of a work such as Edwin Muir's "The Castle" (page 323). Sometimes you will be asked to agree or disagree with a stated interpretation of a work, giving specific evidence to support your position. For example, see the essay topics on pages 478–479, 551, and 718–719.

You will find that there is frequent overlapping of approaches. In discussing a subject, you may draw upon illustration, explanation, analysis, or any other approach that is useful. In comparing or contrasting two works, you may rely on description or interpretation. However, an examination question generally will have a central purpose, and it is important that you focus on this purpose in preparing your answer.

On the following pages you will find some sample examination questions and answers for study and discussion. Note that the assignments (shown in italics) may be phrased as essay topics.

I

QUESTION   *Poe uses irony in "The Cask of Amontillado" (page 58) to heighten the effect of horror. In a paragraph give specific examples of Poe's method.*

METHOD OF ATTACK   This is an exercise in *illustration*. Your aim is to select examples of irony that intensify the terror of the narrative. How will you proceed?

One approach is to consider the kinds of irony Poe uses. You have learned that one common kind of irony is *dramatic irony*, in which the reader knows something that the character is ignorant of (see page 36). Another kind of irony, called *verbal irony*, is a way of saying one thing and meaning the opposite (see page 24). You might decide to focus on examples of these two kinds of irony. You would then need to identify effective examples of each kind in the story.

Once you have chosen an approach, jot down some notes to guide you in writing. These notes can be arranged under two heads:

Dramatic Irony

The reader knows that Montresor is plotting revenge against Fortunato, but Fortunato has no inkling of this. When the two men meet during the carnival, Fortunato is greeted as a friend.

Fortunato is wearing a clown costume. He doesn't realize what the reader knows — that he is being taken for a fool.

These examples reveal Montresor's diabolic character to the reader while hiding the truth from the intended victim.

Verbal Irony

In the vaults the dampness causes Fortunato to cough. He says that a cough will not kill him. Montresor agrees, saying that he will not die of a cough. The statement seems innocent, but the reader knows that the words are menacing.

Montresor drinks to Fortunato's long life, knowing that his hours are numbered.

These examples show Montresor toying with Fortunato before he kills him.

ANSWER   Here is a model paragraph developed from the notes.

Topic sentence restates question.

Subordinate Idea

In "The Cask of Amontillado," Poe uses dramatic and verbal irony to heighten the effect of horror. *His use of dramatic irony reveals Montresor's diabolic character to the reader while hiding the truth from the intended victim, Fortunato. The reader knows from the outset that Montresor has been plotting revenge against*

	Fortunato, but Fortunato is completely ignorant of his intention. When the two meet during the carnival, Montresor greets Fortunato with pretended pleasure. Fortunato is wearing a clown suit. He does not realize what the reader knows—that he is in fact going to play
Supporting Statements	
Subordinate Idea	the fool. *Poe makes use of verbal irony to show Montresor toying with Fortunato before he kills him.* In the vaults the dampness
Supporting Statements	causes Fortunato to cough. He says in jest that the cough will not kill him, and Montresor agrees. His comment, that Fortunato will not die of a cough, appears innocent on the surface, but Montresor really means that Fortunato is going to die in some other way. When they drink a toast, Montresor drinks to Fortunato's long life, knowing full well that his hours are numbered. *The irony in the story*
Concluding Sentence	*heightens the horror because it emphasizes the cruelty of the murderer.*

Length: 200 words

In the assignment, the examiner provided you with a *thesis statement*—that irony in "The Cask of Amontillado" heightens the effect of horror. A thesis statement is a sentence that expresses the *thesis*, or the central idea that gives focus to your paper. The thesis statement indicates what the paper will be about. Although the statement of the thesis appears at the opening of the essay, it represents the end product of thinking. Generally, you will be required to formulate your own thesis statement about a subject.

II

QUESTION	*Analyze the character of the speaker in Frost's "Mending Wall" (page 278).*
METHOD OF ATTACK	This is an exercise in *character analysis.* This assignment is more demanding than the first assignment because you have to exercise your own judgment in setting limits to your answer. The question also requires that you supply your own thesis statement. Your thesis statement should be formulated *after* you have examined the evidence and come to a conclusion about the subject.

Assuming that you have the text of the poem to work from, you might go through it line by line, noting explicit and implicit clues to the speaker's character. You might jot down line references alongside your notes to guide you in writing your paper. As you work, look for major characteristics that will provide a focus for your essay.

This is one way to approach the assignment:

Character of Speaker

Attitude of speaker throughout poem is reflective. He likes to question things.

Speaker seems to have a strong feeling against barriers. He believes "something" in nature rebels against walls (1–4; 9–11).

He qualifies this: Some walls are useful—those that keep hunters out (5–9); those that control livestock (30–31).

He wants to reason with his neighbor about the function of walls (28–34).

He respects the ideas of others. Despite his own beliefs, at spring mending-time, he informs his neighbor of the gaps (11–12).

OPEN MIND

Speaker thinks of the mending as an "outdoor game" (21). He considers business silly and teases his neighbor (25–26).

He feels mischievous and plays with the idea of saying that "elves" are responsible for the pranks (36).

SENSE OF HUMOR

He would like his neighbor to think for himself (28–34).

He suppresses the impulse to impose his own ideas (36–38).

Although he views his neighbor as a "stone savage," blindly following tradition, he does not try to change his mind (38–42).

REALISTIC

What you might conclude from this set of notes is that the speaker is a mature, thoughtful man who has learned to accept and live with the shortcomings of others. Each of the overall characteristics shown in the notes can become the subject of a paragraph.

This is what the final essay might look like.

ANSWER

INTRODUCTION
Thesis Statement

The speaker in Frost's "Mending Wall" is a mature, thoughtful man who has learned to accept and live with the shortcomings of others. It is clear that he has a strong feeling against barriers in nature and barriers in human relationships, yet recognizes that he must be resigned to the existence of such barriers.

BODY
Topic Sentence

The first thing we learn about the speaker is that he admits he doesn't know all the answers and keeps an open mind. There is "something" in nature, he tells us, that rebels against walls. He

Supporting Evidence

doesn't know what this something is, but he is sympathetic to it.

Not that he is inflexible on the subject of walls: he recognizes that some walls, like those that keep hunters and livestock out, are useful and necessary. Unlike his neighbor who clings uncritically to tradition and keeps on repeating "Good fences make good neighbors," the speaker questions the purpose of walls. Yet, he respects the ideas and rights of others. Despite his own beliefs, he feels obligated to respect his neighbor's wishes, and at spring mending-time, the men meet to repair the wall between their properties.

Topic Sentence

Supporting Evidence

The speaker shows himself to be a good-natured man with a sense of humor. He refers to the mending of the wall as "just another kind of outdoor game." In a playful mood he teases his neighbor, telling him that the apple trees will never get across to eat the cones under the pine trees. He admits to feeling mischievous and considers putting the blame for the pranks on elves.

Topic Sentence

Supporting Evidence

The speaker is realistic enough to realize that he cannot change his neighbor's thinking by reasoning with him. He knows that the wall is more than a barrier between their lands; it represents a barrier between their habits of thinking. He suppresses the impulse to put a notion in his neighbor's head: "I'd rather/He said it for himself." Although he views his neighbor as "an old-stone savage armed," blindly following tradition, he does not attempt to impose his own ideas. He knows his neighbor has an unquestioning mind and that it is futile to argue with him.

CONCLUSION

Even though he disagrees with his neighbor's philosophy, we know that the speaker will remain on good terms with him. Undoubtedly he will continue to meet with him at spring mending-time and keep the wall between them as they go.

Length: 396 words

III

QUESTION

The young lovers in Shakespeare's Romeo and Juliet *seem ideally suited to each other because they have so many characteristics in common. Yet Shakespeare has been careful to differentiate them. Write an essay pointing out significant differences in these characters.*

METHOD OF ATTACK

This is an exercise in *contrast*. It is obvious that you will not be able to deal with every significant aspect of the characters; you will have to select a few key aspects to focus on.

Again, begin by taking notes:

Differences

Romeo	Juliet
Seems to be ruled by his emotions. In first act he is melancholy, moody, lovesick over Rosaline. After he meets Juliet he becomes ecstatic.	Juliet appears thoughtful and mature. In her first scene, she is dignified and composed. She reserves judgment until she can see for herself.
He is rash—he kills Tybalt in fury.	In balcony scene she exhibits common sense and practicality. She takes lead in making the arrangements for their marriage.
In Friar's cell, when he hears the Prince's edict of banishment, he loses control of himself.	She is resourceful. She pretends to accept the Nurse's counsel to avoid suspicion.
He depends on others to make decisions for him. He relies on his friends and the Friar to help him resolve his difficulties.	She manages to keep her head under stress. While she and the Friar plot a stratagem to avert the marriage to Paris, she pretends to be ruled by her parents' wishes.

Thesis Statement: Romeo is more emotional and excitable; Juliet is more levelheaded and resourceful.

ANSWER

INTRODUCTION
Restate Question.
Thesis Statement

BODY
Topic Sentence

Supporting Evidence

The young lovers in Shakespeare's *Romeo and Juliet* have many characteristics in common. Yet Shakespeare has been careful to differentiate them. *Romeo is more emotional and impulsive; Juliet more levelheaded and resourceful.*

Romeo seems to be ruled by emotions rather than by reason. When we first meet him in the play, he is lovesick, moody, and restless. He spends his time daydreaming and sighing over Rosaline. Within a short while, he is blissfully ecstatic in declaring his love for Juliet. When he is provoked into a duel by Tybalt, he loses his head and kills him. Then, in the Friar's cell, when he learns that the Prince has banished him, he loses control of himself. He seems dependent upon others to think for him. His friends Benvolio and Mercutio have to help him get over his infatuation with Rosaline. Later, he relies on the Friar's counsel to cope with his grief. He yields easily to despair. When he hears that Juliet is dead, he immediately decides to buy poison and end his own life.

Topic Sentence

While Juliet is every bit as ardent as Romeo and shares his youthful impulsiveness, she exhibits greater thoughtfulness and common sense. When we first meet her, she appears dignified and composed.

Supporting Evidence She does not become excited at having received a proposal of marriage, but reserves judgment until she meets Paris. After she and Romeo declare their love for one another, she takes the lead in arranging for their marriage. When she hears of her cousin Tybalt's death, Juliet is quick to condemn Romeo, then catches herself and checks her outburst. She realizes that Romeo has acted in self-defense. As circumstances threaten to overwhelm her, she shows skill in handling people. When the Nurse, her trusted confidant, suggests that she commit bigamy, Juliet pretends to accept her counsel to avoid suspicion. She manages to keep her head and not alert her family to the stratagem that she and the Friar have plotted to avert her marriage to Paris.

CONCLUSION
Topic Sentence **By means of these differences, Shakespeare makes individuals of his characters.** Romeo and Juliet are not mere stereotypes of young people in love. Because of Shakespeare's skillful characterization, we find their actions and distinct natures true to life.

Length: 368 words

Writing on a Topic of Your Own

Choosing a Topic

At times you may be asked to write an essay on a topic of your own choosing. Often it will be necessary to read a work or group of works more than once before a suitable topic presents itself.

Although any literary subject that interests you is usually acceptable as a topic for study, it is a good idea to steer away from broad topics that invite generalizations and sweeping statements. You may be fascinated by the language of *Romeo and Juliet*, but in a 350–500 word essay, you would be forced to cover the subject too superficially to demonstrate any real mastery of the material. It might be better to restrict yourself to one aspect of the language —for example, images of light—in one scene—the balcony scene of Act Two.

Students sometimes worry that if they choose a narrow topic, they won't have enough to say. This will seldom present a problem if you have developed the habit of digging into a selection and examining it in depth.

A topic may focus on one element or technique in a work. If you are writing about fiction, you might concentrate on some aspect of plot, such as conflict. Or you might concentrate on character, setting, or theme. If you are writing about poetry, you might choose to analyze imagery or figurative language. In writing about drama, you might focus on dramatic irony or stage conventions. A topic may deal with more than one aspect of a work. You might, for example, discuss several elements of a short story in order to show how an idea or theme is developed. Keep the key verbs, such as *analyze, compare, illustrate,* in mind (see pages 743–745) as guides in limiting a topic.

Once you have a topic in mind, your object is to form it into a *thesis,* a controlling idea that represents the conclusion of your findings. This thesis, of course, will appear at the opening of your paper. It may be necessary to read a work several times before you can formulate a thesis. You would then need to present the evidence supporting your position. Here are some examples showing how a thesis differs from a topic:

Topic   The Central Conflict in "Split Cherry Tree" (page 44)

Thesis The central conflict is between two ways of life—an out-of-date tradition of toil and limited education, represented by Pa, and a new way of life based on scientific and technological progress, represented by Professor Herbert.

Topic   Attitudes Toward the Land in "A Mild Attack of Locusts" (page 78)

Thesis Margaret feels that farming is a hopeless business because some disaster is always occurring; Stephen and Richard, on the other hand, expect hardships and accept them without losing heart.

Topic   John Masefield's Diction in "Cargoes" (page 252)

Thesis Masefield has chosen words with both pleasant and unpleasant associations to suggest a contrast between the exotic romance of the old ships and the unromantic utility of modern vessels.

Gathering Evidence

It is a good idea to take notes as you read, even if you do not yet have a topic in mind. Later on, when you have settled on a topic, you can discard any notes that are not relevant. Some people prefer a worksheet, others index cards. In the beginning, you should record all your reactions. A topic may emerge during this early stage. As you continue to read, you will shape your topic into a rough thesis.

When you take notes, make an effort to state ideas in your own words. If a specific phrase or line is so important that it deserves to be quoted directly, be sure to enclose the words in quotation marks. When you transfer your notes to your final paper, be sure to copy quotations exactly.

If you cite lines in a poem, you should enclose the line numbers in parentheses following the quotation. The following note, which is for the *Odyssey* (page 488), shows you how to incorporate two lines of a poem into your own text:

> Odysseus notes that the Cyclopes are barbarians without laws and traditions when he says "Cyclopes have no muster and no meeting,/no consultation or old tribal ways" (lines 99–100).

The slash (/) shows the reader where line 99 ends and line 100 begins. If you cite three or more lines, you should separate the quotation from your own text in this way:

> Upon his return to Ithaca, the goddess Athena appears to Odysseus and transforms him so that he is seen in his former magnificence:
>
> > Lithe and young she made him,
> > ruddy with sun, his jawline clean, the beard
> > no longer gray upon his chin.
> > (lines 856–858)

Sometimes a direct quotation from a literary work can be the springboard to a topic. Consider, for example, a paper based on Odysseus' characterization of himself as "formidable for guile in peace and war."

Let us suppose that you have just concluded the unit on *Great Expectations* (page 556). You are instructed to write an essay of approximately 500 words on a topic of your own choosing.

You haven't any ideas at the outset so you skim through the unit, refreshing your memory of characters and events. You reread notes and questions, sifting through this material for approaches and ideas. You become aware that one of Dickens' important themes in the novel has to do with the need for compassion in human relationships. You believe that exploring this theme will help to clarify Dickens' point of view.

The subject is too broad, however, for an essay of 500 words, so you consider ways to narrow its scope. Should you confine yourself to a chapter or to one of the stages of the novel? Should you focus on a key incident? Each approach is possible. In choosing an approach, be guided by the nature of the problem and by your own interests.

You decide to restrict your study to Pip's relationship with the convict, Abel Magwitch. At this point you begin taking notes.

Do not be concerned about taking too many notes. Until you settle on a clear focus for your paper, you should record all your reactions.

Notes

When the convict returns many years after their meeting on the marshes, Pip thinks of him as a wild animal: "The abhorrence in which I held the man, the dread I had of him, the repugnance with which I shrank from him, could not have been exceeded if he had been some terrible beast" (page 658).

Pip is terrified to be alone with him and locks him in the bedroom.

Pip is disgusted by his manners. He eats "like a hungry old dog" (page 664).

Pip learns that the convict has risked his life in coming back to England. He feels a concern for the convict's safety and plans to get him out of England.

He learns about Magwitch's miserable life and the injustice he has suffered.

He finds out that the convict is Estella's father.

After the accident with the steamer, Pip refuses to abandon Magwitch. He provides him with dry clothes and looks after him. He accompanies him to London. He feels that his place is at Magwitch's side.

Pip recognizes that a change has taken place in his feelings: "For now my repugnance to him had all melted away, and in the hunted, wounded, shackled creature who held my hand in his, I only saw a man who had meant to be my benefactor, and who had felt affectionately, gratefully, and generously toward me with great constancy through a series of years" (page 700).

Pip has nothing to gain, but he does not desert Magwitch. He does not reveal that Magwitch's possessions will be forfeited to the Crown and that all his hopes of making Pip's fortune are gone.

While Magwitch is in the prison infirmary, Pip visits him every day. During the trial Pip holds his hand and comforts him.

After Magwitch is sentenced to death, Pip petitions the Home Secretary of State and others in authority.

When the old man is dying, Pip comforts him by telling him that his child is alive, that she has become a lady, and that he loves her.

From this set of notes we can conclude that Dickens emphasizes the change in Pip's attitude toward the convict Abel Magwitch. We can also derive a thesis statement: *As Pip develops compassion for Magwitch, we witness a reformation in his character.*

Organizing the Material

Before you begin writing, organize your main ideas into an outline. Your outline should provide for an introduction, a body, and a conclusion. The introduction should identify the author(s) and work(s). It should contain a statement of your thesis as well. The body of your paper should present the evidence supporting your thesis. The conclusion should bring together your main ideas.

The outline will grow out of the notes you have compiled. Remember that you need not use *all* the evidence you have collected. You should include material that has bearing on your topic.

This is one kind of outline. It indicates the main idea of each paragraph.

INTRODUCTION

Paragraph 1 *Thesis* As Pip develops compassion for Magwitch, we witness a reformation in his character.

BODY

Paragraph 2 Pip is terrified and repelled when the convict reenters his life many years after their meeting on the marshes.

Paragraph 3 As he learns more about Magwitch, Pip loses his fear and strong aversion to the man.

Paragraph 4 After the accident in which Magwitch is fatally injured, Pip acts out of deep sympathy rather than a sense of obligation.

Paragraph 5 Through his compassion for Magwitch, Pip becomes a more admirable and appealing character.

CONCLUSION

Paragraph 6 Dickens seems to be saying that compassion brings out the best in human nature.

Writing the Essay

Here is a model essay developing the thesis statement.

TITLE	THE THEME OF COMPASSION IN *GREAT EXPECTATIONS*
INTRODUCTION	An important theme in *Great Expectations* is the power of compassion to transform human nature. Dickens makes this clear when Pip undergoes a change in attitude toward his benefactor, the convict Abel Magwitch. *As Pip develops compassion for Magwitch, we witness a reformation in his character.*
Thesis Statement	
BODY	**Pip is terrified and repelled when the convict reenters his life many years after their meeting on the marshes.** Pip thinks of him as a wild animal: "The abhorrence in which I held the man, the dread I had of him, the repugnance with which I shrank from him, could not have been exceeded if he had been some terrible beast" (page 658). He is afraid to be alone with him, and after Magwitch goes to bed, Pip locks him in the bedroom. Pip finds his manners disgusting and watches him eat "like a hungry old dog" (page 664).
Topic Sentence	
Topic Sentence	**As he learns more about Magwitch, Pip loses his fear and strong aversion to the man.** He finds out that Magwitch has suffered great wretchedness and injustice. He also discovers that the convict is Estella's father. Realizing that the convict has risked his life in returning to England, Pip feels it is his duty to get the man out of the country.
Topic Sentence	**After the accident in which Magwitch is fatally injured, Pip acts out of deep sympathy rather than a sense of obligation.** He treats the old man with great kindness, providing him with dry clothing and obtaining comforts for him. He refuses to abandon him and accompanies him to prison in London. Pip recognizes the change in himself: "For now my repugnance to him had all melted away, and in the hunted, wounded, shackled creature who held my hand in his, I only saw a man who had meant to be my benefactor, and who had felt affectionately, gratefully, and generously toward me with great constancy through a series of years" (page 700).
Topic Sentence	**Through his compassion for Magwitch, Pip becomes a more admirable and appealing character.** His final scenes with Magwitch are the most moving passages in the book. While Magwitch is in the prison infirmary, Pip visits him every day. During the trial, Pip holds his hand and comforts him. Out of kindness he does not reveal that Magwitch's possessions will be forfeited to the Crown and that his hopes of making Pip's fortune are gone. After Magwitch receives his death sentence, Pip petitions the Home Secretary for mercy. He

sends out appeals to those in authority. Finally, to ease the old man's death, he tells him that his little girl (Estella) is alive, that she has become a lady, and that he loves her.

CONCLUSION **Dickens seems to be saying that compassion brings out the best in human nature.** Pip outgrows the snobbery that leads him to value appearance rather than substance. In recognizing the good in Magwitch's character, he becomes capable of gratitude and generosity of spirit.

Length: 485 words

Revising Papers

When you write an essay in class, you have a limited amount of time to plan and develop your essay. Nevertheless, you should save a few minutes to read over your work and make necessary corrections.

When an essay is assigned as homework, you have more time to prepare it carefully. Get into the habit of revising your work. A first draft of an essay should be treated as a rough copy of your manuscript. Chances are that reworking your first draft will result in a clearer and stronger paper.

When you revise your paper, examine it critically for awkward sentences, inexact language, errors in capitalization, punctuation, and spelling. Rewrite any passages that are unclear or incomplete.

Here are some guidelines for revision.

Guidelines for Revising a Paper

1. *Check to see that your major point, a thesis, is clearly stated.* In a short essay, the thesis should be stated in the first sentence. In a longer composition, the thesis should appear in the introductory paragraph.

2. *Follow a logical organization.* A long composition should have an introduction, a body, and a conclusion. Each part of the essay should be clearly related to the thesis.

3. *Make sure that ideas are adequately developed.* Support any generalization with specific evidence.

4. *Check for errors in capitalization, punctuation, spelling, and sentence structure.*

Here is an early draft of the model essay on pages 756–757, showing
how it was revised for greater clarity, accuracy, and conciseness.

~~One of the most~~ *An* important theme~~s~~ in ~~the novel~~ Great Expectations is the

power of compassion to transform human nature. ~~We see~~ *Dickens makes clear* this when Pip undergoes

a change in attitude toward Abel Magwitch, the convict ~~who is~~ his benefactor.

As Pip develops compassion for Magwitch, we witness a reformation in his

character.

Pip ~~has not seen the convict since his boyhood on the marshes. When Pip~~ *is terrified and repelled when the convict reenters his life many years after their meeting on the marshes.*

~~recognizes him, he is terrified.~~ Pip thinks of him as a wild animal: "The

abhorrence in which I held the man, the dread I had of him, the repugnance

with which I shrank from him, could not have been exceeded if he had been some

terrible beast" (page 658). ~~Physically he is repelled.~~ He is afraid to be

alone with him, and after Magwitch goes to bed, Pip locks him in the bedroom.

Pip finds his manners disgusting and watches him eat "like a hungry old dog"

(page 664).

~~Pip begins to change~~ *Pip loses his fear and strong aversion to the man.* as he learns *more* about Magwitch~~'s life~~. He finds out

~~how~~ *that* Magwitch has suffered *great wretchedness and injustice.* He also discovers that the convict is Estella's

father. ~~Magwitch~~ *Realizing that the convict* has risked his life in returning to England, Pip feels it is

his duty to get the man out of the country.

After the accident ~~with the steamer, Pip treats the old man more~~ *in which Magwitch is fatally injured, Pip acts out of deep sympathy rather than a sense of obligation.*

~~sympathetically.~~ He provides him with dry clothing and *treats the old man with great kindness, obtaining comforts for him.* ~~looks after him.~~

758   *Reading and Writing About Literature*

He refuses to abandon him and
~~When the old man is taken~~ to prison in London, ~~Pip~~ accompanies him~~.~~

Pip recognizes ~~that~~ _the_ a change ~~has taken place in his feelings~~ _in himself:_ "For

now my repugnance to him had all melted away, and in the hunted,

wounded, shackled creature who held my hand in his, I only saw a man

who had meant to be my benefactor, and who had felt affectionately,

gratefully, and generously toward me with great constancy through a

series of years" (page 700).

✓ His final scenes with Magwitch are the most moving passages in the

book. _While Magwitch is in the prison infirmary,_ Pip visits him ~~in the infirmary~~ every day. During the trial,

Pip holds his hand and comforts him. Through his compassion for

Magwitch, Pip becomes a more admirable and appealing character. _Out of kindness_ He does

reveal _Magwitch's_
not ~~tell Magwitc~~h that ~~his~~ possessions will be forfeited to the Crown and

that his hopes of making Pip's fortune are gone. After Magwitch

petitions the Home Secretary for mercy.
receives his death sentence, Pip ~~does not give up hope of saving him.~~
He sends out appeals to those in authority. Finally, to ease the old man's death,
~~When the old man is dying~~, he tells him that his _little girl (Estella)_ ~~child~~ is alive, that

she has become a lady, and that he loves her.

Dickens seems to be saying that compassion brings out the best in

Pip outgrows the snobbery that leads him to value appearance rather than
human nature. ~~At the end of the book, Pip is no longer a snob.~~ In

recognizing the good in Magwitch's character, he becomes capable of

of spirit
gratitude and generosity.

Rolls for the Czar   *Robin Kinkead*

This is a tale of the days of the Czars, of ermine and gold and pure white bread.

In Saint Petersburg[1] the Czar held his court with pomp and ceremony that dazzled peasants and ambassadors alike. His Winter Palace covered acres by the side of the frozen Neva.[2] It had pillars of lapis lazuli[3] and of rare stone from the Urals. Its halls held treasures from all the world.

Once a year the Czar paid a visit of state to Moscow, where the rich merchants lived, trade center of the Imperial Domain. Here he would sit in the throne room of the Kremlin,[4] where his ancestors once ruled warring Muscovy.[5]

There was another great man in Moscow — a baker, Markov by name. The master bakers of the city were famous, and Markov was prince among them. His cakes and pastry were renowned throughout all the Russias, but his rolls were the best of all: pure white, like the driven snow of the steppes, a crust just hard enough to crunch, the bread not too soft, but soft enough to hold the melted butter.

Merchant princes from the gold rivers of Siberia, chieftains from the Caucasus in high fur hats, nobles from their feudal estates in the country, all came to Moscow to eat Markov's rolls.

The Czar himself was a mighty eater and especially fond of Markov's delicacies. So one day in February, when it came time for a visit to Moscow, he was thinking of Markov and his art, anticipating the rolls. His private car bore the imperial coat of arms. The rest of the train was filled with grand dukes, princes of the blood, and noble ladies. The railroad track ran straight as an arrow five hundred miles through the snow, the white birch forests, and the pines.

The train chuffed into the Moscow station, into a morning of sun and frost. The sun sparkled on the gold domes of churches, it glittered on the cuirasses[6] of a regiment of guards, all men of noble birth. Smoke rose straight up from chimneys. Twin jets of steam snorted from the nostrils of the three horses of the Czar's troika.[7] The Czar had a fine appetite.

The horses' hoofs kicked up gouts of snow as they galloped over the moat and through the gate in the Kremlin wall. The Czar walked up the royal staircase, carpeted in red and lined with bowing servants. He was thinking of the rolls.

He went through the formal greetings with a distracted look, then sat down eagerly at the breakfast table. Not a glance did he give

---

1. **Saint Petersburg:** now known as Leningrad.
2. **Neva** (nē'və, nyĕ-vä'): a river.
3. **lapis lazuli** (lăp'ĭs lăz'yŏŏ-lē): azure-blue gemstone.
4. **Kremlin** (krĕm'lən): the citadel, or fortress, of Moscow.
5. **Muscovy** (mŭs'kə-vē): the Russian Empire.

6. **cuirasses** (kwĭ-răs'əz): The cuirass was a piece of armor for the breast and back.
7. **troika** (troi'kə): a small carriage drawn by a team of three horses.

the caviar, the smoked sterlets,[8] the pheasant in aspic. He watched the door. When a royal footman came through carrying a silver platter loaded with rolls, the Czar smiled. All was well.

The Czar rubbed his hands and took a steaming roll. He broke it open and the smile vanished from his face. A dead fly lay embedded in the bread. Courtiers crowded around to look.

"Bring Markov here!" said the Czar, with one of his terrible glances.

The banquet room was silent in tense horror. Markov came in puffing slightly but bearing himself with the pride of a master artist.

"Look at this, Markov," said the Czar, pointing at the fly, "and tell me what it is."

Markov looked and stood frozen for a moment. Princes, nobles, and servants all leaned forward waiting for doom to strike him. The Czar could bend horseshoes in his bare hands. A word from him and the bleak wastes of Siberia lay waiting.

No man could tell what Markov thought, but they knew that a fly had endangered his life. He reached to the platter and picked up the fly. He put it in his mouth and ate it. Every eye watched him swallow.

"It is a raisin, Sire," he said.

Wrath faded from the Czar's face. He broke out laughing and the nobles relaxed.

"Markov," he said, "we grant you a coat of arms with a fly as the motif.[9] A fly imperiled your life and a fly saved your life."

And the Czar went on with his rolls.

---

8. **sterlets** (stûr′līts): sturgeon from the Black Sea, a source of caviar.

9. **motif** (mō-tēf′): central figure in the design.

FOR STUDY AND DISCUSSION

1. The events of this story take place long before the Russian Revolution of 1917, when the government of the Czars was overthrown. What impression does this story create about "the days of the Czars"?

2. What is the effect of including "pure white bread" along with ermine and gold in the opening sentence?

3. Is Markov an admirable or a despicable figure? Give reasons for your answer.

4. The Czar rewards Markov with a coat of arms, a great honor. What insight does this action give you into the granting of honors by Russian royalty?

5. Is this story merely an amusing anecdote, or does it make a comment on human nature? Support your answer with specific evidence from the story.

SUGGESTIONS FOR WRITING

1. Why does the Czar reward Markov instead of punishing him? Write a brief essay giving your interpretation of this incident.

2. Show how the author conveys the magnificence and splendor of the Russian Empire during the reign of the Czars.

Who's There?   *Arthur C. Clarke*

When satellite control called me, I was writing up the day's progress report in the Observation Bubble—the glass-domed office that juts out from the axis of the Space Station like the hubcap of a wheel. It was not really a good place to work, for the view was too overwhelming. Only a few yards away I could see the construction teams performing their slow-motion ballet as they put the station together like a giant jigsaw puzzle. And beyond them, twenty thousand miles below, was the blue-green glory of the full Earth, floating against the raveled star clouds of the Milky Way.[1]

"Station Supervisor here," I answered. "What's the trouble?"

"Our radar's showing a small echo two miles away, almost stationary, about five degrees west of Sirius.[2] Can you give us a visual report on it?"

Anything matching our orbit so precisely could hardly be a meteor; it would have to be something we'd dropped—perhaps an inadequately secured piece of equipment that had drifted away from the station. So I assumed; but when I pulled out my binoculars and searched the sky around Orion,[3] I soon found my mistake. Though this space traveler was man-made, it had nothing to do with us.

"I've found it," I told Control. "It's someone's test satellite—cone-shaped, four antennas, and what looks like a lens system in its base. Probably U.S. Air Force, early nineteen-sixties, judging by the design. I know they lost track of several when their transmitters failed. There were quite a few attempts to hit this orbit before they finally made it."

After a brief search through the files, Control was able to confirm my guess. It took a little longer to find out that Washington wasn't in the least bit interested in our discovery of a twenty-year-old stray satellite, and would be just as happy if we lost it again.

"Well, we can't do *that*," said Control. "Even if nobody wants it, the thing's a menace to navigation. Someone had better go out and haul it aboard."

That someone, I realized, would have to be me. I dared not detach a man from the closely knit construction teams, for we were already behind schedule—and a single day's delay on this job cost a million dollars. All the radio and TV networks on Earth were waiting impatiently for the moment when they could route their programs through us, and thus provide the first truly global service, spanning the world from Pole to Pole.

"I'll go out and get it," I answered, snapping an elastic band over my papers so that the air currents from the ventilators wouldn't set them wandering around the room. Though I tried to sound as if I was doing everyone a great favor, I was secretly not at all displeased. It had been at least two weeks since I'd been outside; I was getting a little tired of stores schedules, maintenance reports, and all the glamorous ingredients of a Space Station Supervisor's life.

---

1. **Milky Way:** the galaxy in which the solar system is located. In the night sky, it is visible as a broad, shining band, created by billions of stars and clouds of interstellar gas.
2. **Sirius** (sĭr′ē-əs): the "Dog Star," in the constellation Canis Major (kā′nĭs mā′jər) in the Southern Hemisphere. It is the brightest star in the sky.
3. **Orion** (ō-rī′ən): a constellation that the ancient Greeks named for the hunter Orion, because the stars in the constellation form the figure of a man with a belt and a sword.

The only member of the staff I passed on my way to the air lock[4] was Tommy, our recently acquired cat. Pets mean a great deal to men thousands of miles from Earth, but there are not many animals that can adapt themselves to a weightless environment. Tommy mewed plaintively at me as I clambered into my spacesuit, but I was in too much of a hurry to play with him.

At this point, perhaps I should remind you that the suits we use on the station are completely different from the flexible affairs men wear when they want to walk around on the moon. Ours are really baby spaceships, just big enough to hold one man. They are stubby cylinders, about seven feet long, fitted with low-powered propulsion jets, and have a pair of accordion-like sleeves at the upper end for the operator's arms. Normally, however, you keep your hands drawn inside the suit, working the manual controls in front of your chest.

As soon as I'd settled down inside my very exclusive spacecraft, I switched on power and checked the gauges on the tiny instrument panel. There's a magic word, "FORB," that you'll often hear spacemen mutter as they climb into their suits; it reminds them to test fuel, oxygen, radio, batteries. All my needles were well in the safety zone, so I lowered the transparent hemisphere over my head and sealed myself in. For a short trip like this, I did not bother to check the suit's internal lockers, which were used to carry food and special equipment for extended missions.

As the conveyor belt decanted[5] me into the air lock, I felt like an Indian papoose being carried along on its mother's back. Then the pumps brought the pressure down to zero, the outer door opened, and the last traces of air swept me out into the stars, turning very slowly head over heels.

The station was only a dozen feet away, yet I was now an independent planet—a little world of my own. I was sealed up in a tiny, mobile cylinder, with a superb view of the entire universe, but I had practically no freedom of movement inside the suit. The padded seat and safety belts prevented me from turning around, though I could reach all the controls and lockers with my hands or feet.

In space, the great enemy is the sun, which can blast you to blindness in seconds. Very cautiously, I opened up the dark filters on the "night" side of my suit, and turned my head to look out at the stars. At the same time I switched the helmet's external sunshade to automatic, so that whichever way the suit gyrated my eyes would be shielded from that intolerable glare.

Presently, I found my target—a bright fleck of silver whose metallic glint distinguished it clearly from the surrounding stars. I stamped on the jet-control pedal, and felt the mild surge of acceleration as the low-powered rockets set me moving away from the station. After ten seconds of steady thrust, I estimated that my speed was great enough, and cut off the drive. It would take me five minutes to coast the rest of the way, and not much longer to return with my salvage.

And it was at that moment, as I launched myself out into the abyss, that I knew that something was horribly wrong.

It is never completely silent inside a spacesuit; you can always hear the gentle hiss of oxygen, the faint whirr of fans and motors, the susurration[6] of your own breathing—even if you listen carefully enough, the rhythmic

---

4. **air lock:** an airtight compartment, with adjustable pressure, between two places of unequal pressure.
5. **decanted** (dĭ-kănt′əd): unloaded.

6. **susurration** (sōō′sə-rā′shən): soft sound, as a murmur, whisper, or rustle.

thump that is the pounding of your heart. These sounds reverberate through the suit, unable to escape into the surrounding void; they are the unnoticed background of life in space, for you are aware of them only when they change.

They had changed now; to them had been added a sound which I could not identify. It was an intermittent, muffled thudding, sometimes accompanied by a scraping noise, as of metal upon metal.

I froze instantly, holding my breath and trying to locate the alien sound with my ears. The meters on the control board gave no clues; all the needles were rock-steady on their scales, and there were none of the flickering red lights that would warn of impending disaster. That was some comfort, but not much. I had long ago learned to trust my instincts in such matters; their alarm signals were flashing now, telling me to return to the station before it was too late. . . .

Even now, I do not like to recall those next few minutes, as panic slowly flooded into my mind like a rising tide, overwhelming the dams of reason and logic which every man must erect against the mystery of the universe. I knew then what it was like to face insanity; no other explanation fitted the facts.

For it was no longer possible to pretend that the noise disturbing me was that of some faulty mechanism. Though I was in utter isolation, far from any other human being or indeed any material object, I was not alone. The soundless void was bringing to my ears the faint but unmistakable stirrings of life.

In that first, heart-freezing moment it seemed that something was trying to get into my suit—something invisible, seeking shelter from the cruel and pitiless vacuum of space. I whirled madly in my harness, scanning the entire sphere of vision around me except for the blazing, forbidden cone toward the sun. There was nothing there, of course. There could not be—yet that purposeful scrabbling was clearer than ever.

Despite the nonsense that has been written about us, it is not true that spacemen are superstitious. But can you blame me if, as I came to the end of logic's resources, I suddenly remembered how Bernie Summers had died, no farther from the station than I was at this very moment?

It was one of those "impossible" accidents; it always is. Three things had gone wrong at once. Bernie's oxygen regulator had run wild and sent the pressure soaring, the safety valve had failed to blow—and a faulty joint had given way instead. In a fraction of a second, his suit was open to space.

I had never known Bernie, but suddenly his fate became of overwhelming importance to me—for a horrible idea had come into my mind. One does not talk about these things, but a damaged spacesuit is too valuable to be thrown away, even if it has killed its wearer. It is repaired, renumbered—and issued to someone else. . . .

What happens to the soul of a man who dies between the stars, far from his native world? Are you still here, Bernie, clinging to the last object that linked you to your lost and distant home?

As I fought the nightmares that were swirling around me—for now it seemed that the scratchings and soft fumblings were coming from all directions—there was one last hope to which I clung. For the sake of my sanity, I had to prove that this wasn't Bernie's suit— that the metal walls so closely wrapped around me had never been another man's coffin.

It took me several tries before I could press the right button and switch my transmitter to the emergency wave length. "Station!" I gasped. "I'm in trouble! Get records to check my suit history and——"

I never finished; they say my yell wrecked the microphone. But what man alone in the absolute isolation of a spacesuit would *not* have yelled when something patted him softly on the back of the neck?

I must have lunged forward, despite the safety harness, and smashed against the upper edge of the control panel. When the rescue squad reached me a few minutes later, I was still unconscious, with an angry bruise across my forehead.

And so I was the last person in the whole satellite relay system to know what had happened. When I came to my senses an hour later, all our medical staff was gathered around my bed, but it was quite a while before the doctors bothered to look at me. They were much too busy playing with the three cute little kittens our badly misnamed Tommy had been rearing in the seclusion of my spacesuit's Number Five Storage Locker.

FOR STUDY AND DISCUSSION

1. Science fiction typically deals with scientific possibilities of the future. What docs the setting of this story predict about our future life in outer space?

2. Using information provided in the story, explain the narrator's role in the Space Station.

3. Why is it necessary for someone to retrieve the test satellite? Why is the narrator eager to go?

4. Why does the narrator refer to his spacecraft as "very exclusive"?

5. What are the reasons for the narrator's panic? Why does he suddenly remember Bernie Summers?

6. What preparation has Clarke made for the ending of the story? Is it a satisfying conclusion?

SUGGESTIONS FOR WRITING

1. Analyze the way Clarke creates the sense of isolation one feels in outer space.

2. Although the events of this story are fictional, they are so well imagined that they seem authentic. Show how Clarke uses actual scientific developments and projected scientific inventions to create realistic effects.

A Mother in Mannville

Marjorie Kinnan Rawlings

The orphanage is high in the Carolina mountains. Sometimes in winter the snowdrifts are so deep that the institution is cut off from the village below, from all the world. Fog hides the mountain peaks, the snow swirls down the valleys, and a wind blows so bitterly that the orphanage boys who take the milk twice daily to the baby cottage reach the door with fingers stiff in an agony of numbness.

"Or when we carry trays from the cookhouse for the ones that are sick," Jerry said, "we get our faces frostbit, because we can't put our hands over them. I have gloves," he added. "Some of the boys don't have any."

He liked the late spring, he said. The rhododendron was in bloom, a carpet of color, across the mountainsides, soft as the May winds that stirred the hemlocks. He called it laurel.

"It's pretty when the laurel blooms," he said. "Some of it's pink and some of it's white."

I was there in the autumn. I wanted quiet, isolation, to do some troublesome writing. I wanted mountain air to blow out the malaria from too long a time in the subtropics. I was homesick, too, for the flaming of maples in October, and for corn shocks and pumpkins and black-walnut trees and the lift of hills. I found them all, living in a cabin that belonged to the orphanage, half a mile beyond the orphanage farm. When I took the cabin, I asked for a boy or man to come and chop wood for the fireplace. The first few days were warm, I found what wood I needed about the cabin, no one came, and I forgot the order.

I looked up from my typewriter one late afternoon, a little startled. A boy stood at the door, and my pointer dog, my companion, was at his side and had not barked to warn me. The boy was probably twelve years old, but undersized. He wore overalls and a torn shirt, and was barefooted.

He said, "I can chop some wood today."

I said, "But I have a boy coming from the orphanage."

"I'm the boy."

"You? But you're small."

"Size don't matter, chopping wood," he said. "Some of the big boys don't chop good. I've been chopping wood at the orphanage a long time."

I visualized mangled and inadequate branches for my fires. I was well into my work and not inclined to conversation. I was a little blunt.

"Very well. There's the ax. Go ahead and see what you can do."

I went back to work, closing the door. At first the sound of the boy dragging brush annoyed me. Then he began to chop. The blows were rhythmic and steady, and shortly I had forgotten him, the sound no more of an interruption than a consistent rain. I suppose an hour and a half passed, for when I stopped and stretched, and heard the boy's steps on the cabin stoop, the sun was dropping behind the farthest mountain, and the valleys were purple with something deeper than the asters.

The boy said, "I have to go to supper now. I can come again tomorrow evening."

I said, "I'll pay you now for what you've done," thinking I should probably have to insist on an older boy. "Ten cents an hour?"

"Anything is all right."

We went together back of the cabin. An astonishing amount of solid wood had been cut. There were cherry logs and heavy roots of rhododendron, and blocks from the waste pine and oak left from the building of the cabin.

"But you've done as much as a man," I said. "This is a splendid pile."

I looked at him, actually, for the first time. His hair was the color of the corn shocks and his eyes, very direct, were like the mountain sky when rain is pending—gray, with a shadowing of that miraculous blue. As I spoke, a light came over him, as though the setting sun had touched him with the same suffused glory with which it touched the mountains. I gave him a quarter.

"You may come tomorrow," I said, "and thank you very much."

He looked at me, and at the coin, and seemed to want to speak, but could not, and turned away.

"I'll split kindling tomorrow," he said over his thin ragged shoulder. "You'll need kindling and medium wood and logs and backlogs."

At daylight I was half wakened by the sound of chopping. Again it was so even in texture that I went back to sleep. When I left my bed in the cool morning, the boy had come and gone, and a stack of kindling was neat against the cabin wall. He came after school in the afternoon and worked until time to return to the orphanage. His name was Jerry; he was twelve years old, and he had been at the orphanage since he was four. I could picture him at four, with the same grave gray-blue eyes and the same—independence? No, the word that comes to me is "integrity."

The word means something very special to me, and the quality for which I use it is a rare one. My father had it—there is another of whom I am almost sure—but almost no man of my acquaintance possesses it with the clarity, the purity, the simplicity of a mountain stream. But the boy Jerry had it. It is bedded on courage, but it is more than brave. It is honest, but it is more than honesty. The ax handle broke one day. Jerry said the woodshop at the orphanage would repair it. I brought money to pay for the job and he refused it.

"I'll pay for it," he said. "I broke it. I brought the ax down careless."

"But no one hits accurately every time," I told him. "The fault was in the wood of the handle. I'll see the man from whom I bought it."

It was only then that he would take the money. He was standing back of his own carelessness. He was a free-will agent and he chose to do careful work, and if he failed, he took the responsibility without subterfuge.[1]

And he did for me the unnecessary thing, the gracious thing, that we find done only by the great of heart. Things no training can teach, for they are done on the instant, with no predicated[2] experience. He found a cubbyhole beside the fireplace that I had not noticed. There, of his own accord, he put kindling and "medium" wood, so that I might always have dry fire material ready in case of sudden wet weather. A stone was loose in the rough walk to the cabin. He dug a deeper hole and steadied it, although he came, him-

---

1. **subterfuge** (sŭb′tər-fyōōj′): deception.
2. **predicated** (prĕd′ə-kāt′əd): established.

self, by a short cut over the bank. I found that when I tried to return his thoughtfulness with such things as candy and apples, he was wordless. "Thank you" was, perhaps, an expression for which he had had no use, for his courtesy was instinctive. He only looked at the gift and at me, and a curtain lifted, so that I saw deep into the clear well of his eyes, and gratitude was there, and affection, soft over the firm granite of his character.

He made simple excuses to come and sit with me. I could no more have turned him away than if he had been physically hungry. I suggested once that the best time for us to visit was just before supper, when I left off my writing. After that, he waited always until my typewriter had been some time quiet. One day I worked until nearly dark. I went outside the cabin, having forgotten him. I saw him going up over the hill in the twilight toward the orphanage. When I sat down on my stoop, a place was warm from his body where he had been sitting.

He became intimate, of course, with my pointer, Pat. There is a strange communion between a boy and a dog. Perhaps they possess the same singleness of spirit, the same kind of wisdom. It is difficult to explain, but it exists. When I went across the state for a weekend, I left the dog in Jerry's charge. I gave him the dog whistle and the key to the cabin, and left sufficient food. He was to come two or three times a day and let out the dog, feed and exercise him. I should return Sunday night, and Jerry would take out the dog for the last time Sunday afternoon and then leave the key under an agreed hiding place.

My return was belated and fog filled the mountain passes so treacherously that I dared not drive at night. The fog held the next morning, and it was Monday noon before I reached the cabin. The dog had been fed and cared for that morning. Jerry came early in the afternoon, anxious.

"The superintendent said nobody would drive in the fog," he said. "I came just before bedtime last night and you hadn't come. So I brought Pat some of my breakfast this morning. I wouldn't have let anything happen to him."

"I was sure of that. I didn't worry."

"When I heard about the fog, I thought you'd know."

He was needed for work at the orphanage and he had to return at once. I gave him a dollar in payment, and he looked at it and went away. But that night he came in the darkness and knocked at the door.

"Come in, Jerry," I said, "if you're allowed to be away this late."

"I told maybe a story," he said. "I told them I thought you would want to see me."

"That's true," I assured him, and I saw his relief. "I want to hear about how you managed with the dog."

He sat by the fire with me, with no other light, and told me of their two days together. The dog lay close to him, and found a comfort there that I did not have for him. And it seemed to me that being with my dog, and caring for him, had brought the boy and me, too, together, so that he felt that he belonged to me as well as to the animal.

"He stayed right with me," he told me, "except when he ran in the laurel. He likes the laurel. I took him up over the hill and we both ran fast. There was a place where the grass was high and I lay down in it and hid. I could hear Pat hunting for me. He found my trail and he barked. When he found me, he acted crazy, and he ran around and around me, in circles."

We watched the flames.

"That's an apple log," he said. "It burns the prettiest of any wood."

We were very close.

He was suddenly impelled to speak of things he had not spoken of before, nor had I cared to ask him.

"You look a little bit like my mother," he said. "Especially in the dark, by the fire."

"But you were only four, Jerry, when you came here. You have remembered how she looked, all these years?"

"My mother lives in Mannville," he said.

For a moment, finding that he had a mother shocked me as greatly as anything in my life has ever done, and I did not know why it disturbed me. Then I understood my distress. I was filled with a passionate resentment that any woman should go away and leave her son. A fresh anger added itself. A son like this one—The orphanage was a wholesome place, the executives were kind, good people, the food was more than adequate, the boys were healthy, a ragged shirt was no hardship, nor the doing of clean labor. Granted, perhaps, that the boy felt no lack, what blood fed the bowels[3] of a woman who did not yearn over this child's lean body that had come in parturition[4] out of her own? At four he would have looked the same as now. Nothing, I thought, nothing in life could change those eyes. His quality must be apparent to an idiot, a fool. I burned with questions I could not ask. In any, I was afraid, there would be pain.

"Have you seen her, Jerry—lately?"

"I see her every summer. She sends for me."

I wanted to cry out, "Why are you not with her? How can she let you go away again?"

He said, "She comes up here from Mann-

ville whenever she can. She doesn't have a job now."

His face shone in the firelight.

"She wanted to give me a puppy, but they can't let any one boy keep a puppy. You remember the suit I had on last Sunday?" He was plainly proud. "She sent me that for Christmas. The Christmas before that"—he drew a long breath, savoring the memory—"she sent me a pair of skates."

"Roller skates?"

My mind was busy, making pictures of her, trying to understand her. She had not, then, entirely deserted or forgotten him. But why, then—I thought, "I must not condemn her without knowing."

"Roller skates. I let the other boys use them. They're always borrowing them. But they're careful of them."

What circumstances other than poverty—

"I'm going to take the dollar you gave me for taking care of Pat," he said, "and buy her a pair of gloves."

I could only say, "That will be nice. Do you know her size?"

"I think it's 8½," he said.

He looked at my hands.

"Do you wear 8½?" he asked.

"No. I wear a smaller size, a 6."

"Oh! Then I guess her hands are bigger than yours."

I hated her. Poverty or no, there was other food than bread, and the soul could starve as quickly as the body. He was taking his dollar to buy gloves for her big stupid hands, and she lived away from him, in Mannville, and contented herself with sending him skates.

"She likes white gloves," he said. "Do you think I can get them for a dollar?"

"I think so," I said.

I decided that I should not leave the mountains without seeing her and knowing for myself why she had done this thing.

---

3. **bowels:** an archaic meaning. The bowels were once believed to be the seat of pity.
4. **parturition** (pär'tyoo-rish'ən, pär'choo-, pär'too-): childbirth.

The human mind scatters its interests as though made of thistledown, and every wind stirs and moves it. I finished my work. It did not please me, and I gave my thoughts to another field. I should need some Mexican material.

I made arrangements to close my Florida place. Mexico immediately, and doing the writing there, if conditions were favorable. Then, Alaska with my brother. After that, heaven knew what or where.

I did not take time to go to Mannville to see Jerry's mother, nor even to talk with the orphanage officials about her. I was a trifle abstracted about the boy, because of my work and plans. And after my first fury at her—we did not speak of her again—his having a mother, any sort at all, not far away, in Mannville, relieved me of the ache I had about him. He did not question the anomalous[5] relation. He was not lonely. It was none of my concern.

He came every day and cut my wood and did small helpful favors and stayed to talk. The days had become cold, and often I let him come inside the cabin. He would lie on the floor in front of the fire, with one arm across the pointer, and they would both doze and wait quietly for me. Other days they ran with a common ecstasy through the laurel, and since the asters were not gone, he brought me back vermilion maple leaves, and chestnut boughs dripping with imperial yellow. I was ready to go.

I said to him, "You have been my friend, Jerry. I shall often think of you and miss you. Pat will miss you too. I am leaving tomorrow."

He did not answer. When he went away, I remember that a new moon hung over the mountains, and I watched him go in silence up the hill. I expected him the next day, but he did not come. The details of packing my personal belongings, loading my car, arranging the bed over the seat, where the dog would ride, occupied me until late in the day. I closed the cabin and started the car, noticing that the sun was in the west and I should do well to be out of the mountains by nightfall. I stopped by the orphanage and left the cabin key and money for my light bill with Miss Clark.

"And will you call Jerry for me to say good-bye to him?"

"I don't know where he is," she said. "I'm afraid he's not well. He didn't eat his dinner this noon. One of the other boys saw him going over the hill into the laurel. He was supposed to fire the boiler this afternoon. It's not like him; he's unusually reliable."

I was almost relieved, for I knew I should never see him again, and it would be easier not to say goodbye to him.

I said, "I wanted to talk with you about his mother—why he's here—but I'm in more of a hurry than I expected to be. It's out of the question for me to see her now too. But here's some money I'd like to leave with you to buy things for him at Christmas and on his birthday. It will be better than for me to try to send him things. I could so easily duplicate—skates, for instance."

She blinked her honest spinster's eyes.

"There's not much use for skates here," she said.

Her stupidity annoyed me.

"What I mean," I said, "is that I don't want to duplicate things his mother sends him. I might have chosen skates if I didn't know she had already given them to him."

She stared at me.

"I don't understand," she said. "He has no mother. He has no skates."

---

5. **anomalous** (ə-nŏm′ə-ləs); irregular; abnormal.

1. How does the narrator's attitude toward Jerry change during the course of the story?
2. In what way is the relationship that develops between Jerry and the narrator a mother-son relationship? How does the narrator fail to understand Jerry's feelings?
3. The narrator says that Jerry had integrity. Yet he tells a lie. What causes Jerry to lie about his mother?
4. After deciding to see Jerry's mother, the narrator decides against it: "It was none of my concern." How would you describe the conflict within her?

5. Toward the end of the story, did you find the narrator's reaction to Jerry sensitive or insensitive? Explain your answer.

SUGGESTIONS FOR WRITING

1. Describe the various stages of the relationship between the narrator and Jerry.
2. As you have learned, an author reveals what a character is like through methods of direct and indirect characterization (see pages 36, 43, 53, and 796). Show how Rawlings presents and develops the character of Jerry, referring to specific details in the story.

The Eclipse   *Selma Lagerlöf*
Translated by Velma Swanston Howard

There were Stina of Ridgecôte and Lina of Birdsong and Kajsa of Littlemarsh and Maja of Skypeak and Beda of Finn-darkness and Elin, the new wife on the old soldier's place, and two or three other peasant women besides—all of them lived at the far end of the parish, below Storhöjden, in a region so wild and rocky none of the big farm owners had bothered to lay hands on it.

One had her cabin set up on a shelf of rock, another had hers put up at the edge of a bog, while a third had one that stood at the crest of a hill so steep it was a toilsome climb getting to it. If by chance any of the others had a cottage built on more favorable ground, you may be sure it lay so close to the mountain as to shut out the sun from autumn fair time clear up to Annunciation Day.[1]

They each cultivated a little potato patch close by the cabin, though under serious difficulties. To be sure, there were many kinds of soil there at the foot of the mountain, but it was hard work to make the patches of land yield anything. In some places they had to

---

1. **Annunciation Day:** March 25, the day commemorating the appearance of the angel Gabriel to Mary (Luke 1:26–38).

clear away so much stone from their fields, it would have built a cow-house on a manorial estate;[2] in some they had dug ditches as deep as graves, and in others they had brought their earth in sacks and spread it on the bare rocks. Where the soil was not so poor, they were forever fighting the tough thistle and pigweed which sprang up in such profusion you would have thought the whole potato land had been prepared for their benefit.

All the livelong day the women were alone in their cabins; for even where one had a husband and children, the man went off to his work every morning and the children went to school. A few among the older women had grown sons and daughters, but they had gone to America. And some there were with little children, who were always around, of course; but these could hardly be regarded as company.

Being so much alone, it was really necessary that they should meet sometimes over the coffee cups. Not that they got on so very well together, nor had any great love for each other; but some liked to keep posted on what the others were doing, and some grew despondent living like that, in the shadow of the mountain, unless they met people now and then. And there were those, too, who needed to unburden their hearts, and talk about the last letter from America, and those who were naturally talkative and jocular,[3] and who longed for opportunity to make use of these happy God-given talents.

Nor was it any trouble at all to prepare for a little party. Coffeepot and coffee cups they all had of course, and cream could be got at the manor, if one had no cow of one's own to milk; fancy biscuits and small cakes one could, at a pinch, get the dairyman's driver to fetch from the municipal[4] bakery, and country merchants who sold coffee and sugar were to be found everywhere. So, to get up a coffee party was the easiest thing imaginable. The difficulty lay in finding an occasion.

For Stina of Ridgecôte, Lina of Birdsong, Kajsa of Littlemarsh, Maja of Skypeak, Beda of Finn-darkness, and Elin, the new wife at the old soldier's, were all agreed that it would never do for them to celebrate in the midst of the common everyday life. Were they to be that wasteful of the precious hours which never return, they might get a bad name. And to hold coffee parties on Sundays or great Holy Days was out of the question; for then the married women had husband and children at home, which was quite company enough. As for the rest—some liked to attend church, some wished to visit relatives, while a few preferred to spend the day at home, in perfect peace and stillness, that they might really feel it was a Holy Day.

Therefore they were all the more eager to take advantage of every possible opportunity. Most of them gave parties on their name-days,[5] though some celebrated the great event when the wee little one cut its first tooth, or when it took its first steps. For those who received money-letters from America, that was always a convenient excuse, and it was also in order to invite all the women of the neighborhood to come and help tack a quilt or stretch a web just off the loom.

All the same, there were not nearly as many occasions to meet as were needed. One year one of the women was at her wits' end. It was her turn to give a party, and she had no

---

2. **manorial** (mă-nôr′ē-əl) **estate:** The manor was the main house or mansion on a large, landed estate.
3. **jocular** (jŏk′yə-lər): given to joking.

4. **municipal** (myōō-nĭs′ə-pəl): city.
5. **name-days:** The name-day is the feast day of the saint after whom a person is named.

objection to carrying out what was expected of her; but she could not seem to hit upon anything to celebrate. Her own name-day she could not celebrate, being named Beda, as Beda had been stricken out of the almanac. Nor could she celebrate that of any member of her family, for all her dear ones were resting in the churchyard. She was very old, and the quilt she slept under would probably outlast her. She had a cat of which she was very fond. Truth to tell, it drank coffee just as well as she did; but she could hardly bring herself to hold a party for a cat!

Pondering, she searched her almanac again and again, for there she felt she must surely find the solution of her problem.

She began at the beginning, with "The Royal House" and "Signs and Forecasts," and read on, right through to "Markets and Postal Transmittances for 1912," without finding anything.

As she was reading the book for the seventh time, her glance rested on "Eclipses." She noted that that year, which was the year of our Lord nineteen-hundred twelve, on April seventeenth there would be a solar eclipse. It would begin at twenty minutes past high noon and end at 2:40 o'clock, and would cover nine-tenths of the sun's disk.

This she had read before, many times, without attaching any significance to it; but now, all at once, it became dazzlingly clear to her.

"Now I have it!" she exclaimed.

But it was only for a second or two that she felt confident; and then she put the thought away, fearing that the other women would just laugh at her.

The next few days, however, the idea that had come to her when reading her almanac kept recurring to her mind, until at last she began to wonder whether she hadn't better venture.[6] For when she thought about it, what friend had she in all the world she loved better than the Sun? Where her hut lay not a ray of sunlight penetrated her room the whole winter long. She counted the days until the Sun would come back to her in the spring. The Sun was the only one she longed for, the one who was always friendly and gracious to her and of whom she could never see enough.

She looked her years, and felt them, too. Her hands shook as if she were in a perpetual chill and when she saw herself in the looking glass, she appeared so pale and washed out, as if she had been lying out to bleach. It was only when she stood in a strong, warm, down-pouring sunshine that she felt like a live human being and not a walking corpse.

The more she thought about it, the more she felt there was no day in the whole year she would rather celebrate than the one when her friend the Sun battled against darkness, and after a glorious conquest, came forth with new splendor and majesty.

The seventeenth of April was not far away, but there was ample time to make ready for a party. So, on the day of the eclipse Stina, Lina, Kajsa, Maja, and the other women all sat drinking coffee with Beda at Finn-darkness. They drank their second and third cups, and chatted about everything imaginable. For one thing, they said they couldn't for the life of them understand why Beda should be giving a party.

Meanwhile, the eclipse was under way. But they took little notice of it. Only for a moment, when the sky turned blackish gray, when all nature seemed under a leaden pall,[7] and there came driving a howling wind with

---

6. **venture** (věn'chər): dare, take a risk.
7. **leaden pall:** gloomy atmosphere.

sounds as of the Trumpet of Doom and the lamentations of Judgment Day[8]—only then did they pause and feel a bit awed. But here they each had a fresh cup of coffee, and the feeling soon passed.

When all was over, and the Sun stood out in the heavens so beamingly happy—it seemed to them it had not shone with such brilliancy and power the whole year—they saw old Beda go over to the window, and stand with folded hands. Looking out toward the sunlit slope, she sang in her quavering[9] voice:

Thy shining sun goes up again,
I thank Thee, O my Lord!
With new-found courage, strength and hope,
I raise a song of joy.

Thin and transparent, old Beda stood there in the light of the window, and as she sang the sunbeams danced about her, as if wanting

---

8. **Trumpet . . . Day:** the day of God's final judgment.
9. **quavering:** trembling.

to give her, also, of their life and strength and color.

When she had finished the old hymn-verse she turned and looked at her guests, as if in apology.

"You see," she said, "I haven't any better friend than the Sun, and I wanted to give her a party on the day of her eclipse. I felt that we should come together to greet her, when she came out of her darkness."

Now they understood what old Beda meant, and their hearts were touched. They began to speak well of the Sun. "She was kind to rich and poor alike, and when she came peeping into the hut on a winter's day, she was as comforting as a glowing fire on the hearth. Just the sight of her smiling face made life worth living, whatever the troubles one had to bear."

The women went back to their homes after the party, happy and content. They somehow felt richer and more secure in the thought that they had a good, faithful friend in the Sun.

FOR STUDY AND DISCUSSION

1. How does the author convey the hardships that the peasant women have to endure?
2. What is the purpose of the coffee parties?
3. Why does Beda choose a solar eclipse as the occasion for a party?
4. How does the eclipse reaffirm the women's faith in life?

SUGGESTIONS FOR WRITING

1. Show how nature in this story functions as both antagonist and ally in the struggle for life.
2. Behind the events of this story there is a *theme*, a general idea about life (see pages 130, 138, 146, and 813). Discuss the theme of the story, accounting for the key incidents.

A Horseman in the Sky *Ambrose Bierce*

I

One sunny afternoon in the autumn of the year 1861 a soldier lay in a clump of laurel by the side of a road in western Virginia. He lay at full length upon his stomach, his feet resting upon the toes, his head upon the left forearm. His extended right hand loosely grasped his rifle. But for the somewhat methodical disposition of his limbs and a slight rhythmic movement of the cartridge box at the back of his belt he might have been thought to be dead. He was asleep at his post of duty. But if detected he would be dead shortly afterward, death being the just and legal penalty of his crime.

The clump of laurel in which the criminal lay was in the angle of a road which after ascending southward a steep acclivity[1] to that point turned sharply to the west, running along the summit for perhaps one hundred yards. There it turned southward again and went zigzagging downward through the forest. At the salient[2] of that second angle was a large flat rock, jutting out northward, overlooking the deep valley from which the road ascended. The rock capped a high cliff; a stone dropped from its outer edge would have fallen sheer downward one thousand feet to the tops of the pines. The angle where the soldier lay was on another spur of the same cliff. Had he been awake he would have commanded a view, not only of the short arm of the road and the jutting rock, but of the entire profile of the cliff below it. It might well have made him giddy to look.

The country was wooded everywhere except at the bottom of the valley to the northward, where there was a small natural meadow, through which flowed a stream scarcely visible from the valley's rim. This open ground looked hardly larger than an ordinary dooryard, but was really several acres in extent. Its green was more vivid than that of the inclosing forest. Away beyond it rose a line of giant cliffs similar to those upon which we are supposed to stand in our survey of the savage scene, and through which the road had somehow made its climb to the summit. The configuration of the valley, indeed, was such that from this point of observation it seemed entirely shut in, and one could but have wondered how the road which found a way out of it had found a way into it, and whence came and whither went the waters of the stream that parted the meadow more than a thousand feet below.

No country is so wild and difficult but men will make it a theater of war; concealed in the forest at the bottom of that military rattrap, in which half a hundred men in possession of the exits might have starved an army to submission, lay five regiments of Federal infantry. They had marched all the previous day and night and were resting. At nightfall they would take to the road again, climb to the place where their unfaithful sentinel now slept, and descending the other slope of the ridge fall upon a camp of the enemy at about midnight. Their hope was to surprise it, for the road led to the rear of it. In case of failure, their position would be perilous in the extreme; and fail they surely would should accident or vigilance apprise the enemy of the movement.

---

1. **acclivity** (ə-klĭv′ə-tē): upward slope.
2. **salient** (sā′lē-ənt): projecting part.

The sleeping sentinel in the clump of laurel was a young Virginian named Carter Druse. He was the son of wealthy parents, an only child, and had known such ease and cultivation and high living as wealth and taste were able to command in the mountain country of western Virginia. His home was but a few miles from where he now lay. One morning he had risen from the breakfast table and said, quietly but gravely: "Father, a Union regiment has arrived at Grafton. I am going to join it."

The father lifted his leonine[3] head, looked at the son a moment in silence, and replied: "Well, go, sir, and whatever may occur do what you conceive to be your duty. Virginia, to which you are a traitor, must get on without you. Should we both live to the end of the war, we will speak further of the matter. Your mother, as the physician has informed you, is in a most critical condition; at the best she cannot be with us longer than a few weeks, but that time is precious. It would be better not to disturb her."

So Carter Druse, bowing reverently to his father, who returned the salute with a stately courtesy that masked a breaking heart, left the home of his childhood to go soldiering. By conscience and courage, by deeds of devotion and daring, he soon commended himself to his fellows and his officers; and it was to these qualities and to some knowledge of the country that he owed his selection for his present perilous duty at the extreme outpost.

Nevertheless, fatigue had been stronger than resolution and he had fallen asleep. What good or bad angel came in a dream to rouse him from his state of crime, who shall say? Without a movement, without a sound, in the profound silence and the languor of the late afternoon, some invisible messenger of fate touched with unsealing finger the eyes of his consciousness—whispered into the ear of his spirit the mysterious awakening word which no human lips ever have spoken, no human memory ever has recalled. He quietly raised his forehead from his arm and looked between the masking stems of the laurels, instinctively closing his right hand about the stock of his rifle.

His first feeling was a keen artistic delight. On a colossal pedestal, the cliff—motionless at the extreme edge of the capping rock and sharply outlined against the sky—was an equestrian[4] statue of impressive dignity. The figure of the man sat the figure of the horse, straight and soldierly, but with the repose of a Grecian god carved in the marble which limits the suggestion of activity. The gray costume harmonized with its aerial background; the metal of accoutrement[5] and caparison[6] was softened and subdued by the shadow; the animal's skin had no points of high light. A carbine strikingly foreshortened lay across the pommel of the saddle, kept in place by the right hand grasping it at the "grip"; the left hand, holding the bridle rein, was invisible. In silhouette against the sky

---

3. **leonine** (lē′ə-nīn′): characteristic of the lion; here, referring to the father's long hair and imposing appearance.

4. **equestrian** (ĭ-kwĕs′trē-ən): on horseback.
5. **accoutrement** (ə-kōō′trē-mənt): equipment other than weapons and dress issued to a soldier.
6. **caparison** (kə-păr′ə-sən): ornamental cover placed on a horse.

the profile of the horse was cut with the sharpness of a cameo;[7] it looked across the heights of air to the confronting cliffs beyond. The face of the rider, turned slightly away, showed only an outline of temple and beard; he was looking downward to the bottom of the valley. Magnified by its lift against the sky and by the solider's testifying sense of the formidablenessness of a near enemy the group appeared of heroic, almost colossal, size.

For an instant Druse had a strange, half-defined feeling that he had slept to the end of the war and was looking upon a noble work of art reared upon that eminence[8] to commemorate the deeds of an heroic past of which he had been an inglorious part. The feeling was dispelled by a slight movement of the group: the horse, without moving its feet, had drawn its body slightly backward from the verge; the man remained immobile as before. Broad awake and keenly alive to the significance of the situation, Druse now brought the butt of his rifle against his cheek by cautiously pushing the barrel forward through the bushes, cocked the piece, and glancing through the sights covered a vital spot of the horseman's breast. A touch upon the trigger and all would have been well with Carter Druse. At that instant the horseman turned his head and looked in the direction of his concealed foeman—seemed to look into his very face, into his eyes, into his brave, compassionate heart.

Is it then so terrible to kill an enemy in war—an enemy who has surprised a secret vital to the safety of one's self and comrades—an enemy more formidable for his knowledge than all his army for its numbers? Carter Druse grew pale; he shook in every limb,

turned faint, and saw the statuesque group before him as black figures, rising, falling, moving unsteadily in arcs of circles in a fiery sky. His hand fell away from his weapon, his head slowly dropped until his face rested on the leaves in which he lay. This courageous gentleman and hardy soldier was near swooning from intensity of emotion.

It was not for long; in another moment his face was raised from earth, his hands resumed their places on the rifle, his forefinger sought the trigger; mind, heart, and eyes were clear, conscience and reason sound. He could not hope to capture that enemy; to alarm him would but send him dashing to his camp with his fatal news. The duty of the soldier was plain: the man must be shot dead from ambush—without warning, without a moment's spiritual preparation, with never so much as an unspoken prayer, he must be sent to his account. But no—there is a hope; he may have discovered nothing—perhaps he is but admiring the sublimity of the landscape. If permitted, he may turn and ride carelessly away in the direction whence he came. Surely it will be possible to judge at the instant of his withdrawing whether he knows. It may well be that his fixity[9] of attention—Druse turned his head and looked through the deeps of air downward, as from the surface to the bottom of a translucent sea. He saw creeping across the green meadow a sinuous line of figures of men and horses—some foolish commander was permitting the soldiers of his escort to water their beasts in the open, in plain view from a dozen summits!

Druse withdrew his eyes from the valley and fixed them again upon the group of man and horse in the sky, and again it was through

---

7. **cameo** (kăm'ē-ō'): a carving in raised relief, often showing a head in profile.
8. **eminence** (ĕm'ə-nəns): here, raised position.

9. **fixity** (fĭk'sə-tē): steadiness.

the sights of his rifle. But this time his aim was at the horse. In his memory, as if they were a divine mandate,[10] rang the words of his father at their parting: "Whatever may occur, do what you conceive to be your duty." He was calm now. His teeth were firmly but not rigidly closed; his nerves were as tranquil as a sleeping babe's—not a tremor affected any muscle of his body; his breathing, until suspended in the act of taking aim, was regular and slow. Duty had conquered; the spirit had said to the body: "Peace, be still." He fired.

III

An officer of the Federal force, who in a spirit of adventure or in quest of knowledge had left the hidden bivouac[11] in the valley, and with aimless feet had made his way to the lower edge of a small open space near the foot of the cliff, was considering what he had to gain by pushing his exploration further. At a distance of a quarter mile before him, but apparently at a stone's throw, rose from its fringe of pines the gigantic face of rock, towering to so great a height above him that it made him giddy to look up to where its edge cut a sharp, rugged line against the sky. It presented a clean, vertical profile against a background of blue sky to a point half the way down, and of distant hills, hardly less blue, thence to the tops of the trees at its base. Lifting his eyes to the dizzy altitude of its summit the officer saw an astonishing sight—a man on horseback riding down into the valley through the air!

Straight upright sat the rider, in military fashion, with a firm seat in the saddle, a strong clutch upon the rein to hold his charger from too impetuous a plunge. From his bare head his long hair streamed upward, waving like a plume. His hands were concealed in the cloud of the horse's lifted mane.

The animal's body was as level as if every hoof stroke encountered the resistant earth. Its motions were those of a wild gallop, but even as the officer looked they ceased, with all the legs thrown sharply forward as in the act of alighting from a leap. But this was a flight!

Filled with amazement and terror by this apparition of a horseman in the sky—half believing himself the chosen scribe[12] of some new Apocalypse,[13] the officer was overcome by the intensity of his emotions; his legs failed him and he fell. Almost at the same instant he heard a crashing sound in the trees—a sound that died without an echo—and all was still.

The officer rose to his feet, trembling. The familiar sensation of an abraded shin recalled his dazed faculties. Pulling himself together he ran rapidly obliquely away from the cliff to a point distant from its foot; thereabout he expected to find his man; and thereabout he naturally failed. In the fleeting instant of his vision his imagination had been so wrought upon by the apparent grace and ease and intention of the marvelous performance that it did not occur to him that the line of march of aerial cavalry is directly downward,

---

10. **mandate** (măn′dāt′): authoritative command.
11. **bivouac** (bĭv′ōō-ăk, bĭv′wăk): temporary encampment of soldiers in the open.
12. **chosen scribe** (skrīb): writer selected by God.
13. **Apocalypse** (ə-pŏk′ə-lĭps′): revelation; an allusion to the last book of the New Testament.

and that he could find the objects of his search at the very foot of the cliff. A half-hour later he returned to camp.

This officer was a wise man; he knew better than to tell an incredible truth. He said nothing of what he had seen. But when the commander asked him if in his scout he had learned anything of advantage to the expedition he answered:

"Yes, sir; there is no road leading down into this valley from the southward."

The commander, knowing better, smiled.

IV

After firing his shot, Private Carter Druse reloaded his rifle and resumed his watch. Ten minutes had hardly passed when a Federal sergeant crept cautiously to him on hands and knees. Druse neither turned his head nor looked at him, but lay without motion or sign of recognition.

"Did you fire?" the sergeant whispered.

"Yes."

"At what?"

"A horse. It was standing on yonder rock—pretty far out. You see it is no longer there. It went over the cliff."

The man's face was white, but he showed no other sign of emotion. Having answered, he turned away his eyes and said no more. The sergeant did not understand.

"See here, Druse," he said, after a moment's silence, "it's no use making a mystery. I order you to report. Was there anybody on the horse?"

"Yes."

"Well?"

"My father."

"The sergeant rose to his feet and walked away. "Good God!" he said.

FOR STUDY AND DISCUSSION

1. In Part I we learn that five regiments of Federal infantry are camped in a valley. What is their mission? Why are they vulnerable?

2. The sentinel is guarding a road. Why is this road strategically important?

3. In Part II, we learn about the sentinel's background. How does the scene between Carter Druse and his father convince you that both men are high-minded idealists?

4. When Druse sees the figure on the cliff, he hesitates to shoot. What "hope" does he entertain? Why does he decide to fire?

5. In Part III the action is witnessed from the point of view of an unnamed Federal officer. Why is he unnerved by what he sees?

6. What terrible irony is revealed in Part IV? How has Bierce prepared the reader for this ending?

7. In what way does this story make a powerful statement against war?

SUGGESTIONS FOR WRITING

1. Compare Bierce's story with "War" (page 99). Do you think the authors are making a similar statement about war, or different statements? Defend your answer with specific reference to details in both stories.

2. Analyze the character of Carter Druse. In the light of what you learn about him, is what he does believable?

A Song of the Moon *Claude McKay*

The moonlight breaks upon the city's domes,
And falls along cemented steel and stone,
Upon the grayness of a million homes,
Lugubrious° in unchanging monotone.

4. **lugubrious** (lŏŏ-gŏŏ′brē-əs, lŏŏ-gyŏŏ′-): mournful.

Upon the clothes behind the tenement,   5
That hang like ghosts suspended from the lines,
Linking each flat,° but to each indifferent,
Incongruous° and strange the moonlight shines.

7. **flat:** apartment.

8. **incongruous** (ĭn-kŏng′grŏŏ-əs): unsuitable.

There is no magic from your presence here,
So moon, sad moon, tuck up your trailing robe,   10
Whose silver seems antique and too severe
Against the glow of one electric globe.

Go spill your beauty on the laughing faces
Of happy flowers that bloom a thousand hues,
Waiting on tiptoe in the wilding° spaces,   15
To drink your wine mixed with sweet draughts° of dews.

15. **wilding:** uncultivated.
16. **draughts** (drăfts).

FOR STUDY AND DISCUSSION

1. What aspects of urban life are emphasized in the first two stanzas of the poem?
2. What makes the moonlight "incongruous and strange" (line 8)?
3. In line 9 the poet says that there is no magic in the moon's presence. What does he mean by "magic"? Why is it lacking in the scene?
4. Why does the poet address the moon as "sad" in line 10?
5. Where does the poet feel the beauty of moonlight belongs?

SUGGESTION FOR WRITING

Compare and contrast "A Song of the Moon" with "Silver" (page 275). In your essay, be sure to include a discussion of imagery, personification, and mood.

Siren Song   *Margaret Atwood*

This is the one song everyone
would like to learn: the song
that is irresistible:

the song that forces men
to leap overboard in squadrons   5
even though they see the beached skulls

the song nobody knows
because anyone who has heard it
is dead, and the others can't remember.

Shall I tell you the secret   10
and if I do, will you get me
out of this bird suit?

I don't enjoy it here
squatting on this island
looking picturesque and mythical   15

with these two feathery maniacs,
I don't enjoy singing
this trio, fatal and valuable.

I will tell the secret to you,
to you, only to you.   20
Come closer. This song

is a cry for help: Help me!
Only you, only you can,
you are unique

at last. Alas   25
it is a boring song
but it works every time.

FOR STUDY AND DISCUSSION

1. In Greek mythology the Sirens were creatures, half bird and half woman, that lured sailors to their destruction by singing enchanting songs. Which lines in the poem allude to the fate of seamen trapped by the song of the Sirens?

2. To whom is the speaker talking? How does she lure him to his death?

SUGGESTION FOR WRITING

Contrast the approach of this Siren with that of the Sirens in Homer's *Odyssey*, pages 507–508.

This play takes place in France during World War II. In 1940 the Germans invaded France. A government formed under Marshal Pétain surrendered and agreed to collaborate with Hitler. Many French people refused to accept the humiliating terms of the Occupation and formed a resistance movement. They continued to fight for freedom as an underground force.

The Pen of My Aunt   *Gordon Daviot*

Characters

Madame
Stranger
Corporal
Simone

Scene: *A French country house during the Occupation. The lady of the house is seated in her drawing room.*

Simone (*approaching*). Madame! Oh, madame! Madame, have you —

Madame. Simone.

Simone. Madame, have you seen what —

Madame. Simone!

Simone. But madame —

Madame. Simone, this may be an age of barbarism, but I will have none of it inside the walls of this house.

Simone. But madame, there is a — there is a —

Madame (*silencing her*). Simone. France may be an occupied country, a ruined nation, and a conquered race, but we will keep, if you please, the usages of civilization.

Simone. Yes, madame.

Madame. One thing we still possess, thank God; and that is good manners. The enemy never had it; and it is not something they can take from *us*.

Simone. No, madame.

Madame. Go out of the room again. Open the door —

Simone. Oh, *madame!* I wanted to tell you —

Madame. — open the door, shut it behind you — quietly — take two paces into the room, and say what you came to say. (*Simone goes hastily out, shutting the door. She reappears, shuts the door behind her, takes two paces into the room, and waits.*) Yes, Simone?

Simone. I expect it is too late now; they will be here.

Madame. Who will?

Simone. The soldiers who were coming up the avenue.

Madame. After the last few months I should not have thought that soldiers coming up the avenue was a remarkable fact. It is no doubt a party with a billeting order.[1]

Simone (*crossing to the window*). No, madame, it is two soldiers in one of their little cars, with a civilian between them.

Madame. Which civilian?

---

1. **billeting** (bĭl′ĭt-ĭng) **order:** a written order directing that quarters be provided for troops in a private house.

Simone. A stranger, madame.

Madame. A stranger? Are the soldiers from the Combatant branch?

Simone. No, they are those beasts of Administration. Look, they have stopped. They are getting out.

Madame (*at the window*). Yes, it is a stranger. Do you know him, Simone?

Simone. I have never set eyes on him before, madame.

Madame. You would know if he belonged to the district.

Simone. Oh, madame, I know every man between here and St. Estèphe.[2]

Madame (*dryly*). No doubt.

Simone. Oh, merciful God, they are coming up the steps.

Madame. My good Simone, that is what the steps were put there for.

Simone. But they will ring the bell and I shall have to——

Madame. And you will answer it and behave as if you had been trained by a butler and ten upper servants instead of being the charcoal-burner's daughter from over at Les Chênes.[3] (*This is said encouragingly, not in unkindness.*) You will be very calm and correct——

Simone. Calm! Madame! With my inside turning over and over like a wheel at a fair!

Madame. A good servant does not have an inside, merely an exterior. (*Comforting*) Be assured, my child. You have your place here; that is more than those creatures on our doorstep have. Let that hearten you——

Simone. Madame! They are not going to ring. They are coming straight in.

Madame (*bitterly*). Yes. They have forgotten long ago what bells are for.

[*Door opens.*]

Stranger (*in a bright, confident, casual tone*). Ah, there you are, my dear aunt. I am so glad. Come in, my friend, come in. My dear aunt, this gentleman wants you to identify me.

Madame. Identify you?

Corporal. We found this man wandering in the woods——

Stranger. The corporal found it inexplicable that anyone should wander in a wood.

Corporal. And he had no papers on him——

Stranger. And I rightly pointed out that if I carry all the papers one is supposed to these days, I am no good to God or man. If I put them in a hip pocket, I can't bend forward; if I put them in a front pocket, I can't bend at all.

Corporal. He said that he was your nephew, madame, but that did not seem to us very likely, so we brought him here.

[*There is the slightest pause; just one moment of silence.*]

Madame. But of course this is my nephew.

Corporal. He is?

Madame. Certainly.

Corporal. He lives here?

Madame (*assenting*). My nephew lives here.

Corporal. So! (*Recovering*) My apologies, madame. But you will admit that appearances were against the young gentleman.

Madame. Alas, Corporal, my nephew belongs to a generation who delight in flouting appearances. It is what they call "expressing their personality," I understand.

Corporal (*with contempt*). No doubt, madame.

Madame. Convention is anathema[4] to them, and there is no sin like conformity. Even a collar is an offense against their liberty, and a discipline not to be borne by free necks.

---

2. **St. Estèphe** (săn ə-stĕf′).
3. **Les Chênes** (lā shĕn′).

4. **anathema** (ə-năth′ə-mə): something that is cursed or shunned.

Corporal. Ah yes, madame. A little more discipline among your nephew's generation, and we might not be occupying your country today.

Stranger. You think it was that collar of yours that conquered my country? You flatter yourself, Corporal. The only result of wearing a collar like that is varicose veins[5] in the head.

Madame (*repressive*). Please! My dear boy. Let us not descend to personalities.

Stranger. The matter is not personal, my good aunt, but scientific. Wearing a collar like that retards the flow of fresh blood to the head, with the most disastrous consequences to the gray matter[6] of the brain. The hypothetical[7] gray matter. In fact, I have a theory —

Corporal. Monsieur,[8] your theories do not interest me.

Stranger. No? You do not find speculation interesting?

Corporal. In this world one judges by results.

Stranger (*after a slight pause of reflection*). I see. The collared conqueror sits in the high places while the collarless conquered lies about in the woods. And who comes best out of that, would you say? Tell me, Corporal, as man to man, do you never have a mad, secret desire to lie in a wood?

Corporal. I have only one desire, monsieur, and that is to see your papers.

Stranger (*taken off guard and filling in time*). My papers?

Madame. But is that necessary, Corporal? I have already told you that —

---

5. **varicose** (vărʹə-kōsʹ) **veins:** abnormally swollen or enlarged veins.
6. **gray matter:** the nerve tissue of the brain and spinal cord. Informally, the expression refers to brains or intelligence.
7. **hypothetical** (hīʹpə-thĕtʹĭ-kəl): theoretical; based on an assumption.
8. **Monsieur** (mə-syœʹ): a French title of courtesy, like ''Mister'' or ''sir'' in English.

Corporal. I know that madame is a very good collaborator and in good standing —

Madame. In that case —

Corporal. But when we begin an affair we like to finish it. I have asked to see monsieur's papers, and the matter will not be finished until I have seen them.

Madame. You acknowledge that I am in ''good standing,'' Corporal?

Corporal. So I have heard, madame.

Madame. Then I must consider it a discourtesy on your part to demand my nephew's credentials.

Corporal. It is no reflection on madame. It is a matter of routine, nothing more.

Stranger (*murmuring*). The great god Routine.

Madame. To ask for his papers was routine; to insist on their production is discourtesy. I shall say so to your Commanding Officer.

Corporal. Very good, madame. In the meantime, I shall inspect your nephew's papers.

Madame. And what if I —

Stranger (*quietly*). You may as well give it up, my dear. You could as easily turn a steamroller. They have only one idea at a time. If the Corporal's heart is set on seeing my papers, he shall see them. (*Moving towards the door*) I left them in the pocket of my coat.

Simone (*unexpectedly, from the background*). Not in your *linen* coat?

Stranger (*pausing*). Yes. Why?

Simone (*with apparently growing anxiety*). Your *cream* linen coat? The one you were wearing yesterday?

Stranger. Certainly.

Simone. Merciful Heaven! I sent it to the laundry!

Stranger. To the laundry!

Simone. Yes, monsieur; this morning; in the basket.

Stranger (*in incredulous anger*). You sent my coat, *with my papers in the pocket*, to the laundry!

Simone (*defensive and combatant*). I didn't know monsieur's papers were in the pocket.

Stranger. You didn't know! You didn't know that a packet of documents weighing half a ton were in the pocket. An identity card, a *laisser-passer*,[9] a food card, a drink card, an army discharge, a permission to wear civilian clothes, a permission to go farther than ten miles to the east, a permission to go more than ten miles to the west, a permission to—

Simone (*breaking in with spirit*). How was I to know the coat was heavy! I picked it up with the rest of the bundle that was lying on the floor.

Stranger (*snapping her head off*). My coat was on the back of the chair.

Simone. It was on the floor.

Stranger. On the back of the chair!

Simone. It was on the floor with your dirty shirt and your pajamas, and a towel and whatnot. I put my arms around the whole thing and then—woof! into the basket with them.

Stranger. I tell you that coat was on the back of the chair. It was quite clean and was not going to the laundry for two weeks yet—if then. I hung it there myself, and—

Madame. My dear boy, what does it matter? The damage is done now. In any case, they will find the papers when they unpack the basket, and return them tomorrow.

Stranger. If someone doesn't steal them. There are a lot of people who would like to lay hold of a complete set of papers, believe me.

Madame (*reassuring*). Oh, no. Old Fleureau is the soul of honesty. You have no need to worry about them. They will be back first thing tomorrow, you shall see; and then we shall have much pleasure in sending them to the Administration Office for the Corporal's inspection. Unless, of course, the Corporal insists on your personal appearance at the office.

Corporal (*cold and indignant*). I have seen monsieur. All that I want now is to see his papers.

Stranger. You shall see them, Corporal, you shall see them. The whole half ton of them. You may inspect them at your leisure. Provided, that is, that they come back from the laundry to which this idiot has consigned them.

Madame (*again reassuring*). They will come back, never fear. And you must not blame Simone. She is a good child, and does her best.

Simone (*with an air of belated virtue*). I am not one to pry into pockets.

Madame. Simone, show the Corporal out, if you please.

Simone (*natural feeling overcoming her for a moment*). He knows the way out. (*Recovering*) Yes, madame.

Madame. And Corporal, try to take your duties a little less literally in future. My countrymen appreciate the spirit rather than the letter.

Corporal. I have my instructions, madame, and I obey them. Good day, madame. Monsieur.

[*He goes, followed by* Simone—*door closes. There is a moment of silence.*]

Stranger. For a good collaborator, that was a remarkably quick adoption.

Madame. Sit down, young man. I will give you something to drink. I expect your knees are none too well.

Stranger. My knees, madame, are pure gelatine. As for my stomach, it seems to have disappeared.

Madame (*offering him the drink she has poured out*). This will recall it, I hope.

---

9. *laisser-passer* (lĕs′ā-pä-sā′): French for "allow to pass." A *laisser-passer* is a pass used in place of a passport.

Stranger. You are not drinking, madame.

Madame. Thank you, no.

Stranger. Not with strangers. It is certainly no time to drink with strangers. Nevertheless, I drink the health of a collaborator. (*He drinks.*) Tell me, madame, what will happen tomorrow when they find that you have no nephew?

Madame (*surprised*). But of course I have a nephew. I tell lies, my friend; but not *silly* lies. My charming nephew has gone to Bonneval for the day. He finds country life dull.

Stranger. Dull? This—this heaven?

Madame (*dryly*). He likes to talk and here there is no audience. At Headquarters in Bonneval he finds the audience sympathetic.

Stranger (*understanding the implication*). Ah.

Madame. He believes in the Brotherhood of Man—if you can credit it.

Stranger. After the last six months?

Madame. His mother was American, so he has half the Balkans in his blood. To say nothing of Italy, Russia, and the Levant.

Stranger (*half-amused*). I see.

Madame. A silly and worthless creature, but useful.

Stranger. Useful?

Madame. I—borrow his cloak.

Stranger. I see.

Madame. Tonight I shall borrow his identity papers, and tomorrow they will go to the office in St. Estèphe.

Stranger. But—he will have to know.

Madame (*placidly*). Oh, yes, he will know, of course.

Stranger. And how will you persuade such an enthusiastic collaborator to deceive his friends?

Madame. Oh, that is easy. He is my heir.

Stranger (*amused*). Ah.

Madame. He is, also, by the mercy of God, not too unlike you, so that his photograph will

not startle the Corporal too much tomorrow. Now tell me what you were doing in my wood.

Stranger. Resting my feet—I am practically walking on my bones. And waiting for tonight.

Madame. Where are you making for? (*As he does not answer immediately*) The coast? (*He nods.*) That is four days away—five if your feet are bad.

Stranger. I know it.

Madame. Have you friends on the way?

Stranger. I have friends at the coast, who will get me a boat. But no one between here and the sea.

Madame (*rising*). I must consult my list of addresses. (*Pausing*) What was your service?

Stranger. Army.

Madame. Which Regiment?

Stranger. The Seventy-ninth.

Madame (*after the faintest pause*). And your Colonel's name?

Stranger. Delavault was killed in the first week, and Martin took over.

Madame (*going to her desk*). A "good collaborator" cannot be too careful. Now I can consult my notebook. A charming color, is it not? A lovely shade of red.

Stranger. Yes—but what has a red quill pen to do with your notebook?—Ah, you write with it of course—stupid of me.

Madame. Certainly I write with it—but it is also my notebook—look—I only need a hairpin—and then—so—out of my quill pen comes my notebook—a tiny piece of paper—but enough for a list of names.

Stranger. You mean that you keep that list on your desk? (*He sounds disapproving.*)

Madame. Where did you expect me to keep it, young man? In my corset? Did you ever try to get something out of your corset in a hurry? What would you advise as the ideal quality in a hiding place for a list of names?

Stranger. That the thing should be difficult to find, of course.

Madame. Not at all. That it should be easily destroyed in emergency. It is too big for me to swallow—I suspect they do that only in books—and we have no fires to consume it, so I had to think of some other way. I did try to memorize the list, but what I could not be sure of remembering were those that—that had to be scored off. It would be fatal to send someone to an address that—that was no longer available. So I had to keep a written record.

Stranger. And if you neither eat it nor burn it when the moment comes, how do you get rid of it?

Madame. I could, of course, put a match to it, but scraps of freshly burned paper on a desk take a great deal of explaining. If I ceased to be looked on with approval my usefulness would end. It is important therefore that there should be no sign of anxiety on my part: no burned paper, no excuses to leave the room, no nods and becks and winks. I just sit here at my desk and go on with my letters. I tilt my nice big inkwell sideways for a moment and dip the pen into the deep ink at the side. The ink flows into the hollow of the quill, and all is blotted out. (*Consulting the list*) Let me see. It would be good if you could rest your feet for a day or so.

Stranger (*ruefully*). It would.

Madame. There is a farm just beyond the Marnay crossroads on the way to St. Estèphe —(*She pauses to consider.*)

Stranger. St. Estèphe is the home of the single-minded Corporal. I don't want to run into him again.

Madame. No, that might be awkward; but that farm of the Cherfils would be ideal. A good hiding place, and food to spare, and fine people—

Stranger. If your nephew is so friendly with the invader, how is it that the Corporal doesn't know him by sight?

Madame (*absently*). The unit at St. Estèphe is a noncommissioned [10] one.

Stranger. Does the Brotherhood of Man exclude sergeants, then?

Madame. Oh, definitely. Brotherhood does not really begin under field rank,[11] I understand.

Stranger. But the Corporal may still meet your nephew somewhere.

Madame. That is a risk one must take. It is not a very grave one. They change the personnel every few weeks, to prevent them becoming too acclimatized.[12] And even if he met my nephew, he is unlikely to ask for the papers of so obviously well-to-do a citizen. If you could bear to go *back* a little——

Stranger. Not a step! It would be like—like denying God. I have got so far, against all the odds, and I am not going a yard back. Not even to rest my feet!

Madame. I understand; but it is a pity. It is a long way to the Cherfils farm—two miles east of the Marnay crossroads it is, on a little hill.

Stranger. I'll get there; don't worry. If not tonight then tomorrow night. I am used to sleeping in the open by now.

Madame. I wish we could have you here, but it is too dangerous. We are liable to be billeted on at any moment, without notice. However, we can give you a good meal, and a bath. We have no coal, so it will be one of those flat-tin-saucer baths. And if you want to be very

---

10. **noncommissioned:** made up of enlisted men. They are of subordinate ranks.
11. **field rank:** a field officer, such as a major, lieutenant colonel, or colonel, who ranks above a captain.
12. **acclimatized** (ə-klī′mə-tīzd′): accustomed to a new environment.

kind to Simone you might have it somewhere in the kitchen regions and so save her
carrying water upstairs.

Stranger. But of course.

Madame. Before the war I had a staff of twelve.
Now I have Simone. I dust and Simone
sweeps, and between us we keep the dirt at
bay. She has no manners but a great heart,
the child.

Stranger. The heart of a lion.

Madame. Before I put this back you might
memorize these: Forty Avenue Foch, in Crest,
the back entrance.

Stranger. Forty Avenue Foch, the back entrance.

Madame. You may find it difficult to get into
Crest, by the way. It is a closed area. The
potboy [13] at the Red Lion in Mans.

Stranger. The potboy.

Madame. Denis the blacksmith at Laloupe.
And the next night should take you to the
sea and your friends. Are they safely in your
mind?

Stranger. Forty Avenue Foch in Crest; the
potboy at the Red Lion in Mans; and Denis
the blacksmith at Laloupe. And to be careful
getting into Crest.

Madame. Good. Then I can close my notebook – or roll it up, I should say – then – it fits
neatly, does it not? Now let us see about
some food for you. Perhaps I could find you
other clothes. Are these all you —

[*The* Corporal's *voice is heard mingled in
fury with the still more furious tones of*
Simone. *She is yelling:* "Nothing of the sort,
I tell you, nothing of the sort," *but no words
are clearly distinguishable in the angry row.*

The door is flung open, and the Corporal
bursts in dragging a struggling Simone *by
the arm.*]

---

13. **potboy:** a boy who serves pots of beer in an inn.

Simone (*screaming with rage and terror*). Let
me go, you foul fiend, let me go. (*She tries
to kick him.*)

Corporal (*at the same time*). Stop struggling,
you lying deceitful little bit of no-good.

Madame. Will someone explain this extraordinary —

Corporal. This creature —

Madame. Take your hand from my servant's
arm, Corporal. She is not going to run away.

Corporal (*reacting to the voice of authority
and automatically complying*). Your precious
servant was overheard telling the gardener
that she had never set eyes on this man.

Simone. I did not! Why should I say anything
like that?

Corporal. With my own ears I heard her, my
own two ears. Will you kindly explain that
to me if you can.

Madame. You speak our language very well,
Corporal, but perhaps you are not so quick
to understand.

Corporal. I understand perfectly.

Madame. What Simone was saying to the
gardener, was no doubt what she was announcing to all and sundry at the pitch of her
voice this morning.

Corporal (*unbelieving*). And what was that?

Madame. That she *wished* she had never set
eyes on my nephew.

Corporal. And why should she say that?

Madame. My nephew, Corporal, has many
charms, but tidiness is not one of them. As
you may have deduced from the episode of the
coat. He is apt to leave his room —

Simone (*on her cue; in a burst of scornful
rage*). Cigarette ends, pajamas, towels, bed-
clothes, books, papers – all over the floor like
a *flood.* Every morning I tidy up, and in two
hours it is as if a bomb had burst in the room.

Stranger (*testily*). I told you already that I
was sor —

Simone (*interrupting*). As if I had nothing

else to do in this enormous house but wait on you.

Stranger. Haven't I said that I——

Simone. And when I have climbed all the way up from the kitchen with your shaving water, you let it get cold; but will you shave in cold? Oh, no! I have to bring up another——

Stranger. I didn't ask you to climb the stairs, did I?

Simone. And do I get a word of thanks for bringing it? Do I indeed? You say: "*Must* you bring it in that hideous jug; it offends my eyes."

Stranger. So it does offend my eyes!

Madame. Enough, enough! We had enough of that this morning. You see, Corporal?

Corporal. I could have sworn——

Madame. A natural mistake, perhaps. But I think you might have used a little more common sense in the matter. (*Coldly*) And a great deal more dignity. I don't like having my servants manhandled.

Corporal. She refused to come.

Simone. Accusing me of things I never said!

Madame. However, now that you are here again you can make yourself useful. My nephew wants to go into Crest the day after tomorrow, and that requires a special pass. Perhaps you would make one out for him.

Corporal. But I——

Madame. You have a little book of permits in your pocket, haven't you?

Corporal. Yes. I——

Madame. Very well. Better make it valid for two days. He is always changing his mind.

Corporal. But it is not for me to grant a pass.

Madame. You sign them, don't you?

Corporal. Yes, but only when someone tells me to.

Madame. Very well, if it will help you, I tell you to.

Corporal. I mean, permission must be granted before a pass is issued.

Madame. And have you any doubt that a permission will be granted to my nephew?

Corporal. No, of course not, madame.

Madame. Then don't be absurd, Corporal. To be absurd twice in five minutes is too often. You may use my desk—and my own special pen. Isn't it a beautiful quill, Corporal?

Corporal. Thank you, madame, no. *We* Germans have come a long way from the geese.

Madame. Yes?

Corporal. I prefer my fountain pen. It is a more efficient implement. (*He writes.*) For the fifteenth and the sixteenth. "Holder of identity card number——" What is the number of your identity, monsieur?

Stranger. I have not the faintest idea.

Corporal. You do not know?

Stranger. No. The only numbers I take an interest in are lottery numbers.

Simone. I know the number of monsieur's card.

Madame (*afraid that she is going to invent one*). I don't think that likely, Simone.

Simone (*aware of what is in her mistress' mind, and reassuring her*). But I really *do* know, madame. It is the year I was born, with two "ones" after it. Many a time I have seen it on the outside of the card.

Corporal. It is good that someone knows.

Simone. It is—192411.

Corporal. 192411. (*He fills in the dates.*)

Madame (*as he nears the end*). Are you going back to St. Estèphe now, Corporal?

Corporal. Yes, madame.

Madame. Then perhaps you will give my nephew a lift as far as the Marnay crossroads.

Corporal. It is not permitted to take civilians as passengers.

Stranger. But you took me here as a passenger.

Corporal. That was different.

Madame. You mean that when you thought he was a miscreant you took him in your car, but now that you know he is my nephew you refuse?

Corporal. When I brought him here it was on service business.

Madame (*gently reasonable*). Corporal, I think you owe me something for your general lack of tact this afternoon. Would it be too much to ask you to consider my nephew a miscreant for the next hour while you drive him as far as the Marnay crossroads?

Corporal. But——

Madame. Take him to the crossroads with you and I shall agree to forget your—your lack of efficiency. I am sure you are actually a very efficient person, and likely to be a sergeant any day now. We won't let a blunder or two stand in your way.

Corporal. If I am caught giving a lift to a civilian, I shall *never* be a sergeant.

Madame (*still gentle*). If I report on your conduct this afternoon, tomorrow you will be a private.

Corporal (*after a long pause*). Is monsieur ready to come now?

Stranger. Quite ready.

Corporal. You will need a coat.

Madame. Simone, get monsieur's coat from the cupboard in the hall. And when you have seen him off, come back here.

Simone. Yes, madame. (*Exit* Simone.)

Corporal. Madame.

Madame. Good day to you, Corporal.

[*Exit* Corporal.]

Stranger. Your talent for blackmail is remarkable.

Madame. The place has a yellow barn. You had better wait somewhere till evening, when the dogs are chained up.

Stranger. I wish I had an aunt of your caliber. All mine are authorities on crochet.

Madame. I could wish you were my nephew.

Good luck, and be careful. Perhaps one day, you will come back, and dine with me, and tell me the rest of the tale.

[*The sound of a running engine comes from outside.*]

Stranger. Two years today, perhaps?

Madame. One year today.

Stranger (*softly*). Who knows? (*He lifts her hand to his lips.*) Thank you, and *au revoir.*[14] (*Turning at the door*) Being sped on my way by the enemy is a happiness I had not anticipated. I shall never be able to repay you for that. (*He goes out.*) (*Off*) Ah, my coat—thank you, Simone.

[*Sound of car driving off.*

Madame *pours out two glasses. As she finishes,* Simone *comes in, shutting the door correctly behind her and taking two paces into the room.*]

Simone. You wanted me, madame?

Madame. You will drink a glass of wine with me, Simone.

Simone. With you, madame!

Madame. You are a good daughter of France and a good servant to me. We shall drink a toast together.

Simone. Yes, madame.

Madame (*quietly*). To Freedom.

Simone (*repeating*). To Freedom. May I add a bit of my own, madame?

Madame. Certainly.

Simone (*with immense satisfaction*). And a very bad end to that Corporal!

[*Curtain.*]

---

14. *au revoir* (ō rə-vwȧr′): French for "until we meet again."

FOR STUDY AND DISCUSSION

1. What do you learn in the opening speeches about the setting and background of the play?
2. In what ways is the conflict of the play both physical and psychological?
3. Identify the climax of the play.
4. How is the conflict resolved?
5. What does the title of the play refer to?
6. Both Madame and Simone are women of great courage and intelligence. How does the dramatist distinguish them so that they are revealed as individuals?
7. How is the character of Madame's nephew a foil, or contrast, to that of the Stranger?
8. How does the dramatist convince you that the Corporal can be tricked by Madame?
9. Although this play deals specifically with a situation in France during World War II, it makes a statement about human nature that is universal in its relevance. In your own words, tell what the theme of the play is.

SUGGESTIONS FOR WRITING

1. Write an analysis of the Corporal's character. In your essay, include what he reveals about himself through his words and actions as well as what is revealed about him by other characters.
2. In a paragraph explain the details of Madame's plan for the Stranger's escape.
3. Show how dramatic irony is used in this play. Give at least three separate examples in which the reader knows something that a character in the play does not know.
4. In occupied France, some individuals, like Madame, resisted the German invaders; other individuals, like Madame's real nephew, became opportunists who cooperated with their oppressors. This play turns on the contrast between upholding principles, on the one hand, and serving one's own selfish needs, on the other. Discuss this contrast in values as it is developed in the play.

ABOUT THE AUTHORS

Arthur C. Clarke was born in England in 1917. When he was thirteen, he built a telescope in order to study the moon. During World War II he was a flight lieutenant in the R.A.F. He attended King's College, London, where he studied physics and mathematics. He has been a member of several scientific organizations and has written many technical papers. Clarke, a prolific writer, has been called "the colossus of science fiction." His story "The Sentinel" inspired the film *2001: A Space Odyssey*. His collections of short stories include *Across the Sea of Stars, The Other Side of the Sky, The Nine Billion Names of God,* and *Tales of Ten Worlds.* Some well-known novels are *Childhood's End, Earthlight,* and *Islands in the Sky.*

Marjorie Kinnan Rawlings (1896–1953) was born in Washington, D.C. She attended the University of Wisconsin and worked as a journalist. In 1928 she bought an orange grove at Cross Creek in Florida and settled there. The swamplands and back country of Florida became the setting for her stories. She won the Pulitzer prize in 1939 for *The Yearling,* a story of a boy and his pet fawn. Her other books include a collection of short stories, *When the Whippoorwill,* and a collection of remembrances, *Cross Creek.*

Selma Lagerlöf (1858–1940) was born on her father's estate in Värmland, Sweden, where she lived for most of her life. Her books, which include novels, plays, and stories, show that the land and its people were the chief sources of her inspiration as a writer. In 1909 she became the first woman to be awarded the Nobel prize for literature; in 1914 she became the first woman member of the Swedish Academy of Arts and Letters. Her best-known books include *The Story of Gösta Berling*, a two-part novel called *Jerusalem*, and *The Wonderful Adventures of Nils*.

Ambrose Bierce (1842–1914?) was born on an Ohio farm. Although he had no formal education, he read widely in his father's library. During the Civil War he joined the Union army and became an outstanding soldier. After the war he moved to San Francisco and began his career as a journalist. In 1872 he went to London, where he became known as "Bitter Bierce" for his caustic humor. He returned to San Francisco in 1876. His first book of stories, *Tales of Soldiers and Civilians*, appeared in 1891. His most famous work probably is a book of cynical definitions, *The Devil's Dictionary*. In 1913 he left for Mexico and disappeared without a trace.

Claude McKay (1890–1948) was born in Sunny Ville, Jamaica, in the West Indies. He moved to Kingston, where he began to write poems. When he was twenty-two, he published two collections of poetry, which won an award. He emigrated to the United States and attended Tuskegee Institute and Kansas State College. He became a prominent member of the Harlem Renaissance writers. His most important volume of poetry, *Harlem Shadows*, was published in 1922. He also wrote several novels, including *Home to Harlem*.

Margaret Atwood was born in Ottawa, Canada, in 1939. She attended Victoria College at the University of Toronto. Her first collection of poems, *The Circle Game*, published in 1966 when she was twenty-seven, won The Governor General's Award. In addition to poetry she has written novels and literary criticism.

Gordon Daviot (1897–1952) is one of the pen names of Elizabeth MacKintosh, who also wrote under the name of Josephine Tey. She was born in Inverness, Scotland, and attended the Royal Academy. She taught physical education in England before her first novel was published. She wrote many mysteries, including *The Daughter of Time* and *The Franchise Affair*. She also wrote a number of plays. *The Pen of My Aunt* was published posthumously in 1954.

Guide to Literary Terms and Techniques

ALLITERATION *The repetition of similar sounds, usually consonants or consonant clusters, in a group of words.* Common examples are "safe and sound," "brown as a berry," and "the more the merrier." Although most alliteration occurs at the beginning of words, it may occur within words as well. When alliteration occurs at the beginning of words, it is called *initial alliteration;* when it occurs within words, it is called *internal* or *hidden alliteration.*

Alliteration has a wide and persistent appeal. It is frequently used in clichés, such as "a dime a dozen," "bigger and better," and "jump for joy." Because alliteration adds emphasis to a group of words, it is often used in advertising jingles and in political slogans.

In poetry, alliteration can be an effective musical device, as in these lines from Sidney Lanier's "Song of the Chattahoochee":

> The willful waterweeds held me thrall,
> The laving laurel turned my tide.

Alliteration is often combined with **rhyme** and other musical devices, as in this stanza from Edgar Allan Poe's "Eldorado":

> Gaily bedight,
> A gallant knight,
> In sunshine and in shadow,
> Had journeyed long,
> Singing a song
> In search of Eldorado.

See **Repetition.**
See also page 289.

ALLUSION *A reference in one work of literature to a person, place, or event in another work of literature or in history, art, or music.* Allusion can be used equally well in prose or poetry. As it is usually an appeal to the reader to share some experience with the writer, allusion is used to best effect when it refers to something familiar.

Allusions to the Bible are common in literature. In *Great Expectations,* Pip, the narrator, alludes to the Book of Genesis when he describes the Hulks, the prison boat, as a "wicked Noah's ark." Literature is also filled with allusions to the plays of William Shakespeare. In *Great Expectations,* Dickens expects his readers to recognize the allusion to Shakespeare's *Julius Caesar* when he describes Mr. Wopsle as a "ham" actor performing one of the noblest speeches ever written for the theater: "What he did on those occasions was to turn up his cuffs, stick up his hair, and give us Mark Antony's oration over the body of Caesar."

Allusions to ancient Greek and Roman literature are also common. The following poem alludes to a Greek myth. Medusa was one of the Gorgons, three horrible sisters with serpents for hair. Whoever looked at any of them instantly turned to stone. The allusion to Medusa here suggests that something, perhaps death, has brought the speaker's life to a halt, that it no longer has any meaning:

Medusa
Louise Bogan

I had come to the house, in a cave of trees,
Facing a sheer sky.
Everything moved, — a bell hung ready to strike,
Sun and reflection wheeled by.

When the bare eyes were before me
And the hissing hair,
Held up at a window, seen through a door.
The stiff bald eyes, the serpents on the forehead
Formed in the air.

This is a dead scene forever now.
Nothing will ever stir.
The end will never brighten it more than this,
Nor the rain blur.

The water will always fall, and will not fall,
And the tipped bell make no sound.
The grass will always be growing for hay
Deep on the ground.

And I shall stand here like a shadow
Under the great balanced day,
My eyes on the yellow dust, that was lifting in the
    wind,
And does not drift away.

See pages 30, 131, 255.

ANACHRONISM *An event or detail existing out of its proper time in history.* William Shakespeare often uses anachronisms. A classic example is the reference to the game of billiards ("Let us to billiards") in *Antony and Cleopatra,* a play set in ancient times. The game of billiards was not invented until the sixteenth century. The clock that strikes in Shakespeare's *Julius Caesar* is also an anachronism, as there were no striking clocks in ancient Rome. Writers sometimes use anachronisms deliberately, to add humor to a piece of literature or to lend a sense of timelessness — that is, to prevent something from being "dated." In "The Fifty-First Dragon," Heywood Broun uses a number of modern references in a medieval setting. Examples include the character of the Headmaster and the references to faculty members, to campus slang, and to school spirit.

See page 155.

ANALOGY *An extended comparison showing the similarities between two things.* Analogies are often used for illustration (to explain something unfamiliar by comparing it to something familiar) or for argument (to persuade that what holds true for one thing holds true for the thing to which it is compared).

In "The Sound of the Sea," Henry Wadsworth Longfellow describes the sounds of the rising sea-tide in the first eight lines of the poem. In the last six lines, he draws an analogy between the sounds of the sea and inspiration:

So comes to us at times, from the unknown
  And inaccessible solitudes of being,
    The rushing of the sea-tides of the soul;
And inspirations, that we deem our own,
  Are some divine foreshadowing and foreseeing
    Of things beyond our reason or control.

See page 202.

ARGUMENT *A form of discourse in which reason is used to influence or change people's ideas or actions.* Writers practice argument most often when writing nonfiction, particularly essays or speeches. In his famous speech delivered to the House of Burgesses on March 23, 1775, Patrick Henry advances the argument that only by armed resistance can the colonies defend themselves against England and gain their liberty. He concludes: "I know not what course others may take; but as for me, give me liberty or give me death!"

See **Persuasion.**
See also page 161.

ASIDE *Words spoken by a character in a play, usually in an undertone, not intended to be heard by other characters on stage.* The aside is used in the theater to let the audience know what a character is really thinking or feeling as opposed to what he or she pretends to be thinking or feeling to the other characters in the play. Sometimes asides are exchanged between two characters whose dialogue is not meant to be heard by the other characters present. Many examples of this device may be found in the plays of William Shakespeare.

See **Conventions, Monologue, Soliloquy.**
See also page 425.

ASSONANCE *The repetition of similar vowel sounds, usually close together, in a group of words.* Familiar examples are "free and easy," "mad as a hatter," and so on. Assonance is used to please the ear and to emphasize certain sounds. Like other forms of sound repetition, it is mainly a poetic device. Henry Wadsworth Longfellow uses "rising tide" in "The Sound of the Sea." Another example is found in "Mending Wall," where Robert Frost writes: "and I am apple orchard."

See **Alliteration, Onomatopoeia, Repetition.**
See also page 289.

AUTOBIOGRAPHY *A person's account of his or her own life.* An autobiography is generally written in narrative form and includes some introspection. Autobiographies are distinct from diaries, journals, and letters, which are not unified life stories written for publication. Autobiographies are also different from memoirs, which often deal, at least in part, with public events and important persons other than the author. It is not uncommon for anyone who has achieved distinction in life to write an account of his or her experiences. Autobiographies are frequently written by politicians, entertainers, high-ranking members of the services, and literary figures. For example, Winston Churchill's *My Early Life* is a famous autobiography by a political figure.

See **Biography, Nonfiction.**

BALLAD *A story told in verse and usually meant to be sung.* The earliest ballads, known as *folk ballads* or *popular ballads,* were composed anonymously and transmitted orally for generations. The main ballad tradition began in Europe in the late Middle Ages. The material was taken from local and national life, from legend and folklore. The most popular themes, often tragic ones, are disappointed love, jealousy, revenge, sudden disaster, and deeds of adventure and daring. Generally, the language is simple, the rhythm pronounced, and the story told through dialogue and action. A **refrain,** or chorus, is also a common element.

The traditional **ballad stanza** consists of four lines. The first and third lines have four stressed words or syllables; the second and fourth lines have three stresses. The number of unstressed syllables in each line may vary. The second and fourth lines usually rhyme. Here is a ballad stanza from an American folk ballad, "The Lover's Lament":

My deárest deár, the tíme draws néar
When yóu and Í must párt;
But líttle do you knów the gríef or wóe
Of mý poor troúbled heárt.

The folk ballad is still a living tradition in Sicily, Iceland, and many other parts of the world. In America, this tradition has flourished in the Appalachian Mountains, among cowhands, and within labor movements.

Another kind of ballad is the *literary ballad,* in which a known writer imitates the folk ballad. E. E. Cummings' "All in green went my love riding" is a literary ballad. Other distinguished examples include Samuel Taylor Coleridge's "The Rime of the Ancient Mariner," John Keats's "La Belle Dame Sans Merci," and Alfred Noyes's "The Highwayman."

See **Narrative Poetry.**
See also pages 319, 320, 322.

BIOGRAPHY *An account of a person's life written by another person.* Biography is one of the most popular forms of nonfiction. Biographies in English have taken many different forms since they were first written in medieval times to praise the virtues of saints and to celebrate the feats of heroes. The modern biographer aims at accuracy and usually makes an attempt to interpret the personality of the subject. Details of the social and historical circumstances in which the subject lived are often included. A fine example of a detailed biography is James Boswell's *The Life of Samuel Johnson,* written in the eighteenth century and considered by many to have set the tone for modern biography.

See **Autobiography, Nonfiction.**
See also page 205.

BLANK VERSE *Verse written in unrhymed iambic pentameter, where each line usually contains ten syllables and every other syllable is stressed.* Blank verse is the principal English meter, the pattern used in some of the greatest English poetry, including the tragedies of William Shakespeare and the epics of John Milton. Unrhymed iambic lines prove particularly appropriate in treating serious themes. The following lines from Shakespeare's *Romeo and Juliet* are written in blank verse:

Bŭt sóft!/Whăt líght/thrŏugh yón/dĕr wín/dŏw
   breaks?
Ĭt ĭs/thĕ eást,/ănd Júl/ĭet ĭs/thĕ sún!

See **Iambic Pentameter, Meter.**
See also page 425.

CATASTROPHE *The tragic dénouement, or unknotting, of a play or story.* The deaths of Romeo and Juliet represent the final catastrophe of William Shakespeare's play.

See **Plot.**
See also page 449.

CHARACTERIZATION *The personality a character displays; also, the means by which an author reveals that personality.* Generally, a writer develops a character in one or more of the following ways: (1) by showing the character acting and speaking; (2) by giving a physical description of the character; (3) by revealing the character's thoughts; (4) by revealing what other characters think about the character; (5) by commenting directly on the character. The first four methods are *indirect* methods of characterization. The writer shows or dramatizes the character and allows you to draw your own conclusions. The last method is *direct* characterization. The writer tells you directly what a character is like.

Direct characterization is always supported by indirect techniques, as characters must act or speak if the writer is developing a story. Also, if characters are to be believable, the reader must hear or see, rather than simply be told, what the characters think or feel or do.

See **Characters, Point of View.**
See also pages 36, 43, 53.

CHARACTERS *Persons—or animals, things, or natural forces presented as persons—appearing in a short story, novel, play, or narrative poem.* Characters are sometimes described as dynamic or static. *Dynamic characters* experience some change in personality or attitude. This change is an essential one and usually involves more than a mere change in surroundings or condition. In Morley Callaghan's "All the Years of Her Life," Alfred is an example of a character who undergoes a major change. *Static characters* remain the same throughout a narrative. They do not develop or change beyond the way in which they are first presented. Mitty in James Thurber's "The Secret Life of Walter Mitty" is an example of a static character.

Characters in a **novel** are generally more fully developed than those in a short story, for example. Not only does the novelist have room to develop perhaps more than one dynamic character, but he or she may reveal a main character in many different stages of change. Pip, in Charles Dickens' novel *Great Expectations,* is a character who, in the course of growing up, undergoes important and basic changes in personality and outlook.

Characters are sometimes classified as *flat* or *round.* Flat characters have only one or two "sides," representing one or two traits. They are often stereotypes that can be summed up in a few words, for example, an "anxious miser" or a "strong, silent type." Round characters are complex and have many "sides" or traits. Their behavior is unpredictable because they are individuals, and their personalities are fully developed and require lengthy analysis. Flat characters, when developed by a skillful writer, may be as impressive as round characters.

See **Characterization.**
See also pages 43, 53.

CLIMAX *That point of greatest emotional intensity, interest, or suspense in a narrative.* In drama, the climax is often identified with the *crisis,* or *turning point.*

See **Drama.**
See also pages 23, 449.

COMEDY *In general, a literary work that is amusing and ends happily.* Comedy is distinct from **tragedy,** which is generally concerned with a central character who meets an unhappy or disastrous end. The comic hero or heroine may be a person of ordinary character and ability who does not usually achieve the heroic stature of the tragic figure.

Comedies are often concerned, at least in part, with poking fun at romantic attitudes and exposing human folly. They frequently depict a hero or heroine overthrowing rigid social fashions and customs. Wit, humor, and a sense of festivity are found in many comedies.

The term comedy is usually applied to a drama. Dramatic comedy is generally divided into two main sorts: romantic comedy — where there exist joyous situations and where the two chief figures are lovers; and satirical comedy — where the chief characters are held up to ridicule and often come between a pair of young lovers.

Anton Chekhov's *A Marriage Proposal* is an example of another type of comedy known as **farce.** It reveals through exaggerated situations the foolishness in which people can entangle themselves.

See **Drama, Farce, Satire.**
See also page 333.

COMPLICATION *A series of difficulties forming the central action in a narrative.* Complications in a story, for example, make a conflict difficult to resolve and add interest and suspense. In Frank R. Stockton's "The Lady, or the Tiger?" complications include the search for the tiger, the princess' inquiry, and her discovery of the identity of the young woman.

See **Conflict, Plot.**
See also page 23.

CONFLICT *A struggle between two opposing forces or characters in a short story, novel, play, or narrative poem.* Conflict can be *external* or *internal,* and it can take one of these forms: (1) a person against another person; (2) a person against society; (3) a person against nature; (4) two elements or ideas struggling for mastery within a person.

In a narrative there may be a single conflict that is uncomplicated and easy to recognize or there may be several, more subtle conflicts involved. In Jesse Stuart's story "Split Cherry Tree," there is conflict between the students and the farmer and their teacher, between Dave and his father, and between the father and the teacher. There is also a larger conflict in the story between two ways of life.

See **Plot.**
See also page 17.

CONNOTATION *The emotion or association that a word or phrase may arouse.* Connotation is distinct from **denotation,** which is the literal or "dictionary" meaning of a word or phrase.

Words acquire their connotations by the way they've been used in the past and by the circumstances in which they've been used. For example, the word *springtime* literally means that season of the year between the vernal equinox and the summer solstice, but the word usually makes most people think of such things as youth, rebirth, and romance. The word *shroud* literally means a cloth used for burial purposes, or anything that covers or protects. However, most people associate the word *shroud* with death, gloom, darkness, and other unpleasant things. Advertisers are especially sensitive to the connotations of words. For example, a department of a store probably would not be called "Cheap Clothes"; it would more likely be called "Budget Sportswear."

See **Denotation, Diction.**
See also pages 171, 253.

CONVENTIONS *Unrealistic devices or procedures that the reader (or audience) agrees to accept.* In poetry, for example, the use of rhyme is a convention. In drama, the playwright is free to have characters speak aloud without other characters hearing (the aside) or speak aloud while alone on stage (the soliloquy). These are dramatic conventions. The more realistic playwrights wish to be, the fewer dramatic conventions they will use; that is, they will ask the audience to suspend their disbelief as little as possible.

Familiarity with conventions of all forms enables us to know just what is taking place. Through the convention of the "fade in" and "fade out" in film, for example, we know that there has been a shift in time and place.

See **Aside, Monologue, Soliloquy.**
See also page 424.

COUPLET *Two consecutive lines of poetry that rhyme.* Here is the concluding couplet from William Shakespeare's "Sonnet 55":

So, till the judgment that yourself arise,
You live in this, and dwell in lovers' eyes.

This couplet is from Lord Byron's "The Destruction of Sennacherib":

And the might of the Gentile, unsmote by the
     sword,
Hath melted like snow in the glance of the Lord!

See **Heroic Couplet.**
See page 295.

CRISIS or **TURNING POINT** *A point of great tension in a narrative that determines how the action will come out.* In Act Three of William Shakespeare's *Romeo and Juliet,* Tybalt kills Mercutio, and Romeo kills Tybalt. These events mark the turning point of the play's action.

See **Plot.**
See also page 449.

DENOTATION *The literal or "dictionary" meaning of a word.* Denotation is distinct from **connotation,** which is what is suggested by a word beyond its literal meaning. For example, the denotation, or dictionary definition, of the word *star* (as in "movie *star*") is "a prominent actor or actress,"

but the connotation of the word *star* is that of an actor or actress who is adored by fans and who leads a fascinating and glamorous life.

See **Connotation, Diction.**
See also pages 171, 253.

DESCRIPTION *Any careful detailing of a person, place, thing, or event.* Description is one of the four major forms of discourse. We associate the term with prose, both fiction and nonfiction, but poems also use description, if a bit more economically.

Descriptions re-create sensory impressions: sights, sounds, smells, textures, tastes. Some description is direct and factual, but more often, description helps to establish a mood or stir an emotion. Here is part of the famous description of Miss Havisham in her bridal dress from Charles Dickens' novel *Great Expectations:*

But I saw that everything within my view which ought to be white had lost its luster, and was faded and yellow. I saw that the bride within the bridal dress had withered like the dress, and like the flowers, and had no brightness left but the brightness of her sunken eyes. I saw that the dress had been put upon the rounded figure of a young woman, and that the figure upon which it now hung loose had shrunk to skin and bone.

See **Exposition, Narration, Persuasion.**
See also pages 156, 238.

DIALECT *A representation of the speech patterns of a particular region or social group.* Dialect differs from the standard speech of a country in sentence pattern, vocabulary, and pronunciation. Writers often use the distinctive patterns of dialect to establish local color. Among American writers noted for their use of regional speech are James Russell Lowell, for the dialect of rustic New England; James Whitcomb Riley, for the Hoosier dialect of Indiana; Mark Twain, for the dialect of the Mississippi Valley; and Bret Harte, for the dialect of the West.

See pages 54, 97, 311.

DICTION *A writer's choice of words, particularly for clarity, effectiveness, and precision.* A writer's diction can be formal or informal, abstract or concrete. In choosing "the right word," writers must think of their subject and their audience. Words that are appropriate in informal dialogue would not always be appropriate in a formal essay. A writer might have a character use "tubby" in an insulting remark, but the word would be inappropriate in a medical article.

The impact that diction can have on a piece of writing is illustrated by the following versions of a nursery rhyme. The story is the same; the diction is different.

Three blind mice,
See how they run.
They all ran after the farmer's wife,
Who cut off their tails with a carving knife.
Have you ever seen such a sight in your life
As three blind mice?

Three rodents with defective vision,
Observe their rate of motion.
They all pursued an agriculturalist's spouse,
Who severed their spinal extremities with a common kitchen utensil.
Have you ever observed such a phenomenon in the span of your existence
As three rodents with defective vision?

The following poem contains no words or phrases one would consider elegant, yet the poem is eloquent. Note the impact of simple, earthy words like *soap, onions,* and *wet clay,* and their appropriateness in the poem.

Lineage
Margaret Walker

My grandmothers were strong.
They followed plows and bent to toil.
They moved through fields sowing seed.
They touched earth and grain grew.
They were full of sturdiness and singing.
My grandmothers were strong.

My grandmothers are full of memories
Smelling of soap and onions and wet clay
With veins rolling roughly over quick hands
They have many clean words to say.
My grandmothers were strong.
Why am I not as they?

See **Connotation, Denotation.**
See also pages 248, 251.

DRAMA *A story acted out, usually on a stage, by actors and actresses who take the parts of specific characters.* Drama is generally divided into two types: **tragedies,** serious plays in which the central characters meet an unhappy or disastrous end, like William Shakespeare's *Romeo and Juliet;* and **comedies,** humorous plays that end happily, like Shakespeare's *A Midsummer Night's Dream.*

Plot, the sequence of events, is an important element of drama, as is **dialogue,** the conversations held by the characters, which serve to advance the story's action. **Stage directions** are also essential to drama, as they tell actors and actresses how to move or how they should deliver certain lines. The director of a play makes particular use of stage directions.

Exposition, the presentation of important background information, usually occurs at the opening of a drama (but it may occur at any point that the audience needs information about past events). A drama then introduces the **conflict,** or opposition against which the characters must struggle. In most dramas there is a **climax,** a point of great emotional intensity or suspense. Sometimes, the term *climax* is identified with the **crisis,** a decisive **turning point** that determines the outcome of the action. The end of a drama involves the **resolution,** or outcome, usually by death in a tragedy or by marriage in a comedy.

See **Plot.**
See also pages 333, 380.

DRAMATIC IRONY *A device whereby the audience (or reader) understands more of a situation or of what is being said than the character is aware of.* Such speech or action has great significance to the audience or reader and little significance to the character speaking or performing it. The character remains unaware of the real state of affairs. Dramatic irony is a common device for involving the reader in the story's action.

See **Irony.**
See also pages 36, 461.

DRAMATIC POETRY *Poetry in which one or more characters speak.* Each speaker always addresses a specific listener. This listener may be silent (but identifiable), or the listener may be another character who speaks in reply.

In "Lord Randal," there are two speakers, Lord Randal and his mother:

"O where hae ye been, Lord Randal my son?
O where hae ye been, my handsome young man?"
"I hae been to the wild wood, mother, make my bed soon,
For I'm weary wi' hunting, and fain wald lie down."

See **Narrative Poetry, Poetry.**
See also pages 310, 326.

DYNAMIC CHARACTER *A character who undergoes an important and basic change in personality or outlook.*

See **Characters**.
See also page 43.

EPIC *A long narrative poem that relates the deeds of a hero.* Epics incorporate myth, legend, folk tale, and history, and usually reflect the values of the societies from which they originate. The tone is generally grand, and the heroes and their adventures appear larger than life.

Many epics were drawn from an oral tradition and are known as *primary* epics. These were transmitted by song and recitation before they were written down. Two of the most famous primary epics of Western civilization are Homer's *Iliad* and *Odyssey*. Another primary epic is one of the earliest works in history, the *Epic of Gilgamesh*, from ancient Mesopotamia.

A second type of epic is the *literary* or *secondary* epic. These were written down from the start. Examples include the *Aeneid*, Rome's national epic written by the poet Virgil to give the ancient Romans a sense of their own destiny; the *Divine Comedy*, the great epic of the Middle Ages written by the Italian poet Dante; and *Paradise Lost* and *Paradise Regained*, two great epics written by the seventeenth-century English poet John Milton.

See **Narrative Poetry**.
See also page 481.

EPITHET *A descriptive adjective or phrase used to characterize someone or something.* Examples are "yellow-bellied coward," "Catherine the Great," and "Richard the Lion-Hearted." Homer's *Odyssey* is filled with epithets, such as "raider of cities" (a reference to Odysseus) and "father of gods and men" (a reference to Zeus).

See page 545.

ESSAY *A piece of prose writing, usually short, that deals with a subject in a limited way and expresses a particular point of view.* An essay is never a comprehensive treatment of a subject (the word comes from a French word for "attempt" or "try"). An essay may be serious or humorous, tightly organized or rambling, restrained or emotional.

The two general classifications of essay are the *informal essay* (also called the *familiar* or *personal* essay) and the *formal essay*. The informal essay is conversational and personal, often revealing a great deal of the writer's personality. The formal essay is more serious in tone and usually objective. Its topics are often drawn from philosophy, literature, or history. However, many essays cannot be easily pigeonholed. For instance, even where the style is formal and seemingly impersonal, the writer may reveal much of his or her personality and point of view.

See **Exposition, Nonfiction**.
See also pages 161, 166.

EXPOSITION *The kind of writing that is intended primarily to present information.* Exposition is one of the major forms of discourse. Although it is used in fiction as well as nonfiction, the most familiar form it takes is in essays. The commentaries which introduce the major sections in this book are exposition.

Exposition is also that part of a play in which important background information is revealed to the audience. In *Romeo and Juliet*, for example, William Shakespeare begins by giving us essential information about the Montagues and the Capulets. He presents the conflict between these two houses before introducing the love story.

See **Description, Essay, Narration, Persuasion, Plot**.
See also pages, 23, 203, 449.

FABLE *A brief story or poem that is told to present a moral, or practical lesson.* The characters in fables are often animals who speak or act like human beings. The best-known fables are those attributed to Aesop, who is said to have lived around the sixth century B.C. The following fable of the tortoise and the hare is characteristic of Aesop's terse style and clearly stated moral:

> The tortoise and the hare argued about who was swifter, and they agreed to run a race. The hare sprinted out well ahead of the tortoise. Seeing how slow his adversary was, the hare became so confident that he relaxed and even lay down for a nap by the roadside. Meanwhile, the tortoise plodded on without stopping, passed the hare asleep on the road, and got to the finish line first. MORAL: *Slow and steady wins the race.*

Another master of this form is the seventeenth-century French writer Jean de la Fontaine. La Fontaine took many of his stories from Aesop but translated them into verse. "The Fox and the Crow" is a fable that La Fontaine adapted from Aesop. Here a modern poet has translated the fable into English, preserving the wit and charm of La Fontaine's version:

The Fox and the Crow
Marianne Moore

On his airy perch among the branches
    Master Crow was holding cheese in his beak.
Master Fox, whose pose suggested fragrances,
    Said in language which of course I cannot speak,
    "Aha, superb Sir Ebony, well met.
How black! who else boasts your metallic jet!
    If your warbling were unique,
    Rest assured, as you are sleek,
One would say that our wood had hatched nightingales."
All aglow, Master Crow tried to run a few scales,
    Risking trills and intervals,
Dropping the prize as his huge beak sang false.
The fox pounced on the cheese and remarked, "My dear
    sir,
    Learn that every flatterer
    Lives at the flattered listener's cost:
A lesson worth more than the cheese that you lost."
    The tardy learner, smarting under ridicule,
Swore he'd learned his last lesson as somebody's fool.

Essayists and humorists such as James Thurber and E. B. White have added new twists to the fable. In White's "The Wings of Orville," it is through the speech and actions of the animal characters themselves, rather than a concluding statement, that we come to understand the moral.

See pages 168, 171.

FALLING ACTION *All of the action in a play that follows the turning point.* The falling action leads to the **resolution** or conclusion of the play. In William Shakespeare's *Romeo and Juliet*, the fortunes of the two lovers steadily decline following the deaths of Mercutio and of Tybalt in Act Three. The action "falls" until the final catastrophe.

See **Plot**.
See also page 449.

FARCE *A type of comedy based on a farfetched humorous situation, often with ridiculous or stereotyped characters.* The humor in a farce is often slapstick—that is, the clowning frequently involves crude physical action. The characters in a farce are often the butts of practical jokes: pies are thrown at their faces or beds cave in on them.

These elements of exaggeration and absurdity set farce apart from other forms of comedy. Anton Chekhov wrote a number of farces, including *A Marriage Proposal, The Bear*, and *The Anniversary*.

See **Comedy**.
See also pages 333, 343.

FICTION *Anything that is invented or imagined, especially a prose narrative.* Although fiction may be based on actual events or personal experiences, its characters and settings are invented. Even if a story is set in an actual place and involves recognizable characters or details, we understand the story itself to be fictitious. In literature, fiction generally refers to the **novel** or the **short story**.

See page 161.

FIGURATIVE LANGUAGE *Language that is not intended to be interpreted in a literal sense.* Figurative language always makes use of a comparison between different things. By appealing to the imagination, figurative language provides new ways of looking at the world.

The interpretation of a poem often depends upon recognizing its figurative meaning. In the following poem, for example, the "poor chap" has not drowned in water, but in loneliness. He is the "I" who speaks in the first and last stanzas.

Not Waving but Drowning
Stevie Smith

Nobody heard him, the dead man,
But still he lay moaning:
I was much further out than you thought
And not waving but drowning.

Poor chap, he always loved larking
And now he's dead
It must have been too cold for him his heart gave way,
They said.

Oh, no no no, it was too cold always
(Still the dead one lay moaning)
I was much too far out all my life
And not waving but drowning.

Figurative language consists of **figures of speech.** The main figure of speech used in literature is **metaphor.** Metaphor draws a comparison between two unlike things without the use of any special language. Doris Lessing uses a number of metaphors in her story "A Mild Attack of Locusts." For example, she likens a swarm of locusts to a "main army."

Another frequently used figure of speech is **simile**. A simile draws a comparison between two unlike things through the use of the words *like, as, as if, than, such as,* and other specific words of comparison. Similes in everyday speech are common. "His voice sounds *like* a foghorn" is a simile in which the sound of a person's voice is compared to the sound of a foghorn. Other examples are "He eats *like* a bird" and "She was *as* cool *as* a cucumber." A well-known simile from literature is William Wordsworth's line, "I wandered lonely *as* a cloud." Lessing uses similes in her descriptions of the locusts, noting that ". . . the clouds of moving insects thickened and lightened *like* driving rain."

Another form of figurative language is **personification**. Personification invests something nonhuman with human qualities. In "The Day Is Done," Henry Wadsworth Longfellow personifies "cares" by describing them as people who can gather up their belongings and walk away:

> And the cares, that infest the day,
> Shall fold their tents, like the Arabs,
> And as silently steal away.

See pages 84, 111, 269.

FIGURE OF SPEECH   *A term applied to a specific kind of figurative language, such as* metaphor *or* simile. Everyday language abounds with many different figures of speech, in which we say one thing and mean another.

Frequently figures of speech compare some action or feeling to something else, as in, "He eats like a bird." Or they may express exaggeration, as in, "I'll die if I don't go to the dance." They may substitute a part of a thing for a whole, as in using "the stage" to mean the entire theatrical profession. Or they may assign personality to an animal or something that is inanimate, as in "the sea is angry." There are more than two hundred different kinds of figures of speech.

See Figurative Language.
See also page 269.

FLASHBACK   *A scene in a short story, novel, play, or narrative poem that interrupts the action to show an event that happened at an earlier time.* Many narratives present events as they occur in time—that is, in chronological order. Sometimes, however, a writer interrupts this natural sequence of events and "flashes back" to a past event to tell the reader or audience what happened earlier in the story or in a character's life.

Homer uses flashback in the *Odyssey*. Odysseus, before making his return home, recounts to the King of Phaeacia "those years of rough adventure," his journey of ten years.

FOIL   *A character who sets off another character by contrast.* By heightening the differences between two characters, a writer dramatizes the significance of both characters. For example, in the opening scene of William Shakespeare's *Romeo and Juliet,* Benvolio, who attempts to keep peace, is a foil for Tybalt, who wants to continue fighting.

See page 408.

FOLK BALLAD   *A story told in verse that is by an unknown author and meant to be sung.* "Lord Randal" is a famous folk ballad.

See Ballad.
See also pages 319, 320.

FOLK TALE   *An account, legend, or story that is passed along orally from generation to generation.* Folk tales are of unknown authorship. They may be legends connected to historical figures, as is the story of George Washington and the cherry tree, or they may be fanciful accounts of the supernatural. In this last category fall stories of ghosts, of devils and spirits, of witches, of talking animals, and of legendary heroes, such as Paul Bunyan.

See page 125.

FORESHADOWING   *The use of hints or clues in a narrative to suggest what action is to come.* Foreshadowing helps to build suspense in a story because it suggests what is about to happen. It also helps the reader savor all the details of the buildup. Foreshadowing is common in short stories, novels, and drama.

In "The Most Dangerous Game," Richard Connell foreshadows the major action of the story in the conversation between Rainsford and Whitney. Their talk of fear, death, superstition, and evil builds suspense at the outset.

See Plot, Suspense.
See also page 17.

FRAMEWORK STORY   *A narrative that contains another narrative.* Both the framework story and the inner story add meaning to one another, and one is usually important to the outcome of the other. Kurt Vonnegut's story "Tom Edison's Shaggy Dog" contains one story within the framework of another. *The Canterbury Tales,* written by the fourteenth-century English poet Geoffrey Chaucer, is a famous example of several stories within a story.

See page 30.

FREE VERSE *Poetry that has no fixed meter or pattern and that depends on natural speech rhythms.* Free verse may rhyme or not rhyme; its lines may be of different lengths; and like natural speech, it may switch suddenly from one rhythm to another.

When used by a skillful poet, free verse displays special rhythms and melodies unlike any traditional forms. Other than the fact that it is arranged by lines, free verse is very much like rhythmical prose. The following lines are from "The Dismantled Ship," a poem by Walt Whitman, who was the first poet to use free verse extensively.

In some unused lagoon, some nameless bay,
On sluggish, lonesome waters, anchored near the
  shore,
An old, dismasted, gray and battered ship,
  disabled, done,
After free voyages to all the seas of earth, hauled
  up at last and hawsered tight,
Lies rusting, moldering.

See **Meter, Poetry.**
See also page 297.

HEROIC COUPLET *Two consecutive lines of rhyming poetry that are written in iambic pentameter and that contain a complete thought.* In a heroic couplet, there is usually one pause at the end of the first line, and another heavier pause at the end of the second line. The form was often used in England for heroic or epic poetry.

William Shakespeare frequently uses the heroic couplet. Here is an example from Act Two of *Romeo and Juliet:*

Hence will I to my ghostly father's cell,
His help to crave and my dear hap to tell.

See **Couplet.**
See also page 425.

HOMERIC SIMILE *An extended comparison that mounts in excitement and usually ends in a climax.* The Homeric simile is also known as the epic simile.

See Epic, Simile.
See also page 545.

IAMBIC PENTAMETER *The most common verse line in English poetry.* It consists of five verse **feet** (*penta-* is from a Greek word meaning "five"), with each foot an **iamb** — that is, an unstressed syllable followed by a stressed syllable. William Shakespeare's plays are written almost entirely in iambic pentameter. Here is an example from *Romeo and Juliet:*

Ălack / thĕ dáy! / Hĕ's góne, / hĕ's kílled, / hĕ's
déad.

See **Meter, Rhythm.**
See also page 425.

IMAGERY *Language that appeals to any sense or any combination of senses.* Most imagery tends to be visual in nature, but imagery may also suggest the way things sound, smell, taste, or feel to the touch. Imagery is put to particularly effective use in poetry. A skillful poet will carefully choose words that convey the most vivid images. The following poem conveys an experience entirely through images — those of touch, sight, and sound:

The Pond
Amy Lowell

Cold, wet leaves
Floating on moss-colored water,
And the croaking of frogs —
Cracked bell-notes in the twilight.

Writers who use imagery extensively make an experience more intense for us. Good images involve our sensory awareness and help us to be more responsive readers.

See pages 199, 257.

INVERSION *A reversal of the usual order of words to achieve some kind of emphasis.* For example, in "A Narrow Fellow in the Grass," Emily Dickinson writes:

Several of nature's people
I know, and they know me

It would be more common to write: "I know several of nature's people, and they know me."

Inversion usually appears in poetry, but it occurs in prose and in speech as well. The effect of its slightly unexpected quality is to give special importance to a phrase or thought. It may also be used to produce effective rhyme.

See page 251.

IRONY *A contrast or an incongruity between what is stated and what is really meant, or between what is expected to happen and what actually does happen.* Two kinds of irony are: (1) *verbal irony,* in which a writer or speaker says one thing and means something entirely different; and (2) *dramatic irony,* in which a reader or an audience perceives something that a character in the story or play does not know.

The following tongue-in-cheek statement by Mark Twain is an example of verbal irony. Twain's actual meaning is quite different from his surface meaning:

> When I was a boy of fourteen, my father was so ignorant I could hardly stand to have the old man around. But when I got to be twenty-one, I was astonished at how much the old man had learned in seven years.

An example of dramatic irony is found in William Shakespeare's *Romeo and Juliet.* The audience of the play knows that Juliet is not dead but is merely drugged and appears lifeless. Romeo, however, does not know this. Presuming that his young wife is dead, Romeo kills himself.

See pages 24, 36, 130.

LITERAL LANGUAGE *A fact or idea stated directly.* When a writer intends something to be understood exactly as it is written, he or she is using literal, or nonfigurative, language.

See **Figurative Language.**
See also page 84.

LITERARY BALLAD *A story told in verse in which a known writer imitates a folk ballad.* "All in green went my love riding" by E. E. Cummings is a literary ballad.

See **Ballad.**
See also page 322.

LYRIC POETRY *Poetry that expresses a speaker's personal thoughts or feelings.* The elegy, ode, and sonnet are forms of the lyric. As its Greek name indicates, a lyric was originally a poem sung to the accompaniment of a lyre, and lyrics to this day have retained a melodic quality. Lyrics may express a range of emotions and reflections: Robert Burns's "John Anderson My Jo" expresses emo-

tions of deep love, while Robert Frost's lyric "Desert Places" expresses the loneliness and fright the speaker feels when looking at a winter landscape.

See **Poetry, Sonnet.**
See also page 310.

METAPHOR *A comparison between two unlike things with the intent of giving added meaning to one of them.* Metaphor is one of the most important forms of **figurative language.** It is used in virtually all forms of literature. "Life is a dream," "Life is a vale of tears," "Life is a bowl of cherries" are all examples of metaphor. Unlike a **simile,** a metaphor does not use a connective word such as *like, as, than,* or *resembles* to state a comparison.

In the following poem, Eve Merriam does not say that morning is like a new sheet of paper, but rather that morning *is* a new sheet of paper. Her comparison is intended to point out that in every morning we can find a fresh, clean beginning.

> **Metaphor**
> *Eve Merriam*
>
> Morning is
> a new sheet of paper
> for you to write on.
>
> Whatever you want to say,
> all day,
> until night
> folds it up
> and files it away.
>
> The bright words and the dark words
> are gone
> until dawn
> and a new day
> to write on.

Many metaphors are implied, or suggested. An *implied metaphor* does not directly state that one thing is another, different thing. Homer uses an implied metaphor in the *Odyssey* when he describes the dawn as having "fingertips of rose." This implies that dawn is a woman with rose-tipped fingers that stretch across the morning sky.

See **Figurative Language, Simile.**
See also pages 84, 272, 273.

METER *A generally regular pattern of stressed and unstressed syllables in poetry.* In these lines from Edgar Allan Poe's "Eldorado," the stressed syllables are marked (´) and the unstressed (˘):

Gaílў bĕdíght,
Ă gallănt kníght,
Ĭn sunshíne and ĭn shadŏw

Meter is measured in units called **feet**. A foot consists of one stressed syllable and, usually, of one or more unstressed syllables. A line of poetry has as many feet as it has stressed syllables. Standard poetic feet include: **iamb,** one unstressed syllable followed by one stressed syllable (Bŭt sóft!); **trochee,** one stressed syllable followed by one unstressed syllable (gállănt); **dactyl,** one stressed syllable followed by two unstressed syllables (híckŏrў); and **anapest,** two unstressed syllables followed by a stressed syllable (ŭndĕrstánd).

A metrical line is named for its pattern and number of feet: *iambic pentameter* (5 iambs); *trochaic tetrameter* (4 trochees); *dactylic hexameter* (6 dactyls); *anapestic trimeter* (3 anapests), and so on.

See **Rhythm.**
See also page 283.

MONOLOGUE *A long, uninterrupted speech (in a narrative or drama) that is spoken in the presence of other characters.* Unlike a soliloquy and most asides, a monologue is heard by the other characters present. The characters in William Shakespeare's plays often deliver monologues. Mercutio's speech on Queen Mab in Act One, Scene 4 of *Romeo and Juliet* is an example.

See **Aside, Conventions, Soliloquy.**
See also page 425.

NARRATION *The kind of writing or speaking that tells a story (a narrative).* Narration is one of the four major forms of discourse. Any narrative must be delivered by a narrator, whether it is the author or a character created by the author. Narration may take the form of prose or poetry. A narrative may be book length, such as a novel or an epic, or it may be paragraph length, such as a fable or an anecdote. The short stories, the ballads and other narrative poems, the epic, and the novel in this book are all examples of narration.

See **Description, Exposition, Persuasion,**
See also pages 158, 238.

NARRATIVE POETRY *Poetry that tells a story.* One kind of narrative poem is the **epic,** a long poem which sets forth the heroic ideals of a partic-

ular society. Homer's *Odyssey* is an epic. The **ballad** is another kind of narrative poem. "Lord Randal" is an example of a ballad.

See **Ballad, Epic, Poetry.**
See also page 310.

NARRATOR *One who narrates, or tells, a story.* A writer may choose to have a story told by a *first-person* narrator, someone who is either a major or minor character. Or, a writer may choose to use a *third-person* narrator, someone who is not in the story at all. Third-person narrators are often *omniscient,* or "all-knowing"—that is, they are able to enter into the minds of all the characters in the story.

Jesse Stuart's short story "Split Cherry Tree" is told by an "I" who is one of the characters in the story. This narrator can reveal his own thoughts, of course, but he can report only what he thinks goes on in the minds of the other characters. Thus, we know only what the narrator tells us. Frank R. Stockton's short story "The Lady, or the Tiger?" is told by a third-person narrator. The author serves as an omniscient observer who steps outside the action of the story to address the reader.

See **Point of View.**
See also pages 63, 77, 97.

NONFICTION *Any prose narrative that tells about things as they actually happened or that presents factual information about something.* **Autobiography** and **biography** are among the major forms of nonfiction. The purpose of this kind of writing is to give a presumably accurate accounting of a person's life. **Essays** are also common forms of nonfiction. They are generally personal observations on some subject. Other kinds of nonfiction include the stories, editorials, and letters to the editor found in newspapers, as well as diaries, journals, and travel literature.

Writers of nonfiction use the major forms of discourse: description (an impression of the subject); narration (the telling of the story); exposition (explanatory information); and persuasion (an argument to influence people's thinking).

See page 161.

NOVEL *A fictional narrative in prose, generally longer than a short story.* The author is not restricted by historical facts but rather is free to create fictional personalities in a fictional world. The characters may be recognizable and disguised with fictitious names, or the real names of actual historical figures may be used. The setting and action of the story, no matter how detailed, are also invented, but may be based on actual places and drawn from little-known or well-known facts.

The subject matter of the novel is virtually unrestricted, and the forms the novel may take cover a wide range. For example, there are the *historical novel,* in which historical figures appear or in which characters, settings, and periods are drawn in such detail, one feels they are real; the *picaresque novel,* a kind of travel story, often satiric and usually presenting the exploits of a rogue; and the *psychological novel,* in which the characters' complex emotional and intellectual states are the focus. These are but a few of the traditional forms of the novel. Some of the many modern forms include the detective story, the spy thriller, and the science fiction novel. Classifications constantly overlap, and new forms develop. Perhaps no other form of literature has undergone so much change.

> See **Fiction, Short Story.**
> See also page 553.

OCTAVE *The first eight lines of a Petrarchan (or Italian) sonnet.* The octave, from the Latin word for "eight," often has the rhyme scheme *abbaabba.* A thought or idea is often introduced in the octave and further developed in the last six lines, or **sestet,** of the poem.

> See **Sestet, Sonnet.**
> See also page 294.

ONOMATOPOEIA *The use of a word whose sound in some degree imitates or suggests its meaning.* The names of some birds are onomatopoetic, imitating the cry of the bird named: *cuckoo, whippoorwill, owl, crow, towhee, bobwhite.* Some onomatopoetic words are *hiss, clang, rustle,* and *snap.* In this line from Robert Browning's "Meeting at Night," the word *slushy* is onomatopoetic: "And quench its speed i' the *slushy* sand."

> See **Alliteration, Assonance.**
> See also pages 236, 289.

PARALLELISM *The use of phrases, clauses, or sentences that are similar or complementary in structure or in meaning.* In "The Destruction of Sennacherib," Lord Byron constructs the second stanza so that the first line is parallel to the third, and the second line parallel to the fourth:

> Like the leaves of the forest when Summer is green,
> That host with their banners at sunset were seen:
> Like the leaves of the forest when Autumn hath blown,
> That host on the morrow lay withered and strown.

The technique of parallelism is used extensively in the Psalms in the Bible, where the idea of one line is repeated in the next. These lines from Psalm 96 are examples:

> Give unto the Lord glory and strength.
> Give unto the Lord the glory due his name.

> See page 291.

PARAPHRASE *A summary or recapitulation of a piece of literature.* A paraphrase does not enhance a literary work. It merely tells in the simplest form what happened. A paraphrase of Christina Rossetti's poem "Uphill" might go this way:

> A traveler about to make a journey (the journey of life) inquires about the direction of the road and the length of the trip. The answer reveals that the road winds uphill (through life's struggles) and the journey takes "the whole long day" (a lifetime). The traveler next asks if there will be a place to spend the night and is told there will certainly be an inn. Inquiring if there will be others who have made the same trip (through life to death) and what welcome to expect, the traveler is assured of company and a ready greeting. And, in response to questions regarding comfort and the available supply of beds (graves), the traveler is informed that both may be expected by all those who need them.

This summary gives us some essential information and is useful for checking to see just what did happen. But it is also clear that such a paraphrase is not memorable, nor does it produce the powerful symbolic effect of the original poem.

> See page 329.

PERSONIFICATION *A figure of speech in which an animal, an object, a natural force, or an idea is given personality, or described as if it were human.* In the following line from "Dirge," Percy Bysshe Shelley personifies a storm. He addresses it as if it were a person who could feel sadness and shed tears: "Sad storm, whose tears are vain."

> See **Figurative Language, Figures of Speech.**
> See also pages 190, 275.

PERSUASION *The type of speaking or writing that is intended to make its audience adopt a certain opinion or perform an action or do both.* Persuasion is one of the major forms of discourse. Modern examples of persuasion include political speeches, television commercials, and newspaper editorials.

See **Argument, Description, Exposition, Narration.**
See also page 161.

PETRARCHAN SONNET *A fourteen-line lyric poem consisting of two parts: the octave (or first eight lines) and the sestet (or last six lines).* The Petrarchan, or Italian, sonnet originated in Italy in the thirteenth century and was much used by the Italian poet Francesco Petrarch. Its rhyme scheme is *abbaabba cdecde.*

The following poem is a Petrarchan sonnet. Note the variation in the sestet, where the rhyme scheme is *cddccd.*

I Wish I Could Remember That First Day
Christina Rossetti

a   I wish I could remember that first day,
b   First hour, first moment of your meeting me,
b   If bright or dim the season, it might be
a   Summer or Winter for aught I can say;
a   So unrecorded did it slip away,
b   So blind was I to see and to foresee,
b   So dull to mark the budding of my tree
a   That would not blossom yet for many a May.
c   If only I could recollect it, such
d   A day of days! I let it come and go
d   As traceless as a thaw of bygone snow;
c   It seemed to mean so little, meant so much;
c   If only now I could recall that touch,
d   First touch of hand in hand—Did one but know!

See **Sonnet.**
See also page 294.

PLOT *The sequence of events or happenings in a literary work.* Plots may be simple or complex, loosely constructed or close-knit. But every plot is made up of a series of incidents that are related to one another.

Conflict, a struggle of some kind, is the most important element of plot. Conflict may be *external or internal.* External conflict is a clash between two or more characters, between characters and society, or between characters and nature. Internal conflict is a struggle within the mind of a character. There may be more than one form of conflict in a work. All the elements of the conflict are incorporated into the plot. As the plot advances, we learn how the conflict is resolved, either through the action or through major changes in the attitudes or personalities of the characters.

Action is generally introduced by a section of **exposition,** information essential to understanding the work. The exposition is part of the **rising action,** during which there is often a **complication,** a point where the central character meets some opposition. The action rises to a **crisis,** or **turning point.**

The **falling action** follows the turning point. The end of the action is the **dénouement** (literally "unknotting") or **resolution,** the moment in the plot when the conflict ends. Not all plots have a resolution as such. In older stories, there generally is a resolution. But many modern stories end without a resolution. They provide us with enough information so that we may draw our own inferences as to how the conflict will be resolved.

One or several **subplots** may be interwoven with the main action. Several subsidiary plots are common in a novel.

See the terms noted above.
See also pages 1, 23, 449.

POETRY *Traditional poetry is language arranged in lines, with a regular rhythm and often a definite rhyme scheme. Nontraditional poetry does away with regular rhythm and rhyme, although it usually is set up in lines.* The richness of its suggestions, the sounds of its words, and the strong feelings evoked by its lines are often said to be what distinguish poetry from other forms of literature. Poetry is difficult to define, but most people know when they read it.

Lines of poetry are often arranged in **stanzas.** Through the use of **rhyme** and strong **rhythms,** poetry establishes certain feelings and effects; through the use of **imagery,** poetry suggests things we can know through our senses; and through the use of **figurative language,** poetry adds special meanings by comparison. Techniques used to build musicality or to emphasize meaning include **alliteration, assonance, onomatopoeia, repetition,** and **inversion.**

See the terms noted above.
See also page 271.

POINT OF VIEW *The vantage point from which a narrative is told.* There are two basic points of view. In the *first-person point of view,* the story is told by one of the characters in his or her own words, that is from the "I" vantage point. First-person point of view is a limited point of view, since the reader is told only what this character knows and observes. The author's use of this vantage point adds a sense of immediacy to a work. Here is an example of first-person point of view from Charles Dickens' novel *Great Expectations:*

> My father's family name being Pirrip, and my Christian name Philip, my infant tongue could make of both names nothing more explicit than Pip. So I called myself Pip, and came to be called Pip.

In the *third-person point of view*, the narrator tells the story from the vantage point of "he" or "she." The third-person narrator might be an *omniscient*, or all-knowing, observer who can describe all the characters and actions in the story as well as comment on what the characters think and feel. O. Henry's story "The Gift of the Magi" is written from an omniscient point of view:

> Now there were two possessions of the James Dillingham Youngs in which they both took a mighty pride. One was Jim's gold watch that had been his father's and his grandfather's. The other was Della's hair. Had the Queen of Sheba lived in the flat across the air shaft, Della would have let her hair hang out the window someday to dry, just to depreciate Her Majesty's jewels and gifts. Had King Solomon been the janitor, with all his treasures piled up in the basement, Jim would have pulled out his watch every time he passed, just to see him pluck at his beard from envy.

An author might also tell a story in the third-person from the point of view of only one character. A *limited* third-person point of view is used in Doris Lessing's "A Mild Attack of Locusts," in which everything is told from Margaret's vantage point.

See **Narrator.**
See also pages 63, 77, 97.

PUN *Usually, the humorous use of a word or phrase to suggest two or more meanings at the same time.* William Shakespeare's play *Richard III* opens with a famous pun:

> Now is the winter of our discontent
> Made glorious summer by this sun of York.

The "sun of York" is a reference to Edward IV, son of the Duke of York, who also had as his emblem the sun.

Sometimes puns are used seriously. The poet John Donne, in his "Hymn to God the Father," puns on the word *Son* (which has the double meaning of *Christ* and *the sun*) and on the word *done* (which is also the poet's name):

> But swear by Thy self, that at my death Thy Son
> Shall shine as he shines now, and heretofore;
> And having done that, Thou hast done.

See page 477.

QUATRAIN *Usually, a stanza or poem of four lines.* However, a quatrain may also be any group of four lines unified by a rhyme scheme. Quatrains usually follow an *abab, abba,* or *abcb* rhyme scheme. Here is a quatrain from Henry Wadsworth Longfellow's "The Day Is Done":

a   And the night shall be filled with music,
b   And the cares, that infest the day,
c   Shall fold their tents, like the Arabs,
b   And as silently steal away.

Shakespeare's sonnets are always divided into three quatrains and a couplet, or two rhyming lines.

See **Stanza.**
See also page 295.

REFRAIN *A word, phrase, line, or group of lines repeated regularly in a poem, usually at the end of each stanza.* Refrains are often used in ballads and other narrative poems to create a songlike rhythm and to help build suspense. Refrains can also serve to emphasize a particular idea. This refrain is used in "Lord Randal":

> ". . . For I'm weary wi' hunting;
>   and fain wald lie down."

See **Repetition.**
See also page 317.

REPETITION *The return of a word, phrase, stanza form, or effect in any form of literature.* Repetition is an effective literary device that may bring comfort, suggest order, or add special meaning to a piece of literature. Common forms of repetition are **alliteration**, repeating sounds at the beginning, middle, or end of words; **rhyme;** and **refrain.**

One of the great masters of repetition is Edgar Allan Poe, who worked out theories of how poetry affects a reader. He concluded that simple repetition was one of the most important and functional devices a poet could use. In his poem "Eldorado," which is filled with ghostly images, Poe repeats the word *shadow* in every stanza. Such repetitions build emotional tension.

In the following poem, note how the repetition of words and phrases builds tension:

If something should happen

Lucille Clifton

for instance
if the sea should break
and crash against the decks
and below decks break the cargo
against the sides of the sea
or
if the chains should break
and crash against the decks
and below decks break the sides
of the sea
or
if the seas of cities
should crash against each other
and break the chains
and break the walls holding down the cargo
and break the sides of the seas
and all the waters of the earth wash together
in a rush of breaking
where will the captains run and
to what harbor?

Sometimes a poet will repeat a phrase or part of a line, as in these lines from Robert Burns's "Sweet Afton," written after the death of his sweetheart:

Flow gently, sweet Afton, among thy green
    braes!
Flow gently, I'll sing thee a song in thy praise!
My Mary's asleep by thy murmuring stream—
Flow gently, sweet Afton, disturb not her dream!

See **Alliteration, Assonance, Refrain, Rhyme.**

RESOLUTION *The outcome of the conflict in a play or story.* The resolution concludes the falling action.

See **Plot.**
See also pages 24, 449.

RHYME *The repetition of sounds in two or more words or phrases that usually appear close to each other in a poem.* For example: *river/shiver, song/long, leap/deep.* If the rhyme occurs at the ends of lines, it is called *end rhyme.* Here is an example of end rhyme from Ralph Waldo Emerson's "Music":

It is not only in the *rose,*
It is not only in the *bird,*
Not only where the rainbow *glows,*
Nor in the song of woman *heard,*
But in the darkest, meanest *things*
There always, always something *sings.*

If the rhyme occurs within a line, it is called *internal rhyme.* Here is an example of internal rhyme from Alfred, Lord Tennyson's "Bugle Song":

The splendor *falls* on castle *walls*

Approximate rhyme (or *near rhyme* or *partial rhyme*) is rhyme in which the final sounds of the words are similar, but not identical (as opposed to *exact rhyme*). *Cook/look* is an exact rhyme; *cook/lack* is an approximate rhyme. Rudyard Kipling uses approximate rhyme in these lines from "Recessional":

For frantic boast and foolish *word*—
Thy Mercy on Thy People, *Lord!*

Rhymes in the work of any careful poet serve many purposes: one is to increase the musicality of the poem; another is to give delight by fulfilling our expectation of a recurring sound; a third purpose is humor. Clever rhymes, for example those in this limerick, produce a comic effect:

There was a young lady of Lynn
Who was so uncommonly thin
    That when she essayed
    To drink lemonade
She slipped through the straw and fell in.

See **Poetry, Repetition, Rhyme Scheme.**
See also page 287.

RHYME SCHEME *The pattern of rhymes in a poem.* The rhyme scheme (indicated by a different letter of the alphabet for each new rhyme) of the first stanza of William Wordsworth's "I Wandered Lonely as a Cloud" is repeated in each succeeding stanza and gives structure to the poem:

a I wandered lonely as a cloud
b   That floats on high o'er vales and hills,
a When all at once I saw a crowd,
b   A host, of golden daffodils.
c Beside the lake, beneath the trees,
c Fluttering and dancing in the breeze.

See **Poetry, Rhyme.**
See also page 287.

RHYTHM *The arrangement of stressed and unstressed syllables into a pattern.* Rhythm is most apparent in poetry, though it is part of all good writing. Rhythm often gives a poem a certain musical quality. Rhythm may be used to imitate the action being described and thus help to communicate the writer's meaning. In Lord Byron's "The Destruction of Sennacherib," the lines actually imitate the swooping and blowing of a swift, cold wind:

For the Angel of Death spread his wings on the
    blast,
And breathed in the face of the foe as he passed;
And the eyes of the sleepers waxed deadly and
    chill,
And their hearts but once heaved, and forever
    grew still!

When the rhythm of a poem has a regular (instead of an irregular) pattern of stressed (ˊ) and unstressed (˘) syllables, this pattern is called **meter.** Good poets usually put stress on the most important words in the line. Stressed words may be accented by having them also alliterate: *face/foe; hearts/ heaved.*

In addition to meter, poets use other techniques to intensify rhythm. **Rhyme** contributes to rhythm by causing us to feel that a passage has come to an end. When rhymes fall close together, we have the feeling that we must pause in our reading of the lines.

Another powerful means of building rhythm is through **repetition.** In these lines from Sidney Lanier's "Song of the Chattahoochee," the repetition of the word *abide* echoes the plants' and trees' coaxing of the river to stay:

The rushes cried *Abide, abide,*
The willful waterweeds held me thrall,
The laving laurel turned my tide,
The ferns and the fondling grass said
    Stay,
The dewberry dipped for to work delay,
And the little reeds sighed *Abide, abide,*
    Here in the hills of Habersham,
    Here in the valleys of Hall.

See **Meter, Repetition, Rhyme.**
See also page 283.

RISING ACTION *Those events in a play that lead to a turning point in the action.* In William Shakespeare's *Romeo and Juliet,* the rising action begins when Romeo and Juliet declare their love and concludes with the deaths of Mercutio and Tybalt.

See **Plot.**
See also page 449.

SATIRE *A kind of writing that holds up to ridicule or contempt the weaknesses and wrongdoings of individuals, groups, institutions, or humanity in general.* The aim of most satirists is to set a moral standard for society, and they often attempt to persuade the reader to see their point of view through the force of laughter. The laughter may be achieved by a light and witty tone or through bitter irony. In "The Secret Life of Walter Mitty," James Thurber satirizes the modern individual, who daydreams of being a romantic hero while living a humdrum existence. In *Visit to a Small Planet,* Gore Vidal satirizes hypocrisy in human nature.

See **Comedy, Irony.**
See also page 366.

SESTET *The last six lines of a Petrarchan (or Italian) sonnet.* The sestet, from the Latin word for "six," usually has a rhyme scheme of *cdecde.* A thought or idea that is introduced in the first eight lines, or **octave,** of the poem is sometimes further developed in the sestet.

See **Octave, Sonnet.**
See also page 294.

SETTING *The time and place of action in a narrative.* In short stories, novels, poetry, and nonfiction, setting is generally created by description. In drama, setting is usually established by stage directions and dialogue.

Setting can be of great importance in establishing not only physical background but also mood or emotional intensity. In turn, the mood contributes to the plot and theme of the narrative. For example, in the opening chapter of *Great Expectations,* Charles Dickens uses the setting to create a mood of bleakness:

Ours was the marsh country, down by the river, within twenty miles of the sea. My first vivid impression of things seems to me to have been gained on a memorable raw afternoon toward evening. At such a time I found out for certain that this bleak place was the churchyard; and that Philip Pirrip, late of this parish, and Georgiana, wife of the above, were dead and buried. I knew that the dark flat wilderness beyond was the marshes; and that the low leaden line beyond was the river; and that the distant savage lair from which the wind was rushing was the sea; and that the small bundle of shivers growing afraid of it all and beginning to cry was Pip.

See **Plot, Theme.**
See also pages 104, 110.

SHAKESPEAREAN SONNET *A fourteen-line lyric poem consisting of three quatrains (four-line stanzas) and a concluding couplet (two rhyming lines).* The Shakespearean, or English, sonnet was not invented by William Shakespeare, but is named for him because he is its most famous practitioner. Its rhyme scheme is *abab cdcd efef gg.* Here is one of Shakespeare's best-known sonnets:

Sonnet 18

a   Shall I compare thee to a summer's day?
b   Thou art more lovely and more temperate:
a   Rough winds do shake the darling buds of May,
b   And summer's lease hath all too short a date;

c   Sometimes too hot the eye of heaven shines,
d   And often is his gold complexion dimmed;
c   And every fair from fair sometimes declines,
d   By chance, or nature's changing course, untrimmed.

e   But thy eternal summer shall not fade
f   Nor lose possession of that fair thou owest;
e   Nor shall Death brag thou wanderest in his shade,
f   When in eternal lines to time thou growest—

g   So long as men can breathe, or eyes can see,
g   So long lives this, and this gives life to thee.

See **Sonnet.**
See also page 295.

SHORT STORY *Narrative prose fiction that is shorter than a novel.* Biblical stories, Greek myths, legends, and fables are the ancestors of the short story, but the name itself was not used until the nineteenth century. Edgar Allan Poe is regarded by many as the originator of this form as it is known today.

Short stories vary in length. Some are no longer than five hundred words; others run to forty or fifty thousand words. An extended short story is sometimes referred to as a *novelette,* or, when slightly longer, as a *novella.*

The major difference between a short story and longer fictional forms, such as the **novel,** is that the main literary elements—plot, setting, characterization—are used with greater compression in the short story than in the longer forms.

See **Fiction, Novel.**
See also page 1.

SIMILE *A comparison made between two dissimilar things through the use of a specific word of comparison, such as* like, as, than, *or* resembles. The comparison must be between two essentially unlike things. To say "Dorothy is like her grandmother" is not to use a simile. But to say "Dorothy is like a golden flower" is to use a simile. Like all **figures of speech,** similes help us to see things in vivid, new ways.

Note how similes are used in the following poem to emphasize visions of beauty, purity, and tranquillity.

Velvet Shoes
Elinor Wylie

Let us walk in the white snow
  In a soundless space;
With footsteps quiet and slow,
  At a tranquil pace,
  Under veils of white lace.

I shall go shod in silk,
  And you in wool,
White *as* a white cow's milk,
  More beautiful
  Than the breast of a gull.

We shall walk through the still town
  In a windless peace;
We shall step upon white down,
  Upon silver fleece,
  Upon softer than these.

We shall walk in velvet shoes:
  Wherever we go
Silence will fall *like* dews
  On white silence below.
  We shall walk in the snow.

See **Figurative Language, Homeric Simile, Metaphor.**
See also pages 84, 271, 545.

SOLILOQUY *A speech, usually lengthy, in which a character, alone on stage, expresses his or her thoughts aloud.* The soliloquy is a very useful dramatic device, as it allows the dramatist to convey a character's most intimate thoughts and feelings directly to the audience. In Shakespeare's *Romeo and Juliet,* we are introduced to the Friar in Act Two through a soliloquy in which he reveals his knowledge of herbs, thus foreshadowing the plan of the sleeping potion later in the play. One of Shakespeare's masterful uses of soliloquy occurs in Act Four, Scene 3, in Juliet's speech before taking the potion. She reveals her innermost conflicts: first her fear of being poisoned by the Friar, then her terror of awaking in the tomb, and finally her desperate courage, braving death in order to be reunited with Romeo.

See **Aside, Conventions, Monologue.**
See also page 425.

SONNET *A fourteen-line lyric poem, usually written in rhymed iambic pentameter (in lines of ten syllables with a stress on every other syllable).* Sonnets vary in structure and rhyme scheme, but are generally of two types: the *Petrarchan,* or *Italian, sonnet* and the *Shakespearean,* or *English, sonnet.* Sonnets usually express a single theme or idea.

The Italian sonnet is a form that originated in Italy in the thirteenth century. The Italian sonnet has two parts, an **octave** (eight lines) and a **sestet** (six lines). It is usually rhymed *abbaabba cdecde.* The two parts of the Italian sonnet play off each other in a variety of ways. Sometimes the octave raises a question which the sestet answers. Sometimes the sestet opposes what the octave says or extends it.

The Italian sonnet is often called the Petrarchan sonnet because the Italian poet Francesco Petrarch used it so extensively. Petrarch dedicated more than three hundred sonnets to a woman named Laura.

The Shakespearean sonnet, a form made famous by William Shakespeare, consists of three quatrains (four-line stanzas) and a concluding couplet (two rhyming lines), with the rhyme scheme *abab cdcd efef gg.*

The sonnet form lends itself to variations. Many modern poets have experimented with the sonnet form, combining features of the Petrarchan and Shakespearean modes or inventing new patterns.

Here the poet is working with a traditional subject — the intensity of feeling stirred by beautiful music. Note, however, how she has modified the traditional form of the sonnet.

Girl with 'Cello
May Sarton

a	There had been no such music here until
b	A girl came in from falling dark and snow
b	To bring into this house her glowing 'cello
a	As if some silent, magic animal.
a	She sat, head bent, her long hair all a-spill
b	Over the breathing wood, and drew the bow.
a	There had been no such music here until
b	A girl came in from falling dark and snow.
a	And she drew out that sound so like a wail,
b	A rich dark suffering joy, as if to show
b	All that a wrist holds and that fingers know
a	When they caress a magic animal.
a	There had been no such music here until
b	A girl came in from falling dark and snow.

The poet makes use of only two rhymes, including approximate rhyme (or partial rhyme); *until/ animal; wail/animal.* The poet also repeats certain lines as refrains in each stanza. The first quatrain, which rhymes *abba,* is Petrarchan, but the second quatrain, which rhymes *abab,* is Shakespearean. The sestet departs from these traditional forms altogether: *abbaab.*

See page 295.

SPEAKER *The voice in a poem.* The speaker may be the poet or a character created by the poet. The speaker may also be a thing or an animal. For example, the "I" or speaker of Ralph Waldo Emerson's poem "Fable" is a squirrel arguing with a mountain:

> And I think it no disgrace
> To occupy my place.
> If I'm not so large as you,
> You are not so small as I,
> And not half so spry.
> I'll not deny you make
> A very pretty squirrel track;
> Talents differ; all is well and wisely put;
> If I cannot carry forests on my back,
> Neither can you crack a nut.

Identifying the speaker in a poem is a key to understanding the poem's meaning.

See page 242.

STANZA *A group of lines forming a unit in a poem.* Many stanzas have a fixed pattern — that is, the same number of lines and the same rhyme scheme. "I Wandered Lonely as a Cloud" by William Wordsworth has a regular pattern. Each of the four stanzas has six lines composed of a quatrain and a couplet, with the rhyme scheme *ababcc.* Some poems do not repeat the same pattern in each stanza, yet each group of lines is still referred to as a stanza. "The Fawn" by Edna St. Vincent Millay has five stanzas, but there is no regular pattern of line length or rhyme scheme.

A stanza may be as short as the **couplet,** two rhyming lines. A favorite form of many English poets has been the **heroic couplet,** two rhyming lines of iambic pentameter. The **tercet,** or **triplet,** is a stanza of three lines, often with one rhyme. The **quatrain** is a four-line stanza with many patterns of rhyme and rhythm. In ballads, the second and fourth lines are usually rhymed while the first and third lines are unrhymed.

Some stanza forms are named for the poets who devised them. The **Spenserian stanza,** for example, a complex nine-line stanza, with the rhyme scheme *ababbcbcc,* is named for the sixteenth-century English poet Edmund Spenser.

See page 293.

STATIC CHARACTER *A character who remains the same throughout a narrative.* Static characters do not develop or change beyond the way in which they are first presented.

See **Characters.**
See also page 43.

SUBPLOT *Secondary action that is interwoven with the main action in a play or story.* Several subplots are not uncommon in a novel. The effect of one or more subplots may be to provide some comic relief from a more serious main plot, or to create a certain atmosphere or mood, such as suspense or intrigue. *Great Expectations* by Charles Dickens is an example of a novel with several subplots, all related to the main action of Pip's story. For instance, there is the story of Mr. Wemmick's life outside the office, a life that we find surprisingly full and warm. His story is revealed to us through his devotion to his deaf father, the Aged Parent; through his relationship with Miss Skiffins; and through his concern for his small, private home.

See **Plot.**
See also page 553.

SUSPENSE *That quality of a literary work that makes the reader or audience uncertain or tense about the outcome of events.* Suspense makes readers ask, "What will happen next?" or "How will this work out?" and impels them to read on. Suspense is greatest when it focuses attention on a sympathetic character. Thus, the most familiar kind of suspense involves a character hanging from the ledge of a tall building, or tied to railroad tracks as a train approaches, or ascending a staircase to open a suspicious door. But suspense may also arise simply from curiosity, as when a character must make an important decision, or seek an explanation for something. One of the reasons for the popularity of "The Lady, or the Tiger?" is that the author does *not* relieve our suspense. When that story is over, we are still wondering, "What happened?"

Often a writer hints at what is to come. This method of building suspense is known as **foreshadowing.** Foreshadowing helps to establish interest early in a narrative and also prepares the reader for the outcome.

See **Foreshadowing, Plot.**
See also page 17.

SYMBOL *Any object, person, place, or action that has a meaning in itself and that also stands for something larger than itself, such as a quality, an attitude, a belief, or a value.* A rose is often a symbol of love and beauty; a skull is often a symbol of death; spring and winter often symbolize youth and old age; a dove usually symbolizes peace. In "Uphill," Christina Rossetti uses the climb up a hill to symbolize life's journey.

In this poem a game of football is used to symbolize the cycle of life:

In the beginning was the
Lillian Morrison

Kickoff.
The ball flew
spiralling true
into the end zone
where it was snagged,
neatly hugged
by a swivel-hipped back
who ran up the field
and was smeared.

The game has begun.
The game has been won.
The game goes on.
Long live the game.
Gather and lock
tackle and block
move, move,
around the arena
and always the beautiful
trajectories.

See page 279.

THEME *The main idea or the basic meaning of a literary work.* The theme of a work is not the same thing as its subject. In the following poem, for example, the subject is toy bears, but the underlying idea—the theme—is that as the playthings of childhood vanish, youthful innocence is lost forever.

Bears
Adrienne Rich

Wonderful bears that walked my room all night,
Where are you gone, your sleek and fairy fur,
Your eyes' veiled imperious light?

Brown bears as rich as mocha or as musk,
White opalescent bears whose fur stood out
Electric in the deepening dusk,

And great black bears who seemed more blue than
   black,
More violet than blue against the dark —
Where are you now? upon what track

Mutter your muffled paws, that used to tread
So softly, surely, up the creakless stair
While I lay listening in bed?

When did I lose you? whose have you become?
Why do I wait and wait and never hear
Your thick nocturnal pacing in my room?
My bears, who keeps you now, in pride and fear?

Not all literary works can be said to express a
theme. Theme generally is not a concern in those
works that are told primarily for entertainment; it
is of importance in those literary works that comment on or present some insight about the meaning of life.

In some literary works the theme is expressed directly, but more often, theme is *implicit* — that is,
it must be dug out and thought about. A simple
theme can often be stated in a single sentence. But
sometimes a literary work is rich and complex, and
a paragraph or even an essay is needed to state the
theme.

See pages 130, 138, 146.

TONE   *The attitude a writer takes toward his or
her subject, characters, and readers.* Through
tone, a writer can amuse, anger, or shock the
reader. Tone is created through the choice of words
and details. William Shakespeare in *Romeo and
Juliet* and Anton Chekhov in *A Marriage Proposal*
deal with courtship and marriage, but from entirely different perspectives. Shakespeare treats his
young lovers as tragic figures. They have nobility
and dignity, and their declarations of love are
among the most eloquent passages in the play.
Chekhov's play presents a comic misalliance of
two completely unromantic characters who seem
constitutionally incompatible. Shakespeare's tone
might be described as compassionate and tender;
Chekhov's as wry and genially mocking.

TRAGEDY   *In general, a literary work in which
the central character meets an unhappy or disastrous end.* Unlike **comedy**, which often portrays a
central character of weak nature, tragedy often
depicts the problems of a central character of dignified or heroic stature. Through a related series of
events, this main character, the tragic hero or
heroine, is brought to a final downfall. The causes
of the character's downfall vary. In traditional
dramas, the cause is often an error in judgment or a
combination of inexplicable outside forces that
overwhelm the character. In modern dramas, the
causes range from moral or psychological weakness to the evils of society. The tragic hero or
heroine, though defeated, usually gains a measure
of wisdom or self-awareness. There may be more
than one central character in a tragedy. William
Shakespeare's *Romeo and Juliet,* for example, has a
tragic hero and heroine.

See **Drama.**
See also page 333.

TURNING POINT

See **Crisis, Plot.**
See also page 449.

VERSE DRAMA or **VERSE PLAY.** *A play written mostly or entirely in verse.* Verse plays are
often written in **blank verse** (unrhymed iambic
pentameter). William Shakespeare's *Romeo and
Juliet* and Ted Hughes's *Orpheus* are examples of
verse drama.

See **Blank Verse.**

FOR COMPOSITION

1. Compare Louise Bogan's poem "Medusa" (page
794) with Stevie Smith's poem "Not Waving but
Drowning" (page 801). What literary techniques
does each poet use to describe a figurative, as opposed to a literal, death?
2. Of Margaret Walker's poetry, poet Stephen Vincent Benét wrote: ". . . out of deep feeling, Miss
Walker has made living and passionate speech."
Support this statement by analyzing in a brief
essay Walker's diction in "Lineage" (page 799).
Select specific words or phrases and describe their
impact on you.
3. After reading Lucille Clifton's "If something
should happen" (page 809), what emotions do you
feel? How do repeated words and phrases throughout the poem help to build intense feelings?
4. Reread Lillian Morrison's poem "In the beginning was the" (page 813). In a short essay, explain
what each element of the game of football symbolizes in life. For example, "Kickoff" is symbolic of
birth.
5. Select five literary terms or techniques and find
examples of those devices. (A single poem, play, or
piece of prose may illustrate more than one device.) Explain how each term is used in the selections you have chosen.

Glossary

The words listed in the glossary in the following pages are found in the selections in this textbook. You can use this glossary as you would a dictionary – to look up words that are unfamiliar to you. Strictly speaking, the word *glossary* means a collection of technical, obscure, or foreign words found in a certain field of work. Of course, the words in this glossary are not "technical, obscure, or foreign," but are those that might present difficulty as you read the selections in this textbook.

Many words in the English language have several meanings. In this glossary, the meanings given are the ones that apply to the words as they are used in the selections in the textbook. Words closely related in form and meaning are generally listed together in one entry (**commend** and **commendable**), and the definition is given for the first form. Related words that appear as separate entries in dictionaries are listed separately (**allude** and **allusion**). Regular adverbs (ending in *-ly*) are defined in their adjective form, with the adverb form shown at the end of the definition.

The following abbreviations are used:

adj., adjective	*n.*, noun	*v.*, verb
adv., adverb	*prep.*, preposition	

For more information about the words in this glossary, consult a dictionary.

A

abash (ə-băsh') *v.* To make ashamed or ill at ease.
abate (ə-bāt') *v.* To reduce in amount or intensity.
abhor (ăb-bôr') *v.* **1.** To look at with horror. **2.** To hate intensely.
abhorrence (ăb-hôr'əns) *n.* Hatred; disgust.
abhorrent (ăb-hôr'ənt) *adj.* Hateful; disgusting.
abiding (ə-bī'dĭng) *adj.* Lasting.
ablution (ă-bloo'shən) *n.* A washing of the body or part of it.
abscond (ăb-skŏnd') *v.* To go away quickly and secretly.
abstract (ăb-străkt', ăb'străkt') *adj.* Having a geometric pattern or design that does not represent any particular figure.

absurd (ăb-sûrd', -zûrd') *adj.* Ridiculous; laughable.
abut (ə-bŭt') *v.* To border on; be next to.
abysmal (ə-bĭz'məl) *adj.* Extreme; bottomless.
abyss (ə-bĭs') *n.* Any bottomless depth or empty space.
accommodate (ə-kŏm'ə-dāt) *v.* To settle differences; reconcile.
accomplice (ə-kŏm'plĭs) *n.* A partner in an undertaking, particularly of an illegal or secret nature.
accost (ə-kôst', ə-kŏst') *v.* To approach and speak to in a bold way.
accouterments (ə-koo'tər-mənts) *n. pl.* Special clothing or equipment.
acquiesce (ăk'wē-ĕs') *v.* To agree readily.
acrid (ăk'rĭd) *adj.* Harsh or bitter to the taste or smell.
adjoin (ə-join') *v.* To be next to.
adjunct (ăj'ŭngkt') *n.* Something connected to another thing in a helpful, but not necessary, way.
adjure (ə-joor') *v.* To command or appeal to solemnly.
adobe (ə-dō'bē) *n.* Sun-dried brick.
adulation (ăj'ŏo-lā'shən) *n.* Overflowing flattery or praise.
adversary (ăd'vər-sĕr'ē) *n.* An opponent or enemy.
adz (ădz) *n.* An axlike tool.
affable (ăf'ə-bəl) *adj.* Friendly; pleasant.
affirm (ə-fûrm') *v.* To make a solemn and formal declaration to speak the truth without taking an oath.
affluent (ăf'loo-ənt) *adj.* Wealthy. — *n. pl.* Rich people.
aghast (ə-găst') *adj.* Terrified; shocked.
agile (ăj'əl, ăj'īl) *adj.* Active; able to move easily and quickly.
agility (ə-jĭl'ə-tē) *n.* The ability to move quickly and easily.
alacrity (ə-lăk'rə-tē) *n.* Eagerness.
alderman (ôl'dər-mən) *n.* A member of the city government.
allude (ə-lood') *v.* To make a casual or indirect reference.
allusion (ə-loo'zhən) *n.* An indirect but meaningful reference.
altercation (ôl'tər-kā'shən) *n.* A noisy quarrel.
ambiguity (ăm'bĭ-gyoo'ə-tē) *n.* **1.** Something that has two or more meanings. **2.** Mystery.
amble (ăm'bəl) *v.* To walk in a slow, relaxed way.
amend (ə-mĕnd') *v.* To change in order to correct.
amends (ə-mĕndz') *n. pl.* Anything done or given to make up for an injury or loss.
amenity (ə-mĕn'ə-tē, ə-mē'nə-tē) *n.* Something that makes life more comfortable or convenient.

The pronunciation system in this glossary is used by permission from *The American Heritage Dictionary of the English Language.*

ă pat/ā pay/âr care/ä father/b bib/ch church/d deed/ĕ pet/ē be/f fife/g gag/h hat/hw which/ĭ pit/ī pie/îr pier/j judge/k kick/l lid, needle/m mum/ n no, sudden/ng thing/ŏ pot/ō toe/ô paw, for/oi noise/ou out/ŏŏ took/ōō boot/p pop/r roar/s sauce/sh ship, dish/t tight/th thin, path/*th* this, bathe/ ū cut/ûr urge/v valve/w with/y yes/z zebra, size/zh vision/ə about, item, edible, gallop, circus/à *Fr.* ami/œ *Fr.* feu, *Ger.* schön/ü *Fr.* tu, *Ger.* über/ KH *Ger.* ich, *Scot.* loch/N *Fr.* bon.

amicable (ăm′ĭ-kə-bəl) *adj.* Friendly.

amorous (ăm′ər-əs) *adj.* **1.** Loving. **2.** In love.

analogy (ə-năl′ə-jē) *n.* **1.** Some similarity between otherwise different things. **2.** An explanation of one thing by comparing it to another thing.

anguish (ăng′gwĭsh) *n.* Great mental or physical suffering.

animate (ăn′ə-māt′) *v.* To make lively or energetic.

animosity (ăn′ə-mŏs′ə-tē) *n.* Extreme hatred.

anticipate (ăn-tĭs′ə-pāt′) *v.* To use in advance, as an allowance of money or a legacy.

antimony (ăn′tə-mō′nē) *n.* A metallic chemical element used in combination with other metals in order to harden them.

antiquated (ăn′tə-kwā′tĭd) *adj.* Very old; out-of-date.

aperture (ăp′ər-choŏr, -chər) *n.* An opening.

apothecary (ə-pŏth′ə-kĕr′ē) *n.* A person who prepares and sells drugs.

appall (ə-pôl′) *v.* To horrify; shock.

apparition (ăp′ə-rĭsh′ən) *n.* **1.** A ghost. **2.** A strange sight. **3.** A sudden appearance.

appease (ə-pēz′) *v.* To satisfy; relieve.

appellation (ăp′ə-lā′shən) *n.* A name.

appertain (ăp′ər-tān′) *v.* To relate to; belong to.

apportion (ə-pôr′shən, ə-pōr′-) *v.* To assign; divide.

appraise (ə-prāz′) *v.* To evaluate; judge.

apprehend (ăp′rĭ-hĕnd′) *v.* **1.** To capture. **2.** To understand.

apprehension (ăp′rĭ-hĕn′shən) *n.* Anxiety; fear.

apprehensive (ăp′rĭ-hĕn′sĭv) *adj.* Fearful.

apprise (ə-prīz′) *v.* To notify.

appropriate (ə-prō′prē-āt′) *v.* To take possession of something, frequently without permission.

aptitude (ăp′tə-tood′, -tyood) *n.* A natural ability or tendency.

ardor (är′dər) *n.* Great passion; emotional warmth.

array (ə-rā′) *n.* **1.** An orderly display. **2.** Fine clothes and accessories.

arrogant (ăr′ə-gənt) *adj.* Excessively self-important and proud.

artisan (är′tə-zən, -sən) *n.* Someone with an occupation or craft that requires special skill.

ascertain (ăs′ər-tān′) *v.* To make sure through examination.

aspire (ə-spīr′) *v.* To have a grand ambition.

assail (ə-sāl′) *v.* To attack violently.

assent (ə-sĕnt) *n.* Agreement.

assert (ə-sûrt′) *v.* To declare; express.

assertion (ə-sûr′shən) *n.* A declaration without proof.

assumption (ə-sump′shən) *n.* Something taken for granted without proof.

astound (ə-stound′) *v.* To amaze.

asunder (ə-sŭn′dər) *adv.* Apart.

athwart (ə-thwôrt′) *prep.* Across.

attain (ə-tān′) *v.* To arrive at through effort.

audacious (ô-dā′shəs) *adj.* Fearless; rudely bold.

audacity (ô-dăs′ə-tē) *n.* Boldness; daring.

auspicious (ô-spĭsh′əs) *adj.* Lucky; predicting a good future.

austere (ô-stîr′) *adj.* Simple; plain.

automaton (ô-tŏm′ə-tən, -tŏn′) *n.* A person or thing acting in a mechanical way.

aversion (ə-vûr′zhən) *n.* An extreme dislike.

avowal (ə-vou′əl) *n.* An open declaration.

awful (ô′fəl) *adj.* Inspiring a feeling of reverence and wonder.

azure (ăzh′ər) *adj.* Sky-blue.

B

babouche (bə-bŭsh′) *n.* A flat, backless slipper worn in North Africa.

baffle (băf′əl) *v.* To puzzle.

baleful (bāl′fəl) *adj.* Threatening; evil.

bandy (băn′dē) *v.* To converse casually.

banish (băn′ĭsh) *v.* To exile. – **banishment** *n.*

bankrupt (băngk′rŭpt′, -rəpt) *adj.* Having no money; destitute. – *To go bankrupt.*

barbaric (bär-băr′ĭk) *adj.* Wild; uncivilized.

barbarous (bär′bər-əs) *adj.* Uncivilized; cruel.

barricade (băr′ə-kād, băr′ə-kād′) *n.* A structure set up to block a passageway, usually for protection.

battlement (băt′l-mənt) *n.* A wall with open spaces to shoot through, usually on top of a tower.

beguile (bĭ-gīl′) *v.* **1.** To deceive; trick. **2.** To spend time pleasantly.

behest (bĭ-hĕst′) *n.* An order.

belated (bĭ-lā′tĭd) *adj.* Late. – **belatedly** *adv.*

bellow (bĕl′ō) *v.* To roar.

bemuse (bĭ-myooz′) *v.* To stupefy.

benefactor (bĕn′ə-făk′tər) *n.* Someone who helps another person, especially financially.

berate (bĭ-rāt′) *v.* To scold harshly.

bereave (bĭ-rēv′) *v.* To leave sad or forlorn, as by death.

beseech (bĭ-sēch′) *v.* To ask seriously.

bestow (bĭ-stō′) *v.* To give; grant.

bier (bîr) *n.* A structure upon which a corpse, or a coffin, is placed.

bilge (bĭlj) *n.* The water around the lower part of a ship.

bizarre (bĭ-zär′) *adj.* Odd; queer.

blanch (blănch, blänch) *v.* To become pale or white.

bland (blănd) *adj.* Mild; pleasant. – **blandly** *adv.*

blight (blīt) *n.* A plant disease.

blotch (blŏtch) *n.* A spot or mark differing in color from the surrounding area.

bluster (blŭs′tər) *v.* To express oneself in a boastful or bullying way.

boggy (bô′gē, bŏg′ē) *adj.* Swampy.

boisterous (boi′stər-əs, -strəs) *adj.* Stormy; violent.

borough (bûr′ō, bûr′ə) *n.* **1.** A self-governing town. **2.** A unit of a larger city.

boutique (boo-tēk′) *n.* A small shop.

brace (brās) *n.* A rope used to swing or secure the sails of a ship.

brandish (brăn′dĭsh) *v.* To wave or flourish in a menacing way.

bravado (brə-vä′dō) *n.* **1.** A show of false courage. **2.** Defiant behavior.

brazen (brā′zən) *adj.* **1.** Made of or resembling brass in color and hardness. **2.** Shameless; bold.

breach (brēch) *n.* An opening or gap in a wall.

bristle (brĭs′əl) *v.* To rise and stand erect as a result of anger or fear.

broach (brōch) *v.* To bring up a topic for discussion.

brusque (brŭsk) *adj.* Abrupt in behavior or speech; discourteous. — **brusquely** *adv.*

buckler (bŭk-lər) *n.* A small round shield held or worn on the arm.

buffet (bŭf'ĭt) *n.* A punch with the fist.

bulldoze (bŏŏl'dōz') *v. Slang.* To bully.

burgeon (bûr'jən) *v.* To grow rapidly; flourish.

burnish (bûr'nĭsh) *v.* To polish; make smooth and shiny.

butt (bŭt) *n.* The thicker and larger end of an object.

C

cadent (kād'ənt) *adj.* Moving in a rhythmic, measured way.

cajole (kə-jōl') *v.* To coax.

calamity (kə-lăm'ə-tē) *n.* A disaster; misfortune.

candelabra (kăn'də-lä'brə, -läb'rə, -lā'brə) *n.* A large, branched candleholder.

canopy (kăn'ə-pē) *n.* A rooflike covering held or fastened above a person or thing for protection or decoration.

capitalize (kăp'ə-təl-īz') *v.* To profit by.

caprice (kə-prēs') *n.* A sudden, impulsive change of mind or way of thinking.

capricious (kə-prĭsh'əs, -prē'shəs) *adj.* Tending to change one's mind suddenly; flighty.

carbine (kär'bīn', -bēn') *n.* A light shoulder rifle of limited range.

carriage (kăr'ĭj) *n.* The manner of bearing the body; posture.

cascade (kăs-kād') *n.* A waterfall.

catacombs (kăt'ə-kōmz') A series of grave sites in an underground burial place.

catalepsy (kăt'l-ĕp'sē) *n.* A condition in which there is a sudden and temporary loss of consciousness and rigidity of the body. — **cataleptic** *adj.*

catapult (kăt'ə-pŭlt') *n.* Slingshot. — *v.* To leap or spring up suddenly.

causeway (kôz'wā') *n.* A raised road across water or swampland.

cavalier (kăv'ə-lîr') *n.* A courteous, well-dressed gentleman.

cessation (sĕ-sā'shən) *n.* A stopping, either permanent or temporary.

chafe (chāf) *v.* To make sore; irritate.

char (chär) *v.* To scorch.

chide (chīd) *v.* To scold in a mild way.

chipyard (chĭp'yärd') A place where wood is cut for fuel.

chivalry (shĭv'əl-rē) *n.* The noble qualities of courage and honor associated with medieval knights.

chorister (kôr'ĭs-tər, kōr'-, kŏr'-) *n.* A choir singer.

chronic (krŏn'ĭk) *adj.* Continuing; recurrent.

chronicle (krŏn'ĭ-kəl) *n.* A record of events in the order in which they happened.

chronological (krŏn'ə-lŏj'ĭ-kəl, krō'nə-) *adj.* Arranged in the order that the events took place.

churn (chûrn) *v.* To shake or stir forcefully

ciphering (sī'fər-ing) *n.* Arithmetic.

circumscribe (sûr'kəm-skrīb') *v.* To encircle.

civility (sə-vĭl'ə-tē) *n.* Politeness.

clamor (klăm'ər) *v.* To demand or complain noisily; to make a loud, continuous noise. — *n.* noise. — **clamorer** *n.*

cleave (klēv) *v.* To stick to; cling.

cleft (klĕft) *n.* A gap; opening. — *adj.* split.

clemency (klĕm'ən-sē) *n.* Mercy.

cogent (kō'jənt) *adj.* Forceful.

cognomen (kŏg-nō'mən) *n.* A name; nickname.

coherent (kō-hîr'ənt, kō-hĕr'-) *adj.* Logical; consistent in thought.

cohort (kō'hôrt') *n.* A companion; associate.

collision (kə-lĭzh'ən) *n.* A violent coming together; forceful clash.

combatant (kəm-băt'ənt, kŏm'bə-tənt) *n.* Someone taking part in an armed conflict; fighter.

comber (kō'mər) *n.* A large ocean wave.

commence (kə-mĕns') *v.* To begin.

commend (kə-mĕnd') *v.* To give regards, or good wishes, to someone. — **commendable** *adj.*

commiserate (kə-mĭz'ə-rāt') *v.* To sympathize with.

communal (kə-myoon'əl, kŏm'yə-nəl) *adj.* Belonging to the community; shared.

compassion (kəm-păsh'ən) *n.* Pity.

compassionate (kĕm-păsh'ən-ĭt) *adj.* Sympathetic.

compensation (kŏm'pən-sā'shən) *n.* Something of equal worth given to make up for a loss or damage.

compilation (kŏm'pə-lā'shən) *n.* The act of gathering and putting together literary works, statistics, etc.

compose (kəm-pōz') *v.* To calm or quiet oneself.

composure (kəm-pō'zhər) *n.* Calmness.

compound (kŏm'pound) *n.* An enclosed area or group of buildings where people live.

comprise (kəm-prīz') *v.* To consist of.

compromise (kŏm'prə-mīz') *n.* A settlement. — *v.* **1.** To place one's reputation and character in danger. **2.** To settle by having each side give up some demands.

compulsory (kəm-pŭl'sə-rē) *adj.* Required.

conceive (kən-sēv') *v.* To think up.

concentration (kŏn'sən-trā'shən) *n.* **1.** Extreme thoughtfulness. **2.** Focused attention.

conception (kən'sĕp'shən) *n.* A mental picture; idea.

concession (kĕn-sĕsh'ən) *n.* Something yielded or granted.

conciliatory (kən-sĭl'ē-ə-tôr'-ē, -tōr'ē) *adj.* Soothing; friendly.

condescend (kŏn'dĭ-sĕnd') *v.* To come down willingly to the level of someone regarded as inferior.

condone (kən-dōn') *v.* To excuse; overlook.

confectioner (kən-fĕk'shən-ər) *n.* A person who makes or sells sweet foods.

confer (kən-fûr') *v.* To give; grant.

configuration (kən-fĭg'yə-rā'shən) *n.* The form or shape of.

confound (kən-found', kŏn-) *v.* To mix up; confuse.

congregate (kŏng'grə-gāt') *v.* To gather in a crowd.

conjecture (kən-jĕk'chər) *n.* A conclusion based on insufficient evidence.

ă pat/ā pay/âr care/ä father/b bib/ch church/d deed/ĕ pet/ē be/f fife/g gag/h hat/hw which/ĭ pit/ī pie/îr pier/j judge/k kick/l lid, needle/m mum/ n no, sudden/ng thing/ŏ pot/ō toe/ô paw, for/oi noise/ou out/ŏŏ took/ōō boot/p pop/r roar/s sauce/sh ship, dish/t tight/th thin, path/*th* this, bathe/ ū cut/ûr urge/v valve/w with/y yes/z zebra, size/zh vision/ə about, item, edible, gallop, circus/à *Fr.* ami/œ *Fr.* feu, *Ger.* schön/ü *Fr.* tu, *Ger.* über/ кн *Ger.* ich, *Scot.* loch/N *Fr.* bon.

conjure (kŏn′jər, kən-jōōr′) v. To appeal to earnestly. — **conjure up 1.** To bring to mind. **2.** To cause something to happen as by magic.

connoisseurship (kŏn′ə-sûr′shĭp′) n. Expert knowledge in some particular field, often in matters of art or fine foods.

consequence (kŏn′sə-kwĕns) n. Effect; result.

conspire (kən-spīr′) v. **1.** To act together secretly, usually to commit a crime. **2.** To plot or plan something.

consternation (kŏn′stər-nā′shən) n. Amazement; bewilderment.

constraint (kən-strānt′) n. Emotional repression.

contemplate (kŏn′təm-plāt′) v. To think about carefully; look at intently.

contemptible (kən-tĕmp′tə-bəl) adj. Deserving of scorn; worthless.

contemptuous (kən-tĕmp′chōō-əs) adj. Scornful. — **contemptuously** adv.

contend (kən-tĕnd′) v. To struggle against in combat or competition.

contentious (kən-tĕn′shəs) adj. Quarrelsome.

contingent (kən-tĭn′-jənt) adj. Dependent upon something that has not yet happened.

contraption (kən-trăp′shən) n. A device; gadget.

contrite (kən-trīt′, kŏn′trīt′) adj. Feeling very guilty for having done something wrong.

contrive (kən-trīv′) v. To plan cleverly; scheme.

convention (kən-vĕn′shən) n. A thing, behavior, or procedure established by custom and widely used throughout society.

convert (kən-vûrt′) v. To change into another form or thing.

copious (kō′pē-əs) adj. Plentiful.

cordial (kôr′jəl) adj. Friendly; hearty.

cordwood (kôrd′wŏŏd′) n. Wood cut in short lengths to be used for fuel.

corroborate (kə-rŏb′ə-rāt′) v. To confirm.

corrode (kə-rōd′) v. To wear away gradually.

corrupt (kə-rŭpt′) v. To cause to become morally unsound.

cosmopolite (kŏz-mŏp′ə-līt′) n. A person at home anywhere in the world.

council (koun′səl) n. A serious discussion among a group of people.

counsel (koun′səl) n. **1.** Advice. **2.** Legal representation in court. **3.** Ideas; opinions. **4.** Private, unexpressed thoughts. — v. To advise.

countenance (koun′tə-nəns) n. **1.** The face. **2.** The look on a person's face.

counterpart (koun′tər-pärt′) n. A person or thing that closely resembles another.

countinghouse (koun′tĭng-hous′) n. A place in which a business carries out its clerical and financial functions.

courtier (kôr′tē-ər, kōr′-, -tyər) n. **1.** A person who serves at a royal court. **2.** A person who seeks favor through flattery.

couscous (kōōs′kōōs) n. A North African food made of steamed, crushed grain.

cove (kōv) n. A small inlet or bay.

covet (kŭv′ĭt) v. To have a strong desire for something.

cower (kou′ər) v. To shrink away or hide oneself in fear.

coy (koi) adj. Affectedly cute or playful.

craven (krā′vən) adj. Very fearful; cowardly.

credulity (krĭ-dōō′lə-tē, -dyōō′lə-tē) n. A tendency to believe something too quickly.

credulous (krĕj′ōō-ləs) adj. Too easily convinced.

crest (krĕst) n. A cluster of feathers or an emblem decorating the top of a helmet.

crypt (krĭpt) n. An underground chamber used as a burial place.

cryptic (krĭp′tĭk) adj. Having an unclear meaning; mysterious.

cubicle (kyōō′bĭ-kəl) n. A small enclosed space or room.

cull (kŭl) v. To select; gather.

culminate (kŭl′mə-nāt′) v. To come to the highest degree or effect.

cunning (kŭn′ĭng) adj. Clever. — **cunningly** adv.

curfew (kûr′fyōō) n. **1.** A specified time when inhabitants of a town are required to be off the streets. **2.** A bell or other signal announcing this time.

currant (kûr′ənt) n. A seedless raisin.

cutter (kŭt′ər) n. A small boat that moves quickly.

cynical (sĭn′ĭ-kəl) adj. Of the belief that there is no true goodness in anyone; scornful.

D

damask (dăm′əsk) n. A heavy fabric with a woven-in-pattern used for table linen and furniture covers.

dank (dăngk) adj. Miserably damp and chilly.

deal (dēl) n. Pine wood.

debacle (dĭ-bä′kəl, -băk′əl) n. A sudden collapse or break-up.

debauch (dĭ-bôch′) n. An orgy.

decal (dē′kăl′) n. A picture or design transferred onto wood, material, etc., from specially prepared paper.

decanter (dĭ-kăn′tər) n. An ornamental glass bottle used for serving liquids.

deceptive (dĭ-sĕp′tĭv) adj. Deceiving.

declaim (dĭ-klām′) v. To speak loudly; recite dramatically.

declamation (dĕk′lə-mā′shən) n. A speech delivered in a dramatic manner.

decorous (dĕk′ər-əs, dĭ-kôr′əs) adj. Proper; in good taste.

decrepit (dĭ-krĕp′ĭt) adj. Worn out; broken down.

deface (dĭ-fās′) v. To disfigure.

defamation (dĕf′ə-mā′shən) n. The damaging of someone's reputation or character.

deflect (dĭ-flĕkt′) v. To bend; cause to go off to one side.

deft (dĕft) adj. Skillful in a quick and sure way. — **deftly** adv.

degenerate (dĭ-jĕn′ə-rāt′) v. To lower in quality or value; worsen.

dejected (dĭ-jĕk′tĭd) adj. Depressed.

deliberation (dĭ′lĭb′ə-rā′shən) n. Careful and lengthy consideration.

delirious (dĭ-lîr′ē-əs) adj. In a state of wild excitement. — **deliriously** adv.

deliverance (dĭ-lĭv′ər-əns) n. The state or act of being freed.

demeanor (dĭ-mē′nər) n. Behavior; conduct.

dependent (dĭ-pĕn′dənt) adj. Hanging down.

deplorable (dĭ-plôr′ə-bəl, dĭ-plōr′ə-) adj. Regrettable.

depreciate (dĭ-prē′shē-āt′) *v.* To belittle; make seem less valuable.

depreciation (dĭ-prē-shē-ā′shən) *n.* Belittlement.

deprive (dĭ-prīv′) *v.* To deny someone the enjoyment or use of something.

deride (dĭ-rīd′) *v.* To make fun of.

derisive (dĭ-rī′sĭv) *adj.* mocking.

desolate (dĕs′ə-lĭt) *adj.* Deserted; forlorn; lonely. —**desolately** *adv.*

desolation (dĕs′ə-lā′shən) *n.* Misery; loneliness.

despond (dĭ-spŏnd′) *v.* To become discouraged or hopeless.

detestable (dĭ-tĕs′tə-bəl) *adj.* Hateful.

devastate (dĕv′ə-stāt) *v.* To destroy; overwhelm.

devise (dĭ-vīz′) *v.* To plan or create something.

devoid (dĭ-void′) *adj.* Without.

devolve (dĭ-vŏlv′) *v.* To be passed on to another person, as a responsibility.

dexterity (dĕk-stĕr′ə-tē) *n.* Skill; cleverness.

dexterous (dĕk′strəs) *adj.* Skillful.

diabolical (dī′ə-bŏl′ĭ-kəl) *adj.* devilish.

diffidence (dĭf′ə-dəns) *n.* Shyness.

diffuse (dĭ-fyooz′) *v.* To spread out in all directions.

dilapidated (dĭ-lăp′ə-dā′tĭd) *adj.* In a state of disrepair.

diplomacy (dĭ-plō′mə-sē) *n.* The skillful handling of relationships among nations.

dipsomaniac (dĭp′sə-mā′nē-ăc) *n.* A person who craves alcoholic beverages.

dire (dīr) *adj.* Dreadful.

direful (dīr′fəl) *adj.* Frightful.

dirge (dûrj) *n.* A funeral hymn.

disaffection (dĭs′ə-fĕk′shən) *n.* The loss of affection or loyalty.

disapprobation (dĭs-ăp′rə-bā′shən) *n.* Disapproval.

disband (dĭs-bănd′) *v.* To break up, as a group.

discern (dĭ-sûrn′, -zûrn′) *v.* To see clearly.

discernible (dĭ-sûr′nə-bəl) *adj.* Distinguishable.

discomfit (dĭs-kŭm′fĭt) *v.* To make uneasy; embarrass.

discomfiture (dĭs-kŭm′fĭ-choor′) *n.* Embarrassment; uneasiness.

discomposure (dĭs′kəm-pō′zhər) *n.* The lack of calmness.

disconsolate (dĭs-kŏn′sə-lĭt) *adj.* Unable to be comforted; dejected. —**disconsolately** *adv.*

discord (dĭs′kôrd′) *n.* **1.** A conflict or disagreement. **2.** A combination of harsh tones sounded together.

discordant (dĭs-kôr′dənt) *adj.* **1.** Harsh in sound. **2.** Not in agreement; conflicting.

discourse (dĭs′kôrs′, -kōrs′) *n.* A long speech or written piece about a particular subject.

discreet (dĭs-krēt′) *adj.* Careful. —**discreetly** *adv.*

discretion (dĭs-krĕsh′ən) *n.* Caution.

disdain (dĭs-dān′) *v.* **1.** To reject scornfully. **2.** To have an attitude of contempt toward something or someone.

disdainful (dĭs-dān′fəl) *adj.* Scornful.

disintegrate (dĭs-ĭn′tə-grāt′) *v.* To decay.

disinterested (dĭs-ĭn′trĭ-stĭd, -ĭn′tə-rĕs′tĭd) *adj.* Having no selfish interest or motive. —**disinterestedness** *n.*

dislocate (dĭs′lō-kāt′, dĭs-lō′kāt′) *v.* To displace a limb or organ from its normal place in the body. —**dislocation** *n.*

dismay (dĭs-mā′) *n.* Discouragement; alarm.

dismember (dĭs-mĕm′bər) *v.* To remove the limbs from the body.

disparage (dĭs-păr′ĭj) *v.* To belittle.

disparity (dĭs′păr′ə-tē) *n.* Inequality or difference in rank, quality, or age.

disperse (dĭs-pûrs′) *v.* To scatter in various directions.

dispirited (dĭs-pĭr′ĭt-ĭd) *adj.* Sad.

dispose (dĭs-pōz′) *v.* To arrange or settle some important business.

disposition (dĭs′pə-zĭsh′ən) *n.* **1.** A settlement. **2.** A person's temperament. **3.** Inclination.

dissemble (dĭ-sĕm′bəl) *v.* To hide behind a disguise.

dissolution (dĭs′ə-loo′shən) *n.* **1.** Disintegration. **2.** Death.

distill (dĭs-tĭl′) *v.* **1.** To purify or refine. **2.** To increase the strength of a substance.

distort (dĭs-tôrt′) *v.* To twist out of proper shape.

distracted (dĭs-trăk′tĭd) *adj.* **1.** Having one's attention diverted. **2.** Confused or bewildered.

distraught (dĭs-trôt′) *adj.* Troubled; anxious.

divan (dĭ-văn′, dī′văn′) *n.* A long, low couch.

divert (dĭ-vûrt′, dī-) *v.* To entertain.

divine (dĭ-vīn′) *v.* To guess.

dogged (dô′gĭd, dŏg′ĭd) *adj.* Stubborn; persistent. —**doggedly** *adv.*

doleful (dōl′fəl) *adj.* Mournful.

dolt (dōlt) *n.* A stupid person.

domestic (də-mĕs′tĭk) *adj.* Having to do with the family or house.

dote (dōt) *v.* To be extremely fond of.

dowry (dour′ē) *n.* The money or property a woman brings to her husband at marriage.

drawn (drôn) *adj.* Tense.

droll (drōl) *adj.* Comical in a strange way.

drudge (drŭj) *n.* Someone who does hard, tedious work.

dubious (doo′bē-əs, dyoo′-) *adj.* Vague; doubtful. —**dubiously** *adv.*

duct (dŭkt) *n.* A tubular structure in the body through which a substance passes. —**ductal** *adj.*

dullard (dŭl′ərd) *n.* A stupid person.

duly (doo′lē, dyoo′-) *adv.* Rightfully.

dumbwaiter (dŭm′wā′tər) *n.* A portable serving table.

dune (doon, dyoon) *n.* A small hill of windblown sand.

duplication (doo′plĭ-kā′shən, dyoo′-) *n.* An exact copy of something.

duress (doo-rĕs′, dyoo-, door′ĭs, dyoor′-) *n.* The threat of the use of force.

dynamic (dī-năm′ĭk) *adj.* Energetic; forceful,

ă pat/ā pay/âr care/ä father/b bib/ch church/d deed/ĕ pet/ē be/f fife/g gag/h hat/hw which/ĭ pit/ī pie/îr pier/j judge/k kick/l lid, needle/m mum/ n no, sudden/ng thing/ŏ pot/ō toe/ô paw, for/oi noise/ou out/oo took/oo boot/p pop/r roar/s sauce/sh ship, dish/t tight/th thin, path/*th* this, bathe/ ū cut/ûr urge/v valve/w with/y yes/z zebra, size/zh vision/ə about, item, edible, gallop, circus/ā *Fr.* ami/œ *Fr.* feu, *Ger.* schön/ü *Fr.* tu, *Ger.* über/ KH *Ger.* ich, *Scot.* loch/N *Fr.* bon.

E

ebb (ĕb) *n.* A fading away.— *v.* To lessen.

eccentric (ĕk-sĕn′trĭk, ĭk-) *adj.* Unusual in behavior.

ecstatic (ĕk-stăt′ĭk) *adj.* In a state of intense delight.

eddy (ĕd′ē) *v.* A current of air or water moving in a circular motion.

edify (ĕd′ə-fī) *v.* To teach; enlighten.

efficacious (ĕf′ə-kā′shəs) *adj.* Having the ability to accomplish a desired effect or result.

ejaculate (ĭ-jăk′yə-lāte′) *v.* To exclaim suddenly.

elate (ĭ-lāt′) *v.* To make very happy or proud.

elation (ĭ-lā′shən) *n.* A feeling of great joy.

electrum (ĭ-lĕk′trəm) *n.* A light-yellow metal made from combining gold and silver.

elixir (ĭ-lĭk′sər) *n.* A substance that is supposed to extend life indefinitely.

elliptical (ĭ-lĭp′tĭ-kəl) *adj.* Not a perfect circle.

elude (ĭ-lōōd′) *v.* To avoid being caught; escape understanding.

elusive (ĭ-lōō′sĭv) *adj.* Hard to retain or understand.

embellish (ĕm′bĕl′ĭsh, ĭm-) *v.* To improve by adding detail to.

embellishment (ĕm-bĕl′ĭsh-mənt) *n.* Ornamentation.

embezzle (ĕm-bĕz′əl) *v.* To steal money that has been put in one's care.— **embezzlement** *n.*

emblazon (ĕm-blā-zən, ĭm-) *v.* To decorate brightly.

embodiment (ĕm-bŏd′ĭ-mənt, ĭm-) *n.* The bodily or visible form of something.

emboss (ĕm-bôs′, -bŏs′, ĭm-) *v.* To decorate with raised designs or patterns.

emulation (ĕm′yə-lā′shən) *n.* The imitation of another with the idea of equaling or going beyond.

encamp (ĕn-kămp′, ĭn-) *v.* To share living accommodations temporarily.

encompass (ĕn-kŭm′pəs, ĭn-) *v.* To include; enclose.

encrust (ĕn-krŭst′, ĭn-) *v.* To cover with elaborate decoration.— **encrustation** *n.*

endeavor (ĕn-dĕv′ər, ĭn-) *n.* An earnest effort.

endow (ĕn-dou′, ĭn-) *v.* To give money or property.

endurance (ĕn-dŏŏr′əns, -dyŏŏr′əns, ĭn-) *n.* The capacity to bear up under hardship or prolonged stress.

endure (ĕn-dŏŏr′, -dyŏŏr′, ĭn-) *v.* **1.** To last. **2.** To tolerate.

enjoin (ĕn-join′, ĭn-) *v.* To order someone to do something; urge.

enmity (ĕn′mə-tē) *n.* Hostility.

ennui (än′wē) *n.* Boredom.

ensue (ĕn-sōō′, ĭn-) *v.* To follow immediately.

entrails (ĕn′trālz′, -trəlz) *n. pl.* The internal organs of humans or animals.

entrance (en′trăns, -trăns, ĭn-) *v.* To fill with delight; enchant.

environ (ĕn-vī′rən, ĭn-) *v.* To surround.

enzymes (ĕn′zīmz) *n. pl.* Substances in plant and animal cells that help bring about certain chemical processes.

ephemeral (ĭ-fĕm′ər-əl) *adj.* Lasting only a short time.

epistle (ĭ-pĭs′əl) *n.* A letter; message.

epithet (ĕp′ə-thĕt′) *n.* A word or phrase used to describe someone, often insulting.

equity (ĕk′wə-tē) *n.* Fairness; justice.

erode (ĭ-rōd′) *v.* To wear away.

errant (ĕr-ənt) *adj.* Wandering.

erratic (ĭ-răt′ĭk) *adj.* **1.** Wandering. **2.** Irregular.

erudition (ĕr′yŏŏ-dĭsh′ən, ĕr′ŏŏ-) *n.* Extensive knowledge obtained through reading and study.

eruption (ĭ-rŭp′shən) *n.* A sudden bursting out.

essence (ĕs-əns) *n.* A solution containing the fragrance of the plant from which it is taken.

esteem (ĕ-stēm′, ĭ-stēm′) *n.* High rank; renown.

ethical (ĕth′ĭ-kəl) *adj.* Having to do with what is considered to be right or wrong behavior.

ethics (ĕth′ĭks) *n. pl.* **1.** The study of standards of behavior. **2.** Rules governing the conduct of people within certain groups.

ethnic (ĕth′nĭk) *adj.* Characteristic of a particular national, racial, cultural, or religious group.

evasive (ĭ-vā′sĭv) *adj.* Vague; not straightforward.— **evasively** *adv.*

evoke (ĭ-vōk′) *v.* To call forth.

ewe (yōō) *n.* A female sheep.

exact (ĕg-zăkt′, ĭg-) *v.* To force payment or the giving up of something.

exalted (ĕg-zôl′tĭd, ĭg-) *adj.* Of elevated rank or status.

exasperate (ĕg-zăs′pə-rāt′, ĭg-) *v.* To irritate; annoy.

exceeding (ĕk-sē′dĭng, ĭk-) *adj.* Extreme.

excess (ĕk-sĕs′, ĭk-, ĕk′sĕs′) *n.* A quantity that is more than required or desirable.

exclusive (ĕks-klōō′sĭv, ĭks-) *adj.* Not shared with another person.

excruciating (ĕk-skrōō′shē-ā′tĭng, ĭk-) *adj.* Intense.

excursion (ĕk-skûr′zhən, ĭk-) *n.* A round trip, usually very short and taken for pleasure.

execrate (ĕk-sĭ-krāt′) *v.* To curse; denounce.

exhilaration (ĕg-zĭl′ə-rā′shən, ĭg-) *n.* Excitement.

exigency (ĕk′sə-jən-sē) *n.* An emergency.

exorbitant (ĕg-zôr′bə-tənt, ĭg-) *adj.* Unreasonably high.

exotic (ĕg-zŏt′ĭk, ĭg-) *adj.* From a faraway and fantastic place.

expatriate (ĕks-pā′trē-āt′) *v.* To exile.

expeditious (ĕk′spə-dĭsh′əs) *adj.* Fast and efficient.

expend (ĕk-spĕnd′, ĭk-) *v.* To use up.

explicit (ĕk-splĭs′ĭt, ĭk-) *adj.* Definite.

expound (ĕk-spound′) *v.* To explain in detail.

expulsion (ĕk-spŭl′shən, ĭk-) *n.* A forcing out of someone from a group or organization.

exquisite (ĕks′kwĭ-zĭt) *adj.* Intense.— **exquisitely** *adv.*

extravagance (ĕk-străv′ə-gəns, ĭk-) *n.* Wastefulness.

extricate (ĕk′strĭ-kāt′) *v.* To get out of an entanglement.

exuberant (ĕg-zōō′bər-ənt) *adj.* Lively.

exude (ĕg-zōōd′, ĭg-, ĕk-sōōd′, ĭk-) *v.* To give off or emit.

exultant (ĕg-zŭl′tənt, ĭg-) *adj.* Joyful.

F

fabulous (făb′yə-ləs) *adj.* Unbelievable.

fain (fān) *adv.* Gladly.

famished (făm′ĭsht) *adj.* Starving.

fancy (făn′sē) *n.* Imagination; creativeness.

fastidious (fă-stĭd′ē-əs, fə-) *adj.* Extremely fussy about personal cleanliness and appearance.

fealty (fē-əl-tē) *n.* Loyalty.

feasible (fē′zə-bəl) *adj.* Capable of being done.— **feasibility** *n.*

felicitous (fĭ-lĭs′ə-təs) *adj.* Suitable to a specific purpose.

felon (fĕl'ən) *n.* Criminal.

ferocity (fə-rŏs'-ə-tē) *n.* Fierceness.

fervent (fûr'vənt) *adj.* Having or showing intense feeling.

fervid (fûr'vĭd) *adj.* Full of emotion.

fester (fĕs'tər) *v.* To develop pus; rot.

fetter (fĕt'ər) *v.* To chain.

filament (fĭl'ə-mənt) *n.* The fine metal wire in an electric light bulb.

finicky (fĭn'ĭ-kē) *adj.* Extremely fussy. —**finickiness** *n.*

flagon (flăg'ən) *n.* A large container for liquids, as wine or liquor.

flail (flāl) *v.* To strike.

flamboyance (flăm-boi'əns) *n.* Showy behavior.

flare (flâr) *n.* To curve outward.

flax (flăks) *n.* Plants whose seeds produce linseed oil and whose fibers are spun into linen cloth.

florid (flôr'ĭd, flōr'-) *adj.* **1.** Rosy. **2.** Flowery.

flounder (floun'dər) *v.* To move with difficulty, as in mud or water.

flout (flout) *v.* To be scornful of.

folly (fŏl'ē) *n.* Foolishness.

foray (fôr'ā') *n.* A raid.

forestay (fôr'stā', fōr'-) *n.* A rope supporting the front mast of a ship.

forfeit (fôr'fĭt) *n.* Something a person must give up as punishment for breaking the law or rules of a game.

forfeiture (fôr'fĭ-chŏor') *n.* The act of giving up something as a penalty or fine.

formidable (fôr'mə-də-bəl) *adj.* **1.** Causing fear. **2.** Very impressive because of skill or strength.

fortitude (fôr'tə-tōod', -tyōod') *n.* Ability to bear pain and misfortune.

founder (foun'dər) *v.* To sink.

frantic (frăn'tĭk) *adj.* Excessively emotional.

fraternal (frə-tûr'nəl) *adj.* Brotherly.

fray (frā) *n.* A fight.

frugal (frōo'gəl) *adj.* Thrifty.

fuddle (fŭd'l) *n.* Confusion.

furtive (fûr'tĭv) *adj.* Done in a sly or secret way.

fusillade (fyōo'sə-läd', -lăd', fyōo'zə-) *n.* A firing of many firearms, either at the same time or rapidly and continuously.

futile (fyōot'l, fyōo'tĭl') *adj.* Useless.

G

gad (găd) *v.* To wander about seeking amusement.

gait (gāt) *n.* **1.** A particular way of walking or running. **2.** The usual speed at which certain movements are performed.

gamut (găm'ət) *n.* The complete range of something.

garland (gär'lənd) *n.* A circlet or string of flowers.

garret (găr'ĭt) *n.* The attic.

gavel (găv'əl) *n.* A small, wooden hammer used to signal for silence.

genial (jēn'yəl, jē'nē-əl) *adj.* Pleasant; friendly.

gesticulation (jĕ-stĭk'yə-lā'shən) *n.* A movement of a part of the body to express something.

geyser (gī'zər) *n.* A spring that periodically gushes columns of hot water and steam into the air.

gingerly (jĭn'jər-lē) *adv.* With great care or caution.

girdler (gûrd'lər) *n.* One that encircles something.

glade (glād) *n.* An open area in a forest.

glint (glĭnt) *n.* To sparkle.

gloat (glōt) *v.* To feel great pleasure over another's loss or suffering.

gnarled (närld) *adj.* Lumpy and twisted.

gnaw (nô) *v.* To eat away at; torment.

goad (gōd) *v.* To urge on.

gorge (gôrj) *v.* To eat greedily.

gosling (gŏz'lĭng) *n.* A young goose.

graft (grăft, gräft) *v.* To join a part of one plant to another in order to produce a certain kind of fruit or flower.

granite (grăn'ĭt) *n.* A hard, gray rock.

grapple (grăp'əl) *n.* A grip or clutch.

gravity (grăv'ə-tē) *n.* Seriousness.

grimace (grĭ-mās', grĭm'ĭs) *v.* To twist the face in pain or disgust.

grist (grĭst) *n.* **1.** Grain that has been ground. **2.** Something produced by grinding.

groin (groin) *n.* The fold in the body where the trunk meets the thigh.

grotesque (grō-tĕsk') *adj.* Odd; fantastic.

grovel (grŭv'əl, grŏv'-) *v.* To cringe.

guile (gīl) *n.* Cunning; slyness.

guise (gīz) *n.* Style of dress.

gullible (gŭl'ə-bəl) *adj.* Easily fooled or convinced.

gyrate (jī'rāt') *v.* To rotate; whirl.

H

habituate (hə-bĭch'ōo-āt') *v.* To get used to something through frequent and repeated exposure.

haggard (hăg'ərd) *adj.* Having a very exhausted appearance.

halcyon (hăl'sē-ən) *adj.* From an earlier, happier time.

hale (hāl) *adj.* Strong.

haversack (hăv'ər-săk') *n.* A canvas bag used to carry supplies.

hearken (här'kən) *v.* To listen to.

heathen (hē'thən) *n. pl.* People who worship many gods and idols.

heed (hēd) *n.* Careful consideration.

henna (hĕn'ə) *n.* A plant of North Africa and Asia that yields a red dye.

herald (hĕr'əld) *n.* A person or thing that announces important news or events to come.

hermitage (hûr'mə-tĭj) *n.* A place to live that is away from other people.

hew (hyōo) *v.* To make or shape by cutting with an ax.

hoist (hoist) *v.* To lift.

hone (hōn) *v.* To sharpen on a hard stone.

ă pat/ā pay/âr care/ä father/b bib/ch church/d deed/ĕ pet/ē be/f fife/g gag/h hat/hw which/ĭ pit/ī pie/îr pier/j judge/k kick/l lid, needle/m mum/ n no, sudden/ng thing/ŏ pot/ō toe/ô paw, for/oi noise/ou out/ŏo took/ōo boot/p pop/r roar/s sauce/sh ship, dish/t tight/th thin, path/*th* this, bathe/ ū cut/ûr urge/v valve/w with/y yes/z zebra, size/zh vision/ə about, item, edible, gallop, circus/ à *Fr.* ami/œ *Fr.* feu, *Ger.* schön/ü *Fr.* tu, *Ger.* über/ KH *Ger.* ich, *Scot.* loch/N *Fr.* bon.

hover (hŭv′ər, hŏv′-) v. To float in the air or move back and forth near a particular place.

humidor (hyōō′mə-dôr′) n. A case provided with a moisturizing device to keep tobacco products fresh.

humiliate (hyōō-mĭl′ē-āt′) v. To hurt someone's pride or feelings; degrade.

humiliation (hyōō-mĭl′ē-ā′shən) n. Disgrace; shame.

hurtle (hûrt′l) v. To throw with great force.

I

idol (īd′l) n. A false god.

idolatry (ī-dŏl′ə-trē) n. Extreme devotion to a person or thing.

ignominious (ĭg′nō-mĭn′ē-əs) adj. Disgraceful. — **ignominiously** adv.

ignoramus (ĭg′nə-rā′məs) n. A stupid person.

illuminate (ĭ-lōō′mə-nāt′) v. **1.** To explain. **2.** To decorate a handwritten book with colorful designs or pictures.

imbecile (ĭm′bə-sĭl, -səl) n. A severely retarded person.

imminent (ĭm′ə-nənt) adj. About to happen.

immobile (ĭ-mō′bəl, -bēl′) adj. Not moving.

immortals (ĭ-môrt′lz) n. pl. The gods of ancient Greece and Rome.

immune (ĭ-myōōn′) adj. Not affected by something.

impact (ĭm′păkt′) n. A forceful coming together.

impart (ĭm-pärt′) v. **1.** To give. **2.** To make known.

impartial (ĭm-pär′shəl) adj. Showing no favoritism. — **impartiality** (ĭm′pär-shē-ăl′ə-tē) n.

impend (ĭm-pĕnd′) v. To be about to happen; threaten.

impenetrable (ĭm-pĕn′ə-trə-bəl) adj. Unable to be passed through.

imperative (ĭm-pĕr′ə-tĭv) adj. Urgent.

imperceptible (ĭm′pər-sĕp′tə-bəl) adj. Hardly noticeable; gradual. — **imperceptibly** adv.

imperious (ĭm-pîr′ē-əs) adj. Domineering; arrogant.

impetuosity (ĭm-pĕch′ōō-ŏs′ə-tē) n. An impulsive act.

impetuous (ĭm-pĕch′ōō-əs) adj. Acting suddenly without much thought. — **impetuously.** adv.

impinge (ĭm-pĭnj′) v. To make an impression on.

implacable (ĭm-plăk′ə-bəl, -plăk′ə-bəl) adj. **1.** Incapable of being calmed. **2.** Unforgiving.

imply (ĭm-plī′) v. To suggest.

import (ĭm′pôrt′, -pōrt′) n. Significance.

impose (ĭm-pōz′) v. To establish with authority.

impostor (ĭm-pŏs′tər) n. A person who pretends to be something he or she is not.

imprecation (ĭm′prə-ka′shən) n. A curse.

impromptu (ĭm-prŏmp′tōō, -tyōō) adj. Done on the spur of the moment.

imprudent (ĭm-prōō′dənt) adj. Unwise.

impudence (ĭm′-pyə-dəns) n. Bold, shameless behavior.

impudent (ĭm′-pyə-dənt) adj. Disrespectful.

impulse (ĭm′pŭls′) n. A sudden desire to do something.

impunity (ĭm-pyōō′nə-tē) n. Protection against punishment.

inaccessible (ĭn′ăk-sĕs′ə-bəl) adj. Unapproachable. — **Inaccessibility** n.

inadvertent (ĭn′əd-vûr′tənt) adj. Unintentional. — **inadvertently** adv.

inaptitude (ĭn-ăp′tə-tōōd′, -tyōōd′) n. Lack of ability.

incantation (ĭn′kăn-tā′shən) n. The chanting of magical words to cast a spell. — **incantatory** (ĭn′kăn′tə-tôr′e) adj.

incautious (ĭn-kô′shəs) adj. Not careful. — **incautiously** adv.

inception (ĭn-sĕp′shən) n. The origin of something.

incessant (ĭn-sĕs′ənt) adj. Continuous. — **incessantly** adv.

incompatible (ĭn′kəm-păt′ə-bəl) adj. Conflicting.

incomprehensible (ĭn′kŏm-prĭ-hĕn′sə-bəl, ĭn-kŏm′-) adj. Not understandable.

inconceivable (ĭn′kən-sē′və-bəl) adj. Unbelievable.

inconsequential (ĭn-kŏn′sə-kwĕn′shəl) adj. Unimportant.

inconsolable (ĭn′kən-sō′lə-bəl) adj. Unable to be comforted.

incorruptible (ĭn′kə-rŭp′tə-bəl) adj. Not subject to becoming immoral or dishonest.

incredulity (ĭn′krə-dōō′lə-tē, -dyōō′lə-tē) n. Disbelief.

incubation (ĭn′kyə-bā′shən, ĭng′-) n. The period during which eggs are developed and hatched.

incursion (ĭn-kûr′zhən, -shən) n. A sudden entering into.

indecipherable (ĭn′dĭ-sī′fər-ə-bəl) adj. That cannot be made understandable.

indifference (ĭn-dĭf′ər-əns) n. A lack of interest.

indifferent (ĭn-dĭf′ər-ənt) adj. **1.** Without interest in. **2.** Uninvolved.

indignation (ĭn′dĭg-nā′shən) n. Anger.

indiscriminate (ĭn′dĭs-krĭm′ə-nĭt) adj. **1.** Haphazard. **2.** Unrestrained. — **indiscriminately** adv.

indolent (ĭn′də-lənt) adj. Lazy. — **indolently** adv.

ineffectual (ĭn′ĭ-fĕk′chōō-əl) adj. Not producing a desired result. — **ineffectually** adv.

inequity (ĭn-ĕk′wə-tē) n. Unfairness.

inevitable (ĭn-ĕv′ə-tə-bəl) adj. Unavoidable. — **inevitably** adv.

infer (ĭn-fûr′) v. To conclude from available facts.

infernal (ĭn-fûr′nəl) adj. Hellish; fiendish.

infest (ĭn-fĕst′) v. To swarm over in a destructive way.

inflammatory (ĭn-flăm′ə-tôr′ē, -tōr′ē) adj. Fiery.

inflexible (ĭn-flĕk′sə-bəl) adj. Stubborn.

infuse (ĭn-fyōōz′) v. To put into as by pouring.

ingenuity (ĭn′jə-nōō′ə-tē, -nyōō′ə-tē) n. Cleverness.

ingrate (ĭn′grāt) n. An ungrateful person.

injudicious (ĭn′jōō-dĭsh′əs) adj. Unwise.

injunction (ĭn-jŭngk′shən) n. A command.

innards (ĭn′ərdz) n. pl. The intestines and other internal organs of the body.

innovation (ĭn′ə-vā′shən) n. A change.

inscription (ĭn-skrĭp′shən) n. A short message written on or carved into a hard surface.

inscrutable (ĭn-skrōō′tə-bəl) adj. Mysterious.

insidious (ĭn-sĭd′ē-əs) adj. **1.** Treacherous. **2.** Stealthy.

insinuating (ĭn-sĭn′yōō-ā′tĭng) adj. Arousing doubts and suspicions. — **insinuatingly** adv.

insolent (ĭn′sə-lənt) adj. Bold in a reckless way.

insolvent (ĭn-sŏl′vənt) adj. Not able to pay debts.

instigate (ĭn′stĭ-gāt′) v. To stir up.

institute (ĭn′stə-tōōt′, -tyōōt′) v. To start.

insufferable (ĭn-sŭf′ər-ə-bəl) adj. Unbearable. — **insufferably** adv.

insupportable (ĭn′sə-pôr′tə-bəl, -pōr′tə-bəl) adj. Unbearable.

intact (ĭn-tăkt′) adj. Whole; undamaged.

inter (ĭn-tûr′) v. To bury.

interlope (ĭn′tər-lōp′) v. To intrude; meddle. — **interloper** n.

interment (ĭn-tûr′mənt) *n.* Burial.

interpose (ĭn′tər-pōz′) *v.* **1.** To introduce an interrupting remark in a conversation. **2.** To come between as a settling force. — **interposition** (ĭn′tər-pə-zĭsh′ən) *n.*

interstice (ĭn-tûr′stĭs) *n.* A small, narrow space between parts of a thing.

intervene (ĭn′tər-vēn′) *v.* To come in as an influencing force.

intimacy (ĭn′tə-mə-sē) *n.* A close and familiar relationship.

intimate (ĭn′tə-mĭt) *adj.* Close and familiar.

intimate (ĭn′tə-māt′) *v.* To hint.

intolerable (ĭn-tŏl′ər-ə-bəl) *adj.* Unbearable.

intoxicate (ĭn-tŏk′sĭ-kāt′) *v.* To make drunk. **2.** To excite.

intricate (ĭn′trĭ-kĭt) *adj.* Full of detail; complicated.

intrigue (ĭn′trēg′, ĭn-trēg′) *v.* To scheme secretly. — **intriguer** *n.*

intrusion (ĭn-trōō′zhən) *n.* An uninvited or illegal entry.

invariable (ĭn′vâr′ē-ə-bəl) *adj.* Constant- — **invariably** *adv.*

inveterate (ĭn′vĕt′ər-ĭt) *adj.* By custom or habit.

invocation (ĭn′və-kā′shən) *n.* **1.** A serious request. **2.** A prayer asking for help.

iridescent (ĭr′ə-dĕs′ənt) *adj.* Bright and shifting in color.

irrational (ĭ-răsh′ən-əl) *adj.* Senseless. — **irrationally** *adv.*

irresolute (ĭ-rĕz′ə-lōōt) *adj.* Undecided

irrevocable (ĭ-rĕv′ə-kə-bəl) *adj.* Incapable of being undone.

J

jar (jär) *v.* To make an irritating sound.

jostle (jŏs′əl) *v.* To push and shove in a crowd.

joust (jŭst, joust, jōōst) *n.* A fight with lances between two people on horseback.

jubilant (jōō′bə-lənt) *adj.* Joyful. — **jubilantly** *adv.*

judicial (jōō-dĭsh′əl) *adj.* Showing careful consideration of all sides of a problem when making a decision.

K

kibitzer (kĭb′ĭt-sər) *n. Informal.* A meddler who gives unwanted advice.

L

lacerated (lăs′ə-rā′tĭd) *adj.* Wounded; torn.

lair (lâr) *n.* The home of a wild animal.

lament (lə-mĕnt′) *v.* To grieve for.

lamentable (lăm′ən-tə-bəl, lə-mĕn′-) *adj.* Distressing.

lance (lăns, läns) *n.* A thrusting weapon having a wooden shaft and a pointed metal tip.

languish (lăng′gwĭsh) *v.* **1.** To become weak. **2.** To long or pine for something. — *n. Obsolete.* Weakness.

lapse (lăps) *n.* A minor fault or error

larceny (lär′sə-nē) *n.* Theft.

larder (lär′dər) *n.* A storage room for household food supplies.

lascar (lăs′kər) *n.* A sailor from India.

lateral (lăt′ər-əl) *adj.* Situated at the side. — *n.* In football, a pass thrown sidewise. — **laterally** *adv.*

literal (lĭt′ər-əl) *adj.* Real. — **literally** *adv.*

lithe (līth) *adj.* Limber.

loam (lōm) *n.* Rich, dark soil.

loath (lōth, lōth) *adj.* Unwilling.

loathsome (lōth′səm, lōth′-) *adj.* Disgusting.

longitudinal (lŏn′jə-tōōd′n-əl, -tyōōd′n-əl) *adj.* Lengthwise.

lop (lŏp) *v.* To cut off.

lope (lōp) *v.* To move with a steady, easy stride.

lore (lôr, lōr) *n.* The accumulated information on a particular subject.

lounge (lounj) *v.* **1.** To spend time idly. **2.** To move in a related way.

lout (lout) *n.* A stupid person.

lugger (lŭg′ər) *n.* A small sailing vessel.

luminous (lōō′mə-nəs) *adj.* Giving off light.

lunacy (lōō′nə-sē) *n.* **1.** Insanity. **2.** Very foolish behavior.

lunatic (lōō′nə-tĭk) *adj.* **1.** Insane. **2.** Exceedingly foolish.

lurch (lûrch) *v.* To fall and rise abruptly.

lurid (lŏŏr′ĭd) *adj.* Passionate; vivid.

M

magnetize (măg′nə-tīz′) *v.* **1.** To attract. **2.** To have a strong influence upon.

magnanimous (măg-năn′ə-məs) *adj.* Noble in mind and heart.

malevolence (mə-lĕv′ə-ləns) *n.* A feeling of extreme ill will toward others.

malice (măl′ĭs) *n.* A desire to be hurtful to others.

malignant (mə-lĭg′nənt) *adj.* Very harmful.

mammoth (măm′əth) *adj.* Gigantic.

maneuver (mə-nōō′vər) *v.* To move in a purposeful and skilled way for a particular reason.

manacle (măn′ə-kəl) *v.* To handcuff.

martial (mär′shəl) *adj.* Military.

martinet (mär′tə-nĕt′) *n.* Someone who demands very strict observance of rules.

martyr (mär′tər) *v.* To torture.

masonry (mā′sən-rē) *n.* Brickwork or stonework.

massive (măs′ĭv) *adj.* **1.** Very large. **2.** Of such an extent to make a deep impression.

mattock (măt′ək) *n.* A digging tool similar to a pickax.

maudlin (môd′lĭn) *adj.* Tearfully sentimental.

meager (mē′gər) *adj.* A small amount.

medieval (mē′dē-ē′vəl, mēd′ē-′vəl) *adj.* Pertaining to the Middle Ages.

meditate (mĕd′ə-tāt′) *v.* To think deeply about something.

meditation (mĕd′ə-tā′shən) *n.* Deep thoughtfulness.

meditative (mĕd′ə-tā′tĭv) *adj.* In deep thoughtfulness; pensive.

ă pat/ā pay/âr care/ä father/b bib/ch church/d deed/ĕ pet/ē be/f fife/g gag/h hat/hw which/ĭ pit/ī pie/îr pier/j judge/k kick/l lid, needle/m mum/ n no, sudden/ng thing/ŏ pot/ō toe/ô paw, for/oi noise/ou out/ŏŏ took/ōō boot/p pop/r roar/s sauce/sh ship, dish/t tight/th thin, path/*th* this, bathe/ ū cut/ûr urge/v valve/w with/y yes/z zebra, size/zh vision/ə about, item, edible, gallop, circus/ à *Fr.* ami/œ *Fr.* feu, *Ger.* schön/ü *Fr.* tu, *Ger.* über/ кн *Ger.* ich, *Scot.* loch/n *Fr.* bon.

melodramatic (měl′ə-drə-măt′ĭk) *adj.* Highly exciting or emotional.

menace (měn′ĭs) *n.* A harmful person or thing.

mentality (měn-tăl′ə-tē) *n.* Cast of mind.

merit (měr′ĭt) *v.* To deserve.

meteorite (mē′tē-ə-rīt′) *n.* The part of a larger body from outer space that falls to the earth's surface.

meticulous (mə-tĭk′yə-ləs) *adj.* Extremely precise.

mettle (mět′l) *n.* Courage.

mime (mīm) *n.* A form of drama that uses movements of the body instead of words to put across ideas.

minaret (mĭn′ə-rĕt′) *n.* A tall slender tower attached to a mosque.

miscreant (mĭs′krē-ənt) *n.* A wicked person.

moderate (mŏd′ə-rāt′) *v.* To become mild.

modulate (mŏj′ōō-lāt′, mŏd′yə-) *v.* **1.** To regulate or vary the pitch of the voice or a musical instrument. **2.** To change pitch within a musical composition.

momentum (mō-měn′təm) *n.* The force that keeps an object moving.

monitor (mŏn′ə-tər) *n.* A device used to record or regulate the performance of some machine or process.

mooch (mōōch) *v.* To loaf.

moral (môr′l, mŏr′-) *adj.* Concerned with what is right or wrong behavior.

morbid (môr′bĭd) *adj.* Gruesome.

morose (mə-rōs′, mô-) *adj.* Gloomy.

morsel (môr′səl) *n.* A small amount.

mortification (môr′tə-fĭ-kā′shən) *n.* Humiliation.

mortify (môr′tə-fī′) *v.* **1.** To humiliate. **2.** To decay because of injury or disease.

mosaic (mō-zā′ĭk) *n.* A picture or design made by setting small pieces of colored glass or clay in mortar.

mosque (mŏsk) *n.* A Moslem house of worship.

motley (mŏt′lē) *adj.* Composed of many different and unrelated elements or colors. *n.* A clown costume.

mottle (mŏt′l) *v.* To streak or spot with many colors.

multitude (mŭl′tə-tōōd′, -tyōōd′) *n.* A large number of individuals.

muster (mŭs′tər) *v.* To gather together. *— n.* An assembly.

mute (myōōt) *adj.* Unable to speak. *—* **mutely** *adv.*

mutilate (myōōt′l-āt′) *v.* To cut off or make useless a part of the body. *—* **mutilation** *n.*

mutinous (myōōt′n-əs) *adj.* Rebellious.

myriad (mĭr′ē-əd) *adj.* A great number.

mythic (mĭth′ĭk) *adj.* Imaginary.

N

naive (nä-ēv′) *adj.* Not worldly-wise.

niche (nĭch) *n.* A hollow place in a wall.

niggardly (nĭg′ərd-lē) *adj.* Stingy.

ninny (nĭn′ē) *n.* A fool.

niter (nī′tər) *n.* A white or gray hardened form of potassium nitrate.

nomenclature (nō′mən-klā′chər, nō-měn′klə-chər) *n.* A set of names for a particular group of things.

nonchalant (nŏn′shə-länt′) *adj.* Casual; unconcerned.

nuptial (nŭp′shəl) *n.* A wedding.

nurture (nûr′chər) *v.* To nourish.

nuzzle (nŭz′əl) *v.* To snuggle.

nymph (nĭmf) *n.* A nature goddess.

O

obituary (ō-bĭch′ōō-ĕr′-ē) *n.* A death notice that includes a short description of the dead person's life.

oblivious (ə-blĭv′ē-əs) *adj.* Unaware.

obnoxious (ŏb-nŏk′shəs, əb-) *adj.* Hateful.

ocher (ō′kər) *n.* A yellow or reddish-brown color.

ointment (oint′mənt) *n.* A salve.

ominous (ŏm′ə-nəs) *adj.* Threatening. *—* **ominously** *adv.*

omnipotent (ŏm-nĭp′ə-tənt) *adj.* All-powerful.

opaque (ō-pāk′) *adj.* Not letting light through.

opiate (ō′pē-ĭt, -āt′) *n.* Something that soothes or quiets.

oppression (ə-prĕsh′ən) *n.* Something that weighs heavily on the mind, body, or senses.

oppressive (ə-prĕs′ĭv) *adj.* Distressing; hard to bear.

option (ŏp′shən) *n.* A choice.

oracle (ôr′ə-kəl, ŏr′-) *n.* Something or someone believed to be a source of wisdom.

oration (ô-rā′shən, ō-rā′-) *n.* A formal speech given at a formal ceremony.

orator (ôr′ə-tər, ŏr′-) *n.* A skilled public speaker.

orb (ôrb) *n.* An eye.

ordnance (ôrd′nəns) *n.* Military weaponry.

ornamental (ôr′nə-měn′təl) *adj.* Made fancy with decorations.

ornate (ôr-nāt′) *adj.* Heavily decorated.

overweening (ō′vər-wē′nĭng) *adj.* Overbearing.

P

palate (păl′ĭt) *n.* The sense of taste.

palatial (pə-lā′shəl) *adj.* Magnificent, like a palace.

pall (pôl) *n.* Anything dark and gloomy that covers or wraps around something.

palpable (păl′pə-bəl) *adj.* Capable of being touched.

palpitation (păl′pə-tā′shən) *n.* An irregular and rapid beating of the heart.

palter (pôl′tər) *v.* To argue about terms, prices, etc.

pandemonium (păn′də-mō′nē-əm) *n.* Wild noise and disorder.

pantomime (păn′tə-mīm′) *n.* A drama performed solely with actions and gestures.

paradox (păr′ə-dŏks′) *n.* A situation or statement that has contradictory qualities. *—* **paradoxical** *adj.*

paramour (păr′ə-mōōr′) *n.* A lover.

parapet (păr′ə-pĭt, -pĕt′) *n.* A low wall or railing around the edge of a roof or bridge.

parley (pär′lē) *n.* A discussion held to settle a dispute.

paroxysm (păr′ək-sĭz′əm) *n.* A sudden fit or spasm.

partridge (pär′trĭj) *n.* A wild bird hunted for sport or food.

pathetic (pə-thĕt′ĭk) *adj.* Arousing pity. *—* **pathetically** *adv.*

patronize (pā′trə-nīz′, păt′rə-) *v.* To treat others with an air of superiority.

pedigree (pĕd′ə-grē′) *n.* Ancestry.

peeve (pēv) *v.* To annoy.

pelt (pĕlt) *v.* To pound steadily and heavily.

penitent (pĕn′ə-tənt) *adj.* Feeling and expressing shame for having done something wrong. *—* **penintently** *adv.*

penitential (pĕn′ə-tĕn′shəl) *adj.* Expressing remorse for one's wrongs.

pennant (pĕn′ənt) *n.* A flag.

pensive (pĕn′sĭv) *adj.* Thoughtful.

penury (pĕn′yə-rē) *n.* Poverty.

perceive (pər-sēv′) *v.* To become aware of something.

perceptible (pər-sĕp′tə-bəl) *adj.* Noticeable; recognizable.

perception (pər-sĕp′shən) *n.* **1.** Awareness. **2.** Insight or understanding.

perdition (pər-dĭsh′ən) *n.* Hell.

perjury (pûr′jə-rē) *n.* The telling of a lie while swearing to tell the truth.

pernicious (pər-nĭsh′əs) *adj.* Destructive; deadly.

perplex (pər-plĕks′) *v.* To confuse.

persistent (pər-sĭs′tənt, -zĭs′tənt) *adj.* Stubborn. — **persistently** *adv.*

pert (pûrt) *adj.* Saucy.

peruse (pə-rooz′) *v.* To read; study.

perverse (pər-vûrs′) *adj.* Contrary to what is considered to be correct thinking or behavior.

perverted (pər-vûr′tĭd) *adj.* Evil.

petition (pə-tĭsh′ən) *n.* A formal request to a person or group in authority.

pettish (pĕt′ĭsh) *adj.* Irritable. — **pettishly** *adv.*

pewter (pyoo′tər) *n.* A dull, grayish alloy that has tin as its major metal.

phenomenon (fĭ-nŏm′ə-nŏn′) *n.* **1.** Something that can be seen but is difficult to understand. **2.** An unusual occurrence.

philanthropist (fĭ-lăn′thrə-pĭst) *n.* A person of means who helps less fortunate people.

pilgrimage (pĭl′grə-mĭj) *n.* Any long journey for a particular purpose.

pillage (pĭl′ĭj) *v.* To loot; damage.

pinnacle (pĭn′ə-kəl) *n.* A peak.

pious (pī′əs) *adj.* Showing religious devotion.

pique (pēk) *v.* To cause a feeling of resentment.

placable (plăk′ə-bəl, plā′kə-) *adj.* Capable of being calmed or soothed.

placard (plăk′ärd′, -ərd) *n.* A poster used to make a public announcement.

placid (plăs′ĭd) *adj.* Calm. — **placidly** *adv.*

plaintiff (plān′tĭf) *n.* The party that brings suit in court.

plaintive (plān′tĭv) *adj.* Sad. — **plaintively** *adv.*

pliancy (plī′ən-sē) *n.* The quality of being supple or flexible.

pliant (plī′ənt) *adj.* Flexible.

plumb (plŭm) *adv.* Exactly.

plunder (plŭn′dər) *n.* Property taken by force.

poacher (pō′chər) *n.* Someone who hunts or fishes unlawfully on the property of another.

poise (poiz) *n.* Dignified and serene behavior.

pommel (pŭm′əl, pŏm′-) *n.* The rounded, front part of a saddle.

ponderous (pŏn′dər-əs) *adj.* Extremely heavy — **ponderously** *adv.*

portentous (pôr-tĕn′təs, pōr-) *adj.* Threatening.

posture (pŏs′chər) *v.* To take on a bodily or mental attitude to produce a desired effect.

prate (prāt) *v.* To chatter.

precarious (prĭ-kâr′ē-əs) *adj.* **1.** Insecure. **2.** Based on unproved statements or conclusions. — **precariously** *adv.*

preclude (prĭ-klood′) *v.* To make impossible.

predatory (prĕd′ə-tôr′ē) *adj.* Living by catching and eating other animals.

predominate (prĭ-dŏm′ə-nāt′) *v.* To be greater in quantity.

prejudice (prĕj′ə-dĭs) *n.* An opinion, usually unfavorable, formed before knowing all the facts about a person or thing.

preliminary (prĭ-lĭm′ə-nĕr′ē) *adj.* Happening before or leading up to a main action. — **preliminaries** *n. pl.*

premises (prĕm′ĭs-əz) *n. pl.* A building and the area surrounding it.

presentiment (prĭ-zĕn′tə-mənt) *n.* A feeling that a particular thing will happen.

preserve (prĭ-zûrv′) *n.* An area set aside for the protection of wildlife.

preside (prĭ-zīd) *v.* To hold the position of authority.

prevail (prĭ-vāl′) *v.* **1.** To succeed. **2.** To be effective. **3.** To remain in force.

privation (prĭ-vā′shən) *n.* The lack of the basic needs or comforts of life.

probe (prōb) *n.* An instrument used to explore a wound or body cavity.

procure (prō-kyoor′, prə-) *v.* To get.

prodigious (prə-dĭj′əs) *adj.* Enormous. — **prodigiously** *adv.*

profane (prō-fān′, prə-) *v.* To treat sacred things with contempt. — **profaner** *n.*

profanity (prō-făn′ə-tē, prə-) *n.* Disrespectful or irreverent language.

profess (prə-fĕs′, prō-) *v.* To declare openly.

profound (prə-found′, prō-) *adj.* Complete; deep.

profusion (prə-fyoo′zhən, prō-) *n.* An abundance.

proliferate (prō-lĭf′ə-rāt′) *v.* To increase quickly and in great quantity.

promiscuous (prə-mĭs′kyoo-əs) *adj.* In a haphazard way. — **promiscuously** *adv.*

prone (prōn) *adj.* Lying flat.

proposition (prŏp′ə-zĭsh′ən) *n.* **1.** A plan or idea offered for consideration. **2.** In math, a problem to be solved.

proprietor (prə-prī′ə-tər) *n.* An owner.

proprieties (prə-prī′ə-tēz) *n. pl.* Accepted behavior in polite society.

prosperity (prŏs-pĕr′ə-tē) *n.* Wealth; success.

prostrate (prŏs′trāt′) *v.* **1.** To be flat; **2.** To kneel or fall to the ground in humility or surrender. — *adj.* lying flat.

protozoa (prō′tə-zō′ə) *n. pl.* Microscopic organisms.

protract (prō-trăkt′) *v.* To prolong.

protrude (prō-trood′) *v.* To jut out.

provender (prŏv′ən-dər) *n.* Food.

Providence (prŏv′ə-dəns, -dĕns′) *n.* God.

provision (prə-vĭzh′ən) *n.* A stock of food in store for future use.

provoke (prə-vōk′) *v.* To anger.

prow (prou) *n.* The front part of a ship.

ă pat/ā pay/âr care/ä father/b bib/ch church/d deed/ĕ pet/ē be/f fife/g gag/h hat/hw which/ĭ pit/ī pie/îr pier/j judge/k kick/l lid, needle/m mum/ n no, sudden/ng thing/ŏ pot/ō toe/ô paw, for/oi noise/ou out/oo took/oo boot/p pop/r roar/s sauce/sh ship, dish/t tight/th thin, path/*th* this, bathe/ ŭ cut/ûr urge/v valve/w with/y yes/z zebra, size/zh vision/ə about, item, edible, gallop, circus/ à *Fr.* ami/œ *Fr.* feu, *Ger.* schön/ü *Fr.* tu, *Ger.* über/ KH *Ger.* ich, *Scot.* loch/N *Fr.* bon.

prudence (prōod′əns) *n.* Cautious behavior.

prune (prōon) *v.* To cut off dead or live parts of a plant in order to improve growth or shape.

psychological (sī′kə-lŏj′ĭ-kəl) *adj.* Pertaining to the mind.

puke (pyōok) *v.* To vomit.

pungent (pŭn′jənt) *adj.* Sharp or bitter in taste or smell.

Q

quack (kwăk) *n.* Someone who pretends to have a great deal of knowledge and skill in a certain field.

quadruped (kwŏd′rōo-pĕd′) *adj.* Four-footed.

quarry (kwôr′ē, kwŏr′ē) *n.* An animal that is being hunted. **2.** A place where building stone is taken from the ground.

quench (kwĕnch) *v.* To put an end to.

querulous (kwĕr′ə-ləs, kwĕr′yə-) *adj.* Complaining.

quest (kwĕst) *n.* A search.

quibble (kwĭb′əl) *v.* To argue at length the minor details of a topic.

quirk (kwûrk) *n.* A strange character trait or mannerism.

quiver (kwĭv′ər) *n.* A container for arrows.

quizzical (kwĭz′ĭ-kəl) *adj.* In a questioning way. — **quizzically** *adv.*

R

rakish (rā′kĭsh) *adj.* Having a carefree, dashing appearance. — **rakishly** *adv.*

rampart (răm′pärt) *n.* A protective wall encircling a city or fort.

random (răn′dəm) *adj.* Purposeless; haphazard.

rapier (rā′pē-ər) *n.* A long, slender two-edged sword.

rapturous (răp′chər-əs) *adj.* Feeling great joy.

rash (răsh) *adj.* Reckless.

ravage (răv′ĭj) *v.* To destroy; lay waste. — *n.* Destruction.

ravenous (răv′ən-əs) *adj.* Very hungry. — **ravenously** *adv.*

raze (rāz) *v.* To tear down, as a building.

rebuke (rĭ-byōok′) *v.* To scold sharply.

recalcitrant (rĭ-kăl′sə-trənt) *adj.* Difficult to control. — **recalcitrance** *n.*

receptacle (rĭ-sĕp′tə-kəl) *n.* A container.

recess (rē′sĕs′, rĭ-sĕs′) *n.* A hollow place or indentation in a wall.

recline (rĭ-klīn′) *v.* To lie down or lean back.

recoil (rĭ-koil′) *v.* To draw or fall back.

recompense (rĕk′əm-pĕns′) *n.* Payment; reward.

reconcile (rĕk′ən-sīl′) *v.* **1.** To accept or agree to something. **2.** To become friendly again.

reconnoiter (rē′kə-noi′tər, rĕk′ə-) *v.* To explore or inspect in order to seek out information.

recourse (rē-kôrs′) *n.* A turning to someone or something for help.

rectory (rĕk′tə-rē) *n.* The house in which the minister of a church lives.

redress (rĭ-drĕs′) *v.* To set right; make amends. — **redresser** *n.*

reek (rēk) *v.* To give off smoke or steam or odors.

reeve (rēv) *n.* The chief officer of a town.

reflect (rĭ-flĕkt′) *v.* **1.** To think seriously. **2.** To give back a likeness.

reflection (rĭ-flĕk′shən) *n.* **1.** Careful thought. **2.** An image of something.

refute (rĭ-fyōot′) *v.* To prove to be wrong or false.

regalia (rĭ-gāl′yə, -gā′lē-ə) *n.* Magnificent clothes.

regulation (rĕg′yə-lā′shən) *adj.* Required by rule or law.

reiterate (rē-ĭt′ə-rāt′) *v.* To say over and over again.

relay (rē′lā, rĭ-lā′) *n.* A fresh supply of something.

relentless (rĭ-lĕnt′lĭs) *adj.* Unyielding.

relevant (rĕl′ə-vənt) *adj.* Important to the matter under consideration. — **relevancy** *n.*

relinquish (rĭ-lĭng′kwĭsh) *v.* To give up.

relish (rĕl′ĭsh) *v.* To enjoy the taste of; like.

reluctance (rĭ-lŭk′təns) *n.* Nonwillingness.

reluctant (rĭ-lŭk′tənt) *adj.* Unwilling.

remonstrance (rĭ-mŏn′strəns) *n.* Protest.

remonstrate (rĭ-mŏn′strāt′) *v.* To protest.

remorse (rĭ-môrs′) *n.* A feeling of guilt for having done something wrong.

remote (rĭ-mōt′) *adj.* Distant; slight. — **remotely** *adv.*

render (rĕn′dər) *v.* To express in one's own way.

renowned (rĭ-nound′) *adj.* Famous.

reparation (rĕp′ə-rā′shən) *n.* Something paid or given to make up for an injury or loss.

repast (rĭ-păst′, -päst′) *n.* A meal.

repertoire (rĕp′ər-twär, -tôr) *n.* The range of techniques or skills of a particular person or group.

replenish (rĭ-plĕn′ĭsh) *v.* To resupply with fuel.

repose (rĭ-pōz′) *v.* To lie at rest. — *n.* Calmness.

reprimand (rĕp′rə-mănd′, -mänd′) *n.* A severe scolding.

reproach (rĭ-prōch′) *v.* To blame or criticize.

repugnance (rĭ-pŭg′nəns) *n.* A feeling of intense dislike.

resiliency (rĭ-zĭl′yən-sē) *n.* The ability to return quickly to good health and spirits after an illness or tragedy.

resonant (rĕz′ə-nənt) *adj.* Having a full, rich sound.

resort (rĭ-zôrt′) *v.* To go often.

resources (rē′sôrs′əz, -zôrs′əz) *n. pl.* Available money or property.

restitution (rĕs′tə-tōo′shən, -tyōo′shən) *n.* The making good or paying for damage or loss.

restive (rĕs′tĭv) *adj.* Nervous; restless.

restorative (rĭ-stôr′ə-tĭv, rĭ-stōr′-) *n.* Something that brings back life or strength.

retainer (rĭ-tā′nər) *n.* Someone in the service of another.

retort (rĭ-tôrt′) *v.* To answer in a sharp, quick way.

retribution (rĕt′rə-byōo′shən) *n.* Something given or done as a repayment or reward.

retrieve (rĭ-trēv′) *v.* To bring back.

rev (rĕv) *v. Informal.* To cause an engine or motor to go faster.

revel (rĕv′əl) *v.* To take great pleasure in.

revelation (rĕv′ə-lā′shən) *n.* The act of making something known.

revelry (rĕv′əl-rē) *n.* Very loud merrymaking.

reverberate (rĭ-vûr′bə-rāt′) *v.* To make a loud, reechoing sound.

revere (rĭ-vîr′) *v.* To regard with great respect and awe.

reverie (rĕv′ər-ē) *n.* A daydream.

revulsion (rĭ-vŭl′shən) *n.* A feeling of disgust.

rheum (rōom) *n.* A watery discharge from the eyes, mouth, or nose.

richochet (rĭk′ə-shā′, -shĕt′) *v.* To skip off a surface after striking it at an angle.

righteous (rī'chəs) *adj.* Morally right; fair. — **righteously** *adv.* — **righteousness** *n.*

rimy (rīm'ē) *adj.* Frosty.

rite (rīt) A religious or other formal ceremony.

ritual (rĭch'ōō-əl) *n.* A set of actions regularly followed in performing a ceremony.

roan (rōn) *adj.* Reddish-brown.

roister (rois'tər) *v.* To behave in a lively and noisy way.

romp (rŏmp) *v.* To play in a carefree, lively way.

rouble (rōō'bəl) *n.* The basic unit of money in the Soviet Union.

rowel (rou'əl) *n.* A small wheel with sharp teeth on the back of a spur.

ruminate (rōō'mə-nāt') *v.* To think about something over and over again.

rumination (rōō'mə-nā'shən) *n.* **1.** The chewing of cud. **2.** Lengthy thought.

rummage (rŭm'ĭj) *v.* To find by searching through.

runnel (rŭn'əl) *n.* A little stream.

ruse (rōōz) *n.* A trick.

S

saddlebow (săd'l-bō') *n.* The arched front part of a saddle.

sagacious (sə-gā'shəs) *adj.* Knowledgeable.

sage (sāj) *adj.* Wise.

sallow (săl'ō) *adj.* Having a sickly, pale-yellow color.

salvation (săl-vā'shən) *n.* **1.** A rescue from evil or danger. **2.** The person or thing that makes rescue possible. **3.** Redemption.

samovar (săm'ə-vär', săm'ə-vär') *n.* A metal urn with a spigot, used in making tea.

sanctuary (săngk'chōō-ĕr'ē) *n.* A sacred place.

sandalwood (săn'dəl-wŏŏd') *n.* A wood from an Asian tree, used for woodcarving and furniture.

satchel (săch'əl) *n.* A small suitcase or bag.

savor (sā'vər) *n.* A special taste or smell.

sconce (skŏns) *n.* A wall bracket for candles or lights.

screech (skrēch) *n.* To scream in a high-pitched, harsh voice.

scruple (skrōō'pəl) *n.* A feeling of uneasiness about doing things that one thinks are wrong.

scrutiny (skrōōt'n-ē) *n.* A close, careful inspection.

securities (sĭ-kyŏŏr'ə-tēz) *n. pl.* Stocks and bonds.

seethe (sēth) *v.* To boil.

seminary (sĕm'ə-nĕr'ē) *n.* A school where priests, ministers, or rabbis are trained.

sensuous (sĕn'shōō-əs) *adj.* Pleasing to the senses; pleasurable.

sentiment (sĕn'tə-mənt) *n.* The thought or feeling behind a statement or action.

sepulcher (sĕp'əl-kər) *n.* A burial chamber; tomb.

sequin (sē'kwĭn) *n.* A small, shiny metal disk sewn in fabric as decoration.

serene (sĭ-rēn') *adj.* Calm.

serge (sûrj) *n.* A heavy, smooth fabric, usually of wool.

serpentine (sûr'pən-tēn', -tīn') *adj.* Winding.

serrated (sĕr'rā'tĭd) *adj.* Having sawlike edges or surfaces.

shackle (shăk'əl) *n.* A device used to prevent freedom of movement. — *v.* To restrict or confine as with chains or manacles.

shamble (shăm'bəl) *v.* To walk in an awkward, shuffling way.

sheer (shîr) *adj.* Very steep.

shipwright (shĭp'rīt') *n.* A carpenter who builds or repairs ships.

shirk (shûrk) *v.* To put off or avoid doing something that should be done. — **shirker** *n.*

shrift (shrĭft) *n. Archaic.* Confession to a priest.

shroud (shroud) *n.* A burial cloth.

sinewy (sĭn'yōō-ē) *adj.* Muscular.

singular (sĭng'gyə-lər) *adj.* Extraordinary; strange. — **singularly** *adv.*

singularity (sĭng'gyə-lăr'ə-tē) *n.* Distinctness; individuality.

sinister (sĭn'ĭ-stər) *adj.* Appearing evil or wicked.

sinuosity (sĭn'yōō-ŏs'ə-tē) *n.* A winding and twisting in shape or movement.

skeptical (skĕp'tĭ-kəl) *adj.* Doubting; questioning.

slaughter (slô'tər) *v.* To kill violently. — *n.* massacre.

slither (slĭth'ər) *n.* A sliding and gliding movement.

slouch (slouch) *v.* To walk, sit, or stand in a drooping way.

slumbrous (slŭm'brəs) *adj.* Causing one to be sleepy or relaxed.

smite (smīt) *v.* **1.** To afflict. **2.** To strike forcefully. — **smiter** *n.*

smithy (smĭth'ē, smĭth'ē) *n.* A workshop where metal is heated and hammered into particular objects.

sniper (snī'pər) *n.* A person who shoots at others from a hidden position.

solar (sō'lər) *adj.* Coming from the sun.

solemnize (sŏl'əm-nīz') *v.* To perform a formal ceremony.

solicitous (sə-lĭs'ə-təs) *adj.* Showing concern.

solicitude (sə-lĭs'ə-tōōd', -tyōōd') *n.* Concern.

solitary (sŏl'ə-tĕr'ē) *adj.* Alone.

solitude (sŏl'ə-tōōd, -tyōōd) *n.* **1.** Aloneness. **2.** A lonely, out-of-the-way place.

sordid (sôr'dĭd) *adj.* Dirty.

spasmodic (spăz-mŏd'ĭk) *adj.* Characterized by irregular and excitable movements.

spectral (spĕc'trəl) *adj.* Ghostly.

speculation (spĕk'yə-lā'shən) *n.* A theory or conclusion based on guesswork.

spherical (sfîr'ĭ-kəl) *adj.* Round.

spinet (spĭn'ĭt) *n.* A small, upright piano.

spontaneous (spŏn-tā'nē-əs) *adj.* Happening so naturally that there appears to be no outside influence. — **spontaneously** *adv.*

sprint (sprĭnt) *v.* To run a short distance at top speed.

spume (spyōōm) *n.* Foam or froth. *v.* To foam or froth.

ă pat/ā pay/âr care/ä father/b bib/ch church/d deed/ĕ pet/ē be/f fife/g gag/h hat/hw which/ĭ pit/ī pie/îr pier/j judge/k kick/l lid. needle/m mum/ n no. sudden/ng thing/ŏ pot/ō toe/ô paw, for/oi noise/ou out/ŏŏ took/ōō boot/p pop/r roar/s sauce/sh ship. dish/t tight/th thin, path/th this, bathe/ ŭ cut/ûr urge/v valve/w with/y yes/z zebra, size/zh vision/ə about. item. edible, gallop, circus/à *Fr.* ami/œ *Fr.* feu, *Ger.* schön/ü *Fr.* tu, *Ger.* über/ KH *Ger.* ich, *Scot.* loch/N *Fr.* bon.

Glossary 827

squeegee (skwē′jē′) *n.* A T-shaped tool with a rubber blade used to wipe water from a surface.

squirt (skwûrt) *n. Informal.* A small or young person.

staccato (stə-kä′tō) *adj.* Made up of separate, short, distinct sounds.

stamina (stăm′ə-nə) *n.* The ability to resist fatigue, illness, or hardship.

stance (stăns) *n.* The standing posture of a person or animal.

staple (stā′pəl) *n.* A U-shaped piece of metal driven into a surface to keep a hook, bolt, or wiring in place.

statistic (stə-tĭs′-tĭk) *n.* A numerical item of information about a specific subject. — **statistically** *adv.*

stave (stāv) *v.* To break or smash.

steep (stēp) *v.* To immerse; involve.

stipulation (stĭp′yə-lā′shən) *n.* An agreed-upon condition or term, as in a contract.

stockade (stŏk′ād′) *n.* A fort or enclosed area used for protection or imprisonment.

strait (strāt) *n.* A narrow waterway connecting two larger bodies of water.

strategy (străt′ə-jē) *n.* A plan of action or scheme to achieve a specific purpose.

strew (strōō) *v.* To cover by scattering.

sublime (sə-blīm′) *adj.* Inspiring awe; impressive. — **sublimity** (sə-blĭm′ə-tē) *n.*

subordinate (sə-bôr′də-nĭt) *adj.* **1.** Of inferior rank or position. **2.** Under the control or authority of another.

subside (səb-sīd′) *v.* To become less active or intense.

suffice (sə-fīs′) *v.* To be enough.

suffuse (sə-fyōōz′) *v.* To spread through or fill.

sullen (sŭl′ən) *adj.* Gloomy; slow. — **sullenly** *adv.*

sultry (sŭl′trē) Very hot.

sumptuous (sŭmp′chōō-əs) *adj.* Magnificent; having the appearance of being costly.

supercilious (sōō′pər-sĭl′ē-əs) *adj.* Haughty; scornful. — **superciliously** *adv.*

superscription (sōō′pər-skrĭp′shən) *n.* Something written above or outside another thing.

supple (sŭp′əl) *adj.* Able to move and bend easily.

suppliant (sŭp′lĭ-ənt) *n.* A beggar.

supplication (sŭp′lĭ-kā′-shən) *n.* A humble prayer or request.

surmise (sər-mīz′) *v.* To guess.

surmount (sər-mount′) *v.* To be at the top of.

surpassing (sər-păs′ĭng, -päs′ĭng) *adj.* Exceptional. — **surpassingly** *adv.*

sustain (sə-stān′) *v.* To support; encourage.

swarthy (swôr′thē) *adj.* Having a dark complexion.

swirl (swûrl) *v.* To move with a twisting motion.

symmetrical (sĭ-mĕt′rĭ-kəl) *adj.* **1.** Showing exact correspondence in shape, size, and arrangement of elements. **2.** Harmonious in arrangement.

synopsis (sĭ-nŏp′sĭs) *n.* A brief summary.

T

tactics (tăk′tĭks) *n. pl.* Skillful methods used to achieve a specific goal.

taint (tānt) *v.* To infect; spoil.

tally (tăl′ē) *v.* To count.

tamper (tăm′pər) *v.* To interfere with in order to damage.

tangible (tăn′jə-bəl) *adj.* Capable of being touched or seen; real.

taroc (tăr′ək) *n.* A card game.

tedious (tē′dē-əs) *adj.* Tiresome.

tempered (tĕm′pərd) *adj.* Having the proper degree of hardness or elasticity (metal).

tendril (tĕn′drəl) *n.* A long, slender, part of a climbing plant, used for clinging to some object.

tentative (tĕn′tə-tĭv) *adj.* Uncertain. — **tentatively** *adv.*

termination (tûr′mə-nā′shən) *n.* The end of something.

terrain (tə-rān′, tĕ-) *n.* **1.** A particular stretch of land. **2.** Ground.

terse (tûrs) *adj.* Free of unnecessary words.

testy (tĕs′tē) *adj.* Touchy. — **testily** *adv.*

tether (tĕth′ər) *v.* To confine an animal to a certain area by tying or chaining it.

theoretical (thē′ə-rĕt′ĭ-kəl) *adj.* Based on a general plan or idea. — **theoretically** *adv.*

thicket (thĭck′ĭt) *n.* A thick growth of small trees.

thong (thông, thŏng) *n.* A narrow strip of leather or other material used for tying.

thresh (thrĕsh) *v.* To beat grain out of its thick outside covering.

thrive (thrīv) *v.* To prosper.

throes (thrōz) *n. pl.* A condition of painful struggle.

throng (thrŏng) *n.* A very large group of people or things.

throttle (thrŏt′l) *n.* A device that controls the amount of fuel entering an engine.

thwart (thwôrt) *v.* To frustrate; defeat.

tidings (tī′dĭngz) *n. pl.* News.

tier (tîr) *n.* One of a series of rows or layers placed one on top of the other.

timorous (tĭm′ər-əs) *adj.* Timid. — **timorously** *adv.*

titanic (tī-tăn′ĭk) *adj.* Huge.

tithe (tīth) *n.* **1.** A tax or contribution. **2.** One tenth or any small amount.

traipse (trāps) *v. Informal.* To walk.

tranquil (trăn′kwəl) *adj.* Calm; motionless.

transgression (trăns-grĕsh′ən, trănz-) *n.* **1.** The breaking of a law. **2.** The act of going beyond certain limits.

transition (trăn-zĭsh′ən, -sĭsh′ən) *n.* The passing from one condition or form to another.

travail (trə-vāl′, trăv′āl′) *n.* Agony.

treacherous (trĕch′ər-əs) *adj.* **1.** Unreliable; dangerous. **2.** Disloyal.

treachery (trĕch′ə-rē) *n.* Betrayal.

treble (trĕb′əl) *n.* A high-pitched voice.

trellis (trĕl′ĭs) *n.* A frame made of strips of wood crossing each other to form square or diamond patterns.

trespass (trĕs′pəs) *v.* **1.** To enter another's property or land without permission. **2.** To intrude upon another's privacy or time.

tributary (trĭb′yə-tĕr′ē) *n.* A stream flowing into a river.

tripe (trīp) *n.* The stomach lining of cattle, used as food.

trowel (trou′əl) *n.* A flat-bladed tool used for applying plaster.

truculence (trŭk′yə-ləns) *n.* Eagerness to fight.

truffle (trŭf′əl) *n.* A potato-shaped, edible, mushroomlike plant.

tucker (tŭk′ər) *v. Informal.* To tire. — *to tucker out.*

tumult (tōō′məlt, tyōō′-) *n.* **1.** Great noise and confusion. **2.** Emotional disturbance.

tumultous (tə-mŭl′chŏŏ-əs) *adj.* Confused and excited.

turnkey (tûrn′kē) *n.* A person in charge of the keys in a jail.

tyro (tī′rō) *n.* A person with no experience in a particular field.

U

ulterior (ŭl′tîr′ē-ər) *adj.* Remote; beyond what is immediately evident.

uncanny (ŭn′kăn′ē) *adj.* Weird, mysterious.

uncouth (ŭn′kŏŏth) *adj.* **1.** Crude. **2.** Clumsy.

uninhibited (ŭn′ĭn-hĭb′ə-tĭd) *adj.* Unrestrained. — **uninhibitedly** *adv.*

unobtrusive (ŭn′əb-trŏŏ′sĭv) *adj.* Unnoticeable. — **unobtrusively** *adv.*

unparalleled (ŭn′păr′ə-lĕld′) *adj.* Unequaled.

unsavory (ŭn′sā′və-rē) *adj.* Offensive; disagreeable.

unscathed (ŭn′skā*th*d′) *adj.* Unharmed.

unscrupulous (ŭn′skrŏŏ′pyə-ləs) *adj.* Not caring about what is right or wrong.

urbane (ûr′bāne′) *adj.* Polite; refined.

usurp (yŏŏ-sûrp′, -zûrp′) *v.* To seize power or possessions illegally. — **usurper** *n.*

V

vagabond (văg′ə-bŏnd′) *n.* A wanderer.

vague (vāg) *adj.* Unclear in thought or expression.

valedictory (văl′ə-dĭk′tə-rē) *adj.* Pertaining to a parting or farewell.

valiant (văl′yənt) *adj.* Brave.

valor (văl′ər) *n.* Bravery.

variable (vâr′ē-ə-bəl) *adj.* Changeable.

varmint (vär′mənt) *n.* A troublesome person or animal.

vault (vôlt) *v.* To leap. — *n.* **1.** An underground room or cave with an arched ceiling. **2.** A burial chamber.

veery (vîr′ē) *n.* A reddish-brown thrush.

vehement (vē′ə-mənt) *adj.* Expressing intense emotion. — **vehemently** *adv.*

vendor (vĕn′dər) *n.* A person who sells.

venerable (vĕn′ər-ə-bəl) *adj.* Deserving respect because of age and dignity.

vengeance (vĕn′jəns) *n.* The act of punishing another (or desire to do so) in return for an injury or wrong.

verdict (vûr-dĭkt) *n.* A decision.

verily (vĕr′ə-lē) *adv. Archaic.* Truly.

veritable (vĕr′ə-tə-bəl) *adj.* Actual; true. — **veritably** *adv.*

versatile (vûr′sə-təl) *adj.* Having many uses or serving many purposes.

vertical (vûr′tĭ-kəl) *adj.* Going straight up and down.

vestibule (vĕs′tə-byŏŏl′) *n.* A small entrance room.

vex (vĕks) *v.* To irritate.

vexation (vĕk-sā′shən) *n.* Annoyance.

vial (vī′əl) *n.* A small bottle for liquids.

vicarious (vī-kâr′ē-əs, vĭ-) *adj.* Experienced through imagined sharing in another's activities. **vicariously** *adv.*

vicious (vĭsh′əs) *adj.* Evil; dangerous.

victual (vĭt′l) *n.* Food.

vile (vīl) *adj.* Disgusting.

vintage (vĭn′tĭj) *n.* Wine of a particular year and place.

virtually (vûr′chŏŏ-ə-lē) *adv.* Practically; nearly.

vizier (vĭ-zîr′, vĭz′yər) *n.* A high officer in the government of a Moslem country.

W

waddle (wŏd′l) *v.* To walk with short steps that cause the body to sway from side to side.

waft (wäft, wăft) *v.* To carry gently through the air.

wainscot (wān′skət, -skät) *v.* To line a room or a wall with fabric or wood paneling.

waive (wāv) *v.* To put off for another time.

wane (wān) *n.* A gradual dimming or lessening.

wanton (wŏn′tən) *adj.* Unrestrained.

warrant (wôr′ənt, wŏr′-) *n.* An official order authorizing an arrest, search, or seizure.

waver (wā′vər) *v.* To be unsure or unsteady.

wheedle (hwēd′l) *v.* To coax and flatter to get something.

whelm (hwĕlm) *v.* To plunge in water.

whet (hwĕt) *v.* To stimulate. Also **whetten.**

whey (hwā) *n.* The watery part of milk that remains after cheese has been made from it.

whimper (hwĭm′pər) *v.* To cry and sob quietly.

wicket (wĭk′ĭt) *n.* A small gate.

wily (wī′lē) *adj.* Tricky; sly.

wreak (rēk) *v.* **1.** To cause harm to. **2.** To express rage or hostility.

Z

zealous (zĕl′əs) *adj.* Enthusiastically devoted to a particular interest.

zenith (zē′nĭth) *n.* The highest point in the heavens.

ă pat/ā pay/âr care/ä father/b bib/ch church/d deed/ĕ pet/ē be/f fife/g gag/h hat/hw which/ĭ pit/ī pie/îr pier/j judge/k kick/l lid, needle/m mum/ n no, sudden/ng thing/ŏ pot/ō toe/ô paw, for/oi noise/ou out/ŏŏ took/ōō boot/p pop/r roar/s sauce/sh ship, dish/t tight/th thin, path/*th* this, bathe/ ū cut/ûr urge/v valve/w with/y yes/z zebra, size/zh vision/ə about, item, edible, gallop, circus/ à *Fr.* ami/œ *Fr.* feu, *Ger.* schön/ü *Fr.* tu, *Ger.* über/ ĸʜ *Ger.* ich, *Scot.* loch/ɴ *Fr.* bon.

Outline of Skills

Page numbers in italics refer to entries in the Guide to Literary Terms and Techniques.

LITERARY SKILLS

LANGUAGE/VOCABULARY SKILLS

Index of Titles by Themes

Love

Mythology

Nature

Suspense

Values

Index of Fine Art

Photo Credits

Art Credits

Index of Authors and Titles

The page numbers in italics indicate where a brief biography of the author is located.

6
7
E 8
F 9
G 0
H 1
I 2
J 3